IUS COMMUNE CASE
FOR THE COMMON LAW C

CASES, MATERIALS AND TEXT ON NATIONAL,
SUPRANATIONAL AND INTERNATIONAL

NON-DISCRIMINATION LAW

IUS COMMUNE CASEBOOKS
FOR THE COMMON LAW OF EUROPE

General editor
Walter van Gerven

Cases, Materials and Text on National, Supranational and International

Non-Discrimination Law

Editors
Dagmar Schiek, Lisa Waddington and Mark Bell

Coordinator
Dimitri Droshout (Universities of Leuven and Maastricht)

Chapter Authors
Mark Bell (University of Leicester)
Tufyal Choudhury (University of Durham)
Olivier De Schutter (University of Louvain-la-Neuve)
Janneke Gerards (University of Leiden)
Aileen McColgan (King's College, London)
Gay Moon (Head of Equality Project at JUSTICE, London)
Dagmar Schiek (University of Leeds)
Lisa Waddington (Maastricht University)

·HART·
PUBLISHING

OXFORD AND PORTLAND, OREGON
2007

Published in North America (US and Canada) by
Hart Publishing
c/o International Specialized Book Services
920 NE 58th Avenue, Suite 300
Portland, OR 97213-3786
USA
Tel: +1 503 287 3093 or toll-free: (1) 800 944 6190
Fax: +1 503 280 8832
Email: orders@isbs.com
Website: www.isbs.com

Hart Publishing, 16C Worcester Place, Oxford, OX1 2JW
Tel: +44 (0)1865 517530 Fax: +44 (0) 1865 510710
Email: mail@hartpub.co.uk
Website: http://www.hartpub.co.uk

British Library Cataloguing in Publication Data
Data Available

ISBN: 978-1-84113-748-3 (paperback)

Typeset by Forewords, Oxford
Printed and bound in Great Britain by
TJ International Ltd, Padstow, Cornwall

Companion Website

The reader's attention is drawn to a companion website, where additional information about the Ius Commune Casebook series as well as original language versions and hyperlinks to full text versions of the excerpts reproduced in this casebook are available:

http://www.casebooks.eu/nonDiscrimination

This publication is supported by the **European Community Action Programme to combat discrimination (2001-2006)**. This programme was established to support the effective implementation of new EU anti-discrimination legislation. The six-year Programme targeted all stakeholders who could help shape the development of appropriate and effective anti-discrimination legislation and policies, across the EU-25 [EU-27 at the time of publication], EFTA and [the then] EU candidate countries.

The Action Programme has three main objectives. These are:
- To improve the understanding of issues related to discrimination
- To develop the capacity to tackle discrimination effectively
- To promote the values underlying the fight against discrimination

For **more information** see:
http://ec.europa.eu/employment_social/fundamental_rights/

This publication does not necessarily reflect the opinion of the European Commission Directorate-General Employment and Social Affairs. Neither the European Commission nor any person acting on its behalf is responsible for the use which might be made of the information in this publication.

IUS COMMUNE CASEBOOKS
FOR THE COMMON LAW OF EUROPE

www.casebooks.eu

D Schiek, L Waddington and M Bell (eds.), *Cases, Materials and Text on National, Supranational and International Non-Discrimination Law* (Oxford: Hart Publishing, 2007)

J Beatson and E Schrage (eds.), *Cases, Materials and Text on Unjustified Enrichment* (Oxford: Hart Publishing, 2003)

H Beale, H Kötz, A Hartkamp and D Tallon (eds.), *Cases, Materials and Text on Contract Law* (Oxford: Hart Publishing, 2002)

W van Gerven, P Larouche and J Lever, *Cases, Materials and Text on National, Supranational and International Tort Law* (Oxford: Hart Publishing, 2000)

W van Gerven (ed.), *Tort Law – Scope of Protection* (Oxford: Hart Publishing, 1998)

Foreword

A great deal of academic literature already exists on the topics of equality and discrimination, ranging from theoretical discussion of the concept of equality to doctrinal analysis of legal provisions in national, European and international law. This book offers an original contribution by providing an in-depth comparative perspective on European non-discrimination law. It reflects the reality that non-discrimination law in Europe is strongly interconnected. Most notably, domestic legislation and case-law on gender equality has been influenced by European Union law since the 1970s. More recently, a series of Directives since 2000 have provoked wide-ranging reforms of national legislation across various grounds of discrimination, such as ethnic origin and disability. Developments within national law can, in turn, be expected to influence future trends within EU legislation and case-law. Therefore, this book uses a comparative method in order to examine the approaches of different legal systems to key issues within non-discrimination law. In so doing, it reveals the rich variety found within domestic legal orders, but also traces evidence of the cross-border influence of EU law, as well as other European and international legal instruments.

By providing an innovative and comparative perspective on non-discrimination law, this book will be a valuable resource for several audiences. The doctrinal legal materials are analysed in a broader socio-legal context. This book should therefore be a stimulating text for both students and academics. For legal practitioners, judges, activists and policy makers, it offers insights into legislative and judicial responses to common challenges that present themselves within non-discrimination law. The book fits within the broader objectives of the Ius Commune Casebook Project, which is a joint undertaking of Maastricht University (UM) and the University of Leuven (K.U.Leuven). The project's aim is to produce a collection of casebooks, covering each of the main fields of law. The current text is the fourth such book, complementing the existing texts on tort law, contract law and unjustified enrichment. Other casebooks are also in progress on topics such as property law and consumer law. While non-discrimination law is part of private law, it is rooted in human rights law and also applies to special fields such as employment law and administrative law. This is the first volume to take the casebook series beyond the narrow confines of private law.

A feature of the casebook series is the existence of a complementary website: www.casebooks.eu. This site provides access to many of the original language versions of those extracts translated during the compilation of the casebook. In addition, where the full text of an extract (e.g. a court decision) is publicly available, then the relevant hyperlink is available on the casebook website. Therefore, the website provides a living resource to supplement the published text and allows the reader to go further where desired.

One of the most immediate and practical barriers to an extensive comparative study of European legal systems is language. Therefore, an essential element in realising this book was financial support from the European Community Action Programme to Combat Discrimination (2001–2006). Amongst other things, this provided the resources to bring together a group of international experts to work on the book and permitted translation of legislation, case-law and other legal materials from across the 27 EU Member States. Our first step was to assemble a team of chapter authors and national experts.

Each chapter was written independently by one author. The precise delimitation of the chapters is explained in the introduction. To enhance a common perspective, several authors' meetings provided opportunities for team work and in depth discussion of chapters. Ultimately, there remain different approaches within the individual chapters, which reflect not only the different national background of authors based in Belgium (Prof. Olivier De Schutter), Britain (Prof. Aileen McColgan, Prof. Mark Bell, Tufyal Choudhury and Gay Moon), the Netherlands (Prof. Lisa Waddington, Prof. Janneke Gerards) and Germany (Prof. Dagmar Schiek), but also the fact that authors' individual perspectives are coloured by their specific experience relating to human rights law or EC law and to one or several specific grounds for discrimination. The editors wish to express their sincere gratitude to the other chapter authors for their generous cooperation throughout this substantial project.

The role of the national experts was to identify the key legislation and case-law from within their jurisdiction according to the themes examined in each chapter of the book. We extend warm thanks to the following persons (in alphabetical order) for their contributions as national experts. The countries in respect of which they contributed information are listed in brackets after their name and professional affiliation: Zoe Apostolopoulou, e-ISOTIS, Athens (Cyprus), Prof. Susanne Baer, Humboldt Universität zu Berlin (Germany), Fotini Bayeri LL.M, Lawyer (Greece), Dr. Claire de Beausse de La Hougue, Université Paris II (France), Margarida FA Brandão Matias, College of Europe, Bruges (Portugal), Aušrine Burneikienë, Equal Opportunities Ombudsman (Lithuania), Prof. Theresia Degener, Evangelischen Fachhochschule RWL, Bochum (Germany), Zuzana Dlugosova, The Citizen and Democracy (Slovakia), Dr. Tonio Ellul, Ellul Mifsud and DeBono Advocates (Malta), Dr. Gita Feldhune, University of Latvia (Latvia), Dr. Petra Foubert, University of Leuven (K.U.Leuven) (Belgium), Dr. Marianne Gijzen, Maastricht University (Netherlands), Javier Güemes, European Disability Forum (Spain), Rachael Hession, Law Society of Ireland (Ireland), Margarita Ilieva, Attorney-at-law, Bulgarian Helsinki Committee (Bulgaria), Iustina Ionescu, Centre for Legal Resources (Romania), Dovile Juodkaite, Global Initiative on Psychiatry (Lithuania), Dr. András Kádár, Hungarian Helsinki Committee (Hungary), Jaroslaw Kaminski, Polish Disability Forum (Poland), Andrea Kämpf, Icon Institut (Germany), Dr. Kristina Koldinská, Charles University, Prague (Czech Republic), Dr. Karin König, Lawyer, City of Vienna Municipality (Austria), Dr. Rok Lampe,

University of Maribor (Slovenia), Paul Lappalainen, Swedish National Integration Authority (Sweden), Timo Makkonen, Law and Consultancy Firm Timo A Makkonen (Finland), Prof. Aileen McColgan, King's College London (UK), Kasper Nizam, Consultant, Socialt Udviklingscenter (Denmark), Vadim Poleshchuk MA, Legal Information Centre for Human Rights (Estonia), Shivaun Quinlivan, National University of Ireland, Galway (Ireland), Cristina Sosa Erdozain, GLE Services, Brussels (Spain), Dr. Florian Stork, Lawyer (Germany), Véronique van der Plancke, Catholic University of Louvain (UCL) (Belgium), Maria Ventegodt Liisberg, Danish Institute for Human Rights (Denmark), Dr. Małgorzata Zajac Zysk, Mittal Steel Poland SA (Poland). In addition, Prof. Alessandro Simoni (University of Florence, Italy) kindly supplied information on Italy.

From the sources compiled by national experts, a wide range of material was translated into English. These translations were made by a private company, and subject to review by the relevant national expert. Some extracts are also chapter authors' or national experts' own translations or translations that were otherwise publicly available.

Once each chapter of the book was prepared in first draft, it was submitted for review by an Independent Advisory Board. This group of leading experts in non-discrimination law provided excellent feedback and strongly contributed to the quality of the final text. We wish to thank the following persons for their generous participation in the Board's work:

— Dr. Catherine Barnard, University of Cambridge
— Prof. Theresia Degener, Evangelische Fachhochschule RWL
— Prof. Jenny Goldschmidt, University of Utrecht
— Prof. Aart Hendriks, University of Leiden and Dutch Equal Treatment Commission
— Prof. Christopher McCrudden, University of Oxford
— Prof. Luís Miguel Poiares Pessoa Maduro, Advocate-General to the Court of Justice
— Prof. Gerard Quinn, National University of Ireland, Galway
— Hans Ytterberg, Swedish Ombudsman Against Discrimination on Grounds of Sexual Orientation.

A number of other persons provided research and other assistance to individual chapters, and we acknowledge the assistance of the following: Stelios Andreadakis and Pascale Lorber (University of Leicester—chapter two), Katherina Drinkuth LL.M, Franz Ebert (stud iur) and Frauke Remmers (Dipl Oec) (all University of Oldenburg—chapter three), Robin Allen QC (Cloisters Chambers, London—chapter eight).

Through the contributions of national experts and the review by the Independent Advisory Board, every effort has been taken to ensure that the law described in the book is accurate, complete and as up-to-date as possible. Nevertheless, this is a highly fluid area of law and monitoring change across 27 countries with their many different languages has been a genuine challenge. New case-law at domestic and European level in the wake of the 2000 Directives is beginning to trickle out, whilst some Member States are still in the process of revising national legislation. Naturally, responsibility for any errors lies with the authors.

Part of the dynamism of non-discrimination law reflects the fact that it is relatively "young" in many European states. This also posed a challenge in writing this book, because there are some countries where very little case-law exists so far or the core legislation has only been introduced in recent years. This context explains why there is greater reference within this book (compared to others in the Ius Commune series) to decisions of lower courts and also to those of quasi-judicial bodies which specialise in non-discrimination law.

Finally, the editors express great thanks for the financial, academic and administrative support provided across several years by Maastricht University and the Ius Commune Casebook Project. This project was first conceived by Lisa Waddington, who holds the European Disability Forum Chair in European Disability Law in the Faculty of Law at Maastricht University, who succeeded in applying for financial support from the European Commission for the broader project entitled "Stimulating Public Interest Litigation at a Pan-European Level—Raising Knowledge and Imparting Skills", funded by the European Commission within the framework of the Community Action Programme to Combat Discrimination. Besides the casebook, the project comprised a series of summer schools on aspects of non-discrimination law, which complemented the comparative research during the writing of the casebook. Prof. Hildegard Schneider (Maastricht University) and Prof. Gerard Quinn (National University of Ireland, Galway) had the responsibility for this part of the overall project.

During this first stage of the project, when the administrative support structure and the working routine of chapter authors and national experts was established, the editors were generously supported by Dr. Marianne Gijzen. As this book falls within the ius commune series, the editors would also like to acknowledge the contribution of the General Editor of the series, Prof. Walter van Gerven, and Richard Hart of Hart Publishing, who has consistently supported the series. Special thanks go to Dimitri Droshout, the Ius Commune Casebook Project research coordinator. He played a particularly active role in steering this book towards its completion. He provided support above and beyond his normal tasks and guided us in maintaining consistency with the spirit of this series.

There were two principal assistants who played an invaluable role in furthering this book. Moritz Jesse made a leading contribution in the first stage when national experts were collecting materials and then during the translation process. In the later stages of the project, Raluca Rusu ensured that the chapters were transformed from the authors' individual styles into the specific format requirements of the series. Both assistants were constantly available for a wide variety of support tasks and their contributions were instrumental in permitting us to complete this book within the intended timeframe. Finally, there are a range of other persons who also made important individual contributions at different times to the project and we happily acknowledge their support: William Bull (language review), Dr. Simon Duindam,

Hein Kruijt (translation of the annex), Chantal Kuypers, Mariken Lenaerts, Marie-Anne Sarlet, Diana Schabregs, Yleen Simonis.

Dagmar Schiek, Oldenburg
Lisa Waddington, Maastricht
Mark Bell, Leicester

15 January 2007

Contents

**INTRODUCTORY CHAPTER
A COMPARATIVE PERSPECTIVE ON NON-DISCRIMINATION LAW**

CHAPTER TWO
DIRECT DISCRIMINATION

CHAPTER THREE
INDIRECT DISCRIMINATION

CHAPTER FOUR
HARASSMENT

CHAPTER FIVE
INSTRUCTIONS TO DISCRIMINATE AND VICTIMISATION

CHAPTER SIX
REASONABLE ACCOMMODATION

CHAPTER SEVEN
POSITIVE ACTION

CHAPTER EIGHT
ENFORCEMENT BODIES

Table of Abbreviations

ACAS	Advisory Conciliation and Arbitration Service (GB)
ADA	Americans with Disabilities Act of 1990
AGG	General Non-Discrimination Act (Germany)
All ER	All England Law Reports
Art.	Article(s)
BAG	Bundesarbeidsgericht (Germany)
BGB	Bürgerliches Gesetzbuch (Civil Code, Germany)
Camb LJ	Cambridge Law Journal
Cardozo L.Rev.	Cardozo Law Review
Cass.	Cour de cassation (France)
crim.	Criminal Chamber
soc.	Social Chamber
CCPR	International Covenant on Civil and Political Rights
CEDAW	International Convention on the Elimination of All Forms of Discrimination against Women
CEDAW Committee	Committee on the Elimination of Discrimination against Women
CEEP	European Centre of Enterprises with Public Participation
CEHR	Commission for Equality and Human Rights (GB)
CERD	UN Committee on the Elimination of Racial Discrimination
CESCR	International Covenant on Economic, Social and Cultural Rights
CFI	Court of First Instance of the European Communities
CGB	Dutch Equal Treatment Commission
CMLRev	Common Market Law Review
CoE	Council of Europe
Colum. L.Rev.	Columbia Law Review
COM	Document of the European Commission, with reference to year and serial number
CRE	Commission for Racial Equality (GB)
DDA	Disability Discrimination Act 1995 (UK)
DO	Swedish Ombudsman for Ethnic Discrimination
DRC	Disability Rights Commission (GB)
Duke L.J.	Duke Law Journal
EAT	Employment Appeals Tribunal
EC	Treaty establishing the European Community or European Community
ECHR	European Convention on Human Rights
EComHR	European Commission of Human Rights
ECNI	Equality Commission for Northern Ireland

ECtHR	European Court of Human Rights
ECJ	Court of Justice of the European Communities
ECR	Reports of cases before the Court of Justice of the European Communities and the Court of First Instance
ECRI	Council of Europe European Commission against Racism and Intolerance
ECSR	European Committee of Social Rights
ECtHR	European Court of Human Rights
ed.	editor
EDF	European Disability Forum
edn.	edition
EEC	European Economic Community
EEOC	US Equal Employment Opportunity Commission
EFTA	European Free Trade Association
EHRR	European Human Rights Reports
EHRLR	European Human Rights Law Review
ELJ	European Law Journal
ELRev	European Law Review
ENAR	European Network against Racism
EOC	Equal Opportunities Commission (GB)
EQUINET	European Network of Equality Bodies
ETC	Dutch Equal Treatment Commission
EU	European Union or Treaty on European Union
EUMC	European Union Monitoring Centre on Racism
EYMI	European Yearbook of Minority Issues
FRA	Fundamental Rights Agency (EU)
GG	Grundgesetz (Constitution/ Basic Law, Germany)
GOR	Genuine occupational requirements
HALDE	High Authority against Discrimination and For Equality (France)
Harvard L.Rev.	Harvard Law Review
HO	Swedish Ombudsman for the Disabled
HomO	Swedish Ombudsman for Sexual Orientation
HRC	Human Rights Committee
ICERD	International Convention on the Elimination of All Forms of Racial Discrimination
ICJ	International Court of Justice
ICLQ	International and Comparative Law Quarterly
ICR	Industrial Court Reports
IGC	Intergovernmental Conference
IJCLLIR	International Journal of Comparative Labour Law and Industrial Relations
IJDL	International Journal of Discrimination Law
ILJ	Industrial Law Journal
ILO	International Labour Organization
ILR	International Labour Review

ILRR	Industrial and Labor Relations Review
Int'l SSJ	International Social Science Journal
IRLR	Industrial Relations Law Reports
JämO	Swedish Ombudsman for equal opportunities between men and women
JCHR	UK Parliamentary Joint Committee for Human Rights
JLR	Japan Labor Review
JO	Journal Officiel (Official Gazette, France)
LJ	Lord Justice (UK)
Mich. L.Rev.	Michigan Law Review
MJ	Maastricht Journal of European and Comparative Law
MLR	Modern Law Review
NILR	Netherlands International Law Review
No.	Number
NYULR	New York University Law Review
ODEI	The Irish Equality Tribunal (formerly called the Office of the Director of Equality Investigations)
Ohio St.L.J.	Ohio State Law Journal
OJ	Official Journal of the European Communities, with reference to series, issue number and page number
OJ C	Official Journal of the European Communities, Communication
OJ L	Official Journal of the European Communities, Legislation
OJLS	Oxford Journal of Legal Studies
OUP	Oxford University Press
para.	paragraph(s)
PCIJ	Permanent Court of International Justice
Rev. Cons. Stud.	Review of Constitutional Studies
RevESC	Revised European Social Charter
RR	Roma Rights
RRA	Race Relations Act 1976
RRAA	Race Relations Amendment Act 2000
RTDH	Revue trimestrielle des droits de l'homme
SDA	Sex Discrimination Act 1975
Temple L.Rev.	Temple Law Review
UNICE	Union of Industrial and Employer's Confederations of Europe
WLR	Weekly Law Reports
YEL	Yearbook of European Law

Country Codes

The present casebook explores a greater number of jurisdictions than previous volumes in the Ius Commune Casebook series. To avoid confusion, the familiar single-letter country codes have been replaced with two-letter codes. The majority of the country codes below correspond with the appropriate ISO code. However, this book stays closer to natural intuition when referring to the United Kingdom or its constituent countries. In this casebook **GB** merely refers to Great Britain and not, unlike the same ISO country code, to the United Kingdom as a whole. **GB** is used to refer to England, Scotland and Wales, if the law in these jurisdictions differs from that in Northern Ireland. **NIR** is used when reference is made to instruments that are specific to Northern Ireland. Otherwise, i.e. whenever – and only if – the situation is the same in the whole of the United Kingdom, **UK** is used.

This book also discusses a wider variety of instruments originating from the Council of Europe, as opposed to previous volumes which did not go beyond the ECHR and decisions of the European Court of Human Rights in Strasbourg. Therefore the code ECHR has been avoided; instead **CoE** is used to refer to all instruments that are related to the Council of Europe.

AT	Austria
BE	Belgium
BG	Bulgaria
CoE	Council of Europe
CY	Cyprus
DE	Germany
DK	Denmark
EC	European Communities
EE	Estonia
ES	Spain
FI	Finland
FR	France
GB	England, Wales and Scotland
HU	Hungary
IE	Ireland
INT	International
IT	Italy
LT	Lithuania
LU	Luxembourg
LV	Latvia
MT	Malta
NIR	Northern Ireland

NL	The Netherlands
PL	Poland
PT	Portugal
RO	Romania
SE	Sweden
SK	Slovakia
UK	United Kingdom
UN	United Nations
US	United States of America

TABLE OF CASES

The following table contains all cases referred to in this book.
Cases in **bold** are excerpted at the page number indicated in **bold**.

European Jurisdictions

International (in chronological order)

Others (in alphabetical order)

Canada

Hong Kong

Table of Legislative Instruments

The following table contains the legislative instruments (legislative acts, EC legislation, treaties) referred to in this book. Instruments in **bold** are excerpted at the page numbers indicated in **bold**.

European legislation

International (in chronological order)

Others (in alphabetical order)

INTRODUCTORY CHAPTER
A COMPARATIVE PERSPECTIVE ON
NON-DISCRIMINATION LAW

Prof. Dagmar Schiek, Prof. Lisa Waddington and Prof. Mark Bell

1.   PRELIMINARY REMARKS

The aims of this book are manifold. It takes as its starting point the EU legal framework of non-discrimination law. This consists of several layers, including fundamental principles of EU law, EC treaty provisions referring to the internal market and a collection of EC Directives prohibiting discrimination on grounds of sex, racial or ethnic origin, religion or belief, disability, age and sexual orientation. Given the supranational character of EC law and its ensuing supremacy over national law, one would expect non-discrimination law to impact on national law and cases through a top-down model of regulation. As EC law will always be rooted in national traditions, this assumption is false.

Accordingly, the aspirations of this book go beyond an examination of EU Non-Discrimination Law. Being a part of the casebook series, it also examines national legal cultures and their influence on, as well as their response to, the demands of EU law. As indicated by the series title, "Ius Commune Casebooks for the Common Law of Europe", the underlying assumption is that European legal orders are converging towards a "common law of Europe". This common law of Europe is anchored in both traditions of national law and the harmonising effect of EU law. Consequently, national materials are presented and analysed alongside Community law materials. The reader will be enabled to understand how Community non-discrimination law is implemented in different legal orders, and how some legal orders have had more impact on its contents than others.

Finally, non-discrimination law as a field has aspirations beyond Community and national law. It is rooted in international instruments and has wider aims than simply implementing legal principles. Above all, the quest for equality, in which non-discrimination law participates, can be characterised as a basic feature of mature human societies. This means that in this field conceptual themes are common to different legal orders in different parts of the world, while the specific national or regional legal regime for equality will always be coloured by specific national and regional requirements. Accordingly, this "casebook" is not restricted to reports of case-law and legislation. It discusses conceptual issues of non-discrimination law and equality law in relation to the chapter headings, which are again rooted in conceptual problems of the field at large.

This introduction will cover several areas. It aims to provide the reader with an introduction to some of the key concepts used in the field of non-discrimination law. This should enhance the readability of the book for readers who are less familiar with the subject and clarify the conceptual approach for other readers. As a first step, we will explain the relevance of non-discrimination and equality within EU law. We will then briefly introduce the concepts expanded upon in the main chapters, to enhance understanding of their inter-relationship. This section will also be used to give an overview of the content and explain the delimitations of the book. Next, we will introduce the sources of non-discrimination law, including an overview of the body of EU directives in the field and international law sources. This part will also explain the relevance of different enforcement institutions, the "case-law" of which is referred to throughout the chapters. The discussion of EU law includes the explanation of certain choices made in terms of the scope of the book. The penultimate section of the introduction turns to the comparative dimension of non-discrimination law, describing different approaches in different legal and political cultures, and explaining the specific problems that are to be confronted by comparative non-discrimination law and the approach taken in the substantive chapters. Finally, the reader will be made familiar with the concepts and terminology in non-discrimination law. This will enable her to read the following chapters with a critical mind.

2.   NON-DISCRIMINATION LAW IN THE EUROPEAN UNION

The principle of equality (or non-discrimination) is deeply embedded within EU law. At the constitutional level, it is one of the general principles of law upheld by the European Court of Justice (ECJ). This means that respect for the principle of equality is a condition for the legality of any EU legislative instrument or any action by the EU institutions and agencies. Moreover, Member States are obliged to respect this principle when national law falls within the scope of EU law. This general principle of equality is capable of application to a wide range of situations. It can be invoked, inter alia, in relation to discriminatory distinctions between products, companies or natural persons.[1] As such, it extends well beyond non-discrimination law in the sense adopted by this book.

Stemming from this bedrock principle, law relating to equality and non-discrimination can be found in several distinct fields under the EC Treaty. First, there is a large body of internal market law which concerns non-discrimination against goods and services, as well as workers and self-employed persons, the latter in connection with the exercise of free movement rights. Therefore, imported goods should not be subject to discriminatory taxation (Article 90 EC) or, alternatively, there must be no discrimination in employment against workers from other Member States (Article 39(2) EC). Indeed, "any discrimination on grounds of nationality" within the scope of the EC Treaty is prohibited (Article 12 EC). Forbidding such discrimination was clearly functional to the removal of barriers to free movement within the internal

---

[1] G. More, "The Principle of Equal Treatment: from Market Unifier to Fundamental Right?" in P. Craig and G. de Búrca (eds.), *The Evolution of EU Law* (Oxford, Oxford University Press, 1999).

market. If Member States could deter imports through subjecting them to less favourable treatment in comparison to domestic products, then trade would be impeded. Similarly, workers would be dissuaded from exercising their free movement rights if they faced discriminatory treatment compared to national workers in the host Member State.

Non-discrimination on grounds of nationality is also fundamental to Union citizenship. Introduced through the 1993 Treaty on European Union, the Court of Justice has used the right to non-discrimination found in Article 12 EC as a key instrument in strengthening the content of Union citizenship.[2] Specifically, it has been a lever to open access for EU citizens to social welfare benefits previously limited to domestic nationals.[3] Nevertheless, a distinction can be drawn between the use of the principle of non-discrimination within internal market and citizenship law and the separate field of non-discrimination law with which this book is concerned. In the former, non-discrimination appears more instrumental in nature. It has been used as a mechanism to remove barriers to trade and to enhance the status of EU citizenship. Yet, even within citizenship law, there is no opposition to nationality discrimination per se.[4] States remain free to treat their own nationals less favourably than EU citizens, unless this is because their own nationals have exercised free movement rights.[5]

The non-discrimination principle crops up in various other fields of EU law, such as immigration law[6] and labour law.[7] This book focuses, however, on non-discrimination law which flows from Article 13 EC. This states:

> "1. . . . the Council, acting unanimously on a proposal from the Commission and after consulting the European Parliament, may take appropriate action to combat discrimination based on sex, racial or ethnic origin, religion or belief, disability, age or sexual orientation."

The measures taken by the Union to combat discrimination under Article 13 EC, and other related provisions,[8] have the distinguishing characteristic that they aim to combat discrimination based on personal characteristics as an autonomous objective. This differs in nature from the Union's law on nationality discrimination where combating discrimination was, at least initially, a means to an end (constructing the internal market). Clearly, this is not an absolute distinction. The trajectory of

---

[2] D. Kostakopoulou, "Ideas, Norms and European Citizenship: Explaining Institutional Change" (2005) 68 MLR 233.

[3] E.g. Case C–184/99 *Grzelczyk* [2001] ECR I–6913; Case C–456/02 *Trojani* [2004] ECR I–7573.

[4] G. de Búrca, "The Role of Equality in European Community Law" in A. Dashwood and S. O'Leary (eds.), *The Principle of Equal Treatment in EC Law* (London, Sweet & Maxwell, 1997) 27.

[5] E.g. Case C–192/05 *K. Tas-Hagen, R. A. Tas* v. *Raadskammer WUBO van de Pensioen- en Uitkeringsraad*, ECJ judgment of 26 October 2006.

[6] Most notably, Directive 2003/109/EC of 25 November 2003 concerning the status of third country nationals who are long-term residents [2004] OJ L16/44.

[7] E.g. Directive 97/81/EC of 15 December 1997 concerning the framework agreement on part-time work concluded by UNICE, CEEP and the ETUC [1998] OJ L14/9 and Directive 1999/70/EC of 28 June 1999 concerning the framework agreement on fixed-term work concluded by ETUC, UNICE and CEEP [1999] OJ L175/43.

[8] E.g. Art. 141 EC.

nationality discrimination law, particularly in the wake of Union citizenship, has been to reduce the significance of the internal market rationale. Nevertheless, the raison d'être of non-discrimination law under Article 13 EC is different from that found within internal market or citizenship law. By choosing to concentrate on discrimination linked to personal characteristics, this book does not generally consider discrimination between non-persons (e.g. products), legal persons (e.g. companies) or between different types of employment contract (e.g. full-time, part-time, fixed-term).

This delimitation in scope is also justified by the different approach to the principle of non-discrimination evident in internal market, citizenship or labour legislation compared to non-discrimination legislation. In the former, the principle of non-discrimination is typically set out in general terms and not further defined.[9] In contrast, within non-discrimination legislation, the concept of discrimination has been defined in increasing detail, with distinctions drawn between direct and indirect discrimination, harassment and instructions to discriminate. Non-discrimination legislation has also developed specialised rules to assist enforcement, such as shifting the burden of proof or creating equality bodies.

3. STRUCTURE AND DELIMITATIONS OF THE BOOK

This book focuses on the main substantive features of non-discrimination law.

Unlike the constitutions of some Member States, Community discrimination law does not encompass a general, open-ended discrimination clause. Prohibitions to discriminate and (weaker) corresponding obligations to pursue equality are restricted to a closed list of enumerated "discrimination grounds". These grounds are sex, racial and ethnic origin, religion and belief, sexual orientation, disability and age. The "discrimination grounds" delimit the scope of application of Community non-discrimination law. Not all national legislators agreed with these limits. Some drafted open lists and most included additional grounds. The first chapter, written by Prof. Dr. Janneke Gerards (University of Leiden, the Netherlands), focuses on "discrimination grounds". It not only explains the grounds covered by the EC Directives, but includes such grounds as are addressed widely in national legislation even though this is not specifically required by Community law. These additional grounds include nationality and marital status in particular. All discrimination grounds are, in some way, related to each other. The reason for this is that human beings carry all of the discrimination grounds within them; we all have an age, gender, etc. A specific section on "multiple discrimination" in chapter one thus explores whether and how far Community law also addresses discrimination on several grounds at once.

---

[9] E.g. Art. 24, Directive 2004/38/EC on the right of citizens of the Union and their family members to move and reside freely within the territory of the Member States . . . [2004] OJ L229/35.

The following chapters address different forms of discrimination (chapters two to six). The core EC non-discrimination Directives prohibit direct discrimination and indirect discrimination (chapters two and three), these forms of discrimination having been elements of all the EC law concepts of non-discrimination so far.

Chapter two, written by Prof. Mark Bell (University of Leicester, England), discusses direct discrimination. Direct discrimination occurs where someone makes a distinction with direct reference to one of the discrimination grounds. For example, a person is not employed because the employer decides that he does not like "African" hairstyles. As the texture of one's hair is considered as decisive for racial origins by those who still believe in human races, this is direct discrimination on grounds of race. While one tends to assume that this form of discrimination will become less and less relevant, this is not actually the case. New phenomena for the EU, such as segregation, can be covered by this ancient concept. Another reason why direct discrimination still occurs is the fact that all discrimination law regimes accept justifications. EC law only accepts such justifications which it states explicitly. Chapter two explains these justifications and their application by the Community and national courts.

Chapter three, written by Prof. Dr. Dagmar Schiek (University of Oldenburg, Germany), covers indirect discrimination. Indirect discrimination occurs when someone makes a distinction which does not refer directly to a discrimination ground, but still results in disproportionate disadvantage for a group of persons identified by a discrimination ground. For example, a rule that Sunday is the main day of rest, and that all other days need to be working days, would create disproportionate disadvantage for those following a religion that has a different weekly rest day (e.g. Sabbath for Jewish people, which is on a Saturday). Indirect discrimination law assumes that there is a causal link between the discrimination ground (here: religion) and the disadvantage. However, it remains possible to rebut this assumption by bringing forward objective justifications. In our example, a justification could be that it is not possible to create the calm atmosphere necessary for a weekly holiday on several days of the week. The reader will learn in chapter three that this reason is probably insufficient as objective justification.

The core Directives also tackle new forms of discrimination, namely harassment and victimisation, as well as incitement to discriminate. These forms of discrimination are covered by chapters four and five.

Harassment and sexual harassment, which enjoy different protection, are the theme of chapter four, written by Prof. Aileen McColgan (Kings College, London and a practising barrister). Harassment does not require different treatment. It occurs where a person is subjected to an intimidating environment or is violated or insulted because of one of the discrimination grounds. For example, if the few black tenants in a larger block of flats are being subjected to intimidating behaviour and regular searches of their person by "security staff", which goes along with racist remarks, this would constitute racial harassment. Legal protection against harassment has, though, largely developed in the field of gender equality.

Discrimination and harassment do not always occur in a straightforward manner. There are also related forms of behaviour, which address either persons who have complained about discrimination or harassment, or those who seek to compel other persons to engage in discrimination and harassment. The former is named victimisation and the latter incitement to discriminate. Both forms of behaviour have in common that they aim at past or future discrimination. This is the reason why they are covered in one chapter, namely chapter five, written by Tufyal Choudhury (Lecturer, Durham University, England). The core equality Directives make a distinction between these forms of behaviour and harassment. Whereas harassment is named as a form of discrimination, the other behaviour is only deemed to be discrimination.

The last form of discrimination addressed by discrimination law is the denial of reasonable accommodation for persons with different needs. This is covered in chapter six, written by Prof. Dr. Lisa Waddington (University of Maastricht, the Netherlands). The core EC Directives only prohibit denial of reasonable accommodation in relation to disability. Thus, for example, an employer cannot refuse to employ a person in a wheelchair because the relevant office would be on the second floor if there is the possibility of moving an employee from a ground floor office to that office and allocating the ground floor office to the wheelchair user. Directive 2000/78/EC, which contains an obligation to provide reasonable accommodation, does not clearly define its denial as discrimination,[10] which means that it remains disputed whether this is indeed an additional form of discrimination or rather an obligation proactively to further equality. Although EC law only addresses reasonable accommodation in relation to disability, the concept can be applied to other grounds, such as religion, which will be discussed in chapter six.

The two subsequent chapters have in common that they cover different emanations of proactive equality law. Neither the Community core Directives nor national legislation is confined to simply prohibiting different forms of discrimination. The Directives maintain the possibility for Member States to establish "positive action" and oblige them to establish (independent) bodies to supervise non-discrimination law and to propose measures to further the positive aim of equality. The Directives have a few more provisions on "proactivity". For example, Member States should encourage employers to provide equality plans in relation to gender equality in employment and to take up social dialogue. These cautious measures are not covered here.

Chapter seven, written by Prof. Dr. Olivier de Schutter (Catholic University of Louvain, Belgium), explains the different forms and admissibility of positive action. This has been a rather contested field. In particular, in relation to gender equality, there are quite a few decisions resulting from challenges by men against having more opportunities for women for promotion. The chapter also covers general policies to enhance equality of results, such as recruitment strategies, although the author does not consider these as positive action proper. Given that positive action will often require the collection of data concerning the extent of disadvantage suffered, the chapter also contains a section on data protection and equality law.

[10] See M. Gijzen, *Selected Issues in Equal Treatment Law: A Multi-layered Comparison of European, English and Dutch Law* (Maastricht, Intersentia, 2006) 396–8.

Chapter eight, written by Gay Moon (Head of the Equality Project within JUSTICE), discusses the position of bodies for the supervision of non-discrimination legislation. Following the examples of the Scandinavian countries and positive experiences in Britain, the Netherlands and Austria, the Community legislator has obliged Member States to establish bodies to oversee the application of sex equality law and racial equality law. While the provisions in the Directives are not very precise, there is a variety of experiences with these bodies across the Member States. The chapter gives an overview of relevant activities and also discusses whether these bodies are sufficiently independent under international law standards.

Whilst we have endeavoured to make this book as comprehensive as possible, certain topics could not be included. As has been explained above,[11] the book focuses on the discrimination grounds found within Article 13 EC and does not explore in detail law relating to discrimination on other grounds, such as nationality or type of employment contract. Within the field of non-discrimination law, the principal topic which is not examined is remedies. There were several reasons for making this choice. First, this is an area where EC legislation is less prescriptive and more discretion is afforded to national legal traditions. In general, the core Directives do not specify what remedies have to be available in a concrete case of discrimination; instead, they identify the characteristics which national remedies should possess, such as being effective, dissuasive and proportionate.[12] Similarly, other European and international human rights instruments provide less detailed norms on remedies.[13] Secondly, in many Member States, the remedies for a breach of non-discrimination law are simply found within the normal procedures for an action under labour law or civil law. It was evidently beyond the scope of this book to embark upon a comparative analysis of the general systems for enforcing labour law or civil law in Europe. There are, however, a number of Member States where specific bodies have been created for adjudicating on complaints of unlawful discrimination, such as the Equality Tribunal in Ireland or the Equal Treatment Commission in the Netherlands. An analysis of such institutions can be found within chapter eight, on equality bodies. This is one aspect of enforcement which is more peculiar to non-discrimination law and where specific requirements can be found in EC legislation. Therefore, within the broad field of enforcement, this topic was selected to be the subject of an individual chapter.

4.   SOURCES OF NON-DISCRIMINATION LAW

The primary focus of this book is law of the EU and national law within the Member States of the EU. Nevertheless, there are other legal sources referred to across the chapters which are important to understanding the development of

---

[11] See above, Section 2.

[12] E.g. Art. 15 of the Racial Equality Directive (2000/43/EC).

[13] See further, C. McCrudden "International and European Norms Regarding National Legal Remedies for Racial Inequality" in S. Fredman (ed.), *Discrimination and Human Rights—the case of racism* (Oxford, Oxford University Press, 2001).

non-discrimination law and appreciating the full range of influences on domestic legal norms. This section will briefly introduce the main sources of international and European law which are referred to in the chapters. The subsequent section considers different national legal approaches to non-discrimination law.

4.1.   INTERNATIONAL SOURCES OF NON-DISCRIMINATION LAW

Provisions on equality or non-discrimination are firmly embedded in international law, most notably within the key human rights treaties of the United Nations (UN). Indeed, protection against discrimination through international law even predates the creation of the UN; in chapter three, reference is made to several decisions from the Permanent International Court of Justice during the 1920s and 1930s. A distinction can be drawn between general human rights treaties and specialised treaties on discrimination. In the former category, the International Covenant on Civil and Political Rights (ICCPR) and the International Covenant on Economic, Social and Cultural Rights (ICESCR) are obvious points of reference.[14] Each contains several provisions of relevance to equality and non-discrimination, although these differ in their scope.[15] Notably, the ICCPR has a free-standing equality clause in Article 26:

> "All persons are equal before the law and are entitled without any discrimination to the equal protection of the law. In this respect, the law shall prohibit any discrimination and guarantee to all persons equal and effective protection against discrimination on any ground such as race, colour, sex, language, religion, political or other opinion, national or social origin, property, birth or other status."

In contrast, the ICESCR only obliges states to ensure that "the rights enunciated in the present Convention will be exercised without discrimination of any kind . . ." (Article 2(2)). The implementation of both the ICCPR and the ICESCR is monitored by specific treaty bodies: the Human Rights Committee and the Committee on Economic, Social and Cultural Rights respectively. These Committees consider periodic national reports on implementation. In the case of the Human Rights Committee, its role also includes receiving individual communications in respect of those states which have ratified the Optional Protocol to the ICCPR. Article 5(4) of the Optional Protocol specifies that, having considered a communication relating to an alleged violation of the provisions of the ICCPR, the Human Rights Committee "shall forward its views to the State Party concerned and to the individual". As Steiner and Alston note, this does not clarify the legal status which is to be attached to such "views".[16]

---

[14] Both were approved by the UN General Assembly in 1966 and entered into force in 1976.

[15] See further, W. Vandenhole, *Non-discrimination and Equality in the View of the UN Human Rights Treaty Bodies* (Antwerpen, Intersentia, 2005).

[16] H. Steiner and P. Alston, *International Human Rights in Context—Law, Politics and Morals*, 2nd edn (Oxford, Oxford University Press, 2000) 739.

Beyond general human rights instruments, there are also specialised treaties relating to equality and non-discrimination. Here, mention can be made of the International Convention on the Elimination of All Forms of Racial Discrimination (ICERD, 1966) and the Convention on the Elimination of All Forms of Discrimination Against Women (CEDAW, 1979). The right to non-discrimination is also included within the 1989 Convention on the Rights of the Child (Article 2(1)). Finally, on 13 December 2006, the UN General Assembly adopted the Convention on the Rights of Persons with Disabilities.[17] Each of these specialist treaties is supported by an expert committee which monitors implementation. In the case of the Committee on the Elimination of Racial Discrimination (CERD) and the Committee on the Elimination of Discrimination Against Women, individual communications relating to violations can be received. Under ICERD, the Committee can make "suggestions and recommendations" to State parties (Article 14(7)(b)), whilst under the Optional Protocol to CEDAW, the Committee can transmit its "views" and "recommendations" to the parties concerned (Article 7(3)).

Although it is difficult to categorise the exact legal nature of these procedures, the decisions on individual communications provide guidance on the interpretation and application of the conventions. As such, they are referred to in various chapters of this book. For instance, chapter three analyses the decisions of several committees in order to identify their approach to indirect discrimination. In addition, some committees have adopted the practice of issuing general comments or recommendations. These aim to clarify the approach of the committee to the interpretation of specific provisions in the convention or to highlight key issues relevant to the convention's implementation. Chapter one, for example, refers to General Recommendation No. 8 by CERD on "identification with a particular racial or ethnic group".

Finally, it should be mentioned that other international sources can have persuasive value in shaping domestic law on non-discrimination. Chapter eight draws attention to the "Paris Principles" on human rights bodies (adopted by the UN General Assembly) and the benchmarking role they play in relation to national equality bodies.

4.2. NON-DISCRIMINATION AND THE COUNCIL OF EUROPE

Given the European focus of this book, the legal instruments of the Council of Europe are particularly important. All EU states are also members of the Council of Europe. Moreover, the ECJ regularly refers to the treaties and case-law of the Council of Europe, especially that of the European Court of Human Rights. As with the UN, the Council of Europe has both general and specialised instruments of relevance to non-discrimination law.

---

[17] Available on the UN website.

9

Beginning with general instruments, there are two core human rights treaties belonging to the Council of Europe. The first, and most famous, is the European Convention on Human Rights (ECHR). Article 14 of the ECHR provides:

> "The enjoyment of the rights and freedoms set forth in this Convention shall be secured without discrimination on any ground such as sex, race, colour, language, religion, political or other opinion, national or social origin, association with a national minority, property, birth or other status".

The Convention also created the European Court of Human Rights (ECtHR). This court can receive individual complaints and issue legally binding decisions. Indeed, there is a substantial body of case-law under Article 14, which is referred to in most of the chapters of this book.[18]

The sister convention to the ECHR is the European Social Charter (ESC). This was first signed in 1961 and then substantially revised in 1996. Reference to non-discrimination can be found in both the original ESC and the Revised ESC, but with greater clarity in the latter. Article E of the 1996 Revised ESC states:

> "The enjoyment of the rights set forth in this Charter shall be secured without discrimination on any ground such as race, colour, sex, language, religion, political or other opinion, national extraction or social origin, health, association with a national minority, birth or other status."

Implementation of the ESC is monitored by the European Committee on Social Rights (ECSR). Although called a Committee, the Rules of the ECSR make it clear that its task is "to make a legal assessment of the conformity of national situations with the European Social Charter" (Rule 2(1)). For this reason, the Committee views itself as a quasi-judicial body, although this assessment has been questioned by some commentators.[19] Akin to the UN Treaty bodies, the Committee receives periodic national reports and it issues "conclusions" on state compliance with the ESC. A highly distinct feature of the ESC is the possibility for "collective complaints". Three types of organisation have the right to lodge complaints:

— international organisations of employers and trade unions;
— international NGOs with consultative status at the Council of Europe;
— "representative national organisations of employers and trade unions within the jurisdiction of the Contracting Party against which they have lodged a complaint".[20]

---

[18] It should be noted that a free-standing right to non-discrimination is provided under Protocol 12 to the ECHR, which has been in force since 1 April 2005. At the time of writing, this has only been ratified by 14 states.

[19] P. Alston, "Assessing the Strengths and Weaknesses of the European Social Charter's Supervisory System" in G. de Búrca and B. de Witte (eds.), *Social Rights in Europe* (Oxford, Oxford University Press, 2005) 59.

[20] Art. 1, Additional Protocol to the European Social Charter providing for a system of collective complaints, Council of Europe Treaty Series No. 158.

Fourteen states have so far ratified or accepted by declaration the Collective Complaints Protocol. The ECSR issues "decisions" on collective complaints and monitors state compliance with the decision through the ongoing national reporting procedure. The Committee's decisions on collective complaints are assuming an increasing importance in the field of non-discrimination law. For example, several chapters in this book mention the Committee's decision in *Autism-Europe* v. *France*,[21] where it found a breach of Article E of the Revised ESC in France's provision of education to people with autism.

Beyond the ECHR and the ESC, the Council of Europe also possesses some specialised instruments and bodies whose work relates to discrimination. The European Commission on Racism and Intolerance (ECRI) is an expert advisory committee established in 1994 to strengthen the work of the Council of Europe on combating racism. Amongst its activities, it issues "general policy recommendations" to Member States of the Council of Europe. Although not legally binding, these have persuasive value and are mentioned in several chapters in this book. For example, in chapter eight, Gay Moon discusses Recommendation No. 2 on "specialised bodies to combat racism, xenophobia, anti-semitism and intolerance at national level". Finally, another relevant Council of Europe instrument is the 1994 Framework Convention for the Protection of National Minorities, which is monitored by the Advisory Committee. As its title indicates, this Convention lays down a framework of principles on national minorities, rather than individual rights. Indeed, there is no individual complaint procedure linked to this Convention.

4.3. THE EC DIRECTIVES ON NON-DISCRIMINATION

EC legislation on non-discrimination has built up in a piecemeal fashion since a series of gender equality Directives were adopted in the 1970s. Recent years have witnessed a process of extension and consolidation of the legislative framework, following the new legal base of Article 13, inserted in the EC Treaty in 1999. There are now four Directives which are the core of EC non-discrimination legislation. In turn, these core Directives play a large part in shaping the content of national non-discrimination legislation within the 27 Member States. Each is briefly presented below and a more detailed table of comparison is provided in the Annex.

THE RACIAL EQUALITY DIRECTIVE[22]

This Directive prohibits discrimination on grounds of racial or ethnic origin in employment, vocational training, education, social protection, social advantages, and

---

[21] Complaint No. 13/2002, 4 November 2003.
[22] Directive 2000/43/EC of 29 June 2000 implementing the principle of equal treatment between persons irrespective of racial or ethnic origin [2000] OJ L180/22.

access to goods and services, including housing. The deadline for implementation of the Directive expired in 2003.

THE EMPLOYMENT EQUALITY DIRECTIVE[23]

This Directive prohibits discrimination on grounds of religion or belief, disability, age and sexual orientation, but only in respect of employment and vocational training. The deadline for implementation of the Directive expired in 2003, but states had the possibility to extend the implementation period in respect of disability and age until 2006.

THE GENDER EMPLOYMENT DIRECTIVE

Discrimination on grounds of sex in employment and vocational training was first prohibited in Directive 76/207,[24] often referred to as the Equal Treatment Directive. In 2002, this was substantially amended in order to codify some of the case-law of the ECJ and to incorporate many of the new elements found in the Racial Equality and Employment Equality Directives.[25] Despite the 2002 amendments, the legal provisions relating to sex discrimination in employment, vocational training and social security remained scattered over several different Directives. This gave rise to the 2006 Recast Gender Employment Directive,[26] which consolidates the gender equality legislation. Therefore, at the time of writing, Directive 76/207 (as amended) remains the principal piece of legislation on gender equality in employment. This will be repealed on 15 August 2009 and replaced by the Recast Directive.[27] In order to provide the most current information to readers, this book refers to both the gender equality legislation currently in force and the relevant provisions of the Recast Directive.

[23] Directive 2000/78/EC establishing a general framework for equal treatment in employment and occupation [2000] OJ L303/16.

[24] [1976] OJ L39/40.

[25] Directive 2002/73/EC of the European Parliament and of the Council of 23 September 2002 amending Directive 76/207/EEC on the implementation of the principle of equal treatment for men and women as regards access to employment, vocational training and promotion, and working conditions [2002] OJ L269/15.

[26] Directive 2006/54/EC of the European Parliament and of the Council of 5 July 2006 on the implementation of the principle of equal opportunities and equal treatment of men and women in matters of employment and occupation (recast) [2006] OJ L204/23.

[27] Art. 34, *ibid.*

THE GENDER GOODS AND SERVICES DIRECTIVE[28]

This Directive forbids discrimination on grounds of sex in access to and supply of goods and services. The deadline for implementation of the Directive will expire on 21 December 2007. Its provisions will not be affected by the Recast Directive.

5.   COMPARATIVE NON-DISCRIMINATION LAW

As has been said, this book has comparative aspirations. This is particularly difficult in a field such as non-discrimination law. While other more established fields of law, such as contract law or tort law, may be considered as serving as a mere regulatory backdrop for (economic) activities which the law does not aspire to change,[29] or as a necessary compound of any legal order,[30] nobody would regard non-discrimination law similarly. Many doubt whether non-discrimination law is necessary, at least when it goes beyond the narrow confines of constitutional provisions that only apply to state–citizen relations.[31] In addition, non-discrimination law aspires to model social reality. Of course, everyone is aware of the fact that such modelling is never straightforward. Accordingly, concepts of non-discrimination law can never be analysed under legal perspectives only. Comparison

---

[28] Directive 2004/113/EC of 13 December 2004 implementing the principle of equal treatment between men and women in the access to and supply of goods and services [2004] OJ L373/37.

[29] See, e.g. K Zweigert and H Kötz, *Einführung in die Rechtsvergleichung* (Tübingen, Mohr, 3rd edn, 1996) 39, characterising civil law as a "vergleichsweise 'unpolitisches'" (comparatively unpolitical) subject. The same authors acknowledge in the same volume that contract law conveys fundamental political decisions, such as a enshrining as legally binding the political messages of liberalism instead of socialism (see *ibid.*, at 315–17).

[30] The Ius Commune Casebook on *Tort Law* (eds. W. van Gerven, P. Larouche and J. Lever), for example, starts its General Introduction with the following statement: "Persons living together in society are almost bound on occasions to cause each other harm . . . the law of tort is concerned with the prevention of such harm . . . and with the allocation of losses."

[31] These doubts are most serious in Germany, where the implementation of the Directives into fields of law outside employment was so controversial as to delay the implementation process for three years. See, e.g. J. Pickert, "Antidiskriminierungsprogramme im freiheitlichen Privatrecht" in Lorenz (ed.), *Haftung wegen Diskriminierung wegen derzeitigem und zukünftigem Recht, Karlsruher Forum 2004* (Karlsruhe, 2005) 100.

[32] Some of the most prominent comparative lawyers of the past and the present wished this requirement applied to any instance of comparative law (see, e.g. O. Kahn-Freund, "On Uses and Misuses of Comparative Law" (1974) 37 *MLR* 1, 27: "The use of comparative law for practical purposes becomes an abuse . . . if it . . . ignores (the) context of the law"; or M.-A. Glendon, M. Wallace Gordon and C. Osakwe, *Comparative Legal Traditions* (St Paul, MN, West Publishing Company, 1985) 8 ("Ideally, a comparatist should have a grasp of history, law, economics and sociology as well as the necessary foreign language abilities"). However, when it comes to comparing traditional areas of law, such as contract law, between the Member States of the EU that are rather similar as regards degree of industrialisation and cultural orientation, less caution towards an integrated socio-economic and legal study of law applies: K. Zweigert and H. Kötz, *Introduction to Comparative Law*, 3rd edn (translated by T. Weir) (Oxford, Clarendon Press, 1998) 39–40 ("in unpolitical" areas of law a praesumptio similitudinis applies which allows for a rather simple heuristic principle"). It seems no coincidence too that comparative lawyers who demand that comparative law is an interdisciplinary subject generally have a background in one of the areas of law that attain to shape society, e.g. labour law, family law or criminal law.

between political, economic and social backgrounds is essential in order to understand and assess the legal concepts.[32] This again means that comparison of non-discrimination laws not only entails analysis of different fields of law but also requires integration of comparative approaches from other disciplines, most notably political science and sociology, but also economic approaches to reasons for and the persistence of inequality and exclusion.

This book does not achieve all of this. Instead, we use this introduction to give some background to the more detailed comparisons undertaken in the course of the book. For this overview, we will group the Member States.[33] While the traditional division between common law on the one hand and civil law on the other hand is not necessarily an indicator of a common development,[34] this rough grouping seems suited to the field of non-discrimination law. As the common law countries have a much longer tradition in non-discrimination law than most of the civil law countries, their specific legal culture may well colour the field. Besides distinguishing between common and civil law countries, we will dedicate special attention to the Dutch legal order, which, although belonging among the civil law countries, has established non-discrimination law prior to and independent from EU pressure, and to the Nordic countries, which have built up an acknowledged body of (gender) equality law independently from the EU. A full account of non-discrimination law in Member States that have acceded to the EU since 2004 seems premature. While we have been able to present a large number of cases and materials from these Member States in the single chapters, we have not attempted to group them into one family of non-discrimination law regimes.

5.1.   COMMON LAW COUNTRIES

It is no secret that the EC Non-discrimination Directives have been inspired by the ECJ case-law in gender equality issues[35] and free movement of persons.[36] Furthermore, since UK models have inspired EC gender equality legislation, EC non-discrimination law is often aligned to an Anglo-American model of law and legislation.[37] In addition, one has to consider that these Directives were inter alia the

---

[33] On the often criticised concept of families of law, see R. David and J. Brierly, *Major Legal Systems in the World Today. An Introduction to the Comparative Study of Law*, 3rd edn (London, Steens & Sons, 1985); E. Örücü, "Family Trees for Legal Systems: Towards a Contemporary Approach" in M. von Hoecke, *Epistemology and Methodology of Comparative Law* (Oxford, Hart, 2004) 359–75.

[34] See M. MacEwen, "Promoting Equal Opportunity: the Enforcement Agency" in *Ibid.* (ed.), *Anti-Discrimination Law Enforcement. Comparative Approaches* (Aldershot, Ashgate, 1997) 1–15, 1.

[35] See S. Parmar, "The European Court of Justice and Anti-Discrimination Law: Some reflections on the Experience in Gender Equality Jurisprudence for the Future Interpretation of the Racial Equality Directive" in J. Niessen and I. Chopin (eds.), *The Development of Legal Instruments to Combat Racism in a Diverse Europe* (The Hague, Martinus Nijhoff, 2004) 131–54, at 133–7.

[36] See A. Tyson, "The Negotiation of the European Community Directive on Racial Discrimination" in J. Niessen and I. Chopin (eds.), *The Development of Legal Instruments to Combat Racism in a Diverse Europe* (The Hague, Martinus Nijhoff, 2004) 111–30 at 115, with reference to the *O'Flynn* case.

[37] Especially Directive 2000/43/EC has been characterised as "remarkable example of direct legal transplantation": B. Hepple, "Race and Law in Fortress Europe" (2004) 67 *MLR* 1, at 3.

result of intense lobbying of the Starting Line Group,[38] which exercised a decisive influence on the final wording of the "non-discrimination" legislative package.[39] This group is said to have been dominated by Anglo-Dutch intellectual influences.[40] Thus, the model behind the EC non-discrimination Directives emerged against a background of experience with UK and (partly) Dutch non-discrimination law, making the common law countries' conceptions of the field the most prominent influence.

While there are huge differences between legal orders with a longstanding tradition in civil rights and anti-discrimination law, such as the USA, Canada, Australia and the UK, and (more recently) also Ireland, these countries share many features of their approach to non-discrimination law. The foremost commonality is their shared heritage of being common law countries. Smits has found a nice heading for one of the most striking characteristics of the common law: "The Absence of Systemati-sation, or a Desire Thereof".[41] Nevertheless, under the same heading, he duly reports several trends towards systematisation in England as the main common law country. Still, this trait is noticeable and does influence legislative policy. Politicians in common law countries are less inclined to follow systemic approaches when implementing legislation in new policy areas. This makes it easy for them to respond to specific challenges, as well as to keep the resulting legislation from seriously permeating the deep layers of law. It also alleviates adopting wide-ranging exceptions from principles that are otherwise considered as fundamental. For example, UK legislation had provided for an authorisation to discriminate on grounds of sex in any insurance classification because such discrimination had been usual in the trade. It had also provided for small premises exceptions in favour of landlords who did not wish to rent to those considered as belonging to ethnic minorities. Another typical trait of common law non-discrimination law is that it develops ground by ground, as the political pressure demands, and that rulings accepted for one ground, e.g. "race", are not necessarily regarded as binding for another ground, e.g. gender. In most common law countries, legislation on non-discrimination is still ground specific, which results in a patchwork character of law. Remarkably, Irish legislation has been combined into two multi-ground Acts, starting with the Employment Equality Act

---

[38] This lobbying group had been founded in the late 1980s as a coalition of the British Commission for Racial Equality, the Dutch national office against racism and the "Churches Commission for Migrants in Europe". It was based in Brussels and comprised more than 400 NGOs in 1999. In 1993, it issued its first proposal for a directive against racial discrimination. At this time, the membership comprised Barbara John (then City of Berlin's officer for foreign citizens) and the Belgian Centre for equal opportunities and against racism, as well as several organisations with their base in Brussels (inter alia Caritas Europe, The Jewish Information Centre and the Migrants Forum). For a detailed report see I. Chopin, "The Starting Line Group: A Harmonised Approach to Fight Racism and to Promote Equal Treatment" [1999] *EJML* 111.

[39] Tyson, above *n.* 36, 111.

[40] A. Geddes and V. Guiraudon, "Britain France and EU Anti-Discrimination Policy: The Emergence of an EU Policy Paradigm" (2004) 27 *West European Politics* 334, at 340–4.

[41] J. Smits, *The Making of European Private Law: Towards a Jus Commune Europaeum as a Mixed Legal System* (Antwerp *et al*, Intersentia, 2002) 88. Of course, characterising this legal tradition in a few lines is bound to miss many important details. For the purposes of this article, this condensed approach is sufficient.

1998 and continuing with the Equal Status Act 2000 covering non-employment discrimination.[42]

From a socio-economic perspective, the relatively pronounced position of non-discrimination law in the common law countries can be attributed to two different reasons, namely the heightened public awareness of diversity, above all ethnic diversity, and the absence of welfarist traditions. The heightened awareness of diversity is rooted in the fact that most of these countries have a relatively high proportion of non-white population, often summarised under the term "ethnic minorities". In the US and Canada, these comprise native Americans or Canadians, who have been submitted to colonisation, as well as descendants of former slaves.[43] In the US, Canada and the UK, the non-white population has grown with immigration, often from former colonies. This is, however, not the only reason. There are Continental countries with a colonial past, e.g. France and Spain, where awareness of diversity is less developed and a general preference for acculturation of minorities prevails. The common law countries have, even in their relations with former colonies, leaned towards a policy style of tolerating difference. Over time, they have actively promoted a multiculturalist approach, according to which different minorities are perceived as communities with specific agents and cultural notions in their own right.[44] While there is less of a welfare state tradition in these countries than in Continental European countries, there has been a civil rights movement, or its equivalent, within which these minorities claimed their rights of substantive equality. Non-discrimination legislation was one of the answers to these demands.[45] Again, Ireland is a special case, as this country only began to experience a significant influx of immigration since 1996 and has no significant colonial past. It does, though, include an internal ethnic minority referred to as the Traveller Community. When immigration became more relevant and ethnic diversity increased, the country turned towards comprehensive equality legislation instead of welfarist measures to ease upcoming tensions.[46]

Within the framework of judicial and doctrinal exchange between Commonwealth countries, common traits in non-discrimination law evolved. Development was incremental and has been characterised as involving four generations of equality

---

[42] O. Smith, "Ireland's Multiple Ground Anti-Discrimination Framework—Extending the Limitations?" (2005) 8 *IJDL* 7, at 8 with further references.

[43] See, e.g. N. Foner, *In a New Land. A Comparative View of Immigration* (New York, New York University Press, 2005) ch. 9, at 206–24 with further references.

[44] See R. Koopmans, "Partizipation der Migranten, Staatsbürgerschaft und Demokratie: nationale und locale Perspektiven" in M. Pöhl and H. Hartmanns (eds.), *Strategien der Integration* (Berlin, Bertelsmann Stiftung, 2001) 103–11. On negative repercussions of multi-culturalism see F. Glastra, P. Schedler and E. Katz, "Multiculturalism with a Price Tag: On the Theory and Practice of Intercultural Management in the Netherlands" in C. Agocs (ed.), *Work Place Equality. International Perspectives on Legislation, Policy and Practice* (The Hague, Kluwer Law International, 2002) 181–99. It should be noted, however, that the multiculturalist model has been highly debated in recent years within the UK.

[45] On the background of race, sex and disability discrimination law in the UK, see M. Connolly, *Townshend Smith on Discrimination Law: Text, Cases and Materials* (London, Cavendish, 2nd edn, 2004) 3–33, 35–73, 75–9.

[46] See Smith, above n. 42.

law.[47] For the UK, the Race Relations Act 1965 represents the first generation, answering demands for equality by installing special authorities endowed with powers to challenge discriminatory practices. Only the second generation of legislation, modelled upon the Civil Rights Act in the US, empowered individuals to present claims (Race Relations Act 1968, Sex Discrimination Act 1975). The third generation of equality law includes affirmative action in the US and Northern Ireland as well as in Canada and Australia, but only more powers for equality Commissions in the UK, where legislation and case-law were increasingly influenced by EU developments. The fourth generation is said to consist of positive duties on public authorities, employment and pay equity plans, as well as contract compliance regimes. The stress is more on positive obligations than on negative prohibitions.[48]

5.2.   CIVIL LAW COUNTRIES IN EUROPE

As regards Member States from Continental Europe, there is a different history of non-discrimination law from a purely legal perspective as well as from a socio-political perspective.

As regards the general style of the civil law countries, this is usually characterised as more systemic, again in the suggestive headings by Smits: "Systematisation and the Programmatic Desire Thereof".[49] This trait corresponds with a principled approach to the legal system as such, which tends to reject a partitioning of the law, which results from stressing single policy areas, such as non-discrimination, at the expense of others issues, such as, for example, freedom of speech. Another characteristic of civil law jurisdictions is the division of the body of law into two main categories of public and private law.[50] Although this distinction cannot be upheld in "modern" areas of law such as employment law, it is still at the heart of the legal system, making the civil law proper especially resistant to change in some Member States. These structures are influential in the area of non-discrimination law and one of the sources of difficulty to implement the Anglo-American approach.

On a principled level, the civil law countries should experience much fewer difficulties in implementing non-discrimination law than the high number of infringement procedures against these countries[51] seems to indicate. After all, the

---

[47] B. Hepple, M. Coussey, and T. Choudhury (eds.), *Equality: A New Framework. Report of the Independent Review of the Enforcement of UK Anti-Discrimination Legislation* (Oxford, Hart, 2000) 6 with further references.

[48] See Hepple, *above n.* 37, 8–13; J. Shaw "Mainstreaming Equality and Diversity in European Union Law and Politics" (2005) 58 *Current Legal Problems* 255–312.

[49] Smits, *above n.* 41, 79.

[50] Glendon *et al, above n.* 32, 256, stressing the fundamental quality of this schism, and 265, stressing that private law is considered much more resistant to being politically influenced. "The law of the Civil Code is the area of the law where the function of government is limited to the recognition and enforcement of private rights."

[51] The ECJ has decided quite a few cases where the European Commission has initiated proceedings for non-compliance by Member States who have not or not completely implemented Directive 2000/43/EC (see

principle of equality is one of the most prominent principles of Continental constitutional law since the French revolution. Thus, non-discrimination is considered a very important principle of law and part of all Continental constitutions.[52]

This has not, however, led to legal provisions outlawing contractual discrimination in countries such as Germany or France. On the contrary, relegating non-discrimination law to the constitution and thus to public law has enabled courts in civil law countries to not apply fundamental principles such as non-discrimination and equality in the realm of private law, i.e. in areas such as contract law, employment law and insurance law. In particular, in Germany, France and Belgium there are still academics who argue that non-discrimination law and freedom of contract are irreconcilable antonyms.[53] It has been demonstrated in more detail elsewhere that this is in fact not the case. On the contrary, integrating non-discrimination among the principles of contract law seems a logical development following the substantive turn in theories of freedom of contract.[54] If, following the inadequate conservative view, non-discrimination as a principle remains contained within the realm of citizen–state relations, this has severe consequences. For example, access to credit facilities, housing or work can legally be denied on terms that are directly or indirectly discriminating on grounds of race, religion, disability and even gender.[55] The need to implement EC Directives on equal treatment of women and men in employment contributed to a "common-law-like" fragmentation of the law. Employment law regimes now prohibited one form of discrimination but did not address others, while the same forms of discrimination were legitimised in any (other) field of contract law.

Generally, and prior to implementing Community law on sex discrimination, the elevated position of equality and non-discrimination as constitutional principles led some Continental states to implement their international law obligations via criminal

---

Cases C–326/04 *Commission* v. *Greece* [2004] OJ C239/7; C–327/05 *Commission* v. *Finland* [2005] OJ C239/7; C–335/04 *Commission* v. *Austria* [2005] OJ C171/5; C–320/04 *Commission* v. *Luxembourg* [2005] OJ C93/2; C–329/04 *Commission* v. *Germany* [2005] OJ C143/13). While possibly important to convince Member States to complete implementation, these judgments' contents are not spectacular, and publication in the European Court Reports is not envisaged.

[52] See Johanssen, in Niessen and Chopin, above n. 36, 156 –7, in relation to racial discrimination. The implementation reports of the modern day network of experts on non-discrimination place less emphasis on the relevance of the constitutional provisions

[53] Pickert, *above n.* 31; J.M. Binon, "Le Principe d'égalité de traitement en droit européen et ses applications à l'assurance: obligation morale ou croisade idéologique?" in C. van Schoubroek and H. Cousy (eds.) *Discriminatie in verzekering,* 7e Internationaal Colloquium Europees Verzekeringsrecht 2007, at 5.

[54] See extensively, D. Schiek, *Differenzierte Gerechtigkeit—Diskriminierungsschutz und Vertragsrecht,* 2000, at 428–55; see also D. Schiek, "Broadening the Scope and the Norms of EU Gender Equality Law: Towards a Multidimensional Conception of Equality Law" (2005) 12 *MJ* 427, at 433–6. This view is shared, inter alia, by R. Nielssen, *Gender Equality in European Contract Law* (Copenhagen, DØJF, 2004) 115 and C.W. Canaris, "Drittwirkung der gemeinschaftsrechtlichen Grundfreiheiten", in Bauer *et al.* (Hrsg) *Umwelt, Wirtschaft und Recht,* Wissenschaftliches Symposium aus Anlass des 65. Geburtstages von Reiner Schmidt, 16–17 November (2002) 29, at 46 with note 61.

[55] For a defence of constitutionalising European contract law while retaining discrimination at will as one of its principles, see O. Cherednychenko, "EU Fundamental Rights EC Fundamental Freedoms and Private law" (2006) 14 *ERPL* 23, at 41–3, referring to fundamental freedoms and the inherent prohibition to discriminate on grounds of nationality.

law rather than via civil law. Such an approach, while leading to a profound moral statement on discrimination, is not capable of addressing discriminatory business practices. These are often not based on deliberate discrimination, but rather are a consequence of usage and practice being based on institutionalised racism, (dis)abilism or sexism. Thus, the unbelieving statement of a British author that "the French dislike the idea that they could possibly be racist"[56] is partly due to a principled approach to discrimination, which aligns any discriminatory practice with unconstitutional and even criminal behaviour.

This principled approach of civil law countries thus proved less than helpful in pursuing wider socio-economic aims, such as equality or equal opportunities in fact, through the law. This would have required exposing unconscious forms of discrimination, which are by definition outside the reach of criminal law provisions. The common law countries experienced fewer barriers in their legal cultures to addressing these forms of discrimination. The innocent use of criteria resulting in disparate impact due to entrenched social discrimination was tackled by concepts such as the prohibition of indirect discrimination and shifting the burden of proof (third generation legislation), while fourth generation legislation attempts to tackle institutional discrimination. Experience in implementing EU gender equality law suggests that such concepts are not easily transplanted to some civil law countries. As regards indirect discrimination, French courts are especially notorious for misapplying this concept;[57] and similar statements can be made as regards burden of proof.[58]

This reluctance is, however, not only due to legal styles in civil law countries. As mentioned above in relation to common law countries, the approach towards diversity in society is a second decisive variable. Such an approach tends to be predominantly governed by the approach towards minorities, predominantly ethnic minorities.[59] Here, migration research and racial and ethnic studies recount endless evidence of deeply opposed cultures between the Anglo-American world and Continental Europe. In the former, immigration was cherished as a part of one's history and—whether influx resulted from the colonial past or more recent economic success—the resulting diversity of the population was gradually accepted over the years. In contrast, in Continental Europe there was and is a tendency to denounce a history of migration which has been typical for most of these countries.[60] The

---

[56] A. Dummet, "Implementing European Anti-discrimination Law: A Critical Perspective" in Niessen and Chopin, above n. 36, 235–53, at 240.

[57] See, e.g. C. Wallace, "European Integration and Legal Culture: Indirect Sex Discrimination in the French Legal System" (1999) 19 *Legal Studies* 398; K. Berthou, "New Hopes for French Anti-Discrimination Law" (2003) 19 *IJCLLIR* 109, at 110, 117–18.

[58] Berthou, *above n.* 57, 116.

[59] On a new approach, under which minorities encompass "national" (i.e. ethnic, religious and linguistic), political and social minorities, the latter comprising those with minority sexual orientations, see G. Sasse and E. Thielemann, "A Research Agenda for the Study of Migrants and Minorities in Europe" (2005) 43 *JCMS* 655.

[60] See Foner, above n. 43, ch. 9, at 208–12. For an overview of nineteenth- and twentieth-century migration flows into Europe, which resulted in the concept of ethnicity being profoundly artificial, see J. Marko, *Autonomie und Integration* (Wien, Böhlau, 1995) 225–89.

resulting ideology was that of national unity, which proved hostile to acknowledging claims to diversity. Under this ideology, measures stressing that specific groups of the population were to be targeted as primary beneficiaries of equality policies were difficult to justify. This is taken as the reason for a certain reluctance to accept the new non-discrimination law framework.[61] The reluctance is especially strong in France, where the republican ideal of citizenship is, on the one hand, accused of requiring assimilation as a prerequisite of integration and, on the other, praised for refraining from ethnically grounded versions of citizenship.[62] This principle is nicely encompassed in this quotation:[63]

> ". . . (R)epublicanism as a foundational political theory . . . represents the founding principles of the Republic, whereby the individual relates to the state unmediated by other corporate bodies . . . Consequently, the state finds itself 'at once intolerant of constituted groups and inclusive of their constituent members as individuals', leading to an assimilationist model of citizenship, which continues to resonate in French politics and society . . . While the Republic may not have sought officially to eliminate diverse ethnic cultural traditions, the politicization of identities was prohibited . . . The precondition for full citizenship for migrants thus is individual assimilation into a way of life, and *any* individual *in theory* should be capable of full membership upon assimilation, thereby differentiating the French republican ideal from an ethnic model of citizenship. This provides the justification for the refusal to recognize any racial or ethnic differentiation as the basis for group-based political claims . . . (R)epublicanism depends upon a belief in citizenship as a national project in which individuals *in fact* will transcend their particular affiliations, towards full and foundational membership in a wider community of citizens . . . Individuals, but not communities, are the bearers of rights . . . Republicanism thus provides the ideological basis for resistance to any claims to difference, which are constructed as contrary to the Republic itself . . ."

The legal-normative foundation for French anti-discrimination law is the constitutional principle of equality, developed historically from the 1789 Declaration on the rights of man and the citizen.[64] Moreover, the universal principle of the equality of all citizens underpins the constitutional ideology of the French Republic.[65] Article 1 of the 1958 Constitution states:

> "France guarantees equality before the law to all citizens without distinction based on origin, race or religion. She respects all beliefs."[66]

---

[61] A. Geddes and V. Guiraudaon, "Britain, France and EU Anti-Discrimination Policy: The Emergence of an EU Policy Paradigm" (2004) 27 *West European Politics* 334.

[62] See, on the example of gay and lesbian rights, C.F. Stychin, "Civil Solidarity of Fragmented Identities? The Politics of Sexuality and Citizenship in France" (2001) 10 *Social & Legal Studies* 347, at 352–4.

[63] *Ibid.*, at 352–3.

[64] D Borrillo, "Les instruments juridiques français et européens dans la mise en place du principe d'égalité et de non-discrimination" [2002] *Revue français des affaires sociales* 113.

[65] S Latraverse, "Report on Measures to Combat Discrimination: Directive 2000/43/EC and 2000/78/EC. Country Report France" (European Commission, 2005) 3, available on the website of Directorate-General for Employment, Social Affairs and Equal Opportunities.

[66] Translation by S Latraverse, *ibid.*

Although bearing imprints of the Aristotelian model (see below), this legal framework is distinguished from it by a stronger emphasis on equality as the sameness of treatment.[67] For this book, the French reluctance to install any legislation that is modelled upon diversity models is mirrored in most chapters. Many have had difficulties finding illustrative material from France.

5.3.   SPECIAL CASE: THE NETHERLANDS

There is, however, a remarkable exception to the rule: the Netherlands as a civil law country had developed a profound body of non-discrimination legislation prior to and independent of inspirations from the EU. This cannot be due to the fact that the general legal style in this country diverges from what was said above. The reasons are to be sought in the socio-political approach towards equality and discrimination.

The situation is also exceptional insofar as there has been an all-encompassing non-discrimination act since 1994. Initially, the implementation of Community gender equality had been hesitant. However, there seems to be a tendency to define openness to trade, ideas and persons as central to being Dutch within the official discourse. Against the predominance of a rather conservative family ideal and corresponding demands on women, and aided by an active women's movement, this led to implementation of gender equality legislation in the 1970s.[68] As regards the position towards minorities, the Dutch are said to have established a positive position towards diversity and non-discrimination.[69] Without any Community pressure, in 1994 the General Equal Treatment Act (*Algemeen Wet Gelijke Behandeling*) was adopted, not only prohibiting discrimination on most grounds comprising the EC non-discrimination Directives, but also within many areas which are covered by Directive 2000/43/EC.[70] For the implementation of Directive 2000/78/EC, special legislation on disability and age discrimination was needed.[71] The General Equal Treatment Act also established an Equal Treatment Commission, whose tasks encompass quasi-judicial activities. Although its *"oordeelen"* (literally "judgements", officially translated as "opinions") are not considered as legally binding, they enjoy a high authority and are followed in most cases.

A specific feature of the Dutch legislative tradition has endured beyond the advent of the new Community legislation. Possibly due to the tendency to avoid conflict, Dutch law does not prohibit discrimination, but rather prohibits distinction.[72] The

[67] E Dockès, "Equality in Labour Law: an Economically Efficient Human Right? Reflections from a French law Perspective" (2002) 18 *IJCLLIR* 187, at 189.

[68] A. van der Vleuten, "Pincers and Prestige: Explaining the Implementation of EU Gender Equality Legislation" (2005) 3 *Comparative European Politics* 464, at 467.

[69] F. Glastra, P. Schedler and E. Kats, "Between Public Controversy and Market Initiative: The Politics of Employment Equity and Diversity in the Netherlands" in Agocs, *above n.* 44, 165–79.

[70] See S. Burri and F. Dorssemont, "The Transposition of the Race Directive (2000/43/EC) and the Framework Directive on Equal Treatment in Employment (2000/78/EC) into Dutch and Belgian Law" (2005) 21 *IJCLLIR* 537, at 542–4.

[71] *Ibid.*, at 548.

[72] See Gijzen, *above n.* 10, 39–41.

reason behind this peculiar choice is the assumption that there should be a difference in wording between criminal and civil law, and that the use of distinction lowers the threshold towards asking for advice or bringing cases before the Equal Treatment Commission. This specific trait is, however, criticised as distinctions may be easier to justify than discrimination.[73]

Thus we find that civil law countries need not necessarily be reluctant to implement non-discrimination law. We also find that, if they do, non-discrimination attains a more prominent place in the juridical discourse than is the case for the other Member States.

5.4.   NORDIC MEMBER STATES

While the Nordic states, comprising Scandinavia in the geographic sense plus Denmark and Iceland, are often grouped as part of the civil law family,[74] within a European comparison it is certainly justified to treat them as a specific subsystem.[75] These countries are considered to be less inclined towards highly abstract general rules than the other civil law countries, stressing reasonableness and realism instead,[76] with "Scandinavian Realism" being the corresponding school in legal theory.[77] Nordic law does not rely on case-law methodology either. Instead, it is characterised as being based on usage and custom.[78] It thus shares a more pragmatic and unorthodox approach to law and its application with Common Law countries, while its jurists tend to develop principles from a teleological reasoning similar to their colleagues in Civil Law countries.[79] In addition, law evolves through social institutions to a much greater extent than on the continent, with collective bargaining being of utmost importance in areas where it lost its influence on the continent long ago.[80] Also, the system of ombudsmen has a special tradition in the

---

[73] R. Holtmaat, "Stop de Inflatie van het Discriminatiebegrip! Een pleidooi voor het maken van onderscheid tussen discriminatie and ongelijke behandeling" (2003) 25 *Nederlandes Juristenbladet* 1266, at 1268.

[74] See R. David, *Les Grand Systemes de droit comparé* (English edition, 1985) 53, distinguishing between the Romanistic–German family, which includes Nordic law, the common law family, the socialist law family and a loosely knit group of other systems, and Glendon *et al*, *above n.* 32, who just cover civil law, common law and socialist law, while not precisely answering the question whether Nordic law is included under civil law or not.

[75] See Zweigert and Kötz, above n. 32, 73; albeit as a subgroup of civil law systems alongside the Franco-Roman and German families of law (*ibid.*, 277).

[76] *Ibid.*, 281.

[77] See H.P. Graver, "Law, Justice and the State: Nordic Perspectives" in Karlsson and Jónsson (eds.), *Law, Justice and the State IV* (Stuttgart, Franz Steiner publishers, 1995) 23–27.

[78] L.B. Orfield, *The Growth of Scandinavian Law* (Philadelphia, PA, University of Pennsylvania Press, 1953) ix.

[79] L. Gustavsson, *Business Laws in Nordic Countries* (The Hague, Kluwer International, 1995) consequently considers placing Nordic law between Common Law and Civil Law (at 33).

[80] On the significance of collective agreements for Scandinavian Labour Law see R. Fahlbeck, "Industrial Relations and Collective Labour Law: Characteristics, Principles and Basic features" in P. Wahlgreen (ed.), *Stability and Change in Nordic Labour Law (2002)* 43 *Scandinavian Studies in Law* 87.

Nordic Member States, even outside non-discrimination law. This is an institution to which complaints may be directed and, if need be, it can raise a claim against a non-complying institution of its own motion without the need to expose the complainant. It has had a secure position in Scandinavian consumer law since 1971.[81] Thus, implementing the obligations of creating an independent body under Directives 2000/43/EC, 2002/73/EC and 2004/113/EC, the Nordic states can rely on existing institutions.

As regards non-discrimination law, today's Nordic Member States of the EU (Denmark, Sweden and Finland) show some marked similarities, which are due not only to a shared legal legacy, but also to socio-economic similarities. Apart from a minority of Laps living in Sweden and Finland, all of these countries have experienced ethnic diversity only at a relatively late point in their history, with considerable immigration starting only in the 1980s.[82] Secondly, all of these countries have a relatively active women's movement, with Iceland being the prime example as having had a feminist party within the Parliament since 1980.[83] Accordingly, equality legislation (this being the Nordic term for gender equality law) developed rather early and independently of the EU, Denmark being the exception in this respect.[84] The strong impetus to gender equality[85] corresponds to the high level of female participation in employment, which is even more remarkable as in all these countries industrialisation commenced considerably later than in other Member States.[86] Another specific tradition is the legacy of women labour unions, which are still predominant in Denmark today.[87] Despite this dominance of the gender equality paradigm, Nordic Member States extended their appreciation for equality to sexual orientation, ethnic minorities, disability and religion between 1996 and 1999 and thus earlier than required by EU law,[88] Finland being the exception to the rule in this

---

[81] Zweigert and Kötz, above n. 32, 283 with further references.

[82] Lynn Roseberry, "Equal Rights and Discrimination Law in Scandinavia" in Wahlgreen, above n. 80, 215–56, at 246 with further references.

[83] See S. Thorgeisdottir, "Feminist Ethics and Feminist Politics" in Karlsson and Jonsson, above n. 77, 35–9.

[84] According to Lynn Roseberry, Community law obligations may have been decisive (above n. 82, 226), but she admits that there was also considerable pressure from feminist groups (*ibid.*); see on the same lines, Nielssen, *Equality in Law between Men and Women in the European Community: Denmark* (The Hague, Martinus Nijhoff, 1987) 7.

[85] There are relatively few court cases, thus, from an individual justice model perspective, the impact of non-discrimination law may seem negligible: see Roseberry, above n. 82, who gives the impression of missing structures comparable to those known to her from her original homeland in the US (esp at 218). Nevertheless, the general conviction in Scandinavian countries is that women should have equal shares of jobs and income. This aim is pursued through welfare legislation as well as through non-discrimination legislation.

[86] See K. Nousiainen, "Women and Work in Today's Nordic Countries—Introducing the Themes" in Laura Kallimomaa-Puha (ed.), *Perspectives of Equality: Work, Women and Family in the Nordic Countries and the EU* (Copenhagen, Nordic Council of Ministers, 2000) 15–35.

[87] See generally R. Nielssen and M. Halvorsen, "Sex Discrimination: Between the Nordic Model and European Community Law" in N. Bruun et al. (eds.), *The Nordic Labour Relation Model* (Dartmouth, Aldershot, 1992) 183–205.

[88] Roseberry (2002), *above n.* 82, at 252.

respect.[89] The openness to equality principles is not restricted to employment and constitutional law, but has been extended to contract law, and in general before comprehensive legislation was enacted.[90]

All the Nordic Member States have had gender equality legislation prohibiting unequal pay for equal work on grounds of sex and direct and indirect discrimination in other employment matters since the 1970s or 1980s, following which result-oriented measures were installed through later legislation. Even the Danish legislation provided for the possibility to have positive measures acknowledged by the Equality Board, while the more developed Swedish legislation demanded already in 1976 that positive action measures were to be included in each and every collective agreement, and that the Equality Ombudsman was to supervise the collective agreements in this respect.[91] Most notably, positive obligations on social partners and employers themselves have been an element of Swedish law since as early as 1991. At this time, legislation added specific requirements as to the contents of these positive action measures, and introduced employers' obligations to report and survey in 1994. Finally, employers' obligations to actively promote equal pay by regular payroll analyses irrespective of their size and under the supervision of said Ombudsman were introduced in 2001.[92] Thus, what is discussed under the notion of "fourth generation equality law" in the UK has been an element of Swedish law for a long time. Finnish legislation was introduced in 1970 and 1987 respectively, in response to International Labour Organisation obligations. After a longish legislative process, purportedly due to the Anglo-American roots of the legislation,[93] the country emerged with a modern equality act which explicitly aimed at promoting equality between women and men in working life, thus skipping three generations of equality legislation through which Anglo-American countries painfully worked their way, and starting with the "fourth generation model" right away. As in the other Scandinavian countries, an ombudsman and an Equality Commission aid implementation of the law. As regards the other equalities, legislation is less comprehensive, and at times restricted to the third generation model from common law countries. However, the typical Scandinavian feature of creating an enforcement agency in the figure of an ombudsman remains, who is not only entrusted with supervising employers' obligations, but may also take cases to the courts by herself. All countries have also installed Equality Councils or similar bodies, which promote not only gender equality, but also the other equalities.

[89] Thus Finland was the only Nordic Country against which the European Commission started a non-compliance proceedings in relation to Directive 2000/43/EC, albeit only on the grounds of not including the Åland area in the 2001 legislation (see C–327/04 [2005] OJ J93/3 2005).
[90] T. Wilhelmsson, "Contract and Equality" in P. Wahlgreen (ed.), *Legal Theory (2000) 40 Scandinavian Studies in Law* 145.
[91] Roseberry, above *n.* 82, 236.
[92] *Ibid.*, 237–40.
[93] N. Bruun and P. Koskinen, *Jämstelldhetslagen* (Helsinki, Juristförbundes Förlag, 1987), cited in Roseberry, *ibid.*, 242.

5.5. SUMMARY OF COMPARISON AND RELEVANCE FOR REST OF
      THE BOOK

Different legal styles and different approaches towards diversity and gender
equality throughout the EU will make a uniform trans-European non-
discrimination law difficult to achieve. If anything, a flexible approach will best
serve the purpose of installing a substantively equal system of legal redress against
discrimination in all the Member States. In particular, implementation and its
assessment by the EU authorities need to be sensitive to the different legal styles
that prevail throughout the Union. It is of equal importance that implementation takes account of specific structures within certain fields of law in which
non-discrimination as a general principle will become established. While
employment law in most Member States already integrates principles of equality,
this is not always the case with other areas, such as "contract law proper" and
insurance law. Especially as regards gender equality in the Nordic Member States,
there is also the danger that remaining too close to the EU legislative model will
decrease the level of protection.

  With regard to explaining the central concepts of equality law, these different
approaches have been a challenge and a starting point. As we will see later on, EC law
is modelled upon Dutch and British legislation, with a "Nordic" influence on the
institutional side. This is the reason why British, Irish and Dutch cases are
overrepresented in most chapters. These legal orders have more experience with the
specific type of non-discrimination law established by the EC Directives. As has been
said, French examples are difficult to find in many chapters. This is also true for
German examples, as this country has been reluctant to implement Community
equality legislation. Scandinavian cases are not well represented either, partly due to
the relatively small amount of case-law in these countries. We have tried to integrate
as much diverse and illustrative material as possible, and we found quite a few
interesting cases from Member States which have only recently become members of
the EU. We were unable to judge the extent to which EC equality law has influenced
everyday reality in the EU Member States.

6. AIMS AND CONCEPTS OF
      NON-DISCRIMINATION LAW

Non-discrimination law (or discrimination law, as this field of law is sometimes named) is a field of law with a mission, or rather multiple missions. It is
so deeply engrained with meaning that a new reader of discrimination law can
easily get lost in a mire of concepts and aims. This section offers some guidance
through this labyrinth, while also offering the general approach of the editors to
these issues.

6.1.   (NON-)DISCRIMINATION OR EQUALITY?

A first conceptual approach is on the question whether law should be phrased in negative or positive terms. The title of the book chooses a negative term and negates it, which results in engendering a positive notion. Thus, non-discrimination and equality could be considered the same from a semantic approach. In the field of non-discrimination law, these phrases are sometimes given a very different meaning. Some authors contend that a legal ban on discrimination has less aspiring aims than a legal concept of equality.[94] Anti-discrimination legislation is considered to be based upon a "set of negative obligations, focusing on actions that (one) must refrain from".[95] At the same time, this type of legal regime is deemed to have a focus on individual remedies as opposed to group remedies.[96] Equality law regimes in contrast are characterised as not only prohibiting discrimination, but also harassment and victimisation, and as including positive obligations, *inter alia* to establish equality bodies or to make use of positive action.[97]

As has been said, non-discrimination and equality can be considered as having the same meaning, semantically. However, the term discrimination is focused on a specific form of action. Equality describes an ideal. Thus, the positive noun for non-discrimination could well be equal treatment. Nevertheless, it is one of the paradoxes of equality law that equal treatment does not necessarily bring about equality in a substantive sense. This brings us to the first layer of distinguishing conceptual approaches to non-discrimination law: often, a formal approach is contrasted with a substantive approach.

6.2.   FORM AND SUBSTANCE

First of all, not all legal-theoretical approaches to the notion of equality distinguish between equality and equal treatment. The philosophical basis of Western legal theory in this regard goes back to Aristotle. He did not distinguish between equality and equal treatment, as his approach to equality was a formal one. He also perceived equality as the basis of law and justice. This is captured in the following citation:

> "Thus, for example, one takes law (right) for equality, and it is, but equality only for equals, not for all. And thus one takes inequality for law (right), and it is, but not for all, but only for unequals."[98]

---

[94] See Bell, *Anti-Discrimination Law and the European Union* (Oxford, Oxford University Press, 2002) 145–52; Prechal, "Equal Treatment, Non-Discrimination and Social Policy: Achievement in Three Themes" (2004) 41 *CMLR* 533, 537.
[95] Bell, *ibid.*, 148.
[96] *Ibid.*
[97] *Ibid.*, 140.
[98] Aristotle, *Politea*, 1280a (trans T. Saunders, 1995).

As regards equal treatment of persons, Aristotle envisaged a very special kind of equality, which is called arithmetic or proportional equality:

> "Things [and persons] that are alike should be treated alike, while things that are unalike should be treated unalike in proportion to their unalikeness."[99]

While this sounds very familiar, and is the starting point of Western equality doctrine, the formula does not really say very much when it comes to the question which persons should be treated alike. Persons are never alike in all aspects.[100] Accordingly, a decision needs to be made as to which differences matter in order to ascertain whether persons are truly alike. What seems like a straightforward formula, only masks value judgements hidden behind the word "alike". Aristotle himself was not a fan of egalitarianism. Deeply rooted in pre-modern Greece, he considered that slaves were not alike to free men, women were not alike to men and Greeks were not alike to foreigners, to name just a few examples. His formula for equal treatment survived until our times, because it can be adapted to many ideologies and value systems. Once the value judgement has been made that all men are to be considered equal, the formula can be used legally to condemn unequal treatment of men (and women) on grounds of colour, ethnicity, nationality, etc. The formula can also be used to justify unequal treatment on grounds of anything if the value judgement has been made that this "difference" shall be considered as relevant "unalikeness".[101] Formal equality in the sense of the Aristotelian formula is thus indifferent towards social reality. This is particularly so if the second aspect of the principle—not only allowing, but requiring unequal treatment of unequals—is applied, as it is profoundly anti-egalitarian. It can be condensed to the Latin formula "*suum cuique*" (everyone shall be treated as he deserves), again one of the foundations of occidental legal reasoning, which can be utilised for stabilising any given hierarchy.[102] If equal treatment is always denied on grounds of perceived difference, such difference will never cease to matter. In any case, the Aristotelian conception does not require more than "equality as consistency",[103] effectively reducing a grand ideal to a merely formal requirement.

---

[99] Aristotle, *Ethica Nichomacea* 1131a-6 (trans W. Ross, 1925).

[100] This is captured by Radbruch's famous citation "Gleichheit ist immer nur eine Abstraktion von gegebener Ungleichheit" (G. Radbruch, *Rechtsphilosopie* (8th edn, 1973) (commented re-edition from 1956, at 112 ("Equality is nothing more than disregarding existing inequalities for the sake of abstractness"—translation by D.S.).

[101] This critique has been summarised perfectly by the Decision of the Canadian Supreme Court in the Andrew case, which explicitly stressed that the Aristotelian conception can be used to justify the "Nuremberg laws of Adolf Hitler" (referring to the numerous statutes enacted since 1933 which subjected persons considered Jewish to special detrimental treatment) as well as race segregation in US American schools (Canadian Supreme Court (1989), 1989 Dominion Law Reports 4th Series 11, 14f). This view, expressed by McIntyre J, who dissented from the majority on other issues, was shared by the majority; see Wilson J, *ibid.* at 31.

[102] A German version (*Jedem das Seine*) was actually written above the entrance of Buchenwald concentration camp, which is seen as a symbol for the negative connotation of an obligation to tread "unequal persons" unequally (see Osterloh, "Commentary on Article 3 Subsection 1 GG (German Constitution), No 5" in Sachs (ed.) *Grundgesetz, Kommentar*, 3rd edn, 2005).

[103] See, e.g., S. Fredman, *Discrimination Law* (Oxford, Oxford University Press, 2002) 7–11.

Engendering equality in social reality is not an issue of arithmetic equality in the Aristotelian conception. These words signify the starting point of a different perspective on equality as a legal concept, which is termed "substantive" equality. The ideal of substantive equality is mirrored in the grand UN conventions on equality, the ICERD[104] and the CEDAW,[105] which are now accompanied by the Convention on the Rights of Persons with Disabilities.[106] According to these conventions, the term discrimination is defined as meaning

> "Any distinction, exclusion or restriction made on the basis of [the protected ground in question] which has the purpose or effect of impairing or nullifying the recognition, enjoyment or exercise . . .[107] of all human rights and fundamental freedoms in the political, economic, social, cultural, civil or any other field."

The conventions are thus meant to repair factual inequality; they purport equality as a social aim. The aim of substantive equality starts not from a theory of law, but rather from a theory of justice. Equality as a right is meant to create a constitution of inclusion, not only in public, but also in privately governed (economic) relations. Equality as a right being engendered through law creates a substantive perspective on equality law. Substantively, equality through law envisages changes in social structures so as to deprive no one of his or her opportunities due to being grouped into given collectives (such as women, ethnic minorities or people with disabilities).

Substantive equality is not a uniform concept.[108] It comprises equality of result, equality of opportunities, equality in relation to substantive rights such as freedom of profession or capabilities, and equal respect (or a value-driven approach). All these approaches have in common that equality is to be achieved in social reality. As equality is a relational concept, it can only be rooted in social reality by using a medium of comparison: striving for equality, one needs to ask "Equality of What?"[109]

---

[104] International Convention on the Elimination of all Forms of Racial Discrimination, adopted and opened for signature and ratification by General Assembly resolution 2106 (XX) of 21 December 1965.

[105] International Convention on the Elimination of All Forms of Discrimination against Women, adopted and opened for signature by General Assembly resolution 34/180 of 18 December 1979.

[106] This convention was adopted and opened for signature as Resolution 661 by the 61st General Assembly Resolution on 13 December 2006 and is not yet in force.

[107] While the ICERD and the Convention on the Rights of Disabled People address any distinction on the basis of race or disability, the CEDAW goes one step further and prohibits any distinction which has the purpose or effect of impairing the enjoyment of rights by women. This convention is thus phrased asymmetrically.

[108] See Barnard and Hepple, "Substantive Equality" (2000) 59 (3) *CLJ* 562, at 564–6 with further references.

[109] This is the title of one of the chapters in Nobel prize-winning economist Amartya Sen's monograph of 1992, which answers the question with the concept of capabilities (A. Sen, *Inequality Re-examined* (New York, Clarendon Press, 1992).

6.3.   EQUALITY AND DISTRIBUTIVE AND CORRECTIVE JUSTICE

This leads to the second layer of distinguishing opposing approaches in equality law. Again, this distinction refers back to Aristotle's theory of justice. He distinguished between corrective justice, applicable to exchange relations between two parties, and distributive justice, applicable to ongoing relationships within groups or society at large.[110] Corrective justice aims at (re-)establishing the positions of both parties as they were before they entered into their exchange. It presupposes a relationship that is meant to end at a certain point and is thus premised on the image of autonomous individuals, who happen to engage in restricted interaction. For example, the theory of "*iustum pretium*" is based on corrective justice,[111] as it requires that a seller receive a just price for her goods, which then re-establishes the wealth of the seller and buyer as it was before the purchase. Tort law is also based on corrective justice, according an indemnity to balance the loss one has suffered from a tort. Distributive justice, in contrast, aims at an adequate distribution of resources and opportunities in society at large. The sacrifices necessary to achieve this adequate distribution must normally be imposed equally on all citizens—and thus borne by "the public"—and cannot be accorded to single persons. While Aristotelian principles are no longer central to modern contract law, the poles of corrective and distributive justice are still being referred to as appropriate boundaries between private and public rule.[112]

If we apply this duality to equality law, we achieve a dichotomy similar, but not identical, to that between formal and substantive equality.

Pursuing corrective justice, equality law would strive to undo social wrongs that have happened. Thus, if women were not allowed to undergo training as airline pilots in the past, this wrong needs to be corrected. Thus, the opportunity for training should be opened to all women. In addition, age limits for entering the training should not apply in order to avoid punishing women for past denial of training opportunities. Or, if lesbian and gay people had been denied the right to reproductive rights or adoption rights, this wrong needs to be corrected. Corrective justice can be at the heart of remedial regimes. To apply it, one needs to identify the source of an injustice.

Distributive justice can be applied without isolating a single or several specific sources of injustice. Thus, its realisation lends itself to such fields of equality law where public responsibility is rightly taken up. For example, the distribution of educational opportunities should not move along lines of race, ethnic origin or religion, and public resources should be spent in a way that all factions of the population can substantively profit from them. From this perspective, one would consider as discriminatory a higher education system in which children of migrants are less likely to achieve a university degree, and public funding of universities would

---

[110] Aristotle, *Ethica Nicomacea, above n.* 99 (book V, 2–5, 1130a14–1133b28).

[111] See, on the historical traces of this theory in Aristotelian philosophy, J. Gordley, *Foundations of Private Law* (Oxford, Oxford University Press, 2006) 15.

[112] See, in reference to indirect discrimination law, A. Morris "On the Normative Foundations of Indirect Discrimination Law" (1995) 15 *OJLS* 199, 205–6.

have to be adjusted as to encourage them to offer an academic environment in which children of migrants excel as much as their peers whose parents did not migrate.

The duality of corrective and distributive justice may indicate which fields of equality law are rightly applied to non-state (economic) actors and which are only a public responsibility. Certainly, under its conservative interpretation, distributive policies should only be pursued via the channels of direct state action, which is often associated with public law.[113] However, modern welfare state models recognise that, in the age of globalisation, the welfare state needs to change towards a regulatory state. This implies, inter alia, a need to stimulate (economic) activities of citizens in such a way that redistributive effects are achieved horizontally rather than by vertical redistribution. If these theories are accepted, redistribution can become a legitimate aim of contract law.

6.4.   INDIVIDUALS AND GROUPS

Another schism within equality law relates to the protection of individual rights on the one hand and the group-related character of discrimination (and non-discrimination law) on the other: discrimination in societal reality reacts to assumed (or ascribed) group membership. In this sense, a person is subjected to a disadvantage because, for example, another person considers that he is homosexual or she follows a religion which the other person despises. Some authors have accorded to non-discrimination law the aim of improving "the relative position of particular groups".[114] This statement presupposes that it is possible to group humans in accordance with "discrimination grounds". Thus, there would be a group of male persons who have no religion or belief, no sexual orientation, no ethnic or racial origin and no age, or a group of disabled persons who have no sex, no religion and so on. Obviously, this is unrealistic. Human beings combine all the "discrimination grounds".[115] A multifaceted non-discrimination legislation such as that of the EU can never be reduced to the purpose named above; only monodimensional non-discrimination regimes such as the UN ICERD can be so categorised.[116] However, the schism between individual and group dimensions of non-discrimination law is still of relevance to multidimensional non-discrimination law regimes. This relevance lies in the different perspective which legal provisions may aim at.

[113] C.W. Canaris, "Aspekte de iustitia commutative und der iustitia distributive im Vertragsrecht" in L.E. Kotsiris (Hrsg), *Law at the Turn of the 20th Century* (1996) 281*ff*; for a critical position see Bleckmann, *Neue Aspekte der Drittwirkung der Grundrechte*, DVBl 1988, 938, 946.

[114] C. McCrudden, "International and European Norms Regarding National Legal Remedies For Racial Inequality" in S. Fredman (ed.), *Discrimination and Human Rights. The Case of Racism* (Oxford, Oxford University Press, 2001) 251, 255.

[115] For greater detail, see Schiek, "Broadening the Scope", above n. 54, 427.

[116] It is certainly no coincidence that the article cited in favour of the "group justice model" by several authors (inter alia Gijzen, *above n.* 10, 65 with further references) appeared in a volume on racial discrimination.

If non-discrimination law maintains an individualistic perspective, its main ambition is to afford human beings respect as individuals. The aim of a colour blind, gender blind, ability blind etc society can be associated with this perspective.[117] The individualistic turn in non-discrimination law is also related to dignity, with which each human being is endowed for the sake of his or her individuality. At the same time, the individualistic aims of non-discrimination law pursue the aim of an unencumbered self.

This perspective has severe limits.

First of all, it does not recognise that advantage and disadvantage are spread unevenly within sets of discrimination grounds. Disadvantage on grounds of sex is suffered by women; disadvantage on grounds of religion is usually suffered by those associated with a minority religion; and so on. Thus it leads to a symmetrical conception of equality law, while recognising group-related disadvantage will lead to an asymmetric reading of the rights guaranteed.[118]

Secondly, the individualistic perspective has a decisively assimiliationist tendency. The individual that is associated with a minority religion should conform to standards perceived as neutral by those adhering to the majority religion, and only if discrimination occurs in spite of this should legal protection be granted. Thus, the individualistic model of non-discrimination law does not correspond well with the general aim of enhancing (or maintaining) diversity. If the individualistic model aims at making differences between ethnicities, genders, etc invisible, the diversity model cherishes differences and strives to eliminate or diminish social inequality based on these.[119] The diversity model is at the base of minority protection, for example.

Modern non-discrimination law regimes integrate both perspectives. However, to adequately address discrimination in social reality, they need to be sensitive to group dimensions of discrimination while not neglecting the value of individual autonomy. In this regard, different "discrimination grounds" have different value bases. While legislation against discrimination on grounds of sex and sexual orientation aims, inter alia, at freeing the individual from the obligation to conform to group standards, legislation against ethnic discrimination may, if combined with minority protection or identity preservation aims, work into the opposite direction and support gender-specific dress codes, for example, as an expression of cultural diversity. Thus, EC non-discrimination law needs to maintain an adequate balance between group-related and individualistic aims.

6.5.   ENFORCING NON-DISCRIMINATION LAW

Given that non-discrimination law pursues wider socio-economic aims which are partly contrary to existing social practices, effective enforcement becomes a problem.

---

[117] See Gijzen, *above* n. 10, 63.

[118] For more arguments for an asymmetric approach of EU equality law see D. Schiek, "A New Framework of Equal Treatment of Persons in EC Law" (2002) 8 *ELJ* 290, 307–8.

[119] See Schiek, "Broadening the Scope", above n. 54, 442.

Legal provisions that mirror the majority view in society require considerably fewer enforcement policies than provisions seeking to counteract majority morals.[120] Thus, non-discrimination law needs various specific enforcement strategies. Confusingly, what has been described substantively as the schism between individuals and groups is often used in relation to enforcement interchangeably, as if substantive rights and enforcement were synonymous. This is due to non-discrimination law being rooted mainly in common law legal orders, which tend not to distinguish between legal rules and their enforcement ("*ubi ius, ibi remedium*"). In relation to enforcement, the term "individual justice model" is used to describe a legal regime that relies mainly on individual complaints as the enforcement mechanism. This model is sometimes also referred to as second generation equality law. While the first generation did not grant any individual rights, the third generation endeavours to support individual complainants by institutional actors, such as equality agencies. The fourth generation includes proactive enforcement of the law, via positive obligations.[121] This fourth generation model is also referred to as the group justice model.[122] Considered in context with regulation and governance theory at large, the fourth generation of equality rights embodies "new forms of governance" beyond the traditional command and control model.[123] As has been said, the present volume only partly addresses enforcement. Chapter two, discussing direct discrimination, addresses some issues relating to proving discrimination, and chapter eight explains institutional arrangements to enforce equality norms. It is, however, advisable to keep the problem of enforcing rights in mind when reading the chapters on the substantive problems of non-discrimination law.

---

[120] See, from a rather uncritical perspective, J. Griffith, "The Social Workings of Anti-Discrimination Law" in T. Loenen and P. Rodrigues (eds.), *Non-Discrimination Law: Comparative Perspectives* (The Hague, Kluwer, 1999) 313, 327: "To be effective in social life . . . rules must be used by actors in their everyday interactions without the intervention of legal officials."

[121] This form of enforcement has been argued for by S. Fredman, who now takes a more critical position as positive obligations without accompanying individual, enforceable rights tend to remain mere political concepts: S. Fredman, "Transformation or Dilution: Fundamental Rights in the EU Social Space" (2006) 12 *ELJ* 41.

[122] See McCrudden, *The New Concept of Equality*, Conference Paper, Trier, June 2003, available on the website of the Academy of European Law, under III.2.

[123] Schiek, "Broadening the Scope", above n. 54, 433 with further references.

CHAPTER ONE
DISCRIMINATION GROUNDS

Prof. Janneke Gerards

1.1. INTRODUCTION

Non-discrimination legislation in many Member States of the EU contains a long list of prohibited grounds. As a result of the implementation of the relevant Gender Equality and Article 13 Directives, they should at least include gender/sex, race/ethnicity, religion/belief, sexual orientation, disability and age, but in many national texts much longer lists can be found, also mentioning, for example, marital status, birth/descent, nationality, political conviction and income. As a result, the personal scope of such legislation would seem to be quite broad, offering extensive protection against discrimination. In practice, however, it is not as simple as that. The actual scope of non-discrimination law is determined by at least two variables. First, the definition of a certain ground is of importance in determining the scope of non-discrimination legislation. If "race" is also taken to mean "skin colour", "ethnic origin" and "belonging to a national minority", a prohibition of racial discrimination is obviously much more inclusive than if only a narrow definition is given to the notion. Secondly, even if a legislative act enumerates a large number of grounds, and even if these grounds are broadly defined, this does not yet mean that all grounds are protected to the same degree. The degree of protection also depends on the justifications and exceptions the legislation allows for and on their interpretation and application by the courts.[1] To some extent, however, there appears to be a connection between the possibilities for justification and the grounds of discrimination. This is particularly true for legal systems with an open system of justification, as contrasted to closed systems, in which a limited number of carefully drafted exception clauses are provided.[2] In open systems, as are visible in the European Convention of Human Rights and in a number of Member States, the ground of discrimination may to a large extent determine the strictness with which the courts analyse cases of unequal treatment and the arguments advanced in justification. According to well-established case-law of the European Court of Human Rights (ECtHR), for example, "very weighty reasons" must be adduced by the Member States to justify a difference in treatment based on sex, birth, nationality and sexual orientation. By contrast, the intensity of the Court's assessment will be much weaker if an instance of discrimination is based on another ground. The same is true for non-discrimination law in a number of states. It

---

[1] Possibilities for justification and exception clauses are discussed below by M. Bell in Chapter Two: Direct Discrimination and by D. Schiek in Chapter Three: Indirect Discrimination.

[2] See above, Introductory Chapter: A Comparative Perspective on Non-discrimination Law.

appears from national legislation and case-law that discrimination based on specific grounds is regarded as less acceptable than discrimination based on other grounds. Accordingly, the protection offered by non-discrimination law in open systems of justification is dependent not only on the definition and scope of the various grounds of discrimination, but also on the perception of such grounds as unacceptable or "suspect" reasons for distinction.

Because of the importance of the concept of "suspectness" of certain grounds of discrimination, we will start this chapter with a general discussion of this concept and its relevance for the intensity of judicial review (section 1.2).

Subsequently, we will give an overview of the various grounds of discrimination that are protected in the legal systems under study. Section 1.3 will focus on a number of discrimination grounds that are prohibited in almost all legal systems under study. We will discuss the grounds of race, ethnic and national origin, nationality, gender, marital status, sexual orientation, birth, religion and political conviction, disability, age, working time and fixed-term work. This chapter will thus consider a number of grounds which are not covered by the Article 13 and Gender Equality Directives, but which are included in openly formulated legislative or constitutional non-discrimination provisions; in international human rights instruments such as the European Convention of Human Rights (ECHR) or the International Covenant on Civil and Political Rights (ICCRP); or in specific EC legislation. We will therefore devote greater attention in this chapter to the case-law of the ECtHR and international monitoring bodies that provides for explanations and definitions of the various grounds. This is particularly valuable even with regard to the grounds that are covered by the various equal treatment Directives; presently there is little clarity as to the definition of the various grounds contained therein. Indeed, many national legislators and courts appear to rely on the international case-law as an important source of inspiration and it is highly probable that the European Court of Justice (ECJ) will do so as well if asked to provide a definition. This is particularly true for grounds which are closely related to fundamental freedoms, such as the ground of religion, which will probably be interpreted in line with the case-law on Article 9 of the ECHR that is concerned with the definition of the freedom of religion. Furthermore, we will refer to a wide range of national non-discrimination legislation in which the grounds are defined. Because of the relatively recent implementation of the Directive by most states, only limited case-law is available to elucidate the scope and meaning of the various grounds. Such case-law primarily exists in the Netherlands, Ireland, Germany and the UK, where non-discrimination legislation has been in existence for a longer period of time. For that reason, most case-law excerpts will come from these legal systems.

In addition to discussing the definition and interpretation of the various grounds mentioned, we will also address the issue of "suspectness" of each of these grounds, given that some of the grounds are mainly protected in open systems of non-discrimination law.

In section 1.4, the separate issue of discrimination based on assumed characteristics and discrimination by association will be considered: the question is whether and to what extent states only prohibit discrimination that is based on actual, existing personal characteristics or whether they also prohibit discrimination that is based on characteristics that are (rightly or wrongly) attributed to a certain individual.

Section 1.5 will be devoted to a description of the concept of multiple discrimination, i.e. discrimination based on (a close combination of) two or more protected grounds, such as gender and ethnic origin. In this section we will also provide some insight as to the ways in which this concept is dealt with in Europe.

Finally, we will present some concluding thoughts on the convergence of the European legal systems with respect to the definition of the grounds of discrimination and their suspectness in section 1.6.

1.2. "SUSPECT" GROUNDS OF DISCRIMINATION

The notions of discrimination and unequal treatment easily evoke the image of serious cases of discrimination which are based on prejudice and stigma, and which severely harm individual rights and interests. The general principle of equal treatment has a wide reach, however, and also covers such issues as unequal treatment of farmers based on the amount of milk they produce, or distinctions between income groups in the context of income taxation. Especially open-formulated non-discrimination provisions will cover all such forms of unequal treatment, mostly in combination with an undefined, general possibility for justification. In such systems it will be up to the courts to decide if and under what circumstances a case of unequal treatment is acceptable. As has been stressed in the introductory chapter to this casebook, such open systems may be found primarily in broadly defined constitutional prohibitions of discrimination and international human rights treaties, such as the ECHR (Article 14 and Article 1 Twelfth Protocol) and the ICCRP (Article 26). In the EC Treaty, open possibilities for justification are visible as well. Examples may be found in provisions relating to unequal treatment in the field of agriculture (Article 34(2) EC); nationality discrimination (Article 12 EC); (indirect) discrimination relating to the four freedoms; and indirect discrimination in a variety of non-discrimination Directives.[3] In all of these cases, the courts will necessarily have to address the question if a certain difference in treatment is supported by a convincing, objective and reasonable justification in order to decide on its legal acceptability. Although the issue of justification in open systems will not generally be dealt with in this chapter, it may be noted that the justifiability of a difference in treatment may be influenced by the ground on which it is based.[4] Grounds such as race, ethnic origin or gender are

---

[3] For more details, see ch. 3, section 3.3. To some extent, an open system is even provided by the various Equality Directives with respect to direct discrimination. Examples are the possibility for justification of age discrimination provided by the Employment Equality Directive (Art. 6) and the possibility for justification relating to the provision of services and goods primarily or exclusively to members of one sex provided by the Gender Goods and Services Directive (Art. 4(5)).

[4] Next to the ground of discrimination, a variety of other factors may influence the justifiability of a case of (indirect) discrimination. See, in particular, ch. 3, section 3.5.2.B.

rarely considered to constitute reasonable bases for unequal treatment and, accordingly, it will be very difficult to justify a distinction based on such a ground. Indeed, the fact that certain personal characteristics are generally regarded as unreasonable and unacceptable grounds for unequal treatment may have formed an important reason for the introduction of specific non-discrimination legislation with a closed list of exceptions.[5] Such generally unacceptable grounds of discrimination are commonly termed "suspect" grounds, as they immediately raise a suspicion of unreasonableness and prejudice.[6] They may be contrasted with "non-suspect" grounds, which do not immediately evoke such images of unfairness and are usually considered relatively tolerable criteria for distinction—one may think of examples such as intelligence, merit and talent.

The "suspectness" of a ground may have important consequences for the strictness with which a court will review the reasonableness of the discrimination at hand. As stated above, this is especially true in open systems, in which a wide variety of grounds and justifications for discrimination will have to be considered by the courts. The ECtHR in particular, which decides cases under the "open" non-discrimination provision of Article 14 of the ECHR, has used the suspectness of certain grounds of discrimination to determine the proper "level" of review. In general, the ECtHR applies a "very weighty reasons" test if it finds that a ground is commonly held to be suspect by the various Member States or if the ground may be considered suspect for other reasons.[7] In those cases it is very strict and a justification will hardly ever be accepted. This is different for cases in which no suspect ground is present. The ECtHR then generally leaves a certain "margin of appreciation" to the state to determine the necessity of a certain classification or distinction, which means that it will only marginally review the state's justification. In fact, the ECtHR then seems to apply a test which comes close to a general test of arbitrariness. Two examples may serve to illustrate the Court's approach:

---

[5] J.H. Gerards, "Intensity of Review in Equal Treatment Cases" [2004] *NILR* 35.

[6] The terminology of "suspectness" derives from the case-law of the US Supreme Court relating to the Fourteenth Amendment to the US Constitution. Although this terminology is not used by the ECJ or the ECtHR, it constitutes useful shorthand for the perceived unreasonableness and unfairness of unequal treatment based on certain grounds. For that reason, the term will be used throughout this Casebook. It must be remarked, however, that the term is not used to refer to the notion of "suspectness" as it has elaborately been developed in the US, but only to denote the meaning given to it in this casebook.

[7] See, e.g. ECtHR, 28 November 1984, *Abdulaziz, Cabales and Balkandali* v. *the United Kingdom*, Series A, Vol. 87, § 78. See further J.H. Gerards, *Judicial Review in Equal Treatment Cases* (Leiden, Martinus Nijhoff Publishers, 2005) 199*ff*.

ECtHR, 13 December 2005[8]   **1.CoE.1.**
Timishev v. Russia

FREEDOM OF MOVEMENT OF CHECHENS

Timishev

Facts: Timishev, a Chechen lawyer, lives as a forced migrant in Nalchik, in the Kabardino-Balkaria Republic of the Russian Federation. In 1999, the applicant and his driver travelled by car from the Ingushetia Republic to Nalchik. Their car was stopped at the checkpoint and officers of the Inspectorate for Road Safety refused him entry. The refusal appeared to be based on an oral instruction from the Ministry of the Interior of Kabardino-Balkaria not to admit persons of Chechen ethnic origin. Timishev had to turn round and make a detour of 300 kilometres to reach Nalchik through a different checkpoint.

Held: The Court decided that the refusal of entry amounted to a violation of the prohibition of discrimination (Article 14 ECHR), taken in conjunction with the right to liberty of movement (Article 2 of Protocol No. 4).

Judgment: "56. . . . Discrimination on account of one's actual or perceived ethnicity is a form of racial discrimination . . . Racial discrimination is a particularly invidious kind of discrimination and, in view of its perilous consequences, requires from the authorities special vigilance and a vigorous reaction. It is for this reason that the authorities must use all available means to combat racism, thereby reinforcing democracy's vision of a society in which diversity is not perceived as a threat but as a source of enrichment . . .

58. . . . In any event, the Court considers that no difference in treatment which is based exclusively or to a decisive extent on a person's ethnic origin is capable of being objectively justified in a contemporary democratic society built on the principles of pluralism and respect for different cultures."

ECtHR, 21 February 1986[9]   **1.CoE.2.**
James and Others v. the United Kingdom

DIFFERENT TREATMENT OF PROPERTY OWNERS

James

Facts: The complaint in this case arose from a legal provision in the UK concerning long leasehold tenure. The legal system provided for a form of long-term lease whereby the leaseholder had to meet all costs for maintenance and repairs. At the end of the lease the whole property, including improvements and repairs, reverted to the landlord. To eradicate this situation, leasehold reform legislation was introduced. In the new system, a leaseholder with long lease tenure could take over the property for the value of the land when the lease expired. The applicants argued the leasehold reform legislation was discriminatory on the ground of "property", in that, firstly, it was a measure that applied only to a restricted class of property, that is long leasehold houses occupied by the leaseholders; and, secondly, the lower the value of the property, the more harshly the landlord was treated.

Held: The facts of the case did not disclose any breach of Article 14 ECHR, taken in conjunction with the right to property as guaranteed by Article 1 First Protocol.

---

[8] Not yet published. See also below **1.CoE.7.** and **1.CoE.112.**
[9] Series A, Vol. 98.

Judgment: "75. For the purposes of Article 14, a difference of treatment is discriminatory if it has no objective and reasonable justification, that is, if it does not pursue a legitimate aim or if there is not a reasonable relationship of proportionality between the means employed and the aim sought to be realised . . . As in relation to the means for giving effect to the right of property, the Contracting States enjoy a certain margin of appreciation in assessing whether and to what extent differences in otherwise similar situations permit a different treatment in law . . .

76. As to the applicants' first head of complaint, . . . [t]his amounts in substance to the same complaint, albeit seen from another angle, as that which has been examined under Article 1 of Protocol No. 1 . . . The Court sees no cause for arriving at a different conclusion in relation to Article 14 of the Convention: having regard to the margin of appreciation, the United Kingdom legislature did not transgress the principle of proportionality. In the Court's opinion, therefore, the contested distinction drawn in the legislation is reasonably and objectively justified.

77. The second head of complaint must also be examined in the light of the Court's finding under Article 1 of Protocol No. 1 that the United Kingdom Parliament was entitled to consider the scheme embodied in the leasehold reform legislation as a reasonable and appropriate means for achieving the legitimate aim pursued . . . In view of the legitimate objectives being pursued in the public interest and having regard to the respondent State's margin of appreciation, that policy of different treatment cannot be considered as unreasonable or as imposing a disproportionate burden on the applicants . . . The provisions in the legislation entailing progressively disadvantageous treatment for the landlord the lower the value of the property must be deemed to have a reasonable and objective justification and, consequently, are not discriminatory."

Note

In *James*, the ECtHR applied a marginal test, referring to the "margin of appreciation" the states have in the area of regulation of property. The main reason for this would seem to be that the case concerned a difference of treatment in regard to different categories of property owners and was therefore based on property. As the Court does not consider the ground of property to be a suspect ground of discrimination, it did not see the need to apply a strict test. This was clearly different in *Timishev*, where the alleged discrimination was based on ethnic origin. In that case the ECtHR applied a particularly strict test, stating that no difference in treatment which is based exclusively or to a decisive extent on a person's ethnic origin would be capable of being objectively justified. The reason for this was explained in paragraph 56, where the Court stated that racial discrimination is a particularly invidious type of discrimination. It thus clearly regards race and ethnic origin as suspect grounds of discrimination, triggering a very strict assessment of the justification—in fact, in this case no such justification was considered to exist. Hence, these examples show that the ECtHR distinguishes between more "suspect" and "non-suspect" grounds and applies a stricter or more marginal test accordingly.

It is important to note, however, that the intensity of judicial review and the requirements for justifiability will not be influenced by the ground of discrimination alone, not even in open systems of non-discrimination law. Other factors are of relevance too, such as the importance of the individual rights and interests harmed by the difference in treatment; the seriousness of the interference with individual rights and interests; the character of the discretionary powers of the person or institution responsible for the difference in treatment; and even the general policy area in the context of which a distinction is made.[10] In an open system, even discrimination based on a relatively neutral ground (e.g. income) may be subjected to vigorous scrutiny if it interferes with a fundamental right (e.g. the right to vote). Alternatively, classifications based on a suspect ground (e.g. gender) may be reviewed more marginally if they are made in the specific context of social security measures.[11] Nonetheless, it is clear that the ground for discrimination bears important influence on the justifiability of a difference in treatment, especially in open systems of discrimination. For that reason, it is worthwhile to devote some attention to the subject in the context of this chapter. For each of the various grounds discussed in section 1.3, we will investigate the substantive reasons which are given in national and international legislation and case-law to regard certain grounds as a priori "suspect" or, to the contrary, as "non-suspect". As far as possible, we will also consider the extent to which the ECJ in its case-law has varied the intensity of its review with respect to certain grounds of discrimination.

1.3. THE GROUNDS OF DISCRIMINATION

1.3.1. INTRODUCTION

In most Member States, non-discrimination legislation contains a list of prohibited grounds. Currently these should be at least the grounds enumerated in the Employment Equality Directive, the Racial Equality Directive and the various Gender Equality Directives—i.e. gender, racial/ethnic origin, religion/belief, sexual orientation, disability and age. Sometimes grounds have been added which are considered to be of particular importance, but which are not mentioned in the European Directives. Further, a number of states use open-ended lists of grounds, which make it less necessary to give clear definitions of the various grounds. After all, all situations of unequal treatment, regardless of the ground on which it is based, are covered by such lists. In these cases, classification under specific grounds (and thereby definition of the grounds) is only important if there are different exception and justification clauses for discrimination based on specific grounds, or if the courts apply a stricter test to discrimination based on grounds that are considered suspect.

It is mainly in states that prohibit discrimination on a limited number of grounds, however, that the definition of the grounds really matters: the definition is then determinative of the scope of protection. In these states one could therefore expect

---

[10] On this, see more elaborately Gerards, above n. 7.
[11] This is visible, for example, in the context of the objective justification of cases of indirect discrimination on grounds of gender. On this see ch. 3, section 3.5.2.B.

that careful attention would be paid to the formulation and definition of the various grounds of discrimination.[12] In practice, however, a definition of the grounds or an explanation of their meaning has been given only rarely in the legislation itself or in legislative history. Many states appear to find the grounds difficult to define or consider the concepts self-explanatory.[13] Thus, the meaning of most of the grounds will need to be explained by the courts.

This will be a difficult task indeed, as many grounds pose important problems of definition and distinction. This is true in particular for the grounds protected (and, conversely, those *not* protected) by the Employment Equality Directive and the Racial Equality Directive. It is sometimes difficult to distinguish, for example, between such grounds as race and ethnic origin, ethnic origin and national origin, national origin and nationality, ethnic origin and religion, marital status and sexual orientation, or disability and (chronic) illness. Since the Article 13 Directives have only recently been adopted and the resulting national legislation is in many Member States the first anti-discrimination legislation to come into force, limited case-law is presently available in the various Member States to explain the meaning of the grounds and to elucidate the borderlines between them. It is important, however, that the ECJ has indicated that the grounds contained in the Article 13 Directives have to be considered as Community legal concepts which require the development of uniform definitions:

> "It follows from the need for uniform application of Community law and the principle of equality that the terms of a provision of Community law which makes no express reference to the law of the Member States for the purpose of determining its meaning and scope must normally be given an autonomous and uniform interpretation throughout the Community, having regard to the context of the provision and the objective pursued by the legislation in question . . ."[14]

As yet, however, most of the grounds have not been explained by the ECJ. In this chapter, we will therefore mainly revert to court interpretations of legislation that was already in existence before the Article 13 Directives entered into force. Such case-law is available in particular in the Netherlands, the UK, Germany and Ireland. We have furthermore tried to trace as many useable examples as possible of interesting (legislative) definitions given in the Member States; such examples are, however, rare. The discussion of the definition of the various grounds will therefore necessarily remain incomplete for many of the Member States under study.

Furthermore, it has transpired that the case-law of international human rights bodies is of particular importance to the definitions given on the national level. For example, many states have based their definition of race and ethnic origin on

---

[12] See extensively S. Fredman, *Discrimination Law* (Oxford, Oxford University Press, 2002) 68*ff.*

[13] For the latter situation, see, e.g. O. de Schutter, "Report on Measures to Combat Discrimination: Directives 2000/43/EC and 2000/78/EC. Country Report Belgium" (European Commission, 2004) 15, available on the website of Directorate-General for Employment, Social Affairs and Equal Opportunities.

[14] ECJ, Judgment of 11 July 2006, Case C–13/05 *Chacón Navas* [2006] ECR I–6467, para. 40; see below **1.EC.84.**

the ICERD definition, whilst the definition of the ground of religion is often strongly influenced by the case-law of the ECtHR regarding the right to freedom of religion.[15] Expectedly such international materials will also influence the future interpretation of the grounds by the ECJ, either directly or indirectly through the available national definitions. Whenever relevant and available, we will therefore also discuss international materials and case-law.

1.3.2.   RACE; ETHNIC, RACIAL AND NATIONAL ORIGIN; BELONGING TO A NATIONAL OR ETHNIC MINORITY; SKIN COLOUR

1.3.2.A.   DEFINITIONS

RACE

The Racial Equality Directive prohibits discrimination on the grounds of racial or ethnic origin, but neither of these terms have been defined or explained. In the legislation of the various Member States, the grounds of race and ethnic origin are also mentioned, but a variety of definitions have been given here. In most Member States, the definition is inspired by the definition of racial discrimination as contained in the International Convention on the Elimination of All Forms of Racial Discrimination (ICERD).[16] The ECtHR has also used this Convention in interpreting the ECHR[17] and it is probable that the ECJ will be inspired by it if asked to interpret the Racial Equality Directive. The relevant part of Article 1 of this Convention reads as follows:

> "In this Convention the term 'racial discrimination' shall mean any distinction, exclusion, restriction or preference based on race, colour, descent, or national or ethnic origin which has the purpose or effect of nullifying or impairing the recognition, enjoyment or exercise on an equal footing, of human rights and fundamental freedoms in the political, economic, social, cultural or any other field of public law."

The ICERD's definition of racial discrimination thus covers a number of grounds, i.e. race, colour, descent, national origin and ethnic origin. It is perhaps surprising, considering the impact of the provision and the contents of ICERD, that the

---

[15] The latter is witnessed, for example, by the Explanatory Note to the UK Equality Act 2006, in which it is stated that the term religion ". . . has a broad definition in line with the freedom of religion guaranteed by Art. 9 of the ECHR" (para. 155, available on the website of the UK Parliament).

[16] The ICERD definition itself is based on the wording of the Universal Declaration on Human Rights (Art. 2). Other international conventions use similar terminology. See, e.g. the International Covenant on Economic, Social and Cultural Rights (mentioning race, colour and national origin—see Art. 2) and the International Covenant on Civil and Political Rights (also mentioning race, colour and national origin—see Art. 2).

[17] See, e.g. ECtHR, judgment of 23 September 1994, *Jersild* v. *Denmark*, Series A, Vol. 298, para. 30 and ECtHR, judgment of 13 December 2005, *Timishev* v. *Russia*, not yet reported, para. 56.

Convention does not contain a more substantive definition of race. An explanation for this may be found in the particularly sensitive character of the term "race". The principled view is widely expressed that the use of this term in legislation would reinforce the perception that individuals can actually be distinguished according to "race", even though there is no solid scientific or theoretical basis for this.[18] Moreover, all racist theories are based on the perceived existence of different human races.[19] According to some, the use of the term in legislation might be tantamount to accepting such theories.[20] An alternative terminology is therefore often preferred, such as the terms "origin" or "ethnicity".[21]

Nonetheless, many states find it difficult or even undesirable *not* to use the term "race" in legislation. Removing "race" from prohibitions of racial discrimination would easily cause confusion. Furthermore, for some it is of importance to use the word "race" to stress that it is precisely "racism" that has to be combated.[22] A variety of approaches have been chosen to solve this problem. The Racial Equality Directive uses the term "race", but stresses in its preamble that any theory which attempts to determine the existence of separate human races is rejected (Recital 6). The European Commission against Racism and Intolerance (ECRI) has opted for a comparable approach. In a footnote to its General Recommendation on national legislation to combat racism and racial discrimination, it stresses that:

> "[s]ince all human beings belong to the same species, ECRI rejects theories based on the existence of different 'races'. However, in this Recommendation ECRI uses this term in order to ensure that those persons who are generally and erroneously perceived as belonging to 'another race' are not excluded from the protection provided for by the legislation."

A similar approach is adopted by the Austrian legislator, which explains in its explanatory notes to the Equal Treatment Act why it has opted to use the term "race" and how it should be understood:

---

[18] J. Cormack and M. Bell, "Developing Anti-Discrimination Law in Europe. The 25 EU Member States Compared" (European Commission, September 2005) 19.

[19] *Cf.* G. Cardinale, "The Preparation of ECRI General Policy Recommendation No. 7" in J. Niessen and I. Chopin (eds.), *The Development of Legal Instruments to Combat Racism in a Diverse Europe* (Leiden, Martinus Nijhoff, 2004), 84.

[20] A. Tyson, "The Negotiation of the EC Directive on Racial Discrimination" in Niessen and Chopin, above n. 19, 113.

[21] An example of such use is visible, for instance, in Finland; see Finnish Constitution of 2000, s. 6. See also Scheinin, who explains that the term "origin" was chosen to reflect race, colour, ethnicity and social origin (M. Scheinin, "Constitutional Consistence: Minority Rights and Non-Discrimination under the Finnish Constitution" in M. Scheinin and R. Toivanen, *Rethinking Non-Discrimination and Minority Rights* (Turkiv.Åbo: Institute for Human Rights, Åbo Akademi University, 2004) 2.

[22] *Ibid.*, 113.

Austrian Equal Treatment Act (Gleichbehandlungsgesetz),   **1.AT.3.**
Explanatory Notes[23]

"The Directive on anti-racism does not contain a definition of 'race and ethnic origin'. Theories which attempt to determine or separate race are rejected. The use of the term 'race' does not imply an acceptance of such theories. As a benchmark for the interpretation of the open and broad Directive we have to look to international norms, especially the Convention on the Elimination of all Forms of Racial Discrimination CERD. Additionally, Art. 26 of the ICCPR can be used. CERD deals with discrimination based on 'race, colour, descent, or national or ethnic origin', Art. 26 ICCPR obliges the ratifying states to provide protection against discrimination inter alia on the grounds of race, skin-colour, language, religion, and national origin. As a back-up for interpretation, reference shall also be made to ILO Convention Nr. 111, as well as Art. 14 of the Human Rights Convention.

Also Art. IX para. 1 fig. 3 of the Introductory Provisions to the Code of Administrative Procedure (EGVG) provides for an administrative penal sanction for discrimination of a person due to his/her race, skin-colour, national or ethnic origin, religious faith or disability and can therefore also be used to interpret the term 'race'. The use of the term 'race' in the above mentioned instruments shows that the term 'race' is quite commonly used in legal texts, albeit that the terms 'race and ethnic origin'—understood correctly according to international law—cannot be seen in a way that they refer to biological relationships to a distinct ethnic group in the sense of a theory of descent. The above mentioned sources lend rather useful support to a more culturally orientated view of the problem of ethnic discrimination. Addressees of discrimination are persons who are perceived by others as being 'strange' because they are not seen as members of the majority of the regional population due to some distinct differences. Discrimination in these cases is related to differences which are perceived as natural due to myths of descent and affiliation and which cannot be modified by the affected persons."

Note

In these explanatory notes, the Austrian government explained that the notion of "race" as contained in the Austrian Equal Treatment Act should be understood as a purely legal notion, which does not at all refer to any biological distinctions between "races". It also underlined that the term does not imply an acceptance of theories according to which different "races" can be distinguished. In this way, the use of the term is clarified without there being a need to revert to the use of other, possibly less clear notions or terms.

A definition as contained in ICERD is another common solution. No substantive definition of "race" or an explanation of the term is given, but "racial discrimination" is defined as a broad legal category covering a variety of race-related and

---

[23] 307 der Beilagen XXII. GP—Regierungsvorlage—Materialien at 15. The translation given here can be found in D. Schindlauer, "Report on Measures to Combat Discrimination: Directives 2000/43/EC and 2000/78/EC. Country Report Austria" (European Commission, January 2005) 7, available on the website of Directorate-General for Employment, Social Affairs and Equal Opportunities.

ethnic forms of discrimination, encompassing a variety of biological, cultural and historical group characteristics.[24] An example of this approach can be found in the definition proposed for national legislation to combat racism by the ECRI General Policy Recommendation:

European Commission against Racism and Intolerance, **1.CoE.4.**
ECRI General Policy Recommendation No. 7 on national legislation to combat racism and racial discrimination[25]

"1. For the purposes of this Recommendation, the following definitions shall apply:
b) 'direct racial discrimination' shall mean any differential treatment based on a ground such as race, colour, language, religion, nationality or national or ethnic origin, which has no objective and reasonable justification . . ."

Note
The list of grounds comprised under the general umbrella of "racial discrimination" in this General Recommendation is even longer than in ICERD, containing also nationality, language and even religion. The reason for this is to be found in the explanatory memorandum to the Recommendation and relates to the wish to combat all possible instances of racism, xenophobia and intolerance:

"In the Recommendation, the term 'racism' should be understood in a broad sense, including phenomena such as xenophobia, antisemitism and intolerance. As regards the grounds set out in the definitions of racism and direct and indirect racial discrimination (paragraph 1 of the Recommendation), in addition to those grounds generally covered by the relevant legal instruments in the field of combating racism and racial discrimination, such as race, colour and national or ethnic origin, the Recommendation covers language, religion and nationality. The inclusion of these grounds in the definitions of racism and racial discrimination is based on ECRI's mandate, which is to combat racism, antisemitism, xenophobia and intolerance. ECRI considers that these concepts, which vary over time, nowadays cover manifestations targeting persons or groups of persons, on grounds such as race, colour, religion, language, nationality and national and ethnic origin. As a result, the expressions 'racism' and 'racial discrimination' used in the Recommendation encompass all the phenomena covered by ECRI's mandate. National origin is sometimes interpreted as including the concept of nationality. However, in order to ensure that this concept is indeed covered, it is expressly included in the list of grounds, in addition to national origin. The use of the expression 'grounds such as' in the definitions of racism and direct and indirect racial discrimination aims at establishing an open-ended list of grounds, thereby allowing it to evolve with society. However, in criminal law, an

[24] See K. Henrard, *Devising an Adequate System of Minority Protection. Individual Human Rights, Minority Rights and the Right to Self-Determination* (Leiden, Martinus Nijhoff, 2000) 49.
[25] Adopted on 13 December 2002, CRI (2003) 8, available on the website of the Council of Europe, European Commission against Racism and Intolerance.

exhaustive list of grounds could be established in order to respect the principle of foreseeability which governs this branch of the law."[26]

The method of defining "race" by listing a number of more specific grounds has been followed in many of the EU Member States. There appears to be some variation as to exactly which grounds are comprised under the notion of "race", but mostly race, ethnic origin, national origin and colour are included.[27]

EC Implementation Act (EG-Implementatiewet),   **1.NL.5.**
Explanatory Memorandum[28]

... Dutch law proceeds on the basis of the concept of 'race' as such. The concept of race must be broadly interpreted in accordance with the International Convention on the Elimination of All Forms of Racial Discrimination and established precedents and also includes skin colour, origin or national or ethnic descent.

British Race Relations Act 1976[29]   **1.GB.6.**

'Racial grounds' means any of the following grounds, namely colour, race, nationality (including citizenship), ethnic and national origins.

Within the EU, furthermore, there are some states which do not so much include characteristics such as ethnic origin or membership of a national minority within the wide category of "race" as prohibit *both* discrimination based on race *and* discrimination based on ethnicity, colour, national origin or other relevant grounds.[30] In themselves, such variations would not seem to matter much. Most importantly, the relevant prohibitions of discrimination cover all relevant instances of racial discrimination. Still, the results of differences in definition may be far-reaching. The material scope of legislation, the availability of exemptions and the intensity of judicial review are often closely connected with the ground in question and its perceived "suspectness". This can be illustrated by the situation in the UK, where the scope of the racial non-discrimination legislation has been complicated by a number of amendments to implement the Racial Equality Directive. These amendments, which, for instance, have the effect of broadening the material scope of protection, do apply

---

[26] G. Cardinale, "The Preparation of ECRI General Policy Recommendation No. 7" in Niessen and Chopin, above n. 19, 84–5.

[27] J. Cormack and M. Bell, Developing Anti-Discrimination Law in Europe. The 25 EU Member States Compared (European Commission, September 2005) 20.

[28] *Kamerstukken II* 2002/03, 28 770, no 3, at 3.

[29] c. 74, s. 3(1). An identical provision is included in the Race Relations (Northern Ireland) Order 1997, Statutory Rule 2003 No. 341, Art. 5(1).

[30] See in particular Art. 14 ECHR (". . . discrimination on any ground such as . . ., race, colour, language . . . national or social origin, association with a national minority . . .") and the identical list in Art. 1 of Protocol 12 to the ECtHR.

45

to the grounds explicitly connected to the Directive (race and ethnic or national origin), but not to other grounds protected by the UK legislation, such as colour and nationality. As a result, the level of protection is lower with respect to colour and nationality, even if these grounds are commonly regarded as elements of the definition of race.

Finally, the frequent use of "ethnicity" or "ethnic origin" as either an acceptable alternative for "race" or a complementary notion might raise questions as to the difference between race and ethnicity and the definition of ethnicity. Mostly, this question remains unanswered, but in 2005 the ECtHR explicitly addressed the issue.

ECtHR, 13 December 2005[31]   **1.CoE.7.** *
Timishev v. Russia

FREEDOM OF MOVEMENT OF CHECHENS

Timishev

Facts: Timishev, a Chechen lawyer, lives as a forced migrant in Nalchik, in the Kabardino-Balkaria Republic of the Russian Federation. In 1999, the applicant and his driver travelled by car from the Ingushetia Republic to Nalchik. Their car was stopped at the checkpoint and officers of the Inspectorate for Road Safety refused him entry. The refusal appeared to be based on an oral instruction from the Ministry of the Interior of Kabardino-Balkaria not to admit persons of Chechen ethnic origin. Timishev had to turn round and make a detour of 300 kilometres to reach Nalchik through a different checkpoint.

Held: The Court decided that the refusal of entry amounted to a violation of the prohibition of discrimination (Article 14 ECHR), taken in conjunction with the right to liberty of movement (Article 2 of Protocol No. 4).

Judgment: "55. Ethnicity and race are related and overlapping concepts. Whereas the notion of race is rooted in the idea of biological classification of human beings into subspecies according to morphological features such as skin colour or facial characteristics, ethnicity has its origin in the idea of societal groups marked by common nationality, tribal affiliation, religious faith, shared language, or cultural and traditional origins and backgrounds."

Note

The distinction between race and ethnicity made by the ECtHR in *Timishev* seems to be in accordance with the general academic opinion on the subject. From academic literature it was clear already that "race" is mainly used to refer to biological factors, whereas "ethnic origin" is primarily determined by other factors and characteristics, such as geographical, religious and linguistic characteristics. It must be stressed, however, that there is a difference between the definition of "race" given by the ECtHR, which refers to any perceived biological and morphological differences between "races", and the definition of "racial discrimination" given by ICERD and a

---

[31] Not yet published.
* See also above **1.CoE.1.** and below **1.CoE.112.**

number of Member States. It must be recalled that the ICERD definition is a much wider notion that also covers ethnicity, language and other related grounds. Since the wide definition is most accepted in legal discourse, we will further refer to "race" only in this sense.

MEMBERSHIP OF AN ETHNIC OR RACIAL GROUP

Although the definition given by the ECtHR in *Timishev* to the notion of "ethnicity" seems rather clear, it has proven difficult to establish what "ethnicity", "ethnic origin" or "belonging to an ethnic group" mean in practice. An important question here is whether the notion should be interpreted objectively or subjectively. When ethnic origin (or, for that matter, the broad notion of "race" or "racial group") is regarded as an objective category, a number of concrete criteria can be formulated to test whether or not an individual belongs to a specific racial or ethnic group. The ECtHR clearly opts for this approach, referring to objective criteria such as a common nationality, tribal affiliation, religious faith, shared language and cultural and traditional origins and backgrounds. The objective approach is also discernible in the case-law of some Member States, in which similar criteria are mentioned. An example can be found in the following case decided by the Dutch Equal Treatment Commission:

Equal Treatment Commission (Commissie Gelijke Behandeling)   **1.NL.8.**
Opinion 1998-57

ASYLUM SEEKERS ARE NOT MEMBERS OF A "RACIAL GROUP"

Dentistry for asylum seekers

Facts: The applicant, a fifteen-year-old asylum seeker living in a refugee centre in Eindhoven, broke one of his teeth during a sports activity. The respondent, a dentist, refused to treat the boy because he was not accompanied by an employee of the refugee centre. According to the applicant, the respondent thereby made an unlawful distinction based on race.

Held: There is no discrimination against asylum seekers as a racial group, but there is a case of discrimination based on ethnic origin and nationality against the individual asylum seekers which is not compatible with the Equal Treatment Act.

Judgment: ". . . [I]t must first be considered whether there has possibly been unequal treatment for a group of persons which can be regarded as a distinction based on race within the meaning of the Equal Treatment Act.

The Commission feels that the group of asylum seekers as such does not necessarily fall within the concept of race within the meaning of Article 1 of the Equal Treatment Act. After all, there is no question of a cohesive group with shared physical, ethnic, geographical or cultural characteristics. Nor do asylum seekers differ from other population groups through shared characteristics or behaviour patterns."[32]

---

[32] Interestingly, there is some internal debate in the Netherlands on the qualification of asylum seekers as a racial group. In 2000, the Supreme Court handed down a judgment which is clearly contradictory to that

Note

In this case, the Dutch Equal Treatment Commission considered it of importance that the asylum seekers did not belong to a special group with distinct characteristics that could be established in an objective way.

It is also possible to opt for a more subjective interpretation. Such an interpretation would be in line with a recent General Recommendation of the ICERD Committee which is worded as follows:

Committee on the Elimination of Racial Discrimination **1.UN.9.**
General Recommendation No. 08: Identification with a particular racial
or ethnic group (Art.1, par.1&4): 22/08/90[33]

"The Committee on the Elimination of Racial Discrimination, having considered reports from States parties concerning information about the ways in which individuals are identified as being members of a particular racial or ethnic group or groups, is of the opinion that such identification shall, if no justification exists to the contrary, be based upon self-identification by the individual concerned."

In the spirit of this Recommendation, a number of Member States use terms of ethnic affiliation or ethnic belonging instead of "ethnic origin" or "race":

Austria—*Gleichbehandlungsgesetz* (Federal Equal Treatment Act): ethnic affiliation (*ethnische Zugehörigkeit*)
France—*Article 225-I Code pénal* (Criminal Code) and *Article L. 122-45 Code du travail* (Labour Code): membership or non-membership, true or supposed, of a given ethnic group, nation, race or religion (*de leur appurtenance ou de leur non-appartenance, vrai or suppose, à une ethnie, une nation, une race ou une religion déterminée*)
Sweden—*Lagen om åtgärder mot etnisk diskriminering i arbetslivet* (Ethnic Discrimination Act)—ethnic belonging (*etnisk tillhörighet*)

Thus far, it is not quite clear what the practical effect of such alternatives would be, since there is no case-law in these Member States in which explicit questions regarding the definition of racial discrimination were raised. During the deliberations on the Racial Equality Directive it was mentioned, however, that the use of these alternatives might have the consequence of limiting the impact of the non-discrimination provisions. It was suggested that, to succeed in a case of alleged discrimination, a national court might then need to be convinced that the

---

of the Equal Treatment Commission, even though both instances depart from the same criteria. The Supreme Court in its judgment held that ". . . residents of the refugee centre in question do not differ exclusively through their common address but also—as is common knowledge—by their skin colour, national or ethnic descent and/or geographical or cultural origin and in that sense belong to a race in the broad sense of the word . . ."

[33] 38th Session, 1990, Doc A/45/18.

discrimination in question was actually inspired by an idea or supposition about the racial background of the victim.[34] Such might be difficult to prove, as it would require judicial insight into the discriminator's mind.[35] Having regard to the legislative background, however, it is improbable that the ECJ would accept such a burden of proof under the Directive.

Finally, some states have opted for a combination of the subjective and objective approach to the establishment of membership of a racial or ethnic group. A good example of the combined approach can be found in the UK, in which a benchmark decision on the definition of ethnicity was given in a 1983 judgment in the case of *Mandla* v. *Dowell Lee*:[36]

House of Lords, 24 March 1983[37]   **1.GB.10.**
Mandla v. *Dowell Lee*

SIKHS AS AN ETHNIC GROUP

Mandla

Facts: The headmaster of a private school refused to admit as a pupil to the school a boy who was an orthodox Sikh (and wore long hair under a turban), unless he removed the turban and cut his hair. The headmaster's reasons for his refusal were that the wearing of a turban, being a manifestation of the boy's ethnic origins, would accentuate religious and social distinctions in the school which, being a multiracial school based on the Christian faith, the headmaster desired to minimise.

Held: The Sikhs are a group defined by reference to "ethnic origins" for the purpose of the Race Relations Act 1976 ("the 1976 Act"); the "no turban" rule is not "justifiable" within the meaning of the 1976 Act.

Judgment: LORD FRASER OF TULLYBELTON: "My Lords, I recognise that 'ethnic' conveys a flavour of race but it cannot, in my opinion, have been used in the Act of 1976 in a strictly racial or biological sense. For one thing, it would be absurd to suppose that Parliament can have intended that membership of a particular racial group should depend upon scientific proof that a person possessed the relevant distinctive biological characteristics (assuming that such characteristics exist). The practical difficulties of such proof would be prohibitive, and it is clear that Parliament must have used the word in some more popular sense. For another thing, the briefest glance at the evidence in this case is enough to show that, within the human race, there are very few, if any, distinctions which are scientifically recognised as racial . . . In my opinion, the word 'ethnic' still retains a racial flavour but it is used nowadays in an extended sense to include other characteristics which may be commonly thought of as being associated with common racial origin.

---

[34] Tyson, above n. 19, 113.

[35] See also ch. 2, section 2.3.2.A on motive and direct discrimination.

[36] See critically on this decision, which has triggered a number of comparable cases to be brought before the British courts, S. Fredman, *Discrimination Law* (Oxford, Oxford University Press, 2002) 71, who submits that the criteria defined in *Mandla* v. *Lee* are not always applied consistently and convincingly.

[37] [1983] IRLR 209.

For a group to constitute an ethnic group in the sense of the Act of 1976, it must, in my opinion, regard itself, and be regarded by others, as a distinct community by virtue of certain characteristics. Some of these characteristics are essential; others are not essential but one or more of them will commonly be found and will help to distinguish the group from the surrounding community. The conditions which appear to me to be essential are these: (1) a long shared history, of which the group is conscious as distinguishing it from other groups, and the memory of which it keeps alive; (2) a cultural tradition of its own, including family and social customs and manners, often but not necessarily associated with religious observance. In addition to those two essential characteristics the following characteristics are, in my opinion, relevant; (3) either a common geographical origin, or descent from a small number of common ancestors; (4) a common language, not necessarily peculiar to the group; (5) a common literature peculiar to the group; (6) a common religion different from that of neighbouring groups or from the general community surrounding it; (7) being a minority or being an oppressed or a dominant group within a larger community, for example a conquered people (say, the inhabitants of England shortly after the Norman conquest) and their conquerors might both be ethnic groups.

A group defined by reference to enough of these characteristics would be capable of including converts, for example, persons who marry into the group, and of excluding apostates. Provided a person who joins the group feels himself or herself to be a member of it, and is accepted by other members, then he is, for the purposes of the Act, a member ... In my opinion, it is possible for a person to fall into a particular racial group either by birth or by adherence, and it makes no difference, so far as the Act of 1976 is concerned, by which route he finds his way into the group ... A person may treat another relatively unfavourably 'on racial grounds' because he regards that other as being of a particular race, or belonging to a particular racial group, even if his belief is, from a scientific point of view, completely erroneous."

Notes

(1) It is clear from this case that the notion of "ethnic or racial group" is defined objectively by reference to a number of essential criteria, i.e. a long, shared history and a particular cultural tradition. In addition, the group should share a number of other characteristics, such as a common geographical origin or a common language. Whether an individual is really found to belong to such an ethnic group is determined on the basis of whether the individual actually regards himself as forming part of the relevant group. This means that the definition is not completely objective in character, but also has subjective features.

(2) The case of *Mandla* is interesting for other reasons as well. It stresses, for example, that there is no such thing as a "biological race" and that, for that reason, the use of the notion of "ethnic origin" must be preferred over that of "race"—in this regard its reasoning is similar to the legislative approach used in a number of other Member States. The *Mandla* definition of the notion "ethnic origin" furthermore intends to avoid the "racial flavour" that is still inherent in the notion by referring to non-race related, objective group characteristics. The definition also makes clear that one larger ethnic group may comprise a variety of smaller ethnic groups, which have their own particular characteristics.

(3) *Mandla* has triggered a number of comparable cases to be brought before the British courts, which have not always been successful. Rastafarians have not been

considered to constitute an ethnic group, for example, because of a lack of separate identity from the rest of the Afro-Caribbean community[38] and Muslims have not been held to constitute an ethnic group as they are primarily regarded as a religious grouping.[39] These borderline cases make clear that there is much overlap between the grounds of ethnic origin and religion, which has to be duly acknowledged. The problems resulting from this overlap will be discussed further in section 1.5 of this chapter, in which the issue of multiple discrimination will be addressed.

TRAVELLERS AND GYPSIES

Specific examples of the combination between objective and subjective elements of ethnic groups can be found in the case-law that relates to Roma, Sinti, Gypsies and the Traveller Community. Irish legislation, for instance, contains a definition of "Traveller Community" which is apparently based on a combination of subjective and objective factors: according to this definition, "Traveller Community" means "the community of people who are commonly called Travellers and who are identified (both by themselves and others) as people with a shared history, culture and traditions including, historically, a nomadic way of life on the island of Ireland".[40] This definition has been further elaborated and clarified in the following two decisions of the Irish Equality Officer:[41]

Equality Tribunal, 1 June 2001[42]   **1.IE.11.**
Decision DEC-S/2001/003, Connors v. *Molly Heffernan's Public House*

NOMADIC LIFE NO REQUIREMENT FOR ESTABLISHMENT OF TRAVELLER IDENTITY

Molly Heffernan's pub

Facts: On different occasions, the manager of Molly Heffernan's pub refused to offer service to Mr and Mrs Connors. They claim that they were told they were refused because of their membership of the Traveller Community.

Held: The claimants are Travellers as defined by the Act; both of the complainants have been discriminated against on the basis of their membership of the Traveller Community.

Decision: "8. [From the definition in Section 2 of the Equal Status Act] I consider that for someone to be considered as a Traveller within the meaning defined in the Act they must identify themselves as a Traveller and must also be identified by others as a Traveller. From this

---

[38] *Dawkins* v. *Department of the Environment* [1993] IRLR 284, CA.
[39] *CJ H Walker Ltd.* v. *Hussain* [1996] IRLR 11, EAT.
[40] Equal Status Act 2000 (No. 8/2000), s. 2.
[41] In addition to the quoted decision, see on this *Joyce et al.* v. *The Temple Gate Hotel* (DEC-S2001–012), *Maughan* v. *The Glimmer Man* (DEC-S2001–020), *Maughan* v. *Dolly Heffernan's Public House* (DEC-S2002–010v.011).
[42] Available on the website of the Equality Tribunal of Ireland, under the heading Equal Status Decisions.

definition it is clear that for someone to be considered as a member of the Traveller community that they do not have to be actively leading a nomadic way of life. This is because the definition states that Travellers are people with a shared history, culture and traditions '*including historic-ally, a nomadic way of life*' [emphasis in the original]. In my view the reference to the word historically in this context is important and that it was put in the definition to include people who were nomadic in the past but who are now settled and the settled descendants of people who led a nomadic way of life in the past . . .

Mrs Connors stated at the oral hearing that she considers herself to be a Traveller because she has a different culture than settled people. She said that before she got married she lived in a caravan with her parents and led a nomadic life. Since then she has lived in a house as a settled Traveller and for the last ten years this has been in a house in Tallaght . . .

Mr Connors said that he has never led a nomadic life and the he has been settled all of his life, the last 10 years in his current home in Tallaght. He said that his parents were Travellers and that although they were also settled for a long time, when they were young they led a nomadic life with their parents (Mr Connor's grandparents). It is clear to me that Mr Connors has always identified himself as a Traveller . . .

. . . [A]s I said earlier I do not think that actively living a nomadic life is an essential prereq-uisite to establishing a Traveller identity within the meaning defined in the Act. In any event in my mind the claimant clearly satisfies the link to nomadism required by the definition because his parents led a nomadic lifestyle in the past.

I have fully considered the question raised by the respondent as to whether Mr Connors is a Traveller within the meaning defined in the Act and I am satisfied that he is. It is clear to me that Mr Connors has always identified himself as a Traveller and that others, and in particular Mr Kane, also recognised him as such e.g. when he refused him service from the pub."

Equality Tribunal, 20 August 2001[43]   **1.IE.12.**
Decision DEC-S/2001/008, O'Brien v. Killarney Ryan Hotel

IRRELEVANCE OF SUBJECTIVE FEELING OF BELONGING TO THE "TRAVELLER
COMMUNITY"

Travellers in Killarney Ryan Hotel

Facts: Mr O'Brien called for a drink in Killarney Ryan Hotel several times, but was refused service. He claimed that he was later told that the manager had instructed staff not to serve Travellers. The hotel denied that a strict anti-Traveller policy was in place.

Held: The complainant comes within the definition of a member of the Traveller Community contained in the Act, but has not produced sufficient evidence to substantiate his claim that the respondents discrimi-nated against him on the grounds of his imputed membership of the Traveller Community.

Decision: "9.1 [Mr O'Brien] stated [at the hearing] that he personally does not consider himself a Traveller and explained that, while his parents were Travellers and had lived a nomadic life, he himself had never travelled. He said that he and his wife have lived in a private housing estate for almost 30 years and had brought up their family as part of the settled community.

This point raises the question as to whether the complainant is entitled to claim discrimi-nation on the Traveller community ground when he does not see himself as a Traveller . . .

---

[43] Available on the website of the Equality Tribunal of Ireland, under the heading Equal Status Decisions.

Given that the complainant has stated that his parents were members of the Traveller community and that they did indeed travel, I believe that, by imputation, the complainant's status is in keeping with the Act's definition of a member of the Traveller community. For this reason, I believe that the complainant comes within the definition of a member of the Traveller community contained in the Act."

Note

The cited cases disclose an intricate combination of objective and subjective factors. Although objective factors such as leading a nomadic life and coming from a family of Travellers may be of importance in deciding if the complainant can be considered as a member of the Traveller Community, subjective factors may also play a role. Their relevance is limited, however, to the situation in which the complainant actually identifies himself with the Traveller Community. In that situation, the subjective feeling of belonging to the group will even overrule the fact that the complainant does not conform to certain objective criteria, such as leading a nomadic life. On the other hand, from the fact that a complainant does not consider himself a Traveller it may *not* be derived that he does not come within the definition of membership of the Traveller Community. In that situation, objective factors such as a family history of travelling may be of overriding influence to the legal classification. Although this would seem to run counter to the individual desire not to be considered a Traveller, it has the advantage of offering a high level of protection, as it guarantees that individuals are also protected against discrimination if they are assumed to belong to the Traveller Community.

In other EU Member States, non-discrimination law makes no specific mention of Roma, Sinti, Gypsies and Travellers. In these states the relevant groups are protected by such notions as membership of a minority group, ethnic group or racial group. Interestingly, the combination of objective and subjective factors is not always present here, as may be illustrated by one of the leading cases on the issue in the UK:

Court of Appeal[44]   **1.GB.13.**
Commission for Racial Equality v. *Dutton*

GYPSIES AS AN ETHNIC GROUP

Gypsies at the Cat and Mutton pub

Facts: Dutton displayed signs marked "No travellers" at his pub, the Cat and Mutton, following "unpleasant experiences" involving persons from caravans parked nearby: they had caused damage, threatened him and his wife and upset the regular customers.

Held: Gypsies are an identifiable group defined by their ethnic origins for the purposes of the Race Relations Act; there was no evidence to show that the signs were justifiable.

[44] [1989] 1 All ER 306, CA.

Judgment: NICHOLLS LJ: "On the evidence it is clear that . . . gipsies are a minority, with a long-shared history and a common geographical origin. They are a people who originated in northern India. They migrated thence to Europe through Persia in medieval times. They have certain, albeit limited, customs of their own, regarding cooking and the manner of washing. They have a distinctive, traditional style of dressing, with heavy jewellery worn by the women, although this dress is not worn all the time. They also furnish their caravans in a distinctive manner. They have a language or dialect, known as 'pogadi chib', spoken by English gipsies (Romany chals) and Welsh gipsies (Kale) which consists of up to one-fifth of Romany words in place of English words. They do not have a common religion, nor a peculiar, common literature of their own, but they have a repertoire of folktales and music passed on from one generation to the next. No doubt, after all the centuries which have passed since the first gipsies left the Punjab, gipsies are no longer derived from what, in biological terms, is a common racial stock, but that of itself does not prevent them from being a racial group as widely defined in the Act.

I come now to the part of the case which has caused me most difficulty. Gipsies prefer to be called 'travellers' as they think that term is less derogatory. This might suggest a wish to lose their separate, distinctive identity so far as the general public is concerned. Half or more of them now live in houses, like most other people. Have gipsies now lost their separate, group identity, so that they are no longer a community recognisable by ethnic origins within the meaning of the Act? . . .

. . . [W]ith respect to the judge, I do not think that there was before him any evidence justifying his conclusion that gipsies have been absorbed into a larger group, if by that he meant that substantially all gipsies have been so absorbed. The fact that some have been so absorbed and are indistinguishable from any ordinary member of the public, is not sufficient in itself to establish loss of . . . 'an historically determined social identity in [the group's] own eyes and in the eyes of those outside the group.' . . . In my view the evidence was sufficient to establish that, despite their long presence in England, gipsies have not merged wholly in the population, as have the Saxons and the Danes, and altogether lost their separate identity. They, or many of them, have retained separateness, a self-awareness, of still being gipsies . . .

In my view . . . the evidence was still sufficient to establish that gipsies are an identifiable group of persons defined by reference to ethnic origins within the meaning of the Act."

Note
In defining the relevant racial group, Nicholls LJ applied the objective criteria of the above-cited case of *Mandla* v. *Dowell Lee* (**1.UK.10.**). In addition, he discussed the question if Gypsies had lost their separate and distinctive identity, thus making clear that the meaning of the notion of "racial or ethnic group" can vary over time, depending on whether the objective criteria are met in the concrete circumstances. The question whether the concerned individual actually regards himself as being part of the group did not seem to be of any influence at all.

For the Netherlands, the situation is different, as is exemplified by the following case:[45]

---

[45] The decision cited below is well-established case-law of the Dutch Equal Treatment Commission. See also Opinion 1998-99, available on the website of the Dutch Equal Treatment Commission.

Equal Treatment Commission (Commissie Gelijke Behandeling)   **1.NL.14.**
Opinion 1999-65

UNEQUAL TREATMENT OF CARAVAN DWELLERS CONSTITUTES RACIAL
DISCRIMINATION

Baby's furniture for caravan dwellers

Facts: The applicants lived in a caravan placed on an official caravan site and wanted to acquire baby's furniture at a shop that was run by the respondent. The sales person informed them of the fact that the respondent did not deliver any furniture to caravan sites. The reason for this policy was that there had been a number of serious incidents in the past when goods were delivered to caravan sites.

Held: Discrimination against caravan dwellers constitutes indirect racial discrimination. The facts disclose a case of unjustified indirect discrimination which is contrary to the Equal Treatment Act.

Opinion: "4.3 The question arises first of all whether caravan dwellers are covered by the concept of race in terms of the Equal Treatment Act. To answer this question, the legislative history of the Act approving the Convention on the Elimination of all Forms of Racial Discrimination and that of the ban against discrimination under criminal law based thereon, serve as a guideline. Both indicate that when ascertaining whether racial discrimination exists, reference can be made to characteristics that are of a physical, ethnic, geographical, cultural, historic or religious nature.

This interpretation of the concept of race means that the cohesion within the group in question is important to the present consideration. This cohesion may be determined by social, cultural and/or historical backgrounds.

The Commission has already considered that, in principle, the concept of race may cover a group of persons that has manifested itself from generation to generation as caravan dwellers and which regards itself as a population group with a culture to be distinguished from other population groups. This applies the more so because caravan dwellers generally encounter prejudice and unequal treatment from their environment as a special population group.

The Commission finds that the origin of both applicants is characterised by a lengthy tradition of caravan dwelling. Both the parents and grandparents of both of them have already lived on caravan sites and with regard to the applicant—according to oral tradition—this lifestyle goes back to the 18th century.

Both applicants are registered as caravan dwellers. It is clear from the particulars produced that the applicant had a licence under Article 18 Caravan Act (old version) to live in a caravan, through her father. The applicants regard themselves as belonging to the population group of caravan dwellers. They experience their 'own' culture with strong mutual ties between caravan dwellers and with mutual support. As caravan dwellers they claim experiencing relegation and disadvantage through the actions of both the authorities and non-caravan dwellers.

In view of these facts and the circumstances, the Commission feels that the unequal treatment of applicants as caravan dwellers may be regarded as unequal treatment by virtue of their race within the meaning of article 1 AWGB."

Note

It is clear from this opinion that the Dutch Equal Treatment Commission has regard to a combination of objective and subjective factors in determining whether caravan dwellers constitute a racial group. Of relevance are not only factors relating to group cohesion and social, cultural or historical background, but also factors relating to the identification of an individual with the group concerned.

Hence, it is clear that there is but little convergence within the European Union as regards the proper definition of an ethnic or racial group and, in particular, with regard to the definition of the group of Travellers, Gypsies and caravan dwellers—varying criteria to determine group membership are currently in use.

MEMBERSHIP OF A (NATIONAL) MINORITY—NATIONAL ORIGIN

Closely related to the grounds of race and ethnic origin is the notion of national origin or membership of a national minority. According to the drafting history of the ICERD, the term "national origin" is used in the context of a politically organised nation included within a different state, which continues to exist as a nation in the cultural and social sense of the word, even without being a sovereign state.[46] Members of such a nation can be discriminated against, not so much because of their race or ethnic background, but as members of the (former) nation. In this context, the term "national origin" is often used to denote "belonging to a national minority". Reference is also sometimes made in this context to "national self-consciousness", which is connected with a certain political aspiration for a degree of autonomy or even independence.[47] It has proven to be very difficult, however, to arrive at an agreement regarding the precise definition of a "minority". There is presently no generally accepted definition of this notion, either at the European level or at the international level.[48] The controversies relate to all minorities (ethnic, religious, linguistic, national), but the problems are most insoluble with respect to national minorities.[49] The European Framework Convention for the Protection of National Minorities, in which the notion would appear to play a central role, even takes special care not to take any position in this regard:[50]

> *Council of Europe, "European Framework Convention for the*   **1.CoE.15.**
> *Protection of National Minorities", Explanatory Memorandum, 1996*

"12. It should . . . be pointed out that the framework Convention contains no definition of the notion of 'national minority'. It was decided to adopt a pragmatic approach, based on the

---

[46] See N. Lerner, *The UN Convention on the Elimination of all Forms of Racial Discrimination* (Alphen a/d Rijn, Sijthoff and Noordhoff, 1980) 29, referring to a debate in the context of the drafting of CERD (Av.C.3v.SR.1304, pp. 2v.3).

[47] Henrard, above n. 24, 54.

[48] *Ibid.*, 18 and *cf.* N. Lerner, *Group Rights and Discrimination in International Law*, 2nd edn (Leiden, Martinus Nijhoff, 2003) 8–9, mentioning several definitions of a minority group.

[49] *Ibid.*, 27*ff.*

[50] The same is true for the UN Declaration on the Rights of Persons Belonging to National or Ethnic, Religious and Linguistic Minorities, adopted by UN General Assembly, Resolution 47/135 of 18 December 1992.

recognition that at this stage, it is impossible to arrive at a definition capable of mustering general support of all Council of Europe member States.

The lack of any clear definition of a (national) minority may have important consequences for the protection of members of such minorities. Presently, a number of states do not, or only reluctantly, recognise the existence of national minorities in their midst. It is clear that in those cases, the concept of discrimination based on 'national origin' is hardly conceivable. Of course, such denial of the existence of national minorities has clear consequences for the protection against discrimination."

The lack of any clear definition of a (national) minority may have important consequences for the protection of members of such minorities. Presently, a number of states do not, or only reluctantly, recognise the existence of national minorities in their midst. It is clear that in those states a prohibition of discrimination based on "national origin" is hardly conceivable. Indeed, this is illustrated by the legislative situation in certain Member States, such as Greece, which has been criticised precisely for that reason:

> ". . . throughout the 20th Century the existence of racial/ethnic minorities has been viewed by the young (1832–) Greek state as a taboo subject 'with dangerous implications for its ethnic and territorial integrity'. As a consequence, no serious public debate on these matters has ever been initiated by any Greek political party, or any NGO . . . It is also characteristic that a (pending) Bill for the transposition of the Race Directive was brought to surface by the socialist opposition in May 2004, without initiating consultations or non-governmental organizations."[51]

As a result of such problems, there does not seem to be a workable definition of minorities which is agreeable to all the Member States and which could serve as a proper basis for protection against discrimination based on membership of a national minority.

A further problem related to the definition of "national origin" and "membership of a national minority" concerns the term "national" itself. In the first place, the term must be carefully distinguished from the notion of "nationality", which is discussed separately in section 1.3.3 below. This notion refers to citizens of other nation states and is mainly political in character, whereas the notion of national origin refers to autochthon individuals and seems to be more social in nature. Still, both notions are often confused, as the term "national origin" is sometimes used to refer to individuals who are born in another nation state. To that extent, national origin and nationality are overlapping concepts.[52]

In addition, it appears to be difficult to make a clear distinction between "national origin" and "membership of a national minority", and between "ethnic origin" and

---

[51] I. Ktistasis and N. Sitaropoulos, "Discrimination Based on Racial or Ethnic Origin. Executive Summary for Greece" (European Commission, June 2004) 1, available on the website of Directorate-General for Employment, Social Affairs and Equal Opportunities.

[52] This was solved in the ICERD by adding a second and third paragraph to Art. 1, in which it is made clear that the notion of nationality is not covered by the term "racial discrimination". See Lerner, above n. 48, 53.

"membership of an ethnic minority".[53] In Estonia, for example, one of the basic elements of the definition of member of a *national* minority is that "they differ from Estonians by their *ethnic* affiliation, cultural and religious idiosyncrasies, or language [emphasis added]".[54] In this definition, membership of a particular ethnic group is decisive for the qualification of a group as a national minority. In other states, the notion of national origin is formulated more widely, covering both national origin as described above and ethnic origin; this is, for example, the case in Lithuania.[55] Notwithstanding such examples of overlap, it is clear that the notions cannot be used interchangeably—although a member of a national minority may have a different ethnic background than the majority, a person of different ethnic origin does not necessarily mean that an individual is a member of a national minority.[56] Some Member States have endeavoured to prevent any confusion by inserting a clear definition of both notions in the relevant legislation, or even by indicating which groups in the state should be considered national or ethnic minority groups. A good illustration of this approach can be found in the Polish legislation:

Polish National and Ethnic Minorities and Regional   **1.PL.16.**
Languages Act of 6 January 2005[57]

1) A national minority within the meaning of the Act is a group of Polish citizens which jointly satisfies the following criteria:

1.   Is less numerous than the remainder of the Polish population;
2.   Differs in a fundamental way from the remaining citizens, in its language, culture or tradition;
3.   Strives to preserve its language, culture or tradition;
4.   Is aware of its own historical national identity and directs its efforts towards its expression and protection;
5.   Its ancestors have lived in the present Polish territories for at least 100 years;
6.   It identifies with its country's nation.

2) The following are recognised as national minorities:

1.   Belarusian
2.   Czech
3.   Lithuanian

---

[53] Henrard, above n. 24, 54.

[54] Art. 1 of the Law on Cultural Autonomy of National Minorities, cited by V. Poleshchuk, "Report on Measures to Combat Discrimination: Directive 2000/43/EC and 2000/78/EC: Country Report Estonia" (European Commission, February 2005) 10, available on the website of Directorate-General for Employment, Social Affairs and Equal Opportunities.

[55] S. Vindrinskaite, "Report on Measures to Combat Discrimination: Directive 2000/43/EC and 2000/78/EC. Country Report Lithuania (European Commission, December 2004) 6, available on the website of Directorate-General for Employment, Social Affairs and Equal Opportunities.

[56] However, this is a point of debate. It has also been argued that the notion of "national minority" is wider than that of "ethnic minority" and even that "national minority" can be taken to include all ethnic, religious or linguistic minorities. See Henrard, above n. 24, 54.

[57] Art. 2.

4. German
5. Armenian
6. Russian
7. Slovak
8. Ukrainian
9. Jewish

3) An ethnic minority within the meaning of the Act is a group of Polish citizens which jointly satisfies the following criteria:

1. Is less numerous than the remainder of the Polish population;
2. Differs in a fundamental way from the remaining citizens, in its language, culture or tradition;
3. Strives to preserve its language, culture or tradition;
4. Is aware of its own historical ethnic identity and directs its efforts towards its expression and protection;
5. Its ancestors have lived in the present Polish territories for at lest 100 years;
6. It does not identify with its country's nation.

4) The following are recognised as ethnic minorities:

1. Karimians
2. Lemkovians
3. Roma
4. Tatars

Although this approach seems to have the advantage of clarity, it also has its problematic elements, as is made clear by a discussion of this legislative definition in a report of the Polish Parliamentary Office:

Comments of the Polish Parliamentary Office to the   **1.PL.17.**
Draft National Minorities Act[58]

"The Minorities Act as adopted finalises the meaning of the terms 'national minorities' and 'ethnic minorities' and specifies to which groups these terms relate. The first concept applies to ethnic communities which identify themselves with the nations of their own states, while the second one applies to non-national communities. This is a formal division, which simplifies the socially complex ethnic identities of members of minority groups. It has also aroused protests among some minorities. When the *Sejm* adopted the Act in November 2004 and sent it to the Senate, senators received a letter protesting against the division into 'national' and 'ethnic' minorities from the Association of Jewish Confessional Communities in Poland, the Union of Polish Tatars and the Polish Roma Association.

These organisations found the provision 'deeply humiliating' and protested against associating their sense of separate national identity with the existence of the state. Their letter

[58] S. Łodziński, "Wyrównanie czy uprzywilejowanie? Spory dotyczące projektu ustawy o ochronie mniejszości narodowych (1989–2005)", Kancelaria Sejmu Bioro Studiów I Ekspertyz; Wydział Analiz Economicznych I Społecznych, March 2005, Report No. 232, ch. 6.

says 'We experience this as a painful blow to our identities, inflicted on us in a manner which takes no account of the history of the lands in which we have come to live, the history of the nations among which our cultures have developed, or the development of statehood which also includes our history. Irrespective of the existence or non-existence, either now or at any time, of one or more Tatar, Roma or Jewish states, we were and remain nations. No parliament in the world has the power to deprive us of our awareness of this fact.'

The division may also cause bitterness among those who were classified as ethnic minorities, such as the Roma and the Lemkovians, which have limited parliamentary election rights. However, the Minorities Act, although it does not include electoral rights, is designed to guarantee equal rights to both kinds of minorities [references omitted]."

Note
The commentary illustrates that explicit recognition and distinction of ethnic and national minorities is highly controversial, as it may simplify the complex reality in a diverse society and cause unwanted and unnecessary social divisions. For that reason, it is not surprising that most Member States have thus far refrained from adopting the Polish legislative approach and do not clearly distinguish between national and ethnic minorities.

LANGUAGE

It is clear from the definition of racial discrimination given in the legislation of a number of states that language is explicitly covered by the notion of race or ethnic origin. In other states, this point is open to debate. In the Netherlands, for example, a difference is made between a prohibition to speak a foreign language (which would amount to discrimination directly based on race)[59] and a requirement to speak Dutch (which would not amount to direct discrimination based on race, but merely to indirect discrimination).[60] It may be gathered from this that language is only considered to form an actual part of the ground of ethnicity and race if the language concerned is *foreign*.

Further, some states mention language as a separate ground of discrimination, as is the case in the Polish constitution (Article 13) and the Finnish Non-Discrimination Act (section 6). Unfortunately, no materials are presently available in which the meaning of the ground is further explained.

ETHNICITY AND RELIGION

One last difficult question which is relevant to this subsection relates to the distinction between racial or ethnic discrimination and discrimination based on religion. Discrimination against Jews or Muslims, for instance, can easily be

---

[59] See, e.g. Dutch Equal Treatment Commission, Opinion 2001-97.
[60] See, e.g. Dutch Equal Treatment Commission, Opinion 2001-141.

categorised both ways.[61] This causes particular problems if the protection offered against racial discrimination is different from the protection against religious discrimination, as is the case with the protection offered by the Racial Equality Directive and the Employment Equality Directive. This problem will be explored separately in section 1.5, which is devoted to the concept of "multiple" and "intersectional" discrimination.

1.3.2.B. SUSPECTNESS

Race is commonly regarded as a highly suspect ground. Unequal treatment based on such a ground can only rarely be considered acceptable. This finds clear expression in the legislation in the various Member States, which mostly contains absolute or nearly absolute prohibitions on race-based distinctions. Insofar as non-discrimination legislation has an open character (i.e. does not contain an enumerative list of grounds and contains an open possibility for justification), it is usually clear from case-law that race based classifications are suspect and almost impossible to justify. This is particularly clear from the case-law of the European Court of Human Rights. In its case-law on race based discrimination, two different situations can be distinguished. In the first place, the ECtHR has dealt with complaints of racially inspired cases of inhuman and degrading treatment, such as racial police violence. In this context, it has consistently held that discrimination based on race can of itself amount to degrading treatment within the meaning of Article 3 of the Convention.[62] This type of case, in which acts are at stake that are clearly inspired by racism and racial prejudice, can be distinguished from cases that actually concern a *difference in treatment* based on race or ethnic origin. In this type of case, the ECtHR has recently qualified race and ethnic origin as "suspect" grounds of discrimination. This is particularly clear from the *Timishev* case decided in 2005, which has been discussed before (see **1.CoE.1.**). In this case, the Court made it clear that racial discrimination has to be regarded as so invidious that hardly any discrimination based on race or ethnic origin can be considered to be justifiable. This ruling stands in marked contrast to earlier judgments of the ECtHR relating to unequal treatment of Gypsies:

---

[61] See above n. 18, 20.
[62] ECtHR, 6 July 2005, *Nachova and Others* v. *Bulgaria*, not yet published, §§ 145 and 164.

ECtHR, 18 January 2001[63]   **1.CoE.18.**
Chapman v. United Kingdom

NO STRICT TEST APPLIED TO DISCRIMINATION AGAINST GYPSIES[64]

Chapman

Facts: Chapman is a Gypsy by birth and has always travelled in the Hertfordshire area in the UK. In 1985, she bought a piece of land with the intention of giving up her nomadic lifestyle and living quietly in a mobile home place on the land. The County Council, however, told her that she would not be allowed to live on the land, since it was in the Metropolitan Green Belt and national and planning policies overrode Chapman's needs and interests.

Held: As there is no lack of objective and reasonable justification for the measures taken against the applicant, there is no violation of Article 14 of the Convention.

Judgment: "93 . . . The Court observes that there may be said to be an emerging international consensus amongst the Contracting States of the Council of Europe recognising the special needs of minorities and an obligation to protect their security, identity and lifestyle . . ., not only for the purpose of safeguarding the interests but to preserve a cultural diversity of value to the whole community.

94. However, the Court is not persuaded that the consensus is sufficiently concrete for it to derive any guidance as to the conduct or standards which Contracting States consider desirable in any particular situation. The framework convention, for example, sets out general principles and goals but the signatory States were unable to agree on means of implementation. This reinforces the Court's view that the complexity and sensitivity of the issues involved in policies balancing the interests of the general population, in particular with regard to environmental protection, and the interests of a minority with possibly conflicting requirements renders the Court's role a strictly supervisory one.

95. Moreover, to accord to a Gypsy who has unlawfully stationed a caravan site at a particular place different treatment from that accorded to non-Gypsies who have established a caravan site at that place or from that accorded to any individual who has established a house in that particular place would raise substantial problems under Article 14 of the Convention . . .

129. . . . While discrimination may arise where States without an objective and reasonable justification fail to treat differently persons whose situations are significantly different . . . the Court does not find, in the circumstances of this case, any lack of objective and reasonable justification for the measures taken against the applicant."

Notes

(1) Although the ECtHR acknowledged the special character of the problems of Gypsies in this case, this did not lead it to conclude that a case of de facto unequal treatment based on Gypsy status or ethnic origin is suspect, nor did it require very weighty reasons to be adduced in justification. It may be argued, however, that this judgment concerned an atypical case of ethnically inspired unequal treatment, since

---

[63] Reports 2001-I.
[64] See for comparable cases ECtHR, 25 September 1996, *Buckley* v. *UK*, Reports 1996-IV and ECtHR, 18 January 2001, *Jane Smith* v. *UK*, not published.

there was no clear case of disadvantageous treatment of a Gypsy in comparison to a non-Gypsy. On the basis of *Timishev* and earlier case-law of the ECtHR, in which it said "that it is particularly conscious of the vital importance of combating racial discrimination in all its forms and manifestations",[65] it may be expected that the ECtHR will show less deference if it is presented with a more obvious case of unequal treatment of Gypsies.

(2) Having regard to the general perception of suspectness of the grounds of race and ethnicity, it is highly probable that the national courts and the ECJ will strictly review all instances of direct discrimination based on these grounds. However, considering the possible impact of ECtHR precedents such as *Chapman*, and having regard to the lack of consensus on the definition of racial and ethnic groups, it is difficult to predict what will happen if more controversial cases are brought before the courts. A uniform and wide definition provided by the ECJ, accompanied by a clear stance with respect to the level of scrutiny, would be most helpful to guarantee an adequate level of protection against discrimination.

1.3.3.   NATIONALITY

1.3.3.A.   DEFINITION

DIFFERENT SITUATIONS

The ground of nationality poses particular problems for non-discrimination legislation. A distinction is usually made between two different situations. First, an important question is whether non-discrimination legislation applies to non-citizens who are present in a certain Member State, i.e. whether non-citizens have a claim to the protection offered by such legislation. This question seems to be answered in the affirmative for the Article 13 Directives, which both apply to "all persons". This is obviously a notion that is broad enough to cover citizens as well as non-citizens.[66] Indeed, the preambles of both Directives stress that the prohibition of discrimination should also apply to nationals of third countries.[67]

Secondly, it is questionable if non-discrimination law covers all cases of unequal treatment based on nationality. In this respect, the approach towards discrimination based on nationality appears to differ from that towards race and origin, both on the international and European level and on the level of the Member States. ICERD and the Racial Equality Directive do not prohibit the states from making distinctions

---

[65] ECtHR, 23 September 1994, *Jersild* v. *Denmark*, Series A, Vol. 298, para. 30.

[66] See the Racial Equality Directive, Art. 3(1) and the Employment Equality Directive, Art. 3(1). See also S. Parmar, "The European Court of Justice and Anti-Discrimination Law" in J. Niessen and I. Chopin, *The Development of Legal Instruments to Combat Racism in a Diverse Europe* (Leiden, Martinus Nijhoff, 2004) 138.

[67] Recital 13 of the preamble to the Racial Equality Directive, Recital 12 of the preamble to the Employment Equality Directive.

based on this ground,[68] whereas the EU Charter of Fundamental Rights and the EC Treaty contain explicit non-discrimination clauses relating to nationality discrimination.[69] Within the EU, this seeming contradiction may be explained by the background of the various provisions. Article 12 EC[70] is meant to remove all differences in treatment of EU citizens and is usually read in close connection with the EC Treaty provisions relating to free movement. Disadvantageous treatment of citizens of other EU Member States might hamper their rights of free movement within the internal market and should therefore be prevented. A similar need for equal treatment for economic and internal market reasons does not exist with respect to third-country nationals. Accordingly, third-country nationals do not generally fall within the scope of the non-discrimination clauses of the EC Treaty.[71] On these issues, the European Court of Justice has developed an extensive and highly nuanced body of case-law. It is understandable that the Member States, when drafting the Racial Equality Directive, wished to leave this body of case-law intact by exempting nationality discrimination from the scope of the Directive.[72] Thus, it might be said that nationality discrimination continues to be governed by the "regular" provisions of the European Treaties and the ECJ case-law, rather than by the specific equality provisions of the Equality Directives.

As a result of the exclusion of nationality from the scope of the Article 13 Directives, some EU Member States, such as Bulgaria,[73] have refrained from mentioning the ground in their national non-discrimination legislation. Even in these states, however, the level of protection accorded to non-nationals should be equal to the level of protection guaranteed by international treaties such as the ECHR and the ICCRP. In other states, a different choice has been made: a large number of states have added "nationality" to their legislative lists of prohibited grounds.

DEFINITION OF NATIONALITY

The definitions given to the notion of nationality are widely diverging and sometimes confusing. For instance, ICERD defines "nationality" purely as "citizenship", whilst the Racial Equality Directive (in exempting this category) refers to "third country nationals and stateless persons". In the Member States, "nationality" is sometimes

---

[68] See Art. 1(2) and (3) CERD and Art. 3(2) of the Racial Equality Directive.

[69] See Art. 21(2) of the Charter of Fundamental Rights of the European Union and Art. 12 EC.

[70] And, consequently, Art. 21(2) of the Charter of Fundamental Rights—see "Explanation Relating to the Complete Text of the Charter", December 2000, on Art. 21(2).

[71] There are some exceptions, based on a variety of legal constructs. Family members of EU citizens may, for instance, be placed in a different situation, just like employees in the EC service. See on this P. Craig and G. de Búrca, *EU Law. Text, Cases and Materials*, 3rd edn (Oxford, Oxford University Press, 2003) 754.

[72] See critically on this C. Brown, "The Race Directive: Towards Equality for All the Peoples of Europe?" [2002] *YEL* 210.

[73] P. Johansson, "Comparing National and Community Anti-Discrimination Law" in Niessen and Chopin, above n. 66, 189: in Bulgaria, non-nationals are only protected against discrimination on the grounds of nationality in the exercise of basic rights under binding instruments.

used to refer to national minorities and the ground of national origin, mentioning "citizenship" as a separate ground of distinction.[74] A clearer definition can be found in Article 2(a) of the European Convention on Nationality:

> "'Nationality' means the legal bond between a person and a State and does not indicate the person's ethnic origin."

According to this definition, nationality is a purely legal and objective concept which refers to the nationality legislation valid in a certain state. The nationality of a specific individual can be established on the basis of such legislation, thus enabling a determination of whether an individual is discriminated against because of his nationality.

Still, the availability of such a relatively clear definition does not bring an end to the confusion, since it is not always obvious that it is this definition that is meant if a Member State prohibits unequal treatment based on "nationality": the notion is seldom defined and mostly no reference is made to any international definitions. Particularly unclear is whether national non-discrimination legislation which refers to "nationality" must also be held to cover stateless persons (which is a large category in several Eastern European states, such as Estonia and Latvia),[75] or persons whose nationality is difficult to establish as a result of lack of nationality papers. It is thus difficult to give any general overview of the way in which the notion is used throughout Europe.

An additional problem is that the notion of nationality is easily confused with the concept of national or ethnic origin.[76] In many cases, discrimination against non-nationals and discrimination based on national and ethnic origin will coincide, especially since there is a considerable overlap between minority ethnic communities in Europe and communities of third-country nationals.[77] In some cases, "nationality" thus seems to be used not so much to refer to someone's legal nationality, as to someone's country of birth or ethnic background. Having regard to such overlap, it is understandable that the legislation of some Member States comprises the ground of nationality under the scope of the wider notion of "race". In the Irish Equal Status Act of 2000, for instance, the ground of race is defined as including "race, colour, nationality or ethnic or *national* origins".[78] Such definitions still raise the question whether they refer only to nationality in the sense of "national origin", or (also) to the concept of nationality in the form of "citizenship". Indeed, it would seem that both meanings are used, as is made explicit in the comparable definition given to "racial grounds" in UK legislation: "'racial grounds' means any of the following grounds, namely colour, race, nationality (including citizenship), ethnic and national origins".[79]

---

[74] *Cf.* A. Dummett, "Implementing European Anti-Discrimination Law" in Niessen and Chopin, above n. 66, 238.
[75] *Ibid.* at 238–9.
[76] Brown, above n. 72, 210.
[77] See M. Bell, "Setting Standards in the Fight against Racism" in Niessen and Chopin, above n. 66, 218–19.
[78] Art. 3(2)(h), emphasis added.
[79] Race Relations Act 1976, s. 3(1) and Race Relations (Northern Ireland) Order 1977, Art. 5(1).

Notwithstanding such examples, it is clear that the European Directives and a large number of Member States adhere strictly to the distinction between nationality and national or ethnic origin. Any real convergence of legislation is thus not visible in this area.

1.3.3.B.   SUSPECTNESS

The suspectness of nationality as a ground of discrimination is particularly difficult to determine, since nationality is closely connected to national sovereignty. Many states confer privileges, social advantages and rights only to their own citizens, not aliens, rendering nationality a rather common ground of distinction. This is also certainly true for immigration law, where it is widely accepted that non-nationals can be treated differently from nationals. In these cases, concerning what may be termed the "external dimension" of the treatment of non-nationals, nationality is clearly considered a non-suspect ground. Indeed, many of the Member States which have included an explicit prohibition on nationality discrimination allow for wide exceptions to the principle of equal treatment, at least as long as this is compatible with the requirements of the European Convention of Human Rights and Title IV of the EC Treaty.

This is different for cases in which the "internal dimension" of the treatment of non-nationals is at stake. These cases concern classifications based on nationality in a variety of areas, such as employment (e.g. lower payments for non-nationals) or social security (e.g. exclusion from childcare benefits). In cases relating to this "internal dimension", it is more difficult to find a justification for nationality based differences in treatment.[80] The European Court of Human Rights has even accepted nationality as a suspect ground in these cases, which means that a distinction based on these grounds has to be justified by "very weighty reasons":

ECtHR, 16 September 1996[81]   **1.CoE.19.**
Gaygusuz v. *Austria*

"VERY WEIGHTY REASONS" TEST APPLIED TO NATIONALITY DISCRIMINATION

Gaygusuz

Facts: Mr Gaygusuz is of Turkish origin and lives in Austria on the basis of a permanent residence permit. The Austrian authorities refused to grant him emergency assistance, a kind of social advantage, on the ground that he did not have Austrian nationality. Such nationality was one of the legislative conditions for entitlement for an allowance of this type.

Held: The difference in treatment between Austrians and non-Austrians is not based on any objective and reasonable justification and therefore constitutes a violation of Article 14 ECHR.

---

[80] *Cf.* M. Bell, "Setting Standards in the Fight against Racism" in Niessen and Chopin, above n. 66, 218.
[81] Reports 1996-IV.

Judgment: "42 . . . the States enjoy a certain margin of appreciation in assessing whether and to what extent differences in otherwise similar situations justify a different treatment. However, *very weighty reasons* would have to be put forward before the Court could regard a difference exclusively based on the ground of nationality as compatible with the Convention [emphasis added]."

Note

The ECtHR confirmed this holding in the *Koua Poirrez* case of 2003.[82] Unfortunately, in neither case has it explained the reason why nationality should trigger a "very weighty reasons" test. Indeed, it is probable that this case-law is not completely crystallised as yet. This may appear from the following decision:

ECtHR, 25 October 2005[83]   **1.CoE.20.**
Niedzwiecki v. *Germany*

NO "VERY WEIGHTY REASONS" TEST APPLIED TO NATIONALITY DISCRIMINATION

Niedzwiecki

Facts: Mr Niedzwiecki, who is of Polish origin, moved to Germany in 1987. In 1989 he obtained a provisional residence permit; in 1991 he was issued with a limited residence title for exceptional purposes. This residence title was renewed every two years. In 1997, he finally obtained an unlimited residence permit. In 1995, his daughter was born. Niedzwiecki applied for child benefits, which were available under the Federal Child Benefits Act. His request was dismissed, as he only had a limited residence title for exceptional purposes.

Held: Though no "very weighty reasons" test was applied, the Court found that there were no sufficient reasons justifying the different treatment.

Judgment: "32. . . . . The Contracting States enjoy a certain margin of appreciation in assessing whether and to what extent differences in otherwise similar situations justify a different treatment . . .

   33. The Court is not called upon to decide generally to what extent it is justified to make distinctions, in the field of social benefits, between holders of different categories of residence permits. Rather it has to limit itself to the question whether the German law on child benefits as applied in the present case violated the applicant's rights under the Convention . . ."

Note

In *Niedzwiecki*, the ECtHR did not mention the "very weighty reasons" test at all, nor did it refer to its earlier judgments in *Gaygusuz* (**1.CoE.19.**) and *Koua Poirrez*. From § 33, it may even be inferred that the ECtHR is willing to apply a less strict test to cases of nationality discrimination in social security, as it is "not called upon to decide generally to what extent it is justified to make distinctions in the field of social benefits". It is not clear, therefore, if the Court still considers nationality a suspect

<hr/>

[82] ECtHR, 30 September 2003, *Koua Poirrez* v. *France*, Reports 2003-X, para. 46.
[83] Not yet published.

ground of discrimination, nor if it will be stricter or less strict in cases yet to be decided. To this extent, the national courts will find little guidance in this case-law as to the level of scrutiny they will need to apply in cases of nationality discrimination.

The ECJ's case-law on nationality discrimination is even more complicated. Indeed, the ECJ seems to regard nationality as a suspect ground of discrimination in the sphere of employment and social security, especially because of economic and internal market considerations. Discrimination against EU citizens would hamper their access to the employment market of other Member States and would impede their freedom of movement. It is thus well understandable that the ECJ, as much as the ECtHR, has laid down strict requirements to justify classifications based on nationality. Interestingly, the strictness of the ECJ's review is thus based on different considerations than the "very weighty reasons" test applied by the ECtHR. This is apparent, for example, from the following excerpt from an opinion of Advocate General Jacobs:

ECJ, Opinion of Advocate General Jacobs, 20 October 1993[84]   **1.EC.21.**
Joined Cases C–92/92 and C–326/92, Phil Collins v. Imtrat
Handelsgesellschaft mbH and Patricia Im- und Export Verwaltungsgesellschaft
GmbH and Leif Emanuel Kraul v. EMI Electrola GmbH

IMPORTANCE OF THE PROHIBITION OF NATIONALITY DISCRIMINATION

Phil Collins

"The prohibition of discrimination on grounds of nationality is the single most important principle of Community law. It is the leitmotiv of the EEC Treaty . . . It is not difficult to see why the authors of the Treaty attached so much importance to the prohibition of discrimination. The fundamental purpose of the Treaty is to achieve an integrated economy in which the factors of production, as well as the fruits of production, may move freely and without distortion, thus bringing about a more efficient allocation of resources and a more perfect division of labour . . . Although the abolition of discriminatory rules and practices may not be sufficient in itself to achieve the high level of economic integration envisaged by the Treaty, it is clearly an essential prerequisite. The prohibition of discrimination on grounds of nationality is also of great symbolic importance, inasmuch as it demonstrates that the Community is not just a commercial enterprise in which all the citizens of Europe are able to participate as individuals. The nationals of each Member State are entitled to live, work and do business in other Member States on the same terms as the local population. They must not simply be tolerated as aliens, but welcomed by the authorities of the host State as Community nationals who are entitled, 'within the scope of application of the Treaty', to all the privileges and advantaged enjoyed by the nationals of the host State. No other aspect of Community law touches the individual more directly or does more to foster that sense of common identity and shared

---

[84] [1993] ECR I–5145.
[85] Paras 9–11.

destiny without which the 'ever closer union of the peoples of Europe', proclaimed by the preamble to the Treaty, would be an empty slogan."[85]

Note

Thus, according to Advocate General Jacobs, the primary reason for suspectness of nationality discrimination is economic in nature. In addition, he stresses that equal treatment of all EU citizens would foster a sense of common identity, thus giving a more fundamental reason for suspectness as well. It seems clear that the ECJ has been inspired by like considerations, in particular in the line of case-law it developed with respect to the rights related to EU citizenship. A good illustration of the case-law on this issue is the case of *D'Hoop*:

ECJ, 11 July 2002[86]   **1.EC.22.**
Case C–224/98, M.N. D'Hoop v. *Office national de l'emploi*

IMPORTANCE OF PROHIBITION OF NATIONALITY DISCRIMINATION

D'Hoop

Facts: Ms D'Hoop, who has Belgian nationality, completed her secondary education in France. Her diploma was recognised in Belgium as equivalent to the approved certificate of higher secondary education. D'Hoop studied at university in Belgium until 1995. In 1996, she applied for a so-called "tideover allowance", a specific type of unemployment allowance which is granted to young people who have just completed their studies and are seeking their first employment. Her application was refused because she did not fulfil the relevant conditions, one of which was to have completed full-time higher secondary education at an educational establishment run, subsidised or approved by the Belgian authorities.

Held: Community law precludes a Member State from refusing to grant a tideover allowance to one of its nationals, a student seeking her first employment, on the sole ground that that student completed her secondary education in another Member State.

Judgment: "28. Union citizenship is destined to be the fundamental status of nationals of the Member States, enabling those who find themselves in the same situation to enjoy within the scope *ratione materiae* of the Treaty the same treatment in law irrespective of their nationality, subject to such exceptions as are expressly provided for . . .

29. The situations falling within the scope of Community law include those involving the exercise of the fundamental freedoms guaranteed by the Treaty, in particular those involving the freedom to move and reside within the territory of the Member States, as conferred by Article 8a of the EC Treaty (now, after amendment, Article 18 EC) . . .

30. In that a citizen of the Union must be granted in all Member States the same treatment in law as that accorded to the nationals of those Member States who find themselves in the same situation, it would be incompatible with the right of freedom of movement were a citizen, in the Member State of which he is a national, to receive treatment less favourable than he would enjoy if he had not availed himself of the opportunities offered by the Treaty in relation to freedom of movement.

---

[86] [2002] ECR I–6191.

31. Those opportunities could not be fully effective if a national of a Member State could be deterred from availing himself of them by obstacles raised on his return to his country of origin by legislation penalising the fact that he has used them . . ."

Note

It appears from this case that all EU citizens have the right to be treated on the same footing as national citizens and that unequal treatment is only allowed if it is justified by fundamental and compelling reasons. Still, the ECJ's case-law on nationality is nuanced. The strictness of the requirements does not seem to depend only on the suspectness of the ground of nationality, but also on other circumstances, such as the policy field in question. In cases concerning public security or public order, for example, the demands seem to be less stringent.[87]

Hence, it is difficult to state any general conclusions with respect to the level of scrutiny applied to cases of nationality discrimination.

1.3.4.   GENDER, SEX AND RELATED GROUNDS

1.3.4.A.   DEFINITION

GENDER AND SEX

The ground of gender/sex seems only rarely to raise debate, although the terms "sex" and "gender" are sometimes confused. In legal discourse, the term "sex" is used to refer to biological, genetically determined differences between women and men, such as differences related to pregnancy and lactation or average differences in physical strength. Other differences between men and women appear to be more social than biological in nature, such as (perceived) differences in the relation between parent and child. To describe these "social" differences between the sexes, the term "gender" is usually employed. Thus, "sex" refers to a biological reality, whereas "gender" refers to a social reality:

> "Gender refers to the social attributes and opportunities associated with being female and male, and the relationship between women and men, and girls and boys, as well as between women and between men. These attributes, opportunities and relationships are socially constructed and are learned through socialization processes. They are context and time-specific but changeable, since gender determines what is expected, allowed and valued in a woman or a man in a given situation. In most societies, there are differences and inequalities between men and women in the assignment of responsibilities, under-taking of activities, access and control over resources, and decision-making opportunities, with gender part of the broader socio-cultural context . . ."[88]

---

[87] See, e.g. Case 30/77 *Bouchereau* [1977] ECR 1999, paras 28 and 30 and Case C–83/94 *Leifer* [1995] ECR I–3231, para. 35.

[88] A.-M. Mooney-Cotter, *Gender Injustice. An International Comparative Analysis of Equality in Employment* (Aldershot, Ashgate, 2004) 6.

In practice, it is sometimes hard to separate the two notions, as it is not always easy to classify a difference between men and women as either socially constructed or biological in nature. The result is that academic writers, courts and legislators do not always carefully distinguish between the terms, rendering the difference rather fuzzy. Indeed, although the term "gender" is now used more often than "sex", many legal texts still primarily contain the ground "sex". Further, it is important to remember that not all states distinguish between the two notions in their own languages; often, "sex" and "gender" are covered by a single term.

SYMMETRICAL AND ASYMMETRICAL DEFINITIONS

In determining the personal scope of non-discrimination legislation, an important difference may be perceived between symmetrical and asymmetrical non-discrimination provisions. Symmetrical provisions protect against sex or gender discrimination in general, regardless of whether it is a man or a woman that is disadvantaged by the difference in treatment. The various European gender provisions are all formulated in such a symmetrical way, i.e. not referring to one particular sex.[89] Often as a result of implementation of the various Directives, most national legislation in the Member States contains such neutrally formulated provisions as well, as the following examples from Estonia and Germany may illustrate:

Estonian Law on Gender Equality 2004[90]   **1.EE.23.**

The purpose of this Act is to ensure gender equality arising from the Constitution of the Republic of Estonia and to promote equal treatment for men and women as a fundamental human right and for the public good in all areas of social life . . .

German Constitution (Grundgesetz)[91]   **1.DE.24.**

Men and women shall have equal rights. The state shall promote the actual implementation of equal rights for women and men and take steps to eliminate disadvantages that now exist.

At this point, there is an interesting contrast between European and international law. The International Convention on the Elimination of All Forms of Discrimination against Women (CEDAW, 1979) is based on a clearly asymmetrical approach. All of

---

[89] See, e.g. Art. 2 of the Gender Employment Directive (Art. 2 of the Recast Gender Employment Directive).
[90] RT I 2004, 27, 181, Art. 1.
[91] Art. 3(2).

its provisions are meant to protect the position of women, not of men. The main reason for this is that, in general, women find themselves in a disadvantaged position as compared to men and are more often harmed by discriminatory treatment. In order to reduce the factual disadvantages and improve the real participation of women in social, economic and political life, it was considered necessary to provide specific rules that apply to women only. This is clearly expressed in a number of important CEDAW provisions:

International Convention on the Elimination of All Forms of   **1.UN.25.**
Discrimination against Women, 1979

Article 1
For the purposes of the present Convention, the term 'discrimination against women' shall mean any distinction, exclusion or restriction made on the basis of sex which has the effect or purpose of impairing or nullifying the recognition, enjoyment or exercise by women, irrespective of their marital status, on a basis of equality of men and women, of human rights and fundamental freedoms in the political, economic, social, cultural, civil or any other field.

Article 2
States Parties condemn discrimination against women in all its forms, agree to pursue by all appropriate means and without delay a policy of eliminating discrimination against women . . .

Article 3
States Parties shall take in all fields, in particular in the political, social, economic and cultural fields, all appropriate measures, including legislation, to ensure the full development and advancement of women, for the purpose of guaranteeing them the exercise and enjoyment of human rights and fundamental freedoms on a basis of equality with men.

Article 4
1. Adoption by States Parties of temporary special measures aimed at accelerating de facto equality between men and women shall not be considered discrimination as defined in the present Convention, but shall in no way entail as a consequence the maintenance of unequal or separate standards, these measures shall be discontinued when the objectives of equality of opportunity and treatment have been achieved . . .

Note
The difference of approach between CEDAW and the European gender provisions is clearly illustrated by the cited Articles. For the Member States this may be difficult to deal with. If a Member State were to use an asymmetrical approach, as is favoured by CEDAW and many academic writers, they might infringe the strictly symmetrical provisions of the European Directives, especially if the application of the relevant provisions were to cause an interference with the rights and interests of men. Several academic writers have therefore argued that it would be preferable to create more uniformity and consistency in the international and European approaches towards

gender discrimination.[92] At present, however, such harmonisation still seems a distant prospect.

GENDER RELATED GROUNDS—PREGNANCY AND GENDER-SPECIFIC ILLNESS

Although it might seem to be relatively easy to classify a concrete case of discrimination as based on sex or gender, this is more difficult for situations in which the discrimination is not so much based on someone's being a man or a woman, but on closely related grounds, such as pregnancy, childbirth or maternity. European law has been unclear on this point until 1990, when the *Dekker* case was decided:

ECJ, 9 November 1990[93]   **1.EC.26.**
Case C–177/88, Dekker v. *Stichting VJV*

DISCRIMINATION BASED ON PREGNANCY CONSTITUTES SEX DISCRIMINATION

Dekker

Facts: In June 1981 Mrs Dekker applied for the post of instructor at the training centre for young adults run by VJV. She informed the committee dealing with the applications that she was three months' pregnant. The committee nonetheless put her name forward to the board of management of VJV as the most suitable candidate for the job. VJV, however, informed Mrs Dekker that she would not be appointed, because VJV would be financially unable to employ a replacement during Mrs Dekker's absence and would thus be short-staffed.

Held: An employer acts in direct contravention of the principle of gender equality if he refuses to enter into a contract of employment with a female candidate whom he considers to be suitable for the job, where such refusal is based on the possible adverse consequences of employing a pregnant woman.

Judgment: "12. . . . it should be observed that only women can be refused employment on grounds of pregnancy and such a refusal therefore constitutes direct discrimination on grounds of sex. A refusal of employment on account of the financial consequences of absence due to pregnancy must be regarded as based, essentially, on the fact of pregnancy . . ."

Precisely because of the fact that pregnancy and gender are closely correlated concepts, the ECJ held in *Dekker* that the definition of sex also covers pregnancy. In the later case of *Mary Brown*, the Court has broadened the meaning of the ground of sex even further to cover absence during pregnancy:

---

[92] E.g. R. Holtmaat and C. Tobler, "CEDAW and the European Union's Policy in the Field of Combating Gender Discrimination" (2005) 12 *MJ* 421 and J.H. Gerards, "Descriptieve representatie als rechtvaardiging voor voorkeursbeleid. Noot bij *Jacobs/België* (Human Rights Committee 17 augustus 2005)", (2005) 30 *NJCM-Bulletin* 640.

[93] [1990] ECR I–3941.

ECJ, 30 June 1998[94]   **1.EC.27.**
Case C–394/96, Mary Brown v. Rentokil

DISMISSAL BECAUSE OF ABSENCE DURING PREGNANCY IS SEX DISCRIMINATION

Mary Brown

Facts: Mrs Mary Brown informed Rentokil, her employer in August 1990, that she was pregnant. Thereafter she had difficulties associated with her pregnancy. She did not work again after mid-August 1990. According to the employment policy of Rentokil, an employee would be dismissed if he or she were absent because of sickness for more than 26 weeks continuously. Since Mrs Brown did not go back to work, she was dismissed while pregnant in February 1991.

Held: Articles 2(1) and 5(1) of Directive 76/207 preclude dismissal of a female worker at any time during her pregnancy for absences due to incapacity for work caused by illness resulting from that pregnancy.

Judgment: "22. Although pregnancy is not in any way comparable to a pathological condition . . ., the fact remains . . . that pregnancy is a period during which disorders and complications may arise compelling a woman to undergo strict medical supervision and, in some cases, to rest absolutely for all or part of her pregnancy. Those disorders and complications, which may cause incapacity for work, form part of the risks inherent in the condition of pregnancy and are thus a specific feature of that condition . . .
    24. . . . [D]ismissal of a female worker during pregnancy for absences due to incapacity for work resulting from her pregnancy is linked to the occurrence of risks inherent in pregnancy and must therefore be regarded as essentially based on the fact of pregnancy. Such a dismissal can affect only women and therefore constitutes direct discrimination on grounds of sex."

The ECJ held in this case that medical conditions occurring during and attributable to the pregnancy are so closely interconnected with the pregnancy that a distinction based on such a condition constitutes sex based discrimination. This situation may be contrasted to the situation in which a condition or illness is the result of the pregnancy, but occurs after the period of pregnancy and maternity leave. In this situation, the Court has adopted a different stance:

ECJ, 8 November 1990[95]   **1.EC.28.**
Case C–179/88, Handels- og Kontorfunktionaerernes Forbund i Danmark, acting on behalf of Birthe Vibeke Hertz v. Dansk Arbejdsgiverforening

NO SEX DISCRIMINATION IN CASE OF DISMISSAL FOR PREGNANCY-RELATED
REASONS

Hertz

Facts: Mrs Hertz gave birth to a child in 1983 after a pregnancy marked by complications for most of which, with the consent of her employer, she was on sick leave. Mrs Hertz resumed work in late 1983. She had no health problems until 1984, but between 1984 and 1985, she was once more on sick leave for 100

---

[94] [1998] ECR I–4185.
[95] [1990] ECR I–3979.

working days; her illness was a consequence of her pregnancy and confinement. Her employer informed Mrs Hertz that he was terminating her employment contract.

Held: Article 5(1) of Directive 76/207, in conjunction with Article 2(1) thereof, does not preclude dismissals which are the result of absences due to an illness attributable to pregnancy or confinement.

Judgment: "13. It follows from the provisions of the Directive quoted above [76/207/EEC] that the dismissal of a female worker on account of pregnancy constitutes direct discrimination on grounds of sex, as is a refusal to appoint a pregnant woman . . .

14. On the other hand, the dismissal of a female worker on account of repeated periods of sick leave which are not attributable to pregnancy or confinement does not constitute direct discrimination on grounds of sex, inasmuch as such periods of sick leave would lead to the dismissal of a male worker in the same circumstances . . .

17. Male and female workers are equally exposed to illness. Although certain disorders are, it is true, specific to one or other sex, the only question is whether a woman is dismissed on account of absence due to illness in the same circumstances as a man; if that is the case, then there is no direct discrimination on grounds of sex."

Notes

(1) It appears from the case-law of the ECJ that, even if only a man or a woman can develop a certain disease or condition (e.g. prostate or breast cancer), this does not constitute a relevant sex-related difference per se. Although the character of a disease may differ and the development of a disease may be gender-specific, it is clear, according to the ECJ, that men and women are equally prone to illness. This is different with respect to pregnancy, as this is obviously a condition that is particular to women. For that reason, it is understandable that pregnancy discrimination is considered sex discrimination, whereas this is not true for discrimination based on gender-specific illness.

(2) Nonetheless, it seems surprising that pregnancy-related illness is considered as closely linked to one's sex during pregnancy and maternity leave, but not after the period of maternity leave has passed. The reason for this may be found outside the definitional question itself. The ECJ considers it desirable that special protection is given to women during their pregnancy, especially against the harmful effects of the risk of dismissal. That risk does not exist any more after pregnancy, implying that there is less reason to place illness, pregnancy and gender within the same category of prohibited grounds for distinction.

HOMOSEXUALITY AND GENDER

Another interesting issue relates to the question as to where the exact borderline between homosexuality and gender should be drawn. This question became particularly relevant as Community law offered comprehensive protection against gender discrimination in employment, but none against discrimination based on sexual orientation. In a number of factual situations, however, it would seem possible to define discrimination based on sexual orientation in terms of gender discrimination. Gays, lesbians and bisexuals (or, eventually, heterosexuals) would then also profit from the protection offered by European law. The ECJ, however, has blocked this possibility:

ECJ, 17 February 1998[96]   **1.EC.29.**
Case C–249/96, Grant v. South-West Trains

SEX DISCRIMINATION OR DISCRIMINATION BASED ON SEXUAL ORIENTATION

Grant

Facts: Ms Grant was employed by South West Trains (SWT), a railway company. As an employment benefit, all SWT employees and their spouses were granted free and reduced travel concessions. Ms Grant applied in 1995 for travel concessions for her female partner, with whom she declared she had had a meaningful relationship for over two years. SWT refused to allow the benefit sought, on the ground that for unmarried persons travel concessions could be granted only for a partner of the opposite sex.

Held: The refusal by an employer to grant travel concessions to a person of the same sex with whom a worker has a stable relationship, where such concessions are granted to a worker's spouse or to a person of the opposite sex with whom a worker has a stable relationship outside marriage, does not constitute discrimination prohibited by Article 119 of the Treaty or Directive 75/117.

Judgment: "26. The refusal to allow Ms Grant the concessions is based on the fact that she does not satisfy the conditions prescribed in those regulations, more particularly on the fact that she does not live with a 'spouse' or a person of the opposite sex with whom she has had a 'meaningful' relationship for at least two years.

27. That condition, the effect of which is that the worker must live in a stable relationship with a person of the opposite sex in order to benefit from the travel concessions, is, like the other alternative conditions prescribed in the undertaking's regulations, applied regardless of the sex of the worker concerned. Thus travel concessions are refused to a male worker if he is living with a person of the same sex, just as they are to a female worker if she is living with a person of the same sex.

28. Since the condition imposed by the undertaking's regulations applies in the same way to female and male workers, it cannot be regarded as constituting discrimination directly based on sex."

Note

The reasonableness of the distinction between gender and sexual orientation made in *Grant* is heavily debated.[97] Given that protection against gender discrimination is still much stronger than that against discrimination based on sexual orientation, it may be considered unfortunate from a strategic point of view that the ECJ has decided to exclude the possibility of classifying discrimination against gays, lesbians and bisexuals as (at least partly) based on gender.

GENDER/SEX, TRANSSEXUALITY AND INTERSEXUALITY/HERMAPHRODITISM

An interesting debate regarding the definition of gender further relates to the question if transsexuality and intersexuality come under the scope of gender/sex. With respect to transsexualism, the answer to this question is clear, now that the ECJ

---

[96] [1998] ECR I–621.
[97] S. Fredman, *Discrimination Law* (Oxford, Oxford University Press, 2002) 73.

has explicitly accepted that transsexualism is so closely related to sex and gender that a distinction based on this ground can be regarded as a distinction that is directly based on grounds of sex.

ECJ, 30 April 1998[98]   **1.EC.30.**
Case C–13/94, P. v. S. and Cornwall County Council

DISCRIMINATION BASED ON TRANSSEXUALITY CONSTITUTES SEX DISCRIMINATION

P. v. S.

Facts: P. used to work as a manager in an educational establishment operated by Cornwall County Council. In early April 1992, a year after being taken on, P. informed S., the Director of the establishment, of the intention to undergo gender reassignment. This began with a "life test", a period during which P. dressed and behaved as a woman, followed by surgery to give P. the physical attributes of a woman. After undergoing minor surgical operations, P. was given three months' notice, expiring on 31 December 1992.

Held: Article 5(1) of Directive 76/207 precludes dismissal of a transsexual for a reason related to a gender reassignment.

Judgment: "17. The principle of equal treatment 'for men and women' to which the directive [Directive 76/207/EEC] refers in its title, preamble and provisions means, as Articles 2(1) and 3(1) in particular indicate, that there should be 'no discrimination whatsoever on grounds of sex'.

18. Thus, the directive is simply the expression, in the relevant field, of the principle of equality, which is one of the fundamental principles of Community law.

19. Moreover, as the Court has repeatedly held, the right not to be discriminated against on grounds of sex is one of the fundamental human rights whose observance the Court has a duty to ensure . . .

20. Accordingly, the scope of the directive cannot be confined simply to discrimination based on the fact that a person is of one or other sex. In view of its purpose and the nature of the rights which it seeks to safeguard, the scope of the directive is also such as to apply to discrimination arising, as in this case, from the gender reassignment of the person concerned.

21. Such discrimination is based, essentially if not exclusively, on the sex of the person concerned. Where a person is dismissed on the ground that he or she intends to undergo, or has undergone, gender reassignment, he or she is treated unfavourably by comparison with persons of the sex to which he or she was deemed to belong before undergoing gender reassignment."

By now, the various Member States have integrated this decision into their own case-law,[99] or have adopted special legislation to protect transsexuals and regulate legal issues of gender reassignment.[100]

Some related grounds have proven to be more difficult to interpret as being gender-related. This is particularly true when there are problems relating to sexual

---

[98] [1998] ECR I–2143.

[99] See, e.g. Opinion 1998–12 of the Dutch Equal Treatment Commission.

[100] See, e.g. the German *Transsexuellengesetz* (TSG, Transsexuality Act), paras 1, 4, 5, 7, 8 and 10 and the UK Sex Discrimination (Gender Reassignment) Regulations 1999, SI 1999/1102.

differentiation, which may be present with respect to hermaphrodites and inter- or intrasexuals. Case-law in this problematic area, however, is scarce.

DOES HERMAPHRODITISM QUALIFY AS A SEPARATE GENDER?

Hermaphrodites

Facts: A hermaphrodite demanded that the entry under "sex" in the public register of civil status should be "intersexual" or "intrasexual". The registry refused, stating that neither of the terms designated a certain sex.

Held: Neither human dignity nor the right to free development of the personality, nor the principle of equality require the recognition of an additional gender category as capable of being entered under the law on registration of births, deaths and marriages.

Judgment: "a) The term 'hermaphrodite' is taken to refer to living entities which are of both sexes, i.e. they possess male and female sex-organs in equal measure . . . A person is described as 'hermaphrodite', if both testicles and ovaries are present. Only in this case—which occurs with extreme rarity—can one speak of 'genuine hermaphroditism' . . .

The applicant is not a hermaphrodite within the meaning of this definition, since in her case only female and no male sex-glands are present: while she possesses ovaries, she does not possess testicles. In the present case, therefore, it does not have to be decided whether, in the case of genuine hermaphroditism, the sexual designation 'hermaphrodite' could be entered in the Register of Births, Deaths and Marriages.

b) The entry of 'intersexual' or 'intrasexual' as gender identification in the Register of Births, Deaths and Marriages cannot be considered as an option, since these terms do not indicate any specific gender, but are blanket-terms for a series of disorders in sexual differentiation, in which internal and external sexual features develop, in varying degrees of prominence, in contradiction to the chromosomal gender.

Biology and medicine make the assumption that human beings belong to one of two sexes, and consider the various forms of doubtful gender as exceptions to the rule, which arise, due to a variety of malfunctions, in the development of the embryo. Among the manifestations of intersexuality, apart from rare syndromes, science recognises three manifestations of hermaphroditism in particular: genuine hermaphroditism, where both testicular and ovarian tissue is present in the organism, as well as the male and female forms of pseudo-hermaphroditism.

In the latter, which applies to the applicant, male or female gonads of the corresponding chromosome set are present, whereas the external features of the opposite sex are visible . . .

The division of humanity into five genders, as asserted by this appeal, is nothing other than a classification of genuine hermaphroditism, masculine pseudohermaphroditism and feminine pseudohermaphroditism as independent genders. It represents a minority opinion, which—as far as can be ascertained—has as yet found little support except among the group of researchers cited in the grounds for the appeal.

---

[101] NJW-RR 2003, at 1590.

c) Not even from fundamental human rights can any claim to recognition of an additional gender next to 'male' and 'female' be derived in cases such as the present one. Even the Federal German constitution, in Art. 3 II 1, assumes that human beings are divided into two sexes, male and female. This bipolar concept of gender is the basis of the ban on discrimination in Art. 3 III of the *Grundgesetz* [GG, Basic Law], under which regulations which discriminate on the basis of sex are only permissible, to the extent that they are urgently required for the resolving of problems which, by their nature, can only arise in either men or women . . .

Neither the principle of human dignity (Art. 1 I GG) nor the right to free development of the personality (Art. 2 I GG), nor the principle of equality (Art. 3 II GG) require the recognition of an additional gender category as capable of being entered under the law on registration of births, deaths and marriages. Such a category—as explained—does not correspond to the current state of scientific knowledge, is entirely unknown to current German law and would lead to considerable difficulties in the defining of terms and to uncertainties in the law."

Note

According to the Munich regional court, there can exist no other category of sex apart from the male and female sex. In this approach, hermaphroditism and inter/intrasexualism can be considered as different from transsexualism, since a transsexual, after gender reassignment, can still be designated as a man or as a woman. Such a clear placement in the categories of "men" and "women" is not possible with respect to hermaphrodites or inter/intrasexuals. Still, there is a close relation between intersexualism and gender or sex, for which reason it would not be illogical to classify distinctions based on intersexualism or hermaphroditism as being gender based. Some support for this submission can be found in the ECJ's decision in *P. v. S.*, where it considered that "the scope of the directive cannot be confined simply to discrimination based on the fact that a person is of one or other sex".[102] A similar stance seems to have been taken by the German Constitutional Court in a 2005 decision concerning transsexuality, in which it found that it should be acknowledged that not all transsexuals really strive for complete gender reassignment. It thereby seemed to imply that it may be difficult to categorise such persons as either men or women.[103] Thus, both cases would seem to leave some room for legal acknowledgement of transgender categories in the future.

1.3.4.B.   SUSPECTNESS

Sex and gender are generally regarded as suspect grounds of discrimination, both by the European Court of Justice and the European Court of Human Rights. The reasoning that leads both Courts to apply a strict test of gender discrimination seems to be somewhat different, however, as is illustrated by the following two excerpts:

[102] See *P.v.S.*, above **1.EC.30.**, para. 20.
[103] BVerfG, 6 December 2005, 1 BvL 3/03.

ECJ, 30 March 1993[104]   **1.EC.32.**
Case C–328/91, Secretary of State for Social Security v. Thomas and Others

STRICT SCRUTINY IN GENDER DISCRIMINATION CASES

Thomas

Facts: In the UK, the Social Security Act 1975 provided for the grant of severe disability allowances to people who are incapable of working. People who have attained retirement age, which is 65 for men and 60 for women, are not entitled to those benefits. Mrs Thomas was refused severe disability allowance on the ground that she had ceased employment because of invalidity after attaining retirement age.

Held: Where a Member State prescribes different retirement ages for men and women for the purposes of granting old-age and retirement pensions, the scope of the derogation permitted under Directive 79/7 is limited to the forms of discrimination existing under the other benefit schemes which are necessarily and objectively linked to the difference in retirement age.

Judgment: "8. In considering the scope of the derogation provided for . . ., it is to be noted, first, that, in view of the fundamental importance of the principle of equal treatment, which the Court has reaffirmed on numerous occasions, the exception to the prohibition of discrimination on grounds of sex . . . must be interpreted strictly."

ECtHR, 25 May 1985[105]   **1.CoE.33.**
Abdulaziz, Cabales and Balkandali v. the United Kingdom

VERY WEIGHTY REASONS TEST APPLIED TO GENDER DISCRIMINATION

Abdulaziz

Facts: A British law concerning family reunification (the "1984 Act") made it much easier for foreign families where the man was already resident in Britain to be reunited than for families where only the wife lived in Britain.

Held: The applicants have been victims of discrimination on the ground of sex, in violation of Article 14 taken together with Article 8.

Judgment: "78. Although the Contracting States enjoy a 'certain margin of appreciation' in assessing whether and to what extent differences in otherwise similar situations justify a different treatment, the scope of this margin will vary according to the circumstances, the subject-matter and its background. As to the present matter, it can be said that the advancement of the sexes is today a major goal in the Member States of the Council of Europe. This means that very weighty reasons would have to be advanced before a difference of treatment on the ground of sex could be regarded as compatible with the Convention."

Note

It appears from these excerpts that the ECJ bases the suspectness of the ground of gender (mirrored by the strictness of its review) on considerations relating to the

[104] [1993] ECR I–1247.
[105] Series A, Vol. 94.

fundamental character of the right to equal treatment of men and women.[106] This fundamental character has been stressed in a long line of case-law which the ECJ has developed since 1978.[107] The ECtHR, by contrast, primarily seems to apply a "very weighty reasons" test because, throughout the Council of Europe, all states seem to agree that gender is a suspect ground of discrimination. Both reasons are strongly related, however, as the European consensus on the suspectness of the gender ground is evidently inspired by a generally shared perception of sex equality as a fundamental right.

Importantly, the ECJ and the ECtHR do not consider gender discrimination to be suspect in all cases, although the ECJ seems to be more consistent in this respect than the ECtHR. Indeed, the ECJ would not even seem to consider it of any relevance that a gender distinction is made in the context of positive action—the test it applies there is as strict as the one applied to "regular" forms of gender discrimination.[108] Nonetheless, even the ECJ seems to relax its standards sometimes, especially if the area of social security is concerned. To this extent, the approaches of the ECJ and ECtHR appear to be rather similar, as may be illustrated by the following excerpts:

ECJ, 12 July 1984[109]   **1.EC.34.**
Case 184/83, Hofmann v. Barmer Ersatzkasse

LESS INTENSIVE REVIEW OF SOCIAL SECURITY ISSUES

Hofmann

Facts: Mr Hofmann, a German father, obtained unpaid leave from his employer for the period between the expiry of the statutory period of eight weeks which was available to the mother and the day on which the child reached the age of six months. During that time he took care of the child while the mother continued her employment. He submitted to the Barmer Ersatzkasse a claim for payment during that period. His request was refused, as only mothers could claim paid maternity leave under the relevant German legislation.

Held: A Member State may, after the statutory protective period has expired, grant to mothers a period of maternity leave which the State encourages them to take by the payment of an allowance. The Directive

---

[106] There may also be more political reasons for strictly scrutinising gender discrimination. As Ellis has argued, sex equality may have been given priority "because it provides a relatively innocuous, even high sounding, platform by means of which the Community can demonstrate its commitment to social progress" and may constitute political legitimisation of the European Community. She also stresses that an important reason for suspectness of gender discrimination may still be economical in character, as sex equality prevents competitive distortions in highly integrated market. See E. Ellis, *EU Anti-Discrimination Law* (Oxford, Oxford University Press, 2005) 22–3.

[107] In *Defrenne III*, the ECJ held for the first time that the elimination of sex discrimination forms part of the fundamental rights respected by community law (Case 149/77 *Defrenne v. Sabena* [1978] ECR 1365, paras 26 and 27). In *Schröder*, decided in 2001, the ECJ even held that the fundamental rights aspect of the principle of equal treatment of men and women had become more important than the social and economic values it was originally meant to protect (Case C–50/96 *Schröder* [2000] ECR I–743, para. 57).

[108] On this issue, see below, O de Schutter in Chapter Seven: Positive Action, section 7.5.

[109] [1984] ECR 3074.

does not impose on the Member States a requirement that they shall, as an alternative, allow such leave to be granted to fathers, even where the parents so decide.

Judgment: "27. . . .the Directive leaves Member States with discretion as to the social measures which they adopt in order to guarantee, within the framework laid down by the Directive, the protection of women in connection with pregnancy and maternity and to offset the disadvantages which women, by comparison with men, suffer with regard to the retention of employment. Such measures are . . . closely linked to the general system of social protection in the various Member States. It must therefore be concluded that the Member States enjoy a reasonable margin of discretion as regards both the nature of the protective measures and the detailed arrangements for their implementation."

ECtHR, 27 March 1998[110]   **1.CoE.35.**
Petrovic v. Austria

No very weighty reasons required to justify gender discrimination

Petrovic

Facts: According to an Austrian regulation of parental leave allowances, both men and women could take parental leave, but only women came into consideration for a parental leave allowance.

Held: The Austrian authorities' refusal to grant the applicant a parental leave allowance has not exceeded the margin of appreciation left to them and was not discriminatory within the meaning of Article 14.

Judgment: "37. It is true that the advancement of the equality of the sexes is today a major goal in the Member States of the Council of Europe and very weighty reasons would be needed for such a difference in treatment to be regarded as compatible with the Convention . . .

38. However, the Contracting States enjoy a certain margin of appreciation in assessing whether and to what extent differences in otherwise similar situations justify a different treatment in law. The scope of the margin of appreciation will vary according to the circumstances, the subject matter and its back-ground; in this respect, one of the relevant factors may be the existence or non-existence of common ground between the laws of the Contracting States . . .

39. It is clear that at the material time, that is at the end of the 1980s, there was no common standard in this field, as the majority of the Contracting States did not provide for parental leave allowances to be paid to fathers . . .

42. There still remains a very great disparity between the legal systems of the Contracting States in this field. While measures to give fathers an entitlement to parental leave have now been taken by a large number of States, the same is not true of the parental leave allowance, which only a very few States grant to fathers.

43. The Austrian authorities' refusal to grant the applicant a parental leave allowance has not, therefore, exceeded the margin of appreciation allowed to them. Consequently, the difference in treatment complained of was not discriminatory within the meaning of Article 14."

---

[110] Reports 1998-II.

Note

It appears from both *Hofmann* and *Petrovic* that neither the fundamental character of the equality principle nor the existence of a general consensus relating to the suspectness of sex as a ground for classification is always decisive for the strictness of judicial review. The need to leave room for differentiation between and within the Member States, or the lack of common ground in a specific policy field, may override these general notions and may induce a more marginal test.[111]

1.3.5.   SEXUAL ORIENTATION

1.3.5.A.   DEFINITION

SYMMETRICAL OR ASYMMETRICAL APPROACH

As is the case with gender equality, protection against discrimination based on sexual orientation may be based on a symmetrical or an asymmetrical approach. The Employment Equality Directive appears to start from a symmetrical approach, generally prohibiting discrimination based on "sexual orientation". No special protection is thus provided for gays, lesbians and bisexuals, who in practice constitute the group that is most often subjected to discrimination and disadvantage as a result of their sexual orientation. As a result of the implementation of the Directive, a symmetrical approach is also generally adopted in the non-discrimination legislation of the Member States. In several Member States, notably Ireland and the UK, this has been made explicit by mentioning all relevant groups in a legislative definition of the term of sexual orientation:

Irish Equal Status Act 2000[112]   **1.IE.36.**

'Sexual orientation' means heterosexual, homosexual or bisexual orientation.

Employment Equality (Sexual Orientation) Regulations 2003[113]   **1.GB.37.**

In these Regulations, 'sexual orientation' means a sexual orientation towards—

(a)   persons of the same sex;
(b)   persons of the opposite sex; or
(c)   persons of the same sex and of the opposite sex.

---

[111] See in more detail also ch. 3, section 3.5.2.B.
[112] No. 8/2000, Section 2.
[113] SI 2003/1661, Reg. 2.

These legislative examples show that the prohibition of discrimination based on sexual orientation covers discrimination based on homosexual or bisexual orientation as well as on heterosexual orientation.[114]

A different stance seems to be taken in Germany, where the notion of "sexual identity" ("*sexuellen Identität*") is used instead of "sexual orientation" (e.g. Article 1 § 1 of the General Equal Treatment Act (AGG)). The result seems to be an asymmetrical approach:

> "Usually, German legislators use the term 'sexual identity'. This is designed to cover homosexuals, transsexuals and intersexuals. Until today, bisexuals and heterosexuals have not been part of the legal discussion."[115]

As a result, bisexuals and heterosexuals do not seem to be protected by the German legislation against discriminatory treatment.

SEXUAL ORIENTATION, SEXUAL PREFERENCE AND SEXUAL BEHAVIOUR

The Employment Equality Directive prohibits discrimination based on sexual orientation, but the Explanatory Memorandum to the Directive contains an important distinction in this regard:

Explanatory Memorandum to the Employment Equality Directive[116] **1.EC.38.**

"With regard to sexual orientation, a clear dividing line should be drawn between sexual orientation, which is covered by this proposal, and sexual behaviour, which is not."

Unfortunately, the Explanatory Memorandum does not state any reasons for the distinction made between sexual orientation and sexual behaviour.[117] The implementation of the prohibition by the various Member States shows mixed reactions to

---

[114] *Cf.* clearly, e.g. Finland (see T. Makkonen, "Report on Measures to Combat Discrimination: Directive 2000/43/EC and 2000/78/EC. Country Report Finland" (European Commission, 2005) 8, available on the website of Directorate-General for Employment, Social Affairs and Equal Opportunities; (presumably) France (see D. Borrillo, "France" in European Group of Experts on Combating Sexual Orientation Discrimination, *Combating Sexual Orientation Discrimination in Employment: Legislation in Fifteen EU Member States* (Leiden University, 2004) 193); Ireland (see main text); Italy (see A. Simoni, "Report on Measures to Combat Discrimination: Directive 2000/43/EC and 2000/78/EC. Country Report Italy" (European Commission, 2004) 8, available on the website of Directorate-General for Employment, Social Affairs and Equal Opportunities; the Netherlands (see main text); Sweden (see H. Ytterberg, "Sweden" in European Group of Experts, *ibid.*; and the UK (see main text and B. Cohen, "Report on Measures to Combat Discrimination: Directive 2000/43/EC and 2000/78/EC. Country Report United Kingdom" (European Commission, 2005) 9, available on the website of Directorate-General for Employment, Social Affairs and Equal Opportunities).

[115] S. Baer, "Germany" in European Group of Experts, *ibid.*, 218, available on the website of Directorate-General for Employment, Social Affairs and Equal Opportunities.

[116] COM (1999) 565 def, Explanation to Art. 1.

[117] See critically M. Bonini-Baraldi, "European Law" in European Group of Experts, *ibid.*, 25.

this definition. Some Member States have accepted the European Commission's approach by limiting legislative protection to sexual orientation, as is the case in the UK:

"'Sexual orientation' does not include 'sexual practices and preferences (e.g. sado-masochism and paedophilia)'."[118]

Other states do not seem to have paid much attention to the issue and have limited themselves to adding the ground "sexual orientation" to their non-discrimination legislation without giving a legislative definition or referring to the distinction between orientation and behaviour. In these states, clarification will have to be offered by case-law or legislative history, but there are presently only a few examples that disclose explicit consideration of the issue. Such an example may be found in the opinions of the Dutch Equal Treatment Commission, which predate the Employment Equality Directive.

Equal Treatment Commission (*Commissie Gelijke Behandeling*)   **1.NL.39.**
Opinion 2003-150

"SEXUAL ORIENTATION" ALSO COVERS SEXUAL BEHAVIOUR

Lesbian test person

Facts: The defendant party is a research institute that carries out research relating to the development of drugs, thereby making use of test persons. In 2003 the research institute was studying a drug that would be used to treat Alzheimer's disease and was looking for test persons. In its research protocol, it defined the following conditions for suitable test persons: "Female subjects must be non-pregnant, surgically sterile, or, if sexually active, must have a partner who has been vasectomised for at least six months, or agree to utilize [a] form of contraception from screening through completion of the study . . ." The applicant is a lesbian woman, who has applied to participate in the drug study. The research institute excluded her because she does, though sexually active, not use any form of contraception.

Held: As the sexual orientation of the applicant is not pertinent to the aims of the research protocol, there is no justification for the difference in treatment.

Opinion: "5.3. The term heterosexual or homosexual orientation must, according to the legislative history of the Equal Treatment Act, be broadly interpreted and is aimed at a person's orientation in sexual and amatory feelings, expressions and relations . . . The term orientation has been adopted because it covers specific expressions as well as feelings. The term orientation is therefore broader than the term preference . . . It follows that specific behaviour that is generally regarded as an emanation of a person's homosexual (or heterosexual) orientation is protected by the Equal Treatment Act."

Note
It is clear from this case that the Dutch Equal Treatment Commission uses the term "sexual orientation" precisely because of its wide scope, considering that it is

---

[118] UK Employment Equality (Sexual Orientation) Regulations 2003, Explanatory Memorandum, Annex B, para. 5.

sufficiently broad to cover both sexual feelings and expressions. This reading of the term was confirmed by the legislative history of the Dutch implementation of the Employment Equality Directive, in which the government explained its interpretation of the term "sexual orientation" (*seksuele gerichtheid*):

> "The concept of orientation (*gerichtheid*) includes a person's concrete expressions as well as feelings and preferences, so that the term 'orientation'—and consequently also the protection against discrimination—is broader than the concept of preference (*voorkeur*) and the concept of proclivity (*geaardheid*) . . . Replacing the term orientation by the term preference or the term proclivity would restrict the protection that the Equal Treatment Act offers on this point. The government does not intend to reduce the level of protection under the Equal Treatment Act." [119]

As the adoption of the distinction made by the Commission would have reduced the level of protection offered by the Dutch equal treatment legislation, it is understandable that the Dutch government has opted for continued use of the wide notion of "sexual orientation". Similar interpretations have been given in other states, such as Italy and Sweden.[120] These wide definitions do not only provide a higher level of protection against discrimination, but they would also seem to be more in line with the approach taken by the European Court of Human Rights. In several cases, this Court has implicitly accepted that a distinction based on homosexual conduct constitutes a case of unequal treatment under Article 14 ECHR.[121]

OTHER FORMS OF SEXUAL ORIENTATION, PREFERENCE OR BEHAVIOUR

In concrete cases coming before the national courts or equal treatment commissions, questions are sometimes raised regarding behaviour or feelings somehow related to sexual orientation or sexual behaviour, such as transvestism or transsexuality. The question then arises if these forms should be comprised under the notion of sexual orientation. For transsexuality the answer to this question is relatively clear. Since the ECJ's decision in *P. v. S.* (**1.EC.30.**), almost all Member States regard transsexuality as part of the definition of the ground of sex, rather than as discrimination based on sexual orientation. The question of whether transvestism, sadomasochism and paedophilia could be considered as part of the definition of sexual orientation is much more difficult to answer. In most Member States, this question has not been

---

[119] Memorandum of the Government in connection with the Report of the Second Chamber on the EC Implementation Act, *Kamerstukken II* 2002/03, 28 770, no. 5, at 7.

[120] See A. Simoni, "Report on Measures to Combat Discrimination: Directives 2000/43/EC and 2000/78/EC. Country Report Italy" (European Commission, December 2004), available on the website of Directorate-General for Employment, Social Affairs and Equal Opportunities; and H. Ytterberg, "Sweden" in European Group of Experts, *ibid.*, 457–8, available on the website of Directorate-General for Employment, Social Affairs and Equal Opportunities.

[121] See ECtHR, 9 January 2003, *L. and V.* v. *Austria*, Reports 2003-I. Although the ECtHR referred to a distinction based on "sexual orientation", it is clear from the facts that the case concerned not so much homosexual orientation as homosexual conduct: the complaint related to the criminalisation of homosexual acts of adult men with consenting adolescents. See also above Bonini-Baraldi, note 117, at 26.

addressed at all and, to the extent to which the issue has been dealt with, there appears to be little agreement on the appropriate classification. In the Dutch and UK legislative materials, it is explicitly stated that paedophilia is not protected; in the UK, sadomasochism is also mentioned in this respect.[122] The question if transvestism is covered by the notion of sexual orientation is debated:

Equal Treatment Commission (Commissie Gelijke Behandeling)   **1.NL.40.**
Opinion 1996-108

DISCRIMINATION AGAINST TRANSVESTITES IS NOT SEXUAL ORIENTATION
DISCRIMINATION

Homosexual transvestite

Facts: The applicant is a homosexual who practices transvestism. He was in training with the respondent to become a qualified nurse. His practical training period was terminated by the respondent because of complaints by patients and colleagues about perverse and suggestive remarks he had made, which were regarded as shocking and annoying.

Held: It has not been established that the dismissal was based on the applicant's sexual orientation.

Opinion: "7.4. The fact that the applicant told a colleague that he had ordered shoes with stiletto heels partly played a role in the defendant party's decision to terminate the contract of employment. However, this cannot be taken as indicating discrimination based on homosexual orientation, since there has been no sign that transvestism occurs predominantly amongst persons with a homosexual orientation."

Note
It is clear from this opinion that the Dutch Equal Treatment Commission does not see an objective relation between sexual orientation and transvestism, which view has also been expressed in France:

"[T]he concept of sexual orientation does not protect . . .transvestites against discrimi-nation . . . [T]he latter have found protection in the category of 'morals' or, more particularly, in the category of 'physical appearance'."[123]

In other states, however, a wider definition of "sexual orientation" has been given, which does include transvestism. This appears to be the case, for example, in Denmark:

"In the existing Danish law the term 'sexual orientation' is used, which means homo- and heterosexual relations and other kinds of lawful sexual inclinations (like transvestism)."[124]

---

[122] Dutch Memorandum of the Government in connection with the Report of the Second Chamber on the EC Implementation Act, *Kamerstukken II* 2002/03, 28 770, no. 5, at 7 and the Explanatory Memorandum to the UK Employment Equality (Sexual Orientation) Regulations 2003, Annex B, para. 5.
[123] D. Borrillo, "France" in European Group of Experts, *ibid.*, s. 7.2.1.
[124] S. Baatrup, "Denmark" in European Group of Experts, *ibid.*, s. 5.2.2.

Although it is difficult to derive any general conclusions from these examples, there seems to be some agreement as to the fact that forms of sexual inclination other than homo- or heterosexualism are usually excluded from the definition of sexual orientation. As the Equality Employment Directive does not offer any guidance in this respect, interpretative case-law of the ECJ is needed to provide clarity.

1.3.5.B.   SUSPECTNESS

Already in the case of *Dudgeon* v. *the United Kingdom* (1981), the ECtHR held that consensual homosexual behaviour concerned "a most intimate aspect of private life" and that "[a]ccordingly, there must exist particularly serious reasons before interferences on the part of the public authorities can be legitimate . . ."[125] In a later case (*Smith and Grady* v. *UK*), concerning a discharge from the army because of homosexuality, the Court also held that "[c]oncerning as it did a most intimate aspect of an individual's private life, particularly serious reasons by way of justification were required".[126] Both of these cases did not explicitly concern unequal treatment, however, but were mainly about the right to privacy (Article 8 ECHR). Only in the case of *Salgueiro* (1999) did the Court directly address the issue of discrimination based on sexual orientation:

ECtHR, 21 December 1999[127]   **1.CoE.41.**
Salgueiro da Silva Mouta v. *Portugal*

DISADVANTAGE BASED SOLELY ON SEXUAL ORIENTATION IS NOT ACCEPTABLE

Salgueiro

Facts: After his divorce, Salgueiro da Silva Mouta sought an order giving him parental responsibility for his daughter. The Court of First Instance awarded him parental responsibility, holding that he would be, to a greater extent than the mother, "capable of providing her with the balanced conditions she needs and of respecting her right to maintain regular and sustained contact with her mother and maternal grand-parents". This judgment was quashed on appeal and parental responsibility was awarded to the mother. The primary reason for this was contained in the following consideration: "The fact that the child's father, who has come to terms with his homosexuality, wishes to live with another man is a reality which has to be accepted. It is well-known that society is becoming more and more tolerant of such situations. However, it cannot be argued that an environment of this kind is the healthiest and best suited to a child's psychological, social and mental development, especially given the dominant model in our society, as the appellant rightly points out. The child should live in a family environment, a traditional Portuguese family, which is certainly not the set-up her father has decided to enter into, since he is living with another man as if they were man and wife. It is not our task here to determine whether homosexuality is or is not an illness or whether it is a sexual orientation towards persons of the same sex. In both cases it is an abnormality and children should not grow up in the shadow of abnormal situations; such are the dictates of human nature . . ."

---

[125] ECtHR, 22 October 1981, Series A, Vol. 45, para. 52.
[126] ECtHR, 27 September 1999, Reports 1999-VI.
[127] Reports 1999-IX.

Held: The Portuguese Court of Appeal made a distinction based on considerations regarding the applicant's sexual orientation, which is not acceptable under the Convention.

Judgment: "35. It is the Court's view that the above passages from the judgment in question, far
from being merely clumsy or unfortunate as the Government maintained, or mere obiter dicta,
suggest, quite to the contrary, that the applicant's homosexuality was a factor which was
decisive in the final decision . . .

36. The Court is therefore forced to find, in the light of the foregoing, that the Court of
Appeal made a distinction based on considerations regarding the applicant's sexual
orientation, a distinction which is not acceptable under the Convention . . ."

Note

From the wording of this judgment, it might be derived that distinctions and classifications based on sexual orientation will never be accepted under the ECHR. The
Court nuanced this opinion in a later case by stating that such difference in treatment
might be justified by "very weighty reasons":

ECtHR, 9 January 2003[128]   1.CoE.42.
L. and V. v. Austria

VERY WEIGHTY REASONS TEST APPLIED TO SEXUAL ORIENTATION DISCRIMINATION

L. and V.

Facts: L. and V. were convicted under the Austrian Criminal Code (*Strafgesetzbuch*) of homosexual acts
with adolescents. L. was sentenced to one year's imprisonment suspended on probation for a period of
three years; V. was sentenced to six months' imprisonment suspended on probation for a period of three
years. L. and V. complained before the ECtHR of the maintenance in force of Article 209 of the Criminal
Code, which criminalises homosexual acts of adult men with consenting adolescents between the ages of 14
and 18. Heterosexual or lesbian relations between adults and adolescents in the same age bracket were not
punishable.

Held: The Government has not offered convincing and weighty reasons justifying the maintenance in force
of Article 209 of the Criminal Code and, consequently, the applicants' convictions under this provision.

Judgment: "45. The applicants complained of a difference in treatment based on their sexual
orientation. In this connection, the Court reiterates that sexual orientation is a concept covered
by Article 14 . . . Just like differences based on sex, differences based on sexual orientation
require particularly serious reasons by way of justification . . .

49. What is decisive is whether there was an objective and reasonable justification why
young men in the 14 to 18 age bracket needed protection against sexual relationships with adult
men, while young women in the same age bracket did not need such protection against
relations with either adult men or women. In this connection the Court reiterates that the scope
of the margin of appreciation left to the Contracting State will vary according to the circumstances, the subject matter and the background; in this respect, one of the relevant factors may
be the existence or non-existence of common ground between the laws of the Contracting
States . . .

---

[128] Reports 2003-I.

89

50. In the present case the applicants pointed out, and this has not been contested by the Government, that there is an ever growing European consensus to apply equal ages of consent for heterosexual, lesbian and homosexual relations. Similarly, the Commission observed in *Sutherland* . . . that 'equality of treatment in respect of the age of consent is now recognised by the great majority of Member States of the Council of Europe'."

Note

By applying the "very weighty reasons" test, the ECtHR has placed the ground of sexual orientation on the same level as sex and illegitimate birth. The reason for suspectness is the existence of a growing consensus within the various Contracting States of the Council of Europe on the need to treat homosexual relations on the same footing as heterosexual relations.

The ECJ has not yet been offered the opportunity to pronounce itself on the suspectness of the ground of sexual orientation. Having regard to the ECtHR's case-law, it might be expected that the ECJ will award a similar level of protection and will strictly scrutinise any case of discrimination based on sexual orientation. Indeed, the fact that the ground is now explicitly mentioned in the Employment Equality Directive, the EU Fundamental Rights Charter and Article 13 EC may be regarded as recognition of the suspectness of discrimination based on sexual orientation.[129] However, Bell's caveat that sexual orientation discrimination is not yet recognised as creating a barrier to participation in the European labour market and undermining overall economic competitiveness still holds true.[130] Although this is certainly not the only factor which determines the ECJ's intensity of review in discrimination cases, it therefore remains uncertain that the ECJ will provide a level of protection against sexual orientation discrimination that is comparable to that offered to equal treatment based on gender or nationality. It is clear, moreover, from such cases as *Grant* (above, **1.EC.29.**), that the ECJ does not presently recognise the need to treat same-sex partners the same as partners of different sex. The Employment Equality Directive might not lead to a change in this respect, since its material scope is rather limited and does not cover the sensitive and controversial area of family law.[131] Against this background, it would not be surprising if the ECJ chose to decide sexual orientation cases along two different lines: it may regard sexual orientation as a suspect ground of discrimination in those limited areas in which there is clear legislation available (such as in the area of employment), whilst leaving a wide scope of discretion to the states in other, more controversial and unregulated areas, such as family law.

[129] See, on the developments in the EU, in particular with respect to policy measures adopted by the European institutions, M. Bell, "Setting Standards in the Fight against Racism" in Niessen and Chopin, above n. 66, 89*ff.*
[130] *Ibid.*, 119.
[131] However, see Case C–267/06 *Maruko*, lodged with the Court of Justice on 20 June 2006, which concerns surviving partner pensions and their availability to registered (same-sex) partners.

1.3.6. MARITAL AND FAMILY STATUS

1.3.6.A. DEFINITIONS

MARITAL STATUS

The Employment Equality Directive does not contain a prohibition of discrimination based on marital status in the sense of discrimination between married and unmarried couples. Indeed, European law does not really seem to be concerned with discrimination on this basis, even though the Gender Employment Directive mentions the ground as a possible cause of indirect gender discrimination.[132] The little case-law available with respect to marital status is concerned mainly with Regulation No. 1612/68, which provides a number of rights and benefits to workers employed in a different Member State and their family and spouses. In the *Reed* case of 1986, the ECJ denied that an unmarried partner could be brought within the category of "spouse" as contained in this Regulation:

ECJ, 17 April 1986[133]   **1.EC.43.**
Case 59/85, State of the Netherlands v. Ann Florence Reed

NO RESIDENCE PERMIT FOR UNMARRIED PARTNER

Reed

Facts: Ms Reed, an unmarried British national, arrived in the Netherlands in 1981. In 1982 she applied for a residence permit on the ground that she was living with Mr W. Mr W. was also an unmarried British national, who had worked in the Netherlands since 1981 and obtained a residence permit as a national of a member state of the EEC. Miss Reed and Mr W. were living together in the Netherlands and had a stable relationship of some five years' standing. Miss Reed was refused a residence permit on the basis of the Dutch policy on aliens. Although that policy made it possible for aliens to obtain a residence permit in the Netherlands because of a stable relationship (even if the partners were not married), this possibility did not exist for workers residing in the Netherlands on the basis of a residence permit granted to nationals of EEC states.

Held: The relevant provisions must be interpreted as meaning that a Member State which permits the unmarried companions of its nationals, who are not themselves nationals of that Member State, to reside in its territory cannot refuse to grant the same advantage to migrant workers who are nationals of other Member States.

---

[132] Gender Employment Directive, Art. 2 para. 1 (not included in the Recast Gender Employment Directive): "For the purposes of the following provisions, the principle of equal treatment shall mean that there shall be no discrimination whatsoever on grounds of sex either directly or indirectly by reference in particular to marital or family status." On the meaning of this clause, see above Ellis, n. 106, 28.
[133] [1986] ECR 1283.

Judgment: "14. Article 10(1) of Regulation No. 1612/68 provides that certain members of the 'family' of a worker, including his 'spouse', irrespective of their nationality, 'have the right to install themselves with a worker who is a national of one member state and who is employed in the territory of another member state'.

15. In the absence of any indication of a general social development which would justify a broad construction, and in the absence of any indication to the contrary in the regulation, it must be held that the term 'spouse' in Article 10 of the Regulation refers to a marital relationship only . . .

22. It must . . .be ascertained whether the right to be accompanied by an unmarried companion falls within the scope of the Treaty and is thus governed by the principle of non-discrimination laid down by the provisions referred to above . . .

26. As the Court has repeatedly held, the purpose of . . . Regulation No. 1612/68 is to achieve equal treatment, and therefore the concept of social advantage . . .must include all advantages 'which . . . are generally granted to national workers primarily because of their objective status as workers or by virtue of the mere fact of their residence on the national territory and the extension of which to workers who are nationals of other member countries therefore seems suitable to facilitate their mobility within the Community' . . .

28. . . . . it must be recognized that the possibility for a migrant worker of obtaining permission for his unmarried companion to reside with him, where that companion is not a national of the host member state, can assist his integration in the host state and thus contribute to the achievement of freedom of movement for workers. Consequently, that possibility must also be regarded as falling within the concept of a social advantage . . .

29. It must therefore be concluded that the member state which grants such an advantage to its own nationals cannot refuse to grant it to workers who are nationals of other Member States without being guilty of discrimination on grounds of nationality . . .

30. . . . . A member state which permits the unmarried companions of its nationals, who are not themselves nationals of that member state, to reside in its territory, cannot refuse to grant the same advantage to migrant workers who are nationals of other Member States."

Note

In this case the ECJ expressly held that the Regulation only applied to married partners, thereby rejecting the supposition that unequal treatment based on marital status were impermissible under EC law. The ECJ did, however, recognise that if a Member State voluntarily granted similar rights to married and unmarried partners in respect of its own nationals, it should also grant those rights to workers from other Member States. Thus, the Member States were left with a rather wide margin of discretion to decide whether they wanted to prohibit discrimination based on marital or family status and, if they did, how they would interpret the relevant ground.

Fifteen years later, the ECJ's stance has not significantly changed. In the case of *D. and Sweden* v. *Council*, it held once more that it was not the task of the ECJ to widen the scope of such notions as "marriage" in order to cover similar legal arrangements such as registered partnerships:

ECJ, 13 May 2001[134]   **1.EC.44.**
Joined Cases C–122/99 P and C–125/99, P, D. and Sweden v. Council

DISCRIMINATION OF SAME-SEX PARTNERS WITH A REGISTERED PARTNERSHIP

D v. Council

Facts: D., a Swedish EC official working at the Council, registered a partnership with another Swedish national of the same sex in Sweden on 23 June 1995. He applied to the Council for his status as a registered partner to be treated as being equivalent to marriage for the purpose of obtaining the household allowance provided for in the Staff Regulations. The Council rejected the application on the ground that the provisions of the Staff Regulations could not be construed as allowing a registered partnership to be treated as being equivalent to marriage.

Held: The Council could not interpret the Staff Regulations so as to treat D's situation as that of a married official for the purposes of granting a household allowance.

Judgment: "33. . . . As the appellants contend, a stable relationship between partners of the same sex which has only a de facto existence, as was the case in Grant . . . is not necessarily equivalent to a registered partnership under a statutory arrangement, which, as between the persons concerned and as regards third parties, has effects in law akin to those of marriage since it is intended to be comparable.

34. It is not in question that, according to the definition generally accepted by the Member States, the term 'marriage' means a union between two persons of the opposite sex.

35. It is equally true that since 1989 an increasing number of Member States have introduced, along-side marriage, statutory arrangements granting legal recognition to various forms of union between partners of the same sex or of the opposite sex and conferring on such unions certain effects which, both between the partners and as regards third parties, are the same as or comparable to those of marriage.

36. It is clear, however, that apart from their great diversity, such arrangements for registering relation-ships between couples not previously recognised in law are regarded in the Member States concerned as being distinct from marriage.

37. In such circumstances the Community judicature cannot interpret the Staff Regulations in such a way that legal situations distinct from marriage are treated in the same way as marriage. The intention of the Community legislature was to grant entitlement to the household allowance under Article 1(2)(a) of Annex VII to the Staff Regulations only to married couples.

38. Only the legislature can, where appropriate, adopt measures to alter that situation, for example by amending the provisions of the Staff Regulations. However, not only has the Community legislature not shown any intention of adopting such measures, it has even . . . ruled out at this stage any idea of other forms of partnership being assimilated to marriage for the purposes of granting the benefits re-served under the Staff Regulations for married officials, choosing instead to maintain the existing arrangement until the various consequences of such assimilation become clearer.

39. It follows that the fact that, in a limited number of Member States, a registered partnership is assimilated, although incompletely, to marriage cannot have the consequence that, by mere interpretation, persons whose legal status is distinct from that of marriage can be covered by the term 'married official' as used in the Staff Regulations."

---

[134] [2001] ECR I–4319.

Note

D. v. *Council* shows that there may be a strong measure of overlap between the ground of marital status and that of sexual orientation. It seemed to be decisive in the case not that a distinction was made between married partners and partners with a registered partnership, but that a distinction was made between same-sex partners and partners of a different sex. It is far from clear how this case would have been decided if D. had had a registered partnership with an individual of another sex. If that would have resulted in the outcome that a well-established and consistent relationship between unmarried partners ought to be treated the same as the relationship between married partners, such a result would imply that the ground would cover only relations between different-sex partners, not between partners of the same sex. If that were true, this would constitute discrimination based on sexual orientation.[135]

FAMILY STATUS AND MARITAL STATUS

The above has shown that EC law does not provide any guidance as to the way in which the Member States should combat discrimination based on marital status. This is stressed by Recital 22 of the preamble to the Employment Equality Directive, which states that "this Directive is without prejudice to national laws on marital status and the benefits dependent thereon". Many Member States have included the ground of marital status in their non-discrimination legislation, yet the legislative definitions are far from uniform. In some legislation a notion of "family status" is mentioned which encompasses both marital status and related grounds, such as cohabitation with (close) family members, such as parents, siblings or children. An example may be found in the Bulgarian legislation:

The Bulgarian Protection against Discrimination Act[136]   **1.BG.45.**

'Family status' shall mean marital status, or a factual cohabitation with, and a caring responsibility for offspring or parents, including grandchildren and grandparents, or for a collateral relative up to third degree inclusive of those who are dependent due to age or a disability.

Non-discrimination provisions starting from such a wide notion of family status obviously offer stronger protection against unequal treatment than provisions starting from marital status do.

Other Member States make a sharper distinction between family status and marital status. They do not consider "marital status" as part of the definition of

---

[135] *Cf.* O. de Schutter, "The Prohibition of Discrimination under European Human Rights Law. Relevance for EU Racial and Employment Equality Directives" (European Commission, February 2005) 43.

[136] Art. 1, subs 12.

"family status", but define family status as a separate ground with a different meaning. Marital status is then used primarily to refer to the civic relationship of two individuals (married, unmarried, cohabitating), whereas family status is employed to refer to the relationship between an individual and his family members. In this regard, the category of family members may be wide or narrow, the Bulgarian definition quoted above being an example of a wide definition which even encompasses grandparents. The Irish definition is also relatively wide, although it is limited to the relation to minors and other persons needing direct care.[137] This definition was explored further in decisions by the Equality Officer:

Equality Tribunal, 12 September 2003[138]   **1.IE.46.**
Decision DEC-S/2003/109-110, Travers & Maunsell v. *The Ball Alley House*

DEFINITION OF FAMILY STATUS

The Ball Alley House

Facts: Travers and Maunsell complained about the fact that they were asked to leave the Ball Alley House pub at 7.00 pm because they had a sleeping nine-month-old baby with them on the premises. According to the owner of the pub, he acted in accordance with the pub's children's policy, according to which no children were allowed in(to) the pub after 6.00 pm to curtail the annoyance and risks that can arise from the presence of unsupervised children.

Held: The complainants were directly discriminated against on the family status ground contrary to the provisions of the Equal Status Act 2000 in being refused service.

Decision: "7.20 . . . I consider that the 'family status' ground is different to other grounds in so far as a persons family status can change, for the purposes of the Equal Status Act 2000, depending on the circumstances in which they find themselves at a particular time . . . [I]t appears clear to me that the term 'family status' as defined in the Equal Status Act 2000, relates specifically to having responsibility for children under 18 or for a person with a disability. Therefore, for a person to claim that they were discriminated against on the 'family status' ground, I consider that it must be shown that the treatment afforded to them was directly attributable to the fact that that person 'had responsibility' for a child under the age of 18 or for a person with a disability."

Note
It is clear from this case that the notion of "family status" under the Irish Equal Status Act 2000 is rather flexible. Parents will not always be able to invoke the ground, for example when a situation occurs in which they have no responsibility for their child. On the other hand, the notion is relatively wide in that it also covers relations to persons with a disability.

[137] See Equal Status Act 2000 (No. 8/2000), Art. 2 (Interpretation).
[138] Available on the website of the Equality Tribunal of Ireland, under the heading Equal Status Decisions.

By contrast, there are a number of states which use a far more limited definition and in which the refusal of service in a pub because of the presence of a minor would not constitute a prohibited form of discrimination. In the Netherlands, for example, only the ground of "civil status" is covered by the equal treatment legislation, which only concerns legal differences between married and unmarried persons and between registered and non-registered partners.[139] Although distinctions between legitimate, natural and adopted children would appear to fall under the scope of the Dutch notion, discrimination against singles does not qualify as a direct distinction on this ground.[140] Against the background of the wide variety of definitions of family life and marital status in the various Member States, these examples once more stress the lack of common ground and convergence in this area of equal treatment law.

1.3.6.B.   SUSPECTNESS

Just like the exact meaning of "marital status" or "family status", the suspectness of the ground is still undetermined. Both the ECtHR and the ECJ have remained relatively silent on this issue. The ECJ's decisions do seem to make clear, however, that the ECJ does not regard the ground as a highly problematic ground for unequal treatment. This may be different for the ECtHR, but the one decision available does not provide a clear-cut answer to the question of suspectness:

ECtHR, 4 June 2002[141]   **1.CoE.47.**
Wessels-Bergervoet v. *The Netherlands*

VERY WEIGHTY REASONS TEST APPLIED TO DISCRIMINATION BASED ON SEX AND
MARITAL STATUS

Wessels-Bergervoet

Facts: Wessels-Bergervoet and her husband have always lived in the Netherlands. In 1984, Wessels was granted a married man's old-age pension under the General Old Age Pensions Act (AOW). However, his pension was reduced by 38% as neither he nor Wessels-Bergervoet had been insured under the Act during nine periods when he had worked in Germany and had old-age insurance under the German social-security legislation. These nine periods amounted in total to 19 years. After Wessels-Bergervoet reached the age of 65 in 1989, she was granted an old-age pension, which was reduced by 38%, just like her husband's, under a royal decree of 1985, the limitation applying to Wessels also applied to the person married to him.

---

[139] Cabinet view on the evaluation of the Equal Treatment Act by the Equal Treatment Commission, 1999, *Kamerstukken II* 2001–02, 28 481, no. 1, 13.

[140] *Ibid.*

[141] Reports 2002-IV.

Held: The difference in treatment between married women and married men is not based on any objective and reasonable justification and accordingly constitutes a violation of Article 14 of the Convention taken in conjunction with Article 1 of Protocol No. 1.

Judgment: "47. . . .The only reason for the applicant's exclusion from insurance under the AOW for a global period of nineteen years was the fact that she was married to a man who was not insured under the AOW on grounds of his employment abroad. It is undisputed that a married man in the same situation as the applicant would not have been excluded from the AOW insurance scheme in this manner.

48. The Court concludes that the reduction applied to the applicant's AOW benefits was therefore based exclusively on the fact that she is a married woman . . .

49. The Court considers that very strong reasons would have to be put forward before it could regard a difference in treatment based exclusively on the ground of sex and marital status as compatible with the Convention."

Note

It is clear from this judgment that the Court regards discrimination based on combination of sex and marital status as suspect, but it is difficult to conclude from the ruling whether it will also apply a "very weighty reasons" test if a complaint of discrimination is based solely on the ground of marital status. Unfortunately, no other ECtHR judgments are available that give any clue as to the Court's stance on this issue.

1.3.7.   BIRTH, PARENTAGE AND DESCENT

The ground of legitimate or illegitimate birth, parentage or descent is often mentioned in national legislation, but is not included in the list of grounds of the Employment Equality Directive. No definition of these grounds can thus be found in EC law. Although many Member States prohibit discrimination based on birth or parentage, a definition is seldom provided on the domestic level—the national legislators either seem to find the meaning of the grounds rather obvious and further definition superfluous, or they consider it difficult to provide a clear and practical legislative definition.

The ECtHR has paid much attention to the ground of birth as a basis for unequal treatment. In the case-law of this Court, issues of definition and suspectness are closely intertwined; these will therefore not be dealt with separately in this section.

In its famous *Marckx* decision, the Court accepted for the first time that a distinction based on birth in or out of wedlock would be very difficult to justify:

ECtHR, 13 June 1979[142]   **1.CoE.48.**
Marckx v. *Belgium*

ILLEGITIMATE BIRTH AS A SUSPECT GROUND FOR DISCRIMINATION

Marckx

Facts: Alexandra Marckx was born in 1973; she is the daughter of Paula Marckx, who is unmarried. Paula Marckx duly reported Alexandra's birth, recognised the child and thereby became Alexandra's guardian. The procedure concluded with a judgment confirming the adoption, the effect whereof was retroactive to the date of the instrument of adoption. Marckx complained about the Civil Code provisions on the manner of establishing the maternal affiliation of an illegitimate child and on the effects of establishing such affiliation as regards both the extent of the child's family relationships and the patrimonial rights of the child and of his mother. She also raised the issue of whether it is necessary for the mother to adopt the child if she wishes to increase its rights.

Held: The state cannot rely on any general interest or objective and reasonable justification to limit an unmarried mother's right to make gifts or legacies in favour of her child when at the same time a married woman is not subject to any similar restriction. Accordingly, there was a breach of Article 14 of the Convention

Judgment: "41. It is true that, at the time when the Convention of 4 November 1950 was drafted, it was regarded as permissible and normal in many European countries to draw a distinction in this area between the 'illegitimate' and the 'legitimate' family. However, the Court recalls that this Convention must be interpreted in the light of present-day conditions (*Tyrer* judgment of 25 April 1978, Series A no. 26, p. 15, para. 31). In the instant case, the Court cannot but be struck by the fact that the domestic law of the great majority of the Member States of the Council of Europe has evolved and is continuing to evolve, in company with the relevant international instruments, towards full juridical recognition of the maxim 'mater semper certa est'.

Admittedly, of the ten states that drew up the Brussels Convention, only eight have signed and only four have ratified it to date. The European Convention of 15 October 1975 on the Legal Status of Children born out of Wedlock has at present been signed by only ten and ratified by only four members of the Council of Europe. Furthermore, Article 14(1) of the latter Convention permits any State to make, at the most, three reservations, one of which could theoretically concern precisely the manner of establishing the maternal affiliation of a child born out of wedlock (Article 2).

However, this state of affairs cannot be relied on in opposition to the evolution noted above. Both the relevant Conventions are in force and there is no reason to attribute the currently small number of Contracting States to a refusal to admit equality between 'illegitimate' and legitimate' children on the point under consideration. In fact, the existence of these two treaties denotes that there is a clear measure of common ground in this area amongst modern societies.

The official statement of reasons accompanying the Bill submitted by the Belgian Government to the Senate on 15 February 1978 . . . provides an illustration of this evolution of rules and attitudes. Amongst other things, the statement points out that 'in recent years several Western European countries, including the Federal Republic of Germany, Great Britain, the Netherlands, France, Italy and Switzerland, have adopted new legislation radically altering the traditional structure of the law of affiliation and establishing almost complete equality between legitimate and illegitimate children'. It is also noted that 'the desire to put an end to all

---

[142] Series A, Vol. 31.

discrimination and abolish all inequalities based on birth is . . .apparent in the work of various international institutions'. As regards Belgium itself, the statement stresses that the difference of treatment between Belgian citizens, depending on whether their affiliation is established in or out of wedlock, amounts to a 'flagrant exception' to the fundamental principle of the equality of everyone before the law (Article 6 of the Constitution). It adds that 'lawyers and public opinion are becoming increasingly convinced that the discrimination against (illegitimate) children should be ended'."

Note

It is clear from the cited considerations that the Court will not easily accept a justification for a difference in treatment based on legitimate or illegitimate birth, having regard to the growing European consensus regarding the unacceptability of such distinctions. The "common ground" argument is thus the main reason for suspectness in this case. This was stressed by the Court in its later judgment in the *Inze* case:

ECtHR, 28 October 1987[143]   **1.CoE.49.**
Inze v. *Austria*

VERY WEIGHTY REASONS TEST APPLIED TO DISCRIMINATION BASED ON
ILLEGITIMATE BIRTH

Inze

Facts: Mr Inze was born out of wedlock in 1942. Until 1965, he lived on a farm which had belonged first to his maternal grandmother and then to his mother. At the age of 23, he left the farm and later he married and settled down a few kilometres away. The applicant's mother died intestate on 18 April 1975 and left as her heirs, apart from the applicant, her husband and her second son. According to the provisions of the Civil Code, the widower was entitled to a one-fourth part of the inheritance and each of the sons (irrespective of their illegitimate or legitimate birth) to three-eighths thereof. However, the farm in question was subject to special regulations providing that farms of a certain size may not be divided in the case of hereditary succession and that one of the heirs must take over the entire property and pay off the other heirs. Inze had claimed that he should be called to take over his mother's farm as he was the eldest son, but his claim was dismissed: according to national law, precedence should be given to legitimate children.

Held: The reasons advanced by the Government cannot justify the rule at hand; violation of Article 14.

Judgment: "41. The Contracting States enjoy a certain margin of appreciation in assessing whether and to what ex-tent differences in otherwise similar situations justify a different treatment in law; the scope of this margin will vary according to the circumstances, the subject-matter and its background . . .

In this respect, the Court recalls that the Convention is a living instrument, to be interpreted in the light of present-day conditions . . . The question of equality between children born in and children born out of wedlock as regards their civil rights is today given importance in the Member States of the Council of Europe. This is shown by the 1975 European Convention on the Legal Status of Children born out of Wedlock, which is presently in force in respect of nine Member States of the Council of Europe. It was ratified by the Republic of Austria on 28 May 1980, with a reservation which is not relevant to the facts of the present case. Very weighty

---

[143] Series A, Vol. 126.

reasons would accordingly have to be advanced before a difference of treatment on the ground of birth out of wedlock could be regarded as compatible with the Convention . . ."

Note

It is clear from this case that "very weighty reasons" have to be advanced in justification of a distinction based on birth out of wedlock. By now, the "very weighty reasons" test has become part of a well-established line of case-law regarding distinctions based on birth.[144] Discrimination based on this ground is thus clearly considered suspect and its justification will be subjected to very strict scrutiny by the ECtHR.

From the perspective of the definition and meaning of the various grounds of discrimination, it is furthermore interesting to see that the ECtHR has recently applied the "very weighty reasons" test in two related cases of unequal treatment: discrimination against parents of illegitimate children and discrimination against adopted children.

ECtHR, 8 July 2003[145]   1.CoE.50.
Sahin v. *Germany*

DISCRIMINATION AGAINST PARENTS OF ILLEGITIMATE CHILDREN

Sahin

Facts: Mr Sahin is the father of G., who was born out of wedlock in 1988. He acknowledged paternity of the unborn child and undertook to pay maintenance. Sahin applied to the national courts for a decision granting him a right of access to G., but all his requests were dismissed. The main reason was that the courts were convinced that personal contact with her father would not be in the child's best interests. A Chamber of the ECtHR, which dealt with the case in 2001, found a violation of Article 14 because the underlying legislation put fathers of children born out of wedlock in a different, less favourable position than divorced fathers. Unlike the latter, natural fathers had no direct right of access to their children and the mother's refusal of access could only be overridden by a court when access was "in the interests of the child".

Held: The Court does not discern a sufficient justification for the difference in treatment of divorced and natural fathers; the discrimination is accordingly in violation of Article 14 ECHR.

Judgment: "94. The Court has already held that very weighty reasons need to be put forward before a difference in treatment on the ground of birth out of or within wedlock can be regarded as compatible with the Convention . . . The same is true for a difference in the treatment of the father of a child born of a relationship where the parties were living together out of wed-lock as compared with the father of a child born of a marriage-based relationship. The Court discerns no such reasons in the instant case."

---

[144] See also the case of *Camp and Bourimi* v. *the Netherlands*, ECtHR, 3 October 2000, Reports 2000-X.
[145] Not published.

Note

It is clear from this case that the ECtHR not only accepts that a difference in treatment between divorced fathers of legitimate children and fathers of children born out of wedlock is covered by the prohibition of discrimination of Article 14 ECHR, but even that this difference in treatment is included in the same category of suspect grounds, requiring very weighty reasons as justification.[146] The same is true for discrimination against adopted children, as the following excerpt makes clear:

ECtHR, 13 July 2004[147]   **1.CoE.51.**
Pla and Puncernau v. *Andorra*

DISCRIMINATION AGAINST ADOPTED CHILDREN

Pla and Puncernau

Facts: In 1949 Mrs Carolina Pujol Oller died, leaving three children. She settled her estate on her son, Francesc-Xavier, as tenant for life. She indicated that Francesc-Xavier was to transfer the estate to a son or grandson of a lawful and canonical marriage. Francesc-Xavier contracted canonical marriage to the second applicant, Roser Puncernau Pedro. They adopted two children in accordance with the procedure for full adoption. In 1995 Francesc-Xavier made a will in which he left a sum of money to his son and daughter. After his death in 1996 two sisters, the great-grandchildren of the testatrix, brought proceedings to have the codicil declared null and void. The Andorran high court held that a proper interpretation of the will in the context of the legal and social circumstances at the time implied that the testatrix could not have intended that an adopted son could be regarded as 'a son or grandson of a lawful and canonical marriage'. Accordingly, Francesc-Xavier's codicil was declared null and void.

Held: The interpretation given by the national court amounted to a discrimination based on birth and is in contravention of Article 14 ECHR.

Judgment: "61. The Court reiterates that a distinction is discriminatory for the purposes of Article 14 if it has no objective and reasonable justification, that is if it does not pursue a legitimate aim or if there is not a 'reasonable relationship of proportionality between the means employed and the aim sought to be realised' . . . In the present case, the Court does not discern any legitimate aim pursued by the decision in question or any objective and reasonable justification on which the distinction made by the domestic court might be based. In the Court's view, where a child is adopted (under the full adoption procedure, moreover), the child is in the same legal position as a biological child of his or her parents in all respects: relations and consequences connected with his or her family life and the resulting property rights. The Court has stated on many occasions that very weighty reasons need to be put forward before a difference in treatment on the ground of birth out of wedlock can be regarded as compatible with the Convention. Furthermore, there is nothing to suggest that reasons of public policy required the degree of protection afforded by the Andorran appellate court to the appellants to prevail over that afforded to the first applicant.

---

[146] Before the case of *Sahin*, there was some reason to doubt the suspectness of a distinction based on parentage: in the earlier case of *McMichael*, the Court did not apply a very weighty reasons test to a case in which a married father was treated differently from a natural father (ECtHR 24 February 1995, *McMichael* v. *UK*, Series A, Vol. 307-B, paras 97–8).

[147] Reports 2004-VIII.

62. The Court reiterates that the Convention, which is a dynamic text and entails positive obligations for States, is a living instrument, to be interpreted in the light of present-day conditions and that great importance is attached today in the Member States of the Council of Europe to the question of equality between children born in and children born out of wedlock as regards their civil rights . . .Thus, even supposing that the testamentary disposition in question did require an interpretation by the domestic courts, that interpretation could not be made exclusively in the light of the social conditions existing when the will was made or at the time of the testatrix's death, namely in 1939 and 1949, particularly where a period of fifty-seven years had elapsed between the date when the will was made and the date on which the estate passed to the heirs. Where such a long period has elapsed, during which profound social, economic and legal changes have occurred, the courts cannot ignore these new realities. The same is true with regard to wills: any interpretation, if interpretation there must be, should endeavour to ascertain the testator's intention and render the will effective, while bearing in mind that 'the testator cannot be presumed to have meant what he did not say' and without overlooking the importance of interpreting the testamentary disposition in the manner that most closely corresponds to domestic law and to the Convention as interpreted in the Court's case-law.

63. Having regard to the foregoing, the Court considers that there has been a violation of Article 14 of the Convention taken in conjunction with Article 8."

Note

In paragraph 61 of its judgment in *Pla and Puncernau*, the Court seems to classify discrimination based on being an adopted child instead of a biological child as discrimination based on "birth out of wedlock". This may seem an odd classification, but it is probably chosen because of the fact that birth out of wedlock is a suspect ground of discrimination warranting intensive scrutiny, which secures a measure of protection against discrimination the Court wanted to offer to adopted children too.

In conclusion, it seems clear that the notion of "birth" should be given a rather wide definition under the ECHR, including even adopted children and illegitimate fathers, and that distinctions based on this ground should be considered suspect at all times. As a consequence, the domestic courts should adopt a similar approach to the ground.

1.3.8.   RELIGION AND BELIEF; POLITICAL OR PERSONAL CONVICTION

1.3.8.A.   DEFINITION

INTRODUCTION

The Employment Equality Directive prohibits discrimination based on "religion or belief", without giving a definition of these terms. The only thing that is clear from this prohibition is that a difference is perceived between the notions of "religion" and "belief" which is considered meaningful enough to justify separate mention of the notions. The same combination is also often found in national legislation. Many national lists of grounds even contain more or other related grounds, such as conscience and thought, but also political or personal conviction.

Employment Equality (Religion or Belief)   **1.GB.52.**
Regulations 2003[148]

In these Regulations, 'religion or belief' means any religion, religious belief, or similar philosophical belief.

Bulgarian Protection Against Discrimination Act[149]   **1.BG.53.**

All direct or indirect discrimination on the grounds of . . . religion or faith . . . beliefs [and] political affiliation . . . shall be prohibited.

Constitution of Malta[150]   **1.MT.54.**

In this article, the expression 'discriminatory' means affording different treatment to different persons attributable wholly or mainly to their respective descriptions by . . . political opinions . . . [or] creed . . .

These broad lists of grounds are probably inspired by the fact that international legal texts tend to provide a wide definition of the freedom of religion of belief, mentioning far more aspects than religion and belief alone. Both international and regional legislators have shrunk back from explicitly addressing the difficult question regarding the definition of such terms as "religion" and "belief". Instead, they have opted for listing a wide number of related notions, which may have appeared an easier solution than to provide elaborate and disputable definitions.[151]

---

[148] SI 2004/2520, s. 2(1). This definition will be amended when Equality Act 2006 s. 77 enters into force. This clarifies that lack of religion and lack of belief are prohibited grounds of discrimination.
[149] Art. 4(1).
[150] Art. 45(3).
[151] Lerner, above n. 48, 77.

Universal Declaration of Human Rights   **1.UN.55.**
(1948)[152]

Everyone has the right to freedom of thought, conscience and religion; this right includes freedom to change his religion or belief, and freedom, either alone or in community with others and in public or private, to manifest his religion or belief in teaching, practice, worship and observance.

Declaration on the Elimination of All Forms of Intolerance   **1.UN.56.**
and of Discrimination based on Religion and Belief (1981)

1(1)—Everyone shall have the right to freedom of thought, conscience and religion. This right shall include freedom to have a religion or whatever belief of his choice, and freedom, either individually or in community with others and in public or private, to manifest his religion or belief in worship, observance, practices and teaching.

2(1)—No one shall be subject to discrimination by any State, institution, group of persons, or person on the grounds of religion or other belief.

2(2)—For the purposes of the present Declaration, the expression 'intolerance and discrimination based on religion or belief' means any distinction, exclusion, restriction or preference based on religion or belief and having as its purpose or as its effect nullification or impairment of the recognition, enjoyment or exercise of human rights and fundamental freedoms on an equal basis.

European Convention of Human Rights[153]   **1.CoE.57.**

Everyone has the right to freedom of thought, conscience and religion; this right includes freedom to change his religion or belief and freedom, either alone or in community with others and in public or private, to manifest his religion or belief, in worship, teaching, practice and observance.

Charter of Fundamental Rights of the European Union[154]   **1.EC.58.**

1. Everyone has the right to freedom of thought, conscience and religion. This right includes freedom to change religion or belief and freedom, either alone or in community with others and in public or in private, to manifest religion or belief, in worship, teaching, practice and observance.

[152] Art. 18.
[153] Art. 9(1).
[154] Art. 10.

2. The right to conscientious objection is recognised, in accordance with the national laws governing the exercise of this right.

Human Rights Committee, General Comment No. 22: **1.CoE.59.**
The right to freedom of thought, conscience and religion (Article 18)[155]

"1.The right to freedom of thought, conscience and religion (which includes the freedom to hold beliefs) in Article 18.1 is far-reaching and profound; it encompasses freedom of thought on all matters, personal conviction and the commitment to religion or belief, whether manifested individually or in community with others. The Committee draws the attention of States parties to the fact that the freedom of thought and the freedom of conscience are protected equally with the freedom of religion and belief . . .

2. Article 18 protects theistic, non-theistic and atheistic beliefs, as well as the right not to profess any religion or belief. The terms 'belief' and 'religion' are to be broadly construed. Article 18 is not limited in its application to traditional religions and beliefs with institutional characteristics or practices analogous to those of traditional religions . . ."

The variety in grounds covered by such national and international lists makes it interesting to investigate what exactly is the meaning of such terms as "religion", "faith", "belief", "conscience", "thought", "political conviction" and "personal conviction".[156] In this section, we undertake to give an overview of the existing national and international case-law on the matter. We will devote particular attention to the definitions given in international legal texts and case-law relating to the freedom of religion, as the national notions are often interpreted in accordance with international law.[157] For the European Member States, the main source of inspiration is the case-law of the ECtHR on Article 9 ECHR. It is highly probable that future decisions of the ECJ on the Employment Equality Directive will be influenced by this case-law as well. For that reason, we will discuss this case-law in considerable detail.

RELIGION—RECOGNITION AND SECTS

It is clear from the quoted European legislation and case-law that the notion of "religion" itself extends to all existing and recognised religions and faiths. There is some debate, however, about the requirement of a religion being "recognised". Sometimes the requirement seems to be taken literally, in the sense that a religion is

[155] 30 July 1993—ICCRP/C/21/Rev.1/Add.4.
[156] On this see also M.D. Evans, "The Evolution of Religious Freedom in International Law: Present State and Perspectives" in J.-F. Flauss (ed.), *International Protection of Religious Freedom* (Brussels, Bruylant, 2002) 39*ff.*
[157] See, e.g. T. Makkonen, "Discrimination Based on Religion and Belief. Finland", Executive Summary (European Commission, 2004) 3, available on the website of Directorate-General for Employment, Social Affairs and Equal Opportunities and the Explanatory Note to the UK Equality Act 2006, para. 155.

only considered to exist if a religious community is officially recognised by a governmental body. The Danish situation offers a good example of this approach:

N.E. Hansen, "Report on measures to combat discrimination: **1.DK.60.**
Directive 2000/43/EC and 2000/78/EC. Country report Denmark"[158]

"'Religion' is not directly legally defined in Denmark. Indirectly a definition may be found due to the practice of the Danish authorities in relation to the recognition of 'religious communities'. This recognition takes place in order to allow recognised communities to perform marriage ceremonies with legal validity. On the other hand, a number of communities are not recognised by the state, and consequently not a 'religious community' in a legal sense . . .

Religious communities in Denmark may be grouped into four categories: according to section 4 of the Danish Constitution . . . the Evangelical-Lutheran Church is the National Church of Denmark. The status as national church is associated with certain rights, which distinguish the legal position of the Danish national church markedly from that of other religious communities.

The second category of religious communities comprises the so-called recognised religious communities . . . A total of eleven religious communities have been recognised by Royal Decree.

The third category consists of religious communities with only limited recognition . . . Section 16 of the [Danish Formation and Dissolution of Marriage Acts] empowers the Ministry to take administrative action to afford limited competence to ministers of religion, imams and other spiritual leaders of newly arrived religions, to celebrate marriage ceremonies with legal effect, according to civil law. The fact that a minister of religion or an imam has authority to celebrate marriages implies that the religious community in question has obtained a certain degree of recognition . . . [A] Committee decides . . .what constitutes a religious community . . . Presently 56 religious communities are included in the third category.

The fourth category comprises non-recognised religious communities, which are religious communities that either cannot or do not wish to obtain recognition, and therefore do not enjoy the same rights as the religious communities with full or limited recognition . . ."

Note
It is clear that the protection offered by the prohibition of discrimination may vary for each of the different categories distinguished in the Danish legislation. Also, the scope of non-discrimination legislation depends on the willingness of the national authorities to recognise a certain religious group as a religious community.

Different approaches to the recognition of religious communities are also conceivable. A rather loose approach can be found in Italy:

---

[158] (European Commission, 2005) 17, available on the website of Directorate-General for Employment, Social Affairs and Equal Opportunities.

A. Simoni, "Report on measures to combat discrimination: **1.IT.61.**
Directive 2000/43/EC and 2000/78/EC. Country report Italy"[159]

"The main set of standards has been set by the Court in a 1995 case, where it is said that, in the absence of agreements with the State, the character of 'religious denomination' of a social group can be established on the basis of 'public recognitions' (*pubblici riconoscimenti*), or on the basis of its charter (not alone but examined against the backdrop of the actual activity of the organisation) or on the basis of the 'common opinion' (*comune considerazione*). These criteria have been applied and further detailed specially with regard to the case of Scientology, which according to the case-law of the Supreme Court meets the criteria for the inclusion among the 'religious denominations' protected under the Constitution."

Note

It is clear from this excerpt that in Italy there is no need for *official* recognition to be able to speak of a "religious denomination". Instead, the Italian courts appear to rely on general criteria such as public recognition and common opinion as to the religious character of the community. This may lead to a relatively wide definition of the ground of religion, as the example of the acceptance of the Church of Scientology as a religious community shows, though the approach will clearly not result in a wider recognition of religious groups per se—this will depend on the application of such notions as "public recognition" and the extent to which a "common opinion" is easily accepted to exist.

The Italian recognition of the Church of Scientology brings us to the interesting question if minority religions and sects are generally covered by the ground of religion. There does not appear to be a uniform answer to this question in the various Member States. In Belgium, for example, sects are not covered by national legislation:

"The protection from discrimination based on religion will most probably be denied to members of groups defined as 'sects' under the Belgian law of 2 June 1998, which describes these as 'any group with a religious or philosophical vocation, or pretending to have such a vocation, which in its organisation or practice, performs illegal and damaging activities, causes nuisance to individuals or to the community or violates human dignity'."[160]

---

[159] (European Commission, 2004) 8, available on the website of Directorate-General for Employment, Social Affairs and Equal Opportunities.

[160] de Schutter, above n. 13, 16, available on the website of Directorate-General for Employment, Social Affairs and Equal Opportunities.

[161] *Cf.* also N. Gavalas, "Report on Measures to Combat Discrimination: Directive 2000/43/EC and 2000/78/EC. Country Report Greece" (European Commission, 2004), at 16, available on the website of Directorate-General for Employment, Social Affairs and Equal Opportunities, stating that, according to Greek scholars, the Greek Constitution does not recognize "mystical and secret practices and dogmas". Likewise, the Spanish Organic Law on Religious Freedom states that "activities, intentions and entities relating to or engaging in the study of and experimentation on psychic or parapsychological phenomena or the dissemination of humanistic or spiritual values or other similar non-religious aims do not qualify for

Several other Member States seem to exclude sects from a number of advantages available to recognized religious communities as well.[161] As yet it is unclear, however, how sects are generally defined and whether they will always be excluded from the scope of "religion".[162] The Italian and Belgian examples make clear that this will not be the case by definition, but possibly only if the sect performs illegal activities. Indeed, some sect-like organisations, such as the Church of Scientology, are frequently considered to fall under the protection of the freedom of religion. This is apparent from the Italian case-law mentioned above, but also (though more implicitly) from the case-law of the European Commission of Human Rights (EComHR)—a predecessor of the present ECtHR.[163] The EComHR also assumed that other sects, such as Druids and the Divine Light Zentrum, constitute religious organisations, unfortunately without defining criteria which might enable the domestic courts to make or test such classifications.[164] This makes it difficult for the states to give a proper definition of a sect and to reason whether certain sects fall outside the scope of the principle of religion. It has been rightly stressed by the special rapporteur on Freedom of Religion and Belief to the UN Commission on Human Rights that the uncertainty as to the status of such sects may easily lead to unacceptable forms of intolerance and discrimination based on religion.[165]

How to prove the existence of religion?

Closely related to the question if sects or cults come within the scope of religion is the question if someone who professes to have a certain religion, and claims that he has been discriminated on the basis of that religion, really adheres to such a religion. This issue raises difficult issues of proof, as is evidenced by the following case decided by the ECtHR:

the protection provided in this Act" (see L. Cachon, "Report on Measures to Combat Discrimination: Directive 2000/43/EC and 2000/78/EC. Country Report Spain" (European Commission, 2005) t 9, available on the website of Directorate-General for Employment, Social Affairs and Equal Opportunities; it is probable that sects such as the Church of Scientology are implicitly aimed at by this provision. The legislator specifies only what religion is not, not what it is. See more generally A. Amor, "Implementation of the Declaration on the Elimination of Intolerance and of Discrimination Based on Religion or Belief" (1998), Addendum: Visit to Germany, Ev.CN.4v.1998/6.

[162] See, e.g. S. Latraverse, "Report on Measures to Combat Discrimination: Directive 2000/43/EC and 2000/78/EC. Country Report France" (European Commission, 2004) 12, available on the website of Directorate-General for Employment, Social Affairs and Equal Opportunities, stating that there is currently no definition of sects in France.

[163] See *X. and Church of Scientology* v. *Sweden*, App. No. 7805/77, D&R 16, at 68; see further C. Evans, *Freedom of Religion under the European Convention of Human Rights* (Oxford, Oxford University Press, 2001) 55. The ECJ has dealt with national restrictions as regards the Church of Scientology as well, but never explicitly addressed the question whether it should be regarded as a religion (see Case 41/74 *Van Duyn* [1974] ECR 1137 and Case C–54/99 *Association Eglise de scientologie de Paris* [2000] ECR 1335).

[164] See Evans, *ibid.*, 55.

[165] Amor, above n. 161, paras. 94*ff*.

ECtHR, 13 April 2006[166]   **1.CoE.62.**
Kosteski v. *the Former Yugoslav Republic of Macedonia*

PROOF OF ADHERENCE TO A RELIGION

Kosteski

Facts: In 1998, Kosteski did not appear at work at the Electricity Company of Macedonia. He explained that he had wanted to celebrate a religious holiday which was a public holiday for the citizens of Muslim faith under the National Constitution. The disciplinary committee found that he had breached the disciplinary rules of the company and fined him with a cut of 15% in his salary for three months. Later in the same year, the applicant was again fined for not having appeared at work at the time of the celebration of another Muslim religious holiday. The case was brought before the Bitola Municipal Court, which found that the applicant had not given any evidence to corroborate his statement that he was a Muslim. He had never been absent from work at the time of the Muslim religious holidays before 1998. To the contrary: he had celebrated the Christian religious holidays, his parents were Christians and his way of life and diet showed that he was a Christian. The court held that the applicant proclaimed himself a Muslim in order to justify his absence from work.

Held: By requiring the applicant to produce evidence to substantiate his claims, the authorities did not violate the freedom of religion, nor the prohibition of discrimination (Article 14 in conjunction with Article 9 ECHR).

Judgment: "39. Insofar as the applicant has complained that there was an interference with the inner sphere of belief in that he was required to prove his faith, the Court recalls that the courts' decisions on the applicant's appeal against the disciplinary punishment imposed on him made findings effectively that the applicant had not substantiated the genuineness of his claim to be a Muslim and that his conduct on the contrary cast doubt on that claim in that there were no outward signs of his practising the Muslim faith or joining collective Muslim worship. While the notion of the State sitting in judgment on the state of a citizen's inner and personal beliefs is abhorrent and may smack unhappily of past infamous persecutions, the Court observes that this is a case where the applicant sought to enjoy a special right bestowed by Macedonian law which provided that Muslims could take holiday on particular days, including the Bayram festival in issue in the present case . . . In the context of employment, with contracts setting out specific obligations and rights between employer and employee, the Court does not find it unreasonable that an employer may regard absence without permission or apparent justification as a disciplinary matter. Where the employee then seeks to rely on a particular exemption, it is not oppressive or in fundamental conflict with freedom of conscience to require some level of substantiation when that claim concerns a privilege or entitlement not commonly available and, if that substantiation is not forthcoming, to reach a negative conclusion . . . The applicant however was not prepared to produce any evidence that could substantiate his claims. To the extent therefore that the proceedings disclosed an interference with the applicant's freedom of religion, this was not disproportionate and may, in the circum-stances of this case, be regarded as justified in terms of the second paragraph, namely, as prescribed by law and necessary in a democratic society for the protection of the rights of others . . .

45. In the present case, while there is no right as such under Article 9 to have leave from work for particular religious holidays, the Court notes that the courts' decisions on the

---

[166] Not yet published.

applicant's appeal against the disciplinary punishment imposed on him made findings touching on the apparent genuineness of his beliefs. This, in the Court's view, is sufficient to bring the applicant's complaints within the scope of Article 9.

46. However, insofar as the applicant claims that he is the only person of the Muslim faith who has been required to prove his adherence to that religion, the Court considers that any resulting difference of treatment may be regarded as based on objective and reasonable justification. The applicant was making claim to a privilege or exemption to which he was not entitled unless he was a member of the faith concerned and in circumstances which arguably gave rise to doubts as his entitlement. As found above under Article 9, it was not unreasonable or disproportionate to require him to show some level of substantiation of his claim."

Note

The ECtHR found in this case that the requirement to show evidence of the adherence to the Muslim faith touched upon the genuineness of the applicant's religious conviction and thus came within the scope of both the freedom of religion and the prohibition of discrimination based on religion. Although no proof of the existence of a genuine religious conviction may generally be required of an individual, the Court allowed the national courts to ask for such proof if the individual claims a privilege or exemption which itself is based on the freedom of religion. For those cases, "some level of substantiation" may be required of the individual claim of adherence to a certain religion. It remains unclear, however, what kind of evidence would be needed to substantiate such a claim and to what extent having a certain religion can actually be proven. Further decisions by either the ECtHR or the ECJ may elucidate these points.

THE FREEDOM NOT TO HAVE A RELIGION

It is common ground that the notion of "religion" does not only cover adopting or professing a certain religion, but also the freedom not to adopt or profess a religion. In particular, the ECtHR has accepted atheism and agnosticism as part of the wider notions of "thought" and "conscience" and thereby of the right to freedom of religion.[167]

---

[167] This is not self-evident: Evans has pointed out that the issue of whether atheism and agnosticism are included within the definition has been a much debated one and one that has never been conclusively resolved in the UN (Evans, above n. 163, 51).

ECtHR, 18 February 1999[168]   1.CoE.63.
Buscarini et al. v. *San Marino*

FREEDOM OF CONSCIENCE COVERS FREEDOM *NOT* TO HAVE A RELIGION

Buscarini

Facts: Buscarini and Della Balda were elected to the parliament of the Republic of San Marino. The official oath to be taken by members of the Republic's parliament included a reference to the Holy Gospels. The applicants took the oath in the form of words laid down in the decree save for the reference to the Gospels, which they omitted. Afterwards the Secretariat of the parliament gave an opinion on the form of the oath sworn by the applicants to the effect that it was invalid. They were then required to swear allegiance in accordance with the oath on pain of forfeiting their parliamentary seats; in the end, they complied with the requirement.

Held: The requirement to take the oath on the Gospels is tantamount to requiring to swear allegiance to a particular religion, a requirement which is not compatible with Article 9 of the Convention.

Judgment: "34. The Court reiterates that: 'As enshrined in Article 9, freedom of thought, conscience and religion is one of the foundations of a "democratic society" within the meaning of the Convention. It is, in its religious dimension, one of the most vital elements that go to make up the identity of believers and their conception of life, but it is also a precious asset for atheists, agnostics, sceptics and the unconcerned. The pluralism indissociable from a democratic society, which has been dearly won over the centuries, depends on it' . . . That freedom entails, inter alia, freedom to hold or not to hold religious beliefs and to practise or not to practise a religion."

Note

In this case the ECtHR clearly accepted a wide interpretation of the freedom of religion, which finds support in other international materials. The UN Human Rights Committee, for example, has expressed an opinion similar to the ECtHR's in its General Comment to the right to freedom of thought, conscience and religion contained in Article 18 ICCRP:

"5. The Committee observes that the freedom to 'have or to adopt' a religion or belief necessarily entails the freedom to choose a religion or belief, including the right to replace one's current religion or belief with another or to adopt atheistic views, as well as to retain one's religion or belief." [169]

It may be expected that such a wide definition of the freedom of religion will also be applied in the context of non-discrimination law. An example of such application may be found in an opinion of the Dutch Equal Treatment Commission:

---

[168] Reports 1999-I.

[169] General Comment No. 22: The right to freedom of thought, conscience and religion (Art. 18), 30 July 1993, ICCRP/C/21/Rev.1/Add.4.

Equal Treatment Commission (Commissie Gelijke Behandeling)   **1.NL.64.**
Opinion 2003-114

"RELIGION" ENCOMPASSES "NOT HAVING A RELIGION"

Interconfessional school

Facts: The defendant is an organisation based on a Christian foundation, consisting of various schools accessible to all pupils, regardless of their religion or belief. All Christian (interconfessional) schools partic-ipating within the defendant organisation require their teachers to pay respect to the Christian view of life. The participating non-Christian schools do not have a similar requirement, but the organisation still requires that its teachers be willing to accept functions at both the non-Christian and Christian schools. The applicant, who was working in a non-Christian school, was given in 2003 a teaching and coordinating function in one of the Christian schools. He refused as he could not pay due respect to the Christian foundations of the relevant department.

Held: The requirement constitutes indirect discrimination based on religion which could not be justified under the Equal Treatment Act.

Opinion: "5.9 The concept of religion under the Equal Treatment Act must inter alia be inter-preted in accordance with the international human rights treaties, including the European Convention of Human Rights. This means that freedom of religion is aimed not only at possessing or professing a faith but also at not possessing or professing a faith. This implies that failure to cooperate with education on a religious foundation must be regarded as an aspect of freedom of religion and is therefore covered by the concept of religion under the Equal Treatment Act. In the present case, it may therefore also be tested on the grounds of religion for possible discrimination."

Note

It is evident from this case that not having a certain religion is covered by the notion of "religion" in Dutch non-discrimination law and discrimination based on this ground is prohibited.

MANIFESTATION OF RELIGION AND RELIGIOUS EXPRESSIONS

It is widely accepted that religious practice and profession of religion come under the scope of the freedom of religion: the freedom of religion is not limited to the freedom of conscience alone. This is expressly stated in most international fundamental rights texts, and both the ECHR and the EU Charter of Fundamental Rights expressly mention the freedom "either alone or in community with others and in public or private, to manifest his religion or belief, in worship, teaching, practice and observance".[170] The ECtHR has elaborated this notion of religious expression in its *Kokkinakis* case:

---

[170] Evans, above n. 163, 41.

ECtHR, 25 May 1993[171]   **1.CoE.65.**
Kokkinakis v. *Greece*

RELIGIOUS EXPRESSION IS PROTECTED BY THE FREEDOM OF RELIGION

Kokkinakis

Facts: Mr Kokkinakis was born into an Orthodox family. After becoming a Jehovah's Witness in 1936, he was arrested more than 60 times for proselytism. He was also interned and imprisoned on several occasions.

Held: It has not been shown that the applicant's convictions were justified by a pressing social need. There has accordingly been a breach of Article 9 of the Convention.

Judgment: "31. While religious freedom is primarily a matter of individual conscience, it also implies, inter alia, freedom to 'manifest [one's] religion'. Bearing witness in words and deeds is bound up with the existence of religious convictions.

According to Article 9, freedom to manifest one's religion is not only exercisable in community with others, 'in public' and within the circle of those whose faith one shares, but can also be asserted 'alone' and 'in private'; furthermore, it includes in principle the right to try to convince one's neighbour, for example through 'teaching', failing which, moreover, 'freedom to change [one's] religion or belief', enshrined in Article 9, would be likely to remain a dead letter."

The Human Rights Committee has opted for a similarly wide interpretation of the freedom of religion and belief in its aforementioned general comment on Article 18 ICCRP:

Human Rights Committee, General Comment No. 22:   **1.UN.66.**
The right to freedom of thought, conscience and religion[172]

"The freedom to manifest religion or belief may be exercised 'either individually or in community with others and in public or private'. The freedom to manifest religion or belief in worship, observance, practice and teaching encompasses a broad range of acts. The concept of worship extends to ritual and ceremonial acts giving direct expression to belief, as well as various practices integral to such acts, including the building of places of worship, the use of ritual formulae and objects, the display of symbols, and the observance of holidays and days of rest. The observance and practice of religion or belief may include not only ceremonial acts but also such customs as the observance of dietary regulations, the wearing of distinctive clothing or head coverings, participation in rituals associated with certain stages of life, and the use of a particular language customarily spoken by a group. In addition, the practice and teaching of religion or belief includes acts integral to the conduct by religious groups of their basic affairs, such as the freedom to choose their religious leaders, priests and teachers, the freedom to establish seminaries or religious schools and the freedom to prepare and distribute religious texts or publications."

[171] Series A, Vol. 260-A.
[172] 30 July 1993, CPR/C/21/Rev.1/Add.4.

Domestic case-law likewise shows that manifestations of belief are acknowledged to form part of the freedom of religion—in most Member States, cases may be found in which this is established by the courts.[173] It may be derived from these cases and the international materials that the prohibition of religious discrimination will probably be interpreted in line with the right to freedom of religion. Thus, unequal treatment based on manifestations of religion will be unlawful as much as unequal treatment based on having a certain religion as such.

Still, many difficulties appear where a more precise definition of this category is required. With respect to the religious character of such clear examples of religious manifestation as the organisation of religious communities and the building of places of worship, there seems to be a strong consensus that this is part of the freedom of religion.[174] There are, however, many instances of religious manifestation on which opinions may reasonably differ. This is particularly true for religious practices which are not supported by all or even a majority of members of a religious community. It is clear, for example, that religious attire is not regarded as mandatory by all believers: not all Muslim women choose to wear a niqaab or head scarf, nor do all Jewish men wear a yarmulke. The same is true for religious requirements regarding behaviour. There may be Christian nurses who will refuse to assist in an abortion operation because of their religious convictions, whilst others will not regard such assistance as problematic; similarly, some Muslim men will shake hands with a woman, where others will refuse to do so.

The Member States appear to be divided over the question whether it should be *objectively* determined if a certain expression or behaviour can be regarded as part of someone's religion or whether a *subjective* approach should be adopted. In a subjective approach it should be established if the relevant person or group regards his or her behaviour as conforming to a religious prescription, regardless of the lack of support of the practice by other believers. Such a subjective approach is to some degree adopted by the Dutch courts and the Dutch Equal Treatment Commission, as is illustrated by the following excerpt:

Equal Treatment Commission (Commissie Gelijke Behandeling)   **1.NL.67.**
Opinion 1998-18

SUBJECTIVE APPROACH TO RELIGIOUS PRACTICE

Teacher's trainee with head scarf

Facts: The applicant was a trainee teacher who was offered a traineeship with a primary school. Because of her Islamic faith, the applicant wore a head scarf. When the head of the school noticed this, he contacted the applicant's supervisor and told her that it was not desirable for teachers to wear a head scarf in class.

---

[173] See, e.g. BVerfG, 5 February 1991, 2 BvR 263/86 (*Bahá'í*) and the Italian *Corte Costituzionale* 19–27 April 1993, No. 1993/195.

[174] See in particular ECtHR, 26 October 2000, *Hasan and Chaush* v. *Bulgaria*, Reports 2000-XI, para. 62.

The applicant refused to oblige to the request to remove her head scarf and ended her traineeship with the school.

Held: The request constitutes a case of direct discrimination based on religion which is incompatible with the Equal Treatment Act.

Opinion: "With regard to whether the applicant's wearing a head scarf comes within the scope of the concept of 'religion' within the meaning of the Equal Treatment Act and consequently within the scope of that act, the Commission considers as follows.

The term religion included in the Equal Treatment Act as a ground for non-discrimination covers not only the adoption of a religious conviction but also conduct accordingly. Conduct which, having regard to its character and to the significance of the religious rules and provisions, directly expressed the religious conviction is also protected by the ban on discrimination based on religion. The wearing of a head scarf by a Muslim woman or a Muslim girl may be one of these expressions of her religious conviction. The fact that these rules are honoured in different ways and that attitudes to wearing a head scarves (also in Muslim circles) differ, does not detract from this as far as protection for a person against unlawful discrimination within the meaning of the Equal Treatment Act is concerned. The position is different only where there might be an individual, subjective attitude that can no longer be regarded generally as an expression of faith by members of the religious community or a particular persuasion within it. There is no question of the latter with regard to wearing a head scarf. In accordance with long existing precedents of the Supreme Court, it is not up to the Commission to interfere with differences of opinion regarding theological principles and interpretations of the Koran.

The conclusion from the above is that the applicant's wearing a head scarf comes within the scope of the concept of religion as stated in the Equal Treatment Act . . ."

Note

This case discloses a rather subjective approach to religious expression, as the Equal Treatment Commission holds that a certain expression does not need to be regarded as a religious requirement by all members of the religious community. On the other hand, the Commission accepted that an expression or practice should not be completely subjective in character, in the sense that only one or a few individuals regard the expression as a religious prescription. To that extent, the approach is objective in character.

It is clear, however, that opinions on the issue are diverging. In particular, the former EComHR adopted a different stance, which departs from an objective approach:

EComHR, 16 May 1977[175]   **1.CoE.68.**
Arrowsmith v. *UK*

OBJECTIVE APPROACH TO RELIGIOUS PRACTICE

Arrowsmith

Facts: Arrowsmith was arrested when distributing leaflets to troops stationed at an army camp, urging them to desert or refuse orders if they were posted to Northern Ireland. She was convicted under the Incitement to Disaffection Act 1934 and sentenced to 18 months' imprisonment. Arrowsmith alleged a violation of her freedom of religion, contending that the dissemination of the leaflet was a moral imperative flowing from her life-long commitment to the pacifist cause.

Held: The contents of the leaflet and its distribution did not amount to the manifestation of a belief and do not enjoy the protection of Article 9.

Judgment: "3. For the purposes of paragraph 1 of Art. 9 the manifestation has to have some real connection with the belief. The question whether or not a particular manifestation falls within the protection afforded by Art. 9 (1) has to be determined by an objective, not subjective, test. In the present case it has to be determined on the face of the leaflet itself whether or not the contents of that leaflet and the act of its distribution were in fact a manifestation of the belief of pacifism. In fact, the contents of the leaflet and its distribution did not amount to the manifestation of a belief and so did not enjoy the protection of Art. 9 (1)."

Note

The Commission in this case demanded an objective valuation of the available evidence on the character of the manifestation, although it did not formulate criteria as to the classification of a certain expression or manifestation as part of the freedom of religion. From later cases it appears that it has opted for a rather strict approach in this respect.[176] It is rather unclear if the ECtHR will adopt the same approach towards manifestations of religion as the EComHR did. From the important case of *Leyla Sahin* v. *Turkey* it would seem to transpire that it prefers a more subjective interpretation:

ECtHR, 10 November 2005[177]   **1.CoE.69.**
Leyla Sahin v. *Turkey*

HEADSCARF AS RELIGIOUS EXPRESSION

Leyla Sahin

Facts: Leyla Sahin studied medicine at the University of Istanbul. As an expression of her Islamic faith, she wore a head scarf. In 1998 a circular was issued stipulating that students whose head was covered and

---

[175] Appl. No. 7050/75, D&R 8, at 123.
[176] See, e.g. EComHR, 3 December 1996, *Konttinen* v. *Finland*, Appl. No. 24949/94, not published.
[177] Not yet published.

students with beards should not be admitted to lectures, courses and examinations. Leyla Sahin was thereupon refused from enrolling in several courses because of her headscarf. In May 1998 disciplinary proceedings were brought against her as a result of her failure to comply with the dress rules and she was given a warning. At a later point in time, she was suspended from the University, although she was reinstated in 2000 as a result of an amnesty.

Held: The interference at issue was justified in principle and proportionate to the aim pursued and did not constitute a violation of Article 9 ECHR.

Judgment: "78. As to whether there was interference, the Grand Chamber endorses the following findings of the Chamber [see paragraph 71 of the Chamber judgment of 29 June 2004]:

> 'The applicant said that, by wearing the headscarf, she was obeying a religious precept and thereby manifesting her desire to comply strictly with the duties imposed by the Islamic faith. Accordingly, her decision to wear the headscarf may be regarded as motivated or inspired by a religion or belief and, without deciding whether such decisions are in every case taken to fulfil a religious duty, the Court proceeds on the assumption that the regulations in issue, which placed restrictions of place and manner on the right to wear the Islamic headscarf in universities, constituted an interference with the applicant's right to manifest her religion'."

Note

The ECtHR did not pay close attention in this case to the issue of whether the expression actually formed an expression of religion. Instead, it seemed to accept without further ado the individual statement that the wearing of a headscarf was a religious manifestation, which is an approach that is rather subjective in character. It is clear, however, that the case-law of the ECtHR on this point is not yet crystallised, since some recent cases show a strict approach which is closer to that of the EComHR.[178] It is therefore difficult to derive any general conclusions from present case-law as to the exact test that needs to be applied in order to establish if a certain expression is covered.

BELIEF

The Employment Equality Directive and many other national and international instruments mention the ground of belief on the same footing as the ground of religion. Indeed, the two notions are to some extent similar, the most important difference relating to the (assumed) existence of a deity or divine being: whereas this element is always present in the definition of "religion", it is expressly left out of the definition of "belief". Belief should thus be taken to mean a coherent set of fundamental ideas and attitudes to life and human existence, without reference being

---

[178] See, e.g. ECtHR, 13 April 2006, *Kosteski* v. *the Former Yugoslav Republic of Macedonia*, not yet published (above, **1.CoE.62.**). Other cases have confirmed the more subjective approach of the Court, however. In its admissibility decision in the case of *Phull* v. *France* (11 January 2005, appl. no. 35753/03, not published), it assumed, for instance, purely on the basis of the applicant's statement that masculine adherents of the Sikh religion are required to wear a turban, that a demand to remove the turban to undergo a safety check at an airport amounted to an interference with the freedom of religion.

made to a higher being. Indeed, this is the definition most often given by the courts. Two examples may serve to illustrate this:

ECtHR, 25 February 1982[179]   **1.CoE.70.**
Campbell and Cosans v. *UK*

DEFINITION OF "PHILOSOPHICAL CONVICTIONS" AND "BELIEF"

Campbell and Cosans

Facts: In St Matthew's Roman Catholic Primary School, corporal punishment was used in the form of striking the palm of a pupil's hand with a leather strap. Under Scottish law, teachers were invested with the power to administer such punishment in moderation as a disciplinary measure. According to the parents of the applicants, who were pupils of the school in question, this ran counter to their "philosophical convictions" as protected by Article 2 of Protocol 1 to the ECHR.

Held: The philosophical convictions of the parents should have been respected by the school. The omission to do so amounts to a violation of the right to education as protected in Article 2 of Protocol 1.

Judgment: "36 . . . In its ordinary meaning the word 'convictions', taken on its own, is not synonymous with the word 'opinions' and 'ideas', such as are utilized in Article 10 of the Convention, which guarantees freedom of expression; it is more akin to the term 'beliefs' (in the French text: 'convictions') appearing in Article 9—which guarantees freedom of thought, conscience and religion—and denotes views that attain a certain level of cogency, cohesion and importance . . .

Having regard to the Convention as a whole . . . the expression 'philosophical convictions' in the present context denotes, in the Court's opinion, such convictions as are worthy of respect in a 'democratic society' and are not incompatible with human dignity; in addition, they must not conflict with the fundamental right of the child to education . . ."

Equal Treatment Commission (Commissie Gelijke Behandeling) **1.NL.71.**
Opinion 2005-28

DEFINITION OF "BELIEF" AND "RELIGION"

"Nazarene" religious conviction

Facts: One of the employees of a cafeteria refused the applicant access because of his appearance: he looked like a vagabond and stunk fiercely, which had led to disgust and complaints from customers and employees. The applicant contends that his personal appearance is in accordance with his "Nazarene" conviction. He admits that there is no group officially holding and exercising this conviction, and that the views and attitudes related to the conviction are not public and not generally known. He argues that the Nazarene conviction departs from the given that there is an invisible, creative and controlling being which brings happiness. A Nazarene is convinced that the human body is made as it is meant to be and is usually functioning well as long as it is not modified by using such things as a razor. For that reason, the applicant does not shave or cut his hair and he does not use any detergents that may not please the "being", such as water or soap.

---

[179] Series A, Vol. 48.

Held: The case is inadmissible as it has not been shown that the refusal was based on the applicant's religion or belief.

Opinion: "5.3 The question arises firstly whether the applicant can in the present case have recourse to the ground of belief and/or religion.

5.4 Parliament has combined the concepts of religion and belief in one provision under Article 6 of the Constitution [amended in 1983] because religious and humanistic convictions display many gradual overlaps in practice. By placing the concepts of freedom of religion and belief on the same footing, Parliament intended to provide a guideline for interpretation of the then 'new' concept of belief. This equal footing is constitutional by nature and Parliament may not therefore so interpret it that religion and belief are of equal substance. Essential differences between the two would be lost from sight were the essence of religion and belief be ignored.

Recognition that religion and belief each have their specific character as to nature and orientation does not, however, alter the fact that these differences should not have a bearing as far as guaranteeing freedom, protection and equality are concerned. Freedom and protection must therefore be guaranteed for both forms of spiritual life on an equal footing . . .

5.5 According to the established precedents of the Commission, religion incorporates a conviction as to life in which a higher being stands central, while with belief, this supreme being is lacking but a common existential conviction nonetheless exists . . .

5.6 In line with established precedents the Commission takes belief to mean a more or less cohesive system of ideas, concerned with fundamental attitudes to human existence . . .

5.7 The Commission also considers it necessary that this attitude is not individually held but is held by a group . . .

5.8 The Commission considers that it follows from the considerations under 5.4 to 5.7 that, whether or not a higher being exists, both religion and belief imply an existential common conviction, in other words a more or less cohesive system of ideas incorporating fundamental attitudes to human existence that the applicant does not hold individually only.

5.9 Since the applicant argues that the distinction concerns both his religion and his belief, the Commission will for the rest of this Opinion treat this as a single conviction.

5.10 According to the applicant, the knowledge associated with 'Nazareneship' is not generally known or public. The applicant therefore provides no information sources, even after the Commission had requested them in writing, that support his view. The applicant refers to the Bible for the concept of "Nazareneship". The applicant indicates that many people, especially Jews, practice 'Nazareneship'. However, the applicant admits that there is no Dutch organisation with an umbrella function. He has not indicated any others who belong to the same religion or attitude to life, nor has he mentioned third parties who can say something about this religion or attitude to life.

5.11 The Commission arrives at the view that the applicant has been unable to demonstrate that 'Nazareneship' comprises a more or less cohesive system of ideas, concerned with fundamental attitudes to human existence, and that a common attitude therefore exists. The applicant was unwilling to take up the Commission's request to indicate information sources and cannot demonstrate group practice. The applicant was therefore unable to show that 'Nazareneship' in terms of the Bible or otherwise can today be taken as a religion or attitude to life within the meaning of the Equal Treatment Act. The Commission has not otherwise found any indications in public sources as to the existence of such a religion or attitude to life."

Notes

(1) It is clear from both excerpts that coherence and cogency form important aspects in answering the question if someone's convictions can be termed a "belief"

for the purposes of anti-discrimination legislation. The Dutch definition moreover includes a number of additional requirements, such as the presence of fundamental attitudes to human existence and the need for the establishment of group practice. According to the Equal Treatment Commission, a purely individually held belief cannot be qualified as a belief in the sense of non-discrimination legislation. It is uncertain, however, if this requirement complies with the more flexible definition given by the ECtHR.

(2) From *Campbell and Cosans*, it furthermore transpires that any "philosophical convictions" or beliefs must be worthy of respect in a "democratic society" and must be compatible with human dignity in order to be protected by the freedom of religion. This criterion may be an important means to put totalitarian, fascist or Nazi-convictions, or beliefs which imply criminal behaviour, outside the scope of the ground of belief. Unfortunately, the criterion is not further elaborated and the Strasbourg case-law on the issue is somewhat ambiguous.[180] It is clear, however, that the criterion is broadly accepted under international law, as it is also mentioned by the Human Rights Committee in its General Comment on the interpretation of the freedom of religion.[181]

RELATION BETWEEN RELIGION AND BELIEF

Although the discussion of the notions of religion and belief shows that there is an important difference between the two, the practical relevance of the distinction seems relatively limited. The Employment Equality Directive mentions both notions as prohibited grounds of distinction, just like most of the Member States do, which means that there will often be no need to establish whether a concrete case of unequal treatment is based on either religion or belief. This is witnessed by the following decision of the German Federal Administrative Court:

---

[180] The case of *X.* v. *Austria* (EComHR, 13 December 1963, Appl. No. 1747/62, 13 Collections 42 (1963)), for example, concerned Nazism. The EComHR avoided the question regarding the proper classification of this "belief" by moving directly to the question if the interference in question was justified. As is pointed out by Evans (above n. 163, 56), this approach can be taken to imply that Nazism is a belief capable of manifestation, which falls within the scope of the freedom of belief and interferences with which should be justified in accordance with Art. 9(2). It is probable, however, that this judgment is effectively overruled by the Court's *Campbell and Cosans* decision (above, **1.CoE.70.**).

[181] Human Rights Committee, above n. 169, para. 7.

The German Federal Administrative Court   **1.DE.72.**
(Bundesverwaltungsgericht), 27 March 1992[182]

RELIGION OR BELIEF?

Bhagwan

Facts: The applicants in this case are meditation associations that form part of the Osho-movement established by Osho-Rajneesh (before: Bhagwan).

Held: The applicants' religion or belief is covered, in principle, by the freedom of religion as guaranteed by Article 4 German Basic Law.

Judgment: "The terms 'religion' and 'belief' are to be understood as meaning the convictions of a person concerning certain views on the world as a whole, the origin of mankind and the purpose and meaning of life of mankind. Religion is based on a reality that exceeds and surrounds all of mankind ('transcendent'), whereas a belief restricts itself to intrinsic ('immanent') world boundaries. These prerequisites were deemed by the Oberverwaltungsgericht [Higher Administrative Court] to have been fulfilled in this case with the reasoning that in particular the teachings of Oslo-Rajneeshs on the 'enlightenment' speak of the purpose of mankind and contain a comprehensive elucidation on the question of meaning . . . No further categorization of the teachings followed by the applicant, i.e. classification as either religion or belief, is required due to the fact that a belief and a religion are placed on equal terms in Article 4 paragraph 1 of the Grundgesetz [Basic Law]."

Note

In its decision, the Federal Administrative Court did not see a need to categorise the conviction of the applicant associations as either religious or non-religious in character. It is probable that other courts, such as the ECJ, will adopt a similar approach, paying more attention to the similarities between religion and belief (such as there being a shared and coherent set of fundamental attitudes or beliefs) than to the differences.

POLITICAL CONVICTION OR OPINION

The ground of political conviction or political opinion is not explicitly mentioned in the Employment Equality Directive. However, many Member States have included the ground in constitutional or statutory lists of prohibited grounds of discrimination, often placing it in the same category as religion and belief. In Belgium, the omission of the ground of political opinion from the Anti-Discrimination Law even proved to be a reason for the Belgian Arbitration Court to extend the scope of the Act to all possible discrimination grounds.[183]

---

[182] BVerwGE 90, 112.
[183] Court of Arbitration, 6 October 2004, no. 157/2004. See further de Schutter, above n. 160, 11, available on the website of Directorate-General for Employment, Social Affairs and Equal Opportunities.

An interesting interpretative question relating to the Employment Equality Directive is if political conviction can be considered to amount to "belief", which would have the advantage that individuals are protected from being discriminated against not only on the basis of their personal religious beliefs, but also on the basis of their political convictions. Indeed, it is difficult to draw a clear line between belief and political conviction, certainly where a political creed implies a fully fledged view as to the organisation of society and the individual's place in it, as is the case with communism.[184] Unfortunately, few cases are available to provide guidance on this issue. The EComHR case of *Arrowsmith* may offer some clarification:

EComHR, 16 May 1977[185]   **1.CoE.73.**[*]
Arrowsmith v. *UK*

OBJECTIVE APPROACH TO RELIGIOUS PRACTICE

Arrowsmith

Facts: Arrowsmith was arrested when distributing leaflets to troops stationed at an army camp, urging them to desert or refuse orders if they were posted to Northern Ireland. She was convicted under the Incitement to Disaffection Act 1934 and sentenced to 18 months' imprisonment. Arrowsmith alleged a violation of her freedom of religion, contending that the dissemination of the leaflet was a moral imperative flowing from her lifelong commitment to the pacifist cause.

Held: The contents of the leaflet and its distribution did not amount to the manifestation of a belief and do not enjoy the protection of Article 9.

Judgment: "1. Art. 9 applies to religious or other beliefs based on thought and conscience. Beliefs which are not so based are not protected by Art. 9 but their expression may be protected by Art. 10. Pacifism is generally regarded as: 'the policy of avoiding or abolishing war by the use of arbitration in settling international disputes; advocacy or support of the policy or belief in its practicability; often, with depreciatory implication, the advocacy of peace at any price' (Oxford English Dictionary).

Another definition is as follows: 'the doctrine that the abolition of war is both possible and desirable' (Concise Oxford Dictionary).

To the extent to which pacifism may be characterised as a belief based on thought and conscience, paragraph 1 of Art. 9 would apply to it."

Note

Apparently, the EComHR considered a belief to be present as soon as it is based on thought and conscience, even if it seems rather political in nature, as may be the case with a belief such as that of pacifism. This will be a difficult criterion to apply in practice, however, as it places a demand on the courts to establish when a certain expression is really based on thought and conscience.

[184] Lerner, above n. 48, 78, mentioning Nazism as an example of a borderline case and explaining that Nazism expected the German individual to identify fully with the Nazi creed in almost religious terms.
[185] Appl. No. 7050/75, D&R 8, at 123.
[*] See above **1.CoE.68.**

The issue of proper classification is made somewhat easier if political conviction or opinions are explicitly mentioned as protected grounds of discrimination. As in the case of religion and belief, a distinction can be made between *having* and *expressing* a political conviction. Generally, both elements can be considered to form part of the definition of political opinion: clearly, such expressions as membership of a political party come within the scope of this ground.[186] In the Netherlands, however, a line is drawn where criminally punishable behaviour is concerned:

Equal Treatment Commission (Commissie Gelijke Behandeling)   **1.NL.74.**
Opinion 1998-45

"POLITICAL CONVICTION" DOES NOT COVER CRIMINALLY PUNISHABLE BEHAVIOUR

Extremist right wing party

Facts: The applicant, the Nationale Volksunie/CP'86, is an extremist right wing political party. The party tried to open a business bank account with the defendant, but was refused because of the bank's policy not to start relations with persons, companies and organisations whose activities cannot be considered socially acceptable. The bank supported its decision by pointing to a number of offences, intimidation and other criminal acts attributable to the applicant.

Held: The refusal does not constitute discrimination which is unacceptable under the Equal Treatment Commission.

Opinion: "The Commission has found in the past that the concept of political opinion under the Equal Treatment Act includes not only the adoption of a political conviction but also behaviour that may generally be regarded as an expression of such political convictions. The Commission's guiding consideration is that conduct that is criminal is excluded from protection under the Equal Treatment Act. The Commission considers that whether or not the conduct to which the defendant refers should be regarded as criminal, it is in any event so much in conflict with what is legally acceptable that it cannot be regarded as conduct protected by the Equal Treatment Act. This leads to the conclusion that the defendant's refusal to accept the applicant as a customer on grounds of legally unacceptable behaviour does not amount to discrimination on grounds of political conviction within the meaning of the Equal Treatment Act."

Note
The approach taken by the Dutch Equal Treatment Commission seems to be in line with *Campbell and Cosans*, in which the ECtHR held that "philosophical convictions" are only protected if they are not incompatible with human dignity and if they are worthy of respect in a "democratic society". Article 17 of the ECHR, which prohibits the use of fundamental rights where it has the effect of destroying the rights guaranteed by the Convention, would seem to stand in the way of any other interpretation.

---

[186] E.g. Dutch Equal Treatment Commission, Opinion 1997-132: "The Commission notes that political conviction must in any event include membership of a political party."

1.3.8.B.   SUSPECTNESS

It may seem obvious that the ground of religion constitutes a suspect ground of discrimination, since such discrimination touches on the fundamental individual right to freedom of religion. Religion is based on faith and not reason, which makes it an element beyond the individual will that is particularly worthy of protection against outside interference.[187] Furthermore, it is clear that members of religious groups often suffer discrimination as a result of (historical) prejudice, which may give sufficient cause in itself for regarding a religiously based distinction as inherently suspect. It may therefore seem surprising that the suspect character of the grounds of religion and belief is not, or not yet, explicitly confirmed by national and international judicial decisions. In particular, the case-law of the European Court of Human Rights would seem to show some ambiguities. From a case decided by the ECtHR in 1993, it would seem to follow that it regards discrimination based on religion as highly suspect:

ECtHR, 23 June 1993[188]   **1.CoE.75.**
Hoffmann v. *Austria*

RELIGION BASED DISCRIMINATION IS HIGHLY SUSPECT

Hoffmann

Facts: In 1980, Mrs Ingrid Hoffmann married Mr S; two children were born to them. At a certain moment in time, Mrs Hoffmann left the Roman Catholic Church to become a Jehovah's Witness. In 1986, a divorce was pronounced between Hoffmann and S. Both parents applied to the national courts to be granted parental rights over the children. The lower courts granted parental rights to Hoffmann, as the children had stronger emotional ties with her and separation might cause them psychological harm. The Austrian Supreme Court overturned the judgments of the lower courts, granting parental rights to Mr S. instead of the applicant. According to the Supreme Court, the lower courts had not given due consideration to the children's welfare. The Supreme Court stressed that the children would be at risk of becoming social outcasts if educated according to the religious teaching of the Jehovah's Witnesses and their well-being could be in danger because Hoffmann would refuse to consent to the children's receiving a necessary blood transfusion.

Held: As there was no reasonable relationship of proportionality between the difference in treatment and the aim pursued (protection of the welfare of the children), there has been a violation of Article 8 taken in conjunction with Article 14.

Judgment: "33. . . . The European Court . . . accepts that there has been a difference in treatment and that that difference was on the ground of religion; this conclusion is supported by the tone and phrasing of the Supreme Court's considerations regarding the practical conse-quences of the applicant's religion.

Such a difference in treatment is discriminatory in the absence of an 'objective and reasonable justification', that is, if it is not justified by a 'legitimate aim' and if there is no

---

[187] Lerner, above n. 48, 37.
[188] Series A, Vol. 155-C.

'reasonable relationship of proportionality between the means employed and the aim sought to be realised' . . .

36. In so far as the Austrian Supreme Court did not rely solely on the Federal Act on the Religious Education of Children, it weighed the facts differently from the courts below, whose reasoning was moreover supported by psychological expert opinion. Notwithstanding any possible arguments to the contrary, a distinction based essentially on a difference in religion alone is not acceptable . . ."

Note

Judging from the ECtHR's reasoning, the decision would seem to imply that discrimination based on the ground of religion alone cannot ever be justified. This could be considered as the ultimate expression of strictness, which would clearly confirm the highly suspect character of the ground of religion. Nevertheless, it is questionable whether the ECtHR adheres to this strict approach in all cases of discrimination based on religion.[189] In 2003, the ECtHR delivered a judgment which may raise some doubts in this respect:

ECtHR, 16 December 2003[190]   **1.CoE.76.**
Palau-Martinez v. France

MARGIN OF APPRECIATION IN RELIGIOUS DISCRIMINATION CASE

Palau-Martinez

Facts: Mrs Palau-Martinez married in January 1983. She and her husband had two children when her husband left the matrimonial home and moved in with his mistress. The Court of First Instance granted a divorce and decided that the children would reside with their mother. The father was to have visiting and residence rights on an unrestricted basis. Palau-Martinez appealed against this judgment, asking to be given access to the children during the summer (holidays). The Court of Appeal upheld the grant of the divorce but found that the children's place of residence should be their father's home. In support of this, the Court of Appeal referred to the fact that Palau-Martinez was a Jehovah's Witness and the two children were being brought up in accordance with the precepts of her religion. According to the Court of Appeal, it was in the children's best interests to be free from the constraints and prohibitions imposed by a religion whose structure resembled that of a sect.

---

[189] A first case which may cause doubt in this respect is *Thlimmenos* v. *Greece* (*ECtHR*, 6 April 2000, Reports 2000-IV). This is hardly a representative case, however, as it is concerned with the recognition of new legal concepts which may have distracted the Court's attention from the question of suspectness of the ground in question. For a further discussion of the *Thlimmenos*-case, see ch. 2, excerpt **2.CoE.2.**The same holds true for another case decided in 2000: European Court of Human Rights, 27 June 2000, *Cha'are Shalom Ve Tsedek* v. *France* (Reports 2000-IV). The complaint in this case concerned an alleged instance of discrimination based on religion with respect to religious slaughtering. The Court did not apply a strict test to this case but this may, once more, have been the result of the atypical nature of the case, which concerned an interference with the freedom of religion which the Court considered to be limited in scope and impact (para. 87). This in itself may constitute an adequate reason for reduced intensity of review and may serve to explain the fact that the Court did not address the more general question as to the suspectness of the ground of religion.

[190] Reports 2003-XII.

Held: As there was no reasonable relationship between the Court of Appeal's decision and the best interests of the children, the case disclosed a violation of Article 8 of the Convention in conjunction with Article 14.

Judgment: "31. . . . [D]ifferent treatment is discriminatory, for the purposes of Article 14, if it 'has no objective and reasonable justification', that is, if it does not pursue a 'legitimate aim' or if there is not a 'reasonable relationship of proportionality between the means employed and the aim sought to be realised'. Moreover, the Contracting States enjoy a certain margin of appreciation in assessing whether and to what extent differences in otherwise similar situations justify a different treatment . . .

38. There is . . . no doubt, in the Court's view, that the Court of Appeal treated the parents differently on the basis of the applicant's religion, on the strength of a harsh analysis of the principles regarding child-rearing allegedly imposed by this religion . . .

42. The Court notes firstly that the Court of Appeal . . . asserted only generalities concerning Jehovah's Witnesses.

It notes the absence of any direct, concrete evidence demonstrating the influence of the applicant's religion on her two children's upbringing and daily life and, in particular, of the reference which the Government alleged was made in the Court of Appeal's judgment to the fact that the applicant took her children with her when attempting to spread her religious beliefs. In this context, the Court cannot accept that such evidence is constituted by the Court of Appeal's finding that the applicant 'does not deny that she is a Jehovah's Witness or that the two children were being brought up in accordance with the precepts of this religion'.

It further notes that the Court of Appeal did not consider it necessary to grant the applicant's request for a social inquiry report, a common practice in child custody cases; such an inquiry would no doubt have provided tangible information on the children's lives with each of their parents and made it possible to ascertain the impact, if any, of their mother's religious practice on their lives and upbringing during the years following their father's departure when they had lived with her. Accordingly, the Court considers that the Court of Appeal ruled *in abstracto* and on the basis of general considerations, without establishing a link between the children's living conditions with their mother and their real interests. Although relevant, that reasoning was not in the Court's view sufficient.

43. In those circumstances, the Court cannot conclude that there was a reasonably proportionate relationship between the means employed and the legitimate aim pursued. There has accordingly been a violation of Article 8 of the Convention taken in conjunction with Article 14."

Notes

(1) The facts of *Palau-Martinez* are similar to those of *Hoffmann*, in which the Court stated that a distinction based on religion alone could never be acceptable. In *Palau-Martinez*, however, the Court does not mention this very strict approach, nor does it mention a "very weighty reasons" test or a European common ground regarding the unlawfulness of discrimination based on religion. Quite to the contrary, it mentions the fact that states have a margin of appreciation in determining whether discrimination of this kind is permitted (§ 31). From this it must be derived that the ECtHR does not place religion on exactly the same level as grounds such as race, gender or (il)legitimate birth.

(2) It also transpires from the Court's reasoning, however, that the disadvantage complained of was not based primarily on religion, but more generally on the interests of the applicant's children. It cannot be excluded, therefore, that the Court

will revert to its earlier *Hoffmann* ruling in later cases which represent clearer examples of purely religious discrimination. Furthermore, the cited paragraphs do not express a strong degree of deference—the test applied is much stricter than the test of arbitrariness which the use of the "margin of appreciation" formula would seem to imply. Even if the Court does not view religion as a really suspect ground of discrimination, still the case suggests that it at least considers this ground to be "semi-suspect", warranting a stricter test than that applied to non-suspect grounds.

(3) A (relatively) strict approach by the ECHR in the future as well as a strict test to be applied by the ECJ seems the more probable, given the existence of a general consensus on the suspectness of specific aspects of the general ground of religion or belief. It is clear from both the text of Article 9 of the ECHR and other international texts (quoted at the start of this section) that a distinction can be made between the freedom to *manifest* a religion and belief and the freedom to *hold* certain beliefs. Article 9 paragraph 2 ECHR makes clear that interferences with the freedom of religion are only allowed with respect to the *manifestation* of belief—the right to *hold* a certain belief is considered to be inviolable. The same holds true for Article 18 of the ICCRP.[191] It may be derived from this that a discrimination based on the sole fact that someone holds a certain belief or religion has to be considered highly suspect and cannot, in principle, be justified. This may be different for distinctions based on manifestations of religion or belief, as is shown by *Palau-Martinez*. The suspectness of distinctions based on religion and belief may thus be determined on the basis of a kind of "nexus" doctrine, i.e. by determining whether a certain manifestation is close to the core of the freedom of religion, belief or political conviction, or is more peripheral in character.

1.3.9.   DISABILITY AND (CHRONIC) ILLNESS

1.3.9.A.   DEFINITION

As a result of the Employment Equality Directive, all states now prohibit discrimination based on disability. In addition, the scope of protection of both international and domestic legal instruments sometimes includes (chronic) illness, health and genetic features, as may be illustrated by the following excerpts:

Charter of Fundamental Rights of the   **1.EC.77.**
European Union (2000)[192]

Any discrimination based on any ground such as . . . genetic features [and] . . . disability . . . shall be prohibited . . .

---

[191] Human Rights Committee, above n. 169, para. 3.
[192] Art. 21(1).

Convention on Human Rights and Biomedicine (1997)[193]   **1.EC.78.**

Any form of discrimination against a person on grounds of his or her genetic heritage is prohibited.

Finnish Non-Discrimination Act 21/2004[194]   **1.FI.79.**

Nobody may be discriminated against on the basis of . . . health, disability . . . or other personal characteristics . . .

Dutch Act on Equal Treatment on the Grounds of Disability or   **1.NL.80.**
Chronic Illness (2003)[195]

The following definitions apply in this Act:
. . .b. direct unequal treatment: unequal treatment between people on the grounds of a real or supposed disability or chronic illness . . .

As a result of the absence of a definition of the notion of disability in the Employment Equality Directive, many states have refrained from providing a legislative definition. When confronted with concrete questions as regards the meaning of "disability", the courts may therefore be inclined to search for elucidation in other legislation where the notion is used, such as social security legislation relating to disability pensions or benefits. In most of these laws, some definition is given as to the meaning of "disability". Usually, such definitions refer to bodily, mental or psychological impairments with a minimum degree of severity, often expressed in terms of the detrimental influence on normal bodily functions or measured as a percentage of the remaining capacity to work. It must be noted, however, that the context in which such definitions are given is completely different from that of anti-discrimination law. Having regard to its particular aims and its political and socio-economic context, social security legislation relating to disability benefits requires highly specified and narrowly formulated definitions. On the other hand, general equal treatment legislation is meant to offer a high level of protection against social exclusion and discrimination of disabled persons. Having regarded to those aims, the definition of disability will need to be much more inclusive.[196] For that reason, great caution must be exercised in interpreting the notion of disability

---

[193] Art. 11.

[194] Yhdenvertaisuuslaki (21/2004), s. 6(1).

[195] Wet gelijke behandeling op grond van handicap of chronische ziekte, Staatsblad (Official Gazette) 2003, 206, Art. 1.

[196] It may also include provisions relating to discrimination based on assumed disabilities and illness. This issue will be dealt with separately in section 1.4, in which the issue of discrimination by assumption and association is discussed.

contained in equal treatment legislation on the basis of or in line with the definition given in disability insurance regulations; the definition in the latter type of regulation may be regarded as a minimum standard, but should certainly not be taken as a guiding principle. In this section, therefore, we will focus on the definitions contained in legislation and case-law relating to equal treatment based on disability, instead of definitions contained in social security legislation.

HANDICAP OR DISABILITY?

In many legislative texts, academic articles and translations, the terms "handicap" and "disability" are used interchangeably. The desirability of this may be questioned, as both terms have a distinct meaning which may influence the interpretation given to the provision in which the term is used. The difference between the terms is explained clearly in the UN Standard Rules on the Equalization of Opportunities for Persons with Disabilities.

UN General Assembly, "Standard Rules on the Equalization of **1.UN.81.**
Opportunities for Persons with Disabilities"[197]

"17. The term 'disability' summarizes a great number of different functional limitations occurring in any population in any country in the world. People may be disabled by physical, intellectual or sensory impairment, medical conditions or mental illness. Such impairments, conditions or illnesses may be permanent or transitory in nature.

18. The term 'handicap' means the loss or limitation of opportunities to take part in life of the community on an equal level with others. It describes the encounter between the person with a disability and the environment. The purpose of this term is to emphasize the focus on the shortcomings in the environment and in many organized activities in society, for example, information, communication and education, which prevent persons with disabilities from participating on equal terms."

Note
It seems clear from this definition that the term "disability" is used mainly to refer to disability in the medical sense, while the term "handicap" refers to the social aspects of disability (see *infra* for further discussion of this difference). Still, there does not seem to be a general consensus on these definitions and the distinction made between them. In the remainder of this section, we will primarily use the term "disability", as this is the term which is usually employed in the context of European law.

---

[197] A/RES/48/96, December 1993.

Most of the grounds discussed in this chapter have been defined in a symmetrical way in national and international legal instruments and case-law. A group that is normally advantaged by discrimination on a certain ground (e.g. men) is thereby protected to the same degree as a group that is normally disadvantaged (e.g. women). This is different, however, where disability discrimination is concerned. Even though the Employment Equality Directive does not contain a definition of the ground of disability, various commentators have argued that it is only discrimination on grounds of disability, and not on grounds of *not* having a disability, that is prohibited:

> ". . . [I]t must be remembered that with regard to disability the Directive does not operate in the same symmetrical fashion as provisions on sex and race do. It is only discrimination on grounds of disability and not 'non-disability' which is prevented by the Directive. Thus in principle employer or state measures which prefer disabled workers do not constitute unlawful discrimination against non-disabled co-worker or applicants."[198]

Opinions seem to be divided, however, which is understandable as the wording of the Directive itself leaves room for a symmetric as well an asymmetric interpretation. This is clearly shown by Waddington:

> ". . . The Directive provides:
>
> 'The purpose of this Directive is to lay down a general framework for combating discrimination on the ground . . . of . . . disability.
>
>   Direct discrimination shall be taken to occur where one person is treated less favourably than another is, has been or would be treated in a comparable situation, on any of the grounds referred to in Article 1.'
>
> These provisions could be interpreted as embracing a symmetrical approach to disability discrimination, in other words as protecting an individual from discrimination on the grounds that they are disabled as well as discrimination on the grounds that they are not disabled." [199]

As yet it is unclear if a symmetric or an asymmetric interpretation should be preferred. The first decision of the ECJ on the definition of disability (*Chacón Navas*, below **1.EC.84.**) does not provide any clarity on this issue either. As a result of this uncertainty, different approaches can be discerned in national legislative texts. An asymmetrical approach is visible in the UK, Germany and Spain,[200] whereas the Dutch Equal Treatment on grounds of Handicap and Chronic Illness Act seems to start from a symmetrical approach:[201]

---

[198] A.T. Skidmore, "EC Framework Employment Directive on Equal Treatment in Employment: Towards a Comprehensive Community Anti-discrimination Policy?" [2001] *ILJ* 131.

[199] L. Waddington, "Implementing the Disability Provisions of the Framework Employment Directive: Room for Exercising National Discretion" in A. Lawson and C. Gooding (eds.), *Disability Rights in Europe. From Theory to Practice* (Oxford, Hart, 2005) 115.

[200] *Ibid.*, 115.

[201] See M. Gijzen, "Report on Measures to Combat Discrimination: Directive 2000/43/EC and 2000/78/EC. Country Report Netherlands" (European Commission, 2004), para. 2.1.1, available on the website of Directorate-General for Employment, Social Affairs and Equal Opportunities.

"Every citizen enjoys protection on the basis of this bill; this is not about having a handicap or chronic illness, but about being discriminated against as compared to someone who has or does not have such impairment." [202]

The symmetrical character of the Dutch non-discrimination legislation has been confirmed by the Equal Treatment Commission:

"Parliament has not further defined the concepts of handicap and chronic disorder. The ban on distinction on these grounds also includes a ban on a distinction on account of not possessing a handicap or chronic disorder."[203]

Such a symmetrical approach seems to fit best with the approach taken by the ECJ to the grounds of gender and race and is more protective of the rights of non-disabled persons. It is just as clear, however, that an asymmetric approach provides better protection of disabled people, as non-disabled workers are then withheld from challenging forms of positive action.[204] It remains to be seen which approach is favoured by the ECJ on this issue.

SOCIAL CONSTRUCT OR MEDICAL IMPAIRMENT?

In defining "disability", it is further important to note that there are different views with respect to the concept of disability itself, which are usually described in the form of two main theoretical models—the medical model and the social model of disability.[205] The medical model is based on a rather functional view of disability, which regards disability primarily as a physical or psychological impairment impeding someone's daily functioning in society. An example of legislation which is based on the medical model may be found in the UK:

Disability Discrimination Act 2005[206]   **1.UK.82.**

Subject to the provisions of Schedule 1, a person has a disability for the purposes of this Act if he has a physical or mental impairment which has a substantial and long-term adverse effect on his ability to carry out normal day-to-day activities.

Schedule 1—Provisions supplementing Section 1[207]
2.—(1) The effect of an impairment is a long-term effect if—

---

[202] Explanatory Memorandum to the Act on Equal Treatment on the Grounds of Disability or Chronic Illness of 2003, *Kamerstukken II* 2001/02, 28 169, no. 3, at 9.
[203] Dutch Equal Treatment Commission, Opinion 2005–02.
[204] Waddington, above n. 199, 116.
[205] See further below L. Waddington, Chapter Six: Reasonable Accommodation and L. Waddington, *From Rome to Nice in a Wheelchair. The Development of a European Disability Policy*, Inaugural Lecture University of Maastricht 2005 (Groningen, Europa Law Publishing, 2006) 13.
[206] c. 50, s. 1(1).
[207] *Ibid.*, c. 50.

    (a)   it has lasted at least 12 months;

    (b)   the period for which it lasts is likely to be at least 12 months; or

    (c)   it is likely to last for the rest of the life of the person affected.

. . .

4.—(1) An impairment is to be taken to affect the ability of the person concerned to carry out normal day-to-day activities only if it affects one of the following—

    (a)   mobility;

    (b)   manual dexterity;

    (c)   physical co-ordination;

    (d)   continence;

    (e)   ability to lift, carry or otherwise move everyday objects;

    (f)   speech, hearing or eyesight;

    (g)   memory or ability to concentrate, learn or understand; or

    (h)   perception of the risk of physical danger . . .

Note

It is clear that a definition such as that contained in the Disability Discrimination Act 1995 involves determinations of fact. The presence of a disability must be established on the basis of medical proof, for instance in the form of a medical diagnosis, in order to successfully invoke the relevant provisions. As a result, many disability discrimination cases in the UK involve discussions on the basis of expert medical opinions.[208]

The medical definition is often criticised in academic literature, as it is questionable if it provides sufficient protection against disability discrimination. In particular, it has been argued that the medical model focuses too strongly on adaptation to prevailing norms and standards in society, instead of on the failure of the social environment to adjust to the needs and aspirations of people with impairments.[209]

    The social model regards disability as a social construct, being ". . . the result of the impaired individual's situation in his or her environment and in the wider structure of society, which places that individual at a disadvantage".[210]

    According to this perspective, many cases of disability discrimination stem not so much from the actual impairment as from a disabling environment.[211] On this view the concept of "disability" in anti-discrimination legislation needs to be given a different definition, which should not focus on functional impairments alone, but should also take into account the impairments created by society.[212]

    The social model is more in line with the European policy towards disability than the purely medical approach—indeed, the European Action Plan on equal opportunities for people with disabilities (2003) explicitly recognises disability as a "social

---

[208] K. Wells, "The Impact of the Framework Employment Directive on UK Disability Discrimination Law" [2003] *ILJ* 257.

[209] Waddington, *From Rome to Nice*, above n 205, 13.

[210] Wells, above n 208.

[211] Waddington, *From Rome to Nice*, above n 205, 14.

[212] Wells, above n 208, 261.

construct".[213] The approach of the World Health Organisation (WHO) towards disability also recognises the social aspects of the concept of disability. Its influential *International Classification of Functioning, Disability and Health* (ICF), which provides a worldwide standard for the description of health and health-related states, is based on a model of disability which endeavours to include both the medical and the social perspective. In addition, the model encompasses an individual perspective, which means that it recognises that some aspects of disability are almost entirely internal to the person.[214] The model of disability it has thus created is called the "biopsychosocial model" and is explained as follows:

> World Health Organisation, *"Towards a Common Language*   **1.UN.83.**
> *for Functioning, Disability and Health"*[215]

". . . [I]n ICF disability and functioning are viewed as outcomes of interactions between health conditions (diseases, disorders and injuries) and contextual factors.

Among contextual factors are external environmental factors (for example, social attitudes, architectural characteristics, legal and social structures, as well as climate, terrain and so forth); and internal personal factors, which include gender, age, coping styles, social background, education, profession, past and current experience, overall behaviour pattern, character and other factors that influence how disability is experienced by the individual.

[There are] . . . three levels of human functioning classified by ICF: functioning at the level of body or body part, the whole person, and the whole person in a social context. Disability therefore involves dysfunctioning at one or more of these same levels: impairments, activity limitations and participation restrictions. The formal definitions of these components of ICF are provided . . . below . . .

Body Functions are physiological functions of body systems (including psychological functions).
Body Structures are anatomical parts of the body such as organs, limbs and their components.
Impairments are problems in body function or structure such as a significant deviation or loss.
Activity is the execution of a task or action by an individual.
Participation is involvement in a life situation.
Activity Limitations are difficulties an individual may have in executing activities.
Participation Restrictions are problems an individual may experience in involvement in life situations.
Environmental Factors make up the physical, social and attitudinal environment in which people live and conduct their lives."

Various efforts have been made to translate the "social" or "biopsychosocial" model into anti-discrimination legislation. The social aspect of disability is, for instance, well

---

[213] European Commission, Equal Opportunities for People with Disabilities: A European Action Plan, COM (2003) 650 final, at 4.
[214] See World Health Organisation, *Towards a Common Language for Functioning, Disability and Health*, ICF, WHO/EIP/GPE/CAS/01.3 (WHO, Geneva, 2002) 9.
[215] *Ibid.*

articulated in a definition proposed by the European Disability Forum (EDF) in 2004:

> "1. For the purposes of this Directive, the principle of equal treatment shall mean that there shall be no direct or indirect discrimination whatsoever on the grounds of disability and no discrimination in the form of a failure to make a reasonable accommodation . . .
>
> 7. For the purposes of this Directive, a person shall be regarded as having a disability if they currently have a disability, they have had a disability in the past, they may have a disability in the future, they are associated with a person with a disability through a family or other relationship, or they are assumed to fall into one of these categories."[216]

This definition not only cover persons with a current impairment, but also covers persons who have had a disability in the past or may become disabled in the future. Assumed disabilities and discrimination by association are also covered, which results in a provision focusing primarily on the aspect of *discrimination* against disabled persons, instead of the disability itself.[217]

An existing legislative definition which seems to come close to the approach that is proposed by the WHO is contained in the Irish Employment Equality Acts of 1998 to 2004, although the aspect of individuality is not clearly visible therein:

> "'Disability' means:
>
> (a) the total or partial absence of a person's bodily or mental functions, including the absence of a part of a person's body,
>
> (b) the presence in the body of organisms causing, or likely to cause, chronic disease or illness,
>
> (c) the malfunction, malformation or disfigurement of a part of a person's body,
>
> (d) a condition or malfunction which results in a person learning differently from a person without the condition or malfunction, or
>
> (e) a condition, illness or disease which affects a person's thought processes, perception of reality, emotions or Judgment or which results in disturbed behaviour,
>
> and shall be taken to include a disability which exists at present, or which previously existed but no longer exists, or which may exist in the future or which is imputed to a person."[218]

Although this definition seems to be based primarily on the medical model, it also refers to discrimination based on previous and future disabilities and disabilities which are not real, but assumed. Furthermore, it appears from the application of

---

[216] European Disability Forum, *Proposal for a Directive Implementing the Principle of Equal Treatment for Persons with Disabilities*, 12 March 2004, Art. 2, available on the website of European Disability Forum.

[217] These elements have also been mentioned as necessary to the definition of 'disability' in non-discrimination legislation by the EU Network of Independent Experts on Disability Discrimination in their *Baseline Study of Disability Discrimination Law in the EU Member States* (European Commission, November 2004), at 11–12, available on the website of Directorate-General for Employment, Social Affairs and Equal Opportunities.

[218] Irish Employment Equality Acts 1998 to 2004, s. 2 (Interpretation).

these definitions in Irish case-law that the courts will not easily dismiss a claim on the ground that the individual is not disabled, as will be illustrated in more detail hereinafter. To that extent, the Irish definition comes much closer to the WHO and EDF definitions than the aforementioned UK definition does.

Finally, some states have not given a social definition of disability discrimination in their legislative texts, but rather have expressed in explanatory notes that the notion should be defined in accordance with ICF, as is the case in the Netherlands:

> "A conclusive definition of the terms handicap or chronic disease is neither necessary nor desirable, especially because what are concerned are not precisely described characteristics of a person but characteristics in relation to situationally determined restrictions. In general usage, the terms have a sufficiently clear meaning. Contact points can be offered if required by the WCC standard . . . 'Terms for the Handicapped' [a national standard developed by the National Health Council in 1991], the International Classification of Impairments Disabilities and Handicaps (ICIDH) and the International Classification of Functioning, Disability and Health (ICF). In this connection, the government has not considered it plausible, either, that the absence of definitions for the terms handicap and chronic disease will affect the application or implementation of the law."[219]

The Dutch government thus argued that the addressees of non-discrimination legislation will find sufficient guidance to define the notion of disability outside the legislative text, which implied that there was no real need to provide for a definition in the non-discrimination legislation.

A wide definition of disability that leaves sufficient room to take account of the social aspects of disability is to be preferred over a purely medical definition from the perspective of inclusion and effective protection against discrimination. It might therefore be expected that the European Court of Justice will choose an interpretation of the disability ground contained in the Employment Equality Directive which is in line with the social definition of disability. There is reason for doubt here, however, as a result of the first case decided by the ECJ on the meaning of the notion of disability: *Chacón Navas*. In his opinion to the case, Advocate General Geelhoed pleaded for restraint n the interpretation of the Directive, as the understanding of the notion of disability is evolving relatively quickly and the notion may be understood differently from one context to the other. Geelhoed concluded that it would not be advisable to pursue a more or less exhaustive definition of the notion of handicap. Nevertheless, he proceeded to define the notion of disability as follows:

> "76. Disabled people are people with serious functional limitations (disabilities) due to physical, psychological or mental afflictions.
> 77. From this two conclusions can be drawn:
>
> — the cause of the limitations must be a health problem or physiological abnormality which is of a long-term or permanent nature;
> — the health problem as cause of the functional limitation should in principle be distinguished from that limitation.

---

[219] Second Memorandum in Reply with respect to the Act on Equal Treatment on the Grounds of Disability or Chronic Illness of 2003, *Kamerstukken* II 2001/02, 28 169, no. 5, at 16.

78. Consequently, a sickness which causes what may be a disability in the future cannot in principle be equated with a disability. It does not therefore provide a basis for a prohibition of discrimination, as referred to in Article 13 EC in conjunction with Directive 2000/78.

79. An exception to this rule is admissible only if during the course of the sickness permanent functional limitations emerge which must be regarded as disabilities despite the continuing sickness.

80. A dismissal because of sickness can thus constitute discrimination on the grounds of disability, which is prohibited by Directive 2000/78, only if the person concerned is able to make a reasonable case that it is not the sickness itself but the resulting long-term or permanent limitations which are the real reason for the dismissal.

81. I would add, to complete the picture, that in that hypothesis the dismissal may none the less be justified if the functional limitations—the disability—make impossible or seriously restrict the pursuit of the occupation or business concerned."

This definition is highly medical or functional in character, as it only refers to serious functional limitations which are the result of a physical, mental or psychological impairment and find their basis in a medical problem. In its judgment, the ECJ has partly followed the definition proposed by the Advocate General:

ECJ, 11 July 2006   **1.EC.84.**
Sonia Chacón Navas v. Eurest Colectividades SA
DEFINITION OF DISABILITY AND ILLNESS

Chacón Navas

Facts: Ms Chacón Navas was employed by Eurest and was certified as unfit to work on grounds of sickness in 2003. She was on leave of absence from her employment for eight months when she was given notice of her dismissal, which was not supported by reasons. The referring court pointed out that Chacón Navas had to be regarded as having been dismissed solely on account of the fact that she was absent from work because of sickness.

Held: A person who has been dismissed solely on account of sickness does not fall within the general framework laid down for combating discrimination on grounds of disability by the Employment Equality Directive.

Judgment: "39. The concept of 'disability' is not defined by Directive 2000/78 itself. Nor does the directive refer to the laws of the Member States for the definition of that concept.

40. It follows from the need for uniform application of Community law and the principle of equality that the terms of a provision of Community law which makes no express reference to the law of the Member States for the purpose of determining its meaning and scope must normally be given an autonomous and uniform interpretation throughout the Community, having regard to the context of the provision and the objective pursued by the legislation in question . . .

41. As is apparent from Article 1, the purpose of Directive 2000/78 is to lay down a general framework for combating discrimination based on any of the grounds referred to in that article, which include disability, as regards employment and occupation.

42. In the light of that objective, the concept of 'disability' for the purpose of Directive 2000/78 must, in accordance with the rule set out in paragraph 40 of this judgment, be given an autonomous and uniform interpretation.

43. Directive 2000/78 aims to combat certain types of discrimination as regards employment and occupation. In that context, the concept of 'disability' must be understood as referring to a limitation which results in particular from physical, mental or psychological impairments and which hinders the participation of the person concerned in professional life.

44. However, by using the concept of 'disability' in Article 1 of that directive, the legislature deliberately chose a term which differs from 'sickness'. The two concepts cannot therefore simply be treated as being the same.

45. Recital 16 in the preamble to Directive 2000/78 states that the 'provision of measures to accommodate the needs of disabled people at the workplace plays an important role in combating discrimination on grounds of disability'. The importance which the Community legislature attaches to measures for adapting the workplace to the disability demonstrates that it envisaged situations in which participation in professional life is hindered over a long period of time. In order for the limitation to fall within the concept of 'disability', it must therefore be probable that it will last for a long time.

46. There is nothing in Directive 2000/78 to suggest that workers are protected by the prohibition of discrimination on grounds of disability as soon as they develop any type of sickness.

47. It follows from the above considerations that a person who has been dismissed by his employer solely on account of sickness does not fall within the general framework laid down for combating discrimination on grounds of disability by Directive 2000/78."

Notes

(1) Focusing on the difference between "sickness" and "disability", the ECJ formulated a definition of disability in *Chacón Navas* which includes three cumulative requirements:

a.   There must be a limitation which results in particular from physical, mental or psychological impairments;
b.   The limitation must hinder the participation of the person concerned in professional life;
c.   It must be probable that the limitation will last for a long time.

Thus, the ECJ's definition focuses on *present* disability, which is defined in a rather functional and medical fashion. The definition thus seems to be closer to the medical model of disability than to the social model, resembling the definition provided in the UK Disability Discrimination Act. The ECJ did not pronounce itself on the question if future or previous disabilities may be covered by the notion of disability, as the Advocate General did in his opinion to the case. It is probable that it has accepted the Advocate General's invitation to refrain from giving an exhaustive and fixed definition at once, leaving intact the open nature of the term. This has the advantage that the Court can further elucidate and develop its definition in later cases on the basis of concrete national questions and factual situations. It cannot therefore be derived from *Chacón Navas* that the ECJ has completely distanced itself from a more social approach towards the notion of disability—it might, for instance, accept future or previous disability as part of the definition in later judgments which specifically relate to such aspects. Furthermore, it is recalled here that the Member States are allowed to provide a higher level of protection against disability discrimination than is offered by the Employment Equality Directive. Hence, even though the ECJ has given a uniform and autonomous definition of the notion of disability in *Chacón Navas*, a Member State might opt for a more inclusive definition if it would thereby guarantee a higher level of protection against discrimination.

(2) The ECJ's definition of disability does not explain the precise meaning of the various requirements included therein. For example, the minimum duration needed for a limitation to qualify as "lasting for a long time" or the exact meaning of the requirement of "hindrance to the participation in professional life" is uncertain. Furthermore, the distinction the ECJ makes between sickness and disability is an interesting one, especially against the background of the legislation of some Member States in which illness and chronic illness are expressly included. Further elucidation of the meaning of these elements is needed in order to give a truly uniform definition of the ground. In this regard, the legislation and case-law of some of the Member States may be an important source of inspiration for the ECJ. For that reason, we will discuss the most important elements of the definition of disability as it is given in the Member States in the remainder of this section.

PERMANENT OR LONG-TERM PHYSICAL OR MENTAL IMPAIRMENT

Two important elements of the ECJ's definition of disability can also be traced in the legal practice of the Member States, where (present) disability is often defined as a physical or mental impairment which is permanent or at least long-term in character. Interesting examples can be found, for example, in Germany and the Netherlands:

German Federal Constitutional Court (Bundesverfassungsgericht), **1.DE.85.**
8 October 1997[220]

DISABILITY AS A LONG-TERM PHYSICAL, MENTAL OR PSYCHOLOGICAL FUNCTION
IMPAIRMENT

Spina bifida

Facts: The applicant was born in 1984 with spina bifida. Both of her legs are paralysed, just like her bladder and bowels. She also suffers from a disturbance of the coordination of her movements and dysfunction of her speech and locomotion system. The applicant was placed in a primary school, which she finished

---

[220] 1 BvR 7/97.

without any delays. During her time at the primary school, she received special guidance and additional training in mathematics. When she wanted to transfer to an integrated secondary school, it transpired that she would need intensive additional support and training. Against the desire of the parents, the national authorities thereupon decided to place the applicant in a special school for physically disabled children, as it would not be possible to organise the necessary support and additional training at a regular secondary school. According to the applicant, this decision ran counter to Article 3(2) of the German Basic Law, which stipulates that no person shall be disfavoured because of disability.

Held: The placement in a special school amounts to unconstitutional discrimination, as the applicant could have been taught at a regular school by specially trained personnel, the costs could be covered by the school's own means and no other organisational or personal obstacles existed.

Judgment: "C.1.1. a) What is meant by 'disability' [in Art. 3 III 2 GG] cannot be directly inferred from the legislative materials . . . However, it can be seen that the legislator who amended the Basic Law adopted the interpretation of the term that was common at the time when the Basic Law was amended. This understanding of the term disability was expressed particularly in Article 3(I)(1) of the *Schwerbehindertengesetz* (SchwbG, Law on Severely Disabled). According to that law, disability is the effect of an impairment of function that is not purely temporary, and which stems from an anomalous physical, mental or psychological condition. This same interpretation of 'disability' underlies the term 'disabled' in the Third Federal Government Report on the situation of the disabled and the development of rehabilitation, and is consistent with international practice in the defining of terms . . . There is no reason not to start from this definition as a basic principle when interpreting Art. 3 III 2 *Grundgesetz* . . . Whether [Art. 3 III 2 GG] conclusively defines disability does not have to be decided on here. The case of the applicant gives no reason for this."

The Dutch Second Memorandum of Reply with respect to the   **1.NL.86.**
Act on Equal Treatment on the Grounds of Disability or
Chronic Illness of 2003[221]

"Disabilities and chronic diseases may be physical, mental or psychological by nature . . . Brief or lengthy restrictions resulting from an accident do not in principle fall within the protection under this act. The possibility of recovery is an essential element, comparable with the situation of incapacity for work where a person may temporarily be less able to work through an accident but will in due course be able to function again to the full extent of his or her capacity. As stated in the Explanatory Memorandum (page 24), a disability is in principle irreversible."

Note

Both the definition of the German Constitutional Court and the Dutch definition in the *travaux préparatoires* speak of a "physical, mental or psychological impairment" which is long-term in character. The latter element is further defined in the Dutch legislative materials by stating that a disability is irreversible and there is no possibility of recovery—in fact, this comes down to the requirement that the disability is permanent in character. Such a limitation to long-term or permanent disabilities is also visible in other Member States, but it is clear that the protection

---

[221] *Kamerstukken* II 2001/02, 28 169, no. 5, at 16.

139

of a prohibition of discrimination is relatively limited if this requirement is included—after all, it means that negative employment decisions, such as dismissal, are not covered by the legislation if someone is temporary disabled as a result of an accident.

The requirement of a "physical, mental or psychological impairment" is also common in the various Member States. Only rarely is a definition framed differently, as in the Hungarian legislation on the Rights of Disabled Persons:

> "A person is disabled if he/she has a fully or greatly restricted command of organoleptic, locomotor or mental abilities, or is greatly restricted in his/her communication, and this constitutes an enduring obstacle with regard to his/her participation in social life."[222]

It is questionable if a definition such as this one will be in full compliance with the definition provided by the ECJ in *Chacón Navas*, as it is much more specific as regards the various limitations which qualify as disabilities.

LIMITATION TO PARTICIPATION IN SOCIAL OR PROFESSIONAL LIFE

As the ECJ made clear in *Chacón Navas*, an essential element of the definition of a disability is the negative influence of the impairment on the individual's participation in professional life. This requirement is mentioned in the legislation of many Member States, but it is only rarely further explained and the national provisions reveal a wide variety of definitions. Sometimes a negative influence on participation in the employment market is sufficient, while other states demand a substantial reduction of all "normal" functions of life or a restriction of participation in society. A few examples may serve as an illustration of this point:

Executive Regulation adopted on 30 January 2004 by the   **1.BE.87.**
Flemish Government to implement certain provisions of the
Decree of 8 May 2002[223]

. . .2. Persons with a handicap—persons with a physical, sensorial, mental or psychic disturbance or limitation which may constitute an obstacle to fair participation in the employment market.

---

[222] Act XXXVI of 1998 on the Rights of Disabled Persons and Guaranteeing of their Equal Opportunities, Art. 4.

[223] Besluit van de Vlaamse regering tot uitvoering van het decreet van 8 mei 2002 houdende evenredige participatie op de arbeidsmarkt wat betreft de beroepskeuzevoorlichting, beroepsopleiding, loopbaanbegeleiding en arbeidsbemiddeling, N. 2004–786, Belgisch Staatsblad (Belgian Official Gazette) 2004, 12050.

Cypriot Law concerning Persons with Disabilities[224]   **1.CY.88.**

Disability—Any form of deficiency or disadvantage that may cause bodily, mental or psycho-logical limitations which are permanent or of an indefinite duration and which, considering the background and other personal data of the particular person, substantially reduce or exclude the ability of the person to perform one or more activities or functions that are considered normal or substantial for the quality of life of any person of the same age that does not experience the same deficiency or disadvantage.

French Act 2005-102 on the Equality of Rights and Opportunities,   **1.FR.89.**
the Participation and Citizenship of Disabled Persons (2005),
amending Section L. 114-1 of the Social Action and Family Code[225]

The following constitutes a disability according to this code: any limitation on activity or restriction on the ability to participate in society encountered by a person in his or her environment by reason of a substantial, lasting or definitive alteration of one or many physical, sensory, mental, cognitive or psychological faculties, of multiple disabilities or of a disabling illness.

Lithuanian Law on the Social Integration of the Disabled 2004[226]   **1.LT.90.**

Disability—the combination of a person's body structure, functional disorders and unfavourable elements of the environment, which cause exacerbation of long-term health conditions and decrease abilities to participate in public life and activities.

Portuguese Law 38/2004[227]   **1.PT.91.**

A person shall be considered disabled when, as a consequence of congenital or acquired loss or anomaly of functions or body structures, including psychological functions, he/she presents with specific difficulties, in conjunction with circumstantial factors, which limit or hinder activity and participation on equal terms as other persons.

Notes
(1) It is difficult to say if these definitions are all compatible with the definition given by the ECJ in *Chacón Navas*, which only refers to limitations to an individual's

---

[224] Law N. 127(I)/2000 as amended by Law N. 57(1)/2004.
[225] Loi ° 2005/102 pour l'égalité des droits et des chances, la participation et la citoyenneté des personnes handicapées of 11 February 2005, JO 36 of 12 February 2005.
[226] Art. 2(6) (The main concepts of this law).
[227] Lei no. 38/2004 de 18 de Agosto de 2004 define as bases gerais do regime juridico da prevenção, habilitação e participação da pessoa com deficiênda, Art. 2 (Definition).

"participation in professional life". The ECJ's restriction would seem to deprive people of the protection offered by the Directive if they are hindered in some daily activities without there being a loss of ability to perform a certain job or class of jobs. This may be illustrated by the example of a job applicant in a wheelchair who is refused for a job in a call centre because the employer feels that she will probably work less efficiently than an able-bodied person. This clearly constitutes discrimination based on disability, but it is questionable if the situation is covered by the definition given by the ECJ. After all, even though it will be clear that a wheelchair may cause some difficulties in daily life, it is far from certain that this would really hinder her participation in professional life. As the job applicant's disability would thereby fall short of the requirements formulated by the ECJ, her case would not fall within the scope of protection of the Directive.

(2) National definitions which focus on the limitation of "day-to-day activities" or "activities or functions that are considered normal or substantial for the quality of life" would seem to offer stronger protection in this respect, as they cover a larger category of disability. Furthermore, the negative consequences of the limited definition given by the ECJ may be mitigated if the prohibition of discrimination is extended to discrimination based on *assumed* disability, i.e. discrimination based on misconceptions or stereotypical assumptions about the individual's abilities to participate in professional life. This issue will be discussed in more detail in section 1.4.

FUTURE DISABILITY

An important question which was not addressed by the ECJ in *Chacón Navas* relates to whether someone who is likely to acquire a disability in the future is covered by the prohibition of discrimination based on disability. This question is particularly relevant with respect to persons who are genetically predisposed to certain kinds of illness or disability, or have attracted a disease the symptoms of which will only develop in the future (e.g. Huntington's disease or HIV/Aids). In some legal systems future disability is explicitly mentioned as part of the definition of disability, but the criteria that have to be met in order to classify a case as "future disability" are rather unclear:

SGB IX, Social Law Code, Book IX   **1.DE.92.**
(Sozialgesetzbuch, Neuntes Buch)[228]

(2) A person is disabled if his/her bodily functions, mental capabilities or spiritual health deviate with a high degree of probability from the typical condition for the age of the person by at least six months and if as a result this affects the participation of the person in question

---

[228] Sozialgesetzbuch, Neuntes Buch (SGB IX), Rehabilitation und Teilhabe behinderter Menschen of 19 June 2001, BGBl.I.1046, § 2 (Disability).

in daily life. *A person is under threat of becoming disabled if such an influence on daily life is to be expected* [emphasis added].

Swedish Disability Discrimination Act 1999—Section 2   **1.SE.93.**

Disability means every permanent physical, mental or intellectual limitation of a person's functional capacity that, as a consequence of an injury or illness that existed at birth, arose thereafter or *may be expected* to arise [emphasis added].

Note
Both of these definitions make it clear that there must be some objective basis for expecting that the disability will actually occur in the future and will meet the various criteria established for the presence of a disability. How such expectations must be proved before the courts is presently not clear.[229]

CHRONIC ILLNESS, SICKNESS AND HEALTH

In some Member States, legislation is in place which offers specific protection against discrimination based on chronic or long-lasting illness, or even generally sickness or state of health. The national definitions given are highly diverse, as may be illustrated by the following excerpts and those given above (in particular **1.FR.89.**, **1.NL.80.** and **1.PT.91.**):

Hungarian Act CXXV of 2003 on equal treatment and   **1.HU.94.**
on fostering equal opportunities[230]

A provision shall qualify as direct discrimination if it results in less favourable treatment for a person or group than for another person or group in a comparable position, because of their actual or assumed . . .

g)   disability,
h)   health condition . . .

---

[229] In this respect, the case-law in the US relating to the Americans with Disabilities Act (ADA) may be of particular interest. For further information see, e.g. J.H. Gerards, "Regulation of Genetic Information in the United States" in J.H. Gerards, A.W. Heringa and H.L. Janssen, *Genetic Discrimination and Genetic Privacy in a Comparative Perspective* (Antwerp, Intersentia, 2005) 154*ff*.
[230] 2003. évi CXXV. törvény az egyenlő bánásmódról és az esélyegyenlőség előmozdításáról, s. 8.

143

Portuguese Labour Code[231]   **1.PT.95.**

(1) Employers may not practice any direct or indirect discrimination based on, in particular, . . . reduced capacity to work, disability, chronic illness . . .

Note

It appears that some Member States refer to a broad category such as "health condition", but that most legislative texts contain some kind of limitation. The French text, for example, speaks of "disabling illness" (above **1.FR.89.**), and states such as Portugal and the Netherlands have chosen to cover only *chronic* illness (above **1.NL.80.** and **1.PT.91.**). Such legislative choices would seem to create the need to define these notions and to distinguish disabling or chronic illness from other forms of illness.[232] Mostly, however, no such definitions or explanations are given. In the Netherlands, for example, the legislature has refrained from giving a definition of "chronic illness", stating that the term has a clear significance in daily usage. The only clue given as to the definition of the notion is as follows:

Dutch Explanatory Memorandum to the Act on Equal Treatment **1.NL.96.**
on the Grounds of Disability or Chronic Illness of 2003[233]

"A disability is . . . irreversible in principle. A chronic illness is not always so, but is in any event long-lasting by nature."

The Irish definition of "disability" mentions "the malfunction, malformation or disfigurement of a part of a person's body", without explaining if the definition also covers cases of chronic illness or (temporary) sickness. It is clear from a number of decisions of the Irish Equality Officer, however, that the provision must be given a wide interpretation:

Equality Tribunal, 11 December 2002[234]   **1.IE.97.**
Decision DEC-E/2001/052, Fernandez v. *Cable & Wireless*

ILLNESS AS DISABILITY

Fernandez

Facts: Ms Fernandez was given an intravenous penicillin injection to fight a kidney infection in 2001. She had a severe reaction to the injection and had to stay in hospital for a week to recover. After this, and in

---

[231] Art. 23(1).
[232] Although this is less relevant for the Portuguese Labour Code, which does not contain a closed list of grounds and may be interpreted as to cover non-chronic illness as well as chronic illness.
[233] Kamerstukken II, 2001/02, 28 169, no. 3, at 24.
[234] Available on the website of the Equality Tribunal of Ireland, under the heading Employment Equality Decisions.

combination with earlier health problems relating to pregnancy, she was removed from the "24-hour service" at the call centre she was working for with the loss of £5000 per annum. Furthermore, she was advised to follow the established practice with respect to planning of medical appointments, as she had not given adequate notice of such appointments to her team leader. Her team leader warned her that if there were further occurrences of unplanned leave, further action would have to be considered.

Held: In the circumstances of this particular case, the respondent did provide reasonable accommodation in relation to the complainant's medical appointment; the respondent did not directly discriminate against the complainant on the disability ground.

Decision: "5.12 The complainant does not deny that she had a number of sick leave absences but submits that the impact of her absences on the call centre had only minimal effect. I have examined the absence details including sick leave provided by both parties and for the most part, the absences correspond. The respondent submitted that the complainant was removed from the 24-hour shift on 20 August 2001 due to her high level of sick leave absences. It did not dispute the nature of the complainant's illnesses but did not accept that the complainant had proved her case that she had/has a disability as defined by the Act. I have considered the nature of the complainant's illnesses and I accept that the complainant's illnesses amounted to a disability within the meaning of the Act."

The Equality Officer's decision makes clear that any sickness may come within the scope of the definition of disability, regardless of its duration, character or severity. This understanding was confirmed by a more recent decision:

Equality Tribunal, 1 June 2004[235]   **1.IE.98.**
Decision DEC-E/2004/029, A Civil Servant v. The Office of Civil Service and Local Appointments Commissioners

ASTHMA AND IRRITABLE BOWEL SYNDROME AS DISABILITY

Asthmatic civil servant

Facts: The complainant passed an exam and interview in 2001 for the post of Executive Officer. By letter dated 29 November 2001, he was informed that his sick leave record did not fall within the limits specified in Department of Finance Circular 34/76. He was informed that his application had not been successful as he could not be regarded as qualified in terms of health. The complainant submits that he suffers from asthma and irritable bowel syndrome.

Held: In the circumstances of this case, the respondent has successfully rebutted the claim of discrimination on the disability ground.

Decision: "5.5 . . . I have considered . . .various definitions and I am not satisfied that asthma (which according to Butterworths Medical Dictionary is, inter alia, a narrowing of the smaller bronchi and bronchioles of the lungs) amounts to a disability within the definition of subsection (b), *i.e.* the presence in the body of organisms causing, or likely to cause, chronic disease or illness.

5.6 I will now consider the definition of irritable bowel syndrome . . .I have considered the . . . definition and in particular, that it is caused by a disturbance of involuntary muscle

[235] Available on the website of the Equality Tribunal of Ireland, under the heading Employment Equality Decisions.

movement in the large intestine and therefore, I am not satisfied that irritable bowel syndrome is a disability which falls within subsection (b) of the definition of disability and relates to the presence in the body of organisms causing, or likely to cause, chronic disease or illness.

5.7 As stated in the preceding paragraphs, I find it difficult to reconcile the complainant's illnesses with subsection (b) of the definition of disability. However, I will proceed to examine whether the illnesses could fall within any of the other subsections of the definition of disability. Section 2(1) of the Act defines disability in broad terms. It provides at subsection (c) that disability includes 'the malfunction, malformation or disfigurement of a part of a person's body', I have considered a number of Labour Court cases of discriminatory dismissal on the disability ground which concern illnesses such as diabetes, epilepsy, a congenital neuromuscular disease, a hearing difficulty and injuries sustained in a car accident . . . The Court in the case of *Customer Perception Limited* v. *Gemma Leydon* considered in that case whether injuries sustained by the complainant in a road traffic accident amounted to a disability within the meaning of the Employment Equality Act, 1998. It held:

'Taking the ordinary and natural meaning of the term malfunction (connoting a failure to function in a normal manner), the condition from which the complainant suffered in consequences of her accident amounted to a malfunction of parts of her body. It thus constituted a disability within the meaning of the Act. Moreover, in providing that the term comprehends a disability which existed but no longer exists, it is clear that a temporary malfunction comes within the statutory definition.'

In my view, both asthma and irritable bowel syndrome are malfunctions of the airways of the lungs and the intestinal tract respectively and more appropriately fall within the definition contained at subsection (c). I therefore accept that both conditions amount to disabilities within the meaning of the Act."

Notes

(1) The decision in the case of the civil servant confirms that sickness and illness that cannot be considered as chronic in character nevertheless constitute a "disability" within the meaning of the Employment Equality Act if they (temporarily) cause a malfunctioning of parts of the body. This wide definition has also led the Equality Officer to accept that alcoholism forms part of the definition of disability, just like health problems that are the result of work-related stress.[236]

(2) Thus, the Irish definition seems to be more protective than the definition provided by the ECJ in *Chacón Navas*. From this case it transpired, after all, that temporary illness does not come within the scope of "disability", although this may be different for a disabling or chronic illness that meets the requirements of hindering participation in professional life over a long period of time. To that extent, the ECJ's decision would seem to oblige all national laws to provide for some protection against discrimination based on chronic illness.

---

[236] See Equality Officer Decision, 2 May 2003, DEC S/2002/024, *A Complainant* v. *Café Kylemore* (alcoholism) and Equality Officer, 20 November 2003, DEC E/2003v.052, *Mr. O.* v. *A Named Company* (work-related stress).

1.3.9.B.   SUSPECTNESS

While the legislation in many Member States devotes significant attention to the definition of disability, much less information is available with respect to the perceived suspectness of the ground. Because of the inclusion of the ground in the Directive and the many policy efforts made on both the European and domestic level, a consensus might seem to exist on the need to offer strong protection against disability discrimination and to provide for special accommodation to meet the needs of disabled persons. It may thus be concluded that disability is generally considered as a suspect ground for discrimination.

The only clue which is presently available as to the approach that will be taken by the ECJ in this respect can be found in the case of *Mangold*,[237] in which the Court applied a relatively strict test to a distinction based on age. It might be derived from this that the Court will adopt a similar approach towards the ground of disability. There may be some doubt in this regard, however, as Advocate General Geelhoed has argued that an extensive interpretation of the Employment Equality Directive might lead to potentially far-reaching economical and financial consequences for the relations between citizens and between public authorities and citizens.[238] This line of reasoning would seem to imply that the states should generally be afforded a relatively wide margin of appreciation to decide if certain distinctions are reasonable and justifiable. As a result, disability discrimination would not have to be strictly scrutinised on the level of the ECJ, regardless of the suspectness of the ground in question. Of course, this should not be taken to mean that disability cannot be considered suspect on the national level and a strict test cannot be applied by the national courts on their own accord. Nonetheless, the lack of clear approval of the ECJ on the Community level would certainly discourage some national courts from doing so. For that reason, much will depend on the ECJ's willingness to stand by its decision in the *Mangold* case or, alternatively, to follow the proposal made by AG Geelhoed. Unfortunately, the *Chacón Navas* case as it was decided by the ECJ does not offer any more clarity in this respect, as the Court found that the Directive was not applicable to the case at hand and therefore did not address the question about the justifiability of the discrimination that was complained of.

Similarly, no answer to the question of suspectness can be found in the case-law of the ECtHR, as the ECtHR has not yet decided any cases pertaining to disability discrimination.[239]

---

[237] See below **1.EC.101.**

[238] See his opinion in the case of *Chacón Navas*, above **1.EC.84.** and accompanying text.

[239] The reason for this is that the ECtHR has not yet accepted many cases of disability discrimination to come under the scope of one of the substantive provisions of the ECHR; because of the accessory character of the non-discrimination provision contained in Art. 14, this means that it has also proven to be impossible to successfully challenge cases of disability discrimination. For an example, see ECtHR, 11 April 2006, *Molka v. Poland*, Appl. No. 56550/00 (admissibility decision), not published. This might change now that the independent non-discrimination provision of Protocol No. 12 has entered into force. Furthermore, it is important to note that this has not prevented the ECtHR from deciding complaints from disabled persons under the substantive rights protected by the Convention, such as Art. 8 (right to respect

1.3.10. AGE

1.3.10.A. DEFINITION

As with the other grounds contained in the Employment Equality Directive, no definition is provided of the ground of age. The Member States have scarcely made use of the resulting possibility to provide their own definition of the notion: most of the Member States have not given any explanation of the meaning of "age". Indeed, the meaning of the ground would seem to be self-evident, as it would simply seem to refer to distinctions between older and younger persons.[240] Consequently, few national materials are available in which the notion is further explained. A rare exception is the Netherlands, where some attention has been paid to the question if the ground also covers age categories:

> "The notion of 'distinction' includes first of all direct unequal treatment, whereupon age is used directly as the ground for distinction. This is so not only if a distinction is made on grounds of a particular age but also if age categories are adopted. An example of adopting a specific age is the fixing of an age limit in a job advertisement or allowing additional days holiday based on age. An example of the use of age categories may be found in the Dismissals Order. In the light of this Order, age categories may be adopted for group severance when fixing the order of severance. The Order refers to 5 age categories; the youngest category includes employees aged 15 to 25, the oldest, employees aged 55 and over."[241]

Furthermore, some states have found it necessary to explain that the ground of age should be interpreted in a symmetrical manner, thus clarifying that discrimination against both younger and older persons is prohibited. In the Explanatory Notes to the Austrian Equal Treatment Act, it is, for instance, stated that: "The ground 'age' also covers discrimination on the ground of young age."[242]

In other legal systems the symmetrical character of the ground of age seems to have been taken for granted. From the various country reports on measures to combat discrimination it clearly transpires that "age" is supposed to cover younger as well as older persons,[243] but this assumption is seldom expressed in legislation, legislative

---

for private life). For a further analysis, see in particular O. de Schutter, *The Prohibition of Discrimination under European Human Rights Law. Relevance for EU Racial and Employment Equality Directives* (Brussels, European Commission, 2005) 21/23.

[240] Although here, as well as with disability, it is sometimes argued that a distinction should be made between someone's biological age and the social construct of age: societal attitudes, assumptions and barriers may be of importance here as much as with disability. *Cf.* H. Meenan, "Age Equality after the Employment Directive" (2003) 10 *MJ* 13.

[241] Explanatory Memorandum to the Act on Equal Treatment on Grounds of Age, *Kamerstukken II* 2001/02, 28170, no. 3, at 17.

[242] Explanatory Notes to the Austrian Equal Treatment Act, *307 der Beilagen XXII. GP, Regierungsvorlage, Materialien*, at 15.

[243] See generally the website of Directorate-General for Employment, Social Affairs and Equal Opportunities.

materials or case-law. An exception to this general approach can be found in Ireland:

Irish Equal Status Act 2000, as amended by the Equality Act 2004[244] **1.IE.99.**

(3) (a) The age ground applies only in relation to persons above the maximum age at which a person is statutorily obliged to attend school.

(b) Notwithstanding subsection (1) and section 37(2), an employer may set a minimum age, not exceeding 18 years, for recruitment to a post.

(c) Offering a fixed term contract to a person over the compulsory retirement age for that employment or to a particular class or description of employees in that employment shall not be taken as constituting discrimination on the age ground.

Note

The result of the Irish formulation is that only persons over 18 years old are protected against age discrimination. Furthermore, in certain circumstances the non-discrimination legislation does not apply to persons over the compulsory retirement age, which may differ for each employment sector. However, this second exclusion does not so much relate to the *definition* of the ground of age, but can be considered to constitute a general limitation on the scope of the non-discrimination legislation. It is unclear as yet whether such a general exclusion is in compliance with the Employment Equality Directive, which seems to start from the perspective that everyone, regardless of age, should have the same right to equal treatment.[245]

1.3.10.B.   SUSPECTNESS

The suspectness of the ground of age is subject to debate. A number of reasons can be said to raise doubt as to the suspect character of this ground.[246] The relevance and reasonableness of many age-based distinctions is not, or at least not fundament-ally, disputed—examples are age restrictions for smoking, drinking or driving, or age limitations relating to the right to participate in elections.[247] Further, even though there are many cases of unacceptable stereotyping as regards persons belonging to certain age groups,[248] there would not seem to be a degree of social prejudice comparable to that visible with respect to race, ethnic origin, sexual orientation or

---

[244] No. 8/2000, as amended by No. 24/2004, s. 3.

[245] C. O'Cinneide, *Age Discrimination and European Law*, European Commission Report (April 2005) 11, available on the website of the Migration Policy Group.

[246] *Ibid.*, 13.

[247] This is also stated in the preamble to the Employment Equality Directive: in consideration 25, it is stipulated that it is essential to distinguish between situations of justified unequal treatment based on age, and actual age discrimination.

[248] See O'Cinneide, above n. 245, 10.

gender. It has even been argued that the introduction of non-discrimination legislation with respect to the ground of age was primarily inspired by the economically motivated wish to improve employment participation of senior workers, which is necessary to finance the welfare state for an ageing population. Notions relating to fundamental individual rights and human dignity, which form the primary source of inspiration for other non-discrimination provisions, are considered of secondary importance here.[249] For such reasons there might seem to be less need to apply a strict test to age-discrimination than to the other grounds mentioned in the Employment Equality Directive. This view is supported by a decision of the Irish Supreme Court of 1997, which is one of the very few European cases in which express attention is devoted to the issue:

Supreme Court, 15 May 1997   **1.IE.100.**
Case 118/1997, In the Matter of Article 26 and in the Matter of
the Employment Equality Bill 1996

LIMITED SCOPE OF AGE DISCRIMINATION PROHIBITIONS

Age discrimination in the Employment Equality Bill

Facts: In 1996, the Irish parliament (Oireachtas) had drafted an Employment Equality Bill. In 1997, the Irish president referred the Bill to the Supreme Court for a decision on the question as to whether the Bill was repugnant to the Irish Constitution. One of the specific questions that was raised in this case related to the prohibition on age discrimination as contained in the Bill. The Bill excluded persons aged 65 or more and persons under 18 from the scope of the ground of age. Furthermore, the prohibition did not apply to employment in the Defence Forces, the Garda Siochana (the Irish police service) or the prison service. The question was raised if these exclusions were in compliance with the general principle of equal treatment as guaranteed in Article 40.1 of the Irish Constitution, given that not all persons were offered the same level of protection against age discrimination.

Held: The provisions relating to the age ground are not repugnant to the provisions of the Constitution.

Judgment: ". . . The aged are . . . entitled as human beings to protection against laws which discriminate against them, unless the differentiation is related to a legitimate objective and is not arbitrary or irrational. The young are also so entitled, although the need for protection may be less obvious and pressing in their case. There is no question but that the Bill under consideration in seeking to eliminate from the work place so far as practicable is designed to meet an important objective which is enshrined in the Constitution itself . . .

It might be, at first sight, more difficult to defend on constitutional grounds the wide-ranging exclusion from the Bill's provisions of employment in the Defence Forces, the Garda Siochana or the Prison Service. Once, however, it is accepted that discrimination on the grounds of age falls into a different constitutional category from distinction on grounds such as sex or race, the decision of the Oireachtas not to apply the provisions of the Bill to a

---

[249] Although they are certainly of relevance. If a distinction is based on stereotypes or prejudice regarding someone's age, it may well be argued that such a distinction comes into conflict with one's right to respect for human dignity; in addition, such discrimination sometimes deprives persons of important work opportunities. See O'Cinneide, above n. 245, 10.

relatively narrowly defined class of employees in the public service whose duties are of a particular character becomes more understandable . . ."

Note

The excerpt makes clear that the Irish Supreme Court perceives a difference between the age ground and grounds such as sex or race. In the case of unequal treatment based on age, a test of arbitrariness or irrationality is considered sufficient and exclusions from the scope of protection are more readily held to be permissible.

Notwithstanding such assumptions in favour of a more marginal test, it is clear from the ECJ's decision in *Mangold* that a relatively strict test of proportionality will be applied in cases in which a difference in treatment is based on age alone:

ECJ, 22 November 2005[250]　　　　　　**1.EC.101.**
Werner Mangold v. *Rüdiger Helm*

STRICT TEST OF PROPORTIONALITY IN AGE-DISCRIMINATION CASES

Mangold

Facts: In 2003 Mr Mangold, then 56 years old, concluded with Mr Helm a contract that provided the following three points:

1. The employment relationship shall start on 1 July 2003 and last until February 2004.

2. The duration of the contract shall be based on the statutory provision which is intended to make it easier to conclude fixed-term contracts of employment with older workers . . . since the employee is more than 52 years old.

3. The parties have agreed that there is no reason for the fixed term of this contract other than that set out in paragraph 2 above. All other grounds for limiting the term of employment accepted in principle by the legislature are expressly excluded from this agreement.

The contract was based on the Law on part time working and fixed-term contracts, in which it was stated that a fixed-term employment contract shall not require objective justification if at the start of the fixed-term employment relationship the employee has reached the age of 58. The Law also provided that until 31 December 2006 the first sentence could be read as referring to the age of 52 instead of 58.

Held: Community law must be interpreted as precluding a provision of domestic law such as that at issue in the main proceedings.

Judgment: "63. . . . [T]he Member States unarguably enjoy broad discretion in their choice of the measures capable of attaining their objectives in the field of social and employment policy.

64. However, as the national court has pointed out, application of national legislation such as that at issue in the main proceedings leads to a situation in which all workers who have reached the age of 52, without distinction, whether or not they were unemployed before the contract was concluded and whatever the duration of any period of unemployment, may

---

[250] [2005] ECR I–9981.

lawfully, until the age at which they may claim their entitlement to a retirement pension, be offered fixed-term contracts of employment which may be renewed an indefinite number of times. This significant body of workers, determined solely on the basis of age, is thus in danger, during a substantial part of its members' working life, of being excluded from the benefit of stable employment which, however, as the Framework Agreement makes clear, constitutes a major element in the protection of workers.

65. In so far as such legislation takes the age of the worker concerned as the only criterion for the application of a fixed-term contract of employment, when it has not been shown that fixing an age threshold, as such, regardless of any other consideration linked to the structure of the labour market in question or the personal situation of the person concerned, is objectively necessary to the attainment of the objective which is the vocational integration of unemployed older workers, it must be considered to go beyond what is appropriate and necessary in order to attain the objective pursued. Observance of the principle of proportionality requires every derogation from an individual right to reconcile, so far as is possible, the requirements of the principle of equal treatment with those of the aim pursued . . . Such national legislation cannot, therefore, be justified under Article 6(1) of Directive 2000/78."

Note

Although the ECJ did not expressly deal with the issue of suspectness and even stressed that Member States enjoy broad discretion in the field of social and economic policy, it is clear from its decision in *Mangold* that it will not apply a marginal test of arbitrariness to age distinctions. It may be concluded that the ECJ will apply at least an intermediate intensity of review to discrimination based on age, as it concerns a derogation from the individual right to non-discrimination. To this extent, the national courts (such as the Irish Supreme Court) will need to adapt their case-law to meet the standard of review set by the ECJ.

1.3.11.   PART TIME AND FIXED-TERM WORK

1.3.11.A.   DEFINITION

Two European Directives were adopted in the nineties which are devoted to part time workers and workers with fixed-term contracts. Both Directives aim to implement the Framework Agreements on part time work and fixed-term contracts concluded by the Union of Industrial and Employer's Confederations of Europe (UNICE), the European Centre of Enterprises with Public Participation (CEEP) and the European Trade Union Confederation (ETUC). Both Framework Agreements contain express prohibitions of discrimination against part time workers and workers with fixed-term contracts. These prohibitions are formulated asymmetrically, protecting only members of the group that are most often victims of discrimination. The Directives further contain explicit definitions of part-time workers, full-time workers and fixed-term contracts, which sets them apart from the Racial and Employment Equality Directives.

Council Directive 97/81/EC of   **1.EC.102.**
15 December 1997 concerning the Framework Agreement
on part-time work concluded by UNICE, CEEP and ETUC—
Annex (Framework Agreement on Part-Time Work)[251]

For the purposes of this agreement:
1. The term 'part-time worker' refers to an employee whose normal hours of work, calculated on a weekly basis or on average over a period of employment of up to one year, are less than the normal hours of work of a comparable full-time worker.
2. The term 'comparable full-time worker' means a full-time worker in the same establishment having the same type of employment contract or relationship, who is engaged in the same or a similar work/occupation, due regard being given to other considerations which may include seniority and qualification/skills . . .
Clause 4—Principle of non-discrimination
1. In respect of employment conditions, part-time workers shall not be treated in a less favourable manner than comparable full-time workers solely because they work part time unless different treatment is justified on objective grounds.
2. Where appropriate, the principle of *pro rata temporis* shall apply.

Council Directive 1999/70/EC of 28 June 1999 concerning the   **1.EC.103.**
framework agreement on fixed-term work concluded by ETUC, UNICE and
CEEP—Annex (Framework Agreement on Fixed-Term Work)[252]

1. For the purpose of this agreement the term 'fixed-term worker' means a person having an employment contract or relationship entered into directly between an employer and a worker where the end of the employment contract or relationship is determined by objective conditions such as reaching a specific date, completing a specific task, or the occurrence of a specific event.
2. For the purpose of this agreement, the term 'comparable permanent worker' means a worker with an employment contract or relationship of indefinite duration, in the same establishment, engaged in the same or similar work/occupation, due regard being given to qualifications/skills.

Clause 4—Principle of non-discrimination
1. In respect of employment conditions, fixed-term workers shall not be treated in a less favourable manner than comparable permanent workers solely because they have a fixed-term contract or relation unless different treatment is justified on objective grounds . . .

In this section we will provide an overview of the way these provisions have been implemented and interpreted on the international level and in the various Member States. We will start with an explanation of the meaning of the grounds of part-time and full-time work, followed by a discussion of the ground of fixed-term contract.

---

[251] [1998] OJ L 14/12, cl. 3 (Definitions).
[252] [1999] OJ L 175/43, cl. 3 (Definitions).

PART-TIME AND FULL-TIME WORK

The definition provided in the Framework Agreement on Part-Time Work is similar to the definitions contained in International Labour Organisation (ILO) Convention No. 175 concerning part-time work:

ILO Convention No. 175: Part-Time Work Convention[253]   **1.UN.104.**

For the purposes of this Convention:

  (a)   the term 'part-time worker' means an employed person whose normal hours of work are less than those of comparable full-time workers;
  (b)   the normal hours of work referred to in subparagraph (a) may be calculated weekly or on average over a given period of employment;
  (c)   the term 'comparable full-time worker' refers to a full-time worker who:
  (i)   has the same type of employment relationship;
  (ii)   is engaged in the same or a similar type of work or occupation; and
  (iii) is employed in the same establishment or, when there is no comparable full-time worker in that establishment, in the same enterprise or, when there is no comparable full-time worker in that enterprise, in the same branch of activity, as the part-time worker concerned;
  (d)   full-time workers affected by partial unemployment, that is by a collective and temporary reduction in their normal hours of work for economic, technical or structural reasons, are not considered to be part-time workers.

Notes
(1) Just like the European Framework Agreement, the ILO Convention is formulated asymmetrically, protecting only part-time workers against discrimination. This is in line with the common view that part-time employment is "atypical" employment which deviates from the general rule of full-time work.[254] Being the exception, part-time workers need stronger protection against discrimination than full-time workers do.

(2) Furthermore, the definitions are comparable as far as regards the choice of full-time workers as the relevant comparator. Part-time work is defined in relation to full-time work by stipulating that a job is part-time when the number of weekly working hours is considerably less than the number of hours in a comparable full-time job.[255] The reason for mentioning a similar occupation is that the number of

---

[253] Art. 1.
[254] K. Ogura, "International Comparison of Atypical Employment: Differing Concepts and Realities in Industrialized Countries" (2005) 2 *JLR* 6.
[255] A. van Bastelaer et al., *The Definition of Part-Time Work for the Purpose of International Comparisons*, Labour Market and Social Policy Occasional Papers No. 22 (Paris, OECD, 1997) 5–6.

hours per week or month that are regarded as normal for full-time employees may vary considerably according to the profession or activity concerned.[256]

(3) Finally, the definitions in neither the ILO Convention nor the European Framework Agreement distinguish between various types of part-time work, such as job-sharing, combinations between work and training (e.g. traineeships and apprenticeships) and semi-retirement.[257] Hence, all of these forms are presumably covered by the non-discrimination provisions. Only part-time workers who work on a casual basis may be excluded from the scope of the relevant legislation, as is expressly stated in the European Framework Agreement:

> "Member States, after consultation with the social partners in accordance with national law, collective agreements or practice, and/or the social partners at the appropriate level in conformity with national industrial relations practice may, for objective reasons, exclude wholly or partly from the terms of this Agreement part-time workers who work on a casual basis. Such exclusions should be reviewed periodically to establish if the objective reasons for making them remain valid."[258]

According to the *ETUC Guide to the Framework Agreement on Part-time Work*, the term "casual" contained in this definition may be read as to describe short, temporary and non-repetitive contracts.[259]

Within the EU, most Member States strive for equal treatment of part-time workers by other means than by adopting specific non-discrimination legislation, e.g. by concluding collective agreements or amending or supplementing existing employment legislation.[260] Only a few states appear to have implemented the Part-Time Work Directive by extending the scope of their non-discrimination legislation to the ground of part-time/full-time work.[261] These states have sometimes included a definition of part-time and full-time work which is similar to the one contained in the ILO Convention and the Part-Time Work Directive, though a few notable variations and deviations are visible:[262]

---

[256] A.T. Bollé, "Part-time Work: Solution or Trap?" (1997) 136 *ILR* 559.

[257] See A.T. Vielle and A.T. Walthery, *Flexibility and Social Protection, European Foundation for the Improvement of Living and Working Conditions* (Luxembourg, European Communities Publications, 2003) 10.

[258] European Framework Agreement on part-time work, in Vielle and Walthery, above n. 257, cl. 2 (2) (Scope).

[259] See Annex 9 to S. Clauwaert, *Survey on the Implementation of the Part-Time Work Directive v. Agreement in the EU Member States and Selected Applicant Countries* (Brussels, European Trade Union Institute, 2002) 102 (cl. 2, scope).

[260] Further information on the implementation of the Directive can be found in Clauwaert, above n. 259.

[261] Obviously, equal treatment legislation which does not contain a closed list of protected grounds will also include the grounds of working-time and fixed-term work.

[262] See Clauwaert, above n. 259, 30*ff.*

(1) . . .

— 'full-time employee' means an employee who is not a part-time employee;

— 'normal hours of work' means, in relation to an employee, the average number of hours worked by the employee each day during a reference period;

— 'part-time employee' means an employee whose normal hours of work are less than the normal hours of work of an employee who is a comparable employee in relation to him or her;

— 'reference period' means a period which complies with the following conditions:

(a)   the period is of not less than 7 days nor more than 12 months duration,

(b)   the period is the same period by reference to which the normal hours of work of the other employee referred to in the definition of 'part-time employee' in this section is determined, and

(c)   the number of hours worked by the employee concerned in the period constitutes the normal number of hours worked by the employee in a period of that duration; . . .

(2) For the purposes of this Part, an employee is a comparable employee in relation to the employee firstly mentioned in the definition of 'part-time employee' in this section (the 'relevant part-time employee') if—

(a)   the employee and the relevant part-time employee are employed by the same employer or associated employers and one of the conditions referred to in subsection (3) is satisfied in respect of those employees,

(b)   in case paragraph (a) does not apply (including a case where the relevant part-time employee is the sole employee of the employer), the employee is specified in a collective agreement, being an agreement that for the time being has effect in relation to the relevant part-time employee, to be a type of employee who is to be regarded for the purposes of this Part as a comparable employee in relation to the relevant part-time employee, or

(c)   in case neither paragraph (a) nor (b) applies, the employee is employed in the same industry or sector of employment as the relevant part-time employee is employed in and one of the conditions referred to in subsection (3) is satisfied in respect of those employees, and references in this Part to a comparable full-time employee in relation to a part-time employee shall be construed accordingly.

(3) The following are the conditions mentioned in subsection (2)—

(a)   both of the employees concerned perform the same work under the same or similar conditions or each is interchangeable with the other in relation to the work,

(b)   the work performed by one of the employees concerned is of the same or a similar nature to that performed by the other and any differences between the work performed or the conditions under which it is performed by each, either are of small importance in relation to the work as a whole or occur with such irregularity as not to be significant, and

(c)   the work performed by the relevant part-time employee is equal or greater in value to the work performed by the other employee concerned, having regard to such matters as skill, physical or mental requirements, responsibility and working conditions.

---

[263] No. 45/2001, s. 7 (Interpretation).

Note
The Irish definition is far more detailed than the European provisions where the comparator and the definition of "normal working hours" are concerned. It is clear that such an elaborate provision, though rather complex, offers much clarity in respect of the way the notion of "part-time work" will be interpreted by employers and courts.

A definition which clearly deviates from the ILO standards and the Part-Time Work Directive can be found in the UK:

The Part-Time Workers (Prevention of Less Favourable   **1.GB.106.**
Treatment) Regulations 2000[264]

(1) A worker is a full-time worker for the purpose of these Regulations if he is paid wholly or in part by reference to the time he works and, having regard to the custom and practice of the employer in relation to workers employed by the worker's employer under the same type of contract, is identifiable as a full-time worker.
(2) A worker is a part-time worker for the purpose of these Regulations if he is paid wholly or in part by reference to the time he works and, having regard to the custom and practice of the employer in relation to workers employed by the worker's employer under the same type of contract, is not identifiable as a full-time worker.
(3) For the purposes of paragraphs (1) (2) and (4), the following shall be regarded as being employed under different types of contract—

    (a)   employees employed under a contract that is not a contract of apprenticeship;
    (b)   employees employed under a contract of apprenticeship;
    (c)   workers who are not employees;
    (d)   any other description of worker that it is reasonable for the employer to treat differently from other workers on the ground that workers of that description have a different type of contract.

(4) A full-time worker is a comparable full-time worker in relation to a part-time worker if, at the time when the treatment that is alleged to be less favourable to the part-time worker takes place—

    (a)   both workers are—
        (i)   employed by the same employer under the same type of contract, and
        (ii) engaged in the same or broadly similar work having regard, where relevant, to whether they have a similar level of qualification, skills and experience; and
    (b)   the full-time worker works or is based at the same establishment as the part-time worker or, where there is no full-time worker working or based at that establishment who satisfies the requirements of sub-paragraph (a), works or is based at a different establishment and satisfies those requirements.

---

[264] As amended by the Part-time Workers (Prevention of Less Favourable Treatment) Regulations 2000 (Amendment) Regulations 2002, SI 2002/2035, Reg. 2.

Note

This provision makes reference to the "custom and practice of the employer" to define when a worker can be considered to work full-time or part-time. In addition, the UK definition specifies a variety of possible employment contracts to which the regulations apply. Not mentioned in the excerpt are a number of additional provisions which relate to workers becoming part-time and workers returning part-time after absence. The system of legislative definitions thus created has been strongly criticised in the UK since it has led to the exclusion of many part-time workers from the protection offered by the Directive.[265] A House of Lords decision of 2006, however, states that the regulations have to be interpreted broadly rather than narrowly, which suggests that more part-time workers will be covered in the future.[266]

In France, until 2001, protective employment legislation covered only discrimination based on working hours at least one fifth less than the statutory working hours or the working hours determined by agreement for the industry or enterprise.[267] In 2000, the relevant provision of the *Code du travail* was amended by the so-called *Loi Aubry II*:

French Labour Code (Code du travail)[268]   **1.FR.107.**

Article L.212-4-2

Workers are deemed to be part-time if the duration of their work is less than:

— the statutory hours of work or, if such hours are less than the statutory hours, the hours of work determined by agreement for the industry or enterprise or the hours of work applicable in the plant;
— the monthly hours of work ensuing from the application, over that period, of the statutory hours of work or, if these are less, the hours of work determined by agreement for the industry or enterprise or the hours of work applicable in the plant;
— the annual hours of work ensuing from the application, over that period, of the statutory hours of work, i.e. 1600 hours or, if these are less, the hours of work determined by agreement for the industry or enterprise or the hours of work applicable in the plant.

Note

This new definition has clearly brought the French legislation more in line with the European and ILO definitions.[269]

---

[265] See Clauwaert, above n. 259, 33.
[266] *Matthews and others* v. *Kent and Medway Towns Fire Authority and others* [2006] 2 All ER 171.
[267] Art. L.212-4-2 of the French Labour Code (*Code du travail*). See a Clauwaert, above n. 259, 30–1.
[268] As amended by the Loi Aubry II, Loi 2000–37 relative à la réduction négociée du temps de travail (1) of 19 January 2000, JO, 20 January 2000, 975.
[269] A similar definition may be found in Italy; Clauwaert, above n. 259, 31.

Finally, an interesting deviation from the ILO and the European definition can be found in the Dutch Act on Equal Treatment based on Working Hours of 1996, which entered into force before the Part-time Work Directive was adopted:

Dutch Act on Equal Treatment based on   **1.NL.108.**
Working Hours of 1996[270]

It is forbidden to discriminate on the grounds of a difference in working hours, in the conditions under which a contract of employment is entered into, continued or terminated, or in the conditions under which an appointment is made, extended or terminated, unless such unequal treatment is objectively justified . . .

Note
Neither the Dutch Working Hours Act nor its legislative history provide for a definition of the ground of working hours. It is clear, however, that the Act is based on a symmetrical approach, protecting full-time workers as much as part-time workers.[271] For that reason, the relevant comparator is not a full-time employee, but an employee with different working hours. This means that the choice of the comparator depends on the concrete circumstances of the case and the applicable provisions of collective labour agreements.[272] Thus, where necessary or suitable, part-time workers may be compared with other part-time workers to find out if there was a case of unequal treatment based on working hours.[273]

Thus, the various definitions discussed in this subsection show differences both with respect to the precision with which they are formulated and the level of protection they secure: where the Dutch definition even protects full-time workers against discrimination, the scope of protection offered by the UK definition would seem to be much more limited in character. Presently there does not seem to be any real sign of uniformity or convergence in this context, regardless of the definitions provided by the Part-time Work Directive and ILO Convention No. 175.

FIXED-TERM CONTRACTS

Very little information is available on the implementation of the Fixed Term Work Directive in the Member States. As with the Part-time Work Directive, most states have made the choice to supplement or amend their employment legislation instead

---

[270] Staatsblad (Official Gazette) 1996, 391, Art. III(1).
[271] The Netherlands is not unique in this respect; a symmetrical approach can also be found in the Polish Labour Code (Art. 183a).
[272] See S. Burri, *Tijd delen. Deeltijd, gelijkheid en gender in Europees- en nationaalrechtelijk perspectief* (Deventer, Kluwer, 2002) 195.
[273] See Clauwaert, above n. 259, 53.

159

of adopting or amending non-discrimination legislation. Usually, the same definition seems to be used as is contained in the Framework Agreement on fixed-term work, although there are some variations. Ogura has shown, for example, that the term "fixed-term work" means in some countries that the work is temporary in character, where in other states the term is used to refer to a ceiling on the duration of a contract or the length or frequency of contract renewal.[274]

The Netherlands and Poland have included the ground of duration of employment contracts in their equal treatment legislation, placing the ground of fixed-term work on the same level as other grounds discussed in this chapter.[275] The Dutch legislation even provides for the possibility to bring cases of unequal treatment before the Equal Treatment Commission.

The relevant provisions are formulated as follows:

Dutch Act on Equal Treatment   **1.NL.109.**
based on Temporary and Permanent Contracts of 2002[276]

1. Employers may not discriminate between employees in the terms and conditions of employment on the basis of the permanent or temporary nature of the contract of employment, unless such discrimination is objectively justified . . .

4. The provisions of paragraphs 1 to 4 shall not apply to temporary agency work . . .

Polish Labour Code[277]   **1.PL.110.**

The principle of equal treatment of employees shall be applied to the initiation and termination of the employment relationship, employment terms as well as promotion and access to vocational training, irrespective of . . . whether employment is for a specified or an unspecified period of time . . .

Note
Both provisions disclose a symmetric approach, discrimination against workers with a permanent contract being prohibited as strongly as discrimination against workers with fixed-term contracts. The definitions thereby differ from the one contained in the

---

[274] Ogura, above n. 254, 14.

[275] For a comparable (but asymmetric) approach, see Hungarian Act on Equal Treatment and Equal Opportunities of 2003, s. 8(r), which prohibits discrimination of persons based on "definite term or part time nature of their employment contract".

[276] Staatsblad (Official Gazette) 2002, 560, cl. 1 (adding a new Art. 649 to the Dutch Civil Code).

[277] Consolidated text of 23 December 1997 (Dz.U. 1998, No. 21, Item 94), Wording of 2005-2-8, Art. 183a.

Fixed-term Work Directive, which focuses on discrimination against the fixed-term contract and is clearly asymmetric in character.[278]

Further information with respect to the Dutch definition of fixed-term contracts is given in the Explanatory Memorandum to the Act:

Dutch Explanatory Memorandum to the Act on Equal   **1.NL.111.**
Treatment based on Temporary and Permanent Contracts of 2002[279]

. . . This wording [the definition contained in the Framework Agreement] with regard to the termination of the contract of employment for a specified period complies with the criteria applicable in Dutch law concerning fixed-term contracts of employment. For example, according to article 667, book 7, Civil Code, a contract of employment ends *de jure* when the period fixed by the agreement, the law or custom has expired. The period for which a contract of employment has been concluded can therefore be precisely stated. The period can also be made dependent on completing a particular job or another event (employee's recovery from an illness). If the final date is not fixed by the calendar, it must be objectively determinable. If that is not the case, there is no question of a contract of employment for a specified period.

The description of the notion of 'comparable employee in permanent employment' requires no further implementation. Mention is made in Clause 3 (2) in this connection of an employee with a contract of employment or a working relationship for an indeterminate period in the same establishment that undertakes the same or similar work or who undertakes the same or similar duties, with qualifications/skills being taken into account. When considering whether there is equal treatment, a comparable employee with a contract of employment for an unlimited period must be the criterion.

Note
It is clear that the Dutch definition contained in the non-discrimination legislation is based on the regular definition of fixed-term and permanent contracts as are in the Dutch Civil Code. This approach may well be followed in other Member States.

1.3.11.B.   SUSPECTNESS

Compared to such grounds as race, gender and religion, the grounds of part-time work and fixed-term contract can hardly be considered to be "suspect". The prohibitions on less favourable treatment of part-time workers and workers with fixed-term contracts is not inspired by the need to combat deeply-rooted stereotypes and prejudice, nor is it meant to remove historical stigma against vulnerable minority groups. Instead, the Part-time and Fixed-term Work Directives and their national

---

[278] Long-term or permanent employment contracts are considered the "typical" form of employment contract in most industrialized countries; Ogura, above n. 254, 9–10.
[279] Kamerstukken II 2000/01, 27 661, No. 3, at 3.

implementation legislation seem to be inspired mainly by economic and social policy considerations, such as the need to create jobs and the desire to enable workers to combine work and caring responsibilities.[280] Although such considerations are evidently of great importance, they show that unequal treatment based on these grounds cannot be regarded as inherently invidious and suspect, but rather as economically and socially undesirable.

The social policy considerations underlying the Agreements make clear, however, that the situation is more complicated than might appear at first sight. Far more women than men have part-time positions[281] and part-time employment appears to be concentrated at the end (and, to a lesser extent, the beginning) of people's working lives.[282] This means that direct unequal treatment of part-time workers may easily result in indirect discrimination against women and elderly workers. Indeed, some have argued that national efforts to introduce specific legislation to combat discrimination based on part-time work is really an endeavour to combat gender discrimination in the workplace.[283] As gender is obviously a suspect ground, it might be expected that unfavourable treatment of part-time workers, resulting in indirect discrimination against women, will for that reason be subjected to relatively strict scrutiny by the courts. To some degree, this may also be true for fixed-term contracts in relation to the ground of age. As is exemplified by the case of *Mangold*,[284] younger or elderly workers may have fixed-term contracts more frequently than other age groups, and may be subjected to unfavourable treatment more often. In many of these cases it may be possible to find an indirect discrimination based on age, which is arguably a more suspect ground of discrimination and justifies more intensive judicial review.

[280] See S. Sciarra, "New discourses in labour law: part-time work and the paradigm of flexibility" in S. Sciarra et al. (eds.), *Employment Policy and the Regulation of Part-Time Work in the European Union. A Comparative Analysis* (Cambridge, Cambridge University Press, 2004) 22 and A. Jacobs and M. Schmidt, "The Right to Part-time Work: The Netherlands and Germany compared" (2001) 17 *IJCLLIR* 372.

[281] A. van Bastelaer et al., *The Definition of Part-Time Work for the Purpose of International Comparisons*, Labour Market and Social Policy Occasional Papers No. 22 (Paris, OECD, 1997) 9 and, more recently, Ogura, above n. 254, 21.

[282] A. Corral and I. Isusi, *Part-time Work in Europe*, European Foundation for the Improvement of Living and Working Conditions (2004) 4.

[283] A. Jacobs and M. Schmidt, "The Right to Part-time Work: The Netherlands and Germany Compared" (2001) 17 *IJCLLIR* 372.

[284] See above **1.EC.101.**

1.4. DISCRIMINATION ON GROUNDS OF ASSUMED CHARACTERISTICS AND DISCRIMINATION BY ASSOCIATION

1.4.1. DISCRIMINATION ON GROUNDS OF ASSUMED CHARACTERISTICS

In some situations it is clear that a difference in treatment is not so much based on a particular personal characteristic, such as race, gender or religion, but on *assumptions* relating to that characteristic. It is well conceivable, for example, that an employer takes a negative employment decision because he *thinks* that a certain employee is chronically ill and therefore unable to perform his job responsibilities to his satisfaction, or a barman refuses entrance to a young person whom he perceives as belonging to an ethnic minority. An important question is if such cases of unequal treatment are covered by non-discrimination legislation. Mostly this question is answered in the affirmative, as non-discrimination is primarily meant to protect individuals against discrimination. Whether such discrimination is based on real characteristics or on perception is irrelevant.

The Employment and Racial Equality Directives do not contain express references to discrimination on grounds of assumed characteristics. On the other hand, it does not transpire from their content that discrimination by assumption is excluded from its scope. Given the importance of the inclusion of discrimination by assumption, and given the fact that important international instruments seem to offer protection against such discrimination, it must be presumed that both the Employment Equality Directive and the Racial Equality Directive protect individuals against discrimination based on assumed characteristics.

International support for such a wide formulation of the prohibition of discrimination may firstly be found in the interpretation of Article 14 ECHR by the ECtHR:

ECtHR, 13 December 2005   **1.CoE.112.**[*]
Timishev v. *Russia*

FREEDOM OF MOVEMENT OF CHECHENS

Timishev

Facts: Timishev, a Chechen lawyer, lives as a forced migrant in Nalchik, in the Kabardino-Balkaria Republic of the Russian Federation. In 1999, the applicant and his driver travelled by car from the Ingushetia Republic to Nalchik. Their car was stopped at the checkpoint and officers of the Inspectorate for Road Safety refused him entry. The refusal appeared to be based on an oral instruction from the Ministry of the Interior of Kabardino-Balkaria not to admit persons of Chechen ethnic origin.

---

[*] See above **1.CoE.1.** and **1.CoE.7.**

Timishev had to turn round and make a detour of 300 kilometres to reach Nalchik through a different checkpoint.

Held: The Court decided that the refusal of entry amounted to a violation of the prohibition of discrimination (Article 14 ECHR), taken in conjunction with the right to liberty of movement (Article 2 of Protocol No. 4).

Judgment: "54 . . . the Court notes that the Kabardino-Balkarian senior police officer ordered traffic police officers not to admit 'Chechens'. As, in the Government's submission, a person's ethnic origin is not listed anywhere in Russian identity documents, the order barred the passage not only of any person who actually was of Chechen ethnicity, but also of those *who were merely perceived as belonging to that ethnic group* . . . In the Court's view, this represented a clear inequality of treatment in the enjoyment of the right to liberty of movement on account of one's ethnic origin.

    56 . . . Discrimination on account of one's *actual or perceived* ethnicity is a form of racial discrimination . . . [emphasis added]."

Note

It is clear from this case that Article 14 prohibits not only discrimination based on real characteristics, but also discrimination based on *perceived* characteristics, i.e. discrimination by assumption. As a result, even persons who are not really a member of a certain group can be covered by the non-discrimination legislation if they are regarded by others as belonging to that group.

On the national level, a few Member States have expressly prohibited discrimination based on assumption, either by mentioning the concept in the legislative text or by referring to it in legislative history or case-law:

Explanatory Notes to the Austrian   **1.AT.113.**
Equal Treatment Act[285]

The principle of equal treatment is applicable irrespective of the fact whether the reasons for the discrimination (e.g. race or ethnic origin) are factually given or only assumed.

Hungarian Act CXXV. of 2003 on equal treatment and on   **1.HU.114.**
fostering equal opportunities[286]

A provision shall qualify as direct discrimination if it results in a less favourable treatment for a person or group than for another person or group in a comparable position, because of their actual or assumed a) gender; b) racial origin; c) colour of skin; d) nationality; e) belonging to national or ethnic minority; f) mother tongue; g) disability; h) health condition; i) religious or non-confessional conviction; j) political or other opinion; k) family status; l) motherhood

---

[285] See Explanatory Notes, 307 der Beilagen XXII.GP, Regierungsvorlage, Materialien, at 15.
[286] 2003. évi CXXV. törvény az egyenlő bánásmódról és az esélyegyenlőség előmozdításáról, s. 8.

(pregnancy), fatherhood; m) sexual orientation; n) sexual identity; o) age; p) social origin; q) property status; r) definite term or part-time nature of their employment contract; s) association with an interest representing organisation; t) other conditions, properties or characteristics (hereinafter together: characteristics).

Irish Equal Status Act 2000, as amended by the **1.IE.115.**
Equality Act 2004[287]

(1) For the purposes of this Act and without prejudice to its provisions relating to discrimination occurring in particular circumstances discrimination shall be taken to occur where—

(a) a person is treated less favourably than another person is, has been or would be treated in a comparable situation on any of the grounds specified in subsection (2) (in this Act referred to as the 'discriminatory grounds') which—
(i) exists,
(ii) existed but no longer exists,
(iii) may exist in the future, or
(iv) is imputed to the person concerned . . .

Next to these legislative examples, which all refer to assumed or imputed characteristics, there are some examples of cases in which the national courts have held that discrimination by assumption is prohibited. The following excerpt may serve as an illustration:

House of Lords, 24 March 1983[288] **1.GB.116.***
Mandla v. Dowell Lee

SIKHS AS AN ETHNIC GROUP

Mandla

Facts: The headmaster of a private school refused to admit as a pupil to the school a boy who was an orthodox Sikh (and wore long hair under a turban), unless he removed the turban and cut his hair. The headmaster's reasons for his refusal were that the wearing of a turban, being a manifestation of the boy's ethnic origins, would accentuate religious and social distinctions in the school which, being a multiracial school based on the Christian faith, the headmaster desired to minimise.

Held: The Sikhs are a group defined by reference to "ethnic origins" for the purpose of the Race Relations Act 1976 ("the 1976 Act"); the "no turban"rule is not "justifiable" within the meaning of the 1976 Act.

---

[287] No. 8/2000, as amended by No. 24/2000, s. 6.
[288] [1983] IRLR 209.
* See above **1.GB.10.**

Judgment: LORD FRASER OF TULLYBELTON: ". . .In my opinion, it is possible for a person to fall into a particular racial group either by birth or by adherence, and it makes no difference, so far as the Act of 1976 is concerned, by which route he finds his way into the group . . . A person may treat another relatively unfavourably 'on racial grounds' because he regards that other as being of a particular race, or belonging to a particular racial group, even if his belief is, from a scientific point of view, completely erroneous . . ."

Note
It follows from this case that the fact that the individual discriminated against really belongs to a certain group is irrelevant to the determination if such discrimination is covered by the non-discrimination legislation. It suffices to establish that the person who is responsible for the difference in treatment believes that the victim is a member of a protected group.

In other states, discrimination by assumption is expressly protected only with respect to specific grounds, such as race[289] and, in particular, disability.[290] An example of application of such a specific provision may be found in the following opinion of the Dutch Equal Treatment Commission:

Equal Treatment Commission (Commissie Gelijke Behandeling) **1.NL.117.**
Opinion 2004-67

DISCRIMINATION BASED ON ASSUMED DISABILITY

Heart attack

Facts: The applicant was working as a seaman on a transport vessel on the basis of a temporary employment contract. In June 2003, he suffered a heart attack, which made him unfit to work for two months. After this, he started working again, but he received a letter in December 2003 announcing that his temporary employment contract would not be extended, as this would be irresponsible considering his recent medical past.

---

[289] See, e.g. Art. 225-I of the French Penal Code (*Code pénal*) and Art. L. 122–45 of the French Labour Code (*Code du travail*). For a comparable Luxembourg example see F. Moyse, "Report on Measures to Combat Discrimination: Directive 2000/43/EC and 2000/78/EC. Country Report Luxembourg" (European Commission, December 2004) 10, available on the website of Directorate-General for Employment, Social Affairs and Equal Opportunities.

[290] See, e.g. the Dutch Act on Equal Treatment on the Grounds of Disability or Chronic Illness (2003), Art. 1 (b): "Direct unequal treatment: unequal treatment between people on the grounds of *a real or supposed* disability or chronic illness." Other examples may be found in the Maltese Equal Opportunities (Persons with Disabilities) Act 2000, Art. 3(1)(b); see further T. Ellul, "Report on Measures to Combat Discrimination: Directive 2000/43/EC and 2000/78/EC. Country Report Malta" (European Commission, 2005) 6, available on the website of Directorate-General for Employment, Social Affairs and Equal Opportunities and the Slovakian Anti-Discrimination Act (Section 6(3)(d)); see further Z. Dlugosova, "Report on Measures to Combat Discrimination: Directive 2000/43/EC and 2000/78/EC. Country Report Slovakia" (European Commission, 2004/2005) 13–14, available on the website of Directorate-General for Employment, Social Affairs and Equal Opportunities.

Held: The case discloses an instance of direct discrimination which cannot be justified by reasons of health or security and which is, accordingly, in contravention of the Act on Equal Treatment on Grounds of Disability and Chronic Illness.

Opinion: "5.4 . . . [T]he concept of discrimination is not aimed only at an actual handicap or chronic illness but also at an assumed handicap or chronic illness. The concept of assumed handicap or chronic illness is included in the Act on Equal Treatment on Grounds of Disability and Chronic Illness in order to also offer protection against discrimination in cases where it is incorrectly assumed that a person suffers from a handicap or chronic illness. Examples are an ex-cancer patient who is regarded as chronically ill . . .

This implies that recourse can also be had to the ban on discrimination based on a handicap or chronic illness if a person is incorrectly (still) regarded as a patient on account of a sickness or accident in the past. Since the applicant has argued that he has been unable to obtain any new employment on account of his (recent) medical past, more especially a heart attack, he can have recourse to the grounds of discrimination for handicap or chronic illness protected under the Act on Equal Treatment on Grounds of Disability and Chronic Illness."

Notes

(1) It is clear from this opinion that the concept of assumed illness or disability widens the definition of "disability and chronic illness" to a significant degree. As explained in section 1.3.9.A, the Dutch concept of chronic illness will normally only come into play if someone is ill for an undetermined or very long period. If regard is paid to appearances, however, even a non-chronic illness may trigger the application of the non-discrimination legislation, as long as it can be shown that the person responsible for the difference in treatment *regards* the illness as constantly affecting or endangering the victim's health.

(2) By providing this definition, the Dutch legislator and the Equal Treatment Commission have made clear that it is really the discrimination itself that is considered problematic, not so much the ground on which it is based. The effectiveness of the non-discrimination legislation is thereby increased considerably.

An important question with respect to legislation in which the issue of discrimination by assumption is only mentioned in relation to specific grounds is if this should be read so as to exclude the possibility of such a construction with respect to other grounds. Although there is little information available on this issue, it is clear that no such negative inference can be made in the Netherlands. The case-law of the Equal Treatment Commission has shown that assumptions about other grounds than disability may also give rise to a case of discrimination that is covered by the Dutch equal treatment legislation, even if the Equal Treatment Act does not contain an express provision relating to discrimination by assumption. An example of the Dutch approach may be found in the following excerpt:

Equal Treatment Commission (Commissie Gelijke Behandeling) **1.NL.118.**
Opinion 2002-84

ASCRIBED POLITICAL CONVICTION

Discussion about terrorist attacks

Facts: On 11 September 2001, the applicant, who is of Iranian origin, was working as a temporary employee for the defendant party. On that day she had a politically charged discussion with one of her colleagues about the terrorist attacks in the US. When her colleague asked her if she thought Osama Bin Laden was responsible for the attacks, she said that she was not certain, but did not think so: although it had been on the news that the US had proof of Bin Laden's involvement, no one had yet seen this proof. The applicant said that she therefore had a neutral opinion. Three days after the incident, the applicant's temporary contract was terminated. Her colleague had told her group leader that she had found the discussion to be "shocking" and that it had caused her feelings of fear and intimidation. Because the employment contract of the applicant was temporary and the contract of her colleague was permanent, the only solution for the disturbed relations between the two colleagues was to end the applicant's contract.

Held: As the employer has not carefully investigated the complaints of the colleague relating to the political discussion she had had with the applicant, the suspicion of direct discrimination based on political opinion has not been sufficiently rebutted. There has thus been a violation of the Equal Treatment Act by the employer.

Opinion: "5.6 The Commission considers that terrorist attacks are not infrequently based on political motives or convictions that may be included under the concept of 'political opinion' within the meaning of Article 1, preamble and (b) of the Equal Treatment Act. A person's political attitude may, it is said, be expressed in discussions regarding such attacks. There is no doubt that the witness [the applicant's colleague] assumed that the applicant wished to protect the Muslims and that the applicant consequently placed the blame for the attacks on America and not on Bin Laden. Whether or not the applicant actually held this conviction, the Commission feels that in the present case a political opinion within the meaning of the AWGB is under discussion. In the Commission's opinion, this ground also includes the ascribing of a political conviction . . ."

Note

It transpires from this that the Dutch Equal Treatment Commission did not deem it relevant if the individual really held a certain political view, or if it was rather imputed to her by her colleague: in both cases, a case of discrimination based on political opinion could be made out.

In some Member States, the issue of discrimination on grounds of assumed characteristics is still unresolved. Future case-law will have to provide clarity about the extent to which imputed characteristics can be considered to constitute an unlawful basis for unequal treatment. In general, however, it may be expected that widely formulated non-discrimination provisions which generally prohibit discrimination on the basis of a certain ground (i.e. "discrimination on the basis of race, gender, etc.", instead of "discrimination on the basis of *his* or *her* race, gender, etc."), will easily allow for the inclusion of discrimination based on assumed characteristics.[291]

---

[291] T. Makkonen, "Discrimination Based on Religion and Belief. Finland", Executive Summary (European Commission, 2004) 9, available on the website of Directorate-General for Employment, Social Affairs and Equal Opportunities.

1.4.2.   DISCRIMINATION BY ASSOCIATION

Another important concept is discrimination by association, which is a concept that can be interpreted in two different ways. In the first place, it may be understood as to refer to associations of individuals with certain characteristics which are treated unfavourably if compared to other associations. Understood in that way, the concept is closely related to the classic freedom of association.[292] Another, more common reading of the notion is that it relates to the situation where someone is discriminated against not so much because of his or her own characteristics, but because of his or her relations with someone else. An example is that of a non-Roma person who is refused entry to a bar because he is together with a number of people from the Roma community.

The vast majority of Member States have not yet provided a clear answer to the question if discrimination by association is covered by non-discrimination legislation, nor does such an answer clearly follow from the Article 13 Directives. A rare example is Ireland, where the concept is explicitly mentioned in the Equal Status Act 2000 (as amended by the Equality Act 2004):

> "(1) For the purposes of this Act and without prejudice to its provisions relating to discrimination occur-ring in particular circumstances discrimination shall be taken to occur where . . .
> (b) a person who is associated with another person . . .
> (i) is treated, by virtue of that association, less favourably than a person who is not so associated is, has been or would be treated in a comparable situation, and
> (ii) similar treatment of that other person on any of the discriminatory grounds would, by virtue of paragraph (a), constitute discrimination . . ."[293]

A classic example of application of this provision can be found in a decision by the Irish Equality Officer:

Equality Tribunal, 27 January 2004[294]   **1.IE.119.**
Decision DEC-S/2004/009-014, Six Complainants v. *A Public House, Dublin*

DISCRIMINATION BY ASSOCIATION

Drunk or disabled?

Facts: Mr BMcM has a disability which affects his balance, coordination and facial expressions, and causes him at times to display some traits of drunkenness. At the relevant time, Mr BMcM went to a pub in Dublin with his family to celebrate his mother's 50th birthday. They met in the car park and went to enter

---

[292] de Schutter, above n. 13, 19, available on the website of Directorate-General for Employment, Social Affairs and Equal Opportunities.

[293] No. 8/2000, as amended by No. 24/2004, s. 6.

[294] Available on the website of the Equality Tribunal of Ireland, under the heading Equal Status Decisions.

the pub, but were stopped by the doorman who said that they would not be admitted: the owner of the premises had indicated that the group might have consumed alcohol.

Held: Mr BMcM was discriminated against by the refusal on the basis of disability; the remaining five applicants were discriminated against, by association, on the disability ground in terms of the Equal Status Act 2000.

Decision: "7.3 It is quite clear from the evidence provided that the five members of the complainant group, other than Mr. BMcM were not giving any indication that they had any drink taken, and all six complainants were well presented. However, it is also clear that something indefinable about Mr. BMcM drew the attention of the doorman to him specifically, and the doorman singled out Mr. BMcM as the reason for refusing the entire group entry. This is further borne out in the emphasis placed on Mr. BMcM's demeanour and appearance by the respondent in written submissions. Given that Mr. BMcM's disability outwardly affects his facial expressions and at times causes him to stagger, I am satisfied that the visible attributes of his disability are precisely what drew attention to him. These attributes are identical to those which would give the appearance of drunkenness to any person charged with making a snap decision in the matter. The doorman stated that it is his standard practice to speak to potential clients for a short time in circumstances where he suspects that they have drink taken, in order to determine whether his suspicions are well founded. In the instant cases he made no attempt to engage any member of the group in such a conversation . . .

10.1 The complainant, Mr. BMcM was discriminated against by the respondent on the disability ground in terms of Sections 3(1)(a) and 3(2)(g), 5(1) and 4(1) of the Equal Status Act 2000. The remaining five complainants were discriminated against, by association, on the disability ground in terms of Section 3(1)(b) and 3(2)(g), 5(1) and 4(1) of the Equal Status Act 2000."

Note

There was no reason in this case to assume that the five complainants other than Mr BMcM were disabled, but it was clear that they were refused entry because of the fact that they were together with a man who was. This constituted discrimination based on disability as much as when the complainants themselves are disabled.

In other Member States, the issue of whether discrimination by association can be regarded as being based on one of the protected grounds remains generally unresolved. It is to be expected, however, that cases of discrimination by association will be dealt with in much the same manner as that adopted by the Equality Officer.

1.5. MULTIPLE DISCRIMINATION

1.5.1. INTRODUCTION

International treaties, European Directives and national legislation prohibit discrimination on the basis of a variety of personal characteristics, varying from race and age to birth and sexual orientation. However, each individual will unavoidably present a combination of these characteristics and it is thus easily imaginable that concrete cases of unequal treatment are based on a combination of grounds. A woman could be refused for a job because she wears a headscarf out of religious principle, a man could become the victim of harassment because of his ethnic origin in combination with his homosexuality, or an elderly worker with back problems might have difficulties in finding a permanent job because of the combination of age and disability. Such cases disclose examples of what is commonly called "multiple discrimination", i.e. discrimination based on more than one ground.

Within the wider category of multiple discrimination, two subcategories can be distinguished. First, it is possible that a case shows a concurrence of grounds. For example, the case may be that someone has been refused access to a pub because he belongs to the Roma community and is accompanied by a young child—in this case, the grounds of origin and family status have both influenced the negative decision. Another well-known example is that of a police department which uses both a written test in its application procedure that disproportionately affects persons of a different ethnic or national origin and a minimum height requirement that adversely affects women.[295] Such a policy would cause indirect discrimination based on both gender and race. This form of multiple discrimination is often termed "cumulative" or "additive" discrimination.[296]

Secondly, discrimination may be based on a unique combination of factors. A black woman, for example, may have been discriminated against not so much because she is a woman or because she is black, but because she is a *black woman*.[297] Similarly, specific prejudice may exist towards gays of different ethnic origin, or towards female migrants. In these cases, it will not so much be the different grounds in se that cause the discrimination as the unique combination of grounds.[298] This form of multiple discrimination is mostly referred to as "intersectional discrimination", as it is located at the intersection between the individual grounds protected by non-discrimination legislation.[299]

Although the existence of such cases of multiple discrimination is well known, present non-discrimination legislation is hardly apt to solve these issues. Generally, non-discrimination law seems to regard discrimination as a "one-issue" problem. Such instruments as the Racial Equality Directive and ICERD only offer protection against discrimination to persons of different racial or ethnic origin, while the various Gender Equality Directives and CEDAW are exclusively directed at gender-related problems. Although such specific protection against discrimination is highly desirable

---

[295] E.W. Shoben, "Compound Discrimination: The Interaction of Race and Sex in Employment Discrimination" (1980) 55 *NYULR* 793, at 794–5.

[296] See S. Hannett, "Equality at the Intersections: The Legislative and Judicial Failure to Tackle Multiple Discrimination" (2003) 23 *OJLS* 68.

[297] *Ibid.* See also above Shoben, n. 295, 796, giving the example of an oral interview in an application procedure in which black men and white women score well, but black women are disproportionally excluded. It is not then race or gender in itself that is problematic, but the interaction of both characteristics.

[298] *Cf.* e.g. *Gender and Racial Discrimination*, Report of the Expert Group Meeting, 21–24 November 2000, Zagreb.

[299] See S. Fredman, "Double Trouble: Multiple Discrimination and EU Law" [2005] *European Anti-Discrimination Law Review* Issue No. 2, at 13.

and needed, it hardly solves intersectional problems such as those experienced by black women.

In this section, we will provide a short overview of the most important problems resulting from the one-issue approach (section 1.5.2), followed by a discussion of the various ways in which these problems have been acknowledged and approached within the European states (section 1.5.3).

1.5.2.   PROBLEMS OF MULTIPLE DISCRIMINATION

DIFFERENCES IN PERSONAL AND MATERIAL SCOPE

The most important problem relating to multiple discrimination is created by the differences in personal and material scope of non-discrimination legislation. Many non-discrimination laws contain closed lists of grounds, excluding grounds such as political conviction or marital status, and relate only to certain areas (e.g. employment), to the exclusion of others (e.g. provision of services). These differences may have the effect that a case of multiple discrimination is only partly covered by legislation. In addition, it will be hard to determine if there is any legislative protection available if, for example, legislation only offers protection in the field of social services to cases of race based discrimination. This is particularly problematic in cases of intersectional discrimination, where it will be very difficult and often artificial to separate the various grounds and to classify a case as based *primarily* on one ground or the other. This may result in strange and arbitrary classifications, as exemplified by the fact that in the UK Sikhs and Jews have been held to constitute ethnic groups for the purposes of the Race Relations Act 1976, whereas Muslims and Rastafarians have not.[300] Given that such a classification has major consequences for the protection against discrimination, the search for clear line-drawing between the various grounds is highly complex.

The complexities are even more distinct if different enforcement mechanisms are provided for each of the different grounds.[301] A good example of this is Sweden, where there is an Ombudsman system which provides for different protection for gender, disability, ethnic origin and sexual orientation. The UK also had a variety of Commissions to assess cases relating to their specific field of interests and Denmark still has a Commission which has powers only in the field of race discrimination.[302] If such institutions are presented with complaints about multiple discrimination, they may only deal with one aspect of the case. Consequently, there will be no opportunity for them to grasp the full extent of the case of unequal treatment presented and deal with the complex issues of social stereotyping disclosed by such a case.

---

[300] *Ibid.*, 72 and Brown, above n. 72, 204.

[301] For a detailed overview of enforcement bodies, see below, G. Moon, Chapter Eight: Enforcement Bodies.

[302] See further ch. 8 below.

An additional difficulty arises from the differences in exemptions that are available with respect to the various grounds of discrimination. It may be difficult to decide under the Employment Equality Directive if a case of discrimination against an elderly disabled worker must be considered under the more general exemption for age, or the much more narrowly defined exemption for disability. In cases of cumulative discrimination, this may be solved by considering both aspects separately, deciding the cases of disability discrimination and age discrimination on their own merits. In intersectional discrimination cases, where the disadvantage suffered is based on a close combination of grounds, this may be more difficult to do. It is well recognised that the disadvantage suffered by common victims of intersectional discrimination, such as black women, is of a different character than discrimination against black men or white women.[303] In drafting equal treatment legislation, as well as in applying it, it is important to recognise and acknowledge such particularities.

ESTABLISHING (INDIRECT) DISCRIMINATION: WHO IS THE COMPARATOR?

Multiple discrimination may also cause particular problems in establishing a case of indirect discrimination. As Hannett has shown, a job requirement may, for instance, not disproportionately affect either Asian men or white women, but it may have a clearly adverse impact on Asian women:

> "In a claim for indirect race discrimination, the comparison must be made between the proportion of Asians who can comply, compared with the proportion of non-Asians who can comply. Under this test, it may be arguable that *as an Asian* [the woman in question] has not been indirectly discriminated against as she has suffered insufficient disproportionate effect: Asian men, and some Asian women, could comply with the condition. Similarly, in a claim for indirect sex discrimination, the comparison must be made between the proportion of women who can comply, compared with the proportion of men who can comply. Again, under this test, it is at least arguable that as a woman she has not been indirectly discriminated against, as the majority of women could comply. But as *an Asian woman*, the requirement or condition disproportionately impacts upon her."[304]

If such a possible impact on groups sharing multiple characteristics is not accepted, problematic cases of societal discrimination may escape judicial scrutiny.

The problem of establishing discrimination in multiple discrimination cases is thus closely related to the choice of a relevant comparator. In cases of unequal treatment based on a single ground, this is relatively easy—a female employee complaining about unfavourable employment conditions may be compared to a male employee, or a black person complaining about unequal treatment in respect of social advantages may be compared to a white person.[305] In situations of multiple discrimination the

---

[303] Fredman, above n. 299.

[304] Hannett, above n. 296, 73 (emphasis in the original).

[305] Although many problems exist here as well; see further on this below, ch. 2, section 2.3.1.

situation is far more complex, as is demonstrated by the example of the Asian woman.[306] It might seem clear that it is not sufficient to compare her to women or Asian persons alone, but to whom should she be compared instead? Possible comparators might be white women or Asian men, or both, but it is difficult to decide which of these comparators is the most appropriate.[307] Moreover, the establishment of a prima facie case of indirect discrimination will be even further complicated by the lack of availability of statistical information on the complex and highly specific comparator group—though a state may collect information with respect to women or people of different ethnic origin, it will not always be easy to gather relevant and useable information with respect to women of a specific ethnic origin.[308]

1.5.3. PRACTICAL SOLUTIONS TO CASES OF MULTIPLE DISCRIMINATION

All of these problems are well-known by now. The existence of multiple discrimination and the related social problems are even expressly acknowledged in the preamble to the Employment Equality Directive: [309]

"3. In implementing the principle of equal treatment, the Community should, in accordance with Article 3(2) of the EC Treaty, aim to eliminate inequalities, and to promote equality between men and women, especially since women are often the victims of multiple discrimination."

Such recognition is also visible on the international level, as is exemplified by the following two excerpts:

Fourth World Congress on Women,   **1.UN.120.**
Beijing Declaration and Platform for Action[310]

We are determined to: . . .

32. Intensify efforts to ensure equal enjoyment of all human rights and fundamental freedoms for all women and girls who face multiple barriers to their empowerment and advancement because of such factors as their race, age, language, ethnicity, culture, religion, or disability, or because they are indigenous people . . .

---

[306] For a concrete example, see UK Court of Appeal, 30 July 2004, *Bahl* v. *The Law Society* [2004] EWCA Civ 1070 in reaction to UK Employment Appeal Tribunal, 31 July 2003 [2003] UKEAT 1056 01 3107.

[307] An additional complexity here may be that not all states accept hypothetical comparators, or even stipulate which comparators should be chosen in specific cases. On this see Hannett, above n. 296, 83.

[308] See Fredman, above n. 299, 14, referring to an Irish study which demonstrates that there is no statistical information available about ethnic minority people with disabilities, even though it is clear that this group suffers from complex forms of discrimination.

[309] An identical recital is contained in the Racial Equality Directive (para. 14).

[310] 15 September 1995, A/CONF.177/20 (1995) and A/CONF.177/20/Add. 1 (1995).

Committee on the Elimination of Racial Discrimination,   **1.UN.121.**
General Recommendation No. 25: Gender related dimensions of
racial discrimination[311]

1. The Committee notes that racial discrimination does not always affect women and men equally or in the same way. There are circumstances in which racial discrimination only or primarily affects women, or affects women in a different way, or to a different degree than men. Such racial discrimination will often escape detection if there is no explicit recognition or acknowledgement of the different life experiences of women and men, in areas of both public and private law.

   . . .

3. Recognizing that some forms of racial discrimination have a unique and specific impact on women, the Committee will endeavour in its work to take into account gender factors or issues which may be interlinked with racial discrimination. The Committee believes that its practices in this regard would benefit from developing, in conjunction with the States parties, a more systematic and consistent approach to evaluating and monitoring racial discrimination against women, as well as the disadvantages, obstacles and difficulties women face in the full exercise and enjoyment of their civil, political, economic, social and cultural rights on grounds of race, colour, descent, or national or ethnic origin.

4. Accordingly, the Committee, when examining forms of racial discrimination, intends to enhance its efforts to integrate gender perspectives, incorporate gender analysis, and encourage the use of gender-inclusive language in its sessional working methods, including its review of reports submitted by States parties, concluding observations, early warning mechanisms and urgent action procedures, and general recommendations.

Note
Such international and European acknowledgement of the gender and racial aspects of multiple discrimination is extremely important, just like the policy efforts made by the ICERD Committee. Nevertheless, the recognition of the problem has only rarely been followed by the adoption of adequate legal solutions. In legal scholarship it has been stressed that multiple discrimination could effectively be dealt with by developing a harmonised model of equal treatment legislation, featuring a comparable scope of protection and similar exemptions for all grounds and providing sufficient flexibility as regards the choice of a comparator.[312] Such an approach is presently visible in the widely formulated non-discrimination provisions in fundamental rights instruments such as the European Convention on Human Rights. Article 14 of the Convention contains neither a closed list of grounds nor an elaborate system of carefully drafted exception clauses. As a result, it is not necessary under Article 14 to show that a difference in treatment is based on a specific ground and the ECtHR is able to decide each case on its own merits, not being bound by the

---

[311] 20 March 2000, 56th session; available on the website of the Committee on the Elimination of Racial Discrimination.
[312] S. Fredman, *Discrimination Law* (Oxford, Oxford University Press, 2002) 74–5 and Fredman, above n. 299, 17.

limitations of exception clauses. Indeed, it is clear from the ECtHR's case-law that there is no need to reduce a complex case of unequal treatment to one of the grounds expressly mentioned in the Convention:

ECtHR, 28 November 1984[313]   **1.CoE.122.**
Rasmussen v. *Denmark*

INTERSECTIONAL DISCRIMINATION UNDER THE ECHR

Rasmussen

Facts: Mr Rasmussen was married in 1966. During the marriage, two children were born, a boy and a girl. Mr Rasmussen had reason to suspect, even before the birth of the girl in 1971, that another man might be the father; however, in order to save the marriage, he took no steps to have his paternity determined. In 1973, he and his wife applied for and obtained a separation; in 1975, they obtained a divorce. In 1976, Mr Rasmussen finally sought formal leave to institute proceedings to determine the paternity of the girl, previously still having nurtured hopes of preserving the marriage. He was refused such leave for the reason that he had not brought the action within the time limits provided for and there was no cause to grant him an exemption. According to the relevant legislative provision, the time limit to contest paternity only applied to the husband, not to the mother of the child—with respect to women, the choice was made to leave the issue to be decided by the courts.

Held: The competent authorities were entitled to think that, as regards the husband, the aim sought to be realised would be most satisfactorily achieved by the enactment of a statutory rule, whereas as regards the mother it was sufficient to leave the matter to be decided by the courts on a case-by-case basis. The difference of treatment complained of was not discriminatory within the meaning of Article 14.

Judgment: "34. For the purposes of Article 14, the Court . . .finds that there was a difference of treatment as between Mr. Rasmussen and his former wife as regards the possibility of instituting proceedings to contest the former's paternity. There is no call to determine on what ground this difference was based, the list of grounds appearing in Article 14 not being exhaustive."

Notes

(1) In this case it would have been possible to classify the difference in treatment as based on gender, but the Court saw no need to do so. Instead, it focused on the actual difference in treatment between the time limit applying to the husband and that applying to the wife.

(2) Such an approach would seem to solve the issue of intersectional discrimination quite effectively, as a complainant may then allege a case of discrimination based on his being a homosexual black man or an Islamic woman, or any other combination of characteristics. It must be recalled, however, that even with such open lists it may be important to show that a distinction is actually based on a certain ground. It has been shown in this chapter that the ECtHR treats certain grounds of discrimination as suspect, requiring "very weighty reasons" as a justification for a difference of treatment based on such a ground. Thus the ground chosen is still

---

[313] Series A, Vol. 87.

important for the way in which a case is decided, even in open systems of non-discrimination law. Indeed, it is far from certain if the same outcome would have been reached in the case of *Rasmussen* if the Court had accepted that the distinction was actually gender based and applied a "very weighty reasons" test.

(3) For many cases of multiple discrimination this does not seem to pose a real problem, however, as it may be assumed that such cases usually concern at least one suspect personal characteristic (or even more, as in the example of discrimination against a black woman), which may determine the intensity of judicial review. The creation of open lists of grounds, combined with a comparable material scope and comparable exception clauses, thus clearly constitutes an effective remedy to victims of multiple discrimination.

The various European Equality Directives show, however, that streamlining is not an easy task if an elaborate legislative framework is in place which contains detailed provisions and exemptions which are closely fitted to the covered grounds of discrimination. Indeed, it is fully reasonable that there are different possibilities of justification for the various grounds, as each exemption will be the result of a careful weighing of interests and each of the covered grounds is different in character and suspectness. It is also understandable that the EU has adopted an incremental approach as regards the material scope of protection, starting with employment and, to some degree and where feasible, broadening it to social security and provision of services. It is important, however, that any differences are limited to where they are really necessary. It may therefore be worthwhile to investigate the possibilities to opt for a more comprehensive approach on the national level, harmonising the various measures where possible and advisable.[314] As many of the Member States seem to have followed the structure of the Article 13 Directives, however, such harmonisation does not seem to be feasible in the short term.[315]

This situation necessitates the search for a solution within the framework of the existing variety of non-discrimination laws. Indeed, some of the Member States seem to have provided for such a solution. Especially in cases of cumulative discrimination the approach is rather straightforward: as far as possible, all aspects of the complaint are dealt with.[316] Typical examples of this approach can be found in the decisions of the Irish Equality Officer:

---

[314] Fredman, above n. 299, 17.
[315] See Cormack and Bell, above n. 18.
[316] Hannett, above n. 296, 79.

Equality Tribunal, 18 December 2001[317]
DEC-S2001-020, Maughan v. *The Glimmer Man*

CUMULATIVE DISCRIMINATION

The Glimmer Man

Facts: Maughan is visually impaired and is a member of the Traveller Community. When he entered the Glimmer Man pub with his wife (who is also visually impaired), his thirteen-year-old son and his guide dog he was refused service, first because of the presence of the child (the bar had a no-children policy) and then, after he had sent his son home, because of the presence of the dog. Maughan felt that his membership of the Traveller Community might also have influenced the refusal to serve him.

Held: Maughan was discriminated against on the basis of his family status, contrary to the Equal Status Act 2000. He was not discriminated against on the basis of disability or his membership of the Traveller Community on the same day.

Decision: "4 . . . Section 3(2) provides that the discriminatory grounds include the family status ground, disability ground and membership of the Traveller community ground . . . The issues for consideration in this complaint are whether or not The Glimmer Man Ltd discriminated against Mr. John Maughan on the basis of the grounds claimed . . .

6. For the complainant's claim to be upheld on any of the grounds claimed he has to establish *prima facie* evidence of discrimination on that ground. In order for the complainant to establish *prima facie* evidence on a ground he has to show that he was treated less favourably than someone in the same circumstances who is not covered by that ground. If he succeeds in establishing *prima facie* evidence on a ground, the burden of proof then shifts to the respondent to rebut the inference of discrimination on that ground.

The complainant claimed that he was discriminated against on the family status, disability and membership of the Traveller community grounds.

6.1 . . . Both parties agree that when the complainant first entered the pub his thirteen year old son was with him. I am therefore satisfied that the complainant is covered by the family status ground.

6.2 . . . The complainant claims that because of his visual impairment he falls within the scope of this definition and I accept that this is the case.

6.3 . . . At the oral hearing the complainant stated that although he does not lead a nomadic lifestyle at the moment he did so in the past with his parents for a time. He said that he has always considered himself to be a member of the Traveller community and that his relatives also identify themselves as Travellers. He said that he lived on a halting site for a number of years and I consider that he is a member of the Traveller community within the meaning defined in the Act.

[The Equality Officer proceeded by examining, for each of the three grounds, the concrete complaint of discrimination.]

10. Taking account of all the evidence presented it is my decision that Mr John Maughan was discriminated against by The Glimmer Man Ltd on the basis of his family status on 2nd November, 2000, contrary to the Equal Status Act, 2000. It is also my decision that Mr John Maughan was not discriminated against by The Glimmer Man Ltd on the basis of disability or his membership of the Traveller community on the same day . . ."

---

[317] Available on the website of the Equality Tribunal of Ireland, under the heading Equal Status Decisions.

Note

The Equality Officer dealt with each of the grounds separately, not having regard to their possible interrelation or overlap. This enabled him to take account of the different requirements and exemptions available under the Irish Equal Status Act 2000–2004. Thus, all cumulative complaints were effectively dealt with.

As mentioned before, the situation is more difficult with respect to intersectional discrimination, as such cases are not easily identifiable as discrimination based on one particular protected ground. The Dutch Equal Treatment Commission tends to deal with this type of case in the following way:

Equal Treatment Commission (Commissie Gelijke Behandeling) **1.NL.124.**
Opinion 1998-48

INTERSECTIONAL DISCRIMINATION AGAINST A JEWISH EMPLOYEE

Jewish employee

Facts: The applicant, who is of Jewish origin and who has adopted the Jewish faith, worked for a transport company which often deals with countries in the Middle East. The applicant complains of severe forms of anti-Semitism in the workplace, varying from insulting remarks being made about Jews and finding a drawing of a swastika on his desk, to being skipped when coffee was distributed. When he complained about this, the employer took measures and made sure that the responsible colleagues apologised for their behaviour.

Held: As the employer has investigated the complaints about discrimination and has taken effective measures to avoid them, no discrimination can be established contrary to the Equal Treatment Act.

Opinion: "4.5 The applicant is of Jewish origin; his wife and children are Jewish and he has assumed the Jewish faith. At the hearing, the applicant indicated that he identifies with the Jewish people both by religion and by descent.

According to the established precedents of the Supreme Court, discrimination by virtue of Jewish descent also falls within the concept of the concept of race. The Commission will therefore in the present case examine possible unequal treatment based on religion and on race."

Notes

(1) After having decided that it would proceed on the assumption that the distinction was based on both religion and race, the Equal Treatment Commission examined if the allegations of the applicant were sufficiently substantiated and the measures taken by the employer could be considered sufficient to meet his responsibilities in safeguarding a discrimination-free environment. The Commission then concluded that the case did not disclose discrimination based on religion or race. Hence, the Commission did not distinguish between the two grounds in examining the case, but considered the claim in its entirety.

(2) Indeed, this approach was easily possible in this case, as religion and race are both highly suspect grounds and the same obligations for employers exist under the

Dutch legislation with respect to both grounds. It may be more difficult to choose this integrated approach in cases in which scope or suspectness differ with respect to the various grounds invoked.

It might be submitted, in this regard, that a court must in principle apply the legislative provisions which provide most protection to the individual or group concerned. In cases in which the grounds of age and race coincide, for example, this would imply that the courts rely on the Racial Equality Directive instead of the Employment Equality Directive. Indeed, it may be said that, as a general rule, the courts should search for the highest level of protection available. Indeed, this rule is included in the German *Allgemeines Gleichbehandlungsgesetz* (General Equal Treatment Act),[318] which is the only example in Europe of a legislative rule dealing with multiple discrimination:

> "Discrimination based on several of the grounds mentioned in § 1 is only capable of being justified by reference to of §§ 8 to 10 and 20, if the justification applies to all the grounds liable for the difference of treatment."[319]

This provision implies that the justification advanced for a case of multiple discrimination (whether cumulative or intersectional) always needs to be assessed with respect to all grounds alleged. As a consequence the highest level of protection is secured, as this construction means that the requirements of both the most restrictive exception clause and the less restrictive ones must be met. Although this may not solve all problems related to multiple discrimination, it can be regarded as an interesting starting point.

1.6. COMPARATIVE ANALYSIS

In this chapter, we have given an overview of the way in which a variety of grounds of discrimination have been defined and interpreted in European law, the law of the Member States and a number of international instruments. When drafting the Article 13 Directives, the choice was made not to provide a definition of the various grounds protected (race, ethnic origin, religion and belief, sexual orientation, disability and age), thus leaving considerable discretion to the Member States to adopt their own interpretation of the terms. The need to take decisions on the European legislative level about sensitive and controversial issues such as the definition of "race", "membership of an ethnic minority" and "disability" was thereby avoided. The result has been, however, the coming into being of a wide spectrum of national definitions and understandings: the discussion in this chapter discloses a clear lack of common ground with respect to the meaning of many of the grounds, in particular race, ethnic origin, marital status and disability. We have also found that many states have not provided for any interpretation or definition of the grounds at all, limiting themselves

[318] Allgemeines Gleichbehandlungsgesetz (AGG, 2006), BGBl. Teil I 17.8.2006, S. 1897.
[319] *Ibid.* § 4.

to including the various grounds in their national implementation legislation without paying express attention to their meaning. In these states, the personal scope of the non-discrimination legislation will depend on the interpretation and application of the grounds by the national authorities and, eventually, the ECJ.

By contrast, strong convergence and growing uniformity are visible with respect to those aspects of the grounds of discrimination which have been already been addressed by the ECJ. Since the case of *Grant*,[320] for example, it is accepted in all Member States that discrimination against transsexuals should be regarded as discrimination based on gender. Likewise, as a result of the *Dekker*[321] and *Mary Brown*[322] jurisprudence, all Member States place discrimination based on pregnancy and pregnancy-related illness in the same category as gender discrimination.

It is expected that the harmonising influence of the ECJ's case-law will further increase in the future. The ECJ itself has stated in its *Chacón Navas* judgment[323] that there is a clear need for uniform application of Community law and its principle of equality, which requires an autonomous and uniform interpretation of the various grounds that is valid throughout the Community. This fundamental stance will in all probability give rise to a wealth of judgments in the future in which definitions are given of all the grounds protected by the Article 13 Directives and possibly even with respect to Equality Directives that have been drafted outside the context of Article 13 (e.g. the Part-time and Fixed-term Work Directives). The ECJ will probably proceed on a case-by-case basis, as is well illustrated by its approach in *Chacón Navas*. In that case the ECJ provided a uniform, yet rather open-ended, definition of the ground of disability, which can be elaborated and detailed in later cases. The ECJ may thereby find inspiration in the definitions contained in national case-law and legislative materials, which are sometimes highly developed—in the UK, Ireland and the Netherlands, for example, much attention has been given to definitional issues. The ECJ may also find guidance in the wealth of international materials available with respect to the grounds of discrimination. Where the grounds of race and ethnicity are concerned, the ECJ's interpretation may be adapted to the definitions provided by the ICERD Convention and the ECtHR, and to those proposed by ECRI. The understanding of the grounds of religion and belief may be based on the ECtHR's elaborate case-law on the freedom of religion as protected by Article 9 of the ECHR—indeed, the definitions in national legal systems already show such influence, although there are still many variations. The interpretation of the ground of "disability" may be inspired by other international instruments, such as the International Classification of Functioning, Disability and Health (ICF) adopted by the World Health Organisation. Although the ECJ does not mention ICF in *Chacón Navas*, this may be different in later cases where specific aspects of the definition of disability are at stake.

---

[320] See above **1.EC.29.**
[321] See above **1.EC.27.**
[322] See above **1.EC.28.**
[323] See above **1.EC.84.**

Hence, an intricate cycle of mutually influenced interpretations may come into being in which national definitions are tailored to those developed by the ECJ. The ECJ's definitions themselves will be inspired by national understandings and international materials, which in turn are influenced by both national and European developments.

We have further focused on the question if the various grounds discussed are to be considered "suspect". In open systems of non-discrimination law, where there are no limited lists of grounds or closed systems of specific exception clauses, the "suspectness" of the ground will often determine the strictness of the test of justification applied by the courts. It is clear, for example, that the ECtHR requires "very weighty reasons" to be adduced in justification of discrimination based on grounds such as illegitimate birth, gender, sexual orientation and nationality. This means that the ECtHR will closely scrutinise the reasons advanced by the government in favour of such discrimination, which usually results in the finding of a violation of the prohibition of discrimination. Similarly, even though the ECJ does not work with an open system comparable to that of the ECHR, the "suspectness" of the ground in question may also determine the strictness with which the ECJ assesses national allegations about necessity and proportionality of a certain difference in treatment. It must be noted, however, that the suspectness of the various grounds will not always result in strict scrutiny. The case-law of both the ECJ and the ECtHR shows examples where other circumstances were found (such as the context of the case or a lack of consensus in a specific domain) which justified a reduction in the intensity of review. Nonetheless, the suspectness of the ground at hand clearly forms an important reason for intensification of the level of review.

It is clear from the discussion of "suspectness" in this chapter that, as a matter of principle, all of the grounds mentioned in Article 13 EC (gender, race/ethnicity, religion/belief, disability, age and sexual orientation) can be considered as suspect. A possible exception to this rule might be the ground of "age", but this remains uncertain, as the ECJ made clear in *Mangold*.[324] In that case it held that age-discrimination has to be regarded as a derogation from a fundamental individual right and the proportionality test has to be applied in that light. It may be derived from this that the ECJ will at least apply an intermediate level of review in cases of age discrimination.

With respect to grounds which are not included in Article 13 EC, such as nationality, marital or family status, legitimate birth, part-time work and fixed-term work, the perceived suspectness differs. It is well-established case-law of the ECtHR that (il)legitimate birth is a highly suspect ground, but its case-law is less clear and predictable with respect to the grounds of nationality and marital status. No case-law at all is available from which any conclusions may be drawn with respect to the suspectness of the grounds of part-time and fixed-term work, although some general

---

[324] See above **1.EC.101.**

predictions may be made on the basis of the case-law relating to other grounds (see above, section 1.3.11).

Thus, a fair amount of convergence can be discerned with respect to the suspectness of the grounds of discrimination discussed in this chapter. National and European courts may find important guidance in this consensus as to the appropriate intensity of review.

Finally, we have discussed a number of issues in this chapter which are relevant to all grounds of discrimination. First, we have mentioned the possibility of defining the various grounds in a symmetrical or asymmetrical way. The European Directives clearly favour a symmetrical definition, meaning, for example, that the ground of gender must be interpreted to cover both men and women, and the ground of sexual orientation must be read to cover heterosexuals as well as gays and bisexuals. Within the context of the Article 13 Directives, some debate is only possible with respect to the ground of disability, which some authors have stated protects only disabled people. As national legislation shows both symmetrical and asymmetrical definitions here, this controversy needs to be solved by the ECJ.

A second general issue discussed in this chapter relates to discrimination by assumption and by association. Sometimes individuals are not discriminated against because of characteristics they really have, but rather because of characteristics which others impute to them or because of an association with persons with certain characteristics. Although none of the European non-discrimination Directives contains an express prohibition of these forms of discrimination, the legislation and case-law in the various Member States show clear recognition of the need to combat such discrimination. It is expected, for that reason, that the ECJ will adopt a similar approach.

Finally, we have considered the difficult issue of multiple discrimination, which can generally be described as the situation in which a single case of discrimination is based on more than one ground. The differences in material scope and exemptions provided for each ground by the European Equality Directives prove to be particularly problematic in such cases, even if the structure of the Directives has the advantage of providing nuanced and well-fitted solutions for each of the grounds as such. The problems of multiple discrimination have been acknowledged in academic literature and to some degree in national case-law and legislation, but no workable solutions have been offered. The ideal solution would be to create an open system of non-discrimination legislation in which each individual case can be decided on its own merits and account can be taken of particularities such as a unique combination of grounds. However, it is evident that such a system would hardly be compatible with the current system of European non-discrimination law and would unacceptably reduce the degree of clarity and specificity provided by that system. Adequate responses will therefore have to be found within the system itself. A good example of how this could be done is offered by a provision included in the German General Non-Discrimination Act of 2006, which stipulates that in cases of multiple discrimination the justification must meet the requirements of the strictest exception clause applicable to the case at hand. As it is possible to apply this method even without explicit legislative provision, it might be expected that the ECJ will adopt such an approach in future case-law.

Thus, where the interpretation and suspectness of discrimination grounds is at issue, European law will remain an interesting object for the study of the convergence of national legal systems. It is expected that common definitions and understandings of the various grounds and their suspectness will develop over the years under influence of judgments of the ECJ, which itself will be inspired by national and international interpretations and developments. It remains uncertain, however, if this will really lead to uniform and identical definitions throughout Europe. To some degree, national definitions of grounds such as religion or marital status will be inextricably bound up with strong national opinions, traditions and sensitivities. The ECJ will need to respect such national differences and will probably leave some discretion and room for differentiation in these areas, searching for an acceptable balance between the need for differentiation and the need for uniform protection against discrimination.

CHAPTER TWO
DIRECT DISCRIMINATION

Prof. Mark Bell

2.1. INTRODUCTION

When law is deployed to tackle discrimination in society, the first step is normally to prohibit the most overt manifestations of prejudice. These are incidents where individuals or groups are expressly treated less favourably because of a particular characteristic, such as sex or ethnic origin. Two contemporary examples from European case-law serve as good illustrations. In 2002, several Romanian men of Roma ethnic origin entered the "Complex Moldova" bar in Botoşani. They were confronted with a sign stating "we do not serve Roma". On requesting something at the bar, they were refused; the bartender explained that "the owner does not want to have Gypsies in this bar". This refusal of service was subsequently held to constitute unlawful direct discrimination by the National Council for Combating Discrimination in Romania and a fine of around Euro 200 was imposed on the bar.[1]

Elsewhere, a similar set of facts arose in the Italian case of *Zerman*.[2] Here, several North African men were repeatedly refused service in the "Giardino" bar in Verona. On one occasion in 1999, the bartender refused a request for two coffees, stating "this is my house and I give coffees to who I want". In 2005, the Court of Cassation upheld the bar owner's earlier conviction for unlawful racial discrimination.

Such cases may be regarded as classic examples of direct discrimination. There is little controversy over the fact that the individuals have experienced less favourable treatment on grounds of their ethnic origin. If any form of discrimination is to be forbidden in law, such overt expressions of prejudice will certainly be included. These typical examples can lead to the conclusion that direct discrimination is a relatively straightforward legal concept. In contrast, this chapter will highlight various challenges that continue to vex the understanding and application of direct discrimination, even within experienced systems of anti-discrimination law.

First, there is a risk that direct discrimination is equated with overt and intentional forms of discrimination. In the course of this chapter, it will be illustrated that direct discrimination may be both covert and lacking a prejudicial motive. Consider the hypothetical example of a 55-year-old woman who applies for a position as a shop assistant in a clothes store that is mainly aimed at young women in their late teens/early twenties. The store decides to appoint a similarly qualified 25-year-old woman on the basis that she would be more able to understand the needs of the

---

[1] National Council for Combating Discrimination in Romania, 27 May 2003, Decision No. 165, Bucharest.

[2] La Corte Suprema di Cassazione, 5 December 2005, No. 46883/'03 R.G., available on the website of the Dipartimento per i diritti e le pari opportunità.

typical customer. Is this a legitimate commercial consideration or does it reflect ageist stereotyping of the older woman's ability to engage with younger clients?

The second underlying issue for analysis is the ongoing relevance and utility of direct discrimination within more mature systems of anti-discrimination law. If direct discrimination is equated with the most overt forms of discrimination, then these can be expected to diminish in frequency as the law becomes more established. Providing that the sanctions for breach of the law are reasonably effective, most employers or service-providers will seek to conceal discriminatory actions in order to protect themselves against litigation. This has certainly been the experience of courts within the UK. A consistent point of guidance from the Court of Appeal has been the following:

> "It is important to bear in mind that it is unusual to find direct evidence of racial discrimination. Few employers will be prepared to admit such discrimination even to themselves. In some cases the discrimination will not be ill-intentioned but merely based on an assumption 'he or she would not have fitted in'."[3]

The difficulty in ascertaining the reason for less favourable treatment, in the absence of overt evidence, prompts questions around the long-term usefulness of the prohibition of direct discrimination. In various European legal systems, attempts have been made to preserve the vitality of this concept by introducing specific rules relating to evidence and proof. In particular, the effectiveness of the prohibition of direct discrimination has been linked to provisions permitting a shift in the burden of proof from the complainant to the respondent.

The final issue for reflection is when, if ever, should the law permit direct discrimination? Some national legal systems are based on the principle that direct discrimination cannot be justified, although narrow exceptions may be provided within statute. These cover a variety of circumstances, such as the notion of genuine occupational requirements. The latter addresses rare circumstances where the suspect characteristic is relevant to the individual's ability to perform the job or to use the service. For example, consider a cosmetics firm that produces certain hair care products designed for use by women of African or Caribbean origin. In advertising and packaging these products, it is likely to be a genuine occupational requirement to employ models who are also women of African or Caribbean origin. Nevertheless, the extension of anti-discrimination law to a wider range of discrimination grounds puts pressure on the assumption that direct discrimination is subject only to narrow statutory exceptions.

Some states generally allow justification of direct discrimination, whereas in others this is permitted only for specific grounds. On the one hand, the prohibition of age discrimination has often been accompanied by the possibility to justify direct discrimination in a broader range of circumstances. On the other, potential conflicts between discrimination grounds or their engagement with other human rights has sometimes resulted in a more flexible approach to justifying direct discrimination than was hitherto taken in respect of sex or race discrimination. Notably, the tension that can

---

[3] Neill LJ, *King* v. *Great Britain-China Centre* [1992] ICR 516, 528.

arise between freedom of religion and non-discrimination on the ground of sexual orientation has provoked debate in many European legal systems.

This chapter is divided into two main themes. The first theme is the concept of direct discrimination. This part examines the emergence of direct discrimination as a specific concept within case-law and legislation. It considers issues surrounding the application of direct discrimination, such as establishing causation, the role of comparators and the (ir)relevance of motive. It also examines the difficulties in proving direct discrimination and considers the application of direct discrimination to segregationist practices. The second part of the chapter shifts to consider exceptions that may be permitted in legislation and case-law to the prohibition of direct discrimination. These can be separated between open-ended grounds for objective justification and specific exceptions with a narrow scope.

2.2. RECOGNISING DIRECT DISCRIMINATION

In order to commence the analysis of direct discrimination, it is necessary to consider its legal origins. The notion of direct discrimination as a distinct form of discrimination has emerged over time, through both legislation and case-law. Specifically, a transition can be witnessed from generalised prohibitions of discrimination that lack any precise definition of what actually constitutes discrimination towards detailed statutory definitions of direct discrimination, which normally coincide with the introduction of a definition of indirect discrimination. This section begins with an overview of European-level legal instruments from the Council of Europe and the European Union before progressing to consideration of the approach within some national legal systems.

2.2.1.   DISCRIMINATION AND THE COUNCIL OF EUROPE

The Council of Europe has an array of legal instruments that address issues of discrimination. This makes a good starting point for any consideration of the development of discrimination law in Europe. The most well-known instrument is, of course, the European Convention on Human Rights (ECHR), enforced by the European Court of Human Rights (ECtHR). Its case-law exercises a significant influence on both national courts and also the European Union's Court of Justice (ECJ). The specific provision of the Convention dealing with discrimination is Article 14:

> "The enjoyment of the rights and freedoms set forth in this Convention shall be secured without discrimination on any ground such as sex, race, colour, language, religion, political or other opinion, national or social origin, association with a national minority, property, birth or other status."

This does not define discrimination, nor does it distinguish between direct and indirect discrimination. Instead, it has been necessary for case-law to develop a consistent understanding of discrimination. The Court has most commonly explained discrimination as a difference in treatment without any reasonable and objective justification. This approach was clearly established in the *Belgian Linguistics* case.

ECtHR, 23 July 1968[4]   **2.CoE.1.**

Case "relating to certain aspects of the laws on the use of languages in education in Belgium" v. Belgium

THE CONCEPT OF DISCRIMINATION UNDER ARTICLE 14

Belgian linguistics

Facts: The case concerned a number of complaints from French-speaking families about restrictions in different districts of Belgium on access to French-language schools for their children or the limited provision of such schools.

Held: There was a breach of Article 14 in conjunction with Article 2 of Protocol 1 (right to education), in so far as children living in certain districts near Brussels were prevented from attending French-language schools.

Judgment: "10. In spite of the very general wording of the French version ("sans distinction aucune"), Article 14 does not forbid every difference in treatment in the exercise of the rights and freedoms recognised. This version must be read in the light of the more restrictive text of the English version ('without discrimination'). In addition, and in particular, one would reach absurd results were one to give Article 14 an interpretation as wide as that which the French version seems to imply. One would, in effect, be led to judge as contrary to the Convention every one of the many legal or administrative provisions which do not secure to everyone complete equality of treatment in the enjoyment of the rights and freedoms recognised. The competent national authorities are frequently confronted with situations and problems which, on account of differences inherent therein, call for different legal solutions; moreover, certain legal inequalities tend only to correct factual inequalities. The extensive interpretation mentioned above cannot consequently be accepted.

It is important, then, to look for the criteria which enable a determination to be made as to whether or not a given difference in treatment, concerning of course the exercise of one of the rights and freedoms set forth, contravenes Article 14. On this question the Court, following the principles which may be extracted from the legal practice of a large number of democratic States, holds that the principle of equality of treatment is violated if the distinction has no objective and reasonable justification. The existence of such a justification must be assessed in relation to the aim and effects of the measure under consideration, regard being had to the principles which normally prevail in democratic societies. A difference of treatment in the exercise of a right laid down in the Convention must not only pursue a legitimate aim: Article 14 is likewise violated when it is clearly established that there is no reasonable relationship of proportionality between the means employed and the aim sought to be realised."

---

[4] (1979–1980) 1 European Human Rights Reports 252.

Notes

(1) The Court's approach to interpreting Article 14 reflects an Aristotelian concept of equality: like situations should be treated alike.[5] This is in keeping with the approach frequently taken to the interpretation of national constitutional provisions on equality.

(2) Whilst no specific concept of direct discrimination is mentioned, the Court's formula is sufficiently broad to capture such discrimination. Subsequent case-law has regularly confirmed that distinctions resulting in less favourable treatment can be challenged under Article 14. For example, in *Lustig-Prean and Beckett* v. *UK* (1999) 29 EHRR 548, the Court held that the ban on lesbians and gays serving in the UK armed forces was discrimination contrary to Article 14, in conjunction with Article 8 (right to private life). The applicants had been treated less favourably by reason of their sexual orientation.

(3) The Aristotelian concept of equality has two limbs. First, the equal treatment of persons in similar situations, and secondly, the different treatment of persons in dissimilar situations. The Court's case-law has clarified that also the latter falls within the scope of Article 14.

ECtHR, 6 April 2000[6]   **2.CoE.2.**
Thlimmenos v. *Greece*

FAILURE TO TREAT DIFFERENTLY PERSONS IN DIFFERENT SITUATIONS

Thlimmenos

Facts: The applicant, a Jehovah's Witness, received a criminal conviction for refusing an order to wear military uniform; this refusal was motivated by his religious beliefs. Several years later, he passed the examinations to become a chartered accountant, but his appointment was denied on the basis of his criminal record. He argued that the failure to distinguish between persons convicted as a result of their religious beliefs and persons convicted for other reasons was, inter alia, a breach of Articles 9 (freedom of religion) and 14 ECHR.

Held: There was a violation of Article 14 taken in conjunction with Article 9.

Judgment: "44. The Court has so far considered that the right under Article 14 not to be discriminated against in the enjoyment of the rights guaranteed under the Convention is violated when States treat differently persons in analogous situations without providing an objective and reasonable justification . . . However, the Court considers that this is not the only facet of the prohibition of discrimination in Article 14. The right not to be discriminated against in the enjoyment of the rights guaranteed under the Convention is also violated when States without an objective and reasonable justification fail to treat differently persons whose situations are significantly different."

---

[5] On the concept of equality, see above, Introductory Chapter: A Comparative Perspective on Non-discrimination Law.

[6] Reports of Judgements and Decisions 2000-IV.

189

Notes

(1) The definition of discrimination employed in this case is more precise than that adopted in *Belgian Linguistics*. In particular, it is notable that the Court specifies that differential treatment must be between "persons in analogous situations", thereby introducing a comparator element. The need for a comparator has not, though, been consistently required by the Court in its case-law under Article 14.[7]

(2) *Thlimmenos* could be viewed as tantamount to recognising the concept of indirect discrimination.[8] This line of argument would be based on the logic that Jehovah's Witnesses were placed at a particular disadvantage by a facially neutral rule: the apparent requirement for chartered accountants not to have a criminal record. Yet, it is not evident from this case if Jehovah's Witnesses as a group were placed at a disadvantage by this requirement; there was no statistical evidence presented on the prevalence of criminal records within the community of Jehovah's Witnesses linked to pacifistic beliefs. The Court's assessment focuses on the effect of the rule on Mr Thlimmenos as an individual, rather than the group-based disparate impact analysis which would be more typical within indirect discrimination (see further chapter three). Notably, the Court avoids using either the label of "direct" or "indirect" discrimination.[9] Subsequent cases have more clearly recognised indirect discrimination linked to disparate impact.[10]

Given the increasing distinction between direct and indirect discrimination in the Court's case-law, it is perhaps unfortunate that this was not taken further in Protocol 12 to the ECHR. Whereas Article 14 prohibits discrimination within the rights and freedoms provided elsewhere in the Convention, Protocol 12 establishes an autonomous right to non-discrimination. Article 1(1) states:

> "The enjoyment of any right set forth by law shall be secured without discrimination on any ground such as sex, race, colour, language, religion, political or other opinion, national or social origin, association with a national minority, property, birth or other status."

Protocol 12 entered into force on 1 April 2005, but, so far, it has only been ratified by minority of states in the Council of Europe. At the time of writing, the Court has yet to interpret the concept of discrimination within Protocol 12, although it can be anticipated that the Court's gradual differentiation of direct and indirect discrimination will apply also in this context. Indeed, the explanatory report on Protocol 12 stated that "the meaning of the term "discrimination' in Article 1 is intended to be identical to that in Article 14 of the Convention".[11]

---

[7] J. Gerards, *Judicial Review in Equal Treatment Cases* (Leiden, Martinus Nijhoff Publishers, 2005) 130.

[8] O. de Schutter, "The Prohibition of Discrimination under European Human Rights Law—Relevance for EU Racial and Employment Equality Directives" (European Commission, 2005) 16, available on the website of Directorate-General for Employment, Social Affairs and Equal Opportunities.

[9] J. Gerards categorises this case as concerning "substantive equality", see n. 7 above, 116.

[10] E.g. ECtHR, 7 February 2006, *D.H. and others* v. *The Czech Republic*, Application 57325/00. See further below D. Schiek, Chapter Three: Indirect Discrimination, excerpt **3.CoE.11.**

[11] Para. 18, Explanatory report on Protocol 12 to the Convention for the Protection of Human Rights and Fundamental Freedoms (ETS No. 177). Available on the website of the Council of Europe.

A similar transition from a broad, undefined notion of discrimination towards specific concepts of direct and indirect discrimination can be found under the European Social Charter. The 1961 Charter did not contain a specific article on discrimination, although this was mentioned in the preamble. When the Charter was extensively revised in 1996, a dedicated article was added, but this adopted the model found in Article 14 ECHR. Article E states:

> "The enjoyment of the rights set forth in this Charter shall be secured without discrimi-nation on any ground such as race, colour, sex, language, religion, political or other opinion, national extraction or social origin, health, association with a national minority, birth or other status."

The proximity of Article E to Article 14 ECHR was reinforced by an explanatory statement in the Appendix to the Charter: "a differential treatment based on an objective and reasonable justification shall not be deemed to be discriminatory". This formula is broad enough to include less favourable treatment resulting in direct discrimination; case-law from the European Committee of Social Rights has confirmed that indirect discrimination is also covered.[12]

2.2.2. DISCRIMINATION AND THE EUROPEAN UNION

Non-discrimination and equal treatment are legal norms that permeate various levels of EU law, reaching from the general principles of fundamental rights found within the case-law of the ECJ to specific anti-discrimination legislation. As with the Council of Europe instruments discussed above, a trajectory can be traced from general notions of discrimination, sometimes undefined, towards the distinguishing of direct and indirect discrimination.

Looking first at the Court's general principles of law, the principle of equal treatment has been consistently recognised as a requirement for the legality of EC Treaty legislation or actions of the EU institutions.[13] Moreover, respect for fundamental rights, including non-discrimination, is a requirement imposed upon Member States when they are implementing EC Treaty law.[14] Like the ECtHR, the ECJ has adopted an Aristotelian approach to the concepts of equality and non-discrimination. In *Garcia Avello*,[15] a case concerning nationality discrimination, it stated:

> "It is in this regard settled case-law that the principle of non-discrimination requires that comparable situations must not be treated differently and that different situations must

---

[12] European Committee of Social Rights, *Autism-Europe* v. *France*, Complaint No. 13/2002, 4 November 2003, Strasbourg. See also para. 46, European Committee of Social Rights, *European Roma Rights Centre* v. *Italy*, Complaint No. 27/2004, 7 December 2005, Strasbourg.

[13] See further, G. de Búrca, "The Role of Equality in European Community Law" in Dashwood and O'Leary (eds.), *The Principle of Equal Treatment in European Community Law* (London, Sweet & Maxwell, 1997).

[14] Para. 19, *Johnston* v. *Chief Constable of the Royal Ulster Constabulary* [1986] ECR 1651.

[15] Case C–148/02 *Garcia Avello* v. *Belgium* [2003] ECR I–11613.

not be treated in the same way (see, inter alia, Case C–354/95 *National Farmers' Union and Others* [1997] ECR I–4559, paragraph 61). Such treatment may be justified only if it is based on objective considerations independent of the nationality of the persons concerned and is proportionate to the objective being legitimately pursued . . ."[16]

Moreover, the Court has also recognised that this general principle includes indirect discrimination.[17] The differentiation between direct and indirect discrimination within the Court's general principle of non-discrimination was already preceded by a clear dichotomy of these concepts within EC anti-discrimination legislation. As regards sex equality law, Article 119 of the 1957 EEC Treaty stated:

"Each Member State shall during the first stage ensure and subsequently maintain the application of the principle that men and women should receive equal pay for equal work."

This did not define how "equal" pay was to be determined. In Case C–43/75 *Defrenne* v. *SABENA (II)* [1976] ECR 455, the Court suggests a possible distinction between direct and indirect discrimination, without putting real flesh on the bones of these concepts. The case concerned a challenge to various aspects of the pay and working conditions of female air stewards that were less favourable than those enjoyed by their male counterparts. The Court was asked to consider whether Article 119 EEC was sufficiently clear and precise in order to permit individuals to enforce this obligation within their national courts, in other words, the concept of direct effect. The Court held that:

"A distinction must be drawn within the whole area of application of Article 119 between, first, direct and overt discrimination which may be identified solely with the aid of the criteria based on equal work and equal pay referred to by the Article in question and, secondly, indirect and disguised discrimination which can only be identified by reference to more explicit implementing provisions of a Community or national character."[18]

In other words, the Court concluded that only the prohibition of direct discrimination was sufficiently clear and precise from the text of Article 119 EEC in order to sustain the direct effect of this provision. The Court appears to link the existence of direct discrimination to explicit forms of discrimination; however, this restrictive view has not prevailed in subsequent legislation and case-law.[19] The Court's judgment in *Defrenne* arrived within a few months of the adoption of specific legislation to prohibit sex discrimination in all aspects of employment and vocational training. Directive 76/207, hereafter referred to as the Gender Employment Directive, did not include a definition of direct and indirect discrimination, but the distinction between these two concepts was recognized in Article 2(1):

[16] Para. 31. See also para. 39, Case C–292/97 *Karlsson and others* [2000] ECR I– 2737.
[17] Para. 28, Case C–25/02 *Rinke* v. *Ärztekammer Hamburg* [2003] ECR I–8349.
[18] Para. 18, C-43/75 *Defrenne* v. *SABENA (II)* [1976] ECR 455.
[19] E. Ellis, *EU Anti-discrimination Law* (Oxford, Oxford University Press, 2005) 89.

"For the purposes of the following provisions, the principle of equal treatment shall mean that there shall be no discrimination whatsoever on grounds of sex either directly or indirectly by reference in particular to marital or family status."[20]

The failure to define the difference between direct and indirect discrimination effectively delegated this task to the future case-law of the ECJ. In particular, the Court was instrumental in constructing a working definition of indirect discrimination; this is explored in detail in chapter three. In the last decade, there has been a move to incorporate express definitions of direct and indirect discrimination within EC anti-discrimination legislation. This process commenced in 1997 with the introduction of a legislative definition of indirect sex discrimination through the Burden of Proof Directive.[21] Perhaps surprisingly, this was not accompanied by any attempt to write a statutory definition of direct discrimination. In contrast, EC legislation since 2000 has established a common definition of direct discrimination that applies across various grounds of discrimination.

A statutory definition of direct discrimination was first instituted by Directive 2000/43, hereafter referred to as the Racial Equality Directive.[22] Article 2 states:

"1. For the purposes of this Directive, the principle of equal treatment shall mean that there shall be no direct or indirect discrimination based on racial or ethnic origin.
    2. For the purposes of paragraph 1:

(a) direct discrimination shall be taken to occur where one person is treated less favourably than another is, has been or would be treated in a comparable situation on grounds of racial or ethnic origin."

This definition of direct discrimination was subsequently incorporated into Directive 2000/78 (hereafter referred to as the Employment Equality Directive);[23] the Gender Employment Directive (as amended in 2002);[24] and Directive 2004/113 (hereafter the Gender Goods and Services Directive).[25] The same formula is retained in the Recast Gender Employment Directive.[26]

---

[20] Directive 76/207/EEC of 9 February 1976 on the implementation of the principle of equal treatment for men and women as regards access to employment, vocational training and promotion, and working conditions [1976] OJ L39/40.

[21] Directive 97/80/EC of 15 December 1997 on the burden of proof in cases of discrimination based on sex [1998] OJ L14/6.

[22] Directive 2000/43/EC of 29 June 2000 implementing the principle of equal treatment between persons irrespective of racial or ethnic origin [2000] OJ L180/22. This Directive prohibits discrimination on grounds of racial or ethnic origin in employment, vocational training, education, social protection, social advantages, and access to goods and services, including housing.

[23] Art. 2, Directive 2000/78/EC establishing a general framework for equal treatment in employment and occupation [2000] OJ L303/16. This Directive prohibits discrimination on grounds of religion or belief, disability, age and sexual orientation, but only in respect of employment and vocational training.

[24] Art. 2 (as amended), Directive 2002/73/EC of the European Parliament and of the Council of 23 September 2002 amending Directive 76/207/EEC on the implementation of the principle of equal treatment for men and women as regards access to employment, vocational training and promotion, and working conditions [2002] OJ L269/15.

[25] Art. 2(a), Directive 2004/113/EC of 13 December 2004 implementing the principle of equal treatment between men and women in the access to and supply of goods and services [2004] OJ L373/37.

[26] Art. 2(1)(a), Directive 2006/54/EC of the European Parliament and of the Council of 5 July 2006 on the implementation of the principle of equal opportunities and equal treatment of men and women in matters of employment and occupation (recast) [2006] OJ L204/23.

The impact of the anti-discrimination Directives since 2000 has been to codify a consistent statutory definition of direct discrimination. As will be examined further below, this "model" definition has exerted a very substantial influence on national anti-discrimination legislation. Although a consolidated approach now exists in these core Directives, it is worth noting that not all EC legislation dealing with the issue of discrimination contains a specific definition of direct (or indirect) discrimination. For example, Directive 2003/109 on the rights of long-term residents does not contain any definition of discrimination.[27]

2.2.3.   GENERAL CONCEPTS OF DIRECT DISCRIMINATION IN NATIONAL LAW

In defining the general principle of non-discrimination, both the ECtHR and the ECJ have been strongly influenced by national case-law. In *Belgian Linguistics*, the ECtHR stated that it was "following the principles which may be extracted from the legal practice of a large number of democratic States".[28] Similarly, national constitutional provisions are a key source for the ECJ in interpreting the general principles of EC law.[29] The Aristotelian approach to equality, which is clearly evident in the case-law of the ECtHR and the ECJ, is a common point of reference within national case-law on the interpretation of constitutional equality guarantees.[30] As such, constitutions are often the baseline for protection against direct discrimination in national legal orders. The next two extracts are rather typical of the situation in many European states.

O. De Schutter, "Report on measures to combat discrimination: **2.BE.3.**
Directive 2000/43/EC and 2000/78/EC. Country report Belgium"[31]

"Articles 10 and 11 of the Constitution guarantee equality before the law and enjoyment without discrimination of the rights and freedoms recognized to all, without specifying a list of prohibited grounds of discrimination. These equality clauses are applicable generally, without any restriction either as to the grounds on which the discrimination is based (they require that the principle of equality be respected with respect to all grounds) or as to situations concerned

---

[27] Directive 2003/109/EC of 25 November 2003 concerning the status of third-country nationals who are long-term residents [2004] OJ L16/44. Art. 11 of this Directive prohibits discrimination against third country nationals who are recognised as long-term residents in the Union across a range of activities, including employment, education and access to goods and services.
[28] Paragraph 10, ECtHR, 23 July 1968, *Case 'relating to certain aspects of the laws on the use of languages in education in Belgium'* v. *Belgium* (1979–1980) 1 European Human Rights Reports 252.
[29] Para. 13, Case 4/73 *Nold* v. *Commission* [1974] ECR 491.
[30] For a critique, see D. Schiek, "Torn between Arithmetic and Substantive Equality? Perspectives on Equality in German Labour law" (2002) 18 *IJCLLIR* 149 at 150.
[31] (European Commission, 2005) 12–13, available on the website of Directorate-General for Employment, Social Affairs and Equal Opportunities.

(they are applicable to all contexts, going beyond not only employment and occupation, but also the scope of Directive 2000/43/EC).

The notions of equality and non-discrimination under Articles 10 and 11 of the Constitution are interpreted in conformity with the classical understanding of the requirement of non-discrimination in international law, especially as formulated by the European Court of Human Rights: the rules on equality and non-discrimination of the Constitution do not exclude a difference in treatment between certain categories of persons, provided that an objective and reasonable justification may be offered for the criterion of differentiation; the existence of such a justification must be assessed with regard to the aim and the effects of the contested measure and to the nature of the principles applying to the case; the principle of equality is violated where it is established that there exists no reasonable relationship of proportionality between the means used and the aim sought to be realised."

T. Makkonen, "Report on measures to combat discrimination: **2.FI.4.**
Directive 2000/43/EC and 2000/78/EC. Country report Finland"[32]

"Provisions guaranteeing equality and non-discrimination have been given a pride of place in the Constitution, as they are placed first among fundamental rights, starting at section 6. Section 6(1) of (731/1999) Constitution [perustuslaki (731/1999)] reads as follows: 'Everyone is equal before the law.' Corollary to the section 6(1) are sections 6(2) and 6(3):

> 'No one shall, without an acceptable reason, be treated differently from other persons on the ground of sex, age, origin, language, religion, conviction, opinion, health, disability or other reason that concerns his or her person.
>
> Children shall be treated equally and as individuals and they shall be allowed to influence matters pertaining to them to a degree corresponding to their level of development.'

The prohibition of discrimination in section 6(2) is rather general in scope: its field of application has not been limited in any way, it covers both direct and indirect discrimination, and the listing of grounds is open-ended, as was mentioned before. The provision does not use the concept of "discrimination" as such but speaks instead of "differential treatment without an acceptable reason". A reason is acceptable if it serves an objectively justifiable end that serves the objectives of the fundamental rights system, and if the means used are proportionate to the ends. The non-discrimination clause of section 6(2) in combination with the obligation of authorities to promote human rights and fundamental freedoms, as laid down in section 22 of the Constitution, have been taken to mean that the legislator has an obligation to make sure that the legislation does not contain provisions that without an acceptable reason treat people differently on a prohibited ground."

These approaches to equality are summarised by McCrudden as "equality as rationality".[33] The content of the equality guarantee is broad and undefined. It is a

---

[32] (European Commission, 2005) 6–7, available on the website of Directorate-General for Employment, Social Affairs and Equal Opportunities.

[33] C. McCrudden, "Theorizing European Equality Law" in C. Costello and E. Barry (eds.), *Equality in Diversity—the New Equality Directives* (Dublin, Irish Centre for European Law, 2003) 19.

flexible norm that can be applied to a wide range of different scenarios, but the counterbalance to its breadth is the relatively loose level of scrutiny and the open-ended possibility for differential treatment to be justified.[34] Constitutional equality provisions do not typically distinguish between direct and indirect discrimination, let alone provide any definition of these concepts. Instead, specific definitions are more commonly located within legislation. They may be nested within broader sources of law, such as Labour Codes,[35] or alternatively dedicated anti-discrimination legislation. In this area, the 2000 Directives have had a striking impact on shaping national law. All EU Member States have introduced new legal instruments in response to these Directives. Very many states have taken the opportunity to follow the Directives' scheme with regard to defining direct discrimination. Some states chose to "cut and paste" the text of the Directive directly into national law. For example, the definition of direct discrimination in Greece,[36] Italy[37] and Portugal[38] is almost identical to that found in the Directives. In other states, the definition is not "word-for-word" from the Directives, but it conforms to the essential elements required. These may be summarised as the following:

— the need to demonstrate less favourable treatment;
— a requirement for a comparison with another person in a similar situation, but with different characteristics (e.g. ethnic origin, religion, sexual orientation);
— the possibility to use a comparator from the past (e.g. a previous employee) or a hypothetical comparator;
— justification of direct discrimination is only possible by reference to specific, limited exceptions.

Overall, these four elements are generally present in national legislation in Austria, Cyprus, Denmark, Estonia, Finland, Germany, Greece, Italy, Ireland, Latvia, Lithuania, Malta, Portugal, Slovakia, Slovenia, Sweden and the UK.[39] Whilst this suggests a significant degree of convergence within national legal orders in response to the Directives, whether this is realised in practice will depend heavily on the interpretation of such provisions by national courts. It must also be recognised that new, Directive-inspired definitions of direct discrimination often coexist with earlier legal provisions that do not share the same approach. For example, the following

---

[34] See, e.g. the analysis of the Spanish equality provisions in M. Rodríguez-Piñero Bravo-Ferrer and M. Rodrígues-Piñero Royo, "The Principle of Equality in the Labour Market—Reflections on the Spanish Model" (2002) 18 *IJCLLIR* 169.

[35] E.g. definitions of discrimination are located in the Labour Codes of Poland and Estonia.

[36] Arts. 3(1)(a) and 7(1)(a) of Law 3304 of 27 January 2005.

[37] Art. 2, Legislative Decree of 9 July 2003, no. 215, Implementation of Directive 2000/43/EC for the equal treatment of persons irrespective of race and of ethnic origin (Gazzetta Ufficiale no. 186, 12 August 2003); Art. 2, Legislative Decree of 9 July 2003, no. 216, Implementation of Directive 2000/78/EC for equal treatment in relation to employment and working conditions (Gazzetta Ufficiale no. 187, 13 August 2003).

[38] Art. 3(3)(a), Law 18 of 11 May 2004; Art. 32(a), Law 35 of 29 July 2004.

[39] See further, J. Cormack and M. Bell, "Developing Anti-discrimination Law in Europe—the 25 EU Member States Compared" (European Commission, 2005), available on the website of Directorate-General for Employment, Social Affairs and Equal Opportunities.

extract highlights the different definitions of direct discrimination now found within Finnish legislation.

> *T. Makkonen, "Report on measures to combat discrimination:*   **2.FI.5.**
> *Directive 2000/43/EC and 2000/78/EC. Country report Finland"*[40]

"Only the Non-Discrimination Act [yhdenvertaisuuslaki 21/2004)], implementing the two Directives, contains an express definition of direct discrimination. Direct discrimination is defined in section 6(2) of the Act as follows:
  'Discrimination means:
  1) the treatment of a person less favourably than the way another person is treated, has been treated or would be treated in a comparable situation (direct discrimination).'
  Other parts of legislation approach discrimination differently. Section 6(2) of the Constitution [perustuslaki (731/1999)] prohibits 'putting of a person into a different position without an acceptable reason'. Section 11:9 of the Penal Code [rikoslaki (391/1889)] defines discrimination as 'putting a person into a manifestly unequal position or into substantially worse position than the others, without an acceptable reason'. Section 47:3 of the Penal Code defines discrimination in employment as 'putting of an employee or a prospective [sic] into a disadvantageous position without a weighty, acceptable reason'."

Whilst evidence of convergence towards the norm set by the Directives can be identified, it is notable that three significant legal systems, the UK, France and Germany, continue to exhibit considerable differences in this area. The following discussion will also consider the case of the Netherlands, which has certain distinctive features.

2.2.3.A.   UK

The UK possesses a highly fragmented statutory framework of anti-discrimination law. There are different laws governing each ground of discrimination and, in some cases, more than one piece of legislation in relation to a specific ground. For example, discrimination on grounds of religion or belief is prohibited in employment by virtue of the Employment Equality (Religion or Belief) Regulations 2003[41] and discrimination on grounds of religion or belief in specified areas outside employment (e.g. access to goods and services) is prohibited by Part II of the Equality Act 2006. To add to the complexity, most grounds of discrimination are regulated by different legal instruments in respect of Northern Ireland. Notwithstanding this statutory patchwork quilt, the predominant definition of direct discrimination is well-represented in section 1 of the Race Relations Act 1976:

---

[40] (European Commission, 2005) 9, available on the website of Directorate-General for Employment, Social Affairs and Equal Opportunities.
[41] Statutory Instrument (S.I.) 1660.

"(1) A person discriminates against another in any circumstances relevant for the purposes of any provision of this Act if

(a) on racial grounds he treats that other less favourably than he treats or would treat other persons."

This must be read in conjunction with section 3(4), which states:

"A comparison of the case of a person of a particular racial group with that of a person not of that group under section 1(1) . . . must be such that the relevant circumstances in the one case are the same, or not materially different, in the other".

Although not identical, this conforms to the essential requirements for the definition of direct discrimination as found in the Racial Equality Directive. A fairly similar approach to direct discrimination can be found in other British legal provisions.[42] In contrast, the Disability Discrimination Act (DDA) 1995 has pursued a different concept of discrimination. Originally, the Act did not employ the notions of direct and indirect discrimination. Instead, a dichotomy was created between "discrimination for a reason relating to disability" and "failure to make a reasonable adjustment". The decision to adopt a different scheme reflected a concern that the strict comparator approach in direct discrimination would be difficult to apply in disability cases. Unlike sex or race, disability is more likely to have an impact on the way in which a job can be performed. Simply guaranteeing the sameness of treatment will often not result in equality in practice.

In order to comply with the Employment Equality Directive, the DDA was amended in 2004 to insert a specific definition of direct discrimination alongside the other categories of discrimination that already existed. Direct discrimination is prohibited by section 3A(5):

"A person directly discriminates against a disabled person if, on the ground of the disabled person's disability, he treats the disabled person less favourably than he treats or would treat a person not having that particular disability whose relevant circumstances, including his abilities, are the same as, or not materially different from, those of the disabled person."

This form of discrimination is not open to justification; however, its utility is constrained by the requirement for the comparator to have similar abilities to the disabled person. In many cases, a disabled person will be the subject of less favourable treatment because their disability impacts upon the way in which they would be able to perform their job. For example, consider the situation of a person refused a job because it occasionally entails lifting heavy objects and they are unable to carry out this because of a disability (such as an upper limb disorder). Their comparator would be another person who could not lift heavy objects for a reason not connected to disability (e.g. lack of strength). If the employer can demonstrate that he or she would not have recruited any person unable to lift heavy objects, then direct

[42] Sex Discrimination Act 1975, ss. 1(1)(a) and 1(2)(a); Employment Equality (Religion or Belief) Regulations 2003, Reg. 3(1)(a); Employment Equality (Sexual Orientation) Regulations 2003 (S.I. 1661), Reg. 3(1)(a); Equality Act 2006, s. 45(1); Employment Equality (Age) Regulations 2006 (S.I. 1031), Reg. 3.

discrimination has not occurred. The employer may, though, be committing other forms of discrimination under the Act, in particular, a failure to comply with the duty to make reasonable adjustments. An example of direct discrimination which would successfully fall within this section could be the following. A person with disfigurement of their facial skin is not hired for a position as a shop assistant because the employer thinks that this would disturb customers. A person without the disfigurement but with the same abilities would have been appointed, so this would amount to direct discrimination.

The broader counterpart to direct discrimination under the DDA is discrimination for a reason relating to disability. This form of discrimination embraces a mixture of the concepts of direct and indirect discrimination found in other areas of anti-discrimination law. The principal difference is that the comparison needed to demonstrate less favourable treatment is more flexible than that applying to direct discrimination. At the same time, it is open to the employer to justify less favourable treatment related to disability; this option is not open in respect of direct discrimination. Section 3A(1) states:

" . . .a person discriminates against a disabled person if—

(a) for a reason which relates to the disabled person's disability, he treats him less favourably than he treats or would treat others to whom that reason does not or would not apply; and

(b) he cannot show that the treatment in question is justified."

In *Clark* v. *Novacold* [1999] IRLR 318, the Court of Appeal clarified that the appropriate comparator for demonstrating discrimination for a reason relating to disability is not someone with a similar ability unconnected to disability, but simply someone who does not have that disability. The "sick man" comparator was rejected. Essentially, tribunals have to consider how the person would have been treated in the absence of their disability. In this case, the complainant was dismissed following an absence from work caused by a disability. If he had not had the disability, he would not have been absent from work and consequently would not have been dismissed. Therefore, he was treated less favourably for a reason relating to his disability. Whilst the approach of the courts to the identification of a comparator in this context has been broad and flexible, it has been combined with discretion for employers at the justification stage. An employer needs to demonstrate that the reason for the rule or practice was of "real weight and thus be of substance".[43] Yet, it is not required that the employer's practice was the best possible in the circumstances.[44] It remains to be seen how the ECJ will view the different conceptual framework for prohibiting disability discrimination in the UK. Notably, there is no definition of indirect discrimination within the DDA.

---

[43] Arden LJ, *Jones* v. *Post Office* [2001] IRLR 384 CA.
[44] Ibid.

2.2.3.B.   FRANCE

The foundation for French anti-discrimination law is the constitutional principle of equality. This has strong historical roots, developing from the 1789 Declaration on the rights of man and the citizen.[45] Moreover, the universal principle of the equality of all citizens underpins the constitutional ideology of the French Republic.[46] Article 1 of the 1958 Constitution states:

> "France guarantees equality before the law to all citizens without distinction based on origin, race or religion. She respects all beliefs."[47]

The content of the equality principle bears clear imprints of the Aristotelian model. It is, though, distinguished by a stronger emphasis on equality as the sameness of treatment.[48]

Flowing from the general principle of equality, legislative prohibitions of discrimination have traditionally been couched in open terms with no specific reference to direct or indirect discrimination. For example, Article 225-1 of the Penal Code states:

> "Any distinction made between natural persons because of their origin, their sex, their family situation, their pregnancy, their physical appearance, their surname, their state of health, their disability, their genetic characteristics, their way of life, their sexual orientation, their age, their political opinions, their trade union activities, their belonging or non-belonging, real or assumed, to a determined ethnicity, nation, race or religion constitutes discrimination."

Similarly, Article L. 123-1 of the Labour Code on equality between women and men does not expressly refer to direct or indirect discrimination.

The process of implementing the 2000 anti-discrimination Directives stimulated legislative recognition of the direct/indirect discrimination dichotomy. Yet, in contrast to most other EU Member States, France did not choose to include a legislative definition of these concepts. Article L. 122-45 of the Labour Code now provides:

> "No-one can be excluded from a recruitment procedure or access to a work placement or a period of training in a firm; no employee can be disciplined, dismissed or subjected to a discriminatory measure, direct or indirect, notably in relation to remuneration in the sense of Article L. 140-2, or bonus schemes or the distributing of shares, training, alternative employment, assignments, qualifications, classification, professional advancement, variation or renewal of the contract by reason of his origin, sex, way of life, sexual orientation, age, family situation or her pregnancy, his genetic characteristics, his belonging or non-belonging, real or assumed, to a determined ethnicity, nation or race, his political

---

[45] D. Borrillo, "Les instruments juridiques français et européens dans la mise en place du principe d'égalité et de non-discrimination" (2002) *Revue français des affaires socials*, at 113.

[46] S Latraverse, "Report on Measures to Combat Discrimination: Directive 2000/43/EC and 2000/78/EC. Country Report France" (European Commission, 2005) 3, available on the website of Directorate-General for Employment, Social Affairs and Equal Opportunities.

[47] Translation by S. Latraverse, *ibid.*

[48] See Borrillo, above n. 45, 117; E. Dockès, "Equality in Labour Law: an Economically Efficient Human Right? Reflections from a French Law Perspective" (2002) 18 *IJCLLIR* 187, 189. This is discussed further in Introductory Chapter.

opinions, his trade union activities or activities as a member of an association, his religious beliefs, his physical appearance, his surname or by reason of his state of health or his disability."

The meaning of "direct" and "indirect" discrimination have been left for future judicial interpretation.

2.2.3.C.   THE NETHERLANDS

Like the UK, the Netherlands possesses a rather fragmented statutory framework on non-discrimination.[49] On the one hand, the 1994 General Equal Treatment Act is the broadest instrument, prohibiting discrimination in employment and access to goods and services on the grounds of religion, belief, political orientation, race, sex, nationality, sexual orientation and marital status.[50] This is complemented by specific legislation on discrimination on grounds of sex, working time (part-time and temporary workers), disability and chronic illness, and age.[51] A novelty of these provisions is that they do not contain a definition of direct discrimination, nor do they use the term "discrimination"; instead, they refer to "distinction". For example, section 1 of the 1994 General Equal Treatment Act states:

"In this Act and in the provisions based upon this Act the following definitions shall apply:

a.   Distinction: direct and indirect distinction, as well as the instruction to make a distinction;

b.   Direct distinction: distinction between persons on the grounds of religion, belief, political opinion, race, sex, nationality, hetero- or homosexual orientation or marital status; . . ."[52]

The compatibility of this approach with that found within the EC Directives is discussed below.

> M. Gijzen, "Report on measures to combat discrimination: **2.NL.6.**
> Directive 2000/43/EC and 2000/78/EC. Country report Netherlands"[53]

"In order to understand Dutch non discrimination law the following is vital to bear in mind. Article 1 of the Constitution, as well as the relevant Articles in the Criminal Code are centred

---

[49] See further, J. Gerards, "Implementation of the Art. 13 Directives in Dutch Equal Treatment Legislation" (2006) 13 MJ 291; M. Gijzen, *Selected Issues in Equal Treatment Law: a Multi-layered Comparison of European, English and Dutch Law* (Antwerp, Intersentia, 2006).
[50] Algemene Wet Gelijke Behandeling (AWGB), Staatsblad 1994, 230.
[51] See further Gerards, above n. 49.
[52] Source: M. Gijzen, "Report on Measures to Combat Discrimination: Directive 2000/43/EC and 2000/78/EC. Country Report Netherlands" (European Commission, 2005), available on the website of Directorate-General for Employment, Social Affairs and Equal Opportunities.
[53] (European Commission, 2005) 13–14, available on the website of Directorate-General for Employment, Social Affairs and Equal Opportunities.

around a concept of discrimination. In contrast, the Statutory non discrimination Acts are all centred around a prohibition from making distinction [*verbod om onderscheid te maken*]. The Statutory Acts do not therefore employ the term discrimination. What is the difference between discrimination and distinction in the Dutch non discrimination context? Discrimination in Dutch law has a highly pejorative connotation. This means that this concept is strongly linked up with the idea of disadvantage. Connected to that, discrimination mirrors the theory of 'group justice' in the sense that the notion of discrimination is not a neutral notion, but one which is related to the disadvantaged position of the group to which a particular individual applicant belongs. In sharp contrast, the notion distinction is a neutral notion. It does not attach importance to the question, whether the individual applicant belongs to an 'advantaged' or 'disadvantaged' group in society (e.g. to the racial majority, or the racial minority). The explanatory memorandum to the General Equal Treatment Act, clearly states that the prohibition of making distinction is restricted to distinctions which cannot be justified. In other words: only unjustified distinctions are prohibited under the General Equal Treatment Act. This same approach is followed by the Disability Discrimination Act and the Age Discrimination Act which equally focus upon the concept of *onderscheid*.

Given that Directives 2000/43 and 2000/78 employ the notion of discrimination, the transposition of these Directives fuelled a debate in Dutch legal circles, on the use of the correct legal terminology (distinction or discrimination?). Indeed, the Council of State (*Raad van State*), which is the highest advisor of the government in drafting new legislation, had advised the government to abandon the neutral concept distinction and had shown itself advocate of using the more normative concept discrimination. The principal reason for this preference was in order to bring the terminology of Dutch anti-discrimination law in line with EC Equality Law. However, the government has not followed this advice and it has received support for this stance from the Equal Treatment Commission. In the Commission's view, the term *discriminatie* would wrongly give the impression that the alleged discriminator had the intention to discriminate and cause disadvantage. Under both the Article 13 Directives and under the General Equal Treatment Act/ the Disability Discrimination Act/ the Age Discrimination Act, a perpetrator's intention to discriminate is not a material ingredient for the successfulness of a complaint. Thus, rather than being punitive in nature, the law's nature is remedial. As Waaldijk observes in his report on sexual orientation,[54] the government has indicated that no problems have arisen in the case law with regard to the Dutch terminology and, that the European Commission has not pointed at any problems either. In the government's opinion, the neutral term distinction, provides more legal certainty and hence, more legal protection. The government has nevertheless promised that it would look into the question of the most appropriate terminology again. As will be explained below in more detail, it appears that the Dutch term distinction is wider than the Directives' term discrimination. Therefore, the use of the Dutch term is acceptable."

---

[54] K. Waaldijk, "Report of the European Group of Experts on Combating Sexual Orientation Discrimination. The Netherlands" (European Commission, 2004), available on the website of Directorate-General for Employment, Social Affairs and Equal Opportunities.

2.2.3.D.   GERMANY

The final example to consider in this section is that of Germany. The starting point of anti-discrimination law is the constitutional provisions on equality. These are particularly relevant to employment law relationships governed by public law, such as civil servants, where the constitutional provisions are binding and directly applicable.[55] Article 3 states:

> "(1) All persons shall be equal before the law.
> (2) Men and women shall have equal rights. The state shall promote the actual implementation of equal rights for women and men and take steps to eliminate disadvantages that now exist.
> (3) No person shall be favoured or disfavoured because of sex, parentage, race, language, homeland and origin, faith, or religious or political opinions. No person shall be disfavoured because of disability."[56]

Article 3(1) embodies the Aristotelian concept of equality. Peters states that it "requires that those that are relevantly equal must be treated alike, and those that are relevantly unequal must be treated differently. The problem is, of course, to determine the relevant element of comparison."[57] In addition, specific anti-discrimination legislation applies to private sector employment relationships. There are various statutory provisions relating to discrimination, in particular on grounds of sex[58] and serious disability.[59] These do not provide statutory definitions of direct discrimination. Instead, discrimination is prohibited in general terms. The broadest protection (in terms of grounds) is found within the Workplace Constitution Act. This does not, however, create rights for individual employees, but instead binds the employer in respect of the Works Council.

Workplace Constitution Act (Betriebsverfassungsgesetz (BetrVG)) **2.DE.7.**
of 27 July 2001[60]

§ 75 (1) The employer and the works council must ensure that all persons employed within the organisation are treated according to just and equitable principles, and in particular that there is no different treatment of persons due to their race, religion, nationality, origins, political or trade union activity or attitudes or because of their sex or sexual identity. They must ensure that employees are not subjected to discrimination as they exceed certain ages.

---

[55] D. Schiek, *Differenzierte Gerechtigkeit* (Baden-Baden, Nomos, 2000).
[56] Translation in: S. Baer, "Report on Measures to Combat Discrimination: Directive 2000/43/EC and 2000/78/EC. Country Report Germany" (European Commission, 2005) 13, available on the website of Directorate-General for Employment, Social Affairs and Equal Opportunities.
[57] A. Peters, *Women, Quotas and Constitutions* (The Hague, Kluwer Law International, 1999) 149–50.
[58] Sections 611a and 612a, inserted by Equal Treatment (EC) Act, BGB 1980 1, 1308.
[59] Sozialgesetzbuch, Part IX, s. 81(2).
[60] Bundesdesetzblatt Teil I 2001 Nr. 39 27.01.2001 S. 1852.

The process of implementing the Article 13 Directives in Germany was subject to various delays.[61] New legislation was finally adopted in summer 2006. The German Non-discrimination Act 2006 adopts a definition of direct discrimination which is clearly influenced by the approach taken in the Directives:

> "§ 3(1) Direct discrimination occurs when a person experiences, experienced, or would experience a less favourable treatment than another person in a comparable situation on any of the grounds mentioned in § 1. Direct sex discrimination also occurs in . . . the case of less favourable treatment of a pregnant woman or motherhood."

The prohibited grounds of discrimination listed in § 1 are: "race, ethnic origin, gender, religious or other consciously held beliefs, disability, age, or sexual identity".

This section has considered the emergence of direct discrimination out of general, undefined notions of non-discrimination or equality. It has traced the growing recognition of the dichotomy between direct and indirect discrimination, both within the case-law of the ECJ and, more recently, by the ECtHR. The most precise definitions of direct discrimination remain located in legislation. The 2000 anti-discrimination Directives have provided a spur for many European states to introduce statutory definitions of direct discrimination, very often modelled on the text of the Directives. Nonetheless, there are still states, such as France and the Netherlands, where the meaning of direct discrimination has not been codified in legislation.

2.3. ESTABLISHING DIRECT DISCRIMINATION

Even where direct discrimination is defined in statute, its practical implementation throws up several key themes that are central to its effectiveness. These are typically issues addressed through judicial interpretation and which go to the heart of the concept of equality that underpins the legislation. This section first considers questions of causation and the role for comparators in establishing direct discrimination. Secondly, the relevance of intent on the part of the discriminator is assessed, a subject which is closely linked to the law's treatment of stereotyping. Finally, this section examines the notion of less favourable treatment; does this include any differences in treatment or only those imposing a significant detriment on the victim?

---

[61] For discussion of earlier legislative proposals, see F. Stork, "Comments on the Draft of the New German Private Law Anti-discrimination Act: Implementing Directive 2000/43/EC and 2004/113EC in German Private Law" (2005) 6(2) *German Law Journal.*

2.3.1.   CAUSATION AND COMPARATORS

When considering the definition of direct discrimination provided in the anti-discrimination Directives, a core requirement is that the complainant can demonstrate that they have been "treated less favourably than another is, has been or would be treated in a comparable situation".[62] The underlying question in any direct discrimination case is therefore *why* was the person treated less favourably? Was it because of a prohibited characteristic or because of other reasons (e.g. poor performance in the workplace)? The way in which comparators are used within litigation on direct discrimination can be linked back to the concept of equality that underpins the legislation. In particular, an emphasis on identifying a similarly situated comparator reflects the Aristotelian notion that "likes should be treated alike". If two persons are in a comparable situation, then they should be treated in the same way, with no regard to irrelevant characteristics, such as religion or sexual orientation. In the employment context, this means that employers should not take into account such characteristics when making decisions on whom to hire, promote or dismiss. Decisions should be fair and rational, based on "merit".

Superficially, this appears to be a straightforward, logical and even common-sense approach to equality. Yet it is problematic on several levels. The first criticism that has been made concerns the relatively empty nature of the formula "likes should be treated alike".[63] Its meaning and impact depends entirely on when persons are deemed to be in a like situation. This is certainly a problem in direct discrimination cases, where the complainant and respondent will often dispute the identification of the "correct" comparator. Changing the comparator will often change the outcome of the case. As will be illustrated in the cases discussed below, there is a real risk that the courts' choice of comparator becomes rather arbitrary and lacks a consistent rationale. In her analysis of Dutch courts' approach to determining whether a comparable situation exists, Gerards criticises the very limited explanations provided by courts for why a given situation is to be treated as comparable (or not):

> "this is a problem, because the assessment is then highly non-transparent and easily influenced by subjective opinions as a result thereof: it is not possible, or very difficult, to verify the objective basis the court has used in determining comparability."[64]

Secondly, the identified comparator becomes the "norm".[65] As long as the individual complainant has been treated in a similar way to the comparator, then direct discrimination will not be established. This presupposes an inherent neutrality in the standard

---

[62] E.g. Art. 2(2)(a) Racial Equality Directive.

[63] L. Betten, "New Equality Provisions in European Law: some Thoughts on the Fundamental Value of Equality as a Legal Principle" in K. Economides, L. Betten, J. Bridge, A. Tettenborn and V. Shrubsall (eds.), *Fundamental Values* (Oxford, Hart Publishing, 2000) 73.

[64] See Gerards, above n. 7, 566–7.

[65] N. Lacey, *Unspeakable Subjects—Feminist Essays in Legal and Social Theory* (Oxford, Hart, 1998) 24.

of treatment accorded to the comparator. Yet the norm reflected in the comparator may simply enshrine organisational culture or behaviour that runs counter to a substantive notion of equality. Fredman refers to the "powerful conformist pressures" arising from a comparator who is typically the white, male, able-bodied person.[66] For example, if the organisational norm is to work long hours, including overtime at short notice, this will tend to exclude women as they remain disproportionately responsible for caring, both for children and for older relatives. Whilst such practices could be challenged as indirect discrimination, direct discrimination is of little assistance. Here the male "norm" reinforces underlying patterns of inequality.

The third difficulty arising with the comparator requirement is the difficulty in locating a comparator in some situations. On the one hand, this may relate to patterns of segregation. There are well-documented patterns of occupational segregation by gender that militate against an individual finding a comparator.[67] Where a particular sector of employment is dominated by persons of a particular gender, then it may in practice be hard to find any actual comparator. In other situations, the comparator requirement seems artificial and difficult to apply. This is most evident in the context of sex discrimination cases linked to pregnancy. It is manifestly impossible to find a pregnant male comparator and over time courts have been torn between drawing on supposedly comparable situations, such as the "sick man", and rejecting the possibility for comparison altogether. Similarly, comparators in the area of gender reassignment discrimination are problematic. Such examples question the need to impose a comparator requirement for all instances of direct discrimination. On one side, Wintemute argues that "claims of discrimination without comparison are impossible".[68] This line of reasoning contends that it is always necessary to have some external benchmark or reference point by which to evaluate the act or practice being challenged. Here, the comparator is an essential mechanism for distinguishing discriminatory treatment from merely detrimental treatment. For example, if a well-qualified woman has not been given a job promotion, a comparison with a similarly situated man should reveal whether this was a discriminatory decision rather than merely a capricious act on the part of the employer.

Other commentators contest the need for a comparator in every instance of direct discrimination. Bamforth suggests that "discrimination does not, as a social practice, depend on comparisons—rather, members of particular groups are discriminated against because of characteristics society has ascribed to those groups".[69] Izzi argues that there are some situations where direct discrimination is self-evident without the need for a comparator.[70] These are typically scenarios where the less favourable

---

[66] S. Fredman, *Discrimination Law* (Oxford, Oxford University Press, 2002) 98.

[67] U. Behning and A. Pascual, "Comparison of the Adaptation of Gender Mainstreaming in National Employment Strategies" in U. Behning and A.Pascual (eds.), *Gender Mainstreaming in the European Employment Strategy* (Brussels, European Trade Union Institute, 2001) 323.

[68] R. Wintemute, "When is Pregnancy Discrimination Indirect Sex Discrimination?" (1998) 27 *ILJ* 23, 25.

[69] N. Bamforth, "The Changing Concept of Sex Discrimination" (1993) 56 *MLR* 872, 880.

[70] D. Izzi, "Discriminazione senza comparazione? Appunti sulle direttive comunitarie 'di seconda generazione'" (2003) n. 99/100 *Giornale di diritto del lavoro e di relazioni industriali* 423, 426.

treatment is overtly based on a suspect characteristic, for example, a ban on night-working that only applies to women. In such cases, a comparator seems superfluous, even an unwarranted distraction. The following extract provides an illustration of a case where the comparator requirement does not appear helpful to the identification of direct discrimination.

ECJ, 30 April 1996[71]   **2.EC.8.**
Case C–13/94, P v. S and Cornwall County Council

SEX DISCRIMINATION AND TRANSSEXUALS

P v. S

Facts: P informed her employer that she intended to undergo gender reassignment (from male to female). Subsequently, her employer decided to terminate her employment. P argued that her dismissal constituted unlawful sex discrimination.

Held: The Gender Employment Directive precluded the dismissal of a transsexual for a reason related to gender reassignment.

Judgment: "14. The United Kingdom and the Commission submit that to dismiss a person because he or she is a transsexual or because he or she has undergone a gender-reassignment operation does not constitute sex discrimination for the purposes of the Directive.

15. In support of that argument, the United Kingdom points out in particular that it appears from the order for reference that the employer would also have dismissed P. if P. had previously been a woman and had undergone an operation to become a man.

16. The European Court of Human Rights has held that "the term 'transsexual' is usually applied to those who, whilst belonging physically to one sex, feel convinced that they belong to the other; they often seek to achieve a more integrated, unambiguous identity by undergoing medical treatment and surgical operations to adapt their physical characteristics to their psychological nature. Transsexuals who have been operated upon thus form a fairly well-defined and identifiable group" (*Rees* v. *United Kingdom* para. 38, Series A, 106).

17. The principle of equal treatment "for men and women" to which the Directive refers in its title, preamble and provisions means, as Articles 2(1) and 3(1) in particular indicate, that there should be "no discrimination whatsoever on grounds of sex".

18. Thus, the directive is simply the expression, in the relevant field, of the principle of equality, which is one of the fundamental principles of Community law.

19. Moreover, as the Court has repeatedly held, the right not to be discriminated against on grounds of sex is one of the fundamental human rights whose observance the Court has a duty to ensure (see, to that effect, Case 149/77, *Defrenne* v. *SABENA* [1978] E.C.R. 1365, [1978] 3 C.M.L.R. 312, paras 26-27 and Joined Cases 75 & 117/82, *Razzouk and Beydoun* v. *E.C. Commission* [1984] E.C.R. 1509, para. 16.)

20. Accordingly, the scope of the Directive cannot be confined simply to discrimination based on the fact that a person is of one or other sex. In view of its purpose and the nature of the rights which it seeks to safeguard, the scope of the Directive is also such as to apply to discrimination arising, as in this case, from the gender reassignment of the person concerned.

---

[71] [1996] ECR I–2143.

21. Such discrimination is based, essentially if not exclusively, on the sex of the person concerned. Where a person is dismissed on the ground that he or she intends to undergo, or has undergone, gender reassignment, he or she is treated unfavourably by comparison with persons of the sex to which he or she was deemed to belong before undergoing gender reassignment.

22. To tolerate such discrimination would be tantamount, as regards such a person, to a failure to respect the dignity and freedom to which he or she is entitled, and which the Court has a duty to safeguard."

Notes

(1) The Court's decision combines a human rights based analysis with reference to the comparator test. In particular, it clearly rejects the "equal misery" comparator proposed by the UK (paragraph 15) and instead compares *P*'s treatment with that of a man who did not undergo gender reassignment (paragraph 21).

(2) The choice of comparator seems value-driven in this case. The Court cites fundamental human rights as well as individual dignity in supporting its decision. The Court seems to be arguing that the contextual values at stake support using any discretion it enjoys in favour of choosing a comparator which results in protection from discrimination for *P*. In paragraph 17, the Court notes that the Directive required no discrimination whatsoever on grounds of sex.

(3) This case could have been an opportunity to depart from the comparator requirement altogether. After all, is a man who has not undergone gender reassignment really in a similar situation to *P*? Paragraph 21 can also be read as suggesting that the comparator could be *P* herself, prior to undergoing gender reassignment. The choice of comparator in *P* has proven difficult to apply in subsequent cases (see below).

The approach of legal systems to the relevance and importance of a comparator in direct discrimination cases varies considerably. An emphasis on identifying an appropriate comparator is strongest in UK legislation, which goes further than other national and European legislation in specifying the characteristics of the comparator. Section 3(4) of the Race Relations Act 1976 is typical:

> "A comparison of the case of a person of a particular racial group with that of a person not of that group . . . must be such that the relevant circumstances in the one case are the same, or not materially different, in the other".[72]

Consequently, the first step in a direct discrimination case has conventionally been to identify an appropriate comparator.[73] In a complaint of sex discrimination, a woman would therefore look to identify a man in a comparable situation. Having identified the comparator, the courts compare their treatment and, if less favourable treatment

---

[72] The equivalent provisions are: Sex Discrimination Act 1975, s. 5(3); Employment Equality (Religion or Belief) Regulations 2003, Reg. 3(3); Employment Equality (Sexual Orientation) Regulations 2003, Reg. 3(2); Employment Equality (Age) Regulations 2006, Reg. 3(2).

[73] A departure from this approach is suggested by Lord Nicholls in *Shamoon* v. *Chief Constable of the Royal Ulster Constabulary* [2003] 2 All ER 26 HL. His judgment recognizes that in some cases it will be appropriate to examine causation at the same time as considering the appropriate comparator.

is uncovered, seek to identify the reason why the complainant was so treated. The identification of the comparator is consequently an important, although not an absolute, prerequisite to a successful claim for direct discrimination. Many cases stumble at this hurdle. There are some recent signs of a shift away from erecting the identification of the appropriate comparator as the first stage in analysis of direct discrimination.

Unlike the UK, other systems have not placed the same emphasis on identifying a comparator in similar circumstances to the complainant. Instead, the nature of the judicial inquiry proceeds directly to the question of causation, in other words, whether the reason for the treatment was discriminatory. Analysis of the cause of the treatment is therefore intertwined with the consideration of how comparable situations are treated.[74] Within this inquiry, comparators become one avenue to establish causation, but not the exclusive route. This approach can be seen in the case-law of the Court of Cassation in France.

Court of Cassation, Criminal Division, 14 June 2000[75]   **2.FR.9.**
CFDT Inter-Co v. Fort

ROLE FOR COMPARATORS IN IDENTIFYING CAUSE OF TREATMENT

CFDT Inter-Co

Facts: It was alleged that an employee experienced discrimination on the grounds of his trade union activities. Having received positive workplace evaluations prior to becoming a trade union representative, his career did not subsequently progress and he was effectively demoted. The employer contended that his treatment was due to disciplinary problems and poor occupational performance.

Held: Whilst the decision of the Court of Appeal had been favourable to the employer, this was overturned by the Court of Cassation. In particular, the latter noted the failure of the Court of Appeal to compare his treatment with that of another employee with similar qualifications and seniority (but presumably not acting as a trade union representative). This would have been one means of verifying the presence or absence of discrimination.

Judgment: "the Court of Appeal, which has omitted to analyse all the facts presented by the civil party, and has not considered, notably by making a comparative study with another worker of equivalent qualifications and seniority, if during the development of his professional career until 1996 the worker had not been subject to discrimination connected to his trade union role and activities, has not given a legal basis for its decision."

Gerards notes differences within the approach of Dutch courts to the role for comparators. The Dutch Supreme Court, the Central Appeals Tribunal and the Administrative Law Division begin their analysis of equal treatment cases by

---

[74] On the slippage between comparability and justification, see Case C–356/98 *Kaba* [2000] ECR I–2623. See further, G. de Búrca, "Unpacking the Concept of Discrimination in EC and International Trade Law" in C. Barnard and J. Scott, *The Law of the Single European Market—Unpacking the Premises* (Oxford, Hart Publishing, 2002) 193.

[75] No. 99–81108.

searching for the identification of a comparable situation. If comparability is absent, then the difference in treatment is treated as permissible.[76] In contrast, the Equal Treatment Commission proceeds from a focus on disadvantage. This means that the first stage is to consider whether the complainant has been subject to disadvantage and then secondly to consider whether there are any reasons that might justify that disadvantage.[77] Gerards argues that whilst the courts' identification of a comparable situation lacks transparent analytical criteria, and is hence uncertain, the Equal Treatment Commission's focus on disadvantage is more objective.[78]

As many European states do not place the same focus on identifying an appropriate comparator as found in the UK, there is often no substantial body of case-law in this area. Nevertheless, this issue has featured significantly in the case-law of the ECJ, frequently arising from preliminary references from the UK.

2.3.1.A.   CHOOSING THE APPROPRIATE COMPARATOR

The general principle of equal treatment within EC law is closely tied to a classical comparator test. In *A* v. *Commission*, the Court of First Instance summarised the case-law in the following statement:

> "the principle of equal treatment is breached when two categories of persons whose factual and legal circumstances disclose no essential difference are treated differently or where situations which are different are treated in an identical manner."[79]

Consequently, the fortunes of many cases turn on the Court's decision on whether the relative situations of persons or groups of persons are comparable in nature. This is also true for the substantial body of case-law on discrimination between non-physical persons or objects, such as differential treatment of products, producers and companies.[80] The 1976 Gender Employment Directive did not include a statutory definition of direct discrimination. Nevertheless, debates around comparators and sex discrimination have figured prominently in the existing ECJ case-law. This part examines various cases that illustrate wider difficulties with the comparator requirement.

The first set of extracts concern how to choose the "correct" comparator. The malleability of the comparator requirement renders it a flexible instrument for the courts to adapt to specific case circumstances. This can, though, slip into arbitrary and inconsistent reasoning. This danger is displayed in several cases around the boundary between discrimination on grounds of sex, gender reassignment and sexual orientation.

---

[76] See Gerards, above n. 7, 647.
[77] *Ibid.*, 649. See also 561–4.
[78] *Ibid.*, 649.
[79] Case T–10/93 *A* v. *Commission* [1994] ECR II–179, para. 42.
[80] G. More, "The Principle of Equal Treatment: from Market Unifier to Fundamental Right?" in P. Craig and G. de Búrca (eds.), *The Evolution of EU Law* (Oxford University Press, Oxford, 1999).

As discussed above, in *P* v. *S* the ECJ recognised that dismissal for a reason relating to gender reassignment was direct discrimination on grounds of sex. Whilst not completely abandoning the language of comparators, the Court stressed the human rights dimension and, in particular, the principle of human dignity. The next case to reach the ECJ concerning gender reassignment discrimination was Case C–117/01 *KB* v. *NHS Trust Pensions Agency* [2004] ECR I–541. This case concerned a woman (KB) with a transgender male partner. KB worked for the British National Health System (NHS) and was a member of the occupational pension scheme. In the event of her death, a survivor pension would be payable to her spouse. She was not, however, able to marry her partner because he was treated in UK law as a woman (according to his birth certificate). This complex fact scenario presented discrimination in two stages; the fact that the survivor pension was linked to marriage and that marriage, in turn, was not open to a person in KB's situation. Whilst the Advocate-General treated this as direct discrimination,[81] the Court argued that it was closer to indirect discrimination. It considered that the requirement to marry in order to receive the survivor pension applied to all scheme members, but placed persons in the situation of KB at a disadvantage.[82] As in *P* v. *S*, the Court does invoke a comparator test, but alongside a strong emphasis on the human rights dimension (leading it to find in favour of KB).

The next case illustrates the difficulty of applying the *P* v. *S* comparator in other situations of gender reassignment discrimination.

ECJ, 27 April 2006[83]   **2.EC.10.**
Case C–423/04, Richards v. *Secretary of State for Work and Pensions*

SEX DISCRIMINATION AND TRANSSEXUALS

Richards

Facts: The applicant was a male-to-female transsexual who applied to receive a state retirement pension from her 60th birthday. This was refused because (a) only women were entitled to the state retirement pension at 60 (men at 65) and (b) under the domestic law applying at the time in question the applicant was treated as male. She challenged this refusal as sex discrimination contrary to Directive 79/7 on equal treatment for men and women in matters of social security.[84]

Held: Refusal of the pension was contrary to Article 4(1) of the Directive.

Opinion of the Advocate-General: "38. The applicant in the present case is denied her pension in circumstances where, had she been registered as female at birth; she would have been entitled to it. The alleged discrimination accordingly lies in the United Kingdom's failure to recognise a

---

[81] Advocate-General Ruiz-Colomer, Opinion of 10 June 2003, para. 76.
[82] Paras. 29–31.
[83] Not yet reported.
[84] Directive 79/7/EEC of 19 December 1978 on the progressive implementation of the principle of equal treatment for men and women in matters of social security [1979] OJ L6/24.

transsexual person in their acquired gender on equal terms with persons recorded as of that gender at birth.

39. The Court stated in *P* v. *S* that, where a person is dismissed on the ground that he or she intends to undergo, or has undergone, gender reassignment, he or she is treated unfavourably by comparison with persons of the sex to which he or she was deemed to belong before undergoing gender reassignment (Paragraph 21).

40. If that approach were applied in the present case, the correct comparator for the applicant would thus be 'persons of the sex to which he or she was deemed to belong before undergoing gender reassignment'. That class would comprise male pension claimants, who are not entitled to a pension until they reach the age of 65, so that there would be no discrimination.

41. I agree with the Commission however that the reasoning to be used in applying sex discrimination law to the case of transsexual persons should differ from the classical model which is always based on a straightforward comparison between men and women.

42. *P* v. *S* was a particularly clear case of discrimination, since it was accepted that the dismissal was 'for a reason related to a gender reassignment'. Whether the comparator was a man who was not proposing to have gender reassignment surgery or a woman who had not had such surgery, the result would have been the same: in comparison with such a person, the applicant had been disadvantaged . . .

44. In *KB* the situation was different. In arriving at its conclusion that the exclusion of the female-to-male transsexual partner of a female member of the National Health Service Pension Scheme constituted sex discrimination contrary to Article 141 EC, the Court compared the couple to 'a heterosexual couple where neither partner's identity is the result of gender reassignment surgery and the couple are therefore able to marry' (Paragraph 31). The correct comparator in the case of the female-to-male transsexual was therefore a male person whose identity was not the result of gender reassignment surgery.

45. In the present case also that seems to me to be the correct basis of comparison. The applicant is denied her pension in circumstances where, had she been registered as female at birth; she would have been entitled to it. The alleged discrimination accordingly lies in the United Kingdom's failure to recognise a transsexual person in their acquired gender on equal terms with persons recorded as of that gender at birth, precisely the issue in KB. I consider therefore that the correct comparator in the present case concerning a male-to-female transsexual person is a female person whose identity is not the result of gender reassignment surgery.

46. On that basis, I am of the view that it is contrary to Article 4(1) of Directive 79/7 for a Member State to refuse to grant a retirement pension before the age of 65 to a male-to-female transsexual where that person would have been entitled to a pension at the age of 60 had she been regarded as a woman as a matter of national law."

Judgment: "29. Unlike women whose gender is not the result of gender reassignment surgery and who may receive a retirement pension at the age of 60, Ms Richards is not able to fulfil one of the conditions of eligibility for that pension, in this case that relating to retirement age.

30. As it arises from her gender reassignment, the unequal treatment to which Ms Richards was subject must be regarded as discrimination which is precluded by Article 4(1) of Directive 79/7.

31. The Court has already found that national legislation which precludes a transsexual, in the absence of recognition of his new gender, from fulfilling a requirement which must be met in order to be entitled to a right protected by Community law must be regarded as being, in principle, incompatible with the requirements of Community law."

Notes

(1) Advocate-General Jacobs recognises that more than one comparator could be "correct". He also acknowledges the difficulty of fitting gender reassignment cases within the classical model of comparison in sex discrimination. Nevertheless, there is no suggestion that the comparator requirement could be dispensed with. It is difficult to see how the comparator illuminated further the obvious evidence in this case (and the others) of disadvantage experienced by the complainant because of undergoing gender reassignment.

(2) The Court avoids any classification of the discrimination as either direct or indirect, although it implicitly invokes a non-transgender female comparator in paragraph 29. In substance, the Court's judgments in *KB* and *Richards* are heavily influenced by the decision of the ECtHR in *Goodwin* v. *UK*[85] that the inability to amend the birth certificate of a transsexual person breached Article 8 ECHR (private life). The ECJ is arguably approaching these cases more through the lens of its case-law on respect for general principles of fundamental rights within the scope of Community law than as direct (or indirect) discrimination under specific legislation.

(3) The problems experienced in applying the comparator test to gender reassignment cases are also evident at the national level. For example, see *Croft* v. *Post Office* [2003] IRLR 592. In this case, the English Court of Appeal had to consider an employer's refusal to permit an employee to have access to the female toilets when the employee in question was presenting as a woman but had yet to complete gender reassignment surgery.

The approach developed in *P* v. *S* encouraged further litigation to test the limits of sex discrimination law.

ECJ, 17 February 1998[86]   **2.EC.11.**
Case C–249/96 Grant v. South-West Trains

SEX DISCRIMINATION AND SEXUAL ORIENTATION

Grant

Facts: The employer extended travel concessions to certain relatives of employees, worth around GBP £1000 per year. Whereas travel concessions were available in respect of unmarried partners of the opposite-sex, they were not extended to unmarried partners of the same-sex. The applicant argued that the refusal to supply the travel concession in respect of her same-sex partner was in breach of Article 119 EC (now Article 141 EC) on equal pay for women and men.

Held: The refusal to supply travel concessions to the same-sex partner of an employee, where such concessions were provided for opposite-sex partners, whether married or unmarried, was not discrimination prohibited under Article 119.

Judgment: "26. The refusal to allow Ms Grant the concessions is based on the fact that she does not satisfy the conditions prescribed in those regulations, more particularly on the fact that she

---

[85] (2002) 35 EHRR 18, Application 28957/95.
[86] [1998] ECR I–621.

does not live with a 'spouse' or a person of the opposite sex with whom she has had a 'meaningful' relationship for at least two years.

27. That condition, the effect of which is that the worker must live in a stable relationship with a person of the opposite sex in order to benefit from the travel concessions, is, like the other alternative conditions prescribed in the undertaking's regulations, applied regardless of the sex of the worker concerned. Thus travel concessions are refused to a male worker if he is living with a person of the same sex, just as they are to a female worker if she is living with a person of the same sex.

28. Since the condition imposed by the undertaking's regulations applies in the same way to female and male workers, it cannot be regarded as constituting discrimination directly based on sex.

29. Second, the Court must consider whether, with respect to the application of a condition such as that in issue in the main proceedings, persons who have a stable relationship with a partner of the same sex are in the same situation as those who are married or have a stable relationship outside marriage with a partner of the opposite sex . . .

32. As for the laws of the Member States, while in some of them cohabitation by two persons of the same sex is treated as equivalent to marriage, although not completely, in most of them it is treated as equivalent to a stable heterosexual relationship outside marriage only with respect to a limited number of rights, or else is not recognised in any particular way . . .

35. It follows that, in the present state of the law within the Community, stable relationships between two persons of the same sex are not regarded as equivalent to marriages or stable relationships outside marriage between persons of opposite sex. Consequently, an employer is not required by Community law to treat the situation of a person who has a stable relationship with a partner of the same sex as equivalent to that of a person who is married to or has a stable relationship outside marriage with a partner of the opposite sex."

Notes

(1) Unlike *P* v. *S*, in this case, the ECJ adopts an equal misery comparator.[87] Gay men and lesbians are treated equally poorly by their employer, so there is no discrimination on grounds of sex. The value-driven approach that underpinned the reasoning in *P* v. *S* is less evident. This case illustrates the unpredictability of the comparator test. The approach to selecting the "correct" comparator in *P* v. *S* was not applied in *Grant*, even though the decisions were only 2 years apart. Instead, the Court's change in direction seems more explicable by wider policy considerations. In particular, it referred to the (then) imminent amendment of the EC Treaty to insert Article 13. This created a legal competence for the adoption of specific legislation on sexual orientation discrimination (paragraph 48). It seems that the Court was reluctant to pre-empt any future legislation in this area; rather, it was content to defer the matter to the legislature.[88]

(2) The Court's reasoning in *Grant* was also applied by the UK House of Lords following lengthy litigation around whether sexual orientation discrimination was contrary to the Sex Discrimination Act 1975: Joined Cases *Advocate General for*

---

[87] For an argument against this comparator in sexual orientation cases, see R. Wintemute, "Recognising New Kinds of Direct Sex Discrimination: Transsexualism, Sexual Orientation and Dress Codes" (1997) 60 *MLR* 334.

[88] See also discussion of this case above in ch. 1, excerpt **1.EC.30.**

Scotland v. *MacDonald, Pearce* v. *Mayfield Secondary School Governing Body* [2004] 1 All ER 339.

(3) Another element of the Court's decision in *Grant* is its observation that same-sex couples were not in a comparable situation to either married opposite-sex couples or unmarried opposite-sex couples. A similar approach was taken in Case C–122/99P and 125/99P *D and Sweden* v. *Council* [2001] ECR I–4319, where the Court distinguished Swedish registered partnership from (opposite-sex) marriage. Since these decisions, the ECtHR has accepted that unmarried same-sex couples are in a comparable situation to unmarried opposite-sex couples and that a difference in treatment between these two categories must be shown to be necessary.[89]

(4) Nevertheless, the comparability of married opposite-sex and unmarried same-sex couples remains contested. In *R (on the application of Amicus—MSF and others)* v. *Secretary of State for Trade and Industry and others* [2004] IRLR 430, the English High Court considered a legal challenge to an exception within the Employment Equality (Sexual Orientation) Regulations 2003 designed to protect occupational benefits provided to married employees (for example, a surviving spouse pension entitlement). The judge concluded that unmarried same-sex couples were not comparable to married opposite-sex couples.[90] In various cases, the German courts have also upheld the legitimacy of conferring preferential treatment on married couples in comparison to unmarried same-sex couples,[91] even where the latter are in a legally recognised partnership.[92] These issues will be tested again before the ECJ in pending Case 267/06 *Maruko*, which concerns differences in the treatment of married and registered partners in Germany as regards access to surviving spouse pension entitlements.[93]

2.3.1.B.   DIRECT DISCRIMINATION WITHOUT A COMPARATOR

The above cases demonstrate the general difficulty in pinning down the approach to be followed when selecting a comparator, especially where more than one comparator is potentially "correct". In the cases on gender reassignment discrimination, it is arguable that no comparator is completely appropriate. This dilemma is even greater in relation to discrimination against women because of pregnancy. Some cases have suggested that pregnant women could be compared with men off work because of

---

[89] ECtHR, *Karner* v. *Austria*, 24 July 2003, Application 40016/98. The ECtHR did not accept that generalisations about protection of the "traditional family" were a sufficient justification for excluding same-sex couples from legal protections extended to unmarried opposite-sex couples (paras. 37–41).

[90] Para. 164.

[91] P. Skidmore, "Improving the Position of Lesbians and Gay Men at Work in the Light of the Framework Directive for Equal Treatment in Employment—a German Case Study" in A. Dashwood, J. Spencer, A. Ward and C. Hillion (eds.), *Cambridge Yearbook of European Legal Studies*, Vol. 3 (Oxford, Hart Publishing, 2001) 439.

[92] BVerwG 2 C 43.04, 1 January 2006. See further, M. Mahlmann, "Report on Measures to Combat Discrimination: Directive 2000/43/EC and 2000/78/EC. Country Report Germany" (European Commission, forthcoming).

[93] Case C–267/06 *Tadao Maruko* v. *Versorgungsanstalt de deutschen Bühnen*, lodged 20 June 2006.

sickness.[94] Yet this misses the obvious point that both men and women can be sick, whereas only women can experience pregnancy. Moreover, the notion that pregnancy is akin to sickness is itself objectionable. In the following case, the ECJ rejected the need for a comparator in cases of discrimination because of pregnancy.

ECJ, 8 November 1990[95]   **2.EC.12.**
Case C–177/88, Dekker v. VJV Centrum

COMPARATORS AND PREGNANCY DISCRIMINATION

Dekker

Facts: Mrs Dekker applied for a job as an instructor at a youth training centre. She subsequently informed the committee dealing with the applications that she was pregnant. Although the selection committee identified her as the best candidate, the board of management decided not to appoint her because she was pregnant and, for financial reasons, they would be unable to employ a replacement during her maternity leave.

Held: Refusal to employ a woman on account of her pregnancy was a breach of the principle of equal treatment in Directive 76/207.

Judgment: "10. Consideration must be given to the question whether a refusal of employment in the circumstances to which the national court has referred may be regarded as direct discrimination on grounds of sex for the purposes of the Directive. The answer depends on whether the fundamental reason for the refusal of employment is one which applies without distinction to workers of either sex or, conversely, whether it applies exclusively to one sex.

11. The reason given by the employer for refusing to appoint Mrs Dekker is basically that it could not have obtained reimbursement from the Risicofonds of the daily benefits which it would have had to pay her for the duration of her absence due to pregnancy, and yet at the same time it would have been obliged to employ a replacement. That situation arises because, on the one hand, the national scheme in question assimilates pregnancy to sickness and, on the other, the Ziekengeldreglement contains no provision excluding pregnancy from the cases in which the Risicofonds is entitled to refuse reimbursement of the daily benefits.

12. In that regard it should be observed that only women can be refused employment on grounds of pregnancy and such a refusal therefore constitutes direct discrimination on grounds of sex. A refusal of employment on account of the financial consequences of absence due to pregnancy must be regarded as based, essentially, on the fact of pregnancy. Such discrimination cannot be justified on grounds relating to the financial loss which an employer who appointed a pregnant woman would suffer for the duration of her maternity leave."

Note

The apparent clarity of this decision has been muddied by subsequent case-law where the Court has sought to curtail the scope of this legal principle. The logic inherent in *Dekker* is that any less favourable treatment linked to pregnancy is direct sex

---

[94] *Hayes* v. *Malleable Working Men's Club and Institute* [1985] IRLR 367.
[95] [1990] ECR I–3941.

discrimination because only women can experience pregnancy. Yet the Court has distinguished situations where a woman incurs a pregnancy-related illness.[96] Specifically, where a woman incurs a pregnancy-related illness that extends beyond the period of maternity leave, then the Court views her situation as comparable to a male worker absent because of ill-health.[97] Alongside its struggle to maintain consistency in this field,[98] the Court has rejected attempts to extend the *Dekker* approach into other situations not relating to pregnancy.

ECJ, 7 December 2000[99]   **2.EC.13.**
Case C–79/99, Schnorbus v. Land Hessen

MORE FAVOURABLE TREATMENT OF PERSONS HAVING COMPLETED MILITARY
SERVICE

Schnorbus

Facts: The number of qualified applicants exceeded the number of places available on a practical course for trainee lawyers. In selecting within the qualified applicants, initial priority was given to those persons where a delay in starting the course would cause "particular hardship". One category of hardship was individuals who had already completed compulsory military or civilian service. A female candidate whose entry to the course was deferred argued that the priority attached to the completion of compulsory military or civilian service was discrimination on the ground of sex because these categories could only apply to men (no such service obligations applied to women).

Held: The priority attached to those who had completed military or civilian service constituted indirect discrimination. This was, however, capable of objective justification.

Opinion of Advocate-General Jacobs: "33. To state matters simply, it may be said that discrimination on grounds of sex arises where members of one sex are treated more favourably than the other. The discrimination is direct where the difference in treatment is based on a criterion which is either explicitly that of sex or necessarily linked to a characteristic indissociable from sex. It is indirect where some other criterion is applied but a substantially higher proportion of one sex than of the other is in fact affected.

. . .

38. It is true that under German law as it stands women cannot be accorded priority under the rule in issue whereas the overwhelming majority of men can, as a direct result of the fact that the criterion used—completion of compulsory national service—relates to an obligation imposed by law on all men and on men alone.

---

[96] For an overview of the case-law, see E. Ellis, *EU Anti-discrimination Law* (Oxford, Oxford University Press, 2005) 228–36.

[97] Case C–394/9 *Brown v. Rentokill Ltd* [1998] ECR I–4185. See also Case C–191/03 *Northern Western Health Board* v. *McKenna* [2005] 1 CMLR 6. See further above, ch. 1.

[98] For a more detailed discussion, see E. Caracciolo di Torella and A. Masselot, "Pregnancy, Maternity and the Organisation of Family Life: an Attempt to Classify the Case-law of the Court of Justice" (2001) 26 *ELR* 239; G. Mancini and S. O'Leary, "The New Frontiers of Sex Equality Law in the European Union" (1999) 24 *ELR* 331.

[99] [2000] ECR I–10997.

39. This might be compared to the situation as regards pregnancy. The Court has held, in a series of cases starting with *Dekker*, that since only women can be refused employment on grounds of pregnancy, such a refusal constitutes direct discrimination on grounds of sex.

40. However, there is a distinction to be drawn between a criterion based on an obligation imposed by law on one sex alone and a criterion based on a physical characteristic inherent in one sex alone. No amount of legislation can render men capable of bearing children, whereas legislation might readily remove any discrimination between men and women in relation to compulsory national service.

41. In the present case, therefore, there is no direct discrimination because the rule in issue differentiates between those who have and those who have not completed compulsory national service as a result of a statutory obligation and not between men and women as such."

Judgment: "32 . . . Paragraph 14a of the JAO provides for a number of circumstances which may be taken into account for priority access to practical legal training. They include the completion of compulsory military or civilian service. In such a case, the benefit of the priority envisaged by the abovementioned provisions cannot be regarded as being directly based on the sex of the persons concerned.

33. According to the criteria established by the case-law of the Court, only provisions which apply differently according to the sex of the persons concerned can be regarded as constituting discrimination directly based on sex . . ."

Notes

(1) The Court's terse judgment provides little real engagement with the inevitable question why a criterion that exclusively placed men in a more favourable situation does not constitute direct discrimination. The Advocate-General's reasoning (paragraph 40) is not entirely convincing. Even if a change in the law could open national service to women, this is only a hypothetical future possibility and not the factual context that applied to Ms Schnorbus. Moreover, it is not evident why the origin of the gender-specific condition (legal or biological) is relevant to its categorisation as direct or indirect discrimination.

(2) One explanation of the outcome in this case is the possibility to consider objective justification of indirectly discriminatory measures, whereas direct sex discrimination is not open to such justification in EC law. By treating this situation as indirect discrimination, the Court had greater flexibility to consider wider policy justifications. In other cases, the Court has shown a reluctance to impinge upon the organisation of national service.[100]

2.3.1.C.   HYPOTHETICAL COMPARATORS

The difficulties experienced in identifying a comparator have, to some extent, been recognised in the possibility to invoke a hypothetical comparator. This principle is now entrenched in the standard definition of direct discrimination within the anti-discrimination Directives:

---

[100] Case C–186/01 *Dory* [2003] ECR I–2479. See below, section 2.6.3.C.

"direct discrimination shall be taken to occur where one person is treated less favourably than another is, has been or would be treated in a comparable situation".[101]

The express reference to hypothetical comparators has been incorporated into the national legislation of most EU states, although the relevant laws in Spain[102] and Hungary[103] fail to mention this element. The obvious challenge surrounding a hypothetical comparator concerns the need to make an objective assessment in relation to a situation that did not actually exist. The following case from Northern Ireland explores how contextual evidence can assist in constructing a hypothetical comparator.

House of Lords, 27 February 2003[104]   **2.NIR.14.**
Shamoon v. Chief Constable of the Royal Ulster Constabulary

HYPOTHETICAL COMPARATORS

Shamoon

Facts: Ms Shamoon was a chief inspector in the police and as part of her duties she conducted appraisals of other officers. Following complaints about her conduct of the appraisals, she was removed from this duty. She argued that this was direct discrimination on the ground of sex because two other male chief inspectors continued to perform appraisals. The male chief inspectors had not been the subject of complaints. The question arose as to whether they were appropriate comparators.

Held: The House of Lords held that she had not established sufficient evidence of direct discrimination contrary to Article 3(1)(a) of the Sex Discrimination (Northern Ireland) Order 1976.

Judgment: LORD SCOTT: "106. Article 3(1) of the 1976 Order declares that 'a person discriminates against a woman . . . if . . . on the ground of her sex he treats her less favourably than he treats or would treat a man'. And Article 7, headed 'Basis of Comparison', provides that:

'A comparison of the cases of persons of different sex under Article 3(1) . . . must be such that the relevant circumstances in the one case are the same, or not materially different, in the other.'

107. There has been, in my respectful opinion, some confusion about the part to be played by comparators in the reaching of a conclusion as to whether a case of Article 3(1) discrimination—or for that matter a case of discrimination under section 1(1) of the Sex Discrimination Act 1975, or under section 1(1) of the Race Relations Act 1976, or under the comparable provision in any other anti-discrimination legislation—has been made out. Comparators come into play in two distinct and separate respects.

108. First, the statutory definition of what constitutes discrimination involves a comparison: ' . . . treats that other less favourably than he treats or would treat other persons'.

---

[101] Art. 2(2)(a) Racial Equality Directive (emphasis added).
[102] Art. 28(1)(b), Law 62/2003.
[103] Art. 8, Equal Treatment and the Promotion of Equality of Opportunities Act 2003.
[104] [2003] 2 All ER 26, HL.

The comparison is between the treatment of the victim on the one hand and of a comparator on the other hand. The comparator may be actual ("treats") or may be hypothetical ('or would treat') but 'must be such that the relevant circumstances in the one case are the same, or not materially different, in the other' (see Article 7). If there is any material difference between the circumstances of the victim and the circumstances of the comparator, the statutory definition is not being applied. It is possible that, in a particular case, an actual comparator capable of constituting the statutory comparator can be found. But in most cases a suitable actual comparator will not be available and a hypothetical comparator will have to constitute the statutory comparator. In *Khan* [*Chief Constable of the West Yorkshire Police* v. *Khan* [2001] 1 WLR 1947 HL] one of the questions was as to the circumstances that should be attributed to the statutory hypothetical comparator. It is important, in my opinion, to recognise that Article 7 is describing the attributes that the Article 3(1) comparator must possess.

109. But, secondly, comparators have a quite separate evidential role to play. Article 7 has nothing to do with this role. It is neither prescribing nor limiting the evidential comparators that may be adduced by either party. The victim who complains of discrimination must satisfy the fact finding tribunal that, on a balance of probabilities, he or she has suffered discrimination falling within the statutory definition. This may be done by placing before the tribunal evidential material from which an inference can be drawn that the victim was treated less favourably than he or she would have been treated if he or she had not been a member of the protected class. Comparators, which for this purpose are bound to be actual comparators, may of course constitute such evidential material. But they are no more than tools which may or may not justify an inference of discrimination on the relevant prohibited ground e.g.. sex. The usefulness of the tool will, in any particular case, depend upon the extent to which the circumstances relating to the comparator are the same as the circumstances relating to the victim. The more significant the difference or differences the less cogent will be the case for drawing the requisite inference. But the fact that a particular chosen comparator cannot, because of material differences, qualify as the statutory comparator, e.g.. under Article 7, by no means disqualifies it from an evidential role. It may, in conjunction with other material, justify the tribunal in drawing the inference that the victim was treated less favourably than she would have been treated if she had been the Article 7 comparator.

110. In summary, the comparator required for the purpose of the statutory definition of discrimination must be a comparator in the same position in all material respects as the victim save only that he, or she, is not a member of the protected class. But the comparators that can be of evidential value, sometimes determinative of the case, are not so circumscribed. Their evidential value will, however, be variable and will inevitably be weakened by material differences between the circumstances relating to them and the circumstances of the victim."

Notes

(1) Lord Scott expresses the view that "in most cases" a sufficiently similar actual comparator will not be available and, consequently, hypothetical comparators should be commonly used. His judgment argues that the interpretation of how a hypothetical comparator would have been treated can be assisted by reference to the wider context of the case. Even if other persons are not in a sufficiently similar situation to be an actual comparator, their treatment could provide relevant evidence for considering how a hypothetical comparator would have been treated. For example, even though there was no actual comparator for the situation of Ms

Shamoon, it would have been relevant to consider how, in general, complaints about the behaviour of chief inspectors were treated.

(2) Linked to the interpretation of a hypothetical comparator, Lord Scott underlines the potential utility of any other evidence that may assist a court to draw inferences of discrimination; for example, a discriminatory statement or question during the course of a job interview. He argues that such evidence can remove the need for an actual comparator, permitting the court to make the assumption that a hypothetical person with different personal characteristics would not have been so treated (see further paragraph 116). In *Anya* v. *University of Oxford* [2001] IRLR 377, the Court of Appeal held that inferences of discrimination might be drawn where a recruitment exercise has not been conducted in accordance with the employer's normal procedures and where there is evidence of hostility to the individual within the selection panel. The drawing of inferences by courts is considered further in section 2.4.

Hypothetical comparators are frequently deployed in the decisions of the Irish Equality Tribunal. The following case provides a good illustration of their use.

Equality Tribunal, 7 May 2003[105]   **2.IE.15.**
DEC-S/2003/29, O'Brien v. *Iarnród Eireann*

HYPOTHETICAL COMPARATORS

O'Brien

Facts: Mrs O'Brien was taking the train with her children when the bag of another passenger went missing. At a subsequent station, she was asked to leave the train, where she was questioned by the police and had her belongings searched. The missing bag was not found, so she was allowed back on the train. Mrs O'Brien argued that she had been singled out for suspicion because she was a member of Ireland's Traveller Community and that this constituted direct discrimination.

Held: Mrs O'Brien had been subject to unlawful direct discrimination because she was a Traveller.

Decision: "Para. 7.1. There are three key elements which need to be established to show that a prima facie case exists. These are:

(a)   Membership of a discriminatory ground (e.g. the Traveller community ground)
(b)   Evidence of specific treatment by the respondent
(c)   Evidence that the treatment received by the complainant was less favourable than the treatment someone, not covered by that ground, would have received in similar circumstances . . .

7.4 In this particular case, I have not been provided with any comparable situation where a non-Traveller was accused of larceny while a passenger on an Iarnród Eireann service. I, therefore, find that I am unable to compare this case with another 'real-life' situation which has

---

[105] Available on the website of the Equality Tribunal of Ireland under the heading Equal Status Decisions.

occurred in the past. In order to properly evaluate the complainants' case, I believe, therefore, that it is necessary to introduce a hypothetical comparator at this point. The Equal Status Act 2000 provides for the use of a hypothetical comparator in Section 3(1)(a) where it states that discrimination shall be taken to occur where a person is treated less favourably than another person is, has been or would be treated.

7.5 Hypothetical comparators have been introduced in a number of other Equal Status cases in recent years where an actual comparator did not exist . . ."

[The Equality Officer at this point examines in detail certain factual circumstances surrounding the incident]

"7.9 On the basis of the above pieces of evidence, I simply cannot accept that Mr Nolan [the train ticket collector] would have acted in a similar manner if a non-Traveller woman with two children had been accused of larceny.

I believe that, if a non-Traveller had been involved, it is reasonable to expect that the Ticket Collector would have at least asked to speak to the two witnesses who had been identified before agreeing to call the Gardai [police]. Yet, despite the fact that the passenger has said that it was only '50/50' that Mrs O'Brien's children had been involved, Mr Nolan chose not to seek out the two witnesses to confirm their reports. More importantly, Mr Nolan chose not to inform Mrs O'Brien of the allegation against her, which I find hard to believe is standard practice, especially where an unfounded allegation has been made against a passenger. I also cannot accept that Mr Nolan was following standard procedures in not speaking to Mrs O'Brien afterwards or offering her some form of apology. It also appears that Mrs O'Brien was never offered an apology from anyone in Iarnród Eireann over the incident."

Notes

(1) In establishing the hypothetical comparator, the Equality Officer focuses on what would have been "reasonable" or "standard" treatment in the circumstances. He concludes that the treatment accorded to Mrs O'Brien was not in line with what seemed "normal" and this is the basis for a finding of unlawful direct discrimination. The use of the hypothetical comparator is closely intertwined with the provisions on the burden of proof. It allows the Equality Officer to identify a prima facie case of discrimination, which then shifts the burden of proof to the respondents, who were unable to provide a sufficiently persuasive alternative explanation.

(2) The reasoning in this case illustrates the flexibility of the hypothetical comparator. In essence, the question that the Equality Officer is trying to answer is simply whether Mrs O'Brien was treated less favourably because she was a Traveller. His answer is that her treatment does not seem fair in the circumstances and this gives rise to a presumption of discrimination. Here, it seems that a hypothetical comparator amounts to scrutiny of the respondent's actions by a standard of reasonableness. Izzi criticises this element of hypothetical comparators. She argues that their use places too much discretion in the hands of courts and thereby reduces legal certainty.[106]

---

[106] See Izzi, above n. 70, 428.

2.3.1.D.   EQUAL PAY COMPARATORS

Although the potentially valuable contribution of hypothetical comparators is recognised in the three "core" anti-discrimination Directives, it does not extend to EC law on equal pay. Whilst there was previously some doubt as to whether an equal pay comparator had to work for the same employer as the individual complainant,[107] recent case-law has emphasised the need for a single source for the pay of both the complainant and the comparator.

ECJ, 13 January 2004[108]   **2.EC.16.**
Case C–256/01, Allonby v. *Accrington & Rossendale College*

COMPARATORS IN EQUAL PAY

Allonby

Facts: In order to reduce costs, the college dismissed a group of lecturers, including Ms Allonby. She subsequently recommenced working at the college, but her employment was now via an employment agency. The pay rate was lower and various occupational benefits were lost, including access to the occupational pension scheme. Ms Allonby brought an equal pay claim, seeking to compare herself to the full-time lecturers still employed by the college.

Held: The Court held, inter alia, that she could not compare herself with the full-time college employees because they did not share a single source determining their remuneration.

Judgment: "41. The national court submitted the first question to enable it to rule on Ms Allonby's claim for entitlement to remuneration from ELS [the employment agency] equal to that of a male lecturer employed by the College.

42. Accordingly, this question must be construed as seeking to ascertain whether, in circumstances such as those of the main proceedings, Article 141(1) EC must be interpreted as meaning that a woman whose contract of employment with an undertaking has not been renewed and who is immediately made available to her previous employer through another undertaking to provide the same services is entitled to rely, vis-à-vis the intermediary undertaking, on the principle of equal pay, using as a basis for comparison the remuneration received for equal work or work of the same value by a man employed by the woman's previous employer.

43. It must be borne in mind at the outset that Article 141(1) EC can be relied on only by workers within the meaning of that provision.

44. However, even if that condition is satisfied, the first question cannot be answered in the affirmative.

45. Admittedly, there is nothing in the wording of Article 141(1) EC to suggest that the applicability of that provision is limited to situations in which men and women work for the same employer. The principle established by that Article may be invoked before national courts, in particular in cases of discrimination arising directly from legislative provisions or collective labour agreements, as well as in cases in which work is carried out in the same

---

[107] See Ellis, above n. 19, 161.
[108] [2004] ECR I–873.

223

establishment or service, whether private or public (see, inter alia, Case 43/75 *Defrenne II* [1976] ECR 455, paragraph 40, and Case C–320/00 *Lawrence and Others* [2002] ECR I–7325, paragraph 17).

46. However, where the differences identified in the pay conditions of workers performing equal work or work of equal value cannot be attributed to a single source, there is no body which is responsible for the inequality and which could restore equal treatment. Such a situation does not come within the scope of Article 141(1) EC. The work and the pay of those workers cannot therefore be compared on the basis of that provision (*Lawrence*, paragraph 18).

47. It is clear from the order for reference that the male worker referred to by Ms Allonby is paid by the College under conditions determined by the College, whereas ELS agreed with Ms Allonby on the pay which she would receive for each assignment.

48. The fact that the level of pay received by Ms Allonby is influenced by the amount which the College pays ELS is not a sufficient basis for concluding that the College and ELS constitute a single source to which can be attributed the differences identified in Ms Allonby's conditions of pay and those of the male worker paid by the College."

Notes

(1) The Court takes a formalistic view of the source of the employee's pay by focusing on her legal relationship with the agency.[109] Yet the level of fee provided by the College to the agency had a significant influence on the subsequent remuneration then provided by the agency to Ms Allonby.

(2) A subsequent UK case has taken the restrictive approach to equal pay comparators a step further. In *Robertson* v. *Department for Environment, Food and Rural Affairs (DEFRA)* [2005] IRLR 363 CA, six male civil servants working for DEFRA sought to compare their pay with two female civil servants working in the Department of the Environment, Transport and the Regions. The Court of Appeal held that a cross-departmental comparison was not possible because there was no single source responsible for determining the workers' pay. Although they were all government employees, the responsibility for negotiating and determining pay had been devolved to individual government departments. This case raises the worrying prospect that employers in the private sector, particularly in large organisations, could hinder equal pay claims by devolving the determination of workers' pay to sub-divisions of the firm.[110]

2.3.1.E.   COMPARATORS IN AGE DISCRIMINATION

The choice of a comparator in age discrimination cases presents slightly different challenges compared to other grounds of discrimination. Consider the example of a job application process. If a well-qualified woman applies for a job and is unsuccessful, she may want to verify the sex of the person who was awarded the post. If the appointed person was a man, then she may want to learn more about his

---

[109] S. Fredman, "Marginalising Equal Pay Laws" (2004) 33 *ILJ* 281, 282.
[110] I. Steele, "Tracing the Single Source: Choice of Comparators in Equal Pay Claims" (2005) 34 *ILJ* 338, 344.

qualifications in order to be sure that the appointment process was free from discrimination. The rather distinct feature of age is that the successful candidate (to continue
the example) will almost always have a different chronological age to the unsuccessful
candidate (barring the rare circumstance where two job candidates were born on the
same day). This raises the question whether a comparator for age discrimination can
be any person of a different age or whether there needs to be a sufficient distance
between their ages to give rise to a prima facie foundation for claiming age
discrimination.

This issue has been explored in several Irish cases without producing a settled
answer. First, in *Superquinn* v. *Freeman*,[111] the Labour Court held that a difference in
age between a 28 year old and a 31 year old was not enough, in the absence of any
other facts, to give rise to a presumption of discrimination. Yet, in *Reynolds* v.
Limerick County Council,[112] the Equality Tribunal treated a difference of eight years
between the complainant and the comparator as sufficient. The choice of comparator
appears to depend heavily on the facts of the case. In the following case, the Equality
Officer accepted that even a difference in age of two days could be a sufficient
comparison on the facts of the case.

Equality Tribunal, 24 September 2001[113]   **2.IE.17.**
DEC-E/2001/029, Perry v. The Garda Commissioner

HYPOTHETICAL COMPARATORS AND AGE DISCRIMINATION

Perry

Facts: The dispute concerned the conditions of a voluntary early retirement scheme for traffic wardens. One
element of the scheme was a severance payment; the level of this payment differed between workers who
were under 60 and those who were over 60. The complainant, who was 64, compared her situation to that
of a colleague with similar employment history, who was 59. Her severance payment would be almost IR
£11,000 less than the 59-year-old colleague.

Held: Although there was a difference in treatment on the ground of age, this was not unlawful at the time
of the relevant facts due to a transitional period in implementation of the Employment Equality Act as
regards age-related remuneration.

Decision: "Para. 4.13 Employees under the age of 60 who choose Option B receive a severance
gratuity calculated on the basis of two weeks' pay per year of actual service (to a maximum of
2 years' pay). Employees over the age of 60 may only receive Option A, the severance gratuity
element of which is calculated on the basis of two weeks' pay per year of potential service to
age 65 (to a maximum of 18 weeks' pay) . . .

4.14 The respondent has argued that the scheme is designed to reflect the difference in
income forgone by the applicants. The respondent also asserted that an Equality Officer can
only consider the specific facts in a case before him or her. However, I regard it as my

---

[111] AEE/02/8 Determination No. 0211, 14 November 2002.
[112] Para. 5.10, DEC-E2003-032, 7 August 2003.
[113] Available on the website of the Equality Tribunal of Ireland.

responsibility to take into account all matters that I believe relevant to this investigation. In the interest of exploring further the respondent's argument about forgone income, I considered the application of the scheme to two hypothetical employees, with identical service records, Employee X aged 60 years and 1 day and Employee Y aged 59 years 364 days . . .

4.15 If one ignores the elements which either cannot be dealt with or are based on actual service—pension, lump sum and redundancy payment—the inequity of the scheme becomes obvious. The employee aged over 60 can only receive £2,000 as a severance gratuity, while the second employee has an alternative whereby he or she can obtain a severance gratuity worth £8,000."

2.3.2.   INTENT, MOTIVE AND STEREOTYPING

If less favourable treatment on a prohibited ground is established, then the respondent may seek to advance defences for their actions. The specific statutory exceptions are examined later in section 2.6; however, a preliminary issue concerns whether the complainant needs to prove a discriminatory motive on the part of the respondent in order to establish direct discrimination.[114]

Stereotyping occupies a special position within the debate around the relevance of motive. In some cases, the employer or service-provider will argue that there was no malice towards the complainant as an individual, but that they were just acting upon wider generalisations about persons with such characteristics. These preconceived notions of how an individual will behave because of her group characteristics are stereotypes. They may or may not be factually correct. For example, an insurance company that charges higher premiums for male drivers under 25 might justify their actions by reference to statistical data indicating that this group has a higher likelihood to be involved in road traffic accidents. The factual basis of the action does not, though, remove its stereotyping quality. An individual male driver aged 22 might be very skilled and careful in his driving, but he is being treated less favourably because of a group characteristic. The potential for the prohibition of direct discrimination to disrupt stereotyping is crucial to the goal of substantive equality. Stereotypes often underpin patterns of inequality and institutionalised cultures of discrimination.[115]

This section begins by examining the role of motive followed by a consideration of stereotyping and direct discrimination.

---

[114] See also below T.Choudhury, Chapter Five: Instructions to Discriminate and Victimisation, section 5.2.

[115] On institutional racism, see para. 6.34, W. MacPherson, "The Stephen Lawrence Inquiry—Report of an Inquiry" CM 4262-I (London, The Stationery Office, 1999); M. Verlot, "Understanding Institutional Racism" in The Evens Foundation (eds.), *Europe's New Racism: Causes, Manifestations and Solutions* (Oxford, Berghahn Books, 2002).

2.3.2.A.   MOTIVE

At the outset, it is useful to clarify terminology, specifically the distinction between intent and motive. In criminal law, this is fundamental. For example, whether an individual intended to kill another person or was simply reckless as to the other person's safety can be crucial to the offence of murder. In this context, intent might be best described as the aim of the person's actions (did they aim through their actions to bring about another person's death?). This is clearly distinct from motive, which concerns the reason why they undertook that action. Although the language of intent and motive is sometimes confused in discrimination law, this section is mainly concerned with the relevance of a person's *motive* in cases of direct discrimination.

A pattern that can be identified in various legal systems is a transition from treating motive as relevant to subsequently viewing it as irrelevant. For example, Mahlmann argues that the emphasis of the German Federal Constitutional Court on evidence of discriminatory motive has diminished over time.[116] This is also the case in UK case-law. In *Peake* v. *Automotive Products Ltd*, the English Court of Appeal had to consider whether it was direct discrimination on the ground of sex where an employer allowed female factory workers to leave five minutes earlier than men. The practice was held not to be discrimination. Lord Denning argued that:

> "It is not discrimination for mankind to treat womankind with the courtesy and chivalry which we have been taught to believe is right conduct in our society."[117]

There are various problems with this line of reasoning. Most obviously, the decision itself reveals stereotypical attitudes towards women's "vulnerability" within the workplace, reinforcing paternalistic behaviour. In addition, it links direct discrimination to the subjective state of mind of the perpetrator. Imposing such a rule would make it highly difficult to prove direct discrimination. In many circumstances, the victim of discrimination will have no evidence regarding the subjective motive of the discriminator. For example, where a job applicant is simply not called to interview, the employer is likely to explain the decision by reference to better qualified alternative candidates. Whilst the individual might be able to prove, as an objective fact, that other candidates were not better qualified, it is much more difficult for the individual then also to prove that the reason for selecting less qualified candidates was because of a discriminatory motive. This became evident to the English courts and, just two years after the decision in *Peake*, Lord Denning accepted that chivalry could not justify direct sex discrimination.[118]

Case-law from Belgian courts also reveals differences over time with regard to the relevance of motive.

---

[116] See Mahlmann, above n. 92.
[117] *Peake* v. *Automotive Products Ltd* [1978] QB 233 at 238. See further, A. McColgan, *Discrimination Law—Text, Cases and Materials* (Oxford, Hart Publishing, 2005) 40.
[118] *Ministry of Defence* v. *Jeremiah* [1980] QB 87.

Labour Court of Ghent (*Cour du Travail*), 24 January 1985   **2.BE.18.**
MVT v. *G*

THIRD PARTY PRESSURE AND DIRECT DISCRIMINATION

Dismissed Jewish employee

Facts: On two occasions, the employer received threats by telephone from an anonymous caller, allegedly from the Palestine Liberation Organisation, demanding immediate dismissal of "the Jew G", or else the establishment would be blown up and the manager's family was also threatened with death. The employee concerned, who was not actually Jewish, was dismissed. He challenged this as unlawful racial discrimination.

Held: The law on racism did not apply because the reason for his dismissal was not racially motivated.

Judgment: "There is no doubt that respondent could rightly argue illegality if the dismissal had been based on purely racist motives. However, it should be noted in this connection that the respondent's dismissal was not prompted by racial discrimination directed at the appellant but was based exclusively on blackmail and threats made by an unknown person against the appellant.

It should be stressed that the respondent was not a Jew nor possessed Jewish nationality; the appellant certainly had no racial leanings and was not known to have anti-Jewish sympathies, which was undoubtedly the case with the person who proceeded with the distasteful blackmail.

The reason why the appellant proceeded to dismiss its employee undoubtedly originates not in racism but in the threats to the firm, the personnel and the manager's family. The sanctions for which the laws and treaties concerning racism provide cannot therefore be applied."

Notes

(1) A similar willingness to consider motive is evident in the case of *Public Prosecutor's Office* v. *François C.*[119] In this case, a Turkish man was refused permission to hire a motorbike. The sales assistant was prosecuted for racial discrimination. She stated that she felt apprehensive because the customer began speaking in Turkish to another man with him and this was the reason for not renting the motorbike. The Court accepted that this was not a racist motive and discrimination had not been committed.

(2) The difficulty with such decisions is that they place the state of mind of the perpetrator at the centre of the concept of direct discrimination. An alternative approach is to view direct discrimination as an objective question focusing on the *effects* of the perpetrator's actions. In the extract above, the dismissed employee was treated less favourably on racial grounds; had he not been perceived as Jewish, he would not have been dismissed.

(3) Other cases from Belgium indicate a more restrictive attitude to the relevance of motive. In one case, a cafe refused to serve a group of Indian men; the manager argued that this was due to the prejudice of other customers. The Court held that the

---

[119] Criminal Court of Bruges, 25 September 1995.

views of the other customers were irrelevant.[120] Similarly, a bar that sought to limit the number of foreigners permitted entry because of a supposed need to maintain good order was convicted of racial discrimination.[121]

In some states, it is a settled principle of law that motive is not relevant to a finding of direct discrimination. Although this issue has proved troublesome for UK courts,[122] it seems well-established now that "racial discrimination is not negatived by the discriminator's motive or intention or reason or purpose"[123] (see further the Prague Airport case discussed below). The Equal Treatment Commission of the Netherlands has also held that the General Equal Treatment Act "prohibits unequal treatment irrespective of the intention of the person who metes it out".[124]

In other states, it is difficult to be sure that there are no circumstances in which motive will be taken into account. For example, *Zerman* concerned the refusal of a bar owner in Italy to serve several clients of North African origin.[125] The bar owner argued that this was justified by concerns about the need to maintain order in the bar and problems of drunkenness amongst immigrants. This was rejected by the Court of Cassation as unfounded; there was no evidence that the individuals concerned had engaged in disorderly behaviour. Whilst the Court firmly rejects the relevance of the bar owner's motive in this case, it stops short of any general statement of law that motive is irrelevant to a finding of discrimination.

2.3.2.B.   STEREOTYPING

The cases discussed above provide examples of the stereotypes that often arise as explanations for direct discrimination. Employers and service providers may, for example, attribute their actions to the stereotyped preferences of customers. Some of these stereotypes will not be supported by firm evidence and amount to thinly veiled attempts to camouflage the discriminatory motive of the employer or service provider. There are, though, circumstances where the factual basis for the stereotype may be supported by contextual evidence. This scenario is considered in the next two cases, from the UK and Spain.

---

[120] *Public Prosecutor and others* v. *Martine M, Mario G and Marc D*, Court of Appeal, Antwerp, 17 November 1995. Similarly, in Hungary, an employer claimed that clients did not want security guards who were Roma. The Labour Inspectorate rejected the argument that this was a sufficient reason to justify direct discrimination: A. Kádár and L.Farkas, "Report on Measures to Combat Discrimination: Directive 2000/43/EC and 2000/78/EC. Country Report Hungary" (European Commission, 2007), forthcoming.

[121] Criminal Court of Courtrai, 20 October 1999. The Irish Equality Tribunal has also rejected the possibility to justify a limit on the number of Travellers permitted to enter a bar: *McDonagh* v. *The Castle Inn, Birr*, DEC-S2001-022, 19 December 2001.

[122] See further, A. McColgan, *Discrimination Law*, 2nd edn (Oxford, Hart Publishing, 2005) 40–49.

[123] Lord Nicholls, *Nagarajan* v. *London Regional Transport* [2000] ICR 877 at 884.

[124] Opinion 1996-23.

[125] Court of Cassation, judgment of 5 December 2005, No. 46883/03 R.G.

R (European Roma Rights Centre) v. *Immigration Officer at Prague Airport and another*

STEREOTYPING AND DIRECT RACIAL DISCRIMINATION

Prague Airport case

Facts: In an attempt to reduce the number of asylum applications from the Czech Republic (in particular from the Roma community), a scheme was introduced where passengers seeking to travel to the UK would be first examined by UK immigration officials in Prague Airport. It was clear that extra scrutiny was applied to persons appearing to be from the Roma community; statistics showed that only 0.2% of non-Roma Czech passengers were refused leave to enter the UK, compared with a refusal rate of 87% for Roma passengers.

Held: UK immigration officers directly discriminated on racial grounds against Roma persons seeking to travel to the UK at Prague Airport.

Judgment: BARONESS HALE, paragraph 73: "The ingredients of unlawful discrimination are (i) a difference in treatment between one person and another person (real or hypothetical) from a different sex or racial group; (ii) that the treatment is less favourable to one; (iii) that their relevant circumstances are the same or not materially different; and (iv) that the difference in treatment is on sex or racial grounds. However, because people rarely advertise their prejudices and may not even be aware of them, discrimination has normally to be proved by inference rather than direct evidence. Once treatment less favourable than that of a comparable person (ingredients (i) (ii) and (iii)) is shown, the court will look to the alleged discriminator for an explanation. The explanation must, of course, be unrelated to the race or sex of the complainant. If there is no, or no satisfactory explanation, it is legitimate to infer that the less favourable treatment was on racial grounds: see *Glasgow City Council* v. *Zafar* [1997] 1 WLR 1659, approving *King v Great Britain-China Centre* [1992] ICR 516. If the difference is on racial grounds, the reasons or motive behind it are irrelevant: see, for example, *Nagarajan* v. *London Regional Transport* [2000] 1 AC 501.

74. If direct discrimination of this sort is shown, that is that. Save for some very limited exceptions, there is no defence of objective justification. The whole point of the law is to require suppliers to treat each person as an individual, not as a member of a group. The individual should not be assumed to hold the characteristics which the supplier associates with the group, whether or not most members of the group do indeed have such characteristics, a process sometimes referred to as stereotyping. Even if, for example, most women are less strong than most men, it must not be assumed that the individual woman who has applied for the job does not have the strength to do it. Nor, for that matter, should it be assumed that an individual man does have that strength. If strength is a qualification, all applicants should be required to demonstrate that they qualify . . .

81. The Court of Appeal accepted that the judge was entitled to find that the immigration officers tried to give both Roma and non-Roma a fair and equal opportunity to satisfy them that they were coming to the United Kingdom for a permitted purpose and not to claim asylum once here. But they considered it 'wholly inevitable' that, being aware that Roma have a much greater incentive to claim asylum and that the vast majority, if not all, of those seeking asylum from the Czech Republic are Roma, immigration officers will treat their answers with

---

[126] [2005] 2 AC 1.

greater scepticism, will be less easily persuaded that they are coming for a permitted purpose, and that 'generally, therefore, Roma are questioned for longer and more intensively than non-Roma and are more likely to be refused leave to enter than non-Roma': Simon Brown LJ, paras 66-67. Laws LJ referred to the last of these propositions as 'plainly true on the facts of this case': para. 102. Simon Brown LJ, with whom Mantell LJ agreed, held that nevertheless this was not less favourable treatment, or if it was, it was not on racial grounds. The Roma were not being treated differently qua Roma but qua potential asylum-seekers. Laws LJ considered it 'inescapable' that this was less favourable treatment (para. 102). He also concluded, at para. 109, that this was discrimination:

'One asks Lord Steyn's question [in *Nagarajan* v. *London Regional Transport* [2000] 1 AC 501, 521-522]: why did he treat the Roma less favourably? It may be said that there are two possible answers: (1) because he is Roma; (2) because he is more likely to be advancing a false application for leave to enter as a visitor. But it seems to me inescapable that the reality is that the officer treated the Roma less favourably because Roma are (for very well understood reasons) more likely to wish to seek asylum and thus, more likely to put forward a false claim to enter as a visitor. The officer has applied a stereotype; though one which may very likely be true. That is not permissible. More pointedly, he has an entirely proper reason (or motive) for treating the Roma less favourably on racial grounds: his duty to refuse those without a claim under the Rules, manifestly including covert asylum-seekers, and his knowledge that the Roma is more likely to be a covert asylum-seeker. But that is irrelevant to the claim under section 1(1)(a) of the 1976 [Race Relations]Act.'

82. On the factual premises adopted by the Court of Appeal, this conclusion must be correct as a matter of law. The Roma were being treated more sceptically than the non-Roma. There was a good reason for this. How did the immigration officers know to treat them more scepti-cally? Because they were Roma. That is acting on racial grounds. If a person acts on racial grounds, the reason why he does so is irrelevant: see Lord Nicholls of Birkenhead in *Nagarajan*, at p. 511. The law reports are full of examples of obviously discriminatory treatment which was in no way motivated by racism or sexism and often brought about by pressures beyond the discriminators' control: the council which sacked a black road sweeper to whom the union objected in order to avoid industrial action (*R* v. *Commission for Racial Equality, Ex p Westminster City Council* [1985] ICR 827); the council which for historical reasons provided fewer selective school places for girls than for boys: *R* v. *Birmingham City Council, Ex p Equal Opportunities Commission* [1989] AC 1155. But it goes further than this. The person may be acting on belief or assumptions about members of the sex or racial group involved which are often true and which if true would provide a good reason for the less favourable treatment in question. But 'what may be true of a group may not be true of a significant number of individuals within that group': see Hartmann J in *Equal Opportu-nities Commission* v. *Director of Education* [2001] 2 HKLRD 690, para. 86, High Court of Hong Kong. The object of the legislation is to ensure that each person is treated as an individual and not assumed to be like other members of the group. As Laws LJ observed, at para. 108:

'The mistake that might arise in relation to stereotyping would be a supposition that the stereotype is only vicious if it is untrue. But that cannot be right. If it were, it would imply that direct discrimination can be justified . . .'

83. As we have seen, the legislation draws a clear distinction between direct and indirect discrimination and makes no reference at all to justification in relation to direct discrimination."

El Tribunal Constitucional (Spanish Constitutional Court),   **2.ES.20.**
14 December 1992[127]
Rodríguez Valencia

STEREOTYPING AND DIRECT SEX DISCRIMINATION

Ban on women working in mines

Facts: The case concerned a challenge to restrictions on female employment, including restrictions on women working in mines.

Held: The restrictions were unlawful sexual discrimination.

Judgment: "4. The order for non-discrimination due to sex of section 14 E.C. [Spanish Constitution], consistent with the principle of equality of rights between men and women, of course requires the elimination of those legal norms that (with the exception of pregnancy and maternity), although historically responding to a purpose of the protection of women as a physiologically weaker subject, actually authenticate or reinforce a sexist division of jobs and positions by means of the imposition on women of apparently advantageous restrictions but which involve an obstacle for their access to the labour market.

In many cases this originally protective legislation responds to prejudices, to preconceived opinions that play an important role in the creation and persistence of discrimination. In this case that prejudice is the lesser physical strength and greater weakness of women in relation to men, as something that corresponds to the nature of things, and it is from that prejudice that it is possible to understand without grounds that the physical difference that exists between men and women is sufficient to justify a prohibition for women to work inside mines. Whether this be a defective or an erroneous perception or whether it be an antiquated perception in view of social progress, what is certain is that this type of prohibition responds more to a stereotype than to actual natural or biological differences, and in any event it causes discriminatory effects within the labour market, which involve a special restriction or disadvantage for women. Unlike men, women are prohibited from undertaking work inside mines, which establishes an exclusion directly linked to differences of sex.

There are no reasons that lead one to the conclusion that the particularly oppressive conditions of the work inside mines or the risk to health or of accidents are increased in all cases by the constitution and condition of women with respect to those of men. Although the particular severity of this type of work may require certain demands on strength and physical condition, these should be equally indispensable both for men and women, regardless of sex, without it being relevant, with respect to the eventuality, that a greater number of men than women meet these requirements in any given case. If this is verified, there is no reason (apart from a current state of pregnancy or maternity, which is not the case here) that justifies the absolute exclusion of women from this type of work."

Notes

(1) In *Prague Airport*, Baroness Hale argues that "the object of the legislation is to ensure that each person is treated as an individual and not assumed to be like other members of the group" (paragraph 82). This statement reveals a certain tension

---

[127] Sentence 229/1992.

within the objectives of anti-discrimination law. It simultaneously aims to ensure that individuals are treated as individuals whilst recognising the relevance of group membership. In some circumstances, individuals may want to be treated differently because of their group characteristics. For example, persons of a particular religious belief may want to be able to wear different clothes or to take holidays at different times in comparison to other employees. Positive action schemes are also premised on the need to focus on *group* disadvantage. There is often no requirement for the beneficiaries of positive action to demonstrate that they individually suffered discrimination or disadvantage.[128]

(2) It must also be acknowledged that there is a tension between questions of causation and the irrelevance of motive. Often answering the question *why* someone was treated less favourably leads back in the direction of the respondent's motive. Where evidence of (for example) racial prejudice is present, this may indeed contribute to establishing the existence of direct discrimination. Nevertheless, the absence of such proof, or alternatively proof of a non-prejudicial motive, should not be a stumbling block to a finding of direct discrimination.

(3) The decision of the Spanish Constitutional Court is consistent with case-law from the ECJ, which rejected restrictions on night-work by women.[129] Nevertheless, Article 5 of the 2004 Gender Goods and Services Directive permits different treatment of women and men in the provision of financial services (e.g. insurance) where this is supported by actuarial data. This exception effectively authorises gender stereotyping in the setting of individual insurance premiums. In contrast to the cases above, the EU legislature treated this stereotyping as permissible in so far as it was based on factual evidence (see further section 2.6.3.E).

2.3.3.   LESS FAVOURABLE TREATMENT

Another aspect of establishing direct discrimination is the identification of "less favourable treatment". The question arises whether any difference of treatment, however minor, falls within the scope of the law. For example, as discussed above, in *Peake* v. *Automotive Products Ltd* [1978] QB 233 the English Court of Appeal held that reasons of chivalry justified an employer letting female factory workers out from work five minutes earlier than male workers. Although Lord Denning subsequently recanted from the view that chivalry could justify direct sex discrimination, he postulated that, in any case, the difference in treatment should fall outside the scope of the Sex Discrimination Act 1975 on *de minimis* grounds.[130]

The notion that a difference in treatment has to reach a sufficient magnitude in order to infringe the legal prohibition of discrimination is highly questionable. There

---

[128] See further, S. Fredman, "Affirmative Action at the Court of Justice: a Critical Analysis" in J. Shaw (ed.) *Social Law and Policy in an Evolving Union* (Oxford, Hart Publishing, 2000) 183.

[129] Case C–197/96 *Commission* v. *France* [1997] ECR I–1489.

[130] *Ministry of Defence* v. *Jeremiah* [1980] QB 87. The five minutes less worked each day cumulated in a saving for female employees of 2 days of work per year: see McColgan, above n. 122, 41.

is no such qualification found within the text of the EC anti-discrimination Directives. Although this issue does not appear to have been extensively litigated, a difference of approach between states can be identified.

House of Lords, 27 February 2003[131]   **2.NIR.21.**
Shamoon v. Chief Constable of the Royal Ulster Constabulary

THE MEANING OF DETRIMENT

Shamoon

Facts: Ms Shamoon was a chief inspector in the police and as part of her duties she conducted appraisals of other officers. Following complaints about her conduct of the appraisals, she was removed from further appraisals. She argued that this was direct discrimination on the ground of sex because two other male chief inspectors continued to perform appraisals. A preliminary question arose as to whether being removed from appraisal duties was a sufficiently disadvantageous act as to constitute a prohibited "detriment" within the terms of Article 8(2) Sex Discrimination (Northern Ireland) Order 1976.

Held: Although she had been subject to a detriment, the House of Lords held that she had not established sufficient evidence of direct discrimination contrary to Article 3(1)(a) of the Sex Discrimination (Northern Ireland) Order 1976.

Judgment: "This is a test of materiality. Is the treatment of such a kind that a reasonable worker would or might take the view that in all the circumstances it was to his detriment? An unjustified sense of grievance cannot amount to 'detriment': *Barclays Bank plc v. Kapur* (No 2) [1995] IRLR 87. But, contrary to the view that was expressed in *Lord Chancellor v. Coker* [2001] ICR 507 on which the Court of Appeal relied, it is not necessary to demonstrate some physical or economic consequence. As Lord Hoffmann pointed out in *Khan's* case [2001] ICR 1065, 1077, para. 52, the employment tribunal has jurisdiction to award compensation for injury to feelings whether or not compensation is to be awarded under any other head: Race Relations Act 1976, section 57(4); 1976 Order, article 66(4). Compensation for an injury to her feelings was the relief which the applicant was seeking in this case when she lodged her claim with the tribunal. Her complaint was that her role and position had been substantially under-mined and that it was becoming increasingly marginalised.

36. The question then is whether there was a basis in the evidence which was before the tribunal for a finding that the treatment of which the applicant complained was to her detriment or, to put it more accurately as the tribunal did not make any finding on this point, whether a finding that the applicant had been subjected to a detriment could reasonably have been withheld.

37. It is clear that the treatment of which the applicant complains was in the field of her employment. The practice by which she did the appraisals of constables as part of her job in the urban traffic branch had been terminated. As for the question whether a reasonable person in her position might regard this as a detriment, the background is provided by the fact that not only was it the practice for the appraisals to be done by the chief inspectors but this was, as the tribunal put it, endemic in the force. There was evidence that the applicant

---

[131] [2003] 2 All ER 26, HL.

had carried out as many as 35 appraisals since she was promoted to the rank of chief inspector. Once it was known, as it was bound to be, that she had had this part of her normal duties taken away from her following a complaint to the Police Federation, the effect was likely to be to reduce her standing among her colleagues. A reasonable employee in her position might well feel that she was being demeaned in the eyes of those over whom she was in a position of authority . . ."

This judgment suggests courts should be very cautious before dismissing a difference in treatment as not sufficient to qualify as a detriment. In contrast, German law has taken a more restrictive approach to the circumstances in which a discrimination complaint can be brought. This is illustrated in the following case concerning an individual who claimed discrimination in a job recruitment process, but who, even in the absence of discrimination, would not have been the best qualified candidate.

Federal Labour Court (BAG), 12 November 1998[132]   **2.DE.22.**

DETRIMENT AND REJECTED JOB APPLICANTS

Equal opportunities representative

Facts: The Land of North Rhine-Westphalia advertised the position of equal opportunities representative, a post concerned with issues of gender equality. The complainant was a man who made a formal application for this post, although he did not include his curriculum vitae with his application. When he was not awarded the job, he argued that he had been subject to sex discrimination. One question arising in the case was whether he was in a position to make such a claim.

Held: The complaint was not justified, because he was not objectively suitable for the position that he had applied for.

Judgment: "III. However, the plaintiff does not fulfil the further prerequisites according to § 611a para. 2, sentence 1 BGB.

1. According to this, only applicants who are discriminated against at the time of establishment of a working relationship can claim corresponding monetary compensation. It is true that § 611a BGB in association with § 61b ArbGG [German law governing employers] indicate that not only the best-suited applicant in the sense of § 611a para. 2, sentence 1 BGB [German Civil Code] can be discriminated against, but that further applicants can be discriminated against in the same process for filling positions of employment. However, the law does not presuppose participation in the process of filling the post, but the applicant must have been discriminated against in the sense of the law. The protective goal of § 611a para. 2 BGB is compensation of the applicant who is suitable from an objective point of view but who has been subject to sex-related discrimination within the process. As the version of § 611a para. 2 BGB (compare Federal Parliament Journal 12/7333, p. 21) amended by the German parliamentary committee for women and youth states, not 'every' but only 'the' disadvantaged applicant should be able to claim compensation. § 611a para. 2, sentence 1 BGB therefore not only relies on the formal position of a status of 'applicant' only established through the act of

[132] NZA, 1999, 371.

235

submitting a job application, but also refers to the objective suitability as an applicant to be determined in fact. During the selection process, the only persons who can be disadvantaged in a legal sense are those who applied for the position with serious intent and are objectively suitable for it.

2. According to the determination of the facts of the case of the Labour Court, the plaintiff did not apply for the position of equal opportunities representative with serious intent, but from the beginning intended to try and receive compensation for rejection. Because of the unusual form of the application and above all because a curriculum vitae was not included, nor any information relating to the education and previous professional activities of the plaintiff, the question can even be raised as to whether the 'six-line application' of the Plaintiff of 20 September 1995 for the position of a "women's representative" was eventually legally insignificant in the sense of § 118 BGB, as the declaration was given by the plaintiff in the expectation that the lack of seriousness of the application would be recognised by the defendant. In any event, the assessment of the Labour Court, which was not examined in more detail by the Regional Labour Court, can be used as a basis for recognition of the fact that the plaintiff from the beginning did not intend the establishment of a working relationship through the application made to the defendant, but was only aiming at receiving compensation in accordance with § 611a para. 2 BGB. The assumption of the court based on the personal explanation of the plaintiff during the settlement hearing, and the impression made by the plaintiff in the hearings that the plaintiff did not at all wish to accept the position of equal treatment representative, is not subject to doubt as regards the appeal.

3. In addition, the plaintiff was not a suitable applicant for the position of equal opportunities representative from the objective point of view. At the time of his application, the plaintiff could not demonstrate any theoretical and/or practical experience or knowledge which would have enabled him to fill the position of an equal opportunities representative in a town of approximately 37,000 inhabitants. His capabilities and experience did not correspond to those required by the job advertisements. The fact that the plaintiff claims that he has not been aware of the content of these advertisements does not change anything with regard to his lack of suitability which is to be objectively established. From the beginning, the plaintiff could not be considered as a suitable candidate to fill the post of the position advertised. The defendant is therefore not obliged to pay compensation. The complaint is not justified."

Notes

(1) This judgment expresses the view that disadvantage does not exist where the individual applicant did not apply for the job with "serious intent". The Court obviously felt that the complaint was contrived and artificial in nature. In contrast, the ECJ has shown a willingness to consider discrimination complaints, even where these are "manufactured" disputes. Notably, *Mangold* v. *Helm*,[133] a lawyer entered into a fixed-term contract with a worker over the age of 52 with the clear intention of allowing the worker to challenge the provision of German law that permitted the indefinite use of fixed-term contracts for workers over 52 years old (paragraph 32).

---

[133] Case C–144/04 *Mangold* v. *Helm* [2005] ECR I–9981.

Despite the contrived nature of the dispute, the ECJ accepted the preliminary reference from the national court as admissible.

(2) In Case C–180/95 *Draehmpaehl* v. *Urania Immobilienservice OHG* [1997] ECR I–2195, the ECJ held that a job applicant who would not have been successful even in the absence of discrimination was entitled to a remedy, although limits could be placed on the amount of compensation awarded in such circumstances.

(3) Irish case-law has held that a job applicant who experiences discrimination in the recruitment process can bring a complaint even if she is not the best qualified candidate.[134]

(4) Dutch case-law requires evidence of a "genuine disadvantage" in order for a finding of direct discrimination.[135]

2.4. PROVING DIRECT DISCRIMINATION

One of the principal difficulties with direct discrimination is establishing sufficient proof that a person was treated less favourably and that this was because of their sex, race, etc. It can also be difficult to determine the extent to which the less favourable treatment was caused by discriminatory grounds. Discrimination may have played a part in bringing about the less favourable treatment, even if this was not the sole reason. In some cases, there will be overt evidence of discrimination; for example, in Case C–180/95 *Draehmpaehl* v. *Urania Immobilienservice OHG* [1997] ECR I–2195 the job advert specifically requested a "female assistant". Nevertheless, such incontrovertible evidence can be expected to diminish as employers and service-providers become familiar with the risk of litigation. The challenge for the law is how to uncover direct discrimination where this is kept covert and hidden.

One response is to adopt measures that assist litigants in gathering evidence. This approach is illustrated in UK anti-discrimination legislation, which permits a complainant to serve on the respondent a questionnaire. In this questionnaire, the complainant sets out the circumstances in which they believe that they have experienced discrimination. The respondent is then asked to provide an explanation. The importance of the questionnaire lies in the possibility for individual litigants to rely on the responses in subsequent tribunal proceedings. Indeed, a tribunal may draw a negative inference from an employer's failure to respond.[136] Measures such as these can assist the individual in establishing their case, but an astute respondent will naturally seek to avoid any incriminating answers.

Often courts will be faced with evidence suggesting a possibility that discrimination occurred, but which falls short of definitive proof that this was the reason

---

[134] M. Bolger and C. Kimber, *Sex Discrimination Law* (Dublin, Round Hall Sweet & Maxwell, 2000) 401–2.

[135] See Gerards, above n. 7, 576. See also Gijzen, above n. 49, referring to Opinion 2001-143 of the Equal Treatment Commission.

[136] See McColgan, above n. 122, 318–20.

for the respondent's actions. The approach of courts will clearly be conditioned by the branch of law within which the discrimination norms are located. If an action is based in criminal law, then the standard of proof will typically be higher than that applicable to civil law. One response from courts is to draw *inferences* of discrimination. In such cases, there may be no "smoking gun" that unequivocally proves that the respondent acted for discriminatory reasons, but the totality of the evidence permits the court to conclude that this is the probable explanation.

Court of Cassation, Criminal Division, 25 November 1997   **2.FR.23.**
Case 96-85670, Potier

NO EXPLANATION OTHER THAN DIRECT DISCRIMINATION

Potier

Facts: Having signed a contract of tenancy for a furnished property with the complainants, the landlord learnt that one of the complainants was living with AIDS. Forty-eight hours before the exchange of the keys, the landlord requested a series of additional financial guarantees that were impossible to arrange within such a short time period. The complainants argued that they had been discriminated against on grounds of "state of health".

Held: The landlord had committed unlawful discrimination, inter alia, in breach of Article 225-2 of the Penal Code.

Judgment: "Considering that it arises from the contested Judgment that, by contract of 28 August 1992, Louis Poitier agreed with X . . . and Y . . . a lease relating to furnished premises, in exchange for the immediate payment of a guarantee deposit of 2,360 francs and the production of various documentation relating to the resources of the leaseholders and to the appointment of a third party in the capacity as guarantor; that on this occasion the lessor learned that one of its contractors was suffering from AIDS; that, by an amendment to the contract, drawn up on the following 29 September, he demanded the provision by the tenants, before 5 October, of two additional guarantees, bound to produce three pay slips in addition to a record of civil status; that, not being in a position to satisfy these obligations, the tenants ended the lease on 6 October 1992;

Considering that at the end of a judicial enquiry opened for the complaint with the victim's application to join the proceedings as civil party lodged by the latter, Louis Poitier was brought before the criminal court on the charge of discrimination, based on the former sections 416, 225-1 and 225-2, 1, of the Criminal Code, for having refused to provide a good or a service to people for reasons of their health or their morals; . . .

Whereas, on the one hand, the claimant put forward in his written evidence that the contract was not subject to the common law of leases, since it concerned the hiring of furnished premises, so that the additional guarantees requested by the lessor on 29 September 1992 were by no means irregular, the aforementioned lessor being limited to requesting a second guarantee likely to guarantee not only the rents, but also the inventory of the fixtures; that while not responding to this argument (see p.4 of the claims), the Court violates section 593 of the Code of Criminal Procedure;

. . .

Considering that, to declare Louis Poitier guilty of the offence prosecuted, not on the basis of section 225-2, 1, of the Criminal Code, relating to prevention, but by reference to part 4 of this same text, which punishes the act of subordinating the supply of a good or a service to a condition based, in particular, on the state of health, the Court of Appeal notes that the defendant, who reacted sharply to the announcement of the affliction of Y . . ., imposed on the leaseholders, 48 hours before the handing-over of the keys and the taking of possession of the premises, additional obligations, the nature and the exorbitant completion period of which had no justification other than the defective health of one of them;

Considering that in the case of these reasons, proceeding from a tribunal assessment of the elements of the facts and evidence discussed in the presence of the parties involved, the Court of Appeal, which responded as it should to the claims submitted to it, justified its decision without incurring the alleged objections;

From which it follows that the argument cannot be admitted."

By drawing inferences based on the balance of the evidence, courts can prevent the absence of express evidence of discrimination from becoming a barrier to successful litigation. Indeed, the possibility for courts to draw inferences of discrimination has been widely used by UK courts.[137] This approach remains, though, an option for courts, rather than an obligation. In contrast, many legal systems now require the burden of proof to shift from the complainant to the respondent once a prima facie case has been established. This procedure is evident in national legal systems, as well as EC law. One of the key issues in shifting the burden of proof is determining how much evidence the complainant needs to present in order to trigger the shift. This section will conclude by examining the role of statistics and situation testing, which are being explored in some legal systems as methods of triggering the shift in the burden of proof in cases of direct discrimination.

2.4.1.   SHIFTING THE BURDEN OF PROOF

2.4.1.A.   EUROPEAN UNION

Although measures to alleviate the problems of proof in discrimination litigation have been developed within various national jurisdictions, EC law has exercised a decisive influence on shaping a common approach. This can be traced back to case-law from the ECJ, particularly in the field of equal pay.

---

[137] See further *Glasgow City Council* v. *Zafar* [1998] ICR 120.

ECJ, 17 October 1989[138]   **2.EC.24.**
Case 109/88 Handels- og Kontorfunktionærernes Forbund I Danmark v. Dansk Arbejdsgiverforening acting on behalf of Danfoss

EQUAL PAY AND THE BURDEN OF PROOF

Danfoss

Facts: The case concerned a challenge to a system of additional payments that the employer could make to employees within the same pay grade. Statistical evidence demonstrated that the additional payments resulted in a higher average wage for men than women. Yet it was unclear from the evidence on what basis additional payments were awarded.

Held: The principle of effectiveness required adjustments to national rules on the burden of proof. In particular, where there is evidence that a pay system places women at a disadvantage and that system is non-transparent, then it is for the employer to demonstrate that it is not discriminatory.

Judgment: "10. It is apparent from the documents before the Court that the issue between the parties to the main proceedings has its origin in the fact that the system of individual supplements applied to basic pay is implemented in such a way that a woman is unable to identify the reasons for a difference between her pay and that of a man doing the same work. Employees do not know what criteria in the matter of supplements are applied to them and how they are applied. They know only the amount of their supplemented pay without being able to determine the effect of the individual criteria. Those who are in a particular wage group are thus unable to compare the various components of their pay with those of the pay of their colleagues who are in the same wage group.

11. In those circumstances the questions put by the national court must be understood as asking whether the Equal Pay Directive [Directive 75/117 of 10 February 1975 on the approximation of the laws of the Member States relating to the application of the principle of equal pay for men and women [1975] OJ L45/19] must be interpreted as meaning that where an undertaking applies a system of pay which is totally lacking in transparency, it is for the employer to prove that his practice in the matter of wages is not discriminatory, if a female worker establishes, in relation to a relatively large number of employees, that the average pay for women is less than that for men.

12. In that respect it must first be borne in mind that in its judgment of 30 June 1988 in Case 318/86 *Commission* v. *France* [1988] ECR 3559, paragraph 27, the Court condemned a system of recruitment, characterized by a lack of transparency, as being contrary to the principle of equal access to employment on the ground that the lack of transparency prevented any form of supervision by the national courts.

13. It should next be pointed out that in a situation where a system of individual pay supplements which is completely lacking in transparency is at issue, female employees can establish differences only so far as average pay is concerned. They would be deprived of any effective means of enforcing the principle of equal pay before the national courts if the effect of adducing such evidence was not to impose upon the employer the burden of proving that his practice in the matter of wages is not in fact discriminatory.

14. Finally, it should be noted that under Article 6 of the Equal Pay Directive Member States must, in accordance with their national circumstances and legal systems, take the measures necessary to ensure that the principle of equal pay is applied and that effective means

---

[138] [1989] ECR 3199.

are available to ensure that it is observed. The concern for effectiveness which thus underlies the Directive means that it must be interpreted as implying adjustments to national rules on the burden of proof in special cases where such adjustments are necessary for the effective implementation of the principle of equality.

15. To show that his practice in the matter of wages does not systematically work to the disadvantage of female employees the employer will have to indicate how he has applied the criteria concerning supplements and will thus be forced to make his system of pay transparent."

The principle of shifting the burden of proof was reaffirmed in further case-law, notably Case C–127/92 *Enderby* v. *Frenchay Health Authority* [1993] ECR I–5535.[139] Subsequently, it was codified in legislation through the Burden of Proof Directive:

Directive 97/80/EC of 15 December 1997 on the burden of proof   **2.EC.25.**
in cases of discrimination based on sex[140]

Article 3(2):
This Directive shall not apply to criminal procedures, unless otherwise provided by the Member States.

Article 4:
1. Member States shall take such measures as are necessary, in accordance with their national judicial systems, to ensure that, when persons who consider themselves wronged because the principle of equal treatment has not been applied to them establish, before a court or other competent authority, facts from which it may be presumed that there has been direct or indirect discrimination, it shall be for the respondent to prove that there has been no breach of the principle of equal treatment.

2. This Directive shall not prevent Member States from introducing rules of evidence which are more favourable to plaintiffs.

3. Member States need not apply paragraph 1 to proceedings in which it is for the court or competent body to investigate the facts of the case.

Notes

(1) The definition of the shift in the burden of proof was modelled on section 611a(1) of the German Civil Code. This provides that where an employee substantiates by prima facie evidence facts from which it may be presumed that there has been less favourable treatment on grounds of sex, it shall be for the employer to prove that this treatment is justified by objective reasons other than sex.

(2) Paragraph 3 of Article 4 remains an area of ambiguity. National legal procedures vary and the extent to which it is for the court or other competent body to investigate the facts is not always clear. For example, Schiek highlights initial arguments from the German government that the burden of proof rules should not

---

[139] See Ellis, above n. 19, 100.
[140] [1998] OJ L14/6.

apply to cases relating to civil servants. These are dealt with by the Administrative Courts, which the government argued had the duty to investigate the facts.[141] For the same reasons, in France, the burden of proof does not apply to Administrative Courts.[142]

(3) An equivalent provision on shifting the burden of proof has been included within the other "core" anti-discrimination Directives, specifically, Article 8 Racial Equality Directive, Article 10 Employment Equality Directive and Article 9 Gender Goods and Services Directive. The provision on the burden of proof has now been re-enacted in Article 19 of the Recast Gender Employment Directive.

2.4.1.B.   NATIONAL LAW AND THE BURDEN OF PROOF

The approach of national law to the burden of proof in discrimination cases is strongly influenced by the EC case-law and legislation discussed above. Nevertheless, the precise articulation of the concept is often adapted to the national legal context. Several examples will be examined in this section.

UNITED KINGDOM

As mentioned earlier, British courts had an established body of case-law on when it was permissible to draw an inference of discrimination. The need to implement the Burden of Proof Directive and, later, the 2000 anti-discrimination Directives required the introduction of statutory definitions of the rules on the burden of proof. The statutory definition was first introduced in the Sex Discrimination Act 1975. Section 63A states:

> "(2) Where, on the hearing of the complaint, the complainant proves facts from which the tribunal could, apart from this section, conclude in the absence of an adequate explanation that the respondent—
>
> (a) has committed an act of discrimination or harassment against the complainant which is unlawful . . . or
>
> (b) is . . . to be treated as having committed such an act of discrimination or harassment against the complainant,
>
> the tribunal shall uphold the complaint unless the respondent proves that he did not commit, or, as the case may be, is not to be treated as having committed, that act."

Equivalent definitions have been inserted in legislation on discrimination on grounds of race, religion or belief, disability, sexual orientation and age.[143] In *Barton* v. *Investec*

---

[141] D. Schiek, "Germany" [2005] *Bulletin on Legal Issues in Equality* No. 1, 32.

[142] Latraverse, above n. 46, 19.

[143] Race Relations Act 1976, s, 54A(2); Disability Discrimination Act 1995, s. 17A(1C); Employment Equality (Religion or Belief) Regulations 2003, Reg. 29(2); Employment Equality (Sexual Orientation) Regulations 2003, Reg. 29(2); Employment Equality (Age) Regulations 2006, Reg. 37.

[2003] IRLR 332, an employee challenged a non-transparent bonus payment system that resulted in substantially higher payments for male colleagues. The Employment Appeal Tribunal took the opportunity to issue an extensive clarification on how the burden of proof rules should be applied, building on the pre-existing case-law on drawing inferences of discrimination. These guidelines were subsequently approved, with modification, by the Court of Appeal in the following decision.

Court of Appeal, 18 February 2005[144]   **2.GB.26.**
Igen Ltd (Formerly Leeds Careers Guidance) and Others v. *Wong; Chamberlin and Another* v. *Emokpae; Webster* v. *Brunel University*

GUIDANCE ON THE APPLICATION OF THE BURDEN OF PROOF

Igen v. Wong

Facts: This was a series of joined cases at the Court of Appeal, all of which raised questions relating to the application of the statutory provisions on the burden of proof. Each of the cases concerned direct discrimination on grounds of sex or race.

Held: Whilst the factual decision on each case varied, the Court of Appeal took the opportunity to issue guidance on the application of the burden of proof provisions.

Judgment: paragraph 76, Annex
"(1) Pursuant to section 63A of the 1975 Act, it is for the claimant who complains of sex discrimination to prove on the balance of probabilities facts from which the tribunal could conclude, in the absence of an adequate explanation, that the employer has committed an act of discrimination against the claimant which is unlawful by virtue of Part 2, or which, by virtue of section 41 or section 42 of the 1975 Act, is to be treated as having been committed against the claimant. These are referred to below as 'such facts'.

(2) If the claimant does not prove such facts he or she will fail.

(3) It is important to bear in mind in deciding whether the claimant has proved such facts that it is unusual to find direct evidence of sex discrimination. Few employers would be prepared to admit such discrimination, even to themselves. In some cases the discrimination will not be an intention but merely based on the assumption that 'he or she would not have fitted in'.

(4) In deciding whether the claimant has proved such facts, it is important to remember that the outcome at this stage of the analysis by the tribunal will therefore usually depend on what inferences it is proper to draw from the primary facts found by the tribunal.

(5) It is important to note the word 'could' in section 63A(2). At this stage the tribunal does not have to reach a definitive determination that such facts would lead it to the conclusion that there was an act of unlawful discrimination. At this stage a tribunal is looking at the primary facts before it to see what inferences of secondary fact could be drawn from them.

(6) In considering what inferences or conclusions can be drawn from the primary facts, the tribunal must assume that there is no adequate explanation for those facts.

(7) These inferences can include, in appropriate cases, any inferences that it is just and equitable to draw in accordance with section 74(2)(b) of the 1975 Act from an evasive or

---

[144] [2005] 3 All ER 812.

equivocal reply to a questionnaire or any other questions that fall within section 74(2) of the 1975 Act.

(8) Likewise, the tribunal must decide whether any provision of any relevant code of practice is relevant and, if so, take it into account in determining such facts pursuant to section 56A(10) of the 1975 Act. This means that inferences may also be drawn from any failure to comply with any relevant code of practice.

(9) Where the claimant has proved facts from which conclusions could be drawn that the employer has treated the claimant less favourably on the ground of sex, then the burden of proof moves to the employer.

(10) It is then for the employer to prove that he did not commit, or as the case may be, is not to be treated as having committed, that act.

(11) To discharge that burden it is necessary for the employer to prove, on the balance of probabilities, that the treatment was in no sense whatsoever on the grounds of sex, since 'no discrimination whatsoever' is compatible with the Burden of Proof Directive.

(12) That requires a tribunal to assess not merely whether the employer has proved an explanation for the facts from which such inferences can be drawn, but further that it is adequate to discharge the burden of proof on the balance of probabilities that sex was not a ground for the treatment in question.

(13) Since the facts necessary to prove an explanation would normally be in the possession of the respondent, a tribunal would normally expect cogent evidence to discharge that burden of proof. In particular, the tribunal will need to examine carefully explanations for failure to deal with the questionnaire procedure and/or code of practice."

Notes

(1) The court's guidance links the triggering of a shift in the burden of proof to other elements of the statutory framework, such as the questionnaire procedure (discussed earlier in this section) and codes of practice. The latter are issued, with parliamentary approval, by the statutory equality commissions.[145] They aim to provide practical guidance on meeting the requirements of the legislation and shall be taken into account by tribunals where appropriate.

(2) In one of the joined cases, *Webster* v. *Brunel University*, the complainant was a woman of Asian origin who worked on the IT helpdesk. During a telephone call with the university accommodation office, she heard someone say "Paki" in the background (a derogatory term for people of Pakistani origin). She brought a complaint of racial discrimination against the university, based on its vicarious liability for the actions of its employees. The university argued that the accommodation office was a busy public space and the overheard comment could have been made by someone other than a university employee (e.g. a student). The Court of Appeal held that the onus was on the complainant to prove that the acts alleged were actually committed by the respondent (paragraph 28).

---

[145] Currently, these are the Commission for Racial Equality, Equal Opportunities Commission and Disability Rights Commission. The Commissions will be replaced during 2007–2009 by the Commission for Equality and Human Rights. See further below, G. Moon, Chapter Eight: Enforcement Bodies.

As discussed in section 2.2.3.B, French legislation is underpinned by the general principle of equality rather than specific definitions of direct or indirect discrimination. Although a lengthy list of prohibited discrimination grounds is contained with Article L. 122-45 of the Labour Code, this is not exhaustive; distinctions on non-enumerated grounds may nonetheless violate the constitutional principle of equality. In this regard, Dockès underlines the connection between the grounds specifically mentioned in the Labour Code and the burden of proof:

> "Ultimately, the role played by the list of prohibited criteria is merely that of organising the system of proof though, of course, in practice this will often be a decisive role. If the different treatment is based upon a criterion expressly prohibited under Article L. 122-45, the employee must demonstrate the difference in treatment and the employer will have to justify it. If the different treatment is not based on a prohibited ground, the employee will have to show not only that she was treated differently but also that the reason for such different treatment is unjustified."[146]

A statutory provision for shifting the burden of proof in discrimination cases was introduced by Law 2001-1066 on the fight against discrimination.[147] This inserted the following amendment to Article L. 123-1 of the Labour Code:

> "When a dispute is brought before the court, the employee or the applicant for a job, internship or vocational training shall present factual evidence supporting the assumption that discrimination, either direct or indirect, has occurred. Taking the factual evidence into account, the respondent has to prove that his/her decision was justified on the basis of objective considerations lacking any intent to discriminate. The court shall decide after having asked for any measure of instruction that it considers useful for rendering its judgment."[148]

Article L. 123-1 applies to equality between women and men. An equivalent provision applying to a long list of prohibited discrimination grounds can be found in Article L. 122-45 of the Labour Code. In fact, French courts had already begun to apply the principles on the shift in the burden of proof in response to the ECJ case-law.[149] It may be problematic that this definition refers to an absence of intent to discriminate. This could be misinterpreted as linking direct discrimination with the need for evidence of discriminatory motive.

---

[146] E. Dockès, "Equality in Labour Law: an Economically Efficient Human Right? Reflections from a French Law Perspective" (2002) 18 *IJCLLIR* 187, 192.

[147] Law 2001-1066 of 16 November 2001 concerning the fight against discrimination, JO, no. 267 of 17 November 2001, at 18311.

[148] Translation provided in M.-T. Lanquetin, "France" [2002] *Bulletin on Legal Issues in Equality* No. 1, 18.

[149] D. Borrillo, "Les instruments juridiques français et européens dans la mise en place du principe d'égalité et de non-discrimination" [2002] *Revue français des affaires sociales* 113, 125.

THE NETHERLANDS

Provisions on the shift in the burden of proof have also been developed through a combination of case-law and statute in the Netherlands.

Equal Treatment Commission (Commissie Gelijke Behandeling)   **2.NL.27.**
Opinion 2003-41

RACIAL DISCRIMINATION AND THE BURDEN OF PROOF

Turkish temporary contract worker

Facts: The applicant complained of various acts of racial discrimination by the employer, including the decision not to convert his temporary contract into a permanent contract. The employer argued that this was due to the applicant's poor performance in the workplace.

Held: A direct distinction on the ground of race was made in the decision not to offer the applicant a permanent contract.

Opinion: "5.20 An employer who states that the temporary contract of employment will not be converted into a permanent contract on account of an employee's poor performance must demonstrate such poor performance. Written reports of performance interviews may contribute to such evidence insofar as they may be taken to show that, in any event, that the malfunctioning of the employee was discussed. If the method of assessment was opaque, unverifiable and non-systematic, it is difficult to disentangle the various factors that played a role in an employer's decision.

5.21 The fact that the respondent advised the applicant even before the second annual contract was entered into that this annual contract would not be extended on account of the applicant's poor performance strengthens the impression that the respondent's actions were not considered in a clear, verifiable and systematic way. The Commission does not consider it plausible that an employee's temporary contract should be extended and that, after this, his performance should have deteriorated so much after that the respondent is not prepared to employ the applicant further on expiry of the second annual contract. The absence of reports on the performance interviews makes it impossible to ascertain whether only criticism of the applicant's performance alone that led to the respondent's decision.

5.22 In the light of the above, the Commission concludes that the respondent has insufficiently demonstrated that the decision not to convert the temporary contract into a permanent one is based only on objective reasons. The respondent has insufficiently refuted that the applicant's origin also played a role. The respondent therefore made a direct distinction on grounds of race."

Notes

(1) This decision draws attention to a lack of transparency in the employer's decision-making, as well as behaviour that seems objectively unreasonable. These features shift the burden of proof to the employer.

(2) Paragraph 5.15 mentions that the Commission's inquiry was to establish if the applicant's origin "played a role" in the non-renewal of his contract. The following

decision illustrates that a finding of discrimination can be made even where this was not the exclusive reason for the employer's actions.

Equal Treatment Commission (Commissie Gelijke Behandeling) **2.NL.28.**
Opinion 2004-67

DISABILITY DISCRIMINATION AND THE BURDEN OF PROOF

Contract worker with a heart condition

Facts: The applicant had previously suffered a heart attack. At the end of his fixed-term contract of employment, the employer decided neither to extend the contract, nor to convert it into a permanent contract. Although the applicant had received a letter from the personnel department stating that his contract would not be extended because of his medical history, the employer argued that this was a "communication error" and a reduced supply of work was the basis for the decision not to extend the contract.

Held: The decision not to extend his contract was a direct distinction on the grounds of disability or chronic disease.

Opinion: "5.5 Pursuant to the rules concerning the allocation of proof laid down in article 10 WGB h/cz [the Equal Treatment (Handicap or Chronic Illness) Act 2003] the applicant must put forward facts that lead one to suspect that a distinction is made on grounds of handicap or chronic illness. If he succeeds in doing so, the respondent must prove that he has not acted in conflict with WGB h/cz.

5.9 The above defence cannot hold water. The applicant has argued and the respondent has not denied that the recent medical past was mentioned not only in the letter of 17 December 2003, but already raised earlier—namely during the discussion on 27 October 2003—as a reason for not concluding a new contract of employment. The fact that the statement in the letter was based on a communication error between the management and the personnel department makes no difference in this regard, the more so since the respondent in its defence has indicated that the applicant's medical past was not the sole reason for not concluding a new contract of employment. It is the Commission's established case-law (CGB 23 March 2004, Opinion 2004-26 and CGB 6 August 2001, Opinion 2001-79) that a direct distinction is also present if the grounds for discrimination concerned, in the present case a disability or chronic illness were part of the reason for the impugned actions.

In the light of what the respondent has asserted, the Commission cannot but conclude that the applicant's presumed disability or chronic illness played a role in addition to business considerations. It consequently considers that it is not proved that the respondent did not act in conflict with the WGB h/cz, and that there was a direct distinction based on handicap or chronic disease."

Notes

(1) French case-law has also recognised that a finding of discrimination can be made even where this was not the exclusive reason for the employer's actions: Court of Cassation, Criminal Chamber, 14 June 2000, no. 99-81108, *CFDT Inter-co* (discrimination on the ground of trade union activities).

(2) Similarly, in Germany, the Federal Constitutional Court has accepted that discrimination can occur even where this is just one part of a "bundle of motives".[150]

(3) A statutory definition of the rules on shifting the burden of proof is now present in Dutch equal treatment legislation. For example, Article 10(1) of the General Equal Treatment Act provides

> "if a person who considers herself to have been wronged through 'distinction' as referred to in this Act established before a court facts from which it may be presumed that distinction has taken place, it shall be for the respondent to prove that the contested act was not in contravention of this Act".[151]

The rules on shifting the burden of proof do not apply to the Equal Treatment Commission because of its investigatory function. Nonetheless, the Commission continues to apply the shift in the burden of proof on a voluntary basis within its case-law.[152]

The EC Directives will require all Member States to introduce specific rules on shifting the burden of proof. Initial assessments indicate that implementation of this aspect of the Directives remains patchy and incomplete.[153] In some states, the rule in national legislation does not appear compatible with the Directives' definition. The case of Italy can be provided as an illustration.

A. Simoni, "Report on measures to combat discrimination: **2.IT.29.**
Directive 2000/43/EC and 2000/78/EC. Country report Italy"[154]

"The major weakness in the procedural system assisting the anti-discrimination legislation lies in the rule on the burden of proof, where the legislator continues to be very prudent. According to the Decrees [see above Article 2, Legislative Decree of 9 July 2003, no. 215, Implementation of Directive 2000/43/EC for the equal treatment of persons irrespective of race and of ethnic origin (Gazzetta Ufficiale no. 186, 12 August 2003); Article 2, Legislative Decree of 9 July 2003, no. 216, Implementation of Directive 2000/78/EC for equal treatment in relation to employment and working conditions (Gazzetta Ufficiale no. 187, 13 August 2003)] (identical wording, Articles 4.3 and 4.4 respectively), if the person who considers himself or herself wronged by discrimination submits elements of fact suitable to establish "serious, exact and consistent elements" about the existence of a direct or indirect discrimination, also on the basis of statistical data, the judge can evaluate such elements on the basis of the rule of the Civil Code (Article 2729) allowing a 'prudent appreciation' of presumptions. The absence of an explicit shift in the burden of proof has been raised in parliament by members of the majority, but without significant impact on the final text. The absence of decisions on the basis of the

---

[150] BVerfGE 89, 276 (289). See Mahlmann, above n. 92.
[151] Translation provided: Gijzen, above n. 52, 53.
[152] Ibid.
[153] Cormack and Bell, above n. 39, 70–71. See also D. Houtzager, "Changing Perspectives: Shifting the Burden of Proof in Racial Equality Cases" (Brussels, European Network Against Racism, 2006).
[154] (European Commission, 2005) 28–29, available on the website of Directorate-General for Employment, Social Affairs and Equal Opportunities.

new decree does not allow to evaluate which approach the judges will have in evaluating evidence . . .

That the approach of the legislator has been particularly prudent, is particularly evident if compared to the provision on gender discrimination of Article 4 of Act 125/1991 (on positive actions), which introduces a partial shift of the burden of proof toward the respondent. Indeed Article 4(6) indicates that the complainant must show factual elements suitable for clearly establishing the presumption of the existence of the discriminatory behaviour; the respondent has thus the burden to prove that the discrimination is not existing. The exact definition is 'presunzione precisa e concordante', that is to say precise and non-contradictory presumption, which is more favourable for the complainant than the formula of Article 2729 of the Civil Code [references omitted]."

2.4.1.C.   COUNCIL OF EUROPE

There are no specific rules on shifting the burden of proof within the ECHR. Nonetheless, a series of recent cases have placed the spotlight on whether and when the burden of proof can shift in a complaint of discrimination under Article 14. In considering these cases, the ECtHR has made express reference to the rule on shifting the burden of proof found within the EC anti-discrimination Directives. It has, though, shown more caution about applying this approach within the context of the Convention.

ECtHR [Grand Chamber], 6 July 2005[155]   **2.CoE.30.**
Nachova and others v. *Bulgaria*

ARTICLE 14 ECHR AND THE BURDEN OF PROOF

Nachova

Facts: Two Bulgarian nationals of Roma origin were conscripts in the army. They had a record of going absent without leave. On the occasion in question, they deserted their place of work and, during the subsequent attempt to arrest them, they were both shot dead by the military police. They were both unarmed. The case against Bulgaria argued breaches of both Article 2 (right to life) and Article 14. In particular, it was alleged that such force would not have been used to apprehend a non-Roma Bulgarian and that the officer who shot the men referred to "damn Gypsies" immediately after the killing.

Held: There was a breach of Article 2. Article 14 was breached in the failure to carry out a sufficient investigation into the possible racist motive for the killings. There was not, however, sufficient evidence that the actual killings were racially motivated.

Judgment: "147. It notes in this connection that in assessing evidence, the Court has adopted the standard of proof "beyond reasonable doubt". However, it has never been its purpose to borrow the approach of the national legal systems that use that standard. Its role is not to rule on criminal guilt or civil liability but on Contracting States' responsibility under the

---

[155] Applications 43577/98 and 43579/98.

Convention. The specificity of its task under Article 19 of the Convention—to ensure the observance by the Contracting States of their engagement to secure the fundamental rights enshrined in the Convention—conditions its approach to the issues of evidence and proof. In the proceedings before the Court, there are no procedural barriers to the admissibility of evidence or pre-determined formulae for its assessment. It adopts the conclusions that are, in its view, supported by the free evaluation of all evidence, including such inferences as may flow from the facts and the parties' submissions. According to its established case-law, proof may follow from the coexistence of sufficiently strong, clear and concordant inferences or of similar unrebutted presumptions of fact. Moreover, the level of persuasion necessary for reaching a particular conclusion and, in this connection, the distribution of the burden of proof are intrinsically linked to the specificity of the facts, the nature of the allegation made and the Convention right at stake. The Court is also attentive to the seriousness that attaches to a ruling that a Contracting State has violated fundamental rights . . .

153. The applicants referred to the statement given by Mr M. M., a neighbour of one of the victims, who reported that Major G. had shouted at him 'you damn Gypsies' immediately after the shooting. While such evidence of a racial slur being uttered in connection with a violent act should have led the authorities in this case to verify Mr M.M.'s statement, that statement is of itself an insufficient basis for concluding that the respondent State is liable for a racist killing.

154. Lastly, the applicants relied on information about numerous incidents involving the use of force against Roma by Bulgarian law enforcement officers that had not resulted in the conviction of those responsible.

155. It is true that a number of organisations, including intergovernmental bodies, have expressed concern about the occurrence of such incidents (see paragraphs 55-59 above). However, the Court cannot lose sight of the fact that its sole concern is to ascertain whether in the case at hand the killing of Mr Angelov and Mr Petkov was motivated by racism.

156. In its judgment the Chamber decided to shift the burden of proof to the respondent Government on account of the authorities' failure to carry out an effective investigation into the alleged racist motive for the killing. The inability of the Government to satisfy the Chamber that the events complained of were not shaped by racism resulted in its finding a substantive violation of Article 14 of the Convention, taken together with Article 2.

157. The Grand Chamber reiterates that in certain circumstances, where the events lie wholly, or in large part, within the exclusive knowledge of the authorities, as in the case of death of a person within their control in custody, the burden of proof may be regarded as resting on the authorities to provide a satisfactory and convincing explanation of, in particular, the causes of the detained person's death (see *Salman* v. *Turkey* [GC], no. 21986/93, § 100, ECHR 2000-VII). The Grand Chamber cannot exclude the possibility that in certain cases of alleged discrimination it may require the respondent Government to disprove an arguable allegation of discrimination and—if they fail to do so—find a violation of Article 14 of the Convention on that basis. However, where it is alleged—as here—that a violent act was motivated by racial prejudice, such an approach would amount to requiring the respondent Government to prove the absence of a particular subjective attitude on the part of the person concerned. While in the legal systems of many countries proof of the discriminatory effect of a policy or decision will dispense with the need to prove intent in respect of alleged discrimination in employment or the provision of services, that approach is difficult to transpose to a case where it is alleged that an act of violence was racially motivated. The Grand Chamber, departing from the Chamber's approach, does not consider that the alleged failure of the authorities to carry out an effective investigation into the alleged racist motive for the killing should shift the burden of proof to the respondent Government with regard to the alleged

violation of Article 14 in conjunction with the substantive aspect of Article 2 of the Convention. The question of the authorities' compliance with their procedural obligation is a separate issue, to which the Court will revert below.

158. In sum, having assessed all relevant elements, the Court does not consider that it has been established that racist attitudes played a role in Mr Angelov's and Mr Petkov's deaths."

Notes

(1) The Court notes the distinct nature of proceedings under the Convention, which concern state responsibility (paragraph 147). The process is not designed to determine the criminal liability of individuals and, as such, this would be an argument in favour of permitting a shift in the burden of proof. Nonetheless, had the Court found a substantive violation of Article 14, this would have implied that the individuals involved did, on the balance of probabilities, commit a racist murder.

(2) The judgment places a recurrent emphasis on evidence of a racist motive and prejudice (paragraphs 155 and 157). As discussed in section 2.3.2, overt evidence of racist prejudice is frequently difficult to obtain. In practice, individuals are likely to seek to conceal discriminatory motives. In this case, there was direct evidence from one witness of a racist statement, combined with contextual information on the propensity of Bulgarian law enforcement agencies to use excessive force against Roma with little official accountability. By refusing to shift the burden of proof in this context, the Court sets a high threshold for establishing a substantive violation of Article 14 in relation to unlawful killings. It seems that only abundant, clear-cut evidence of a racist motive will suffice.

(3) *Bekos and Koutropoulos v. Greece*, Application 15250/02, 13 December 2005 also concerned the maltreatment of Roma by law enforcement agencies. The court followed the same approach as in *Nachova*, emphasizing that evidence of motive was needed in cases of alleged racist violence (paragraph 65).[156] The next case, however, provides an example of a situation where the court was willing to draw an inference of discrimination.

ECtHR, 13 December 2005   **2.CoE.31.**
Timishev v. Russia

ARTICLE 14 AND THE BURDEN OF PROOF

Timishev

Facts: The applicant was a Russian national of Chechen ethnic origin. Part of his complaint related to an attempt in June 1999 to cross the border from the Ingushetia Republic into the Kabardino-Balkaria Republic (both within Russia). The applicant claimed that he was subject to racial discrimination when he was denied permission to cross the border because the Ministry of Interior of Kabardino-Balkaria had

---

[156] See also ECtHR, *Ognyanova and Choban v. Bulgaria*, 23 May 2006, Application 46317/99.

issued an instruction not to permit the entry of any Chechens. The officers at the checkpoint claimed he was initially refused entry because he attempted to jump a long queue of cars.

Held: There was a breach of Article 14 in conjunction with Article 2 of Protocol 4 to the ECHR on freedom of movement for those lawfully within the territory of a state.

Judgment: "40. The applicant maintained that he and his driver, both being of Chechen ethnic origin, had been denied access to Kabardino-Balkaria through the Urukh checkpoint because the traffic police had acted on an oral instruction to refuse entry to Chechens travelling by private car.

41. The applicant's submissions were corroborated by the report on a violation of constitutional rights, enclosed with the prosecutor's letter of 1 February 2000, and the summary of the findings of an internal inquiry, approved by the head and deputy head of the internal security police department and the Minister of the Interior. It was established that the instruction in question had originated from the deputy head of the public safety police of the Kabardino-Balkaria Ministry of the Interior and had been transmitted down to rank-and-file traffic police officers.

42. The Government insisted that the applicant had attempted to jump the queue of vehicles but, having been refused priority treatment, had left the checkpoint of his own will. They prayed in aid the judgment of the Nalchik Town Court of 25 August 1999, upheld on appeal by the Supreme Court of Kabardino-Balkaria on 21 September 1999.

43. The Court, however, is not persuaded that the Town Court's judgment laid down a reliable factual basis for this assessment because its findings of fact appear inconsistent and fraught with contradictions. For example, the Town Court found that reinforced controls of vehicles on 19 June 1999 had been introduced by a police order (no. 68) which had only been issued two days later, on 21 June 1999. It also found that the applicant had refused to show his passport or some other identity document. However, if the applicant did not wait in the queue for his turn and left of his own will, then the failure to produce documents could not be held against him. Alternatively, if the police asked for his documents that suggests, by converse implication, that it was his turn in the queue or else that he was granted priority treatment. Furthermore, the Town Court established that the applicant had shown his advocate's card but failed to explain the relevance of its finding that the card had been issued in Grozny rather than in Nalchik (a finding which is, moreover, refuted by a copy of the card produced by the applicant in evidence). The judgment of the Supreme Court of Kabardino-Balkaria of 21 September 1999 did nothing to eliminate these discrepancies.

44. In these circumstances, the Court gives credence to the applicant's version of events, which has been corroborated by independent inquiries carried out by the prosecution and police authorities. It finds that the traffic police at the Urukh checkpoint prevented the applicant from crossing the administrative border between two Russian regions, Ingushetia and Kabardino-Balkaria. There has therefore been a restriction on the applicant's right to liberty of movement within the territory of the respondent State, within the meaning of Article 2 § 1 of Protocol No. 4."

The approach currently adopted by the ECtHR seems similar to the initial steps taken by national courts. There is no firm rule that the burden of proof shifts to the respondent once the applicant presents a prima facie case of discrimination. Instead, the ECtHR has developed a discretionary norm that permits it to draw inferences of discrimination depending on the facts and the particular part of the Convention which is engaged.

2.4.2.   TRIGGERING A SHIFT IN THE BURDEN OF PROOF

For the individual litigant, it will be crucial to know how much evidence it is necessary to provide before the burden of proof shifts to the respondent in direct discrimination cases. Will it be sufficient simply to demonstrate that the complainant was treated less favourably than a person of a different sex/race/religion/etc.? Inevitably, the required level of proof will, to some extent, be contingent on the facts of the specific case before a court. Case-law in the UK and Ireland has required more than a mere difference in treatment combined with a difference between the comparators. In *University of Huddersfield* v. *Wolff* [2004] ICR 828, a female member of staff was not awarded a job promotion; she sought to compare herself with a male colleague who was promoted. Although there was less favourable treatment (non-promotion) and a relevant difference between the comparators (sex), the English Employment Appeals Tribunal held that, in order to shift the burden of proof, the complainant had to provide (some) evidence that the reason for the less favourable treatment was on grounds of sex. Alternatively, in *Margetts* v. *Graham Anthony*,[157] the Irish Equality Tribunal held that the mere fact that the comparators were different in age was not sufficient to shift the burden of proof.

If courts will require something more to indicate the possibility of discrimination, then attention turns to what this could be. Interestingly, the Belgian Federal Law of 25 February 2003 identified two instruments that could be used to trigger a shift in the burden of proof: statistics and situation testing.[158] Each is considered below.

2.4.2.A.   STATISTICS

The collection of statistical data has a significant role to play in various aspects of anti-discrimination law, most notably in relation to indirect discrimination (in terms of establishing disparate impact) and positive action (as part of strategies to monitor progress in achieving equality and setting targets for change). Both of these issues will be examined further in chapters three and seven; therefore, this chapter will only briefly mention the role of statistics in relation to direct discrimination.

Case-law from the UK illustrates how statistical information on the wider context to the individual dispute can be used to trigger a shift in the burden of proof. Where an individual has been treated less favourably than other persons of a different sex/race/etc. and statistics show that persons with the same characteristics are systematically under-represented, then this can be sufficient to transfer the burden of proof to the respondent to show that the less favourable treatment was not due to discriminatory reasons.

---

[157] Para. 4.11, DEC-E2002-050, 27 November 2002.

[158] Arts. 19(3)-(4), Law of 25 February 2003 on the fight against discrimination and modifying the law of 15 February 1993 creating a Centre for Equal Opportunities and the Fight against Racism (Moniteur Belge, 13 May 2003, at 23578).

STATISTICS AND EVIDENCE OF DIRECT RACIAL DISCRIMINATION

Rihal

Facts: The applicant was an Indian-born Sikh, but who had lived in the UK for many years. Over a period of several years, he was not promoted to several vacancies in senior management posts. In contrast, white colleagues did receive promotions. He argued that there was direct discrimination contrary to the Race Relations Act 1976.

Held: Direct discrimination on racial grounds had occurred.

Judgment: LORD JUSTICE SEDLEY: "52. The ethnic audit figures produced by Ealing for the tribunal hearing and summarised in paragraph 43 of the employment tribunal's reasons are disturbing . . . In the housing department of the local authority of a multi-racial borough they portray an almost complete racial divide between upper management and the remainder of the staff. With the single exception of Ms Gomer (whose elevation the tribunal found explicable without negativing their general finding) the entire managerial team was white: this in a borough 40 per cent of whose population is from ethnic minorities, and in a local authority whose other departmental senior management teams typically contain about 25 per cent from ethnic minorities. These figures in themselves rightly put the tribunal on inquiry, because they suggested a clear possibility that there was a culture of white elitism in the upper echelon of the housing department. Such a culture, as the tribunal will have been well aware, can exercise a potent influence on individual decision-makers, of which they themselves may be aware faintly or not at all.

53. Ms Grewal, for the local authority, has relied upon what Balcombe LJ said in *Chapman* v. *Simon* [1994] IRLR 124, para. 33:

'In order to justify an inference, a tribunal must first make findings of primary fact from which it is legitimate to draw the inference. If there are no such findings, then there can be no inference: what is done can at best be speculation.'

What her argument overlooks is that there was no such want of primary facts here. The sharp ethnic imbalance revealed by Ealing's own figures was enough to entitle — indeed arguably to require — the tribunal to look for a convincing non-racial reason. In a well-run organisation there will be procedures, training and monitoring data capable of reassuring a tribunal that everyone has been treated on an equal footing and that any imbalances are caused by fortuitous or extraneous factors. When the tribunal failed to find an acceptable non-racial reason for the imbalance of which Mr Rihal's history formed part, they were entitled to infer that there was none: see *West Midlands PTE* v. *Singh* [1988] ICR 614, 619. Their inference was supported by Mr Rihal's own history of persistent non-promotion."

Notes

(1) The Employment Tribunal decision in this case concluded that the organisational culture was such that the management could not picture "a turban wearing Sikh with a pronounced accent in the managerial roles" (cited at paragraph 21 of the

---

[159] [2004] IRLR 642 CA.

Court of Appeal judgment). This emphasizes the deeply engrained resistance to "difference" within the organisation, rather than displays of overt prejudice.

(2) The ability of individual litigants to rely on statistics to trigger a shift in the burden of proof in direct discrimination cases will depend heavily on the availability of such statistical information. In many EU Member States, there is very limited data collection, especially for grounds such as racial or ethnic origin, religion or belief, disability and sexual orientation.[160]

2.4.2.B.   SITUATION TESTING

An alternative route to trigger a shift in the burden of proof is situation testing. This involves a real-life test of how organisations treat two persons or groups of persons in a similar situation, but with different personal characteristics. For example, an international ILO research project tested employers' behaviour by sending equivalent job applications to firms, but where it was evident that the applicants were of different ethnic origins.[161] Whilst this was purely for the purposes of research into the extent of discrimination, situation testing has also been used as the foundation for legal cases of direct discrimination.[162]

Kisvárda Town Court (Kisvárdai Városi Bíróság),   **2.HU.33.**
28 November 2000[163]

RACIAL DISCRIMINATION IN ENTRY TO DISCO

K.L. disco

Facts: The applicants were several persons of Roma origin who produced evidence based on situation testing that they had been refused entry to "K.L. disco" because they were Roma.

Held: The applicants' personal rights under Hungarian law had been violated by unlawful racial discrimination.

Judgment: "Upon the initiation of the Gypsy Minority Local Government, the Legal Defence Bureau for National and Ethnic Minorities, has carried out a test in the K.L. disco on the

---

[160] See further, Commission, "Comparative Study on the Collection of Data to Measure the Extent and Impact of Discrimination within the United States, Canada, Australia, the UK and the Netherlands" (Luxembourg, Office for the Official Publications of the European Communities, 2004); N. Reuter, T. Makkonen and O. Oosi, "Study on Data Collection to Measure the Extent and Impact of Discrimination in Europe" (European Commission, 2004), available on the website of Directorate-General for Employment, Social Affairs and Equal Opportunities.

[161] E.g. E. Allasino, E. Reyneri, A. Venturini, G. Zincone, "Labour Market Discrimination against Migrant Workers in Italy", International Migration Papers No. 67 (2004), available on the website of the International Labour Organisation.

[162] See further, I. Rorive, "Situation Tests in Europe: Myths and Realities" [2006] *European Anti-Discrimination Law Review* Issue 3, 31.

[163] 11.P.20 450/2000/15.

1 April 2000. On this occasion, M. and B., both residents of Demecser, arrived at the village of D.

In the evening, at around 8 pm, they both attempted to enter. They purchased tickets at the entrance and entered the premises with their tickets. About 20-30 minutes later, one of the club employees handed over membership cards to B. and M., and entered their names in the membership registry. He told them that it was necessary "because of the Gypsies".

Thereafter, the plaintiffs in the first and second degree have attempted to enter, together with Be., as a witness. Be. is of Romany origin and he works at the Roma Press Centre.

They were not granted entry at the entrance; they were refused entry unless they could produce their membership cards. Witness Be. asked how could they obtain a membership card. The employees of the club submit an application to the management of the club, together with a CV and recommendations by two existing members, during weekdays . . .

The plaintiffs' claim is partially founded, according to the following. According to sub-section (1) of Section 75 of the Civil Code (the Ptk.), everybody must respect inherent personal rights. These rights are protected by law. According to section 76 of the Ptk., the following constitute particular violations of inherent personal rights: discrimination of private individuals on the basis of their gender, race, nationality or religion, furthermore the violation of the freedom of their conscience and the illegal restriction of their personal freedom, any damage to their physical safety or health, violation of their honour or human dignity . . .

Witnesses B., M. and Be. all participated in the test as activists of the Legal Defence Bureau for National and Ethnic Minorities. This, however, does not qualify them as biased witnesses. The defendants were not able to contradict the three witness statements satisfactorily. Therefore, the Court accepted these as the basis for judgment."

Notes

(1) This judgment was later upheld by the Hungarian Supreme Court: *Legfelsőbb Bíróság,* Legf. Bír. Pfv. IV. 21.269/2001. sz.

(2) Situation testing has also been accepted by French courts in discrimination cases. In *Fardeau and others,*[164] entry to a nightclub was refused to two small groups of young men of North African origin, whereas entry was permitted to other groups of persons of European origin. The club argued that they were refused entry because they were groups of men and they were not regulars at the establishment. This explanation was rejected by the Court of Cassation based on the evidence presented by the testing.

(3) Situation testing was one element of the evidence presented in *R (European Roma Rights Centre)* v. *Immigration Officer at Prague Airport and another* [2005] 2 AC 1. The House of Lords did not question its admissibility.

(4) Situation testing has also been used within both criminal and civil litigation on discrimination in the Netherlands.[165]

Several states have attempted to incorporate situation testing into anti-discrimination legislation. As mentioned earlier, Article 19(3) of the Belgian Federal Law of

[164] Court of Cassation, Criminal Chamber, 12 September 2000, no. 99–87251.
[165] See further, R. Holtmaat, "Report on Measures to Combat Discrimination: Directives 2000/43/EC and 2000/78/EC. Country Report the Netherlands" (European Commission, forthcoming).

25 February 2003 provided that evidence from situation testing could be used by judges to shift the burden of proof to the respondent. This provision was to be operationalised by a Royal Decree setting out the specific modalities. The negotiations on implementing this part of the law have proven complex and it has not yet been completed:

> "These consultations seem to have highlighted the difficulty there is in pursuing simultaneously two partially incompatible objectives: first, the 'situation tests' should be strictly codified, and their methodology ascertained, to ensure that they will not lead to abuse by alleged victims of discrimination, but also to encourage the judge before which the results of such tests are presented to accept that this will result in the reversal of the burden of proof; second however, such 'situation tests' must not be too burdensome to perform, and they should remain a relatively accessible means by which a presumption of discrimination may be established."[166]

In Hungary, legislation has been introduced permitting the Equal Treatment Authority to organise situational testing, although there is very limited experience of how this will function in practice.[167] Similarly, in France, the 2006 Law on Equality of Opportunity authorises the High Authority on the Fight against Discrimination and for Equality to conduct situation testing (Article 41). In addition, Article 45 of the 2006 law inserts a new provision in the Penal Code confirming that evidence from situation testing is admissible:

> "Art. 225-3-1. The offences covered by the present section are equally constituted if they have been committed against one or more persons who have sought one of the goods, acts, services or contracts mentioned in Article 225-2 with the aim of demonstrating the existence of discriminatory behaviour in order that the proof of this behaviour is established."[168]

The role for equality bodies in conducting situation testing is explored further in chapter eight.

2.5. SEGREGATION

The previous sections have considered the key elements required to establish direct discrimination and the problems of proof that can arise. Before considering exceptions to the prohibition of direct discrimination, this section considers briefly whether a specific manifestation of discrimination, namely segregation, can be treated as direct discrimination.

---

[166] O. de Schutter, "Report on Measures to Combat Discrimination: Directive 2000/43/EC and 2000/78/EC. Country Report Belgium" (European Commission, 2005) 54, available on the website of Directorate-General for Employment, Social Affairs and Equal Opportunities.

[167] Decree 362/2004 on the Equal Treatment Authority and detailed rules of its procedure; see A. Kádár and L. Farkas, "Report on Measures to Combat Discrimination: Directive 2000/43/EC and 2000/78/EC. Country Report Hungary" (European Commission, forthcoming).

[168] Law No. 2006-396 of 31 March 2006 on equality of opportunity (JO no. 79, 2 April 2006, at 4950).

Segregation is not mentioned in the ECHR, the European Social Charter or the EC Directives. Yet cases concerning segregation on grounds of sex or race have arisen under all these instruments.[169] In recent years, growing attention has been paid to segregation, most notably in relation to the treatment of Roma communities.[170] This is not, though, a phenomenon limited to central and eastern European states. Segregation of Roma communities is also evident in western European states,[171] whilst concerns have been expressed about urban segregation of communities of migrant origin.[172] Segregation is often linked to issues around racial discrimination, but it also impinges upon other equality grounds, for example, the segregation of children with disabilities in education.[173]

Segregation can be difficult to classify within the traditional legal framework of discrimination. The first question that arises is whether the mere fact of segregation amounts to direct discrimination. If Roma children are educated separately from non-Roma children, is this per se direct discrimination or is it also necessary to show less favourable treatment? Namely, would it be required to demonstrate that the education provided to Roma children was of a lower quality than that provided to the non-Roma children? In the famous case of *Brown* v. *Board of Education*,[174] the US Supreme Court rejected the idea of "separate but equal".

The second conceptual challenge is distinguishing between voluntary and involuntary segregation. Parents may choose, for example, to send their children to separate schools based on a particular religious ethos. Similarly, national minority communities may seek a measure of isolation within educational and other institutions in order to preserve and promote minority culture, especially minority languages. In respect of other equality grounds, girls-only or boys-only schools continue to exist in Europe and some parents might prefer to have their child educated in a specialist school limited to children with a particular disability. A simple diagnosis would be to treat voluntary segregation as permissible, whereas involuntary segregation is prohibited. Yet the reality of "choice" may be difficult to ascertain. The parent of a Roma child might prefer that she is educated in a

---

[169] In respect of the European Social Charter, see European Committee of Social Rights, *European Roma Rights Centre* v. *Greece*, Complaint No. 15/2003, 8 December 2004, Strasbourg; European Committee of Social Rights, *European Roma Rights Centre* v. *Italy*, Complaint No. 27/2004, 7 December 2005, Strasbourg.

[170] European Commission, "The Situation of Roma in an Enlarged European Union" (Luxembourg, Office for the Official Publications of the European Communities, 2004); European Union Monitoring Centre on Racism and Xenophobia (EUMC), "Roma and Travellers in Public Education" (Vienna, EUMC, 2006).

[171] N. Sigona, "Locating 'the Gypsy Problem'. The Roma in Italy: Stereotyping, Labelling and 'Nomad Camps'" (2005) 31 *Journal of Ethnic and Migration Studies* 741.

[172] T. Phillips, "After 7/7: Sleepwalking to Segregation" (22 September 2005), speech available on the website of the Commission for Racial Equality.

[173] See further, J. Schoonheim and D. Ruebain, "Reflections on Inclusion and Accommodation in Childhood Education: from International Standard Setting to National Implementation" in C. Gooding and A. Lawson (eds.), *Disability Rights in Europe—from Theory to Practice* (Oxford, Hart Publishing, 2005).

[174] 347 US 483 (1954).

mainstream school, but could be deterred if her daughter will be isolated in the school and vulnerable to harassment.

Finally, in the context of this chapter, it is important to underline the difficulty of classifying segregation as either direct or indirect discrimination. If an employer specifically allocates only immigrant workers to a particular task, then this could be direct nationality discrimination. On the other hand, if the concentration of immigrant workers in a particular part of the firm results from facially neutral criteria, such as specific qualification requirements, the segregationist effect of the criteria could be challenged as indirect discrimination. The boundary between these two scenarios may often be less clear in practice. Segregation can become institution-alised and self-perpetuating. This poses the question whether public and private actors should have a positive obligation to combat patterns of segregation.

The following discussion considers segregation within international, European and national legal instruments. This is followed by a review of European and national case-law in this area.

2.5.1.   INTERNATIONAL, EUROPEAN AND NATIONAL LEGAL INSTRUMENTS

The UN International Convention on the Elimination of Racial Discrimination (ICERD) was signed in 1965 against the backdrop of Apartheid policies in South Africa and controversies over the segregation of black people in the USA.[175] A distinctive feature of ICERD in comparison to other international human rights instruments is its express condemnation of segregation. Article 3 provides:

> "States Parties particularly condemn racial segregation and apartheid and undertake to prevent, prohibit and eradicate all practices of this nature in territories under their jurisdiction."

In the framework of ICERD, segregation is identified as a distinct harm, alongside racial discrimination. This approach can also be found within the work of the Council of Europe's European Commission on Racism and Intolerance (ECRI). In 2002, ECRI issued a general policy recommendation setting out a compre-hensive scheme of model legislation on racism that all states should seek to enact. This specified that national law should treat segregation as a specific form of discrimination.[176] Segregation was defined in the explanatory report on the recommendation:

> "Segregation is the act by which a (natural or legal) person separates other persons on the basis of one of the enumerated grounds without an objective and reasonable justification,

---

[175] See further K. Boyle and A. Baldaccini, "A Critical Evaluation of International Human Rights Approaches to Racism" in S. Fredman (ed.), *Discrimination and Human Rights—the Case of Racism* (Oxford, Oxford University Press, 2001).

[176] Para. 6, ECRI general policy recommendation no. 7 on national legislation to combat racism and racial discrimination, CRI (2002) 41, 13 December 2002.

in conformity with the proposed definition of discrimination. As a result, the voluntary act of separating oneself from other persons on the basis of one of the enumerated grounds does not constitute segregation."[177]

Whilst neither ICERD nor ECRI's recommendation defines segregation as direct or indirect discrimination, the British Race Relations Act 1976 draws a clear link between segregation and direct discrimination. Section 1(2) states:

> "It is hereby declared that, for the purposes of this Act, segregating a person from other persons on racial grounds is treating him less favourably than they are treated."

Segregation is also specifically prohibited as a form of discrimination in the Hungarian Equal Treatment Act.[178] Unlike the Race Relations Act, this applies to a long list of discrimination grounds. The prohibition of segregation is subject to exceptions:

A. Kádár and L. Farkas, "Report on measures to combat   **2.HU.34.**
discrimination: Directive 2000/43/EC and 2000/78/EC.
Country report Hungary"[179]

"Pursuant to Article 28 paragraph (1) if the education is only organised for students of one sex, it does not violate the principle of equal treatment, provided that participation in such an education is voluntary, and will not result in any disadvantages for the participants. Similarly to voluntary single sex education, under paragraph 2 voluntary religious education may be taken to conform to the principle of equal treatment if (in elementary and higher education, at the initiation and by the voluntary choice of the parents, at college or university by the students' voluntary participation) education based on religious or other ideological conviction, or education for ethnic or other minorities is organised in a way that the goal or the curriculum of the education justifies the creation of separated classes or groups; provided that this does not result in any disadvantage for those participating in such an education, and the education complies with the requirements approved, laid down and subsidised by the State.

Although it is included in the text of the law quoted above, we would like to underline the fact that such separated education is deemed compatible with the principle of non-discrimination only if participation is voluntary. At the elementary and secondary level, the pupils' and students' parents have to initiate the forming of such classes or groups on a voluntary basis, whereas in higher education it shall be based on the students' voluntary participation. A further condition is that such education shall be of equal value with ordinary (i.e. not separated) education. (This exception was necessary because the Minorities Act, for example, contains the possibility for minority parents to initiate the formulation of separated minority classes for their children, where they can learn the minority language and minority culture. To maintain the legality of such classes, an exempting rule had to be inserted. This is however, only a possibility and not anything compulsory.)"

---

[177] Para. 16, Explanatory report, *ibid.*
[178] Art. 7(1).
[179] (European Commission, 2005) 24–5, available on the website of Directorate-General for Employment, Social Affairs and Equal Opportunities.

Whilst exceptions to the prohibition of direct discrimination will be examined in the next part of this chapter, it can be noted that exceptions for sex-specific education are found in other Member States, such as the Netherlands.[180] Although it does not apply to education, the 2004 Gender Goods and Services Directive contains a broad exception for sex-specific services:

> "Article 4(5)
> This Directive shall not preclude differences in treatment, if the provision of the goods and services exclusively or primarily to members of one sex is justified by a legitimate aim and the means of achieving that aim are appropriate and necessary."

This exception can, in part, be attributed to the need to balance competing human rights claims. In particular, the rights of a single-sex private club to freedom of association may collide with the right to non-discrimination. A tension also exists here between combating discriminatory exclusions and protecting services targeted at groups of people vulnerable to discrimination (e.g. a shelter for female victims of domestic violence). Exceptions based on human rights claims are examined further in section 2.6.3.B of this chapter.

2.5.2. CASE-LAW ON SEGREGATION

The relationship of segregation to direct discrimination has not been extensively explored within European case-law. The most significant decisions relate to issues of racial discrimination. Indeed, attitudes towards segregation appear to differ greatly depending on the ground of discrimination in question. This is already evident from some of the legislative provisions cited above; separate treatment of women and men is regarded as justifiable in a significant range of circumstances. This view can also be identified within the following case at the ECJ.

ECJ, 10 March 2005[181] **2.EC.35.**
Case C–196/02, Nikoloudi v. Organismos Tilepikinonion Ellados AE (OTE)

SEX-SPECIFIC CATEGORY OF WORKERS

OTE

Facts: OTE employed temporary and established workers. To become established, a worker had to be engaged on a full-time basis. Ms Nikoloudi was employed as a part-time cleaner. Prior to 1996, part-time work was not counted when determining length of service for occupational benefits. The company's regulations specified that only women could be employed as cleaners. Ms Nikoloudi argued that sex

---

[180] General Equal Treatment Act 1994, s. 7(2).
[181] [2005] ECR I–1789.

261

discrimination was present because only women could be part-time cleaners under the company's rules and part-time workers were treated less favourably in calculating length of service.

Held: Given that the post of part-time cleaner was reserved to women in the company's rules and part-time workers could not become established employees, there was direct discrimination on the ground of sex contrary to Directive 76/207.

Judgment: "33. OTE submits in the present case that the post of part time cleaner, which is justified by the existence of premises having a small area for cleaning, was reserved for women in order to assist them and meet their specific needs.

34. While it is true that categories of workers composed of persons of a single sex are permitted, in particular by Article 2(2) and (4) of Directive 76/207, and that the creation of a category of exclusively female workers therefore does not constitute in itself direct discrimination against women, the subsequent introduction of unfavourable treatment by reference to that category, whether relating to equal treatment or to equal pay, could, however, amount to such discrimination.

35. So far as concerns, first, equal treatment, in the main proceedings every worker having a contract of indefinite duration with the exception of those working part time, namely female cleaners, was appointed as an established member of staff.

36. It follows that while the criterion of a full time job, as a precondition for appointment as an established member of staff, is ostensibly neutral as to the worker's sex, it effectively excludes a category of workers which, by virtue of Article 3(v)(d) of the General Staff Regulations of OTE read in conjunction with Article 24a(2) thereof, can only be composed of women. Where such a criterion does not render incomparable, with regard to establishment, two situations which as for the rest are comparable, it constitutes direct discrimination on grounds of sex."

Notes

(1) The Court accepts that gender segregation per se is not direct discrimination; this only arises once segregation leads to less favourable treatment.

(2) It argues that categories of work reserved to members of one sex are permitted by Articles 2(2) and (4) of the Gender Employment Directive (prior to amendment). Article 2(2) is an exception for posts where sex is a genuine occupational requirement and Article 2(4) is an exception for positive action. Sex is undoubtedly not a genuine occupational requirement for a job as a cleaner and reserving low pay, manual work to women seems entirely inconsistent with any notion of positive action.

(3) The Court's reasoning in this case is not consistent with its decision in *Schnorbus* (see section 2.3.1.B). In *OTE*, it is willing to accept the presence of direct discrimination because part-time workers were treated less favourably and this category was reserved exclusively to women. Yet, in *Schnorbus*, the Court considered that more favourable treatment of those having completed national service, a category reserved exclusively to men, could only be viewed as indirect sex discrimination.

Even where national legislation specifically prohibits segregation, its application has been difficult. In Britain, there is little recorded case-law on section 1(2) of the Race Relations Act 1976. The most commonly cited case was not successful.

Employment Appeals Tribunal, 14 November 1979[182]   **2.GB.36.**
Pel Ltd v. Modgill and others

RACIAL SEGREGATION IN EMPLOYMENT

Modgill

Facts: Pel Ltd. produced metal furniture. The evidence showed that only Asian workers were employed in the paint spray shop, which was an unpleasant job. Mr Modgill and others challenged this as unlawful racial segregation, which was upheld by the Industrial Tribunal.

Held: The Employment Appeals Tribunal reversed the decision of the Industrial Tribunal, finding that there was not segregation contrary to section 1(2) of the Race Relations Act 1976.

Judgment: JUSTICE SLYNN: "34. Had it here been clear that there was this policy of the company, and had the facts been that through the personnel department only Asians had been sent to this particular section of the factory, it seems to us that there would have been evidence upon which the Tribunal could have reached the conclusion which it did in fact reach. But that is not the way that the Tribunal, at the end of the day, put it. They had evidence which they appear to have accepted, in the body of their decision, that when vacancies arose in the paint shop they were filled by persons introduced by those who were already working there or those who were leaving. The Tribunal recite evidence that relatives had been introduced into this shop by those already working there. Indeed, the evidence was that, in a significant number of cases, people had applied for employment even before the company knew that there was either a vacancy or was about to be a vacancy because one of the Asian workers was to leave. The evidence even went further than that. Mr Barron, who was in charge of this shop, gave evidence, which the Tribunal appear to have accepted, that over the past 12 months or more, when a vacancy occurred in the department, someone came to him and asked about the job—on one occasion it was one of the existing personnel who came to ask; sometimes before he knew that a particular man was going to leave. Mr Barron agreed, so the Tribunal recite in their decision, that he had not had from the personnel department any applicants during the past two years, except in one instance when white persons were sent to him but they were persons who were not interested in the job. And so the facts appear to be that here, for a period of something like two years, the personnel department of the company had not had to select or interview persons for employment in this particular area. Those who worked there had produced candidates for appointment to Mr Barron and he had found men who were able and willing to take on the job. It seems to us that the Tribunal accepted that there arose a situation, really by the acts of those working in the paint shop itself, that all the workers were in fact Asian. This had not always been the position. A few years ago there had been a number of white men working there, and there had been some coloured, non-Asian workers there as well. But over a period the position had changed and, by the introduction of cousins and friends, Asians alone worked there.

35. The Tribunal, as we read their decision, really decided the case on the basis that there had been what they called 'indirect' or 'secondary' discrimination because the company had not had a more positive employment policy which would have removed any element of factual segregation, or suspicion of it, arising in the paint shop. This appears to suggest that it was the opinion of the Industrial Tribunal, not so much that the company had by its own acts segregated these men in this particular area away from others, but that it had not prevented the

---

[182] [1980] IRLR 142 EAT.

men themselves from coming together in this way. What appears to be suggested is that the company ought to have taken steps to ensure that for some of these jobs, white or non-Asian or coloured men were put in, and that Asians were not allowed to take on these jobs on the grounds of their colour, in order to prevent this segregation in fact arising. We repeat that had there been here evidence of a policy to segregate, and of the fact of segregation arising as a result of the company's acts, that might well have constituted a breach of the legislation; but it does not seem to us that there was evidence to support that position. We do not consider that the failure of the company to intervene and to insist on white or non-Asian workers going into the shop, contrary to the wishes of the men to introduce their friends, itself constituted the act of segregating persons on racial grounds within the meaning of s.1(2) of the Act."

Notes

(1) The Employment Appeals Tribunal did not inquire *why* Asian workers should choose to orient towards this unpleasant working environment. Were there barriers to their employment in other, more desirable parts of the enterprise?

(2) The UN Committee for the Elimination of Racial Discrimination takes the view that states have positive obligations to counteract racial segregation, even where this arises from the actions of private individuals:

> "The Committee therefore affirms that a condition of racial segregation can also arise without any initiative or direct involvement by the public authorities. It invites States parties to monitor all trends which can give rise to racial segregation, to work for the eradication of any negative consequences that ensure, and to describe any such action in their periodic reports."[183]

If segregation is classified as direct discrimination, then this will significantly restrict the possibility to justify segregationist practices. This is a key issue in cases of educational segregation, where it is often argued that children are allocated to different classes because of different learning abilities.

Nyíregyháza Town Court, 1 December 1998[184]   **2.HU.37.**
Anonymous Plaintiffs v. Local Government of Tiszavasvári Town

ROMA SEGREGATION IN EDUCATION

School Farewell Ceremony

Facts: The case concerned the situation of Roma children in a Hungarian school. The Roma children were around 50% of all pupils. First, the plaintiffs argued that the existence of special classes within the primary school composed only of Roma children breached their inherent personal rights under Hungarian law. These special classes were located in a different building from the main school building and not accessible to the main school canteen. They were designed for "cumulatively disadvantaged" students. In its statement of

---

[183] Para. 4, General Recommendation XIX (47) on Art. 3, adopted at 1125th meeting, 17 August 1995; Annex VII, Report of the Committee on the Elimination of Racial Discrimination, A/50/18, 22 September 1995.

[184] 16. P. 25.191./1997/ISSUE No. 12.

the facts, the Court noted that "both Gypsy and Hungarian pupils may study in classes with normal curriculum, whilst the composition of special classes is quite homogeneous; only Gypsy pupils may study there."

Secondly, the plaintiffs challenged the specific decision to hold a separate "Farewell Ceremony" for Roma children. This event marked the end of the children's primary school education. The school contended that the separate Farewell Ceremony was required because of public health concerns arising from long-standing problems of hair lice amongst Roma pupils. This was also the explanation for why children in special classes had been prohibited from using the school gymnasium.

Held: The children's rights had been breached as regards the Farewell Ceremony and the ban on using the gymnasium, but not in respect of the organisation of the special classes.

Judgment: "According to the views of the Court, the correct interpretation of the provisions of the law referred to above is that any distinction is prohibited, i.e. qualifies as discrimination, if it is unreasonable, cannot be justified in a satisfactory and objective manner, and the methods applied are not in proportion with the purpose. It is a prohibited distinction, i.e. discrimination, if there is no reasonable proportional relationship between the purpose and the measures taken, and if the discrimination is done arbitrarily in the interest of an illegitimate purpose.

Having considered the circumstances and the interests of the parties in the matter, the Court stated that from the list of claims submitted by the plaintiffs, the prohibited discrimination was committed by organising their Farewell Ceremony in a segregated way from the Hungarian pupils, and also by the fact that the plaintiffs were deprived, throughout their primary school education, from using the school's gymnasium.

With regard to the Year's long-standing infestation problem of the Gypsy children claimed also by the defendant, it was unreasonable to deprive the pupils of Class 8/C from attending the traditional school closing and Farewell Ceremony in 1997, contrary to the practice of previous years, by organising a segregated event for them at a different time. The practice of previous years makes this fact and behaviour against the plaintiffs unjustified. The purpose of the segregation, the reference to public health reasons, do not qualify as legitimate just because such problems require health measures, and as the case documents state, there could have been a solution to resolve this issue with appropriate public health measures.

The fact that the plaintiffs were not allowed to use the gymnasium during their entire primary education constitutes to be, with similar reasons, another case of prohibited discrimination. It cannot be reasonably justified that nearly 50% of primary school pupils who are Gypsy children, including the plaintiffs and who are studying under a special education program, are prevented from using a public room of the school, the gymnasium in this case, without any formal decision and any actual public health measures taken. These facts violated the inherent personal rights of the Plaintiffs, who were protected by provisions of Section 76. of the Civil Code (hereinafter: the Ptk.), which need to be rectified even if there is no such person who can be made directly responsible for it. The defendant, as the authority maintaining the school, is obliged to bear the legal consequences of any breach of the law, irrespective whether they are culpable, guilty or irrespective of their intentions . . .

On the basis of data available, the Court has found the plaintiffs' reference to discrimination unfounded in respect of the segregated education in separate buildings, the prevention from the use of the school canteen, and the separate registration and marking of the Gypsy pupils. The defendant has provided reasonable and objectively acceptable reasons regarding the 'distinction' stating that the use of the canteen shop is only unavailable for children learning in the Petőfi Street building, because the length of the school breaks and accessibility of the other building justify that.

In view of the fact, that the plaintiffs had been having their classes in the Kossuth Street building for several years, during which time the canteen shop was available to them, therefore no discrimination can be established in this case. Their separation by classes is reasonably justified from the teaching aspect that follows the particular educational programme of the special classes."

Notes

(1) The judgment is based on a general principle of non-discrimination and there is no attempt to distinguish direct and indirect discrimination within the school's practice. Nonetheless, the reasoning in relation to the separate Farewell Ceremony and the restriction on using the gym approximates to a direct discrimination analysis. Motive is treated as not relevant, a point confirmed on appeal to the Supreme Court. It held that

> "the fact that the defendant and the school wanted to protect the health of the other pupils with this decision is irrelevant when the determination of the discrimination is assessed. It is clear that the school must protect the rights and interests of every pupil, but the school cannot comply with this obligation by regularly discriminating the minority to protect the majority."[185]

(2) Educational reasons are held to justify the separate special classes, although there is little scrutiny of the content of these reasons. A similar issue arose in *D.H. and others* v. *The Czech Republic*, ECtHR, Application 57325/00, 7 February 2006. This was a case of indirect discrimination; the application of educational selection tests led to a very substantial over-representation of Roma children in special classes. The ECtHR adopted a deferential attitude towards tests devised by "experts in educational psychology" (paragraph 49). Notwithstanding the statistical evidence of disproportionate disadvantage and suggestions that the tests were not appropriate for Roma children (paragraph 26), the Court did not find any breach of Article 14. In particular, it argued that there was no "concrete evidence" of "racial prejudice" (paragraph 52). As with *Nachova* v. *Bulgaria* (discussed in section 2.4.1.C), the Court linked a finding of discrimination to evidence of discriminatory motive.

(3) The final two cases to be examined in this section also concern segregation in education and the boundary between direct and indirect discrimination.

---

[185] Legfelsőbb Bíróság, Legf. Bír. Pfv. IV. 22.408/1999. sz.

National Council for Combating Discrimination, 23 June 2003   **2.RO.38.**
*Decision No. 218 on Petition No. 1704/12.05.2003 from the Roma Centre for
Social Intervention and Research (Romani CRISS) in relation to Cehei School*

ROMA SEGREGATION IN EDUCATION

Cehei school

Facts (from the Decision): "De facto the school in Cehei consists of two buildings. The main building houses Grades 1 to 8, and classes have Romanian children exclusively. Starting with the second term of school year 2002/2003, the main building also houses Roma children in Grades 7 and 8. In the extension are housed Roma children in Grades 5 and 6. Allocation to classes is not based on academic results.

Roma children in Grades 5 to 8 come from Pusta Valea, county of Sălaj. According to teaching staff there is a very small number of Roma children from Cehei in the classes made up of Romanian children from Cehei, in Grades 1 to 8—but these children do not admit to being ethnic Roma. Conditions for study are better in the main building than in the extension."

Held: The school's actions were unlawful discrimination.

Decision: "De jure according to Art. 2. paragraph 2 of Government Ordinance No. 137/2000 on the Prevention and Punishment of All Forms of Discrimination passed and amended by Law 48/2002: 'Any active or passive behaviour which due to its effect unjustly favours or does not favour, or subjects to an unjust or degrading treatment, a person, a group of persons or a community, in relation to other persons, groups of persons or communities' constitutes an administrative offence and will be punished as such . . .

The Steering Committee decides:
1. That the facts presented constitute discriminatory acts in accordance with Art. 2, paragraph 2 of Government Ordinance 137/2000 passed and amended by Law 48/2002;
2. That the school in Cehei will be issued with a Warning . . ."

Note

The decision treats the school's practices as indirect discrimination. Yet it also recognises that some classes are composed exclusively of Roma children and that allocation to these classes is not based on academic results. Arguably, this is less favourable treatment on the ground of ethnic origin and more appropriately characterised as direct discrimination.

National Council for Combating Discrimination,   **2.RO.39.**
25 May 2004
Decision No. 160 on Petition No. 1174/11.05.2004

ROMA SEGREGATION IN EDUCATION

Class V-B

Facts: The applicants argued that the existence of school classes composed exclusively of Roma children was unlawful racial discrimination.

Held: There was not sufficient evidence of unlawful racial discrimination.

Decision: "In the village of [anonymous] lives 'a community of Rudari gipsies'. This village only has a primary school. In order to continue their education children have to walk 6 km to the village of [anonymous], which has a comprehensive school, with Grades 1 to 8. Class V-B is segregated from the other classes in the sense that these pupils have their 'classroom' in the nursery school building, in the school hall. This class consists exclusively of ethnic Roma pupils from the village of [anonymous].

In the meeting of 19.05.2004 the Steering Committee decided to conduct an on-site investigation. The investigation team, consisting of Anamaria Dumitrean and Gheorghe Ioniþã (members of the Steering Committee) and Silvia Dumitrache (counsellor in the Law and Inspection Department), put forward the following conclusions:

a) the school has four classrooms used for morning classes by Grades 1 to 4 and afternoon classes by Grades 5 to 8;

b) 160 pupils study at the school: 51 pupils in Grades 1 to 4 and 109 pupils in Grades 5 to 8;

c) classes are housed as follows:
— Grades 1 to 4 in the school building
— Grades 6 to 8 and Class V-A in the school building
— Class V-B in the nursery-school building, in the school hall.

d) the pupils in class V-B live in the village of [anonymous] and belong to ethnic Roma families;

e) in class V-A and the other classes (Grades 6 to 8), which have afternoon classes, there are also ethnic Roma pupils both from the village of [anonymous] and the village of [anonymous];

f) in Grades 5 to 8 there are 50 pupils from the village of [anonymous], out of which 19 are in Class V-B;

g) the investigation team is of the opinion that the segregation of class V-B in a building other than the school building is not of a discriminatory nature as there are Roma ethnic pupils, both from the village of [anonymous] and the village of [anonymous], in the other classes, and punishes Ms Elena Ionescu, the Headmistress of the school investigated, with a fine of ROL 5 millions (as she refused to give information and explanations and to ensure the support and conditions necessary for the investigation of Ms [anonymous]'s petition), pursuant to Art. 20 paragraph 6 of Government Ordinance No. 137/2000 with the subsequent amendments and supplements.

The Steering Committee adopts the investigation team's conclusions."

Notes

(1) This decision does not clearly distinguish whether the alleged discrimination was direct or indirect. Class V-B was composed exclusively of Roma children and it was spatially segregated from the other classes. Contrary to the reasoning of the decision, the presence of some Roma children in other classes does not take away from the less favourable treatment experienced by the children of Class V-B.

(2) In order to determine whether the Roma children of Class V-B were subject to direct or indirect discrimination in relation to their segregation, it would be necessary to know the basis upon which children were allocated to different classes.

The various cases examined above illustrate the difficulty of locating segregation within the typical legal framework on discrimination. Some instruments treat it as a distinct wrong, whereas others attempt to address it under the concepts of direct and indirect discrimination. Given the higher profile of segregation issues in the enlarged European Union, courts are likely to face further difficult choices on how to respond to such cases. The EU's Network of Independent Experts on Fundamental Rights has argued that the situation of Roma communities in Europe warrants a dedicated Directive on Roma integration.[186]

2.6. JUSTIFICATIONS AND EXCEPTIONS

2.6.1. INTRODUCTION

When legislators decide to prohibit discrimination, they are simultaneously faced with the dilemma of whether and when to permit any derogations from this prohibition. In fact, all European states permit departures from the norm of non-discrimination, so the real question is how broad or narrow any exceptions should be. In many European states, the scope of these exceptions is a quality that distinguishes direct from indirect discrimination. A traditional analysis would propose the following dichotomy.[187] On the one hand, direct discrimination is subject to limited exceptions and these are expressly written into statute in order to provide certainty and clarity. On the other, indirect discrimination is open to objective justification. This traditional dichotomy is well reflected in EC legislation on sex and race discrimination. It is also the dominant model found with EU Member States' anti-discrimination legislation. Nevertheless, it is not the only approach, nor one that applies to all branches of anti-discrimination law. Within EC legislation, rather different models can be identified where direct discrimination is also open to objective justification; this is true in respect of age discrimination. Moreover, some national jurisdictions permit the objective justification of direct discrimination on all grounds. This is also generally true for the European Convention on Human Rights (but see further below).

A preliminary question to consider is why direct discrimination should be subject to a restrictive scheme of narrow exceptions in contrast to indirect discrimination.[188] An effects-based analysis would query the rationale for this bifurcation. As already

---

[186] EU Network of Independent Experts on Fundamental Rights "Report on the Situation of Fundamental Rights in the European Union in 2004" (European Commission, 2005) 93, available on the website of Directorate-General for Freedom, Security and Justice.

[187] This has been described as the "orthodox view" in the context of EC law: T. Hervey, "EC Law on Justifications for Sex Discrimination in Working Life" in R. Blanpain (ed.) *Collective Bargaining, Discrimination, Social Security and European Integration* (Alphen a/d Rijn, Kluwer Law International, 2003) 108.

[188] On this debate, see J. Bowers and E. Moran, "Justification in Direct Sex Discrimination Law: Breaking the Taboo" (2002) 31 ILJ 307; T. Gill and K. Monaghan, "Justification in Direct Sex Discrimination Law: Taboo Upheld" (2003) 32 ILJ 115.

discussed in this chapter, the boundary between direct and indirect discrimination can be rather thin on occasions. For example, in *Schnorbus*,[189] more favourable treatment of persons having completed national service was viewed as indirect discrimination even though only men were eligible to perform national service. Instead, the rationale for the distinction lies in the scope of the rules and practices caught by anti-discrimination law. Direct discrimination tackles less favourable treatment specifically because of a suspect characteristic, such as race, sex, etc. The perpetrator is directly using the prohibited ground as the basis for treating a person or a group in a detrimental manner. This may be overt or covert, but in either case the differential treatment is because of the characteristic. The law treats this as taking into account irrelevant considerations and hence it contravenes the basic principle of formal equality that likes should be treated alike.[190] The fact that one candidate for a job is a Muslim and the other is a Christian is viewed as irrelevant; both are in a like situation regardless of their religious beliefs. Law's opposition to formal inequality means that only in narrowly defined circumstances should suspect characteristics be deemed to be relevant considerations that may genuinely differentiate persons and groups.

The inability to justify direct discrimination also serves to advance substantive equality. As discussed in section 2.3.2.B, direct discrimination is often intertwined with stereotyping. These generalisations may or may not be factually accurate, but in either situation they constitute direct discrimination. If justification of direct discrimination is permitted, then courts will be drawn into the thorny task of deciding when stereotypes may be upheld. By excluding the justification of direct discrimination, the law becomes a potent weapon to deconstruct such stereotypes.[191] Even where only limited exceptions are permitted, there is a risk that these perpetuate stereotyping (see below section 2.6.3.E).

This section will make reference to both "exceptions" and "justifications". These categories are sometimes less than clear-cut. Where legislation provides a very loose "exception" to the prohibition of direct discrimination, then there may be little difference in substance from a "justification". The difference between a justification and an exception seems more in the nature of a continuum than a fundamental division. *Justification* can be defined as the open-ended possibility for a perpetrator of direct discrimination to propose a good reason why their actions should not be treated as unlawful. The perpetrator will normally be required to identify the legitimate aim pursued and the necessary nexus between that aim and the measures actually adopted. *Exceptions* are specific circumstances identified in law where acts that would otherwise be unlawful direct discrimination will not be so treated. The perpetrator is not free to propose any legitimate aim for their actions; the law has already identified the conditions within which exceptions can be permitted. Exceptions will normally identify a specific objective that is permissible and courts will have to consider whether the individual case fits within that objective.

---

[189] Case C–79/99 *Schnorbus* v. *Land Hessen* [2000] ECR I–10997.
[190] S. Fredman, *Discrimination Law* (Oxford, Oxford University Press, 2002) 103.
[191] See Gill and Monaghan, above n. 188, 116. See, e.g. *R (European Roma Rights Centre)* v. *Immigration Officer at Prague Airport and another* [2005] 2 AC 1.

In addition, it is relevant to note that legislation may also include *exclusions*. These can be viewed as questions concerning the personal and material scope of the law, rather than exceptions. Nevertheless, specific exclusions within the general field covered by the law can be difficult to distinguish in substance from an exception. An exclusion might take the form of identifying a specific occupational category (such as the military) which is not covered by a law that generally prohibits discrimination in employment.[192] Article 3(2) of the Racial Equality Directive provides another type of exclusion by limiting the scope of the grounds of "racial or ethnic origin". This provision states:

> "This Directive does not cover difference of treatment based on nationality and is without prejudice to provisions and conditions relating to the entry into and residence of third-country nationals and stateless persons on the territory of Member States, and to any treatment which arises from the legal status of the third-country nationals and stateless persons concerned."[193]

Chapter one explores further the difficult distinction between racial or ethnic origin and nationality. Exclusions tend to be absolute in nature; there is no scope for courts to consider whether it is reasonable for the defendant to rely on it in the specific circumstances of the case. Once it is identified that the facts lie within the scope of the exclusion, then the case falls outside the law.

This section will begin by considering, in general terms, whether and when European and national jurisdictions permit justification of direct discrimination. The chapter will then consider the most common exceptions that apply in respect of all or several grounds of discrimination. This part will examine exceptions relating to genuine occupational requirements; respect for human rights and freedoms; public security; health and safety; and provision of financial services. Following this discussion, there is an examination of exceptions provided in respect of individual grounds of discrimination, in particular, sex, religion and age. A frequent issue concerning exceptions to direct discrimination is the scope for positive action schemes. This will be dealt with separately in chapter seven.

2.6.2. JUSTIFICATION OF DIRECT DISCRIMINATION

The approach of individual legal systems to justification and direct discrimination initially depends on whether a distinction between direct and indirect discrimination is recognised in law. As discussed in section 2.2, most European states have now identified a distinct concept of direct discrimination within national legislation, often on the spur of EC Directives. This section starts by considering Council of Europe legal instruments before turning to EC law and national jurisdictions.

---

[192] For example, Art. 3(4) of the Employment Equality Directive states: "Member States may provide that this Directive, in so far as it relates to discrimination on the grounds of disability and age, shall not apply to the armed forces."

[193] A similar provision can be found in Art. 3(2) of the Employment Equality Directive.

2.6.2.A.   COUNCIL OF EUROPE

Neither the European Convention on Human Rights nor the European Social Charter expressly distinguishes direct and indirect discrimination. The general formula of the ECtHR is the following:

> "discrimination means treating differently, without an objective and reasonable justification, persons in relevantly similar situations . . . The Contracting States enjoy a certain margin of appreciation in assessing whether and to what extent differences in otherwise similar situations justify a difference in treatment . . . but the final decision as to observance of the Convention's requirements rests with the Court."[194]

This approach is also endorsed in the 1996 Revised European Social Charter.[195] On the face of it, this permits direct discrimination to be justified. The flexibility found under Article 14 ECHR can be explained by its breadth. The list of discrimination grounds protected is non-exhaustive and it applies throughout the wide material scope of the Convention. In this respect, Article 14 is akin to constitutional equality clauses, which often also permit the justification of direct discrimination.[196] Nevertheless, it is possible to identify developments in the Court's case-law that suggest a more restrictive approach to justifying discrimination.

First, in *Lustig-Prean and Beckett* v. *UK* (1999) 29 EHRR 548, the Court rejects the possibility for justifications which are themselves based on discriminatory reasons. The case concerned the UK's ban on lesbians and gays serving in the armed forces. Part of the government's justification for the policy was the claimed adverse reactions that there would be from other personnel to working alongside lesbians or gay men in often intimate conditions. Such arguments were dispatched by the Court:

> "to the extent they represent a predisposed bias on the part of a heterosexual majority against a homosexual minority, these negative attitudes cannot, of themselves, be considered by the Court to amount to sufficient justification for the interferences with the applicants' rights" (paragraph 90).

This decision can be viewed as restricting the scope for justification,[197] but it certainly does not call into question the very principle of being able to justify direct discrimination. In contrast, *Timishev* v. *Russia*[198] takes a step further. The Court was required to consider whether security considerations could justify direct discrimination on the grounds of ethnic origin where ethnic Chechens were subject to restrictions when moving within Russian territory. The Court rejects the possibility for justification:

---

[194] Para. 44, *D.H. and others* v. *The Czech Republic*, ECtHR, Application 57325/00, 7 February 2006.

[195] The Appendix states "a differential treatment based on an objective and reasonable justification shall not be deemed to be discriminatory".

[196] See, e.g. case-law of the Estonian Supreme Court: V. Poleshchuk, "Report on Measures to Combat Discrimination: Directive 2000/43/EC and 2000/78/EC. Country Report Estonia" (European Commission, 2005) 7, available on the website of Directorate-General for Employment, Social Affairs and Equal Opportunities.

[197] See also para. 41, *Karner* v. *Austria*, ECtHR, Application 40016/98, 24 July 2003.

[198] ECtHR, 13 December 2005, Applications 55762/00 and 55974/00.

"the Court considers that no difference in treatment which is based exclusively or to a decisive extent on a person's ethnic origin is capable of being objectively justified in a contemporary democratic society built on the principles of pluralism and respect for different cultures."[199]

This is a recent decision of a chamber of the Court, so it would be rash to assume a new principle that direct discrimination, at least on grounds of ethnicity, cannot be justified. Yet it may signal that the Court's gradual recognition of the separate concepts of direct and indirect discrimination will also lead to a reconsideration of the flexibility for justifying direct discrimination. Cases such as the above also reveal the relevance of the *ground* of discrimination to setting the threshold for justifying direct discrimination under the European Convention on Human Rights. Certain grounds, such as sex, sexual orientation or ethnicity, have been treated as highly suspect and hence the Court requires "very weighty reasons" before justification is permitted. The role that the "suspectness" of the ground plays in justification is explored in depth in chapter one.

2.6.2.B.   EUROPEAN UNION

EC anti-discrimination Directives, like most national legislation, do not expressly declare that direct discrimination cannot be justified. Rather, this is implicit from the absence of any textual reference to justification (unlike indirect discrimination, where objective justification is specifically mentioned). Judicial practice has largely conformed to the notion that justifications cannot be advanced in respect of direct discrimination. For example, once the ECJ determined that the dismissal of a woman because of pregnancy was direct discrimination, it rejected the employer's argument that this could be justified because of the financial costs to the firm.[200]

Nonetheless, there are situations where EC legislation does permit the justification of direct discrimination. The first is the treatment of age discrimination within the Employment Equality Directive. Direct discrimination on grounds of age is prohibited in the same terms as the other grounds found within the Directive,[201] but this is subject to the possibility of justifying direct and indirect age discrimination in Article 6(1):

"Member States may provide that differences of treatment on grounds of age shall not constitute discrimination, if, within the context of national law, they are objectively and reasonably justified by a legitimate aim, including legitimate employment policy, labour market and vocational training objectives, and if the means of achieving that aim are appropriate and necessary."

---

[199] Para. 58.
[200] Case C–177/88 *Dekker* v. *VJV Centrum* [1990] ECR I–3941. See also Case C–109/00 *Tele Danmark A/S* v. *Handels-og Kontorfunktionaerernes Forbund I Danmark (HK)* [2001] ECR I–6993 at 7025.
[201] Art. 2(2)(a).

There are various reasons why this cannot be classified as an "exception", as defined in section 2.6.1. First, this provision applies to both direct and indirect discrimination. Secondly, it adopts very similar language to the justification test also present in the definition of indirect discrimination (Article 2(2)(b)). Finally, it is open-ended in nature, providing substantial discretion for court interpretation. The approach of the ECJ and national courts to age-based justifications for direct discrimination will be examined further in section 2.6.4.C.

A greater willingness to accept justifications for direct discrimination can also be detected in the Gender Goods and Services Directive. There are two provisions within this Directive that are broader than traditional exceptions whilst not amounting to open-ended justifications. First, Article 4(5):

> "This Directive shall not preclude differences in treatment, if the provision of the goods and services exclusively or primarily to members of one sex is justified by a legitimate aim and the means of achieving that aim are appropriate and necessary."[202]

This provision circumscribes its aim, which is to permit sex-specific provision of goods and services, but it provides an open-ended justification test in relation to the application of that aim. Secondly, Article 5(2) provides an exception for the use of sex as an actuarial factor in insurance and financial services. This issue is considered further in section 2.6.3.E.

2.6.2.C.   NATIONAL JURISDICTIONS

In many EU Member States, legislation follows the pattern found in the Directives. Although the exact content of exceptions varies, the general principle that direct discrimination is not open to justification is respected. This is broadly the case in the UK,[203] the Netherlands,[204] France[205] and the German Non-Discrimination Act 2006. Although there is no definition of direct discrimination provided in French legislation, the prohibition of discrimination is accompanied by some specific statutory exceptions.

Several states have departed from the Directives' framework and national legislation expressly permits the justification of direct discrimination. In Hungary, Article 7(2) of the Equal Treatment Act 2003 provides:

> "an action, conduct, omission, requirement, order or practice (hereinafter: action) based on a characteristic listed in Article 8 shall not be taken to violate the requirement of equal treatment if it is found by objective consideration to have a reasonable ground directly related to the relevant legal relation."[206]

---

[202] Recitals 16 and 17 added further clarification on the intended application of this provision.
[203] Fredman, above n. 190, 103, argues that UK (and EC) law on equal pay permits justification of direct discrimination.
[204] See Gijzen, above n. 52, 17.
[205] See Latraverse, above n. 46, 13.
[206] See Kádár and Farkas, above n. 167, 9–10.

The Polish Labour Code also permits justification of direct discrimination for objective reasons.[207] In both Hungary and Poland, the possibility for justifying direct discrimination can be linked to the long list of prohibited grounds of discrimination. These go beyond the grounds found in the Directives and, in the case of Hungary, go beyond the material scope of the Directives. These states have balanced a broad scope for anti-discrimination law by maintaining flexibility for the courts in considering possible justifications. This does not seem compatible, however, with the requirements of the EC Directives.

This dilemma is also found within the Belgian Federal Law of 25 February 2003. It covers a wide range of discrimination grounds, and direct discrimination is defined as a "difference in treatment lacking objective and reasonable justification".[208] Article 2(5) seeks to limit the scope for justification of direct discrimination in employment in order to comply with the EC Directives. No corresponding limitation exists in respect of justifications for direct racial discrimination outside employment, which conflicts with the requirements of the Racial Equality Directive.[209] By contrast, the Belgian Federal Law of 7 May 1999 on equal treatment of men and women is a rare example of legislation expressly excluding the justification of direct discrimination.[210]

2.6.3.   EXCEPTIONS APPLYING TO SEVERAL DISCRIMINATION GROUNDS

Whilst recognising differences in approach, the predominant framework is to combine the prohibition of direct discrimination with specified exceptions. These take a wide variety of forms across the European Union and it is not possible to provide a comprehensive inventory of all exceptions in respect of all grounds. There are, though, certain exceptions that are frequently present in national legislation, often inspired by EC law. In surveying these exceptions, it is sensible to begin with those that apply across a range of discrimination grounds before proceeding to examine those limited to individual grounds.

2.6.3.A.   GENUINE OCCUPATIONAL REQUIREMENTS

The principle of formal equality underpinning the prohibition of direct discrimination treats characteristics such as sex and race as irrelevant to a person's ability to

---

[207] Art. 18(3b)(1), Labour Code. See further, P. Filipek and M. Pamula, "Report on Measures to Combat Discrimination: Directive 2000/43/EC and 2000/78/EC. Country Report Poland" (European Commission, 2005), available on the website of Directorate-General for Employment, Social Affairs and Equal Opportunities.

[208] Art. 2(2).

[209] See de Schutter, above n. 166, 21.

[210] Art. 4 states "direct discrimination can under no circumstances be justified".

perform a job; therefore these characteristics should not be taken into account in decision-making. Nonetheless, there are narrow circumstances where the suspect characteristic can be relevant. Most European states have sought to make provision for this by including a legislative exception for "genuine occupational requirements" (GOR).

Strictly speaking, most of the situations arising under the GOR exception are not instances where a person with different characteristics would be *unable* to perform the job. Instead, their ability to perform the job *effectively* would be substantially reduced in comparison to another. For example, in making a film of the life of Martin Luther King, it would be a GOR to require the lead actor to share a similar ethnic origin to the role he was playing. Clearly, a white actor could play the role, but given the centrality of Martin Luther King's ethnicity to his life story, a white actor might seem unconvincing and inappropriate to audiences. Whilst this example is relatively clear-cut, it is difficult to find the objective limits to the GOR concept. Female actresses sometimes play male roles within theatre. Crossing established gender or ethnic boundaries can be a vital way of challenging preconceived stereotypes.[211] At its core, the GOR exception often rests on rather vague notions of perceived suitability, which may change over time.

Two principal approaches to the GOR exception can be identified. The first approach is to identify specific occupations where the suspect characteristic may be lawfully treated as relevant. This was the philosophy underpinning the 1976 Gender Employment Directive. Article 2(2) stated:

> "This Directive shall be without prejudice to the right of Member States to exclude from its field of application those occupational activities and, where appropriate, the training leading thereto, for which, by reason of their nature or the context in which they are carried out, the sex of the worker constitutes a determining factor."

Some states have left a margin of discretion to national courts in interpreting the application of this principle. In Germany, paragraph 611a BGB permits exceptions where sex is an "indispensable element and condition" for the post in question. Other states have chosen to identify through legislation a list of occupations where sex can be a GOR. In the Netherlands, a rather complex system of statutory GORs exists. Under the General Equal Treatment Act of 1994, an exception is provided for cases "in which sex is a determining factor" (Article 2(2)(a)). This is elaborated through a Decree on Equal Treatment of 18 August 1994 (Law Gazette 657). The Decree identifies various circumstances where direct distinctions between women and men can be justified, for example, in beauty contests or sports activities. In relation to employment, the 1980 Act of Equal Treatment between Men and Women provides specific rules which take priority in relation to any overlap with the 1994 General Equal Treatment Act.[212] Pursuant to the 1980 Act, a Decree was issued on activities for which sex is a genuine occupational requirement.

---

[211] Skinner notes that "non-traditional casting" policies are frequently found in North American theatres: O. Skinner, "The Role of Race" [2006] *Catalyst* March, 21.

[212] Art. 4a, General Equal Treatment Act.

Dutch Decree of 19 May 1989 concerning the establishment of   **2.NL.40.**
*a governmental decree regarding occupational activities for which sex
can be determinant*[213]

Article 1
Only activities that belong to training for one or more of the following categories are regarded as occupational activities, and as training to be provided for them where sex is decisive, where applicable, on account of their nature or the conditions for undertaking them:

a. occupational activities that for physical reasons can exclusively be undertaken by persons of a particular sex;
b. occupational activities of a male or female model who must demonstrate certain garments by wearing them;
c. the occupational activities of models for fine artists, photographers, film-makers, hairdressers, and make-up and beauty specialists;
d. occupational activities within private households that imply personal service, care, nursing or raising or providing help to one or more persons;
e. occupational activities that imply personal care, nursing or raising or giving help to persons where the proper discharge of the position concerned within the work organisation as a whole requires it to be undertaken by a person of a particular sex;
f. occupational activities that imply the handling or treatment of persons, where the proper discharge of the position offered within the work organisation as a whole requires it to be undertaken by a person of a particular sex on account of serious feelings of modesty amongst such persons;
g. occupational activities whose pursuit or discharge by persons of a particular sex is effectively hampered by legal provisions concerning the protection of persons of that sex during working;
h. occupational activities pursued abroad, if under the laws locally applying such occupational activities are reserved to persons of a particular sex;
i. occupational activities with the Marine Corps and the Submarine Service.

Notes
(1) A similar approach can be found in various European legal systems, including Flanders[214] and Bulgaria.[215] In France, Article L. 123-1 of the Labour Code provides for a Decree to be issued determining the list of jobs and professional activities where sex is a determining condition. In accordance with this provision, Decree 84-395 of 25 May 1984 (JO of 27 May 1984) identified the following occupational activities where sex is a determining condition: performers required to play a male or female role; male and female models, including for the display of clothes (Article 1).

[213] Staatsblad, 1989, 207.
[214] See de Schutter, above n. 166, 40.
[215] See Ordinance No. 4 of 30 March 2004 on the types of occupation or activity for which, by their nature or the conditions under which they are conducted, sex is a genuine and determining occupational requirement within the meaning of Art. 7, para. 1, point 2 of the Anti-Discrimination Law; Official Gazette No. 40 of 14 May 2004.

(2) In Britain, a GOR exception was included within the text of the Sex Discrimination Act 1975. This identifies various circumstances where sex can be a GOR, such as reasons of authenticity in dramatic performances.[216]

The difficulty with the list approach lies in the institutionalisation of categories of activity where the suspect characteristic can be treated as relevant. Unless the categories are carefully tailored and regularly reviewed, they risk reinforcing stereotypes that the law is meant to counter. For example, the British Race Relations Act 1976 includes the following GOR exception in relation to discrimination on the grounds of colour or nationality:

> "the job involves working in a place where food or drink is (for payment or not) provided to and consumed by members of the public or a section of the public in a particular setting for which, in that job, a person of that racial group is required for reasons of authenticity . . ."[217]

This exception illustrates the weak link that there may be between a GOR exception and the ability of a person to perform the job. The ultimate test for the authenticity of any restaurant lies in the quality of its food, rather than the ethnic characteristics of the person preparing or serving that food. Nevertheless, this exception gives licence to discrimination in order to convey a certain image within the restaurant. Commercially, this may be a well-founded strategy, but it is difficult to reconcile with the underlying goal of eliminating discrimination and stereotyping.

The 2000 anti-discrimination Directives moved away from the occupational list approach and instead proposed a flexible test, based on a case-by-case assessment. Article 4 of the Racial Equality Directive provides:

> ". . . Member States may provide that a difference of treatment which is based on a characteristic related to racial or ethnic origin shall not constitute discrimination where, by reason of the nature of the particular occupational activities concerned or of the context in which they are carried out, such a characteristic constitutes a genuine and determining occupational requirement, provided that the objective is legitimate and the requirement is proportionate."

A similar provision can be found in the Employment Equality Directive (Article 4(1)), albeit supplemented with a specific GOR in relation to religious ethos organisations. This will be examined in section 2.6.4.B. The Gender Employment Directive was amended in 2002 in order to replace the original GOR exception with a text similar to that found in the Racial Equality Directive (new Article 2(6)[218]). On the one hand, this leaves a consistent legislative approach to GORs across the various EC Directives. On the other, the practical application of the GOR test in respect of different grounds of discrimination tends to diverge. In relation to sex and race, the visibility of these characteristics explains some instances where the GOR exception is typically applied, such as acting or modelling. In contrast, characteristics such as

---

[216] Section 7.
[217] Section 5(2)(c).
[218] This is now found in Art. 14(2) of the Recast Gender Employment Directive.

religion or sexual orientation are comparatively less visible, although they may be conveyed by a person's clothing and appearance. The use of sexual orientation as a GOR is particularly contentious. This may be permissible in limited circumstances under some national legislation. For example, the *travaux préparatoires* of the Swedish Sexual Orientation Discrimination Act indicate that sexual orientation could be a GOR for "a vital position" within an organisation working on lesbian or gay rights.[219] A difficulty arises, however, where an employer is permitted to require an employee to be lesbian, gay, bisexual or heterosexual. This presupposes some mechanism through which the employee's sexual orientation can be verified, which risks clashing with the right to respect for private life under Article 8 ECHR.[220] In *Lustig-Prean and Beckett* v. *UK* (1999) 29 EHRR 548 the UK's ban on lesbians and gays within the armed forces violated Article 8 in part because of the intrusive investigations by the military in order to establish whether individuals were lesbian or gay.

The response of the Member States to the use of GORs across a wider range of discrimination grounds has varied.

Many states have chosen to apply a single GOR test to all grounds found within the 2000 Directives.[221] For example, § 8 paragraph 1 of the German Non-discrimination Act 2006 states:

> "Distinction based on any of the grounds mentioned in § 1 is admissible if this reason represents a major and decisive occupational requirement due to the type of activity to be exercised or the conditions in which it is exercised, insofar as the purpose is legal and the requirement is reasonable."

In contrast, France has chosen not to include any GOR exception beyond the pre-existing provisions in relation to sex. The situation in the UK shows how the Directives' standard test can intermingle with specific national approaches. In one respect, the UK has been rather faithful to the Directives' requirements. A specific GOR exception in similar language to that found within the Directives has been included in the Race Relations Act (section 4A); the Employment Equality (Religion or Belief) Regulations (Regulation 7(2)); the Employment Equality (Sexual Orientation) Regulations (Regulation 7(2)) and the Employment Equality (Age) Regulations (Regulation 8). There are, though, peculiarities in relation to individual grounds of discrimination. First, the Race Relations Act retains specific occupational GORs for discrimination on grounds of nationality and colour, such as the "authentic restaurant" GOR discussed above.[222] Secondly, there is no GOR exception in the Disability Discrimination Act 1995. This reflects the asymmetrical structure of the Act; discrimination against disabled persons is unlawful, but there is no

---

[219] See further, H. Ytterberg, "Sweden" in K. Waaldijk and M. Bonini-Baraldi, *Combating Sexual Orientation Discrimination in Employment: Legislation in Fifteen EU Member States* (Leiden, Universiteit Leiden, 2004) 465.

[220] For a discussion, see paras. 80–82, *R (Amicus-MSF and others)* v. *Secretary of State for Trade and Industry and Christian Action Research Education and others* [2004] IRLR 430.

[221] See Cormack and Bell, above n. 39, 48.

[222] On the complex differentiation within the Race Relations Act between nationality and colour discrimination and discrimination on grounds of race, ethnic and national origins, see M. Bell, "A Patchwork of Protection: the New Anti-discrimination Law Framework" (2004) 67 *MLR* 465, 467.

corresponding protection for those who are not disabled.[223] It will not be unlawful discrimination to provide preferential treatment for disabled persons. Thirdly, the general GOR for sexual orientation is supplemented by a provision specifying the circumstances where organised religions can make a requirement concerning the sexual orientation of their employees. Regulation 7(3) of the Employment Equality (Sexual Orientation) Regulations states:

"This paragraph applies where—

(a) the employment is for the purposes of an organised religion;
(b) the employer applies a requirement related to sexual orientation –
  (i)   so as to comply with the doctrines of the religion, or
  (ii) because of the nature of the employment and the context in which it is carried out, so as to avoid conflicting with the strongly held religious convictions of a significant number of the religion's followers; and
(c) either—
  (i)   the person to whom that requirement is applied does not meet it, or
  (ii) the employer is not satisfied, and in all the circumstances it is reasonable for him not to be satisfied, that that person meets it."

This exception was controversial. It adopts broad language, the meaning of which is far from clear (e.g. "a significant number of the religion's followers"). Moreover, it is not designed to provide a religious ethos exception; this exists elsewhere in British legislation.[224] In effect, it was an attempt to provide a detailed legislative interpretation of one instance where a sexual orientation GOR would be permitted under Article 4(1) of the Employment Equality Directive. This was challenged in a judicial review action.

High Court, 26 April 2004[225]   **2.GB.41.**
R (Amicus-MSF and others) v. Secretary of State for Trade and Industry and Christian Action Research Education and others

SEXUAL ORIENTATION REQUIREMENTS AND ORGANISED RELIGIONS

Amicus

Facts: A group of trade unions sought a judicial review of, inter alia, Regulation 7(3) of the Employment Equality (Sexual Orientation) Regulations 2003 on various grounds, including the argument that this provision went beyond the permitted scope of Article 4(1) of the Employment Equality Directive.

Held: The High Court rejected the unions' arguments, but on the basis that Regulation 7(3) had to be interpreted narrowly.

Judgment: MR JUSTICE RICHARDS: "I think it clear from the Parliamentary material that the exception was intended to be very narrow; and in my view it is, on its proper construction, very

---

[223] Section 3A.
[224] Employment Equality (Religion or Belief) Regulations 2003, Reg. 7(3).
[225] [2004] IRLR 430.

narrow. It has to be construed strictly since it is a derogation from the principle of equal treatment; and it has to be construed purposively so as to ensure, so far as possible, compatibility with the Directive. When its terms are considered in the light of those interpretative principles, they can be seen to afford an exception only in very limited circumstances.

116. The fact that the exception applies, by Regulation 7(3)(a), only to employment 'for purposes of an organised religion' is an important initial limitation. I accept Miss Carss-Frisk's submission that that is a narrower expression than 'for purposes of a religious organisation', or the expression 'where an employer has an ethos based on religion or belief', as used in the corresponding regulations relating to discrimination on grounds of religion or belief. I also accept the example she gave, that employment as a teacher in a faith school is likely to be 'for purposes of a religious organisation' but not 'for purposes of an organised religion'.

117. The conditions in Regulation 7(3)(b) impose very real additional limitations. In my view the condition in Regulation 7(3)(b)(i), that the employer must apply the requirement 'so as to comply with the doctrines of the religion', is to be read not as a subjective test concerning the motivation of the employer, but as an objective test whereby it must be shown that employment of a person not meeting the requirement would be incompatible with the doctrines of the religion. That is very narrow in scope. Admittedly the alternative in Regulation 7(3)(b)(ii) is wider; but even that is hemmed about by restrictive language. The condition must be applied 'because of the nature of the employment and the context in which it is carried out' — which requires careful examination of the precise nature of the employment —'so as to avoid conflicting with the strongly held religious convictions of a significant number of the religion's followers'. Again this is in my view an objective, not subjective, test. Further, the conflict to be avoided is with religious convictions, which must be strongly held; and they must be the convictions of a significant number of the religion's followers. This is going to be a very far from easy test to satisfy in practice.

118. The fact that reference is made to 'a significant number' rather than to all or the majority of a religion's followers not only reflects the desirability of avoiding detailed statistical analysis, to which Lord Sainsbury referred in the Parliamentary debate, but also ensures that proper account is taken of the existence of differing bodies of opinion even within an organised religion. Sexual orientation is a matter on which some followers of a religion may hold stronger religious convictions than others. In my view it is legitimate to allow for the possibility of applying a relevant requirement even if the convictions in question are held only by a significant minority of followers."

British anti-discrimination legislation reveals the difficulties that arise from a "one size fits all" approach to GORs. The legislator has tried to go beyond a general test for all grounds, but the result is rather disparate provisions that vary considerably. A similar model can be found in the Netherlands.

> M. Gijzen, "Report on measures to combat discrimination: **2.NL.42.**
> Directive 2000/43/EC and 2000/78/EC. Country report Netherlands"[226]

"*Race and ethnic origin*
The exception in Article 4 of Directive 2000/43 is mirrored in new subsection '*b*' of Article 2(4) of the General Equal Treatment Act [footnote omitted]. Article 2(4) 'b' reads as follows:

[226] (European Commission, 2005) 39–40, available on the website of Directorate-General for Employment, Social Affairs and Equal Opportunities.

*'The prohibition of making distinctions on the grounds of race as it is contained in this Act,
shall not apply:*

a.   . . .

b.   *if the distinction concerns a person's [outer] racial appearance and constitutes, by reason
of the nature of the particular occupational activity concerned, or of the context in which
it is carried out, a genuine and determining occupational requirement, provided that the
objective is legitimate and the requirement is proportionate to that objective.'*

In contrast to Article 4 of Directive 2000/43 that speaks of a *characteristic related to racial or
ethnic origin*, the Dutch provision specifies that only *[outer] racial appearances may constitute
a genuine occupational requirement.*[227] This means that *race in se* is not regarded as a permissible ground for a given distinction.[228] Only *physical differences* (skin colour, hair type etc.) may
form a basis for a distinction, to the exclusion of *sociological differences* . . .

Article 2(4) subsection *'a'* enshrines an equivalent subsection to subsection 'b', however
outside the employment sphere. Directive 2000/43 does not enshrine an equivalent exception
out with the sphere of employment. The subsection a exception, already exists since 1994. The
EC Implementation Act has added a 'proportionality requirement'. It reads as follows:

*'The prohibition of making distinction on the grounds of race as it is contained in this Act,
shall not apply:*

a.   *in cases where a person's racial appearance is a determining factor, provided that the aim
is legitimate and the requirement is proportionate to that aim'* . . .

The exceptions under *a* and *b* have been elaborated in a governmental decree of 1994.[229] The
Decree exhaustively indicates to which categories the Article 2(4) exceptions apply. These are:

a.   *The profession or activity of actor, dancer or artist insofar that the profession or activity
regards the performance of a certain role (elaboration of subsection 'b');*
b.   *Mannequins, models for photographers, artists etc., insofar as in reasonableness requirements can be imposed upon outer appearances (elaboration of subsection 'b');*
c.   *Participation in beauty contests insofar as appearances connected with a person's race,
are vital in the light of the contest's aims (elaboration of subsection 'a');*
d.   *The provision of services that can only be provided to persons having certain outer
appearances (elaboration of subsection 'a'). (The examples given by the government are
special hair dress services for people with 'afro-hair' or skin treatment for persons with a
particular skin type.)*

Religion, belief, sexual orientation
Although Directive 2000/78 would have allowed for it (Article 4(1) of the Directive) no genuine
occupational requirements exception has been enshrined in the General Equal Treatment Act
for these grounds. In fact, the Act only allows for such a defence with regard to the grounds
race and sex. However, in the context of the exceptions of Article 5(2) of the GETA,

---

[227] Explanatory Memorandum to the EC Implementation Act, Second Chamber of Parliament
2002–2003, 28 770, no. 3, at 10.
[228] J.H. Gerards and A.W. Heringa, *Wetgeving Gelijke Behandeling* (Deventer: Kluwer, 2003) 129.
[229] Besluit Gelijke Behandeling van 18 Augustus 1994, Stb 657 (Governmental Decree on Equal
Treatment of 18 August 1994, Law Gazette 657).

institutions founded on religious principles, or on political principles, or schools founded on the basis of religious denomination may impose requirements on the occupancy of a post which, in view of the organisation's purpose, are necessary to live up to its founding principles. The Article 5(2) exceptions are not so much rationalised by the idea of 'genuine occupational requirements' though. *They were regarded necessary in order to reconcile the constitutional principle of equality with other constitutional principles, namely the freedom of religion and the freedom of education as well as the freedom of political opinion.*

Disability

Genuine and occupational requirements have not been defined under the Disability Discrimination Act. The government's view is that, in contrast to race and sex, no scenario is imaginable in which 'disability' would constitute a genuine occupational requirement.[230] An amendment was submitted by a Member of Parliament in this respect, however, without any effect.[231]

Age

Since Age Discrimination Act makes no distinction as between 'direct' and 'indirect' distinction, and since 'objective justification' is provided for both types of 'distinction' (Article 7(1) 'c' of the Act), the government considered a separately enshrined exception regarding 'genuine occupational requirements', a redundant exercise. In this view, in cases in which 'age' is considered a genuine occupational requirement, this can be assessed via the objective justification test."[232]

The case-by-case assessment of GORs now required under the anti-discrimination Directives emphasizes the central role for courts in elaborating how this exception should be applied. The ECJ has considered the GOR exception on several occasions in the context of the Gender Employment Directive.[233] It has stressed the need for this exception to be given a narrow interpretation.

ECJ, 15 May 1986[234]   **2.EC.43.**

Case 222/84, Johnston v. Chief Constable of the Royal Ulster Constabulary (RUC)

GOR EXCEPTION AND SEX DISCRIMINATION IN POLICING

Johnston

Facts: Male police officers in Northern Ireland carried firearms, whilst female police officers did not. In 1980, the Chief Constable decided that general police duties, which frequently required the carrying of firearms, would no longer be assigned to women. As a consequence of this policy, Mrs Johnson's three-year

---

[230] Equal treatment on the ground of disability and chronic disease, Explanatory Memorandum, Second Chamber of Parliament, 2001–2002, 28 169, no. 3 at 35.

[231] Amendment Terpstra, Second Chamber of Parliament, 2001–2002, 28 169, no. 11 of 26–06–02). This amendment was rejected.

[232] Explanatory Memorandum to the Act on Equal Treatment on the Ground of Age in Employment, Occupation and Vocational Training, Second Chamber of Parliament, 2001–2002, 28 170, no. 3 at 35.

[233] See Ellis, above n. 19, 272–82.

[234] [1986] ECR 1651.

contract as a full-time member of the RUC Reserve was not renewed upon completion. She challenged the non-renewal of her contract and the refusal to give her training in handling firearms as unlawful sex discrimination. The Industrial Tribunal referred several questions to the ECJ, including the appropriate interpretation to be given to Article 2(2) of the 1976 Gender Employment Directive.

Held: Public safety considerations may be taken into consideration when relying on the Article 2(2) exception.

Judgment: "35. As is clear from the Industrial Tribunal's decision, the policy towards women in the RUC full time reserve was adopted by the Chief Constable because he considered that if women were armed they might become a more frequent target for assassination and their fire-arms could fall into the hands of their assailants, that the public would not welcome the carrying of fire-arms by women, which would conflict too much with the ideal of an unarmed police force, and that armed policewomen would be less effective in police work in the social field with families and children in which the services of policewomen are particularly appreciated. The reasons which the Chief Constable thus gave for his policy were related to the special conditions in which the police must work in the situation existing in Northern Ireland, having regard to the requirements of the protection of public safety in a context of serious internal disturbances.

36. As regards the question whether such reasons may be covered by Article 2(2) of the Directive, it should first be observed that that provision, being a derogation from an individual right laid down in the Directive, must be interpreted strictly. However, it must be recognized that the context in which the occupational activity of members of an armed police force are carried out is determined by the environment in which that activity is carried out. In this regard, the possibility cannot be excluded that in a situation characterized by serious internal disturbances the carrying of fire-arms by policewomen might create additional risks of their being assassinated and might therefore be contrary to the requirements of public safety.

37. In such circumstances, the context of certain policing activities may be such that the sex of police officers constitutes a determining factor for carrying them out. If that is so, a Member State may therefore restrict such tasks, and the training leading thereto, to men. In such a case, as is clear from Article 9(2) of the Directive, the Member States have a duty to assess periodically the activities concerned in order to decide whether, in the light of social developments, the derogation from the general scheme of the Directive may still be maintained.

38. It must also be borne in mind that, in determining the scope of any derogation from an individual right such as the equal treatment of men and women provided for by the Directive, the principle of proportionality, one of the general principles of law underlying the Community legal order, must be observed. That principle requires that derogations remain within the limits of what is appropriate and necessary for achieving the aim in view and requires the principle of equal treatment to be reconciled as far as possible with the requirements of public safety which constitute the decisive factor as regards the context of the activity in question."

Notes

(1) The Court's emphasis on the principle of proportionality within the assessment of GOR exceptions was applied in Case C–285/98 *Kreil* v. *Germany* [2000] ECR I–69. This concerned a challenge to a German restriction on women serving in any military position involving the use of arms. This had the effect of excluding women from most parts of the armed forces, except those in the medical and military-music services. The Court held that the breadth of this restriction took it beyond the scope of a

legitimate GOR exception (paragraph 27). As regards restrictions on the use of arms by women, it noted that those women who were admitted to the medical and music sections were provided with training in the use of arms, so this was not a sufficient basis for a blanket exclusion from all other parts of the armed forces (paragraph 27).

(2) Alongside proportionality, the Court has stressed the need for any GOR exceptions to be transparent in nature. In Case 318/86 *Commission* v. *France* [1998] ECR 3559, the Court had to consider a series of French rules mandating separate recruitment of men and women to specific occupations, such as prison wardens and the police. In relation to police recruitment, the French government argued that the effectiveness of public order control demanded a minimum proportion of male officers (paragraph 21). The Court held that the GOR exception could only apply in respect of the specific activities where sex was a determining factor; this did not apply to all police functions. The lack of transparency in the French rules meant that there was an insufficient basis for separate recruitment of men and women.

(3) Case C–273/97 *Sirdar* v. *The Army Board and Secretary of State for Defence* [1999] ECR I–7403 provides an example of a situation where the Court viewed the exception as sufficiently narrow for it to be permissible. The complainant was refused a position as a chef in the Royal Marines because women were excluded from this regiment (paragraph 9). The government argued that this was necessary because all personnel in the Royal Marines had to be able to fight in a commando unit in a crisis situation (the principle of interoperability). The Court noted that the Royal Marines were a "small force and are intended to be the first line of attack" (paragraph 30). In this specific context, the requirement for interoperability justified the men-only rule. The judgment does not probe very deeply into the justification for assuming that women could not be an effective part of the commando unit during its fighting function. Hervey suggests that the decision is better explained by reference to privacy considerations given the difficult conditions under which a small fighting force could be required to operate.[235]

It is significant that most of the ECJ case-law around GORs raises issues of public security. As discussed in section 2.6.3.C, the Court's reluctance to entertain general security-based exceptions to the principle of equal treatment has required such cases to be argued as GOR exceptions. Such cases tend to conflict with the pursuit of substantive equality for women. In particular, there is a risk of reinforcing stereotypes concerning women's "weakness" or "vulnerability". This is not, though, the only direction in which the GOR exception can operate. Another utilisation of GORs is akin to positive action and more consistent with substantive equality goals. This vision of the GOR exception is partially contained in the British Race Relations Act 1976. Section 5(2)(d) provides a GOR exception for situations where:

---

[235] See Hervey, above n. 187, 113.

"the holder of the job provides persons of that racial group with personal services promoting their welfare, and those services can most effectively be provided by a person of that racial group".

The following case set limits on how far this exception could be stretched.

Court of Appeal, 4 April 1990[236]   **2.GB.44.**
Lambeth London Borough Council v. *Commission for Racial Equality (CRE)*

ETHNICITY REQUIREMENTS AND GOR EXCEPTIONS

Lambeth v. CRE

Facts: Over half of all tenants in the Council district were Afro-Caribbean or Asian. The Council was concerned that not all tenants were aware of their full social security entitlements in relation to housing benefit. In order to make the Council's housing service more sensitive to the needs of minority ethnic communities, it reserved certain posts to minorities. In line with this initiative, it advertised two posts in the housing benefits department which were only available to Afro-Caribbean and Asian persons. These posts did not, however, involve substantial contact with the public. In response to a legal challenge from the CRE, the Council tried to rely on the section 5(2)(d) exception.

Held: The Court of Appeal held that jobs in question did not fall within the limits of the GOR exception.

Judgment: BALCOMBE LJ: "The services provided by the local authority's housing benefits department undoubtedly promote the welfare of the recipients of those benefits, but the rest of the phrase is qualified by the word 'personal'. 'Personal' is defined by the Oxford English Dictionary as

'Of, pertaining to, concerning or affecting the individual or self (as opposed, variously, to other persons, the general community, etc. . . . .); individual; private; one's own.'

The use of the word 'personal' indicates that the identity of the giver and the recipient of the services is important. I agree with the appeal tribunal [1989] I.C.R. 641, 647, when they say that the Act appears to contemplate direct contact between the giver and the recipient—mainly face-to-face or where there could be susceptibility in personal, physical contact. Where language or a knowledge and understanding of cultural and religious background are of importance, then those services may be most effectively provided by a person of a particular racial group . . .

However, I also agree with the appeal tribunal that the decision in any particular case whether the holder of a particular job provides persons of a particular group with personal services promoting their welfare is a question of mixed law and fact, and that unless the industrial tribunal have come to a decision which is wrong in law, neither the appeal tribunal nor this court can interfere. The industrial tribunal held that the holders of the jobs advertised, being managerial positions, did not provide personal services promoting the welfare of persons of a particular racial group. I can find no error of law in that decision. On this ground alone I would dismiss this appeal."[237]

---

[236] [1990] ICR 768.
[237] At 774–5.

Notes

(1) The difficulty of defining the limits to a welfare-provision exception such as that in section 5(2)(d) were also explored in *Tottenham Green Under Five's Centre* v. *Marshall* [1989] ICR 214. This concerned a nursery that advertised for an "Afro-Caribbean worker". The nursery sought to maintain an ethnic balance between its staff and the children. It wanted a staff member who could speak in Caribbean dialect and who would know how to care for African-Caribbean hair and health. This raised questions about how effectively these functions could be performed by a person of different ethnic origin and whether these were essential or merely desirable qualities. The Employment Appeal Tribunal indicated a willingness to defer to the employer where it was a "genuinely held and reasonably based opinion that a genuine occupational requirement will best promote the welfare of the recipient".[238]

(2) An issue comparable to the welfare-provision exception is whether posts as equal opportunities officers can be reserved for women or minority groups. This issue arose in the following case concerning the post of equal opportunities representative for Land of North Rhine-Westphalia.

Federal Labour Court (BAG), 12 November 1998[239]   **2.DE.45.**
Anonymous

SEX AS A GENUINE OCCUPATIONAL REQUIREMENT

Equal opportunities representative

Facts: The Land of North Rhine-Westphalia advertised the position of equal opportunities representative, a post concerned with issues of gender equality. The complainant was a man who made a formal application for this post, although he did not include his curriculum vitae with his application. When he was not awarded the job, he argued that he had been subject to sex discrimination (see further section 2.3.3). One question arising in the case was whether the position in question could lawfully be reserved to women.

Held: The Regional Labour Court had misinterpreted the relevant legal provisions as reserving this post to women. In any case, there were not sufficient grounds for such a restriction.

Judgment: "1. § 611a, para. 1, sentence 2 BGB allows differentiation on ground of gender only if the differentiation is based on the professional activity to be carried out and if a certain gender is an "indispensable element and condition" for this activity. The text of this law is unambiguous in this respect and corresponds to the requirement of European law, which only allows differentiation if a certain gender is an "indispensable element and condition" for the particular professional activity. (Art. 2(2) of the Equal Treatment Directive 76/207/EEC of 9 February 1976). An absolute requirement in this sense sets considerable requirements as regards the weight of the circumstance which justifies the unequal treatment in terms of justification in fact, as the gender is only an indispensable condition if a member of respective opposite sex would not be able to fulfil the necessary contractual performance, and this inability is based on reasons which for their own part fulfil the legal constitutional values regarding equal treatment of both sexes . . .

---

[238] At 219. See further on this case, McColgan, above n. 122, 555.
[239] NZA, 1999, 371.

287

3. The prerequisite for the indispensability of the female sex for filling the position of an equal opportunities representative for the defendant is therefore not proven by the defendant who is responsible for presentation of the proof.

a) In particular, the indispensability does not result from the Local Government Code of the Land of North Rhine-Westphalia (Gemeindeordnung NW). The task of the equal opportunities representative according to the Gemeindeordnung NW is to participate in all projects and measures of the local authority which relate to women's matters and which have an effect on the equal treatment of women and men and the recognition of their equal status within society, and this task leaves it open as to whether it could only be exercised by members of the female sex. It is rather the case that, by law, no specific knowledge or experience is required of the holder of the position. Therefore, no Judgment can be made as to whether these prerequisites alone can only be fulfilled by the member of a certain sex or possibly only a part of the members of a certain sex. If the latter should be the case, the differentiating criterion would not be the sex, but the presence of specific knowledge and experience."

The following case from the Netherlands concerned a post that was subject to both a sex and ethnic occupational requirement.

Equal Treatment Commission (Commissie Gelijke Behandeling) **2.NL.46.**
Opinion 1997-51

ADVERT FOR MOROCCAN MALE YOUTH OFFICER

Youth worker

Facts: An advertisement for a post as a youth worker expressed a preference for a Moroccan male, given that the post would mainly involve work with boys of Moroccan background. This was challenged as discrimination on grounds of sex and race.

Held: The requirement for a male worker was justified, but not the requirement that the worker be Moroccan.

Opinion: "5.11. The Commission for equal treatment of men and women and the Equal Treatment Commission have already held on various occasions that, when considering whether a specific case falls within the terms of the exceptions as elaborated in the AMVB [Act on Equal Treatment between Men and Women], it must be carefully examined whether all requirements are satisfied.

Exceptions to the precept of equal treatment should generally be restrictively interpreted, in order to prevent this precept from being eroded too much. The Commission for equal treatment of men and women has held that it is up to the party invoking an exception to indicate on what arguments this is based, having regard to the AMVB, and they must at least make a reasonable case that the strict requirements contained therein have been met.

5.12. The respondent underpins her position that the job is a gender specific one by arguments drawn from the specific nature of the problems of the Moroccan boys in question. It is essential for the job that the youth worker to be appointed is able to build up a relationship based on trust with the boys, so that they will put their problems to him.

5.13. The Commission feels that—having regard to the above objectives of the respondent and the specific situation of the boys in question, as also stated in the research report of the respondent—the respondent has made it sufficiently plausible that it is of essential importance to the proper discharge of the duties in this case for the youth worker to be of the male sex . . .

5.16. With regard to the racial specificity of the position, the Commission considers as follows:

The respondent has stated in this connection that she has preference for a Moroccan, on account of the need to employ someone who enjoys the respect of the boys concerned and who can serve as an example for them.

5.17. Pursuant to article 2 (4) AWGB [General Equal Treatment Act], the Equal Treatment Order has exhaustively listed the situations where race may be considered decisive. The Commission finds that this list of occupational activities includes no exception that allow for recruitment of persons who come from the target group, in order to provide assistance to persons of a specific ethnic background. Since Parliament has not made provision for this, the Commission cannot, in view of the restricted scope of the statutory exceptions, conclude other than that the respondent cannot successfully rely on the racial specificity of the position in question. This implies that insofar as the advertisement asks for a specific ethnic origin, this conflicts with the AWGB [references omitted]."

Notes

(1) The reasoning of the Equal Treatment Commission might be interpreted as a "sex-plus" approach to the GOR. The reference to the "problems of Moroccan boys" suggests that the job holder's sex was relevant to working with Moroccan boys rather than boys in general.

(2) The difficulty in using GORs as a mechanism for positive action exposes the tensions between formal and substantive equality. The GOR exception reflects a limited departure from the objective of formal equality. Broadening the GOR exception in order to permit more favourable treatment of persons from disadvantaged communities would be consistent with the pursuit of substantive equality. This would, however, challenge the symmetrical nature of protection against discrimination. With the exception of disability, the dominant model across European states is to protect all persons from direct discrimination irrespective of their characteristics. Therefore, non-appointment of a Dutch person to a post working with Moroccan youths is treated by the law as equally reprehensible to the non-appointment of a Moroccan person to the post.

2.6.3.B.   RESPECT FOR HUMAN RIGHTS AND FREEDOMS

In nearly all European states, the principle of equality is recognised as a constitutional value. The right to non-discrimination is also entrenched within human rights instruments, notably both the European Convention on Human Rights and the Revised European Social Charter. Although there can be no doubting the fundamental status of equality and non-discrimination within European legal systems, on occasions, this clashes with other fundamental rights and values. Frequently, there is no express exception to the prohibition of direct discrimination in relation to conflicts with other human rights or other fundamental interests. Yet case-law reveals that courts may, in practice, use these to place limits on non-discrimination. This issue is openly addressed in the Employment Equality Directive, which contains an exception in Article 2(5):

> "This Directive shall be without prejudice to measures laid down by national law which, in a democratic society, are necessary for public security, for the maintenance of public order and the prevention of criminal offences, for the protection of health and for the protection of the rights and freedoms of others."

This exception can be divided into three parts: public security and related issues; protection of health; other people's rights and freedoms. This section will concentrate on the latter, whilst security and health issues are examined later in this chapter.

Beginning with discrimination in the field of employment and occupation, conflicts can arise between the right to non-discrimination and the right to respect for privacy under Article 8 ECHR. Although not mentioned in the 1976 Gender Employment Directive, the constraints imposed by respect for privacy were recognised by the ECJ.

ECJ, 8 November 1983[240]   **2.EC.47.**
Case 165/82, Commission v. UK

PRIVACY AND THE RIGHT TO NON-DISCRIMINATION

Private household exception

Facts: The Sex Discrimination Act 1975 contained an exception for employment in a private household and employment in small undertakings with no more than five employees.

Held: The small employer exception was not compatible with the Gender Employment Directive.

Judgment: "12. According to the United Kingdom, the exclusions from the prohibition of discrimination provided for in section 6(3) of the 1975 Act in the case of employment in a private household or in undertakings where the number of persons employed does not exceed five are justified by the exception provided for in Article 2(2) of the Directive itself, according to which:

'this Directive shall be without prejudice to the right of Member States to exclude from its field of application those occupational activities and, where appropriate, the training leading thereto, for which, by reason of their nature or the context in which they are carried out, the sex of the worker constitutes a determining factor.'

13. It must be recognized that the provision of the 1975 Act in question is intended, in so far as it refers to employment in a private household, to reconcile the principle of equality of treatment with the principle of respect for private life, which is also fundamental. Reconciliation of that kind is one of the factors which must be taken into consideration in determining the scope of the exception provided for in Article 2(2) of the Directive.

14. Whilst it is undeniable that, for certain kinds of employment in private households, that consideration may be decisive, that is not the case for all the kinds of employment in question.

---

[240] [1983] ECR 3431.

15. As regards small undertakings with not more than five employees, the United Kingdom has not put forward any argument to show that in any undertaking of that size the sex of the worker would be a determining factor by reason of the nature of his activities or the context in which they are carried out."

Notes

(1) The GOR exception in the Directive included references to the "context" in which work is conducted and this permitted the Court to incorporate considerations relating to the right to privacy.[241] This would presumably also be the legal foundation for sex-specific exceptions relating to intimate work (e.g. law enforcement officials required to conduct intimate body searches).

(2) Privacy is not the only human right that may conflict with non-discrimination in the employment field. Freedom of association will be relevant in respect of the internal rules of trade unions, employers' associations and professional bodies. In particular, tensions can arise between the prohibition of direct discrimination and positive action measures within trade unions, such as guaranteed gender or ethnic representation on executive decision-making bodies. Recital 4 of the Racial Equality Directive refers to respect for freedom of association and this is also mentioned in Recital 7 of the 2002 amendments to the Gender Employment Directive:[242]

> "This Directive does not prejudice freedom of association, including the right to establish unions with others and to join unions to defend one's interests. Measures within the meaning of Article 141(4) of the Treaty[243] may include membership or the continuation of the activity of organisations or unions whose main objective is the promotion in practice of the principle of equal treatment between women and men."

This would appear to permit special arrangements, such as women-only sections within trade unions, designed to redress situations where there has been historic (or ongoing) under-representation of women within trade unions, especially at senior levels.

(3) Another area of potential conflict with the right to non-discrimination is freedom of religion (Article 9 ECHR). Insofar as Article 9 ECHR embraces the collective organisation of religions,[244] this is likely to impinge upon the conditions for employment within organised religions. Again there is an overlap here with genuine occupational requirements. A requirement for Catholic priests to be practising

[241] The Irish Employment Equality Acts 1998–2004 include an exception in respect of access to employment where "a person is employed in another person's home for the provision of personal services for persons residing in that home where the services affect the private or family life of those persons" (s. 2(1)).

[242] This is now Recital 20 in the Recast Gender Employment Directive.

[243] Art. 141(4) EC states "With a view to ensuring full equality in practice between men and women in working life, the principle of equal treatment shall not prevent any Member State from maintaining or adopting measures providing for specific advantages in order to make it easier for the underrepresented sex to pursue a vocational activity or to prevent or compensate for disadvantages in professional careers".

[244] See further, R. Allen and G. Moon, "Substantive Rights and Equal Treatment in Respect of Religion and Belief: Towards a Better Understanding of the Rights, and their Implications" [2000] *European Human Rights Law Review* 580.

Catholics can be explained both as a GOR and as an expression of the Catholic Church's Article 9 rights. These issues are discussed further in section 2.6.4.B.

Human rights considerations are also relevant to the prohibition of discrimination outside employment. Similar issues in relation to privacy, freedom of association[245] and freedom of religion can be identified. The Racial Equality Directive does not contain any specific exceptions, but several provisions in the preamble are instructive:

> "Recital 4:
> It is important to respect fundamental rights and freedoms, including the right to freedom of association. It is also important, in the context of access to and provision of goods and services, to respect the protection of private and family life and transactions carried out in this context.
>
> Recital 17:
> The prohibition of discrimination should be without prejudice to the maintenance or adoption of measures intended to prevent or compensate for disadvantages suffered by a group of persons of a particular racial or ethnic origin, and such measures may permit organisations of persons of a particular racial or ethnic origin where their main object is the promotion of the special needs of those persons."[246]

Recital 4 will clearly be relevant to the possible justification of exceptions found within national legislation relating to the renting of rooms within the family home.[247] The balance between privacy and non-discrimination has provoked a particularly shrill debate within Germany which contributed to the delays in agreeing how to transpose the Racial Equality Directive.[248] This may have influenced the even broader provisions found within the text of the Gender Goods and Services Directive. The material scope of the Directive is limited to goods and services "which are offered outside the area of private and family life and the transactions carried out in this context".[249] In relation to freedom of association, Article 4(5) states:

> "This Directive shall not preclude differences in treatment, if the provision of the goods and services exclusively or primarily to members of one sex is justified by a legitimate aim and the means of achieving that aim are appropriate and necessary."

Recitals 16 and 17 of the Directive provide certain examples of differences that could be justified, such as single-sex voluntary bodies or single-sex private clubs. The difficulty for courts lies in identifying the relative weight to be attached to

---

[245] E.g. Art. 30(2) of the Hungarian Equal Treatment Act states: "Entry into premises established for a group defined by characteristics listed in Art. 8 [discrimination grounds] for the purposes of preserving traditions or maintaining cultural and self identity and open to the immediate public may be limited or subject to membership or specific conditions."

[246] See similarly Recital 26, Employment Equality Directive.

[247] § 19 para. 5 of the German Non-Discrimination Act 2006 states: "The regulations of this chapter do not apply to obligations under civil law that are substantiated by a specific close or trust relationship between the parties or their relatives. In tenancies, this may be specifically the case if parties or their relatives use living space on the same estate."

[248] See further, European Commission, "Critical Review of Academic Literature Relating to the EU Directives to Combat Discrimination" (Brussels, European Commission, 2004) 15.

[249] Art. 3(1).

non-discrimination in contrast to other rights, in this case, freedom of association. This dilemma has been exposed in litigation on private associations under the Irish Equal Status Acts 2000–2004. Discriminating private clubs are not prohibited per se, but such clubs may have their certificate of registration suspended or ultimately revoked. This is subject to an exception in section 9(1)(a):

"... a club shall not be considered to be a discriminating club by reason only that—

(a) if its principal purpose is to cater only for the needs of—

   (i)   persons of a particular gender, marital status, family status, sexual orientation, religious belief, age, disability, nationality or ethnic or national origin,
   (ii) persons who are members of the Traveller community, or
   (iii) persons who have no religious belief,

it refuses membership to other persons."

The scope of this exception was tested in the following case.

High Court, 10 June 2005[250]   **2.IE.48.**
The Equality Authority v. *Portmarnock Golf Club and others*

SEX DISCRIMINATION IN MEMBERSHIP OF A GOLF CLUB

Portmarnock Golf Club

Facts: The Equality Authority brought a case challenging Portmarnock Golf Club's rule that only men could become members or associate members of the club. Women could use the facilities to play golf, but could not become members. The golf club argued that its principal purpose was to cater for the needs of male golfers and as such it could rely upon the section 9 exception. The Equality Authority contended that there must be a logical connection between the objects of the club and gender in order to rely on the section 9 exception.

Held: The High Court held that the golf club could rely on the section 9 exception and therefore restricting its membership to men was not unlawful.

Judgment: O'HIGGINS J: "The interpretation contended for by the Golf Club makes for an intelligible reading of s. 9 of the Equal Status Act, 2004. It is straight-forward and easy to reconcile with the purposes of the Act. In particular, it does not undermine the provisions of s. 8 of the Act [the standard provisions on discrimination by clubs], but qualifies them in an understandable way in relation to clubs coming within particular defined categories. On the other hand the court was given no example of an existing club falling within the exemption of s. 9 if the interpretation of the Equality Authority is correct. The court was not given any plausible example of any club—which might, in theory, fall within their definition. A purposive interpretation of the Act affords scant assistance in the present case. The interpretation contended for by the Authority cannot be said to be required either explicitly or implicitly by the Act itself. The legislation does not warrant or mandate the reading into the interpretation of s. 9 words such as 'provided that such clubs exist only for purposes with a logical connection to the grounds of exception' or some such formula. The purpose of the

---

[250] [2005] IEHC 235. Available on the website of the British and Irish Legal Information Institute.

furtherance of equality is not of assistance in interpreting the section because of the fact that exclusion on the gender grounds from the parameters of s. 8 of the Act is not confined to men only clubs but applies equally to women only clubs. In those circumstances, there is no justification for invoking the principle of equality in interpreting the section. Likewise a purposive interpretation, based on the remedial purpose of the Act, which is to be expressed inter alia, to prohibit 'types of discrimination', is not of assistance. I reject also the assertion that the interpretation contended for defeats the purpose of the Act. Section 8 of the Act continues to be an effective and discriminatory provision, regardless of the interpretations of s. 9.

The promotion of equality and the prohibition of types of discrimination—the express purposes of the Act are legitimate and laudable goals of legislation. The interpretation of s. 9 of the Act as contended for by the golf club does not in my view in any way undermine those aims, but rather recognises the fact that there is nothing inherently undesirable with persons seeking—in a social context—the society of persons of the same gender or the same nationality or the same religion. In a tolerant and free and increasingly diverse society, it is not surprising that the type of exemptions envisaged in s. 9 were enacted—as a result of which—in terms of registered clubs—it is permissible to have—exclusively—a bridge club for Bulgarians, a chess club for Catholics, a wine club for women and a golf club for gentlemen. In my view too, the significant omission from the s. 9 based exceptions of exceptions based on race and colour serves to reinforce the plaintiffs' argument for their interpretation of the section. In my view therefore on a correct interpretation of the section Portmarnock Golf Club—whose principal purpose is to cater only for the needs of male golfers comes within the exceptions of s. 8 of the Equality Act provided for by s. 9."

Notes

(1) The judge interprets section 9 from the perspective of formal equality. No sex discrimination exists if both men-only and women-only clubs are permitted. This overlooks the substantive equality context to the case. The perpetuation of men-only clubs could serve to reinforce the historic exclusion of women from informal sites of considerable political and economic power. By contrast, a women-only club could, depending on the facts, be accepted as a necessary mechanism to assist women in overcoming the effects of past and present inequality.

(2) The golf club had alternatively argued that the Act breached the constitutional protection of freedom of association. The High Court rejected this argument and upheld the right of the legislature "to legislate positively to vindicate and promote the value of equality in the legislation promoting those values that may legitimately have an effect on private individuals".

(3) This decision has been appealed to the Supreme Court.

2.6.3.C.   PUBLIC SECURITY ISSUES

Article 2(5) of the Employment Equality Directive is distinguished from the Racial Equality and Gender Directives by the express inclusion of a public security exception. Nevertheless, the ECJ has confronted arguments around discrimination and security on several occasions. In *Johnson*,[251] the UK government argued that direct sex discrimination contrary to the Gender Employment Directive could be justified by broader considerations of public safety, finding their source elsewhere in the EC Treaty. The Court rejected this approach:

> "It must be observed in this regard that the only articles in which the Treaty provides for derogations applicable in situations which may involve public safety are Articles 36, 48, 56, 223 and 224 which deal with exceptional and clearly defined cases. Because of their limited character those Articles do not lend themselves to a wide interpretation and it is not possible to infer from them that there is inherent in the Treaty a general proviso covering all measures taken for reasons of public safety. If every provision of Community law were held to be subject to a general proviso, regardless of the specific requirements laid down by the provisions of the Treaty, this might impair the binding nature of Community law and its uniform application."[252]

This formula was reiterated in other cases concerning public security and sex discrimination.[253] Yet, in the following case, the Court held that "choices of military organisation" could be treated as falling outside the scope of EC law.

ECJ, 11 March 2003[254]   **2.EC.49.**
Case C–186/01, Dory v. Germany

NATIONAL SERVICE AND SEX DISCRIMINATION

Dory

Facts: Mr Dory was called for compulsory military service in Germany, which in principle applies to all men and not to women. He argued that such service limited his access to employment and, as such, was direct sex discrimination contrary to the Gender Employment Directive.

Held: The choice of military organisation by a state falls outside the scope of Community law.

Judgment: "35. Certainly, decisions of the Member States concerning the organisation of their armed forces cannot be completely excluded from the application of Community law, particularly where observance of the principle of equal treatment of men and women in connection with employment, including access to military posts, is concerned. But it does not follow that Community law governs the Member States' choices of military organisation for the defence of their territory or of their essential interests.

36. It is for the Member States, which have to adopt appropriate measures to ensure their internal and external security, to take decisions on the organisation of their armed forces, as the Court observed in *Sirdar*, and *Kreil*.

37. The German Government submits that compulsory military service is of great importance in Germany, both politically and in terms of the organisation of the armed forces. It stated, in its written observations and at the hearing, that the institution of such service makes a contribution to the democratic transparency of the military, national integration, the

---

[251] Case 222/84 *Johnston* v. *Chief Constable of the RUC* [1986] ECR 1651.
[252] Para. 26.
[253] E.g. Para. 16, Case C–285/98 *Kreil* v. *Germany* [2000] ECR I–69.
[254] [2003] ECR I–2479.

295

link between the armed forces and the population, and the mobilisation of the manpower needed by the armed forces in the event of a conflict.

38. Such a choice, enshrined in the Grundgesetz, consists in imposing an obligation to serve the interests of territorial security, albeit in many cases to the detriment of access of young people to the labour market. It thus takes precedence over the objectives of policies aimed at the work prospects of young people.

39. The decision of Germany to ensure its defence in part by compulsory military service is the expression of such a choice of military organisation to which Community law is consequently not applicable.

40. It is true that limitation of compulsory military service to men will generally entail a delay in the progress of the careers of those concerned, even if military service allows some of them to acquire further vocational training or subsequently to take up a military career.

41. Nevertheless, the delay in the careers of persons called up for military service is an inevitable consequence of the choice made by the Member State regarding military organi-sation and does not mean that that choice comes within the scope of Community law. The existence of adverse consequences for access to employment cannot, without encroaching on the competences of the Member States, have the effect of compelling the Member State in question either to extend the obligation of military service to women, thus imposing on them the same disadvantages with regard to access to employment, or to abolish compulsory military service.

42. In the light of all the foregoing, the answer to the National Court's question must be that Community law does not preclude compulsory military service being reserved to men [references omitted]."

Ellis describes the logic of this decision as "elusive".[255] It appears to reflect a political reluctance on the part of the Court to confront the institution of national service, a caution also witnessed in *Schnorbus*.[256]

The approach in national law to security-based exceptions varies greatly. Some states, such as France and the Netherlands, have not included any express public security or public order exception. Others, such as Cyprus[257] and Malta,[258] have chosen to follow the model of the Employment Equality Directive and have included provisions similar to Article 2(5). The UK has included public security exceptions within its anti-discrimination legislation, but not in the terms used by the Directive. Section 42 of the Race Relations Act 1976 states: "Nothing in Parts II to IV shall render unlawful an act done for the purpose of safeguarding national security if the doing of the act was justified by that purpose."[259]

---

[255] See Ellis, above n. 19, 282.

[256] Case C–79/99 *Schnorbus* v. *Land Hessen* [2000] ECR I–10997.

[257] Art. 5(3)(b), Equal Treatment in Employment and Occupation, Law No. 58 (1)/2004 (31.3.2004). See further, N. Trimikliniotis, "Report on Measures to Combat Discrimination: Directive 2000/43/EC and 2000/78/EC. Country Report Cyprus" (European Commission, 2005) 40, available on the website of Directorate-General for Employment, Social Affairs and Equal Opportunities.

[258] Legal Notice 461 of 2004, Reg. 1(6)(a), cited in T. Ellul, "Report on Measures to Combat Discrimi-nation: Directive 2000/43/EC and 2000/78/EC. Country Report Malta" (European Commission, 2005) 25, available on the website of Directorate-General for Employment, Social Affairs and Equal Opportunities.

[259] Similar provisions can be found in Sex Discrimination Act 1975, s. 52; Disability Discrimination Act 1995, s. 59(3); Employment Equality (Sexual Orientation) Regulations 2003, Reg. 24; Employment Equality (Religion or Belief) Regulations 2003, Reg. 24; Employment Equality (Age) Regulations 2006, Reg. 28.

2.6.3.D.   HEALTH AND SAFETY

Specific exceptions relating to health and safety can be located in European and national legislation on sex and disability discrimination. In addition, there is some evidence from national jurisdictions that such considerations can be relevant to cases of age and religious discrimination.

Beginning with sex discrimination, the 1976 Gender Employment Directive included the following proviso:

> "This Directive shall be without prejudice to provisions concerning the protection of women, particularly as regards pregnancy and maternity."[260]

In *Johnson*, the ECJ clarified the limited circumstances in which this protection exception could be invoked. The UK government argued that the policy of the police in Northern Ireland not to provide firearms to women could be justified by reference to this exception; it was a measure designed to protect women from the risk of assassination. This logic was rejected by the Court, which emphasised that this exception was primarily concerned with gender-specific protection reasons:

> "44. It must be observed in this regard that, like Article 2(2) of the Directive, Article 2(3), which also determines the scope of Article 3(2)(c), must be interpreted strictly. It is clear from the express reference to pregnancy and maternity that the Directive is intended to protect a woman's biological condition and the special relationship which exists between a woman and her child. That provision of the Directive does not therefore allow women to be excluded from a certain type of employment on the ground that public opinion demands that women be given greater protection than men against risks which affect men and women in the same way and which are distinct from women's specific needs of protection, such as those expressly mentioned.
>
> 45. It does not appear that the risks and dangers to which women are exposed when performing their duties in the police force in a situation such as exists in Northern Ireland are different from those to which any man is also exposed when performing the same duties. A total exclusion of women from such an occupational activity which, owing to a general risk not specific to women, is imposed for reasons of public safety is not one of the differences in treatment that Article 2(3) of the Directive allows out of a concern to protect women."[261]

The Court identifies two dimensions to the protection exception; protection of a woman's "biological condition" and the "special relationship" between mother and child. The former can be aligned to a health and safety rationale, whereas the latter addresses broader social factors concerning the maternal role (examined further in section 2.6.4.A). The protection exception is now found in Article 2(7) of the amended Gender Employment Directive.[262] This also specifies that the prohibition of sex discrimination is without prejudice to the specific provisions in Directive 92/85/EEC of 19 October 1992 on the introduction of measures to encourage

---

[260] Art. 2(3).
[261] Case 222/84 *Johnston* v. *Chief Constable of the RUC* [1986] ECR 1651.
[262] Art. 28(1) Recast Gender Employment Directive.

improvements in the safety and health at work of pregnant workers and workers who have recently given birth or are breastfeeding.[263] This Directive creates an obligation for employers to conduct a risk assessment if any work activities are liable to pose a risk to the health of women in these categories (for example, where the job involves working with biological agents). Depending on the outcome of such assessments, the employer may temporarily adjust the woman's working arrangements or, in a case of last resort, grant the woman leave for the relevant period.[264]

The Employment Equality Directive also addresses health and safety issues, with specific reference to disability. Article 7(2) states:

> "With regard to disabled persons, the principle of equal treatment shall be without prejudice to the right of Member States to maintain or adopt provisions on the protection of health and safety at work or to measures aimed at creating or maintaining provisions or facilities for safeguarding or promoting their integration into the working environment."

This provision is oddly situated under the heading "positive action". Whilst the second part of Article 7(2) may be interpreted as authorising positive action for disabled persons, it is difficult to view the saving clause for health and safety as akin to positive action. Rather, health and safety considerations are more likely to impose restrictions on disabled persons' access to employment and thereby come into conflict with the non-discrimination objective. Some national legislation takes a more overt approach to the fact that health and safety considerations can operate as an exception to non-discrimination. In France, the Penal Code prohibition of discrimination does not apply in relation to discrimination based on state of health or handicap where the individual is refused a job, or dismissed from a job, on grounds of medical unfitness.[265] In addition, discrimination on the ground of state of health is not unlawful where the actions concerned are designed to prevent risks to physical integrity.[266] In Cyprus, the Law on Persons with Disabilities provides that "the principle of equal treatment does not prevent the maintenance or introduction of regulations for the protection of health and safety at the workplace".[267]

In the Netherlands, Article 3(1) of the Disability Discrimination Act states "The prohibition of distinction shall not apply if: a. the distinction is necessary for the protection of public security and health".[268] The Equal Treatment Commission has clarified, however, that a high threshold is required to justify disability discrimination on grounds of health and safety.

---

[263] [1992] OJ L348/1.

[264] Art. 5.

[265] Art. 225–3(2) CP.

[266] Art. 225–3(1) CP. In relation to Germany, see §20 para. 1 of the Non-Discrimination Act 2006.

[267] Law on Persons with Disabilities, 57(I)/2004 (31.03.2004), s. 4(1), amending s. 3B(2) of Law 127(I)/2000. See Trimikliniotis, above n. 257, 41.

[268] See Gijzen, above n. 52, 47.

Equal Treatment Commission (Commissie Gelijke Behandeling) **2.NL.50.**
Opinion 2004-67

DISABILITY DISCRIMINATION AND THE BURDEN OF PROOF

Contract worker with a heart condition

Facts: The applicant had previously suffered a heart attack. At the end of his fixed-term contract of employment, the employer decided neither to extend the contract, nor to convert it into a permanent contract. Although the applicant had received a letter from the personnel department stating that his contract would not be extended because of his medical history, the employer argued that this was a "communication error" and a reduced supply of work was the basis for the decision not to extend the contract.

Held: The decision not to extend his contract was a direct distinction on the grounds of disability or chronic disease.

Opinion: "5.11 Article 3(a) WGB h/cz [Act on equal treatment on the ground of disability or chronic disease] states that the ban on distinctions does not apply if a distinction is necessary to protect health and safety. The government considered it necessary to include this exclusion having regard to the possible risks inherent in participation by disabled or chronically ill persons in all social activities, including work. Health and safety risks may affect both the disabled or chronically ill and persons in their immediate environment.

However, recourse should not be had to this exception too easily. After all, the distinction must be necessary. Recourse to this exception therefore makes high demands on the substantiation that there was indeed a real danger to health and safety. If this risk can be eliminated by ensuring effective accommodation, the distinction is no longer necessary and not, therefore, justified either (Parliamentary Documents (Kamerstukken) II 2001/02, 28 169, No. 3, p. 31).

5.12 The respondent has asserted that she has a duty of care towards her employees and may therefore decide not to extend the applicant's contract of employment because this harbours too great a risk. However, the respondent has not adduced arguments and reasons which make clear that and for which reason concluding a new contract of employment with the applicant would give rise to a real danger to the applicant and other employees on board a ship. An appeal by the applicant to this exception cannot therefore be successful."

In the UK, there is no specific health and safety exception within the Disability Discrimination Act 1995. It is, however, possible for an employer to justify discrimination for a reason relating to disability.[269] Section 3A (2) defines this justification test in rather open terms:

"Treatment is justified . . . if, but only if, the reason for it is both material to the circumstances of the particular case and substantial".

In the following case, the Court of Appeal had to consider the justification for restrictions imposed by an employer on an employee with diabetes. The Court affords a broad discretion for the employer where these restrictions are grounded in health and safety considerations.

---

[269] Section 3A(1).

Court of Appeal, 11 April 2001[270]   **2.UK.51.**
Jones v. Post Office

DISABILITY DISCRIMINATION AND HEALTH AND SAFETY

Jones

Facts: Mr Jones delivered post to a rural area by driving a delivery van. He had diabetes and this eventually required him to commence insulin treatment. At this point, he was removed from driving duties. The post office was later willing to allow him to resume driving duties, so long as this was limited to maximum periods of two hours. Mr Jones challenged this restriction as less favourable treatment for a reason relating to disability. At first instance, the employment tribunal held that the medical evidence did not reasonably justify such a restriction on his driving. The case turned on the standard for justifying less favourable treatment under section 3A(2) of the DDA (then section 5(3)).

Held: The Court of Appeal held that the employment tribunal was incorrect to insert its own evaluation of the risk assessment for that of the employer. The test for justification under section 5(3) only permitted the tribunal to consider whether the employer had a material and substantial reason for his or her decision, even if the tribunal would have reached a different evaluation based on the same medical evidence.

Judgment: PILL LJ: "Para. 24. I have to say that I have found little assistance, upon the construction of section 5(3), in other cases or in the wording of other statutes. I do find force in a consideration of the employer's general duties under statute and at common law, in effect acknowledged by Mummery LJ in the Clark case and asserted in the submissions of Mr Griffith-Jones. The 1995 Act is plainly intended to create rights for the disabled and to protect their position as employees but those intentions must be considered in the context of the employer's duties to employees generally and to the general public. I cannot accept, in a case such as the present, involving an assessment of risk, that Parliament intended in the wording adopted to confer on employment tribunals a general power and duty to decide whether the employer's assessment of risk is correct. The issue is a different one from whether a person has a disability, within the meaning of section 1 of the Act, which is to be determined by the employment tribunal: *Goodwin* v. *Patent Office* [1999] ICR 302.

25. Upon a consideration of the wording of section 5(3) in context, I conclude that the employment tribunal are confined to considering whether the reason given for the less favourable treatment can properly be described as both material to the circumstances of the particular case and substantial. The less favourable treatment in the present case is the limit upon the hours of driving. The reason given for it is the risk arising from longer periods of driving. The employer obtained what are admitted to be suitably qualified and expert medical opinions. Upon the basis of those opinions the employer decided that the risk was such as to require the less favourable treatment. In order to rely on section 5(3) it is not enough for the employer to assert that his conduct was reasonable in a general way; he has to establish that the reason given satisfies the statutory criteria. The employer asserted in this case that the risk arising from the presence of diabetes is material to the circumstance of the particular case and is substantial. Where a properly conducted risk assessment provides a reason which is on its face both material and substantial, and is not irrational, the tribunal cannot substitute its own appraisal. The employment tribunal must consider whether the reason meets the statutory criteria; it does not have the more general power to make its own appraisal of the medical evidence and conclude that the

[270] [2001] IRLR 384.

evidence from admittedly competent medical witnesses was incorrect or make its own risk assessment."

Health and safety requirements may also produce conflicts with non-discrimination on other grounds. In relation to religious discrimination, the conflicts are likely to arise in cases of indirect discrimination. Employers may have rules inspired by health and safety considerations on workplace dress, personal appearance or the wearing of safety equipment that conflict with religious practices. For example, the Sikh practice of wearing turbans may be difficult to reconcile with an employer's requirement to wear safety headgear. Assuming that the employer's rules will apply to all employees, then the matter will be treated as possible indirect discrimination if it places persons of a particular religion at a particular disadvantage.[271] In contrast, such health and safety considerations have been assimilated to genuine occupational requirements within Austrian legislation. Although not mentioned in the text of the Equal Treatment Act, the explanatory notes accompanying the GOR exception state:

> "The exception also comprises the areas of health and safety. This comprises especially those protective provisions regulating a duty to wear uniforms or helmets for reasons of safety."[272]

Health and safety requirements arising in relation to age are more likely to amount to direct discrimination. For example, it would be direct age discrimination if an employer only required workplace medical assessments for workers over a particular age. Alternatively, an adventure holiday company that imposed an age limit on its clients would also commit direct age discrimination. The possibility to justify direct discrimination on the ground of age, both in the Employment Equality Directive (Article 6) and most national legislation, eschews the need for a specific health and safety exception to be written into legislation. Nevertheless, courts are likely to be confronted with health and safety arguments in age discrimination litigation. Although not a case under anti-discrimination legislation, the German Labour Court has accepted the health and safety rationale for an age limit of 60 on airline cockpit crew.[273]

2.6.3.E.   PROVISION OF FINANCIAL SERVICES

Both EC and national legislation occasionally provide exceptions in relation to the provision of financial services. These exceptions typically allow the prohibited ground to be taken into account through the use of "actuarial factors". This means that in

---

[271] E.g. Reg. 26(1) of the British Employment Equality (Religion of Belief) Regulations specify that requiring a turban-wearing Sikh to wear a safety helmet is indirect discrimination that cannot be justified.
[272] 307 der Beilagen XXII. GP—Regierungsvorlage—Materialien, at 16. Cited in D. Schindlauer, "Report on Measures to Combat Discrimination: Directive 2000/43/EC and 2000/78/EC. Country Report Austria" (European Commission, 2005) 20, available on the website of Directorate-General for Employment, Social Affairs and Equal Opportunities.
[273] BAG 25 February 1998, NZA 1998, 715.

calculating risk assessments (which will determine the premium paid by the individual customer) the service provider can take into account statistical information disaggregated by characteristics such as sex or age. In effect, this is a form of stereo-typing that is sometimes allowed by law.

Within EC legislation, there is a marked disparity between the different Directives on the permissibility of such an exception. The material scope of the Racial Equality Directive covers the provision of services, but there is no exception that would permit statistical data based on racial or ethnic origin to be used in the calculation of customer premiums. Accordingly, in an early case under the Cypriot legislation implementing the Directive, the Commissioner responsible for complaints of discrimination held unlawful the practice of some Cypriot car insurers to charge higher premiums or to refuse insurance for persons of non-Cypriot origin, in particular Pontian Greeks.[274]

When the Commission subsequently proposed to prohibit sex discrimination in the provision of services, it acknowledged the diversity of practice within the Member States in this area. Whilst insurance providers in some states, such as France, had moved towards unisex tariffs, in other states, such as Germany, sex was frequently used as an actuarial factor in calculating premiums.[275] In some cases, states that had prohibited discrimination in the provision of services made this subject to exceptions permitting the continued use of actuarial factors. This is the case in the UK, where legislation on both sex and disability discrimination contains such exceptions.[276] In Ireland, the Equal Status Acts 2000–2004 provide an exception for the use of "actuarial or statistical data" which applies to all grounds of prohibited discrimination.[277]

The Commission's core argument rested on the fundamental nature of the right to non-discrimination.[278] It also argued that characteristics such as sex were not necessarily as important to risk assessment as other lifestyle variables, such as diet and smoking.[279] Nevertheless, there was strong resistance from insurance companies to removing sex as an actuarial factor. One of the political difficulties encountered with the proposal was the mixed impact it could have on women. In some circumstances, women actually benefited from having sex taken into account; this is often the case with car insurance. In the UK, the Equal Opportunities Commission favoured restrictions on when insurers could use sex rather than a total prohibition.[280] Ultimately, the Member States could not agree to exclude the use of sex as an

[274] See Trimikliniotis, above n. 257, 8.
[275] European Commission, "Explanatory Memorandum Accompanying the Proposal for a Council Directive Implementing the Principle of Equal Treatment between Women and Men in the Access to and Supply of Goods and Services" COM (2003) 657 at 6.
[276] Sex Discrimination Act 1975, s. 45; Disability Discrimination (Services and Premises) Regulations 1996, Reg. 2(2).
[277] Section 5(2)(d).
[278] See European Commission, above n. 275, 7.
[279] Ibid.
[280] See McColgan, above n. 122, 271.

actuarial factor and a rather complex exception was included in the Gender Goods and Services Directive:

> "Article 5: Actuarial factors
> 1. Member States shall ensure that in all new contracts concluded after 21 December 2007 at the latest, the use of sex as a factor in the calculation of premiums and benefits for the purposes of insurance and related financial services shall not result in differences in individuals' premiums and benefits.
> 2. Notwithstanding paragraph 1, Member States may decide before 21 December 2007 to permit proportionate differences in individuals' premiums and benefits where the use of sex is a determining factor in the assessment of risk based on relevant and accurate actuarial and statistical data. The Member States concerned shall inform the Commission and ensure that accurate data relevant to the use of sex as a determining actuarial factor are compiled, published and regularly updated. These Member States shall review their decision five years after 21 December 2007, taking into account the Commission report referred to in Article 16, and shall forward the results of this review to the Commission.
> 3. In any event, costs related to pregnancy and maternity shall not result in differences in individuals' premiums and benefits.
> Member States may defer implementation of the measures necessary to comply with this paragraph until two years after 21 December 2007 at the latest. In that case the Member States concerned shall immediately inform the Commission."

It is difficult to find any principled basis for why EC legislation treats sex stereotyping in insurance as permissible whilst ethnic stereotyping is unlawful. The Employment Equality Directive extends this inconsistency further by providing a specific exception for using age as an actuarial factor within occupational social security schemes.[281] The example set by EC law has evidently influenced the content of the German Non-Discrimination Act 2006. This prohibits discrimination contracts for "private law insurance" (§ 19 paragraph 1 no. 2), but this is subject to the following exception:

> § 20 para. 2: "Distinction on grounds of sex is only admissible in the meaning of § 19 para. 1 no. 2 for premiums and benefits, if gender consideration in risk evaluation is based on relevant and exact actuarial and statistical data and is a determining factor. Costs in connection with pregnancy and motherhood may not under any circumstances result in different premiums or benefits. Discrimination on the grounds of religious or any other held beliefs, disability, age, or sexual orientation is only admissible in the meaning of § 19 para. 1 no. 2 if it is based on recognised principles of risk-adequate calculation, especially on risk evaluation ascertained through actuarial and statistical data collection."

In the following extract, Schiek highlights the risk that such exceptions institutionalise direct discrimination.[282]

---

[281] Art. 6(2).
[282] See also D. Schiek, "Broadening the Scope and the Norms of EU Gender Equality Law: Towards a Multidimensional Conception of Equality Law" (2005) 12 *MJ* 427, 435–436.

D. Schiek, *"Freedom of contract and a non-discrimination*   **2.EC.52.**
principle—irreconcilable antonyms?"[283]

"Even more troubling is the justification of direct discrimination through the use of actuarial techniques. Actuarial techniques provide a seemingly neutral way of assessing risk according—for example—to gender or 'race' and ethnicity. Thus differentiation in health and life insurance charges between men and women and in motor vehicle liability insurance charges for the majority and minority populations are quite usual all over Europe. However, it is doubtful whether there are biological reasons for the average higher health costs and longer life spans of Western women. More probably these are results of gender specific behaviour towards health care. That minorities are at a higher risk of having car accidents not because of biological but because of social reasons, is obvious.

The neutrality of actuarial techniques is an ideological farce. The statistical relevance of ascribed personal characteristics stems from societal discrimination on the grounds of these characteristics. Therefore actuarial criteria stabilise discriminatory hierarchies. What is worrying is that with standardisation of contract procedures, actuarial practices become applicable outside the realm of insurance. Thus even direct discrimination against 'other persons' may become acceptable as long as there is a large enough number of similar contracts to build reliable statistics. If it is accepted that women pay higher health insurance rates—why not charge them additional interest to cover for their higher health risk which may endanger their solvency? Reflections like these lead to intentional discrimination without any sense of guilt. Actors may even believe that they cannot escape market pressures to discriminate. Standardisation thus reinforces the need for a prohibition of unintentional and indirect discrimination in contracting. It stresses the importance of including equality as a right to non-discrimination among the principles of contact law [references omitted]."

2.6.4. EXCEPTIONS APPLYING TO SPECIFIC GROUNDS OF DISCRIMINATION

The previous section identified a number of exceptions that are commonly applied to more than one ground of discrimination. In addition, European and national legislation contain a variety of exceptions to the prohibition of direct discrimination which are limited to specific grounds. This section will not provide an exhaustive analysis of all such exceptions; some are peculiar to national or regional circumstances, such as the exceptions to religious discrimination in relation to policing and teaching in Northern Ireland.[284] Instead, this section highlights ground-specific exceptions that are common within the EU Member States, taking the anti-discrimination Directives as a starting point.

---

[283] In T. Loenen and P. Rodrigues (eds.), *Non-discrimination Law: Comparative Perspectives* (The Hague, Kluwer, 1999) 84–5.
[284] Art. 15, Employment Equality Directive.

2.6.4.A.   SEX

As already discussed in section 2.6.3.D, Article 2(7) of the Gender Employment Directive states:

"This Directive shall be without prejudice to provisions concerning the protection of women, particularly as regards pregnancy and maternity."

One element of this protection concerns health and safety issues that specifically affect women, which are further regulated by Directive 92/85. This exception extends, though, beyond physical health and safety and also encompasses, in the words of the ECJ, protection linked to "the special relationship between the woman and her child".[285] The difficulty with this broader category of protection lies in the risk of reinforcing stereotypical notions of women's maternal role, thereby legitimising the unequal division of caring responsibilities between women and men. This danger was highlighted in the Court's judgment in the following case.[286]

ECJ, 12 July 1984[287]   **2.EC.53.**
Case 184/83, Hofmann v. *Barmer Ersatzkasse*

SEX DISCRIMINATION AND PAID MATERNITY LEAVE

Hofmann

Facts: German law provided two periods of paid maternity leave. The first period was for eight weeks after childbirth and this was compulsory. The second period lasted until the child was six months old and this was optional. Mr Hofmann was a father who stayed at home during the optional period of maternity leave to care for his child, whilst the child's mother returned to work. He was not able to receive maternity pay for this period as this was reserved to mothers. He argued that this restriction constituted direct sex discrimination contrary to the Gender Employment Directive.

Held: The optional period of paid maternity leave was justified by the exception for the protection of women in the Gender Employment Directive.

Judgment: Having set out the relevant provisions of the Directive, the Court turned to its conclusions: "24. It is apparent from the above analysis that the Directive is not designed to settle questions concerned with the organization of the family, or to alter the division of responsibility between parents.

25. It should further be added, with particular reference to paragraph (3), that, by reserving to Member States the right to retain, or introduce provisions which are intended to protect women in connection with 'pregnancy and maternity', the Directive recognizes the legitimacy, in terms of the principle of equal treatment, of protecting a woman's needs in two respects. First, it is legitimate to ensure the protection of a woman's biological condition during pregnancy and thereafter until such time as her physiological and mental functions have returned to normal after childbirth; secondly, it is legitimate to protect the special relationship

---

[285] Para. 45, Case 222/84 *Johnson* v. *Chief Constable of the RUC* [1986] ECR 1651.
[286] See also discussion of this case above in ch. 1, excerpt **1.EC.34.**
[287] [1984] ECR 3047.

305

between a woman and her child over the period which follows pregnancy and childbirth, by preventing that relationship from being disturbed by the multiple burdens which would result from the simultaneous pursuit of employment.

26. In principle, therefore, a measure such as maternity leave granted to a woman on expiry of the statutory protective period falls within the scope of Article 2(3) of Directive 76/207, inasmuch as it seeks to protect a woman in connection with the effects of pregnancy and motherhood. That being so, such leave may legitimately be reserved to the mother to the exclusion of any other person, in view of the fact that it is only the mother who may find herself subject to undesirable pressures to return to work prematurely.

27. Furthermore, it should be pointed out that the Directive leaves Member States with a discretion as to the social measures which they adopt in order to guarantee, within the framework laid down by the Directive, the protection of women in connection with pregnancy and maternity and to offset the disadvantages which women, by comparison with men, suffer with regard to the retention of employment. Such measures are, as the government of the United Kingdom has rightly observed, closely linked to the general system of social protection in the various Member States. It must therefore be concluded that the Member States enjoy a reasonable margin of discretion as regards both the nature of the protective measures and the detailed arrangements for their implementation."

Notes

(1) McGlynn has criticised the Court's "ideology of motherhood" that arises from this and other decisions.[288] It tends to reify the mother–child relationship and consequently sidelines the role of fathers. Hervey argues that Court conflates the protection of pregnancy with motherhood.[289] Whilst pregnancy is unique to women and hence requires gender-specific protection measures, motherhood is part of the broader realm of parental responsibilities that are shared with men.

(2) Whilst some of these cases rely on the protection of women exception, others are dealt with by reference to the comparator test. In Case C–218/98 *Abdoulaye* v. *Renault* [1999] ECR I–5723, a lump sum payment was made to women on maternity leave, but not to men who became fathers. The Court held that women on maternity leave were not in a comparable situation to men, so direct discrimination did not arise (paragraph 20).[290]

2.6.4.B.   RELIGION

National legislation frequently includes specific exceptions in relation to discrimination on the grounds of religion or belief. These spring from the need to balance freedom of religion with the right to non-discrimination. Freedom of religion implies a degree of latitude for religions to organise their internal affairs in accordance within

---

[288] C. McGlynn, "Ideologies of Motherhood in European Community Sex Equality Law" (2000) 6 *ELJ* 29.

[289] See Hervey, above n. 187, 123.

[290] See also Case 2003–86 *Negotiating Organisation of Healthcare and Social Workers, TSN ry* v. *Social Service Employers' Association ry*, Finnish Labour Court, 24 November 2003: the situation of a woman on maternity leave cannot be compared to that of a man or a woman on sick leave.

their religious beliefs. It will also be engaged where individuals and groups seek to manifest their beliefs—for example, through the manner in which a particular service is delivered. Difficulties arise where the exercise of freedom of religion collides with the right to non-discrimination. This will be the case where organisations wish to impose upon their employees, or clients, requirements relating to religious belief and practice. The content of specific religious beliefs may provoke conflicts with other grounds of discrimination. If the religious belief is hostile to pregnancy outside marriage or homosexuality, then requirements imposed on employees could give rise to sex or sexual orientation discrimination.

In seeking to analyse this complex area, two preliminary points can be made. First, some of the matters described above can be dealt with under the general exception for genuine occupational requirements. As suggested earlier, a requirement for a Catholic priest to be a practising Catholic should be regarded as a GOR. The need for additional exceptions arises in situations where religious requirements are not essential to the person's ability to perform the job or use the service, but where the organisation wishes to impose such requirements in order to maintain a particular ethos. For example, a Lutheran nursing home might require its nurses to be practising Lutherans, even though the specific function of nursing could be performed regardless of the person's religious beliefs.

Secondly, national legal systems vary considerably in the degree to which law provides an autonomous space for religions to regulate their internal affairs. In some states, anti-discrimination law has a broad scope of application and it applies to persons holding religious posts such as ministers.[291] For example, the Finnish Supreme Court has held that the Act on Equality between Women and Men could apply to the recruitment of an assistant pastor.[292] In other states, exclusions are applied that limit the application of anti-discrimination law. In the Netherlands, Article 3 of the General Equal Treatment Act provides that it does not apply to:

> "a. legal relations within religious communities and independent sections thereof and within other associations of a spiritual nature;
> b.   the office of minister of religion."

This exclusion does not extend to organisations such as religious schools, but it does cover some relationships within churches.[293] The autonomy of religious bodies is also entrenched in German constitutional law.[294] This has a significant impact on the application of employment rights to those working in organisations with a religious ethos, such as residential care facilities run by religious charities. Such organisations, "tendency employers", will not be bound by the non-discrimination provision in

---

[291] The application of the Sex Discrimination Act 1975 to employment in the Church of Scotland was recently confirmed by the House of Lords: *Percy* v. *Church of Scotland Board of National Mission (Scotland)* [2006] IRLR 195.

[292] Case 2001-9.

[293] See further, J. Gerards, "Implementation of Article 13 in Dutch Equal Treatment Legislation" (2006) 13 *MJ* 291, 306.

[294] P. Skidmore, "Improving the position of lesbians and gay men at work in the light of the Framework Directive for equal treatment in employment—a German case study" in Dashwood *et al.*, above n. 91, 448.

paragraph 75 of the Workplace Constitution Act insofar as this conflicts within the maintenance of their ethos. Employees will be under obligations to behave in a manner consistent with the organisation's ethos, which can stretch into the conduct of employees' private lives.[295]

The Employment Equality Directive attempts to balance freedom of religion and non-discrimination through the inclusion of an exception for organisations with an ethos based on religion or belief. Article 4(2) states:

> "Member States may maintain existing national legislation or provide for future legislation incorporating existing national practices pursuant to which, in the case of churches or other public or private organisations the ethos of which is based on religion or belief, as regards the occupational activities within those organisations, a difference of treatment based on a person's religion or belief shall not constitute discrimination where, by reason of the nature of these activities or of the context in which they are carried out, a person's religion or belief constitute a genuine, legitimate and justified occupational requirement, having regard to the organisation's ethos. This difference of treatment shall be implemented taking account of Member States' constitutional provisions and principles, as well as the general principles of Community law, and should not justify discrimination on another ground.
>
> Provided that its provisions are otherwise complied with, this Directive shall thus not prejudice the right of churches and other public or private organisations, the ethos of which is based on religion or belief, acting in conformity with national constitutions and laws, to require individuals working for them to act in good faith and with loyalty to the organisation's ethos."

There are two elements to this long and convoluted exception. The first paragraph permits organisations with an ethos based on religion or belief to treat a person's religion or belief as an occupational requirement where justified by virtue of the nature or context of the activities. Therefore, a school managed by a religious order might require teachers to practice the religion of the school. The school would have to demonstrate that the nature and context of teachers' activities required them to share the school's religion in order to maintain its ethos. This might be the case if all teachers were regularly required to lead worship or to incorporate religious teaching into their pastoral care for students. This paragraph is, however, subject to the exception that it "should not justify discrimination on another ground". In principle, therefore, the religious school might be entitled to refuse to employ a teacher of a different religion, but not because the teacher was lesbian or gay. This balancing approach finds a strong echo in Dutch law, which is examined further below.

The second paragraph permits organisations with an ethos based on religion or belief to impose requirements on employees in relation to their behaviour and conduct, which should be in keeping with the organisation's ethos. This is, however, subject to the proviso that the provisions of the Directive must be "otherwise complied with", which seems to exclude the possibility that a requirement which discriminated on grounds of sexual orientation (for example) could be justified under this paragraph. In particular, the interpretation of this provision will have to be

---

[295] *Ibid.* at 449.

balanced with the right to respect for private life under Article 8 ECHR and there are obvious tensions where the organisation's ethos disapproves of same-sex relationships.

Member States' responses to Article 4(2) vary considerably. Some states have chosen not to avail themselves of the possibility to include this exception in anti-discrimination legislation. No such provision can be found in the French Labour Code. This fits with a decision by the Court of Cassation in 1991.[296] In the case in question, the Fraternité Saint-Pie X had employed P as a sacristan since 1985. P was a gay man, but maintained his privacy and this was not known to either his employer or to the vast majority of church-goers. Following an indiscretion, his sexual orientation came to the knowledge of the Fraternité and he was dismissed in June 1987. The Court of Cassation held that, as the dismissal was based solely on his *mœurs*,[297] it was contrary to Articles L. 122-35 and L. 122-45 of the Labour Code. Similarly, in Finland, no religious ethos exception was included when implementing the Directives. In 2004, an Administrative Court held that it was unlawful discrimination for the Evangelical Lutheran Church to refuse to appoint a woman as a chaplain on the basis that she was living in a same-sex relationship.[298]

Many other states have included or retained exceptions relating to religious ethos requirements.[299] The Netherlands is a particularly interesting example because such exceptions have generated litigation. Article 5(2) of the General Equal Treatment Act 1994 states that the prohibition of discrimination in employment shall not apply to:

> "the freedom of an institution founded on religious or ideological principles to impose requirements which, having regard to the institution's purpose, are necessary for the carrying out of the duties attached to a post; such requirements may not lead to discrimination on the sole grounds of political opinion, race, sex, nationality, heterosexual or homosexual orientation or civil status."

An equivalent exception applies in respect of admission to and participation in private educational establishments.[300] Two scenarios arise under these exceptions: first, where an organisation directly discriminates against a person on grounds of religion or belief; and, secondly, where such discrimination is connected to other personal characteristics, such as sexual orientation. In the following case, the Equal Treatment Commission clarified the circumstances where direct discrimination on grounds of religion and belief could be justified by the religious ethos exception.

---

[296] *P. v. Association Fraternité Saint-Pie X.* (1991) II Juris classeur périodique, no 21724, 303.

[297] '*Mœurs*' may be defined as morals or habits, *un mode de vie*. In this case, it was interpreted as extending to sexual orientation.

[298] Vaasa Administrative Court, 27 August 2004, Ref. No. 04/0253/3. See further, T. Makkonen, "Report on Measures to Combat Discrimination: Directive 2000/43/EC and 2000/78/EC. Country Report Finland" (European Commission, 2005) 4, available on the website of Directorate-General for Employment, Social Affairs and Equal Opportunities.

[299] E.g. such exceptions can be found in Reg. 7(3) of the British Employment Equality (Religion or Belief) Regulations 2003; s. 37(1) of the Irish Employment Equality Act 1998; and § 9 of the German Non-Discrimination Act 2006.

[300] Art. 7(2).

Equal Treatment Commission (Commissie Gelijke Behandeling) **2.NL.54.**
Opinion 2003-112

RESTRICTIONS ON WEARING RELIGIOUS SYMBOLS

Dutch headscarf case

Facts: This case concerned a challenge to a school's rule that did not permit wearing a headscarf within the school's building. In line with its religious ethos, the wearing of any clothing associated with non-Catholic or non-Christian convictions was prohibited.

Held: Although the rule constituted direct discrimination on the ground of religious beliefs, it was lawful by virtue of statutory exceptions for institutions with a religious ethos.

Opinion: "5.7 According to Article 1 AWGB [General Equal Treatment Act], a distinction may be both direct and indirect. A direct distinction is a distinction where reference is directly made to one of the grounds for discrimination protected by the AWGB, including religion. The AWGB bans any direct distinction, unless the Act contains a specific possibility for exception.

5.8 The wearing of clothing that may be associated with non-Catholic or non-Christian convictions is prohibited in the student rules. By reason of the school's constitution, no expression may be given to any other than the Catholic religion, such as Islam. The respondent therefore refers directly to the ground of religion. The Commission therefore finds that the respondent is making a direct distinction.

5.9 Direct distinctions are prohibited unless a statutory ground for exception applies, as included in article 7 (2) AWGB. This article permits an institution for special education [e.g. a private educational establishment with a particular religious ethos] to impose rules for admission and regarding participation in education, which are essential to achieve its constitutional aims, having regard to the objects of the institution. These rules may not, however, result in a distinction based on the sole ground of political conviction, race, sex, nationality, heterosexual or homosexual alignment or civic status. The latter does not apply to religion.

5.10 This provision is connected with article 23 Constitution, which guarantees freedom of education. This freedom of education implies that institutions of special education may set requirements to fulfil their identity as long as they make no distinction in doing so that is not justified by the attitudes characteristic to this identity (Parliamentary documents (Kamerstukken) II 1990/91, 22 014, No. 3, p. 17). The requirements made of pupils or other participants in education regarding fulfilment of the foundation will be less stringent than those for the institution's personnel (Parliamentary documents II 1990/91, 22 014, No. 3, p. 22). . . .

5.14 It is an established fact in this case that the school has Catholic leanings and that the parents/guardians of each prospective pupil are asked to subscribe to the school's foundation. This is clear from the school guide and is also laid down in the school's tuition contract. In addition, the student rules further explain the school's identity and mission. The respondent has stated that as part of the subject of divinity/bible knowledge, all observances, forms of worship and associated attendance are mandatory for the first to fourth years. In addition, the respondent has provided reasoned argument that the school's Catholic leanings are regularly and effectively observed, such as during Lent, religious worship and festivals. In addition, the school maintains relations with the diocese, is recognised by the Netherlands Catholic Schools Council and has a school chaplain.

5.15 The Commission finds in the light of the above that the respondent is in practice giving expression to the school's identity and consistently maintains this identity. The fact that not every pupil actually has Catholic leanings makes no difference here, since the parents/guardians of every pupil are asked to subscribe to the school's foundation. Having a certain (Catholic) foundation and conducting a consistent policy in this connection does not rule out that the school admits pupils from another religion."

Notes

(1) This decision provides a broad discretion for actions connected to the religious ethos of the school. The Equal Treatment Commission does not scrutinise in detail the necessity of the ban on the headscarf to upholding the school's ethos. In fact, the decision noted elsewhere that other schools managed by the same respondent adopted a different policy and did permit students to wear the headscarf.

(2) In Opinion 2001-09 (26 January 2001), the Equal Treatment Commission held that a Protestant school was entitled not to appoint a teaching assistant who was not an active member of the church. It described its inquiry as seeking to discover "whether there is an objective link between the conviction on which the [organisation's] aims are based and the occupational requirement derived from it" (paragraph 4.6).

(3) In Case 2003-145 (1 December 2003), a newspaper photographer was dismissed after he changed church. The employer argued that the newspaper was ideologically based on a church community that accepts the Bible and the "Three Formulae of Unity" as the basis for its beliefs (paragraph 5.6). The complainant offered to give up his role on the editorial team and, in any case, argued that his role as a photographer was of less significance to the newspaper's content. In contrast, the employer contended that the photographer's work was integral to the identity of the newspaper. The Equal Treatment Commission agreed and held that his dismissal was justified by the religious ethos exception in Article 5(2) of the General Equal Treatment Act.

The proviso to the religious ethos exception in Article 5(2) of the General Equal Treatment Act is that this should not give rise to discrimination on the "sole ground" of race, sex, etc. This attempts to strike a delicate balance between permitting differences of treatment required by the organisation's religious ethos and not providing a carte blanche for other forms of discrimination under the cover of religious ethos. As such, it parallels the second paragraph of Article 4(2) of the Employment Equality Directive, albeit worded in slightly different terms. The following case provides an example of how this has been interpreted by the Equal Treatment Commission.

Equal Treatment Commission (Commissie Gelijke Behandeling) **2.NL.55.**
Opinion 1999-38

RELIGIOUS ETHOS EXCEPTION AND SEXUAL ORIENTATION

Job applicant in a same-sex relationship

Facts: A primary school based on Reformed Church principles did not appoint to a teaching post a gay man living in a same-sex relationship. The school's board requested the opinion of the Equal Treatment

Commission on whether this action was compatible with the religious ethos exception in Article 5(2) of the General Equal Treatment Act.

Held: The school had made a direct distinction based on sexual orientation and this was not compatible with the Act.

Opinion: ". . . When interpreting the legislation, it is not obvious, therefore, that one should assume that any homosexual teacher, whether or not cohabiting, can automatically be excluded from particular positions. It must certainly be clear from the start what demands teachers who apply for a vacancy must meet. These demands may be connected with the way in which the teacher gives shape to his personal life but may not go so far as to consider homosexual cohabiting automatically as a ground for rejection in all circumstances. The statutory ban on distinction based on 'the sole ground' applies to all institutions for special education, i.e. also to those educational institutions where rejection of homosexual orientation or homosexual cohabiting results from their foundation. The AWGB [General Equal Treatment Act], after all, contains no further exception regarding these teaching establishments.

The same applies to positions where—as in the present case—standards and values are taught in accordance with the school's foundation. With regard to these positions, as well, the ban on distinction based on the sole ground of homosexual orientation is fully applicable. The AWGB is therefore based on the assumption that the appointment of a homosexual teacher or a teacher cohabiting unmarried must in principle be regarded as possible at an institution for special education. As far as this is concerned, the distinction in this case must be regarded as unlawful. However, this may be different if there are 'additional circumstances'.

4.9. In this connection, the Commission considers the following in the present case. The sole ground-construction provides the possibility of a balancing of interests where so-called 'additional circumstances' are concerned. The legislator was confident that this balancing exercise would in practice result in a satisfactory situation, as far as the adoption of a personnel policy is concerned that results in the appointment of persons that fit within the institution.

Within the framework of the AWGB, therefore, a diligent attitude is expected from the educational establishment regarding any homosexual applicant or one cohabiting while unmarried. Since recourse has been had to the sole ground-construction, it must be shown that a balance of interests was made in which the person of the teacher concerned and his conduct or possible attitudes towards the institution's foundation and the way in which the duties must be performed, give rise to the conclusion that there were additional circumstances that result in no distinction was made based on the sole ground of homosexual orientation. It is reasonable, therefore, that the applicants must in any event make it plausible that the teacher concerned did not in this respect fit within the school, having regard to the foundation of the educational establishment. This implies that the teacher concerned must at least be given the opportunity to explain how he can reconcile his or her sexual orientation or way of cohabiting with the objectives of the educational establishment. The educational establishment may then consider whether circumstances may exist that make the person of the teacher concerned incompatible with his job performance within the establishment [references omitted]."

Notes

(1) This opinion is carefully nuanced and illustrates the difficulty in practice of avoiding discrimination on the "sole ground" of sexual orientation whilst also permitting differences in treatment based on maintaining the employer's religious ethos.

(2) The Equal Treatment Commission starts from the premise that an automatic rule excluding any lesbian or gay applicant or even any applicant in a same-sex relationship would be unlawful discrimination on grounds of sexual orientation. This premise can be dislodged if the employer identifies "additional circumstances". These are not clearly defined in the opinion, but a hypothetical example could be a lesbian or gay applicant who is also a well-known and public critic of the particular church's teaching on homosexuality. This might indicate a greater conflict between the individual and the organisation's ethos than the "sole ground" of the individual's sexual orientation.

(3) The Equal Treatment Commission emphasizes the necessity of dialogue to allow the individual to present their own point of view on how they could "reconcile" their sexual orientation with the organisation's ethos. This seems a constructive approach, albeit one that is not guaranteed to resolve conflicts in every case.

2.6.4.C.   AGE

The Employment Equality Directive distinguishes age from the other grounds of discrimination by permitting the justification of direct discrimination. Article 6(1) states:

"Notwithstanding Article 2(2), Member States may provide that differences of treatment on grounds of age shall not constitute discrimination, if, within the context of national law, they are objectively and reasonably justified by a legitimate aim, including legitimate employment policy, labour market and vocational training objectives, and if the means of achieving that aim are appropriate and necessary. Such differences of treatment may include, among others:

(a) the setting of special conditions on access to employment and vocational training, employment and occupation, including dismissal and remuneration conditions, for young people, older workers and persons with caring responsibilities in order to promote their vocational integration or ensure their protection;
(b) the fixing of minimum conditions of age, professional experience or seniority in service for access to employment or to certain advantages linked to employment;
(c) the fixing of a maximum age for recruitment which is based on the training requirements of the post in question or the need for a reasonable period of employment before retirement."

This provision has been criticised for its breadth and inherent flexibility.[301] By linking justifications for age discrimination to wider employment policy objectives, Article 6(1) created the risk that age could be treated as qualitatively different to other discrimination grounds. This looser framework for justifying direct discrimination might have been interpreted as akin to a low threshold of rationality demanding

---

[301] H. Meenan, "Age Equality after the Employment Directive" (2003) 10 *MJ* 9, 23.

limited judicial scrutiny. Nevertheless, in its first decision interpreting this part of the Directive, the ECJ sought to establish limits to the scope for justifying direct discrimination. In particular, it has indicated that direct discrimination exclusively on the ground of age will be subject to strict review.

ECJ, 22 November 2005   **2.EC.56.**
Case C–144/04, Mangold v. *Helm*

AGE DISCRIMINATION IN EMPLOYMENT CONTRACTS

Mangold

Facts: In order to combat unemployment amongst older workers, German labour law on fixed-term contracts was amended. Whereas fixed-term contracts are normally subject to a maximum number of renewals, a temporary derogation was created for employees over the age of 52. In respect of these workers, the unlimited successive use of fixed-term contracts was permitted. Mr Mangold, aged 56, was employed by Mr Helm on a fixed-term contract. He argued, inter alia, that the legal provision permitting recourse to a fixed-term contract was direct discrimination contrary to the Employment Equality Directive.

Held: The relevant provision of German law was unlawful direct age discrimination.

Judgment: "Para. 56. In this regard, it is to be noted that, in accordance with Article 1, the purpose of Directive 2000/78 is to lay down a general framework for combating discrimination on any of the grounds referred to in that article, which include age, as regards employment and occupation.

57. Paragraph 14(3) of the TzBfG, however, by permitting employers to conclude without restriction fixed-term contracts of employment with workers over the age of 52, introduces a difference of treatment on the grounds directly of age . . .

59. As is clear from the documents sent to the Court by the national court, the purpose of that legislation is plainly to promote the vocational integration of unemployed older workers, in so far as they encounter considerable difficulties in finding work.

60. The legitimacy of such a public-interest objective cannot reasonably be thrown in doubt, as indeed the Commission itself has admitted.

61. An objective of that kind must as a rule, therefore, be regarded as justifying, 'objectively and reasonably', as provided for by the first subparagraph of Article 6(1) of Directive 2000/78, a difference of treatment on grounds of age laid down by Member States.

62. It still remains to be established whether, according to the actual wording of that provision, the means used to achieve that legitimate objective are 'appropriate and necessary'.

63. In this respect the Member States unarguably enjoy broad discretion in their choice of the measures capable of attaining their objectives in the field of social and employment policy.

64. However, as the national court has pointed out, application of national legislation such as that at issue in the main proceedings leads to a situation in which all workers who have reached the age of 52, without distinction, whether or not they were unemployed before the contract was concluded and whatever the duration of any period of unemployment, may lawfully, until the age at which they may claim their entitlement to a retirement pension, be offered fixed-term contracts of employment which may be renewed an indefinite number of times. This significant body of workers, determined solely on the basis of age, is thus in danger, during a substantial part of its members' working life, of being excluded from the benefit of

stable employment which, however, as the Framework Agreement makes clear, constitutes a major element in the protection of workers.

65. In so far as such legislation takes the age of the worker concerned as the only criterion for the application of a fixed-term contract of employment, when it has not been shown that fixing an age threshold, as such, regardless of any other consideration linked to the structure of the labour market in question or the personal situation of the person concerned, is objectively necessary to the attainment of the objective which is the vocational integration of unemployed older workers, it must be considered to go beyond what is appropriate and necessary in order to attain the objective pursued. Observance of the principle of proportionality requires every derogation from an individual right to reconcile, so far as is possible, the requirements of the principle of equal treatment with those of the aim pursued (see, to that effect, Case C–476/99 *Lommers* [2002] ECR I–2891, paragraph 39). Such national legislation cannot, therefore, be justified under Article 6(1) of Directive 2000/78."

Notes

(1) The Court's judgment indicates that it does not view age discrimination as a special ground where a different approach is warranted. Instead, it declares that "the principle of non-discrimination on grounds of age must thus be regarded as a general principle of Community law" (paragraph 75). In this way, the Court locates age within its fundamental rights case-law and reinforces the need for any derogation to be closely scrutinised.

(2) This decision exposes the tensions that can arise between employment policy and combating age discrimination. The German labour market reforms were nested within the flexibility agenda of the EU Employment Strategy.[302] A similar debate surrounded the "contrat première embauche" in France.[303] This sought to combat youth unemployment through removing protection from unfair dismissal for persons aged under 26 during the first two years of the employment contract. Following widespread protests, the French government agreed to repeal this provision.

(3) The Irish Employment Equality Acts 1998–2004 include the following exception: "offering a fixed term contract to a person over the compulsory retirement age for that employment or to a particular class or description of employees in that employment shall not be taken as constituting discrimination on the age ground".[304] From one perspective, this could be viewed as encouraging employers to keep in employment workers beyond retirement age, without assuming an indefinite contractual obligation. Yet the rationale in *Mangold* suggests that such measures expose workers to a reduced level of employment protection exclusively on the grounds of their age. Its legality would seem to depend on whether the courts will make a distinction between a *Mangold*-type rule concerning pre-retirement older

---

[302] See further, P. Skidmore, "The European Employment Strategy and Labour Law: a German Case-study" (2004) 29 *ELR* 52.

[303] Art. 8, Law No. 2006-396 of 31 March 2006 on equality of opportunity (J.O. no. 79, 2 April 2006, at 4950).

[304] Section 6(3) as amended.

workers and measures that only apply in respect of workers over the compulsory retirement age.

Mangold concerned a situation where barriers to the employment of older persons were tackled through reductions in labour law protection. Another strategy is positive actions to encourage older workers to remain in the labour market. These measures typically aim to facilitate a transition into retirement, or "flexible" retirement, such as additional holidays and reduced working hours. To the extent that such measures constitute more favourable treatment of older workers, then they risk being challenged as direct discrimination. This was considered by the Equal Treatment Commission in the following case.

Equal Treatment Commission (Commissie Gelijke Behandeling)   **2.NL.57.**
Opinion 2004-118

JUSTIFICATION FOR AGE DISCRIMINATION

Benefits for older workers

Facts: The employer offered a package of benefits for older workers. The three elements were: (1) additional leave for those over 45, 50 and 55; (2) additional leave for those with 10, 15 and 20 years of service; (3) optional reduction in working hours for those over 60. Numbers 1 and 3 were challenged as direct age discrimination against younger workers, whereas number 2 was challenged as indirect age discrimination (also against younger workers who were less likely to have accrued the length of service required).

Held: The three measures constituted direct and indirect discrimination respectively and were not justified.

Opinion: "4.2 Article 1(1) WGB 1 [Act on equal treatment on the ground of age in employment, occupation and vocational training] states that a distinction based on age means a distinction based on age or based on other capacities or conduct resulting in a distinction based on age. Pursuant to article 3, preamble and (e), WGB 1, a distinction based on age is prohibited in conditions of employment. The three mentioned regulations concern working conditions.
    4.3 Under Article 7(1), preamble and (c), WGB1, making a distinction based on age may be objectively justified in certain circumstances. Whether an objective justification exists in a specific case must be examined by considering the objective of the distinction and the means for achieving this objective. The objective must be legitimate in the sense of being sufficiently important or responding to a real need. A legitimate objective requires further that there may be no discriminatory intent. The means used must be appropriate and necessary. A means is appropriate if it is suitable for achieving the objective. A means is necessary if the objective cannot be achieved by other means that do not result in a distinction, or at least are less onerous, and the means stands in a reasonable relationship of proportionality to the objective. Only when all these conditions are met does the distinction not conflict with the equal treatment legislation . . .
    4.5 Article 14.2.3. of the conditions of employment regulations state that employees aged 45, 50 and 55 will be granted additional days' leave. A distinction is thereby made between, among others, staff aged 45 and over and those that are less than 45 years old. The conclusion is that Article 14.2.3 makes a distinction based on age.

316

4.6 The applicant has adduced as an objective justification that the purpose of the above regulation is to be able to maintain the deployment of older workers by giving them rather more opportunity to rest, so that the individual stress limit will be less rapidly reached, if at all . . .

4.10 The written documents and explanations given at the hearing have not shown that there are physically greatly demanding jobs with the applicant's organisation. The applicant stated at the hearing that warehousemen may certainly undertake physically demanding work but these jobs are not so physically burdensome that age plays a role. In addition, the applicant has taken a number of steps precisely with respect to these jobs to make the burden more tolerable by e.g. making work in the warehouses more varied, partly by organising a different distribution of responsibilities. In addition, the applicant has indicated that the jobs of a buyer and salesman, in particular, are psychologically demanding but not to such an extent that they result in higher absenteeism. Where there is a difference in absenteeism, this is due to personal circumstances and through increasing work pressure. Age plays no role here. The applicant was unable to say whether the extra days' leave from age 45 really contribute to the individual tolerance limit being reached less quickly.

4.11 The applicant has further argued that the additional days' leave have already been allowed for more than 20 years, that the arrangement is regarded as positive by staff, and that the rule was introduced as a result of a social trend. However, these are general arguments that do not justify a distinction based on age. Generally speaking, vague, generalising arguments provide inadequate justification (see: Parliamentary documents II 2001/02, 28 170, No. 3, p. 25 and European Court of Justice 13 July 1989, Case C–171/88 (*Rinner-Kühn*), Jur. 1989, p. 2743).

4.12 It is clear from the above that there is no question in the present case of an actual need in the organisation to give workers aged 45 and over (slightly) more opportunity for rest. The purpose of the provision therefore fails to meet an real need within the applicant's organisation and is not therefore legitimate . . .

4.25 Article 7.4.1. states that employees aged 60 and over may be eligible for reduced working hours with retention of salary, provided that the time not worked is paid at 65% of the normal gross hourly wage. A distinction is thereby made between employees aged 60 and over and those who are less than 60 years old. This leads to the conclusion that clause 7.4.1 of the rules of work makes a direct distinction based on age.

4.26 The applicant has adduced as an objective justification of the distinction based on age that the purpose of the above rule is threefold. Firstly, the applicant hereby wishes to ensure that older employees continue to participate for as long as possible in employment. Secondly, this rule ensures an effective and uniform transfer of tasks and/or familiarisation period for the next generation and thirdly the applicant hereby wishes to achieve that older employees slowly reduce their activities in preparation for life with more leisure time. With regard to this objective of older employees participating in employment, the applicant has indicated that it considers it important that employees aged 60 or over should work fewer hours per week due to their reduced stress resistance. The same applies in this connection as considered under 4.6 to 4.11 above. To that extent, the Commission considers the objective of older employees participating in work as not legitimate, since this is not a real need on the part of the organisation."

Notes

(1) In relation to the seniority-related leave entitlement, this was held to be indirect discrimination without justification. The Equal Treatment Commission argued that

there were other ways in which the company could stimulate staff motivation and reward loyalty, such as performance-related bonus systems (paragraph 4.23).

(2) Although this decision precedes *Mangold*, it likewise adopts a strict standard when considering justification of direct age discrimination. Again, there is evidence of conflict between employment policy objectives and non-discrimination. In particular, the Equal Treatment Commission does not regard the retention of older workers in the labour market as a legitimate aim for a private company to pursue (paragraph 4.26). This is implicitly treated as a public policy objective, which is not essential for any individual company.

(3) The decision emphasizes the importance of formal equality between older and younger workers, but there is little consideration of the role for positive action. A substantive equality analysis would argue that older workers are not always in the same position as younger workers. Statistical evidence reveals disadvantage for older workers within the labour market, as illustrated by consistently lower rates of employment amongst this category.[305] Breaking the pattern of older workers' early exit from the labour market may require positive interventions. Whilst the decision in this case focuses on affirming the equal capacity of older workers, it restricts the space for a private employer to promote older people's employment by conferring certain advantages on this category of workers.

(4) Following this case, the Equal Treatment Commission decided to commission further scientific research on whether there was an objective link between age and the need for reduced working pressures. This research reached a different conclusion to that cited in the above case, finding that there was a basis for reducing work pressures in respect of older workers. Consequently, the Equal Treatment Commission has stayed all cases around reduced work entitlements for older workers until December 2006 in order to permit employers and trade unions to reconsider the position.[306]

Many states have chosen to incorporate Article 6 of the Employment Equality Directive, or a version thereof, into national anti-discrimination legislation.[307] In France, Article L. 122-45-3 states:

"Differences of treatment based on age do not constitute discrimination when they are objectively and reasonably justified by a legitimate objective, particularly employment policy objectives, and when the means of realising this objective are appropriate and necessary.

These differences can in particular consist of:

— the restriction of access to employment or the implementation of special working conditions in order to ensure the protection of young and old workers;

---

[305] See European Commission, "Employment in Europe", 2005, Statistical Annex: Key Employment Indicators, at 2, available on the website of Directorate-General for Employment, Social Affairs and Equal Opportunities.
[306] See further, Gijzen, above n. 49.
[307] See, e.g. § 10 of the German Non-discrimination Act (Allgemeines Gleichbehandlungsgesetz (AGG), BGBl. Teil I 17.8.2006, S. 1897.

— the fixing of a maximum age for recruitment, based on the training required for the post concerned or the necessity of a reasonable period of employment before retirement."

The first draft of the British Employment Equality (Age) Regulations 2006 also chose to list examples of situations where age discrimination could be justified. These were, however, removed in the final text. Regulation 3(1) states:

"For the purposes of these Regulations, a person ('A') discriminates against another person ('B') if—

(a) on grounds of B's age, A treats B less favourably than he treats or would treat other persons . . .

and A cannot show the treatment or, as the case may be, provision, criterion or practice to be a proportionate means of achieving a legitimate aim."

An issue of particular importance within age discrimination law is retirement. Where national law or an individual employer compels an employee to retire at a given age, this is direct age discrimination. Some doubt over the need to justify this form of direct discrimination is created by Recital 14 in the Employment Equality Directive, which states: "this Directive shall be without prejudice to national provisions laying down retirement ages". This could be read as an exclusion from the scope of the Directive, but it is located in the preamble rather than the main body of the Directive.[308] Therefore, compulsory retirement could, in principle, be challenged as direct discrimination, but Recital 14 may persuade the ECJ to treat this as a justified form of direct discrimination.[309]

Practice amongst national courts varies on this issue. The German Federal Labour Court has, in the past, upheld automatic retirement at 65 for a public sector employee,[310] and the Polish Supreme Court held in 2003 that:

"the fact that an employee has reached retirement age constitutes an independent cause justifying termination of a contract of employment, and does not constitute discrimination against an employee who has acquired pension rights."[311]

Occasionally, other courts have been willing to challenge compulsory retirement in the form of maximum age limits.

---

[308] A similar issue arises in relation to Recital 22: "This Directive is without prejudice to national laws on marital status and the benefits dependent thereon." This will be relevant to potential litigation challenging workplace benefits limited to married employees as indirect discrimination against employees in same-sex relationships. With the exception of the Netherlands, Belgium and Spain, same-sex couples cannot get married in the Member States.

[309] The legality of compulsory retirement is raised in the following cases pending at the Court of Justice: Case C–87/06 *Vincente Pascual García v Confederación Hidrográfica del Duero* 14 February 2006, [2006] OJ C 121/2; Case C–411/05 *Félix Palacios de la Villa v Cortefiel Servicios SA, José María Sanz Corral and Martin Tebar Less*, 22 November 2005, [2006] OJ C 36/20.

[310] BAG, 21 April 1977 BAGE 29, at 133.

[311] Section 1. Decision of 26 November 2003, PK 616/02, Pr. Pracy 2004/6/34. See further, M. Zysk, "Age Discrimination Law in a Country with a Communist History: the Example of Poland" (2006) 12 *ELJ* 371, 387.

G. Feldhune, "Report on measures to combat   **2.LV.58.**
discrimination: Directive 2000/43/EC and 2000/78/EC.
Country report Latvia"[312]

"1) in the 20.05.2003 decision in the case No. 2002-21-01, available electronically at http://www.satv.tiesa.gov.lv/Eng/Spriedumi/21-01(02).htm

The provisions of the law setting the age-limit of 65 for occupying the post of university professor or associated professor, as well as highest administrative positions in universities and scientific institutions was invalidated as discriminatory. The challenge was based on non-discrimination article and article on right to work (Art. 106 'Everyone has the right to freely choose their employment and workplace according to their abilities and qualifications'); the main arguments were that to limit the right to work based on age, not abilities or qualifications, as provided for by Art. 106, is contrary to this article, and that the process of assessing of abilities should be individualized, not using the age as proxy. The Constitutional Court held that the restrictions were not proportionate, as the evidence showed they were not suitable for attaining the aim sought, namely, failed to attract young people to the academia. Since the Constitutional Court held that the restrictions violated the right to work and thus were invalid, it did not consider whether they were also discriminatory.

2) in the 18.12.2003 decision in the case No. 2003-12-01, available electronically at http://www.satv.tiesa.gov.lv/Eng/Spriedumi/12-01(03).htm

The provision of State Civil Service Law providing that upon reaching the pensioning age the person has to retire from the civil service unless the superior decides otherwise was upheld. The challenge concerned right to work (Art. 106), right to hold a position in civil service (Art. 101) and right not to be discriminated against (Art. 91). The main argument related to discrimination was that persons of comparable qualifications are treated differently based on whether they have reached pensioning age, and also that gender-based discrimination had taken place, as pensioning age still differs for men and women. The Constitutional Court held that the regulation of civil service relationships may differ from that of employment relationships and that restrictions were proportionate, keeping in mind the necessity to ensure good administration and the interest of the society in ensuring that the corps of civil servants does not age and the age equilibrium in it is maintained. One of the arguments of the court was that it is also the question of employment policy and that by restricting the right to work of persons who have other source of income—namely, the pension—the possibilities to work of persons who can only earn their living by work are broadened. The court also took into account the empirical evidence that showed that only about 1/7 of the persons concerned by the norm where actually dismissed from the service, while the other 5/6 continued to work."

Notes

(1) In 2005, the Belgian Court of Arbitration held unlawful a provision of a Flemish law setting a maximum age limit of 75 for members of Church Councils.[313]

---

[312] (European Commission, 2005) 4, available on the website of Directorate-General for Employment, Social Affairs and Equal Opportunities.

[313] *A. Geensens and others* v. *Flemish Region*, no. 152/2005, Court of Arbitration, 5 October 2005.

(2) The British Employment Equality (Age) Regulations 2006 permit employers to dismiss employees at the age of 65.[314] For such a dismissal to be lawful, various procedural steps must first be completed.[315] In particular, employees must be informed of the intended date for retirement and given an opportunity to request to continue working beyond this date. The employer has a duty to consider this request, but ultimately it can be refused.

2.7. COMPARATIVE ANALYSIS

Taking an overview, a number of concluding observations can be made. First, it is evident that direct discrimination as a distinct dimension to the broader concept of "discrimination" is recognised in the national legislation of most European states. A significant influence in stimulating this recognition has been the EC anti-discrimination Directives. The Directives adopted since 2000 have provoked most states to include a specific definition of direct discrimination within national legislation. Whilst this is evidence of convergence across European laws on discrimination, specific national traits remain visible. The UK model, with its strong emphasis on the preliminary task of finding an appropriate comparator, is not reflected in other Member States. For many, the new legislative definitions of direct discrimination remain untested before national courts. This means that, in practice, approaches to direct discrimination might continue to vary considerably. Key issues within the concept of direct discrimination, such as the relevance or irrelevance of motive, substantially depend on the stance that will be adopted by national courts, as well as their desire to engage with the ECJ in resolving such ambiguities.

Over time, it is crucial to maintain the vitality of direct discrimination as an utilisable protection. It is reasonable to assume that rational actors will seek to conceal evidence of direct discrimination; therefore, the most overt and straightforward cases will diminish as the legal obligations become embedded. This gives rise to the next challenge, which is to recognise that direct discrimination extends beyond obvious and intentional examples of prejudice. In particular, direct discrimination is instrumental in tackling entrenched stereotypes which may simply be taken for granted as conventional "truths". For example, in the Prague Airport case,[316] the English Court of Appeal adopted the stance that it was self-evident that Czech Roma should be less trusted by immigration officials than non-Roma. In a telling example, Lord Justice Simon Brown argued

---

[314] Reg. 30. An employer could dismiss an employee at a younger age if this can be objectively justified direct discrimination.

[315] Reg. 47 (Sch. 6).

[316] *R (European Roma Rights Centre)* v. *Immigration Officer at Prague Airport and another* [2005] 2 AC 1 HL.

"If a terrorist outrage were committed on our streets today, would the police not be entitled to question more suspiciously those in the vicinity appearing to come from an Islamic background?"[317]

This approach, which treats direct discrimination as almost "natural", conflicts with one of the underlying aims of formal equality, which is to ensure that individuals are not treated differently solely by virtue of their sex, race, religion, etc.

Tackling deep-seated practices, such as stereotypes, has proven difficult, not least because of problems of proof. European legal systems have been gradually turning towards modifications in the burden of proof as a means to facilitate discrimination litigation, including in relation to direct discrimination. Such measures hold considerable promise, but in most states there is only limited judicial experience in applying these rules. Many questions remain surrounding the mechanics of shifting the burden of proof in individual cases. For example, the point at which there is sufficient evidence to trigger a shift in the burden of proof from the complainant to the respondent remains contested. The use of statistics or situation testing represent interesting mechanisms both to trigger a shift in the burden of proof and also to link individual direct discrimination cases to broader patterns of inequality. Such tools illustrate the potential to move direct discrimination beyond a narrow concern for formal equality between individuals and instead to connect this with the pursuit of substantive equality.

Contemporary trends in anti-discrimination law pose certain challenges for the concept of direct discrimination. These arise both from the extension in the list of prohibited grounds and from the extension in the material scope of anti-discrimination legislation. Earlier legislation that was tailored to sex and race discrimination, mainly in employment, was more amenable to the exhaustive listing of specific exceptions. This underpins those systems where direct discrimination is not open to justification. As the grounds and scope of anti-discrimination law expand, the inability to justify direct discrimination comes under more pressure. On the one hand, some grounds are more recent incorporations and states have been reluctant to restrict flexibility; this is evident in relation to age. On the other, conflicts between grounds produce dilemmas for anti-discrimination law, such as the balancing of claims based on sexual orientation and religion. More generally, the expanded reach of the right to non-discrimination brushes up against other fundamental rights and freedoms, such as freedom of association. Whilst some Member States, such as the UK and the Netherlands, possess a considerable body of case-law that explores some of these tensions, for many European states this remains relatively new terrain. Given the overarching influence of the EC Directives, as well as the European Convention of Human Rights, an active cross-border judicial dialogue will be a vital element in adapting direct discrimination to the changed legal context.

---

[317] Para. 88, *R (European Roma Rights Centre)* v. *Immigration Officer at Prague Airport and another* [2003] 4 All E.R. 247 CA.

CHAPTER THREE
INDIRECT DISCRIMINATION

Prof. Dagmar Schiek

3.1. INTRODUCTION

Most non-discrimination law regimes are not confined to a mere prohibition of direct discrimination, but include a prohibition of indirect discrimination as well. Indirect discrimination is defined differently in different jurisdictions and at different times. The definition in the EC Racial Equality Directive may serve as an example:

> "Indirect discrimination shall be taken to occur where an apparently neutral provision, criterion or practice would put persons of a racial or ethnic origin at a particular disadvantage compared with other persons, unless that provision, criterion or practice is objectively justified by a legitimate aim and the means of achieving that aim are appropriate and necessary."[1]

In a nutshell, the concept of indirect discrimination law says that discrimination on any of the "discrimination grounds"[2] may be present in a rule or practice which does not even mention the ground in question, but which has a detrimental effect on persons meant to be protected against discrimination. An early example of detrimental effect on grounds of race in the US was the requirement of a high-school diploma even for unskilled jobs where literacy was barely a necessity, which practically excluded most black applicants.[3] In European Community law, frequent examples include neglecting any seniority gained while working in other Member States as a form of indirect discrimination on grounds of nationality[4] and denying part-time employees equal employment opportunities as a form of discrimination on grounds of sex.[5] However, detrimental effect on its own does not constitute indirect discrimination. If the rule or practice serves a legitimate aim unconnected with prohibited discrimination and does not go over and above what is necessary to achieve that aim, the detrimental effect is "objectively justified", and the rule may be applied.

In common with non-discrimination law in general, the notion of indirect discrimination is coloured by international and EU law obligations, which makes restricting

---

[1] Directive 2000/43/EC of 29 June 2000 implementing the principle of equal treatment between persons irrespective of racial or ethnic origin [2000] OJ L180/22, Art. 2 para. 2.

[2] See J. Gerards, Chapter One: Discrimination Grounds, section 1.3.1.

[3] US Supreme Court, Judgment of 8 March 1971, *Griggs* v. *Duke Power Co* 401 US 424 (1971); see below **3.US.13.**

[4] ECJ, Judgment of 15 January 1998, C–15/96 *Schöning-Kougebetopoulou v. Freie und Hansestadt Hamburg* [1998] ECR I–47; ECJ, Judgment of 30 November 2000, C–195/98 *Österreichischer Gewerkschaftsbund* [2000] ECR I–10497.

[5] ECJ, Judgment of 13 May 1986, 170/84 *Bilka—Kaufhaus GmbH v. Karin Weber von Hartz* [1986] ECR 1607; see below **3.EC.16.**

its study to the comparison of national jurisdictions impossible. Some national jurisdictions only introduced the notion when implementing EU law, while others were familiar with the concept before it was applied by the European Court of Justice (ECJ) or found its way into the EU statute book. The ECJ and national courts, while applying the concept, amalgamated notions and judicial techniques stemming from diverse legal cultures, the result being a new and specifically European legal instrument. To a certain extent, all this is true for most legal concepts that have become part of the EU legal order.[6]

Still, the prohibition of indirect discrimination is a special case. Although its earliest roots are to be found in public international law from the pre-UN era, its more developed forms have a clear and decisive national origin in US case-law and UK and Irish legislation and case-law. Accordingly, the concept is one of the rare cases of a legal transplant from the Anglo-American legal order into Continental legal orders. This has not been without its problems, resulting in a very mixed reception of the concept in different legal orders. In addition to its being structurally alien to Continental legal orders, difficulties associated with implementing indirect discrimination law result from the different, at times even contradictory, rationales and conceptions on which this body of law is premised.

The consequence for this chapter is that we will start with a section on rationales and conceptual issues (section 3.2), continue by recounting the emergence of the legal concept of indirect discrimination (section 3.3) and then explain some problems related to a comparative approach (section 3.4), before starting the actual comparison (section 3.5). In the closing section (section 3.6) we will attempt to outline the most important issues when developing the concept within a framework of a multi-ground non-discrimination law.

3.2. RATIONALES AND CONCEPTIONS OF INDIRECT DISCRIMINATION LAW

3.2.1. RATIONALES

Why would a legislator introduce a concept as complicated as indirect discrimination? There are basically two rationales: one, to prevent circumvention of one or several specific prohibitions to discriminate; and two, to aid the attainment of the wider goals of discrimination law in social reality.

---

[6] See generally K. Lenaerts, "Interlocking Legal Orders in the European Union and Comparative Law" (2003) 52 *International & Comparative Law Quarterly* 873–906.

3.2.1.A.   PREVENTING CIRCUMVENTION OF PROHIBITION

This first rationale is vital for any legal regime which prohibits discrimination for a closed list of grounds.[7] For example, if a distinction based on language differences will produce nearly the same effects as a distinction based on ethnic origin, circumventing a prohibition to discriminate on grounds of ethnic origin will be ridiculously easy. To avoid such circumvention, effects of a rule or practice instead of its motives are considered, rendering purpose to discriminate entirely irrelevant.

This legislative technique is not unique to non-discrimination law. Rather, we can find it in any field of law that attains to structure socio-economic reality. For example, in competition law, the prohibition of cartels captures any agreement which has the purpose or effect of distorting competition (e.g. Article 81 EC).[8] Similarly, the prohibition on restricting imports (Article 28 EC) is not limited to purposive restrictions, but also applies to indistinctly applicable measures not intended to have any effect on intra-Community trade, though still liable to restrict imports.[9] These prohibitions are as effects orientated as any prohibition of indirect discrimination.

We also find other similarities. Effects-orientated rules will apply to any innocent behaviour that results in the same impact as the intentional behaviour at which the rule is actually aimed. For example, a prohibition of cartels effectively distorting competition will also apply to a decision adopted by the Dutch bar to prohibit partnerships between solicitors and chartered accountants for the purpose of avoiding conflict of interests and unprofessional conduct.[10] A prohibition of any rule having an effect equivalent to a quantitative restriction despite being indistinctively applicable will capture any rule establishing safety measures for working equipment as such rules are bound to be different in different Member States and thus will have negative effects on imports from other Member States.[11] In relation to non-discrimination law, a requirement for an air pilot to have the relevant licence in order to assure the safety of equipment and passengers will exclude a disproportionate number of women, as most airlines denied training opportunities to women in the past. Still the requirement might be viewed as decisive for passenger safety.

---

[7] See ch. 1, section 1.3.1, using the term "limited number of grounds" versus "open-ended lists of grounds". EC law is generally based on closed lists of grounds; see Directives 2000/43/EC, 2000/78/EC and 76/207/EEC (amended by Directive 2002/73 and to be replaced by Directive 2006/54/EC by August 2008).

[8] It is worth noting that the equivalent provision of the ECSC Treaty (Art. 65) actually required agreements "tending directly or indirectly" to the prevention, restriction or distortion of competition; see D.G. Goyder, *EC Competition Law*, 4th edn (Oxford, Oxford University Press, 2003) 96. See *ibid.* for the case-law constructing the meaning of effect.

[9] The basis of this doctrine is the case-law of the European Court of Justice, starting with the "*Cassis*" case (ECJ, Judgment of 20 February 1979, Case 120/78 *Rewe-Zentrale AG* v. *Bundesmonopolverwaltung für Branntwein* [1979] ECR 649). On the relation between non-discrimination principles in social and economic law, see P. Norberg, "Non-discrimination as a Social and a Free Market Value" in A. Numhauser-Henning (ed.), *Legal Perspectives on Equal Treatment and Non-Discrimination* (Alphen a/d Rijn, Kluwer Law International, 2001) 65–90. This author considers the prohibition of indistinctly applicable measures of equivalent effect as a prohibition of indirect discrimination (*ibid.*, 72–4).

[10] ECJ, Judgment of 19 February 2002, C–309/99 *J.C.J. Wouters, J.W. Savelbergh, Price Waterhouse Belastingadviseurs BV* [2002] ECR I–1577.

[11] ECJ, Judgment of 28 January 1986, Case 188/84 *Commission* v. *France* [1986] ECR 419.

Outlawing all of these measures is a very effective means of avoiding circum-vention of the prohibition of cartels, restrictions of imports or discrimination, but might go beyond what is necessary to achieve that aim. Accordingly, justification is an important element.[12] Eventually, doctrine chooses terminology other than justifi-cation. For example, in competition law, reducing the scope of application of Article 81 resulted in the invention of the concept of ancillary restraints and more recently the as yet uncategorised "*Wouters*-approach".[13] But the basic scheme remains: if one chooses to catch effects of human action that may well be aimed at totally different issues under the notion of discrimination, such as distortion of competition or restriction of intra-Community trade, there needs to be some opportunity to balance the real purpose of the measure with the purposes of non-discrimination law, competition law or free movement of goods law. Thus, there is the possibility of justifying measures resulting in discrimination, restriction of competition or restriction of intra-Community trade by reference to a purpose unconnected to the former, and by demonstrating that the measure in question is indeed indispensable to achieving its aim. The possibility of justification is, however, denied for measures that have the purpose to discriminate, distort competition or restrict intra-Community trade.

It should be noted that prohibiting indirect discrimination becomes superfluous from this perspective if discrimination is prohibited not only in relation to specific grounds, but generally (open-list technique[14]). In the latter case, any differentiation on any ground requires justification irrespective of whether the discrimination is direct

---

[12] See the extensive report on examples for justifying indistinctly applicable measures of equivalent effect given by S. Weatherill, *Cases and Materials on EU Law*, 7th edn (Oxford, Oxford University Press, 2006) 405–14.

[13] See Goyder, above n. 8, 100–2, for ancillary restraints. The ECJ's *Wouters* decision, cited above at n. 10, is difficult to categorise within the categories hitherto accepted in EC competition law. The Court, although a prohibition for solicitors to enter into partnerships with registered accountants restricts competition while preventing the "production" of combined services of chartered accountants and solicitors, held that it did not violate Art. 81, as not all agreements restricting the freedom to act for market participants were anti-competitive (No. 97). Rather, to assess anti-competitiveness, recourse must be had to the circumstances of an agreement or decision, and in particular its objectives (No. 97). Having found that these objectives include preserving the professional conduct of solicitors and chartered accountants alike (Nos. 107–8), the Court decreed that the decision does not go over and above what is necessary and is thus not a restriction of competition (No. 109). Some authors appreciate this reasoning and categorise it as introducing into European competition law a "European rule of reason" (G. Monti "Article 81 EC and Public Policy" (2002) 39 *CMLRev* 1057, 1086–90) or the mandatory requirement exception developed in the Court's case-law on the fundamental freedoms (A. Momninos "Non-competition Concerns: Resolution of Conflicts in the Integrated Article 81 EC", The University of Oxford Centre for Competition Law and Policy, Working Paper (L) 08/05, 11–12) or to widen the category of ancillary restraints to include "regulatory ancillarity" (R. Whish, *Competition Law*, 5th edn (London, Butterworths, 2003), 121–2; others urge the Court not to continue this line of reasoning (E. Loozen "Professional Ethics and Restraints of Competition" (2006) 31 (1) *ELRev* 28). In any case, it is possibly too early to see whether *Wouters* is "an exotic curiosity without lineal descendants" or "a moment in which a new a fresh slope of history begins" (I. Forrester "Where Law Meets Competition: Is Wouters Like a Cassis de Dijon or like a platypus?" in C. Ehlermann and I. Atanasiu (eds.), *European Competition Law Annual 2004: The Relationship between Competition Law and the Liberal Professions* (Oxford, Hart Publishing, 2006) 271–94).

[14] On different techniques for structuring discrimination law, see above, J. Gerards, Chapter One, section 3.1. On the irrelevance of an indirect discrimination in this context, see generally J. Gerards, *Judicial Review in Equal Treatment Cases* (Leiden, Martinus Nijhoff, 2005) 13.

or indirect. As such, a ban on discrimination in the "open-list technique" tends to lean towards accepting justification of any discrimination. This is explained by the fact that the prohibition would be too wide-reaching without this possibility. For example, a prohibition to discriminate on any grounds would ban any distinction between children born to married and to unmarried mothers (see below, **3.UN.5.**). As there may be good reasons for such differentiation, a justification will be accepted. In contrast, a legal norm which only bans discrimination on a limited number of grounds will remain operable, even if justifications are not generally permitted. The existence of an "objective justification" can then remain specific to the prohibition of indirect discrimination.

3.2.1.B.   SOCIAL ENGINEERING

The second rationale for prohibiting indirect discrimination may be referred to as a *social engineering perspective*. As an overall perspective on discrimination law, the *social engineering perspective* proceeds beyond a merely *formal* conception of law, but rather aims at *substantively* moulding societal relations differently from how they would have developed spontaneously. "Social engineering" denotes that non-discrimination law is meant to change society, and to overcome discrimination in socio-economic reality. Of course, "social engineering" by legal provisions and/or case-law is never straightforward, a well-known fact in legal sociology. However, the general idea behind a body of law such as discrimination law is that legal norms will have some effect on social reality. This overall aim is also relevant as a rationale for indirect discrimination law.

Relying on this rationale, one may stress that indirect discrimination law "takes as a starting-point a belief that economic power . . . should in an ideal world be equally redistributed between different relevant groups".[15] If we assume that discrimination can be perceived as being entrenched in social institutions, it follows that it is important to expose discriminatory structures. Accordingly, the prohibition of indirect discrimination starts from the assumption that—given the social division along the dividing lines defined by grounds of discrimination—any structural detriment for those protected against discrimination ensuing from facially neutral distinctions is usually not coincidental, but a result of this social division. Therefore, any such rule or practice is to be subjected to scrutiny by courts.

However, not each and every practice resulting in disadvantage is outlawed by indirect discrimination law even under the social engineering perspective. While there is an assumption that increased disadvantage is caused by structural discrimination in general, a single (economic) actor may rebut the assumption that the specific requirements or general practices she applies are really the cause of the increase in question. Under the social engineering perspective, the possibility to justify

---

[15] R. Townshend-Smith, "Justifying indirect Discrimination in English and American Law: How Stringent should the Test Be?" (1995) 1 *IJDL* 103, 105.

detrimental effects serves to refute the general assumption of a causal link between disadvantage and discrimination ground.

Above all, the social engineering perspective as a rationale for indirect discrimination law requires linking socio-economic reality and the law. Establishing this link is not easy, and is tied to the conceptual issues connected to indirect discrimination law.

3.2.2.   CONCEPTUAL ISSUES

3.2.2.A.   FORM AND SUBSTANCE

A prohibition of indirect discrimination law is sometimes related to the aim of substantive equality, while a prohibition of direct discrimination is equated with aiming at formal equality.[16] This oppositional approach is not quite appropriate.[17] Certainly a prohibition of indirect discrimination goes beyond a merely formal approach to law, as its application depends on effects of differentiation in socio-economic reality. However, recognising direct discrimination may also require acknowledging social reality in practice. The first decision of the Spanish Constitutional Court on equal pay irrespective of gender, which is also its first decision expressly acknowledging indirect discrimination, illustrates the fact that substantive equality will embrace indirect discrimination law, but is not exclusive to this field.

El Tribunal Constitucional (Spanish Constitutional Court),   **3.ES.1.**
1 July 1991
Case 145/91, Pilar Rodriguez de la Fuente and 138 others v. *City of Madrid*

DISCRIMINATION BY ASSIGNING EMPLOYEES TO DIFFERENT EMPLOYMENT
CATEGORIES PER GENDER

Hospital cleaners

Facts: One hundred and thirty-eight women employed as cleaners in a Madrid hospital challenged their wage, as they were remunerated in accordance with the category of "cleaners" in the relevant collective agreement, while men, also engaged in cleaning in the hospital, received higher wages because they were categorised as "manual workers" under the same collective agreement, being described as "unskilled workers, offering their physical strength and providing non-specialised work".

Held: The Court of First Instance found that women were doing the same work as the men, but received lower salaries; thus this was a case of sex discrimination. The Court of Second Instance considered that the difference in pay was justified by categorising the jobs differently, and disregarded the fact that women actually did the same work as men. The Constitutional Court reversed the judgment of the second instance, as the difference between the workers clearly resulted from sex.

[16] See, e.g. E. Ellis, *EU—Anti-discrimination Law* (Oxford, Oxford University Press, 2005) 87–8.
[17] See further above M. Bell, Chapter Two: Direct Discrimination, section 2.3.2.A.

Judgment: "The relevance of Article 14 C.E. (Spanish Constitution) is not only that it establishes the general principle of equality, but it also pursues the prohibition of specific, historically deeply entrenched distinctions, which have resulted in positioning large sectors of the populace in a social position which is not only disadvantageous but also openly contravenes human dignity as recognised by Article 10 C.E., and this positioning is as much due to actions by public bodies as to social practices.

This affirmation . . . which in some cases has allowed to consider some legislative measures in favour of these traditionally disadvantaged groups as compatible with article 14 C.E., also has important effects when deciding whether a difference disadvantaging those groups is compatible with Article 14 C.E. or not.

The constitutional prohibition of discrimination on grounds of personal characteristics is also linked to a substantive notion of equality. This is especially so in relation to sex, which functions as a signifier of women belonging to a social group that is historically subjected to social, economic and legal devaluation. This makes it possible to expand and enrich the notion of discrimination itself, to include not only the notion of direct discrimination, in other words, a detrimental differentiated treatment on grounds of gender where this is a matter of direct consideration, but also the notion of indirect discrimination, which includes formally non-discriminatory treatments which, for reasons of factual differences arising between workers of different genders, result in detrimental, unequal consequences because of the differentiated and unfavourable impact which formally equal treatments or reasonably unequal treatments have on workers of one gender or another as a result of such difference . . ."

Note: substantive equality and indirect discrimination law

(1) Although the Constitutional Court was actually aware that this was not a case of indirect discrimination and decided accordingly, it also issued some fundamental statements in relation to the concept of discrimination under Spanish Constitutional law at large, including a notion of indirect discrimination.

(2) In particular, it mentions the notion of substantive equality in relation to indirect discrimination, but does not actually say that indirect discrimination is the only form of discrimination which is linked to substantive equality. It rather expresses the view that a notion of substantive equality also requires one to acknowledge indirect discrimination.

Other examples where direct discrimination cases involve acknowledging substantive equality include the pregnancy discrimination cases, where some Advocates General before the ECJ referred to substantive equality in order to maintain that any discrimination on grounds of motherhood or pregnancy is direct discrimination on grounds of sex and as such not justifiable, although a man can never be in a situation comparable to that of a pregnant woman.[18] Substantive equality is also pursued by other concepts, such as positive action,[19] and as such is not specific to indirect discrimination law.

---

[18] See, e.g. AG Tesauro in his opinion in Case C–421/92 *Habermann-Beltermann* [1994] ECR I–1657 and AG Ruiz-Jarobo Colomer in Case C–136/95 *Caisse nationale d'assurance vieillesses de travaileurs salaries (CNAVIS)* v. *Evelyne Thibault.* [1998] ECR I–2011. For further on this, see above, M. Bell, Chapter 2: Direct Discrimination, section 2.3.1.

[19] See below, O. Schutter, Chapter Seven: Positive Action.

On the other hand, indirect discrimination law also retains formal elements, which safeguard the neutrality of the concept towards economic choices. This accounts for it being placed between the two poles of distributive and corrective justice.

3.2.2.B.   DISTRIBUTIVE AND CORRECTIVE JUSTICE

Indirect discrimination law, if based on the social engineering rationale, clearly is infected by the larger aims of distributive justice. It elevates the distribution of opportunities (e.g. positions on the employment market) or resources (e.g. credit facilities) in proportion to a group's share in the population to the yardstick of justice. However, indirect discrimination law also allows for justification of such measures or procedures that result in unequal distribution of resources or opportunities. These objective justifications are not a regrettable limitation of the concept, but rather a precondition for its application to private (economic) actors in a market economy. The foundational idea of the market economy is that private economic actors' choices are superior to public planning in achieving adequate distributions. Thus, their choices should not be bound to achieve any of the numerous aims pursued in the name of distributive justice. Accordingly, the requirements of indirect discrimination law do not constitute an "imposition of liability for criteria over the existence of which the employer has no direct control".[20] They only require the employer or any other economic actor to prove that it did not exploit the disadvantaged situation of persons who are subjected to socio-economic discrimination. In other words, indirect discrimination law makes it unlawful to profit from discriminatory structures, even if someone else has established them.

Again, we find that indirect discrimination law cannot be aligned neatly with one of the two poles of distributive or corrective justice.

3.2.2.C.   GROUPS AND INDIVIDUALS

Indirect discrimination law is also often said to correspond to a notion of group justice, as opposed to individual justice.[21] Certainly, group disadvantage is the starting point of indirect discrimination law. However, indirect discrimination law has never established group rights. The concept rather provides for remedies to individuals, who suffer from disadvantage due to their ascribed group membership, although the practice or measure in question does not explicitly refer to that group membership. In addition, just establishing group disadvantage is not enough to establish a claim for indirect discrimination. First, there must be a link between the employer's or other economic actor's practice and individual disadvantage. Secondly, the assumption of

---

[20] See M. Connolly and R. Townshend-Smith, *Discrimination Law*, 2nd edn (London, Cavendish Publishing, 2004) 240.
[21] See Connolly and Townshend-Smith, *ibid.*, 238; C. Barnard and B. Hepple, "Substantive Equality" (2000) 59 *Camb LJ* 562, 568.

the disadvantageous practice being discriminatory can be refuted by proving that it was necessary to attain one of the aims chosen by the economic actor. Accordingly, indirect discrimination law continues to guarantee individual justice, albeit in relation to disadvantage suffered for group related reasons.

This raises the question as to how far claimants in indirect discrimination cases must be required to act as group representatives rather than as individuals. Some authors demand that indirect discrimination law be based on group membership rather than on individuality. This seems to be the background to Barnard and Hepple's criticism of the EC Racial Equality Directive's definition of indirect discrimination. They state that:

> ". . . the focus of the definition in the Race Directive is on the disadvantage suffered by individuals rather than by a particular racial or ethnic group to which an individual belongs. Literally interpreted, there will be discrimination if two or more individuals 'of a racial or ethnic group' . . . suffer a particular disadvantage, even without evidence that the racial or ethnic group as such suffers from that disadvantage. This interpretation would conflate the concepts of direct and indirect discrimination."[22]

On the other hand, it is also possible to consider the group aspect of indirect discrimination law as one of its detriments. Karen Lundstrøm, for example, warns:

> "The Court's requirement of comprehensive statistical evidence means that women are deprived of their individual right to equal treatment. Every woman who considers that she is in any way being subjected to (indirect) sex discrimination must prove that not only she herself, but also a large number of other women, and considerably more women than men, have been discriminated against by formally sexually neutral regulations or practices. In this way women have been effectively changed from individuals to a collective, whereas the aim of all anti-discrimination legislation is the opposite: to change collectives into individuals."[23]

The opinion of this author is that indirect discrimination law should steer a middle course between group and individual. While no discrimination in social reality can be understood without reference to ascribed group membership, remedies against indirect discrimination should not be dependent on the applicant taking up a representative role. From this perspective, it would appear that the definition in the new equal treatment Directive[24] corresponds to the aim of indirect discrimination law to guarantee individual justice in spite of ascribed group membership, as opposed to enforcing ascribed group membership in order to establish discrimination claims.

In any case, we can again conclude that indirect discrimination law is positioned in-between group justice and individual justice.

---

[22] See Barnard and Hepple, above n. 21, 568–9.
[23] K. Lundström, "Indirect Sex Discrimination in the European Court of Justice's Version" in A. Numhauser-Henning (ed.), *Legal Perspectives on Equal Treatment and Non-discrimination* (The Hague, Kluwer, 2001) 143, 159.
[24] For the text, see the text accompanying n. 86 below; see also **3. EC.18.**

3.2.2.D.   CONCEPTUAL HYBRIDISM OF INDIRECT DISCRIMINATION LAW

All in all, indirect discrimination law is a conceptual hybrid.[25] It guarantees an individual right while acknowledging that discrimination in social reality is group related. It corresponds to the concept of corrective justice, while taking wider aims of distributive justice as standard for legally acceptable behaviour. It requires remedying a specific individual situation, which results from group-related disadvantage. Above all, indirect discrimination law is linked to substantive equality, while not providing for measures to achieve this aim.

3.2.3.   LIMITS OF INDIRECT DISCRIMINATION LAW

The conceptual hybridism of indirect discrimination law is the source of its perceived limits . Cases based on this concept have the potential to expose discriminatory structures. Hence, the prohibition of indirect discrimination has been praised as a "revolutionary novelty"[26] and applauded as having the "capacity . . . to challenge practices which serve to perpetuate the effects of past disadvantages and unequal life chances".[27] There are, however, those who seem disappointed with the results of its practical application, especially against the background of Britain, where the concept has been applied for more than 30 years.[28] Some criticise the very possibility of justifying rules that result in a detrimental effect as reducing the impact of the concept.[29] This criticism is understandable, given the hybrid character of indirect discrimination law. It requires acknowledging the effect of seemingly neutral distinctions on distribution of wealth, opportunities, etc. per alleged race, ethnic origin, gender, etc., while not burdening any economic actor with the obligation positively to balance disadvantage qua "grounds". Indirect discrimination law is restricted to a prohibition to exploit existing inequalities and to stabilise further or even increase them. Positive duties to combat structural disadvantage remain with public institutions or such social institutions that are under a specific responsibility,[30] the latter category becoming less relevant as boundaries between public and private are increasingly blurred. Thus, any disappointment is due to overburdening the

---

[25] D. Schiek, *Differenzierte Gerechtigkeit? Diskriminierungsschutz und Vertragsrecht* (Baden-Baden, Nomos, 2000) 67–70.

[26] S. Prechal, "Equality of Treatment, Non-Discrimination and Social Policy: Achievements in Three Themes" (2004) 41 *CMLRev* 533.

[27] A. McColgan, *Discrimination Law*, 2nd edn (Oxford, Hart Publishing, 2005) 73.

[28] See, e.g. S. Fredman, "The Age of Equality" in S. Fredman and S. Spencer (eds.), *Age as an Equality Issue* (Oxford, Hart Publishing, 2003) 58, stating that "existing indirect discrimination provisions in the sex and race discrimination legislation have proved difficult"; see Barnard and Hepple, above n. 21, 584, concluding that the present frameworks of EC and UK legislation "are not in themselves capable of leading to greater substantive equality".

[29] See, e.g. S. Wilborn "The Disparate Impact Model of Discrimination: Theory and Limits" (1985) 34 *American UL Review* 799, 801.

[30] On the relation of indirect discrimination and positive action, see McColgan, above n. 27, 139–42.

prohibition of indirect discrimination with the expectation of achieving all the substantive aims of discrimination law and policy at large, although indirect discrimination law is only a small part of equality law and policy in their entirety. This does not mean, however, that indirect discrimination law should not be developed to fulfil its potential in unmasking seemingly neutral policies, which are in fact emanations of structural discrimination. However, indirect discrimination law will never bring about the changes required to eliminate structural discrimination, but only allows individuals to challenge the results of such practices in limited circumstances. The Swedish writer Karen Lundstrøm has captured the potential of indirect discrimination law, referring to gender equality:

K. Lundstrøm, *"Indirect Sex Discrimination in the*   **3.SE.2.**
European Court of Justice's Vision"[31]

"Since the concept of indirect discrimination opens up the possibility to prove that apparently sexually neutral and objective requirements, conditions and regulations can, in fact, be discriminating, and are thus not sexually neutral and objective at all, it has at least the theoretical potential . . . If it can be shown that certain practices and regulations are not objective, the masculine norms on which these rest will be revealed and the norms will become open to change."

3.3. ORIGINS OF INDIRECT DISCRIMINATION LAW

While in most writings on indirect discrimination the origins in US case-law are stressed,[32] there are indeed some earlier emanations in pre-UN international law, which again lead to the assumption that the modern UN Conventions against discrimination are linked to these. We will thus start with a short account of the predecessors of the concept in public international law and the present provisions of the UN Conventions, explaining whether and how far these instruments require the introduction of an explicit prohibition of indirect discrimination as known by EC law. The next step is to relate the origins of the Community law concept in US case-law and the adoption of this concept into UK and Irish legislation. Only as a third part can we relate the development of the concept in EU non-discrimination law. Before we start presenting comparative legal material analysing the present content of the prohibition of indirect discrimination in the national legal orders of the EU Member States, we will highlight some specific limits of comparison. We will also explain our choice of key legal orders for this chapter.

---

[31] In A. Numhauser-Henning, *Legal Perspectives on Equal Treatment and Non-Discrimination* (The Hague, Kluwer International, 2001) 143, 147–8.
[32] See, e.g. Connolly and *Townshend-Smith,* above n. 20, 240; S. Fredman, *Discrimination Law* (Oxford, Oxford University Press, 2002) 106; McColgan, above n. 27, 73.

3.3.1.   INTERNATIONAL HUMAN RIGHTS LAW

3.3.1.A.   EARLIER EMANATIONS OF THE CONCEPT

The earliest traces of indirect discrimination law can be found in pre-UN international law. The *Déclaration de Droits Internationaux d'Homme* from 1929 reads in Article 5:

> "L'egalité . . . exclude toute discrimination directe ou indirecte".

However, as this document was a mere declaration, it is impossible to know what exactly was meant by "discrimination indirecte".

As regards some even older instruments, there has been some case-law that is being cited as the origin of indirect discrimination law in International Human Rights Law.[33] Most of these instruments are treaties aimed at protecting national minorities. For example, the *Treaty on the Protection of Polish Minorities of 1919*, signed together with the Treaty of Versailles, provided in its Article 8:

> "Polish nationals who belong to national, religious or linguistic minorities shall enjoy the same treatment and security in law and in fact as the other Polish nationals."

Permanent International Court of Justice, 10 September 1923[34]   **3.UN.3.**
Poland

WHETHER EVACUATION ORDER VIOLATES THE TREATY ON PROTECTION FOR
POLISH MINORITIES

German settlers in Poland

Facts: The Permanent International Court of Justice had to give an opinion on a piece of legislation concerning the ownership of land formerly owned by the German Crown or any other emanation of the German Reich and which was allocated to Poland in the Treaty of Versailles. The second article of this act deemed any transfer from the German crown or other emanation of the Reich after November 11, 1918 invalid, and the land would fall back to Poland. Article 5 empowered the treasury to oust the occupants of any land who relied on any such transfer. A group of settlers of German origin, who had acquired Polish citizenship after 1919, occupied their holdings under "Rentengutsverträge", which had been concluded with the German authorities and not been correctly notified in the land registry by an "Auflassung" before the land was allocated to Poland. Some settlers had leased land from the German authorities and were using that land in accordance with the lease.

While in a few instances working to the detriment of Polish citizens who do not belong to a national and/or linguistic minority, the act mainly works to the disadvantage of citizens belonging to the German minority. It is thus discrimination in fact and contrary to Article 8 of the Treaty on the protection of Polish minorities.

---

[33] D. Schindler, *Gleichberechtigung von Individuen als Problem des Völkerrechts* (Zürich, Polygraph, 1957) 143–5.

[34] [1923] PCJI 3. The main relevance of this case in international law is not the indirect discrimination issue, but rather the question of sovereignty of (rather young) states under the regime of early emanations of human rights law (see F. Morrison, "Between a Rock and a Hard Place: Sovereignty and International Protection" (2005) 80 *Chicago-Kent Law Review* 31, 35–7.

Held: The court, in its advisory opinion applied for by Poland, mainly considered whether the League of Nations has any competence at all in this matter. Only a minor part of the judgment is dedicated to equal protection. In this regard, the Court held that applying the legislation as Poland did at the time amount to racial discrimination contrary to the above provision, although there was no direct discrimination.

Judgment: "While under the terms of the Minorities Treaty it necessarily rests with the Council in the first instance to determine whether an infraction or danger of infraction exists, the Court is of opinion that upon the facts before it the existence of such a condition clearly appears.

As has been seen, Article 7 of the treaty provides that all Polish nationals shall be equal before the law and shall enjoy the same civil and political rights without distinction as to race, language or religion. The expression "civil rights" in the Treaty must include rights acquired under a contract for the possession or use of property, whether such property be immoveable or moveable.

Article 8 of the Treaty guarantees to racial minorities the same treatment and security "in law and in fact" as to other Polish nationals. The fact that no racial discrimination appears in the text of the law of July 14th, 1920, and that in a few instances the law applies to non-German Polish nationals who took, as purchasers from original holders of German race, make no substantial difference. Article 8 is designed to meet precisely such complaints as are made in the present case. There must be equality in fact as well as ostensible legal equality in the sense of the absence of discrimination in the words of the law.

Although the law does not expressly declare that persons who are to be ousted from the lands are persons of the German race, the inference that they are so is to be drawn even from the terms of the law. This is also clearly established by the proofs before the Court."

Notes

(1) As has been said, this case is considered—along with similar rulings in relation to international treaties on minority protection such as "Polish minorities in Danzig"[35] and "Minority Schools in Albany"[36]—as an early emanation of indirect discrimination law. However, the Permanent International Court of Justice does not apply anything close to the complicated EC law definition cited above. The judges rather reason on the basis whether equal treatment in fact (as opposed to equal treatment in law) is effectively guaranteed.[37]

(2) While the distinction between equality in fact and equality in law is different from the distinction between direct and indirect discrimination, there are also links between the two. As has been mentioned, a prohibition of indirect discrimination inter alia takes the degree to which equality in fact has been achieved as a point of reference for a presumption of unlawful discrimination. The statistical data to be established under such prohibition may often contribute towards recognising which practices will result in factual inequality. However, the prohibition of indirect discrimination does not establish a positive duty to strive towards equality in fact, as it allows justification and thus the weighing of equality in law against equality in fact. Thus, equality in fact is not the same as indirect discrimination. From a modern perspective

---

[35] PCIJ, Case *Polish Nationals in Danzig*, Advisory Opinion of 4 February 1932 [1932] PCIJ 1.
[36] PCIJ, Case *Minority Schools in Albania*, Advisory Opinion of 6 April 1935 [1935] PCIJ 1.
[37] See Schindler, above n. 33, 142, where Schindler equates the prohibition of indirect discrimination with ensuring equality in fact, while he considers that the prohibition of direct discrimination amounts to ensuring equality in law.

on discrimination law, these early judgments are still enlightening, as they demonstrate that both are conceptually connected.

3.3.1.B.   MODERN INTERNATIONAL LAW AND INDIRECT DISCRIMINATION—UNITED NATIONS

As regards modern public international law, the concept of equality and non-discrimination is central to many of its provisions. It is useful to distinguish between general human rights instruments and such instruments that are explicitly aimed at combating discrimination, though.

GENERAL HUMAN RIGHTS PACTS

The grand conventions implementing the UN Declaration of Human Rights, the International Covenant on Civil and Political Rights (ICCPR) and International Covenant on Economic, Social and Cultural Rights (ICESCR), stress the relevance of non-discrimination as principles. The ICCPR states in Article 2 that human rights must be respected and ensured "without distinction of any kind, such as race, colour, sex, language, religion, political or other opinion, national or social origin, property, birth or other status". Similarly, the ICESCR obliges the signatory states to guarantee that the rights ensured by it are "exercised without discrimination of any kind as to race, colour, sex, language, religion, political or other opinion, national or social origin, property, birth or other status". The ICCPR also contains a specific equality clause. None of these general acts contain a definition of discrimination. Nonetheless, the concept of indirect discrimination has been referred to in international human rights case-law.

International Covenant on Civil and Political Rights (UN)   **3.UN.4.**

Article 26
All persons are equal before the law and are entitled without any discrimination to the equal protection of the law. In this respect, the law shall prohibit any discrimination and guarantee to all persons equal and effective protection against discrimination on any ground such as race, colour, sex, language, religion, political or other opinion, national or social origin, property, birth or other status.

Note
Application of the ICCRP is supervised by the Human Rights Committee (HRC), which delivers communications inter alia. The HRC does not consider Article 26 as absolute prohibition to discriminate, but accepts justifications of any form of discrimination. It has also acknowledged the concept of indirect discrimination in

relation to Article 26, although the Article as such does not differentiate between direct and indirect discrimination.

UN Human Rights Committee, 8 August 2003[38]   **3.UN.5.**
Communication No. 998/2001, Althammer v. Austria

INDIRECT DISCRIMINATION AGAINST PENSIONERS

Althammer

Facts: Mr. Althammer *et al.* are pensioners who worked for the Salzburg Social Insurance Board. Pensioners and active employees used to receive a household allowance of 220 ATS, and 260 ATS children benefit for each child up to age 27. In 1996, the household allowance was abolished and the children benefit raised to 380 ATS per child up to age 27. Althammer *et al.* considered this discriminatory, as most pensioners would not profit from the children benefit, although most of them had a spouse who had to be maintained.

Held: There is no discrimination contrary to Article 26 ICCRP.

Judgment: "10.2 . . . The Committee recalls that a violation of Article 26 can also result from the discriminatory effect of a rule or measure that is neutral at face value or without intent to discriminate . . . However, such indirect discrimination can only be said to be based on the grounds enumerated in Article 26 of the Covenant if the detrimental effects of a rule or decision exclusively or disproportionately affect persons having a particular race, colour, sex, language, religion, political or other opinion, national or social origin, property, birth or other status. Furthermore, rules or decisions with such an impact do not amount to discrimination if they are based on objective and reasonable grounds. In the circumstances of the instant case, the abolition of monthly household payments combined with an increase of children's benefits is not only detrimental for retirees but also for active employees not (yet or no longer) having children in the relevant age bracket, and the authors have not shown that the impact of this measure on them was disproportionate. Even assuming, . . ., that such impact could be shown, the Committee considers that the measure . . . was based on objective and reasonable grounds. For these reasons, the Committee concludes that, in the circumstances of the instant case, the abolition of monthly household payments . . . does not amount to discrimination as prohibited in Article 26 of the Covenant."

Notes

(1) As we have seen, an open-ended list of grounds is not conducive for a prohibition of indirect discrimination. However, the list of grounds in Article 26 ICCRP leads to the enumerated grounds being taken more seriously. In its general comments No. 18, the HRC specified that ". . . .different treatment based on one of the specific grounds enumerated in Article 26 . . . places a heavy burden on the State Party to explain the reason for the differentiation".[39]

---

[38] Available on the website of the United Nations.

[39] Office of the High Commissioner for Human Rights, General Comment 18, Non-discrimination, 10 November 1989, ICCRP General Comment No. 18, UN GAOR, Human Rights Committee, 37th session, UN Doc. HRI/GEN/1/Rev. 1, para. 6 available on the website of the Office of the United Nations High Commissioner for Human Rights.

(2) From *Althammer* one might well be led to conclude that indirect discrimination under Article 26 ICCRP is only actionable if a neutrally worded rule impacts negatively on a group circumscribed by one of the grounds explicitly mentioned in Article 26 ICCRP.

(3) The further application of the definition of indirect discrimination, which the HRC developed in *Althammer*, is, however, slightly contradictory. In line with its *Althammer* definition, the HRC has refuted the notion of indirect discrimination in relation to distinctions between owners of plots designated as "building land" and "rural land".[40] However, in contrast to its *Althammer* definition, the HRC has held that a rule distinguishing between children born out of wedlock before 1 July 1996 and after that date amounts to indirect discrimination as it is not based on reasonable criteria.[41] In this case, the reference to indirect discrimination seemed irritating. Children born out of wedlock before a certain date are certainly not sharing a status equivalent to those enumerated in Article 26 ICCRP. The HRC is rather criticising an arbitrary distinction. It could have done so under its general formula for Article 26 ICCRP, which does not distinguish between direct and indirect discrimination. This case also demonstrates that this lack of clarity harbours the danger of introducing a general justification for any form of discrimination, be it direct or indirect.

SPECIFIC UN NON-DISCRIMINATION CONVENTIONS

In contrast to the general human rights instruments, specific non-discrimination pacts of the UN, the International Convention on the Elimination of All Forms of Racial Discrimination (ICERD, 1965) and the Convention on the Elimination of All Forms of Discrimination against Women (CEDAW, 1979) aim at combating discrimination in relation to one or a cluster of grounds. These pacts do define discrimination.

International Convention on the Elimination of   **3.UN.6.**
All Forms of Racial Discrimination adopted and opened for signature
and ratification by General Assembly resolution 2106 (XX) of 21 December 1965

Article 1
In this Convention, the term 'racial discrimination' shall mean any distinction, exclusion, restriction or preference based on race, colour, descent, or national or ethnic origin which has the purpose or effect of nullifying or impairing the recognition, enjoyment or exercise, on an equal footing, of rights and fundamental freedoms in the political, economic, social, cultural or any other field of public life.

---

[40] Communication No. 1106/2003 (*Godfried et al.* v. *Austria*).
[41] August 2004, *Derksen* v. *The Netherlands*, Communication No. 976/2001, UN Doc. ICCRP/C/80/D/976/2001 (2004), available on the website of the Office of the United Nations High Commissioner for Human Rights.

Convention on the Elimination of All Forms of Discrimination   **3.UN.7.**
against Women adopted and opened for signature, ratification and accession by
General Assembly resolution 34/180 of 18 December 1979

Article 1:
For the purposes of the present Convention, the term 'discrimination against women' shall mean any distinction, exclusion or restriction made on the basis of sex which has the effect or purpose of impairing or nullifying the recognition, enjoyment or exercise by women, irrespective of their marital status, on a basis of equality of men and women, of human rights and fundamental freedoms in the political, economic, social, cultural, civil or any other field.

Note
We find a regulatory technique that we associated with competition law earlier on. The Convention prohibits certain behaviour whether it has the purpose or effect of achieving a certain aim. Here, the purpose or effect refers to the recognition, enjoyment or exercise of rights and freedoms, not to the act of discrimination as such. As regards discrimination, the conventions require that a distinction be based on the ground of discrimination addressed, without specifying whether "basing" includes an indirect relation between a distinction and a ground.

As regards ICERD, Article 2(1)(c) specifies an obligation of states, which might be fulfilled by effectively outlawing indirect discrimination:

"(c) Each State Party shall take effective measures to review governmental, national and local policies, and to amend, rescind or nullify any laws and regulations which have the effect of creating or perpetuating racial discrimination wherever it exists."

This latter provision, which does not find a parallel in CEDAW, implies that a regulation which has the effect of perpetuating racial discrimination shall be considered as discriminatory. Introducing a prohibition of indirect discrimination, signatory states would be able to discharge part of this obligation. Accordingly, the CERD (the Committee supervising the ICERD) has in several cases explicitly welcomed national legislation prohibiting not only direct but also indirect discrimination and even required states to prohibit indirect discrimination in some cases.[42]

The CERD has also had the opportunity to consider a definition of indirect discrimination.

[42] W. Vandenhole, *Non-Discrimination and Equality in the View of UN Human Rights Treaty Bodies* (Antwerp, Intersentia, 2005) 41.

Committee on the Elimination of Racial Discrimination,   **3.UN.8.**
5 August 2003
*Communication No. 31/2003, L.R. et al. (represented by European Roma
Rights Centre)* v. *Slovakia*

INDIRECT ETHNIC DISCRIMINATION—CITY COUNCIL WITHDRAWING FUNDING
PROGRAMME FAVOURING ROMA FAMILIES IN RESPONSE TO A RACIST MOTION BY
MAJORITY CITIZENS

L.R. v. Slovakia

Facts: The petitioners, represented inter alia by the European Roma Rights Centre, call for an investigation of certain actions by Slovakian authorities in relation to a low-cost housing programme. The city council of Dobšinà had applied to participate in such a programme, which was explicitly aimed at providing Roma with suitable housing. Upon receipt of a petition opposing the "influx of . . . inadaptable citizens of Gypsy origin", signed by 2700 inhabitants of Dobšinà, the city council cancelled its earlier resolution to apply for the funds. The petitioners sought to argue that the cancellation of the decision was indirectly discriminatory, being based on a discriminatory petition. In defending its non-action, the State Party argued that only a resolution of a city council that was racist on its face would qualify as discriminatory.

Held: As there is no right to appeal against a city council decision that lacks individual relevance, there was not the possibility to exhaust domestic remedies in this case. The applicants had applied to the police and the Attorney of State to initiate proceedings against the council for violating the law but without success, as the desired actions were inadmissible under domestic law. The Court held that there was discrimination and a violation of CERD.

Judgment: "The Committee recalls that the definition of racial discrimination in Article 1 expressly extends beyond measures which are explicitly discriminatory, to encompass measures which are not discriminatory at face value but are discriminatory in fact and effect, that is, if they amount to indirect discrimination. In assessing such indirect discrimination, the Committee must take full account of the particular context and circumstances of the petition, as by definition indirect discrimination can only be demonstrated circumstantially."

Note
Responding to the petitioners' request to rescind the council's decision, the CERD acknowledged indirect discrimination and delivered something close to a definition. It equates indirect discrimination with factual discrimination, which is in line with the effects-oriented definition given by the international rights instruments of discrimination generally. There is a lack of preparedness to respond to the detailed argument of the petitioners, although the CERD recognises that the conduct of the State Party is discriminatory. The Committee also does not seem prepared to define indirect discrimination clearly for the purposes of CERD.

The CEDAW Committee has in numerous cases applied the concept of indirect discrimination.[43] It has to be noted that, similar to the CERD, the CEDAW Committee does not deliver a clear legal definition of indirect discrimination. This is already apparent from its general definition, delivered in the end note to the general recommendation No. 25:

---

[43] For numerous references see Vandenhole, above n. 42, 74–7.

General Recommendation No. 25, on Article 4, paragraph 1   **3.UN.9.**
of the Convention on the Elimination of All Forms of Discrimination
against Women, on temporary special measures[44]

"Indirect discrimination against women may occur when laws, policies and programmes are based on seemingly gender-neutral criteria which in their actual effect have a detrimental impact on women. Gender-neutral laws, policies and programmes unintentionally may perpetuate the consequences of past discrimination. They may be inadvertently modelled on male lifestyles and thus fail to take into account aspects of women's life experiences which may differ from those of men. These differences may exist because of stereotypical expectations, attitudes and behaviour directed towards women which are based on the biological differences between women and men. They may also exist because of the generally existing subordination of women by men."

As in the older case-law of the Permanent International Court of Justice (PICJ), the CEDAW Committee equalises de facto inequality and indirect discrimination. Accordingly, in cases which were categorised as indirect discrimination cases, the facts show that these should rather be considered as cases where State Parties neglected their obligation to improve the situation of women.[45] For example, the Committee held China responsible for violating CEDAW for its failure to take active measures to enhance women's participation in public life and used the concept of indirect discrimination in this context.[46]

All in all, the UN Human Rights law, while formally acknowledging the concept of indirect discrimination law, does not in fact distinguish between direct and indirect discrimination in relation to ICCRP, nor between indirect discrimination and a State Party obligation for positive measures in relation to CERD and CEDAW. Due to the open-ended norm in Article 26 ICCRP and the contextualised approach towards discrimination in the ICERD and CEDAW, a detailed conception of indirect discrimination law may seem less important under UN International Human Rights Law. However, the fact that the human rights committees have used the concept demonstrates that it is perceived as relevant.

3.3.1.C.   EUROPEAN HUMAN RIGHTS LAW AND INDIRECT DISCRIMINATION

As regards European Human Rights law, there are no specific non-discrimination conventions. However, the European Convention of Human Rights (ECHR) and the

---

[44] At 9, available on the website of the United Nations, Division for the Advancement of Women, Department of Economic and Social Affairs.

[45] See on this R. Holtmaat and Ch. Tobler "CEDAW and the EU's Policy in the Field of Combating Gender Discrimination" (2005) 12 *MJ* 399, 413–15.

[46] Office of the High Commissioner for Human Rights, *Women and Health*: 2 February 1999, CEDAW General Recom. 24 (Art. 12) issued by CEDAW Monitoring Committee on 2 February 1999 during its 20th session (UN GAOR, 1999, Doc. No. A/54/38/Rev. 1 (part I) para. 319 (China Hongkong).

Revised European Social Charter of 1996 refer to protection against discrimination. Article 14 of the European Convention of Human Rights provides that:

> "The enjoyment of the rights and freedoms set forth in this Convention shall be secured without discrimination on any ground such as sex, race, colour, language, religion . . ."

As there was a general desire to overcome the lack of a free-standing equality clause in the ECHR, Protocol No. 12 to the ECHR was adopted. However, it does not provide any definition of indirect discrimination either, but rather only states that the enjoyment of any right or freedom shall be secured without discrimination on any ground such as those already enumerated in Article 14. The European Social Charter (ESC) of 1961 does not contain any non-discrimination clause, while the Revised European Social Charter (RevESC) of 1996 contains a new Article E in part V, which resembles Article 14 ECHR:

> "The enjoyment of rights set forth in this Charter shall be secured without discrimination on any grounds such as race, colour, sex, language, religion, political or other opinion, national extraction or social origin, health, association with a national minority, birth or other status."

All three of these clauses are open-ended norms, where we might not necessarily expect the development of indirect discrimination law. However, both the European Court of Human Rights (ECtHR) and the European Committee of Social Rights (ECSR) have after being reluctant for a long while[47] acknowledged the concept, partly relying on ECJ case-law.

For the ECtHR case-law, the decision in *Thlimmennos* v. *Greece*[48] is sometimes mentioned as an example for indirect discrimination.[49] The decision specifies that Article 14 ECHR obliges State Parties not only to treat equals equally, but also to treat unequal cases differently, thus demonstrating that formally neutral provisions may be considered as discrimination under the ECHR without using the concept of indirect discrimination.[50] This case is analysed in the context of direct discrimination.[51]

Indirect discrimination was first acknowledged with explicit reference to the ECJ in an extensive *obiter dictum* for a case rejected for inadmissibility.

---

[47] See Gerards, above n. 14, 113–15; Fredman, above n. 32, 108 with reference to *Abdoulaziz* case.

[48] ECtHR 6 April 2000, Application No. 34369/97.

[49] O. de Schutter, *The EU Equality Directives in the Context of the Prohibition of Discrimination under European Human Rights Law* (Brussels, Human European Consultancy, 2004) 10–11.

[50] See L. Waddington and A. Hendricks, "The Expanding Concept of Employment Discrimination in Europe: From Direct and Indirect Discrimination to Reasonable Accommodation Discrimination" (2002)18 *IJCLLIR* 403, 420–1.

[51] See M. Bell, Chapter 2: Direct Discrimination, excerpt number **2.COE.2**.

ECtHR, 6 January 2005[52]   **3.CoE.10.**
Hoogendijk v. *The Netherlands*

WHETHER SUBMITTING A CLAIM FOR A SOCIAL BENEFIT TO A MEANS TEST
CONSTITUTES SEX DISCRIMINATION

Hoogendijk

Facts: Ms. Hoogendijk had suffered a severe accident at the age of 28 and was no longer able to work full-time after this. In October 1976, Dutch law introduced a disability allowance by national legislation named "AAWW". Ms. Hoogendijk's application for this benefit was rejected on the grounds that the disability benefit was means tested and her husband was earning enough money. Originally, the AAWW had excluded married women entirely from the benefit. This was successfully challenged under European Community sex discrimination law. When the Netherlands included married women within the personal scope of application, a means test was introduced in order to prevent an undue increase in expenses. This means test took into account not only the earnings of the applicant, but also earnings of any family member who was obliged to contribute to their maintenance. The main question before the ECtHR was whether Ms. Hoogendijk was deprived of her property rights contrary to the first protocol attached to the ECHR. However, she also submitted that the legislation constituted violation of Article 14 ECHR.

Held: The claim is inadmissible.

Judgment: "Although the amended rules were formulated in a neutral manner, it did in fact result in more (married) women than men losing their AAWW benefits . . .

In so far as the applicant's claim of discrimination is based on the fact that the implementation of the income requirement under the AAW scheme affected more women than men, the Court considers that where a general policy or measure has disproportionately prejudicial effects on a particular group, it is not excluded that this may be regarded as discriminatory notwithstanding that it is not specifically aimed or directed at that group.

Although statistics in themselves are not automatically sufficient . . ., the Court cannot ignore that, according to the results of the research carried out by the Social Insurance Council on the effect of the implementation of the AAW Reparation Act of 3 May 1989 as submitted by the applicant, a group of about 5,100 persons lost their entitlement to AAW benefits on account of failure to meet the income requirement and that this group consisted of about 3,300 women and 1,800 men.

. . . [T]he Court considers that where an applicant is able to show, on the basis of undisputed official statistics, the existence of a prima facie indication that a specific rule—although formulated in a neutral manner—in fact affects a clearly higher percentage of women than men, it is for the respondent Government to show that this is the result of objective factors unrelated to any discrimination on grounds of sex. If the onus . . . does not shift to the respondent Government, it will be in practice extremely difficult for applicants to prove indirect discrimination. As no such objective factors have appeared or have been submitted by the respondent Government, the Court accepts as sufficiently demonstrated that the introduction of the income requirement in the AAW scheme did in fact have an indirect discriminatory effect in respect of married or divorced women having become incapacitated for work at a time when it was not common in the Netherlands for married women to earn an own income from work.

---

[52] Application 5864/00, (2005) 40 EHRR SE22.

The question therefore arises whether there is a reasonable and objective justification for the introduction of the income requirement under the AAW.

The Court notes that the income requirement—applicable to both men and women and irrespective of their marital status—was introduced in the AAW scheme in order to remove the discriminatory exclusion of married women from this scheme whilst seeking to keep the costs of the AAW scheme within acceptable limits. The Court accepts that this constitutes a reasonable and objective justification."

Note: does the ECtHR acknowledge a prohibition of indirect discrimination?
In this case the ECtHR seems to embrace the concept of indirect discrimination as established by the ECJ case-law. However, there are a few *caveats* against assuming that indirect discrimination is now firmly embedded in ECHR law. First of all, the case concerns a piece of legislation which had been invalidated by the ECJ precisely on the grounds that there was indirect discrimination. Despite this, the ECtHR has recourse to its *Thlimmenos* decision, which did not apply the logic of indirect discrimination. In addition, the ECtHR does not seem to be prepared to treat the detrimental effect of a legislative measure as suspect in itself. Instead, it allows the government to revert to objective factors at two stages. First, the government may maintain that the detrimental effect is the result of objective factors unrelated to sex. Secondly, and over and above this, the government is given the opportunity to advance a reasonable and objective justification. The ECtHR has thus considered embracing the concept of indirect discrimination, but in effect it does not share the assumption that any detrimental effect is deemed to be based on discrimination if not objectively justified.

In a more recent case, the ECtHR repeated its apparent acknowledgement of a prohibition of indirect discrimination being included in Article 14 ECHR, although again in this case the result was not in favour of the applicants.

ECtHR, 7 February 2006[53]   **3.CoE.11.**
D.H and others v. *Czech Republic*

WHETHER ARTICLE 14 INCLUDES PROHIBITION TO INDIRECTLY DISCRIMINATE

Roma children in special schools

Facts: The applicants are 14 children from Roma families who were educated in special schools for children with learning deficiencies, in some cases initially, in other cases after starting in a regular school. The applicants' representative, the European Roma Rights Centre and other human rights organisations argued that sending Roma children to special schools would amount to indirect discrimination, relying on statistics which indeed demonstrated that the percentage of Roma children in special schools was higher than that of other children. They challenged the "general functioning of the educational system" in the Czech Republic for being indirectly discriminatory against Roma children. The school authority countered that the specific decisions were taken after careful consideration of school staff and with the consent of the parents.

[53] Application 57325/00, available from the ECtHR website.

Held: After pursuing their case unsuccessfully before the national constitutional court, the Roma Rights Centre raised the issue before the ECtHR. The ECtHR dismissed the claim, but reiterated the definition of indirect discrimination developed in the *Hoogendijk* case:

Judgment: "45. The Court notes that the applicants' complaint under Article 14 of the Convention, taken together with Article 2 of Protocol No. 1, is based on a number of serious arguments . . . The Court points out, however, that . . . it is not its task to assess the overall social context. Its sole task in the instant case is to examine the individual applications before it and to establish on the basis of the relevant facts whether the reason for the applicants' placement in the special schools was their ethnic or racial origin.

46. In that connection, the Court observes that, if a policy or general measure has disproportionately prejudicial effects on a group of people, the possibility of its being considered discriminatory cannot be ruled out even if it is not specifically aimed or directed at that group. However, statistics are not by themselves sufficient to disclose a practice which could be classified as discriminatory (*Hugh Jordan v. the United Kingdom*, no. 24746/94, § 154).

With regard to pupils with special needs, the Court . . . wishes to reiterate with regard to the States' margin of appreciation in the education sphere that the States cannot be prohibited from setting up different types of school for children with difficulties or implementing special educational programmes to respond to special needs . . .

49. The Court observes that the rules governing children's placement in special schools do not refer to the pupils' ethnic origin, but pursue the legitimate aim of adapting the education system to the needs and aptitudes or disabilities of the children. Since these are not legal concepts, it is only right that experts in educational psychology should be responsible for identifying them . . .

52. Thus, while acknowledging that these statistics disclose figures that are worrying and that the general situation in the Czech Republic concerning the education of Roma children is by no means perfect, the Court cannot in the circumstances find that the measures taken against the applicants were discriminatory. Although the applicants may have lacked information about the national education system or found themselves in a climate of mistrust, the concrete evidence before the Court in the present case does not enable it to conclude that the applicants' placement or, in some instances, continued placement, in special schools was the result of racial prejudice, as they have alleged."

Note

Again, the ECtHR concedes that statistics may prove discrimination, but allows the State Party to justify the detrimental effect at two stages. In the first place, they need to cite a legitimate aim. If that aim is accepted, it then apparently falls on the applicants to prove that there was racial prejudice in spite of the aim. This means that the reluctance to apply indirect discrimination law before the ECtHR prevails, although it facially acknowledges the concept.

Application of the RevESC with its new equality clause is supervised by the ECSR. This body inter alia receives collective complaints (Additional Protocol to the ESC of 1995 providing for a system of collective complaints), which are referred to as "decisions". The ECSR's approach to indirect discrimination is similar to that of the ECtHR, although its first application has had a positive result for the complaining party.

European Committee on Social Rights, 10 March 2004[54]   **3.CoE.12.**
International Association Autism—Europe (IAAE) v. *France*

WHETHER DENYING AUTISTIC CHILDREN ADEQUATE SCHOOLING
(INCLUDING ACCESS TO MAINSTREAM SCHOOLS) AMOUNTS TO (INTER ALIA)
DISCRIMINATION

Autism

Facts: Autism France raised proceedings because they considered that autistic children were denied adequate schooling, either (and preferably) in mainstream school, where necessary with special support, or in special schools.

Held: The main issues were integration of the disabled access to education and others. However, the Committee also held that the insufficient attention to the needs of autistic children in the educational system amounted to indirect discrimination.

Decision: "52. The Committee observes further that the wording of Article E is almost identical to the wording of Article 14 of the European Convention on Human Rights. As the European Court of Human Rights has repeatedly stressed in interpreting Article 14 and most recently in the Thlimmenos case [*Thlimmenos c. Grèce* [GC], no 34369/97, CEDH 2000-IV, § 44)], the principle of equality that is reflected therein means treating equals equally and unequals unequally . . . In other words, human difference in a democratic society should not only be viewed positively but should be responded to with discernment in order to ensure real and effective equality.

In this regard, the Committee considers that Article E not only prohibits direct discrimination but also all forms of indirect discrimination. Such indirect discrimination may arise by failing to take due and positive account of all relevant differences or by failing to take adequate steps to ensure that the rights and collective advantages that are open to all are genuinely accessible by and to all."

Note: is using the term indirect discrimination the same as acknowledging the concept? In contrast to the ECtHR, the ECSR uses the term indirect discrimination. The concept is, however, not defined specifically. Similarly to the CERD and CEDAW Committee, the ECSR seems to consider that indirect discrimination occurs when a State Party fails to effectively provide opportunities for equal enjoyment of Convention rights in practice for all. Nevertheless, this case raised the hopes of disability lawyers of having the concept of reasonable accommodation included under the notion of indirect discrimination.[55]

---

[54] Resolution ResCH(2004), Collective complaint No.13/2002, available on the website of the Council of Europe.
[55] See further below L.Waddington, Chapter Six: Reasonable Accommodation, section 6.5.2.

3.3.1.D.   SUMMARY ON INTERNATIONAL LAW

All in all, international human rights law provides effects oriented definitions of discrimination. Discrimination will occur not only when State Parties treat citizens differently, but also if they fail to ensure equal enjoyment of Convention rights. This does not oblige State Parties to introduce a specific prohibition of indirect discrimination. From this perspective, it is not surprising that the supervising committees for the ICERD, CEDAW and the ICCRP have been haphazard in their approach towards indirect discrimination law. After all, prohibiting indirect discrimination is not the only way to bring about equal enjoyment of human rights in practice.

Given the complex structure of indirect discrimination law, some authors would prefer to abandon the concept altogether, referring to the Canadian legal order as an example.[56] The Canadian Charter of Fundamental Rights provides in its section 15(1):

> "Every individual is equal before and under the law and has the right to the equal protection and equal benefit of the law without discrimination and, in particular, without discrimination based on race, national or ethnic origin, colour, religion, sex, age or mental or physical disability."

As the ECHR and the ICCRP, this article provides for a prohibition of discrimination with an open list of grounds. According to its interpretation by the Canadian Supreme Court since the Andrews case,[57] this means that any form of disadvantage related to one of the expressly named grounds or any equivalent ground will suffice to establish a claim of discrimination. This example seems to demonstrate that prohibiting indirect discrimination is not the only way of making non-discrimination law effective. However, it has only been employed in constitutional cases, and not in employment and other cases between private parties, where even in Canada a closed list of grounds and accordingly a prohibition of indirect discrimination has been acknowledged.

We have seen that UN and CoE Committees and the ECtHR have been led towards acknowledging the prohibition of indirect discrimination, although they have not developed a clear definition of the concept. Their case-law may thus encourage State Parties to explicitly acknowledge a prohibition to discriminate indirectly. We will see in the following chapters that the concept of indirect discrimination was more explicitly developed in EC law (following the example of US and UK law). The reader will explore many cases in national and EC law, where indirect discrimination as a concept is successfully used to challenge discriminatory structures or to go beyond mere formal conceptions of discrimination. While we leave it to the reader's own judgement whether this concept is still needed for the future of non-discrimination law, we can definitely say that it is an established element of European non-discrimination law.

---

[56] C. Tobler, *Indirect Discrimination. A Case Study into the Development of the Legal Concept of Indirect Discrimination under EC Law* (Antwerp, Intersentia, 2005) 432–6, with further references.

[57] Canadian Supreme Court, Judgment of 2 February 1989, *Andrews v. Law Society of British Columbia* [1989] 1 SCR 143.

3.3.2.   ORIGINS OF MODERN INDIRECT DISCRIMINATION LAW: US,
UK AND IRISH LAW

The origin of the concept of indirect discrimination, as applied to discrimination
against natural persons,[58] can be found in US case-law, with the case of *Griggs* v.
Duke Power of 1971 marking the point of departure for further development.[59] The
case concerned racial discrimination in employment, which had been prohibited by
the Civil Rights Act 1964.

U.S. Supreme Court, Co 401 U.S. 424 (1971)[60]   **3.US.13.**
Griggs et al. v. *Duke Power Co.*

REQUIRING HIGH SCORE IN TESTS AND HIGH SCHOOL DIPLOMA AS INDIRECT
RACIAL DISCRIMINATION

Griggs

Facts: The Duke Power Corporation had a history of racially segregated employment politics. After the US
Congress passed Title VII of the Civil Rights Act (1964) that prohibited overt discrimination on grounds of
race, the company introduced a neutrally formulated policy. All employees except those in the least
qualified jobs, who also had the lowest wages, were required to have completed high school successfully and
to achieve satisfactory results on two aptitude tests. As it happened, 12% of black males but 36% of white
males fulfilled the first criterion, and as regards the tests, 6% of blacks but 58% of whites achieved satisfactory results. Accordingly, the new policy led to the same result as overt discrimination in the past: black
workers were only employed in low-skilled jobs requiring heavy physical work, which were poorly paid.

Held: The lower courts had both found that there was no illegal racial discrimination. The District Court
had denied any relevance of former discrimination. The Court of Appeal had acknowledged that prior
practices were not insulated from remedial action under Title VII, but considered that there should have
been an element of discriminatory purpose for the use of the requirements to be banned. The Supreme
Court disagreed, developing the concept of indirect discrimination.

Judgment: "The objective of Congress . . . was to achieve equality of employment opportunities and to remove barriers that have operated in the past to favour an identifiable group of
white employees over other employees. Under the Act, practices, procedures or tests, neutral on
their face and even neutral in terms of intent, cannot be maintained if they operate to 'freeze'
the *status quo* of prior discriminatory employment practices . . . The Act proscribes . . . also
practices that are fair in form but discriminatory in operation. The touchstone is business
necessity. If an employee practice, which operates to exclude Negroes, cannot be shown to be

---

[58] At the time when the US Supreme Court decided *Griggs*, the ECJ had already developed notions
similar to indirect discrimination law in its case-law on goods; see Tobler, above n. 56, 111–13, referring to
the ECJ case Case 2/56 *Geitling* [1957/58] ECR 3.

[59] Naturally, this case did not come about unprecedented. Gerards, above n. 14, 372–4, traces the
concept of indirect discrimination in US law back to the 1939 US supreme court decision *Wilson* v. *Lane*
(307 US 268 (1939)), concerning the registration for elections only imposed on those who were not on the
electorate register in 1914, while Schindler, above n. 33, 145, refers to the *Oyama* decision of 1948 (322 US
633 (1948)), concerning the prohibitions for aliens ineligible for American citizenship to buy land.
However, it is rightly characterized as "pioneering" (Fredman, above n. 32, 109) or landmark case (Tobler,
above n. 56, 93).

[60] Argued 14 December 1970, decided 8 March 1971.

related to job performance, the practice is prohibited. [Neither] the high school completion requirement nor the general intelligence test is shown to bear a demonstrable relationship to successful performance of the jobs for which it was used. Both were adopted . . . without meaningful study of their relationship to job-performance ability . . . Congress directed the thrust of the Act to the consequences of employment practices, not simply the motivation. More than that, Congress has placed on the employer the burden of showing that any given requirement must have a manifest relationship to the employment in question."

Notes: historical and continuing relevance of Griggs

(1) The Civil Rights Act did not contain a specific clause saying the indirect discrimination was prohibited and much less defined the concept. Confronted with the above set of facts, the Supreme Court established that the Act did prohibit indirect discrimination and defined the concept. The historical relevance of the case was mainly that continuing discriminatory practices under different headings would not be accepted, even if the employers were wise enough to not show any actionable intent to discriminate.

(2) The ongoing relevance of the decision is the two-tier test of indirect discrimination developed by the Supreme Court which is applied until the present day. As the first step, an employment practice is suspect if it operates to exclude persons protected against discrimination (here: Black Americans) although it is formally fair. Secondly, the suspicion that there is indeed discrimination can be rebutted by objectively justifying the practice, referring to business necessity. The potential of disparate impact discrimination, or indirect discrimination, as defined in this landmark case, was rather far-reaching.[61]

The concept was soon imported to Europe, where the British legislator referred to it in the Sex Discrimination Act 1975 and the Race Relation Act 1976,[62] while the ECJ explicitly referred to *Griggs* in its decision in *Jenkins*.[63] When transplanting the *Griggs* formula, the British legislator changed its content. According to the original definition of the Sex Discrimination Act (1974), a person would be held to discriminate against a woman on grounds of sex if

"he applies to her a requirement or condition which he applies or would apply equally to a man but which is such that the proportion of women who can comply with it is considerably smaller than the proportion of men who can comply with it, and which he cannot show to be justifiable irrespective of the sex of the person to whom it is applied and which is to her detriment because she cannot comply with it."[64]

Similarly, the 1977 Irish Employment Equality Act defined as discrimination the case

---

[61] T. Loenen, "Indirect Discrimination: Oscillating between Containment and Revolution" in T. Loenen and P. Rodriguez (eds.) *Non-Discrimination Law: Comparative Perspectives* (Leiden, Martinus Nijhoff, 1999) 199, 200; R. Sedler, "The Role of Intent in Discrimination Analysis", in *ibid.*, 91, 94 subs.

[62] See Fredman, above n. 32, 106–7.

[63] For development of ECJ case-law, see below section 3.3.3.

[64] See Fredman, above n. 32, 106. The definition has been changed in response to EU case-law and legislation.

"where because of his sex or marital status a person is obliged to comply with a requirement, relating to employment or membership of a body, which is not an essential requirement for such employment or membership and in respect of which the proportion of the other sex or (as the case may be) of a different marital status but of the same sex able to comply is substantially higher."[65]

Both these definitions seem narrower than the Griggs formula. They require any potential claimant to isolate a specific requirement or condition applied to him or her to which disparate impact was attributable. By contrast, the US Supreme Court in *Griggs* seemed to accept adverse effects of any employment practice. A practice, however, can consist of a combination of requirements or even be unwritten and difficult to detect. Still, the reasoning of the *Griggs* decision rested on a logic similar to that of the British and Irish legislation. Where Chief Justice Burger referred to "barriers" that needed to be removed; the British legislator speaks of specific requirements.

In addition, development in US law did not stop with *Griggs*. Especially for employment law, i.e. Title VII cases, the Supreme Court changed its concept of disparate impact discrimination along the lines of British and Irish legislation in *Wards Cove*.[66] In this decision, the Supreme Court held that a claimant needed to demonstrate racial imbalance statistically, and that he needed to establish a particular employment practice to which this disparate impact was to be attributed. In the same decision, the Supreme Court applied a wide definition of business practice. The legislator corrected the latter detail with the 1991 amendment to the Civil Rights Act.[67] This amendment introduced a statutory definition of indirect discrimination, which is valid until the present day. According to the reformed Title VII, there are now two ways to establish a claim based on indirect discrimination. The claimant may, on the one hand, show that "a particular employment practice causes a disparate impact on the basis of race, colour, religion, sex or national origin", in which case it falls upon the respondent to demonstrate that the challenged practice is job related and consistent with business necessity. On the other hand, the claimant may also establish that there is a less discriminatory alternative to satisfy the business necessity on grounds of which an employment practice that impacts disparately on a protected group is based. Congress clarified that as far as business necessity and less discriminatory alternatives are concerned, the law as it stood before 1989 (i.e. before *Wards Cove*) would apply. However, the statutory definition still requires the isolation of a specific practice to which the

[65] Sec. 2 (c) Cited from D. Curtin, *Irish Employment Equality Law* (Dublin, Round Hall, 1989) 236. The legislation has since been changed.

[66] US Supreme Court, Judgment of 5 June 1989, case *Wards Cove Packing Co.* v. *Atonio*, 460 US 642 (1989).

[67] Amendment by Pub. L. 102–166 effective 21 November 1991, except as otherwise provided; see s. 402 of Pub. L. 102–166. Congress explicitly stated in its finding preceding this piece of legislation that "the decision of the Supreme Court in *Wards Cove Packing Co.* v. *Antonio*, 490 US 642 (1989) has weakened the scope and effectiveness of Federal civil rights protections" and states as one of the Act's purposes "to codify the concepts of 'business necessity' and 'job related' enunciated by the Supreme Court in *Griggs* v. *Duke Power Co.*, 401 US 424 (1971), and in the other Supreme Court decisions prior to *Wards Cove Packing*".

disparate impact must be accorded. Unsurprisingly, cases on indirect discrimination are becoming increasingly expensive and time-consuming in modern US law. This results in fewer claimants taking cases to the courts and in even fewer parties being successful in disparate impact cases.[68]

This demonstrates that there was no fundamental difference between the definition of indirect discrimination in US case-law and the earlier UK legislation.[69] Whether demanding a specific employment practice or a specific requirement, the legislator reduces indirect discrimination law to a narrow approach with a tendency to overlook structural discrimination not capable of being boiled down to one specific requirement.

From a less critical perspective, one could classify the definition of indirect discrimination in US, British and Irish legislation as based on the courtroom procedure, as seems befitting for common law jurisdictions, with their focus on case-law. Viewed as an attempt to provide a procedure for determining whether discriminatory effects can be attributed to a certain practice used by a private employer, these legal orders' definition of indirect discrimination appears as an elaborated rule on the burden of proof. The onus of providing the starting material for an assumption of discrimination is on the claimant, who is expected to bring forward statistics establishing disparate impact. The onus then shifts to the defendant, who is expected to make his or her case on business necessity or any other defence. It is then for the claimant again to point to a less discriminatory alternative or to demonstrate in another way that business necessity does not actually require the restrictive requirement or employment practice. The heavy reliance on statistics, which is implicit in this approach,[70] has been praised[71] and criticised;[72] both positions will be covered below (3.5.1.B). The close link between indirect discrimination law and sociological research (quantitative and qualitative) is responsible for the supposed success of the concept within a certain time span in the jurisdictions referred to above. It appears that effective anti-discrimination institutions in these countries have been able to use the concept to induce analysis of socio-economic institutions that might have a structurally discriminating effect.

---

[68] See C. Brors, "Trial und Error im Diskriminierungsschutz: Die Rechtsprechung zum amerikanischen Arbeitsrecht im Jahr 2001 bis 2002" [2003] *Recht der Arbeit* 223, 226–7.

[69] Some assume that US law is more demanding than UK law nowadays at least in relation to race discrimination; see Townshend-Smith, above n. 15, 121–2.

[70] *Ibid.*, 105 ("fundamentally and unavoidably a statistical notion").

[71] See, e.g.. P. Simon, *Comparative Study on the Collection of Data to Measure the Extent and Impact of Discrimination within the United States, Canada, Australia, Great-Britain and the Netherlands* (Brussels, European Commission, 2004).

[72] See, e.g. S. Baer, *Würde oder Gleichheit* (Baden-Baden, Nomos, 1995) 243, who characterises the reliance on number games (*Zahlenspiele*) implicit in applying the prohibition as contempt of human beings (*menschenverachtend*).

3.3.3. INDIRECT DISCRIMINATION IN EUROPEAN COMMUNITY LAW—DEVELOPING THE DEFINITION

3.3.3.A. INDIRECT DISCRIMINATION IN INTERNAL MARKET LAW AND IN EQUALITY LAW

As any notion of discrimination, the concept of indirect discrimination is not restricted to being used in relation to human beings. Discrimination (or unequal treatment) may also occur between situations, commodities, services and so on. Especially in EC law, the concept of indirect discrimination has for a long time played a vital role in the application of the fundamental freedoms. It was used to counteract measures by Member States that resulted in unequal access of goods, services or persons to national markets. Following the doctrinal development in the area of free movement of goods, where the concept of restriction along with the differentiation between distinctly and indistinctly applicable measures has become the main point of reference since the end of the 1980s,[73] the ECJ is increasingly replacing the prohibition of indirect discrimination with the more general concept of restriction.[74] Within the framework of establishing an internal market, the move from non-discrimination towards restriction denotes a move from anti-protectionism towards economic liberalism;[75] its importance cannot be underestimated. However, in legal provisions referring only to equality between human beings, and not to their role as market participants, there is no concept of restriction to fall back on.[76] In addition, as regards equality of persons, the ECJ continues to use the concept of indirect discrimination on grounds of nationality.[77] As this book refers only to equality between human beings and investigates the body of discrimination law in that respect, we will largely disregard the case-law referring to internal market law. In some instances, however, this is not possible, as the Community institutions, above all the ECJ in its case-law, frequently transpose concepts developed in internal market law to other fields of law. Accordingly, such decisions from the field of internal

---

[73] See P. Olivier, *Free Movement of Goods in the European Community*, 4th edn (London, Sweet & Maxwell, 2003) 6.36–6.48, on the remaining relevance of de facto discrimination in deciding upon the application of the so-called "*Keck*-Formula" 6.57–6.68. There are, however, still authors who apply the concept of indirect discrimination to goods and services case-law: G. Davies, *Nationality Discrimination in the European Internal Market* (The Hague, Kluwer International, 2003) 33–4, and with a fervent plea to continue to use discrimination with priority in ch. 6 at 106–15.

[74] C. Barnard, *The Substantive Law of the EU. The Four Freedoms* (Oxford, Oxford University Press, 2004) 256–63; Tobler, above n. 56, 76–7, with examples for case-law at 408–14, and the conclusion that for free movement cases the prohibition of indirect discrimination is indeed superfluous at 431–2.

[75] See M. Poiares Maduro, *We The Court—The European Court of Justice and the European Economic Constitution. A Critical Reading of Art. 30 of the EC Treaty* (Oxford, Hart Publishing, 1998) 35–60; more recently on the relevance of economic integration to constitution-making in the EU, *ibid.*, "The Double Constitutional Life of the Charter" in T. Hervey and J. Kenner (eds.), *Economic and Social Rights under the EU Charter of Fundamental Rights—A Legal Perspective* (Oxford, Hart Publishing, 2003) 269, 271–3.

[76] This point is convincingly made by Tobler, above n. 56, 432.

[77] See AG Tizzano, opinion in *Caixa-Bank France* v. Ministère de l'Économie, des Finances et de l'Industrie (Case C–442/02) ECR 2004 I-8961, No. 47.

market law will be cited which contributed towards the development of indirect discrimination in the realm of equality law.

3.3.3.B.   INDIRECT DISCRIMINATION IN EQUALITY LAW: CASE-LAW AND LEGISLATIVE DEFINITIONS

As in US law, the Community law definition of a prohibition of indirect discrimination developed in case-law before any statutory definition was framed. The legislative definitions resulted from codifying case-law. It has been noted that, in the US, the case-law on indirect discrimination first developed in race discrimination cases. When the prohibition of indirect discrimination crossed the Atlantic, indirect discrimination cases before courts more frequently concerned sex discrimination. This happened notwithstanding the fact that British equality legislation had addressed racial injustice prior to gender imbalances.

ESTABLISHING THE CONCEPT BY CASE-LAW

The first case on indirect discrimination against natural persons before the ECJ concerned discrimination on grounds of nationality under what is today Article 39 EC.

ECJ, 12 February 1974[78]   **3.EC.14.**
Case 152/73, Sotgiu v. Deutsche Post

WHETHER DISADVANTAGE ON GROUNDS OF PERMANENT RESIDENCE OUTSIDE
GERMANY AMOUNTS TO DISCRIMINATION ON GROUNDS OF NATIONALITY

Sotgiu

Facts: In *Sotgiu*, an Italian worker employed in Germany by the Federal Post Office complained that he received a lower "separation allowance" than his German colleagues. In fact, the separation allowance for those with a family home in another Member State was lower than for those with a family home in Germany, but on the other hand those residing in Germany were obliged to move to their place of employment as soon as a suitable home could be made available.

Held: The requirement of having a home in Germany is, while neutral on its face, such that it will be detrimental to foreign workers disproportionately. Article 48 EEC (now 39 EC) prohibits not only overt discrimination but also covert discrimination, which exists if a criterion is liable to disproportionately disadvantage foreign workers, and is not objectively justified. It is left to the national court to decide whether there is an objective justification of the requirement.

Judgment: "11. The rules regarding equality of treatment . . .forbid not only overt discrimination by reason of nationality but also all covert forms of discrimination, which, by the

---

[78] [1974] ECR 153.

application of other criteria of differentiation, lead in fact to the same result. This interpretation . . . is necessary to ensure the effective working of one of the fundamental principles of the Community . . . It may therefore be that criteria such as place of origin or residence of a worker may . . . be tantamount, as regards their practical effect, to discrimination on the grounds of nationality, such as is prohibited by the Treaty and the Regulation.

12. However this would not be the case with a separation allowance the conditions of allotment . . . of which took account of objective differences which the situation of workers may involve according to whether their residence, at the time their taking up a given post, is within the territory of the state in question or abroad. In this respect the fact that, for workers whose home is within the territory of the state concerned payment of the separation allowance is only temporary and is bound up with an obligation to transfer the residence to the place of employment whilst the same allowance is paid for an indefinite period and is not bound up with any such obligation in the case of workers whose residence is abroad . . . may be a valid reason for differentiating between the amounts paid."

Notes

(1) The ECJ referred to the *effet utile* of the principle of discrimination to conclude that it should embrace covert discrimination as well as overt discrimination, as is illustrated by the above citation.

(2) Slightly more generous than the subsequent national legislation in Britain and Ireland, the ECJ held that the main criterion for indirect discrimination was the practical effect of criterion in question. It also held that discriminatory effect could only establish a presumption of discrimination that could be rebutted by the objective justification test. Thus, as in US case-law, the ECJ case-law established a two-tier test of indirect discrimination.

As regards sex discrimination, the ECJ tackled the issue of discrimination in relation to equal pay seven years after *Sotgiu*, in the *Jenkins* case.

ECJ, 31 March 1981[79]   **3.EC.15.**
Case 96/80, Jenkins v. *Kingsgate (ClothingProductions) Ltd.*

WHETHER LOWER HOURLY RATES FOR PART-TIME WORK CONSTITUTE SEX
DISCRIMINATION

Jenkins

Facts: Ms. Jenkins was paid a lower hourly rate than a colleague doing equal work. The English Industrial Tribunal to which she complained held that the employer could rely on her working time being only 75% of the full working hours as a material difference other than sex to justify the unequal pay. The history of the pay difference between part-timers and full-timers with that employer seemed revealing: before the British Equal Pay Act established the principle of equal pay for equal work irrespective of sex as legally binding, part-timers and full-timers had been paid the same hourly rates, but women had been paid 90% of male

---

[79] [1981] ECR 911.

wages. After 1975, women and men were paid the same wages for like work, but part-timers were paid 90% of full-timers' wages. All the part-timers were female with the exception of one man who, after retirement, was allowed to continue work on an irregular basis.

Held: The Industrial Tribunal referred the case to the ECJ, asking whether this constituted sex discrimination. The Court of Justice did not deliver a clear answer, but reserved the last decision for the national court. It did, however, deliver some arguments.

Judgment: "10 . . . The differences in pay prohibited by Article 119 EEC [now Article 141 EC] are therefore exclusively those based on the difference of the sex of the workers. Consequently the fact that part time work is paid at an hourly rate lower than pay for full-time work does not amount per se to discrimination prohibited by Article 119 . . .

11 . . . The fact that work paid at time rates is remunerated at an hourly rate which varies according to the number of hours worked per week does not offend against the principle of equal pay . . . in so far as the difference in pay between part time work and full-time work is attributable to factors which are objectively justified and are in no way related to any discrimination based on sex.

12 . . . in particular, when . . . the employer is endeavouring, on economic grounds which may be objectively justified, to encourage full-time work irrespective of the sex of the worker.

13. By contrast, if it is established that a considerably smaller percentage of women than of men perform the minimum number of weekly working hours required in order to be able to claim the full-time hourly rate of pay, the inequality in pay will be contrary to Article 119 of the Treaty where, regard being had to the difficulties encountered by women in arranging to work that minimum number of hours per week, the pay policy of the undertaking in question cannot be explained by factors other than discrimination based on sex.

14 . . . [I]t is for the national courts to decide in each individual case whether, regard being had to the facts of the case, its history and the employer's intention, a pay policy such as that which is at issue in the main proceedings although represented as a difference based on weekly working hours is or is not in reality discrimination based on the sex of the worker.

15 . . . [A] difference in pay between full-time workers and part time workers does not amount to discrimination prohibited by Article 119 of the treaty unless it is in reality merely an indirect way of reducing the level of pay of part time workers on the ground that that group of workers is composed exclusively or predominantly of women."

Note: relevance of Jenkins to developing the definition, although the Court upheld the intent requirement

(1) Having to address the still dominant theme of indirect gender discrimination, i.e. discrimination on grounds of part-time work, the ECJ was reluctant to establish a principle of indirect discrimination.

(2) In this decision, the Court considered intent as a necessary element of a prohibition of indirect discrimination. While some of the elements of the prohibition as developed in US, British and Irish law were mentioned, the definition is certainly not fleshed out clearly here.

It took another five years for the Court to develop a true definition of indirect sex discrimination, when deciding in *Bilka* upon reference from the German Federal Labour Court.

ECJ, 13 May 1986[80]   **3.EC.16.**
Case 170/84, Bilka—Kaufhaus GmbH v. *Karin Weber von Hartz*

WHETHER REQUIRING FULL-TIME WORK TO BE INCLUDED IN AN OCCUPATIONAL
PENSION SCHEME IS INDIRECT DISCRIMINATION

Bilka

Facts: Bilka Kaufhaus GmbH operated a supplementary pension scheme for its employees. The scheme was based on an agreement between the works council and the employer, and its provisions were deemed to be an integral part of the employees' contracts of employment. The scheme was changed several times. According to the version in force from 26 October 1973, part-time employees would only receive an occupational pension if they had worked full-time for at least 15 years within a total period of 20 years. Ms. Weber worked for Bilka as a sales assistant from 1961 to 1976, working part-time from October 1972. Thus she did not qualify for an occupational pension. She initiated proceedings before German labour courts, challenging the legality of the occupational pension scheme inter alia because it violated the principle of equal pay. Among the employees of Bilka, 75% of the women worked part-time, but only 10% of the men.

Held: Article 119 of the EEC Treaty is infringed by a department store company which excludes part-time employees from its occupational pension scheme where that exclusion affects a far greater number of women than men, unless the undertaking shows that the exclusion is based on objectively justified factors unrelated to any discrimination on grounds of sex. [The] department store company may justify the . . . policy . . . on the ground that it seeks to employ as few part-time workers as possible, where it is found that the means chosen for achieving that objective correspond to a real need on the part of the undertaking, are appropriate with a view to achieving the objective in question and are necessary to that end.

Judgment: "24. In the first of its questions the national court asks whether a staff policy pursued by a department store company excluding part time employees from an occupational pension scheme constitutes discrimination contrary to Article 119 where that exclusion affects a far greater number of women than men.

25 . . . Reference must be made to the Judgment (in *Jenkins*).

26. In that judgment the court considered the question whether the payment of a lower hourly rate for part time work than for full-time work was compatible with Article 119 . . .

28. The conclusion reached by the Court in its judgment of 31 March 1981 is therefore equally valid in the context of this case.

29. If, therefore, it should be found that a much lower proportion of women than of men work full time, the exclusion of part time workers from the occupational pension scheme would be contrary to Article 119 of the Treaty where, taking into account the difficulties encountered by women workers in working full-time, that measure could not be explained by factors which exclude any discrimination on grounds of sex.

30. However, if the undertaking is able to show that its pay practice may be explained by objectively justified factors unrelated to any discrimination on grounds of sex there is no breach of Article 119 . . .

32 . . . [W]hether the reasons put forward by Bilka to explain its pay policy may be regarded as 'objectively justified economic grounds' . . .

33 . . . Bilka argues that the exclusion of part time workers from the occupational pension scheme is intended solely to discourage part time work, since in general part time workers refuse to work in the late afternoon and on Saturdays . . . It was therefore necessary to make full-time work more attractive than part time work, by making the occupational pension scheme open only to full-time workers . . .

---

[80] [1986] ECR 1607.

36. It is for the national court, which has sole jurisdiction to make findings of fact, to determine whether and to what extent the grounds put forward by an employer to explain the adoption of a pay practice which applies independently of a worker's sex but in fact affects more women than men may be regarded as objectively justified economic grounds. If the national court finds that the measures chosen by Bilka correspond to a real need on the part of the undertaking, are appropriate with a view to achieving the objectives pursued and are necessary to that end, the fact that the measures affect a far greater number of women than men is not sufficient to show that they constitute an infringement of Article 119."

Notes: continuing relevance of the Bilka decision

(1) Although the ECJ referred extensively to its decision in *Jenkins,* it went a decisive step further in abandoning the requirement of intent.

(2) The case also established a three element test for any objective justification: the employer, to justify any policy that affects more women than men, needs to show that the aims pursued correspond to a real need, and that the distinction is appropriate and necessary. From this, one can conclude that, where there is a less discriminatory alternative, the measure is not objectively justified. The court also established the principle that it is for the national court to decide whether the objective justification is sufficient.

(3) Upon receiving the ECJ decision, the Federal Labour Court held that this was not the case, as employing part-time employees was economically preferable in a department store, and thus the motive cited was not corresponding to a real need.[81]

(4) It should be noted that the ECJ already established a first difference to the British statutory definition by referring to a pay practice rather than a differentiating criterion. This is not surprising, as the AG referred to the *Griggs* decision in his argument, which is also mirrored in the result.

As a result of this case-law, the definition of indirect discrimination in EC law consisted of two main elements: first, a neutrally worded distinction resulting in disparate impact for nationals of other Member States or women or men respectively; and secondly, there was no objective justification for the use of a distinction. There were two differences between indirect discrimination on grounds of nationality and on grounds of sex. As regards nationality, the Court never required a precise proportion of nationals and non-nationals to be established. The *Bilka* test for sex discrimination, however, was based on statistics. Secondly, only in sex discrimination cases did the Court insist on the objective justification being unrelated to any discrimination on grounds of sex.

CODIFYING THE DEFINITION

The first legislative definition in Community law of the prohibition to discriminate indirectly was established by Directive 97/80/EC[82] on the burden of proof in the area of sex discrimination law. Its Article 2(2) defined indirect discrimination as follows:

---

[81] BAG, 14 October 1986, 3 AZR 66/83 BAGE 53, 161.

"[F]or the purposes of the principle of equal treatment [on grounds of sex D.S.] indirect discrimination shall exist where an apparently neutral provision, criterion or practice disadvantages a substantially higher proportion of the members of one sex unless that provision, criterion or practice is appropriate and necessary and can be justified by objective factors unrelated to sex."

This definition corresponded with the ECJ case-law on indirect sex discrimination, where the use of statistics had been deemed decisive, whereas the ECJ had not argued on a numerical basis in its case-law on indirect nationality discrimination, e.g. in the *Sotgiu* case (above **3.EC.14.**). According to Directive 97/80/EC, the use of statistics remained decisive in establishing indirect gender discrimination, which meant that some cases were lost due to insufficient statistical material (see below 3.5.1.B).

The four Directives on equal treatment of persons contain a slightly different definition of the concept. These definitions read:

Directive 2000/43/EC of 29 June 2000   **3.EC.17.**
implementing the principle of equal treatment between
persons irrespective of racial or ethnic origin (Racial Equality Directive)[83]

Article 2(2)
Indirect discrimination shall be taken to occur where an apparently neutral provision, criterion or practice would put persons of a racial or ethnic origin at a particular disadvantage compared with other persons, unless that provision, criterion or practice is objectively justified by a legitimate aim and the means of achieving that aim are appropriate and necessary.

Directive 2000/78/EC establishing a general framework for equal   **3.EC.18.**
treatment in employment and occupation (Employment Equality Directive)[84]

Article 2(2)
b) indirect discrimination shall be taken to occur where an apparently neutral provision, criterion or practice would put persons having a particular religion or belief, a particular disability, a particular age, or a particular sexual orientation at a particular disadvantage compared with other persons unless:

(i)   that provision, criterion or practice is objectively justified by a legitimate aim and the means of achieving that aim are appropriate and necessary, or
(ii) as regards persons with a particular disability, the employer or any person or organisa-tion to whom this Directive applies, is obliged, under national legislation, to take appropriate measures in line with the principles contained in Article 5 in order to elim-inate disadvantages entailed by such provision, criterion or practice.

---

[82] Directive 97/80/EC of 15 December 1997 on the burden of proof in cases of discrimination based on sex [1998] OJ L14/6. This directive will expire with effect of 15 August 2009 (Art. 34 Directive 2006/54/EC, [2006] OJ L204/23).
[83] [2000] OJ L180/22
[84] [2000] OJ L303/16.

> *Directive 76/207/EEC of 9 February 1976 on the implementation*   **3.EC.19.**
> *of the principle of equal treatment for men and women as regards access to*
> *employment, vocational training and promotion, and working conditions,*[85]
> *amended by Directive 2002/73/EC of the European Parliament and of the*
> *Council of 23 September 2002 (Gender Employment Directive)*[86]

2. For the purposes of this Directive, the following definitions shall apply: . . . indirect discrimination: where an apparently neutral provision, criterion or practice would put persons of one sex at a particular disadvantage compared with persons of the other sex, unless that provision, criterion or practice is objectively justified by a legitimate aim, and the means of achieving that aim are appropriate and necessary [This definition is repeated literally in Directive 2004/113/EC (Gender Goods and Services Directive) Article 2, and will not be changed by Directive 2006/54/EC].

These codifications harmonise previous legislation and case-law. There are, however, a few specific issues to be noted. All the definitions diverge from Directive 97/80/EC insofar as they replace the "disadvantage (for) a substantial higher proportion" by "particular disadvantage". This difference was introduced in order to avoid the necessity to establish statistical evidence, especially for sensitive areas such as sexual orientation or race. There is some argument as to whether the precise wording amounts to throwing the baby out with the bathwater insofar as indirect discrimination is now no longer defined as being aimed at group justice.[87] The Directives' text does not specify that such statistical evidence will be possible in all Member States. The younger Directives also do not state explicitly that the objective justification must be unrelated to any of the discrimination grounds. A third difference from the wording seems to be that the younger Directives require a comparison, whereas Directive 97/80/EC only refers to a higher proportion. This difference in wording may, however, be a consequence of omitting the requirement for statistics. A numerical approach to detrimental effect, at least if one assumes that there are only two subgroups of sex, will always involve a comparison between women and men. The last difference in wording is the specific link of indirect discrimination against disabled persons with positive measures in Article 2(2)(b)ii of the Framework Directive. The conceptual consequences of the new legislation cannot be assessed in full yet, as there is no case-law on these. We will, however, present some material which will allow cautious conclusions to their future applications.

3.4. PROBLEMS OF COMPARISON

As we have seen, indirect discrimination law has been developed in common law jurisdictions: originating in US case-law on racial discrimination, it was adopted in

---

[85] [1976] OJ L39/40.
[86] [2002] OJ L269/15.
[87] See Barnard and Hepple, above n. 21.

UK and Irish discrimination law and thus found its way to Europe, although the ECJ first developed the definitions of indirect discrimination on grounds of nationality and sex in cases it had to decide upon references from German courts. ECJ case-law incrementally specified different elements of the definition, in discourse with national courts, which referred questions to it. The interim result is a codification of this case-law, which all Member States are now obliged to implement into their legal systems.

Thus, European indirect discrimination law serves as a medium to transplant a statutory concept from common law jurisdictions into the majority of Continental legal orders, including some Eastern European legal orders since 2005, and of course into the Scandinavian legal order. In comparative law, there is sometimes scepticism towards legal transplants,[88] although some authors stress that transplanting and the resulting fine-tuning of legal concepts to other legal orders is the most common route of developing legal systems.[89] Especially in the case of indirect discrimination law, there has been a certain degree of reluctance by some legal orders to accept this specific legal transplant.

3.4.1. INDIRECT DISCRIMINATION IN FRENCH LAW

This is particularly so for the French legal order, where, prior to the new legislation implementing Directives 2000/43/EC and 2000/78/EC in 2001,[90] only few cases on indirect discrimination were to be found. Besides the structure of the French legal system, specific approaches to equality policy and integration of minorities, especially racial minorities, may have been more influential. Several authors point to the republican principle of one nation that is threatened by acknowledging that there are different partitions of society which might warrant specific statistical attention.[91]

Geddes and Guiraudon[92] even consider the issue of indirect (racial) discrimination as a dividing line between the French and the UK approach to migration. They connect the reluctance of the French legislature and judiciary towards this concept with differences in approaches to racial discrimination in Europe. The Directives

---

[88] P. Legrand, "The Impossibility of Legal Transplants" (1997) 4 *MJ* 111, revised version under the title "What "Legal Transplants?" in D. Neelken, J. Feest (eds.), *Adapting Legal Cultures* (Oxford, Hart Publishing, 2001) 55–70.

[89] Alan Watson, *Legal Transplants: An Approach to Comparative Law*, 2nd edn (Athens, GA, University of Georgia Press, 1993) concludes that legal transplants are surprisingly common and work well in most cases. The image of fine tuning as a new challenge for comparative law is also used in that regard (E. Örücü, "Critical Comparative Law: Considering Paradoxes for Legal Systems in Transition" (2000) 4(1) *EJCL* (electronic publication, article source: <http://www.ejcl.org/41/art41-1.html>).

[90] K. Berthou, "New Hopes for French Anti-Discrimination Law" (2003) 19 *IJCLLIR* 109, 111, 117.

[91] See Berthou, *ibid.*, 118; see also Ch. Wallace, "European Integration and Legal Culture: Indirect Sex Discrimination in the French Legal System" (1999) 19 *Legal Studies* 397, with the proposition that certainty as a legal principle leads to a reluctance to pursue equality in fact through means of law.

[92] A. Geddes and V.Guiraudon, "Britain, France and EU Anti-Discrimination Policy: The Emergence of an EU Policy Paradigm" (2004) 27 *West European Politics* 334.

have, in their account, been lobbied for by "networks with strong Anglo-Dutch intellectual influences". The policy concept cherished by these networks were based on acknowledging the diversity of a country's population and the existence of visible minorities, and resonated with the statistical approach to discrimination law that lies at the heart of a prohibition to indirect discrimination. Other networks, based in Germany and France, were more concerned about citizenship and immigration rights and less concerned about a group-based approach to non-discrimination law. If this account is realistic, France may not be the only country where the concept of indirect discrimination will only reluctantly be applied to racial and ethnic discrimination. The prevailing reluctance of French courts to apply the concept of indirect discrimination even to gender cases leads to French cases being largely absent from the detailed analysis. Instead, we present some case-law in this section to illustrate the point made in doctrine regarding the difficulties of French courts in applying the concept.

The first series of cases in which French courts applied the concept of indirect discrimination were the *Sunday trading* cases, decided by the criminal section of the Cour de Cassation in 1995.

Court of Cassation, Criminal Section (Cass.crim.), 10 January 1995[93] **3.FR.20.**
Case 92-82490, Baggio

RULE OF SUNDAY REST AS INDIRECT SEX DISCRIMINATION

Baggio

Facts: Mr. Baggio Daniel was ordered to pay three fines of 1500 francs each for the infringement of the rule of Sunday rest, because he employed women working on Sundays. He appealed against this judgment, claiming that the Sunday rest rule was to the detriment of women because most part-time workers were women, and therefore it was indirect sex discrimination, applying for a reference to the ECJ on interpretation of Directive 76/207/EEC.

Held: The Court of Nimes, Criminal Division ordered Mr. Baggio to pay the fines. His appeal is dismissed, as the rule of Sunday rest does not constitute any discrimination on grounds of sex, direct or indirect, as a piece of legislation that aims at protecting employees from disadvantages can never be discriminatory.

Judgment: ". . . Considering that, if the judges wrongly declared the plea lodged by the defendant as inadmissible, pursuant to section 386 of the Code of criminal procedure, the contested Judgment will however not incur the motion of censure, as the plea is without basis; That indeed, the rule which sets Sunday as the weekly rest day was taken in the sole interest of workers, men or women, and constitutes a social advantage; that, consequently, its application cannot, by nature, involve a direct or indirect discrimination to the detriment of one or the other . . ."

The second *Sunday rest* case had no different outcome, but provided a definition of indirect discrimination developed by the *Cour de Cassation*.

[93] Bull. des arrêts de la Cour de Cassation. Chambre criminelle, 1995, No. 9.

Court of Cassation, Criminal Section *(Cass.crim.)*, 27 June 1995[94] **3.FR.21.**
Mme Marrie et Sauty

RULE OF SUNDAY REST AS INDIRECT SEX DISCRIMINATION

Marrie

Facts: Mrs. Marrie was accused of having employed female part-time workers for work on a Sunday.

Held: Mrs. Marrie was fined for infringing the rule of Sunday rest and appealed against that judgment. The Court of Appeal displayed a rather critical stand towards the concept of indirect discrimination in the first place, which seems partly like an ironic approach to applying it in the specific circumstances at hand:

Judgment: "As Article L-221-5 Code du Travail applies to female and male employees indistinctively, and does thus neither in law nor in fact qualify Sunday work as male work or disadvantage women in their access to employment, and if, on the other hand, as the claimant submits, employment opportunities on Sundays are predominantly occupied by female personnel, taking advantage of specific arrangements, repealing the legislation on the weekly rest period might result in creating indirect discrimination to the disadvantage of male employment."

Notes commenting on Marrie

(1) The Court did not follow the argument of the claimants, who—in line with European law—argued that discrimination may exist in the following circumstances:

". . .when a piece of national legislation has the effect of disadvantaging female workers by reason of the simple fact that they represent a smaller percentage of a category of worker benefiting from advantages, or a higher percentage of a category of workers treated less favourably . . . if on grounds of the predominance of women in commercial activity during Sundays, the prohibition to open shops on this day results in an indirect discrimination to the detriment of women in access to employment and remuneration . . ."

(2) The Cour de Cassation does not apply the concept of objective justification though, but merely repeats its finding from *Baggio* that a legislative provision meant for the protection of workers cannot, by its nature, be considered as indirect discrimination under French law.

Concluding notes: evaluation of the Sunday trading cases
These decisions have been cited as examples of the distance of the French judiciary from the concept of indirect discrimination.[95] However, we have to admit that the reasoning to bring the cases under sex discrimination law was not in line with its basic concepts. The claimant did not substantiate the negative effect a prohibition of Sunday work would have especially on women. In addition, the argument that Sunday rest is in the interest of workers could have been brought under the "objective justification test" if applied correctly. If one argued that, due to the rhythmic human

[94] JCP édE 1996 767 (annotation by J.H. Robert).
[95] See Wallace, above n. 91, 397, 401–2.

constitution, a day's rest after six days contributes to human health generally, and that Sunday rest was indispensable to achieve this, an objective justification would have been given.

In essence, all we can derive from these cases is that the French judges were not prepared to apply the concept of indirect discrimination on a rather far-fetched factual basis. Later cases, however, demonstrate more clearly that French courts were not prepared to find indirect discrimination even when confronted with a set of facts that could be characterised as a model of indirect discrimination, namely denial of participation in a promotion procedure on grounds of part-time work.

Court of Cassation, Social Section (Cass. Soc.), 9 April 1996[96] **3.FR.22.**
Case 92—41103, Soufflet v. CPAM

DISCRIMINATION AGAINST PART-TIME WORKERS AND (INDIRECT) SEX
DISCRIMINATION

Soufflet

Facts: Mrs. Soufflet entered the service of Caisse primaire d'assurances maladie de la Marne (Local Health Insurance Fund) in April 1983 and was admitted to the national examination for technicians in December 1984. From November 1987 she worked, at her own request, part-time. After a training course in November 1989 she was appointed as technician with CoEfficient 128, with retroactive effect from 1 July 1989. However, a promotion with the rank of qualified agent with CoEfficient 132 was denied to her because her professional practical time was insufficient.

Held: Mrs. Soufflet brought proceedings and lost her case both before the Court of First Instance and the regional court (Cour d'appel de Metz). She then raised a further appeal to the Cour de Cassation. The Court of Appeal held that the extension of the required minimum seniority for participating in promotion procedures for part-time employees corresponding to the degree of reduction of working time does not constitute indirect discrimination against women.

Judgment: ". . . that the provision of section 5 of the Protocol of 20 July 1976 relating to reduced working time in social security organisations, according to which the periods of professional practice planned for various uses of the classification must be increased to the same extent of the reduction of working time, constitutes a method of a contractual nature for exercising the right to promotion, within the meaning of subparagraph 8 of section L. 212-4-2 of the Labour Code, which does not undermine the principle of equal rights between part time employees and full-time employees laid down by the same text; . . . and . . . that the Court of Appeal, upon investigating whether this provision could constitute discrimination, albeit indirect discrimination, quite rightly denied that this was the case."

Note

It is rather conspicuous how the Cour de Cassation did not at all apply the French definition of indirect discrimination as developed in *Marrie*. Although that definition was developed by a different chamber, such outright denial of the existence of the concept seems surprising, to say the least.

---

[96] Recueil Dalloz 1996 No. 20 IR p. 136.

There had been an earlier case where the Cour de Cassation had acknowledged indirect discrimination on grounds of sex for denying a woman the opportunity to undergo special assessment for a promotion because she was on maternity leave. Again, this case demonstrates that the Cour de Cassation defines indirect discrimination very differently from the ECJ, which has categorised discrimination on grounds of pregnancy as direct discrimination.

Court of Cassation, Social Section (Cass. Soc.), 28 March 1995[97] **3.FR.23.**
Case 94-3154, CNAV v. Thibault

PERFORMANCE EVALUATION AND PREGNANCY DISCRIMINATION

Thibault

Facts: The Cour de Cassation had to decide upon the problems of Madame Thibault, who worked for a public body as legal drafter and whose eligibility for promotion was thus subject to a special assessment procedure know as "la notation". She was denied participation in the annual "la notation" because she had been absent for more than six months in the relevant year, partly because she had taken maternity leave.

Held: The Court of First Instance considered that she had been discriminated against on grounds of sex. The Cour de Cassation actually considered this as a case of indirect discrimination, as is demonstrated by the questions it referred to the ECJ.

Judgment: "1. Is depriving an employee of the possibility of professional promotion which concerns only female workers against the principle of equality in promotion (art. 1 paragraph 1 of EC Directive 76/207)?

2. Is the refusal of eligibility for performance assessment on grounds because of maternity leave an indirect discrimination (Art. 2 paragraph 1)?

3. Which is related to the working conditions (art. 5 paragraph 1)?"

Note

Unsurprisingly, the ECJ decided that such a rule was contrary to EC law as being directly discriminatory.[98] While it seemed to be a fixed rule for a long time under EC law that pregnancy discrimination is direct discrimination on grounds of sex, admittedly the rule in question was applicable to men and women alike. In *Schnorbus*,[99] the ECJ chose to consider different treatment on grounds of compulsory military service as indirect instead of direct discrimination, although only men have to register for compulsory military service. With hindsight, the Cour de Cassation's approach to pregnancy discrimination may not seem so far off the mark.

Taken together, these cases and the *Sunday rest* decisions indicate a certain tendency of the French judiciary to resolve problems of gender discrimination

---

[97] Unfortunately, the wording of the question is neither reproduced in the ECJ case nor in the publication of the reference by the Cour de Cassation ([1995] Droit Social 1036). It is thus cited here from an annotation by M.A. Moreau ([1995] 4 *Droit Social* 1037.

[98] ECJ, Judgment of 30 April 1998, Case C–136/95 *Thibault* [1998] ECR I–2011.

[99] ECJ, Judgment of 7 December 2000, Case C–79/99 *Schnorbus* [2000] ECR I–10997; for more details see above ch. 2, excerpt number **2.EC.13.**

preferably under different headings. This tendency is described by an insider to the French system in the following words.

Ph. Martin, "Droit social et discriminations sexuelles: **3.FR.24.**
à propos des discriminations générées par la loi"[100]

"Any conclusion that the theory of indirect discrimination is insufficiently effective in our domestic legal order would be based on its being ignored in practice by the national judge. This ignorance is, above all, the result of a certain reluctance to argue on an unfamiliar terrain. The national judge is at times tempted to use other means or other legal techniques suitable to achieve equivalent effects as would using the concept of indirect discrimination. It [i.e. the concept of indirect discrimination] remains an alien element for the French judge who is little inclined to reason on a terrain that is by far too sociological. It is noticeable, though, that in certain cases other legal techniques permit to pursue discrimination. For example, when an employer implements (several) dismissals for economic reasons, he must refer to objective criteria which allow him to establish an order of dismissals. May he nevertheless refer to criteria for choosing employees for dismissal which could in effect frustrate protective legislation? The question has been posed to the judge following the dismissal of several employees on parental leave who theoretically should have benefited from employment protection by virtue of Article L 122-28-3 Code du Travail. The Cour de Cassation has held that an employer who dismisses these persons with priority violates Article L 122-28-3. The Court thus, as a result, condemned the employer to award the employees compensation for unfair dismissal. For this it did not reason at all on terms of direct or indirect discrimination as the Community Court had invited it to do."

In more recent judgments, there still seems to be an awkward approach towards indirect discrimination in case-law, although the concept is now mentioned, albeit not defined, in French legislation.

Court of Appeal (Cour d'Appel Rennes), 5 February 2002[101]   **3.FR.25.**
Case 01/00393, S.A. Cogifer v. Ferre, Gruel, Robert et Tarib

REDUCTION IN WORKING TIME AND INDIRECT DISCRIMINATION

Ferre et autres

Facts: The enterprise S.A. Cogifer Val de Rennes reduced, according to Law Aubry II, the weekly working time from 39 to 35 hours, without a reduction in pay. Mr. Ferre and three of his colleagues started working for S.A. Cogifer just after the reduction in working time and were only paid for the 35 hours they were actually working, the firm claiming that the other tariff applied only to those workers who were employed at the time the reduction in working time took place.

---

[100] In [1996] *Droit Social* 562, 563–4.
[101] Numéro JurisData: 2002-169733.

365

Held: Mr. Ferre and his colleagues won in first instance, but the enterprise appealed. The Court of Second Instance in Rennes upheld the first instance decision, relying on the principle of equal pay and the prohibition of indirect discrimination.

Judgment: "(On the application of the Loi Aubry II and its article 32): Considering that all employers are under an obligation to assure equality of remuneration among all employees in their enterprise in equal conditions, especially with equal work, by virtue of the Universal Declaration of Human Rights, the International Covenant of 1966, Article 119 of the EC Treaty, Directive 75/117/EEC on approximation of national laws in relation to applying the principle of equal remuneration which affirms the right of all workers to an equal remuneration for work of equal value, and the equality principle 'equal pay for equal work', established by Articles L 133-5-4 and L 136-2-8 Code du Travail, and thus have to justify differences in remuneration among their employees by recourse to objective factors without any discrimination. Considering that respecting the principle 'equal pay for equal work' in the presence of an indirect discrimination resulting from applying a collective agreement, a usage or a legislative provision . . . the court is obliged to turn down the disputed rule which will have the effect of establishing unequal treatment between employees of the same category, doing the same work and of comparable seniority, and to apply the same scheme of remuneration to the disadvantaged employees as applies to the other employees."

Note

While this is one of the few cases where a French court has relied explicitly on a notion of indirect discrimination, the analysis is devoid of any attempt at ascertaining detrimental effect of a neutral measure. The Court rather seems to establish a principle of equal pay for equal work generally, without any reference to discrimination grounds. It thus avoids the question whether among the newly employed those disadvantaged for reasons of a certain discrimination ground, e.g. ethnic minority workers, were over-represented. The mentioning of indirect discrimination does not seem to contribute to the merits of the case.

In other cases, claims based on indirect discrimination failed due to reasons unrelated to indirect discrimination law. For example, a recent claim by an organisation operating against racism before the Conseil d'Etat[102] failed on the grounds that French procedural law does not provide for an "action populaire", although there might be a good argument that the decree attacked was an example of indirect discrimination: according to this decree, free health services for poor citizens were to be withheld from those not legally resident in France for at least three months.[103] In the 1993 *Alitalia* decision,[104] the principle of indirect discrimination derived from Article 39 EC is applied in relation to a collective agreement placing employees

---

[102] Conseil d'Etat, Juge des référés, Judgment of 21 Octobre 2005, No. 285577, *AIDES* v. *Ministere de l'emploi, de la cohesion sociale et du logement.*

[103] Upon collective complaint of FIDH to the European Committee of Social Rights, a violation of Art. 17 of the Revised Charter of European Social Rights, which guarantees children's rights, was found. The European Committee of Social Rights, Collective Complaint No. 14/2003, *International Federation of Human Rights Leagues (FIDH)* v. *France* Resolution of the Committee of Ministers ResChS(2005)6, available on the website of the Council of Europe.

[104] Cour de Cassation, Judgment of 17 June 2003, No. 01-41.557, *Bruno Gasperini et autres* v. *Société Alitalia et autres.*

resident in France in a more detrimental position than employees resident in Italy. This decision does not refer to the reasons covered by Article 13 (i.e. race, ethnic origin, sex, religion and belief, disability, sexual orientation and age), but is still a sign of hope for acknowledgement of indirect discrimination as a concept in French law.

3.4.2. INDIRECT DISCRIMINATION IN SCANDINAVIAN LAW

The predominant influence of British and Dutch law on younger equality legislation in the Community must not obscure the fact that other Member States have specific traditions even in the area of indirect discrimination law. Especially for Scandinavian law, it is reported that non-discrimination law, although considered as contrary to the tradition of self-regulation especially in labour law, gained in acceptance under the influence of the women's movement and international law, although the extension of equality law to other grounds such as race, ethnicity, disability and sexual orientation is said to have been spurred by Community law developments.[105] However, the prohibitions of discrimination, including that of indirect discrimination, were introduced well before any Community law obligation, most notably so in the case of Sweden. There, a 1991 Act defined sex discrimination as follows:

> "Sex discrimination occurs when someone is disadvantaged in situations where the disadvantage has a direct or indirect connection with the person's sex".[106]

This definition resembles the regulatory technique in international law much more than the recent EC law definition. Other early Scandinavian pieces of legislation mirrored a similar approach, while the legislation has now been converted in line with the more restrictive EC legislation. Focusing on disadvantage and its being connected with any of the forbidden grounds, the original Scandinavian definitions of indirect discrimination allow a more holistic approach than a definition focusing on a single requirement. It is not surprising that, from a Scandinavian perspective, the ECJ case-law on indirect discrimination does not appear as great an achievement as from a UK perspective. With regard to the Finnish legislation prior to the latest development in Community Law, Karoliina Athela specifies:

K. Ahtela, "The Revised Provisions on Sex Discrimination in **3.FI.26.**
European Community Law: A Critical Assessment"[107]

"Unfortunately, the concept of indirect discrimination, obviously influenced by a process of dialogue between the British courts and the Court of Justice, may seem partial and restrictive when looking from the point of view of other legal structures.

---

[105] L. Roseberry, "Equal Rights and Discrimination Law in Sweden" in P. Wahlgreen (ed.), *Stability and Change in Nordic Labour Law* (2002) 43 *Scandinavian Studies in Law* 215.
[106] Section 15 Jämstelldhetslag SFS 1991, 433, translation from Roseberry, *ibid.*, 238, note 132d.
[107] (2005) 11 *ELJ* 57, 71–2.

Section 7 in the Finnish Equality Act is worded as follows:

Direct or indirect discrimination on the basis of sex is prohibited. For the purposes of this Act, discrimination on the basis of sex means:

(1) treating men and women differently on the basis of sex;
(2) treating women differently for reasons of pregnancy or childbirth; or
(3) treating people differently on the basis of parenthood, family responsibilities or for some other reason related to sex.

Discrimination is also involved in any procedure whereby people are *de facto* assigned a different status in relation to each other for the reasons mentioned in paragraph 2.

Even if not explicitly stated, direct discrimination refers to clauses 1 and 2 in the second paragraph, and indirect discrimination to clause 3 in the second paragraph, as well as to the third paragraph. Thus indirect discrimination is defined in two ways: (1) unequal treatment on the basis of a reason related to sex, such as parenthood or family responsibility, or (2) neutral treatment that *de facto* leads to different outcome on the basis of sex or a reason based on sex.
   The definition of indirect discrimination in the Directive [the article analyses Directive 2002/73/EC] . . . is more restrictive in four respects: 1. The Community definition does not allow comparisons between two groups which have both women and men as members . . . 2. The Community definition . . . requires a greater difference in treatment (particular disadvantage), 3. The Community definition requires that provision, criterion or practice be apparently neutral, whereas he Finnish definition does not require that 4. The Community definition includes a justification, whereas the Finnish definition does not.
   The Commission on the Reform of the Equality Act selected to suggest keeping the Act unchanged regarding points 1 and 2, and inserting Community legislation's features, presented in points 3 and 4, into the law proposal. This might reflect the confusion over the meaning of the definitions: should they be taken as such into national legislation or should national legislation ensure that the same protection be given, at least, against discrimination? It was proposed the type of indirect discrimination as forbidden in Clause 3 in the second paragraph, to be left in the law, because the level of protection against discrimination cannot be decreased in connection with the implementation of the Directive. However, the question emerged: Should the justification also be attached to the provision in Clause 3 in the second paragraph? The Commission on the Reform of the Equality Act decided to suggest this, obviously so as not to have to distinguish between two kinds of indirect discrimination, one justifiable, another not. This notwithstanding, the result is clumsy, and some cases of indirect discrimination, as recognised by the Equality Act, simply must be interpreted into the suggested provision—it was not possible simultaneously to keep with the wording of the Community definition and to express all the contents of the prior national provision."

Note

This disappointment expressed at the content of Community law mirrors the fundamentally different approaches between the English lawyer, who focuses on small details, and the Nordic lawyer, who focuses on the general purpose of the law and wishes to see social progress aided by it. Accordingly, lawyers from the Nordic family of law often take a collective approach, considering whether a bundle of rules used in an institution impacts negatively on the situation of women or ethnic minorities. This specific approach to indirect discrimination law is worth considering as a special contribution in as many instances as possible. Unfortunately, due to the less than adversarial Scandinavian tradition of resolving conflict, there are fewer court cases than would be desirable for illustrating practical consequences of such an approach.

3.4.3. INDIRECT DISCRIMINATION IN GERMAN LAW

As regards the large families of law, the inclusion of Germany as a model jurisdiction is possible in the area of indirect discrimination law, although there are some caveats. First, the statutory definition of indirect discrimination at Federal level was only introduced with the late implementation of non-discrimination Directives by the General Equal Treatment Act (Allgemeines Gleichbehandlungsgesetz (AGG) 2006).[108] The definition in § 3 (3) AGG literally copies the German text of the Directives. Prior to implementation, there were definitions in the field of gender equality law in some of the 17 gender equality acts covering the public servants of Länder and Bund,[109] but these are only rarely relevant before courts. Notwithstanding this, case-law has firmly established the concept of indirect discrimination, with references by the Labour Courts having contributed towards development of case-law of the ECJ in the area.

The relatively recent introduction of a statutory definition and the fact that the concept had only been discussed since the 1970s often lead to the assumption that this is truly an imported concept in Germany. The Constitutional Court, however, when deciding upon a constitutional claim of the employer *Bilka*, whose occupational pension scheme was held to be indirectly discriminatory following the ECJ decision in *Bilka* (see above **3.EC.16.**), against the final decision of the Federal Labour Court, grasped the opportunity to base the concept on traditional German constitutional law.

Federal Constitutional Court—1st Senate 2nd chamber   **3.DE.27.**
(BVerfG 1. Senat 2. Kammer), 28 September1992[110]
1 BvR 496/87, Anonymous

WHETHER THE FEDERAL LABOUR COURT'S JUDGMENT FOLLOWING THE ECJ
JUDGMENT IN BILKA VIOLATES CONSTITUTIONALLY PROTECTED RIGHTS

BVerfG Bilka follow up

Facts: The applicant, following the final judgment of the Federal Labour Court, relies on the constitu-tionally guaranteed "Rechtsstaatsprinzip" (rule of law) in challenging this judgment as being too surprising

---

[108] AGG, BGBl. Teil I, 17 August 2006, S. 1897; amendment BGBl. Teil I, 11 December 2006, S. 2745.
[109] On these see D.Schiek et al., *Frauengleichstellungsgesetze des Bundes und der Länder*, 2nd edn (Frankfurt, Bund-Verlag, 2002).
[110] NZA 1993, 213.

for subjecting the company to substantive financial obligations, which resulted from being obliged to grant occupational pensions to all former part-time employees.

Held: The Constitutional Court rejected the application.

Judgment: ". . .The applicant's reliance on the legality of their occupational pension scheme was not established enough to oblige the Federal Labour Court to restrict the effect of its own Judgment to future cases . . . Even at the time when the occupational pension scheme was first created, the legal position was less uncontroversial than suggested . . . The fact that the term 'indirect discrimination' was only beginning to be employed within employment law discourses after this concept had been explicitly stated for the first time in Directive 76/207/EC . . . does not change this. The Constitutional Court had expressed, in general terms, the deliberation behind the concept as early as 1958 in its first Judgment on funding of political parties. It held that an Act of Parliament, which avoids unequal treatment in its wording and defines its scope of application in an abstract and general manner, contradicts the constitutional equality clause if its practical application results in obvious inequality and this unequal effect must be attributed to the specific legal construct . . . Hanau and Preis rightly argue that the application of these principles on indirect sex discrimination is rather self evident . . ."

Note on definition of indirect discrimination by the German Constitutional Court

(1) This is not a full judgment of the Constitutional Court, but rather a chamber decision on the question whether the Constitutional Court will accept the application for substantial decision. The chamber rejected this, because it held that the principles behind indirect discrimination law are not alien to German constitutional law.

(2) In particular, the chamber concludes that the ECJ's decision should not have been surprising to the employer. Referring to the Constitutional Court's case-law on funding of political parties; the chamber finds that the principles behind indirect discrimination law have always been part and parcel of German law.

(3) When the Constitutional Court referred to indirect discrimination in its substantive case-law later on, it did not refer to these German roots of the concept. For example, in its decision of the Hamburg pension scheme, which excluded part-time employees, the Court held that Article 3 paragraph 3 Grundgesetz contains a prohibition of indirect discrimination as it had been acknowledged in the case-law of the ECJ and the Federal Labour Court.[111] Thus, the chamber decision of 1993 remains the only one linking indirect discrimination law to established principles of German constitutional law.

In Germany, the concept of indirect discrimination is nearly exclusively applied to sex discrimination, and is barely accepted as a possibility in other areas of discrimination law. The German case will thus only be partly relevant to this chapter, but will be integrated wherever possible.

---

[111] BVerfG 27.11.1997—1 BvL 12/91, BVerfGE 97, 35 (marginal no. 34 of the judgment). The Constitutional Court considered that excluding part-time employees did not amount do indirect discrimination, because the claimants had not brought convincing statistics to prove their case of detrimental effect. On establishing detrimental effects by statistics, see 3.5.1.B.

3.4.4.   INDIRECT DISCRIMINATION IN BRITISH AND IRISH LAW

Last but not least, we have to take into account that British and Irish concepts of indirect discrimination law, although having been the model for the Community law concept, have been influenced by Community law profoundly. The ECJ approaches any concept, including indirect discrimination law, in a more functional manner than is typical for a common law jurisdiction. Accordingly, *Kilpatrick* considers that, especially for British law, the Community influence has made the concept more practically relevant than it would have been without this influence.[112] These jurisdictions will also be referred to in their relation to Community law.

3.4.5.   INDIRECT DISCRIMINATION IN DUTCH LAW

Having embraced the so-called Anglo-American model of non-discrimination law, but nevertheless being rooted in a Continental legal tradition, Dutch law attains a special place in indirect discrimination law. Here we find many cases, most of them decided not by regular courts, but in the framework of the Equal Treatment Commission's quasi-judicial activity.[113] In contrast to UK tribunals and courts, the Equal Treatment Commission decisions tend to take a less formal approach, while still establishing a dogmatically inclined body of case-law geared to include issues of substantive equality. The Dutch system may be taken as an example of merging common law and Continental approaches towards indirect discrimination law.

3.4.6.   INDIRECT DISCRIMINATION IN OTHER MEMBER STATES

The majority of EU Member States have neither the specific reluctance we find in France nor the specifically positive approach to a group-based concept of discrimination we find in Scandinavia, which differs from the Community law definition. Many Member States, especially those which acceded to the EU only in 2004, copied the EU definition into national instruments, and it is as yet difficult to see whether and how the concept will be applied in practice. It is thus not only due to language difficulties that there are many Member States from which no cases are to be found in this chapter.

[112] C. Kilpatrick, "Community or Communities of Courts in European Integration? Sex Equality Dialogues Between UK Courts and the ECJ" (1998) 4 ELJ 121, 142.
[113] See below G. Moon, Chapter Eight: Enforcement Bodies, section 8.5.2.A.

3.5. INDIRECT DISCRIMINATION—SPECIFIC ELEMENTS

As has become apparent, the approaches to indirect discrimination vary between international and EU law, and there is even more variation within national law. For a comparative analysis it is important to isolate the main elements in such a way that each national approach is mirrored adequately. Focusing exclusively on the elements provided in the youngest EC legislative definitions of the concept is thus not appropriate. Of course, we will consider whether specific national developments are to be considered as conflicting with this definition.

Starting from a definition suitable for all legal orders, we find that there are only few undisputed issues in indirect discrimination law. It is agreed that a prohibition of indirect discrimination consists of two main elements. The first element is the existence of detrimental effect, which is the term we are going to use for a situation in which a rule, a set of rules, a single requirement or a practice disproportionately disadvantages persons of a specific race, ethnicity, religion or belief, sexual orientation or gender, etc. The second element is objective justification, i.e. there is no prohibited indirect discrimination if the measure or practice or the whole structure is objectively justified. Everything else is characterised by a great diversity.

3.5.1. ESTABLISHING DETRIMENTAL EFFECT

In this regard, two basic questions need to be solved.

The first one is to what exactly the detrimental effect is to be attributed. Is the claimant required to establish a specific requirement which causes detrimental effect or—at the other end of the spectrum—do we classify any structure which results in ground specific disadvantage as suspect? It will come as no surprise that the younger EC legislation actually occupies a middle position, which still needs to be carved out by case-law.

The second question is how exactly to establish detrimental effect. Here, a statistical approach competes with a qualitative approach.

Some remarks on terminology are in order at this stage. In Europe, the term "disparate impact" has traditionally been used to characterise indirect discrimination in general. It is thus capable of integrating a non-numerical approach to disparate impact, for which the younger discrimination Directives allow. However, in the US there has never been a move away from a statistical notion, and thus disparate impact signifies statistically disparate impact in their legal order. To avoid confusion especially for those who read US law, the term "disparate impact" will be used not as an overriding notion in this chapter, but only in relation to detrimental effect that is established statistically or quantitatively. As an overriding notion, the term "detrimental effect" will be used. This serves also to link EC indirect discrimination law with international human rights law.

As we have seen, indirect discrimination law developed from a rule on the burden of proof in the US, which is still reflected in its application. Under the burden of proof approach, indirect discrimination law amounts to accepting statistical proof.[114] In indirect discrimination cases, proving detrimental effect is the task of the applicant. Once detrimental effect is proved, the burden of proof shifts to the defendant, who needs to rebut the second-stage requirement (objective justification).

3.5.1.A.   TO WHAT IS THE DETRIMENTAL EFFECT ATTRIBUTED?

SPECIFIC REQUIREMENT OR CONDITION

As has been noted when tracing the origins of indirect discrimination law, British and Irish legislation as well as younger US case-law took a very narrow approach towards the cause of disparate impact. The claimant has to isolate a specific requirement or condition to which he or she is subjected and which disparately impacts upon the members of a "protected group".

Court of Appeal, 1 February 1983[115]   3.GB.28.
Perera v. The Civil Service Commission and The Department of Customs and Excise

WHETHER REFERRING TO THREE CRITERIA IS SUFFICIENT TO ESTABLISH A
"SPECIFIC REQUIREMENT"

Perera

Facts: Mr. Perera, aged 42, had applied for the position of legal assistant in the Civil Service, which was his third attempt to attain such a position. As a qualified lawyer in Sri Lanka, he had been admitted to the English bar four years before his application and thus fulfilled the requirement of being a qualified lawyer and barrister. He was not chosen for the position, though, after having been interviewed. He claimed that this was due to four additional requirements that were taken into account—experience in the UK, command of English, British nationality and age—and that these requirements were such that fewer applicants from ethnic minorities could comply with them than applicants from the ethnic majority. The board, however, did not decide exclusively on these criteria, but only took them into account, when assessing the applicants' qualifications under the four headings "personal qualities", "ability to communicate", "intellectual capacity" and "potential".

Held: The Industrial Tribunal concluded that the claimant had failed to show that that he was subjected to a specific requirement with which he could not comply. Rather, the lack of satisfying the additional requirements named by the claimant would not have constituted an absolute bar to being accepted for the position. Thus, the other issues of indirect discrimination were not discussed as the decision was based on the qualifications and not the requirements named by the claimant. Although these were taken into account, the claimant had failed to show that they had actually been applied. The Employment Appeal Tribunal (EAT) upheld this decision.

---

[114] See above M. Bell, Chapter 2: Direct Discrimination, section 2.4.2.A for statistical proof of direct discrimination.

[115] [1983] ICR 428.

Judgment: STEPHENSEN J.: ". . .The matters which have to be established by an applicant who claims that he has been discriminated against indirectly are, first of all, that there has been a requirement or condition, as the complainant put it, a 'must': something which has to be complied with. Here there was a requirement or condition for candidates for the post of legal assistant in the Civil Service: it was that the candidate should be either a qualified member of the English Bar or a qualified solicitor of the Supreme Court of this country . . . [T]hose . . . were fulfilled by the complainant. But . . . there is no other express requirement or condition, and he has to find a requirement or condition in the general combination of factors which he says the interview board took into account . . . That is the hurdle which, as it seems to me, he is unable to get over. If he were able to prove a particular requirement or condition, he would then have to prove that it had been applied by the board . . . in my opinion none of those factors could possibly be regarded as a requirement or a condition in the sense that the lack of it, whether of British nationality or even of the ability to communicate well in English, would be an absolute bar. The whole of the evidence indicates that a brilliant man whose personal qualities made him suitable as a legal assistant might well have been sent forward on a short list by the interview board in spite of being, perhaps, below standard on his knowledge of English and his ability to communicate in that language . . . I agree . . .that there was no application here of any requirement or condition, and no evidence of it. In my judgment the complainant has failed to prove what he has to prove in order to show a case of indirect discrimination.

O'CONNOR J.: It is only necessary to look at the request made by the commission to the interview board. In making their assessment, they were asked to give their opinion, individually, of the personal qualities of the applicant, his ability to communicate, his intellectual capacity and his potential; and in order to help the members of the board to form an opinion, the four categories were further particularised. For example, in considering their opinion on personal qualities they were asked to apply their minds to maturity, common sense and ability to get on with people; and, in expressing their opinion, limiting it to whether it was very good, good, fair or poor. In my judgment it is quite impossible to say that that exercise was imposing any condition or requirement on the board in making up their mind or in giving their opinion. The evidence . . . shows that in their general look at the applicants, and perhaps particularly at those applicants from overseas, they directed themselves that they should ask themselves whether the applicant had a good command of the English language, whether the applicant had British nationality or intended to apply for it, and the age of the applicant. Once again, it seems to me that none of those is a condition or a requirement; they are merely further examples of the means by which the individual members of the interview board were forming their opinion of an applicant. The fact that some applicants had opinions expressed about them which led to their not going forward on the short list is one of the facts of life; . . . and it is not the application of any condition or requirement."

Note

The decision in *Perera* has been widely criticised, especially as Stephenson LJ failed to realise that submitting an ethnic minority applicant to the additional requirement of being "brilliant" in order to overcome insufficiencies in the other requirements that might have detrimental effect actually proved the relevance of these requirements.[116]

---

[116] See McColgan, above n. 27, 80; Connolly, above n. 20, 245.

Thus, the *Perera* decision is an example of the detrimental effects of the requirement approach on the field of indirect discrimination law.

Equality Tribunal, 27 February 2003[117]   **3.IE.29.**
DEC-S-2003-016/017, Bukola Ogunlade and Sola Oyefeso v. *Michael Guiney Limited Cork*

INDIRECT RACIAL DISCRIMINATION BY DENYING ACCESS TO PERSONS ON THEIR
IDENTIFICATION AS PAST TROUBLEMAKERS

Ogunlade

Facts: The applicants complained of not having been served in or being denied access to the defendant's department store due to their race. The defendant's personnel had not denied the fact of denying service or access, but stated that this was due to the applicants being past troublemakers.

Held: The Equality Tribunal could not find indirect discrimination in basing access policy on staff assumptions as to the applicants having been troublemakers.

Judgment: "The complainants' representatives submitted that this was a case of mistaken identity and that the complainants by virtue of their colour were more difficult to identify than white people . . . The complainants both belong to a category of persons who share a common characteristic, their colour. In a situation where a past troublemaker is black, then avoidance of being recognised as that troublemaker is more difficult for black people by virtue of their colour. This is based on the assumption that one accepts it is easier for the indigenous population to recognise members of their own group because of the familiarity with their features. However, it is a moot point whether or not a person's identification or non-identification as troublemaker is something with which they have to comply . . .the burden of proof is on the person alleging the indirect discrimination that such is the case . . ."

Note
The Equality Tribunal was confronted with a difficult case. Instead of evaluating whether facial controls on entry might be a practice impacting negatively on those deemed to belong to an ethnic minority, the Equality Tribunal preferred a narrow approach to the "requirement": by doubting whether "being identified as a troublemaker" was such a requirement, instead of realising that making service contingent on anyone successfully passing a face control, the tribunal could use the requirement approach to steer away from difficult reasoning.

Despite these difficulties, the Court of Appeal followed the *Perera* approach in several decisions. However, the approach was then questioned before the ECJ in one of the strategic references by an English court.

---

[117] Available on the website of the Equality Tribunal of Ireland, under the heading Equal Status Decisions.

ECJ, 27 October 1993[118]   **3.EC.30.**
C-127/92, Enderby v. Frenchay Health Authority

INDIRECT WAGE DISCRIMINATION BY APPLYING DIFFERENT COLLECTIVE
AGREEMENTS TO PREDOMINANTLY FEMALE AND MALE GROUPS OF EMPLOYEES
RESPECTIVELY

Enderby

Facts: Pamela Enderby was employed as a speech therapist by the Frenchay Health Authority. She
considered herself a victim of gender pay discrimination because at her level of seniority within the
National Health Service (Chief III), speech therapists received considerably less pay (£ 10,106 p.a.) than
clinical psychologists and principal pharmacists (£ 12,527 and £ 14,106 p.a., respectively). Most of the
speech therapists at level Chief III were female, whereas in the other two groups most of the employees at
level Chief III were male. The Employment Appeal Tribunal, before referring the case to the ECJ, assumed
that speech therapists, clinical psychologists and pharmacists performed work of equal value. The questions
before the ECJ were whether the employee can establish a prima facie case of indirect pay discrimination by
pointing to pay differentials between different professions where one of those is predominantly female and
the others predominantly male and, if so, whether the employer could rely on the fact that the pay was
negotiated with different unions or on the tighter market for clinical psychologists and principal pharmacists as objective justifications of unequal pay.

Held: Ms. Enderby's claim was dismissed by the Industrial Tribunal on the grounds that the difference in
pay was based on collective agreements in the drafting of which there was no discrimination. The EAT
upholds that finding, adding that market forces contributed to the difference in earnings. The Court of
Appeal, however, referred several questions to the ECJ.

Enderby touches upon several aspects of non-discrimination law. In relation to the
"specific requirement", only the first question is relevant. This reads:

Judgment: ". . .Question 1
Does the principle of equal pay enshrined in Article 119 of the Treaty of Rome require the
employer to justify objectively the difference in pay between job A and job B?"
". . .14 . . . Accordingly, when a measure distinguishing between employees on the basis of
their hours of work has in practice an adverse impact on substantially more members of one or
other sex, that measure must be regarded as contrary to the objective pursued by Article 119 of
the Treaty, unless the employer shows that it is based on objectively justified factors unrelated
to any discrimination on grounds of sex (reference to *Bilka*, para. 31 et al) . . .
15. In this case, as both the FHA and the United Kingdom observe, the circumstances are
not exactly the same as in the cases just mentioned. First, it is not a question of *de facto*
discrimination arising from a particular sort of arrangement such as may apply, for example, in
the case of part time workers . . .
16. However, if the pay of speech therapists is significantly lower than that of pharmacists
and if the former are almost exclusively women while the latter are predominantly men, there is
a *prima facie* case of sex discrimination, at least where the two jobs in question are of equal
value and the statistics describing that situation are valid.

---

[118] [1993] ECR I–5535.

17. It is for the national court to assess whether it may take into account those statistics, that is to say, whether they cover enough individuals, whether they illustrate purely fortuitous or short-term phenomena, and whether, in general, they appear to be significant."

Notes on Enderby and specific requirements

(1) The ECJ distinguished this case from the former cases, such as *Bilka*, where there was a single requirement to which disparate impact could be attributed. Its reasoning is such that British courts concluded that *Perera* could no longer be upheld.

(2) The ECJ held that it is possible to regard a pay system as indirectly discriminatory in the absence of any isolated "specific requirement". Accordingly, the ECJ relinquished the prerequisite of isolating a "specific requirement" operating as a barrier to equality.

(3) This prerequisite had been decisive in English law to prove indirect discrimination. Thus, the ECJ decision in *Enderby* paved the way for a more collective reading of a prohibition of indirect discrimination by English and other courts in the EU.

The Court of Appeal applied a different approach with direct reliance on *Enderby* in the decision *Allonby* v. *Accrington and Rosendale College*.

Court of Appeal, 23 March 2001[119]   **3.GB.31.**
Allonby v. *Accrington and Rossendale College*

WHETHER "DOWNGRADING" PART-TIME LECTURERS TO SELF-EMPLOYED SERVICE
PROVIDERS CONSTITUTES INDIRECT DISCRIMINATION

Allonby (CA)

Facts: Ms. Allonby was employed by the Accrington and Rossendale College as a part-time lecturer on a succession of fixed-term contracts from 1990 until 1996. At that time, the college decided not to renew any contracts of part-time lecturers but to offer them to continue lecturing on the basis of self-employed service provision. Ms. Allonby considered that, as among part-time lecturers the percentage of women was higher than among lecturers on a whole, this amounted to indirect discrimination on grounds of sex.

Held: Both the Industrial Tribunal (IT) and the Employment Appeal Tribunal rejected the claim. The IT held that disparate impact was justifiable, but the EAT considered that there was no requirement. The Court of Appeal allowed the appeal in relation to this argument and remitted the case for rehearing. Again, several issues were relevant. We will focus on the specific requirement issue.

Judgment: SEDLEY LJ: "It is for the applicant to identify the requirement or condition which she seeks to impugn. These words are not terms of art: they are overlapping concepts and are not to be narrowly construed. If the applicant can realistically identify a requirement or condition capable of supporting her case, as Ms. Allonby did here to the Employment Tribunal's satisfaction, it is nothing to the point that her employer can with equal cogency derive from the facts a different and unobjectionable requirement or condition. The only authority

---

[119] [2001] ICR 1189.

which offers support to Mr. Jeans' argument is the decision of the Employment Appeal Tribunal in *Brook* v. *London Borough of Haringey*. There it was submitted, . . ."that there was indirect discrimination because Haringey have applied a requirement or condition that unless someone was a member of one of the trades whose members were not included in the compulsory pool [for redundancy], they were at risk of redundancy and because there happen to have been more men than women in those other trades there is discrimination which requires justification" . . . The [EAT] said: "We cannot think that what occurred constituted the erection of a rule or barrier which had the effect of discriminating against women. Those trades were open to women. There are no biological or social elements concerned. These submissions are not dissimilar to those considered in *Enderby v. Frenchay Health Authority*. If this submission is well founded, namely that the mere holding of a job or position can constitute a requirement or condition, and is *prima facie* discriminatory requiring justification, it could be applied to whole factories."

There are two reasons why *Brook* must be regarded as wrongly decided. One is that the reasoning in Enderby, on which it is explicitly founded, was overset by the European Court of Justice. Applying Article 119 of the EC Treaty (Articles 117 to 120 of the EC Treaty have been replaced by Articles 136 EC to 143 EC) to a national pay structure which gave a predominantly female sector of the health service lower pay than a predominantly male sector doing work of equal value (a situation in any event entirely different from the present one), the ECJ held that this was enough to require the employer to show that it was not discriminatory . . .

WARD LJ: . . . Firstly, as to the requirement or condition which the college applied to her: Her case, as recorded by the industrial tribunal, was that: 'the college had indirectly discriminated against her inasmuch as it imposed a requirement or condition for continuous employment with the college in the academic year 1996/1997 for an employee to have previously been employed either on a full-time basis or under a contract of employment which conferred proportionate benefits of a full-time contract.' Mr. Jeans QC submits that the college was not applying to her any requirement or condition but merely implementing a decision about the way in which to run its business. He submits that the indirect discrimination provisions are addressed to cases where, for example, an employer stipulates that certain criteria must be met in order that a person can be appointed to a post, e.g. the erstwhile minimum height required to work in the police force, or a requirement that a person have a degree in a particular subject. He submits the law should not be contorted so that every commercial decision can be described as applying a requirement or condition. The tribunal rejected that submission, dealing with the problem of good business reasons under the issue of justifiability. It concluded that: 'The changes, namely the requirement that hourly paid contract workers would in future only be employed through ELS, was the application of a requirement or condition.' . . .

In my judgment, they were fully entitled so to regard it. The reality is that the college told its former employee that it was no longer willing to accept her back as a part time lecturer unless she came either on a full-time basis or through ELS. Although the imposition of that threshold may well have been the implementation of a commercial decision forced upon it by changes in the law, it nonetheless was a threshold for her to cross and it was in that sense a requirement or condition which they applied to her when considering upon what terms she would be permitted to resume her teaching. I see no error in their approach and like my Lords I reject Mr. Jeans's submissions."

Notes

(1) The Court of Appeal thus referred to *Enderby* in adapting the test for indirect discrimination. Unfortunately, the wording of the reasons do not allow an exact conclusion of what the court would consider as sufficient to establish a prima facie case of indirect discrimination.

(2) Ms. Allonby would possibly have profited more from a litigation strategy not focusing exclusively on sex discrimination, but including discrimination of part-time employees, which is also outlawed under EC law (Directive 97/81/EC).[120] However, counsel for Ms. Enderby chose not to pursue this option.

British legislation has, since this judgment, established new standards for indirect discrimination in line with younger EC Directives. These, however, only apply in relation to discrimination on grounds of sex, sexual orientation, religion or belief, and age in employment and vocational training, and to discrimination on grounds of race, ethnic and national origins within the scope of application of Directive 2000/43/EC (i.e. not covering areas of the Race Relations Act[121] that are outside the material scope of the Directive). The definition from the Race Relations Act may be considered as a sufficient example here:

Race Relations Act as amended by The Race Relations Act 1976 **3.GB.32.**
(Amendment) Regulations 2003 Statutory Instrument 2003 No. 1626

(1A) A person also discriminates against another if . . . he applies to that other a provision, criterion or practice which he applies or would apply equally to persons not of the same race or ethnic or national origins as that other, but—

(a)   which puts or would put persons of the same race or ethnic or national origins as that other at a particular disadvantage when compared with other persons;
(b)   which puts that other at that disadvantage, and
(c)   which he cannot show to be a proportionate means of achieving a legitimate aim.

This contrasts with the original definition in the Race Relations Act 1976, according to which indirect discrimination required that a person "applies to that other a requirement or condition which he applies or would apply equally to persons not of the same racial group . . .". The amendment includes the term "practice" in addition to the terms "requirement" and "condition". This allows to include measures other than specific hurdles. However, as regards discrimination on

---

[120]   On coverage of part-time discrimination in national law, see above J. Gerards, Chapter 1: Discrimination Grounds, section 1.3.11.B, with excerpt **1.UK.104.**

[121]   The definition of discrimination in the RRA embraces colour explicitly and may thus seem wider than that of Directive 2000/43/EC. On the British distinction between race and colour, while most Member States consider colour an element of race, see above J. Gerards, Chapter 1: Discrimination Grounds, section 1.3.2.A, text following excerpts **1.NL.5.** and **1.UK.6.**

grounds of colour and nationality, sex discrimination outside employment and so on, the old statutory definition still applies, the reading of which is still not entirely clear following *Allonby*.

A WIDER APPROACH (A COLLECTIVE APPROACH)

The approach contrary to that of demanding a specific requirement to which disparate impact can be accorded would be to regard disadvantage for those belonging to a protected group in a certain employment setting as sufficient to establish a prima facie case of indirect discrimination. This collective approach effectively considers the sum of decisions taken in a specific environment as a whole. The collective approach to establishing detrimental effect is typical for Scandinavian jurisdictions. A particularly illustrative example comes from Finland.

Finnish Supreme Court (Korkein Oikeus Högsta Domstolen),   **3.FI.33.**
14 June 2004
Case 59/2004, Employees v. *Town of Kajaani*

INDIRECT DISCRIMINATION, LAYING OFF A SIGNIFICANT NUMBER OF STAFF

Kajaani

Facts: The town of Kajaani was forced by its weak financial situation to lay off a significant number of personnel. The collective redundancy was effected in respect of the staff categories of social security officials and workers. In these staff categories 93.5% of staff was female, while the overall percentage of female employees was 59.7%.

Held: The District Court had found indirect discrimination, a concept which it defined as "involving any action which is formally based on objective and acceptable grounds but will in fact lead to a situation where the opposite gender would be in a disadvantaged position". The City of Kajaani appealed against this decision. The Supreme Court held that the dismissal did constitute detrimental effect, but was objectively justified and thus not discriminatory.

Judgment: ". . .4. According to the Act on Equality between Women and Men, section 7, discrimination either directly or indirectly is prohibited . . . Indirect discrimination involves an action where as a consequence women and men are left on an unequal footing (section 7 para. 3 Act on Equality between women and men) based on some factor relating to gender.

5. The Act on Equality between Women and Men, section 8, defines at a minimum which kind of action by an employer is considered discrimination as mentioned in section 7. Based on section 8, . . . the action by an employer has to be considered discrimination for example if the employer lays-off workers based on their gender. The Supreme Court states that here the expression based on their gender also includes both direct and indirect forms.

6. In this case it is not that those targeted to be laid-off would have been directly selected based on their gender but whether the female officials and workers in this sector of basic social services have in fact been discriminated against based on their gender as a consequence of the targeting of the lay-offs.

7 . . .The lay-offs have been directed at a significant number of the female dominated staff in the basic social service sector. At the same time no lay-off actions have been implemented in other less wholly female or more male dominated working sectors of the town or at least not on any equivalent scale. As the lay-offs implemented by the town have thus been directed at clearly one of the most female dominated sectors and therefore affecting a relatively larger number of women than men, the Supreme Court considers that the action by the town has to be seen as discrimination as stated in section 8, paragraph 2, point 6 of the Act on Equality Between Women and Men unless the town, in accordance with section 8, paragraph 3, can show that its action has been based on acceptable grounds and not gender."

Notes

(1) This approach is in stark contrast to that taken by the English Courts. Under the *Perera* formula (which has been overruled by *Allonby*), the result of a collective redundancy action would never have qualified as a "requirement or condition". It remains doubtful whether the approach taken in *Allonby* would have led to a different result.

(2) The Finnish Supreme Court does not require any specific single rule to find a prima facie case of indirect discrimination. Any "action" by an employer which would result in disadvantage for women is enough to trigger judicial scrutiny under the heading of indirect discrimination. The Court thus prefers an entirely collective approach to the problem of indirect discrimination. There is not even the need to identify a specific employment practice to which the resulting disadvantage can be attributed.

Interestingly, the German Federal Labour Court was confronted with a very similar set of facts, but arrived at the opposite result.

Federal Labour Court (BAG), 8 February 2003[122]   **3.DE.34.**
9AZR 272/01, A Claimant v. Freie Hanse Stadt Hamburg

INDIRECT DISCRIMINATION: DENYING FULL-TIME EMPLOYMENT TO PRE-SCHOOL TEACHERS

Hamburg pre-school teachers

Facts: The City of Hamburg needed to respond to budgetary constraints created by the statutory obligation to offer kindergarten education to all children for at least three hours a day. One of the measures taken was to reduce daily lessons offered in pre-schools from five hours a day to four hours a day, and to offer only part-time contracts to the pre-school teachers. The result was that pre-schools could be categorised as kindergartens for the purposes of the statutory obligation, and that more kindergarten teachers could be employed due to savings on remuneration for pre-school teachers, thus enabling Hamburg to actually meet its obligations. The requirement to accept a part-time contract applied even in cases where the applicant would have preferred full-time work. Of 198 Hamburg pre-school teachers, only two were male. The claimant and her union challenged this, relying on indirect discrimination law.

---

[122] BAGE 102, 123–32.

381

Held: Both the First Instance Court and the Regional Labour Court considered that subjecting a certain class of employees, who are predominantly female, to part-time employment, amounts to indirect discrimination. They reasoned that the claimant's class of employees had been placed in a disadvantageous situation compared with other employees who had also studied for four years at a polytechnic university to gain their qualifications. They considered that there was no objective justification other than budgetary constraints, which could not be used as justification. The Federal Labour Court allowed the appeal.

Judgment: ". . .§ 611 a Civil Code entails a prohibition of discrimination on grounds of sex by employers . . . It covers direct and indirect discrimination on grounds of sex . . . If a measure is applied equally to men and women, it may still constitute indirect disadvantage, if a detrimental criterion is not directly connected to sex, but where it is complied with predominantly by persons of one sex . . . It is not sufficient, however, that the result is predominantly negative for women. Detriment must be established by comparing with the sex which allegedly profits from the employer's measure . . . The facts established by the regional labour court are not such that the claimant suffers direct or indirect discrimination. The defendant has advertised and filled the positions for pre-school teachers in a gender neutral way. As a result of filling these positions, there are not advantaged persons, but—as far as being employed part time is considered as a disadvantage—only disadvantaged persons . . . There is no rule of law obliging an employer to offer a certain category of employment as full time employment only because in that category of employment female labour prevails."

Note on Hamburg pre-school teacher
The Federal Labour Court has not considered the comparison made by the Regional Labour Court between different categories of employment offered by the City of Hamburg to different classes of employees, which were composed differently qua gender. This comparison would have enabled the Court to establish whether submitting a certain category of employees to the requirement to work part-time only disparately impacts upon women. The Court has not considered that the way in which employment is offered may be sufficient to satisfy the definition of requirement, condition or policy. However, the Regional Labour Court had accepted this as a possibility, thus approaching the matter in a similar way to the Finnish Court.

One of the few French cases on indirect discrimination also dealt with dismissal.

Court of Cassation, Social Chamber (Cass. Soc.), 9 June 1998[123]   **3.FR.35.**
Case No. 96-40390, Société Bureau moderne informatique et négoce
interprofessionnel (BMINI) v. Mme Gaborit

WHETHER DISMISSAL FROM A POSITION USUALLY OCCUPIED BY WOMEN IS
INDIRECT DISCRIMINATION

Gaborit

Facts: Ms. Gaborit was appointed on 26 September 1988 as a salesperson. BMINI dismissed her, referring to economic reasons, on 28 December 1993.

---

[123] *Semaine juridique JCP G édition génerale* 1998, 1507.

Held: Ms. Gaborit claimed an indemnity for unfair and discriminatory dismissal before the Labour Court and the Court of Appeal. Both allowed the claim. BMINI appealed on grounds of law to the Cour de Cassation, which, however, rejected the appeal of the employer.

Judgment: ". . .Whereas the court of appeal found that the employer had eliminated, without any objective reason, a post that was specifically a woman's one and that it was thus solely because of her gender that Mrs. Gaborit had been dismissed."

Note

Due to the reluctant acceptance of the principle of indirect discrimination in French law and the general avoidance of longish reasoning, the decision seems less than enlightening. It even seems to imply that this is a case of direct rather than indirect discrimination.

Another case in which a collective approach to establishing detrimental effect was taken is a very early case from the Netherlands, in which the Hoge Raad established discrimination by a housing association relying on statistical data.

Supreme Court (Hoge Raad), 10 December 1982[124]   **3.NL.36.**
Van Binderen v. *Kaya*

WHETHER A HOUSING ASSOCIATION IS GUILTY OF INDIRECT ETHNIC
DISCRIMINATION WHEN GRANTING A DISPROPORTIONATELY LOW PERCENTAGE OF
THEIR TENANCIES TO FOREIGN WORKERS

Binderen/Kaya

Facts: The applicant in the first instance, Mr. Kaya, was of Turkish origin and had been living lawfully in the Netherlands since 1973. Since 3 February 1977 he had been registered as seeking rented accommodation in Helmond. However, he was still living with his wife and four-year-old daughter in a bedsit at the time of the judgment. His claim was to be assigned a flat by Binderen housing association, which has been denied to him on grounds of discrimination until the time of the appeal. Kaya had gathered statistics on the letting policy of the Binderen housing association. According to these, Binderen had concluded new tenancies for 543 flats in the period between 1975 and 1980, but only one of these had been allocated to a "foreign" household. By comparison, other housing associations in Helmond had allocated just above 7% of their housing stock to "foreign" families. Also, the rate of foreigners seeking accommodation from Binderen (just above 10%) was considerably higher than the proportion of foreign tenants in their housing estates (3 out of 1788).

Held: The Court of First Instance denied Kaya's claim. The Court of Appeal (Hof van Beroep) allowed his appeal on the basis of the statistics cited above. Van Binderen housing association appealed this decision on grounds of law. The fact that the Kaya family was still homeless was no longer in dispute. Van Binderen appealed on grounds of law, as they considered that a judgment of discrimination could not have been based on the statistical arguments delivered by Kaya. The Hoge Raad (Dutch Supreme Court) dismissed Binderen's appeal and upheld the second instance decision in favour of Kaya.

Judgment: "4.1 Parts 1, 2 and 3 of the grounds of appeal in cassation are based on the assumption that Kaya—beside the fact that he had urgent need of housing—did not state more and the Court of Appeal did not take into consideration more than the 'fact that Binderen,

---

[124] NJ 1983, 687.

383

compared to the percentage of foreigners among those seeking rented accommodation, and compared to the number of tenancies awarded to foreign tenants by the five other housing association in Helmond between 1975 and 1980, had let a very minor proportion of its apartments to foreigners.' . . . There is no rule of law, for that matter, which prevents the courts from considering numerical, statistical differences such as presented in this case as sufficient reason for a finding of discrimination, neither is there any rule of law that prevents the courts from deriving from such difference a (strong) presumption of discrimination and from requiring purely on basis of this presumption that the one accused of discrimination show that the disadvantage he is blamed with is based on legally acceptable grounds . . .

4.5 . . . According to para. 25 of its judgment, the Court of Appeal has considered as important the fact that Binderen—who had access to the relevant data from actually allocating the apartments and who could reasonably have been expected to have done so—has failed to substantiate by arguments 'directed specifically at the situation of Kaya' on which lawful basis the fact of not allocating an apartment to him had been founded. The judgment does not show any incorrect application of the law . . .

5.1 . . . As appears from the above considerations, the Court of Appeal's judgment is to be understood as meaning that the facts concerning Kaya's need of a home during the relevant period as established before the Court of Appeal, were of such a nature that, given the fact that Binderen has not rebutted the 'serious presumption' of discrimination, neither in general nor specifically in relation to Kaya, it has to be assumed that Binderen has refrained from allocating an apartment to Kaya purely on grounds of his origin."

Note

The Dutch Supreme Court did not follow Binderen's argument that Kaya failed to specify which requirement he was submitted to, and that there could be no finding of (indirect) discrimination. The Court found that, in order to establish a presumption of discrimination, it was sufficient to show that a large number of decisions on the allocation tenancies tended to prefer non-foreign parties. Today, this would be considered a prima facie case of indirect discrimination. According to the reasoning of the *Hoge Raad*, there is no need to isolate a specific requirement. It finds that the detrimental effect of Binderen's housing policy in its entirety shifts the burden of proof. It would have been Binderen's task to disclose the principles behind its policy of assigning tenancies in order to rebut the assumption of discrimination.

WHAT IS THE PRECISE FACTOR FROM WHICH DETRIMENTAL EFFECT FLOWS IN EQUAL PAY CASES?

A less strict approach to the "requirement-problem" lends itself to adjudicating equal pay cases, which have until now only occurred in relation to sex discrimination on the basis of Article 141 EC and Directive 75/117/EC. However, the equal pay principle will have to be applied to all the other grounds as well in the future, as Directive 2000/43/EC and Directive 2000/78/EC explicitly apply to pay (Article 3 paragraph 1c).[125]

---

[125] For an account of possible difficulties, see D. Houtzager "Unequal Pay in Sex and Race Cases: Same Problems, Same Remedies?" in Dutch Equal Treatment Commission (ed.), *Equal Pay and Working Conditions. Towards the uniform and dynamic implementation of EU Anti-Discrimination Law: The Role of Specialised Bodies* (Brussels, Migration Policy Group, 2004) 64–71.

Special quality of equal pay cases and relevance of indirect discrimination

There is some justification for categorising equal pay cases outside the framework of equal treatment law.[126]

The first sentence of Article 141 EC manages to lay down the equal pay principle without even mentioning the term "discrimination", by stating: "Each Member State shall ensure that the principle of equal pay for male and female workers for equal work or work of equal value is applied." The next sentence clarifies that equal pay for equal work or work of equal value for women and men means the same as equal pay without any discrimination on grounds of sex. Establishing an equal pay claim, a woman has to name a male comparator earning more than herself and to allege that the work to which she and her comparator are obliged is equal or of equal value. If the work is unequal or of unequal value, the distinction between the remuneration is deemed to be based on an objective factor other than sex. We can see that the structure of an equal pay claim is somewhat different from the structure of a claim for equal treatment: instead of showing that there has been a detriment related to sex or another discrimination ground, the onus on the applicant focuses on the nature of the work and the pay. If there is a difference in the pay, but not in the nature of the work, and the comparator is different as regards a discrimination ground, the equal pay claim should succeed.

Some authors doubt whether the prohibition of indirect discrimination actually applies in assessing whether work is of equal value.[127] However, the ECJ has applied indirect discrimination law to numerous pay cases (see below **3.EC.38–40.**) and this has been reflected in national case-law. With the ECJ, we will proceed on the assumption that indirect discrimination may occur in relation to pay, and also in relation to equal value claims.

Still, there are specific characteristics in the field of equal pay.[128] They are related to the complex regulation of pay. Remuneration of employees is usually determined by a variety of factors. In most Member States, collective agreements are still decisive for the basic pay. In addition to these, employer-specific bonuses and also individually agreed remuneration packages may impact on individual remuneration. Accordingly, an equal pay case in the field of indirect discrimination law will often confront a web of pay policies at different levels (and by different authors). Courts will often be reluctant to analyse the single elements of this web separately, let alone establish new rules.

---

[126] Books on EU labour law or discrimination law often cover equal pay and equal treatment in different chapters (see, e.g. Ellis, above n. 16 or C. Barnard, *EC Employment Law*, 3rd edn (Oxford, Oxford University Press, 2006).

[127] Veldman seems to imply that the prohibition of indirect discrimination and the right to equal pay for work of equal value are fundamentally different (E.G. Veldman, "Strengthening the Effects of Community Equal Pay Legislation, or Why Established Equal Pay Standards Have Little Impact on the Pay Gap in the EU Labour Market" in Dutch Equal Treatment Commission, above n. 125, 19, 20–1).

[128] See, with enlightening examples from different fields, S. Burri, "Indirect Sex Discrimination in Pay and Working Conditions: The Application of a Potentially Dynamic Concept" in Dutch Equal Treatment Commission, above n. 125, 28.

In order to further evaluate the special characteristics of the field in relation to indirect discrimination law, it is useful to distinguish between two types of claims. On the one hand, there are claims relating to specific bonuses or other pay elements that are granted to all employees of an employer or within the scope of application of a collective agreement. These pay elements comprise participation in occupational pension schemes, severance payments upon dismissal and end-of-year payments. These are the easier cases, as only one knot of the net of pay regulations needs to be adjusted. For example, where all part-time employees suffer a wage deduction across all tasks, they need to be paid without the reduction;[129] where part-time workers are denied a special benefit payable upon termination of the employment relationship, they need to be granted that benefit;[130] and if part-time workers are denied access to the occupational pension scheme, this access is to be given.[131] On the other hand, there are claims challenging pay systems as a whole, thus attempting to challenge what is known as gender pay gap among economists and sociologists—a term which will have to be supplemented by ethnic, religious, ability-related, etc. pay gap. The term "gender pay gap" applies to the absolute difference in remuneration between women and men, which ranges between 5 and 25% depending on the Member State in question.[132] Certainly, not all of this is due to wage discrimination, as a great deal is the consequence of employment discrimination, i.e. the refusal to employ women in positions categorised as male or to give them equal opportunities regarding promotion. Challenging one's remuneration on the grounds that the difference to remuneration of a specific comparator (with equal work) is based on direct discrimination seems easy if compared to the task of challenging one's remuneration on the grounds that the average pay of women in a given branch, plant or national wage agreement is lower than that of men. This amounts to finding the part of the gender pay gap which is rooted in indirect discrimination.

It is in this field where what we have labelled a "collective approach" to indirect discrimination law[133] lends itself as an instrument of analysis. To challenge pay discrimination related to evaluation of tasks, the law needs to "start at the end of the process and look back".[134] Applying this method to cases of unequal pay of different work, one uses the collective approach to indirect discrimination law.

---

[129] ECJ, Judgment of 31 March 1981, Case 96/80 *Jenkins* v. *Kingsgate (Clothing Productions) Ltd.* [1981] ECR 911; see above **3.EC. 15.**

[130] ECJ, Judgment of 27 June 1990, Case C–33/89 *Maria Kowalska* v. *Freie und Hansestadt Hamburg* [1990] ECR I–2591.

[131] ECJ, Judgment of 13 May 1986, Case 170/84 *Bilka*; see above **3.EC.16.**

[132] The Eurostat database "gender pay gap in an unadjusted form" is regularly updated and freely accessible. It relies only on gross hourly earnings and excludes earnings of those working less than 15 hours a week, which means that a large proportion of underpaid female work is disregarded. Available on the website of EUROSTAT.

[133] See above **3.FI.33.–3.NL.36.**

[134] See Veldman, above n. 125.

ECJ case-law

The ECJ, in its early case-law on equal pay, had seemingly agreed to the assumption that the concept of indirect discrimination under EC law was also capable of covering discriminatory wage systems as a whole.

ECJ, 1 July 1986[135]   **3.EC.37.**
Case 237/85, Rummler v. *Dato Druck*

INDIRECT DISCRIMINATION: WORK REQUIRING LESS MUSCLE POWER IN A LOWER
WAGE GROUP

Rummler

Facts: Gisela Rummler tackled the issue of so called "light work wage groups" before the Oldenburg Labour Court. This case was part of a union campaign to question the practice of establishing light work wage groups. These light work wage groups ("Leichtlohngruppen") had been considered a direct result of the early case-law of the Federal Labour Court, in which it was held that collective agreements were bound by the German constitution's equality clause. The Federal Labour Court had in fact expressly named the difference in physical strength needed to discharge tasks as a criterion that would distinguish work sufficiently to justify pay differences. In the case at hand, the applicant and her union challenged the framework wage-rate agreement for workers of the printing industry, according to which employees were to be remunerated in accordance with one of seven wage groups, the classifying criteria being degree of knowledge, concentration, muscular demand or effort and responsibility with group VII being the highest. The claimant was classified in wage group III and considered that the correct wage group should be IV. That group is described as requiring previous knowledge on the basis of on-the-job-training or experience, occasionally a fair degree of occupational experience requiring moderate accuracy, involving moderate and occasionally great physical effort, particularly as a result of work dependent on machines and involving moderate responsibility. It is specified that the evaluation criteria must not be regarded as cumulative in all cases. The defendant disputed that the applicant had to exert great physical effort in her work, to which the applicant responded that she did occasionally lift parcels of 20 kg, which was heavy work from her perspective.

Held: The then first instance judge Ninon Colneric from Oldenburg Labour Court referred to the ECJ several questions on indirect discrimination by wage systems, inter alia whether the heaviness of the work could be a factor for deciding on wages at all as men were on average stronger than women and thus could fulfil this requirement more easily. The ECJ rejected this, but it held that a wage system as a whole could be indirectly discriminatory if it stressed requirements that men could typically fulfil more easily, such as muscular strength, and, at the same time, ignored requirements that women could typically fulfil more easily, such as dexterity.

Judgment: ". . .7 By its first question the national court seeks to ascertain whether a job classification system based on the criteria of muscle demand or muscular effort and the heaviness of the work is compatible with the principle of equal pay for men and women . . . 11 . . . [R]eference must .. be made to . . . article 1 of Directive 75/117, which provides for the elimination of all discrimination on grounds of sex with regard to all aspects and conditions of remuneration for the same work or for work to which equal value is attributed [and to] . . .12 . . . The second paragraph of article 1, which provides that a job classification system ' must be based on the same criteria for both men and women and so drawn up as to exclude any discrimination on grounds of sex '. 13 It follows that the principle of equal pay requires essentially that

---

[135] [1986] ECR 2101.

387

the nature of the work to be carried out be considered objectively. Consequently, the same work or work to which equal value is attributed must be remunerated in the same manner whether it is carried out by a man or by a woman. Where a job classification system is used in determining remuneration, that system must be based on criteria which do not differ according to whether the work is carried out by a man or by a woman and must not be organized, as a whole, in such a manner that it has the practical effect of discriminating generally against workers of one sex.

14 Consequently, criteria corresponding to the duties performed meet the requirements of article 1 of the directive where those duties by their nature require particular physical effort or are physically heavy. In differentiating rates of pay, it is consistent with the principle of non-discrimination to use a criterion based on the objectively measurable expenditure of effort necessary in carrying out the work or the degree to which, reviewed objectively, the work is physically heavy.

15 Even where a particular criterion, such as that of demand on the muscles, may in fact tend to favour male workers, since it may be assumed that in general they are physically stronger than female workers, it must, in order to determine whether or not it is discriminatory, be considered in the context of the whole job classification system, having regard to other criteria influencing rates of pay. A system is not necessarily discriminatory simply because one of its criteria makes reference to attributes more characteristic of men. In order for a job classification system as a whole to be non-discriminatory and thus to comply with the principles of the directive, it must, however, be established in such a manner that it includes, if the nature of the tasks in question so permits, jobs to which equal value is attributed and for which regard is had to other criteria in relation to which women workers may have a particular aptitude.

17 The answer to question (1) must therefore be that [Community law] does not prohibit the use, in a job classification system for the purpose of determining rates of pay, of the criterion of muscle demand or muscular effort or that of the heaviness of the work if, in view of the nature of the tasks involved, the work to be performed does require the use of a certain degree of physical strength, so long as the system as a whole, by taking into account other criteria, precludes any discrimination on grounds of sex."

Notes

(1) Here the Court apparently gave up the individualistic approach of isolated "requirements" altogether in favour of a collective approach to indirect discrimination: a wage classification system in its entirety should provide for equal opportunities in fact for women and men to achieve on average the same pay to avoid being considered as indirectly discriminatory.

(2) Obviously, this differs from the approach described above under which a single criterion needs to be isolated. However, the judgment in *Rummler* is today considered as having been overruled by a succession of judgments that were referred to the ECJ by Danish pay tribunals and originated from claims brought by Danish unions or (more recently) the Jämstellhedsombudsmannen (JämO[136]). These claimants applied an entirely collective approach to the matter of equal pay, relying on the fact that there was an average pay difference between their female and male members or women and men at a specific work place.

---

[136] See below G. Moon, Chapter 8: Enforcement Bodies, section 8.3.1.

When the relevant union challenged a pay system at the Danish shipyard Danfoss, the ECJ gave up its *Rummler* approach in favour of a more individualistic definition of indirect discrimination.

ECJ, 17 October 1989[137]   **3.EC.38.**

C–109/88, Handels- og Kontorfunktionærernes Forbund I Danmark v. *Dansk Arbejdsgiverforening, acting on behalf of Danfoss*

WHETHER A GENDER PAY GAP RESULTING FROM A SYSTEM OF BONUSES
ESTABLISHES DETRIMENTAL EFFECT

Danfoss

Facts: Danfoss A/S paid each employee in the same wage group of the relevant collective agreement the same basic wage, but made use of the possibility left open by Article 9 of the same agreement to award individual pay supplements. A Danish trade union (Handels og Kontorfunktionarernes Forbund) brought Danfoss A/S before the Industrial Arbitration Board, alleging that two of their female members suffered pay discrimination contrary to the Danish legislation implementing the Equal Pay Directive, as they were paid lower wages than male colleagues in the same wage group. The union based this allegation on the fact that on a basis of 157 workers the average pay for men was 6.84% higher than that of women in the same wage groups. This was due to differences in the individual pay supplements. These were based on criteria such as mobility, training and seniority. The individual employees, however, did not know which factors were decisive for the total amount of their individual pay supplements. It should be added that one of the reasons for the union to attack this bonus system was that it had not been agreed upon with them.

Held: The Danish trade union challenged the system before the relevant court in Denmark, as they considered that the average pay differential would be enough to establish a prima facie case of indirect discrimination against its female members. The Industrial Arbitration Board referred questions on the interpretation of Article 119 EEC (now 141 EC) to the ECJ. The case covered a number of issues. Focusing on establishing detrimental effect, only a part of the questions and the corresponding judgment are relevant.

Judgment: ". . .Questions 1 (a) Where it is established that a male and female employee do the same work of equal value, who, in the view of the Court of Justice, is the person (employer or employee) on whom the burden lies of proving that a differentiation in pay between the two employees is attributable/not attributable to considerations determined by sex?

1 (b) Is it incompatible with the directive on equal pay to give higher pay to male employees, who do the same work as female employees or work of equal value, solely by reference to subjective criteria—for example, staff mobility?

2 (a) Is it contrary to the directive to give to employees of a different sex who do the same work or work of equal value, over and above the basic pay for the job, special supplements for length of service, training, etc .? . . .

3 (a) Can an employee or an employees' organization, by proving that an undertaking with a large number of employees (e.g . at least 100) engaged in work of the same nature or value pays on average the women less than the men, establish that the directive is thereby infringed?

. . .

---

[137] [1989] ECR 3199.

The burden of proof (Questions 1 (a) and 3 (a))
10 It is apparent from the documents before the Court that the issue between the parties to the main proceedings has its origin in the fact that the system of individual supplements applied to basic pay is implemented in such a way that a woman is unable to identify the reasons for a difference between her pay and that of a man doing the same work . . .

11 In those circumstances the [question is] whether the Equal Pay Directive must be interpreted as meaning that where an undertaking applies a system of pay which is totally lacking in transparency, it is for the employer to prove that his practice in the matter of wages is not discriminatory, if a female worker establishes, in relation to a relatively large number of employees, that the average pay for women is less than that for men . . ..

13 It should next be pointed out that in a situation where a system of individual pay supplements which is completely lacking in transparency is at issue, female employees can establish differences only so far as average pay is concerned. They would be deprived of any effective means of enforcing the principle of equal pay before the national courts if the effect of adducing such evidence was not to impose upon the employer the burden of proving that his practice in the matter of wages is not in fact discriminatory.

15 To show that his practice in the matter of wages does not systematically work to the disadvantage of female employees the employer will have to indicate how he has applied the criteria concerning supplements and will thus be forced to make his system of pay transparent.

16 . . . [T]he answers to Questions 1 (a) and 3 (a) must be that . . . where an undertaking applies a system of pay which is totally lacking in transparency, it is for the employer to prove that his practice in the matter of wages is not discriminatory, if a female worker establishes, in relation to a relatively large number of employees, that the average pay for women is less than that for men.

The lawfulness of the contested criteria relating to supplements in question (Questions 1 (b) and 2 (a) and (c))
17 These questions ask in essence whether the directive must be interpreted as meaning that where it appears that the application of the criteria relating to supplements, such as mobility, training or length of service, systematically works to the disadvantage of female employees, the employer may, none the less, and if so on what conditions, justify its use. To answer that question it is necessary to consider each of the criteria separately."

Note
The Danish trade union considered that where there was an average pay differential this would be enough to establish disparate impact and thus a presumption of indirect discrimination. The reasoning is roughly comparable to the litigation strategy by Kaya that led to the Dutch *Binderen* judgment.[138] While the ECJ held that under these specific circumstances it was for the employer to bring forward the facts proving the non-discriminatory nature of the bonus system, the Court did not follow the union's line of argument. In contrast to *Rummler*, the Court no longer assumed that a pay system needed to be structured in such a way that it achieves equality of results for women and men. *Danfoss* is rather the origin of the EC case-law doctrine that each single variable of a wage system needs to be tested for indirect discrimination separately.

---

[138] See above **3.EC.39.**

Still, *Danfoss* seemed to imply that the *Binderen* principle can be relied on in equal pay cases before the ECJ. This assumption was tested in a 1993 case, again upon initiative by Danish trade unions.

ECJ, 31 May 1995[139]   **3.EC.39.**
C–400/93, Specialarbejderforbundet i Danmark v. Dansk Industri, formerly Industriens Arbejdsgivere, acting for Royal Copenhagen A/S

WHETHER STATISTICAL DIFFERENCES IN PAY BETWEEN THREE GROUPS
OF WORKERS ARE SUFFICIENT TO ESTABLISH DETRIMENTAL EFFECT OF A
PAY SYSTEM

Royal Copenhagen

Facts: The case is based at the famous Danish porcelain factory then employing 1150 workers, working either in the turning department, forming and moulding plates, cups and figures with the help of machines; in the painting department, colouring porcelain; or as unskilled workers, manning the kilns and transporting raw materials and intermediate products from one place to another. To all these the same collective agreement applies, which gives workers an option to choose between piece rate and hourly flat rate. This option is used by 70% of the workers in all departments. The union raised a claim in favour of its female members alleging that the piece rate remuneration discriminated indirectly on grounds of sex. To substantiate their claim, they chose three comparator groups. From the group of turners they chose the 26 auto-machine operators, representing 18% of this group, and from the department of painters the blue-pattern painters, who decorate the products by brush, and ornamental-plate painters, who spray-paint ornamental plates which already have a pattern and then remove the paint from certain parts of the pattern with a sponge. The 156 blue pattern painters represent 49% of the painters under piece rate pay, are all female save one worker and need to be trained for 18 months in order to accurately paint fine figures on the porcelain. The 51 spray painters, an all-female group, represent 16% of all painters under piece rate payment and need a training period of only three months. The auto-machine operators receive an average hourly remuneration of 103 DKr, the blue-pattern painters receive 91 DKr and the spray painters 116.20 DKr. The union considers that, according to dexterity and knowledge, the blue pattern painters should receive the highest salary. Relying on the difference between the wages of blue pattern painters and turners, they raised an equal pay claim.

Held: The unions brought the case before an Industrial Arbitration Board (Faglige Voldgiftsret), which referred several questions to the ECJ.

Judgment: "... 15 The reply to the first question (is) ... that Article 119 EEC [today: 141 EC] ... apply to piece-work pay schemes in which pay depends entirely or in large measure on the individual output of each worker ...

16 Before turning to consider the other questions, it must be stressed that the pay at issue in the main proceedings does not depend exclusively on the individual work of each worker but includes a fixed element consisting of a basic hourly wage which is not the same for the different groups of workers concerned.

17 It is for the national court to assess the extent to which it is necessary to take that factor into account in reaching a decision in the main proceedings ...

19 The national court's second question and paragraphs (c) (d) (e) and (g) of its fourth question, which it is appropriate to consider together, ask, first, whether the principle of equal

---

[139] [1995] ECR Royal I–01275.

pay . . . applies where, in a piece-work pay scheme, the average pay of one group of workers consisting predominantly of women carrying out one type of work is appreciably lower than the average pay of a group of workers consisting predominantly of men carrying out another type of work to which equal value is attributed, and, secondly, what is the significance of factors such as those referred to in paragraphs (c) (d) (e) and (g) of the fourth question [these factors are differences in choice of work rate, differences within each group, difference in the fixed rate and intransparency of the entirety of decisive factors, D.S.].

20 It follows . . . that in a piece-work pay scheme the principle of equal pay requires that the pay of two groups of workers, one consisting predominantly of men and the other predominantly of women, is to be calculated on the basis of the same unit of measurement.

21 Where the unit of measurement . . . is objectively capable of ensuring that the total individual pay of workers in the two groups is the same for work which, although different, is considered to be of equal value, the principle of equal pay does not prohibit workers belonging to one or the other group from receiving different total pay if that is due to their different individual output.

22 It follows that in a piece-work pay scheme the mere finding that there is a difference in the average pay of two groups of workers, calculated on the basis of the total individual pay of all the workers belonging to one or the other group, does not suffice to establish that there is discrimination with regard to pay . . .

25 Admittedly, in a piece-work pay scheme such a *prima facie* case of discrimination does not arise solely because significant statistics disclose appreciable differences between the average pay of two groups of workers, since those difference may be due to differences in individual output of the workers constituting the two groups.

26 If however, in a system such as that in the main proceedings . . . it is not possible to identify the factors which determined the rates or units of measurement used to calculate the variable element in the pay . . ., the objective of not depriving workers of any effective means of enforcing the principle of equal pay may require the employer to bear the burden of proving that the differences found are not due to sex discrimination.

27 It is for the national court to ascertain whether . . . the conditions for so shifting the burden of proof are satisfied in the main proceedings . . ."

Note

As in *Danfoss*, the ECJ envisaged a shift of the burden of proof resulting from a less than transparent remuneration system. In *Royal Copenhagen*, the Court was much more adamant that shifting the burden of proof is a different exercise from establishing the precise criteria, requirement or practice to which detrimental effect shall be attributed. The national court is required to look at the unit of measurement and to isolate the degree to which pay differences are dependent on individual output of workers. Thus, the Court effectively denies the underlying assumption that a pay system as a whole should on average lead to gender equality in result. Rather, there remains the opportunity for an employer to establish as a given that male workers have a higher output. In any case, *Royal Copenhagen* shows that the ECJ rejects the collective approach to indirect equal pay discrimination.

National case-law

National case-law took partly different and more open approaches.

Federal Labour Court (BAG), 23 September 1992[140]　　　**3.DE.40.**
4 AZR 30/92, An Applicant v. A defendant

WHETHER CATEGORISING MOST MEN IN A HIGHER WAGE GROUP THAN MOST
WOMEN AMOUNTS TO INDIRECT DISCRIMINATION

Warehouse workers

Façts: The claimants are employed as order pickers in warehouse I of the respondent, in which ironmongery and household items are stored. Four of them are remunerated in accordance with wage group 2 of the relevant collective agreement, and one of them receives remuneration in accordance with wage group 3. Five other female workers are also remunerated in accordance with wage group 2. Of 13 male workers with comparable work, six receive remuneration in accordance with wage group 2 and seven are remunerated in accordance with wage group 3. The claimants consider that grouping the majority of women in wage group 2 and the majority of men in wage group 3 constitutes indirect discrimination, as the work is at least of equal value, if not the same work.

Held: Similarly to the Labour Court of First Instance and the Regional Labour Court, the Federal Labour Court considered that there was indirect discrimination, except in the case of one of the male workers, whose status as former head warehouse worker was protected for social reasons.

Judgment: ". . . (59) An infringement against section 612 paragraph 3 BGB does not require that all male employees with the same work duties as the applicants are paid better than the applicants. Moreover, such an infringement can already exist if the wages policy of the respondent disadvantageously affects a comparatively significantly higher number of female order pickers than male order pickers.

(60) . . . A wages policy can be discriminatory if there are significant differences between the distribution of members of both genders within the group of persons benefiting from the policy and within the group of persons disadvantaged by the policy. In this respect it is irrelevant whether the differences in wages paid are based on rules, regardless of whether these rules are universal throughout the company or merely refer to company or plant, or merely result from the wage policy used by the respondent."

Notes

(1) Here, the Federal Labour Court did not refer to any specific requirement, as the distribution of workers over the wage groups appeared to be arbitrary. The Court interpreted the concept of disparate impact in a more holistic way.

(2) Its reasoning acknowledged that there need not necessarily be a specific requirement but that a policy as a whole may create detrimental effect. This comes close to a merely collective or statistical approach, which is, however, not quite adopted. Rather, the "warehouse worker approach" still requires that a certain policy be isolated, adding to the list of "requirement or condition" a third element, the

---

[140] BAGE 71, 195.

policy. Compared with the *Rummler* approach, the warehouse worker approach seems narrower, as the Federal Labour Court only looked into the question why the male workers were categorised in wage group 3 and the majority of the female workers in wage group 2 instead of considering the effects of the entire collective agreement.

The Spanish Constitutional Court judgment on different pay for equal work[141] was followed by two judgments on different pay for work of equal value. Both the *Antonio Puig* judgment and the *Gomyatex* judgment in fact come close to the *Rummler* criteria, while not citing this old decision. They are thus worth reporting.

Spanish Constitutional Court (El Tribunal Constitucional),   **3.ES.41.**
28 February 1994
Case 58/1994, Works council de Antonio Puig S.A. on behalf of 140 workers v.
Antonio Puig S.A.

WAGE CATEGORIES AND (INDIRECT) SEX DISCRIMINATION

Antonio Puig

Facts: The works council at the undertaking Antonio Puig SA raised an equal pay claim on behalf of 140 female unskilled workers employed in the departments for packing and distribution. These workers have been categorised in equivalent or even higher categories of the relevant collective agreement than a number of male colleagues who, in spite of this, continue to receive higher monthly wages. Traditionally, Antonio Puig has accorded the categories of unskilled worker (*peon*) and qualified auxiliary (*ayudante especialisado*) to men only, whereas the categories of apprenticed worker (*oficiales*) is traditionally allocated to women. However, there are no physical barriers to women performing the tasks traditionally allocated to men only, although the tasks are different in character. If the 140 female workers had been paid correctly in accordance with the collective agreement, they should have received higher remuneration than the male comparators. While the basic salary was the same, additional allowances such as "daily allowance for quality and quantity" were higher. The Constitutional Court lists precisely the different tasks allocated to women and men, from which it transpires that "male" tasks require more bodily strength whereas the women discharge a wider variety of tasks, which require more training, experience and skill.

Held: This was found discriminatory at first instance but then reversed by the Court of Appeal, which held: (1) that the salary depended on a collective agreement, signed by the claimants themselves and therefore could not be discriminatory; and (2) that the employer had proved that the difference in salary depended on the different professional categories. The Constitutional Court considered that this was a case of indirect sex discrimination in the area of pay, effectively applying the principles developed by the Court of Justice in its decision in *Enderby*.

Judgment: ". . .a) If it is the case that there are categories in which mainly workers of one or the other sex are employed, which are unequally paid, and there is no transparency in the determination of the employed criteria, it is obviously the duty of the employer to prove named criteria, to exclude every suspicion that the sex could have been the decisive factor for the difference (reference to *Enderby*). b) To completely understand the incidence to which the claim refers it is not sufficient to point to the differences between the tasks performed. The parameter of equality here is not the equality of tasks but the equal value of the work, this is the only

---

[141] See above **3.ES.1.**

element to be used to assess whether a difference in remuneration is reasonable or not. c) While evaluating the work it must be guaranteed and demanded, that the very criteria used to evaluate the work are not in themselves discriminatory. Therefore it must be ensured that the evaluation criteria are neutral and guarantee the same conditions for workers of both sexes, except in exceptional circumstances and for reasons of the special nature of the work, where different evaluation criteria are required . This is because the prohibition of sex discrimination in salary is also violated when labour is overrated due to only taking such qualities into account as are inherent in one of the sexes, to the detriment of the other (reference to Constitutional Court Case 145/1991 and Directive 75/117/EEC).

Only the composition of these rules makes it possible to decide whether the judgment of equality was taken correctly and whether, as a consequence, the existence or non-existence of discrimination was adequately recognized, given the ones affected, the protection which the courts, as public institutions, are obligated to give."

Spanish Constitutional Court (El Tribunal Constitucional),   **3.ES.42.**
16 October 1995
Case 147/1995, E.S.K.—C.U.I.S. representing 25 workers v. Gomaytex S.A.

WHETHER GRANTING LOWER REMUNERATION TO STAFF IN DEPARTMENTS
PREDOMINANTLY STAFFED BY WOMEN AMOUNTS TO INDIRECT PAY DISCRIMINATION

Gomaytex

Facts: The trade union "ESK-CUIS" challenged in the name of 25 female workers of the employer Gomyatex the judgment of the Basque Regional Labour Court of 2 February 1993 because it did not reverse the violation of their right to equal treatment under Article 14 C.E. (Spanish Constitution) through the submission of the female workers to a lower wage than male workers, although they were performing work of equal value to these. It was uncontroversial that the 25 female workers were employed in the packing and statistical control departments, which were staffed almost exclusively by women, while male staff were employed predominantly in the blending, moulding and varnishing departments. The work in these departments had little in common, except forming part of the same production process. The differences in payment resulted from different wage groups assigned to the female and male workers under collective agreements.

Held: The judge at first instance had allowed the claim, based on the firm's own evaluation of the work discharged with in the different departments. The assessment was based on the factors of knowledge, dexterity and mental, visual and physical effort. The evaluation arrived at a total of 13 points for work in the departments of statistical control, blending and moulding, whereas work in the packing department was rated at 12 and that in the varnishing department at 11 points. The Employment Appeal Tribunal for the Basque Country reversed this judgment, mainly for two reasons. First, it considered that the different categorisation resulted from a collective agreement and that women were not barred, in fact, from working in the "male" departments. Secondly, it considered the differences to be justified by the fact that the women's work was less painful, required less physical strength and was carried out during the day (in two shifts), whereas the male workers had to be prepared to work nights.

Judgment: ". . . Article 14 C.E. prohibits specifically sex discrimination, be it in its more open form as making sex a direct consideration or in its more subtle (and widespread) form as taking recourse to seemingly formally non discriminatory criteria which nonetheless have disadvantageous consequences on a socially depriviledged group, which is generally feminine. In relation to remuneration, this principle of non discrimination requires that . . . a work to which equal value is attributed, must correspond to equal remuneration, which excludes to take into consideration, be it directly or indirectly, the sex as determinant factor of the remuneration criteria. If it is the case that the different salary is apparently covered by assigning different categories, it is obviously not sufficient to ascertain that the tasks discharged of are different. The guarantee of equality under Article 14 C.E. requires to verify whether the criteria used for the assignment of categories are not discriminatory. It is for the employer to discharge of the burden of proof that its employment practice does not systematically disadvantage the remuneration category ascribed a lower value, by establishing the criteria which determine the higher remuneration of the privileged sector and, at the very least, to ensure that its remuneration system transparent. (citing *Danfoss*). At the same time, and corresponding to this (the employer) must show that it takes recourse to value neutral criteria, which guarantee equal conditions for workers of either sex (STC 58/1994). One must not consider as neutral such factors or qualities which are predominantly possessed by the male sex, except when the nature of the work requires such factors and the specific work has a special different value. In principle, and above all, one must not apply as the dominant criterion of evaluation and with the effect of granting a higher remuneration, physical strength, which corresponds to the average features of male work, while neglecting other characteristics which are more common in their impact on both sexes . . .

The analysis shows that the tasks performed by the workers in department where we find only women . . . and by workers in departments set aside for men . . . have little in common, except that they form a part of the same production process. However, this simple statement does not discharge of analyzing the criteria for establishing the value of the work done by the comparator workers. As stated in an earlier judgment, acknowledging functional differences between positions in each of the departments does not establish a reason for valuing one of the tasks—predominantly occupied by men—higher than others—predominantly occupied by women—(STC 58/1994). If assigning different tasks to personnel in different sections only masks discrimination, the resulting wage difference will have to be considered as contravening Article 14 C.E. All this requires that the criteria of job evaluation are assessed carefully. It will be necessary to verify whether some activities have been valued higher than others and whether one has resorted to discriminatory factors, using in an unjustified form, as yardstick qualities predominantly represented by one ex, or, on the contrary, common elements . . . In the present case, certainly, the facts are not the same as those contemplated in the STC 145/1991, where the use of the alluded categories only manifested a disguise of discrimination . . . But certainly there is no proof that the criteria used to justify the wage difference were actually neutral, and applied the concepts of effort and painfulness in a gender neutral way. In addition, these factors have not been complemented by other which also occur in relation to the work in question, with which the evaluation carried out by the employer and confirmed by the Employment Appeal Tribunal is far from being objective and transparent and does not achieve to dispel the discriminatory appearance that is rightly pointed at by the Union."

Note to Antonio Puig and Gomyatex
These cases demonstrate the willingness of the Spanish Constitutional Court to summarily assume that criteria such as physical effort and painfulness must not be used in evaluating the quality of work without being balanced by other criteria which are more typical for female work. In contrast to the result-oriented approach of Scandinavian courts, the Spanish court seems prepared to start only from the result of different payment between typically female and male sectors, but relies on effectively outlawing gendered remuneration criteria instead. Thus, it seems that in Spain *Rummler* is still good law.

CONCLUSIONS AND PRESENT DEFINITION IN EC LAW

We can conclude that the very first step to establish indirect discrimination is already decisive for the effectiveness of the concept. If, as in the former case-law and legislation in the UK, only specific requirements and conditions that establish a hurdle may be invoked, there are only few indirect discrimination cases. If, on the other hand, the result of a process, policy or long-standing business practice is taken as a yardstick, the concept of indirect discrimination is applied more widely, and its potential to expose discriminatory effects is enhanced. The collective approach, labelled "result oriented" by some,[142] may even motivate employers to engage in positive action in order to avoid indirect discrimination claims.

As has been said, EC legislation today has found a compromise between both poles. It requires a criterion, rule or practice to which the disparate impact could be attributed. Returning to the warehouse worker case, which is in a way comparable to *Danfoss*, one could probably argue that the new position of EC legislation would cover them, as there was a specific practice (distributing wage groups or bonuses arbitrarily or not in a fully transparent way) which resulted in disparate impact. It is, however, questionable whether the new definition would capture a collective case such as *Kajaani*, *Binderen* or even *Gomyatex*. Reading the new definitions in accordance with the Directives' objectives, which include putting equal treatment into practice, the collective approach is supported. This can be brought about by a wide reading of the notion of practice. It remains to be seen how the ECJ and national courts will interpret the new legislation.

3.5.1.B.   HOW IS DETRIMENTAL EFFECT ESTABLISHED?

Once a requirement, criterion or practice—possibly a wage system, a redundancy policy or a hiring policy in its entirety—has been established, the detrimental effect which is caused by this requirement needs to be ascertained. There are different problems at this stage. The main problem is whether the approach to establishing detrimental effect is statistical (disparate impact in the narrow sense of the word) or rather qualitative (disparate impact in the wider sense of the word).

STATISTICAL AND OTHER APPROACHES—THE POLICY DEBATE

The statistical approach to establishing disparate impact has been preferred not only by US courts, but also by UK courts. Above all, the ECJ's approach to indirect discrimination on grounds of sex has been based upon statistics.

Generally, indirect discrimination law has been characterised as "fundamentally and unavoidably a statistical notion".[143] In a way, this has been seen as one of its

---

[142] See Connolly and Townshend-Smith, above n. 20, 252–4.
[143] See Townshend-Smith, above n. 15, 105.

advantages. Using statistics to establish a case of indirect discrimination may serve a wider focus in exposing structural disadvantage that would not be perceptible without the numerical information. An overview is given by the authors of a Commission study on collection of data in relation to discrimination:

"The indirect discrimination concept requires statistical reasoning. Beyond intentional acts and explicit provisions, research into unfavourable treatment requires a comparison between the situation of a protected group and that of a benchmark group. If the protected group finds employment less often or occupies lesser positions although their qualifications were adequate, the hiring process will be considered suspicious. The discriminatory effect of apparently neutral procedures is only exposed through the impact they have on protected groups. The significance of negative consequences resulting from procedures is evaluated by means of indicators and indices, which have been subjected to unsophisticated statistical tests . . . Indeed, to be equitable is to ensure the proportional representation of protected groups when the relevant criteria to obtain the occupation, the goods or the services have been fulfilled. The theory adopted by the American legislation is that in absence of discrimination, and in relation to their skills, qualifications and merits, members of protected groups should be present in employment at the level their potential deserves. To ensure the equity of the systems, it is important to record personal characteristics through continuous monitoring in companies and recruitment zones. The role of statistics is all the more central to the anti-discrimination scheme, as all trials and selections can be monitored by technical statistics. Recruitment, promotion, training access, salaries, terminations, the professional positions occupied, exposure to hard or dangerous tasks, etc. most of these parameters can be examined in employee files. The same can be effected in the case of education or access to housing by using relevant indicators for describing selection situations where differentials are expressed".[144]

These authors view the statistical approach towards discrimination law as entirely positive. Other authors even consider that statistics have in themselves a considerable power to mobilise against discrimination.[145]

Statistical information can certainly contribute to unmasking discrimination. However, such information will often not be available, especially when non-discrimination law expands to grounds other than sex and gender. While there is little resistance revealing one's assigned sex—not least because it is obvious—revealing one's sexual orientation will be seen as a problem by many. In this, and other fields, data protection law limits gathering of statistics in many states.[146] Specific legislation in some Member States prohibits[147] or restricts[148] sampling of statistical information

---

[144] P. Simon, *Comparative Study on the Collection of Data to Measure the Extent and Impact of Discrimination within the United States, Canada, Australia, Great-Britain and the Netherlands—Medis Project* (Brussels, European Commission, 2004) 17, 27.

[145] J. Stavo-Dabauge, "Mobilising Statistical Powers for Action against Discrimination: the Case of the UK" (2005) 57 *International Social Science Journal* 43–53; M. Potvin, "The Role of Statistics on Ethnic Origin and Race in Canadian Anti-discrimination Policy" (2005) 57 *International Social Science Journal* 27–42.

[146] See O. De Schutter, Chapter 7: Positive Action.

[147] See Berthou, above n. 90, 118 with notes 52, 53 for France.

[148] See L. Farkas, "Will Women be the Easier Case? A Comparison of Race and Sex Discrimination Litigation in Hungary" in Dutch Equal Treatment Commission, above n. 125, 72–89, 75: in Hungary, sampling of ethnic data is dependent on the consent of all, including by those who profit from ethnic discrimination.

considering racial or ethnic origin; in others there is reluctance to (re-)introduce such statistics. Even in the absence of explicit legal barriers, statistics will be rare for "new" discrimination grounds or in relation to persons at intersections of grounds, such as ethnic minority women or lesbian Muslims. Over-reliance on statistics may thus lead to specific hierarchies in protecting against discrimination.

There are severe disadvantages to a predominantly statistic approach. Its long development in US and UK case-law has ensured that manifold requirements must be fulfilled by an applicant before she can even so much as establish a disparate impact claim (prima facie claim of indirect discrimination). Quite a few cases on indirect sex discrimination were lost before the ECJ and UK courts because the applicants were unable to gather the data required by the courts. This was not always due solely to insufficient knowledge of the law, but at times also to the fact that the relevant statistics did not exist and their compilation would be too costly. Above all, a purely statistical approach to indirect discrimination law leads to complicating this field to a degree that a successful claim becomes ever more difficult. All these criticisms are the reasons why the definition of indirect discrimination in the younger EC legislation does not exclusively rely on statistical proof.

DISPARATE IMPACT ESTABLISHED BY STATISTICS

The principles behind statistical proof of disparate impact can be condensed to the following: statistics are used to establish a prima facie case of indirect discrimination. Where a rule, practice or condition factually only affects those deemed to be members of a protected group negatively, one needs to discuss whether this is not a case of direct discrimination.[149] In the typical prima facie case of indirect discrimination we find that a condition, rule or practice does not divide the persons in its pool of application neatly into all kinds of relevant groups, but that one group finds itself disproportionately in a disadvantaged position. That disadvantage is to be demonstrated numerically.

Overview

The general aim of any of these statistical exercises is to compare the relative possibility of each of the groups, e.g. ethnic majority and ethnic minority, to belong to the (dis)advantaged group. For convenience, the "warehouse workers case" from the German Federal Labour Court may be used to illustrate the overall problem.

---

[149] See above M.Bell: Chapter 2: Direct discrimination, discussing excerpts **2.EC.12.**, **2.EC.13.** and **2.EC.35.**

Federal Labour Court (BAG), 23 September 1992[150]   **3.DE.43.***
4 AZR 30/92, An Applicant v. A Defendant

WHETHER CATEGORISING MOST MEN IN A HIGHER WAGE GROUP THAN MOST
WOMEN AMOUNTS TO INDIRECT DISCRIMINATION

Warehouse workers

Facts and *Held*: The question is whether a remuneration system according to which 1 of 10 female workers, but 7 of 13 male workers in the same department receive the higher of two wage groups is discriminatory. As to the disparate impact, the Federal Labour Court explains:

Judgment: "62. In the case on hand the group of persons disadvantageously affected by the wage policy of the respondent contains significantly more women than men.

63 . . . of 10 female order pickers, nine (i.e. 90%) were classified in group 2. Only the applicant to 3) (i.e. 10%) has been paid under group 3 classification since 1st November 1990. To the contrary, half of the male order pickers (nine) are paid under wage group 2 classification and the other half under wage group 3 classification. If 90% of female employees are being paid on the basis of the lower wage group but only 50% of male employees are being paid on the basis of the same lower wage group, the wage policy of the respondent is, comparatively speaking, significantly more disadvantageous for women than men."

Note

In this case, it was not particularly difficult to establish the relevant statistics, as only a small number of employees (23 taken together) were within the pool compared. However, under more recent standards set by the ECJ as regards the "pool of comparators", the applicants and their union would have had some difficulties, as they did not compare the fate of all the women and men to which this employer applied its system of allocating them into the wage groups of the collective agreement, but focused on a small faction instead. The next step is then to establish the degree of disadvantage. The Federal Labour Court focused on the negative effect, thus being able to conclude that women were indeed disadvantaged: they were 1.8 times as likely to be negatively affected. As we will see, the degree of disadvantage is influenced by the method of calculating it, i.e. whether one compares those negatively or positively affected. For the German case-law, this is the lowest degree of being disadvantaged ever accepted as sufficient to establish a prima facie case of indirect discrimination. There are considerable discussions as to what constitutes "considerable disadvantage" in different legal orders. The last step, which is not required by EC law and was thus not applied by the German court here but is being applied in some national jurisdictions, would have been the question whether the disadvantage is really caused by the discrimination ground in question, i.e. here sex. This additional causality test can be required under different headings, e.g. the heading of whether someone "can comply" with the rule in question due to one of the discrimination

---

[150] BAGE 71, 195–212.
* See above **3.DE.40.**

grounds or the heading whether the disadvantage is truly caused by the discrimination ground.

Choosing the pool of comparators

The first task to be mastered in establishing such proof is to convey the appropriate pool of comparators. There are different possibilities in principle. First, one can debate whether—in employment cases—the pool of comparators must be chosen from the immediate work place (such as in **3.DE.40.** and **3.DE.43.**), from all the employees employed by the employer or from all the potential employees. More generally, one could distinguish between those to whom the rule in question is applicable as the pool of comparators or a sample of those affected which demonstrates the discriminatory potential of the rule. Choosing the pool of comparators carefully is decisive for success of an indirect discrimination claim where a strictly statistically established disparate impact is required.[151]

ECJ, 30 November 1993[152]   **3.EC.44.**
C—189/91, Kirsammer-Hack v. *Sidal*

WHETHER EXEMPTING ESTABLISHMENTS WITH FEWER THAN FIVE EMPLOYEES
FROM STATUTORY EMPLOYMENT PROTECTION IS INDIRECT SEX DISCRIMINATION IF
EMPLOYEES WORKING LESS THAN 10 HOURS A WEEK DO NOT COUNT TOWARDS THE
MINIMUM

Kirsammer-Hack

Facts: Ms. Kirsammer-Hack was dismissed from her job as a dental assistant on grounds of alleged unpunctuality, lack of reliability and unsatisfactory quality of work. She claimed indirect discrimination because she could not rely on the Employment Protection Act (KSchG) as the dentist in question only employed two persons working more than 10 hours per week besides four persons working fewer hours. According to § 23(1) KSchG as it was worded then, this piece of protective legislation applied only to employees working in establishments employing more than five employees working more than 10 hours per week or 45 hours per month. Ms. Kirsammer-Hack worked more than 10 hours per week.

Held: The First Instance Labour Court of Bremen referred to the ECJ inter alia the question whether by exempting undertakings employing five employees or less from employment protection legislation, German law had violated the prohibition of indirect discrimination on grounds of sex. The Court relied especially on the fact that those employed for less than 10 hours per week or 45 hours per month were not counted as employees, and that the majority of these employees (nearly 90%) were female.

Judgment: "22 The Court has consistently held that national rules discriminate indirectly against women where, although worded in neutral terms, they are more disadvantageous to women than men, unless that difference in treatment is justified by objective factors unrelated

---

[151] See for the UK context McColgan, above n. 27, 86.
[152] [1993] ECR I–6185.

to any discrimination on grounds of sex (judgment in Case 171/88 Rinner-Kuehn [1989] ECR 2743, paragraph 12).

23 In the present case, the second sentence of Paragraph 23(1) of the KSchG restricts the application of the system of protection against unfair dismissal to businesses which employ more than five workers, while the third sentence states that part time employees are not taken into account in determining the number of persons employed for the purpose of the second sentence.

24 In that respect, it should be noted that the mere fact of not being taken into account in determining whether or not the national system of protection must be applied to the undertaking is not, in itself, disadvantageous for part time employees.

25 It is only under the combined provisions of the second and third sentences of Paragraph 23(1) of the KSchG that undertakings which employ a number of employees below the stipulated threshold are not subject to the national system of protection and that their employees therefore suffer the disadvantage of being excluded from that system.

26 The combination of the two sentences in question thus leads to a difference in treatment not between part time employees and others but between all workers employed in small businesses not subject to the system of protection and all workers employed in undertakings which, by reason of the fact that they employ a greater number of employees, are subject to it . . .

28 Thus, workers such as the claimant in the main proceedings do not benefit from protection against unfair dismissal although they do not work part time. Conversely, part time employees benefit from the system of protection when they are employed in undertakings subject to that system.

29 The proportion of women among part time employees in Germany to which the national court refers does not therefore justify the conclusion that the provision in question constitutes indirect discrimination against women contrary to Articles 2(1) and 5(1) of the Directive.

30 There would be such discrimination only if it were established that small businesses employ a considerably higher percentage of women than men.

31 In the present case, the information provided to the Court does not establish such a disproportion."

Note

The ECJ's conclusion that the statistics before the national court were not conclusive rests on the logic that, to establish disparate impact, it is necessary to consider all employees affected by the national rule in question. While this is a convincing argument in principle, finding the relevant statistics is not without difficulty. Statistical proof could presently be brought for the number of women working in establishments with less than 20 employees, but the detailed number of hours worked by each worker is not part of the national statistical package. Thus, even if the national court had applied the correct standard, this case would have failed.

ECJ, 31 May 1995[153]   **3.EC.45.**[*]

C—400/93, *Specialarbejderforbundet i Danmark v. Dansk Industri, formerly Industriens Arbejdsgivere, acting for Royal Copenhagen A/S*

WHETHER STATISTICAL DIFFERENCES IN PAY BETWEEN THREE GROUPS
OF WORKERS ARE SUFFICIENT TO ESTABLISH DETRIMENTAL EFFECT OF A
PAY SYSTEM

Royal Copenhagen

Facts and *Held*: See above **3.EC.39.** Within this set of facts, the issue of statistical evidence became relevant. The ECJ was of the opinion that the union should have been more diligent in choosing the comparator group.

Judgment: "31 . . . the third question, which has two limbs, arises because the pay discrimination complained of by the claimant in the main proceedings concerns the automatic-machine operators' group and the blue-pattern painters' group, which in fact are simply subgroups of two larger groups, turners and painters. The claimant argues that its choice of two relatively small groups is justified because in order to compare pay it is necessary to have homogeneous groups, particularly as regards the training of the workers involved. The national court's third question read as a whole asks whether, in a piece-work pay scheme, the composition of the groups of workers whose average pay is to be compared in order to ascertain whether there is any sex discrimination must be determined by reference to specific criteria, in particular as to the number of workers in the group and the proportion which they represent of the total workforce; alternatively, may those groups, through the selection of arbitrary criteria, be so formed as to consist exclusively of men or of women so that in certain circumstances a comparison of two groups of workers made up of men and of women respectively may entail equalizing the pay of two groups of workers made up of women where the average pay of one such group of women is lower and that of the other higher than the pay of the group made up of men.

32 Consideration of whether the principle of equal pay has been observed requires a comparison between the pay of workers of different sexes for the same work or for work to which equal value is attributed . . .

34 The comparison must moreover cover a relatively large number of workers in order to ensure that the differences found are not due to purely fortuitous or short-term factors or to differences in the individual output of the workers concerned.

35 It is for the national court to make the necessary assessments of the facts of the main proceedings in the light of the abovementioned criteria."

Note on Royal Copenhagen re statistical evidence
As a result, the trade union's task would have been Herculean. Before bringing an equal pay claim based on indirect discrimination for a single department, any job in the whole factory would have had to be evaluated, and each single criterion decisive for remuneration isolated and evaluated specifically. Only this would allow the proper composition of a pool of comparators in the eyes of the ECJ.

[153] [1995] ECR Royal I–01275.
[*] See above **3.EC.39.**

The judicial finding that the proper pool of comparators was lacking led to refusal of indirect discrimination claims in national jurisdictions. Two examples may suffice in this regard.

Federal Constitutional Court (BVerfG), 27 November1997[154]   **3.DE.46.**
1 BvL 12/91, An applicant v. City of Hamburg

WHETHER EXCLUDING PART-TIME EMPLOYEES WORKING LESS THAN 18 HOURS A WEEK FROM AN ADDITIONAL PENSION SCHEME CONSTITUTES INDIRECT SEX DISCRIMINATION

Hamburg occupational pension

Facts: The City of Hamburg offered its employees an additional occupational pension scheme in order to approximate pensions received by former employees to those received by former public servants. Access to this scheme was initially excluded for any part-time worker. Since 1986, access was opened to part-time employees working at least 50% of the regular working time, with retroactive effect. This threshold was defined as 18 hours per week in 1991. In 1995, the threshold was lowered to 10 hours a week, as employees working less would not build up a claim to a social security pension. The applicant had been working for 17 hours a week from 1970 to 1979 and for at least 20 hours a week from 1979 to 1989. Upon receiving a reduced special pension due to 9 years of employment being disregarded, she raised a claim to the Hamburg Labour Court on grounds of violation of Article 3 Grundgesetz, which inter alia contains the constitutional gender equality clause.

Held: The Labour Court referred the case to the Constitutional Court, as it considered the rules in question incompatible with Article 3 GG. The Constitutional Court denied a claim based on indirect gender discrimination relating to insufficient statistics

Judgment: "33. The regulation being assessed is partly incompatible with the constitution . . . There is no incompatibility with Article 3 Paragraph 3 sentence 1 *Grundgesetz* (GG) . . .

34 1. Among other things, Article 3 Paragraph 3 sentence 1 GG prohibits discrimination on grounds of gender. In principle, gender must not be linked in any way to an unequal treatment of a person. This also applies if a rule is not designed to impose such unequal treatment but rather pursues other aims [citation omitted]. In accordance with legal precedent; discrimination on the basis of gender can also exist if a gender-neutrally worded regulation mainly affects women and if this is attributable to natural or social differences between the genders [reference to ECJ decisions in Bilka, Kowalska and Enderby as well as Federal Labour Court case-law]. This issue does not require detailed examination in this case because factual disadvantage against women by the regulation has not been established. According to the statistical material of the Free and Hanseatic City of Hamburg for the period up to 1979, the proportion of women in the group of employees employed for less than 50% of the usual working hours was not higher than the proportion of women in the group of other part time workers and the group of full-time workers. There was also no adequate evidence that women employed for less than 50% of the usual working hours were typically more dependent on additional occupational pension schemes than men in the same situation."

---

[154] BVerfGE 97, 35–49.

Note

This case demonstrates a certain unfamiliarity of the Constitutional Court with applying the EC law concept of indirect discrimination. The question that should have been asked was not whether the proportion of women excluded from the additional pension was higher than the proportion of women among the part-timers. The relevant comparison should rather have been made between the proportion of women and men among all employees of the city of Hamburg, among those employees who received an additional pension and among those who did not due to not having worked at least 50% of the regular working time.

Court of Appeal, 21 December 1992[155]   **3.GB.47.**
Jones v. *University of Manchester*

WHETHER A REQUIREMENT FOR A UNIVERSITY GRADUATE CAREER ADVISER
TO BE AGED 27–35 INDIRECTLY DISCRIMINATED AGAINST WOMEN

Jones v. University of Manchester

Facts: Manchester University wished to employ a career adviser and required applicants to have a university degree, experience in service settings and to be between 27 and 35 years of age, the justification being that they should be close in age to graduates to ease communication. Ms. Jones stated that there were more female than male mature students, and thus older graduates, and therefore that the age requirement would have discriminatory effects.

Held: The Court of First Instance (then the Industrial Tribunal) found for the applicant, mainly on the basis that the relevant pool of comparators should have been all graduates who had obtained their degree as mature students, i.e. at the age of 25 or above. Having been presented with evidence that 3.3% of male first degree entrants were between 25 and 29 compared with 2.8% of women, and that 2.1% of male students were age 30 and over compared with 3.7% of women, the Tribunal held that for a candidate to be within the age range was a requirement "such that the proportion of women graduates, having obtained their degrees at 25 years or over, i.e. as mature students, who could comply with it would be considerably smaller than the proportion of male graduates". The Employment Appeal Tribunal overturned the first instance decision, but allowed the appeal. The Court of Appeal upheld the EAT finding on the basis that the Industrial Tribunal had used the wrong pool of comparators.

Judgment: "In order to compare the proportion of women who can comply with a requirement with the proportion of men who can comply with it, it is necessary to determine the relevant total. The relevant total is the number of men and women to whom the person, i.e. the employer in this case, applies or would apply the requirement. In the present case, that meant all men and women graduates with the relevant experience. The relevant total is not all men and women, since the employer would have no occasion to apply the requirement to any men or women other than those who are able to comply with the requirements of the advertisement other than the requirement in question. Nor is the relevant total merely of those men and women who can comply with the requirement, since the section refers to the proportion of men and women who can comply. That shows that those who can comply with the requirement are to be considered as a proportion of the total of men and women to whom the requirement is or would be applied . . . The case for Miss Jones, therefore, as prepared with the help of the EOC, was directed to proving not that the proportion of

[155] [1993] IRLR 218.

women graduates who could comply with the age requirement was considerably smaller than the proportion of men who could comply with it, as required by the section, but to proving that the proportion of women mature graduates who could comply with the age requirement was considerably smaller, etc."

Note on Jones v. Manchester

The case demonstrates that the strict statistical requirements establish a high hurdle to be jumped by any applicant, which seems difficult even if the individual is supported by the main body responsible for equal opportunity issues, in this case the Equal Opportunities Commission. The English Employment Appeal Tribunal had attempted to ease this burden by, inter alia, categorising the choice of comparator pools as a matter of fact to be assessed by the Employment Tribunal (Court of First Instance)[156] or by requiring the defendant employer to bring forth convincing statistics in support of their own case.[157] However, the courts of law continue to apply a strict requirement.

To sum up, both EC law and national law apply strict requirements for establishing the relevant pool of comparators, especially in indirect sex discrimination cases. Under this strict approach, the pool of comparators may well be the whole population, if the rule in question is a generally applicable piece of legislation. Similarly, the pool of comparators will comprise all employees of a branch if the rule in question is part of a collective agreement applied to a branch. If the rule in question is specific to an employer or a landlord, the pool of comparators will only consist of the employees or tenants of this entity. There is not much case-law on indirect discrimination cases concerning access to employment, let alone goods and services. Thus, the question is how the pool of comparators would have to be established in these cases. The Dutch Supreme Court, in its *van Binderen/Kaya* judgment,[158] has considered the population of a town to be the correct pool of comparators for access to tenancies. In access to employment cases, one could have recourse to all applicants, which is the reason why English employers engage in statistical exercises at the application stage. For an applicant in an indirect discrimination case, these data are not accessible, which would mean that averages of compositions of applicant pools should be sufficient.

To establish disparate impact, a comparison must be made between a reference group and the whole pool of comparators. The reference group may be composed of those individuals who do not fulfil the requirement or condition or do not profit from the practice (disadvantaged group). For both the pool of comparator and the reference groups, the proportions of women, those of a specific ethnic minority, those of a specific religious belief or those of a specific sexual orientation, on the one hand, and of men, those of other ethnic backgrounds, those of other specific religious beliefs and so on, on the other, will have to be established. Which numbers are to be compared exactly is discussed in the next subsection.

---

[156] EAT, *Greater Manchester Police Authority* v. *Leas* [1990] IRLR 372, para. 11.
[157] *Ibid.*, para. 13.
[158] See above **3.NL.36.**

There are some open questions when choosing the pool of comparators. We suggest that these should be solved with a view towards applying indirect discrimination law effectively. In accordance with this principle, overly large pools of comparators should be avoided. If, for example, application of a collective agreement with a national scope of applicants leads to disparate impact within one employer or for one region, an employer specific or region specific case of indirect discrimination should be considered. It may well be that the application within this smaller pool of comparators is discriminatory, while the instrument as such is not. While this approach seems to contrast with the younger case-law of the ECJ, it is in line with some national case-law. In the warehouse workers case, the German Federal Labour Court referred only to the employees actually working in the warehouse, and in the *Antonio Puig* case, the Spanish Constitutional Court considered only those workers employed by Antonio Puig in ascertaining the detrimental effect of using criteria such as physical strength.

Establishing disparate impact (which numbers are to be compared exactly?)

Once the correct pool of comparators has been chosen, the next problem is to establish the actual statistical disadvantage at which point even more indirect discrimination cases fail.

When establishing disparate impact, it is not enough to rely on absolute numbers, as one looks for disproportionate disadvantage of individuals to whom one discrimination ground applies in comparison to other individuals. Thus, finding that a rule excludes 50 persons of minority background but 150 persons of ethnic majority background does nothing to prove that those of minority background have not been disadvantaged. The comparison is between proportions, as has been said. Once the proportion in the pool of comparators has been established, one needs to build the reference group and establish the proportion within it. The reference group may consist of those who are advantaged or those who are disadvantaged by the requirement, provision or practice. Both options have been accepted by the ECJ and national courts, but the emphasis has been on the disadvantaged group in most cases.

ECJ, 9 September 1999[159]   **3.EC.48.**
C—281/97, Krüger v. Kreiskrankenhaus Eberswalde

WHETHER DENYING A YEAR-END BONUS TO PART-TIME EMPLOYEES WORKING LESS THAN 10 HOURS A WEEK CONSTITUTES INDIRECT GENDER DISCRIMINATION

Krüger

Facts: Andrea Krüger had worked for Kreiskrankenhaus Eberswalde as a part-time cleaner for less than 45 hours a month. Accordingly, she was not covered by the supplementary collective agreement which

---

[159] [1999] ECR I–5127.

provided for a substantial year-end bonus, which equalled a full monthly wage for employees covered by this agreement. She challenged the denial of the bonus as indirectly discriminatory.

Held: The Munich Labour Court (Court of First Instance) referred to the ECJ some questions in relation to the indirectly discriminatory nature of this measure. As a result, the discrimination claim succeeded before the national court.

Judgment: "26 The exclusion of persons in minor employment from a collective agreement providing for the grant of a special annual bonus constitutes treatment which is different from that for full-time workers. If the national court, which alone has jurisdiction to assess the facts, were to find that that exclusion, although it applies independently of the sex of the worker, actually affects a considerably higher percentage of women than men, it would have to conclude that the collective agreement concerned constitutes indirect discrimination within the meaning of Article 119 of the Treaty."

ECJ, 23 October 2003[160]   **3.EC.49.**

C—4/02, C—5/02, Hilde Schönheit v. *Stadt Frankfurt a. M. and Sylvia Becker* v. *Land Hessen*

WHETHER DEGRESSIVELY REDUCING A PUBLIC SERVANT'S PENSION FOR YEARS
WORKED PART-TIME CONSTITUTES INDIRECT SEX DISCRIMINATION

Schönheit

Facts: Mrs. Schönheit and Mrs. Becker were both public servants in Hessen and had worked part-time and full-time successively. Upon retirement, their pensions were calculated in accordance with a formula that provided for a "Versorgungsabschlag" (pension abatement) for each year worked part-time. This method of calculation meant that the pension received for each year of part-time work would be reduced more than just *pro rata tempore*.

Held: The Verwaltungsgericht Frankfurt referred to the ECJ some questions concerning the indirectly discriminatory nature of this statutory pension scheme.

Judgment: ". . .Therefore it is necessary to determine whether the statistics available indicate that a considerably higher percentage of women than men is affected by the provisions of the BeamtVG entailing a reduction in the pensions of civil servants who have worked part time for at least a part of their career. Such a situation would be evidence of apparent discrimination on grounds of sex unless the provisions at issue were justified by objective factors unrelated to any discrimination based on sex. In this instance, it is apparent from the orders for reference that a considerably higher percentage of female than male civil servants works part time and is therefore affected by the relevant provisions of the BeamtVG. In those circumstances, it must be held, on the basis of the information provided in this regard by the referring court, that provisions such as those at issue in the main proceedings may result in discrimination against women by comparison with men in breach of the principle of equal pay for men and women for equal work, unless the provisions are justified by objective factors unrelated to any discrimination on grounds of sex."

---

[160] [2003] ECR I–12575.

Note

In its decision on the case of *Seymour-Smith and Perez* (ECJ), which will be dealt with in more detail below (see below, **3.EC.54.**), the ECJ deviated slightly from this formula and explained:

> "59 . . . [T]he best approach to the comparison of statistics is to consider, on the one hand, the respective proportions of men in the workforce able to satisfy the requirement of two years' employment under the disputed rule and of those unable to do so, and, on the other, to compare those proportions as regards women in the workforce. It is not sufficient to consider the number of persons affected, since that depends on the number of working people in the Member State as a whole as well as the percentages of men and women employed in that State."

Note on Krüger, Schönheit and Seymour-Smith and Perez (ECJ) regarding mode of comparison

It seems that the ECJ prefers the formula in accordance with which the percentage of the members of the disadvantaged group in the pool of comparators and the percentage in the reference group that is actually disadvantaged by the requirement, condition or policy needs to be assessed. It must be stressed that the ECJ has always left the final decision to the national court, at least in younger cases, such as *Seymour-Smith* and *Perez*.[161] Accordingly, the House of Lords found, upon receiving the judgment, that it was not strictly bound by the seemingly new approach, as Lord Nicholls's speech for the majority revealed:

> "The court commented that, on its face, those statistics did not appear to show that a considerably smaller percentage of women than men was able to fulfil the extended requirement. In its formal answer to the referred question in para. 65, the court repeated the considerably smaller percentage test already stated in para. 60. However, I cannot believe that in doing so the court intended to repudiate the approach stated in para. 61. Nor do I think this can be taken as an indication by the court that the para. 61 approach was inapplicable in this case."[162]

In addition, relying on the disadvantaged group would be more in line with the *effet utile* of Community law, as such reading will actually be more favourable to those seeking judicial protection against discrimination. The mathematical exercise has been demonstrated in a fashion digestible for lawyers in a UK decision.

---

[161] ECJ, 9 February 1999, C–167/97 *Regina v Secretary of State for Employment, ex parte Nicole Seymour-Smith and Laura Perez* [1999] ECR I–623, No. 65. For more details, see below **3.EC.54.**
[162] House of Lords, 17 February 2000, [2000] 1 All ER 857; for more details, see below **3.GB.55.**

House of Lords, 22 July 1999[163]   **3.GB.50.**
Barry v. *Midland Bank Plc*

WHETHER PAYING LESS SEVERANCE GRANT TO THOSE WHO HAVE WORKED
PART-TIME CONSTITUTES INDIRECT SEX DISCRIMINATION

Barry

Facts: Ms. Barry had been working with Midlands Bank from 1970 to 1993, before she chose to terminate the working relationship. As this decision was induced by the company, which had announced that it was relocating to different premises which would have resulted in difficulties for Ms. Barry to reconcile work and care of her pre-school child, she was entitled to a severance payment by the collective agreement. This agreement, however, provided that the severance payment was shortened for each year worked part-time.

Held: The IT and the EAT dismissed the claim while the House of Lords allowed the appeal on questions of law.

Judgment: Lord Nichols of Birkenhead: "In order to decide whether the bank's scheme has a disparately adverse impact on women, a comparison must be made between, on the one hand, the respective proportions of men in the bank who are not disadvantaged by the difference in treatment of which complaint is made and those who are disadvantaged and, on the other hand, the like proportions regarding women in the workforce (reference to Seymour Smith). These proportions by themselves can be misleading, because they are affected by the comparative sizes of the non-disadvantaged group and the disadvantaged group. The smaller the disadvantaged group in proportionate terms, the narrower will be the differential. Take an employer whose workforce of 1,000 comprises an equal number of men and women. 10% of the staff (100 employees) work part time and of these 90% are women. A scheme which disadvantages part timers will disadvantage 10 men (2% of the male employees) and 90 women (18% of female employees). If the figures were the same save that the total workforce was 10,000 employees, the disadvantaged part timers would comprise 10 men (0.2% of male employees) and 90 women (1.8% of female employees). A better guide will often be found in expressing the proportions in the disadvantaged group as a ratio of each other. In both my examples the ratio is 9:1. For every man adversely affected there are nine women. Absolute size, in terms of numbers, remains relevant, since a low ratio may be of little significance in a small company but of considerable significance in a large company."

Note

The wise part of these deliberations is that which points to the decisiveness of the disadvantage. Pursuing the example a little further and giving the proportion of women in the entire workforce and then among the disadvantaged shows disadvantage even on a non-comparative basis. If there are 10% of part-time employees in the entire staff, the overall probability of being excluded from the severance payment is also 10%. However, for women, although they comprise 50% of the workforce, their probability to be excluded is 18%, thus 1.8 times as high as it should be were substantive equality to prevail. Comparing the position of women and men in the advantaged group will, however, show a less pronounced disadvantage: 82% of the female employees and 92% of the male employees (90% of

---

[163] [1999] 3 All ER 974.

all employees) take advantage of the severance payment, i.e. are able to fulfil the requirement.

The same point was made in a case decided by the Court of Appeal around the same time:

Court of Appeal, 21 May 1998[164]   **3.GB.51.**
London Underground Ltd v. Edwards

WHETHER CHANGING A TRAIN OPERATOR'S ROSTERING SCHEME IS INDIRECT
DISCRIMINATION

London Underground v. Edwards

Facts: Mrs. Edwards, a single parent with a young child, was employed as a train driver. Her roster arrangements allowed her to be at home in the mornings and evenings to attend to her son. She generally worked between 8 a.m. and 4 p.m. or from 8.30 a.m. to 4.30 p.m., with Saturday as a rest day. However, because of her working hours she did not receive shift bonuses for unsocial hours (i.e. working between 6 p.m. and 7 a.m.). In 1991the employers announced a new flexible shift system, under which duties were to begin at 4.45 a.m. and were to include Sundays. Avoiding early and late work, employees would work longer shifts for the same money. Mrs. Edwards was not prepared to work the new system and when negotiations between management and the unions about special arrangements for single parents proposed by the employers did not reach agreement, she resigned and claimed unlawful sex discrimination.

Held: The Industrial Tribunal allowed her claim as they found that a considerably smaller number of female single parents than male single parents could comply with the new roster. The EAT allowed the employer's appeal on the grounds that restricting the pool of comparators to single parents was wrong. The second Industrial Tribunal found that, considering all employees, all male train drivers (i.e. 100%) and all but one female train drivers (95.2%) could comply with the new requirements, and considered that this small difference was sufficient given that it was common knowledge that more single mothers would have difficulties. The EAT dismissed the employers' appeal. London Underground appealed on the point of law of whether these numbers established sufficiently adverse impact. The CA dismissed the appeal, inter alia relying on the fact that in Britain there are 10 single mothers for every single father.

Judgment: Simon Brown LJ: ". . . can it properly be said that 95.2% is a 'considerably smaller' proportion than 100% within the meaning of s. 1(1)(b)(i) of the Act? . . . Mr. Allen's second and principal argument is that, . . . assuming . . . that 95% of the women in the group could comply with the new roster requirement, that proportion could properly be held to be considerably smaller than the 100% proportion of men. It is not to be overlooked, he submits, that at the other end of the scale 5% of the women were disadvantaged as against 0% of the men, a very considerable difference indeed . . . I can state my conclusions really quite shortly. Given that this legislation is concerned essentially to contrast the impact of a given requirement or condition as between men and women rather than as between the women in the group, it would seem to me wrong to ignore entirely the striking fact here that not a single man was disadvantaged by this requirement despite the vast preponderance of men within the group. Looked at in the round, this requirement clearly bore disproportionately as between men and women, even though only one woman was affected by it . . . Once, then, one departs from the purely mechanistic approach contended for by the appellants, and has regard to other facts besides merely a comparison between 95% and 100%, the respondent's argument becomes compelling:

[164] [1999] ICR 494.

no other fact could be more relevant than that, whereas 5% of the women were disadvantaged, not one of the 2,023 men was. That further consideration in my judgment supports the industrial tribunal's finding here."

Notes

(1) The example of the facts of this case demonstrates that using the disadvantaged as the reference group is particularly useful in such cases where those habitually discriminated against (e.g. women, ethnic minorities, lesbian, gay and bisexual people) are in an extreme minority position. In these cases, a comparison of those advantaged by a rule and the pool of comparators will show next to no difference. Thus, using the disadvantaged group as the reference group (or making a disadvantage-led comparison) would seem more appropriate in order to safeguard the effective working of discrimination law.

(2) For Britain, it should be noted that the House of Lords has preferred an advantage-led comparison in the more recent case of *Rutherford (2)*,[165] concerning statutory age-limits for redundancy payment in case of dismissal. Their Lordships seemed partly concerned not to convert age discrimination (which was not unlawful in 2002, when the case was tried) into sex discrimination.[166] In addition, some of them stressed they would prefer a disadvantage-led approach in cases where those habitually disadvantaged by discrimination (i.e. in sex discrimination cases women) suffer a detriment.[167] The majority did not wish to apply indirect discrimination law to an advantage most employees would not choose (i.e. the opportunity to work beyond 65).[168] The *Rutherford (2)* case thus seems a specific one. It remains to be seen whether the reasoning in *Barry* will be used in other cases.

In Dutch and German law, the disadvantage-led approach seems to prevail.

Equal Treatment Commission (Commissie Gelijke Behandeling)   **3.NL.52.**
Opinion 1997-4

INDIRECT SEX DISCRIMINATION BY DISREGARDING SENIORITY OF FORMER
STANDBY STEWARDESSES WHO PROCEED TO REGULAR EMPLOYMENT

Stand-by stewardesses

Facts: The applicants had been working for the defendant as part-time stewardesses, but had been employed on an on-call basis before. The relevant collective agreement provides for regular promotion in line with

[165] *Secretary of State for Trade and Industry* v. *Rutherford (No. 2)*, *Same* v. *Bentley* [2006] ICR 785 (HL).
[166] Lord Scott of Foscote: "a difference in treatment of individuals that is based on age cannot be transformed by statistics from age discrimination, which it certainly is, to sex discrimination" (at 791).
[167] Lord Walter of Gestingthorpe: "I can imagine . . . cases in which a disadvantage –led approach would serve as an alert to the likelihood of objectionable discrimination. If . . . the advantaged 95% were split equally between men and women, but the disadvantaged 5% were all women, the very strong disparity of disadvantage would . . . make it a special case . . ." (at 805).
[168] Baroness Hale of Richmond, at 808, following Lord Scott of Foscote and Lord Rodger of Earlsferry.

seniority. However, any professional experience gained while working on an on-call basis was disregarded. The applicants considered this as indirect discrimination. The cabin personnel of the applicant was composed of 680 men and 3996 women working part-time, but those who had changed from on-call work to regular work on a part-time basis comprised 76 women and one man.

Held: The Commission considered that the exclusion of former on-call work professional work was illegal indirect discrimination.

Opinion: "4.5 Generally, the Commission relies on relative data when assessing whether a provision makes an indirect distinction on grounds of sex, as this takes into account the relative share of women and men respectively in the relevant part of the respondent's workforce. In a workforce where men and women are not roughly equally represented (as in the present case), absolute data would convey a distorted picture. The relative test means that one needs to establish how may female stand-by stewardesses are disadvantaged by the rule in comparison with all female members of the cabin crew, as well as how many male stand-by stewards are disadvantaged if compared with all male members of the cabin crew . . .Considering the numbers given above, it transpires that in 1993 (1:681) * 100% = 0.15% of male pursers have been disadvantaged. Out of the female stewardesses (76:4072) * 100%=1.87% are disadvantaged. This means that (1.87: 0.15=) 12.47 times as many women are disadvantaged than men. In the assessment of the Commission this leads to the conclusion that women are disproportionately disadvantaged and that there is thus a case of indirect distinction."

Federal Labour Court (BAG), 20 August 2002[169]   **3.DE.53.**
9 AZR 750/00, An applicant v. A defendant

WHETHER EXCLUDING FROM THE RIGHT TO REDUCE WORKING TIME UPON
REACHING THE AGE OF 60 SUCH EMPLOYEES AS CAN CLAIM A PENSION IS INDIRECT
SEX DISCRIMINATION

Old-age working time reduction

Facts: The Claimant, born on 12 October 1938, has been an employee of the Defendant for more than 20 years. The collective agreement for employees within the confectionery industry applies to the employment relationship. This agreement provides in its § 3, headed "Release of older employees from work" that employees, upon turning 60, 61 and 62 years old, may claim additional holidays for each full year of employment following their sixtieth birthday, provided they have been employed with the company for at least 12 years. The same provision contains an exception to the detriment of those employees who are already able to claim a pension. In the German pension system, several groups of employees can claim a pension at 60: women born no later than 1950, women or men who are severely disabled, and persons who have been paying pension contributions for 40 years at the age of 60. Both among the severely disabled in employment and the last group, the proportion of men is slightly higher then that of women. However, among all those who can claim a pension at 60, there were overwhelmingly more women than men at the time of the proceedings in the first instance (1998).

Held: The Court of First Instance allowed the claim but the Regional Labour Court rejected it, relying on objective justification. The Federal Labour Court restored the decision of the First Instance Court, and had to react to the employer's suggestion that not even a prima facie case of indirect discrimination had been established.

Judgment: "An indirectly discriminatory rule anyway does not relate to the sex of 'woman' but to characteristics which may be present in both sexes, but which in fact are generally not

---

[169] BAGE 102, 269.

413

exhibited by women. Generally speaking, statistical comparisons form the bases of a decision as to whether indirect discrimination is present . . . The group which is disadvantaged by application of the criterion is compared with the entire group of those to whom the criterion can be applied. If, when this method is applied, considerably fewer women than men actually receive the benefit, this rule is described as 'probably based on differences in sex' . . . The fact that the exclusion of benefits primarily affects women, however, is not yet sufficient. Rather, the relationship expressed in numbers amongst those who benefit must differ considerably from the relationship expressed in numbers amongst those who do not benefit . . ."

Note
While the focus on disadvantage is generally to be cherished, there remains a problem in these gender-focused cases. Both courts compare the gender relation in the disadvantaged and the advantaged group, instead of the gender relation in the disadvantaged and the whole group. While this approach is rather efficient in gender cases, it ceases to be so in all fields where there are several groups divided by one criterion (e.g. ethnicity, religion). In these fields comparison of the entirety of employees and the disadvantaged group will often be easier to establish than a detailed picture on the situation of all ethnicities or religions. As shown above, this method will also bring about convincing results if there really is statistical disadvantage.

Degree of adversity ("considerably higher")

There is as yet no generally accepted yardstick as to the meaning of "considerably higher". Although some cases in gender equality failed to fulfil this requirement, this field is still open to development.

British equality lawyers with their specific strength in strategic litigation were fastest in finding a case to bring the question of the required degree of adversity before the ECJ.

ECJ, 9 February 1999[170]   **3.EC.54.**
C—167/97, Regina v. *Secretary of State for Employment, ex parte*
Nicole Seymour-Smith and Laura Perez

TWO-YEAR QUALIFICATION PERIOD FOR EMPLOYMENT PROTECTION AS INDIRECT
SEX DISCRIMINATION

Seymour-Smith and Perez (ECJ)

Facts: Ms. Seymour-Smith and Ms. Perez were dismissed by different employers. They raised complaints of unfair dismissal and applied for compensation under the British Employment Protection Act. These complaints were rejected as inadmissible by the Industrial Tribunal because they had not completed the

---

[170] [1999] ECR 623.

relevant period of service of two years. Given leave for judicial review, they challenged the provision of the Employment Protection Act as being indirectly discriminatory, because in 1985, 13.8% of all male employees but 19.2% of all female employees would have been denied applicability of the Employment Protection Act to their dismissal because they did not fulfil the qualification period. The claimants alternatively relied on the percentage of male and female employees who would have fulfilled the two-year qualification period in 1985 (77.4 and 68.9% respectively).

Held: The High Court dismissed the claimant's application for judicial review because it found that, while the rule affected more women than men, this statistical difference was not disproportionate. The Court of Appeal held that the rule contravened Directive 76/207/EEC, but did not treat the issue as an equal pay case. Both the Secretary of State and the applicants in the original action appealed to the House of Lords, which referred a few questions to the ECJ. Some of these address the problem whether the case is rather equal treatment or equal pay, which is not covered here. There were also some questions regarding objective justification, to which we will return in the relevant section. The main issue relevant for this part is whether the disparate impact is really sufficient, to which questions three and four are relevant, which the ECJ answered in reverse order.

Judgment: "42 By its fourth question, which it is appropriate to answer at this stage, the national court asks essentially whether the legality of a rule of the kind at issue must be assessed as at the time of its adoption, the time when it entered into force or the time when the employee is dismissed . . .

46 . . . the point in time at which the legality of a rule of the kind at issue in this case is to be assessed by the national court may depend on various circumstances, both legal and factual . . .

49 With regard, in particular, to statistics, it may be appropriate to take into account not only the statistics available at the point in time at which the act was adopted, but also statistics compiled subsequently which are likely to provide an indication of its impact on men and on women.

51 By its third question, the national court seeks to ascertain the legal test for establishing whether a measure adopted by a Member State has disparate effect as between men and women to such a degree as to amount to indirect discrimination . . .

54 The applicants in the main proceedings . . .

55 [i]n particular . . . claim that where there are statistics which are significant, cover the entire workforce, and demonstrate long-term phenomena that cannot be explained as fortuitous, anything more than a minimal difference in impact would infringe the obligation to give effect to the principle of equal treatment . . .

60 As the Court has stated on several occasions, it must be ascertained whether the statistics available indicate that a considerably smaller percentage of women than men is able to satisfy the condition of two years' employment required by the disputed rule. That situation would be evidence of apparent sex discrimination unless the disputed rule were justified by objective factors unrelated to any discrimination based on sex.

61 That could also be the case if the statistical evidence revealed a lesser but persistent and relatively constant disparity over a long period between men and women who satisfy the requirement of two years' employment. It would, however, be for the national court to determine the conclusions to be drawn from such statistics.

62 It is also for the national court to assess whether the statistics concerning the situation of the workforce are valid and can be taken into account, that is to say, whether they cover enough individuals, whether they illustrate purely fortuitous or short-term phenomena, and whether, in general, they appear to be significant (reference to Enderby, paragraph 17) . . .

63 In this case, it appears from the order for reference that in 1985, the year in which the requirement of two years' employment was introduced, 77.4% of men and 68.9% of women fulfilled that condition.

64 Such statistics do not appear, on the face of it, to show that a considerably smaller percentage of women than men is able to fulfil the requirement imposed by the disputed rule.

65 Accordingly, the answer to the third question must be that in order to establish whether a measure adopted by a Member State has disparate effect as between men and women to such a degree as to amount to indirect discrimination . . . the national court must verify whether the statistics available indicate that a considerably smaller percentage of women than men is able to fulfil the requirement imposed by that measure. If that is the case, there is indirect sex discrimination, unless that measure is justified by objective factors unrelated to any discrimination based on sex."

Notes

(1) The result achieved by the ECJ seems rather cautious. However, it also presents incremental progress compared with former case-law and also with the approach of the European Commission taken in this case. The UK had rightly cited some former case-law and pointed to the fact that "marked difference" was required. The Commission had actually suggested that "statistically significant evidence" was needed, which could be understood as requiring claimants in indirect discrimination cases to employ a qualified sociologist in addition to a lawyer. The Court had, in its answer to the fourth question, indicated that claimants could rely on available statistics. It had also indicated that where the development of the impact showed an increase in disadvantage, less adversity was required (see paragraph 61). However, in the end the ECJ found that the statistical evidence was inconclusive, while leaving the final assessment to the national court.

(2) The House of Lords took the opportunity to apply the reasoning given under paragraph 61 of the judgment, when it finally decided the case in 2000.

House of Lords, 17 February 2000[171] **3.GB.55.**
R v. Secretary of State for Employment, ex parte Seymour-Smith and another

TWO-YEAR QUALIFICATION PERIOD FOR EMPLOYMENT PROTECTION AS INDIRECT
SEX DISCRIMINATION

Seymour-Smith and Perez (HL)

Facts and *Held*: The facts of the case and the different judgments given are recounted above (see above, **3.EC.54.**). Their Lordships were divided on how to assess the matter. With Lord Slynn and Lord Steyn disagreeing, the majority found that there was indeed a prima facie case of indirect discrimination.

Judgment: Lord Nicholson for the majority: "One of the questions referred . . . to the Court of Justice sought guidance on the legal test for establishing whether a measure adopted by a member state has such a degree of disparate effect as between men and women as to amount to indirect discrimination . . . The view of the Court of Justice is set out in paras 60 to 65 of its judgment . . . The Court of Justice . . . wavered uncertainly between what must be established as a substantive criterion and the evidence needed for that purpose . . . As I see it, the reasoning

---

[171] [2000] 1 All ER 857.

underlying these paragraphs is that, in the case of indirect discrimination, the obligation to avoid discrimination does not consist of applying requirements having precisely the same impact on men and women employees. The obligation is to avoid applying unjustifiable requirements having a considerable disparity of impact . . . A considerable disparity can be more readily established if the statistical evidence covers a long period and the figures show a persistent and relatively constant disparity. In such a case a lesser statistical disparity may suffice to show that the disparity is considerable than if the statistics cover only a short period or if they present an uneven picture. Before your Lordships it was common ground that 1991, not 1985, was the relevant date for the purpose of the issue now being considered. The position at this later date was not considered by the Court of Justice. I turn to the available statistics, covering the period from 1985 to 1993, extracted from the annual labour force surveys. These figures show that over the period of seven years, from 1985 up to and including 1991, the ratio of men and women who qualified was roughly 10:9. For every ten men who qualified, only nine women did so. This disparity was remarkably constant for the six years from 1985 to 1990, but it began to diminish in 1991 These figures are in borderline country. The question under consideration is one of degree . . . I find myself driven to the conclusion that a persistent and constant disparity of the order just mentioned in respect of the entire male and female labour forces of the country, over a period of seven years, cannot be brushed aside and dismissed as insignificant or inconsiderable. I agree with the Court of Appeal ([1996] All ER (EC) 1, [1995] ICR 889) that, given the context of equality of pay or treatment, the latitude afforded by the word considerably should not be exaggerated. I think these figures are adequate to demonstrate that the extension of the qualifying period had a considerably greater adverse impact on women than men . . . The reduction in the disparity, which started in 1991, continued in 1992 and 1993. By 1993 the ratio of men and women qualifiers was about 20:19. But, looking at the overall picture, I do not think the diminished disparity after 1991 is sufficient to displace the message of the figures for the earlier years. Accordingly it is for the government to show that the extension of the qualifying period was justified, to use the accepted nomenclature, by objective factors unrelated to any discrimination based on sex . . ."

Note

Thus, the effect of *Seymour-Smith and Perez* (ECJ) was less serious than it seemed from the ECJ judgment, due to "liberal interpretation of the Court's decision"[172] by their Lordships. The ECJ, however, remained true to its restrictive approach in later decisions. For example, in *Jørgensen*,[173] it held that a measure that was detrimental to 22 medical practitioners, among them 14 women (about 64%), from a total of 1680 medical practitioners, among them 302 women (about 18%), was not indirectly discriminatory due to the fact that the statistics were not sufficiently representative (No. 34).

The statistical assessment of disparate impact is dependent on the correct application of mathematical principles, which is not always guaranteed in legal proceedings. For example, the Dutch Equal Treatment Commission had to decide on the question whether, in the case of collective redundancies, making employees redundant in accordance with their length of service might constitute indirect discrimination.

---

[172] See Barnard and Hepple, above n. 21, 567.
[173] ECJ, Judgment of 6 April 2000, C–226/98 *Birgitte Jørgensen* [2000] ECR I–2447.

Equal Treatment Commission (Commissie Gelijke Behandeling)   **3.NL.56.**
Opinion 1998–66

INDIRECT SEX DISCRIMINATION BY COMPOSING A REDUNDANCY LIST IN ACCOR-
DANCE WITH SENIORITY

Redundancy list composition

Facts: The applicant was employed as a teacher. As a result of decreasing numbers of pupils and a budgetary deficit, the employer decided to reduce the number of teachers. According to a collective agreement, the decisions on dismissal should be made in accordance with redundancy lists, established for each school sector. Within each sector, the main criterion for the position on a redundancy list was length of service (seniority), but whether a person was put on a redundancy list would equally depend on the question whether the sector in question was considered as carrying a risk.

Held: The applicant submitted that the composition of the redundancy list would have a detrimental effect on women due to seniority being the main criterion. She did not, however, establish any specific statistics in regard to seniority, but rather relied on the overall effect of the policy.

Opinion: "4.1. The question is at issue whether the defendant has made a distinction based on sex to the disadvantage of applicant by applying the criterion 'length of service' when ascertaining the sequence on the redundancy list.

4.2. The following legal provisions are relevant in this connection. Article 7:646(1) Civil Code (CC) states that an employer may not distinguish between men and women when, amongst other things, terminating the contract of employment. Article 7:646 CC states that 'distinction between men and women' in this article means 'direct and indirect distinction between men and women'. 'Direct distinction' also means distinction based on pregnancy, confinement and maternity. 'Indirect distinction' means a distinction based on other attributes than sex, for example marital status or family circumstances, resulting in a distinction based on sex. Article 7:646(6) CC states that the ban laid down in paragraph 1 on gender based distinctions does not apply to indirect distinctions that are objectively justified.

4.4 . . . The Commission must therefore ascertain whether application of the criterion 'service with the authority' in this case results in indirect distinction based on sex. The Commission considers as follows in this connection. Indirect distinction arises if on applying the above criterion persons of one sex are predominantly affected. In order to ascertain whether this has occurred in the present case, the Commission considers whether application of this criterion within the circle of the respondent's employees has a detrimental effect predominantly for persons of one sex. The Commission adopts relative figures for this purpose . . .

4.5 . . . There must therefore be a *substantial difference* between the two sexes. The respondent employed at total of 226 male and 117 female teachers as of February 1998. Initially, 3.4% of the women and 4.9% of the men of the teaching staff were expected to be made redundant at 1 August 1998. In fact, however, slightly more than 12% of the men and slightly more than 1% of the women were severed. These figures do not give a picture where it can be said that there is a substantial difference between male and female teachers. The criterion of 'service with the authority' cannot therefore be regarded as one that results in a distinction based on sex, within the meaning of Article 7:646(5) CC This also applies to the relationship of men and women in the bottom part of the redundancy list (the first employees to be affected by redundancy). A proportion of 8 men compared with 5 women in the present case do not create such a significant difference between men and women that there is any question of a preponderant disadvantage for women.

418

The Commission holds that the applicant did not make any distinction based on sex to the disadvantage of the defendant as is prohibited by Article 7:646 Civil Code [emphasis in original]."

Note

Accordingly, the Commission first considers that nearly equal numbers of women and men respectively could well mirror disparate impact. However, in the end it denies this effect, although only 2.2% of men as compared to 3.3% of women are represented at the "bottom end" of the redundancy list. This case is possibly an illustration of the sentence "*judex non calculat*".

Special causation requirements

When disparate impact has been established statistically, there is sometimes an argument that this should still not be regarded as sufficient to establish a prima facie case of indirect discrimination. Such attempts have been documented especially in the UK and in Germany.

In the UK the statutory definitions prior to implementing Directives 2000/43/EC, 2000/78/EC and 2004/113/EC contained the word "can comply". For example, the Race Relation Act insofar as it has not been brought in line with the Directives, states that "a person discriminates . . . if . . . he applies . . . a requirement or condition . . . which is such that the proportion of persons of the same racial group as that other who can comply with it is considerably smaller than the proportion . . ."

There has been some case-law regarding the "can comply" requirement in which this requirement is used to disqualify a prima facie finding of indirect discrimination. However, it has been found that this reading of even the old statutory provisions is incompatible with their wider aims.

Employment Appeal Tribunal, 15 July 1977[174]   **3.GB.57.**
Price v. Civil Service Commission

INDIRECT SEX DISCRIMINATION BY MAXIMUM AGE LIMIT IN RELATION TO CIVIL SERVICE POSTS

Price

Facts: Price, a 35-year-old woman, challenged a maximum age limit of 28 imposed in relation to a Civil Service post. She argued that the age limit discriminated indirectly against women, many women being engaged in child bearing in their later twenties.

Held: Her claim was dismissed by a tribunal on the ground that the words "can comply" had to be interpreted strictly and, given that it was theoretically possible for any woman between 17½ and 28 to apply, the

---

[174] [1978] 1 All ER 1228.

proportion of those able to do so was not considerably smaller than the proportion of men also so able. Ms. Price appealed to EAT.

Judgment: Phillips J: "In one sense it can be said that any female applicant can comply with the condition. She is not obliged to marry, or to have children, or to mind children; she may find somebody to look after them, and as a last resort she may put them into care. In this sense . . . any female applicant can comply with the condition. Such a construction appears to us to be wholly out of sympathy with the spirit and intent of the 1975 Act. Further, it should be repeated that compliance with sub-para. (i) is only a preliminary step, which does not lead to a finding that an act is one of discrimination unless the person acting fails to show that it is justi-fiable. 'Can' is . . . a word with many shades of meaning, and we are satisfied that it should not be too narrowly, or too broadly, construed in its context in s. 1(1)(b)(i). It should not be said that a person 'can' do something merely because it is theoretically possible for him to do so: it is necessary to see whether he can do so in practice. Applying this approach to the circum-stances of this case, it is relevant in determining whether women can comply with the condition to take into account the current usual behaviour of women in this respect, as observed in practice, putting on one side behaviour and responses which are unusual or extreme.

Knowledge and experience suggest that a considerable number of women between the mid-twenties and the mid-thirties are engaged in bearing children and in minding children, and that while many find it possible to take up employment many others, while desiring to do so, find it impossible, and that many of the latter as their children get older find that they can follow their wish and seek employment . . . we should have no hesitation in concluding that our own knowledge and experience is confirmed, and that it is safe to say that the condition is one which it is in practice harder for women to comply with than it is for men. We should be inclined to go further and say that there are undoubtedly women of whom it may be properly said in the terms of s1(1)(b)(i) that they 'cannot' comply with the condition, because they are women; that is to say because of their involvement with their children."

German doctrine, having been forced to acknowledge the concept of indirect discrim-ination by ECJ case-law and a Federal Labour Court open to its implementation into German law, invented another route. Alleging that statistical evidence so typical for indirect discrimination claims might well establish nonsense-relations between economically justifiable employer conduct and discriminatory effects due to other factors, these authors required an additional hurdle to be jumped, the hurdle of "causation". This reasoning had also been adopted by some of the Federal Labour Court's senates.[175] In its decision following the ECJ decision in *Nimz*,[176] the 4th Senate rejected this line of case-law.

---

[175] The German Federal Labour Court sits in different senates, which tend to develop specific views on the law. To avoid divergence, the Grand Senate can be appealed to by each senate in order to unify case-law.

[176] ECJ, 7 February 1992 C–184/89 *Helga Nimz* v. *Freie und Hansestadt Hamburg* [1992] ECR I 297.

Federal Labour Court (BAG), 2 December 1992[177] **3.DE.58.**
4 AZR 52/92, A Claimant v. *Freie und Hanse Stadt Hamburg*

WHETHER EXCLUDING PART-TIME EMPLOYEES FROM REGULAR PROMOTIONS
CONSTITUTES INDIRECT SEX DISCRIMINATON

Nimz follow-up

Facts: Maria Nimz had been excluded from regular promotions in line with the general agreement on employee remuneration with public servants (BAT). The relevant clause in § 23 a) BAT provided that any employee who was entitled to promotion on grounds of average performance after a certain time ("Bewährungsaufstieg") could not rely on months in which she had worked part-time as qualifying periods.

Held: The Labour Court Hamburg had referred the case to the ECJ, which had returned the judgment that such exclusion was indeed contrary to Article 119 EEC Treaty (now Article 141 EC) as it constituted indirect sex discrimination. Accordingly, the Labour Court allowed the claim, against which the City of Hamburg appealed to the Regional Labour Court and the Federal Labour Court. Both dismissed the appeal.

Judgment: ". . . In accordance with ECJ case-law, a legal provision which applies equally to women and men constitutes indirect discrimination contrary to Article 119 EEC on grounds of sex, if it puts at a disadvantage a disproportionately high number of members of one sex and cannot be justified objectively by factors unrelated to sex . . . The third senate and, consequently, the fifth senate, have required in addition that the detrimental effect in disfavour of one sex is founded on sex-specific reasons. Accordingly, it should have been assessed whether the detrimental effect could be explained by factors other than sex. This, however, should be answered in the negative in relation to part time work, as part time work was women's work.

It is doubtful, whether this additional requirement can be derived from Article 119 EEC. The ECJ has in its judgment of 13 May 1986 (reference to *Bilka*), which was based on a reference by the third senate, expanded the following:

'If, therefore, it should be found that a much lower proportion of women than of men work full time, the exclusion of part time workers from the occupational pension scheme would be contrary to article 119 of the Treaty where, taking into account the difficulties encountered by women workers in working full-time, that measure could not be explained by factors which exclude any discrimination on grounds of sex.'

. . . The ECJ had, however, not stated its reference to gender roles as an additional requirement for establishing indirect discrimination. It has rather included it into the part of the sentence that is concerned with the establishing proportionality in relation to justification. In this regard the third senate had explicitly asked whether a rule disadvantaging part time employees was capable of being justified with reference to an employer's desire to employ as few part time employees as possible. Thus the reasoning of the European Court of Justice is meant . . . as a specific reference to the specific case."

Note on Price and Nimz follow-up
Additional requirements to question a finding of disparate impact based on statistics disregard the genius of non-discrimination law. This genius lies in the fact that detrimental effects are prima facie deemed to be linked to social discrimination.

---

[177] BAGE 72, 64.

Nothing more than real-life experience is required to establish this prima facie case. Accordingly, the findings rejecting this doctrine must be welcomed.

Agreement on disparate impact

Because establishing disparate impact statistically is so complicated, a successful litigation strategy may depend on agreement on this very fact. Such technique was used in one of the few Swedish cases, which later led to a finding of the Labour Court against the employer.

Labour Court (Arbetsdomstolen), 21 September 2005[178]   **3.SE.59.**
*AD 87/05, Equal Opportunity Ombudsman (JämO) v. Teknikarbeitsgivarna and
Volvo Car Co.*

WHETHER REQUIRING A HEIGHT BETWEEN 163 AND 195 CM INDIRECTLY
DISCRIMINATES AGAINST WOMEN

Volvo

Facts: A-C. N. had applied for a position in the body workshop, the paint shop or the assembly shop of a Volvo factory, and indicated her height as being 159.7 cm. The employer rejected her application on the ground of her height, stating that it did not fit the margin between 163 and 195 cm. The employer relied on health and safety reasons for objective justification (see below). To be successful, A-C. N. would have had to pass an aptitude test, to which she was, however, not admitted. As her union would not represent her the case was taken up by the JämO. The JämO challenged the height criterion as indirectly discriminatory.

Held: The Labour Court found in favour of the applicant, because the distinction based on height was not justifiable.

Judgment: "Points of departure in the case: . . . Against the background of the information that has been given in the case, it is clear that many women are excluded from employment in the Company through the imposition of the height-requirement established by the Company and which means that a job-applicant, in order to be considered for employment, must be between 163 and 195 cm tall. The parties are agreed that the height-requirement entails the exclusion of about 25 per cent of women from employment with the Company, while only 2 per cent of men are excluded. The difference is due to the fact that women are typically shorter than men and therefore to a significantly greater extent fail to reach the lower limit of the height-requirement, i.e. 163 cm. The parties are agreed that the difference is so significant that the imposition of the height-requirement in practice specifically disadvantages against women."

A similar technique was used in *Seymour-Smith and Perez* (HL), albeit only before the Court of Last Instance, in order to avoid a new finding of facts.

---

[178] Case A 192/03, Judgment 87/05, available on the website of the Swedish Labour Court.

QUALITATIVE ARGUMENTS TO ESTABLISH DETRIMENTAL EFFECT

The alternative to the statistical method to establish detrimental effect as disparate impact is a qualitative assessment that a certain practice will probably work to the detriment of a discriminated group.

The new formula in the recent Directives and its background

The younger EC Directives on Equality establish the opportunity to find for disparate impact upon non-statistical arguments, by stating that to establish a prima facie case of indirect discrimination it is sufficient that "a provision, criterion or practice would put persons of a racial or ethnic origin at a particular disadvantage compared to other persons". In contrast to the Burden of Proof Directive, there is no mention of "substantial higher proportions". Accordingly, the new definition abandons the necessity to establish a prima facie case of indirect discrimination on a statistical basis. This conclusion is supported by the recitals of the Directives, which explicitly state that national rules "may provide in particular for indirect discrimination to be established by any means, including on the basis of statistical evidence".[179]

The basis for this legislative development was a reference to the ECJ by a British court.

ECJ, 23 May 1996[180] **3.EC.60.**
C—237/94, O'Flynn v. *Adjudication Officer*

WHETHER REQUIREMENT OF A BURIAL TO BE WITHIN A COUNTRY INDIRECTLY
DISCRIMINATES AGAINST NATIONALS FROM OTHER MEMBER STATES

O'Flynn

Facts: Mr. O'Flynn was Irish, but had moved to the UK as an employee and remained there after retirement. When his son died, he had a service held in the UK, but the body was transferred to Irish soil for burial. His application for a funeral payment to the UK local authority was rejected on the grounds that the actual burial had taken place outside the UK. Mr. O'Flynn challenged that decision because he felt himself indirectly discriminated against on grounds of nationality.

Held: The adjudication officer referred to the ECJ a number of questions relating to establishing a claim of indirect discrimination without having produced adequate statistics. Relying on national law approaches towards sex and ethnic discrimination, the respondent authorities considered that the condition of the funeral taking place in the UK could only establish a prima facie case of indirect discrimination if it was shown that it was substantially more difficult for migrant workers than for national workers to satisfy it, having regard inter alia to their customs. For that, it was necessary to show that the condition at issue was satisfied only by a substantially lower proportion of workers from all the other Member States than of national workers.

[179] Recital 15 of Directive 2000/43/EC and Directive 2000/78/EC respectively.
[180] [1996] ECR I–02617.

423

Judgment: "17 The Court has consistently held that the equal treatment rule laid down in Article 48 of the Treaty (today: Article 39 EC) and in Article 7 of Regulation No 1612/68 prohibits not only overt discrimination by reason of nationality but also all covert forms of discrimination which, by the application of other distinguishing criteria, lead in fact to the same result . . .

18 Accordingly, conditions imposed by national law must be regarded as indirectly discriminatory where, although applicable irrespective of nationality, they affect essentially migrant workers . . . . or the great majority of those affected are migrant workers . . . where they are indistinctly applicable but can more easily be satisfied by national workers than by migrant workers . . .

20 It follows from all the foregoing case-law that, unless objectively justified and proportionate to its aim, a provision of national law must be regarded as indirectly discriminatory if it is intrinsically liable to affect migrant workers more than national workers and if there is a consequent risk that it will place the former at a particular disadvantage.

21 It is not necessary in this respect to find that the provision in question does in practice affect a substantially higher proportion of migrant workers. It is sufficient that it is liable to have such an effect [references omitted]."

Note

The new definition of indirect discrimination entailed in the 2000 Directives was intended to mirror this judgment. The result of the legislative process, however, is a little different from the "Flynn formula" insofar as the ECJ referred to migrant workers in the plural, and not to single persons, thus stressing the individual aspects of indirect discrimination more than the Directives.

There are diverging views on the desirability of the new formula.[181] On the one hand, statistical proof has been considered a viable tool to expose practices having detrimental effects. On the other hand, there are cases in which the relevant statistics are just not available, although it is reasonable to assume that detrimental effects are occurring. The new formula will make bringing a claim for indirect discrimination easier in these cases, enabling the applicant to rely on related statistics instead of forcing them to conduct fully fledged quantitative research. Last but not least, qualitative arguments will be admitted in addition to quantitative arguments. At first sight, it might seem that this possibility enables the judge to decide on a qualified guess. However, there are quite a few circumstances where it really is apparent that a criterion, rule or practice disparately impacts upon a protected group. In such circumstances, the courts both at EU and national level have tended to assume that there is detrimental effect without statistical evidence, even before any new formula was relevant. There may now be new cases where applicants may succeed in proving indirect discrimination based on qualitative arguments.

---

[181] See above section 3.5.1.B, text accompanying notes 143–8.

Factors where detrimental effect has been assumed prior to implementation of younger Directives

In the practical application of indirect discrimination law in the past, certain fields had established where the courts would assume detrimental effect without specific reference to statistical material.

This even occurred in the ECJ case-law relating to sex discrimination.

ECJ, 17 October 1989[182]   **3.EC.61.**[*]
C-109/88, Handels- og Kontorfunktionærernes Forbund I Danmark v. Dansk Arbejdsgiverforening, acting on behalf of Danfoss

WHETHER A GENDER PAY GAP RESULTING FROM A SYSTEM OF BONUSES
ESTABLISHES DETRIMENTAL EFFECT

Danfoss (continued 1)

Facts and *Held*: As may be remembered, the Danish trade union acting on behalf of two of their female members had challenged a system of individual bonuses. The ECJ had established the principle that—where a remuneration system lacks any transparency—a prima facie case of indirect discrimination is established by showing that the average pay for women is less than for men. It then addressed the question whether the use of such criteria for awarding bonuses as were known to disparately impact on women—inter alia mobility, training and seniority—could be objectively justified. Within this part of the judgment, the Court made a general assumption on the disparate impact of the said criteria, without taking any recourse to statistics.

Judgment: (continued) "21 . . . If it (the criterion of mobility) is understood as covering the employee's adaptability to variable hours and varying places of work, the criterion of mobility may also work to the disadvantage of female employees, who, because of household and family duties for which they are frequently responsible, are not as able as men to organize their working time flexibly . . .

23 . . . as regards the criterion of training, it is not be excluded that it may work to the disadvantage of women in so far as they have had less opportunity than men for training or have taken less advantage of such opportunity . . .

24 . . . as regards the criterion of length of service, it is also not to be excluded, as with training, that it may involve less advantageous treatment of women than of men in so far as women have entered the labour market more recently than men or more frequently suffer an interruption of their career."

Note

These deliberations may be considered as demonstrating the disadvantage of not relying on statistics, as the ECJ seems to be doing little more than applying commonly held prejudices about women. Especially as regards seniority, there may be cases where women acquire higher seniority on average as, due to gender discrimination,

---

[182] [1989] ECR 3199.

[*] See above **3.EC.38.** and below **3.EC.71.**

they receive fewer offers by other employers. This is one of the reasons why the German system of enhancing the remuneration of university professors with each offer of a position with another university disparately impacts upon women.[183] However, the deliberations also show that sometimes common sense does allow a sensible judgment.

Less critically, the ECJ nowadays simply assumes that disadvantage for part-time employees works to the detriment of women. For example, in the *Kachelmann* case, to be covered below (**3.EC.76.**), the ECJ wastes no time on statistical evidence, but simply states: "It is common ground that in Germany part-time workers are far more likely to be women than men."[184]

Likewise, national law may refer to the general assumption by the ECJ and consider detrimental effect as given without any further deliberations on statistical proof.

Equal Treatment Commission (Commissie Gelijke Behandeling)   **3.NL.62.**
Opinion 1996-56

WHETHER AN OCCUPATIONAL DOCTOR MAY BE DENIED WORKING TIME
REDUCTION FOR STUDY PURPOSES ON THE GROUNDS THAT SHE
WORKS PART-TIME

GGD te Breda

Facts: The Applicant is an occupational doctor with the occupational health service of the "stadsgewest" Breda. In contrast to her full-time colleagues, who were granted working time reduction for attending specialisation courses, as a part-timer she was denied this.

Held: The CGB finds that this amounts to indirect discrimination.

Opinion: "4.3 When applying the equal treatment legislation, regard must be had to the case-law of the ECJ . . . In line with the established case-law of the ECJ, different treatment of full time and part time employees is prohibited if it transpires that such a rule disadvantages considerably more women then men without objective justification . . . As demonstrated by the ECJ judgments cited in footnote 3, the prohibition of indirect discrimination on grounds of sex laid down in EC law excludes a measure which provides full compensation for full time employees when participating in training courses providing necessary knowledge and which are organised during normal office hours and restricts compensation for part time workers to their individual working time."

---

[183] D. Schiek and A. Kirschbaum, "New Governance for Higher Education Institutions, Prospects for Female University Careers and Equality Law" in A. Numhauser-Henning (ed.), *Women in Academia—Aiming High and Falling Short?* Bulletin of Comparative Law Labour Relations, No. 57 (The Hague, Kluwer Law International, 2005), 57, 69 with further references.
[184] ECJ, C–322/98 [2000] ECR I–7505, No. 24.

Note

The assumption that part-time work is a factor which, when used as a criterion for distinction, will disparately impact on women is not specific to the Netherlands, but rather common all over Europe. In establishing detrimental effect of part-time work, most courts will not require detailed statistics.

Similarly, in equal pay cases, courts may well accept without statistical proof that a requirement of physical strength will have a detrimental effect on women. This can be demonstrated by one of the Spanish Constitutional Court cases to which we referred above.

Spanish Constitutional Court (El Tribunal Constitucional),   **3.ES.63.**[*]
28 February 1994
Case 58/1994 Works council de Antonio Puig S.A. on behalf of 140 workers v.
Antonio Puig S.A.

WAGE CATEGORIES AND (INDIRECT) SEX DISCRIMINATION

Antonio Puig

Facts: As may be remembered, the case concerned the practice of categorising manual workers into wage groups of the relevant collective agreement at Antonio Puig S.A. Inter alia, the Constitutional Court listed precisely the different tasks allocated to women and men, from which it transpires that "male" tasks require more bodily strength, whereas the women were charged with a wider variety of tasks that required more training, experience and skill.

Held: This was finally held to be unconstitutional discrimination on grounds of gender by the Constitutional Court.

Judgment: "The sole listing of different tasks is only a descriptive argument and although indispensable as a first step it does not give any reasons why some tasks that are performed by men were valued higher than others, performed mostly by women, concerning the salary. On the contrary, it is right then, when the criteria used must be made transparent, subjecting the employer to the duty to demonstrate which criteria it uses and their neutrality with a view to Art. 14 C.E.. Physical strength, as a quality of human activity which could be projected over a determined task, may be taken into consideration, however its clear lack of neutrality because of the different impact it produces in the two sexes, requires the judicial organs to employ a special scrutiny while judging the allegations and the evidence brought forward by who wants to defend his virtue to justify a difference in pay. Because of this scrutiny the addition of criteria of this nature is only possible, if it is undoubted that the physical strength is a absolute determining element for the suitability for the task, or at least that it is a essential part of it, being precise, in those cases that it is combined with other, typical neutral qualities, from the point of view which is to be considered."

As regards ethnic origin and religion and belief, courts have also been prepared to accept detrimental effects of certain requirements without further statistical proof.

---

[*] See **3.ES.41.**

Equality Tribunal, 6 February 2004[185]   **3.IE.64.**
DEC-S-2004-017, Martin McDonagh v. Navan Hire Limited

WHETHER NOT HIRING A SANDING MACHINE TO CUSTOMERS WITHOUT A
PERMANENT ADDRESS IS INDIRECT RACIAL DISCRIMINATION

Sanding machine

Facts: The complainant had unsuccessfully tried to rent a sanding machine at the defendants do-it-yourself-shop. The clerk had already given the Complainant instructions on how to use the machine and had satisfied himself that the machine worked properly, when the complainant started filling out the hiring form. When he gave as his address halting site of a traveller community, the hiring contract was not concluded. The shop owner stated that his hiring policy includes demanding a permanent address and a landline telephone number, and that he does not consider a traveller site a permanent address.

Held: This requirement established a prima facie case of indirect discrimination even in the absence of statistical evidence.

Judgment: "In my view this case should be considered within the above section as the respondent imposed a condition (that is being able to provide a permanent address which is not a halting site address) which substantially fewer Travellers than non-Travellers would be able to satisfy. While the complainant has not produced any statistical evidence to support this contention it is obvious that halting sites are specifically designed for Travellers and that Travellers are substantially more likely to live on halting sites than non-Travellers. In considering this point concerning statistical evidence, I have referred to the Labour Court decision in an employment case, *NBK Designs Ltd v Inoue ED/02/34 Determination No. 0212*. In this Decision, the Labour Court held that an expert tribunal like the Labour Court could take into account, even in the absence of specific evidence, matters such as risk of disparate impact on a protected ground under the Act which are well established and are obvious from its specialist experience. In *Inoue*, the Labour Court held that it was obvious that measures impacting on part time workers, or on those caring for small children, would impact disproportionately on women. It would be reasonable therefore to infer from this rationale that an expert tribunal, such as the Equality Tribunal, can similarly take account of matters such as the number of Travellers living on halting sites in comparison to the number of non-Travellers, matters which are obvious from the Tribunal's specialist experience."

Note

The careful reasoning demonstrates the advantages of according judicial autonomy to tribunals in assessing facts. Three criteria to which detrimental effect is summarily accorded are cited: any measure impacting on part-time work and child care obligations will have a detrimental effect on women; and any measure impacting on those without a permanent address will have a detrimental effect on travellers.

Another field where detrimental effect is often assumed is the controversial issue of women wearing headscarves. There are quite a few judgments where courts have assumed that a policy requiring persons not to wear a headscarf or not to wear any headgear will disparately impact on Muslims.

---

[185] Available on the website of the Equality Tribunal of Ireland, under the heading Equal Status Decisions.

Equal Treatment Commission (Commissie Gelijke Behandeling) **3.NL.65.**
Opinion 1996-109

INDIRECT RELIGIOUS DISCRIMINATION BY REFERRING TO HEADSCARF

Headscarf—employment agency

Facts: The applicant is of Moroccan origin and, in line with her reading of the Qur'an, wears a headscarf in public. She registered with the respondent's employment agency, but was not given work as a data typist or a production helper although these positions were advertised by the respondent. She assumed that this was not due to the reasons given (insufficient typing speed and body height respectively), but rather to her wearing the headscarf. This is based on the fact that during the registration process she had been asked whether she would consider working without a headscarf and upon answering this in the negative, advised that placements might be more difficult as a result. The hearing established that the respondent's employment agency indeed took into account requirements of employers not to send employees wearing a headscarf.

Held: The commission found indirect discrimination on grounds of religion

Opinion: "4.3 . . . The respondent has stated at the hearing that, upon seeing the applicant's headscarf, she has told her in general terms that some employers would not consider persons wearing a headscarf as representative. As this requirement is made generally, and no further specified considerations of a representative appearance are made, a presumption arises of indirect distinction on grounds of religion. This is the case if disproportionately more persons wearing a headscarf in line with their religious convictions as Muslims than others would be affected by these considerations, which are neutral on their face, without there being an objective justification for the distinction. The Commission considers on the basis of witness statements that this is the case. A general reference to unspecified requirements of representativeness, where these requirements have not been elaborated, cannot be considered as objective justification in the Commission's opinion."

Note

The CGB assumed that not offering a job to someone wearing a hijab is only indirect discrimination on grounds of religion. This is hardly convincing. There is no question that any head-covering will be criticised, other than a hijab worn by Muslim women in line with their reading of the Qur'an. Accordingly, there is not a neutral requirement to which the applicant is subjected, but a religiously tainted one. This case should have been considered as one of direct discrimination.

Equal Treatment Commission (Commissie Gelijke Behandeling) **3.NL.66.**
Opinion 2004-112

INDIRECT DISCRIMINATION ON GROUNDS OF RELIGION BY REFUSING TO SERVE
PERSONS WEARING HEAD-COVERINGS

Headscarf—restaurant

Facts: The applicants had visited the restaurant owned by the defendant, in decent clothing but wearing a Muslim headscarf. The defendant operates a policy not to serve clients wearing sport shoes and/or head-coverings. When the applicants, on different occasions, refused to remove their headscarves, they were denied service. The defendant stressed that the Qur'an does not strictly require Muslim women to wear a headscarf.

Held: There was indirect discrimination on grounds of religion.

Opinion: "Following the policy of the defendant, anyone is required to visit her restaurant bareheaded . . . For (the applicants) it is not possible to take off their headscarves without infringing their religious obligations . . . In this regard, the policy has detrimental effect on the applicants . . . Persons, who do not want to take off their head-covering on grounds of their religious convictions such as the applicants are excluded from visiting the defendant's restaurants by this policy."

Notes

(1) In this example, there is indeed indirect discrimination, as the owner had framed her policy in general terms and also wished to exclude other groups, e.g. persons coming into her restaurant wearing a baseball cap.

(2) The case is interesting insofar as one could question whether the applicants could not comply with the policy of the restaurant owner. This forms a parallel with the *Mandla* v. *Lee* case,[186] where it was assumed that a Sikh boy could not, on the basis of religious convictions, comply with the requirement to take off his turban while at school.

Assessing detrimental effect without statistical evidence following the younger Directives

While there is as yet no ECJ case-law on these issues, the first decisions under national legislation after the coming into force of the Directives have been made. Interestingly, comparable summary findings of discrimination were applied in two cases from the Netherlands and Sweden respectively in relation to the requirement to speak the language of the country without any foreign accent, made by a telephone marketing company.

---

[186] [1983] IRLR 209 (HL), reported as excerpt **1.GB.10.** in ch. 1above.

Equal Treatment Commission (Commissie Gelijke Behandeling)   **3.NL.67.**
Opinion 2004-143

WHETHER REQUIRING AN EMPLOYEE FOR TELEPHONE MARKETING TO SPEAK
DUTCH WITHOUT A FOREIGN ACCENT CONSTITUTES INDIRECT RACIAL
DISCRIMINATON

Telephone marketing

Facts: The applicant is born in Leeuwarden and has Dutch nationality, while his parents immigrated from Morocco. He applied for a vacancy advertised by the defendant on a website by filling in an electronic form. The envisaged occupation was that of a telephone advertiser for safety systems. Following a test telephone interview, he was told that his application was successful, and was asked to come to the office to fill in the necessary forms. When he arrived at the office, he was told that he would not be employed due to his foreign accent.

Held: There was unlawful indirect discrimination.

Opinion: "5.6 The requirement of speaking Dutch without a foreign accent does not constitute a direct distinction on grounds of race . . . There are, after all, persons of foreign origin who speak Dutch without an accent, and there are persons of Dutch origin who speak Dutch with a foreign accent.

5.7 However, it is a generally acknowledged fact that the requirement to speak Dutch without a foreign accent will affect persons of non-Dutch origin to a disproportionate extent compared with persons of Dutch origin. Accordingly, the requirement of speaking Dutch without a foreign accent establishes an indirect distinction on grounds of race."

Labour Court (Arbetsdomstolen), 4 December 2002[187]   **3.SE.68.**
Case AD 128/2002, Ombudsman ethnic discrimination (DO) v. *Tjänsföretagens Arbetsgivarförbund and GfK Sv. Aktiebolag*

WHETHER REQUIRING A TELEPHONE INTERVIEWER TO SPEAK SWEDISH
WITHOUT A FOREIGN ACCENT AMOUNTS TO INDIRECT DISCRIMINATION ON
GROUNDS OF RACE

Telephone interviewer

Facts: Susanna D applied for the vacancy of a telephone interviewer advertised by GfK. The application procedure involved three successive test sessions, including trial interviews. After the first round of interviews she attempted to arrange a date for the following session by telephone. Helena L, the manager of the call centre, answered the phone call and mentioned that Susanna D spoke Swedish with a foreign accent and that this could be a problem. Susanna D became angry and an argument ensued. After the telephone conversation, the application procedure was discontinued. While the parties could not agree on who broke off the procedure, the company explained that they have a general requirement for staff to speak clear and correct Swedish, and that they had found that Susanna D, due to her foreign accent, did not fulfil that requirement.

---

[187] Available on the website of the Swedish Labour Court.

Held: It was considered that the employer broke off the application procedure, as it seems unlikely that Susanna D, who had applied on her own initiative, would have done so. While it may well be that she became angry and lost her temper, it would have been the responsibility of the experienced personnel handling the application procedure to clarify that she was welcome to continue the procedure. In addition, the statements of the company underlined that the requirement to speak Swedish without a foreign accent had been decisive for not employing Susanna D. There was unlawful indirect discrimination on grounds of ethnic origin.

Judgment: ". . . The rules on ethnic discrimination are found in the law (1999:130) concerning measures against ethnic discrimination in working life. Under § 10, ethnic discrimination is forbidden in a number of different situations, including when an employer makes a decision on a question of recruitment, invites a job-applicant to a recruitment interview, or takes other steps in the recruitment process. The law distinguishes between direct and indirect discrimination . . . under § 9 section 1, an employer must not disadvantage a job-applicant or employee by imposing a condition, a criterion or a work procedure, which appears neutral but which, in practice, specifically disadvantages persons of a particular ethnicity (indirect discrimination). The legislative materials related to the Act point out suitability tests; the language knowledge requirements and educational standards as examples of the kind of thing that can disadvantage persons of a certain ethnicity. At the same time the Act stresses that it is permissible to impose, for example, a language requirement . . .

[T]here can be no question of any direct discrimination within the meaning of § 8 of the law on measures against ethnic discrimination in working life. In accordance with the position taken by the court in the foregoing, Helena L's conduct was in any case partly based on a requirement for clear and correct Swedish. Such a requirement is obviously one of those that appears neutral but which in practice places persons of a certain ethnicity at a disadvantage. This means that an application of this requirement is only acceptable if the purpose of the company's requirement can be justified by objective reasons and if the measure was appropriate and necessary for the fulfilment of this purpose."

Note on both foreign accent cases

Both these cases are surprisingly similar, and also based on new legislation implementing Directive 2000/43/EC, in the Swedish case prematurely, and in the Dutch case at a time when the implementation process had not yet been completed. As with the headscarf cases reported above, one could doubt whether the line between direct (covert) discrimination and indirect discrimination had been drawn correctly insofar as in both cases reference was made to a foreign accent. Even if that had been so, a requirement for a person whose employment tasks involved telephone interviews or marketing to speak in a clear and distinctive way could qualify as occupational requirement, leading this to be a case of justifiable direct discrimination.

Court of Appeal (Hof van Bewep, Antwerpen), 14 June 2005[188]   **3.BE.69.**
9 appellants v. *Provincial Administration of Limburg*

PROHIBITING WEARING ANY HEAD-COVERINGS AS INDIRECT DISCRIMINATION ON
GROUNDS OF RELIGION

Headscarf—Belgian school

Facts: The applicants claim to be discriminated against on grounds of their religion as a result of new college rules which prohibit the wearing of any head-coverings in the classroom, the study room and the dining hall of a Provincial Commercial College in Hasselt. The explanatory letter specifies that "headscarves may not therefore be worn during lessons". The college rules establish other rules as well, such as a prohibition to eat and drink in class, to wear excessive piercing, to use walkmans and mobiles in the classroom, study room or dining hall and to organise parties in the name of the college without permission of the head teacher.

Held: Even if there was detrimental effect, this was objectively justified.

Judgment: "Whereas there may well be indirect discrimination if an apparently neutral provision, requirement or attitude has a harmful effect as such on persons, unless such provision, requirement or attitude is objectively and reasonably justified; the ban on headscarves has therefore to pursue a legal objective (i.e. objective grounds for justification) and a position of proportionality must exist between the restrictive measure (i.e. the measure making a distinction) and this objective; in actual fact, we must see whether the ban is or is not justified in the light of a general interest or to protect third party rights (E. BREMS, "The headscarf as constitutional head-care", T.B.P., 2004, p. 356); what must be central in this case, however, is that any manifestly arbitrary distinction must be prohibited (J. VRIELINK, S. SOTTIAUX, and D. DE PRINS, "The Anti-Discrimination Act. An analysis article by article", NjW 2003, No. 41 p. 267) A ban on headscarves must therefore be permitted under three conditions; firstly, it must be based on a general rule that is sufficiently clear and accessible; secondly, it must pursue an objective of general interest or the protection of the rights of others; finally, it must be a measure that is not more restrictive than necessary in order to achieve this objective, in other words it must meet the requirement for proportionality [E. BREMS, "The headscarf as constitutional head care", T.B.P., 2004, p. 347]."

Notes

(1) This case was decided on the basis of the Belgian implementation of Directives 2000/43/EC and 2000/78/EC and is thus one of the first examples of whether and how these Directives impact on the headscarf case.

(2) The Court here does not, in fact, discuss whether there is indeed disparate impact. It just assumes that there is a possibility and therefore that objective justification must be considered. Under the circumstances, it is rather doubtful whether the measure was indeed neutral as regards religion, as parents were explicitly alerted to the fact that headscarves are prohibited.

(3) In addition, one of the events that had triggered the establishment of the new rules had been the activities of a group of Muslim pupils wearing headscarves who had criticised their assessments as being tainted by discrimination and also harassed

---

[188] AR/2004/2811.

other Muslim girls who would not wear a headscarf. Accordingly, this might also have been a case of direct religious discrimination. Framed as indirect discrimination, the objective justification becomes decisive, to which we will return under the next subheading.

L. Roseberry, "Tørklædediskrimination på arbejdsmarkedet"[189]   **3.DK.70.**

This article discusses three cases decided by the High Court for Eastern Denmark on the question whether Muslim women may be prohibited to wear headscarves at work, all of which were decided in accordance with legislation prior to implementation of the Directive. The *Fotex* decision of 2003 is still under review by the Supreme Court. In all the cases discussed, the courts denied that a prohibition to wear a headscarf at work could be qualified as not legally acceptable, relying on a weighing of religious freedom of the employee and business necessities of the employer. Lynn Roseberry discusses the prospects of similar cases after proper implementation of the Directives.

> "The definition in the Equal Treatment Act of indirect discrimination has been interpreted to mean that statistical information is required as evidence. It would probably have been difficult and expensive for the claimants in these cases to acquire such information. This was perhaps why the claimants in the three cases did not make a claim of sexual discrimination. The actual situation as regards evidence could however give rise to doubt regarding the need for statistical information.
>
> If the claimants had invoked the Equal Treatment Act, the Østre Landsret (Eastern Division of the High Court) would presumably have applied the Equal Treatment Act's conditions for justification of indirect discrimination. If this had been the case neither Toms nor Føtex would have been acquitted. The probability of such a result in cases of this nature is increased because § 16a of the Equal Treatment Act concerning the sharing of the burden of proof would have been applied.
>
> The new Directives are intended to, and should, make a difference in headscarf cases with respect to these points. The definition of indirect discrimination in Directive 2002/73/EC abolishes the requirement for statistical information in sexual discrimination cases. The same definition is found in the two other new Directives concerning discrimination on grounds of criteria other than gender. All three Directives contain the conditions referred to above for justification of indirect discrimination. The law recently passed on the amendment of the Differential Treatment Act implements the Directives in Danish Law with effect from 8th April 2004. The wording of the act defines indirect discrimination fully in accordance with the Directives and is to be interpreted in conformity with the Directives. On the basis of the preceding discussion it may therefore be assumed that in today's situation the courts would find the clothing regulations of Toms Fabrikker and Føtex to be unlawful, even without regard to the comments on the law to amend the Differential Treatment Act. If the courts are in any doubt regarding the correct interpretation of the Directives and therefore the amending law, they may put a prejudicial question to the European Court of Justice."

---

[189]   (2004) Ugeskrift for Retsvæsen at 189.

434

ASSESSMENT

The non-statistical approach to indirect discrimination law avoids the numerous problems with statistics. Some authors expect that this will make it easier to find indirect discrimination, for example, in cases such as those concerning headscarf-related issues, not only on grounds of religion, but also on grounds of sex. The suggestion is that it is difficult to come by exact numbers in these cases, while reasonable judgement would lead to acknowledging that a requirement not to cover one's head would put women of ethnic minority background at a particular disadvantage.[190]

A non-statistical approach may, however, also create new problems. Rejecting the objectivity of data, discrimination cases might be decided through reliance on stereotypes. It appears that statistics, if properly established, may in some circumstances contribute to overcoming bias. For example, in sex discrimination law, one often assumes that disadvantaging part-time employees will on average disparately impact upon women. However, more detailed statistical research in the UK has demonstrated that this assumption is only true for ethnic majority women, but fails to mirror the reality of women from some ethnic minorities.[191] There might be other cases in which such differences arise, i.e. where ethnic minority women's situation is merged with the situation of ethnic majority women and thus effectively neglected.

3.5.2.   OBJECTIVE JUSTIFICATION

As regards the second element of a definition of indirect discrimination, national legal orders (and doctrine) differ as to whether this is a "justification proper" or whether the objective justification test rebuts the assumption that there is indeed discrimination, i.e. is an element of proof of causation. The main issue in many practical cases is the exact application of the principle of proportionality, which will be dealt with under the heading "standards of scrutiny". In younger case-law, there has been a tendency to deny indirect discrimination because situations were not comparable. As this argument in practice replaces objective justification, it is also discussed here. Last but not least, some examples for acceptable and non-acceptable objective justifications are given.

---

[190]   *Ibid.*

[191]   Ashiagbor, "The intersection between Gender and Race in the Labour Market: Consequences for Anti-Discrimination Law" in A. Morris and T. O'Donnel (eds.), *Feminist Perspectives on Employment Law* (London, Cavendish, 1999) 139–63.

3.5.2.A.   A "JUSTIFICATION PROPER" OR AN ELEMENT OF CAUSATION?

OBJECTIVE JUSTIFICATION AS "JUSTIFICATION PROPER"

The concept of "justification proper" is explained by Tobler as involving a balancing of the general goal to avoid discrimination and other, conflicting goals.[192] Under this doctrine, different treatment and disparate impact alike are capable of being justified generally or for specific reasons, and the difference between both concepts diminishes. "Justification proper" may be used to balance business need and the goal to avoid discriminatory effects in a global way, which does not take into account a strict application of the principle of proportionality. In the early case-law of the ECJ on sex discrimination, there were some examples of such an approach. One may suffice as illustration here.

ECJ, 17 October 1989   **3.EC.71.**[*]
C-109/88, Handels- og Kontorfunktionærernes Forbund I Danmark v. *Dansk Arbejdsgiverforening, acting on behalf of Danfoss*

WHETHER A GENDER PAY GAP RESULTING FROM A SYSTEM OF BONUSES
ESTABLISHES DETRIMENTAL EFFECT

Danfoss (continued 2)

Facts and *Held*: As may be remembered, the Danish trade union, acting on behalf of two of its female members, had challenged a system of individual bonuses. The ECJ had established the principle that—where a remuneration system lacks any transparency—a prima facie case of indirect discrimination is established by showing that the average pay for women is less than for men. It then addressed the question whether the use of such criteria for awarding bonuses as were known to disparately impact on women inter alia mobility, training and seniority could be objectively justified. Within this part of the judgment, the Court made a general assumption on the disparate impact of the said criteria. It also discussed objective justification.

Judgment: (continued) "18 As regards, in the first place, the criterion of mobility, the documents before the Court do not clearly disclose what is to be meant by this . At the hearing the Employers' Association stated that willingness to work different hours did not in itself justify a wage supplement. In applying the criterion of mobility the employer makes a global assessment of the quality of work done by his employees. For that purpose he takes account, in particular, of their enthusiasm for their work, their sense of initiative and the amount of work done.

19 In those circumstances a distinction must be made according to whether the criterion of mobility is employed to reward the quality of work done by the employee or is used to reward the employee's adaptability to variable hours and varying places of work.

20 In the first case the criterion of mobility is undoubtedly wholly neutral from the point of view of sex. Where it systematically works to the disadvantage of women that can only be because the employer has misapplied it. It is inconceivable that the quality of work done by

---

[192] See Tobler, above n. 56, 83.
 [*] See above **3.EC.38** and **3.EC.61.**

women should generally be less good. The employer cannot therefore justify applying the criterion of mobility, so understood, where its application proves to work systematically to the disadvantage of women.

21 The position is different in the second case. If it is understood as covering the employee's adaptability to variable hours and varying places of work, the criterion of mobility may also work to the disadvantage of female employees, who, because of household and family duties for which they are frequently responsible, are not as able as men to organize their working time flexibly . . .

22 . . . The employer may . . . justify the remuneration of such adaptability by showing it is of importance for the performance of specific tasks entrusted to the employee.

23 In the second place, as regards the criterion of training, it is not be excluded that it may work to the disadvantage of women in so far as they have had less opportunity than men for training or have taken less advantage of such opportunity. Nevertheless, in view of the considerations set out in the aforementioned judgment of 13 May 1986 the employer may justify remuneration of special training by showing that it is of importance for the performance of specific tasks entrusted to the employee.

24 In the third place, as regards the criterion of length of service, it is also not to be excluded, as with training, that it may involve less advantageous treatment of women than of men in so far as women have entered the labour market more recently than men or more frequently suffer an interruption of their career . Nevertheless, since length of service goes hand in hand with experience and since experience generally enables the employee to perform his duties better, the employer is free to reward it without having to establish the importance it has in the performance of specific tasks entrusted to the employee."

Notes on Danfoss—global justification

(1) Here, the ECJ obviously considered that objective justification was not a way to rebut an assumption of discrimination. This can be seen from the fact that the Court distinguished between a neutral, i.e. non-discriminatory, application of the criterion of mobility and a discriminatory one. Where any differences between male and female wages resulted from applying the criterion of mobility, the criterion was neutral. Where mobility was connected to the gendered notion of an autonomous employee, the Court held that this notion would have to be taken as disparately impacting upon women (without having recourse to any statistical argument, by the way). Despite this, it considered that overriding business interest was capable of justifying the criterion. The objective justification proper is here applied in parallel to the occupational requirement, to which an employer can have recourse in order to justify direct sex discrimination.[193] Similarly, the Court assumes that more women than men were denied training and could accrue seniority and that in this regard, disparate impact can be assumed. However, it also applied the occupational requirement strategy to these criteria.

(2) The *Danfoss* case had seemed to imply that seniority would almost automatically be justified as a criterion for granting bonuses. In a recent English reference to the ECJ, this presumption was challenged. The Court of Appeal framed the reference question in *Cadman*[194] carefully:

---

[193] See above M. Bell, Chapter 2: Direct Discrimination, section 2.6.3.A.
[194] ECJ, 3 October 2006, C–17/05 *B.F. Cadman* v. *Health & Safety Executive.*

"Where the use by an employer of the criterion length of service as a determinant of pay has a disparate impact as between relevant male and female employees, does Article 141 EC require the employer to provide specific justification for recourse to that criterion?"

In its answer, the ECJ repeated its argument from *Danfoss* that normally length of service is an indicator of experience and thus higher qualification. However, the Court also held that in exceptional circumstances, where an employee brings evidence suggesting that length of service is an inadequate criterion for granting bonuses, the employer would be under an obligation to objectively justify this choice.[195]

In national law, the clearest example of a legal order relying explicitly on the dualist approach towards objective justification is the Netherlands. The Dutch Equal Treatment Act defines the concept as follows:

Dutch Equal Treatment Act   **3.NL.72.**

§ 1. General provisions
Section 1

For the purposes of this Act and the provisions based upon it the following definitions shall apply: a. distinction: direct and indirect distinction, as well as the instruction to discriminate; . . .

c. indirect distinction: distinction on the grounds of other characteristics or behaviour than those meant under (b), resulting in direct distinction.
§ 2. General exceptions

Section 2

1. The prohibition on distinction contained in this Act shall not apply to indirect distinction if the distinction is objectively justified by a legitimate aim and the means used to achieve that aim are appropriate and necessary.

Equal Treatment Commission (Commissie Gelijke Behandeling) **3.NL.73.**[*]
Opinion 1997-4

INDIRECT SEX DISCRIMINATION BY DISREGARDING SENIORITY OF FORMER
STANDBY STEWARDESSES WHO PROCEED TO REGULAR EMPLOYMENT

Stand-by stewardesses (continued)

Facts and *Held*: As may be remembered, the question was whether stand-by stewardesses could generally be excluded from the scope of application of a collective agreement granting promotions without violating the prohibition of indirect sex discrimination. The CGB had asserted that this rule led to detrimental effects and now had to assess whether it was objectively justified.

---

[195] No. 38 of the judgment.
[*] See above **3.NL.52.**

Opinion: "4.6 . . . the aim pursued must be unrelated to any discrimination; the measures applied to achieve that aim must correspond to a real need; and these measures must be suitable and necessary to achieve that aim . . . The aim pursued by the system of wage classification and promotions is to honour relevant work experience. The Commission finds that this aim is untainted with discrimination.

4.7 The measure adopted to achieve that aim is to disregard the experience gained by stand-by work when switching to a position with the cabin crew, because the number of flight hours worked by stand-by's and their continuity is not substantial enough to be taken into account and their involvement with the company is also otherwise insufficient. The parties have not disputed and the Commission finds it plausible that this corresponds to a real need of the respondent . . ..

4.8 The respondent has stressed the importance of sustained experience and the regularity of the duties discharged by the stand-by's . . . The respondent acknowledges that among the stand-by's there is a top group . . . in relation to which the experience in the job is relevant to being honoured, in accordance with the respondent's criteria, with respect to wage classification and promotions with the cabin crew. This leads to the conclusion that the measure adopted by the respondent . . . is neither suitable nor necessary to achieve the aim."

Notes to standby stewardesses re objective justification

(1) The CGB explicitly refers to the test applied by the ECJ re objective justification. This test, however, deviates from the Dutch legislation insofar as the objective justification can be used to refute the presumption of discrimination. The CGB has thus applied a "justification proper" test instead of their national law.

(2) Relying on the strict test linked to the "justification proper" method, the CGB is able to "screen out" such employment policies as are not tailored exactly to the business needs and are thus over-inclusive and unnecessarily discriminatory.

"OBJECTIVE JUSTIFICATION" AS CAUSAL LINK TEST—AN INTEGRATED APPROACH

On the other hand, the "objective justification" may be used to rebut the presumption that there is indeed a causal link between the criterion, rule or practice or a mere structure and the disparate impact. "Objective justification" is then not a justification comparable to the genuine business requirement in direct discrimination cases. It is instead used to establish a causal link between discriminatory effects and the criterion, rule or practice which led to the discriminatory effect.

This has been called the "causation approach" to indirect discrimination.[196] While in direct discrimination cases the causal link between disadvantage and discrimination ground is established by the explicit reference to the discrimination ground, the causal link between disadvantage and discrimination ground is to be established in a different way in indirect discrimination cases. Disparate impact or factual disadvantage only establishes a presumption of discrimination, which can be rebutted. Using "objective justification" as a means to establish a causal link enables

---

[196] See above **3.NL.51.**

indirect discrimination law to refrain from charging a defendant with responsibility for discriminatory effects which have been caused by someone else or which she cannot influence. This is best explained in the words of E. Ellis, who coined the term "causation approach". She writes: "Where an employer 'justifies' apparent indirect discrimination, there is proof that the disadvantage is attributable to some other cause than sex, such as the efficient running of a business."[197] If there is no objective justification, it must be concluded that the discriminatory effect of a neutrally worded policy is attributable to the person or institution which issued the rule, practice or criterion.

If justification is used as a causal link, direct and indirect discrimination are concepts to be carefully distinguished. Adopting this approach, one may never use the term "discrimination" in relation to disparate impact. An obvious advantage of the causation approach is the clear distinction between the two concepts. If, on the other hand, a "justification proper" is accepted in cases of indirect discrimination, it is difficult to defend the present position of Community law only to allow justification of direct discrimination in very limited cases.[198] If a general justification is open for indirect discrimination, denying this opportunity in direct discrimination cases becomes less convincing.

The causation approach is reflected in Sedley LJ's reasoning in *Allonby* (CA).[199]

Court of Appeal, 23 March 2001[200]   **3.GB.74.**[*]
Allonby v. *Accrington and Rossendale College*

WHETHER "DOWNGRADING" PART-TIME LECTURERS TO SELF EMPLOYED SERVICE PROVIDERS CONSTITUTES INDIRECT DISCRIMINIATION

Allonby (CA)

Facts and *Held*: As may be remembered, the question was whether by discontinuing the employment of part-time lecturers and offering them to work as freelancers through a certain agency, Rossendale College had violated the prohibition of indirect sex discrimination. That case mainly established the principle that even in UK law a policy (as opposed to a requirement or condition) might be a sufficient basis for an indirect discrimination claim. In that regard, the question arose to which of the two approaches was more appropriate. In refuting the narrower approach taken by the CA itself in former cases, Sedley LJ explains:

Judgment: "The other reason is that the decision of the EAT in Brook is based on an erroneous understanding of the Sex Discrimination Act's concept of indirect discrimination, an understanding which conflates it with direct discrimination. The fact — if it is a fact — that a section of a workforce facing some disadvantage 'happens to be' predominantly female may be crucial to the question of direct discrimination, but has no bearing on either the initial element of

---

[197] E. Ellis [1994] *CMLRev* 387, 391.
[198] See the controversy between T. Gill and K. Monaghan, "Justification in Direct Sex Discrimination Law: Taboo Upheld" (2003) 32 *ILJ* 115 and J. Bowers et al., "Justification in Direct Sex Discrimination: A Reply" (2003) 32 *ILJ* 185.
[199] CA *Allonby* v. *Accrington and Rossendale College and other* [2001] IRLR 364.
[200] [2001] 2 CMLRev 27.
[*] See above **3.UK.31.**

indirect discrimination under s. 1(1)(b)(i) (unequal impact) or the third element under s. 1(1)(b)(iii) (consequent detriment). The establishment of the requirement or condition and the evaluation of its proportional impact depend upon an exact reading of the evidence and nothing more. To say that those affected happen to be, rather than are, predominantly or exclusively men or women is to say nothing which at this stage is material. Nor does it matter that the outcome may affect a whole factory: in such cases as Clarke v Eley (IMI) Kynoch (above) that is exactly what happened . . .. (I)f the requirement or condition is objectively justified notwithstanding its differential impact on men and women, then it can be fairly said that those disadvantaged simply happen to be women. But that is a conclusion, not a premise . . ."

Note on Allonby (CA) (continued)
This reasoning clearly shows that there is a difference between applying justification proper and the causation approach. Accepting such "objective justifications" that are themselves connected with the discrimination ground is not possible under the causation approach. For example, measures that have detrimental effects on women must not be justified by reference to imposed gender roles, e.g. the "breadwinner model" in the case of disadvantage for part-time employees.

Another example is that the rejection of women wearing a headscarf, a requirement that disparately impacts upon ethnic minority women, must not be justified by reference to expectations of customers to being served by ethnic majority personnel. In practice, the last mentioned justification was indeed used by the Federal Labour Court in Germany when deciding its first headscarf case.[201] The Federal Labour Court actually allowed the claim of a saleswoman of Turkish origin who had been dismissed for wearing a headscarf, considering that the employee's right to freedom of religion had to be balanced against the employer's economic interests. The employer had alleged that he feared for loss of sales if he allowed headscarves to be worn in the cosmetic department, as such dress would not be in line with local standards. The Federal Labour Court held that the mere apprehension of loss would not be sufficient to justify dismissal. However, had the employer been able to prove that there was indeed a decrease in sales after the employee returned from parental leave wearing a headscarf, the balancing of interests could have led to a different result. The Federal Labour Court decided this case not in application of non-discrimination principles, but solely as involving conflicting freedoms on the part of an employee (religious freedom) and an employer (economic freedom). From that perspective, the result is not to be criticised. From a non-discrimination perspective, however, it is questionable whether fear of losing customers who object to being served by a person looking different than those from the majority population "in a small town in Hesse" is indeed unrelated to discrimination on grounds of ethnic origin. Under a causation test of indirect discrimination, such objective justification could not be used to rebut the assumption of causal relation between detrimental effect and the protected ground.

---

[201] BAG, 10 October 2002—2 AZR 472/01, NJW 2003, 1685, annotation by D. Schiek, "Just a Piece of Cloth? German Courts and Employees with Headscarves" (2004) 33 *ILJ* 68.

ASSESSMENT

Having stressed the advantages of the causation approach, its critics should not be overlooked. Tobler points to the fact that applying a "proper justification test" would prompt courts towards applying stricter standards. If the "justification" of indirect discrimination is seen in parallel to explicitly allowed justifications of direct discrimination, she argues, certainly the rule that exceptions have to be read narrowly and justifications to be applied strictly will apply. In addition, she holds—concurring with other authors—that the dualist approach serves to acknowledge detrimental effects even in such cases where the measures are objectively justified. This would be more satisfactory to those complaining of discrimination. She also claims that the practical differences are not too large, anyway.[202] The first argument is, however, refuted by Tobler's own deliberations. She rightly holds that, following the unified model, justifying indirect discrimination could be paralleled to the arguments used in free movement of goods law to conclude that indistinctly applicable measures that are objectively justified by overriding general interests are not measures of equivalent effect to quantitative restrictions.[203] However, the case-law of the ECJ in applying the relevant test can certainly not be accused of being too lenient towards Member States. The second argument is, in this author's view, not convincing.

On the contrary, it proves that the causation approach is more in line with the conceptual aspirations of a prohibition of indirect discrimination. The legal concept has been characterised as a hybrid between formal and substantial and individualistic and group-orientated conceptions of equality.[204] In this author's view, the genius of indirect discrimination law lies exactly in the fact that the concept can be placed at a crossing between protection of individual autonomy against being forcibly ascribed membership of a group, the striving for factual equality and protection against being forced to assimilate to a dominant group or standard. Taking disparate impact as a starting point, indirect discrimination law rests on the assumption that reality is moulded by group membership. Thus there is an assumption that a rule resulting in group-related disadvantage is suspect. However, this claim can be rebutted by the objective justification test. This element ensures that responsibility for enhancing or perpetuating disadvantage is laid only on a person who or institution that has control over the cause of disadvantage. Both disparate impact and objective justification must be required as preconditions for discrimination if indirect discrimination law is to maintain its ability to expose structural discrimination in an acceptable way. In other words, this approach allows for the alignment of the structural analysis of discriminatory institutions with a balanced approach to responsibility for these institutions.

In addition, if the law accepts that detrimental effects on their own deserve the verdict of being classed as discriminatory, and further accept that any reason

---

[202] See Tobler, above n. 56, 254–8.
[203] See above section 3.2.1.A.
[204] A. Morris, "On the Normative Foundations of Indirect Discrimination Law: Understanding the Competing Models of Discrimination Law as Aristotelian Forms of Justice" (1995) 15 *OJLS* 199, 203.

unrelated to discrimination grounds can justify such discrimination, it cannot convincingly refuse to allow any reason to justify direct discrimination.[205] Applying the dualist test will thus ultimately lead to there being a unified test of discrimination, opening up a wealth of justifications for direct discrimination even in such legal orders which—like Community law—as yet do not accept these. Accordingly, the integrated approach is to be preferred on a policy basis.

From the EC law definition, it is not entirely clear whether the approach to objective justification is dualist or integrated. Accordingly, both views can be defended formally. Considering the wider aim of discrimination law, which is to overcome discrimination in socio-economic reality,[206] an integrated approach seems preferable. This conclusion is also supported by the fact that—in contrast to direct discrimination law—the list of possible objective justifications for rules having detrimental effects is an open one. This supports the view that EC law leans towards a causation test of objective justification.

3.5.2.B.   STANDARDS OF SCRUTINY

The decisive detail of objective justification is, however, how strict the standard of scrutiny must be.

COMMUNITY LAW AND ECJ CASE-LAW

Strict standard of scrutiny in relation to employers (sex equality law)

In the definition of indirect sex discrimination, as developed in ECJ case-law from *Bilka*, and which still applies within the scope of application of Article 141 EC, the standard of scrutiny was a strict one. In the *Bilka* judgment (above **3.EC.16.**), the ECJ stressed that employers could not rely on any aim or policy that was related to sex for justification, and that their justification arguments were tested under a strict standard of scrutiny. For a measure with detrimental effect on one of the sexes not to be found to be indirectly discriminatory, the employer was required to explain the practice by reference to "objectively justified factors unrelated to any discrimination on grounds of sex".[207] Whether the facts indeed satisfied the test of objective justification was a matter for the national court to decide, but the ECJ decided on the test to be applied: the national court has to consider whether "the measures chosen . . . corresponded to a real need on the part of the undertaking, are appropriate with a view to achieving the objectives pursued and are necessary to that end". This constituted a strict standard of proportionality. The younger Directives change this in

---

[205] On the principled position of EC law against justifying direct discrimination see above M. Bell, Chapter 2: Direct Discrimination, section 2.6.3.E, text preceding note 113.

[206] On the wider aims of non-discrimination law, see above Introductory Chapter, section 6.

[207] ECJ, Case 170/84 *Bilka—Kaufhaus GmbH* v. *Karin Weber von Hartz* [1986] ECR 1607, No. 30.

two aspects: first of all, the aims that can be pursued by a provision, criterion or practice are no longer restricted to business needs, but rather any legitimate aim can be chosen. Secondly, nowhere is it said explicitly that the aim needs to be unrelated to the discrimination ground in question.[208] However, a teleological reading of the Directives would imply that the presumption of discrimination must not be rebutted by referring to discriminatory criteria. Any criterion referring to the grounds of discrimination themselves cannot be considered other than discriminatory, though. It is to be hoped that the ECJ does not soften the approach to justifying indirect discrimination on the grounds of the Directives' new wording.

A loose standard in relation to Member States

The ECJ has in younger case-law shown an increasing tendency to lower its standard of scrutiny in indirect gender discrimination cases. Again, the decisions of both the ECJ and the HL in *Seymour-Smith and Perez* are illustrative.

ECJ, 9 February 1999[209]   **3.EC.75.**[*]
C—167/97, Regina v. Secretary of State for Employment, ex parte
Nicole Seymour-Smith and Laura Perez

TWO-YEAR QUALIFICATION PERIOD FOR EMPLOYMENT PROTECTION AS INDIRECT
SEX DISCRIMINATION

Seymour-Smith and Perez (ECJ)

Facts and *Held*: As may be recalled, the question in this case was whether prolonging the qualification period for employment protection from six months to two years is indirectly discriminatory. The House of Lords had requested some clarification of the objective justification test to be applied in case they found detrimental effect.

Judgment: "66 By its fifth question the national court seeks to ascertain the legal criteria for establishing the objective justification, for the purposes of indirect discrimination . . ., of a measure adopted by a Member State in pursuance of its social policy . . .

69 It is settled case-law that if a Member State is able to show that the measures chosen reflect a necessary aim of its social policy and are suitable and necessary for achieving that aim, the mere fact that the legislative provision affects far more women than men at work cannot be regarded as a breach of (Community Law) . . .

70 In this case, the United Kingdom Government contends that . . . the qualifying period for protection against dismissal would stimulate recruitment.

71 It cannot be disputed that the encouragement of recruitment constitutes a legitimate aim of social policy.

---

[208] See Barnard, above n. 126, 332, 402, who assumes that justifications directly related to the prohibited grounds might be accepted in the future.
[209] [1999] ECR 623.
[*] See above **3.EC.54.** and below **3.EC.77.**

72 It must also be ascertained, in the light of all the relevant factors and taking into account the possibility of achieving the social policy aim in question by other means, whether such an aim appears to be unrelated to any discrimination based on sex and whether the disputed rule, as a means to its achievement, is capable of advancing that aim.

73 In that connection, the United Kingdom Government maintains that a Member State should merely have to show that it was reasonably entitled to consider that the measure would advance a social policy aim. It relies to that end on Case C–317/93 Nolte [1995] ECR I–4625 . . .

74 It is true that in paragraph 33 of the Nolte case the Court observed that, in choosing the measures capable of achieving the aims of their social and employment policy, the Member States have a broad margin of discretion.

75 However, although social policy is essentially a matter for the Member States under Community law as it stands, the fact remains that the broad margin of discretion available to the Member States in that connection cannot have the effect of frustrating the implementation of a fundamental principle of Community law such as that of equal pay for men and women.

76 Mere generalisations concerning the capacity of a specific measure to encourage recruitment are not enough to show that the aim of the disputed rule is unrelated to any discrimination based on sex nor to provide evidence on the basis of which it could reasonably be considered that the means chosen were suitable for achieving that aim.

77 Accordingly, the answer to the fifth question must be that if a considerably smaller percentage of women than men is capable of fulfilling the requirement of two years' employment imposed by the disputed rule, it is for the Member State, as the author of the allegedly discriminatory rule, to show that the said rule reflects a legitimate aim of its social policy, that that aim is unrelated to any discrimination based on sex, and that it could reasonably consider that the means chosen were suitable for attaining that aim."

Similarly, the ECJ had allowed the national court to take a broad approach towards justifying detrimental effects on part-time employees by reducing their employment protection in Germany.

ECJ, 26 September 2000[210]　　　　　　**3.EC.76.**
C–322/98, Kachelmann v. Bankhaus Lampe

INDIRECT SEX DISCRIMINATION BY REDUCING THE POOL OF COMPARABLE
EMPLOYEES FOR PART-TIME EMPLOYEES TO OTHER PART-TIME EMPLOYEES IN CASES
OF DISMISSAL FOR ECONOMIC REASONS

Kachelmann

Facts: Ms. Kachelmann, a single mother of three children, one of whom is severely disabled, had worked for Bankhaus Lampe (Hamburg) from 1 April 1991 to 30 September 1996, when her dismissal for economic reasons became effective. She worked 30 hours a week instead of 38, the number of working hours considered as full-time by the relevant collective agreement. Her tasks as a case manager with bilingual drafting skills were not comparable to the tasks of any of the other four part-time employees of Bankhaus Lampe, but were to those of a full-time employee, who was less vulnerable to dismissal due to her lower

---

[210] [2000] ECR I–7505.

number of dependent children. Although Ms. Kachelmann was prepared to work full-time instead of part-time, she was dismissed.

Held: The Court of First Instance dismissed the claim, in line with national law—as interpreted by the Federal Labour Court. The Regional Labour Court found that it too would have to dismiss the claim, were it to base its reasoning on the interpretation of the Employment Protection Act by the Federal Labour Court. It referred some questions to the ECJ as to whether this interpretation amounted to indirect sex discrimination. The relevant provisions of national law were §§ 1 paragraphs 1 and 3 of the *Kündigungs-schutzgesetz* (Law on Employment Protection, 'the KSchG). They provide:

"1. The dismissal of an employee whose contract has continued for more than six consecutive months with the same company shall be legally ineffective where it lacks social justification.

2. A dismissal lacks social justification where it is not based on reasons connected with the person or conduct of the employee or with serious constraints affecting the company which make it impossible to retain the employee's post in that company . . .

3. If an employee is dismissed due to serious constraints affecting the company within the meaning of Article 1(2), the dismissal shall nevertheless lack social justification if, in selecting the worker, the employer did not take social factors into account, or did not do so sufficiently . . ."

While social justification requires an equitable selection among workers, this selection process is obviously restricted to those workers which discharge of comparable tasks. The case-law of the Federal Labour Court also requires that full-time employees be compared only to full-time employees and part-time employees only to part-time employees. This was the reason why both courts came to the conclusion that Ms. Kachelmann had no claim under § 1 KSchG.

Judgment: "23. It should be remembered at the outset that it is well settled that where national rules, although worded in neutral terms, work to the disadvantage of a much higher percentage of women than men, they discriminate indirectly against women, unless that difference in treatment is justified by objective factors unrelated to any discrimination on grounds of sex (see, in particular, Case C–226/98 Jørgensen [2000] ECR I–0000, paragraph 29)

. . .

29 . . ., it is necessary to determine whether such a difference in treatment is justified by objective factors unrelated to any discrimination on grounds of sex . . .

30. As Community law stands at present, social policy is a matter for the Member States, which enjoy a reasonable margin of discretion as regards the nature of social protection measures and the detailed arrangements for their implementation. If such measures meet a legitimate aim of social policy, are suitable and requisite for attaining that end and are therefore justified by reasons unrelated to discrimination on grounds of sex, they cannot be regarded as being contrary to the principle of equal treatment (Jørgensen, cited above, paragraph 41).

31. It appears from the case-file that the purpose of the German legislation in question is to protect workers facing dismissal whilst at the same time taking account of the undertaking's operational and economic needs.

32. In that regard, it is clear from the observations submitted to the Court that job comparability is determined according to the actual content of the respective employment contracts, by assessing whether the worker whose job is being abolished for reasons peculiar to the undertaking would be capable, having regard to his professional qualifications and the activities he has hitherto been carrying out within the undertaking, of carrying out the different but equivalent work done by other workers.

33. Application of those criteria may well create an indirect disadvantage for part time workers because their jobs cannot be compared with those of full-time workers. However, as the German Government has pointed out, if job comparability between full-time and part time workers were to be introduced in the selection process on the basis of social criteria under

Article 1(3) of the KSchG, that would have the effect of placing part time workers at an advantage, while putting full-time workers at a disadvantage. In the event of their jobs being abolished, part time workers would have to be offered a full-time job, even if their employment contract did not entitle them to one.

34. The question whether part time workers should enjoy such an advantage is a matter for the national legislature, which alone must find a fair balance in employment law between the various interests concerned. In this case, that assessment has been based on considerations unrelated to the sex of the workers.

35. In those circumstances, the answer must be that Articles 2(1) and 5(1) of the Directive is to be interpreted as not precluding an interpretation of a national rule, such as that contained in Article 1(3) of the KSchG, which proceeds on the general basis that part time workers are not to be compared with full-time workers when an employer has to proceed to selection on the basis of social criteria when abolishing a part time job on economic grounds."

Notes on Kachelmann and Seymour-Smith and Perez

(1) The Court and its AG disagreed on the matter of objective justification. One of the reasons given by the government was that part-time employees would normally not agree to change their weekly hours. AG Saggio considered that the assumption about changing the number of hours worked by a part-time employee was not correct in all cases, which at the same time imports that the measure of excluding their comparability with full-time employees is not necessary to achieve its aim. Accordingly, it could not serve as objective justification of the rule in question.

(2) Both cases reflect the ECJ's reluctance to submit Member States to the same strict requirements it has been applying to employers and confirm a less than bold approach towards indirect discrimination by social policy measures. However, the Court still requires Member States to justify rules that have a detrimental effect. They are, however, only required to base their policy on reasonable assumptions as to whether the means are suitable for attaining that aim. There is no test of necessity. It remains to be seen whether the Court will retain this position when addressing discrimination on other grounds, or whether widening the scope of Community non-discrimination law will encourage the Court to take a more courageous stance.

NATIONAL CASE-LAW

As regards national case-law, objective justification is the second and often decisive hurdle for a indirect discrimination claim. As the decision on these questions is reserved to the national court, the field will continue to be characterised by a certain degree of diversity. This also implies that this section cannot possibly give a full overview and at the same time reduce the material to such an amount that comparative analysis is still possible.

The response of the UK House of Lords to the ECJ decision in *Seymour-Smith* may serve as an example of how a loose standard of scrutiny affects the working of indirect discrimination law. Relieving the British government of any obligation to show that there was indeed some of the desired effect on the employment market that would objectively justify the discriminatory effect, the House of Lords allowed the Crown's appeal.

House of Lords, 17 February 2000[211]   **3.GB.77.**[*]
R v. Secretary of State for Employment, ex parte Seymour-Smith and another

TWO-YEAR QUALIFICATION PERIOD FOR EMPLOYMENT PROTECTION AS INDIRECT SEX DISCRIMINATION

Seymour-Smith and Perez (HL) continued

Facts and *Held*: As may be remembered, the question before the HL was whether extending the qualification period for employment protection in the UK to two years had a negative impact on women and, if so, whether this should be justified.

Judgment: LORD NICHOLSON: "Objective justification falls to be determined . . . as at 1991 . . . That was the date when the 1985 order was applied to the two claimants . . . But objective justification cannot be assessed in 1991 without regard to how the situation in 1991 came about. Thus . . . (it) has to be approached in two stages. The first stage is to consider whether the government was justified in introducing the 1985 order . . . The second stage is to consider whether the government was justified in keeping the order in force six years later . . .

The Divisional Court and the Court of Appeal held that the Secretary of State had failed to discharge the burden of proving that the 1985 order was objectively justified . . . the test applied . . .was whether the order was shown to be a suitable and requisite means to achieve the admittedly legitimate aim of encouraging employment. Thus . . .whether the threshold of two years had been 'proved to result' in greater availability of employment than would have been the case without it. The Court of Appeal declined to incorporate into this formulation any margin of appreciation: [1996] All ER (EC) 1 at 29, [1995] ICR 889 at 955). The answer given by the Court of Justice to the fifth question . . . has now shown that this test was too stringent. . . . The onus is on the member state to show (1) that the allegedly discriminatory rule reflects a legitimate aim of its social policy (2) that this aim is unrelated to any discrimination based on sex, and (3) that the member state could reasonably consider that the means chosen were suitable for attaining that aim.

There is no difficulty with the first two requirements. The object of the 1985 order was to encourage recruitment by employers. This was a legitimate aim . . . unrelated to any sex discrimination. Whether the third requirement was satisfied in 1985 is more debatable. In March 1985 the Secretary of State, Mr. Tom King, stated with regard to the proposed change in the qualifying period: 'The risks of unjustified involvement with tribunals in unfair dismissal cases and the cost of such involvement are often cited as deterring employers from giving more people jobs. This change which now puts all new employees on the same basis as that already existing for those in small firms, should help reduce the reluctance of employers to take on more people . . .' The relevant question is whether the Secretary of State was reasonably entitled to consider that the extension of the qualifying period should help reduce the reluctance of employers to take on more people.

---

[211] [2000] 1 All ER 857.
[*] See above **3.GB.55.**

448

This question raises an issue of fact, to be decided on the basis of the extensive documentary evidence adduced by the parties. The Secretary of State relied on several reports. These are itemised in the judgment of Balcombe LJ ([1995] ICR 889 at 907). One report, 'Burdens on Business', was published by the Department of Trade and Industry in March 1985. This report identified, as one of the available options, increasing employees' qualifying periods in unfair dismissal cases from one year to two years in firms employing more than 20 employees: . . .' (t)his is not a case of a mere generalised assumption . . . Here, there was some supporting factual evidence. To condemn the minister for failing to carry out further research or prepare an impact analysis, as recommended in 'Burdens on Business', would be unreasonable.

The requirements of Community law must be complied with at all relevant times. A measure may satisfy Community law when adopted, because at that stage the minister was reasonably entitled to consider the measure was a suitable means for achieving a legitimate aim. But . . . in course of time the measure may be found to be unsuited for its intended purpose . . . In such a case a measure, lawful when adopted, may become unlawful . . . Ought the government to have taken steps to repeal the 1985 order before 1991? In other words, had the order, lawful at its inception, become unlawful by 1991? Here again, the matter is debatable. As time passed, the persistently adverse impact on women became apparent. But, as with the broad margin of discretion afforded to governments when adopting measures of this type, so with the duty of governments to monitor the implementation of such measures: the practicalities of government must be borne in mind. The benefits of the 1985 order could not be expected to materialise . . . in a matter of months. The government was entitled to allow a reasonable period to elapse before deciding whether the order had achieved its objective . . . Time would then be needed to implement any decision. I do not think the government could reasonably be expected to complete all these steps in six years, failing which it was in breach of Community law . . . I too would allow this appeal."

By contrast, the case-law of the Dutch Equal Treatment Commission could be cited as a model for dealing with objective justification and applying a strict standard of proportionality. We shall take as an example one of the cases which we have referred to above.

Equal Treatment Commission (Commissie Gelijke Behandeling) **3.NL.78.**[*]
Opinion 1996-56

WHETHER AN OCCUPATIONAL DOCTOR MAY BE DENIED WORKING TIME REDUCTION
FOR STUDY PURPOSES ON THE GROUNDS THAT SHE WORKS PART-TIME

GGD te Breda

Facts and *Held*: As may be remembered, the applicant, an occupational doctor, had been denied a reduction in working time in response to undertaking further training. The CGB had assumed that subjecting part-time employees to a detriment would disproportionately affect women. The thrust of the decision was thus on objective justification.

[*] See above **3.NL.62.**

Opinion: "4.10 The aim pursued by the respondent is to contribute to further training and studies of her staff, inter alia to such courses which are of relevance to the discharge of their duties. The Commission finds that this aim is free of any discrimination. The Commission establishes that the means employed by the respondent to achieve this aim include conferring advantages which differ for such civil servants who work less than 19 hours on the one hand and those who work between 19 and 31 hours or more on the other hand. The Commission considers that the defendant has established these rules in order to ensure the continuation of its services. The Commission finds it plausible that these means correspond to a real need on the part of the respondent.

As regards the suitability of the measure the Commission considers that the manner in which study leave is granted in itself enhances the availability of part time staff. The Commission thus finds that the measure may be suitable to achieve its aims. At the same time, the rules have the effect that civil servants working 32 or more hours a week de facto receive more compensation than those working less hours.

As regards the necessity of the measure, the Commission considers as follows. The defendant did not explain why the alternative rules proposed in the Order on Study Facilities 1998, which provides for equal treatment of full- and part timers *pro rata tempore*, cannot be applied in full and why it must necessarily be replaced by a rule which makes a distinction. The defendant has not given any reasons from which it expires that rule chosen . . .corresponds better to office requirements . . . The Commission concludes . . . that there is no objective justification and the respondent thus made an indirect distinction based on grounds of sex in granting study leaves which is in violation of the equal treatment legislation."

Note
The Commission actually applies a strict standard of proportionality. While not questioning the motives of the employer, it diligently examines its reasoning in order to find whether a less discriminatory alternative might be used to achieve these aims. It finds this alternative in a government order on study leave, which would provide for *pro rata tempore* working time reduction for any employee.

Labour Court (Arbetsdomstolen), 21 September 2005[212]   **3.SE.79.**[*]
Equal Opportunity Ombudsman (JämO) v. Teknikarbeitsgivarna and Volvo Car Co.

WHETHER REQUIRING A HEIGHT BETWEEN 163 AND 195 CM INDIRECTLY
DISCRIMINATES AGAINST WOMEN

Volvo

Facts and *Held*: The employer Volvo had actually introduced their height requirement for the following reasons. First, they wished to build rather large cars as these were very marketable. Secondly, the production stations thus required employees to reach up high, and this led to advice by the occupational doctor to employ only persons of a certain height.

[212] Case A 192/03, Judgment 87/05.
[*] See above **3.SE.59.**

Judgment: ". . . The employer parties believe that the height-requirement is appropriate for achieving the objective of reducing the risk of strain injuries. They further maintain that the requirement is necessary since there is no other way of achieving this objective.

The JämO has asserted that the height-requirement is inappropriate since it is too crude a criterion to fulfil its purpose of reducing strain injuries . . .

The examination of this disputed question consists, among other things, of the investigations that have been carried out, and the questioning of professors R.K. and J.F . . .,

R.K. has drawn the following conclusions . . . Work in the workshops entails the less tall operators and fitters (roughly in the range of 160-165 cm) being forced to adopt inappropriate working postures . . . In general, the working postures are not harmful in themselves unless they occur in conjunction with other aggravating circumstances, above all that of exposure for too long a period . . . It is not possible to say that the lower limit should be exactly 163 cm, but there is nothing that proves this is an unreasonable figure . . .

J.E. has commented on R.K.'s investigation. In the main, his conclusions are these. Current research in the field of ergonomics shows that there are many different causes for an employee to suffer strain injury. Many consider that the psycho-social causes are at least of equal importance as physical strains. It is important to lay out and organise a workplace in the best possible way from an ergonomic point of view. Only if that is inadequate, does it become a question of screening, i.e. of rejecting employees who run a greater risk than others of incurring an industrial injury. In a selection process of this kind it is appropriate to weigh up a number of factors, including age, height, muscular strength, body-weight, smoking habits, previous strain complaints, physical exercise and condition, illnesses, coordination and range of movement. Different factors have different degrees of importance. Through judicious assessment an employer has a greater chance of finding the most suitable workforce. Furthermore, in this way a better and more accurate assessment can be made of whether a particular employee runs the risk of incurring an industrial injury. A procedure of this kind should, in his view, lead to more women being considered for employment . . .

Seen in the light of the present evidence, it is undoubtedly the case that the Company's requirement for a specific height has been dictated by a genuine ambition to minimise the risk of strain-injuries among its employees.

The investigation shows that the disputed height-requirement began to be imposed during 2000 and that it applied to all three workshops. However, the investigation is not able to obtain any clear understanding of what more detailed considerations lie behind the requirement. E.Ö. and L.B., among others, have in general terms stated that the height-requirement was probably laid down after a recommendation from the Company's health department. Neither they nor anyone else questioned have been able to say why the lower limit of the height-requirement was fixed at 163 cm . . .

When considering the actual conditions within the Company it appears from the investigation that there are employees who are shorter than 163 cm. .. Employees C.S. and E.S., both of whom are shorter than 163 cm, have told us that for their part they have not experienced any work-tasks that have caused them physical complaints. R.J. has stated that ergonomic problems arise for the employees regardless of their height and that he has the impression that those problems occur to the same extent among those who are 170-180 cm tall as among those who are shorter . . .

In the opinion of the Labour Court, neither the evidence given nor anything else that has emerged from the enquiry gives an unambiguous picture of the importance of the height-requirement in reducing the risk of strain-injury among the workforce. The imposition of the lower limit of the height-requirement has a clearly negative effect on female job-seekers, who, if they do not meet this requirement, are automatically screened out and thus are wholly excluded from the opportunity to undergo further tests in the recruitment process. In the opinion of the court, the Company cannot be considered to have shown in a convincing manner, through the explanation that has been put forward, that the height-requirement was so appropriate and necessary a means of achieving the Company's objective, that the measure, despite its negative effect on women, should be regarded as permissible . . . By applying the height-requirement with respect to A-C.N. when she was seeking work with the Company, the Company has thus been guilty of indirect discrimination within the meaning of § 16 of the law on equal opportunity."

Notes

(1) The reasoning of the Swedish Labour Court sets standards in a careful application of the proportionality principle. The medical evidence for and against height requirements is carefully weighed. In particular, the Court stops short of requiring the employer to offer reasonable accommodation for employees shorter than 163 cm, for example by providing more job rotation possibilities or building smaller cars. Still, it achieves significantly more employment opportunities for those shorter than 163 cm.

(2) It should be noted that not only women, but also persons of specific ethnic origins, are within the group profiting from the relaxation of the height requirement. In the light of the relevance of height requirements for sex and ethnic discrimination, it is troubling that British legislation continues to provide an exception for height requirements for prison officers, thus establishing a permanent objective justification for indirect sex discrimination by a policy that was successfully challenged here (Section 18 Sex Discrimination Act).

3.5.2.C.   OBJECTIVE JUSTIFICATION—PRACTICAL EXAMPLES AND
                APPLICATION AT NATIONAL LEVEL

With the multiplying of grounds for discrimination, cases of indirect discrimination will also abound, and in these cases objective justification will become the most decisive part of the decisions. Thus, this section will attempt to analyse the cases discussed above in this respect, where the case did overcome the hurdle of establishing disparate impact. Case-law on objective justification will, however, remain a scattered area, especially at national level, until the field of non-discrimination law has settled down and established itself across the Member States.

ECONOMIC ARGUMENTS AS OBJECTIVE JUSTIFICATION

EC law

In some cases on indirect sex discrimination, the ECJ established the rule that Member States were banned from citing budgetary constraints as reasons for justifying indirectly discriminatory measures.[213] This line of case-law clearly has its origins in the case-law on the free movement provisions, where the Court has repeatedly held that Member States may not avoid their obligations under internal market law by reference to budgetary constraints.[214] As the internal market is the prime aim of the Community, which often needs to be pursued against the policies of Member States, one would assume that the Court would uphold this kind of argument strictly. However, not even in the law of the internal market is this the case, as the Court has accepted the closely related defences of "cohesion of a tax system"[215] or the "risk of seriously undermining the financial balance of the social security system".[216] Accordingly, one should not expect too much continuity in this area in relation to non-discrimination law, especially once it expands from sex equality to other equalities and is thus bound to affect an increasing number of national policy fields. In addition, this case-law had never been expanded to apply to economic actors. However, economic reasons to justify measures having a detrimental effect should be expected to be particularly difficult to be accepted as objective justifications. The reason for this is that any public or private body always has a variety of ways to cut costs, which in turn means that there will often be a less discriminatory alternative.

ECJ, 6 April 2000[217]   **3.EC.80.**

C—226/98, Birgitte Jørgensen v. Foreningen af Speciallæger (FS) and
Sygesikringens Forhandlingsudvalg (SF)

WHETHER FORCIBLE RECLASSIFICATION OF MEDICAL PRACTICES TO PART-TIME
FOLLOWING DECREASE OF TURNOVER INDIRECTLY DISCRIMINATES AGAINST
WOMEN

Jørgensen

Facts: The proceedings before the national court are between Ms. Jørgensen, a rheumatologist, and the Danish Association of specialised Medical Practitioners (FS) and the Health Insurance Negotiation Committee (SF). Ms. Jørgensen, as a member of FS, is bound by its agreements with SF as far as remuneration for treatments under the National Health Insurance is concerned, which in turn represents almost the only source of income from a medical practice in Denmark. The agreements between FS and SF distinguish between full-time practitioners and part-time special medical practitioners, the latter being engaged in another medical activity outside their practice, e.g. as hospital doctor. A 1990 agreement between SF and

---

[213] ECJ, Case C–343/92 (*Roks*) [1994] ECR I–571; ECJ, Case C–226/98, No. 35 subsq (*Jørgensen*) [2000] ECR I–2447, No. 39 subsq, ECJ, Case C–77/02 (*Steinicke*) [2003] ECR I–9027, No. 66; ECJ, Case C–4/02 (*Schönheit*) [2003] ECR I–12575.

[214] See, for example, ECJ, Case C–352/85 (*Bond van Adverteenders*) [1988] ECR 208, No. 34.

[215] ECJ, Case C–118/96 (*Safir*) [1998] ECR I–1897.

[216] ECJ, Case C–158/96 (*Kohll*) [1998] ECR I–1931.

[217] [2000] ECR I–2447.

453

FS had the explicit aim of reducing expenditure incurred by specialised medical practitioners. To that end, payments to such practitioners with above-average turnover were capped, and the activities of part-time medical practitioners were discouraged by a cap on their annual income of between 400,000 DKr and 500,000 DKr. At the same time, a reclassification scheme was introduced, enabling enforced reclassification of practices. Such practices the turnover of which fell below DKr 400,000 and 500,000 in a specific period were to be reclassified as part-time practices. While the individual doctors would remain able to raise their income, their practices upon sale would not be reclassified as full-time and any successor would be unable to earn more than DKr 500,000 annually. Ms. Jørgensen had always been a full-time practitioner, i.e. she had no income from another medical activity besides her practice. However, due to family commitments, her income in the decisive years for reclassification fell to 425,000 DKr. She maintains that the consequent reclassification of her practice to part-time frustrates her investments in her practice and endangers her income once she is retired, and considers that, since women are more often in her situation then men, the agreement constituted indirect discrimination in violation of either Directive 76/207/EEC on equal treatment of women and men in employment and occupation or Directive 86/613/EEC on equal treatment of self-employed women and men.

Held: Ms. Jørgensen has opposed the decision and unsuccessfully appealed to the Specialised Medical Practitioners Cooperation Committee for her district, upon which she raised proceedings before the Eastern Regional Court of Denmark (Østre Landsret). The Østre Landsret referred several questions to the ECJ. The ECJ held that, on the basis of the statistical evidence before it, disparate impact of the measure is established. Thus, objective justification became decisive in this case.

Judgment: "37 By its second question, the national court asks whether considerations relating to budgetary stringency, savings or medical practice planning may be regarded as objective considerations such as to justify a measure which adversely affects a larger number of women than men . . .

39 . . . It must be observed . . . that, although budgetary considerations may underlie a Member State's choice of social policy and influence the nature or scope of the social protection measures . . ., they do not in themselves constitute an aim pursued by that policy and cannot therefore justify discrimination against one of the sexes. Moreover, to concede that budgetary considerations may justify a difference in treatment between men and women which would otherwise constitute indirect discrimination on grounds of sex would mean that the application and scope of a rule of Community law as fundamental as that of equal treatment between men and women might vary in time and place according to the state of the public finances of Member States.

40. However, . . . reasons relating to the need to ensure sound management of public expenditure on specialised medical care and to guarantee people's access to such care are legitimate and may justify measures of social policy.

41 As Community law stands at present, social policy is a matter for the Member States, which enjoy a reasonable margin of discretion as regards the nature of social protection measures and the detailed arrangements for their implementation . . . If they meet a legitimate aim of social policy, are suitable and requisite for attaining that end and are therefore justified by reasons unrelated to discrimination on grounds of sex, such measures cannot be regarded as being contrary to the principle of equal treatment . . ."

ECJ, 23 October 2003   **3.EC.81.**[*]
C–4/02, C–5/02, *Hilde Schönheit* v. *Stadt Frankfurt a. M. and Sylvia Becker* v. *Land Hessen*

WHETHER DEGRESSIVELY REDUCING A PUBLIC SERVANT'S PENSION FOR YEARS
WORKED PART-TIME CONSTITUTES INDIRECT SEX DISCRIMINATION

Schönheit

Facts and *Held*: As may be recalled, the case concerned a pension abatement ("Versorgungsabschlag") to the disadvantage of public servants who had worked part-time or taken special leave for child care reasons, provided for by German law. The public servants affected were predominantly female.

Judgment: "75. By its third to ninth questions . . . the referring court is essentially asking, . . . in what conditions legislation (such as that at issue) . . . could be regarded as justified by objective factors unrelated to any discrimination on grounds of sex.

77 In the German Government's submission, reasons other than restricting public expenditure, which was the reason stated in the explanatory memorandum to the national legislation, are also capable of justifying indirect discrimination, the national court also being required to take into account reasons deriving from the broad logic of the provisions at issue . . .

84. It must be observed at the outset that the aim of restricting public expenditure, which, according to the national court, was invoked by the State when the pension abatement first become part of national law, cannot be relied on for the purpose of justifying a difference in treatment on grounds of sex.

85. The Court has already held that budgetary considerations cannot justify discrimination against one of the sexes. To concede that such considerations may justify a difference in treatment between men and women which would otherwise constitute indirect discrimination on grounds of sex would mean that the application and scope of a rule of Community law as fundamental as that of equal treatment between men and women might vary in time and place according to the state of the public finances of Member States . . .

86. However, a difference in treatment between men and women may be justified, depending on the circumstances, by reasons other than those put forward when the measure introducing the differential treatment was adopted.

87. It is for the Member State which has introduced such a measure, or the party to the main proceedings who invokes it, to establish before the national court that there are objective reasons unrelated to any discrimination on grounds of sex such as to justify the measure concerned . . . and they are not bound in that respect by the intention expressed when the measure was adopted.

88. The German Government submits that the pension abatement . . . is a corrective mechanism inherent in the pension scheme, whose aim is to prevent civil servants employed on a part time basis from being placed at an advantage by comparison with those employed on a full-time basis as a result of the operation of the earlier regressive pension scale . . .

96. The pension abatement does not actually ensure that that objective is achieved. As is clear from points 60 to 63 and point 100 of the Advocate General's Opinion, where, over their careers as a whole, a part time official and a full-time official have worked the same number of hours, application to the part time official of the pension abatement rule is liable to result in his

[*] See above **3.EC.49.**

being awarded a lower rate of pension than that awarded to the full-time official under the old version of Paragraph 14 of the BeamtVG. In fact, the effect of introducing the pension abatement was to curtail the advantages for part time officials of the regressive pension scale, whilst full-time officials continued to be able to enjoy those advantages, particularly if they liquidated their pension rights after the first years of service, giving higher annual pension entitlements than those awarded over subsequent years.

97. It follows from the foregoing considerations that the third to ninth questions must be answered as follows:—national legislation, such as that deriving from Paragraph 85 of the BeamtVG in conjunction with the old version of Paragraph 14 thereof, which has the effect of reducing a worker's retirement pension by a proportion greater than that resulting when his periods of part time work are taken into account cannot be regarded as objectively justified by the fact that the pension is in that case consideration for less work or on the ground that its aim is to prevent civil servants employed on a part time basis from being placed at an advantage in comparison with those employed on a full-time basis."

Notes on Jørgensen and Schönheit

(1) In both these cases the ECJ repeated the formula that budgetary restrictions are unable to objectively justify detrimental effect. The first argument given for this, that budgetary constraints will never be the sole motive of a national measure, is obviously aberrant in times of ever-shrinking public budgets. The second argument is the basis for the ECJ's strict approach towards budgetary constraints: the principle of equal treatment between women and men shall not be more effective in rich Member States or municipalities than in poor ones. Thus the ECJ seems to defend equal treatment as the sole strand of social policy the Community has consistently been able to claim as its own against being disrupted by increasing divergence of the Member States. The arguments in *Schönheit*, in addition, are one of the few examples where the ECJ has held that a national measure does not satisfy the requirement of necessity. The principle of budgetary restrictions not being able to justify disparate impact is thus upheld.

(2) However, by allowing objective justifications by reasons such as "sound management of budgetary expenditure", the Court has reopened the floodgates it had previously been closing. In practice, the question must always be whether a measure having a detrimental effect on persons who differ from others by virtue of a specific discrimination ground is the only way to achieve "sound management of budgetary expenditure" or whether there are (less discriminatory) alternatives.

National law

Obviously, under national law, any arguments as to the relative weaker position of a principle of equal treatment in different Member States do not apply. The question whether economic justifications are permitted boils down to two basic elements: (1) whether public (or private) entities are able to defend their autonomy in budgetary issues even against overriding aims of equal treatment law; and (2) whether there is a less discriminatory alternative of saving money, i.e. whether the policy is necessary.

Two cases from Finland and Germany respectively may serve as an illustration of these matters.

Finnish Supreme Court (Korkein Oikeus Högsta Domstolen),   3.FI.82.*
4 June 2004
Case 59/2004, Employees v. Town of Kajaani

INDIRECT DISCRIMINATION, LAYING OFF A SIGNIFICANT NUMBER OF STAFF

Kajaani

Facts and *Held*: This case concerned collective redundancies by the city of Kajaani which affected only two departments which were staffed predominantly with women. The Court had established detrimental effect to the disadvantage of women. The reasoning on objective justification was thus decisive for the result of the case, in which the Constitutional Court held that there was no unlawful discrimination.

Judgment: "10. The self-determination right of the county as regards its budget is an essential part of a self-governing municipality. However, the town of Kajaani cannot be released from the presumption of discrimination based only on the fact that the lay-offs directed at the female dominated basic social security sector have been founded on a mandatory budget. Therefore it is necessary to examine whether the grounds set for the savings aims as such to discriminate against a female dominated work sector or whether different actions have been implemented on different working sectors without any acceptable grounds.

11. First of all the town has indicated that the basic social security sector was the only working sector of the town which significantly exceeded its budget during the two previous years i.e. during 1997 and 1998. The need for savings had essentially been caused by the fact that the share by the state allocated to the town as regards its social and health sector had been reduced from 160 million Finnish marks to about 81 million marks per year during the period of 1993—1999. In addition the costs of the basic social security sector had exceeded the grounds of the calculated state share for the operating costs of the social and health care sector by about 10 percent. Based on the Act (Act on the planning of social and health care and the share of the state, Chapter 3), the size of the population, age structure and morbidity have already been included in the cost-calculation grounds. Exceeding the costs has meant that it has been necessary to cover a larger proportion than average of basic social security sector costs by using the town's own funds. The essential purpose of the savings target set for the basic social security sector in the Kajaani town budget has, in fact, been to set the costs at a level which would correspond to the calculated grounds accepted nationwide for the state share system. The validity of the aforementioned economic factors has not been disputed.

12. There have been no similar financial problems in the other working sectors of the town. Nor has it been shown that the town would have applied, or would in an equivalent financial situation have applied, any different practice as regards the staff of the other working sectors . . .

17. Therefore even though the savings operations were directed at some significantly female dominated working sectors at this time it cannot as such yet be considered discriminatory if objective grounds for the municipality management of the finances exist for this. In this case the town of Kajaani has shown such acceptable grounds for its action. The situation could be

* See above **3.FI.33.**

assessed differently if different actions were to be implemented without any objectively acceptable reason in another less female dominated or more male dominated working sector in an equal financial situation. There is nothing to indicate that the town would have treated different staff groups unfairly in this context.

18. The Supreme Court also considers that the lay-offs implemented in the basic social security sector of the town has not, particularly considering the duration of the laying off, been unreasonable as regards the aim set for the lay-offs nor unreasonable in comparison with the position of the staff in other working sectors.

19. Based on the aforementioned grounds the Supreme Court considers that the town of Kajaani has shown that its action has been based on acceptable grounds other than the gender of the laid off officials and workers in the basic social security sector."

Notes

(1) The reasoning of the Finnish Constitutional Court falls short of phrasing the issue of implementing a mandatory budget in the language of objective justification. The argument seems less convincing where the Court considers that the only threshold for the measure (laying off a significant number of women and thus reducing the proportion of female employees significantly) to be lawful is to avoid arbitrarily targeting a predominantly female work sector or favouring the other work sectors. Rather, it needs to be asked what exactly the aim of the measure is and whether this aim could have been achieved in a different way, rendering the lay-offs unnecessary.

(2) However, had the Court applied these principles, the result would not have been very different. The city implemented national measures on communal budgets. As it happened—and was typical for Eastern Germany and other parts of the former "Eastern Bloc"—these measures targeted social services and were aimed at spending less money in this field. Unsurprisingly, these measures disproportionately endangered female employment. The question before the city was whether they could counteract the discriminatory effects of these national requirements, possibly by rearranging the gender composition of their staff in different departments prior to downsizing the social services. However, indirect discrimination law does not require employers to undertake such proactive measures. The correct addressee for this indirect discrimination claim was thus not the City of Kajaani, but rather the author of the "Act on the planning of social and health care and the share of the state, Chapter 3".

(3) The case has been compared to the German Federal Labour Court decision to introduce mandatory part-time employment in a predominantly female sector of Hamburg education services above (**3.DE.34.**). As the Federal Labour Court did not find detrimental effect in this case, the question of objective justification did not arise. This is all the more regrettable, as this would have been a case where the body against which the action was directed (i.e. the City of Hamburg) had more leeway in responding to budgetary constraints established by the obligation on municipalities to provide "kindergarten" education for each child from the age of three. The City would have had to prove that there was no other way than reducing the working time of pre-school teachers to gather enough funds. This would possibly have been

difficult. It should be added, however, that such litigation strategies are without precedent as yet.

Federal Labour Court (BAG), 26 January 2005[218]   **3.DE.83.**
4 AZR 509/03, Anonymous

WHETHER REDUCING WAGES IN A PREDOMINANTLY FEMALE SECTOR IN ORDER TO
AVOID OUTSOURCING AMOUNTS TO INDIRECT SEX DISCRIMINATION

Diakonisches Werk

Facts: The defendant is a member of the "Diakonische Werk", an organisation within the Protestant church the purpose of which is to offer charitable social services. The "Diakonische Werk" had established a new remuneration system that resulted in the establishment of a new wage group range "W" for untrained workers in auxiliary departments at the defendant's hospital. Most of these departments comprise "domestic services". The proportion of women among the untrained staff is much higher than that of men. Those affected by the measures were previously paid under wage group range "H", as were other untrained workers which were not from auxiliary but from main departments. The applicant was employed as an untrained worker. Prior to the changes, she was allocated to the wage group H2 and re-allocated to the wage group range W, resulting in loss of income. She claimed that establishing this specific "light work wage group" amounted to indirect discrimination on grounds of sex.

Held: Her claim was dismissed by the Court of First Instance and the Regional Labour Court. The Federal Labour Court dismissed her appeal. The Federal Labour Court assessed the claim as an equal pay claim. This did not exactly meet the claimant's argument, though. She argued that establishing a new wage group disparately impacts upon women, which could be read as meaning that rearranging wage groups to introduce more differentiation than before has a negative effect on the working conditions of women predominantly. After rebutting her equal pay claim for want of a comparator, the Federal Labour Court assumed that her labour was of equal value with all other employees in her former wage group in order to deliberate whether the measure would be discriminatory.

Judgment: "Even if it is assumed that within the group of cleaning personnel under wage group W the number of female workers is significantly higher than in other group of workers . . . there is no indirect discrimination on grounds of sex. (referring to ECJ case-law and concluding, that the case would turn on objective justification). The purpose of introducing wage group W . . . is stated in the introduction to the wage group regulation. Its aim is to create a remuneration rate close enough to its equivalent system in commercial enterprises to avoid outsourcing of sectors from the "Diakonische Werk" in the future. This danger does not exist as regards other workers. Introducing wage group range W was thus meant to maintain jobs within economic sectors within the Diakonische Werk. Any suspicion that this is not the real aim of the measures is misplaced. In addition, the introduction of wage group range 'W' is suitable and necessary to achieve that aim. The resulting cost reductions diminish the motive to reduce costs by way of outsourcing . . . There is no sign of misuse of the measure. The introduction of wage group range 'W' is thus justified by objective factors unrelated to sex . . . There is no indirect discrimination on grounds of sex."

---

[218] Juris database (partly parallel decision to BAG 4 AZR 171/03, BAGE 113, 276–90).

Note

This is a set of facts where budgetary measures were indeed not an aim in themselves, but had another motive rooted in the charitable character of the "Diakonische Werk". The economic reasoning of the organization was such that unfortunately their predominantly female staff was earning more than in commercial enterprises, which in turn led to budgetary pressures as the "Diakonische Werk" is not only working in a charitable way, but in fact dependent on winning public tenders, often in competition with commercial organizations. The idea was to retain the employees within the "community". This seems to be a set of facts beyond the reach of indirect discrimination law, although the resulting wage reduction mirrors the weaker market position of female labour under the reality of structural wage discrimination.

OBJECTIVE JUSTIFICATION IRRESPECTIVE OF "GROUNDS", TRULY NEUTRAL JUSTIFICATIONS

As has been said, while the original case-law definition of indirect discrimination was insistent upon the justification being unrelated to the discrimination ground, this detail is missing from the younger EC Directives. The purpose of the Directives would, however, suggest that, in order to be truly neutral, justifications should not refer (directly or indirectly) to the ground in question. This reading is supported by the usage of the term "objective justification", which implies that the justification must also be neutral in relation to the discrimination grounds. The decisions discussed in this section illustrate the difficulties of achieving this aim. At the same time, they comprise cases on "new grounds", in contrast to the overwhelming presence of sex discrimination in the foregoing sections.

Headscarf cases

Appeal Court of Antwerp (Hof van Bewep, Antwerpen),   **3.BE.84.**[*]
14 June 2005[219]
9 appellants v. *Provincial Administration of Limburg*

PROHIBITING WEARING ANY HEAD-COVERINGS AS INDIRECT DISCRIMINATION ON
GROUNDS OF RELIGION

Headscarf—Belgian school

Facts and *Held*: The Provincial Commercial College in Hasselt issued rules on manners, attitude and behaviour, according to which pupils may not wear head-coverings in the classroom, in the study room or in the dining hall. Twenty girls of Islamic faith attended the school, of whom 10 originally objected to the rule, while only four refused to sign a letter saying that they agreed to these conditions and were thus prevented

---

[219] AR/2004/2811.
[*] See above **3.BE.69.**

from attending classes. The Court held that imposing a ban on wearing headscarves in such a way disparately impacts upon Muslim girls, but is objectively justified and thus not discriminatory.

Judgment: "A ban on headscarves must therefore be permitted under three conditions: Firstly,
it must be based on a general rule that is sufficiently clear and accessible, secondly, it must
pursue an objective of general interest or the protection of the rights of others, finally, it must
be a measure that is not more restrictive than is necessary in order to achieve this objective, in
other words, it must meet the requirements for proportionality.

Whereas it is not disputed that the rules in question of the Provincial Commercial College
are general (in the sense that they apply to all pupils) clear and accessible; it is also clear that
the ban on head scarves was introduced as a result of the disruption arising in the school at the
end of 2003 as a result of militant action by a number of Muslim girls, who moreover form a
minority within the group of girls that are of the Muslim faith; in this case, they acted not only
provocatively towards the teaching body, who according to newspaper articles submitted by the
respondent (Het Belang van Limburg of 14 November 2003 and 9 December 2003, and De
Weekkrant) was accused of giving less good marks on racist grounds to girls who wore a head
scarf, but also with regard to other Muslim girls who support more discrete behaviour; it may
and must therefore be assumed that the head scarf, the conduct of the appellants or their
daughters apart, in the specific context of the Provincial Commercial College gave cause for
serious disruption or disturbance of the normal course of educational activities and that the
general ban on head coverings is therefore justified; the conduct of certain persons may after
all appear as a provocation to other religious convictions and other Muslim girls who are
progressive or less conservative; the head scarf ban, which is in fact expressly limited to the
classroom, the study room and dining hall, is chiefly directed at the excessive behaviour that
disturbs the peace and quiet in the school and teaching, and is aimed at ensuring peaceful
CoExistence of different cultures and beliefs in the school; any excess is the expression of
provocation, rejection of others, and denial of the educational project aimed at preparing
pupils for an active social life;

Such integration does not militate against a belief in a particular God or religion or in
another philosophical conviction, nor does it imply that a particular religious or philosophical
conviction is treated in a more undervalued way; the neutrality of the education provided by
the Provincial Commercial College must be regarded as respect for the variety of attitudes to
life, but is not a green light for any behaviour that may disrupt the educational activities or
encroach on the dignity or the freedom of other members of the college community; neutrality
within the meaning of "secular attitudes" requires an effort both by the religions and as such
from every individual; within the framework of neutral education, some distance must be
allowed from religious tradition without this entailing self-denial; the limited ban on
headscarves introduced by the respondent is therefore justified both objectively and reasonably
and shows no token of any arbitrariness, so that a cease and desist order is or would be
unfounded in any event; . . ."

Notes

(1) The Court accepts the reasoning that a ban on headscarves had to be
introduced to avoid disruption arising in the school. The girls were accused of
accusing a teacher of lowering their marks because they wore the headscarf, and they
were also accused of bullying other girls of Muslim faith who did not wear their
headscarves to school. The Court also considered that by limiting the ban to
certain rooms, even though these were rooms that none of the pupils and teachers

could avoid, the school remained within the boundaries of the principle of proportionality.

(2) This is an example of where the reasoning would have profited from applying the rule that the objective justification must not be connected with the forbidden ground in question. While the Court considered Muslim girls as the specifically protected group, the objective justification is linked to behaving like a conservative or even fundamentalist Muslim woman. In addition, there might be a case of victimisation: the girls were reproached for complaining about discriminatory marks.

(3) This critical assessment does not mean that a specific school policy on dress codes or even a school uniform, which inter alia aims at integrating persons of different ethnic and religious background, can never be justified. Any clothing policy will disparately impact upon women and girls, because women and girls are subjected to more rules on their outer appearance than men and boys. They are thus more likely to be subjected to conflicting rules. However, a carefully weighed dress code or a widely discussed school uniform could be defended as a means to establish the opportunity of accommodating different groups. In addition, minimum communicative standards could be cited. The recent decision of the House of Lords in *S.B.*, which was not argued as a discrimination case, but rather on religious freedom,[220] may serve as an example. The school had refused to admit a pupil to class wearing a full-length jilbab, i.e. a garment covering the person from head to toe. The basis of this refusal was a school uniform which had been established by a working party, in which all ethnic and religious groups in the school's catchment area had been involved. The purposes of maintaining a school uniform had included serving the needs of a diverse community, promoting a positive sense of communal identity and avoiding manifest disparities of wealth and style. Such a policy could objectively justify disparate impact of the uniform on Muslim girls, or even be accepted as proportionate positive action.

Headscarf—employment agency, restaurant   3.NL.85–3.NL.86[*]

Additional note re neutral justifications
Both the Dutch cases, mentioned above as excerpts **3.NL.65.** and **3.NL.66.**, were less spectacular, as the defendants had not brought forward any arguments justifying their policy. The employment agency was of the opinion that acquiescing in the wishes of their clients by not sending employees with headscarves was better for all parties, and was not aware of this being discriminatory. The owner of the restaurant relied on the reasoning that it was up to her to determine who enters her restaurant, which could not qualify as objective justification.

---

[220] *R (On the Application of S.B)* v. *Headteacher, Governors of Denbigh High School* [2006] All ER 487.
[*] See above **3.NL.65. and 3.NL.66.** respectively.

Neutral justifications in relation to ethnic origin—language requirements

Equal Treatment Commission (*Commissie Gelijke Behandeling*)   3.NL.87.[*]
Opinion 2004-143

WHETHER REQUIRING AN EMPLOYEE FOR TELEPHONE MARKETING TO SPEAK
DUTCH WITHOUT A FOREIGN ACCENT CONSTITUTES INDIRECT RACIAL
DISCRIMINATON

Telephone marketing

Facts and *Held*: The applicant was denied a position as telephone marketer on the grounds that he spoke Dutch with a foreign accent. The CGB concluded that there was indirect discrimination. However, the reasoning showed that it also considered that there could be a justification for such a business practice.

Opinion: "In this regard, the suitability of the requirement will be questioned insofar as there must be no suspicion that the applicant was not rejected on criteria other than such as are connected with his future function. In this case this would have required that one could establish the use of Dutch without a foreign accent as urgent requirement for the adequate functioning of the undertaking. The defendant has not submitted facts to establish this."

Labour Court (*Arbetsdomstolen*), 4 December 2002   3.SE.88.[**]
Case 128/2002, Ombudsman ethnic discrimination (DO) v. *Tjänsföretagens
Arbetsgivarförbund and GfK Sv. Aktiebolag*

WHETHER REQUIRING A TELEPHONE INTERVIEWER TO SPEAK SWEDISH
WITHOUT A FOREIGN ACCENT AMOUNTS TO INDIRECT DISCRIMINATION ON
GROUNDS OF RACE

Telephone interviewer

Facts and *Held*: An applicant was denied a job as a telephone interviewer, also on the grounds that she had a foreign accent. The Labour Court found in favour of the employee, but rather on the burden of proof:

Judgment: "The Labour Court finds that there is, prima facie, an objective justification that a company that carries out market-research surveys requires that its telephone interviewers have a good knowledge of the Swedish language and are able to express themselves in clear and comprehensible manner. As has been touched on in the foregoing, it is very probable that Susanna D's accent was one reason for the company's failure to complete the recruitment process, that is to say that during the recruitment process the company formed the opinion that Susanna D did not meet the linguistic requirement to a reasonable extent. However, the employer parties did not, in the case, raise any objection that is founded on this standpoint. In

---

[*] See above **3.NL.67.**
[**] See above **3.SE.68.**

other words, they have not challenged the DO's statement that Susanna D fulfilled to a reasonable extent the requirement for clear and correct Swedish."

Note on language cases

As has been said, in both these cases one could doubt whether they were about direct or indirect discrimination cases. The suspicious absence of any comprehensive argument about objective justification confirms this view. However, the judgments also show that while the correctness of language may be demanded, a language requirement must not go over and above what is needed for the employment in question.

Neutral justification in relation to different grounds with contradictory results

For objective justification to indeed be objective it would seem necessary that the concept is used consistently in respect of different grounds. This requirement is, of course, linked to the approach defended earlier that "objective justification" in indirect discrimination cases serves to rebut a presumption of discrimination and thus to establish causation. If that is so, this leaves no room to differentiate in "objective justification". If, on the other hand, one follows the opposing view, which will ultimately conflate direct and indirect discrimination into one concept, different standards of justification for grounds can be justified in line with different degrees of "suspectness".[221] Under the approach defended here, such differentiations are not justifiable.

There are two German cases which are illustrative for this not always being the case. Both cases concern the question whether collective agreement clauses on reduction in working time based on age are indirectly discriminatory. Reduction in working time based on age has been introduced in order to allow older employees to phase out from working life in an economically comfortable way, while ensuring that the reduction in working time is used to reduce unemployment. The legislation devised a complicated system of funding reduced working time in connection with an obligation on the employer to take on an unemployed person to make up for the reductions. For the employee, reduced working time on grounds of age resulted in fewer working hours for the same income. In order to avoid unwelcome side effects, legislation or collective agreements implementing the relevant legislation excluded any employees who had a claim to a statutory pension. This applied to women and disabled persons who could claim statutory pension at the age of 60 instead of 65.

---

[221] See Gerards, above n. 14.

Federal Labour Court (BAG)[222]   **3.DE.89.**[*]
9 AZR 750/00, An applicant v. A defendant

WHETHER EXCLUDING FROM THE RIGHT TO REDUCE WORKING TIME UPON
REACHING THE AGE OF 60 SUCH EMPLOYEES AS CAN CLAIM A PENSION IS INDIRECT
SEX DISCRIMINATION

Old-age working time reduction

Facts and *Held*: As may be recalled, the parties disagree on the claimant's entitlement to reduced working hours based on age. The relevant collective agreement grants employees upon their 60th, 61st or 62nd birthday a right to additional releases from work for each year following their 60th birthday, if these employees had been working for the same employer for 12 years or longer. The entitlement to additional holidays is excluded for any employee who is able to claim an early retirement pension. The Court had established that this requirement disparately impacts on women. The Court did not accept the numerous arguments advanced as objective justification, and held that this measure was indeed indirectly discriminatory.

Judgment: ". . . c) The Regional Labour Court basically justified the . . . exclusion . . . by referring to the law relating to pensions. If the different pensionable age for men and women is acceptable according to the constitution, this should also be true for the industry-wide collective agreement . . . The Senate which is solely responsible for the law regarding reduction in working hours based on age does not recognise this. § 3 II Para. 2 N. 2 MTV disadvantages older women because of their sex . . . it is recognised that rules relating to labour law which are related to state pension law and the different pensionable ages which are laid down in it, can be justified . . . it is therefore not excluded as a matter of principle that the fact that women enjoy advantages from the point of view of social law is a disadvantage from the point of view of labour law. The legal reason for permissible different treatment of men and women is therefore not only reference to the rule under social law and the fact that it accords with the constitution. The decisive factor is rather if there is a relationship between the performance due from the employer and the pension rights of the employee referred to which exists in fact. A decision is made in this regard based on the aim which is followed with the performance of the employer . . . The additional paid release from work which is owed by the employer as from completion of the 60th year of life is intended to reflect the fact that the employee is only capable of reduced working performance as from completion of the 60th year of life. The employee is granted additional free time above and beyond the 30 days allowed by the wage tariff in order that he or she can recover from the stresses associated with work. This need for recovery exists for all older employees who work beyond the 60th year of life. The right to claim a pension does not change this. The reduction in working hours based on age does not serve to compensate for economic disadvantage resulting from loss of employment."

Note

The main question in this judgment was whether the disparately impacting measure was objectively justified. The Court considered that differences in statutory pension age as such were no justification, as the purposes of social security law and employment law, here in the form of a collective agreement, were different. It then

---

[222] BAGE 102, 269.
[*] See above **3.DE.53.**

went on to consider how to establish objective justification. The starting point is, according to the Court, the aim of the rule in question, which is found to be offering compensation for having become less resistant to stress during a long working life which was spent to a large extent with this specific employer. The Court then considered whether this aim could be better achieved better when treating those able to claim a pension differently to those who were not. The Court finds in the negative.

Federal Labour Court (BAG)[223]   **3.DE.90.**[*]
9 AZR 122/03, Anonymous

WHETHER DENYING PART-TIME WORK ON GROUNDS OF AGE TO A DISABLED PERSON
ENTITLED TO A PENSION IS INDIRECT DISCRIMINATION

60 years pension and part-time—disabled persons

Facts: The parties are in dispute on the applicant's entitlement to a reduction in working time on grounds of age. His application was rejected on the grounds that he was entitled to a full pension at the age of 60 due to his severe disability. The collective agreement, which corresponds with numerous similar agreements, relies on Section 5 of the Partial Retirement Act according to which the Federal Employment Agency does not fund age-induced part-time working when the beneficiary is entitled to a full pension. Again, the reason behind this is the assumption that age-induced part-time working should establish an additional incentive to leave one's position on the labour market prematurely, which is not necessary when one is entitled to a full pension.

Held: The court held that there was no indirect discrimination, as the rule was objectively justified.

Judgment: "60 b) In comparison with other employees without severe disabilities, the applicant has been treated differently. In contrast to these other employees, the applicant has no entitlement to semi-retirement beyond the age of 60 . . .

61 The refusal to conclude a contract on semi-retirement which will be effective until the regular statutory retirement age, although similar agreements have been concluded with other employees, is, however, not directly attributed to the fact that the applicant is severely disabled . . . The provision may, however, lead to a severely disabled person being subjected to a specific detriment. Therefore it constitutes indirect discrimination in the sense of Article 2 Paragraph 2 letter b) i) of the Framework Directive [Directive 2000/78/EC—added by translator for clarity].

62 According to this provision, a prohibited indirect discrimination occurs where an employee is indirectly disadvantaged "on grounds of his disability", insofar as this disadvantage can not be objectively justified by a legitimate aim and insofar as the means of achieving this aim are appropriate and necessary. This is implemented by section 81 subsection 2 sentence 2 no. 1 sentence 3 1st alternative SGB IX. This provision stipulates that such cases of indirect disadvantage are permissible, if and insofar as there are 'objective reasons' not related to the disability that justify the unequal treatment.

63 c) Such objective reasons do exist in this case

68 (1) The parties to the collective labour agreement invoke section 5 subsection 1 no. 2 of the Altersteilzeitgesetz (Partial Retirement Act, abbr. AltTZG or ATG), which regulates the

---

[223]   BAGE 108, 133.
[*]   See above **3.DE.53.**

question in which cases semi-retirement can no longer be funded by the Bundesanstalt für Arbeit (Federal Institute for Employment, abbr. BA). This rule must be understood within the framework of the ATG in its entirety, which not only looks to promote and encourage the smooth transition of older employees into retirement (section 1 subsection 1 ATG) but also seeks to actively combat unemployment (cf. Bundestag, Drucksache (Federal Parliament, Document no.) 13/4336 pg. 25 and following) Hence, any funding by the BA under the ATG requires that the employer takes on a new employee (section 3 subsection 1 no. 2 ATG). The demarcation of the prerequisites for funding in accordance with ATG therefore serves to encourage employment. This purpose of the legislation may constitute an objective justification for indirect discrimination, if and when the principle of equal treatment is not eroded as a result. For this reason it is not sufficient to proffer mere assertions that a rule is designed to encourage employment. There have to be specific indications which can reasonably justify the assumption that the selected means are appropriate for achieving this aim.

69 (2) The promotion of semi-retirement by the ATG objectively serves the aim of stimulating new employment. The legislation expressly requires the taking on new employees as a prerequisite of the semi-retirement being funded. It can therefore reasonably be assumed that the collectively agreed rules are appropriate for the realisation of this goal of encouraging the appointment of new employees.

70 There is also an internal connection between this aim and the withdrawal of funding for the employees who are entitled to claim maximum old-age pension. This funding is aimed to encourage the dismissal of employees in a socially acceptable way. Additional support during the time in which an employee is entitled to claim maximum old-age pension benefits, and who is therefore adequately protected by the social security system, encourages the employee to remain on the labour market until a higher pensionable age has been reached. This would contradict the aim of stimulating employment by enabling the appointment of new employees as quickly as possible in accordance with the principles of social contract and would be 'counterproductive' with regard to the use of the available social benefits. Overall it is of great significance that the social protection of severely disabled persons is provided on their part from public funds and on the basis of a rule that balances the disadvantages connected with their disabilities in working life and on the employment market with premature social security benefits."

Note

The court considers that the parties to the collective agreement rightly supported the specific legislation's general aim. This decision by the Federal Labour Court must also be seen as a response to the ECJ judgment in *Kutz-Bauer*.[224] Upon reference of the Hamburg Labour Court, the ECJ had held that excluding part-time employees from old-age part-time work could be justified if the measure was indeed proportionate. Explicitly, the Court stated:

"It follows . . . mere generalisations concerning the capacity of a specific measure to encourage recruitment are not enough to show that the aim of the disputed provisions is unrelated to any discrimination based on sex or to provide evidence on the basis of which it could reasonably be considered that the means chosen are or could be suitable for achieving that aim."

It is left to the reader's judgement whether the Federal Labour Court in this case goes beyond "mere generalisations" in its argument.

[224] ECJ, Case C–187/00 [2003] ECR I–2741.

3.5.2.D.   COMPARABILITY OF SITUATIONS AS A NEW AND SPECIAL HURDLE

Another way of depriving the prohibition of indirect discrimination of its effectiveness is to reintroduce the concept of comparability, which is, according to the younger Directives' definition, only applicable in cases of direct discrimination. Here, we shall consider two decisions of the ECJ.

Also in the area of dismissal, but dealing with a redundancy payment and thus pay, the Court had to decide on differentiation between persons serving with the armed forces and those taking parental leave upon reference of the Austrian Federal Court in *Österreichischer Gewerkschaftsbund* (ÖGB).

ECJ, 8 June 2004[225]   **3.EC.91.**
C–220/02 Österreichischer Gewerkschaftsbund, Gewerkschaft der
Privatangestellten v. *Wirtschaftskammer Österreich*

ÖGB—parental leave and military service

Facts: Under Austrian legislation, each employee who is dismissed without his or her fault is entitled to a redundancy payment, the amount of which is calculated in accordance to length of service. Services in the armed forces, during which the employment relationship in civilian life is stalled, count towards the calculation of redundancy payments. This is also true for services performed on a non-compulsory basis, which is a possibility for women and men alike. Maternity leave, which is obligatory under Austrian law, is also taken into account. However, voluntary parental leave, which is used by mothers instead of fathers in most cases, is not.

Held: Upon a collective claim by the ÖGB (Austrian Trade Union Congress), the national court referred to the ECJ the question whether the differentiation between military services (obligatory or not) and obligatory maternity leave on the one hand and parental leave on the other hand constituted indirect gender discrimination. Again, the case turned on objective justification.

Judgment: "59 As regards the question put by the national court concerning the difference in treatment, from the point of view of termination payments, between workers who take parental leave and those who perform military or civilian service, it must be recalled that the principle of equal pay enshrined in Article 141 EC and Directive 75/117, like the principle of non-discrimination of which it is a specific expression, assumes that the male and female workers whom it benefits are in comparable situations . . .

60 In the present case, parental leave is leave taken voluntarily by a worker in order to bring up a child. The voluntary nature of such leave is not lost because of difficulties in finding appropriate structures for looking after a very young child, however regrettable such a situation may be. Parental leave does not have the same purpose as maternity leave; it is regulated by different legislation, and may moreover be taken at periods other than those following maternity leave.

61 The performance of national service, on the other hand, corresponds to a civic obligation laid down by law and is not governed by the individual interests of the worker. The constraint imposed in the public interest on the contract of employment is of a general nature, whatever the size of the undertaking and the employee's length of service may be.

---

[225] [2004] ECR I–5907.

62 In the context of national service, the person called up is at the disposal of the armed forces, at a time which he does not choose. The specific character of the obligation to do military service has, moreover, led the Court to rule that Community law does not preclude that obligation being reserved, in a Member State, to men (the *Dory* judgment).

63 The circumstance that that service can be extended voluntarily does not deprive it of its character or change its purpose. Even though the extension of military service rests on a voluntary basis, such an extension is still dictated by the satisfaction of a requirement of a public nature by virtue of the APSG, which makes the possibility of extension subject to military requirements (Paragraph 8 of the APSG and Paragraphs 19, 20, 23 and 37 of the Wehrgesetz).

64 In each case, the suspension of the contract of employment is thus based on particular reasons, more precisely the interests of the worker and family in the case of parental leave and the collective interests of the nation in the case of national service. As those reasons are of a different nature, the workers who benefit are not in comparable situations.

65 Accordingly, the answer to Questions 2 and 3 must be that Article 141 EC and Directive 75/117 do not preclude the calculation of a termination payment from taking into account, as length of service, the duration of periods of military service or the civilian equivalent performed mainly by men but not of parental leave taken most often by women."

Note

This time, the ECJ seemed to revive a feminist classic, the differentiation between private and public interest, considering that military and civilian services, even if done voluntarily, are in the public interest, whereas taking leave to spend more time with one's child is a private affair. Following AG Kokott, the Court did not frame its findings in the language of objective justification. Instead, it focused on the argument that workers performing military or civilian services and those taking parental leave were not in a comparable situation. It thus introduced a third step into the two-tier test of indirect discrimination, i.e. the question whether the two groups were in a comparable situation.

A similar reasoning was applied in *Wippel*.

ECJ, 12 October 2004[226]   **3.EC.92.**
Case C–313/02, Wippel v. Peek and Cloppenburg

LEGISLATION PROVIDING FOR MINIMUM AND MAXIMUM WORKING
TIME—EXCEPTION FOR PART-TIME

Wippel

Facts: The claimant was employed as an on-call employee with the defendant. The contract of employment did not provide a minimum or maximum weekly working time or a maximum time frame in which to achieve any average working time. In line with the business of the defendant, the claimant was working less and less. She claims back pay.

---

[226] [2004] ECR I–9483.

Held: There is no indirect discrimination, as the on-call worker is not comparable with a normal worker.

Judgment: "52 By the third question the referring court is asking . . . whether . . . Articles 2(1) and 5(1) of Directive 76/207 must be construed as precluding a contract for part-time employment . . . under which weekly working time and the organisation of working time are not fixed but are dependent on quantitative requirements in terms of the work to be performed, which are to be determined on a case-by-case basis, with the workers concerned having the choice to accept or refuse such work.

53 That question is raised in the circumstances of the main proceedings in which . . . Ms. Wippel's contract of employment ought in her view to have contained a clause stipulating a fixed weekly working time with a predetermined salary, whether the person concerned had or had not worked for the whole of that working time.

. . .

55 Secondly . . . national provisions discriminate indirectly against women where, although worded in neutral terms, they operate to the disadvantage of a much higher percentage of women than men, unless that difference in treatment is justified by objective factors unrelated to any discrimination on grounds of sex. The same is true of a contract of employment such as that in the main proceedings.

56 The prohibition on discrimination enunciated in the abovementioned provisions is merely a particular expression of a fundamental principle of Community law, namely the general principle of equality under which comparable situations may not be treated differently unless the difference is objectively justified (see Case C–381/99 *Brunnhofer* [2001] ECR I–4961, paragraph 28, and Case C–320/00 *Lawrence and Others* [2002] ECR I–7325, paragraph 12). That principle can therefore apply only to persons in comparable situations (Joined Cases C–122/99 P and C–125/99 P *D and Sweden* v *Council* [2001] ECR I–4319, paragraph 48).

57 Accordingly, it must first be examined whether a contract of part-time employment according to need . . . results in less favourable treatment of a worker such as Ms. Wippel than of full-time workers in a situation comparable to hers . . .

. . .

59 A part-time employee working according to need, such as Ms. Wippel, works under a contract which stipulates neither the weekly hours of work nor the manner in which working time is to be organised, but it leaves her the choice of whether to accept or refuse the work offered by P&C. The work is remunerated by the hour only for hours actually worked.

60 A full-time worker works under a contract which fixes a working week of 38.5 hours, fixing the organisation of the working week and salary, and which requires him to work for P&C for the whole working time thus determined without the possibility of refusing that work even if the worker cannot or does not wish to do it.

61 Under those circumstances, the employment relationship referred to in the preceding paragraph hereof differs, as to subject-matter and basis, from that of a worker such as Ms. Wippel. It follows that no full-time worker in the same establishment has the same type of contract or employment relationship as Ms. Wippel. It is apparent from the file that in the circumstances of the main proceedings, the same is true of all the full-time workers, in respect of whom the applicable collective agreement provides for a working week of 38.5 hours.

62 In the circumstances of the main proceedings, there is therefore no full-time worker comparable to Ms. Wippel . . . It follows that a contract of part-time employment according to need which makes provision for neither the length of weekly working time nor the organisation of working time does not result in less favourable treatment within the meaning of Clause 4 of the Framework Agreement."

Opinion: AG KOKOTT: "2. Prohibition of discrimination on grounds of sex

90. If one accepts the view of the referring court, Austrian law affords different treatment to full-time and part time workers. By providing for normal working time of 40 hours a week and eight hours a day, Paragraph 3 AZG makes specific provision for full-time workers without including any provision—even of subsidiary application—on working time for part timers.

91. The wording of the AZG is gender neutral in this respect. It is well settled, however, that where national rules, although worded in neutral terms, work to the disadvantage of a much higher percentage of persons of one sex, they constitute indirect discrimination unless that difference in treatment is justified by objective factors unrelated to any discrimination on grounds of sex. 92. According to the information provided by the referring court, full-time workers in Austria are made up of approximately 60% men and 40% women whilst 90% of part timers are women and only 10% are men. The absence of a provision on working time for part time workers—even of subsidiary application—therefore has a considerably greater impact on women than on men.

93. As the Commission rightly states, however, full-time workers and part time workers are not at all comparable in this specific context. As far as the amount of working time is concerned, full-time work in Austria is quite impervious to individual contractual provision: the number of hours to be worked is determined according to normal statutory working time under Paragraph 3 AZG (or any more favourable provision in a collective agreement). Part time employment, on the other hand, presupposes a contractual agreement on working time, whether in the form of a fixed number of regular hours or in the form of a variable number of hours according to the concept of work on demand."

Note

This is, with all respect to the learned jurists at the ECJ, erroneous. One of the decisive differences between the prohibition of direct discrimination and indirect discrimination is that in the first case the impact is on different treatment (and thus allows for the introduction of a comparator or the test of comparable situations) and in the latter case the emphasis is on effects (and thus there is no place to introduce comparator arguments). Introducing the category of comparability into the indirect discrimination test conflates the two and is dogmatically unsound.[227]

3.5.2.E.   ASSESSMENT

The possibility of objectively justifying a neutral measure which disparately impacts on those deemed to be members of a specific group has not yet been carved out satisfactorily in the ECJ case-law. Unsurprisingly, national case-law differs on the matter. The decisive measure to achieve the aims of non-discrimination law is to apply a strict standard, while allowing enough leeway for business needs to be advanced.

---

[227] The same position is taken in Barnard and Hepple (2000 above n. 21) 570.

3.6. COMPARATIVE ANALYSIS

3.6.1. INDIRECT DISCRIMINATION LAW BETWEEN LEGAL TRANSPLANT AND IUS COMMUNE

By sampling and evaluating a massive amount of Community law and national material, this chapter has at least proved that indirect discrimination law is a complex area and far from being consolidated. It is difficult as yet to assess whether indirect discrimination law, often viewed as "legal transplant", will truly take hold in all the national legal orders within the Community. Only when this has been achieved, will all the different emanations of the concept in national law start to influence each other and the concept gradually develop into an integral part of the *"ius commune"*. As said in the beginning, it is not only due to restricted language abilities that only few legal orders were presented in this chapter. The other reason is that most Member States which have already implemented Directives 2000/43/EC and 2000/78/EC have done so by repeating the relevant definitions word for word. This has led to reducing differences in the wording of some statutory clauses at the expense of other phrasings which may have been less narrowly focused.

Indirect discrimination law, however, is not only a "legal transplant" from the Anglo-American legal culture. Its roots in international law at worldwide and European level point towards a conceptual background slightly different from the Community legislative framework. International human rights committees tend to stress the notion of discriminatory effects instead of developing methods of establishing disparate impact, at the same time focusing more on objective justification of measures that have discriminatory effects (see above **3.UN.5.**). Notably in the ECtHR case-law, a judicial dialogue with the ECJ case-law on indirect discrimination law has started, although the ECtHR has been reluctant to accept the concept. While citing the Community case-law in reference, it has introduced additional opportunities for State Parties to justify provisions having discriminatory effects. The Court has thus at times disappointed expectations in the possibilities of judicial campaigning. (see above **3.CoE.10.**)

The development of the concept of indirect discrimination in the Community legal order has seen a movement from internal market and free movement of persons law on the one hand and sex equality law on the other hand towards a legislative consolidation within a framework for equal treatment of persons. It is to be expected that ECJ case-law will start to develop within a few years, hopefully contributing to a coherent development of the field, avoiding a further expansion of pure policy-oriented justification of rules and practices that have detrimental effects.

3.6.2.   CONSOLIDATION OF THE CONCEPT IN NATIONAL AND COMMUNITY LAW

Reflecting on the developments within Member States, one cannot help but notice the vast differences in the amount of case-law, public and academic discourse and social movement towards non-discrimination and equality. While institutions in some Member States, such as the UK and Germany, produce vast amounts of case-law, the input into developing the concept of indirect discrimination is limited at times. We could not help but being impressed, on the other hand, by the few judgments from Scandinavian countries, which combine careful reasoning and an approach to law rooted in social reality. All this leads us to notice some aspects that should be observed carefully within the next few years.

3.6.2.A.   ESTABLISHING DISADVANTAGE—STATISTICAL AND NON-STATISTICAL APPROACHES

The first step in establishing a case of indirect discrimination law is to establish that a neutrally phrased rule or practice results in disproportionate disadvantage in relation to one of the discrimination grounds.

This first sentence is already phrased in accordance with the definition in recent EC legislation. This definition seems to restrict indirect discrimination analysis towards investigating single requirements or practices for adverse effects. Under national (constitutional) law, Scandinavian, Spanish, Dutch and German courts applied a more collective approach at times. This collective approach would allow the courts to assess the potentially adverse impact of complex policy regimes. Examples of this include wage systems (see above **3.DE.40.**, **3.ES.41.–42.**), redundancy policies (see above **3.FI.33.**) and tenancy policies (see above **3.NL.36.**). Subjecting such schemes to the scrutiny of indirect discrimination law, courts would be able to expose discriminatory structures while deciding individual cases. In this way, judicial campaigning might be used to engender change of norms that deepen discrimination in social reality. Hopefully, these more encompassing approaches will not lose relevance due to the narrow formulation of the EC law definition.

As regards establishing disadvantage, the new legislative definition of indirect discrimination enables judges and administrative bodies to establish a finding of indirect discrimination without detailed statistics. Given the discouraging experiences with gathering huge amounts of data only to be told by courts that these are not sufficient (see above **3.EC.45.**, **3.NL.56.**), the prospect of establishing detrimental effects without such exercises seems comforting.

There are, however, risks in two aspects.

On the one hand, the qualitative approach to establishing detrimental effect lends itself to blurring the borders between direct and indirect discrimination, with a tendency to categorise direct discrimination cases as indirect ones. For example, in the cases reported under **2.NL.54.** and **3.BE.84.**, discrimination on grounds of wearing a religious symbol was considered as indirect instead of direct discrimination on grounds of religion. The temptation to merge direct and indirect discrimination is large, as this offers the opportunity to engage in a policy oriented evaluation exercise even in cases where justification of direct discrimination measures is not an option. However, non-discrimination law would suffer from a loss of credibility if courts and advisory bodies failed to see that criteria such as "no foreign accent accepted" (**3.NL.67.**, **3.SE.68.**) or "head coverings not welcome" (**3.NL.66.**) may only thinly mask direct ethnic discrimination.

On the other hand, the qualitative approach might lead to rejecting the possibility of proving indirect discrimination statistically. Undoubtedly, the need for statistical proof has its disadvantages. However, compiling statistical evidence is often an important step towards raising awareness of discriminatory structures. Often, such evidence will not be made available if there is no judicial procedure (or the realistic threat to raise one). Statistical proof should therefore remain available to those campaigning for discrimination.

Once the concept of indirect discrimination is more widely applied than in sex and nationality cases, more examples of adverse effects of neutrally phrased measures will emerge. This will also reduce the complexity of proving disproportionate disadvantage. Just as part-time work discrimination is an acknowledged case of potential for indirect discrimination, height requirements, clothing restrictions, language requirements and many other issues will emerge as suspect neutral grounds, which will trigger indirect discrimination analysis.

3.6.2.B.   OBJECTIVE JUSTIFICATION

As regards the second stage of indirect discrimination, the objective justification problem, there is a great deal of need for consolidation here.

First, the specific characteristic of indirect discrimination law needs to be acknowledged more widely. This specific characteristic lies in the fact that disproportionate disadvantage leads to the presumption that there is a causal link between using a certain criterion or practice or implementing a set of policies and disadvantage related to discrimination grounds, but that this presumption can be rebutted. Applying the objective justification test, one tests this causal link. The causation approach to indirect discrimination would contribute to maintain the distinction between direct and indirect discrimination, which is vital in order to maintain the strictness of the former prohibition.

Secondly, applying the proportionality test in relation to "objective justification" thoroughly needs to become the accepted practice of indirect discrimination law. Some of the Dutch Equal Treatment Commission cases (see above **3.NL.78.**) and the few Swedish cases (see above **3.SE.79.**) can serve as models in this respect. The ECJ has been less diligent in applying the objective justification test especially when social policy choices of Member States were at issue (see above **3.EC.75.**, **3.EC.76.**)

Thirdly, in framing the new Directives, Community institutions seem to have overlooked the necessity to exclude objective justifications relating to discrimination grounds. While a teological reading of the Directives would lead to rejecting justifications related to discrimination grounds as not objective ones, this view needs to be consolidated. Court decisions which justify a prohibition of wearing a piece of garment to which a strong ethnic dimension is ascribed, with reference to ethnicity, although as yet isolated, are troubling (**3.BE.84.**, **3.NL.85.**). The balance between realistically assessing the potential of law to intervene in social conflicts and the danger of courts becoming the advocates of those working against integration needs to be maintained.

3.6.3.   CHALLENGES

One of the major challenges, which could not be addressed in this chapter, is the problem of multiple and intersected identities and their relation towards indirect discrimination law. Especially polarised issues such as headscarves, family rights of disabled women and requirements to integrate religious communities and life styles not adhering to fixed gender roles affect those at intersections. There has in the second half of the last century been a phase when attempts to utilise indirect discrimination law in favour of those suffering multiple disadvantage failed.[228] In order not to not repeat this development, there is a need to discuss questions of intersected identities and group protection, inter alia in the framework of indirect discrimination law.

The field of indirect discrimination lends itself to judicial campaigning to a certain degree. This is not necessarily an advantage. The arguments raised in indirect discrimination claims have the potential to expose structural disadvantage. They may thus lead to policy changes. However, judicial procedures do not necessarily have the potential to repair disadvantage. It is to be desired that the arguments derived from indirect discrimination can be used in fora truly suitable to instil social change.

---

[228] For further references see D. Schiek, "Broadening the Scope and the Norms of EU Gender Equality Law: Towards a Multidimensional Conception of Equality Law" (2005) 12 MJ 427.

CHAPTER FOUR
HARASSMENT

Prof. Aileen McColgan

4.1. INTRODUCTION

"Harassment" and "sexual harassment" pose significant problems in the working environment, as they do elsewhere. Sexual harassment can take the form of

> "insults, remarks, jokes, insinuations and inappropriate comments on a person's dress, physique, age, family situation, and a condescending or paternalistic attitude undermining dignity, unwelcome invitations or requests that are implicit or explicit whether or not accompanied by threats, lascivious looks or other gestures associated with sexuality, unnecessary physical contact such as touching, caresses, pinching or assault".[1]

Harassment is not limited to "sexual harassment" but can relate to other "protected" grounds such as race, disability and sexual orientation,[2] or to unprotected grounds (arbitrary personal dislike, for example). Harassment connected with sex, race and other protected grounds may serve to maintain the homogeneity of (for example) male or white jobs or workplaces by discouraging "outsiders" from entry. It is, perhaps, no coincidence that sexual harassment tends to be particularly prevalent in traditionally male sectors, such as fire-fighting, police jobs and the military, where the entrance of women into very masculinised environments can be seen as a threat to cohesion and morale.

We shall see below that some forms of harassment have been regarded as a species of discrimination, and actionable as such, for almost 30 years in the US, and at least half that long in parts of the EU. Because "discrimination" is frequently regarded as a relative concept (that is, one which requires some form of comparison to establish *less favourable* treatment on grounds of sex or race, etc.), the regulation of harassment in this manner has resulted in gaps in legal protection where (for example) the harasser claims that he or she would have treated a man as badly as he treated a woman complainant, or that he or she would have subjected a man to the same unwanted sexual advances as the woman complainant was subjected to.[3] In the UK, for example, *discrimination* law only protected against harassment when the claimant established that harassing behaviour was either motivated by his or her sex or other protected factor, or was qualitatively different and less favourable than the type of treatment which a person of the other sex (different race, etc.) would have received. The fit between "discrimination" defined as "less favourable treatment" and "harassment" was never complete, but discrimination law was used in an attempt to

---

[1] ILO Committee of Experts 1988 General Survey.
[2] See above J. Gerards, Chapter One: Discrimination Grounds.
[3] Or vice versa where the claimant is a man.

provide a remedy for behaviour which would frequently have otherwise gone unchecked in the absence of explicit regulation of harassment.

Elsewhere harassment (and/or sexual harassment) has been dealt with predominantly as a workplace violence/health and safety problem. Where this has been the case, the focus has been less on analysing the fine legal distinctions which bedevil the regulation of harassment as a form of *less favourable* treatment and more on questions of prevention and on the creation of a benign and healthy working environment.

Sexual harassment is generally subcategorised into "quid pro quo" and "hostile environment" harassment. The former occurs where access to a job-related benefit (including continued employment) is made conditional on a worker's subjection to unwelcome sexual advances. The latter occurs where a worker is subjected to comments of a sexual nature, offensive sexist materials or unwelcome physical contact as part of the working environment. Sexual harassment of the latter type might be explicitly sexual or not: it could, for example, consist simply in bad treatment of an apparently sex-neutral variety which is in fact motivated by hostility towards persons of the claimant's sex, or (more commonly) to persons of that sex in the particular job or workplace. So, for example, women who enter very predominantly male jobs as police officers or fire-fighters frequently find themselves subject not only to explicit sexual taunting, sexual overtures and, not infrequently, sexual assault; but also to non-"sexual" bullying, physical abuse and being undermined, for example, by persistently being required to engage in trivial, low-status or particularly demanding tasks.

Quid pro quo harassment will almost invariably be of a sexual nature, concerned as it is with sexual contact as a job condition.[4] But "hostile environment" harassment can relate to grounds other than sex just as readily as it can to sex itself. A worker may be singled out for ill-treatment by supervisors or colleagues because she is a wheelchair user or a Muslim woman, or because he is a gay man, black or of the Roma community. US law recognised racial harassment as a form of race discrimination even before it recognised sexual harassment as a form of sex discrimination. The *explicit* regulation of harassment other than sexual harassment also predated that of sexual harassment in the EU, although sexual harassment had in fact been recognised as a form of discrimination in the EU at least since 1988.

Directives 2000/43 of 29 June 2000 (the Racial Equality Directive)[5] and 2000/78 of 27 November 2000 (the Employment Equality Directive),[6] which were the first EU provisions explicitly to regulate harassment as a form of discrimination, provide as follows:

---

[4] It will not always be motivated by sex as such: a person may be targeted for sexual contact because of his or her sexual orientation, race or specific disability in which case the harassment may amount to discrimination on one of these grounds as well as quid pro quo sexual harassment.

[5] [2000] OJ L180/22.

[6] [2000] OJ L303/16.

Directive 2000/43/EC of 29 June 2000 implementing the principle **4.EC.1.**
of equal treatment between persons irrespective of racial or ethnic origin and
Directive 2000/78/EC of 27 November 2000 establishing a general framework for
equal treatment in employment and occupation

Article 2
Harassment shall be deemed to be discrimination . . . when an unwanted conduct related to [a protected ground] takes place with the purpose or effect of violating the dignity of a person and of creating an intimidating, hostile, degrading, humiliating or offensive environment. In this context, the concept of harassment may be defined in accordance with the national laws and practice of the Member States.

The Racial Equality Directive prohibits harassment related to racial or ethnic origin in the context of employment, self-employment, vocational guidance and training etc., membership of trade unions and similar organisations, and (by contrast with the Employment Equality Directive) in relation to "social protection, including social security and healthcare", "social advantages", "education" and "access to and supply of goods and services which are available to the public, including housing" (Article 3). The Directives provide that:

Directive 2000/43/EC of 29 June 2000 implementing the principle **4.EC.2.**
of equal treatment between persons irrespective of racial or ethnic origin and
Directive 2000/78/EC of 27 November 2000 establishing a general framework for
equal treatment in employment and occupation[7]

Article 2
1. For the purposes of this Directive, the principle of equal treatment shall mean that there shall be no direct or indirect discrimination based on [the prohibited grounds].

Articles 7 and 9
1. Member States shall ensure that judicial and/or administrative procedures, including where they deem it appropriate conciliation procedures, for the enforcement of obligations under this Directive are available to all persons who consider themselves wronged by failure to apply the principle of equal treatment to them, even after the relationship in which the discrimination is alleged to have occurred has ended . . .

Articles 8 and 10
1. Member States shall take such measures as are necessary, in accordance with their national judicial systems, to ensure that, when persons who consider themselves wronged because the principle of equal treatment has not been applied to them establish, before a court or other competent authority, facts from which it may be presumed that there has been direct or indirect discrimination, it shall be for the respondent to prove that there has been no breach of the principle of equal treatment.

[7] See also above **4.EC.1.**

2. Paragraph 1 shall not prevent Member States from introducing rules of evidence which are more favourable to plaintiffs.

Articles 15 and 17
Member States shall lay down the rules on sanctions applicable to infringements of the national provisions adopted pursuant to this Directive and shall take all measures necessary to ensure that they are applied. The sanctions, which may comprise the payment of compensation to the victim, must be effective, proportionate and dissuasive . . .

What is perhaps most noteworthy about the approach taken by the Directives to harassment is that it defines harassment as discrimination per se, rather than tying such definition to any finding of *less favourable* treatment. It is to be noted, however, that the provisions allow harassment to be defined "in accordance with the national laws and practice of the Member States". The scope for divergence left by this provision is uncertain. We shall see, below, that the German transposing measure requires intention on the part of the harasser, a requirement which appears on its face inconsistent with the definition of harassment as "unwanted conduct . . . [which] takes place with the purpose or *effect* of violating the dignity of a person" etc. [emphasis added]. There may be some room for divergence of approaches as regards the extent of employer liability for harassment by staff and third parties. Even here, however, and despite the fact that the Directives are silent as to the extent of employer liability required by transposing measures, the requirement for "effective, proportionate and dissuasive" sanctions may be taken to suggest that employers should be held liable for harassment within their control, at least in the absence of penal sanctions against individual harassers many of whom are unlikely to have the financial resources to pay significant financial compensation. Questions of fault and liability are further considered below.

The Gender Employment Directive (Directive 76/207/EEC) was amended by Directive 2002/73 and will be replaced from 2009 by the Recast Gender Employment Directive (Directive 2006/54/EC), which brings together the Gender Employment Directive, Council Directive 86/378/EEC (on equal treatment in occupational social security schemes), Council Directive 75/117/EEC (the Equal Pay Directive), and Council Directive 97/80/EC (the Burden of Proof Directive). The Recast Gender Employment Directive now provides as follows:

Directive 2006/54/EC of the European Parliament and of the   **4.EC.3.**
Council of 5 July 2006 on the implementation of the principle of equal opportunities and equal treatment of men and women in matters of employment and occupation (recast)[8]

Article 2
1. For the purposes of this Directive, the following definitions shall apply . . .

[8] [2006] OJ L204/23.

(c) 'harassment': where unwanted conduct related to the sex of a person occurs with the purpose or effect of violating the dignity of a person, and of creating an intimidating, hostile, degrading, humiliating or offensive environment,

(d) 'sexual harassment': where any form of unwanted verbal, non-verbal or physical conduct of a sexual nature occurs, with the purpose or effect of violating the dignity of a person, in particular when creating an intimidating, hostile, degrading, humiliating or offensive environment . . .

2. For the purposes of this Directive, discrimination includes:

(a) harassment and sexual harassment, as well as any less favourable treatment based on a person's rejection of or submission to such conduct . . .

A person's rejection of, or submission to, such conduct may not be used as a basis for a decision affecting that person.

It is interesting to note that the Directives concept of sexual harassment, unlike that of harassment, does not require the violation of dignity and the creation of an "intimidating, hostile, degrading, humiliating or offensive environment" (in each case either as a purpose or an effect) as cumulative conditions, referring instead to the creation of such an environment as a particular example of the violation of dignity. In this it echoes the approach taken by the original EU definition of "sexual harassment" set out in the European Commission's 1991 Recommendation, which provided as follows:

Commission Recommendation of 27 November 1991 on the **4.EC.4.**
protection of the dignity of women and men at work (92/131/EEC)[9]

Article 1

. . . conduct of a sexual nature and other conduct based on sex affecting the dignity of women and men at work, including conduct of superiors and colleagues, is unacceptable, if:

(a) such conduct is unwelcome, unreasonable and offensive to the recipient;

(b) a person's rejection of, or submission to, such conduct on the part of the employers or workers (including superiors or colleagues) is used explicitly or implicitly as a basis for a decision which affects that person's access to vocational training, access to employment, continued employment, promotion, salary or any other employment decisions; and/or

(c) such conduct creates an intimidating, hostile or humiliating working environment for the recipient.

This definition, like that adopted by the amended Equal Treatment Directive, embraces both "quid pro quo" and "hostile environment" sexual harassment. The 1991 Recommendation (Article 1) urged Member States to "take action to promote awareness that conduct" of the type outlined above was unacceptable, "and that such conduct may, in certain circumstances, be contrary to the principle of equal treatment" and recommended that Member States:

[9] [1992] OJ L49/1.

481

Article 2

. . .take action, in the public sector, to implement the Commission's code of practice on the protection of the dignity of women and men at work, annexed hereto. The action of the Member States, in thus initiating and pursuing positive measures designed to create a climate at work in which women and men respect one another's human integrity, should serve as an example to the private sector . . .

Article 3

. . . encourage employers and employee representatives to develop measures to implement the Commission's code of practice on the protection of the dignity of women and men at work . . .

Article 4

. . . inform the Commission within three years of the date of this recommendation of the measures taken to give effect to it, in order to allow the Commission to draw up a report on all such measures . . .

The Code of Practice annexed to the Recommendation stated that sexual harassment could be "physical, verbal or non-verbal". Seven years after the publication of the Recommendation and Code of Practice, the European Commission published *Sexual harassment in the workplace in the European Union* (1998), which highlighted in its Executive Summary the lack of a universal definition of sexual harassment despite the lapse of time since the Commission's 1991 Recommendation. The report noted that sexual harassment was commonplace across the EU. The studies detailed in the report suggested that almost two-thirds of women employees had experienced verbal sexual harassment, unsolicited physical contacts also being commonplace, with up to 5% of women reporting workplace-related sexual assaults/rapes. Around 1 in 10 men in Northern Europe were estimated to have been subject to sexual harassment.

One of the interesting aspects of the 1998 survey concerned the differences it threw up between Northern and Southern Member States (the former defined to include Austria, Belgium, Denmark, Finland, Germany, Ireland, Luxembourg, the Netherlands, Norway, Sweden and the UK, the latter France, Italy, Spain, Greece and Portugal). Whereas sexual harassment was common across the board, only France and Italy of the southern countries demonstrated high levels of awareness of the problem and an inclination to treat it as a serious problem.

[10] See also above **4.EC.4.**

Commission of the European Communities,   **4.EC.6.**
Sexual harassment in the Workplace in the European Union"[11]

"229–231
Research at national level has been carried out only in France and Portugal. The study indicates that an international comparison is scarcely possible, given that the methodology employed to gauge the extent of the problem is not consistent and that, for several countries, there are no surveys at national level.

The researchers nevertheless consider that the results provided by the different studies show that the percentage of women claiming to have received unwanted sexual proposals may be situated between 30% and 84%. However, they also show that this percentage falls sharply to between 25% and 45% when the women are asked if they have been harassed or if they have been subjected to advances or solicitations of a sexual nature. However, the distinguishing criterion does not seem to be very clear.

The researchers conclude from these surveys that, in the southern countries, sexual harassment at workplaces is not an occasional occurrence but, on the contrary, is something which happens all the time, and which the women themselves accept as something they have to put up with because it is part and parcel of being a woman . . .

From the surveys carried out, some conclusions can be drawn for each country. In *Spain*, it seems that sexual harassment is very frequent and that the women who suffer it generally see it as inevitable. Similarly, the male harassers tend to regard their behaviour as natural. The women who suffer most from sexual harassment are those who work in socially and economically low-status sectors, as well as single women.

In *France*, sexual harassment takes many forms, although the non-verbal variety is less frequent. On the other hand, verbal expressions of harassment in the form of sexual requests are experienced by more than one woman in two. Physical harassment (bodily contact, fondling) is mentioned by more than one woman in three. One woman in ten claims to have been the victim of rape or attempted rape.

The employment-related implications for a person suffering harassment are clear.

According to one study, 71% of those claiming to have suffered sexual harassment lose their job, through resignation (as a result of difficulties in performing their work) or dismissal. Those who keep their jobs are for the most part employed in the public sector. The repercussions career-wise are also a source of complaint. Related effects on health give rise to frequent absence from work as a result of sickness (sleeping disorders, weight fluctuations, anxiety, sexual problems). The most frequently cited effects on a personal level are loss of self-esteem and a feeling of being a sex object.

Unlike the situation in Spain, in France it does not appear that the majority of women suffering harassment are from the most disadvantaged groups socially or economically. The range is much wider. Many of the women are well educated and have professional experience. They are neither very young nor very old.

The handful of surveys carried out in *Greece* are based on very low samples. What can be gleaned, however, is that sexual harassment affects more than 70% of women, is generally perpetrated by superiors in the hierarchy, is not perceived as such by the harassers and is rarely denounced for fear of dismissal.

---

[11] (European Commission, 1998) 229, available on the website of Directorate-General for Employment, Social Affairs and Equal Opportunities.

In *Italy*, the surveys show that sexual harassment occurs a lot, with the verbal form being the most widespread; the most serious cases involve superiors in the hierarchy. Responses to sexual harassment appear to vary, depending on whether it has to do with a hierarchical superior or a colleague. In the former case it is denounced, whereas in the second case the women's attitude tends to be more passive. Sexual harassment mainly affects very young women or single or separated women. The employers' reaction seems to be to 'cover up' sexual harassment, especially in the case of small businesses; in large companies, it is increasingly common for the dispute to end with the dismissal of the person suffering harassment, i.e. the person who is perceived as potentially being most troublesome for the company.

In *Portugal*, the surveys which have been carried out are too specific and are based on samples which are too small to provide a comparison. It appears, though, that a perpetrator of sexual harassment is never penalised, on the grounds that there is no reference in labour law to this type of behaviour, nor is there a definition of sexual harassment at the workplace. It is interesting to note that a survey has also been conducted in conjunction with the study carried out for the Commission. One of the main points emerging is that persons suffering harassment are, for the most part, to be found in insecure employment (fixed-duration contracts, dependence on the harasser for promotion or contract renewal)."

Companies had taken action on sexual harassment "on a large scale only in northern countries", where third parties such as patients and clients were the harassers in 16% of incidents (in up to 50% of incidents involving employees having frequent contact with, for example, patients and clients).

Below I consider in more detail the approach to harassment taken by EU Member States both prior to and in order to implement the various Directives' provisions. First, however, it is important to sketch the historical developments in this area. As will become apparent immediately below, the discussion begins in the US, which first witnessed concerted attempts to use the law to challenge harassment and sexual harassment. After I have considered the historical development of concepts of harassment and sexual harassment in the US and (then) international law, I will discuss early initiatives by the EU and EU Member States in this area, drawing attention to the wide variety of legal approaches adopted (penal, civil, labour law and health and safety provisions, as well as discrimination provisions and specific measures to regulate "harassment" and/or "sexual harassment"). The discussion aims to tease out the strengths and shortcomings of these different approaches to the legal regulation of harassment/sexual harassment.

The final substantive section of the chapter (section 4.4) deals with the impact of implementation across a number of EU Member States, drawing attention to a variety of approaches taken to questions such as the relationship between "harassment" and "discrimination", and who may be held responsible for harassment by employees, clients, etc.

4.2. HISTORICAL DEVELOPMENT

As mentioned above, the focus here is for the most part on developments in the US, as it was here that sexual and other forms of harassment and, more specifically, legal challenges to such behaviour, first came to prominence. Many of the questions which currently arise in relation to harassment and sexual harassment in Europe were the subject of early case-law in the US. Much of the discussion in the following section relates to sexual harassment in particular. The reason for this is simple: whereas sexual harassment has been the subject of discussion and study, if not legal regulation, for some four decades, the application of the term "harassment" to conduct other than conduct of a sexual nature has, for the most part, been much more recent, though we shall see that in the US "harassment" was first the subject of successful legal challenge in the context of race.

This is not to say that such (non-sexual) harassment has not generated concern. But this concern has regularly been subsumed within a wider focus on "workplace violence" (psychological as well as physical), rather than being considered as an aspect of "discrimination" on particular grounds, although attention has been directed from time to time on grounds-based harassment. A survey carried out by the British non-government organisation Stonewall in 1993, for example, disclosed very high levels of workplace harassment of gay men and lesbian women (52% of them had been harassed at work due to their sexual orientation),[12] a finding given support by more recent surveys carried out by the UK Trade Union Congress and Lesbian and Gay Employment Rights organisation.[13]

4.2.1. THE LEGAL RECOGNITION OF RACIAL AND "SEXUAL HARASSMENT" IN THE US

The term "sexual harassment" was coined in the US in the 1960s. The phenomenon was generally considered at this time to be connected with questions of sexual attraction and pursuit, but feminists argued that sexual harassment was about power rather than about sex, activists/theorists including Catherine MacKinnon and Susan Brownmiller categorising sexual harassment as a species of sex discrimination which operated to keep women in their traditional place, rather than of "normal", if misguided, male–female interactions.[14]

In 1975 sexual harassment did not feature in most analyses of women at work.[15] But sexual harassment had begun even then to be challenged in the US by feminists.

[12] A. Palmer, *Less Equal than Others: A Survey of Lesbians and Gay Men at Work* (London, Stonewall, 1993), cited by V. Di Martino, H. Hoel and C.L. Cooper, *Preventing violence and harassment in the workplace* (Luxembourg, Office for Official Publications of the European Communities, 2003) 30, available on the website of the European Foundation for the Improvement of Living and Working Conditions.
[13] TUC (Trades Unions Congress), *Straight up! Why the Law should Protect Lesbian and Gay Workers* (London, TUC, April 2000); LAGER, "Profile of Users: A Report Based on Statistical Monitoring of LAGER Case-files" (Lesbian and Gay Employment Rights, London, March 2002), cited by Di Martino *et al.*, above n. 12, 30.
[14] C.A. MacKinnon (with T. Emerson), *Sexual Harassment of Working Women: A Case of Discrimination* (New Haven, Ct, Yale University Press, 1979); S. Brownmiller, *Against Our Will: Men, Women, and Rape* (New York, Simon & Schuster, 1975).
[15] See, e.g. the article by ILO lawyer F. Morgenstern, "Women Workers and the Courts" (1975) 112 *ILR* 15.

Title VII of the Civil Rights Act 1964 prohibited employment-related discrimination on grounds of race, colour, religion, sex or national origin, Section 703(a)(1) providing that it shall be an unlawful employment practice for an employer

> "to fail or refuse to hire or to discharge any individual, or otherwise to discriminate against any individual with respect to his compensation, terms, conditions, or privileges of employment, because of such individual's race, colour, religion, sex, or national origin."

In the 1970s, racial harassment was recognised by the US courts as a form of discrimination actionable under Title VII.

Fifth Circuit Court of Appeals, 454 F.2d 234 (1971)   **4.US.7.**
Rogers v. EEOC

RACIAL HARASSMENT AS ACTIONABLE RACE DISCRIMINATION

Rogers

Facts: The claimant, a "Spanish surnamed American", alleged that she had been subject to race discrimination on grounds, inter alia, that her employers had segregated patients on racial grounds. A procedural issue arose as to whether her complaint could amount to a complaint of race discrimination under Title VII of the US Civil Rights Act 1964, which regulates discrimination in employment.

Held: A lower court had ruled that it could not be characterised as relating to an unlawful employment practice within the meaning of Section 703(a), 42 USCA § 2000e-2(a), which provides that it shall be an unlawful employment practice for an employer "to fail or refuse to hire or to discharge any individual, or otherwise to discriminate against any individual with respect to his compensation, terms, conditions, or privileges of employment, because of such individual's race, colour, religion, sex, or national origin."

Judgment: GOLDBERG J: "In the words of the trial court:

'. . . Accepting arguendo . . . that if Petitioners in fact 'segregated the patients' then such a practice might be so offensive to Mrs Chavez's sensibilities as to make her uncomfortable in her job, there still is no showing that she is 'aggrieved' in the sense contemplated by . . . the employer's pursuit of an 'unlawful employment practice' within § 703.' . . .

I disagree fundamentally with this position. While the district court may have viewed lightly the connection between the petitioners' alleged discrimination against its patients and Mrs Chavez's sensibilities, I think that the relationship between an employee and his working environment is of such significance as to be entitled to statutory protection.

Th[e] language [of section 703(a)] evinces a Congressional intention to define discrimination in the broadest possible terms. Congress chose neither to enumerate specific discriminatory practices, nor to elucidate *in extenso* the parameter of such nefarious activities. Rather, it pursued the path of wisdom by being unconstructive, knowing that constant change is the order of our day and that the seemingly reasonable practices of the present can easily become the injustices of the morrow. Time was when employment discrimination tended to be viewed as a series of isolated and distinguishable events, manifesting itself, for example, in an employer's practices of hiring, firing, and promoting. But today employment discrimination is a far more complex and pervasive phenomenon, as the nuances and subtleties of discriminatory employment practices are no longer confined to bread and butter issues. As wages and hours of employment take subordinate roles in management-labour relationships, the modern employee makes ever-increasing demands in the nature of intangible fringe benefits. Recognizing the importance of these benefits, we should neither ignore their need for protection, nor blind ourselves to their potential misuse.

We must be acutely conscious of the fact that Title VII of the Civil Rights Act of 1964 should be accorded a liberal interpretation in order to effectuate the purpose of Congress to eliminate the inconvenience, unfairness, and humiliation of ethnic discrimination . . . Furthermore, I regard this broad-gauged innovation legislation as a charter of principles which are to be elucidated and explicated by experience, time, and expertise. Therefore, it is my belief that employees' psychological as well as economic fringes are statutorily entitled to protection from employer abuse, and that the phrase 'terms, conditions, or privileges of employment' in Section 703 is an expansive concept which sweeps within its protective ambit the practice of creating a working environment heavily charged with ethnic or racial discrimination. I do not wish to be interpreted as holding that an employer's mere utterance of an ethnic or racial epithet which engenders offensive feelings in an employee falls within the proscription of Section 703. But by the same token I am simply not willing to hold that a discriminatory atmosphere could under no set of circumstances ever constitute an unlawful employment practice. One can readily envision working environments so heavily polluted with discrimination as to destroy completely the emotional and psychological stability of minority group workers, and I think Section 703 of Title VII was aimed at the eradication of such noxious practices.

Petitioners urge, nevertheless, that the second portion of Mrs Chavez's charge could not relate to an unlawful employment practice because it alleges discrimination directed toward petitioners' patients and not toward any employee. Essentially petitioners' contention is that their discriminatory treatment or classification of patients is not a practice directed toward any employee and that because of such discrimination Mrs Chavez cannot complain that she is treated any differently than any other employee. However, petitioners' eisegesis is not consistent with the interpretation recently accorded Title VII by the Supreme Court. In Griggs v. Duke Power Co., 1971, 401 U.S. 424, the Court held that the absence of discriminatory intent by an employer does not redeem an otherwise unlawful employment practice, and that the thrust of Title VII's proscriptions is aimed at the consequences or effects of an employment practice and not at the employer's motivation. Hence, petitioners' failure to direct intentionally any discriminatory treatment toward Mrs Chavez is simply not material to the finding of an unlawful employment practice. Moreover, I believe that petitioners' argument does not countenance the distinct possibility that an employer's patient discrimination may constitute a subtle scheme designed to create a working environment imbued with discrimination and directed ultimately at minority group employees. As patently discriminatory practices become outlawed, those employers bent on pursuing a general policy declared illegal by Congressional mandate will undoubtedly devise more sophisticated methods to perpetuate discrimination among employees. The petitioners' alleged patient discrimination may very well be just such a sophisticated method and, if so, then Mrs Chavez, as the primary object of the discriminatory treatment, suffers directly the consequences of such a practice and is entitled to protection in accordance with the provisions of Title VII."

The "harassment" at issue in the *Barnes* case was of a subtle form. No allegations were made of explicit racial verbal abuse or ill-treatment, or of any practice directed towards the claimant, her complaint being concerned with the creation of a working environment which she regarded as hostile to her as a "Spanish surnamed American" worker.

A number of attempts were made in the early 1970s to use the Title VII against repeated verbal and physical advances by supervisors towards women workers. In 1974, a District Court in Arizona refused to hold an employer liable for sexual harassment by the claimant's supervisor because the conduct "served no policy of the employer and in no way benefited the employer".[16] But the tide gradually turned and in 1976 a lower court in Washington, D.C. recognized quid pro quo sexual harassment as discrimination in *Williams* v. *Saxbe.*[17] A year later the District of Columbia Circuit Court of Appeal ruled that the dismissal of a woman who rejected a superior's sexual advances constituted sex discrimination.

District of Columbia Circuit Court of Appeal, 561 F.2d 983 (1977) **4.US.8.**
Barnes v. *Costle*

QUID PRO QUO SEXUAL HARASSMENT AS ACTIONABLE SEX DISCRIMINATION

Barnes

Facts: The claimant worked as the administrative assistant to the director of the employer's equal employment opportunity division. She claimed that he "repeatedly solicit[ed her] to join him for social activities after office hours, notwithstanding [her] repeated refusal to do so", that he "ma[de] repeated remarks to [her] which were sexual in nature" and that he "repeatedly suggest[ed] to [her] that if she cooperated with him in a sexual affair, her employment status would be enhanced". She claimed that she "continually resisted [his] overtures . . . and finally advised him that notwithstanding his stated belief that many executives 'have affairs with their personnel', she preferred that their relationship remain a strictly professional one", after which she claimed he "began a conscious campaign to belittle [her], to harass her and to strip her of her job duties, all culminating in the decision . . . to abolish [her] job in retaliation for [her] refusal to grant him sexual favours". This, she claimed, "would not have occurred but for [her] sex . . ."

Held: The Court of Appeal reversed the decision of the lower court, which had ruled that that the Equal Employment Opportunity Act of 1972, which extended the reach of Title VII into public sector employment, did not protect the claimant.

Judgment: SPOTTSWOOD W. ROBINSON, III: "We start with the statute as written, and, so measured, we think the discrimination as portrayed was plainly based on appellant's gender. Her thesis, in substance, is that her supervisor retaliated by abolishing her job when she resisted his sexual advances. More particularly, she states that he repeatedly told her that indulgence in a sexual affair would enhance her employment status; that he endeavoured affirmatively but futilely to consummate his proposition; and that, upon her refusal to accede, he campaigned against her continued employment in his department and succeeded eventually in liquidating her position. So it was, by her version, that retention of her job was conditioned upon submission to sexual relations an exaction which the supervisor would not have sought from any male. It is much too late in the day to contend that Title VII does not outlaw terms of employment for women which differ appreciably from those set for men, and which are not genuinely and reasonably related to performance on the job.

[16] *Barnes* v. *Train, Corne* and *De Vane* v. *Bausch and Lomb, Inc.* 13 Fair Employment Practice Case (BNA) 123 DCC, 9 August 1974; discussed in J. Aeberhard-Hodges, "Sexual harassment in employment: recent judicial and arbitral trends" (1996) 135 *ILR* 510.
[17] (DDC 1976), 413 F.Supp. 654.

The District Court felt, however, that appellant's suit amounted to no more than a claim 'that she was discriminated against, not because she was a woman, but because she refused to engage in a sexual affair with her supervisor.' In similar vein, appellee has argued that '(a)ppellant was allegedly denied employment enhancement not because she was a woman, but rather because she decided not to furnish the sexual consideration claimed to have been demanded.' We cannot accept this analysis of the situation charged by appellant. But for her womanhood, from aught that appears, her participation in sexual activity would never have been solicited. To say, then, that she was victimized in her employment simply because she declined the invitation is to ignore the asserted fact that she was invited only because she was a woman subordinate to the inviter in the hierarchy of agency personnel. Put another way, she became the target of her superior's sexual desires because she was a woman, and was asked to bow to his demands as the price for holding her job. The circumstance imparting high visibility to the role of gender in the affair is that no male employee was susceptible to such an approach by appellant's supervisor. Thus gender cannot be eliminated from the formulation which appellant advocates, and that formulation advances a prima facie case of sex discrimination within the purview of Title VII. [According to footnote 55 of the judgment: "It is no answer to say that a similar condition could be imposed on a male subordinate by a heterosexual female superior, or upon a subordinate of either gender by a homosexual superior of the same gender. In each instance, the legal problem would be identical to that confronting us now the exaction of a condition which, but for his or her sex, the employee would not have faced. These situations, like that at bar, are to be distinguished from a bisexual superior who conditions the employment opportunities of a subordinate of either gender upon participation in a sexual affair. In the case of the bisexual superior, the insistence upon sexual favours would not constitute gender discrimination because it would apply to male and female employees alike".]

It is clear that the statutory embargo on sex discrimination in employment is not confined to differentials founded wholly upon an employee's gender. On the contrary, it is enough that gender is a factor contributing to the discrimination in a substantial way. That this was the intent of Congress is readily apparent from a small but highly significant facet of the legislative history of Title VII. When the bill incorporating Title VII was under consideration in 1964, an amendment that would have expressly restricted the sex ban to discrimination based solely on gender was defeated on the floor of the House. Like the Fifth Circuit, we take this as an indication of congressional awareness of the debilitating effect that such a limitation would have had on any attempt to stamp out sex-based factors irrelevant to job competence . . . Appellant's gender, just as much as her cooperation, was an indispensable factor in the job-retention condition of which she complains, absent a showing that the supervisor imposed a similar condition upon a male co-employee . . .

A sex-founded impediment to equal employment opportunity succumbs to Title VII even though less than all employees of the claimant's gender are affected. The protections afforded by Title VII against sex discrimination are extended to the individual, and 'a single instance of discrimination may form the basis of a private suit.' To briefly illustrate, suits have been entertained where a woman charged that she was fired because she was pregnant and unmarried, notwithstanding the fact that no other woman was discharged for that reason, and where a male nurse asserted that he was denied assignments to care for female patients, although no allegations were made with respect to the assignment of other male nurses. Close analogies emerge from situations wherein a black woman was terminated ostensibly for personality conflicts but allegedly was told that she probably did not need the job anyway because she was married to a white male, and where a white woman attributed loss of her job to her relationship with a black man. In each of these instances, a cause of action was recognized although it did not appear that any other individual of the same gender or race had been mistreated by the employer."

Developments in relation to sexual harassment were not confined to the courtroom. The year 1978 saw the publication of Lin Farley's *The Sexual Harassment of Women at Work* and, the following year, Catherine McKinnon's enormously influential *Sexual Harassment of Working Women: A Case of Discrimination* was published. In the same year (1979) Congressional hearings were held to investigate sexual harassment in the federal government, and a directive prohibiting sexual harassment was published by the White House Office of Personnel. In 1980 sexual harassment of state employees was banned in Illinois and the Federal Equal Employment Opportunity Commission (EEOC) published guidelines on sexual harassment. The guidelines, although not legally binding, proved influential even in the Supreme Court.[18]

Equal Employment Opportunity Commission,   **4.US.9.**
"Guidelines on Sexual Harassment"[19]

Unwelcome sexual advances, requests for sexual favors, and other verbal or physical conduct of a sexual nature constitute sexual harassment when

(1) submission to such conduct is made either explicitly or implicitly a term or condition of an individual's employment,

(2) submission to or rejection of such conduct by an individual is used as the basis for employment decisions affecting such individual, or

(3) such conduct has the purpose or effect of unreasonably interfering with an individual's work performance or creating an intimidating, hostile, or offensive working environment.

Early cases recognising sexual harassment as a form of unlawful discrimination had involved quid pro quo harassment ((1) and (2) in the EEOC Guidelines above), although they did not use the term which was coined by Catherine McKinnon in her 1979 book. But in 1980 the beginnings of the expansion of the concept to include hostile environment cases ((3) above) were seen in *Brown* v. *City of Gutherie*,[20] and in *Bundy* v. *Jackson* (1981) the District of Columbia Circuit Court of Appeal, which had in 1977 insisted on actual employment repercussions as a precondition for a finding of harassment-related discrimination under Title VII, ruled that subjection to sexual insults and propositions was actionable as sex discrimination without proof of actual loss.[21] In 1982 the EEOC Guidelines were relied upon by the Eleventh Circuit Court of Appeal in *Henson* v. *City of Dundee* in classifying hostile environment sexual

---

[18] *Meritor Savings Bank FSV* v. *Vinson* 477 US 57 (1986), see below **4.US.11.**
[19] 29 CFR § 1604.11(a) (1980).
[20] 30 EPD P 33, 031 (W.D. Okla. 1980).
[21] 641 F.2d 934.

harassment as a form of sex discrimination, as were decisions including that in *Rogers* v. *EEOC*.

Eleventh Circuit Court of Appeals, 682 F.2d 897 C.A.Fla (1982)   **4.US.10.**
Henson v. *City of Dundee*

"HOSTILE ENVIRONMENT" HARASSMENT AS ACTIONABLE SEX DISCRIMINATION

Henson

Facts: The claimant, a former police dispatcher, claimed a breach of Title VII after she was subjected by her supervisor to "numerous harangues of demeaning sexual inquiries and vulgarities" over a period of two years, as well as repeated requests for sexual relations and victimisation connected with her refusal of these requests.

Held: A lower court had dismissed her claim on the basis that Title VII did not cover "hostile and demeaning work environment" harassment "standing alone", and that

"although Henson's supervisor, Sellgren, subjected her and her female co-worker to 'crude and vulgar language, almost daily inquiring of these two women employees as to their sexual habits and proclivities,' . . . there was no violation of Title VII unless Sellgren's conduct inflicted upon Henson some tangible job detriment."

The lower court did not accept that the claimant resigned because of "an intolerable, sexually demeaning work environment" or that she had been mistreated as a result of her refusal of sexual relations with her supervisor. The Court of Appeal allowed her appeal.

Judgment: VANCE J: "Henson contends that a plaintiff states a claim under Title VII by alleging that sexual harassment perpetrated or condoned by an employer has created a hostile or offensive work environment. She argues that the trial court erred by holding that a Title VII plaintiff must allege in addition that she suffered some tangible job detriment as a result of working in such an environment. We agree that under certain circumstances the creation of an offensive or hostile work environment due to sexual harassment can violate Title VII irrespective of whether the complainant suffers tangible job detriment . . .

Title VII prohibits employment discrimination on the basis of gender, and seeks to remove arbitrary barriers to sexual equality at the workplace with respect to 'compensation, terms, conditions, or privileges of employment.' . . . The former fifth circuit has held that 'terms, conditions, or privileges of employment' include the state of psychological well being at the workplace. In the area of race discrimination, Judge Goldberg stated: the phrase 'terms, conditions, or privileges of employment' in (Title VII) is an expansive concept which sweeps within its protective ambit the practice of creating a working environment heavily charged with ethnic or racial discrimination [citing *Rogers* v. *EEOC*, above **4.US.7.**]. Therefore, courts have held that an employer violates Title VII simply by creating or condoning an environment at the workplace which significantly and adversely affects an employee because of his race or ethnicity, regardless of any other tangible job detriment to the protected employee . . .

Sexual harassment which creates a hostile or offensive environment for members of one sex is every bit the arbitrary barrier to sexual equality at the workplace that racial harassment is to racial equality. Surely, a requirement that a man or woman run a gauntlet of sexual abuse in return for the privilege of being allowed to work and make a living can be as demeaning and disconcerting as the harshest of racial epithets. [Referring to the hearings of the Senate Committee on Labor and Human Resources (Sex Discrimination in the Workplace, 1981,

Hearings Before the Senate Comm. on Labor and Human Resources, 97th Cong., 1st Sess. 336) and the evidence given thereto by the chairman of the Equal Employment Opportunity Commission about "the rising number of charges filed with the agency that complained of sexual harassment".] A pattern of sexual harassment inflicted upon an employee because of her sex is a pattern of behaviour that inflicts disparate treatment upon a member of one sex with respect to terms, conditions, or privileges of employment. There is no requirement that an employee subjected to such disparate treatment prove in addition that she has suffered tangible job detriment.

Of course, neither the courts nor the E.E.O.C. have suggested that every instance of sexual harassment gives rise to a Title VII claim against an employer for a hostile work environment. Rather, the plaintiff must allege and prove a number of elements in order to establish her claim. These elements include the following:

(1) The employee belongs to a protected group. As in other cases of sexual discrimination, this requires a simple stipulation that the employee is a man or a woman.

(2) The employee was subject to unwelcome sexual harassment. The E.E.O.C. regulations helpfully define the type of conduct that may constitute sexual harassment: 'sexual advances, requests for sexual favors, and other verbal or physical conduct of a sexual nature . . ..' In order to constitute harassment, this conduct must be unwelcome in the sense that the employee did not solicit or incite it, and in the sense that the employee regarded the conduct as undesirable or offensive . . .

(3) The harassment complained of was based upon sex. The essence of a disparate treatment claim under Title VII is that an employee or applicant is intentionally singled out for adverse treatment on the basis of a prohibited criterion . . . In proving a claim for a hostile work environment due to sexual harassment, therefore, the plaintiff must show that but for the fact of her sex, she would not have been the object of harassment.

In the typical case in which a male supervisor makes sexual overtures to a female worker, it is obvious that the supervisor did not treat male employees in a similar fashion. It will therefore be a simple matter for the plaintiff to prove that but for her sex, she would not have been subjected to sexual harassment . . . However, there may be cases in which a supervisor makes sexual overtures to workers of both sexes or where the conduct complained of is equally offensive to male and female workers [citing *Barnes* v. *Costle*, above **4.US.8.**]. In such cases, the sexual harassment would not be based upon sex because men and women are accorded like treatment. Although the plaintiff might have a remedy under state law in such a situation, the plaintiff would have no remedy under Title VII . . .

(4) The harassment complained of affected a 'term, condition, or privilege' of employment. The former fifth circuit has held that the state of psychological well being is a term, condition, or privilege of employment within the meaning of Title VII . . . The court in *Rogers* made it clear, however, that the 'mere utterance of an ethnic or racial epithet which engenders offensive feelings in an employee' does not affect the terms, conditions, or privileges of employment to a sufficiently significant degree to violate Title VII . . . For sexual harassment to state a claim under Title VII, it must be sufficiently pervasive so as to alter the conditions of employment and create an abusive working environment. Whether sexual harassment at the workplace is sufficiently severe and persistent to affect seriously the psychological well being of employees is a question to be determined with regard to the totality of the circumstances . . .

(5) *Respondent superior.* Where, as here, the plaintiff seeks to hold the employer responsible for the hostile environment created by the plaintiff's supervisor or co-worker, she must show that the employer knew or should have known of the harassment in question and failed to take prompt remedial action . . ."

In many ways *Henson* is the classic statement of the US approach to harassment as a species of discrimination, particularly in the emphasis (paragraph (3) above) on disparate (less favourable) treatment. The US Supreme Court did not recognise "hostile environment" harassment for a further four years, when it decided the *Meritor Savings Bank* case.

US Supreme Court, 477 US 57 (1986)   **4.US.11.**
Meritor Savings Bank v. *Vinson*

"HOSTILE ENVIRONMENT" HARASSMENT AS ACTIONABLE SEX DISCRIMINATION

Meritor Savings Bank

Facts: A former employee of the bank brought a Title VII action against the bank and her former manager, claiming that she had been subjected to sexual harassment by the manager who had repeatedly pressurised her to have sex with him, which she did on 40 or 50 occasions out of fear of losing her job. It was also alleged that he fondled her in front of other employees, followed her into the women's bathroom when she went there alone, exposed himself to her, and even forcibly raped her on several occasions.

Held: A lower court ruled that any sexual relationship between the claimant and her former manager was voluntary and had nothing to do with her continued employment, and that she was not therefore the victim of sexual harassment. The Court of Appeals and Supreme Court disagreed, the latter stressing that the relevant question was whether sexual contact was "unwanted", rather than whether it was voluntary. The Supreme Court did not require, in relation to "hostile environment" sexual harassment, that a claimant establish economic loss, although it did demand that the harassment "be sufficiently severe or pervasive as to alter the conditions of the victim's employment".

Judgment: REHNQUIST J: "Respondent argues, and the Court of Appeals held, that unwelcome sexual advances that create an offensive or hostile working environment violate Title VII. Without question, when a supervisor sexually harasses a subordinate because of the subordinate's sex, that supervisor 'discriminate[s]' on the basis of sex. Petitioner apparently does not challenge this proposition. It contends instead that in prohibiting discrimination with respect to 'compensation, terms, conditions, or privileges' of employment, Congress was concerned with what petitioner describes as 'tangible loss' of 'an economic character,' not 'purely psychological aspects of the workplace environment.' . . .

We reject petitioner's view. First, the language of Title VII is not limited to 'economic' or 'tangible' discrimination. The phrase 'terms, conditions, or privileges of employment' evinces a congressional intent 'to strike at the entire spectrum of disparate treatment of men and women' in employment . . . Petitioner has pointed to nothing in the Act to suggest that Congress contemplated the limitation urged here.

Second, in 1980 the EEOC issued Guidelines specifying that 'sexual harassment,' as there defined, is a form of sex discrimination prohibited by Title VII . . . The EEOC Guidelines fully support the view that harassment leading to non-economic injury can violate Title VII.

In defining 'sexual harassment,' the Guidelines first describe the kinds of workplace conduct that may be actionable under Title VII. These include '[u]nwelcome sexual advances, requests for sexual favors, and other verbal or physical conduct of a sexual nature.' Relevant to the charges at issue in this case, the Guidelines provide that such sexual misconduct constitutes prohibited 'sexual harassment,' whether or not it is directly linked to the grant or denial of an economic quid pro quo, where 'such conduct has the purpose or effect of unreasonably interfering with an individual's work performance or creating an intimidating, hostile, or offensive working environment.'

In concluding that so-called 'hostile environment' (i.e., *non quid pro quo*) harassment violates Title VII, the EEOC drew upon a substantial body of judicial decisions and EEOC precedent holding that Title VII affords employees the right to work in an environment free from discriminatory intimidation, ridicule, and insult . . .

Of course, as the courts in both *Rogers* and *Henson* recognized, not all workplace conduct that may be described as 'harassment' affects a 'term, condition, or privilege' of employment within the meaning of Title VII . . . For sexual harassment to be actionable, it must be sufficiently severe or pervasive 'to alter the conditions of [the victim's] employment and create an abusive working environment." Respondent's allegations in this case—which include not only pervasive harassment but also criminal conduct of the most serious nature—are plainly sufficient to state a claim for 'hostile environment' sexual harassment.

The question remains, however, whether the District Court's ultimate finding that respondent 'was not the victim of sexual harassment,' . . . effectively disposed of respondent's claim. The Court of Appeals recognized, we think correctly, that this ultimate finding was likely based on one or both of two erroneous views of the law. First, the District Court apparently believed that a claim for sexual harassment will not lie absent an economic effect on the complainant's employment . . . Since it appears that the District Court made its findings without ever considering the 'hostile environment' theory of sexual harassment, the Court of Appeals' decision to remand was correct.

Second, the District Court's conclusion that no actionable harassment occurred might have rested on its earlier 'finding' that '[i]f [respondent] and Taylor did engage in an intimate or sexual relationship . . ., that relationship was a voluntary one.' . . . But the fact that sex-related conduct was 'voluntary,' in the sense that the complainant was not forced to participate against her will, is not a defense to a sexual harassment suit brought under Title VII. The gravamen of any sexual harassment claim is that the alleged sexual advances were 'unwelcome.' While the question whether particular conduct was indeed unwelcome presents difficult problems of proof and turns largely on credibility determinations committed to the trier of fact, the District Court in this case erroneously focused on the 'voluntariness' of respondent's partici-pation in the claimed sexual episodes. The correct inquiry is whether respondent by her conduct indicated that the alleged sexual advances were unwelcome, not whether her actual participation in sexual intercourse was voluntary".

Litigation arising in the aftermath of *Meritor* concerned matters such as the steps which could and should be taken in respect of alleged harassers.[22] Many of the other questions which have arisen across those jurisdictions in which sexual harassment is regulated have been the subject of litigation in the US, amongst them:

— whether the alleged victim's past conduct excludes her from legal protection against sexual harassment (no);[23]
— whether a claim of sexual harassment can succeed based on the fact that the claimant was disadvantaged by comparison with a co-worker who engaged in a sexual relationship with a supervisor (yes);[24]

---

[22] *Ellison* v. *Brady* 9th C-A, 23 January 1991 and *Strochmann Bakeries Inc.* v. *Teamsters Local* 776 969 F.2nd 1442 (CA-3, 1992), discussed by Aeberhard-Hodges, above n. 16, 510–11.
[23] *Katz* v. *Dole* 709 F.2d 251 (4th Cir. 1983).
[24] *Toscano* v. *Nimmo* 570 F.Supp. 1197 (D.C.Del. 1983), 31 August 1983.

— whether non-sexual physical violence to which a person of the other sex than the claimant would not have been subjected amounts to actionable sexual harassment (yes);[25]
— whether the display of sexually explicit or otherwise provocative pictures can amount to sexual harassment (yes);[26]
— whose standard prevails in determining whether conduct was sufficiently severe or pervasive to create a hostile work environment (that of a "reasonable woman" where the complainant is a woman, or of a "reasonable man" where the complainant is a man);[27]
— whether same-sex sexual harassment is actionable as sex discrimination (yes);[28]
— the extent of an employer's vicarious liability for harassment by its staff;[29] and
— under what circumstances employers may be liable for sexual harassment by third parties.[30]

Many of these questions concern sexual harassment in particular, although others are of relevance to harassment more generally.

In 1991 sexual harassment became a focus of national attention in the US as a result of the confidential affidavit submitted by Professor Anita Hill to the Senate Judiciary Committee which alleged that Supreme Court nominee Clarence Thomas had sexually harassed her between 1981 and 1983, when he was Director of the EEOC. Senate hearings on the matter were held in October 1991 and the following year the EEOC reported a 62% increase in the number of harassment complaints received between 1991 and 1992.[31] In 1992 four senators were accused of sexual harassment, Senator Brock Adams terminating a bid for re-election as a result,[32] and the following year the US Defence Department issued a report on sexual harassment which had taken place during a 1991 naval convention. The report implicated no fewer than 117 naval officers in the sexual abuse of 83 women and seven men, and accused a further 51 officers of lying to investigators. Only seven officers were disciplined, but the Secretary of the Navy resigned at the request of Secretary of Defense and the Assistant Chief of Naval Operations retired at reduced rank because of his lack of effort to stop the harassment.[33] Two years later, US law firm Baker & McKenzie found themselves at the wrong end of an award of $7.1 million punitive damages when it failed to end harassment against the claimant secretary.[34] Small

[25] *McKinney* v. *Dole* 765 F.2d 1129 (D.C.Cir. 1985).
[26] The Sixth Circuit Court ruled in *Robinson* v. *Jacksonville Shipyards* 760 F.Supp. 1486, 1524 (M.D.Fla. 1991) that all pictures—not limited to pornography—in which the model "is posed for the obvious purpose of displaying or drawing attention to private portions of his or her body" constitute a hostile environment.
[27] In *Ellison* v. *Brady*, above n. 22, the Ninth Circuit Court adopted a reasonable woman standard as the appropriate test to be applied in determining whether conduct is sufficiently severe or pervasive to create a hostile work environment.
[28] *Oncale* v. *Sundowner Offshore Services* 523 U.S. 75 (1998).
[29] *Faragher* v. *City of Boca Raton, Burlington* v. *Ellerth* 524 U.S. 742, 761 (1998).
[30] *Davis* v. *Monroe County Board of Education, et al.* 526 U.S. 629 (1999).
[31] Available on the website of Information on Sexual Harassment.
[32] *Ibid.*
[33] *Ibid.*
[34] *Ibid.*

wonder it was, then, that, as we shall see below, a number of European countries balked at opening the "Pandora's box" of sexual harassment litigation.

It should be emphasised that sexual and racial harassment are actionable under Title VII only where they amount to less favourable treatment on grounds of sex or race. This was emphasised by the Supreme Court in *Oncale* v. *Sundowner Offshore Servs., Inc.*, in which it accepted that same-sex sexual harassment could breach Title VII's prohibition on sex discrimination.

US Supreme Court, 523 US 75 (1998)   **4.US.12.**
Oncale v. Sundowner Offshore Servs., Inc.

SAME-SEX SEXUAL HARASSMENT AS SEX DISCRIMINATION

Oncale

Facts: The claimant, who had been employed on an oil rig, complained that he had been subjected to sex-related, humiliating actions against him by fellow workers, including sexual assault and threatened rape. His complaints to management produced no remedial action, instead resulting in victimisation by the company's Safety Compliance Clerk. The first instance District Court and Appeal Court ruled that same-sex harassment could not breach Title VII. The Supreme Court allowed his appeal.

Held: Proof of sexual motivation was unnecessary to establish sex discrimination by way of sexual harassment. For sexual harassment to breach Title VII, however, it must be motivated by the recipient's gender. This could be established by offering "credible evidence that the harasser was actually motivated by sexual desire toward members of his own gender"; by offering "proof of gender-specific statements from which an inference can be drawn that 'the harasser is motivated by general hostility to the presence of members of the same sex in the workplace"; or by offering "comparative evidence showing differences in how the harasser treated members of both sexes in the workplace".

Judgment: JUSTICE SCALIA: "Title VII's prohibition of discrimination 'because of . . . sex' protects men as well as women . . . and in the related context of racial discrimination in the workplace we have rejected any conclusive presumption that an employer will not discriminate against members of his own race. 'Because of the many facets of human motivation, it would be unwise to presume as a matter of law that human beings of one definable group will not discriminate against other members of their group.' . . . If our precedents leave any doubt on the question, we hold today that nothing in Title VII necessarily bars a claim of discrimination 'because of . . . sex' merely because the plaintiff and the defendant (or the person charged with acting on behalf of the defendant) are of the same sex.

Courts have had little trouble with that principle in cases . . . where an employee claims to have been passed over for a job or promotion. But when the issue arises in the context of a 'hostile environment' sexual harassment claim, the state and federal courts have taken a bewildering variety of stances. Some, like the Fifth Circuit in this case, have held that same-sex sexual harassment claims are never cognizable under Title VII . . . Other decisions say that such claims are actionable only if the plaintiff can prove that the harasser is homosexual (and thus presumably motivated by sexual desire) . . . Still others suggest that workplace harassment that is sexual in content is always actionable, regardless of the harasser's sex, sexual orientation, or motivations . . .

We see no justification in the statutory language or our precedents for a categorical rule excluding same-sex harassment claims from the coverage of Title VII. As some courts have

496

observed, male-on-male sexual harassment in the workplace was assuredly not the principal evil Congress was concerned with when it enacted Title VII. But statutory prohibitions often go beyond the principal evil to cover reasonably comparable evils, and it is ultimately the provisions of our laws rather than the principal concerns of our legislators by which we are governed. Title VII prohibits 'discriminat[ion] . . . because of . . . sex' in the 'terms' or 'conditions' of employment. Our holding that this includes sexual harassment must extend to sexual harassment of any kind that meets the statutory requirements.

Respondents and their *amici* contend that recognizing liability for same-sex harassment will transform Title VII into a general civility code for the American workplace. But that risk is no greater for same-sex than for opposite-sex harassment, and is adequately met by careful attention to the requirements of the statute. Title VII does not prohibit all verbal or physical harassment in the workplace; it is directed only at 'discriminat[ion] . . . because of . . . sex.' We have never held that workplace harassment, even harassment between men and women, is automatically discrimination because of sex merely because the words used have sexual content or connotations. 'The critical issue, Title VII's text indicates, is whether members of one sex are exposed to disadvantageous terms or conditions of employment to which members of the other sex are not exposed.' . . .

Courts and juries have found the inference of discrimination easy to draw in most male-female sexual harassment situations, because the challenged conduct typically involves explicit or implicit proposals of sexual activity; it is reasonable to assume those proposals would not have been made to someone of the same sex. The same chain of inference would be available to a plaintiff alleging same-sex harassment, if there were credible evidence that the harasser was homosexual. But harassing conduct need not be motivated by sexual desire to support an inference of discrimination on the basis of sex. A trier of fact might reasonably find such discrimination, for example, if a female victim is harassed in such sex-specific and derogatory terms by another woman as to make it clear that the harasser is motivated by general hostility to the presence of women in the workplace. A same-sex harassment plaintiff may also, of course, offer direct comparative evidence about how the alleged harasser treated members of both sexes in a mixed-sex workplace. Whatever evidentiary route the plaintiff chooses to follow, he or she must always prove that the conduct at issue was not merely tinged with offensive sexual connotations, but actually constituted 'discriminat[ion] . . . because of . . . sex.'

And there is another requirement that prevents Title VII from expanding into a general civility code: As we emphasized in *Meritor* and *Harris*, the statute does not reach genuine but innocuous differences in the ways men and women routinely interact with members of the same sex and of the opposite sex. The prohibition of harassment on the basis of sex requires neither asexuality nor androgyny in the workplace; it forbids only behavior so objectively offensive as to alter the 'conditions' of the victim's employment. 'Conduct that is not severe or pervasive enough to create an objectively hostile or abusive work environment—an environment that a reasonable person would find hostile or abusive—is beyond Title VII's purview.' . . . We have always regarded that requirement as crucial, and as sufficient to ensure that courts and juries do not mistake ordinary socializing in the workplace—such as male-on-male horseplay or intersexual flirtation—for discriminatory 'conditions of employment.'

We have emphasized, moreover, that the objective severity of harassment should be judged from the perspective of a reasonable person in the plaintiff's position, considering 'all the circumstances.' . . . . In same-sex (as in all) harassment cases, that inquiry requires careful consideration of the social context in which particular behavior occurs and is experienced by its target. A professional football player's working environment is not severely or pervasively abusive, for example, if the coach smacks him on the buttocks as he heads onto the field—even if the same behavior would reasonably be experienced as abusive by the coach's secretary (male or female) back at the office. The real social impact of workplace behavior often depends on a constellation of surrounding circumstances, expectations, and relationships which are not fully captured by a simple recitation of the words used or the physical acts performed. Common sense, and an appropriate sensitivity to social context, will enable courts and juries to distinguish between simple teasing or roughhousing among members of the same sex, and conduct which a reasonable person in the plaintiff's position would find severely hostile or abusive."

In *Price Waterhouse* v. *Hopkins* 490 US 228 (1989) the Supreme Court ruled that a claim of sex discrimination could be made out by a woman who was discriminated against for failing to conform to gender stereotypes (she had been denied promotion in part because of perceptions that she was "macho", that she "overcompensated for being a woman", and that she was "a lady using foul language". She had, further, been advised to take "a course at charm school", and to "walk more femininely, talk more femininely, dress more femininely, wear make-up, have her hair styled, and wear jewellery"). In *Jones* v. *Pacific Rail Services* (2001) a District Court in Illinois relied on *Price Waterhouse* to rule that the *Oncale* requirement for proof of motivation based on gender could be satisfied by evidence that the claimant was targeted for a failure to comply with gender-based stereotypes. But the US courts are for the most part very careful not to find a breach of Title VII where the harassment at issue is seen to relate to the claimant's sexual orientation, rather than his or her sex. Typical of the general approach is the decision below.

Seventh Circuit Court of Appeals, 231 F.3d 1080 (2000)   **4.US.13.**
Spearman v. *Ford Motor Co.*

HARASSMENT BASED ON SEXUAL ORIENTATION NOT SEX DISCRIMINATION

Spearman

Facts: The claimant complained of harassment, which consisted of his being referred to as a "bitch", compared to a famous drag queen, assigned tasks "traditionally reserved for women", called "gay" and "fag", and accused by his colleagues of looking at them "like a man would take a full look at a woman". He claimed that the harassment was because his "co-workers perceived him to be too feminine to fit the male image" at his workplace.

Held: The treatment was motivated by the claimant's homosexuality and not by his sex.

Judgment: CIRCUIT JUDGE MANION: "While sexually explicit language may constitute evidence of sexual harassment, it is not 'always actionable, regardless of the harasser's sex, sexual orientation, or motivations' [citing *Oncale*]. The plaintiff must still show that he was harassed because of his sex. Similarly, while sex stereotyping may constitute evidence of sex discrimination, '[r]emarks at work that are based on sex-stereotypes do not inevitably prove that gender played a part in a particular employment decision. The plaintiff must show that the employer actually relied on [the plaintiff's] gender in making its decision.' [citing *Price Waterhouse*]. Therefore, according to *Oncale* and *Price Waterhouse*, we must consider any sexually explicit language or stereotypical statements within the context of all

498

of the evidence of harassment in the case, and then determine whether the evidence as a whole creates a reasonable inference that the plaintiff was discriminated against because of his sex.

Here, the record clearly demonstrates that Spearman's problems resulted from his altercations with co-workers over work issues, and because of his apparent homosexuality. But he was not harassed because of his sex (i.e. not because he is a man). His harassers used sexually explicit, vulgar insults to express their anger at him over work-related conflicts. However, these conflicts did not arise because he is a man . . . It is clear that Curtis and Pearson lodged sexually explicit insults at Spearman to express their acrimony over work-related disputes and not to harass him because he is a man; and such conduct does not constitute sexual harassment . . .

The record also shows that Spearman's co-workers maligned him because of his apparent homosexuality, and not because of his sex. The testimonies of [his harassers] clearly demonstrate that Spearman's harassers were motivated by their suspicion of Spearman's sexual orientation and his perceived desire for some sort of physical intimacy with them . . . Moreover, Spearman's co-workers directed stereotypical statements at him to express their hostility to his perceived homosexuality, and not to harass him because he is a man . . . [One] called him a 'bitch' which, according to [another], means a 'woman,' or a 'faggot.' And the graffiti that specifically stated that Spearman is 'gay,' a 'fag,' and compared him to a drag queen confirms that some of his co-workers were hostile to his sexual orientation, and not to his sex.

VII is not a 'general civility code' for the workplace . . . it does not prohibit harassment in general or of one's homosexuality in particular. Likewise, sexually explicit insults that arise solely from altercations over work-related issues, while certainly unpleasant, do not violate Title VII. Because Spearman was not harassed because of his sex, his hostile environment claim fails."

In *Hamm v. Weyauwega Milk Products, Inc.* 332 F.3d 1058 the same court attributed the treatment of the plaintiff (a heterosexual man) to his perceived sexual orientation rather than his failure to conform to gender stereotypes, although it acknowledged that

> "distinguishing between failure to adhere to sex stereotypes (a sexual stereotyping claim permissible under Title VII) and discrimination based on sexual orientation (a claim not covered by Title VII) may be difficult. This is especially true in cases in which a perception of homosexuality itself may result from an impression of non-conformance with sexual stereotypes".

The claimant had been called a "faggot", "bisexual" and a "girl scout", and accused by his colleagues of "sizing [them] up". The Court refused to distinguish *Spearman* on the basis of the claimant's actual sexual orientation and ruled that Hamm had "not present[ed.] evidence to establish that the conduct he complains of 'was not merely tinged with offensive sexual connotations, but actually constituted 'discrimination because of sex'" (citing *Oncale*, above **4.US.12.**).[35]

Despite the strides made in relation to gender-stereotyping, the position for claimants who are (regarded to be) gay or lesbian has in many respects not improved significantly from that which prevailed prior to *Oncale*. Now, as then, it is next to

---

[35] This because other men had also been referred to as girl scouts by the harasser.

impossible for gay men or lesbians (or even someone suspected of being either) to convince a court that workplace harassment was because of their sex rather than (or as well as) their *sexual orientation*.

4.2.2. THE RECOGNITION OF HARASSMENT AND SEXUAL HARASSMENT IN INTERNATIONAL LAW

European courts lagged well behind those in the US in regulating sexual harassment, but the 1980s saw the start of significant activity at the international level, most particularly on the part of the International Labour Organisation (ILO) and the Committee for the Elimination of Discrimination against Women (the body which monitors compliance with the Convention on the Elimination of all forms of Discrimination against Women, CEDAW).

ILO Convention No. 111 of 1958, on Discrimination (Employment and Occupation), does not specifically mention sexual harassment. It does, however, prohibit "discrimination", which is defined to include "any distinction, exclusion or preference made on the basis of . . . sex . . . which has the effect of nullifying or impairing equality of opportunity or treatment in employment or occupation". In 1985 the International Labour Conference resolution on equal opportunity and equal treatment for men and women in employment recognised that sexual harassment at work was detrimental to employees' working conditions and to their employment and promotion prospects, and called for the inclusion of measures to combat and prevent it in policies for the advancement of equality.

In 1988, in its *General Survey* on the Convention, the ILO Committee of Experts on the Application of Conventions and Recommendations categorised sexual harassment as a form of sex discrimination and listed as examples of sexual harassment in employment the behaviours mentioned in section 4.1 above. According to the Committee, these forms of behaviour only amounted to "harassment" where they were justifiably perceived as a condition of employment or a precondition for employment; where they influenced decisions taken in relation to employment or prejudiced occupational performance; or where they humiliated, insulted or intimidated the person suffering from such acts.[36]

In 1989 the ILO also categorised sexual harassment as a health and safety matter[37] and the Committee on the Elimination of Discrimination against Women recognised sexual harassment as a form of violence against women contrary to CEDAW. CEDAW, which was adopted in 1979 by the UN General Assembly, does not mention

---

[36] This approach was reiterated in 1995 when the ILO Committee of Experts' Special Survey on Convention No. 111 provided additional examples of sexual harassment in the employment context, stressing that the unwelcome nature of such behaviour and the direct or indirect impact it has on the working relationship resulted in its recognition as form of sex discrimination contrary to Article 1 of the Convention. And in 2001, the ILO produced a definition of sexual harassment applicable to its entire staff in its *Collective Agreement on the Prevention and Resolution of Harassment-related Grievances*(ILO, 2001).

[37] 1989 Meeting of Experts on Special Protective Measures for Women and Equality of Opportunity and Treatment.

sexual harassment explicitly but prohibits "discrimination against women" and sets out standards for national action designed to end such discrimination.

In 1989 the Committee on the Elimination of Discrimination against Women also recommended that States Parties should include information about sexual harassment in the workplace in their periodic reports to the Committee.[38] Two years later, at its tenth session, the Committee "decided to allocate part of the eleventh session to a discussion and study on article 6 and other articles of the Convention relating to violence towards women and the sexual harassment and exploitation of women",[39] and the following year (1992) the Committee observed that "Equality in employment can be seriously impaired when women are subjected to gender-specific violence, such as sexual harassment in the workplace".[40]

Committee on the Elimination of Discrimination against Women **4.UN.14.**
General Recommendation No. 19 (11th session, 1992): Violence against women[41]

"3. At its tenth session in 1991, it was decided to allocate part of the eleventh session to a discussion and study on article 6 and other articles of the Convention relating to violence towards women and the sexual harassment and exploitation of women. That subject was chosen in anticipation of the 1993 World Conference on Human Rights, convened by the General Assembly by its resolution 45/155 of 18 December 1990 . . .

6. The Convention in article 1 defines discrimination against women. The definition of discrimination includes gender-based violence, that is, violence that is directed against a woman because she is a woman or that affects women disproportionately. It includes acts that inflict physical, mental or sexual harm or suffering, threats of such acts, coercion and other deprivations of liberty. Gender-based violence may breach specific provisions of the Convention, regardless of whether those provisions expressly mention violence.

17. Equality in employment can be seriously impaired when women are subjected to gender-specific violence, such as sexual harassment in the workplace.

18. Sexual harassment includes such unwelcome sexually determined behaviour as physical contact and advances, sexually coloured remarks, showing pornography and sexual demand, whether by words or actions. Such conduct can be humiliating and may constitute a health and safety problem; it is discriminatory when the woman has reasonable grounds to believe that her objection would disadvantage her in connection with her employment, including recruitment or promotion, or when it creates a hostile working environment . . .

24. In light of these comments, the Committee on the Elimination of Discrimination against Women recommends that:

(a) States parties should take appropriate and effective measures to overcome all forms of gender-based violence, whether by public or private act . . .

---

[38] General Recommendation No. 12, available on the UN website, Division for the Advancement of Women, Department of Economic and Social Affairs.
[39] General Recommendation No.19, para. 3 (11th session, 1992): "Violence against Women", available on the UN website, Division for the Advancement of Women, Department of Economic and Social Affairs.
[40] *Ibid.*
[41] *Ibid.*

(j) States parties should include in their reports information on sexual harassment, and on measures to protect women from sexual harassment and other forms of violence of coercion in the workplace . . .

(t) That States parties should take all legal and other measures that are necessary to provide effective protection of women against gender-based violence, including, *inter alia*:

(i) Effective legal measures, including penal sanctions, civil remedies and compensatory provisions to protect women against all kinds of violence, including, *inter alia*, violence and abuse in the family, sexual assault and sexual harassment in the workplace . . ."

In 1995 international attention was focused on sexual harassment as a result of the Fourth World Conference on Women held in Beijing. But for all the mentions and recommendations discussed above, the only international instrument expressly to refer to sexual harassment until the amendment of the Equal Treatment Directive in 2002 was the ILO's Convention No. 169 (the Indigenous and Tribal Peoples Convention, 1989), which deals in terms with sexual harassment against indigenous women.[42] Notwithstanding the flurry of activity at the international and (see below) national levels, Jane Aeberhard-Hodges, of the Equality and Human Rights Coordination Branch of the ILO, remarked in 1997 that "a perusal of the States' reports submitted to CEDAW under the Convention over the last five years reveals that very few governments do in fact include information about sexual harassment either in general or in employment" and that "the experts sitting on CEDAW make few comments concerning sexual harassment in general or in the workplace".[43] More recently, however, the UN Committee on the Elimination of Race Discrimination, which is responsible for adjudications under International Convention on the Elimination of All Forms of Racial Discrimination (ICERD), found that Australia breached the Convention by exposing an Aboriginal man to the word "Nigger".

Committee on the Elimination of Race Discrimination,   **4.UN.15.**
CERD/C/62/D/26/2002 (2002)[44]
Hagan v. *Australia*

EXPOSURE TO RACIALLY OFFENSIVE MATERIAL AMOUNTS TO DISCRIMINATION

Hagan

Facts: In 1960, the grandstand of an important sporting ground in Queensland was named the "E.S. 'Nigger' Brown Stand", in honour of a well-known sporting and civic personality, Mr E.S. Brown. The word "Nigger" was the nickname of Mr Brown, who was white. It was displayed on a large sign on the stand and repeated orally in public announcements relating to facilities at the ground and in match commentaries.

The complainant, an Aboriginal man, asked the trustees of the sports ground to remove the offending

---

[42] Article 20(3)(d).
[43] See Aeberhard-Hodges, above n. 16, 506.
[44] Available on the website of the High Commissioner for Human Rights.

term, which he found objectionable and offensive. The trustees consulted numerous members of the community, who did not object to the term and refused to remove it. The complainant's attempts to obtain a court order for the removal of the sign failed in Australia, the domestic courts ruling that he had not demonstrated that the decision was an act "reasonably likely in all the circumstances to offend, insult, humiliate or intimidate an indigenous Australian or indigenous Australians generally". Nor did the courts accept that the refusal to remove the sign was an act, in the words of the statutory language, "done because of the race . . . of the people of the group". Finally, the domestic courts took the view that Australian law did not protect the "personal sensitivities of individuals", as it considered to be the case here, but rather "render[ed] acts against individuals unlawful only where those acts involve treating the individual differently and less advantageously than other persons who do not share the membership of the complainant's racial, national or ethnic group". The complainant sought a ruling that Australia had discriminated against him contrary to ICERD.

Held: The display of the word "Nigger" was incompatible with Australia's obligations under ICERD to eliminate race discrimination.

Judgment: "The petitioner contends . . . that the term is 'the most racially offensive, or one of the most racially offensive, words in the English language'. Accordingly, he and his family are offended by its use at the ground and are unable to attend functions at what is the area's most important football venue. He argues that whatever may have been the position in 1960, contemporary display and use of the offending term is 'extremely offensive, especially to the Aboriginal people, and falls within the definition of racial discrimination in Article 1' of the Convention.

He clarifies that he has no objection to honouring Mr Brown or naming a football stand in his honour, but that at the time the nickname 'Nigger' was applied to Mr Brown, non-Aboriginal Australians 'either were not aware of or were insensitive to the hurt and offence that term caused to Aboriginal people'. He argues further that it is not necessary to repeat Mr Brown's nickname in order to honour him, for other stadia named after well-known athletes utilize their ordinary names, rather than their nicknames.

He argues that . . . any State party to the Convention has an obligation to amend laws having the effect of perpetuating racial discrimination. He contends that use of words such as the offending term in a very public way provides the term with formal sanction or approval. Words convey ideas and power, and influence thoughts and beliefs. They may perpetuate racism and reinforce prejudices leading to racial discrimination . . .

The Committee has taken due account of the context within which the sign bearing the offending term was originally erected in 1960, in particular the fact that the offending term, as a nickname probably with reference to a shoeshine brand, was not designed to demean or diminish its bearer, Mr Brown, who was neither black nor of aboriginal descent. Furthermore, for significant periods neither Mr Brown (for 12 years until his death) nor the wider public (for 39 years until the petitioner's complaint) objected to the presence of the sign.

Nevertheless, the Committee considers that that use and maintenance of the offending term can at the present time be considered offensive and insulting, even if for an extended period it may not have necessarily been so regarded. The Committee considers, in fact, that the Convention, as a living instrument, must be interpreted and applied taking into the circumstances of contemporary society. In this context, the Committee considers it to be its duty to recall the increased sensitivities in respect of words such as the offending term appertaining today.

The Committee . . . considers that the memory of a distinguished sportsperson may be honoured in ways other than by maintaining and displaying a public sign considered to be racially offensive. The Committee recommends that the State party take the necessary measures to secure the removal of the offending term from the sign in question and to inform the Committee of such action it takes in this respect."

Forms of harassment other than sexual harassment have more generally been dealt with by international bodies as instances of workplace violence rather than as examples of discrimination. In 1998, for example, the ILO published a major study which drew attention to "the emotional and psychological abuse referred to as 'bullying' and 'mobbing' [which], rather than the physical violence . . . represents the greatest threat to most workers".[45]

H. Hoel, K. Sparks & C.L. Cooper,   **4.INT.16.**
"The Cost of Violence/Stress at Work and the Benefits of
a Violence/Stress-free Working Environment"[46]

[Having pointed out that research into "bullying" at work has become much more prevalent in recent years]
" . . . the large number of 'labels' in use has so far made it difficult to get an overview of the problem and its prevalence. For example, whilst 'bullying' is the term most frequently used in the UK and Australia, this behaviour is referred to as 'mobbing' in Scandinavia and German speaking countries. Furthermore, in the US a similar phenomenon has been labelled 'workplace harassment' or 'mistreatment' and, most recently, 'emotional abuse'.

Research into the issue of workplace bullying started in Scandinavia in the 1980's. As part of a growing interest in work-related research in general, an early recognition of the importance of work-related stress had emerged. It is, therefore, not surprising that the first evidence of the problem of bullying, or 'mobbing' as it is referred to in Scandinavia and German speaking countries, emerged in Sweden and subsequently in Norway and Finland . . . some writers make a distinction between 'mobbing' and 'bullying', with 'mobbing' referring to those incidents of harassment where a group of people gang up on a single individual . . .

A widely used definition of bullying is:

'Bullying emerges when one or several individuals persistently over a period of time perceive themselves to be on the receiving end of negative actions from one or several persons, in a situation where the one at the receiving end has difficulties in defending him/herself against these actions'. [Adopting S. Einarsen, B.I. Raknes, S.B. Mathiesen & O.H. Hellesøy, *Mobbing og Harde Personkonflikter. Helsefarlig samspill på arbeidsplassen* (London, Sigma Forlag, 1994).]

Typical behaviours which may fall under the category of bullying are 'withholding information which may affect someone's work', 'attempts to find fault with someone's work', 'public humiliation', 'gossiping' and social exclusion or isolation. Whilst it may be unpleasant to be at the receiving end of someone's negative acts, even if it is a one-off event, such behaviour normally will fall outside the scope of the definition. The exception here may be negative acts of a nature and a severity which permanently instil fear in the recipient. It is worth noting that the definition relates to process development and victimisation, which is considered important for the effect it may have on the target and the surroundings and, therefore, for the costs it may cause or bring about."

---

[45] (University of Manchester Institute of Science and Technology, 1998), available from the ILO's website.
[46] *Ibid.*, 18–20.

On this definition, the authors concluded, from surveys carried out in Sweden, Austria, the UK, Ireland, the EU, Australia, the US and South Africa, that "at least 10% can be considered as being currently subjected to bullying".[47] They found it very difficult to estimate the prevalence of sexual and, in particular, racial harassment from the empirical research, the difficulties including the fact that "Where such studies are reported they are very often based on self-selected samples".[48] The authors cited studies conducted in the US (one of "'ethnic harassment' . . . (defined as verbal abuse and exclusionary conduct due to ethnicity)" found that 40–70% of Hispanic workers reported having experienced such behaviour within the last 24 months),[49] the EU, the UK (where a "significant proportion of participants reported to have experienced or to have witnessed racial harassment within the last 12 months"),[50] Germany, Bulgaria and Korea, reporting that "it is difficult to draw conclusions with regard to the current scale of sexual and racial harassment. However, it appears to be beyond doubt that these forms of violence represent a hazard to a considerable number of people."[51]

Di Martino, Hoel and Cooper remarked, in 2003, that "The original conceptual distinction between bullying (primarily referring to situations of individual harassment) and mobbing (primarily covering situations of collective harassment) is now giving way to a conceptual assimilation of these two terms":

V. Di Martino, H. Hoel and C.L. Cooper,   **4. INT.17.**
"Preventing violence and harassment in the workplace"[52]

"In the past, some researchers . . . have made a distinction between bullying and mobbing, arguing that mobbing is often concerned with aggression from a group of people and that this aggression tends to be directed towards one single person. Similarly, the ILO refers to mobbing as 'ganging-up or mobbing a target employee and subjecting that person to psychological harassment' [Citing D. Chappell and V. Di Martino, Violence at Work, Second Edition (Geneva: International Labour Organisation, 2000)]. However, most researchers now make no distinction between bullying and mobbing with regard to the number of perpetrators or targets involved. One may argue that even if a distinction was accepted, the psychological processes involved appear to be the same.

Both mobbing and bullying involve offensive behaviour through vindictive, cruel, malicious or humiliating attempts to undermine an individual or group of workers. These persistently

---

[47] *Ibid.*, 21.
[48] *Ibid.*, 23.
[49] K.T. Schneider, R.T. Hitlan and AT Radhakrishnan, "An Examination of the Nature of Correlates of Ethnic Harassment Experiences in Multiple Contexts" (2000) 85 *Journal of Applied Psychology* 3, cited by Hoel *et al.*, above n. 12, 22.
[50] Lemos and Crane (2000), "Tackling Racial Harassment in the NHS: Evaluating Black and Minority Ethnic Staff's Attitudes and Experiences" (unpublished NHS report), cited by Hoel *et al.*, above n. 12, 24.
[51] See Hoel *et al.*, above n. 12, 4–6.
[52] *Ibid.*

negative attacks on their personal and professional performance are typically unpredictable, irrational and unfair.

This progressive assimilation of mobbing and bullying does not mean, however, that the two terms are used interchangeably all around Europe. In some countries, such as Germany or the Nordic countries, the term 'mobbing' is the prevalent one, while for the same type of behaviour the word 'bullying' is used in Britain and Ireland. Even in countries with their own terms (such as *harcèlement moral* in France, *acoso or maltrato psicológico* in Spain, *coacção moral* in Portugal or *molestie psicologiche* in Italy), the two English terms, particularly mobbing, are becoming increasingly popular . . .

The variety of behaviours that constitute bullying/mobbing is so large that it is impossible to list them all. The fact is that much behaviour may or may not constitute bullying/mobbing, depending on the way it is carried out and its combination with other behaviours. Despite these difficulties in describing such behaviours, a large area of convergence can be detected across Europe . . ."

The documents which the authors rely on to show this convergence include *Guidance on Bullying*, issued in the UK by the major public sector union, UNISON, in 1996; the *Report of the Task Force on the Prevention of Workplace Bullying*, published in Ireland in 2001; and the 1993 Ordinance of the Swedish National Board of Occupational Safety and Health Containing Provisions on Measures against Victimisation at Work. What is notable about these definitions, reproduced below, is their focus on the nature of the behaviour rather than (as would be the case with the regulation of grounds-based harassment) on the reasons behind the behaviour. Thus, for example, the UNISON guidelines list "bullying" behaviour to include:

Guidance on Bullying, UNISON, 1996 **4.GB.18.**

"— . . . making life difficult for those who have the potential to do the bully's job better than
    the bully;
— punishing others for being too competent by constant criticism or by removing their
    responsibilities, often giving them trivial tasks to do instead;
— refusing to delegate because they feel they cannot trust anyone else;
— shouting at staff to get things done;
— persistently picking on people in front of others or in private;
— insisting that a way of doing things is always right;
— keeping individuals in their place by blocking their promotion;
— if someone challenges a bully's authority, overloading them with work and reducing the
    deadlines, hoping that they will fail at what they do;
— feeling envious of another's professional or social ability, so setting out to make them
    appear incompetent, or make their lives miserable, in the hope of getting them dismissed
    or making them resign.

The Irish report lists, inter alia, "undermining an individual's right to dignity at work; humiliation; intimidation; verbal abuse [and] repeated unreasonable assignments to duties which are obviously unfavourable to one individual". Only the Swedish

Ordinance explicitly makes the connection between bullying and (sexual) harassment, listing, as well as slander, deliberate withholding of work-related information, "persecution in various forms, threats and the inspiration of fear, degradation, e.g. sexual harassment". But it is clear that the types of behaviour listed in the Ordinance and in the UK and Irish materials are capable, if connected with a protected ground, of amounting to "harassment" within the definitions set out in the 2000 and 2002 Directives.

Di Martino *et al.*'s study of violence and harassment in the workplace recognised the particular vulnerability of some groups to workplace violence, and referred to a "progressive recognition that sexual and racial harassment [including jokes and sexual innuendos] are not 'lesser offences' and like all other forms of workplace violence, they constitute an affront to dignity at work". They go on to cite an observation made in the European Foundation for the Improvement of Living and Working Conditions' *Third European Survey on Working Conditions 2000* about the limited research carried out into harassment based on sexual orientation and race, and the focus there called for on the "specific characteristics" of workers in analyses of workplace violence, and continued:

V. Di Martino, H. Hoel and C.L. Cooper,   **4.INT.19.**
"Preventing violence and harassment in the workplace"[53]

"Increasing vulnerability appears a key factor in this area. This concept is capable of cutting across traditional boundaries and stereotypes to offer a new understanding of violence based on the specific characteristics of workers and group of workers within their workplaces, rather than just on their sector of activity, occupation or sex. By re-assembling the information on workplace violence around the concept of vulnerability, the current picture of violence at work might be substantially reshaped and a more effective means of action offered to policy-makers and the interested parties within the EU".

There is perhaps a certain tension between this perspective, with its concern for the experiences of those in particularly vulnerable groups, and that suggested by the 2001 working paper of the Directorate General for Research of the European Parliament in 2001, which remarked that:

"In most Member States . . . the legal remedies for bullied employees exist only insofar as certain isolated acts of the bullying process can be identified as general offences, such as an insult, libel or (sexual) harassment. The most typical actions of workplace bullying are much more subtle, thus undermining the legal protection available for the person concerned."[54]

---

[53] See V. Di Martino *et al.*, above n. 12.
[54] European Parliament, Directorate General for Research, "Bullying at Work" (Working Paper, Social Affairs Series, SOCI 108 EN, August 200), cited by Di Martino *et al.*, above n. 12, 49.

The resolution of this apparent tension may perhaps lie in the dual recognition that vulnerability to "bullying" and/or "harassment" at work is associated with factors such as race, sex, sexual orientation, religion or belief, age and disability (as well as, for example, appearance, low hierarchical status and a variety of other factors), but that it is not exclusive to those rendered especially vulnerable by their characterisation according to these or other factors, and that protection is required from "bullying" and "harassment" regardless of the "discriminatory" or "non-discriminatory" nature of the behaviour. It is equally the case, however, that the selection of persons for "bullying" or "harassment" by reference to protected grounds may be regarded as aggravating that "bullying" or "harassment", and that it may properly give rise to the additional protections afforded in relation to discrimination on protected grounds (these include, for example, favourable rules on the burden of proof and remedies).

During the 1980s and 1990s national legislatures began to take steps to regulate sexual harassment. In 1992, seven of 23 industrialised countries surveyed by the ILO had specific laws on sexual harassment (Australia, Canada, France, New Zealand, Spain, Sweden and the US). Between 1992 and 1996, Argentina, Chile, Costa Rica, the Philippines, New Zealand, South Africa, Austria, Belgium, Finland, France, Germany, Ireland, Italy, Malta and Switzerland all took or initiated steps to regulate sexual harassment,[55] and by 1997, Aeberhard-Hodges notes, 36 countries had legislation specifically targeting sexual harassment, while in many other jurisdictions health and safety legislation could be applied in respect of sexual harassment at work and/or remedies were available for sexual harassment in the context of "workers' compensation legislation".[56] These legislative responses took a variety of forms:

J. Aeberhard-Hodges, **4.INT.20.**
"Sexual harassment in employment: Recent judicial and arbitral trends"[57]

" . . .many jurisdictions are adopting the approach taken by the United States courts, namely that sexual harassment should be clearly identified as a form of sexual discrimination and, as such, a barrier to women's integration in the labour market. In that sense, in the United States decisions have exerted a strong influence on those in other jurisdictions. However, national law approaches remain remarkably different: France's recourse to penal sanctions, Spain's use of health and safety legislation, and the ongoing debate in South Africa about the need to prove fault for tort liability show that different legal systems are prepared to experiment with different legal standards in the attempt to establish the unacceptability of certain behaviour . . .

   Depending on the type of legal framework used, victims of harassment may obtain widely different results. Employment opportunity laws may be advantageous to complainants

---

[55] See Aeberhard-Hodges, above n. 16.
[56] J.Aeberhard-Hodges, interviewed in *ILO World of Work* (No. 19, March 1997).
[57] See Aeberhard-Hodges, above n. 16.

because special procedures for judicial action are usually in place and specialized bodies having expertise in discrimination based on sex are better able to judge both the facts presented to them and the law in reaching their findings. In countries where sexual harassment is considered to be a labour law matter, the impact of the law may be confined to instances of quid pro quo harassment, thus imposing on the complainant the requirement to prove some actual—or, in more recent cases, threatened—employment disadvantage based on the behaviour. Some European labour law provisions on constructive or unfair dismissal are used to protect against sexual harassment. The use of criminal law in this context can be problematic because of the strictness of the burden of proof and because in most systems espousing the presumption of innocence this rests squarely on the shoulders of the party making the allegation."

4.3. THE REGULATION OF HARASSMENT AND SEXUAL HARASSMENT IN THE EU AND ITS MEMBER STATES PRIOR TO 2000

France implemented laws against sexual harassment in 1992, and 10 years later against other forms of harassment. But prior to the implementation of the 2000 Directives by Decree in 2003, many EU Member States did not regulate harassment or sexual harassment as such at all. This lack of legal regulation did not, however, necessarily mean that harassment/sexual harassment were regarded with complacency. This is reflected in the EC Commission report on sexual harassment of 1998.

Commission of the European Communities   **4.EC.21.**
"Sexual harassment in the workplace in the European Union"[58]

"1. THE DEBATE ON SEXUAL HARASSMENT
    Sexual harassment at work started becoming an issue towards the end of the 80s, especially in France and Italy; in the other countries it was not yet really on the agenda. Nevertheless, that does not mean that the scale of the phenomenon was any smaller, merely that there was very little interest in, information about and awareness of it . . .
    However, the nature of the debate conducted in the two countries differs considerably. Whilst in France it focuses on the need for legislation, in Italy it has taken on a more ideological note and concentrates more on research into the causes of the phenomenon and political discussion of the concept used by European documents.
    French feminist associations were the first to call for legal sanctions against sexual harassment in 1990, putting forward a definition inspired by European Community texts and North American ideas. As a result, the phenomenon quickly moved on to the parliamentary agenda, which steered the debate along more traditional political lines. Surveys carried out whilst the debate was going on were also confined to establishing the impact or scale of the

---

[58] (European Commission, 1998), Directorate-General for Employment, Social Affairs and Equal Opportunities, Unit V/D.5.

phenomenon, without any attempt being made to reveal its true complexity. At that time too, the women's movement in France was more of a hostage to the parliamentary political system than in Italy . . .

In Italy, however, the government's insensitivity to the problem—it had not even provided the European Union with statistics or data on the scale of the phenomenon—brought greater involvement in the debate for the women's movement, which gave it a completely different tone.

The search for 'exemplary cases' first conducted by the communication media claimed to be intended to make up for the lack of knowledge and analysis on the subject as it was so new. This led women journalists and programme presenters to ask about the deeper motives for the spread of harassment and women's tendency to keep quiet about their traumatic experiences. Many of them wondered whether the problem of sexual harassment should not be placed in the historical context of the only very recent emancipation of women in Italy. For them 'finding work was like winning the lottery' and being tolerant towards 'male gallantry', as long as it was not disagreeable or vulgar, seemed to be one of the rules of the game.

Other women journalists, who were also looking at the problem from the point of view of the labour market and particularly the recent integration of women at work, explained the phenomenon by comparing the situation in the past—when women who worked were considered as having lax morals—with the current situation—where a woman was no longer criticised (at least not openly) for abandoning her role of spouse and mother—which unleashed a symbolic struggle to reappraise the value of individuals and led men, who felt threatened, to fall back on and even to reinforce the old stereotypes.

Finally, others focused on the fact that women were discriminated against at work. Here, proper recognition for work done by women was said to be needed to combat inequality between the sexes and prevent women having to cope with blackmail linked with sexual harassment, and also to form healthier working and legal relations in a wider perspective.

It was in this context that the need for a law to protect against sexual harassment emerged. Three different positions vis-à-vis the law could be identified:

— there were those who thought a law was vital as a means of protecting women;
— those who, on the basis of the American experience, feared that a law would trigger a sort of war between the sexes; and
— those who regarded it as more important to see how women could cope with the conflict with men without being obliged to play the part of victims.

The women's movement expressed its opposition to a law to protect against harassment using similar arguments to those put forward in the debate on the law against rape. Their reservations were not very different from those expressed on the advisability of promoting legislation on sexual harassment based on the definition in the Michael Rubenstein report. According to this report, sexual harassment is verbal or physical sexual behaviour which the perpetrator knows (or ought to know) is an affront to the victim, i.e. is unwelcome.

This definition (male intentions faced with a refusal expressed by a woman) excludes one fundamental aspect of harassment: the woman's subjective perception of it. The assumption that behaviour can be identified as sexual harassment only when it is defined as such by a woman turns the current legal thinking on its heads and focuses attention on the unquestioned legitimacy of the female experience, irrespective of men's stated intentions.

In this sense the results of the research show clearly that the harasser's and the victim's perceptions of harassment always differ. The fact is that men perceive, justify and present such behaviour completely differently from women. 'As a result, what men regard as legitimate, natural, inevitable and even agreeable for a woman, women feel to be illegitimate, arbitrary, displeasing and an affront to their freedom and dignity' . . .

The debate surrounding the definition of sexual harassment proposed in the Rubenstein report showed not only that it was necessary to find a more precise definition but above all that the definition of harassment was crucial in identifying legal solutions and standards to be adopted to cope with this problem. It was then obvious that more in-depth knowledge of and information on the subjective perception of sexual harassment was needed in order to find ways of solving the problem by legislation.

This was why the establishment of gendered legislation intended to promote women's self-determination occupied the stage from the beginning of the 90s, lawyers, trade unionists and politicians being involved as well as researchers. The definition drafted by the European Commission in 1991 (Recommendation 92/131 to which the Code of Practice is appended) identifies sexual harassment as 'unwanted conduct of a sexual nature, or other conduct based on sex affecting the dignity of women and men at work. This can include unwelcome physical, verbal or non-verbal conduct'. This definition gave rise to various proposals for laws and helped to standardise public administration collective agreements. It also influenced the law on positive action of 1991 which covers discrimination.

The debate which took place in Italy after the EC Recommendation was not confined to legal sanctions and focused mainly on the definition of sexual harassment. The definition in the European Recommendation gave rise to differing views from legal specialists.

Some regarded it as a major step forward in terms of the guidance it gave to the courts, since it placed the emphasis on the 'undesirability' of the conduct and made no attempt to give an objective typology because it could be interpreted differently by the person it is aimed at.

However, other specialists said that the 'undesirability' aspect did not take due account of the complexity of the relations between the sexes, since there were cases where, despite the fact that the victim did not object to certain actions, it could be shown that she was not consenting to them. Others too thought it was non-specific and vague and did not constitute a clear legal definition, which was contrary to the principle of the certainty of law . . .

From the 90s onwards in Italy, the discussion on the definition of sexual harassment and on whether a law was needed to combat it showed no signs of abating. Its intensity was such that the legislative procedure was blocked. At the beginning of the 90s, members of parliament said that there were profound differences of opinion, not only between the various political parties but also in the ranks of the progressives. The debate mainly centred on adoption of the subjective viewpoint because, even though it could well be a reliable means of plotting a course for women's policy, it might also prove inadequate as a yardstick or standard in judicial proceedings. The fear was that in practice—in order to eliminate potential conflicts of legal interpretation—'correct' behaviour, i.e. rules on normal sexual behaviour, would have to be defined precisely. Since such a definition would be governed by the authority 'which historically had patriarchal leanings', the law would end up backfiring on women.

Another key issue was the unlawfulness of sexual harassment. There were many doubts and conflicting opinions about including sexual harassment in criminal law but they did not differ greatly from those expressed with regard to the law against sexual violence. The main reservation hinged on the effectiveness of prosecution, since legislation alone could not resolve a problem of such a scale and with such complex origins. This point of view was shared fairly widely by women, even from a variety of political and cultural factions.

Other specialists pointed out, however, that it was incorrect to penalise and punish interpersonal communication and feared that sexuality would become the target of increasingly widespread condemnation. They were particularly reluctant to see the complexity of communication between the sexes subject to criminal law. Another issue was whether punitive legislation helped to assert women's rights to freedom. Despite negative reactions and doubts as to the advisability of a law on sexual harassment, those who participated in drawing up the proposal for a law did not think that it could be seen as infringing the principle of self-determination for women, as it guaranteed protection for it. Their argument was that offering protection—even under criminal law—was not a sign of weakness but, on the contrary, could make women aware of their rights and empower them instead of being a disincentive to standing up for them.

Others, without denying the importance of a law on sexual harassment at work, pointed out that an effective technical means of defending women's rights when they have been infringed was vital. In civil law, a change in women's favour has, in fact, already been seen, namely the reversal of the burden of proof, which can be applied to sexual harassment where it is regarded as an instance of discrimination."

We shall see below that other states were significantly less concerned about sexual harassment than were either France or Italy.

4.3.1.   HARASSMENT AND SEXUAL HARASSMENT IN THE EU

The European Parliament had in 1986 adopted a Resolution on violence against women, and on 27 November 1991 the European Commission's Recommendation on the protection of the dignity of women and men at work and an associated Code of Practice on measures to combat sexual harassment were adopted. A further Resolution was adopted by the Parliament in 1994 which concerned the creation of a new post of "confidential counsellor" in the workplace, and, in its 1995 fourth medium-term Community action programme on equal opportunities for men and women, the European Commission undertook to work towards a binding instrument on sexual harassment at work.[59] In 1998 the Commission published *Sexual harassment in the workplace in the European Union*, which detailed all relevant research projects which had been carried out across the EU between 1987 and 1997. The foreword by Pádraig Flynn, then Economic and Social Affairs Commissioner, cited the text of the 1991 Commission Recommendation on the protection of the dignity of women and men at work to the effect that: "Unwanted conduct of a sexual nature, or other conduct based on sex affecting the dignity of women and men at work, including the conduct of superiors and colleagues, is unacceptable."

Commission of the European Communities   **4.EC.22.**
"Sexual harassment in the workplace in the European Union"[60]

"FOREWORD
This assertion . . . . should be regarded as a statement of the obvious. To tolerate such conduct would be tantamount to a failure to respect the dignity and freedom to which every human

---

[59] [1995] OJ L335/37.
[60] See above **4.EC.21.**

being is entitled. All those who believe that this right to dignity is a universal fundamental value cannot accept the idea that the Community remains silent and inactive on this issue.

It has to be accepted—and the studies support the fact—that sexual harassment is still endemic, often hidden, affecting all Member States and existing in all kinds of companies. Yet it is still not viewed as a problem which has to be systematically tackled. Despite the absence of an universal definition and despite the various methods used to measure sexual harassment, figures show that between 30% and 50% of female employees still experience some form of sexual harassment . . .

One of the first things which struck me while reading these reports is the poor level of awareness, at all levels, in most of the Member States . . . Another element stressed by these studies and which caused me some dismay is the fact that it is still usually the harassed employee, rather than the harasser, whose career is negatively affected. This situation definitely deserves more attention and action. This need for further attention is reinforced by the fact that the studies have shown that where they exist actual means to combat sexual harassment do not always prove effective . . .

EXECUTIVE SUMMARY
The lack of an universal definition
The Commission definition, found in its 1991 Recommendation, is not known throughout Europe, especially in southern Member States. Furthermore, it is not accepted in all Member States and is not necessarily used in studies trying to measure sexual harassment.

The debate about what constitutes sexual harassment is still going on among researchers and at least one Member State (France) has concluded that the definition of sexual harassment as sexual discrimination is inadequate. It should also be pointed out that the same conclusion can be drawn as regards people surveyed. Not surprisingly men tend to confine sexual harassment to its most serious forms (physical assault), but even among women there are varying perceptions of what constitutes sexual harassment."

According to the findings of the 1998 report, sexual harassment was most commonly dealt with (when it was accepted as having occurred) by the administration of a formal or informal warning to the harasser and with no further action being taken. In the UK, according to a 1991 survey studied for the 1998 report: "The next most likely outcome was no action whatsoever. Furthermore, the victim of sexual harassment had a greater likelihood of being relocated as compared to the harasser." Nor were the UK results atypical. A Belgian national study conducted in the early 1990s[61] found that most complaints were resolved informally even where the harassment was of "the more severe physical forms", perpetrator receiving warnings rather than official sanctions. A Dutch study of harassment of home care workers demonstrated that harassing clients were warned or assigned different home care workers rather than having the provision of services to them terminated.[62] And a Dutch national

---

[61] A. Garcia, G. Colard-Dutry and C. Tholl, "Etude portant sur la mise en place des directives decoulant de l'A.R. de 18 septembre 1992 visant la protection des travailleurs contre le harcelement sexual sur les lieux de travail" (Louvain-La-Neuve, 1994), cited in *Sexual harassment in the workplace in the European Union*, above n. 58, 40.

[62] S. Dijkstra, "Ongewenste intimiteiten in de gezinszorg, de noodzaak van een helder beleid, Stichting tot wetenschappelijk Onderzoek omtrent Sekualiteit en Geweld" (Utrecht, 1992), cited in *Sexual harassment in the workplace in the European Union*, above n. 58.

study published in 1993 found that "dismissal or relocation of a harasser was not always [regarded as] practicable, for instance because of the high position of the harasser within the organisation".[63]

Following the publication of the 1998 report, the Commission in 2000 published proposals for Directives on race equality, employment equality and amendments to the Equal Treatment Directive (these proposals eventually being adopted as Directives 2000/43, 2000/78 and 2006/54 respectively). The proposals dealt with harassment on each of the protected grounds (racial or ethnic origin, religion or belief, disability, age and sexual orientation) as a form of discrimination, and the original proposal for amendment to the Equal Treatment Directive (see now the recast Gender Employment Directive) suggested the prohibition of "sexual harassment", which it defined as

> "unwanted conduct related to sex takes place with the purposes or effect of affecting the dignity of a person and/or creating an intimidating, hostile, offensive or disturbing environment, in particular if a person's rejection of, or submission to, such conduct is used as a basis for a decision which affects that person."

The Common Position adopted by the Council on the proposed Directive in July 2001 widened the approach by embracing a concept of "harassment" which was defined as "unwanted conduct related to the sex of a person [which] takes place with the purpose or effect of violating the dignity of a person and of creating an intimidating, hostile, degrading, humiliating or offensive environment", in addition to "sexual harassment", which referred specifically to "unwanted conduct of a sexual nature". In addition, the Common Position specified that "A person's rejection of, or submission to, such conduct may not be used as a basis for a decision affecting that person". That provision, which clarifies that "quid pro quo" sexual harassment is contrary to EU law, is now new Article 2.2(a) of the Recast Gender Employment Directive (Directive 2006/54/EC). Article 2.2 also provides that harassment and sexual harassment are "discrimination" for the purposes of the Directive.

The definitions of harassment and sexual harassment eventually adopted by the 2000 and 2006 Directives are set out in section 4.1 above. Questions of implementation are turned to below. It is useful here to point out, however, in view of the discussion in section 4.2.2 above as to the relationship between various forms of "harassment" and broader questions of workplace violence, the adoption in 2001 by the European Commission's Advisory Committee on Safety, Hygiene and Health Protection of an "Opinion on Violence at the Workplace".

---

[63] R. van Amstel and H.J. Volkers, "Seksuele intimidatie: voorkomen en beleid voeren, Ervaringen bij 50 arbeidsorganisaties, Onderzoek uitgevoerd in opdracht van het Directoraat-Generaal van de Arbeid door het Nederlands Instituut voor Arbeidsomstandigheden" (Den Haag, 1993), cited in *Sexual harassment in the workplace in the European Union*, above n. 58.

European Commission's Advisory Committee on Safety,   **4.EC.23.**
Hygiene and Health Protection, Opinion on Violence at the Workplace[64]

"Violence can be defined as a form of negative behaviour or action in the relations between two or more people, characterised by aggressiveness, sometimes repeated, sometimes unexpected, which has harmful effects on the safety, health and wellbeing of employees at their place of work.

Aggressiveness may take the form of body language indicating intimidation, contempt or disdain, or of actual physical or verbal violence.

Violence manifests itself in many ways, ranging from physical aggression to verbal insults, bullying, mobbing and sexual harassment, discrimination on grounds of religion, race, disability, sex or, in any event, difference, and may be inflicted by persons both outside and inside the working environment. It is important to bear in mind that physical violence can have consequences that are not only physical but also psychological, which can be immediate or delayed.

Unlike sexual harassment, which is defined in Directive 2000/78/EC, psychological violence, and mobbing in particular, is more difficult to describe. Let us just say that mobbing is a negative form of behaviour, between colleagues or between hierarchical superiors and subordinates, whereby the person concerned is repeatedly humiliated and attacked directly or indirectly by one or more persons for the purpose and with the effect of alienating him or her. This behaviour may take the form of sarcasm, criticism and gossip or lead to limitation of freedom of opinion or reduction of social prestige. The final outcome, which is not necessarily intended, is isolation from the working environment or alienation from the workplace or even the employment relationship.

While physical violence is fairly easy to identify on account of the obvious external signs, the same cannot be said of mental violence, the effects of which may often be denied or distorted.

Violence at the workplace, in all its forms and irrespective of whether it originates inside or outside the workplace itself, is a risk factor which the employer, whether public or private, has a duty to assess and prevent or reduce by means of specific measures in the same way as all other risk factors, pursuant to Article 6 of framework Directive 89/391/EEC. Indeed, under the terms of Article 6(1), the employer is obliged to assess all the risks, and the list of the risks related to chemical agents, work equipment, etc. is not exhaustive.

. . . the perception of this specific problem differs considerably from one Member State to another. There are countries which have enacted a law on the subject, others which have tackled the problem of violence with non-legislative measures, yet others which consider only internal violence as a workplace risk, whereas external violence is regarded as a general risk to the population and hence a problem of public order, and, lastly, others which have yet to develop an awareness of the problem.

. . . there is considerable reluctance to report cases of violence and . . . although there are few comparable national statistics on the subject, the phenomenon seems to be on the increase in all sectors.

Bearing in mind that this risk factor has already been referred to by the provisions of framework Directive 89/391/EEC, and in view of the situation illustrated by the abovementioned studies, we endorse the Commission's proposal for a recommendation on this subject. Such an initiative could provide effective encouragement to undertake a sound

---

[64] Adopted 29 November 2001, DOC 1564/2/01 EN.

assessment of the nature and scale of the problem, and to counter the lack of information on effective preventive measures.

The Commission should therefore draft guidelines based on the definition of the phenomenon in all its various forms and on its inclusion among the risk factors that employers are obliged to assess under the terms of the framework Directive. A model for the assessment of the specific risk as part of the overall assessment would therefore be useful.

The guideline should be based on an essentially preventive approach and therefore set out measures designed to head off the problem. The focus should therefore be on working conditions, work organisation, promoting a good working climate, and good cooperation between management and labour.

Training programmes for managers and workers would be particularly useful in order to draw attention to the problem and identify the appropriate conduct to be maintained in relations with the victims of violence.

While preventive measures should be the priority, they need to be accompanied by psychological and other support for the victims . . .

This initiative should also be accompanied by an awareness raising and information campaign to draw more attention to the problem and to the need to head off violence at work. The campaign should be focused on large, small and medium-sized enterprises and the public sector and be backed up by information material that is practical and easy to understand on good practice with regard to preventive and remedial approaches, as well as sanctions, which are needed whenever the other measures prove to be insufficient.

It would be preferable for the definition of the indicators of the quality of work to take account of the mental and psychosocial factors related to the working environment.

Given the seriousness and extent of the phenomenon of violence at work, it would be useful for the recommendation to be adopted by the Council so that it carries greater political weight with the Member States."

Also in 2001, the European Parliament called for the prioritisation of efforts to tackle workplace harassment, including bullying and sexual harassment, in its Resolution on Harassment at the Workplace, calling on Member States "with a view to counteracting bullying and sexual harassment at work, to review and, if appropriate, to supplement their existing legislation and to review and standardise the definition of bullying", and urging the Commission

> "to consider a clarification or extension of the scope of the framework directive on health and safety at work or, alternatively, the drafting of a new framework directive as a legal instrument to combat bullying and as a means of ensuring respect for the worker's human dignity, privacy and integrity."[65]

The Resolution "emphasize[d] in this connection the importance of systematic work on health and safety and of preventive action". More recently, the Commission stressed the need to adapt the legal framework to cover the emerging psycho-social risks:

[65] 2001/2339 (INI).

Commission of the European Communities, Communication **4.EC.24.**
from the Commission: Adapting To Change In Work And Society:
A New Community Strategy On Health And Safety At Work[66]

"The increase in psycho-social problems and illnesses is posing a new challenge to health and safety at work and is compromising moves to improve well-being at work. The various forms of psychological harassment and violence at work likewise pose a special problem nowadays, requiring legislative action. Any such action will be able to build on the *acquis* of recently adopted directives rooted in Article 13 of the EC Treaty, which defines what is meant by harassment, and make provision for redress. The Commission will examine the appropriateness and the scope of a Community instrument on psychological harassment and violence at work."

4.3.2. HARASSMENT AND SEXUAL HARASSMENT IN THE EU MEMBER STATES

Member States took a variety of approaches to the regulation of harassment/sexual harassment prior to the implementation of the 2000 Directives, and continue to do so notwithstanding a degree of convergence associated with the transposition of those Directives. Below we will consider the early impact of implementation on some of these legal approaches. First it is useful to consider the variety of pre-implementation approaches in more detail. Much of what is discussed in this section is specific to sexual harassment, few Member States having made any attempt to regulate "harassment" more generally prior to being required to do so by the 2000 Directives. It also concerns only a number of Member States, others having made little or no progress on legal measures against harassment/sexual harassment prior to transposition. We saw, above, the general lack of legal regulation amongst Southern European States. The following extract concerns attitudes in former Eastern bloc states:

"Sexual Harassment in Post-Communist Countries"[67] **4.EC.25.**

"A recent study commissioned by the Czech daily, Lidove Noviny indicated that almost half of the country's working women have been subjected to sexual harassment in the workplace. Reports from other post-Communist countries indicate that sexual harassment, though seldom identified as such, is widespread. The study found that 45 percent of Czech women had been sexually harassed, many of them repeatedly. Women's rights advocates said that the real figures are probably higher.

'Sexual harassment is something like folklore in the Czech Republic,' said Lenka Simerska, a sociologist at the Gender Studies Center in Prague. 'It's omnipresent, but it's not considered a

---

[66] 2002–2006 Com (2002) 118 Final.
[67] *New York Times*, 11 July 2000.

serious problem. You're supposed to laugh about it and say that it's a stupid invention of hysterical American feminists, and that actually, it does not exist here at all.'

But it does. Obscene jokes, suggestive remarks, unwelcome advances, gentle slaps on the buttocks—these are all part of a regular day for many working women who do not complain for fear of ridicule or losing their jobs.

The term often used for sexual harassment in the Czech Republic, 'sexualni haraseni,' discourages serious discussion. Coined by an exiled Czech writer, Joseph Skvorecky in the early 1990's, *sexualni haraseni* (phonetically similar to the English term) translates as 'sexual buzz' or 'sexual rumble,' with the tacit understanding that whoever complains about harassment is making an unnecessary fuss.

Discussion of sex is not considered taboo in this country. But the concept of sexual harassment is widely seen as a Western plague that threatens to spoil 'natural' relations between men and women. The few recent lawsuits reported in central Europe show that women have a very spare legal arsenal at their disposal. Since the country has laws against sexual harassment, victims usually sue for violation of the labor code, which provides a vaguely defined right to a harmless work environment.

Centrum Praw Kobiet, the women's rights center in Poland, has counseled dozens of sexual harassment victims but only one of them could claim any sort of legal success. The harassed woman, an employee of a large multinational corporation, won a payment equal to a year's salary as compensation, but she was still forced to leave her job.

'This one was lucky, because the company was international and was concerned about its reputation,' said Eleonara Zielinska, a law professor from Warsaw. Usually the compensation is about three months' pay, far less than in the West. And women must agree to leave their jobs before they can get any compensation at all.

Some things are gradually changing as some post-Communist countries have begun the process of passing laws to combat sexual harassment that would place them in step with the European Union, which they aspire to join. Slovenia hopes to pass a law in the spring, while the Czech government just sent a draft law for its first to reading Parliament. The task still lies ahead for Poland, Hungary and Slovakia, not to mention Balkan countries. And legal protection will not immediately change the deeply rooted attitudes and social climate."

A number of interesting questions arise concerning legal approaches to harassment and sexual harassment adopted across the various Member States. Most, post-implementation of the Directives, follow the definitions of harassment and sexual harassment therein fairly closely, although there are significant variations as regards important questions such as who is liable for harassment, what level of fault is required for liability, and what sanctions and/or remedies apply in respect of it. A much greater variety of approach characterised pre-implementation law. A number of Member States regulated sexual harassment and behaviour variously described as "mobbing", "bullying", "moral harassment" and "workplace violence" (any of these latter four categories of behaviour could include some forms of sexual harassment, and, depending in particular on the scope of the notion of "violence", much harassment related to sex and other subsequently protected grounds). But others did not make use of the terms "harassment" or "sexual harassment" in legislation, with the effect that the relevant legal questions were not so much "what is harassment?" or "what is sexual harassment?", but rather "what behaviour contravenes other workplace or general regulations?" Below we will consider a variety of approaches taken by Member States to harassment/sexual harassment before and after the transposition of the three discrimination Directives, the primary focus of our attention being on the extent to which victims of harassment were and are now afforded real and effective legal protection.

4.3.3. ADDRESSING HARASSMENT AND SEXUAL HARASSMENT OUTSIDE THE FRAMEWORK OF DISCRIMINATION LAW

Most national legal orders did not address harassment or sexual harassment in the context of discrimination law. This did not mean, however, that legal protections were entirely absent.

4.3.3.A. PENAL PROVISIONS

Some instances of sexual and other harassment will typically amount to criminal offences, whether or not of a kind which the authorities are quick to prosecute. Among these, generally, will be rape, other sexual and non-sexual assaults of a physical nature, and perhaps threatening behaviour and sexual contact resulting from threats or blackmail. A provision such as Article 154 of Portugal's Penal Code, for example, will regulate some instances of quid pro quo sexual harassment, while Article 181 of the same Code, which regulates verbal abuse, may capture other examples of sexual and other harassment.

Portuguese Penal Code   4.PT.26.

Article 154
Forcing a person into an action or an omission or support of an activity by means of violence or threats of grievous harm, shall be punished by a prison sentence of three years or a fine.

Article 181
Causing injury to a person by addressing remarks which are an affront to his or her honour and dignity shall be punished by a prison sentence of three months or a fine amounting to 120 days pay.

These and similar provisions are capable of being used to punish harassers, even absent any specific criminal provisions on harassment such as those found in France's Penal Code, or in the UK's Protection from Harassment Act 1997 (see further below). They will, however, be applicable only in respect of a small fraction of harassing behaviour, given their prohibition of specific types of abusive behaviour. Harassment and sexual harassment, on the other hand, may consist in subjection to a course of action in which individual instances of behaviour do not, taken out of context, appear abusive, but where the motivation for them, or the accumulation of many

519

episodes or examples of behaviour, transforms them into abusive treatment. The examples of bullying used in the UNISON guidance, for example, include "making life difficult", "constant criticism", the removal of responsibilities or allocation of "trivial tasks", refusals to delegate and the assignment of excessive work or inadequate deadlines, as well as "shouting" and "persistently picking on people in front of others or in private". It is difficult to see how these former examples, in particular, could be caught by non-targeted penal provisions.

It is worth noting in this context, also, that the application of criminal provisions against sexual harassment, in particular, appears to be unusual. Reliance on penal provisions is problematic in any event given the difficulties of proof generally associated with criminal liability (the shift in the burden of proof required by the discrimination Directives does not, for example, apply to criminal procedures). Victims of most forms of harassment may be disinclined to take legal action which results in criminal penalties rather than compensation or other remedy for claimants themselves. And criminal procedures are significantly less within the control of claimants than are civil proceedings, decisions as to prosecution typically resting with the police or prosecuting authorities rather than with the victims of crime, whose role is generally reduced to that of mere witness to proceedings.

4.3.3.B.   CIVIL PROVISIONS

Some examples of sexual and other harassment will breach civil laws regulating violent, threatening and/or coercive behaviour, and (perhaps) the securing of sexual contact in an abusive or exploitative way. In Italy, for example, where there was no express statutory regulation of harassment or sexual harassment prior to the transposition of the 2000 Directives, the law had "developed a set of principles which to a considerable extent corresponded to the idea of harassment, and provided protection in situations comparable to those foreseen by the Directives".[68]

> *A. Simoni, "Report on Measures to Combat Discrimination:*   **4.IT.27.**
> *Directives 2000/43/EC and 2000/78/EC. Country Report Italy"*

"Notwithstanding the lack until recently of statutory definitions, scholars and case-law, however, previously developed a set of principles which to a considerable extent corresponded to the idea of harassment, and provided protection in situations comparable to those foreseen by the Directives. Much has been done for instance under the label of 'mobbing' . . . since the courts have identified a ground for civil liability in article 2087 of the Civil Code [which provides that employers 'must adopt, in the exercise of the business, and according to the nature of the work, the experience and the technique, the necessary measures to protect the

---

[68] A.Simoni, "Report on Measures to Combat Discrimination: Directives 2000/43/EC and 2000/78/EC. Country Report Italy" (European Commission, 2004) 11, available on the website of Directorate-General for Employment, Social Affairs and Equal Opportunities.

physical integrity and the moral personality of the workers'] and 2103 [which provides that 'The worker must be assigned to the tasks [*mansioni*, i.e. the position and all the activities which make up that position] for which he was recruited, or to the tasks related to the superior category successively reached . . . '] of the Civil Code . . . (as well as article 2043 on damage compensation) . . .''

Portugal's Civil Code specifically provides the following.

Portuguese Civil Code **4.PT.28.**

Article 70 1, Book I, Title II, Chapter I, Section II
The law protects individuals against any unlawful offence or offensive threat to their physical or mental integrity.

Article 483 1, Book II, Chapter I, Section V, Subsection I.
Anyone who unlawfully infringes the right of others or any legal provision designed to protect the interests of others shall be obliged to compensate the person for the damages resulting from such infringement.

Provisions such as these, which do not define or regulate harassment or sexual harassment per se, do not give rise to significant litigation in connection with such harassment. And in France, although harassing behaviour ought on normal principles to give rise to liability in tort, it was remarked in 1997 that "until now no Court has ruled in that sense", perhaps because, as the commentator further points out, "Claimants have to make their own complaints, whether to the police or the courts, and risk a counterclaim for defamation".[69]

4.3.3.C. HEALTH AND SAFETY PROVISIONS

A further non-specific legal weapon against harassment and sexual harassment consists in health and safety law, of which employers may also fall foul by permitting harassment to occur or to continue.[70] In Portugal, while there was no explicit regulation of harassment or sexual harassment as such prior to the transposition of the 2000 Directives, national labour law imposed on employers "the obligation to organise good working conditions for workers, from both the physical and mental point of view",[71] and provided that "[w]ork must be organised and carried out in conditions of discipline, safety, health and moral conduct". Employers were, further, obliged "to institute disciplinary penalties or to dismiss workers of either sex who, by their conduct, cause or threaten to cause demoralisation of their colleagues, especially

---

[69] C. Goette, "Sexual Harassment in the Workplace in France and the USA" (1997, spring) National Lawyers' Association Review.
[70] Di Martino *et al.*, above n. 12, 4, points this out in relation to France.
[71] Art. 19(c) of Decree-Law 49 408 of 24 November 1969.

women and minors",[72] or who infringed the rights or guarantees of the workers in the enterprise or were responsible for physical violence, abuse or other offences prohibited by the law against workers in the enterprise.[73]

The regulation of sexual and other harassment as a health and safety issue can be valuable as a preventative measure, though such provisions do not necessarily give rise to any entitlement to compensation on the part of the victim. As part of a package of legal measures to deal with harassment/sexual harassment, health and safety provisions may have an important role. But in the absence of explicit prohibitions of harassment/sexual harassment, health and safety measures may have limited effect since those responsible for securing appropriate standards may fail to recognise that harassing behaviour entails physical and psychological violence. It is this very recognition which is crucial to an adequate legal and social response to harassment and sexual harassment, which are regularly trivialised as something that has to be "put up with", "natural behaviour", "inevitable", etc.[74]

4.3.3.D.   GENERAL LABOUR LAW PROVISIONS

The fourth non-specific line of defence against harassment and sexual harassment consists in general labour law. The resignation of a harassed employee may, in particular, be regarded as a dismissal for the purposes of general labour law protection, including protection from unfair dismissal. In Belgium, for example, prior to the implementation of legislation explicitly regulating harassment, the Labour Appeal Court of Liège confirmed that the dismissal of a woman who had made a written complaint about sexual harassment by her manager was unfair where the employer failed to explain the reason for dismissal or to bring other evidence to refute her claim.[75] And in Portugal, where legislation provided that "The right to work assumes the absence of any discrimination at all based on sex, be it direct or indirect, principally with reference to marital status or family situation",[76] workers were permitted to terminate their employment contracts without notice if they were subject to unlawful "violations of their physical integrity, liberty, honour or dignity caused by a head of enterprise or his legal representatives",[77] and in such cases were entitled to compensation.[78]

Absent any clear provisions prohibiting sexual and other harassment, however, protections against dismissal are as likely to benefit harassers as they are their victims. So, for example, in the French case of *SA Rockwell International* v. *Loiseau*, an employer was penalised for dismissing an alleged harasser with insufficient reasons to

---

[72] Art. 40.
[73] Decree-Law 64-A/89 of 27 February 1989.
[74] See above **4.EC.21.**, 161.
[75] See Aeberhard-Hodges, above n. 16.
[76] Art. 3(1) of Decree-Law 392/79 of 20 September 1979.
[77] Decree-Law 64-A/89, Art. 35(1)(e) and (f.).
[78] Art. 36.

allow him to prepare a defence.[79] A further difficulty is (as mentioned above) that, absent clear recognition of the wrong of harassment—in particular sexual harassment—and definition of its contours, harassing behaviour is readily trivialised and the perspective of the harasser privileged over that of the harassee.

Commission of the European Communities, **4.EC.29.**
"Sexual harassment in the workplace in the European Union"[80]

"The absence of any legal definition of sexual harassment poses problems in analysing and handling the phenomenon in legal and social terms. This vacuum in Portuguese law makes it impossible for the labour administration or the courts to tackle this problem properly, particularly when it affects fundamental rights like the right to work and the right not to be discriminated against at work on the grounds of sex."

4.3.4. HARASSMENT AND SEXUAL HARASSMENT WITHIN THE CONTEXT OF DISCRIMINATION LAW

Last, but not least, the courts in a number of jurisdictions carved some measure of protection from sexual and (less commonly) other forms of harassment from legislative provisions directed against discrimination. The strong advantage of this approach from the claimant's point of view is that it provides access to enhanced remedies[81] and the reversed burden of proof provided for by EC discrimination law. In Denmark, Ruth Nielsen records that the courts have accepted at least since 1992 that sexual harassment amounts to a breach of the Danish Equal Treatment Act (originally 1978), which prohibits (section 1), "direct discrimination and indirect discrimination" on grounds of sex",[82] although it was not until 2004 that sexual harassment was expressly regulated by the Equality of Women and Men Act.[83] Other forms of harassment may be regulated by section 2 of the Labour Market

---

[79] Nancy, 23 November 1992, discussed by Aeberhard-Hodges, above n. 16, 516.

[80] See above n. 58, 193.

[81] Note the ruling of the ECJ in Case C–271/91 *Marshall* v. *Southampton and South-West Hampshire Area Health Authority* [1993] ECR I–04367 that Art. 6 of the Equal Treatment Directive, which required that "Member States shall introduce into their national legal systems such measures as are necessary to enable all persons who consider themselves wronged by failure to reply to apply to them the principle of equal treatment . . . to pursue their claims by judicial process after possible recourse to other competent authorities", required that "if financial compensation is to be awarded where there has been discriminatory dismissal . . . such compensation must be adequate, in that it must enable the loss and damage actually sustained as a result of the discriminatory dismissal to be made good in full in accordance with the applicable national rules", and that no upper limit to compensation could be imposed by national law.

[82] R. Nielsen, "Danish Labour Law in a Period of Transition" in Dahl *et al.* (eds.), *Danish Law in a European Perspective* (Copenhagen, Thomson Publishers, 2002).

[83] Amended by L 2003-04-25 nr. 286 and L 2004-05-05 nr. 321.

Discrimination Act 1996,[84] which prohibits the employer from discriminating on grounds of race, colour, religion, political belief, sexual orientation or national, ethnic or social origin in relation to "labour conditions". The 1996 Act did not regulate "harassment" as such but, according to Ruth Nielsen: "It is assumed that harassment is covered by the Act as a form of discrimination"[85] (this by analogy with the jurisprudence on sex discrimination).

In the UK, prior to the transposition of the 2000 and 2002 Directives, harassment and sexual harassment were actionable for the most part only where they entailed *less favourable* treatment on a protected ground.[86] Sexual and other harassment not having been regulated by labour law as such, the courts began to provide a remedy to harassed employees by means of discrimination legislation. In *Strathclyde Regional Council* v. *Porcelli*,[87] which was for many years the leading case on harassment, Scotland's appeal court (the Court of Session) recognised that sexual harassment could amount to sex discrimination contrary to the Sex Discrimination Act.

Sex Discrimination Act 1975   **4.GB.30.**

Section 1(1)
In any circumstances relevant for the purposes of any provision of this Act . . . a person discriminates against a woman if— (a) on the ground of her sex he treats her less favourably than he treats or would treat a man . . .

Section 6
(2) It is unlawful for a person, in the case of a woman employed by him at an establishment in Great Britain, to discriminate against her . . .
    (b) by dismissing her, or subjecting her to any other detriment.

Court of Session: First Division, 14 January 1986[88]   **4.GB.31.**
Strathclyde Regional Council v. *Porcelli*

SEXUAL HARASSMENT CAN AMOUNT TO SEX DISCRIMINATION

Porcelli

Facts: The claimant, a laboratory technician driven from her job by the sustained verbal and physical harassment, of a sexual nature, to which male colleagues had subjected her, claimed that she was the victim of sex discrimination contrary to sections 1(1)(a) and 6(2)(b) of the Sex Discrimination Act.

---

  [84] Law No. 459 of 12 June 1996, as amended by Act No. 253 of 7 April 2004.
  [85] *Ibid.*
  [86] Though harassment might breach the Protection from Harassment Act 1997 or found a claim for (unfair) constructive dismissal. See *Majrowski* v. *Guy's and St Thomas's NHS Trust* [2006] UKHL 34, [2006] 3 WLR 125.
  [87] [1986] ICR 564.
  [88] *Ibid.*

Held: A tribunal rejected her sex discrimination claim on the grounds that the reason for the harassment lay in her aggressors' dislike of her, and that a man who was so disliked by them would have been treated equally badly. On this ground the tribunal found that she had not been treated less favourably than an (equally disliked) man would have been and had not, therefore, been discriminated against on the ground of sex. EAT allowed an appeal, a decision upheld by the Court of Session.

Judgment: LORD EMSLIE: " . . .in some cases it will be obvious that there is a sex related purpose in the mind of a person who indulges in unwanted and objectionable sexual overtures to a woman or exposes her to offensive sexual jokes or observations that is not this case. But it does not follow that because the campaign pursued against Mrs Porcelli as a whole had no sex related motive or objective, the treatment of Mrs Porcelli by Coles, which was of the nature of 'sexual harassment' is not to be regarded as having been 'on the ground of her sex' within the meaning of s.1(1)(a). In my opinion this particular part of the campaign was plainly adopted against Mrs Porcelli because she was a woman. It was a particular kind of weapon, based upon the sex of the victim, which . . . would not have been used against an equally disliked man [emphasis added].

The Industrial Tribunal reached their decision by finding that Coles' and Reid's treatment of an equally disliked male colleague would have been just as unpleasant. Where they went wrong, however, was in failing to notice that a material part of the campaign against Mrs Porcelli consisted of 'sexual harassment', a particularly degrading and unacceptable form of treatment which it must be taken to have been the intention of Parliament to restrain. From their reasons it is to be understood that they were satisfied that this form of treatment—sexual harassment in any form—would not have figured in a campaign by Coles and Reid directed against a man. In this situation the treatment of Mrs Porcelli fell to be seen as very different in a material respect from that which would have been inflicted on a male colleague, regardless of equality of overall unpleasantness . . ."

LORD GRIEVE: "In order to decide whether there ha[s] been a breach of s.1(1)(a) consideration . . . ha[s] to be given . . . to the weapons used against the complainer. If any could be identified as what I called 'a sexual sword', and it was clear that the wound it inflicted was more than a mere scratch, the conclusion must be that the sword had been unsheathed and used because the victim was a woman. In such a circumstance there would have been a breach of s.1(1)(a)."

The *Porcelli* judgment was widely followed and was useful in its recognition that at least some episodes of sexual harassment would amount to sex discrimination. But the limitations of an approach which requires differential treatment on grounds of sex as an element of actionable sexual harassment were made evident by a number of cases in which employers have been able to argue that the same "weapon" would have been used on a person of the opposite sex. The classic example put forward on legal argument relates to a supervisory employee who claims that he subjected, or would have subjected, a male employee to the same type of behaviour as he subjected the claimant (whether the behaviour complained of consisted in a physical assault, exposure to offensive language or pictures or, in the case of a bisexual supervisor, unwanted sexual advances).

"PIN UPS" DID NOT DISCRIMINATE AGAINST WOMEN

Stewart

Facts: The claimant claimed to have been constructively dismissed because she was subjected to the display of pictures of semi-naked women in a workplace in which "[t]he conditions . . . tended to be suggestive of the treatment of women as sex objects, not as people" and "[m]anagement had encouraged a general ethos that was male orientated".

Held: The sex discrimination claim failed on the ground that "A man might well [have found the material] as offensive as the claimant did".

Judgment: MUMMERY J: "This is an appeal from the decision of the Industrial Tribunal . . . that the respondents . . . did not discriminate against the applicant . . . on the ground of her sex in the course of her employment: 'by subjecting her to a detriment, namely by continuing to permit the display of pictures of partially clothed and nude women in her workplace when they knew that the display was offensive to her or by failing to deal with her complaints properly or at all.'

The three judgments in *Porcelli* [1986] IRLR 134 contain an illuminating analysis of the relevant provisions of the 1975 Act. The following points on the interpretation of the provisions are relevant to the present case.

(1) In a case of alleged sexual harassment the relevant question, in statutory terms, is: 'Was the applicant less favourably treated on the ground of her sex than a man was or would have been treated?' As Lord Brand observed [in *Porcelli*] 'If that question is answered in the affirmative, there was discrimination within the meaning of the Act and it was conceded by counsel for the employers that, in the present case, if there was discrimination, it was to the detriment of the applicant.'

(2) That primary question can be helpfully broken down into three separate but interrelated elements.

(a) Treatment: What was the treatment meted out to the applicant?

(b) Comparator. Was the treatment meted out to the applicant less favourable than was or would have been meted out to a man in a similar position to her?

(c) Sex: Was the treatment, or any material part of it, meted out to the applicant less favourable on the ground of her sex, i.e. 'because she was a woman'?

(3) The provisions are concerned with less favourable treatment on the ground of sex, *not* with the motive or objective of the person responsible for the treatment . . .

The Tribunal accepted Miss Stewart's complaint that the company had, through its male employees, subjected her to detriment within the meaning of s.6(2)(b) of the 1975 Act, but rejected her complaint of discrimination . . . The detriment relied upon took two forms. (1) Miss Stewart had to work in areas of the workplace where male fellow employees displayed pictures of naked and semi-naked women which she genuinely and reasonably found offensive. (2) When Miss Stewart made a complaint about the display of the pictures to the management of the company, they failed: (a) to deal with the complaint properly or within a reasonable time; and (b) to deal with the hostility to and ridicule of Miss Stewart by the others when they

[89] [1996] ICR 535.

knew about her complaint . . . Those heads of detriment constitute a contravention of the 1975 Act, however, only if they involved discrimination. The Tribunal rejected the complaint of direct discrimination on the ground that Miss Stewart had not established that the company had treated her less favourably than they had treated or would treat a man. The decision of the Tribunal on this point may be summarised as follows.

(1) Display of pictures. The display of the pictures was 'neutral'. The Tribunal said: 'A man might well find this sort of display as offensive as the applicant did . . . We are driven to the conclusion that the nature of the treatment by way of display of the pictures would have been the same to men and women.'

(2) Treatment of complaint. As regards the company's treatment of Miss Stewart's complaint about the display of the pictures, the Tribunal concluded that the company 'would have treated a man just as badly whether he was complaining about the display of nude women or nude men'. There was, therefore, no question of less favourable treatment of Miss Stewart on the ground of her sex . . .

The main issue in this appeal is whether the display of the pictures of women '*in the circumstances of this case* constituted less favourable treatment of the appellant on the ground of her sex'. It cannot be stated too emphatically that the decision in every case of this kind must turn on its particular circumstances. It is important to state what this case does *not* decide. The decision to dismiss this appeal does *not* mean that it is *never* an act of sex discrimination for a company to allow its male employees to display pictures of that kind in the workplace. A decision to allow this appeal would *not* mean that such an employer would in *every* such case be liable for sex discrimination. The crucial point is to clarify the legal position by stating that whether or not there has been less favourable treatment of a woman on the ground of her sex must depend upon the particular facts of every case . . .

The Industrial Tribunal correctly directed itself on the relevant law. Reference was made to the case of *Porcelli* . . . The Tribunal correctly directed itself to the relevant factors identified in that decision: the Tribunal identified the treatment as continuing to permit the display of the pictures and failing to deal with Miss Stewart's complaint properly. The Tribunal asked whether that treatment was less favourable to Miss Stewart than it was or would have been to a man. It held that it was not."

Employment Appeal Tribunal, 27 July 2004[90]   **4.GB.33.**
Brumfitt v. *Ministry of Defence*

SEXUAL ABUSE DID NOT DISCRIMINATE AGAINST WOMEN

Brumfitt

Facts: The claimant, who served in the Royal Air Force, complained of sex discrimination after she attended a training course at which the instructor continually used the words "fuck" and "cunt", as well as wielding a torch covered with a condom smeared in ketchup. An employment tribunal decided that although the applicant found the language to which she had been exposed "offensive and humiliating to her as a woman", she had not been exposed to it because of her sex, but because, like others of both sexes, she had been required to attend the training course. Therefore, it could not be said that "but for her sex", she would not have suffered the treatment complained of or been treated any differently.

---

[90] [2005] IRLR 4.

Held: EAT rejected her appeal, ruling that she had not been subject to "less favourable treatment on the ground of her sex" as men at the course had also been exposed to the behaviour.[91]

Judgment: JUDGE BIRTLES: "There is no doubt whatsoever that Sergeant Fitzpatrick [the instructor] was known for inappropriate and offensive language. Leaving aside the merits of this decision, we are all appalled by the apparent failure of the appropriate RAF authorities to deal with the problems caused by Sergeant Fitzpatrick. The history recounted in the employment tribunal's decision reflects no credit on the service or on any officer involved in this affair . . .

The employment tribunal concluded . . . that the appellant's . . . complaints of sex discrimination in relation to (i) Sergeant Fitzpatrick's offensive and humiliating language (ii) the inadequate investigation by the respondent could not be decided in her favour as she had not been discriminated against on account of her sex because it could not be said that 'but for her sex' the appellant would not have suffered the treatment complained of or been treated any differently. The tribunal decided that the appellant suffered the exposure to the language of the Sergeant at the training course not because of her gender but because, like others of both genders, she had the misfortune of being required to attend the training course. Furthermore, there was no basis on which it could be concluded or inferred that the inadequate investigation of the appellant's complaint of sex discrimination was because of her gender, or that a male complainant in similar circumstances would have been dealt with more favourably . . .

Mr Clarke [for the claimant] submits that the gender-specific nature of the second respondent's misconduct was inherently more offensive to women than to men and was such that the tribunal ought to have inferred that the misconduct occurred on the grounds of the appellant's sex . . .

Mr Sales [for the employer] submitted that [this] misconceived because it failed to consider the treatment to which the appellant was subjected but considered only the effects on her of that treatment, and it also failed to compare the treatment to which the appellant was subjected with the treatment to which an appropriate comparator was or would have been subjected . . .

We agree with Mr Sales . . . Mr Clarke's submission flies in the face of the specific finding of the employment tribunal that the language used by the second respondent was not gender specific . . .

In our judgment the relevant questions in any claim of direct discrimination are (i) has the complainant been treated less favourably than the comparator with whom she falls to be compared and (ii) has she been so treated on the grounds of her sex. The fact that a man uses offensive words of a sexual nature in conversation with a woman does not constitute discrimination unless it can be shown or inferred that this was less-favourable treatment than the man would have meted out to another man in a comparable situation. In this case the tribunal addressed these questions correctly and came to the unequivocal conclusion on the facts that the appellant had not been treated less favourably than any male who attended the course . . .

Mr Clarke submits that the tribunal erred in law by failing to hold the facts as found met the definition of sexual harassment under European Union law. In particular, it failed to have sufficient regard to the amending Directive 2002/73/EC which consolidated and redefined existing principles of EU law. It also ignored the European Commission's Code of Practice 92/131/EEC which refers to unwanted conduct of a sexual nature which affects the dignity of a woman at work. That definition includes unwelcome physical, verbal or non-verbal conduct.

Mr Sales submits that the tribunal in fact made no findings on this issue but simply pointed out that the Member States are not required to give effect to Directive 2002/73/EC until

---

[91] Citing *Pearce*, below: **4.GB.34.**

October 2005 and that the UK has not yet done so. He also made submissions upon whether or not the Directive 'consolidates' or 'codifies' existing principles of EU law or whether it makes a substantive change in the law.

In our judgment the employment tribunal correctly stated that Member States are not required to give effect to Directive 2002/73/EC until October 2005 and that the UK had not yet done so. Furthermore, we accept Mr Sales' submission that the Directive did not merely consolidate or codify existing principles of EU law but change them by introducing a definition of sexual harassment which did not require a comparator. We reject Mr Clarke's submission that sexual harassment, as defined in that instrument, can already form the subject of a complaint under the Equal Treatment Directive . . ."

There were a number of cases in which the UK courts accepted that sex or race "specific" conduct could amount to discrimination without any need to show "less favourable treatment" than a comparator of a different sex or race. But this embryonic development was halted by the House of Lords in the following case, which also cast doubt on the *Porcelli* decision.

House of Lords, 31 July 2001[92]   **4.GB.34.**
Pearce v. Governing Body of Mayfield School

HOMOPHOBIC HARASSMENT IS NOT SEX DISCRIMINATION

Pearce

Facts: The case concerned complaints of sex discrimination based on the subjection of a lesbian teacher to sustained harassment which included the use of taunts such as "lesbian", "dyke", "lesbian shit", "lemon", "lezzie" and "lez". The argument that discrimination on grounds of sexual orientation could and should be regarded as discrimination on grounds of sex was comprehensively rejected by the lower courts and, in turn, by the House of Lords. But a subsidiary argument made by Ms Pearce was that the use by her harassers of gender-specific taunts itself amounted to less favourable treatment on grounds of sex.

Held: The House of Lords rule that Ms Pearce had not been subject to sex discrimination because there was no evidence that she was treated less favourably than a gay man would have been.

Judgment: LORD NICHOLL: "In any case where discrimination is established, this exercise must involve comparing two forms of treatment which are different, whether in kind or in degree. It also involves the tribunal in evaluating the differences and deciding which form of treatment is less favourable.

The suggestion in some cases that if the form of the harassment is sexual or gender-specific, such as verbal abuse in explicitly sexual terms, that of itself constitutes less favourable treatment on the ground of sex, could not be reconciled with the language or the scheme of the statute. The fact that harassment is gender-specific in form cannot be regarded as of itself establishing conclusively that the reason for the harassment is gender-based, 'on the ground of her sex'. It will be evidence, whose weight will depend on the circumstances, that the reason for the harassment was the sex of the victim, although in some circumstances, the inference may readily be drawn that the reason for the harassment was gender-based, as where a male employee subjects a female colleague to persistent, unwanted sexual overtures. In such a case,

---

[92] [2003] ICR 937.

the male employee's treatment of the woman is compared with his treatment of men, even though the comparison may be self-evident. However, the observation of Lord Brand in *Strathclyde Regional Council* v. *Porcelli* that if a form of unfavourable treatment is meted out to a woman to which a man would not have been vulnerable, she has been discriminated against, and the observation of Lord Grieve in the same case that treatment meted out to a woman on the ground of her sex would fall to be regarded as less favourable treatment simply because it was sexually oriented, could not be approved insofar as they were suggesting that it was not relevant whether the claimant was treated less favourably than a man where the harassment is sexually oriented . . .

In the case of Ms Pearce, the natural inference to be drawn from the homophobic terms of abuse was that the reason for this treatment was her sexual orientation, even though the form which the abuse took was specific to her gender. The issue under s.1(1)(a) cannot turn on a minute examination of the precise terms of the abuse. Ms Pearce had not put forward any evidence that a male homosexual teacher would have been treated differently. Therefore, she did not establish that the harassment was on the ground of her sex."

The regulation of harassment only where it also amounts to discrimination in the sense of "less favourable treatment" on a protected ground is problematic for claimants whose employers argue what became known in the UK as the "bastard defence" ("Yes I/my employees treated the claimant badly. But I/they would have treated a person of the other sex/a different race, etc. equally badly"). Such a defence is excluded by an approach which focuses on the nature of the conduct complained of (as in Germany) rather than its motivation. And in France sexual harassment (and now harassment more generally) has deliberately been regulated other than as a form of discrimination. Political emphasis on the fact that men as well as women suffered sexual harassment, and the conclusion drawn therefore that sexual harassment was neither "violence against women" as such, nor a type of sex discrimination, had the result that the penal provisions on sexual harassment were positioned within a section on "sexual aggression" in the chapter on "violations of physical or mental personal integrity" rather than, as was originally intended, in the section on "discrimination" in the chapter on "affronts to personal dignity".[93]

4.3.5.   EXPRESS REGULATION OF SEXUAL AND OTHER HARASSMENT

The particular difficulties which arise where penal provisions are relied upon to target (sexual) harassment are referred to above. But even where the non-targeted provisions relied upon to challenge sexual harassment consist of civil, health and safety or labour law, the absence of any express definition of the wrong may render claims difficult. A Hungarian labour judge who stated at the Ninth Meeting of European Labour Law Judges in 2001 that the state's labour and occupational health and safety

---

[93] See above n. 58, 188.

provisions were "enough to regulate sexual harassment"[94] went on to declare that in 10 years on the bench he had never actually come across a sexual harassment claim. And in Denmark, where it has been long accepted (see above section 4.3.4) that sexual harassment amounts to a breach of the Danish Equal Treatment Act, the category of actionable sexual harassment appears to be narrow. Ruth Nielsen acknowledges that Danish "Case-law on [harassment] is very limited". In one Danish case, prior to the adoption of express legislative prohibition on harassment other than sexual harassment, the High Court ruled that an employee who was called "an Arabic pig" by his employer had not been, by virtue of that single statement, subjected to racial harassment.[95] An equally narrow approach was taken in the following sexual harassment case.

Østre Landsret (High Court for Eastern Denmark),   **4.DK.35.**
31 October 2001[96]

SEXUALLY EXPLICIT INSULTS NOT SEX DISCRIMINATION

The bakery case

Facts: The claimant, who was employed at a bakery run by the 22-year-old defendant, resigned after an incident in which it was accepted by the Danish court that her employer had asked her whether she had had "too much cock" the night before.

Held: The claimant had not been subject to sex discrimination.

Judgment: " . . . it may be taken as given that the appellant experienced wording on the part of the employer that embarrassed her and which she for her part perceived as sexual harassment. It cannot be taken as given that she objected in this connection or confided in anyone at the place of work. The appellant's dissatisfaction only emerged after B had contacted the appellant at her residence by phone on that particularly busy Shrovetide Monday morning because she failed to turn up for work as he had been led to expect from the messages he had received. During the days that followed, the mood between the appellant and B was 'bad', which resulted in the conversation on Friday, 27 February 1998 and in the appellant handing in her notice. None of the other eight employees who have given evidence during this court case, and a number of whom were quite young, like the appellant, felt violated or embarrassed by B or—apart from N . . .—has spoken out in support of B having behaved in a sexually offensive manner towards the women and girls employed . . .

The High Court is satisfied only that when the appellant looked tired as she turned up for work one morning, B said to her: 'Did you have too much cock last night?' While admittedly crude, in the particular situation—when witness N was also present—such an isolated statement, which may very well have been uttered because B, as the employer, was reacting to

---

[94] Hungarian response to a questionnaire circulated at the Ninth Meeting of the European Labour Law Judges (Geneva, December 2001).

[95] Discussed by N. Hansen, "Report on Measures to Combat Discrimination: Directive 2000/43/EC and 2000/78/EC. Country Report Denmark" (European Commission, 2005) 22, available on the website of the Directorate-General for Employment, Social Affairs and Equal Opportunities.

[96] *Forsikrings- og Erstatningsretlig Domssamling* (2001) 2549.

the appellant arriving for work off-colour, is nevertheless not sexual harassment. She is not, therefore, entitled to compensation in pursuance of Section 14 of the Equal Treatment Act, cf. Section 4."

Contrasts can be drawn between the case-law in Denmark and Hungary and that in Ireland, where there have been express legislative prohibitions on harassment and sexual harassment since 1998, and where the general approach of the courts to sexual harassment has been relatively broad.

Irish Employment Equality Acts 1998 to 2004   **4.IE.36.**

Section 23

(3) For the purposes of this Act—

  (a) any act of physical intimacy by B towards A,
  (b) any request by B for sexual favours from A, or
  (c) any other act or conduct of B (including, without prejudice to the generality, spoken words, gestures or the production, display or circulation of written words, pictures or other material),

shall constitute sexual harassment of A by B if the act, request or conduct is unwelcome to A and could reasonably be regarded as sexually, or otherwise on the gender ground, offensive, humiliating or intimidating to A.

This legislative definition clarifies that sexual harassment covers a broad category of treatment, including that which is not sexually motivated. The breadth of the Irish approach is illustrated by the following case.

Equality Tribunal[97]   **4.IE.37.**
DEC-E 2002-014, A Complainant v. *A Company*

"ONLY A FOOLING GIRL"

"Fooling girl"

Facts: The claimant complained that she had been repeatedly referred to by a colleague as "only a young fooling girl more inexperienced than he". She complained that, when she approached him on work-related matters, he would either ignore her request or respond by shouting at her, incorporating her age and work experience into the insults. One example of the behaviour of which she complained was when Mr A "jumped from his chair and lunged at her with his hand raised. He came within inches of the complainant's face and began shouting that he would not f*cking listen to her and that she thought she knew it all." She further stated that Mr A

  "shouted that she was a very foolish girl who hadn't spent forty years working like him and when she had maybe then she could talk to him . . . point[ed] his finger directly into her face and said that she

---

[97] Available on the website of the Equality Tribunal of Ireland, under the heading Employment Equality Decisions.

532

had a 'lack of people skills' and that she was 'completely inexperienced in the workplace' [and] . . . followed her [into her office] continuing to insult her and saying that she was a 'f*cking know all' . . . [and] 'f*cking unbelievable' . . ."

The employer argued that the claimant, whose position was senior to that of Mr A, took a "somewhat confrontational and irrational" approach to her job and overreacted to what they regarded as trivial misdemeanours on the part of Mr A. It further alleged that the claimant acted in a "provocative manner, seeking confrontation on even the most insignificant matters and elevating out of all proportions those occasions when Mr A told her to stop annoying him with her tantrums". It put the difficulties down to a "clash of personalities between the complainant and Mr A".

Held: The claimant had been subject to harassment connected with her age and sex.

Judgment: "I am satisfied that the nature of the verbal abuse was intended to intimidate the complainant. It was designed to 'put her down'. I am also satisfied that it was offensive and humiliating to her. On this basis, therefore, I find that Mr A did verbally harass the complainant. It was not merely a personality clash as suggested by the respondent . . ."

The express statutory regulation of harassment and/or sexual harassment does not, of course, of itself guarantee an effective legal remedy for harassing behaviour. In the first place, legislation can adopt a narrow definition of the legal wrong for which it provides a remedy. Secondly, the application of legislative provisions by the courts can be undermined by broader social attitudes towards harassing behaviour. To take one example, French criminal law prohibited sexual harassment prior to the adoption of the 2000 and 2002 Directives:

French Penal Code[98]　　　　　　　　　　　　　　　　**4.FR.38.**

Article 222-33
The harassment of another person for the purpose of obtaining favours of a sexual nature is punished by one year's imprisonment and a fine of €15,000.

Article 222-33, however, incorporates a very narrow conception of sexual harassment, applying only to quid pro quo harassment, and then only to harassment taking the form of "orders, threats or constraint". The wrong of sexual harassment under the 1992 Law was the abuse of authority with a view to obtaining sexual favours, rather than as sex discrimination. By 1996 there had been no resort to the French provisions passed four years before, this despite harassment being a significant problem in France.[99]

　　French employment and civil law also regulated sexual harassment as a result of the 1992 Act. The Labour Code, like the Penal Code, regulates only quid pro quo harassment, although it defines the abuse of power more widely than the Penal Code to cover "all types of pressure". But prior to the enactment of the Law of 17 January 2002, which transposed the 2000 Directives by imposing liability for

---

[98] Act No. 92–1179 of 2 November 1992.
[99] Aeberhard-Hodges, above n. 16. A 1999 report by Debout to the Economic and Social Council indicated that harassment was a significant problem in France.

"moral harassment" (see below section 4.4.1), "sexual harassment" prohibited under the Labour Code did not apply to:

— sexual blackmail by a person who was of the same rank or lower;
— unwelcome sexual behaviour which affected the working atmosphere, especially sexist remarks, obscene jokes and pornographic pin-ups which were not aimed at any person in particular;
— verbal or physical behaviour of a sexual nature, especially sexist insults and contact, the intention or effect of which was to humiliate a person.[100]

Unwanted sexual behaviour by colleagues was not defined as sexual harassment prior to the implementation of the Directives, the victims of such behaviour being regarded as free to reject it.

Narrow approaches to sexual harassment and to harassment were also taken by the UK's Protection from Harassment Act 1997 and by German law prior to the implementation of the 2000 and 2002 Directives (in 2006). The 1997 UK Act defines "harassment" as "a course of conduct" which in turn "must involve conduct on at least two occasions" (sections 1 and 8). And German Law defined the "sexual annoyance" which it prohibited as:

German Law for the protection of the persons employed   **4.DE.39.**
from sexual annoyance on the job of 24 June 1994

Section 2(2)
. . . deliberate, sexually determined behaviour, which infringes the dignity of persons employed on the job. This includes:
1. sexual actions and behaviours prohibited by criminal law, like
2. other sexual actions and requests for such actions, sexually determined bodily contacts, remarks of a sexual nature as well as showing or affixing on a visible place of pornographic images which are clearly repudiated by the concerned exposed person.

Section 4 of the Act provided that a person subject to sexual harassment has the right to refuse to work without being subject to penalty. The focus on behaviour, rather than motivation, had the effect that the Act of 1994 could be applied to behaviour which consisted of sexualised, albeit not sexually *motivated*, behaviour. But the Act did not apply to harassment which took the form of non-sexualised behaviour, prohibiting intentional, expressly unwanted and explicitly sexual harassment only. And even in relation to the forms of harassment it did cover, the application of the 1994 legislation was problematic. According to a representative study commissioned by the Federal Government in 2002, the Act generated less than 100 cases in the eight years of its operation to that date. The study concluded, inter alia, that sexual harassment was regularly regarded, by legal professionals as well as by employers, as a misdemeanour rather than as an instance of sex discrimination. And the 2005

---

[100] See above n. 58, 189.

German Country Report on Measures to Combat Discrimination reports the frequent application by the courts applying the Act of "problematic if not discriminatory assumptions about 'normal behaviour'".[101]

German and French approaches to "sexual harassment" were narrow. At the other end of the scale, the Belgian Federal Law of 2002 defined "sexual harassment at work" as:

> *Belgian Federal Act of 11 June 2002 on violence, mobbing*   **4.BE.40.**
> *and sexual harassment at work*

Article 5 . . .
. . . any form of verbal, non-verbal or physical conduct of a sexual nature, which the perpetrator knows, or should know, will affect the dignity of men and women at the workplace.

Di Martino *et al.* report that the Belgian definition was "intentionally wide in order to avoid behaviour not expressly mentioned from escaping the coverage of the discipline". Swedish law, which expressly regulated sexual harassment for the first time in 1998, adopted a similarly broad approach, defining sexual harassment as:

> *The Swedish Equal Opportunities Act 1991 (as amended in 1998)*[102] **4.SE.41.**

Section 6
Such unwanted conduct based on sex or unwanted conduct of a sexual nature that violates the integrity of the employee at work.

Section 22 of the Act went on to provide that:

An employer may not subject an employee to harassment on the grounds that the employee has rejected the employer's sexual advances or has reported the employer for sex discrimination.

Harassment on grounds other than sex was regulated in Sweden in 1999 by the implementation of a number of Acts dealing with discrimination on grounds of "ethnicity and religion", disability and sexual orientation.[103] By contrast, Belgian law coupled its prohibition on sexual harassment with a broad ban on "moral harassment" defined as:

---

[101] S. Baer, "Report on Measures to Combat Discrimination: Directives 2000/43/EC and 2000/78/EC. Country Report Germany" (European Commission, 2005) 21, available on the website of Directorate-General for Employment, Social Affairs and Equal Opportunities.
[102] SFS 1991:433.
[103] The law banning discrimination in working life due to ethnicity and religion or other belief, the law banning disability discrimination in working life, and the law banning sexual orientation discrimination in working life.

Article 5 . . .
Repeated abusive conduct of whatever origin, whether from inside or outside a company or institution, manifested in particular by behaviour, words, threats, actions, unilateral gestures or writings which have the purpose or effect of violating the personality, the dignity or the physical or psychological integrity of a worker or any other person to whom this chapter applies, in the conduct of their work, placing their employment in jeopardy or creating an intimidating, hostile, degrading, humiliating or approaches offensive environment.

The concept of "moral harassment", which was introduced in 2002, did not require a link to any regulated ground of discrimination, though it does require that acts complained of be "repeated" (as does the French concept of moral harassment). The 2002 Act further prohibits "violence at work", which it defines as occurring "where a worker or any other person, to whom this chapter applies, is persecuted, threatened or attacked psychologically or physically during work".

4.3.6.   ENFORCING PROHIBITIONS ON HARASSMENT AND SEXUAL HARASSMENT: PROBLEMS OF VICARIOUS AND DIRECT LIABILITY

Much of the focus on sexual and other forms of harassment concerns the employment sphere, although harassment can and does also occur in other contexts, housing and education in particular. Whatever the context, a significant question which arises is whether liability for harassing behaviour can be attributed to a harasser's employer, whether on the basis of vicarious liability (i.e. the employer is held liable for actions taken by the employee in the course (broadly speaking) of his or her employment) or direct liability (the employer being held responsible for failure to discharge a legal responsibility to prevent harassment or, more generally, to employees, tenants, clients, etc. with particular standards of treatment).

Litigation concerning the extent of employer responsibility for the actions of staff is not unique to harassment, discrimination or employment law, arising also where employees are injured by falling off ladders or being physically attacked by clients, etc., and where third parties are injured by the actions of employees. But denial of liability is much more frequent in cases of harassment than in cases where, for example, discrimination in the form of a failure to appoint or promote is alleged, because the temptation in harassment cases is for employers to claim that harassment is at most a wrong by individual employees or clients acting without the authority or approval of employers and that they (the employers) should not therefore be held responsible for it. Unless liability can be pinned on employers, however, any financial remedy may prove illusory and employers will not be provided with incentives to prevent harassment occurring or continuing.

The general position where penal liability is at issue is that an employer will not become vicariously liable for the actions of an employee, though the employer may itself be criminally liable for failing to provide a safe environment for workers, or for conspiring in or facilitating the criminal actions of another. The position at civil law is more varied, as the following case extracts show. The question with which all of them deal is whether, where harassment has been established as having taken place, the employer can be held responsible for it.

High Court[104]   **4.IE.43.**
BC v. *A Health Board*

SEXUAL ASSAULT NOT "WITHIN THE COURSE OF EMPLOYMENT"

BC

Facts: The claimant had been subject to sexual harassment, including a sexual assault, by co-workers. She sued her employer for sex discrimination (the case pre-dating the explicit statutory regulation of sexual harassment).

Held: The employer was not liable for the sexual harassment which had taken place, the acts of which the claimant complained not having been "within the scope of" the harassers' employment.

Judgment: "An employer may, of course, be vicariously liable when his employee is acting negligently, or even criminally . . . But I cannot envisage any employment in which they were engaged in respect of which a sexual assault could be regarded as so connected with it as to amount to an act within its scope."

Similar problems beset the early application of the UK discrimination provisions but were resolved by a decision of the Court of Appeal which drew attention to the difference between the common law approach to vicarious liability and the specific statutory test established by the discrimination legislation.

Race Relations Act 1975   **4.GB.44.**

Section 32
(1) Anything done by a person in the course of his employment shall be treated for the purposes of this Act (except as regards offences thereunder) as done by his employer as well as by him, whether or not it was done with the employer's knowledge or approval . . .
(2) In proceedings brought under this Act against any person in respect of an act alleged to have been done by an employee of his it shall be a defence for that person to prove that he took such steps as were reasonably practicable to prevent the employee from doing that act, or from doing in the course of his employment acts of that description.

---

[104] [1994] ELR 27.

Court of Appeal[105]   **4.GB.45.**
Jones v. *Tower Boot Co Ltd*

WHETHER EMPLOYER IS LIABLE FOR ABUSIVE CONDUCT OF FELLOW EMPLOYEES

Jones

Facts: The claimant complained that he had been repeatedly called "chimp", "monkey" and "baboon", had been attacked and burnt with a hot screwdriver, had metal bolts thrown at his head, had been whipped and had a notice pinned on his back reading "Chipmonks are go".

Held: A lower court applied the common law test under which an employer would be liable only for "acts actually authorised by him . . . [and] acts which he has not authorised, provided they are so connected with acts which he has authorised that they may rightly be regarded as modes—although improper modes—of doing them", and ruled that the acts complained of could not be described, by any stretch of the imagination, as an improper mode of performing authorised tasks and that the employers were not, accordingly, liable for them. The Court of Appeal allowed Mr Jones's appeal, pointing out that the wording of section 32(1) of the Race Relations Act imposed a different test and that the approach adopted by EAT would have the effect that:

Judgment: WAITE LJ: " . . .the more heinous the act of discrimination, the less likely it will be that the employer would be liable . . . [This would] cut[] across the whole legislative scheme and underlying policy of s32 (and its counterpart in sex discrimination), which is to deter racial and sexual harassment in the workplace through a widening of the net of responsibility beyond the guilty employees themselves, by making all employers additionally liable for such harassment, and then supplying them with the reasonable steps defence under s32(3) which will exonerate the conscientious employer who has used his best endeavours to prevent such harassment, and will encourage all employers who have not yet undertaken such endeavours to take the steps necessary to make the same defence available in their own workplace."

In Ireland the decision in *A* v. *A Health Board* resulted in an amendment to the Act by the Employment Equality Act 1998 which provided a statutory definition of vicarious liability, coupled with a "due diligence" defence, in materially identical terms to those of the British Race Relations Act. The application of the statutory test is illustrated below:

Labour Court (An Chúirt Oibreachais),   **4.IE.46.**
AEE/02/6 Determination No. 029, 9 October 2002[106]
A Hospital v. *An Appellant*

EMPLOYERS' LIABILITY FOR HARASSMENT

"A hospital"

Facts: The appellant was employed in the hospital since 1984. In 1997 she commenced working in the catering department as a kitchen porter. In October 1999 and November 1999, the appellant reported to the assistant catering officer that she had been sexually harassed in her place of work over a period of time. She

---

[105] [1997] ICR 254.
[106] Available on the website of the Irish Labour Court.

informed the assistant catering officer that the harassment consisted of serious sexual abuse, and of the dates, times and locations on and in which the incidents occurred, but did not name the alleged harasser for some months, during which she received counselling to assist her to do this. Her difficulties as regards naming her abuser were connected with a history of abuse in her childhood.

The assistant catering officer brought the complaint to the attention of the Catering Manager and the Personnel Manager, who arranged for the appellant to attend an assertiveness course paid for by the respondent. Some seven months after her initial report she named her harasser, who was immediately suspended.

Held: A tribunal ruled that the employer, which had a clear policy on sexual harassment and had trained its staff on the issue, and had undertaken adequate investigations and appropriate disciplinary action, could not be held liable for its actions prior to suspension. The Labour Court disagreed on appeal, ruling that the duty on the employer under section 8 of the Act to ensure that the complainant was in a position to avail of working conditions free from discrimination required the employer to take additional measures to protect this employee.

Judgment: "The Court is of the view that there are three periods in this case which deserve separate examination by the Court:—

(i) The period before October, 1999, when sexual harassment was alleged to have taken place.

(ii) The period between October, 1999, and June, 2000, when a serious complaint of sexual harassment was made without identifying the harasser.

(iii) The period post 7th June, 2000, when the appellant named the alleged harasser.

Period (i): The respondent does not deny that the harassment took place. Therefore, the only defence open to the employer under section 23 is to prove that it took such steps as were reasonably practicable to prevent the harassment. In this case, the employer had a policy on sexual harassment in place and the harasser had been sent on a course outlining his responsibilities in relation to sexual harassment. While the mere act of having a policy on sexual harassment in place without further proactive steps being taken would not in the view of this Court be sufficient to render an employer immune from liability under this Act, nevertheless, the fact that the employer both had a policy in place and had sent the alleged harasser on the course does, in the Court's view, constitute sufficient steps to allow the employer to avail of the defence that he took such steps as were reasonably practicable in relation to the period prior to the harassment being reported under section 23(5).

Period (ii): The situation during this period was different. The Court accepts that Section 23 does not appear to apply to a situation where the harassment has occurred and been reported, save insofar as there is a duty on the employer, if the employee has been treated differently as a result of reporting the harassment, to do all that is reasonable to reverse the effects of such treatment. The Court accepts therefore that the appellant cannot rely on the provisions of section 23 in bringing a claim in respect of this period.

This however is not sufficient to dispose of the matter. There still remains a general duty on the employer under section 8(1)(b) to provide conditions of employment free from discrimination. It is the opinion of the Court that the employer, during this period did not provide conditions of employment to the employee, which was free from discrimination.

In the opinion of the Court, during this period i.e. between October, 1999, and 7th June, 2000, the employer had a duty, on being informed of the harassment, to put in place such procedures as would enable the appellant to avail of working conditions free from discrimination. The Court is of the view that the employer, in the circumstances of this particular case, in particular the very serious nature of the allegations and the appellant's history, should have taken proactive measures including the following:—

— contacted the *gardai* [police]
— contacted the appellant's Union official

— spoken to co-workers to seek to establish the truth or otherwise of the allegations
— transferred the appellant to another working area
— explained its Anti-Bullying/Harassment Policy to her and provided her with a copy of the policy.

By its failure to take these steps, the employer failed to provide the employee with working conditions free from discrimination and accordingly was in breach of its duty to the appellant under section 8(1) of the Act.

The Court wishes to emphasise that it is not suggesting that any or all of these steps should be taken in every case of sexual harassment. The appropriate response to each case must be studied by the employer who should then put in place procedures proportionate with the gravity of the offence . . ."

A somewhat less generous approach to vicarious liability is evident in the following decision of the Dutch Equal Treatment Commission.

Equal Treatment Commission (Commissie Gelijke Behandeling)   **4.NL.47.**
Opinion 1997-122

EMPLOYER'S LIABILITY FOR HARASSMENT

Policy failings forgiven

Facts: The claimant reported sick following sexual intimidation by a colleague, alleging that her employer's handling of the complaint involved unlawful direct sex discrimination against her. She claimed that an alleged lack of an adequate policy in the area of sexual intimidation was in conflict with Dutch laws concerning equal treatment

Held: Although the employer's policies on sexual harassment were inadequate, it did respond to the claim-ant's complaints when she raised them adequately and so could not be regarded as having treated female staff less favourably.

Opinion: "4.2 . . . no distinction may be made in terms of employment between men and women . . .

The Commission adopts a broad attitude to the concept of conditions of work, namely the possibility of a person being able to develop him or herself at work and gaining experience in consequence. This dovetails with the fact that the ban on making a distinction is directed at all aspects of the working relationship, including the working sphere, which partly determines the development and functioning of persons. A working sphere that intimidates and discriminates against women implies that the employee discriminated against is unable to do her work in the same way as her colleagues, which may detrimentally influence performance. The ban on discrimination in relation to working conditions extends to these circumstances. The employer's obligation to refrain from discrimination in employment implies that the employer must ensure that those over whom he has authority also refrain from discrimination.

The question at issue is therefore whether the respondent has sufficiently discharged this obligation, i.e. whether she has responded adequately to the complaints from the applicant and has treated these complaints with sufficient care.

4.3 . . . The respondent was aware of the outspoken conduct in the past of the employee subsequently accused by the applicant of sexual intimidation. She did pay attention to this. The question arises whether the signs in the past that there might be sexual intimidation were sufficiently picked up. The fact is that the respondent did not have an adequate structure that made it possible to react to these signs. The claimant's complaint of harassment indicates that policy shortcomings resulted in the harassment being tolerated. It has also been established that the applicant did not at the time clearly raise her complaints concerning sexual harassment at the time. Where she had doubts about approaching the assistant manager, it would have been possible to approach another member of the management team. The applicant explicitly indicated only some time after the situation had escalated that this conflict was due (partly) to sexual harassment by a male colleague.

When confronted by the applicant with the occurrence of sexual harassment, the respondent called in an independent agency to conduct an independent investigation. It also declared its willingness to implement the advice resulting from this investigation regarding the introduction of such a policy and associated structure. It recognised in so doing that it had a responsibility towards the applicant.

The respondent never implemented its intention, formed before it became aware of the sexual harassment, to dismiss the applicant because of her involvement in the conflict with a female colleague. The respondent showed itself willing at the hearing to cooperate with the reintegration of the applicant at her own workplace.

In view of the above, the Commission notes that any negligence on the part of the respondent was insufficient to amount to discrimination, and was due to a lack of clarity in the past about the policy regarding sexual intimidation. On the other hand, it was also the responsibility of the applicant to make her complaints known to the respondent. The Commission notes that the respondent took initiatives to make good this neglect as soon as it was aware of it. The earlier neglect in setting up an adequate structure for dealing with complaints of this kind is not considered so serious by the Commission that the simple absence of such a structure is sufficient for concluding distinction based on sex.

On this basis, the Commission concludes that there is no question of unequal treatment of female staff in the sense that the other party made an insufficient effort to combat and prevent sexual harassment."

It is clear from this decision that the Dutch employer was under no obligation to take steps to prevent harassment occurring. The contrast with the position in Britain and Ireland is noteworthy: under the statutory provisions adopted in the latter jurisdictions, liability vests with the employer unless "he took such steps as were reasonably practicable to prevent the employee" from committing the act of harassment. The question whether the victim of harassment "clearly raised her complaints concerning sexual harassment at the time" would not, under the statutory test, be relevant to the establishment of liability in a case such as this, where "a lack of policy in . . . respect [of sexual harassment] resulted in undesirable approaches being tolerated". However, although narrower in some respects than Irish and British approaches, the Dutch approach to employer liability for harassment did permit employers to be pinned with responsibility for harassment by third parties.

Equal Treatment Commission *(Commissie Gelijke Behandeling)*   **4.NL.48.**
Opinion 1997-82

LIABILITY FOR HARASSMENT BY THIRD PARTY

The racist patient

Facts: The case concerned a complaint by a nurse who had been subjected to a campaign of racial harassment by a patient at the defendant hospital. The nurse had brought the behaviour to the attention of her managers on more than one occasion.

Held: The employer had failed to comply with its obligation to prevent discrimination.

Judgment: "4. Considerations by the Commission

4.4. The obligation on the employer to refrain from discrimination in the area of work implies that the employer must ensure that those over whom he has authority also refrain from discrimination.

4.5. The present case is not concerned with discrimination against an employee by another or other employe(es), but with the way in which a nurse is treated by a patient. In such cases, too, the respondent is in a position to remedy the situation, e.g. by imposing binding rules of conduct or by taking other steps regarding the patient. This means that, having regard to the statutory equality provisions, ensuring that patients refrain from discriminatory conduct is in the present case just as much an obligation of the respondent.

In certain circumstances the employer may also be required to offer the member of staff concerned alternative work of equal value, so that the staff member is no longer exposed to improper action by the patient. Failing to meet these obligations amounts to action in conflict with article 5 (1) d. AWGB.

4.6. It is undisputed that continuing insults and threats by a patient in the applicant's workplace resulted in an impossible situation for the applicant. These insults are also of a racist and discriminatory nature. The patient's intention in this case is unimportant. We are not, after all, concerned with what intentions lay behind the remarks, but the words that he used in them. The verbal abuse refers to the applicant's skin colour.

4.7. With regard to the obligations mentioned under 4.5., the respondent has stated that the patient was approached regarding his conduct, but no change in attitude can be expected. However, it was ascertained at the hearing that this did not take place in a forceful way. The respondent also takes the view that the patient cannot be transferred, because he uses a room especially adapted for him. The respondent consequently took no steps that were sufficiently adequate to protect the applicant in the work area concerned against discriminatory treatment by the patient in question.

4.8. The respondent therefore has an obligation in the given circumstances to offer the applicant substitute work of equal value. The Commission notes that the respondent offered the applicant—who in her many years of service works exclusively at night substitute work which, however, had to be done during the day. When the applicant refused this offer, the respondent then suggested that she was not adequately cooperating in finding a solution. This opinion is also partly based on the request for release subsequently submitted to the cantonal court.

As held by the Cantonal court, the applicant is entitled in a certain sense to work exclusively on night shift because of the fact that she had already done so for many years. This entitlement is not affected by the fact that, according to the respondent, the most obvious change of activities is impracticable because the nurse concerned, just like the applicant, is of immigrant origin.

The respondent consequently did not offer the applicant substitute work of equal value.

4.9. In view of all of the above, the Commission comes to the conclusion that the respondent failed in her responsibility to find a suitable solution for the applicant. This means that the respondent did not meet the obligation mentioned above to protect the applicant against discrimination in her work area. The Commission therefore feels that the respondent did not safeguard the applicant from discrimination in the workplace.

4.10. The Commission would perhaps unnecessarily comment that the above obligation on the employer does not flow from the statutory equality rules alone. The Cantonal Court also indicated that the respondent has a duty of care here regarding its employees' welfare, as laid down in article 7A:1638x and 7A:1638z Civil Code and article 3 (1) and (4) of the Working Conditions Act."

The contrast with the UK position is stark. In the UK an employer can at present be held liable for harassing behaviour by a client only if the employer's own actions amount to less favourable treatment (if, for example, it takes less seriously a complaint of sexual harassment from a man than it would take a complaint from a woman or vice versa, or if it acts on complaints of racial harassment by white but not by black staff). A decision of the Employment Appeal Tribunal in 1996 (*Burton & Rhule* v. *De Vere Hotels* [1996] IRLR 596) had suggested that employers could be held liable for harassment by others which was within the power of the employer to prevent. But this case was overruled by the House of Lords in the *Pearce* decision.

House of Lords, 31 July 2001[107]　　　　　　　　**4.GB.49.**[*]
Pearce v. *Governing Body of Mayfield School*

LIABILITY FOR HARASSMENT BY THIRD PARTIES

Pearce

Facts: The claimant was subject to abuse as a lesbian by students whom she taught.

Held: Not only did the harassment in this case not amount to sex discrimination, since there was no evidence that she was treated less favourably than a gay man would have been, but the school authorities were not in any event responsible for the campaign of abuse merely because (on the tribunal's findings) they could and should have taken steps to shield the employee. An employer's failure to take reasonable steps to protect employees from racial or sexual abuse by third parties did not amount to discrimination if the failure had nothing to do with the sex or race of the employees.

Judgment: LORD NICHOLLS: "In *Burton* v *De Vere Hotels Ltd* . . . two black waitresses, clearing tables in the banqueting hall of a hotel, were the butt of racist and sexist jibes made by a guest speaker entertaining the assembled all-male company at a private dinner party. The Employment Appeal Tribunal held that the employer of the waitresses had racially discriminated against the waitresses. Had the assistant managers in charge for the evening been properly instructed, the two young women would not have suffered embarrassment. They could, and should, have been withdrawn from the room.

---

[107] [2003] ICR 937.
[*] See also above **4.GB.34.**

This is not a satisfactory decision . . . Viewed in the broadest terms, the *Burton* decision has much to commend it. There is, surely, everything to be said in favour of a conclusion which requires employers to take reasonable steps to protect employees from racial or sexual abuse by third parties. But is a failure to do so 'discrimination' by the employer? Where the *Burton* decision is, indeed, vulnerable is that it treats an employer's inadvertent failure to take such steps as discrimination even though the failure had nothing to do with the sex or race of the employees. In this crucially important respect the decision gives insufficient heed to the statutory discrimination provisions. An essential element of 'direct' sex discrimination by an employer is that, on the grounds of sex, the employer treats the employee less favourably than he treats or would treat an employee of the opposite sex. Similarly with 'direct' racial discrimi-nation: the 'less favourable treatment' comparison is an essential ingredient of the statutory wrong . . . Unless the employer's conduct satisfies this 'less favourable treatment' test, the employer is not guilty of direct sex or racial discrimination. In making this comparison acts of persons for whose conduct an employer is vicariously responsible are to be attributed to the employer. It is otherwise in respect of acts of third parties for whose conduct the employer is not vicariously liable . . .

I turn to the facts in the *Burton* case. The employment tribunal found that although the hotel manager should have instructed his assistant managers to protect the waitresses from the predictably offensive content of the comedian's speech, the manager's failure to do so was not 'less favourable treatment on racial grounds'. His failure to give any thought to what might happen to the waitresses that night was not connected with their ethnic origin. By implication, the tribunal thought the employer would have treated white waitresses in the same way . . . As I see it, these findings negatived racial discrimination on the part of the employer. The hotel's failure to plan ahead properly may have fallen short of the standards required by good employment practice, but it was not racial discrimination. I consider the case was wrongly decided by the Employment Appeal Tribunal . . ."

Even as regards the behaviour of employees, an approach based on vicarious liability (as in Ireland and the UK) may have the effect that employers are not liable for harassment outside the workplace, such harassment generally not being carried out "in the course of [the harasser's] employment". A more generous approach applies under Swedish legislation, which is based on a health and safety model.

The Swedish Equal Opportunities Act 1991 (as amended in 1998) [108] **4.SE.50.**

Section 22a
An employer who becomes aware that an employee considers her or himself to have been exposed to sexual harassment by another employee shall investigate the circumstances surrounding the said harassment and if it has occurred implement the measures that may reasonably be required to prevent continuance of the sexual harassment.

Section 27A
If the employer does not fulfil the employer's obligations pursuant to Section 22a, the employer shall pay damages to the employee for the violation caused by the omission.

[108] SFS 1991:433.

It should be noted that section 22a (to which each of the discrimination Acts has an equivalent provision) applies regardless of whether the employer would have been liable for the original act of harassment.

General Report on Developments in EU Gender Equality Law of   **4.EC.51.**
the Commission's Network of Legal Experts in the Fields of Employment, Social Affairs and Equality between Men and Women (June 2004–May 2005) [109]

" . . . an employer had to pay damages in a case where a rape took place outside the work place, namely when the female applicant made a private visit to the offender's home. Interestingly, the Labour Court found that despite the fact that in this case there was no obligation upon the employer to investigate the rape as such—this was a matter for the police—there was a duty to further investigate the situation at the work place following the report of the rape. The employer did not do so. This negligence was regarded as incompliance with the duty according to Sec. 22a of the Equal Opportunities Act, namely to investigate the circumstances and take reasonable action to prevent further harassment."

Absent a breach of section 22a and its equivalent provisions, Swedish employers are not per se liable for harassment of employees by their colleagues, though they may be liable for failures to prevent such harassment occurring:

The Swedish Equal Opportunities Act 1991 (as amended in 1998) [110] **4.SE.52.**

Section 6
The employer shall take measures to prevent and preclude an employee being subjected to sexual harassment or harassment resulting from a complaint about sex discrimination.

Section 22a equally does not apply in respect of harassment by third parties, but as early as 1993, two Swedish ordinances imposed proactive duties on employers in relation to workplace "violence and menaces" and "victimisation".

V. Di Martino, H. Hoel and C.L. Cooper,   **4.INT.53.**
"Preventing violence and harassment in the workplace" [111]

"In both instruments, the emphasis is on combining prevention strategies to deal with violence from environmental and organisational issues, rather than containing violence at the individual level. The ordinances require employers to plan and organise work in a way that seeks to

---

[109] Available on the website of the European Commission, Directorate-General for Employment, Social Affairs and Equal Opportunities at 21.
[110] SFS 1991:433.
[111] Above n. 12, 50.

prevent the occurrence of violence and victimisation. Employers must also make clear that violence will not be tolerated at the workplace.

The two ordinances refer to the Swedish Work Environment Act, in which physical and psychological factors at work are given special attention and responsibilities for these are devolved to employers. Chapter 3, Section 2 of the Act indicates as part of such responsibility the following obligations:
— To develop a work environment policy declaring the employer's general aims, intentions and attitude to the employees.
— To design procedures to ensure that psychological and social work environment conditions, including personal response, work situation and work organisation, are as good as possible.
— To take steps to prevent people meeting with a negative response at work, e.g. by creating norms which encourage a friendly and respectful climate at the workplace. It is above all the employer and the employer's representatives who must set an example to others in creating a good working climate.
— To give managers and supervisors training and guidance on matters relating to labour law, the effect of different working conditions on people's experiences of work, the effect of interaction and conflict risks in groups, and the skills to be able to respond rapidly to people in situations of stress and crisis.
— To provide a good induction that will enable a new employee to adjust well to the working group and understand the rules governing the workplace.
— To give each employee the best possible knowledge of their activities and objectives. Regular information and workplace meetings will help to achieve this.
— To give all employees information about and involvement in decisions about how to prevent victimisation.
— To try to ensure that work responsibilities have substance and meaning, and that the capacity and knowledge of the individual are utilised.
— To give employees opportunities to develop their knowledge and their jobs, and encourage them to pursue this end."

A failure to take steps in relation to harassment by third parties may well breach the 1977 Work Environment Act, though such a breach would not give rise to a claim for discrimination-related damages. This health and safety approach to workplace violence, including psychological violence, is complemented by discrimination provisions discussed immediately above.

Similarly, although Belgian law imposes vicarious liability only for the actions of employees (except in the case of harassment by school children, in respect of whose actions liability is imposed on school teachers), it also imposes strong obligations on employers to take proactive measures to combat harassment, rather than simply holding them responsible for harassment when it occurs. So, for example, the Belgian Royal Decree which first explicitly regulated sexual harassment imposed positive obligations on employers to have a statement of principle, a confidential counsellor, a grievance procedure and sanctions in respect of sexual harassment. These obligations were extended to the broader concept of workplace violence by the law of 11 June 2002, which required employers to take positive steps to reduce the risk of violence in the workplace, including measures relating to the physical organisation of the working environment, the provision of assistance and support to victims of workplace violence, the introduction of advisors on prevention (*conseiller en prévention*), the quick and impartial investigation of cases of workplace violence, and the provision of information and training about workplace violence.

The Belgian Act of 2002 emphasises the responsibility of the management at all levels in preventing stress and protects workers who complain of workplace violence from victimisation during any complaints procedure. Similarly, France's law of 2 November 1992 obliged employers to take positive steps to prevent sexual harassment (albeit very narrowly defined) by including in their employment regulations[112] the sexual harassment provisions of the Labour Code, by posting the regulations in the workplace and by (Article L122-48 of the Labour Code) "tak[ing] any necessary measures to prevent" sexual harassment.[113] Article L122-48 of the Code allowed a civil claim in respect of a failure to take steps when a case of sexual harassment is brought to the employer's notice; employers could become liable under general civil liability rules for damage caused by their own deeds or negligence or the deeds of persons for whom they were responsible, and could be liable under the Penal Code for complicity in the offence of sexual harassment and/or for discrimination linked with sexual harassment.

4.4. REGULATION OF HARASSMENT AND SEXUAL HARASSMENT AFTER IMPLEMENTATION OF DIRECTIVES 2004/43/EC, 2000/78/EC AND 2002/73/EC

Many Member States (in particular the 2004 accession states) had few or no legal measures regulating harassment prior to accession, and transposed the 2000 and 2003 Directives by means of a "copy out" approach. Too little time has passed to make any comment on the jurisprudence which has developed under these provisions, and it is not my intention to provide a comprehensive account of the various shortcomings of transposing legislation across the Member States. I will, instead, focus on a number of issues raised by transposition in some of those states which did provide some degree of legal protection in relation to harassment and/or sexual harassment as such prior to their implementation of the Directives.

4.4.1. DEFINITIONS OF "HARASSMENT" AND "SEXUAL HARASSMENT"

The approach taken by the Directives to harassment and sexual harassment was outlined above, particular attention being drawn to the breadth of the definitions

---

[112] A mandatory written document for enterprises employing at least 20 people.
[113] See Di Martino *et al.*, above n. 12.

(sexual harassment, for example, includes hostile environment as well as quid pro quo harassment), while there is no need for a comparator in order to prove either harassment or sexual harassment. The narrowness of the approach taken by French law to sexual harassment prior to the implementation of the 2000 Regulations was also mentioned above. A law of 17 January 2002 introduced the concept of moral harassment ("harcèlement moral") into both the Penal and the Labour Code, and amended the definition of sexual harassment in the Labour Code (by Article 122-46) to cover "the behaviour of any person which aims at obtaining sexual favours for one's own benefit or that of a third party". This approach is wider than that which prevailed before in that it captures harassing behaviour by colleagues as well as by superiors, although it still applies only in relation to quid pro quo harassment and imposes a high standard of fault as a condition for liability.

Some hostile environment harassment (whether sexual or otherwise), and some harassment and sexual harassment which is non-intentional, will breach the newly enacted penal and other prohibitions on "harcèlement moral", which is defined (section 222-33-2) as "repeated actions with the object or effect of a degradation of the working conditions likely to infringe upon their rights and dignity, to deteriorate their physical or mental health or to compromise their professional future". That provision makes moral harassment a criminal offence punishable by a one-year prison sentence and a fine of 15,000 euros. In addition, the Labour Code includes the following provision:

French Labour Code   **4.FR.54.**

L122-46

No employee, no recruitment candidate, during a period of probation or training within the company, may be punished, dismissed or be the subject of a discriminatory measure, whether direct or indirect, in particular with regard to remuneration, training, regarding, appointment, qualification, classification, professional promotion, transfer or renewal of contract, for having undergone or refused to undergo actions of harassment by any person, the purpose of which is to obtain favours of sexual nature for their benefit or the benefit of a third party.

No employee may be punished, dismissed or be the subject of a discriminatory measure for having testified to the actions stipulated in the preceding subparagraph or for having reported them.

Any disposal or act to the contrary is legally null and void.

L 122-49

No employee should have to suffer repeated acts of moral harassment which have for their purpose or effect a degradation of his working conditions liable to violate his rights and his dignity and to alter his physical and mental health or to compromise his professional future.

Much harassment in connection with race, disability, etc., will fall within this definition, as will some "hostile environment" sexual harassment. It is worth noting, however, that it applies only to repeated acts of harassment, as defined by the Directives. In Belgium, by contrast, whereas the Act of 2002 similarly defined moral harassment to require repeated actions, the legislation passed to implement the 2000 Directives defines harassment as follows:

Belgian Act to combat discrimination of 25 February 2003[114] **4.BE.55.**

Article 2, § 6

... undesired behaviour connected to the discrimination grounds summarised under §1" ['sex, so-called race, colour, descent, national or ethnic origin, sexual orientation, marital status, birth, fortune, age, religion or belief, current and future state of health, a disability or physical characteristic'] aimed at or affecting the dignity of a person and creating a threatening, hostile, insulting, demeaning or offensive environment.

Like the French concept of "moral harassment", Belgian "harassment" does not require intention on the part of the harasser. It is wider than the French law (and the Belgian non-ground-specific "moral harassment") in that it incorporates no requirement for repetition where the harassment complained of is on a protected ground.[115]

As a result of the transposition of the Directives, Article 1a of the Dutch General Equal Treatment Act, which has been inserted by the EC Implementation Act, provides that:

The Dutch General Equal Treatment Act[116] **4.NL.56.**

Article 1a

1. The prohibition of distinction laid down in this Act shall also include a prohibition of harassment.

2. Harassment as referred to in the first subsection shall mean conduct related to the characteristics or behaviour as referred to in Article 1 under 'b' [the grounds covered by the Act including race, religion, sexual orientation] and, which has the purpose or effect of violating the dignity of a person and [emphasis added] creating an intimidating, hostile, degrading, humiliating or offensive environment.

Materially similar provision is made in relation to disability by Article 1a of the Disability Discrimination Act, which was also amended by the EC Implementation Act), and in Article 2 of the Age Discrimination Act. The Equal Treatment

---

[114] Loi du 25 février 2003 tendant à lutter contre la discrimination et modifiant la loi du 15 février 1993 créant un Centre pour l'égalité des chances et la lutte contre le racisme, Moniteur belge, 17 March 2003.

[115] The 2003 Act further provides that the criminal penalties for harassment under Belgium's Penal Code may be doubled when the harassment committed is motivated by the victim's identification by particular characteristics.

[116] Algemene Wet Gelijke Behandeling [General Equal Treatment Act] of 1994, Stb. [Staatsblad=Law Gazette] 230.

Commission had advised the government to use the term "or" instead of the "and" emphasised above, but this suggestion was rejected.[117] But:

M. Gijzen, *"Report on Measures to Combat Discrimination:* **4.NL.57.** *Directives 2000/43/EC and 2000/78/EC. Country Report Netherlands"*[118]

"Para 2.4.
. . . it follows from the Commission's case-law pre implementation, that the infringement of a person's dignity in itself was sufficient to establish a case of harassment (i.e. of unlawful distinction with regard to the 'employment conditions'). Thus, discriminatory/harassing insults were by themselves sufficient ground to make out a case. In the new definitions, the alleged victim must also prove the element of 'creating an intimidating, etc. environment'. Therefore in my view, the accumulative conditions appear to fall short of the Directives' 'non regression clause'."[119]

Prior to the implementation of the Directives, the Dutch Act of 2 March 1994 laying down general rules for the protection against discrimination regulated the "making of distinctions" in relation, inter alia, to "working conditions", although "harassment" was not as such defined as a concept in Dutch equal treatment law. The Dutch Equal Treatment Commission "attached a broad meaning to the notion of 'employment conditions', ruling that 'right to equality and non discrimination in regard to "employment conditions" including "working conditions", encapsulates a person's right to be freed from "ground-related" harassment in the workplace".[120]

A different question mark hangs over the transposition in Italy of Directive 2000/43. Prior to the transposition of the Directives, Italy had no express provisions dealing with harassment. The Decrees of August 2003 transposed Directives 2000/43 and 2000/78, respectively. But whereas the Decree concerning Directive 78/2000 uses the same wording as the Directive, defining harassment, further, as a form of discrimination, the Decree concerning Directive 2000/43 provides that the unwanted conduct must have the effect of "creating an intimidating, hostile, degrading, humiliating *and* [emphasis added: rather than "or"] offensive environment".

The difference between the Decrees was, it has been suggested, readily classifiable as "a pure *lapsus calami* without implications for interpretation". But, according to the Italian Country Report on Measures to Combat Discrimination (2005), "This

---

[117] Commentary by the Equal Treatment Commission on the implementation of the common provisions of the Employment Framework Directive and the Racial Equality Directive, available on the website of the Dutch Equal Treatment Commission.

[118] (European Commission, 2004) 24, available on the website of Directorate-General for Employment, Social Affairs and Equal Opportunities.

[119] See also D. Houtzager and N. Bochhah, "Onderscheid op grond van ras bij de arbeid: nieuwe ontwikkelingen" (2004) 7/8 *Sociaal Recht* 272, 274.

[120] See above **4.NL.57.**, para. 2.4.

view must now probably be revised if one considers that a recent decree[121] corrected some other formal mistakes of both decrees . . . without making mention of this point". And in Spain, where sexual and moral harassment were expressly regulated for the first time by the transposition of the 2000 Directives, the Law of 62/2003 on fiscal, administrative and social measures defines "harassment" in line with those Directives, save that the Spanish definition does not include the words "hostile" and "degrading", defining "harassment" instead as

> "all unwanted conduct related to racial or ethnic origin, religion or convictions, disability, age or sexual orientation that takes place with the purpose or effect of violating the dignity of a person and creating an intimidating, humiliating or offensive environment."[122]

The Irish definition of sexual harassment has not been substantively changed by the implementation of the 2000 or 2002 Directives, although sections 23 and 32 (which dealt with sexual harassment and harassment) have been repealed and replaced by a new section 14A of the Employment Equality Act 1998 which provides as follows:

Irish Employment Equality Acts 1998 to 2004[123]   **4.IE.58.**

Section 14A
(3) A person's rejection of, or submission to, harassment or sexual harassment may not be used by an employer as a basis for a decision affecting that person.
(7)(a) In this section—

(i) references to harassment are to any form of unwanted conduct related to any of the discriminatory grounds [gender, marital status, family status, sexual orientation, religion, age, disability, race, colour, nationality or ethnic or national origins, membership of the traveller community], and
(ii) references to sexual harassment are to any form of unwanted verbal, non-verbal or physical conduct of a sexual nature, being conduct which in either case has the purpose or effect of violating a person's dignity and creating an intimidating, hostile, degrading, humiliating or offensive environment for the person.

(b) Without prejudice to the generality of paragraph (a), such unwanted conduct may consist of acts, requests, spoken words, gestures or the production, display or circulation of written words, pictures or other material.

It is perhaps noteworthy that both Irish and Danish law, in common with the transposing provisions of many other states, use the terms "in relation to" or "related

---

[121] Decreto legislativo 2 agosto 2004, n. 256, 'Correzione di errori materiali nei decreti legislativi 9 luglio 2003, n. 215 e n. 216, concernenti disposizioni per la parità di trattamento tra le persone indipendentemente dalla razza e dall'origine etnica, nonché in materia di occupazione e condizioni di lavoro', in Gazzetta Ufficiale n. 244 del 16 ottobre 2004.
[122] Art. 28.d, discussed by L. Cachón, "Report on Measures to Combat Discrimination: Directives 2000/43/EC and 2000/78/EC. Country Report Spain" (European Commission, 2005) 24, available on the website of Directorate-General for Employment, Social Affairs and Equal Opportunities.
[123] The Equal Status Acts 1998–2004 adopt similar definitions outside the employment sphere.

to" (or, in Sweden, "based on" or "in connection with"), while the equivalent UK law defines harassment (other than sexual harassment/harassment based on sex) as follows:

Race Relations Act 1976   **4.GB.59.**

Section 4A

(1) A person subjects another to harassment in any circumstances relevant for the purposes of any provision referred to in section 1(1B) where, on grounds of race or ethnic or national origins, he engages in unwanted conduct which has the purpose or effect of –

    (a)   violating that other person's dignity, or
    (b)   creating an intimidating, hostile, degrading, humiliating or offensive environment for him.

(2) Conduct shall be regarded as having the effect specified in paragraph (a) or (b) of subsection (1) only if, having regard to all the circumstances, including in particular the perception of that other person, it should reasonably be considered as having that effect.

The Sex Discrimination Act 1975, as amended in order to transpose the 2002 Directive, refers to "sexual harassment" as such only in the title of section 4A:

Sex Discrimination Act 1975   **4.GB.60.**

Section 4A[124]

Harassment, including sexual harassment

For the purposes of this Act, a person subjects a woman to harassment if—

(a) on the ground of her sex, he engages in unwanted conduct that has the purpose or effect—

    (i)   of violating her dignity, or
    (ii) of creating an intimidating, hostile, degrading, humiliating or offensive environment for her,

(b) he engages in any form of unwanted verbal, non-verbal or physical conduct of a sexual nature that has the purpose or effect—

    (i)   of violating her dignity, or
    (ii) of creating an intimidating, hostile, degrading, humiliating or offensive environment for her, or

(c) on the ground of her rejection of or submission to unwanted conduct of a kind mentioned in paragraph (a) or (b), he treats her less favourably than he would treat her had she not rejected, or submitted to, the conduct.

---

[124] The other discrimination provisions (the Sex Discrimination Act 1975, Disability Discrimination Act 1995, Employment Equality (Sexual Orientation) Regulations 2003 and Employment Equality (Religion or Belief) Regulations 2003 all contain materially similar provisions.

(2) Conduct shall be regarded as having the effect mentioned in sub-paragraph (i) or (ii) of subsection (1)(a) or (b) only if, having regard to all the circumstances, including in particular the perception of the woman, it should reasonably be considered as having that effect . . .

(5) Subsection (1) is to be read as applying equally to the harassment of men, and for that purpose shall have effect with such modifications as are requisite.

The replacement of the word "or" for the Directives' "and" in the definitions of harassment was in order to avoid regression, the case-law which had developed under the discrimination provisions being inconsistent with a requirement for both a violation of dignity and the creation of an "intimidating, hostile, degrading, humiliating or offensive environment". There was concern, however, that the term "on grounds of" rather than "in relation to", "relating to", etc. may have the effect of maintaining the position in the UK which prevailed prior to the transposition of the Directives, that is, regulating harassment only where it takes the form of "less favourable treatment" on the relevant ground. In *R(EOC) v Secretary for Trade and Industry* [2007] EWHC (Admin) the High Court ruled that the UK had failed adequately to transpose the Directive, in part because of this.

4.4.2. "HARASSMENT" AND "DISCRIMINATION"

It was noted above that the 2000 Directives regulate harassment as a form of discrimination. Even since the transposition of the Directives, however, neither sexual nor moral harassment are regarded as species of "discrimination" for the purposes of French law, but rather as violations of physical and psychological integrity (though, having said this, as the France Country Report on Measures to Combat Discrimination points out (2004), that "in the present state of the law, discrimination taking the form of harassment could very well be considered by the courts as covered by the prohibition of direct discrimination under article 122-45" of the Labour Code).[125]

In France the refusal to regard harassment as a form of discrimination appears a matter of high principle. In Belgium, by contrast, and in Ireland, a variety of approaches to this question may be found within a single state. In Belgium, most employment-related matters are covered by Federal law whose provisions on harassment and sexual harassment have been considered above. Some matters, though, still remain within the authority of the regional authorities. And, whereas under the 2003 Federal law and the law governing delegated matters in the German speaking Community, harassment (*harcèlement, pesterijen, Belästigung*), which is defined in accordance with the 2000 Directives, is identified as a form of discrimination, the Flemish Decree of 8 May 2002, which follows the wording of the Directives in defining harassment (*intimidatie*), goes on to state that "The principle of equal treatment implies the absence of any form of direct or indirect discrimination

---

[125] S. Latraverse, "Report on Measures to Combat Discrimination: Directives 2000/43/EC and 2000/78/EC. Country Report France" (European Commission, 2004) 15, available on the website of Directorate-General for Employment, Social Affairs and Equal Opportunities.

or of harassment" [emphasis added].[126] This implies that "harassment" is conceptually distinct from "discrimination", something which has practical significance
under the Flemish Decree, which prohibits "discrimination", rather than "discrimination and harassment", in a number of contexts and provides for sanctions in
relation to "discrimination" alone.

In the UK, legislative provisions dealing with discrimination falling within the
subject matter of the 2000 and 2002 Directives treat "harassment" with (although not
as a form of) discrimination for the purposes of burden of proof, sanctions,
prohibitions on victimisation, etc. Thus, for example:

Disability Discrimination Act 1995   **4.UK.61.**

Section 4 (as amended to incorporate Directive 2000/78)
(1) It is unlawful for an employer to discriminate against a disabled person—

    (a)   in the arrangements which he makes for the purpose of determining to whom he
           should offer employment;
    (b)   in the terms on which he offers that person employment; or
    (c)   by refusing to offer, or deliberately not offering, him employment.

(2) It is unlawful for an employer to discriminate against a disabled person whom he employs—

    (a)   in the terms of employment which he affords him;
    (b)   in the opportunities which he affords him for promotion, a transfer, training or receiv-
           ing any other benefit;
    (c)   by refusing to afford him, or deliberately not affording him, any such opportunity; or
    (d)   by dismissing him, or subjecting him to any other detriment.

(3) It is also unlawful for an employer, in relation to employment by him, to subject to
harassment—

    (a)   a disabled person whom he employs; or
    (b)   a disabled person who has applied to him for employment.[127]

4.4.3.   LIABILITY FOR HARASSMENT

The approach taken in Denmark to sexual and other harassment prior to the transposition of the 2000 Directives was mentioned above. The Danish Labour Market
Discrimination Act, which regulates discrimination on grounds of race, colour,
religion, political belief, sexual orientation or national, ethnic or social origin, and the
Ethnic Equal Treatment Act (which regulate discrimination on grounds of "race or
ethnic origin") now provide, respectively, as follows:

---

[126] Article 5(1), 2°.
[127] The provision is typical of those dealing with employment in the Sex Discrimination Act, Race
Relations Act and provisions transposing the sexual orientation and religion and belief provisions of the
Directive 2000/78.

The Danish Labour Market Discrimination Act   **4.DK.62.**

Chapter 1
Section 1.4.
Harassment shall be regarded as discrimination where undesired behaviour in relation to a person's race, colour, religion or faith, political views, sexual orientation, age, disability or national, social or ethnic origins takes place with the purpose or the effect of violating a person's dignity and creating a threatening, hostile, demeaning, humiliating or unpleasant atmosphere for the person in question.
Section 3.4
Harassment shall be regarded as discrimination where behaviour in relation to race or ethnic origins takes place with the purpose or the effect of violating a person's dignity and creating a threatening, hostile, demeaning, humiliating or unpleasant atmosphere for the person in question.

These definitions are very similar to those set out in the 2000 Directives. However, it is not clear whether and to what extent the protection from harassment applies in relation to harassment by third parties such as clients and patients. The Danish Parliament confirmed that section 1.4 of the Labour Market Discrimination Act was to be interpreted consistent with the judicial approach to sexual harassment, which, according to the 2005 Danish Country Report on Measures to Combat Discrimi-nation, "includes a duty for the employer to provide work conditions free of harassment, whether this harassment be from the employer or from other employees", breach of which duty will give rise to liability for compensation on the part of the employer.[128] According to that Report:

N.E. Hansen, "Report on Measures to Combat Discrimination: **4.DK.63.**
Directives 2000/43/EC and 2000/78/EC. Country Report Denmark"[129]

"Paras. 2.4, 3.1.3
No comments are made in relation to the question of whether the employer is also responsible in relation to harassment coming from clients, patients, etc. This may, thus be up to the Danish courts to interpret . . .

As a general rule an employer is responsible for what his employees do when they act in his Service . . . [but]. If a sub-contractor is an independent legal entity, person or company, the responsibility lies with the subcontractor and not with the contractor . . . Harassment by [peer-workers and other workers as well who are employed by a firm] is not a part of their job performance, and will not therefore be considered to be included in, or to be a part of, the employer's responsibility, unless he has neglected his duty to instruct or correct his personnel as a good employer ought to do to avoid harassment among the employees . . ."[130]

---

[128] See above n. 95 at 23.
[129] *Ibid.*
[130] *Ibid.* at 23–25.

A question has also arisen, in connection with the transposition of the Directives into Dutch law, as to which persons are governed by the prohibition on harassment. Having made the point that the Directives provide for their application to "all persons" (Article 3(1) of Directive 2000/43 and 2000/78), the Dutch Country Report suggests that:

> *M. Gijzen, "Report on Measures to Combat Discrimination:*   **4.NL.64.**
> *Directive 2000/43/EC and 2000/78/EC. Country Report Netherlands"*[131]

"Para 3.1.3

. . . 'all persons' is sufficiently ample to cover in the context of employment: employers, employees and third persons. All may subject another person to discriminatory or harassing treatment connected to a covered non-discrimination ground. Since Directive 2000/43 goes beyond employment, 'all persons' is ample enough in my view, to cover landlords, schools, hospitals and so forth . . .

. . . nothing is specifically said in the Directives on the matter of vicarious liability which, it seems, remains a matter of the Member States' autonomy. However, Member States must guarantee that sanctions are effective, proportionate and dissuasive as follows from Article 15 of Directive 2000/43 and Article 17 of Directive 2000/78)."

The Report goes on to note, however, that while the Dutch discrimination provisions are silent as to "personal applicability", and while, as regards employment:

" . . . the central norm is addressed not only to private and public employers, but also to *organisations from employers, organisations of workers, employment offices (public) job agencies, pension funds, some external advisors ('liberal') professionals, bodies of liberal professionals, training institutions, schools, universities etc* . . . from this it is not clear whether colleague workers or third persons can be held liable under the Acts? The matter was explicitly raised in the Parliamentary discussions on the implementation of the Directives. *It follows clearly from these discussions that the government has not intended to render the non discrimination Acts applicable in relationships between colleagues, let alone in relationships with third persons.* The government defends this by noting that between colleagues *inter se*, there is no contract or relationship of authority. However, it was indicated by the government that those employees who in name of their employer, exercise authority over their co-employees are addressees of the central norm. De facto, such an employee functions in the capacity of employer . . .

The purported inapplicability of the Dutch Acts in relationships between colleagues inter se, appears particularly problematic in the context of work-related *harassment*. In its current format and in the light of the Parliamentary comments, the law prevents an alleged victim of harassment from holding a colleague or a third person directly liable for the contested acts. The only way to do this would be by seeking recourse to the general provisions of *tort law* enshrined in the Dutch Civil Code.

However, and this also follows from the Equal Treatment Commission's case-law *pre implementation* of the Directives, there rests a general *duty of care* upon the employer to maintain a discrimination-free and safe workplace. An employee's right not to be discriminated

---

[131] See above **4.NL.57.**

against in this employment and working conditions, embraces the right to be free from discrimination and harassment at the workplace. In opinion 2004/11 for example, the Equal Treatment Commission inter alia ruled upon the applicant's complaint of racial harassment by a colleague worker. The Commission considered that '. . . *the employer's duty to refrain from distinction in employment also includes the duty to supervise that those who are under his authority refrain from and are protected against discrimination*' (para. 5.8). An employer's failure to do so, results in principle in an act of distinction by the employer.

The employer's vicarious liability for harassing acts by a *third* person was for example at stake in opinion 97/82. The case concerned racial harassment of a nurse, by a patient. The Commission repeated its stance that the employer is under a legal duty to prevent from occurring acts of harassment done by persons under his supervision. The Commission took the view that, although the alleged harassing acts were not done by a colleague worker but by a third person, this did not circumscribe whatsoever the employer's duty of care . . .

Beyond the scope of Dutch equal treatment legislation, the following is essential to take account of. The employer may be held vicariously liable for discriminatory or harassing acts done by colleague workers *under general private employment law*. The relevant Articles upon which a claim can be based are 1. *the good employer's practice (*goedwerkgeversschap, *Article 7:611 of the Civil Code); 2. the employer's general duty of care (i.e. the employer's liability for damages suffered by an employee in the performance of job-related duties, laid down in Article 7:658 of the Civil Code).* Both of these Articles are directed at the employer's liability for acts done by the employer himself, or by others over whom the employer has control. It is disputed in legal circles whether Article 7:658, can form the legal basis for claims that regard *mere psychological damage, rather than physical damage* . . .

Although the Dutch Supreme Court has given no decisive answer, the lower courts have been prepared to accept Article 7:658 Civil Code, in cases of sexual harassment, as a basis for financial compensation of psychological damage resulting from sexually harassing acts [emphasis in original]." (Para 3.1.3)

It appears from this that employers may be held liable for harassment by third parties even if the third parties themselves could not be. In the UK, as we saw above (*Pearce v. Mayfield School*), employers are not liable for the actions of third parties (as distinct from employees). Pre-implementation of the Directives, an employer could be held responsible for allowing harassment by third parties if, *by so allowing*, the employer was treating the harassed employee less favourably in connection with a protected ground (i.e. if the employer allowed women to be subjected to harassment which he would not have permitted in the case of men, etc.). The differential treatment would have amounted to direct discrimination by the employer and, if the harasser's own conduct also amounted to discrimination (because he would not have sexually harassed men, would not have subjected white staff to racial harassment, etc.), the harasser might be held liable for assisting the employer in the employer's own act of discrimination.[132]

---

[132] The relevant provision of the discrimination legislation (applicable in respect of each of the protected grounds) provides that: "(1) A person who knowingly aids another person to do an act made unlawful by this Act shall be treated for the purposes of this Act as himself doing an unlawful act of the like description".

The transposing legislation in the UK did not alter the position as regards liability for harassment by third parties, for which employers will be pinned with liability only insofar as, by permitting the harassment to occur, the employer itself can be regarded as having either discriminated against the employee (as above) or having harassed the employee. It was accepted by the High Court in *R(EOC) v Secretary for Trade and Industry* [2007] EWHC 483 that the failure of the UK Government to prohibit harassment "related to" sex as distinct from the narrower harassment "on grounds of" sex breached the Directive, and that adoption of the broader test might impose liability on employers for some third-party harassment. The government has yet, at the time of writing, to amend the legislation in response to the judgment.

Prior to its amendment, Ireland's Employment Equality Act had provided for vicarious liability as outlined at **4.IE.59.** above. The Equality Act 2004, which transposed the 2000 and 2002 Directives, inserted into the 1998 Act the following provisions:

Irish Employment Equality Acts 1998 to 2004   **4.IE.65.**

"Section 14A[133]
(1) For the purposes of this Act, where—
(a) an employee (in this section referred to as 'the victim') is harassed or sexually harassed either at a place where the employee is employed (in this section referred to as 'the workplace') or otherwise in the course of his or her employment by a person who is—

  (i)   employed at that place or by the same employer,
  (ii) the victim's employer, or
  (iii) a client, customer or other business contact of the victim's employer and the circumstances of the harassment are such that the employer ought reasonably to have taken steps to prevent it, or

(b) without prejudice to the generality of paragraph (a)—

  (i) such harassment has occurred, and
  (ii) either—
    (I) the victim is treated differently in the workplace or otherwise in the course of his or her employment by reason of rejecting or accepting the harassment, or
    (II) it could reasonably be anticipated that he or she would be so treated,

the harassment or sexual harassment constitutes discrimination by the victim's employer in relation to the victim's conditions of employment.
(2) If harassment or sexual harassment of the victim by a person other than his or her employer would, but for this subsection, be regarded as discrimination by the employer under subsection (1), it is a defence for the employer to prove that the employer took such steps as are reasonably practicable—

---

[133] The Equal Status Acts 1998–2004 adopt similar definitions outside the employment sphere.

(a) in a case where subsection (1)(a) applies (whether or not subsection (1)(b) also applies), to prevent the person from harassing or sexually harassing the victim or any class of persons which includes the victim, and

(b) in a case where subsection (1)(b) applies, to prevent the victim from being treated differently in the workplace or otherwise in the course of the victim's employment and, if and so far as any such treatment has occurred, to reverse its effects.

(3) A person's rejection of, or submission to, harassment or sexual harassment may not be used by an employer as a basis for a decision affecting that person.

(4) The reference in subsection (1)(a)(iii) to a client, customer or other business contact of the victim's employer includes a reference to any other person with whom the employer might reasonably expect the victim to come into contact in the workplace or otherwise in the course of his or her employment . . ."

This "belt and braces" approach to harassment certainly complies with the obligations imposed by the Directives, which provide, in relation to employment, as follows:

Directives 2000/43/EC and 2000/78/EC[134]   **4.EC.66.**

Article 3
1. Within the limits of the areas of competence conferred on the Community, this Directive shall apply to all persons, as regards both the public and private sectors, including public bodies, in relation to . . .

(c) employment and working conditions, including dismissals and pay . . .

Harassment which takes place in connection with work certainly impacts on the worker's "working conditions", whether it emanates from the employer, from co-workers or from clients. The circumstances under which liability can be imposed upon an employer for the actions of third parties may justifiably vary between member states (the focus might be, for example, on whether the employer had control of the situation, whether it had actual or constructive knowledge of the harassment, or whether there were steps it could have taken to avoid the harassment or to stop it at an early stage). The Irish approach restricts liability for harassment by third parties to cases where "the employer ought reasonably to have taken steps to prevent it". Whether it is consistent with the Directives to exclude liability for harassment by third parties is questionable.

4.5. COMPARATIVE ANALYSIS

The express recognition and regulation of harassment and sexual harassment by the EU have been relatively recent developments, particularly in the case of harassment other than sexual harassment. The regulation of harassing behaviour gives rise to a

---

[134] See above **4.EC.1.** and **4.EC.2.**

number of practical and conceptual dilemmas which have been responded to in different ways by different national legal orders both inside and outside the EU. The US was an early player in the recognition and regulation of both racial and sexual harassment, but US law is locked into a discrimination model the effect of which is to leave harassment on unprotected grounds (notably sexual orientation and religion or belief) unregulated. Many of the questions which currently bedevil legal responses to harassment and sexual harassment featured in early US case-law, though the high profile of a number of US sexual harassment cases caused something of a backlash in a number of EU Member States which associated the US approach to sexual harassment with a puritanical moral stance which regarded workplace sexual relationships with distaste. So, for example, while UK developments have fairly closely mirrored the US approach, France and Italy in particular resisted pressures towards the regulation of sexual harassment along US lines, and elsewhere in Europe many jurisdictions appeared to regard sexual harassment with complacency. This is not to say that no harassing behaviour could be captured by law: some such harassment includes physical and/or sexual assaults which would breach both criminal and civil standards of behaviour. But, as we saw above, in the absence of express definitions and prohibitions of (sexually) harassing behaviour, legal redress is problematic, not least given difficulties of criminal proof and employment-related protections applicable to harassers as well as their victims.

The implementation of the 2000 and 2002 Directives has taken place too recently to enable any conclusions to be drawn as to the effectiveness of transposing legislation. Suffice to say at this point that a number of interesting questions have been raised by transposing legislation as regards the circumstances in which liability for the actions of staff and third parties can be imposed on employers. Besides this question of general interest, more specific questions arise in a number of cases as to whether the definitions adopted by transposing legislation are adequate in terms of the Directives themselves (the UK, Germany, France and Italy, for example) or to avoid a breach of the principle of non-regression (the Netherlands). A number of these questions are likely to be answered by the domestic courts in the first instance, whether by means of Directive-compatible interpretations or declarations that the transposing legislation requires amendment. Other cases will find their way to the ECJ in the fullness of time.

CHAPTER FIVE
INSTRUCTIONS TO DISCRIMINATE AND VICTIMISATION

Tufyal Choudhury

5.1. INSTRUCTIONS TO DISCRIMINATE

This chapter examines two issues: instructions to discriminate and victimisation. Neither are the central focus of discrimination law, as they are not "discrimination proper" but rather related phenomena. The first, instructions to discriminate, is a "precursor" to discrimination; the law here is trying to address action that could generate discrimination in the future. The second, victimisation, is a "postscript" to discrimination: actions that could dissuade or prevent individuals from seeking redress for the discrimination that they face. In relation to both issues there is a possibility of addressing the phenomena through general principles of law: instructions to do a prohibited action, or victimisation of a person that has asserted their legal rights. As we will see in this chapter, the route chosen in EU discrimination law has been to treat instructions to discriminate as a form of discrimination, whereas victimisation is only outlawed in general and not equated with discrimination.

5.1.1.   DEVELOPMENT OF EUROPEAN AND INTERNATIONAL LAW

This section on instructions to discriminate introduces a new perspective. The chapters thus far have examined the manner in which anti-discrimination law regulates and prescribes the actions of those who discriminate, whether directly or indirectly, or by harassing a person. In these instances, the law is concerned with the liability of those immediately involved in the discriminatory conduct or vicariously liable for the actions of those who are so involved. Establishing a prohibition of instructions to discriminate, EU law addresses the actions of individuals who could be described as accomplices to discrimination but who are not immediately involved. The section explores how international, European and national law addresses the position of accomplices to discrimination. If the central relationship that anti-discrimination law is concerned with is that of the victim of discrimination and the person immediately involved in discriminatory conduct, then this chapter is concerned with the liability of "third parties".

5.1.1.A.   INCITEMENT TO DISCRIMINATE

Many EU Members States have provisions that prohibit incitement to discriminate. Such provisions may have been introduced in response to their obligations under international human rights treaties, in particular under the International Covenant on Civil and Political Rights (ICCPR) and the International Convention on the Elimination of All Forms of Racial Discrimination (ICERD). The provisions of these treaties require State Parties to address incitement of hatred and violence.

International Covenant on Civil and Political Rights[1]   **5.UN.1.**

Article 20
1. Any propaganda for war shall be prohibited by law
2. Any advocacy of national, racial or religious hatred that constitutes incitement to discrimination, hostility or violence shall be prohibited by law.

Incitement to discriminate, alongside incitement to hostility and incitement to violence, is identified here as a particular way in which national, racial and religious hatred can occur. The UN Human Rights Committee has primary responsibility for monitoring compliance by State Parties with their obligations under the ICCPR. In addition to this, the Committee is able to issue General Comments to elaborate on the meaning of specific treaty articles. These are, however, not legally binding on signatory states. Thus, in General Comment 11 the Committee sets out further details reflecting its understanding of State Parties' obligations under Article 20.

Human Rights Committee, General Comment No. 11:   **5.UN.2.**
Prohibition of propaganda for war and inciting national,
racial or religious hatred (Art.20): 29/07/83
Article 20 (Nineteenth session, 1983)[2]

". . . 2. Article 20 of the Covenant states that any propaganda for war and any advocacy of national, racial or religious hatred that constitutes incitement to discrimination, hostility or violence shall be prohibited by law. In the opinion of the Committee, these required prohibitions are fully compatible with the right of freedom of expression as contained in article 19, the exercise of which carries with it special duties and responsibilities. The prohibition under paragraph 1 extends to all forms of propaganda threatening or resulting in an act of aggression or breach of the peace contrary to the Charter of the United Nations, while paragraph 2 is directed against any advocacy of national, racial or religious hatred that constitutes incitement to discrimination, hostility or violence, whether such propaganda or advocacy has aims which are internal or external to the State concerned. The provisions of article 20, paragraph 1 do not prohibit advocacy of the sovereign right of self-defence or the right of peoples to self-determination and independence in accordance with the Charter of the United Nations. For article 20 to become fully effective there ought to be a law making it clear that propaganda and advocacy as described therein are contrary to public policy and providing for an appropriate sanction in

---

[1] 999 UNTS 171.
[2] In *Compilation of General Comments and General Recommendations Adopted by Human Rights Treaty Bodies*, UN Doc. HRI\GEN\1\Rev.1 at 12 (1994).

case of violation. The Committee, therefore, believes that States parties which have not yet done so should take the measures necessary to fulfil the obligations contained in article 20, and should themselves refrain from any such propaganda or advocacy."

The Committee stresses the need for legislation that makes clear that incitement to discriminate is contrary to public policy. The General Comment refers to the tensions between freedom of expression and provisions on incitement to hatred and discrimination. The Committee takes the view that these provisions are not in conflict with the right to freedom of expression.

While the ICCPR is a broad-ranging document, some states have committed themselves to more specific and detailed obligations in relation to combating particular forms of discrimination through specialised Conventions on discrimination. Thus, more detailed provisions on incitement to discriminate can be found in the ICERD.

Convention on the Elimination of Racial Discrimination[3]   **5.UN.3.**

Article 4
States Parties condemn all propaganda and all organizations . . . which attempt to justify or promote racial hatred and discrimination in any form, and undertake to adopt immediate and positive measures designed to eradicate all incitement to, or acts of, such discrimination and, to this end, with due regard to the principles embodied in the Universal Declaration of Human Rights . . . *inter alia*:
(a) Shall declare an offence punishable by law all dissemination of ideas based on racial superiority or hatred, incitement to racial discrimination, as well as all acts of violence or incitement to such acts against any race or group of persons of another colour or ethnic origin, and also the provision of any assistance to racist activities, including the financing thereof;
(b) Shall declare illegal and prohibit organizations, and also organized and all other propaganda activities, which promote and incite racial discrimination, and shall recognize participation in such organizations or activities as an offence punishable by law;
(c) Shall not permit public authorities or public institutions, national or local, to promote or incite racial discrimination.

State Parties' compliance with their obligations under ICERD is monitored by the Committee on the Elimination of Racial Discrimination. The Committee is able to elaborate on State Parties' obligations under specific articles of the Convention by issuing General Recommendations. General Recommendation 15 concerns the Committee's understanding of Article 4 of ICERD.

[3] 660 UNTS 195.

Committee on the Elimination of Racial Discrimination,   **5.UN.4.**
General Recommendation 15, Measures to eradicate incitement to
or acts of discrimination (Forty-second session, 1993)[4]

"3. Article 4 (a) requires States parties to penalize four categories of misconduct: (i) dissemination of ideas based upon racial superiority or hatred; (ii) incitement to racial hatred; (iii) acts of violence against any race or group of persons of another colour or ethnic origin; and (iv) incitement to such acts.

4. In the opinion of the Committee, the prohibition of the dissemination of all ideas based upon racial superiority or hatred is compatible with the right to freedom of opinion and expression. This right is embodied in article 19 of the Universal Declaration of Human Rights and is recalled in article 5 (d) (viii) of the International Convention on the Elimination of All Forms of Racial Discrimination. Its relevance to article 4 is noted in the article itself. The citizen's exercise of this right carries special duties and responsibilities, specified in article 29, paragraph 2, of the Universal Declaration, among which the obligation not to disseminate racist ideas is of particular importance. The Committee wishes, furthermore, to draw to the attention of States parties article 20 of the International Covenant on Civil and Political Rights, according to which any advocacy of national, racial or religious hatred that constitutes incitement to discrimination, hostility or violence shall be prohibited by law.

. . .

6. Some States have maintained that in their legal order it is inappropriate to declare illegal an organization before its members have promoted or incited racial discrimination. The Committee is of the opinion that article 4 (b) places a greater burden upon such States to be vigilant in proceeding against such organizations at the earliest moment. These organizations, as well as organized and other propaganda activities, have to be declared illegal and prohibited. Participation in these organizations is, of itself, to be punished."

The provisions of ICERD Article 4 address incitement to discriminate and incitement to hatred in the same provision; this reflects the close relationship between the two. The link between incitement to discriminate and instructions to discriminate lies in the fact that incitement concerns expressions of A to B that in turn affect C. Such expressions can take the form of instructions by A to B. ICERD requires State Parties to make incitement to racial discrimination an offence punishable by law. Article 4(b) requires State Parties to declare illegal and prohibit organisations that incite racial discrimination.

Several states (including Belgium, France, Ireland, Italy and the UK) have entered reservations in respect of this provision and have expressed concerns about the extent to which requirements to prohibit incitement to discriminate undermines freedom of expression. For example, France, in its reservation to the Convention, states that "it interprets the reference made [in Article 4] to the Universal Declaration of Human Rights . . . as releasing the States Parties from the obligation to enact anti-discrimination legislation which is incompatible with freedom of expression and association". The UK states that

---

[4] UN Doc. A/48/18 at 114 (1994), reprinted in *Compilation of General Comments and General Recommendations Adopted by Human Rights Treaty Bodies*, UN Doc. HRI\GEN\1\Rev.6 at 204 (2003).

"it interprets article 4 as requiring a party to the Convention to adopt further legislative measures in the fields covered by sub-paragraphs (a), (b) and (c) of that article only in so far as it may consider [necessary] with due regard to the principles embodied in the Universal Declaration of Human Rights . . . (in particular the right to freedom of opinion and expression and the right to freedom of peaceful assembly and association)."

These international law provisions have also influenced the development of law at European level, both in the Council of Europe and at the European Union. The Council of Europe's Commission of Racism and Intolerance recalled the provisions in ICERD in the preamble to its General Policy Recommendation 7, on national legislation to combat racism and racial discrimination, adopted in December 2002. Paragraph 18 of the recommendation provides that national laws should penalise public incitement to discriminate, when committed intentionally. Paragraph 20 provides that national laws should prohibit "intentionally instigating, aiding, abetting, or attempting to" publicly incite discrimination.

At EU level, the Council adopted, on 15 July 1996, a Joint Action concerning action to combat racism and xenophobia on the basis of Article K.3 of the EU Treaty (now: Article 31 TEU). Its main objective was to ensure effective legal cooperation between Member States in combating racism and xenophobia. The Joint Action stressed the need to prevent the perpetrators of such offences from benefiting from the fact that they are treated differently in the Member States by moving from one country to another to avoid prosecution. In particular, under the principle of double criminality Member States may refuse cooperation on the grounds that conduct, though illegal in the state requesting assistance, is not illegal in the requested state. Member States were asked to ensure that racist and xenophobic behaviours of the type listed in the Joint Action be punishable as criminal offences or, failing that, and pending the adoption of any necessary provisions, be derogated from the principle of double criminality for such behaviours. Title I.A of the Joint Action makes reference to prohibition of incitement to discriminate.

The Council of the European Union, 96/443/JHA: **5.EC.5.**
Joint Action of 15 July 1996 adopted by the Council on the basis of
Article K.3 of the Treaty on European Union, concerning action to combat
racism and xenophobia[5]

"In the interests of combating racism and xenophobia, each Member State shall undertake, in accordance with the procedure laid down in Title II, to ensure effective judicial cooperation in respect of offences based on the following types of behaviour, and if necessary for the purposes of that cooperation, either to take steps to see that such behaviour is punishable as a criminal offence or, failing that, and pending the adoption of an necessary provisions, to derogate from the principle of double criminality for such behaviour:

[5] [1996] OJ L185/5.

(a) public incitement to discrimination, violence or racial hatred in respect of a group of persons or a member of such a group defined by reference to colour, race, religion or national or ethnic origin; . . ."

In developing the Framework Decision on Racism and Xenophobia[6] to take forward the Joint Action programme, the Council considered whether provisions on incitement to discriminate were needed. This had to be considered in light of the adoption of the Race Directive, which covers instructions to discriminate.

The Commission took the view that the Framework Decision did not need a provision on "incitement" to discriminate, as the Racial Equality Directive[7] provisions on instructions to discriminate covered a substantial part of this. However, the Commission concluded that the prohibition on instructions to discriminate in the Racial Equality Directive did not capture the entire range of conduct covered by incitement to discriminate in the Joint Action of 1996. In their view, Article 2(4) of the Directive does not, for example, cover the publication and general distribution of leaflets inciting discrimination. For this reason, the Commission recommended that the Framework Decision, in addition to prohibiting "public incitement to violence or hatred", should also extend to "any other racist or xenophobic behaviour which may cause substantive damage to individuals or groups concerned".

European Commission, Staff Working Paper,   **5.EC.6.**
*"Legal reasoning for not referring to the concept of 'public incitement to
discrimination' in the Commission's proposal for a Council Framework Decision
on combating racism and xenophobia"*[8]

"During discussion on the above initiative at the Council Working Group 'Substantive Criminal Law', the Presidency asked the Commission services to present their position regarding the legal reasoning for not referring to the concept of 'public incitement to discrimination' in the Commission's proposal for a Council Framework Decision on combating racism and xenophobia (COM (2001) 664 final) . . . the Commission services are of the view that Member States are already obliged by Article 15 of the Directive 2000/43/EC to provide for criminal sanctions, where it is considered that criminal sanctions sufficiently effective and dissuasive, are necessary in order to guarantee the respect of Community obligations regarding the regulated behaviour, in this case to prohibit *'an instruction to discriminate against persons on grounds of racial or ethnic origin'*. Therefore, it would not be legally correct and contrary to Article 47 EU, which states the primacy of the EC Treaty towards the EU Treaty, to provide specifically for criminalisation of an instruction to discriminate in a third pillar instrument.

---

[6] COM (2001) 644 final, [2002] OJ C75/E/269.
[7] Directive 2000/43/EC of 29 June 2000 implementing the principle of equal treatment between persons irrespective of racial or ethnic origin [2000] OJ L180/22.
[8] SEC (2002) 375/1 of 3 April 2002.

3. Complementarily of First Pillar and 3rd Pillar instruments.

It is—in the view of the Commission services—clear that the prohibition of *'an instruction to discriminate against persons on grounds of racial or ethnic origin'* seek to combat discrimination. However, the Council Directive 2000/43/EC does not capture in its entirety the behaviour covered by the Joint Action of 1996 (i.e.: *'public incitement to discrimination . . . in respect of a group of persons or a member of such a group defined by reference to colour, race, religion or national or ethnic origin;'*). *'Incitement'* is a wider concept than *'instruction'*. The Directive does not extend to activities falling within Community's competence. Article 2(4) of the Directive does not cover, for example, the publication and general distribution of leaflets inciting discrimination.

Against this background, the Commission proposes the wording *'any other racist or xenophobic behaviour which may cause substantive damage to individuals or groups concerned'*, which would ensure that situations outside the limits of the powers conferred upon the Community and not captured by the Directive would fall under the scope of the Framework Decision in order to avoid any loopholes."

The Commission's view seems to have prevailed and is reflected in Article 4 of the Council Framework Decision on Combating Racism and Xenophobia.

Council of the European Union, Proposal for a   **5.EC.7.**
Council Framework Decision on Combating Racism and Xenophobia[9]

"Article 4 Offences concerning racism and xenophobia.

Member States shall ensure that the following intentional conduct committed by any means is punishable as a criminal offence:

(a) public incitement to violence or hatred for a racist or xenophobic purpose or to any other racist or xenophobic behaviour which may cause substantial damage to individuals or groups concerned . . .

Article 5

. . . that instigating, aiding, abetting or attempting to commit an offence referred to in Article 4 is punishable'."

Despite intense negotiations, no agreement was reached by Member States on the draft Framework decision. In February 2005, the Council instructed the working group on substantive criminal law to resume negotiations on the draft Framework Decision. No text was agreed by the time of the Justice and Home Affairs Council Meeting in June 2005. In 2006, the Austrian presidency hosted a conference to review progress with a view to reopening the discussion on the proposal for a Framework Decision.

[9] COM (2001) 644 final, [2002] OJ C75/E/269.

5.1.1.B.   INSTRUCTIONS TO DISCRIMINATE

The concept of instructions to discriminate, as a specific form of discrimination, was first introduced into EC law with the two Article 13 Directives, 2000/43/EC[10] and 2000/78/EC.[11] The earlier Directives on equal treatment between men and women did not cover instructions to discriminate. In fact, the Directive on equal treatment between men and women was amended in 2002 to include instructions to discriminate.[12] An examination of some of the background discussion to the formulation of the EC Directives suggests that the provision on instructions to discriminate is one tool that has been developed as part of the broader legal and policy response to tackling racism and xenophobia.

  The extract below is the relevant provisions from the Racial Equality Directive that requires Member States to prohibit instructions to discriminate. The provisions in the other Directives are identical in substance; they each provide that instructions to discriminate are deemed to be discrimination.

Council Directive 2000/43 of 29 June 2000 implementing the   **5.EC.8.**
principle of equal treatment between persons irrespective of racial or ethnic origin[13]

Article 2
Concept of discrimination
1. For the purposes of this Directive, the principle of equal treatment shall mean that there shall be no direct or indirect discrimination based on racial or ethnic origin.
    . . .
4. An instruction to discriminate against persons on grounds of racial or ethnic origin shall be deemed to be discrimination within the meaning of paragraph 1.

The prohibition on instructions to discriminate applies to all areas of activities within the scope of each Directive. It therefore covers any instructions given in the employment context. The Directives do not provide a definition of what constitutes an instruction to discriminate. The approach taken is to "deem" an instruction to discriminate to be a form of discrimination. This opaque formulation leaves significant issues to Member States and the ECJ to interpret.

---

[10] Directive 2000/43/EC of 29 June 2000 implementing the principle of equal treatment between persons irrespective of racial or ethnic origin [2000] OJ L180/22.
[11] Directive 2000/78/EC of 27 November 2002 establishing a general framework for equal treatment in employment and occupation [2000] OJ L303/16.
[12] Directive 2002/73/EC of the European Parliament and of the Council of 23 September 2002 amending Directive 76/207/EEC on the implementation of the principle of equal treatment for men and women as regards access to employment, vocational training and promotion, and working conditions [2002] OJ L269/15.
[13] [2000] OJ L180/22.

5.1.2.   NATIONAL LAW

5.1.2.A.   INSTRUCTIONS TO DISCRIMINATE AS PART OF INCITEMENT TO
            DISCRIMINATE

In several instances an instruction to discriminate can come within the scope of
provisions on incitement to discriminate. The examination of these provisions in this
section suggests that in many instances such provisions do not cover the full range of
behaviour that comes within the scope of the provisions on instructions to
discriminate under the Directives.

In most instances, provisions on incitement contained in national laws are
concerned with discrimination on grounds of race and ethnicity. Such provisions do
not provide protection for all the grounds contained in the Employment Equality
Directive. Furthermore, provisions on incitement often only prohibit acts done in
public and via specific means.

Lithuanian Penal Code   **5.LT.9.**

Article 170. Incitement against National, Racial, Ethnic, Religious or Other Groups of
Residents
(1) A person who, by making public statements orally, in writing, or by using the public media,
ridicules, expresses contempt of, urges hatred towards or encourages discrimination against a
group of residents or against a specific person, on account of the fact that they belong to a
specific national, racial, ethnic, religious or other group, shall be published with (a) a fine (b)
detention or (c) imprisonment of up to two years.

Here the definition of incitement specifically extends to encouraging discrimination,
which would encompass a person who instructs another to discriminate. However, the
Lithuanian Penal Code only covers encouragements to discriminate that are done
though public statements or through the public media. It would therefore not cover
instructions given in private.

Council of State, Opinion of 7 December 2004   **5.LU.10.**

"In conformity with the directive, the notion of discrimination extends under both bills [under
consideration by the Council of State] to any behaviour which consists in instructing anybody
to discriminate against a person on one of the grounds mentioned in the law. This provision
sanctioning the instruction to discriminate in civil law and labour law corresponds to the provisions in article 457-1 of the Penal Code."

The Luxembourg Council of State, in its opinion on the transposition of the EU
Directive, suggests that provisions in the Anti-Discrimination Act covering

instructions to discriminate should be understood as analogous with the provisions in the Luxembourg Penal Code on incitement to discriminate (Article 457-1).

The provisions in Belgium provide an illustration of the complex interplay between civil law and criminal law provisions on incitement to discriminate and the extent to which this provides coverage for instances concerning instructions to discriminate. Prior to the implementation of the EU Directives, the criminal law covered discrimination on the grounds of race, colour, descent, or national or ethnic origin.

Belgian Act of 30 July 1981 on the punishment of certain acts   **5.BE.11.**
motivated by racism or xenophobia[14]

Article 1
By 'discrimination' in this Act is meant any form of distinction, exclusion, restriction or preference, whose purpose or whose result is or could be to destroy, compromise or limit the equal recognition, enjoyment or exercise of human rights and the fundamental freedoms on a political, economic, social or cultural level, or in any other area of social life.

The following shall be punished by a prison sentence of one month to one year and by a fine of fifty francs to one thousand francs, or by one of these punishments alone:

1. Whoever, in one of the circumstances set out in Article 444 of the Penal Code, incites discrimination, hatred or violence against a person on the grounds of his or her race, colour, descent or national or ethnic origin.

2. Whoever, in one of the circumstances set out in Article 444 of the Penal Code, incites discrimination, segregation, hatred or violence against a group, community or members of it on the grounds of race, colour, descent, or national or ethnic origin of its members of some of them.

3. Whoever, in one of the circumstances set out in Article 444 of the Penal Code, announces publicly intent to perpetrate discrimination, hatred or violence against a person on the grounds of his or her race, colour, descent origin or nationality.

4. Whoever, in one of the circumstances set out in Article 444 of the Penal Code, announces publicly intent to perpetrate discrimination, hatred or violence against a group, community or members of it on the grounds of race, colour, descent, origin or nationality of its members, or some of them.

The Belgian law here creates two distinct offences, one of incitement to discriminate, the other of manifesting intent to discriminate. Furthermore, the provisions are not aimed at covering racist abuse or insult. Article 444 of the Penal Code requires the incitement to take place in some public forum:

Belgian Penal Code   **5.BE.12.**

Article 444
The guilty party shall be punished by a prison sentence of eight days to one year and by a fine of twenty six francs to two hundred francs, when the charges have been committed: either in

---

[14] Available on the website of the Centre for Equal Opportunities and Opposition to Racism in Belgium.

public meetings or places; or in the presence of several people, in a place that is not public but accessible to a number of people who are entitled to meet or visit there; or in any place in the presence of the offended person and in front of witnesses; or through documents, printed or otherwise, illustrations or symbols that have been displayed, distributed, sold, offered for sale, or publicly exhibited; or finally by documents that have not been made public but which have been sent or communicated to several people.

The potential for this provision to cover situations in which instructions to discriminate are given is illustrated by some examples from the case-law.

Criminal court (Correctionele rechtbank van Hasselt),   **5.BE.13.**
27 March 1995
Openbaar Ministerie, Hamid B, Stephan A, George S, Azeen M, Singh R,
CGKR v. Martine M, Mario G, Marc D

AN INSTRUCTION BY A BAR MANAGER TO HIS EMPLOYEES NOT TO SERVE FOREIGNERS IN ORDER TO INCITE THEM TO LEAVE THE PLACE CONSTITUTES A VIOLATION OF ARTICLE 1.2° OF THE "ACT OF 30 JULY 1981 ON THE PUNISHMENT OF CERTAIN ACTS MOTIVATED BY RACISM OR XENOPHOBIA"

Belgian waiters case

Facts: The first two defendants gave instructions to their personnel not to serve Indians and to ask Indians to leave the cafe because of the reaction from other customers.

Held: On March 27, 1995, the *correctionnele rechtbank* (i.e. a court dealing with criminal matters) of Hasselt convicted both the waiter and the manager of discrimination.

Judgment: "The requirements made by Article 1.2° have been met in this case:
   a) The first and second defendants instructed their personnel not to serve Indians and therefore incited them to specific acts of discrimination.
   b) The attitude of the first and second defendants is an act of discrimination. The civil parties were undesirable on grounds of their race, skin colour and nationality, and were not served. Although the defendants provide a different version at the hearing, it must be said that the civil parties did not act incorrectly at the time of the events. In his statement of 18.10.1993, the third defendant says: 'The Indians did not annoy the customers present'.
   c) Incitement to discriminate occurred in a public place, namely an inn where other customers were also present. The first defendant repeatedly stated in the presence of the reporting officers that the Indians were not served and had to leave the business.
   d) Discrimination shown towards the Indian community. Indians for present purposes means all persons of the Indian race and extends to other nationalities, namely Pakistanis etc . . ."

Note
The instructions that the defendants gave to their personnel to discriminate were the basis for finding that there was an offence of incitement to discriminate. However, the offence also requires that the incitement occur in a public place. The case here

suggests that the instruction to discriminate in this instance met this requirement because the instructions were given in "an inn where other customers were also present". This implies that instruction given in private, or in an employment context where customers or members of the public are not present, would not be covered by the legislation. In that case, the prohibition to incite racial hatred and discrimination are not a full equivalent to the prohibition of instructions to discriminate in the European Directives.

Criminal Court (Correctionele rechtbank van Dendermonde), **5.BE.14.**
24 December 2002
Openbaar Ministerie, Saida K, Hatem H, Mohmed H, Abdelgaafer H
v. *AVH, police Commissioner; 2. (. . .); 3.KDB, politie-inspecteur*

VIOLATION OF ARTICLES 1.2° AND 4 OF THE "ACT OF 30 JULY 1981 ON THE
PUNISHMENT OF CERTAIN ACTS MOTIVATED BY RACISM OR XENOPHOBIA"

Belgian police case

Facts: Evidence from witnesses indicates that the defendant, a police officer, held racist views and incited other colleagues to act in a discriminatory fashion. He is reported to have said, in relation to immigrants that were arrested: "you should press the crap in their body until they die" and "you should beat them up until they die otherwise you won't have done a good job".

Held: The *correctionele rechtbank* of Dendermonde sentenced the defendant to a deferred sentence of 5 years imprisonment for inciting the members of his corps to violence against immigrants and inciting his police officers to commit acts of discrimination.

Judgment: "There can be no denying that a police policy that amounts without any justification to treating migrants differently from native citizens in comparable circumstances must be regarded as discriminatory . . . The term 'incite' as used in Article 1 of the Act of 30 July 1981 points to the necessarily intentional nature of the offence. Incitement to discriminatory action will exist only if the incitement is of sufficient strength, in such a way that the stated practices are encouraged or invoked. There is no need for the incitement to be positively followed up [references omitted]. To be punishable, third parties must be incited to pursue discriminatory acts of racial segregation or xenophobia. An intention must be evident of a desire to persuade third parties to pursue such conduct.

. . . The argument of the first defendant is that he advocates only a hard approach to migrants who cause problems, without his being a racial bigot in any way . . . It is incontrovertibly clear from statements made by several members of the police unit . . . that the superintendent went much further than simply advocating a hard approach to young migrants who had committed offences, but clearly adopted a discriminatory policy towards migrants whereupon members of his unit were incited to hit the migrants concerned.

Reference may be made in this connection to the following statements:

Assistant superintendent JP declared that the superintendent preaches a hard approach. According to JP, KDB is sometimes given to racist talk and KDB could have made the utterances described in the anonymous letter. The superintendent, too, is said to reveal such an attitude. JP confirmed that the superintendent had told him that he should 'grab' them (the migrants) 'by the neck until the shit runs out of them', and made comments to the effect that 'just beat them till they're dead'. JP repeated that the super-intendent had repeatedly told members of the investigating team and also other members of personnel, that they had to come down hard and violently on migrants and that they had to hit them.

Warrant officer CT declared that he had also witnessed the superintendent showing his contempt for migrants during briefings and calling them 'nignogs'. He preached a hard approach to migrants and was followed in this by KDB . . . Taking these statements together, it is clear that the first defendant, Superintendent AVH, incited members of his unit to act discri-minatingly . . . and that he had shown discrimination towards migrants in pursuit of his office as a police superintendent . . ."

Note

The Belgian cases illustrate how provisions on incitement to discriminate may not cover the full range of behaviour that comes within the scope of the provisions on instructions to discriminate under the Directives. In the Belgian police case, the court emphasised the importance of intention in the Penal Code provisions. In particular, the court noted that the term "incite", as used in the Belgian Penal Code, "points to the necessarily intentional nature of the offence" and that "an intention must be evident of the desire to persuade third parties to pursue such conduct". This requirement of intention is not found in the provisions of the Directive concerning instructions to discriminate.

5.1.2.B.   PENAL CODE PROVISIONS ON ACCOMPLICES

Instructions to discriminate can also be captured by criminal law provisions that prohibit discrimination when combined with provisions on liability of accomplices.

In France, instructions to discriminate are not covered as such by the Labour Code, the Civil Code or the Penal Code. However, Article 225 of the Penal Code does cover discrimination, saying that:

French Penal Code   **5.FR.15.**

Article 225-1
Any distinction made between natural persons because of their origin, sex, family situation, pregnancy, physical appearance, surname, state of health, disability, genetic characteristics, way of life, sexual orientation, age, political opinions, trade union activities, [or] belonging or not belonging, in reality or assumed, to a specific ethnic group, nation, race or religion consti-tutes discrimination . . .

Discrimination also comprises any distinction applied between legal persons by reason of the origin, sex, family situation, physical appearance or patronymic, state of health, handicap, genetic characteristics, sexual morals or orientation, political opinions, union activities,

573

membership or non-membership, true or supposed, of a given ethnic group, nation, race or religion of one or more members of these legal persons.

The provision on the Penal Code on liability of accomplices includes those that give instructions to commit any offence and would therefore cover instructions that contravene the provisions in the Penal Code in relation to discrimination.

French Penal Code   **5.FR.16.**

Article 121-2
Juridical persons, with the exception of the State, are criminally liable for the offences committed on their account by their organs or representatives, according to the distinctions set out in articles 121-4 and 121-7.

However, local public authorities and their associations incur criminal liability only for offences committed in the course of their activities which may be exercised through public service delegation conventions.

The criminal liability of legal persons does not exclude that of the natural persons who are perpetrators or accomplices to the same act, subject to the provisions of the fourth paragraph of article 121-3.

Article 121-6
The accomplice to the offence, in the meaning of article 121-7, is punishable as a perpetrator.

Article 121-7
The accomplice to a felony or a misdemeanour is the person who knowingly, by aiding and abetting, facilitates its preparation or commission.

Any person who, by means of a gift, promise, threat, order, or an abuse of authority or powers, provokes the commission of an offence or gives instructions to commit it, is also an accomplice.

Note
The French Penal Code in Article 121-7 provides an initial definition of an accomplice as someone who knowingly, by aiding or abetting, facilitates the preparation of a felony or misdemeanour. The code then elaborates upon its definition of an accomplice. It provides that an accomplice is someone who provokes the commission of an offence or gives instructions to commit an offence. It is not clear whether a significant distinction is intended to be made between those who instruct and those who provoke the unlawful act. The code identifies several methods by which an accomplice can provoke or instruct discrimination.

Those who issue instructions to discriminate and thereby cause discrimination to occur can also find themselves liable as accomplices under Article 23 of the French law on the freedom of the press which prohibits provocation of racial discrimination.

French law on press freedom of 29 July 1881   **5.FR.17.**

Article 23

The persons who will be penalised as accomplices to an action qualified as a crime or an offence will be those who, either through speeches, calls or threats uttered in public places and meetings; or through writings, prints, drawings, engravings, paintings, emblems, images or any other form of writing, sold or distributed words or images, sold or exhibited in public places or meetings; or through placards or posters exhibited in public view; or through any method of communication to the public by electronic means, that have directly caused the author or the authors to commit the aforementioned action, if the provocation has been followed by an effect.

This provision will also be applicable when the provocation has only been followed by an attempt at a crime provided for in section 2 of the Penal Code . . .

Those who, through one of the means stated in section 23, have caused the discrimination, hatred or violence toward a person or a group of people for reasons of their origin or their affiliation or their non-affiliation to an ethnic group, nation, race or specified religion, will be penalised by a year of imprisonment and a 45000 Euro fine or by one of these two penalties only . . .

Article 24

. . . Those who, through one of the means stated in section 23, have caused the discrimination, hatred or violence toward a person or a group of people for reasons of their origin or their affiliation or their non-affiliation to an ethnic group, nation, race or specified religion, will be penalised by a year of imprisonment and a 45000 Euro fine or by one of these two penalties only.

Notes

(1) Actions under the law of 1881 can be taken by the victim, the public prosecutor or organisations that are created for the purpose of fighting racism or helping the victims of discrimination (Article 48 of the law of 1881). The penalty for violation of Article 23 is a fine of up 45,000 euros or up to one year of imprisonment.

(2) Article 23 requires the instructions that incite discrimination to be given in public. An action is considered to be public if it is through

"speeches, calls or threats uttered in public places and meetings; or through writings, prints, drawings, engravings, paintings, emblems, images or any other form of writing, sold or distributed words or images, sold or exhibited in public places or meetings; or through placards or posters exhibited in public view; or through any method of communication to the public by electronic means."

(3) Furthermore, the incitement will only attract liability if it leads to an act of discrimination or an attempt at discrimination. Merely giving an instruction would not, in this context, be sufficient. Incitement by itself without any further action is not an offence. Where the incitement takes place in the manner required by Article 23 and results in some action, then the perpetrator of the direct incitement may be punished as an accessory to the discrimination. If the incitement is not in public, then reliance is placed on the provision on discrimination in the criminal code.

In Finland, chapter 11 section 9 of the Penal Code prohibits discrimination in the provision of services to the public and in the exercise of official authority; furthermore, chapter 47 section 3 covers discrimination by an employer. Instructions to discriminate in relation to these provisions are covered by the Penal Code when these provisions are read in conjunction with chapter 5 section 2 of the Penal Code, which provides that "He who orders, hires, harasses or otherwise intentionally incites or compels another person to a crime shall be punished if the crime is fulfilled or remains as a attempt, as if he himself had been the actor". Under the provisions of the Penal Code, an incitement to discriminate by itself is not sufficient; the incitement can only be punished if the incitement leads to an actual discrimination or at least an attempt at discrimination. This contrasts with the provisions of Article 6(2)4 of the Non-Discrimination Act that an instruction or order to discriminate is deemed to be discrimination. The *travaux* to section 6(2)4 of the Non-Discrimination Act make it clear that the essential criteria of an "instruction to discriminate" may be fulfilled even if no one takes any discriminatory action in pursuance of the instructions:

"Preparatory Works to the Finnish Non-Discrimination Act,   **5.FI.18.**
HE 44/2003 [Government Proposal 44/2003], extract concerning section 6"

In some cases, an instruction or order to discriminate against people of a particular ethnic origin given in public or, for example, in the workplace in the hearing of staff, may meet the criteria for discrimination, despite the fact that no-one would in fact have acted in accordance with the instruction or order. These kinds of instructions and orders would also be covered by the provisions on supervision provided by the Act. However, with regard to the sanction of compensation, in cases of this type the question could be chiefly one of harassment under Section 6(2) 3, rather than discrimination based on an instruction or order to discriminate as provided by Section 6(2) 4, which could, as breach of Section 6(2) 4, lead to compensation being payable under Section 9.

Article 152 of the Estonian Penal Code of 6 June 2001, provides that:

"unlawful restriction of the rights of the person or granting of unlawful preferences to a person on the basis of his or her nationality, race, colour, sex, language, origin, religion, political opinion, financial or social status is publishable by a fine . . . or by detention."

Instructions to commit this offence can come within the scope of criminal law when combined with Article 22(2) of the Penal Code on accomplices, which provides that "an abettor is a person who intentionally induces another person to commit an unlawful act".

In Latvia, the Penal Code of 17 June 1998 makes it an offence for a person to knowingly restrict, directly or indirectly, the economic, political or social rights of individuals. Instructions to commit this offence can come within the scope of the criminal law when combined with section 20 of the criminal law on joint participation, which provides that "a person who has induced another person to commit a criminal offence shall be considered as an instigator".

In Slovakia instructions that result in discrimination on the grounds of racial or ethnic origin, if given publicly, can be an offence under the Penal Code provisions on incitement to ethnic and racial hatred (Penal Code section 198a).

Penal provisions on accomplices, while providing important protection from instructions to discriminate in some areas, do not always provide the level of protection required against instructions to discriminate in all areas within the scope of the Directives. For example under the French law on press freedom and the provisions of the Finnish Penal Code, instructions or incitement to discriminate will only attract liability if it leads to an act of discrimination or an attempt at discrimination. Merely giving an instruction would not, in this context, be sufficient. By contrast, the Directive prohibits instructions alone, even if they do not lead to an act of discrimination. Incitement by itself without any further action is not an offence. In other instances, the scope of Penal Code provisions on accomplices is limited by their attachment to a substantive offence found in the Penal Code which requires a specific intent to discriminate. The provisions in the Directive are broader as they do not require this specific intention.

5.1.2.C.   INSTRUCTIONS TO DISCRIMINATE AS A FORM OF DISCRIMINATION

The prohibition on instructions to discriminate aims to cover the actions of third parties, namely those who do not themselves carry out the discrimination but whose actions cause others to discriminate. The EU Directives use the term "instruction" to discriminate, and in several Member States this term is used when transposing the Directives.

As noted earlier, the Directives do not provide a definition of what constitutes an instruction to discriminate. Their approach, to "deem" an instruction to discriminate to be a form of discrimination, is an opaque formulation that leaves significant issues for Member States to resolve. In fact, most Member States chose to replicate rather than confront the ambiguities and uncertainties of the Directives. In a significant number of Member States, the legal provisions merely provide that instructions to discriminate are "deemed"[15] to be a form of discrimination, are "considered"[16] as discrimination, "constitute"[17] discrimination or are "included"[18] in the term discrimination.

Two cases from the UK indicate that provisions aimed at prohibiting direct discrimination can be used to challenge instructions to discriminate by those who are the objects (the persons that instructions are about) and subjects (the persons given the instructions) of such instructions. The first case, *B.L. Cars* (below **5.GB.20.**), shows how those who are the objects of instructions can cite the instructions as an

---

[15] Law of the Republic of Estonia on Employment Contracts, passed 15 April 1992, Art. 10 and Greece, Law No. 3304/2005 Art. 2.
[16] Latvia, Labour Law, 6 July 2000, s. 29.
[17] Lithuania, Law on Equal Treatment, 18 November 2003, Art. 2(6).
[18] Ireland, Equality Act 2004, s. 3(b).

example of less favourable treatment in a claim for direct discrimination. In the second case, *Showboat* (below **5.GB.21.**), a person who receives adverse treatment because of a failure to follow instructions to discriminate can also claim to have received less favourable treatment on racial grounds.

Race Relations Act 1976   **5.GB.19.**

Section 1(1)
A person discriminates against another . . . if
  (a) on racial grounds he treats that other less favourably than he treats or would treat other persons . . .

Employment Appeal Tribunal, 15 November 1982[19]   **5.GB.20.**
B.L. Cars Ltd and another (appellants) v. *Brown and others (respondents)*

INSTRUCTIONS TO DISCRIMINATE CAN ALSO AMOUNT TO A DETRIMENT IN A CLAIM
FOR DIRECT DISCRIMINATION

B.L. Cars Ltd

Facts: The respondents were employees who were employed on the premises of B.L. Cars Ltd. A theft occurred at the premises and a black employee was arrested. The appellants believed that the individual who had been arrested would attempt to re-enter their premises using a false identity. The chief security officer for the premises issued instructions to those responsible for the gates through which employees entered which required them to check thoroughly the identity of every black employee trying to enter the premises. The aim of this instruction was to ensure that the black employee charged with theft would not be able to re-enter the plant. Proceedings under section 30 of the Race Relations Act 1976 (RRA), which prohibits instructions to discriminate, were initiated by the Commission for Racial Equality. In addition to this, 28 black employees claimed direct discrimination; they claimed that the instructions to discriminate, given to the security guards, constituted "detriment" to them for the purposes of a claim of direct discrimination.

Held: At first instance the Industrial Tribunal was asked to address the preliminary issues of whether the mere issuing of a written instruction could occasion detriment to individual employees. The tribunal held that the issuing of the written instruction was in itself an act which subjected all black employees at the premises to a detriment. The Employment Appeal Tribunal upheld the decision of the Industrial Tribunal and dismissed the appeal. Having established that issuing instructions can be a detriment for a claim of discrimination, the case was returned to the Industrial Tribunal to decide if on the facts the actions of the appellants amounted to discrimination.

Judgment: WATERHOUSE J: ". . . circulation of the instructions to the gate officers and the setting up of a regime under which black employees would have to undergo special interrogation before they could have access to their place of work were plainly capable of amounting to a detriment to those employees. Whether or not a specific employee was subjected to a detriment depends up on all the facts related to the issuing of the instructions and the particular circumstances of the employee, including his knowledge or means of knowledge of the instructions and his intention before and after they were issued. Publicity associated with

[19] [1983] IRLR 192.

578

the instructions may be relevant not only to the incidence of detriment, subject to detailed consideration of the chain of causation."

Note

In Great Britain, under the Sex Discrimination Act 1975 (SDA), the RRA and the Equality Act 2006 a claim for instructions to discriminate can only be brought by the statutory commissions. Thus employees cannot directly bring a claim for violation of the legislative provisions against instructions to discriminate. However, this case indicates that where an employer issues instructions to discriminate, employees who are the object of the instructions can cite the instructions as an example of detriment or less favourable treatment in a claim for direct discrimination.

Employment Appeal Tribunal, 23 October 1983[20]   **5.GB.21.**
Showboat Entertainment Centre Ltd v. *Owens*

AN EMPLOYEE, WHO IS DISMISSED FOR FAILING TO FOLLOW INSTRUCTIONS TO DISCRIMINATE AGAINST CUSTOMERS ON THE GROUNDS OF RACE CAN MAKE A CLAIM FOR DIRECT DISCRIMINATION ON THE GROUNDS OF RACE

Showboat Entertainment

Facts: Mr. Owens, who was white, was the manager of an amusement centre. He was given instructions, by his employer Showboat Entertainment, to exclude black customers from the centre. He refused to follow these instructions and was dismissed from his employment.

Held: Mr. Owens faced direct discrimination on the grounds of race.

Judgment: BROWNE-WILKINSON J: ". . . the words 'on racial grounds' are perfectly capable in their ordinary sense of covering any reason or action based on race, whether it be the race of the person affected by the action or others . . . We therefore see nothing in the wording of the Act which makes it clear that the words 'on racial grounds' cover only the race of the claimant . . ..We find it impossible to believe that Parliament intended that a person dismissed for refusing to obey an unlawful discriminatory instruction should be without a remedy. It places an employee in an impossible position if he has to choose between being party to an illegality and losing his job. It seems to us that Parliament must have intended such an employee to be protected so far as possible from the consequences of doing his lawful duty by refusing to obey such an instruction . . .Nor do we think the existence of the Commission for Racial Equality's right to enforce section 30 affects our view: there is no reason why the individual's right to complain of the wrong done to him and the Commission's right to stop unlawful acts generally by injunction should not co-exist. We therefore conclude that section 1(1)(a) covers all cases of discrimination on racial grounds whether the racial characteristics in question are those of the person treated less favourably or of some other person."

---

[20] [1984] IRLR 7.

Notes

(1) Mr. Owens was not facing discrimination because of *his* racial or ethnic origin; he was facing less favourable treatment because he refused to follow instructions to discriminate against black people. The court held that the prohibition on direct discrimination covered less favourable treatment because of refusal to follow instructions to discriminate against others as this was still treatment "on racial grounds". The provisions in the RRA can be contrasted to the SDA, where direct discrimination is defined as less favourable treatment of a person "on the grounds of *her* sex [emphasis added]". This would suggest that if, in *Showboat*, the applicant was asked by his employers to exclude female customers from the premises and was dismissed as a consequence of failing to follow this instruction, then he would not succeed in a claim for direct sex discrimination because the treatment he faced would not be related to *his* sex. The definition of direct discrimination in the Employment Equality (Sexual Orientation) Regulations 2003 (SI 1661) and the Employment Equality (Religion and Belief) Regulations 2003 (SI 1660) use the phrase "on grounds of" sexual orientation and religion or belief, and so do not require the adverse treatment to relate to the sexual orientation or religion or belief of the person facing adverse treatment.

(2) This interpretation of the Race Relations Act 1976 was approved by the Court of Appeal in the later case of *Weathersfield Ltd* v. *Sargent*,[21] in which the applicant resigned from a job as a receptionist for a vehicle hire company after she was told that the company's policy was to refuse to provide a service to black drivers.

In a recent German case, a Court of First Instance addressed a similar situation, of an employee facing adverse consequences from a failure to follow instructions to discriminate. In the absence of the transposition of the Directives into German law, the court relied on constitutional principles.

Labour Court (Arbeitsgericht Wuppertal), 3rd Chamber,   **5.DE.22.**
10 December 2003[22]

AN INSTRUCTION NOT TO EMPLOY TURKS IF THERE ARE SUFFICIENT APPLICANTS OF OTHER BACKGROUNDS IS NOT UNLAWFUL

The Cosmetics Company and Turkish employees case

Facts: The defendant is a cosmetic manufacturing company with a workforce that includes 120 female part-time workers, around a quarter of whom were Turkish. The claimant had responsibilities for hiring staff. In September 2003 advertisements were placed in newspapers to recruit workers for the defendant company. The company's chief executive instructed the claimant that, in view of the large number of applicants, no Turkish workers were to be employed. The claimant informed the defendant that he did not intend to follow the instruction. He believed that jobs should be allocated on a "first come, first served" basis. The chief executive asserted his right to decide on who should be employed, and his expectation that the

[21] [1999] IRLR 94.
[22] 3 Ca 4927/03, LAGE § 626 BGB Nr. 2a.

claimant should carry out his instructions. The claimant was warned that if he refused to carry out the instructions then it would be impossible for them to continue to work together and the claimant would have to leave the company. The defendant then terminated the claimant's employment contract on the basis that he was refusing the do the work required of him. The claimant challenged the dismissal. Before the Labour Court, the defendant declared that he had issued general instructions not to employ Turkish workers except in exceptional circumstances; he argued that these instructions were based on past experience of conflict with family members of Turkish women who were employed on a part-time basis.

Held: Germany at this time has not introduced legislation that transposed the Racial Equality Directive into domestic law. Reliance was therefore placed upon Article 3 paragraph 3 of the German Constitution. The Court held that the constitutional provisions do not apply directly between private parties, but can have indirect effect in the area of private law. However, in this case the defendant's reasons for the instructions were "justifiable and understandable", therefore the defendants were justified in their action of an ordinary termination of the claimant's employment with notice. The defendant was not justified in "extraordinary" termination without notice.

Judgment: "According to § 626 BGB, dismissal is justified, among other things, if it results from causes which originate in the behaviour of the employee.

It is undisputed that the claimant permanently refuses to follow the employer's instruction not to employ Turks if there are sufficient other applicants. The claimant refuses to follow the instruction, which is issued by the employer within the framework of his 'right to issue instructions which the employee is obliged to follow' (*Direktionsrecht*), although the consequences of not following the instruction, namely ending of the contract of employment, have been communicated to him.

The claimant cannot appeal to the fact that the instruction not to employ any Turks was not binding on him. It is true that according to consistent rulings by the courts, the right to issue instructions which the employee is obliged to follow must be exercised in a way that appears just and fair according to § 315 BGB, hereby taking into consideration the basic circumstances of the case and taking the interests of both sides into account. For example, any instruction that the employer issues by relying on his right to issue instructions which the employee has to follow must be in accordance with the law. The instruction which is in dispute here does not offend against the law, and is also not immoral. Art. 3 para. 3 GG [German Constitution], whereby no person may be discriminated against or accorded special advantages because of his gender, origin, race, language, homeland and mother country or because of his belief or religious or political views, does contain a prohibition against discrimination, but this basic right is only directly applicable in the relationship between the individual and the state and does not affect directly the relationships between private parties, i.e. Art. 3 para. 2 and 3 GG are not directly applicable in private law. However, it is recognised that Art. 3 para. 2 and 3 GG can develop an indirect effect in the form of prohibitions against discrimination within private law, based on the Constitution. For example the basic right to equal treatment within labour law is also based on Art. 3 GG. However, it is only possible to violate the prohibition to discriminate in a case where a legal relationship exists between employer and employee. But before an employment contract is established, even when preparations are already being made for such a contract, there is yet no right to equal treatment on the part of those who have already been offered employment or other applicants. This means, that at the time when the contract is being prepared for, business freedom, protected by Art. 12 para. 1 sentence 2, 19 para. 3 GG has priority. It is for the businessman alone to decide whom he will employ, and there is no obligation to form a contract. Conversion of the Anti-discrimination Directive 2000/43/EC, which should have been implemented in national law by now, will not be able to restrict business freedom when selecting which applicants to employ. However, the legislature could issue a prohibition on discrimination corresponding to the gender-based prohibition according to § 611 a BGB with the result that in case of infringement claims for compensation could be enforced against the person discriminated against. However, the legislature has not yet issued such an anti-discrimination law.

Although in the present case it does not have to be decided whether the claimant's refusal to follow the employer's instructions was justified, the defendant presented reasons to justify its instructions which were perfectly logical and understandable. It is undisputed that there were no immediate problems with Turkish employees in the defendant's factory. However, according to the defendant, there were problems with relatives of the female Turkish employees which went so far that the Chief Executive's family was threatened with violence. This statement of the defendant, which is disputed by the claimant, is certainly credible. Cases are known to the court in which there were disagreements between employers and female Turkish employees with the result that fathers, brothers or other relatives appeared in the factory in order to represent the interests of the female employees in an extreme form, even against the employees' wishes. For similar reasons, club and discotheque owners often refuse entry to young men of certain nationalities, in order to prevent violence between the members of these nationalities. In these cases too, the rights of the landlord within his own premises are stronger than the prohibition on discrimination described in Art. 3 para3 GG, which also does not take direct effect between private parties.

It is also recognised that the basic/fundamental rights of the employee have to be taken into account when weighing the interests of both parties and when considering the reasonableness of instructions which are issued. The general right of each person for respect and development of his personality which follow from Art. 2 para. 1 of the Constitution as well as the freedom of conscience of the employee according to Art. 4 para. 66 GG are considered to be of particular relevance here.

The general right for respect and development of his personality of the claimant according to Art. 2 para. 1 GG is not infringed by the disputed instruction. In addition, the instruction does not require anything from the claimant which could objectively lead to a conflict of conscience, as the defendant is not requiring anything unlawful from the claimant. The defendant is simply requiring the claimant to carry out an instruction which is permissible within the framework of a businessman's freedom of action; he is not requiring that the claimant should identify with the instruction. As regards the outside world, the claimant is acting in the name of the defendant. Only the defendant will be called upon to defend his actions, not the claimant himself.

In conclusion it can be stated that the claimant refused to follow the permissible instruction of the defendant, refused to carry out the task allotted to him, can no longer fulfil the human resource management responsibilities entrusted to him with regard to engagement of part-time workers in the sense of the defendant, and that he was rightfully dismissed based on his behaviour. The claimant can also not demand of the defendant that he removes these responsibilities from him permanently. The task has been the responsibility of the claimant for a considerable period of time. There is no reason to limit the sphere of responsibility of the claimant and his work performance for the defendant permanently according to the wishes of the claimant."

Note

The facts in this case are similar to those in the *Showboat* case, and so it may be instructive to compare the outcome of these two cases. The defendant in this case has issued instructions that the claimant, in carrying out his duty of hiring employees, should not hire Turkish women. The defendant argues that the instructions are based on his previous experience of part-time female workers of Turkish origin. It is difficult to see how this practice is anything other that discrimination based on national origin; decisions about individual female Turkish workers are being made on the basis of stereotypes about women from that group. In light of this, it is difficult to understand the position taken by the court that the instructions here were not illegal or immoral. A significant difference between the facts in this case and *Showboat* may be found in the attempt by the employer here to justify the instructions. The defendant here points to his previous experience with female Turkish workers as the basis for justifying their discriminatory instructions. The court appears not only to accept this justification but adds its own anecdotal evidence in support of the employer's position. Thus, the court states that it had experience of other cases in which disagreement between female Turkish workers and their employers led to interventions by the women's male relatives. The court appears to further endorse discriminatory practices based on stereotypes when it notes, without any disapproval, that "clubs and discotheque owners often refuse entry to young men of certain nationalities, in order to prevent violence between members of these nationalities".

The prohibition of discrimination in the private sphere concerns the correct balance between the freedom of the individual, whether an employer or service provider, to act as they wish and the wider social interest to prevent discrimination against individuals on prohibited grounds. The German Labour Court in this case appears to place too much weight on the importance of the freedom of the employer; it holds that the right to equal treatment under labour law is only in existence once there is a contract of employment; it does not apply to discrimination in hiring or recruitment. As a consequence, instructions to discriminate in relation to recruitment are not prohibited. The case was based on general employment law provisions (§§ 626 BGB and 315 BGB) which were read in the light of the German Constitution because at the time Germany had not transposed the Racial Equality Directive into its national law. The judge acknowledges that the situation could have been different if the Directive had been transposed into national law, and he notes that

> "the legislature could issue a prohibition on discrimination corresponding to the gender based prohibition according to § 611 a BGB with the result that in case of infringement, claims for compensation could be enforced against the person discriminated against. However, the legislature has not yet issued such an anti-discrimination law."

While this implies that the recent German legislation will be mirrored in future judgments of this specific court, the reasoning also demonstrates a regrettable negation of a judge's Community law obligations. These could well have been met by reading the general provisions not only in line with the Constitution, but also in the light of Directive 2000/43/EC, as well as reading the Constitution in line with EC law.

5.1.2.D.   BEYOND INSTRUCTIONS TO DISCRIMINATE

A survey of Member States' legislation reveals that a wide variety of terms are used to describe the actions of persons who do not themselves discriminate but "instruct" or in some other way affect the behaviour of the person who is discriminating. A crucial issue is whether these different terms broaden the scope of liability of such third parties and provide any further clarification of what constitutes an instruction to discriminate.

In the Czech Republic, the Labour Code (section 2 paragraph 3) covers "instigating, instructing and inciting pressure" to discriminate. Similar terms are used in the Armed Forces Act (section 77 paragraph 2). The Finnish Non-Discrimination Act (section 6(2) paragraph 4) covers both "instructions" and "order" to discriminate. The distinction between an "instruction" and an "order" is not clear. However, the author of the EU report on the implementation of the Directive in Finland suggests that the inclusion of the term "order" takes the Finnish legislative provision beyond the requirements of the EU Directive.[23] The variety of terms used to cover the actions of those who do not directly discriminate but are indirectly involved is revealed in an examination of UK legislation.

Sex Discrimination Act 1975[24]   **5.GB.23.**

Pressure to discriminate
s.40 (1) It is unlawful to induce, or attempt to induce, a person to do any act which contravenes Part II or III by—
   (a) providing or offering to provide him with any benefit; or
   (b) subjecting or threatening to subject him to any detriment.
(2) An offer or a threat is not prevented from falling within this subsection (1) because it is not made directly to the person in question, if it is made in such a way that he is likely to hear of it.

Instructions to discriminate [a similar provision is found in the RRA s.30, Disability Discrimination Act 1995 s.16C(1)]
s.39(1) It is unlawful for a person—
   (a) who has authority over another person; or
   (b) in accordance with whose wishes that other person is accustomed to act, to instruct him to do any act which is unlawful [discrimination], or to procure or attempt to procure the doing by him of any such act.

Race Relation Act 1976   **5.GB.24.**

Pressure to discriminate
s.31 (1) It is unlawful to induce, or attempt to induce, a person to do any act which contravenes Part II or III.

---

[23] T. Makkonen, "Report on Measures to Combat Discrimination: Directive 2000/43/EC and 2000/78/EC. Country Report Finland" (European Commission, 2004) 13, available on the website of Directorate-General for Employment, Social Affairs and Equal Opportunities.
[24] A similar provision is found in the Disability Discrimination Act 1995 s. 16C(2).

(2) An attempted inducement is not prevented from falling within subsection (1) because it is not made directly to the person in question, if it is made in such a way that he is likely to hear of it.

The relationship between the legislative provisions on instructions to discriminate and pressure to discriminate was considered by the Employment Appeal Tribunal in Britain.

Employment Appeal Tribunal, 17 December 1982[25]   **5.GB.25.**
*The Commission for Racial Equality v. The Imperial Society of
Teachers of Dancing*

MEANING OF INDUCING OR ATTEMPTING TO INDUCE A PERSON TO DISCRIMINATE;
MEANING OF PROCURING OR ATTEMPTING TO PROCURE

The Imperial Society of Teachers of Dancing

Facts: The Imperial Society needed to hire an office filing clerk. Their secretary, Mrs McBride, telephoned the careers adviser at a local school to see if the school could recommend anyone. It was alleged that, in the course of the telephone conversation, Mrs McBride told the school that she would rather that they did not send a black person as they would feel out of place in an environment where everyone else was white.

Held: At first instance, the Industrial Tribunal held there were no violations of either section 30 (instructions to discriminate) or section 31 (pressure to discriminate) of the Race Relations Act. On appeal, the Employment Appeal Tribunal held there were no unlawful instructions, as the secretary of the Imperial Society has no authority over the school. However, reversing the decision of the Industrial Tribunal, the Employment Appeal Tribunal held that there was a contravention of section 31.

An inducement to discriminate does not require the offer of a benefit or a threat of a detriment. Procure or attempt to procure discrimination includes the use of words to bring about or attempt to bring about a course of action.

Judgment: NEILL J: "The Industrial Tribunal state their conclusion on this part of the case in paragraph 2 of their reasons as follows: 'We think the word "induce" must imply an element of "stick or carrot", a mere request which is the highest that Mrs McBride's words could be put at, comes far short of an effort to induce as covered by the section.'

With great respect to the Industrial Tribunal we for our part do not consider that the word 'induce' in s.31 can be so limited. There may be cases where inducement involves the offer of some benefit or the threat of some detriment, but in their ordinary meaning the words 'to induce' mean 'to persuade or to prevail upon or to bring about'. In our judgment the intimation by Mrs McBride that 'she would rather the school did not send anyone coloured' as 'that person would feel out of place as there were no other coloured employees' did constitute an attempt to induce Mrs Patterson not to send coloured applicants for interview. We consider that the words 'induce' is apt to cover the facts found to by the Industrial Tribunal in the present case; we see no reason to construe the word narrowly or in a restricted sense . . . we should say something about the word 'procure'. The Industrial Tribunal came to the conclusion that an expression of a preference was not an attempt to procure. On this matter we

---

[25] [1983] IRLR 315.

585

regret to say that we disagree with the Industrial Tribunal. It seems to us that in the context the words 'procure' or 'attempt to procure' have a wider meaning and are apt to include the use of words which bring about or attempt to bring about a certain course of action. [However, the Race Relations Act] requires that there should be some relationship between the person giving the instruction or doing the procuring and the other person. The second person is the person accustomed to act in accordance with the wishes of the first person. In the phrase 'in accordance with whose wishes' we would underline the word 'whose'. It does not seem to us to be possible to construe the section as meaning that it is sufficient to show that the other person is accustomed to act in the same position as the person giving the instructions . . . if there were evidence that Mrs Patterson had been accustomed to acting in accordance with the wishes of the Society it would not matter that Mrs McBride has never spoken to Mrs Patterson before. But the mere fact that the Society was an employer and that other employers had approached Mrs Patterson in the past did not result in our view in the Society of Mrs McBride being a person in accordance with whose wishes Mrs Patterson was accustomed to act [emphasis in original]."

Note
The Employment Appeal Tribunal is here trying to draw out the distinctions between the provisions on instructions to discriminate and the provisions on pressure to discriminate. The facts in the above case were sufficient for the court to find that there had been pressure to discriminate but not sufficient for there to be an "instruction" to discriminate. The critical difference lay in the fact that the latter required a relationship in which the person receiving an instruction was accustomed to act in accordance with the wishes of the person giving an instruction. Pressure to discriminate is defined in the RRA as inducing or attempting to induce a person to discriminate. Liability for pressure to discriminate does not require a relationship in which the person receiving the "instruction" is accustomed to act in accordance with the requirements of a person giving an instruction. In the context of the RRA, the tribunal held that inducing a person to discriminate does not require "the offer of some benefit or the threat of some detriment". The provision in the SDA differs in this respect from that in the RRA. In particular, the section 40 of the SDA provides that an inducement requires the offer of a benefit or a threat of a detriment.

The RRA, the SDA and the Disability Discrimination Act (DDA) treat instructions to discriminate and pressure to discriminate as distinct. Pressure to discriminate covers inducing or attempting to induce a person to discriminate, while instructions to discriminate includes instructing, attempting to instruct, procuring or attempting to procure a person to discriminate. The Northern Ireland Fair Employment And Treatment Order does not employ the term "instructs"; instead, in its terminology, Article 35 covers aiding, inciting, directing, procuring or inducing another to discriminate.

Fair Employment and Treatment (Northern Ireland) Order[26] **5.NIR.26.**

Accessories and incitement
35.—(1) Any person who—
    (a) knowingly aids or incites; or
    (b) directs, procures or induces, another to do an act which is unlawful by virtue of any provision of Part III or IV or Article 34 shall be treated for the purposes of this Order as if he, as well as that other, had done that act"

The Equality Act 2006 section 55 prohibits "instructing, causing or inducing" another to discriminate on the grounds of religion or belief. The need for this new concept of "causing" discrimination was raised during the parliamentary scrutiny of the Equality Bill.

Equality Act 2006 **5.GB.27.**

s. 53 Discriminatory practices
(1) It is unlawful for a person to operate a practice which would be likely to result in unlawful discrimination if applied to persons of any religion or belief.
(2) It is unlawful for a person to adopt or maintain a practice or arrangement in accordance with which in certain circumstances a practice would be operated in contravention of subsection (1).
(3) In this section 'unlawful discrimination' means discrimination which is unlawful by virtue of any of sections 46 to 52.
(4) Proceedings in respect of a contravention of this section may be brought only—
    (a)   by the Commission for Equality and Human Rights, and
    (b)   in accordance with sections 20 to 24.

s. 55 Instructing or causing discrimination
(1) It is unlawful for a person to instruct another to unlawfully discriminate.
(2) It is unlawful for a person to cause or attempt to cause another to unlawfully discriminate.
(3) It is unlawful for a person to induce or attempt to induce another to unlawfully discriminate.
(4) For the purposes of subsection (3) inducement may be direct or indirect.
(5) In this section a reference to unlawful discrimination is a reference to discrimination which is unlawful by virtue of any of sections 46 to 52.
(6) Proceedings in respect of a contravention of this section may be brought only—
    (a)   by the Commission for Equality and Human Rights, and
    (b)   in accordance with section 25.

---

[26] SI 3162 (NI 21).

MR GRIEVE: "I have nothing against the clause, but is there a difference between causing and inducing someone to do something? . . . I think that inducing encompasses causing, although it is just arguable that causing does not encompass inducing. Whichever way round it is, I should be jolly grateful if the Minister would tell me why both subsections (2) and (3) are thought necessary. There is perhaps a certain amount of overkill here. If a person induces, or attempts to induce, someone to do something, they are causing, or attempting to cause, someone to do something.

PAUL GOGGINS: . . . Clearly, it is wrong to instruct someone to do an unlawful act—I do not think that anyone disputes that—and that is covered by subsection (1). It is also clearly wrong to cause someone to do an unlawful act; that, we believe, requires a significant degree of influence. It is clearly wrong for people to influence others in that way. That is covered by subsection (2). We say that persuading a person to do an unlawful act, even when one has no power to cause them to do so, is wrong, too. The distinctive aspect of subsection (3) is that it deals with the fact that a person need not have the power to make discrimination happen in order to encourage it. We should not allow people to encourage unlawful behaviour. The hon. Gentleman may feel that we have gone in for overkill, but I think that we are making sure that every angle of the issue is covered. I would have thought that he would be enthusiastic to make sure that there were no loopholes through which people could wriggle. The provision is genuinely an attempt to eliminate the possibility of people influencing others to do unlawful things. Through the three measures that I have just set out, we seek to cover each and every angle, so that no one can escape the law.

MR GRIEVE: I am grateful to the Minister for his response. I can understand his reasoning, but I did not infer that 'cause' required the exercise of a power to make something happen. The Minister confirms what I already thought: that inducing encompasses causing. To that extent, what I said originally was right. The phrase 'it is unlawful for a person to induce' would also cover subsection (2). While I am a great believer in keeping legislation short and the impact of the provision might be sufficiently marginal for us not to worry about it."

In the various UK provisions concerning instructing discrimination there is a requirement for there to be a relationship of authority between the person instructing and the person being instructed. Either the instructor must have authority over the person receiving the instructions or the latter must be accustomed to act in accordance with his wishes. By contrast, liability for pressure to discriminate does not require that there be any relationship of authority between the person applying the pressure and the person subject to the pressure.

In Slovakian legislation, the need for a pre-existing relationship based on unequal power is also salient in the distinction between instructions to discriminate and incitement to discriminate. Section 2 paragraph 6 of the Slovakian Act No. 365/2004 on Equal Treatment in Certain Areas and Protection against

---

[27] Available on the website of the UK Parliament.

Discrimination defines discrimination to mean "conduct consisting in the abuse of subordinate position of a person for the purpose of discriminating against a third person". This is distinguished from "incitement to discriminate", which is defined in section 2 paragraph 7 as "persuading, affirming or inciting a person to discriminate against a third person".

The requirements for unlawful pressure differ within British legislation. The SDA and DDA require that pressure be applied through the offer of a benefit or the threat of a detriment. The RRA is not constrained in this way. This was made clear by the Employment Appeal Tribunal in the opinion of Neill J in the *Imperial Society of Teachers of Dancing* case,[28] where he said that: "There may be cases where inducement involves the offer of some benefit or the threat of some detriment, but in their ordinary meaning the words 'to induce' mean 'to persuade or to prevail upon or to bring about'."

Article 38 of the Fair Employment Treatment Order (FETO) allows individuals to bring a complaint before a tribunal alleging that another is unlawfully inciting, procuring, inducing, or aiding discrimination. Under the RRA, SDA and DDA an action against an instruction to discriminate can only be taken by the statutory enforcement bodies: at the time the regulations prohibiting discrimination on the grounds of religion or belief and sexual orientation were enacted, there was no enforcement body to cover discrimination on those grounds. The regulation therefore did not have specific provision on instructions to discriminate on those grounds. The Equality Act 2006 creates a new Commission for Equality and Human Rights, which will have enforcement powers in relation to discrimination on the grounds of religion and belief and sexual orientation.

In Ireland, section 14 of the Employment Equality Act 1998 and section 13 of the Equal Status Act prohibit what is termed the procuring of discrimination. The Employment Equality Act also prohibits procuring of victimisation. The sections criminalise the conduct of anyone who procures someone to discriminate. But the actual conduct of discrimination is not *criminal* under the legislation. This makes it significantly different from the approach in Member States, where actions amounting to an instruction to discriminate are covered by either (1) Penal Code provisions on incitement to discriminate or (2) a substantive criminal offence of discrimination combined with a provision on accomplices.

Irish Employment Equality Act 1998   **5.IE.29.**

s. 8(4) A person who is an employer shall not, in relation to employees or employment—
   (a) have rules or instructions which would result in discrimination against an employee or class of employees

[28] Employment Appeal Tribunal, *Commission for Racial Equality* v. *Imperial Society of Teachers of Dancing*, 17 December 1982, [1983] ICR 473.

s. 14

A person who procures or attempts to procure another person to do anything which—

    (a)   which constitutes discrimination which is unlawful under this act, or

    (b)   constitutes victimisation for the purposes of Part VII

shall be guilty of an offence.

    100.—(1) A person who is guilty of an offence under any provision of this Act shall be liable—

    (a)   on summary conviction, to a fine not exceeding £1,500 or to imprisonment for a term not exceeding 1 year or both, or

    (b)   on conviction on indictment, to a fine not exceeding £25,000 or to imprisonment for a term not exceeding 2 years or both.

(2) If the contravention in respect of which a person is convicted of an offence under any provision of this Act is continued after the conviction, that person shall be guilty of a further offence on every day on which the contravention continues and for each such offence shall be liable on summary conviction to a fine not exceeding £250 or, on conviction on indictment, to a fine not exceeding £1,500.

(3) Summary proceedings for an offence under any provision of this Act may be instituted by the Minister or the Authority.

(4) Notwithstanding section 10(4) of the Petty Sessions (Ireland) Act, 1851, summary proceedings for an offence under any provision of this Act may be instituted within 12 months from the date of the offence.

Irish Equal Status Act 2000   **5.IE.30.**

s.13 (1) A person shall not procure or attempt to procure another person to engage in prohibited conduct.

(2) A persons who contravenes subsection 1 shall be guilty of an offence.

Thus we see that various formulations have been developed to capture within the legal prohibitions actions that aim to cause a person to discriminate.

5.1.2.E.   AIDING UNLAWFUL ACTS

In the employment context, employers are usually responsible for the actions of their employees where those employees are carrying out their duties. However, employees who receive instructions to discriminate may also be liable for that discrimination or for aiding their employer in unlawful discrimination if they carry out the instructions they have received. To provide a clearer indication of the balance of liability between employers and employees, legislation in the UK and in Hungary sets out the situations in which an employee or a person in the position of an employee would avoid liability for following the instructions of their employer.

The Hungarian law on equal treatment prohibits instructions to discriminate (direct and indirect), and instructions to segregation, harassment and victimisation. As noted above, provisions on instructions to discriminate often require the existence of a relationship between the person giving the instruction and the person receiving the instruction. Legislation in Hungary places specific obligations on those receiving instructions, including instructions to discriminate.

Hungarian Act CXXV of 2003 on equal   **5.HU.31.**
treatment and on fostering
equal opportunities

Section 7
(1) Direct discrimination, indirect discrimination, harassment, segregation, victimization and instructions to carry out such action constitute a breach of the provisions of equal treatment, with special regard to the provisions of Chapter III . . .

Hungarian Act XXII of 1992 on the Labour Code   **5.HU.32.**

Section 104
(1) The employee must work according to the instructions of his/her employer.
(2) The employee is not obliged to comply with the instructions, if compliance with such instructions constitutes a breach of the legislation or infringes employment regulations. If compliance with the instruction may cause damage, and the employee may expect this to occur, he/she is obliged to draw the employer's attention to this fact. However, in the latter case, he/she is not entitled to refuse the compliance with the instructions

. . .

(5) If the employee does not carry out the work due to the lawful refusal of the instructions, he/she is entitled to an absence fee in respect of the time lost.

Hungarian Act XXIII of 1992 on the legal status of civil servants **5.HU.33.**

Section 38
(1) The civil servant must comply with the instructions of his/her superior.
(2) The civil servant must refuse the compliance with his/her superior's instructions, if carrying out of such instructions would:

    a)   constitute a criminal act or a petty offence;
    b)   directly and seriously endanger the life, the physical safety or the health of others.

. . . (4) If the instructions, or the carrying out thereof are in breach of the legislation or may cause damage, and the civil servant expects such damage to occur or may cause hurt to the rightful interest of those involved if carried out, the civil servant must draw his/her superior's attention to such facts, and may, at the same time, ask to state the instructions in writing. The superior may not refuse to put the instructions in writing. The civil servant may not be victimised for asking to state the instructions in writing.

. . . (6) The civil servant may state his/her own opinion in writing if he/she disagrees with the decision or the instructions of his/her superior. He/she must not be victimised for this.

Hungarian Act XLIII of 1996 on the service status of   **5.HU.34.**
professional members of the armed services

Section 69

(1) During the course of the service, the member of the professional forces must fulfil the orders of his/her superior, except if such constitutes a criminal act.

(2) With the exception contained in sub-section (1), the member of the professional forces must not refuse the fulfilment of a command or an order, even if it is in breach of the law. If the illegal nature of the command is recognised by him/her, he/she must draw the attention of his/her superior to this fact immediately. If the superior nevertheless maintains the command or order, it must be put in writing if requested. The person who issues the illegal command or order shall be responsible for the fulfilment thereof.

Hungarian Act IV of 1959 on the Civil Code   **5.HU.35.**

Section 392

(1) The contractor shall proceed according to the instructions of the client. Instructions may not relate to the organisation of the work, and may not make the completion thereof more burdensome. The parties may deviate from these provisions.

(3) If the client supplies unsuitable materials or gives instructions that are either impractical or professionally incorrect, the contractor must remind the client thereof. Damage caused by the failure to give such reminder shall be the responsibility of the contractor. If the client maintains his/her instructions despite the reminder, or fails to supply adequate materials, the contractor has a right to terminate the contract. If the contractor chooses not to terminate the contract, he/she is obliged to carry out the task with the materials provided, or according to the instructions, at the risk of the client.

(4) The contractor must not accept the task with the material provided, or according to the client's instructions, if this leads to a breach of legislation, official regulations or any damage to the safety of life or property.

Section 395.

(1) The client is entitled to terminate a contract at any time. However, he/she is under the obligation to provide compensation for the contractor's damages.

Section 474.

(1) On the basis of a contract of agency, the agent is obliged to meet the task assigned to them.

(2) The agency must be undertaken according to the instructions and in the interest of the principal.

Section 476.
If the principal gives instructions, which are either unpractical or professionally incorrect, the agent is obliged to remind him/her of such facts; if the principal insists on his/her instructions despite the reminder, he/she shall be responsible for the damages arising from these instructions.

Section 483.
(1) The principal shall be entitled to terminate the contract at any time with immediate effect. However, the principal is liable for all the obligations already accepted by the agent.

The Hungarian Labour Code section 104 provides that, as a general rule, an employee is required to follow the instructions of his or her employer. Where an instruction of an employer breaches the law, then the employee is not required to follow the instructions. However, the Labour Code appears to draw a distinction between instructions that breach legislation, including employment regulations, and instructions that are likely to cause damage. It is not clear from this provision what that damage would consist of. Where an employee thinks that following instructions is likely to cause damage, the employee is under a duty to inform the employer of this possibility, but once they have done so, if the instructions stand, they are required to follow the instructions. By contrast, civil servants and members of the armed forces are required to follow instructions unless the instructions constitute a criminal act or endanger the life and the health and safety of others. Where instructions given to a civil servant may infringe on the rights of others, the civil servant is under a duty to bring this possibility to the attention of his or her superior and can request the instructions to be given in writing. The civil servant is nonetheless required to carry out the instructions. Members of the armed forces are required to carry out instructions even if they are a breach of the law unless they constitute a criminal act. It would seem, therefore, that civil servants and members of the armed forces are required to carry out instructions to discriminate.

Where the relationship that gives rise to an instruction to discriminate is not that of an employer and employee, but between a contractor and agent, the provisions of the Civil Code section 392 apply. Where a contractor, e.g. an employment agency, is given instructions that are discriminatory, it has a duty to inform the client of this and have a right to terminate the contract. There is a duty on contractors not to accept instructions that lead to a breach of legislation or regulations. Where the relationship is one of a principal and agent, provisions of the Civil Code section 476 and 483 apply.

In the UK provisions in the anti-discrimination legislation make it unlawful to "knowingly aid" another person to do an act of unlawful discrimination. Under subsection 2 of these provisions an individual who carries out discriminatory instructions for which the employer is liable will be deemed to have aided the employer. An employee who carries out instructions to discriminate has a defence if he or she acted in reliance upon a statement that the instructions were not unlawful and it was reasonable for the employee to rely on the those statements.

Race Relations Act 1975   **5.GB.36.**

Section 33
Aiding Unlawful Acts
(1) A person who knowingly aids another person to do an act made unlawful by this Act shall be treated for the purposes of this Act as himself doing the unlawful act of the like description.
(2) For the purposes of subsection (1) an employee or agent for whose act the employer is liable under [reference omitted] (or would be so liable but for section) [reference omitted to provision on vicarious liability of employers] shall be deemed to aid the doing of the act by the employer or principle.
(3) For the purposes of this section, a person does not knowingly aid another to do an unlawful act if—

    (a)   he acts in reliance on a statement made to him by that other person that, because of any provision of this Act, the act would not be unlawful; and
    (b)   it is reasonable for him to rely on the statement.

(4) A person who knowingly or recklessly makes such a statement which is false or misleading in a material respect is guilty of an offence.
(5) Any person guilty of an offence under subsection (4) shall be liable on summary conviction to a fine not exceeding level 5 on the standard scale.[29]

Fair Employment and Treatment (Northern Ireland) Order[30]   **5.NIR.37.**

Accessories and incitement
35.—(1) Any person who—

    (a)   knowingly aids or incites; or
    (b)   directs, procures or induces, another to do an act which is unlawful by virtue of any provision of Part III or IV or Article 34 shall be treated for the purposes of this Order as if he, as well as that other, had done that act.

(2) For the purposes of paragraph (1) an employee or agent for whose act the employer or principal is liable under Article 36 (or would be so liable but for Article 36(4)) shall be taken to have aided the employer or principal to do the act.
(3) A person does not under this Article knowingly aid another to do an unlawful act if—

    (a)   he acts in reliance on a statement made to him by that other person that, by reason of any provision of this Order, the act which he aids would not be unlawful; and
    (b)   it is reasonable for him to rely on the statement.

---

[29] A section in these terms is found in the RRA, SDA, religion and belief, and sexual orientation regulations.
[30] SI 3162 (NI 21).

(4) A person who knowingly or recklessly makes a statement such as is referred to in paragraph (3)(a) which in a material respect is false or misleading shall be guilty of an offence and liable on summary conviction to a fine not exceeding level 5 on the standard scale.
(5) An inducement consisting of an offer of benefit or a threat of detriment is not prevented from falling within paragraph (1) because the offer or threat was not made directly to the person in question.

The UK House of Lords had the opportunity to explore in detail the meaning of section 33 of the RRA. In particular, the focus in this case was on the degree of knowledge of the consequences of one's actions that was needed to show that one has knowingly aided another to discriminate.

House of Lords, 22 March 2001[31]   **5.GB.38.**
Hallam and another (Appellants) v. *Cheltenham Borough Council and others (Respondents)*

A DEGREE OF KNOWLEDGE OF THE CONSEQUENCES OF ONE'S ACTIONS IS NEEDED TO SHOW THAT ONE HAS "KNOWINGLY AIDED" ANOTHER TO DISCRIMINATE

Roma/Gypsy wedding reception case

Facts: The applicants, of Romany gipsy decent, hired premises from Cheltenham Borough Council for a wedding reception to be held in August 1997. Police officers from the local police force expressed concerns to the Council that there might be disorder at the reception. Their opinion was based on incidents that had involved Roma gipsies earlier in 1997. As a consequence of the police intervention the local authority reconsidered its position and imposed new contract terms on the applicants, including a requirement to restrict entry to the reception to those with pre-issued tickets. The applicants found these conditions unacceptable and discriminatory.

Held: The applicants succeeded in a claim for racial discrimination against the local authority. They also made a claim against the police officers, arguing that the police officers had knowingly aided the discrimination against them. At first instance, in the County Court, the judge held that

"both police officers undoubtedly aided the council by providing them with information but that is not, in my judgment, enough. The Act requires them to have *knowingly* aided the council *to do an act* made unlawful by the Act. It seems to me that there needs to be some element of joint enterprise—an active assistance of the council to do the act in question . . . Here neither officer was a party to the decision taken by the council. They were not involved in that decision. I have come to the conclusion, with some hesitation, that the actions of these two defendants do not fall within section 33 of the Act and that therefore the claims against them must fail."

The Court of Appeal and House of Lords found that the police officers did not have the knowledge required to be liable for knowingly aiding the local authority to discriminate.

Judgment: LORD BINGHAM OF CORNHILL: ". . . did the police officers aid the council to do that unlawful act? . . . The judge [at first instance in the County Court] recognised, as was obviously true, that the police officers were, in a general sense, being helpful to the council. They had supplied the council with information to alert it to what the police officers considered a serious potential problem, and their general relations with the council were friendly and co-operative, as one would hope. But the judge was at pains to point out that section 33(1) required more

[31] [2001] UKHL 15.

than a general attitude of helpfulness and co-operation. As he accurately put it, 'The Act requires them to have knowingly aided the council to do an act made unlawful by the Act.' The judge there highlighted the important point that it is aid to another to do the unlawful act in question which must be shown, and this is what the appellants had failed to establish against the police officers. The judge concluded . . . [reference omitted] that the appellants had failed to show that the police officers had aided the council to do the unlawful act in question because neither officer was a party to or involved in the making of the council's decision. There were plainly a number of different ways in which the council could have reacted to the information supplied by the police officers, if the council chose to react at all, several of which responses would have been lawful. The judge's decision was open to him on the evidence, and there are no grounds on which the House could properly disturb it.

It does not follow from this conclusion that where a party gives information to another on which that other relies in doing an unlawful discriminatory act the first party can never be liable under section 33(1). That would be to treat the judge's factual conclusion, based on a correct legal self-direction, as if it were itself a legal proposition. It is not, and the judge's hesitation makes plain that there was room for a conclusion other than that which he reached. Subject always to a correct understanding of the subsection, the outcome of cases such as this will almost always turn on the facts properly found."

LORD MILLET (agreeing): ". . . the giving of information to another on which that other relies in doing an unlawful act may amount to aiding that other to do that act. I would take a simple example. Suppose a gang of youths, brandishing weapons and shouting racist abuse, find a suitable victim and chase after him. He evades their pursuit and finds a place to hide. Suppose too that a bystander, seeing what is happening and realising what the youths intend, betrays the victim's hiding place to them. In those circumstances I have no doubt that the bystander would be aiding the youths to do their victim injury, if that is what they do.

But this shows the importance of correctly identifying the act of the principal which the accessory is alleged to have aided. In the present case the police provided information which helped the council to reach a decision what to do about the situation; but this is not the act which the statute makes unlawful. The information which the police provided did nothing to help the council to carry out their decision, whether to cancel the reservation of the Pump Room for the wedding reception or to impose conditions on entry. That was the act which the statute made unlawful, and in doing it the council neither needed nor obtained the aid of the police. The distinction may appear narrow and even technical, but it is neither. The man who helps another to make up his mind does not thereby and without more help the other to do that which he decides to do. He may advise, encourage, incite or induce him to do the act; but he does not aid him to do it . . .[reference omitted] aiding requires a much closer involvement in the actual act of the principal than do either encouraging or inducing on the one hand or causing or procuring on the other."

Note

In his opinion, Lord Millet explored the relationship between aiding and other forms of actions by third parties. He argues that aiding unlawful discrimination is not instructing, inducing or procuring unlawful discrimination; aiding unlawful discrimination requires a much closer involvement in the actual act of a person carrying out the discrimination. A key element in this closer relationship is the link between the aiding act and the discriminatory act. In the case before him, Lord Millet found that the information provided by the police was aiding the council in making its decision.

But crucially there was no certainty that the council would then decide that placing discriminatory requirements on the appellants was the correct course of action to take. Thus, as there were a range of options open to the council in responding to the police's information, and as they did not know beforehand which of those options the council were going to take, it could not be said that the police "knowingly aided" the council in their discriminatory action. In his judgment, Lord Bingham also accepted that the information the police provided contributed to the council's decision of what course of action to take. However, he found that it was difficult to establish that the police "knowingly aided" the council to do an unlawful act, as several options, including lawful measures, were open to the council in reaching its decision on what action they should take. According to Lord Millet, where a person assists another to make a decision there may be a possibility that the secondary party is encouraging, inciting or inducing the principal towards discriminatory conduct. But the secondary party may only be liable for aiding where the principal has made the decision to pursue a course of action involving a discriminatory act.

The UK House of Lords had a further opportunity to discuss the meaning of section 33 of the RRA on aiding discrimination in the case of *Anyanwu*. Here there was an opportunity to distinguish the concept of "aiding" from those of "instructing" and "inciting" found in sections 30 and 31 of the Act.

House of Lords, 22 March 2001[32]   **5.GB.39.**
Anyanwu and another (Appellants) v. South Bank University Students Union and
South Bank University (Respondents), Commission for Racial Equality (Interveners)

DISTINGUISHING AIDING DISCRIMINATION FROM INDUCING OR PROCURING
DISCRIMINATION

Anyanwu v. Southbank University

Facts: In August 1995, the applicants, Mr. Anyanwu and Mr. Ebuzoeme, were students elected as officers to the South Bank University Student's Union. In March 1996 they were expelled from the university following investigations into serious allegations against them relating to their conduct. The appellants were unsuccessful in a judicial review of the university's decision to expel them. As a result of the expulsion the appellants were banned from the university's premises, including the student union offices. As a result of this they were unable to perform their duties as student union officers. The union treated their employment as at an end. The appellants issued a claim of discrimination against the union. They also claimed that the university knowingly aided the unlawful discrimination, to the extent that they brought about the situation which led to the ending of their employment with the union.

Held: An Employment Tribunal dismissed the claim against the university as an abuse of process, as the complaints had been or should have been the subject of a previous adjudication. The appellants appealed to the Employment Appeal Tribunal. The Employment Appeal Tribunal ruled that the proceedings against the university should not have been struck out on the grounds of *res judicata*. The university challenged the ruling in the Court of Appeal. The Court of Appeal focused on whether, assuming the appellant's account of the facts are correct, the university could be said to have knowingly aided the student union to dismiss

---

[32] [2001] UKHL 14.

the appellants. A majority in the Court of Appeal found that this was not the case and so allowed the appeal by the respondents to have the claim against them struck out. The House of Lords reversed the Court of Appeal decision.

Judgment: LORD BINGHAM OF CORNHILL: "The expression 'aids' in section 33(1) is a familiar word in everyday use and it bears no technical or special meaning in this context. A person aids another if he helps or assists him. He does so whether his help is substantial and productive or whether it is not, provided the help is not so insignificant as to be negligible. While any gloss on the clear statutory language is better avoided, the subsection points towards a relationship of cooperation or collaboration; it does not matter who instigates or initiates the relationship. It is plain that, depending on the facts, a party who aids another to do an unlawful act may also procure or induce that other to do it. But the expressions 'procure' and 'induce' are found in sections 30 and 31, not section 33, and are differently enforced; they mean something different from 'aids' and there is no warrant to interpreting 'aids' as comprising these other expressions . . . It is plain that a party who causes another to do an unlawful act does not necessarily aid him to do it. A farmer who starves his sheepdog, with the result that the ravening dog savages a new-born lamb, may reasonably be said to have caused the death of the lamb, but he could not be said to have aided the dog to kill the lamb. In the present appeal no issue arises on the meaning of "knowingly" in this context and it is unnecessary to consider what an aider must know to be liable under section 33(1)."

LORD STEYN (agreeing): "The proposition that as a matter of law a prime mover cannot be said to be under section 33(1) was at the core of the reasoning of Laws LJ. It was the basis of his decision that the university did not aid the dismissal of the appellants . . . The correct approach is to construe the words of section 33(1) in its contextual setting. It creates a form of derivative liability predicated on the commission of an unlawful act by another person. For present purposes the unlawful act against which section 33(1) must be considered is the alleged dismissal of the appellants by their employers (the student union) on discriminatory racial grounds. The issue of knowledge does not need to be considered on the present appeal. Focusing on the concept of knowingly aiding, the word is used in its ordinary sense. While there is no exact synonym the words help, assist, co-operate, or collaborate, convey more or less the right nuance. The word 'aid' is therefore not used in either an extensive or a restrictive sense. The critical question is: Does the word aid in its contextual sense cover the conduct of the secondary party? It follows that it is wrong to be diverted by any inquiries not mandated by the statute as to whether the alleged aider was or was not a prime mover or a free agent. I would therefore hold that interpretation of section 33(1) adopted by the majority in the Court of Appeal ought not to be accepted."

LORD HOPE OF CRAIGHEAD (concurring): "The critical words in section 33(1) are contained in the phrase 'who knowingly aids another person to do an act made unlawful by this Act'. The state of mind that is referred to here is actual knowledge, in contrast to that referred to in section 33(4) which uses the phrase 'knowingly or recklessly'. The activity which is indicated by the word 'aids' is best understood by reading it together with the words 'to do an act' which appear in the same phrase. It can be contrasted with the words 'instruct' and 'induce' which are used in sections 30 and 31. The word 'instructs' in section 30 is used to describe something done by a person with authority or influence. It is used in the sense of issuing an order which the other person must, or can be persuaded to, obey. A person who in that sense instructs, induces or causes another person to do an act may also knowingly aid him to do that act, or he may not. This is because the word 'aids' indicates an act of a different kind from that which may have caused the person to do the unlawful act. It indicates the giving of some kind of assistance to the other person which helps him to do it. The amount or value of that help or assistance is of no importance. Nor is the time at which it is given. It may or may not have been necessary. All that is needed is an act of some kind, done knowingly, which helps the other person to do the unlawful act . . .

. . . it is enough to say that the word 'aids' should be given its plain and ordinary meaning. It requires that the facts be examined to provide the answers to two questions: (i) what was the act done by the other person which was made unlawful by the Act? (ii) did the act which is in question aid the other person to do that act?"

LORD MILLET: "The university may have encouraged, induced or incited the union to dismiss them; these concepts are closely similar and merge imperceptibly into one another. Indeed, the university may well have gone further and caused or procured the union to dismiss the appellants; concepts which are distinct from but also closely related to each other. But aiding is a very different concept from encouraging or inducing on the one hand and causing or procuring on the other. It requires a much closer involvement in the act of the principal.

In my opinion it is, however, unhelpful to have regard to words like 'co-operate' or 'collaborate', which introduce a different concept in which both parties are principals. Such words serve only to confuse the issue, since they distract attention from the particular act of the principal which the accessory is alleged to have aided. Where two parties join together to achieve a common purpose, they may no doubt be said to aid each other in achieving that purpose. But, in the course of their co-operation, each may play his separate part unaided by the other. I take a simple example. Suppose A and B decide to let a bull loose from a field. A opens the gate and B drives the bull out of the field. They co-operate in letting the bull loose. A may without inaccuracy also be said to have aided B to let the bull loose. But B can hardly be said to have aided A to open the gate. This serves to demonstrate the importance of identifying with precision the act of the principal to which the accessory is alleged to have lent his aid."

Notes

(1) Prior to the RRA 1976, under section 12 of the Race Relations Act 1968, those who deliberately aided, induced or incited another person to do an act made unlawful by Part I of that Act were to be treated as themselves doing that act, but they could not be subjected to proceedings at the direct suit of the injured party. Under the RRA 1976, the injured party could pursue a claim against those who intentionally aid unlawful discrimination, while the Commission for Racial Equality, the body set up to monitor and enforce parts of the legislation, is able to bring proceedings for instructing or inciting discrimination.

(2) According to the appellants in this case, there was an atmosphere of racial prejudice at the university, which the union was unable or unwilling to resist. Their allegations were not only that the university's actions aimed to cause the removal of the appellants from their union positions, but that the university was acting in a closer fashion with the union to remove the officers. As evidence, they point to the fact that, by 22 March 1996, the university's board of governors had approved a new interim constitution for the students' union. The effect of this constitution would be to take control of the union away from the elected officials and place it with a board of trustees appointed by the university. The letter terminating the appellants' employment with the union, which was sent in April 1996, came from one of the university's newly appointed trustees. Lord Hope, in allowing the appeal, noted that these facts, although not yet proven, showed that there was an arguable case and were therefore sufficient to allow the appeal.

(3) At the Court of Appeal, Laws LJ for the majority held:

"The question for this court, as it seems to me, is whether on those alleged facts the university can conceivably be said to have 'knowingly aided' the [appellants'] dismissal by the union. In expelling the [appellants] and barring them from the union premises, the university brought about a state of affairs in which the employment contracts were bound to be terminated. In my judgment it is a plain affront to the language of the Act of 1976 to suggest that in such circumstances the university 'aided' the dismissal of the [appellants]. The verb 'aid' (to which no special definition is ascribed by the statute) means 'help' or 'assist'. Its use contemplates a state of affairs in which one party, being a free agent in the matter, sets out to do an act or achieve a result and another party helps him to do it. The first party is the primary actor. The other is a secondary actor. The simplest example may be found in the criminal law. A breaks into a house in order to burgle it. B keeps watch outside or is ready to drive off the get-away car. Plainly B 'aids' A. But here, the university is the prime mover. It did not 'aid' (or 'help') the union to dismiss the [appellants]. It may well be said that it brought about their dismissal. But that is altogether a different thing".

(4) Butler Sloss LJ, agreeing, argued that she was

"unable, in applying the natural meaning to the word 'aids', to attribute to it a meaning which distorts it. In ordinary language a person who aids another person is one who helps, supports or assists the prime mover to do the act. On the present facts the university took steps to expel the [appellants] for its own reasons, justified or unjustified. Those expulsions, carrying with them the prohibition against entering any part of the university buildings including the students' union, cannot in ordinary language be said to be knowingly aiding the students' union to dismiss the [appellants] within section 33(1). In this case the prime mover of the dismissal of the [appellants] was the students' union but its acts were effectively dictated to it by the prior decision of the university to expel the [appellants]. It seems clear to me that the students' union had no alternative but to dismiss the [appellants] after the university expelled them. In ordinary language can that conceivably be said to be knowingly aiding? I would answer 'No'."

(5) However, Pill LJ, dissenting, held:

"Even taking a narrow definition of the word 'aids', the acts complained of, suspension, expulsion and dismissal, and the alleged conduct of the university and the union which preceded each of them, are so entangled upon the facts alleged that it would not be appropriate to separate them at this stage. On any view, the dismissal is intimately connected with the suspension and expulsion. An environment of racial prejudice is alleged to have been 'encouraged and allowed to thrive by the university and the union' (Mr. Anyanwu). The union are alleged to have been 'conniving with the university to remove me' (Mr. Ebuzoeme). In further and better particulars given at the request of the university, Mr. Anyanwu said that 'in all cases the acts of racial discrimination were carried out collectively by the respondents' (that is the university and the union)."

The House of Lords attempts to provide a guide through the different concepts employed by the legislation in this area. In particular, the judgments focus on the concept of "aiding" discrimination and try to delineate with more precision the nature of this concept. Lord Bingham suggests that "aiding" an unlawful act is distinct from inducing or procuring it. He also distinguishes aiding an unlawful act from causing it to occur. In Lord Bingham's view, "causing" an unlawful action to occur is a broader notion than aiding it. Lord Millet is also clear that the concept of aiding is "encouraging or inducing on the one hand and causing or procuring on the other". Similarly, Lord Hope sought to draw out the distinctions between these different concepts while acknowledging the overlap that existed between them. He notes that the person who "instructs, induces or causes another person to do an act may also knowingly aid him to do that act, or he may not". This, he emphasises, is because "the word 'aids' indicates an action of a different kind from that which may have caused the person to do the unlawful act". While the Law Lords are clear that aiding as a concept is distinct from those of inciting, inducing or causing, the judgments provide less insight into the content and nature of this concept. The detailed analysis of the different terms found in the legislation stands in stark contrast to the discussion in Parliament during the recent passage of the Equality Act 2006 (above **5.GB.27.**), where the opposition sought clarification of whether the term "inducing" a person to discriminate was contained within the broader concept of "causing" a person to discriminate. In defending these separate provisions, the government minister suggested that their focus was to ensure that the legislation covered "every possible angle" and "left no loophole" to escape liability.

5.1.3.   COMPARATIVE OVERVIEW

This section has focused on examining the many ways in which international law, the European Directives and the different national legal orders have attempted to attach liability to those who, while not the actual discriminators, have some manner of what Lord Steyn in *Anyanwu* v. *Southbank University* (above **5.GB.39.**) referred to as "derivative liability". Both the Employment Equality and the Racial Equality Directives confine such liability to those who issue "instructions to discriminate". In elegant and simple language, the Directives merely state that "an instruction to discriminate . . . shall be deemed to be discrimination". The text of the Directive provides no further clues as to how this provision is to be understood, interpreted or transposed. In the absence of further guidance, many Member States have opted to simply replicate the words of the Directive without further gloss or details.

Some insight into the harm that the EU Directives are trying to address can be gained by an examination of the wider legal and political context out of which the Directives emerged. In particular, it is suggested here that the Directives' provisions on instructions to discriminate can, in part, find their roots in broader EU measures for tackling racism and xenophobia, which in turn are shaped by various international human rights obligations to prohibit the incitement of racial hatred which encompasses incitement to racial discrimination.

Thus, the origins to the Directives' provisions on instructions to discriminate are complex and diverse. Several Member States, prior to the transposition of the Directive, had in place legal provisions that sought to give effect to their obligations in international law under ICERD to prohibit incitement to racial hatred. The examination of these provisions suggests that while they often cover many instances where a person issues instructions to discriminate, the coverage does not meet the requirements of the Directive in full. In particular, criminal law provisions prohibiting incitement to discriminate, reflecting their focus on maintaining public order, often require the instructions to be given in public. Thus, for example, in the *Belgian waiters* case (above **5.BE.13.**), a prosecution was successful because the instructions were given in "an inn where other customers were also present". The possibility remains that had the instruction been given in private, or in an employment context where customers or members of the public were not present, they would not be covered by the legislation. In that case, the prohibitions to incite hatred and discrimination are not a full equivalent to the prohibition of instructions to discriminate in the European Directives. Furthermore, as such provisions give effect to States Parties' obligations under ICERD, the national laws are restricted to incitement to racial discrimination and therefore do not fully cover the wider set of grounds included in the Employment Equality Directive.

Coverage of instructions to discriminate for a wider range of grounds of discrimination is possible where a penal law prohibition on discrimination is combined with provisions on liability of accomplices. Thus, the French Penal Code provision on discrimination in Article 225-1 (above **5.FR.15.**), which covers 16 different grounds, can cover instructions to discriminate on those grounds when combined with the Penal Code's provisions on accomplices in Article 121-7, which provides that a person who "gives instructions to [commit an offence] is also an accomplice". A similar prohibition of discrimination on a broad range of grounds is found in the Estonian Penal Code, Article 152. Again, this can cover instructions to discriminate when combined with Article 22(2) of the Penal Code, which brings within its scope those who "intentionally induce" another person to intentionally commit an unlawful act. The example of the domestic law in Finland shows some of the difficulties that may be encountered when liability for instructions to discriminate is dependent on broader criminal law provisions concerning accomplices to an unlawful act. Under the provisions of the Finnish Penal Code, incitement to an unlawful act, when combined with the Penal Code prohibition on discrimination, covers instructions to discriminate. However, an offence only occurs where the instructions lead to actual instances of discrimination or, at least, an attempt at discrimination. Thus, an incitement to discriminate, by itself, is not sufficient for liability.

In the case of Finland, this gap in protection is filled by the Non-Discrimination Act, which seeks to transpose the Employment Equality Directive into domestic law. Under this Act an instruction or order to discriminate is deemed to be discrimination. It is clear from the *travaux* to the Act that, unlike the Finnish Penal Code provisions, there is liability for issuing an instruction to discriminate even when the instruction does not lead to any actions.

How exactly instructions to discriminate fit into the non-discrimination framework has yet to be resolved satisfactorily by the Directives on non-discrimination law and their implementation. As this is a common trend of both a prohibition of instructions and victimisation, this will be addressed in the concluding comparative analysis.

5.2. VICTIMISATION

A prohibition on victimisation is aimed at providing protection to those involved in a complaint of discrimination from facing adverse consequences as a result of their involvement in that claim. The prohibition of victimisation is therefore crucial in protecting the integrity of anti-discrimination laws. If a person faces adverse consequences because they have brought a discrimination complaint or provided evidence, acted as a witness or acted in support of another person bringing a claim, then individuals will become very reluctant to bring or be involved in discrimination cases. If people are fearful of the consequences of their involvement in a discrimination claim, in whatever capacity, then enforcement of the law will become impossible. Thus, protection against victimisation is critical to maintaining the integrity and effectiveness of the law.

5.2.1. DEVELOPMENT OF EC LAW

The protection against victimisation in EC law can be traced back to the 1976 Equal Treatment Directive and has been repeated in subsequent directives. They are reproduced here for completeness and also to allow the differences in the formulation to be examined.

Council Directive 76/207/EEC of   **5.EC.40.**
9 February 1976 on the implementation of
the principle of equal treatment for men and women
as regards access to employment, vocational training and promotion,
and working conditions[33]

Article 7
Member States shall take the necessary measures to protect employees against any dismissal by the employer as a reaction to a complaint within the undertaking or to any legal proceedings aimed as enforcing compliance with the principle of equal treatment.

---

[33] [1976] OJ L39/40.

Council Directive 86/378/EEC of 24 July 1986 on the   **5.EC.41.**
implementation of the principle of equal treatment for men and women in
occupational social security schemes[34]

Article 11
Member States shall take necessary steps to protect workers against dismissal where this constitutes a response on the part of the employer to a complaint made at undertaking level or to the institution of legal proceedings aimed at enforcing compliance with the principle of equal treatment.

Council Directive 2000/43 of 29 June 2000 implementing the   **5.EC.42.**
principle of equal treatment between persons irrespective of racial
or ethnic origin[35]

Recital 20
The effective implementation of the principle of equality requires adequate judicial protection against victimisation . . .

Article 9
Member States shall introduce into their national legal systems such measures as are necessary to protect individuals from any adverse treatment or adverse consequence as a reaction to a complaint or to proceedings aimed at enforcing compliance with the principle of equal treatment.

Council Directive 2000/78 of 27 November 2000 establishing a   **5.EC.43.**
general framework for equal treatment in employment and occupation[36]

Article 11
Member States shall introduce into their national legal systems such measures as are necessary to protect employees against dismissal or other adverse treatment by the employer as a reaction to a complaint within the undertaking or to any legal proceedings aimed at enforcing compliance with the principle of equal treatment.

Council Directive of 9 February 1976 on the implementation   **5.EC.44.**
of the principle of equal treatment for men and women as regards access to

---

[34] [1986] OJ L225/40.
[35] [2000] OJ L180/22.
[36] [2000] OJ L303/16.

*employment, vocational training and promotion and working conditions
(76/207/EEC) as amended by Directive 2002/73[37]*

Recital 17
The Court of Justice has ruled that, having regard to the fundamental nature of the right to effective judicial protection, employees enjoy such protection even after the employment relationship has ended [reference omitted]. An employee defending or giving evidence on behalf of a person protected under this Directive should be entitled to the same protection.

Amended Article 7
Member State shall introduce into their national legal systems such measures as are necessary to protect employees, including those who are employees' representatives provided for by national laws and/or practices, against dismissal or other adverse treatment by the employer as a reaction to a complaint within the undertaking or to any legal proceedings aimed at enforcing compliance with the principle of equal treatment.

Notes
   (1) The Directives differ in their references to the protected acts, the narrowest formulation being found in 76/207 and 86/378, which only refer to "dismissal". Directives 2000/78 and 76/207/EEC, as amended by 2002/73 and 2006/54, refer to "dismissal or other adverse treatment", while the broadest formulation is found in Directive 2000/43: "any adverse treatment or adverse consequence".
   (2) The causal link is also framed in almost identical terms in the Directives; the adverse treatment must be a "reaction to" a complaint or legal proceedings.
   (3) Directives 76/207/EEC and 2000/78 limit protection to employees, while Directive 86/378 refers to workers and Directive 2000/43 requires Member States to protect "individuals". These differences in scope of the person protected from victimisation reflect the differences in the material scope of each directive. However, in the most recent Directives, 2002/73 and 2006/54, the text explicitly provides that the term "employee" includes "those who are employee's representatives". The protection of employee's representatives may have been latent in the previous Directives, since these placed an obligation on states to take measures that are "necessary" to protect those covered by the Directives. Thus, measures to protect an employee's representative can be viewed as measures necessary to protect the interests of the employee. The explicit reference to employee's representatives does not operate to preclude Member States from expanding the scope of their legislative protection to other participants in a discrimination claim, e.g. witnesses. It is less clear to what extent it requires Member States to extend protection to such participants in the complaints process.

The issue of the scope of the protection from victimisations in the Directives was considered by the ECJ in the case of *Coote* v. *Granada Hospitality*.

---

[37] [2002] OJ L269/15.

C–185/1997, Belinda Jane Coote v. *Granada Hospitality Limited*

VICTIMISATIONS COVERS THE EMPLOYER'S ACTIONS IN RELATION TO THE EMPLOYEE AFTER THE EMPLOYMENT RELATIONSHIP HAS ENDED

Coote v. Granada Hospitality Ltd.

Facts: Ms. Coote was employed by Granada from December 1992 to September 1993. In 1993 she brought a claim for sex discrimination against Granada, alleging that she had been dismissed because of pregnancy. That claim was settled, and Ms. Coote's employment with Granada ended by mutual agreement on 7 September 1993. In July 1994 Ms. Coote, seeking new employment, had recourse to two employment agencies. She considers that her difficulties in finding employment were due to Granada's failure to provide a reference to one of the employment agencies; Granada disputes this. Ms. Coote then brought a further claim against Granada before the Industrial Tribunal, claiming that she had been victimised by Granada's refusal to supply a reference to the employment agency. She alleged that the refusal was a reaction to the claim which she had previously brought against her former employer. That claim was dismissed on the grounds that the alleged discrimination had taken place after her employment with Granada had ended and that, in any event, the alleged detriment had arisen after that date. The Industrial Tribunal considered that the SDA was to be interpreted as prohibiting only retaliatory measures whose prejudicial effect appears during the employment relationship. The Employment Appeal Tribunal stayed proceedings and referred a number of questions to the ECJ, by which it sought to clarify whether withholding a reference, to which an employee is not entitled under national law, may be considered as an act of victimisation.

Held: Article 6 of Council Directive 76/207/EEC of 9 February 1976 on the implementation of the principle of equal treatment for men and women as regards access to employment, vocational training and promotion, and working conditions requires Member States to introduce into their national legal systems such measures as are necessary to ensure judicial protection for workers whose employer, after the employment relationship has ended, refuses to provide references as a reaction to legal proceedings brought to enforce compliance with the principle of equal treatment within the meaning of that Directive.

Judgment: "It should be noted that Article 6 of the Directive requires Member States to introduce into their national legal systems such measures as are necessary to enable all persons who consider themselves the victims of discrimination 'to pursue their claims by judicial process'. It follows from that provision that the Member States must take measures which are sufficiently effective to achieve the aim of the Directive and that they must ensure that the rights thus conferred can be effectively relied upon before the national courts by the persons concerned [references omitted].

21. The requirement laid down by that article that recourse be available to the courts reflects a general principle of law which underlies the constitutional traditions common to the Member States and which is also enshrined in Article 6 of the European Convention for the Protection of Human Rights and Fundamental Freedoms of 4 November 1950 [reference omitted].

22. By virtue of Article 6 of the Directive, interpreted in the light of the general principle stated above, all persons have the right to obtain an effective remedy in a competent court against measures which they consider to interfere with the equal treatment for men and women laid down in the Directive. It is for the Member States to ensure effective judicial control of compliance with the applicable provisions of Community law and of national legislation intended to give effect to the rights for which the Directive provides [reference omitted].

23. As the Court has also held [reference omitted] Article 6 of the Directive is an essential factor for attaining the fundamental objective of equal treatment for men and women, which,

---

[38] [1998] ECR I–5199.

as the Court has repeatedly held [reference omitted], is one of the fundamental human rights whose observance the Court has a duty to ensure.

24. The principle of effective judicial control laid down in Article 6 of the Directive would be deprived of an essential part of its effectiveness if the protection which it provides did not cover measures which, as in the main proceedings in this case, an employer might take as a reaction to legal proceedings brought by an employee with the aim of enforcing compliance with the principle of equal treatment. Fear of such measures, where no legal remedy is available against them, might deter workers who considered themselves the victims of discrimination from pursuing their claims by judicial process, and would consequently be liable seriously to jeopardise implementation of the aim pursued by the Directive.

25. In those circumstances, it is not possible to accept the United Kingdom Government's argument that measures taken by an employer against an employee as a reaction to legal proceedings brought to enforce compliance with the principle of equal treatment do not fall within the scope of the Directive if they are taken after the employment relationship has ended.

26. It is true that, as the United Kingdom Government also stresses, Article 7 of the Directive expressly requires Member States to take the necessary measures to protect employees against dismissal by the employer as a reaction to any legal proceedings aimed at enforcing compliance with the principle of equal treatment.

27. However, contrary to that Government's submissions, having regard to the objective of the Directive, which is to arrive at real equality of opportunity for men and women [reference omitted] and to the fundamental nature of the right to effective judicial protection, it is not, in the absence of a clear indication to the contrary, to be inferred from Article 7 of the Directive that the legislature's intention was to limit the protection of workers against retaliatory measures decided on by the employer solely to cases of dismissal, which, although an exceptionally serious measure, is not the only measure which may effectively deter a worker from making use of the right to judicial protection. Such deterrent measures include *inter alia* those which, as in the present case, are taken as a reaction to proceedings brought against an employer and are intended to obstruct the dismissed employee's attempts to find new employment.

28. In those circumstances, the answer to the questions put by the national court must be that Article 6 of the Directive requires Member States to introduce into their national legal systems such measures as are necessary to ensure judicial protection for workers whose employer, after the employment relationship has ended, refuses to provide references as a reaction to legal proceedings brought to enforce compliance with the principle of equal treatment within the meaning of the Directive."

Notes

(1) Following the ECJ's ruling, in *Coote* v. *Granada Hospitality Ltd. (No. 2)*[39] the Employment Appeal Tribunal held that section 6(2) of the Sex Discrimination Act Great Britain covered former employees. The House of Lords in *Rhys-Harper* v. *Relaxation Group plc*[40] confirmed that other UK discrimination legislation also covered discriminatory conduct (including victimisation) that takes place after the employment relationship has ended.

---

[39] [1999] ICR 942.

(2) Slovenia provides an example of an approach found in many other EU Member States whereby employment law, in this case the Employment Relations Act Article 76, places duties on the employer to issue the ex-employee with references that certify the kind of work that the employee was doing and not to include in the reference any material that would make it more difficult for them to secure a new job.

(3) The ECJ reasoning is focused on the need to provide protection against any measure that "will effectively deter a worker" from making use of their right to judicial protection. The ECJ recognises the importance of providing protection from victimisation to maintaining the effectiveness and integrity of the law against discrimination, as "fear of such measures . . . might deter workers who consider themselves victims of discrimination from pursuing their claims . . . and would consequently . . . seriously . . . jeopardise implementation of the aim pursued by the Directive."

The need to protect against victimisation has been recognised in the development of the EC Racial and Employment Equality Directives. The extract below is from a publication by the European Network Against Racism (ENAR). ENAR played a crucial role as a non-governmental organisation (NGO) in maintaining pressure on EU governments and lobbying them to ensure that they address issues of racism and xenophobia.

M.M. Sierra (ed.), "Towards Equal Treatment: **5.EC.46.**
Transposing the Directive—Analysis and Proposals"[41]

"B. Need for the concept
To make the implementation of the principle of equal treatment more effective, it seems essential to provide legal protection against victimisation. In fact, it is not sufficient simply to have anti-discrimination legislation: the victims must be empowered to make use of the legislation without fear of reprisals. Indeed, this is one of the factors which explain the ineffectiveness of anti-discrimination legislation. All too often, very few proceedings are initiated on the basis of discrimination experienced in the workplace, even though in an action before an industrial tribunal it is legally possible to assert the rights of individuals discriminated against to obtain compensation. However, the individuals involved, whether they are victims or witnesses to instances of discrimination, fear they might lose their jobs or be hindered in their careers."

5.2.2.   NATIONAL LEGISLATION AND CASE-LAW

Research and comments from tribunals at the national level also emphasise the importance of protecting individuals from victimisation.

[40] [2003] IRLR 483.
[41] (European Network Against Racism, March 2002), available on the website of European Network Against Racism.

SERIOUSNESS OF VICTIMISATION

The claimant who reapplies to a department store

Facts: In May 1999 the claimant applied unsuccessfully for a position with the respondent. She contacted the Equality Authority in December 1999 to seek advice on her allegation that, in rejecting her application, the respondents had discriminated against her on the grounds of disability, because of the fact that she attended a school for children with learning disabilities. The Equality Authority informed her that there was no action they could take to support her as the complaint related to actions that took place before the Employment Equality Act 1998 came into force. The claimant sought further advice from the Equality Authority about a conversation she alleged she had had with the respondent's personnel officer in December 1999. The Authority contacted the respondent about this in January 2000 and they replied denying the conversation took place. The claimant continued to apply for jobs with the respondent and in March 2000 received a letter from one of the respondent's store managers stating that "in view of the untrue and unfounded allegations that you have made to the Employment Equality Authority . . . we are not for the foreseeable future going to accept any application from you for employment in our store or indeed any other branch [of the department store]."

Held: The tribunal found that the department store had penalised the claimant in circumstances amounting to victimisation, contrary to the provisions of section 74(1) of the Employment Equality Act 1998. The respondent department store was ordered to pay 12,700 euros to the claimant.

Judgment: ANNE-MARIE LYNCH (Equality Officer): "I would like to emphasise here that victimisation is a matter that must be considered very seriously. To allow victimisation of claimants under the Act would be to subvert the legislation. The purpose of section 74(1) is to protect those who consider they have been victims of discrimination. If this protection is not supported in Equality Officer decisions, the legislation will be ineffective and the rights of the individuals concerned will be compromised. As stated earlier, the complaint of discrimination on the ground of disability made by the claimant was not upheld. If the respondent had not acted as it did, this matter would have concluded with it having successfully vindicated its position in relation to the allegations of discrimination.

As a demonstration of how seriously I consider the consequences of such victimisation, I am satisfied that the claimant should be awarded significant compensation for the actions of the respondent. Section 82(4) of the Act provides that the maximum amount that may be awarded to a successful claimant, not in receipt of remuneration at the date of the referral of the case, shall be 12,700 euros, and I am therefore satisfied that it is an appropriate level of compensation for the claimant in the matter."

Notes

(1) The Irish Equality Tribunal judgment rightly emphasises the importance of providing protection for those who seek to use equality legislation. That protection must be available whether individuals are successful or unsuccessful in their claims.

(2) Lord Steyn in *Nagarajan* (above **5.GB.56.**) noted that the

"primary purpose [of the legislative provision on victimisation] is to give to persons victimised on account of their reliance on rights under the Act effective civil remedies, thereby also creating a culture which may deter individuals from penalising those who seek to enforce their rights."

In the case of *Aziz* v. *Trinity Street Taxis*,[42] Slade LJ in the UK Court of Appeal stated that the "clear legislative purpose of [reference to legislative provision on victimisations—omitted][was] . . . to ensure, so far as possible, that victims of racial discrimination shall not be deterred from" seeking redress.

(3) Even when legislation is in place, providing effective protection from victimisation is still difficult. A study by Professor Jeanne Gregory of 106 unsuccessful applicants in discrimination cases found that over half subsequently experienced deterioration in their working relationship with their employer or manager.[43] The range of actions included the employees feeling that they had reduced or no prospects of promotion to reduced pay rises and selection for redundancy. This echoes an earlier study by Alice Leonard, who found that between 1980 and 1984 only 17 out of 70 successful claimants remained with their employer beyond two years.[44] Similarly, a study of the Netherlands found that almost half of claimants who submitted a complaint against their employer encountered disadvantages at work, and one-third changed jobs because of the complaint.[45]

Victimisation is a complex issue because it emerges from a situation where A (the person claiming victimisation) and B (the alleged perpetrator) continue in a relationship (usually, an employment relationship), notwithstanding the fact that A is involved (as a claimant or in some other capacity) in an anti-discrimination claim concerning B. The difficulty is in isolating those actions emerging from the continuing relationship that are instances of victimisation from those that are merely part of the continued relationship between the two parties. In prohibiting victimisation we see that national legislation is different. European states vary in the scope of protection that they offer.

Finnish Non-Discrimination Act 21/2004   **5.FI.48.**

Section 8: Prohibition of victimisation
No one may be placed in an unfavourable position or treated in such a way that they suffer adverse consequences because of having complained or taken action to safeguard equality.

---

[42] [1989] 1 QB 463.

[43] J. Gregory, *Trial by Ordeal: A Study of People Who Lost Sex Discrimination Cases in the Industrial Tribunals in 1985 & 1986* (Manchester, Equal Opportunities Commission Research Series, 1989).

[44] A. Leonard, *Pyrrhic Victories: Winning Sex Discrimination and Equal Pay Cases in the Industrial Tribunals, 1980–1984* (London, HMSO, 1987).

[45] See I.P. Asscher-Vonk and C.A. Groenendijk (eds.), *Gelijke behandeling: regels en realiteit. Een juridische en rechtssociologische analyse van de gelijke-behandelingswetgeving* (Den Haag, SDU Uitgevers, 1999) 526.

Finnish Act on Equality Between Women and Men   **5.FI.49.**

Section 8a
The action of an employer is to be deemed discrimination prohibited under this Act, if a person is dismissed or otherwise placed in an unfavourable position after having exercised the rights or obligations provided by this Act or taken part in investigating a case of sexual discrimination.

Dutch General Equal Treatment Act   **5.NL.50.**

Article 8(1) If an employer terminates an employee's employment in contravention of section 5, on the grounds that the employee has invoked article 5, either at law or otherwise, or has provided assistance in relation to it, such termination shall be invalid.

Article 8a
Adverse treatment in reaction to a person's reliance either at law or otherwise on this Act or provision of assistance in relation to it shall be prohibited.

Note
Much of the legislation on victimisation focuses on the employment relationship and, within this context, protection as a minimum covers dismissal of an employee. Both the Dutch and the Finnish legislation are explicit in their coverage of the dismissal and termination of the employment contact. In some jurisdictions dismissal is the only action covered by victimisation provisions. For example, in Poland legal protection for victimisation is limited to renunciation or dissolution of an employment contract but does not extent to other detrimental treatment. In other jurisdictions protection goes beyond dismissal to other actions. The extent of protection beyond dismissal varies within and between different EU states. For example, the Estonian Law on Gender Equality Article 6(2) finds that there is victimisation if an employer "downgrades the working conditions of an employee or terminates an employment relationship with him or her". In other instances the legislation is drawn more broadly; the legislation in Finland covers action that places a person in an "unfavourable position" or includes treating them in such a way that they suffer "adverse consequences" and the Dutch Equal Treatment Act provides protection from "adverse treatment".

Not all actions by A (the person claiming victimisation) are protected. It is therefore important to identify the kinds of actions by A that are protected by provisions on victimisation. Most legislation will identify some "protected acts".

Section 74(2)
For the purposes of this Part victimisation occurs where dismissal or other adverse treatment of an employee by his or her employer occurs as a reaction to—

  (a)   a complaint of discrimination made by the employee to the employer,
  (b)   any proceedings by the complainant,
  (c)   an employee having represented or otherwise supported a complainant
  (d)   the work of an employee having been compared with that of another employee for any of the purposes of this Act . . .
  (e)   an employee having been a witness in any proceedings under this Act . . .
  (f)   an employee having opposed by lawful means an act which is unlawful under this Act
  (g)   an employee having given notice of an intention to take any of the actions mentioned in the preceding paragraphs.

Section 98
(1) If an employee is dismissed in circumstances amounting to victimisation, the employee's employer shall be guilty of an offence and if, in a prosecution for an offence under this section, it is proved—

  (a)   that the employee was dismissed, and
  (b)   that the employee, in good faith, did one or more of the acts specified in paragraphs (a) to (g) of section 74(2),

that proof shall, without more, be evidence until the contrary is proved, that the sole or main reason for the dismissal of the employee was that the employee, in good faith, did one or more of those acts.

. . .

(3) . . . the court . . . may, if it thinks fit, in addition to imposing a fine for the offence, order the employer to pay to the employee concerned such amount of compensation as, . . . the court considers appropriate, having regard to any evidence and to any representations that are made by or on behalf of the employer or the employee concerned.

Irish Equal Status Act 2000   **5.IE.52.**

(2) As between any two persons, the discriminatory grounds (and the descriptions of those grounds for the purposes of this Act) are:

. . .

(j) that one—

  (i)   has in good faith applied for any determination or redress provided for in Part II or III,
  (ii)   has attended as a witness before the Authority, the Director or a court in connection with any inquiry or proceedings under this Act,
  (iii) has given evidence in any criminal proceedings under this Act,
  (iv) has opposed by lawful means an act which is unlawful under this Act, or

(v)   has given notice of an intention to take any of the actions specified in subparagraphs
      (i) to (iv),

and the other has not (the 'victimisation ground').

Notes

(1) In Ireland the seriousness with which dismissal is treated is reflected in the fact that where victimisation amounts to dismissal, under the Employment Equality Act (section 98) this is treated as a criminal offence and there are no financial limits in the amount of compensation awards for victimisation.

(2) Most legislation provides protection for certain acts; the most basic "protected act" is seeking to bring a discrimination claim. The Irish legislation provides protection to those who seek "redress under the Act". The Finnish Non-Discrimination Act provides protection for those who have "complained or taken action to safeguard equality" and under the Act on Equality Between Men and Women it covers those who have "exercised the rights and obligations provided by the legislation", while the Dutch Equal Treatment Act covers those who have "invoked" the equal treatment legislation. However, protection often goes further than this.

(3) A narrowly defined provision on victimisation is restricted to the protection of those who bring a complaint of discrimination. In the cases of Belgium, Greece, Poland and Portugal protection from victimisation is limited to "employees" who have filed a complaint of discrimination or brought legal action.

(4) A wider provision recognises the need to provide protection to others involved in the process—for example, those who provide support to the person bringing the claim. The most obvious example would be trade union representatives or others providing advice and information. The underlying rationale for this is a recognition that, for rights to be effective, real people must have access to advice and information about those rights. Thus, effective victimisation provisions require protection of those who provide that advice and information. Further categories of individuals are witnesses or other employees asked to give evidence in relation to the claim. The Austrian Equal Treatment Act covers the person bringing a claim and other employees who act as witnesses or support the complaint of a victimisation case. In the Finnish Non-Discrimination Act the scope of persons protected is wide. It covers those who have engaged in the proceedings and those who have supported persons claiming discrimination, including trade union representatives, witnesses, legal advisers and representatives of NGOs. In France, the protection from victimisation for witnesses appears to be broader than protection for those who face the initial discrimination. The latter are only protected from dismissal; witnesses are protected from "sanctions, dismissal or any other discriminatory measure". It is, however, possible for a victim to also be a witness and receive the protection available to witnesses. In the Netherlands the Dutch Equal Treatment Commission ruled that someone who is a witness to discrimination can file a complaint and is protected by the provisions on victimisation (see Opinion 2000/73). The Finnish Act on Equality between men and women extends protection to those who have "taken part in investigating a case of sexual discrimination", while the Dutch legislation extends it to cover

those who provide assistance in relation to a claim under the equality legislation. In Ireland, protection extends beyond those who give evidence in a discrimination claim to cover those who may be used as a comparator in a discrimination claim.

(5) The need for protection from victimisation also extends to actions by individuals which may not lead to individual complaints of discrimination but may lead to other enforcement action, for example an investigation by an equality enforcement agency. In many cases the concept of victimisation relates only to actions concerning an individual complaint. However, there are instances where a broader definition is given. In Greece, the definition of victimisation refers to "adverse treatment by an employer to . . . any legal proceedings aimed at enforcing compliance with the principle of equal treatment". In Malta, the Employment and Industrial Relations Act covers victimisation of a person who (a) files a complaint to the lawful authorities or initiates or participates in proceedings for redress on grounds of alleged breach of the provisions of the Act; or (b) discloses information, confidential or otherwise, to a designated public regulating body, regarding illegal or corrupt activities being committed by his employer.

Court of Appeal, 3 July 1997[46]   **5.GB.53.**
Waters v. Commissioner of Police of the Metropolis

PROTECTION FROM VICTIMISATION REQUIRES THE CLAIMANT TO REVEAL FACTS
CAPABLE IN LAW OF AMOUNTING TO AN ACT OF DISCRIMINATION

Waters v. Commissioner of Police

Facts: WPC Waters alleged that she had been raped by a fellow police officer T while they were off-duty. She claimed that as a consequence of her complaint of rape she faced detrimental treatment from her employers. This included being transferred between police stations without consultation or the normal periods of notice, not having her complaint properly investigated, transfer from police to civilian duties, denial of appropriate time off, applications for particular placements refused, being "harassed and unfairly treated" by her superiors, being told that "she should leave the police force before she is forced to go", being subjected to pornography by fellow officers, being threatened with violence by her Chief Superintendent and "quite unjustifiably and with a view to intimidating and harassing her" was required to undergo "psychological analysis" to see if she was "fit for duty". She was advised to leave by a colleague in his capacity as Police Federation representative. She eventually took sick leave. WPC Water's claim for victimisation depended on whether the original complaint that she made concerning the rape provided the basis for a claim of discrimination against the employer that amounted to a contravention of the relevant Act. The court accepted that the sexual harassment or abuse of a woman employee by a male colleague is capable in law of amounting, in a case where the employer's responsibility for it can be established, to discrimination within the terms of sex discrimination legislation. Furthermore, it was accepted that the employer may be vicariously liable for the actions of an employee. The issue before the tribunal was whether the complaint of sexual assault by T was capable of amounting to an allegation within the terms of section 4(1)(d).

Held: The Court of Appeal dismissed the appeal by Waters. They held that as the employer would not have been held vicariously liable for the acts of the employees in this situation, the facts did not reveal a basis for a claim of discrimination in contravention of the SDA which could form the basis of the claim for victimisation.

---

[46] [1997] ICR 1073.

Judgment: WAITES LJ: "Mr. Allen (lawyer for Waters) relies on: (1) The need (already mentioned as being common ground in this case) to construe discrimination legislation purposively in accordance with its objects and (so far as possible) those of the Equal Rights Directive. (2) The breadth of language employed by S 4 itself. Here he prays in aid S 4(2), and (reading 4(1)(d) and (2) together) points out the wide range of allegation that may be included—allegations that allege a contravention of the Act expressly, allegations that make no reference to the Act at all, false allegations (provided they are made in good faith), and true allegations (even if made in bad faith). The Equal Pay Act 1970 is legislation which, as is well known, provides a protean opportunity for complaint in widely varying terms. The specific inclusion of complaints under that Act within the regime of S 4 accordingly provides further indication of intention that the range of potential complaint qualifying for protection should be widely, and not narrowly, drawn. (3) The genus of complaint with which the section is concerned. Any complaint requiring protection from future victimisation is likely, in the nature of things, to have been made spontaneously at a moment of stress or crisis, and without time or opportunity for legal advice. It would be an unreal and unduly restrictive intention, therefore, to attribute to Parliament that every complaint should, as a condition of protection from future victimisation, spell out the relevant allegation in language so unequivocal as to leave no room for doubt in the mind of the employer that the complaint is founded upon discrimination on the ground of sex. With those considerations in mind, the intention properly to be attributed to Parliament is, Mr. Allen submits, the following:

'S 4(1)(d) has to be construed in such a way as to treat as protected acts any allegations which, objectively considered, are aimed at claiming (i.e. provide the basis for development of a claim for) protection under the equality legislation (Sex Discrimination or Equal Pay Act).'

Judged by that yardstick the complaint in this case was clearly, he submits, within the sub-section. The act complained of (serious sexual harassment) was indisputably capable of constituting treatment which subjects a woman to detriment within the terms of S 6(2)(b). It makes no difference that the complaint, had it been carried through to hearing before an Industrial Tribunal, would have been bound to fail because some essential element (such as liability of the employer under S 41) could not be established. If the foundations are laid, it matters not that no house could lawfully be built upon them. That is because Parliament must have intended, if the prohibition against victimisation was to have any real value at all, that protection should arise from the making of the complaint, and should not depend upon the terms in which it is articulated.

That submission fails, in my judgment, for this reason. True it is that the legislation must be construed in a sense favourable to its important public purpose. But there is another principle involved—also essential to that same purpose. Charges of race or sex discrimination are hurtful and damaging and not always easy to refute. In justice, therefore, to those against whom they are brought, it is vital that discrimination (including victimisation) should be defined in language sufficiently precise to enable people to know where they stand before the law. Precision of language is also necessary to prevent the valuable purpose of combating discrimination from becoming frustrated or brought into disrepute through the use of language which encourages unscrupulous or vexatious recourse to the machinery provided by the Discrimination Acts. The interpretation proposed by Mr. Allen would involve an imprecision of language leaving employers in a state of uncertainty as to how they should respond to a particular complaint, and would place the machinery of the Acts at serious risk of abuse. It is better, and safer, to give the words of the sub-section their clear and literal meaning. The allegation relied on need not state explicitly that an act of discrimination has occurred—that is clear from the words in brackets in S 4(1)(d). All that is required is that the allegation relied on should have asserted facts capable of amounting in law to an act of discrimination by an employer within the terms of S 6(2)(b). The facts alleged by the complaint in this case were incapable in law of amounting to an act of discrimination by the Commissioner because they were not done by him, and they cannot (because the alleged perpetrator was not acting in the course of his employment) be treated as done by him for the purposes of S 41. I would accordingly dismiss the sex discrimination appeal."

Notes

(1) What cannot be denied in this case is that the claimant Waters alleged significant acts of reprisal in retaliation and response to her allegation of rape. She reported the incident in the belief that there was some liability or duty on the employer to take action in response; the fact that the employer has no liability (as the actions were outside the employment relationship) should not provide a lacuna for allowing acts of victimisation to be perpetrated. In his judgment Lord Justice Waites appears to place too little emphasis on the experience of the victimised and on the need for deterring victimising behaviour.

(2) In its subsequent review of the discrimination law, the Commission for Racial Equality called for a change in the law to reverse the decision in *Waters*, to allow a victimisation finding where "the initial complaint of discrimination is . . . made in good faith but . . . because of the limitations of the Act, is held not to constitute a complaint in proceeding under the Act".

A further issue that national courts are required to consider is the causal relationship between A's and B's actions. Prior to its amendment by the Employment Equality Act 2004, the legislation in Ireland created the threshold test by which a claim of victimisation required that the dismissal or penalisation was "solely or mainly" because the applicant has done one of a series of "protected acts". This created a presumption that where a person faces dismissal or penalisation and they have done one of the protected acts, then the dismissal or penalisation was "solely or mainly" because they had done the protected act. The 2004 amendment, however, provides that victimisation occurs where the dismissal or other adverse treatment "occurs as a reaction to" the claimant doing one of the protected acts.

Employment Equality (Religion and Belief) Regulations 2003   **5.GB.54.**

Discrimination by way of victimisation

4.—(1) For the purposes of these Regulations, a person ('A') discriminates against another person ('B') if he treats B less favourably than he treats or would treat other persons in the same circumstances, and does so by reason that B has—

    (a) brought proceedings against A or any other person under these Regulations;

(b)   given evidence or information in connection with proceedings brought by any person against A or any other person under these Regulations;

(c)   otherwise done anything under or by reference to these Regulations in relation to A or any other person; or

(d)   alleged that A or any other person has committed an act which (whether or not the allegation so states) would amount to a contravention of these Regulations,

or by reason that A knows that B intends to do any of those things, or suspects that B has done or intends to do any of them.

(2) Paragraph (1) does not apply to treatment of B by reason of any allegation made by him, or evidence or information given by him, if the allegation, evidence or information was false and not made (or, as the case may be, given) in good faith.

German General Equal Treatment Act   **5.DE.55.**
((Allgemeines Gleichbehandlungsgesetz (AGG)), 2006[47]

Article 16
Prohibition of victimisation
(1) The employer must not discriminate against employees resorting to rights under this chapter or refusing to carry out instructions in breach of this chapter. The same applies to persons supporting the employee or testifying as witnesses.
(2) Rejection of tolerance of discriminatory behaviours by concerned employees must not be used as a basis for decisions affecting those employees. Paragraph 1 second sentence shall apply mutatis mutandis.
(3) § 22 [on burden of proof] shall apply mutatis mutandis.

Note
In both Germany and in the UK, victimisation is regarded as a form of discrimination. The German legislation provides that an employer must not discriminate against an employee resorting to their rights in anti-discrimination laws. It does not say what form this discrimination should take; Article 3 of the German Act indicates that it covers direct and indirect discrimination as well as harassment or instructions to discriminate. The provisions on victimisation in the UK appear to be restricted to direct discrimination as they only cover the situation where A treats B less favourably than he would do a person in the same circumstances. This formulation has forced the courts to consider who the appropriate comparator is in a victimisation case. In *Kirby* v. *Manpower Services Commission*,[48] the Employment Appeal Tribunal held that the appropriate comparator was a person who had acted in a way that was similar to the applicant but whose actions did not relate to the relevant equality legislation. In this case, the applicant Mr. Kirby reported the discriminatory actions of his clients to the Community Relations Council, and in doing so he breached his duty of confidentiality towards his clients. The EAT accepted that the appropriate comparator was

---

[47]   AGG, BGBl. Teil I 17.8.2006, s. 1897.
[48]   [1980] ICR 420.

617

someone who had given out similar types of information in breach of their duty of confidence and held that Kirby was treated no less favourably than such a person.

The issue was then considered by the Court of Appeal in the case of *Aziz* v. *Trinity Street Taxis*.[49] The applicant in this case, Mr. Aziz, was a taxi driver who was a member of Trinity Street Taxis (TST), a company that represented the interest of taxi drivers in Coventry. Mr. Aziz believed that he was not being treated fairly by TST. In order to gather evidence, he secretly recorded conversations with other members of TST. The existence of these recordings came to light in a subsequent unsuccessful claim for race discrimination Mr. Aziz brought against TST. As a consequence of making these recordings, Mr. Aziz was expelled from TST. The expulsion was the basis of his claim for victimisation. Slade LJ found that

> "[a] complaint made in reliance on s. 2 necessarily presupposes that the claimant has done a protected act . . . If the doing of such an act itself constitutes part of the relevant circumstances, a claimant would necessarily fail to establish discrimination if the alleged discriminator could show that he treated or would treat all other persons who did the like protected act with equal intolerance. This would be an absurd result."

Slade LJ held that the less favourable treatment suffered by Mr. Aziz could not be regarded as having been

> "by reason that the appellant had [reference omitted] 'otherwise done anything under or by reference to' the RRA . . . on the true construction of s.2(1), if the necessary causal link is to be established, it must be shown that the very fact that the protected act was done by the claimant 'under or by reference to' that legislation, influenced the alleged discriminator in his unfavourable treatment of the claimant".

Despite their criticisms of the EAT approach in *Kirby*, the approach advocated by the Court of Appeal in *Aziz* would not lead to a significantly different outcome. The approach of the Court of Appeal sets a very high test; a claim for victimisation seems to require the claimant to show that the doing of the protected act influenced the less favourable treatment. The Court of Appeal found that the expulsion was not because of his race discrimination claim but due to the breach of trust involved in making the recordings. The House of Lords in two later decisions examined the causal relationship that needs to be established between the protected act and the less favourable treatment.

---

[49] [1988] ICR 534.

House of Lords, 16 July 1999[50]   **5.GB.56.**
Swiggs and Others v. *Nagarajan*

MOTIVATION OF DISCRIMINATOR IRRELEVANT TO A VICTIMISATION CLAIM

Nagarajan

Facts: The claimant worked for a number of years for the respondents. During this time he brought race discrimination claims, some of which were successful and some unsuccessful. In December 1992 he applied for a travel information post. He was interviewed for this post in 1993 but was unsuccessful. He then made a claim of victimisation. At first instance the Employment Tribunal upheld the victimisation claim. In particular, it noted that, in the interview process, the score of one out of ten for the criterion of ability to communicate effectively verbally was "plainly ridiculous", and so the tribunal drew the inference that the interviewers "were consciously or subconsciously influenced by the fact that the applicant had previously brought proceedings against the respondents". The focus of the appeals was on the issue of whether it is sufficient that the respondents' actions were influenced "subconsciously" by the fact that the claimant had previously made discrimination claims against the employers.

Held: The Employment Appeal Tribunal held that "there must be a motive that is consciously connected to the race relations legislation". The Court of Appeal, dismissing the appeal by Mr. Nagarajan, also held that in order for there to be discrimination by way of victimisation the protected act must constitute one of the reasons for the less favourable treatment. That requires conscious motivation. It is not sufficient that the discriminator was consciously aware of the protected acts in treating him less favourably. The mere fact that a person has knowledge of the protected acts cannot in itself justify an inference that he was thereby consciously motivated to treat the claimant less favourably.

Judgment: LORD STEYN (majority opinion): "Section 2(1) in effect provides that in order for there to be unlawful victimisation, the protected act must constitute the 'reason' for the less favourable treatment. The contextual meaning of the words 'by reason that' is at stake. The interpretation upheld by the Court of Appeal requires that under section 2(1) a claimant must prove that the alleged discriminator had a motive which is consciously connected with the race relations legislation. On the other hand, the interpretation put forward by the appellant merely requires that a claimant must prove that the principal or at least an important or significant cause of the less favourable treatment is the fact that the alleged discriminator has done a protected act . . .

As the analysis of the effect of the two contrasting interpretations was explored in oral argument it became clear that the House was not confronted with a simple choice between a subjective and an objective interpretation. It is true that the interpretation upheld by the Court of Appeal requires proof of a subjective state of mind, viz conscious motivation. On the other hand, it would be misleading to describe the appellant's interpretation as objective. This interpretation contemplates that the discriminator had knowledge of the protected act and that such knowledge caused or influenced the discriminator to treat the victimised person less favourably than he would treat other persons. In other words, it postulates that the discriminator's knowledge of the protected act had a subjective impact on his mind. But, unlike the first interpretation, it is a broader construction inasmuch as it does not require the Tribunal to distinguish between conscious and sub-conscious motivation . . . The question is whether there is any policy justification for the interpretation upheld by the Court of Appeal. The purpose of section 2(1) is clear. Its primary purpose is to give to persons victimised on account of their reliance on rights under the Act effective civil remedies, thereby also creating a culture which may deter individuals from penalising those who seek to enforce their rights under the

---

[50] [1999] UKHL 36.

Act. Despite valiant efforts counsel for L.R.T. was unable to point to any plausible policy reason for requiring conscious motivation under section 2(1) but not under section 1(1)(a). On the contrary, counsel for L.R.T. accepted that victimisation is as serious a mischief as direct discrimination. In these circumstances policy considerations point towards similar interpretations.

For my part, it is not the logic of symmetry that requires the two provisions to be given parallel interpretations. It is rather a pragmatic consideration. Quite sensibly in section 1(1)(a) cases the Tribunal simply has to pose the question: Why did the defendant treat the employee less favourably? They do not have to consider whether a defendant was consciously motivated in his unequal treatment of an employee. That is a straightforward way of carrying out its task in a section 1(1)(a) case. Common sense suggests that the Tribunal should also perform its functions in a section 2(1) case by asking the equally straightforward question: Did the defendant treat the employee less favourably because of his knowledge of a protected act? Given that it is unnecessary in section 1(1)(a) cases to distinguish between conscious and sub-conscious motivation, there is no sensible reason for requiring it in section 2(1) cases. Moreover, the threshold requirement laid down by the Court of Appeal in respect of section 2(1) cases would tend to complicate the task of the Tribunal. It would render the protection of the rights guaranteed by section 2(1) less effective."

LORD NICHOLLS OF BIRKENHEAD (concurring): "Direct evidence of a decision to discriminate on racial grounds will seldom be forthcoming. Usually the grounds of the decision will have to be deduced, or inferred, from the surrounding circumstances . . . Racial discrimination is not negatived by the discriminator's motive or intention or reason or purpose (the words are inter-changeable in this context) in treating another person less favourably on racial grounds. In particular, if the reason why the alleged discriminator rejected the complainant's job application was racial, it matters not that his intention may have been benign . . .

I turn to the question of subconscious motivation. All human beings have preconceptions, beliefs, attitudes and prejudices on many subjects. It is part of our make-up. Moreover, we do not always recognise our own prejudices. Many people are unable, or unwilling, to admit even to themselves that actions of theirs may be racially motivated. An employer may genuinely believe that the reason why he rejected an applicant had nothing to do with the applicant's race. After careful and thorough investigation of a claim members of an employment tribunal may decide that the proper inference to be drawn from the evidence is that, whether the employer realised it at the time or not, race was the reason why he acted as he did. It goes without saying that in order to justify such an inference the tribunal must first make findings of primary fact from which the inference may properly be drawn. Conduct of this nature by an employer, when the inference is legitimately drawn, falls squarely within the language of section 1(1)(a). The employer treated the complainant less favourably on racial grounds. Such conduct also falls within the purpose of the legislation. Members of racial groups need protection from conduct driven by unrecognised prejudice as much as from conscious and deliberate discrimination . . .

. . . Thus far I have been considering the position under section 1(1)(a) [section on direct discrimination]. I can see no reason to apply a different approach to section 2 [on victimi-sation]. 'On [racial] grounds' in section 1(1)(a) and 'by reason that' in section 2(1) are interchangeable expressions in this context. The key question under section 2 is the same as under section 1(1)(a): why did the complainant receive less favourable treatment? The consider-ations mentioned above regarding direct discrimination under section 1(1)(a) are correspondingly appropriate under section 2. If the answer to this question is that the discriminator treated the person victimised less favourably by reason of his having done one of the acts ('protected acts') listed in section 2(1), the case falls within the section. It does so, even if the discriminator did not consciously realise that, for example, he was prejudiced because the job applicant had previously brought claims against him under the Act . . .

Decisions are frequently reached for more than one reason. Discrimination may be on racial grounds even though it is not the sole ground for the decision. A variety of phrases, with different shades of meaning, have been used to explain how the legislation applies in such cases: discrimination requires that racial grounds were a cause, the activating cause, a substantial and effective cause, a substantial reason, an important factor. No one phrase is obviously preferable to all others, although in the application of this legislation legalistic phrases, as well as subtle distinctions, are better avoided so far as possible. If racial grounds or protected acts had a significant influence on the outcome, discrimination is made out."

LORD BROWN WILKINSON (dissenting): "The question is whether it is enough for the claimant to show that the interviewers were 'subconsciously' influenced (as the Industrial Tribunal and the majority of your Lordships consider) or whether (as the Employment Appeal Tribunal and Court of Appeal considered) it is necessary to show that the alleged discriminator was conscious of such influence if it is to constitute discrimination against victims within section 2 . . . Approaching the matter first without regard to authority, as a simple matter of construction I would have no doubt that under section 2 the relevant question is whether the reason why the discriminator treats the person victimised less favourably is that the latter has done one of those things specified in paragraphs (a)-(d) ('protected acts'). This is a wholly subjective question directed specifically to the mental state of the alleged discriminator: why did he treat the claimant less favourably? Looking at the language of section 2(1) the subject of the sentence is the alleged discriminator. It is he who must treat the person victimised less favourably. It is he who must treat the victim less favourably 'by reason that' the victim has done protected acts. There is no authority on the construction of section 2(1) which leads to a contrary conclusion and I would therefore give the section its obvious meaning, viz., it must be shown that the conscious reason why the defendant has selectively imposed discriminatory adverse treatment on the applicant is that he wishes, knowingly, to punish the claimant as a victim. I do not understand how one can victimise someone 'subconsciously' . . . the question is essentially a subjective one: why did the alleged discriminator act as he did . . . My Lords it is this very clarity of the statutory words which require the court to determine the reason why the alleged discriminator treated the claimant less favourably that makes it difficult to understand why in some of the authorities and in your Lordships' judgments the question is often posed, not subjectively, but objectively: 'was a substantial cause of less favourable treatment the race or sex of the claimant or (for section 2 cases) the fact that he had done a protected act?' . . . If it be right that the statutory test requires the court to consider, subjectively, what was the reason or one of the reasons which led the defendant to treat the claimant less favourably, it seems to me that any factor relied upon has to be consciously present in the defendant's mind. A matter which is not consciously taken into account by the defendant cannot in my judgment be a ground on which he acted (within section 1(1)) or one of his reasons for acting (within section 2(1)) . . . I find it regrettable that L.R.T. and the members of the interviewing committee should be found to have been guilty of victimisation, a most serious charge, if the relevance (if any) of the applicant's earlier proceedings was not present to their conscious minds when they took the decision. The Race and Sex Discrimination Acts are of great social importance. Their success depends to a substantial extent on their acceptance by the community. To introduce something akin to strict liability into the Acts which will lead to individuals being stamped as racially discriminatory or victimisers where these matters were not consciously in their minds when they acted as they did is unlikely to recommend the legislation to the public as being fair and proper protection for the minorities that they are seeking to protect."

Notes

(1) The approach of the Court of Appeal both in *Nagarajan* and in *Trinity Street Taxis* suggested that there needed to be some conscious motivation in the mind of the alleged discriminator which caused him to treat the claimant less favourably than others. By contrast, Lord Steyn's approach in *Nagarajan* appears to suggest that motivation is irrelevant to a victimisation claim. In his view, the approach taken to victimisation should mirror the approach to direct discrimination, in which there is no need to draw a distinction between conscious and unconscious motivation. Lord Nicholls was clear that motive, intention and reason or purpose were "interchangeable" terms in this context. Furthermore, he argued that motivation was irrelevant to the question of whether a person had been treated favourably on racial grounds. He was also sceptical of the possibility of distinguishing between conscious and unconscious motivation, noting that "people are unable, or unwilling, to admit even to themselves that actions of theirs may be racially motivated". He recognised that there can be a plurality of reasons for action, and held that as long as "protected acts had a significant influence on the outcome, discrimination is made out". This is particularly important as in the earlier decisions in *Kirby* and *Trinity Street Taxis* liability appeared to be evaded because there was another plausible reason for the actions of the employers.

(2) However, the clarity of this approach has been muddied by the House of Lords decision in *Chief Constable of West Yorkshire* v. *Khan*.[51] In that case the claimant, Sergeant Khan, was involved in a race discrimination claim against his employer, the respondent. While the race discrimination claim was pending he applied for a post with another police force and requested a reference from his employer. The respondent's refusal to provide a reference was the basis of a victimisation claim. The employer argued that he could not provide a reference because any further comment on the claimant would prejudice the race discrimination claim before the tribunal. The tribunal at first instance accepted the victimisation claim. The House of Lords accepted that Sergeant Khan had been treated less favourably than a person who had not made a discrimination claim. However, the reason for this less favourable treatment was in their view not because he had done one of the protected acts, namely brought proceedings against his employer, rather the employer was acting to protect his position in relation to the proceedings. Lord Nicholls in this case found that

> "employers, acting honestly and reasonably, ought to be able to take steps to preserve their position in pending discrimination proceedings without laying themselves open to a charge of victimisation. This accords with the spirit and purpose of the Act. Moreover, the statute accommodates this approach without straining the language. An employer who conducts himself in this way is not doing so because of the fact that the claimant has brought discrimination proceedings. He is doing so because currently and temporarily he needs to take steps to preserve his position in the outstanding proceedings."

---

[51] [2001] ICR 1065.

Lord Nicholls drew a distinction between actions that were the consequence of the *existence* of legal proceedings and those that were a consequence of the claimant's conduct in *bringing* the proceedings. Lord Scott argued that the finding of victimisation required the tribunal to identify the "real reason, the core reason, the *causa causans*, the motive, for the treatment complained of".

(3) Much of the argument in *Nagarajan* was based on the premise that the interpretation of section 1 of the RRA, dealing with direct discrimination, was the same as the interpretation of section 2, the provision on victimisation. However, Lord Hoffman in *Khan* suggested that the "but for" test applied to determine causation in direct discrimination cases was distinct from the test in victimisation. While there were parallels between the two sections, the causal questions that they raised were not identical:

> "one can not simply say that Mr. Khan would not have been treated less favourably if he had not brought proceedings. It does not follow that his bringing proceedings was a reason (conscious or unconscious) why he was treated less favourably . . . once proceedings have been commenced, a new relationship is created between the parties. They are not only employer and employee but also adversaries in litigation. The existence of that adversarial relationship may reasonably cause the employer to behave in a way which treats the employee less favourably than someone who had not commenced such proceedings. But the treatment need not be, consciously or unconsciously, a response to the commencement of proceedings. It may simply be a reasonable response to the need to protect the employer's interest as a party to the litigation."

The difficulties that the House of Lords has found itself in arise in part from the legislative approach to addressing victimisation as a form of discrimination. As a consequence of defining victimisation in this way, the legislation adopted the definition of direct discrimination according to which there could be no justification for any less favourable treatment based on race. In respect of direct discrimination, however, the absolute nature of this provision is balanced by the specific exemptions, situations where direct discrimination is permitted. In transposing this approach into the arena of victimisation, no exceptions were created. The pressure placed on the interpretation of section 2 of the RRA would have been eased if the legislation had identified exemptions.

(4) In principle, an employee should receive protection from victimisation, however much time has lapsed since the original complaint was made. The issue of the temporal scope of victimisation provisions therefore relate closely to the creation, by legislation, of a presumption that any adverse treatment of the person concerned is related to their involvement in the discrimination claim. In such a situation it is for the employer to show that the adverse action taken against the employee is unrelated to this discrimination claim. Often the presumption that action taken against an employee was because of his or her involvement in a discrimination claim is for a limited period of time. For example, in Belgium, the Flemish Decree provides that in the 12 months after a complaint of discrimination has been filed, or when a legal suit has been introduced during the three months after the final decision has been adopted, there is a presumption that any dismissal or unilateral changes in the terms

and conditions of employment are a form of victimisation of the claimant. It is for the employer during this period to show that the dismissal or changes in the terms and conditions of employment are unrelated to the discrimination claim.

5.2.3. COMPARATIVE OVERVIEW

Protection from victimisation remains a complex and important area. The provisions of European and national legislation have changed over time to extend the scope and nature of the protection offered. From initial protection limited to the protection of employers from dismissal, European discrimination law today covers those providing advice, information and representation, as well as witnesses, and, in the case of Ireland, even those who are used as comparators in a discrimination claim. Protection initially limited to dismissal now extends in many states to cover any adverse treatment. The scope of protection that is offered by the ECJ has also been extended beyond the employment relationship. This is particularly important for employees in such Member States where no mutual obligations exist between employer and employee after the employment relationship has ended. In many Members States, however, employment law generates mutual duties beyond its duration, including the duty of the employer to provide a reference to the employee and to refrain from unfairly commenting on the employee's conduct. Nevertheless, even these employees will now be able to rely on discrimination law as additional protection.

5.3. COMPARATIVE ANALYSIS

5.3.1. COMMONALITIES BETWEEN INSTRUCTION AND VICTIMISATION

The two areas examined in this chapter, instructions to discriminate and victimisation, are connected because of their attempts to address the actions that surround the actual incident of discrimination. The prohibition of instructions to discriminate seeks to prevent third parties from causing discrimination to take place, while the prohibition of victimisation seeks to protect those who are involved in claims seeking redress for discrimination.

The obligations to tranpose the EU Directives have provided the impetus in several instances for national legislation to ensure protection in both these areas. However, in relation to both the prohibition of instructions to discriminate and victimisation, the Directives have left crucial issues unresolved. This has ensured that across different EU Member States there is a variable geometry of protection, oscillating between the framework of discrimination law and more general principles of law.

In both fields of law covered in this chapter, power imbalances between those suffering discrimination and those engaging in discrimination may arise in specific ways, over and above the social reality of discrimination in general. The question whether these power imbalances are best adressed within or without the non-discrimination framework and how they should be addressed effectively provides a further connecting factor between these two fields.

5.3.2. MEMBER STATES' RESPONSES TOWARDS UNSOLVED ISSUES

While the issues left unresolved by the directives differ, there are some commonalities in Member States' responses. In both fields, some Member States have placed the regulation more within the framework of non-discrimination law, while others have chosen a more general approach. Both ways have advantages and disadvantages.

As regards instructions to discriminate, the Directives state only that instructions to discriminate are deemed to be discrimination. In several jurisdictions, implementing legislation repeats this statement. How an instruction to discriminate will fit into the Directives framework on discrimination is less clear both under the Directives and under the legislation in these national jurisdictions.

Some insight into the possible approaches is gained by consideration of the UK case-law, where the courts have considered how to fit instructions to discriminate within the framework of direct and indirect discrimination. The case of *B.L. Cars* (above **5.GB.20.**) shows that those who are the objects of an instruction to discriminate can cite the instructions as an example of less favourable treatment in a claim for direct discrimination. Where a person is the subject of an instruction to discriminate (i.e. given a discriminatory instruction to follow), the situation may be more complex, as the person may be in a relationship where they are normally expected to follow the instructions they receive from the person issuing the instructions to discriminate. The case of *Showboat Entertainment* (above **5.GB.21.**) shows that a person who is the subject of an instruction and who faces adverse treatment because of a failure to follow instructions to discriminate against another on a prohibited ground can claim that they face direct discrimination.

The consideration of a similar employment situation by the German Labour Court of Wuppertal, however, led to a very different result. The court in the *Cosmetics Company and Turkish Employee's* case (above **5.DE.22.**) exposed the tensions, central to cases involving instructions to discriminate, between the freedom of an employer to organise their business in a manner of their choosing and the wider social interest in preventing discrimination. In this instance, the court appeared to place the freedom of the employer to issue discriminatory instructions and to have those instructions followed by his employees above the right of those receiving those instructions to disobey them without adverse consequences. The case is a reminder that liability must be considered in the context in which those power relations operate.

By contrast, in the case of prohibiting victimisation the directives do not explicitly say that victimisation is deemed to be discrimination. Again, this elicits different responses by Member States.

Although no link with the concept of discrimination is required, German legislation adds a specific prohibition of discriminating against the victim and other persons claiming rights under non-discrimination law. In contrast, UK case-law has interpreted the legislation as only prohibiting victimisation on grounds of direct discrimination. The resulting difficulties in UK law seem to indicate that the Directives were right to address victimisation as prohibited in general rather than to treat it as a form of discrimination. The case-law from the UK, where legislation treats victimisations as a form of discrimination, indicates the difficulties that arise from this approach.

However, the Directive's requirement to treat instructions to discriminate as a form of discrimination may be one that needs to be reconsidered. The provisions of the Directive leave too many questions for Member States and the ECJ to answer. On the one hand, treating instructions to discriminate as a form of discrimination ensures that all the special safeguards in discrimination law, such as the burden of proof, apply automatically. On the other hand, identifying instructions to discriminate as an independent tort that is not dependent on being a form of discrimination allows the context in which a third party acts to cause discrimination to be taken into account.

5.3.3.   POWER RELATIONS CAUSED BY DISCRIMINATION AND INSTRUCTIONS TO DISCRIMINATE

The issue of the power imbalance between someone suffering discrimination and someone engaging in discrimination has been recognised as a further connecting field.

In relation to victimisation, this seems to be straightforward: those having been victims of discrimination are clearly in a disadvantaged situation already and thus more prone to find themselves in a powerless situation. The developments of European law, pushing further the scope of legislative protection, recognise the challenges and difficulties for those bringing a claim of discrimination. They seek to redress the imbalance of power between the employer and employee. However, the gap between the number of claims of victimisation compared to the extent to which victimisations occurs, as suggested by some of the research studies considered here, may be one that cannot be bridged by further or better legislation that continues to rely on individuals bringing cases of discrimination. Given the already disadvantaged situation of those who face discrimination, it is important to empower agents and agencies involved in providing protection from discrimination. Thus, it remains important to extend the scope of application accorded to the prohibition to discriminate. If individual agents who act in favour of those actually discriminated against, e.g. works council members, union officials or sympathetic colleagues, remain unprotected by victimisation provisions, the law will remain less effective. Thus, developments in legal orders such as Ireland are encouraging.

The context of power relations are also important when considering the wide variety of terms that are used to describe the actions of persons who do not themselves discriminate but "instruct" or in some other way affect the behaviour of a person who is discriminating. As well as broadening the scope of liability, these different concepts and terms seek to set out with more care where the balance of responsibility lies between the persons issuing an "instruction" and the person receiving it. The UK legislation, for example, offers a distinction between pressure to discriminate and instructions to discriminate. Liability for an instruction to discriminate only occurs where there is a relationship of authority between the person giving the instructions and the person receiving the instructions, the paradigm for this being an employer–employee relationship.

The Hungarian legislation in this area recognises this and as a general rule requires an employee to follow the instructions of their employer. However, where the instructions involve a violation of the law, including equality law, then the employee is not required to follow instructions. The Hungarian law varies this responsibility depending on the nature of the employment. In particular, civil servants and members of the armed forces are required to follow instructions unless the instructions constitute a criminal act or endanger the life and the health and safety of others.

In the absence of a superior–subordinate relationship, the person merely receiving an instruction to discriminate is expected to assume responsibility for the decision whether to follow such an instruction or not. However, such statements may also amount to pressure to discriminate. Here the UK legislation on sex discrimination suggests an expectation that a person takes responsibility for resisting such pressure, and will only attach liability to the person applying the pressure where they do so by an offer of a benefit or threat of a detriment. The allocation of responsibility between the different parties also underpins the UK case concerning liability for "intentionally aiding" unlawful discrimination. In the *Roma/Gypsy Wedding Reception Case* (above **5.GB.38.**) there is no liability where the party (to whom the information which is alleged to have aided discrimination is given) has yet to decide on a course of action and several options remain open to that person, including measures that do not involve unlawful discrimination.

It seems that the issue of power imbalance indirectly rather than directly connected to discrimination needs to be theorised further in order to make full use of the potential of discrimination law.

CHAPTER SIX
REASONABLE ACCOMMODATION

Prof. Lisa Waddington

6.1. INTRODUCTION

Non-discrimination law commonly makes a distinction between direct and indirect discrimination. In addition, some jurisdictions nowadays recognise that the failure to provide a reasonable accommodation also constitutes discrimination, unless implementing this accommodation would impose an undue hardship or disproportionate burden. In the context of disability, this trend has now received global recognition through the United Nations Convention on the Rights of Persons with Disabilities, which defines discrimination as including a failure to make a "reasonable accommodation".[1] Furthermore, in the European context, the issue of reasonable accommodation is topical, given that the Employment Equality Directive expressly requires employers to make a reasonable accommodation for persons with disabilities.

Council Directive 2000/78/EC of 27 November 2000 establishing   6.EC.1.
a general framework for equal treatment in employment and occupation[2]

Article 5
Reasonable accommodation for disabled persons
In order to guarantee compliance with the principle of equal treatment in relation to persons with disabilities, reasonable accommodation shall be provided. This means that employers shall take appropriate measures, where needed in a particular case, to enable a person with a disability to have access to, participate in, or advance in employment, or to undergo training, unless such measures would impose a disproportionate burden on the employer. This burden shall not be disproportionate when it is sufficiently remedied by measures existing within the framework of the disability policy of the Member State concerned.

Prior to the adoption of the Directive, only three Member States (the UK,[3] Ireland[4] and Sweden[5]) expressly recognised an obligation to provide reasonable

---

[1] The Convention was adopted by the UN General Assembly on 13 December 2006. Art. 2 of the Convention provides, inter alia: "'Discrimination on the basis of disability' means any distinction, exclusion or restriction on the basis of disability which has the purpose or effect of impairing or nullifying the recognition, enjoyment or exercise, on an equal basis with others, of all human rights and fundamental freedoms in the political, economic, social, cultural, civil or any other field. It includes all forms of discrimination, including denial of reasonable accommodation."

[2] [2000] OJ L303/16.

[3] Disability Discrimination Act 1995, s. 3A(2).

[4] Employment Equality Act 1998, s. 16 and Equal Status Act 2000, s. 4.

[5] Disability Discrimination Act 1999, s. 6.

accommodations to meet the needs of individuals with disabilities. Today, the vast majority of Member States[6] provide for such an obligation. However, given the relative novelty of the requirement, case-law in many European jurisdictions is limited or non-existent.[7] In addition, the European Court of Justice has thus far only briefly referred to the obligation,[8] and reasonable accommodation is not expressly provided for in the European Convention of Human Rights[9] or the European Social Charter.[10] For that reason, frequent reference will be made to (recently adopted) national legislation in this chapter, as well as case-law from the UK and Ireland, where the obligation already had statutory recognition prior to the adoption of the Directive. Material from two of the other key jurisdictions covered in this casebook, namely Germany and, in particular, France, is limited, and for this reason these jurisdictions receive less attention in this chapter than is the case elsewhere in this book.

Whilst the obligation to provide a reasonable accommodation is a relatively new phenomenon in much of Europe, non-European jurisdictions, such as the US and Canada, have long-standing statutory provisions requiring that reasonable accommodations be made for individuals with disabilities and, in some cases, individuals with other characteristics. Indeed, the concept was first applied in the context of religious discrimination under US law.[11] However, the most well known of these statutes is the Americans with Disabilities Act 1990.[12] Indeed, it is probably no exaggeration to say that this statute brought the issue of reasonable accommodations for individuals with

---

[6] At the time of writing, not all Member States had fully transposed the Directive by creating a legal duty to provide reasonable accommodation for disabled individuals with regard to employment.

[7] Given that the requirement to make reasonable accommodations in favour of disabled people was already recognised in UK and Irish law prior to the adoption of the Directive, case-law is quite extensive in these jurisdictions (although in the third Member State which recognised such a requirement, Sweden, case-law is limited). Of the Member States that recognised the requirement only after the adoption of the Directive, the Netherlands seems to be developing case-law most rapidly. Incidental cases are being reported in some other Member States. This is reflected in the extracts used in this chapter.

[8] Case C–13/05 *Sonia Chacón Navas* v. *Eurest Colectividades*, see below **6.EC.46.**

[9] But see O. De Schutter, "Reasonable Accommodations and Positive Obligations in the European Convention of Human Rights" in A. Lawson and C. Gooding (eds.), *Disability Rights in Europe. From Theory to Practice* (Oxford, Hart, 2005) 35–63.

[10] However, it has been argued that the European Committee of Social Rights now interprets Art. 15 of the (revised) Social Charter in combination with Art. E to "require reasonable accommodation". Gerard Quinn argues that the Committee views disability non-discrimination legislation as essential to comply with Art. 15(2) of the 1961 Charter, and that the Committee had in mind the obligation to provide for reasonable accommodations when it concluded against Denmark in 2003 on the grounds that it did not have disability employment non-discrimination legislation in place. Quinn also notes that the Committee adopted this approach with regard to Art. 15 (on disability) and Art. E (on non-discrimination) of the revised Charter in its Conclusion's with respect to France in 2003. Indeed, the Committee asked France to provide further information on how the "concept of reasonable accommodation is incorporated in legislation" in the context of employment non-discrimination legislation. See G. Quinn, "The European Social Charter and EU Anti-Discrimination Law in the Field of Disability: Two Gravitational Fields with one Common Purpose" in G. de Búrca and B. de Witte (eds.), *Social Rights in Europe* (Oxford, Oxford University Press, 2005) 279–304.

[11] The Civil Rights Act of 1964 that first prohibited religious discrimination in employment was amended in 1972 to include a duty on the employer to accommodate the religious practices of employees, as long as to do so did not cause undue hardship to the employer.

[12] This Act was itself partially modelled on the earlier Rehabilitation Act of 1973.

disabilities to the attention of policy-makers and disability activists on a global scale, including those within the EU. This chapter therefore will also draw on US case-law in discussing some of the issues raised by the reasonable accommodation requirement.

It is undoubtedly true that Article 5 of the Employment Equality Directive has been the dominant influence on European legislators with regard to the creation of an obligation to provide reasonable accommodations, and, as a result, much of the material covered in this chapter relates to employment accommodations for people with disabilities. However, there is also a patchwork of material covering non-employment-related accommodations for individuals with disabilities, and accommodations provided on the grounds of religion. Every effort has been made to include such material in the chapter, although it has not proved possible to follow the systematic approach adopted in the case of employment-related disability accommo-dations because of a lack of relevant material. Finally, one can envisage that the issue of accommodation also arises for individuals and groups other than those covered in this chapter—such as pregnant women and recent immigrants. In practice, such issues may be dealt with through other tools—such as legislation conferring specific rights on pregnant women or via the more general route of indirect discrimination. Since research revealed no evidence of explicit reasonable accommodation provisions for such individuals, they were not covered in this chapter.

6.1.1.   THE DUTY TO MAKE A REASONABLE ACCOMMODATION—THEORETICAL BACKGROUND[13]

The obligation to make a reasonable accommodation is based on the recognition that, on occasions, the interaction between an individual's inherent characteristics, such as impairment, sex, religion or belief, and the physical or social environment can result in the inability to perform a particular function or job in the conventional manner.[14] The characteristic is therefore relevant in that it can lead to an individual being faced with a barrier that prevents him or her from benefiting from an employment opportunity that is open to others who do not share that characteristic. The resulting disadvantage is exclusion from the job market, or a restricted set of employment opportunities.

However, non-discrimination law is traditionally underpinned by the idea that the protected characteristic, such as race or gender, is rarely relevant to the employment decision and only in exceptional circumstances, such as the bona fide occupational qualification situation, does it allow for unequal treatment. The protected

---

[13] Sections of this paragraph and the next draw on L. Waddington and A. Hendriks, "The Expanding Concept of Employment Discrimination in Europe: From Direct and Indirect Discrimination to Reasonable Accommodation Discrimination" (2002) 18 *IJCLLIR* 403–27.

[14] This statement only relates to an employment-related obligation. However, an obligation to provide reasonable accommodation which is imposed on, for example, providers of goods and services can be justified in the same way.

characteristic should therefore be ignored—the race or gender of a job applicant should play no part, positive or negative, in the decision whether to award the individual the job or not. This is in fact the general position of EC Equality Law. However, as noted above, ignoring, by failing to accommodate, the characteristic can result in denying an individual equal employment opportunities. In this respect, in the specific case of disability, Fredman has argued:

"Characterising disability as an irrelevant characteristic removes the underlying justification for detrimental treatment, but insisting on similar treatment simply reinforces a particular norm and perpetuates disadvantage".[15]

A reasonable accommodation requirement in the employment context therefore prohibits an employer from denying an individual with a disability or other relevant characteristic an employment opportunity by failing to take account of the characteristic, when taking account of it—in terms of changing tasks or the physical environment of the workplace—would enable the individual to do the work.[16] Employers are required to recognise the characteristic and to consider what changes they could make to the work environment to allow an individual to carry out the work to the required standard. Again, in the case of disability,

"Instead of requiring disabled people to conform to existing norms, the aim is to develop a concept of equality which requires adaptation and change".[17]

6.1.2. REASONABLE ACCOMMODATION AND THE NON-DISCRIMINATION REQUIREMENT

As noted above, according to the Directive, the obligation to make a reasonable accommodation is necessary "in order to guarantee compliance with the principle of equal treatment".[18] In the early proposals for the Directive the link between the reasonable accommodation requirement and the non-discrimination norm was even more direct, as the obligation to provide a reasonable accommodation was initially included in Article 2 of the Directive,[19] which contains the other non-discrimination provisions. At a subsequent point, in order not to overload Article 2 with ground specific provisions, the reasonable accommodation was moved to a separate Article, but the reference to "the principle of equal treatment" was retained in order to

[15] S. Fredman, "Disability Equality, A Challenge to the Existing Anti-Discrimination Paradigm?" in Lawson and Gooding, above n. 9, 199–203.
[16] P.S. Karlan and G. Rutherglen, "Disabilities, Discrimination and Reasonable Accommodation" (1996) 46 *Duke LJ* 9.
[17] Fredman, above n. 15, 203.
[18] Council Directive 2000/78/EC of 27 November 2000 establishing a general framework for equal treatment in employment and occupation [2000] OJ L303/16, Art. 5.
[19] The original proposal for Art. 2(4) read: "In order to guarantee compliance with the principle of equal treatment for persons with disability, reasonable accommodation shall be provided, where needed, to enable such persons to have access to, participate in, or advance in employment, unless this requirement creates as undue hardship." See Council of the European Union, Working Party on Social Questions, 11 January 2000, Brussels (31 January 2000) 5231/00.

maintain the organic link between the new Article 5 and Article 2.[20] A similar sentiment can be found in General Comment No. 5 (1994), Persons with disabilities, of the UN Committee on Economic, Social and Cultural Rights.[21] According to this authoritative interpretation of the International Covenant on Economic, Social and Cultural Rights, the term "disability based discrimination" includes any distinction, exclusion or preference, or denial of reasonable accommodation based on disability which has the effect of nullifying or impairing the recognition, enjoyment or exercise of economic, social or cultural rights.[22] Furthermore, as noted above, the UN Convention on the Rights of Persons with Disabilities now defines discrimination as including a failure to make a "reasonable accommodation" in Article 2.

Whilst, unlike the UN instruments referred to above, Article 5 of the Employment Equality Directive does not specifically define an unjustified failure to make a reasonable accommodation as a form of discrimination, there are numerous instances of national non-discrimination law, in both Europe and elsewhere, which do classify such a failure as a form of discrimination.[23] Moreover, in some jurisdictions this obligation is not confined to people with disabilities, but also applies to members of (minority) religions or even to all individuals covered by broadly worded non-discrimination provisions.

6.1.3.   GOALS OF THIS CHAPTER

This chapter will examine and comment on the reasonable accommodation requirement as it has been recognised in European and, where this will add to an understanding of the situation in Europe, non-European jurisdictions. It should be noted that, in spite of the Employment Equality Directive providing the inspiration for much of the relevant legislation, terminology is not uniform across Europe with regard to this obligation. In some instances the different terminology does not reflect a different approach in the application of the requirement to provide a reasonable accommodation, although in some instances it does. These differences, whether they be merely in phrasing, or also substantive, will be noted. In addition, some Member States provide for a broader duty to accommodate than that found in European law—either providing that the duty is owed to a broader group of people, or that it extends beyond the area of employment with regard to people with disabilities.

The chapter therefore seeks to answer the following general questions:

(1)   What is a "reasonable accommodation"? (section 6.2)
(2)   Who is entitled to claim a "reasonable accommodation", and under what conditions? (section 6.3)

---

[20]   Which also refers to the "principle of equal treatment".
[21]   UN Doc. E/C.12/1994/13.
[22]   Para. 15.
[23]   See section 6.5 of this chapter for further discussion of this point.

(3) On what grounds may an employer or other covered party justifiably refuse to make a "reasonable accommodation"? (section 6.4)

(4) What is the relationship between the requirement to make a "reasonable accommodation" and (other) forms of discrimination, and between "reasonable accommodation" and positive action? (sections 6.5 and 6.6)

In many cases these questions are difficult to answer on the basis of the legislative provisions in force in the Member States. Article 5 of the Employment Equality Directive has frequently been transposed simply by incorporating the relevant language version of the Article in the national legislation. Given the brevity of the Article, and the scarcity of case-law from the European Court of Justice related to it, a wide-ranging and authoritative interpretation of the provision does not yet exist. However, a number of Member States have opted for a more "thoughtful" transposition, whilst others had pre-existing provisions concerning reasonable accommodation, and this legislation, as well case-law from those jurisdictions (European and non-European) where the matter has been litigated, will provide the basis for the discussion which follows.

6.2. THE MEANING OF THE TERM "REASONABLE ACCOMMODATION"

This section considers the meaning of the term "reasonable accommodation", as well as examining alternative terms that convey the equivalent meaning or otherwise replace one or other of the two terms in legislation. Whilst the concept of an "accommodation" is generally not controversial, and many statutes and other documents provide illustrative lists of the kinds of measures that are regarded as "accommodations", the meaning of the term "reasonable" is less clear. A number of meanings have been attributed to this term in anti-discrimination legislation and case-law, and this is well illustrated by US case-law in particular. Perhaps in order to reduce the uncertainty that seems to attach itself to the use of the term "reasonable" in this context, some European legislators have chosen to use alternative terminology when transposing Article 5 of the Directive.

This section will address first the term "reasonable". Secondly, the more straightforward concept of "accommodation" will be considered. The choice has been made to address the topics in this order given that a detailed understanding of the notion of an accommodation is not required in order to appreciate the different meanings attributed to the word reasonable in various jurisdictions. Indeed, as will be seen below, the reasonableness of any accommodation is sometimes judged according to the cost or disruption resulting from the change, rather than from any quality attached to the accommodation as such. Much of the material focuses on measures which have been adopted to transpose Article 5 of the Employment Directive; however, extracts pre-dating the Directive and extracts related to accommodation with regard to religious practices are also covered.

6.2.1.   THE MEANING OF THE TERM "REASONABLE"

The term "reasonable", or any alternative term selected by legislators which is used in conjunction with the obligation to make an accommodation, serves the role of a modifier to the requirement to provide an "accommodation". One can identify two ways in which the term can modify the requirement to make an accommodation: first, the term "reasonable" implies that an employer is only obliged to take action which does not result in excessive difficulties or problems; alternatively, or in addition, the term "reasonable", or another selected adjective, relates to the quality of the accommodation itself and means, for example, that the accommodation must be "effective". Therefore, in the first instance, the term modifies the requirement to make the accommodation that is imposed on the employer, whilst in the second, the term is a modifier with regard to the actual accommodation. In many instances the term is (arguably confusingly) used to convey both meanings.

     This section will begin by examining material that illustrates the proposition that a "reasonable" accommodation is one that does not result in "excessive" difficulties being experienced by the employer, and whereby the term modifies the obligation imposed on the employer. Following this, attention will be paid to an alternative interpretation, whereby a "reasonable" accommodation is one that is effective in allowing an individual with a disability (or other covered individual) to carry out a particular set of (employment-related) tasks, i.e. the term becomes a modifier for the accommodation as such. On occasions, different terminology is used to convey this second meaning. Lastly, attention will be paid to those jurisdictions where the term is used to convey both the requirement that the accommodation must not result in excessive difficulties, or a disproportionate burden, for the employer, and must be "effective".

6.2.1.A.   AN ACCOMMODATION THAT DOES NOT RESULT IN EXCESSIVE
             DIFFICULTIES FOR THE EMPLOYER

In this section extracts will be examined which reveal how the term "reasonable" can be used to limit the obligation imposed on employers or other covered parties, by only requiring them to make accommodations which do not result in excessive costs or inconvenience.

Finnish Non-Discrimination Act 21/2004[24]   **6.FI.2.**

Section 5—Improving the access to employment and training of persons with disabilities
     In order to foster equality . . ., a person commissioning work or arranging training shall where necessary take any reasonable steps to help a person with disabilities to gain access to

----

[24] Unofficial translation by the Finnish Ministry of Labour.

work or training, to cope at work and to advance in their career. In assessing what constitutes reasonable, particular attention shall be devoted to the costs of the steps, the financial position of the person commissioning work or arranging training, and the possibility of support from public funds or elsewhere towards the costs involved.

Extracts from the Preparatory Works to the Finnish   **6.FI.3.**
Non-Discrimination Act, HE 44/2003 [Government proposal 44/2003]
concerning Section 5

"In order to guarantee compliance with the principle of equal treatment . . ., a person commissioning work or arranging training would, where necessary, have to take such steps required to enable a person with disabilities to gain access to work or training as are not considered unreasonable for the employer or arranger of training . . .

The provision would not require implementing unreasonable arrangements. When assessing the reasonableness of the arrangements from the point of view of the employer, the financial costs incurred by the arrangements, the size of the organisation or business and its financial position and the availability of public funding or other support, e.g. for re-arranging working conditions, for example, should be taken into account. Furthermore, arrangements could be deemed unreasonable in situations in which such arrangements would excessively change the activities of the workplace and at the same time could endanger compliance with workplace safety legislation, for example."

Notes

(1) The Finnish Non-Discrimination Act lists the following factors which will determine whether any accommodation (or "step") is reasonable: the cost of the accommodation; the financial position of the employer or trainer; and the possibility to obtain a subsidy. In addition, the Preparatory Works refer to excessive changes to the activities of the workplace combined with compliance with workplace safety legislation as relevant factors.

(2) Unusually, Finnish legislation does not expressly refer to the notion of "disproportionate burden", but relies solely on the notion of "reasonableness". Therefore, employers are required to take "steps" to enable an individual with a disability to pursue employment-related activities unless this would be unreasonable, as defined in the statute and preparatory works. The reasonableness test is therefore a substitute for the disproportionate burden defence that is found in most other jurisdictions.

(3) The statute provides very limited information on the kinds of "steps" which can be required of the employer, although it does specify the goals which such steps should achieve.

Irish Equal Status Act 2000   **6.IE.4.**

4. (1) For the purposes of this Act discrimination includes a refusal or failure by the provider of a service to do all that is reasonable to accommodate the needs of a person with a disability

by providing special treatment or facilities, if without such special treatment or facilities it would be impossible or unduly difficult for the person to avail himself or herself of the service.

(2) A refusal or failure to provide the special treatment or facilities to which subsection (1) refers shall not be deemed reasonable unless such provision would give rise to a cost, other than a nominal cost, to the provider of the service in question.

Irish Employment Equality Act 1998   **6.IE.5.**

Section 16, Nature and extent of employer's obligations in certain cases
(3) (a) For the purposes of this Act, a person who has a disability shall not be regarded as other than fully competent to undertake, and fully capable of undertaking, any duties if, with the assistance of special treatment or facilities, such person would be fully competent to undertake, and be fully capable of undertaking, those duties.

(b) An employer shall do all that is reasonable to accommodate the needs of a person who has a disability by providing special treatment or facilities to which paragraph (a) relates.

(c) A refusal or failure to provide for special treatment or facilities to which paragraph (a) relates shall not be deemed reasonable unless such provision would give rise to a cost, other than a nominal cost, to the employer.

Notes
(1) The only factor which is mentioned as justifying a finding that an accommodation is not reasonable is cost. Therefore, an accommodation will not be reasonable if it leads to a cost for the service provider or employer. However, if the cost is only "nominal" then it will still be reasonable to expect the covered party to make the accommodation.

(2) The ceiling of "nominal cost" was imposed by a Supreme Court judgment which effectively decided that requiring employers to make a "reasonable accommodation" amounted to an unjustified "taking" of an employer's property.[25]

(3) The Employment Equality Act 1998 has now been amended by the Equality Act 2004 that was adopted to bring Irish non-discrimination legislation into line with the two Equality Directives. As a consequence, there have been important changes to the requirement to make a reasonable accommodation with regard to individuals with disabilities in the area of employment,[26] and the provision quoted directly above is no longer in force. In contrast, the Equal Status Act 2000 addresses discrimination with regard to access to goods and services, and has been unaffected by the adoption of the Employment Equality Directive.

(4) The "reasonableness" requirement in both statutes was/is clearly used as a modifier to the obligation on the covered party to make an accommodation, and related to what can be expected of the covered party.

[25] See section 6.4.2.B for an extract from the relevant case and further commentary.
[26] See section 6.2.1.B.

In spite of the significant limitation on the requirement to make a reasonable accommodation found in paragraph (3) of section 16 of (Irish) Employment Equality Act, 1998 (that an employer is not required to make an accommodation if it would give rise to more than a nominal cost), individuals with disabilities were able to establish that covered parties had breached the provision by failing to "do all that is reasonable" to accommodate their needs. The following case illustrates this point.

Labour Court, 23 January 2002   **6.IE.6.**
A Company (represented by the Irish Business and Employers' Confederation) v.
A Worker (represented by Irish Municipal, Public and Civil Trade Union)

FAILURE TO DO ALL THAT IS REASONABLE TO ACCOMMODATE AN
EMPLOYEE—FAILURE TO REASSIGN TASKS AND PROVIDE PARKING SPACE

A Company v. A Worker

Facts: The complainant, who had cerebral palsy, worked as a secretary for the defendant organisation. She was assigned the job of sorting internal mail on a temporary basis, but found this task difficult to carry out as a result of her disability. She requested, on a number of occasions, that this task be reassigned to another employee. The task was not reassigned for some time, and the complaints led to tensions between the complainant and her colleagues (e.g. she was excluded from the staff Christmas party) and a poor periodic appraisal for the complainant.

    In addition, the complainant requested a parking space close to her office, as she had difficulty walking. Such a parking space was not provided. Ultimately the complainant resigned from her job and submitted a claim for compensation for constructive dismissal.[27]

Held: The employer had not done all that was reasonable to accommodate the claimant's needs and a constructive dismissal had occurred.

Judgment: ". . . The Court is satisfied that management was aware at all times of the complainant's disability. The employing organisation is a specialist in this particular disability and had the expertise to understand the capabilities of the complainant to perform tasks . . . [A]n assessment was not carried out prior to her commencement of employment, nor at a later time when the complainant complained about her ability to perform certain tasks expected of her. It was only in late 2000 that an assessment was offered but was not taken up.

    Having regard to Section 16 of the 1998 Act, the Court is of the view that the organisation did not fulfil its obligation and provide her with her appropriate needs. While the organisation did respond to her request not to perform certain tasks due to her disability, they considered further requests of this nature to be a form of whinging and had the effect of sending her to 'Coventry' [a colloquial expression implying that management deliberately refused to speak to the complainant] and expected her to sort that out herself . . .

    The Court is satisfied that the car parking difficulties and the social isolation at Christmas were so upsetting for the complainant that coupled with the difficulties experienced in

---

[27] A constructive dismissal occurs where an employee resigns because of some action by the employer which leads the employee to conclude that continued employment with this employer is impossible.

attempting to have the matter of the internal post finally sorted, this represented the last straw for the complainant.

Due to her understandable complaints concerning her inability to carry out the internal postal duties, tensions arose between her and the other colleagues in the team which management did not address. This situation could have been defused at no cost in accordance with the 'Administration Support Team—Division of Workload' which referred to all staff carrying out the duties on a rotational basis.

It is difficult to understand why she was not allowed to park in the designated disabled parking spaces when such spaces were available. This Court cannot accept the contention that users of the services are permitted to use these spaces while a disabled employee is refused permission to do so. It appears to the Court that this attitude, given what had gone before concerning the postal duty problems, led to a situation where the employee felt the situation was untenable.

The Court is satisfied that she had utilized all internal grievance procedures, had referred her case to a number of different managers, and was given the impression that it would be unwise to pursue her grievance any further. The Court notes that promises were given that the situation would be rectified. These were not fulfilled.

In a situation where she found herself unsupported by management and her colleagues, and the problems were continuing to exist, the Court is of the view that it was reasonable in those circumstances for the complainant to terminate her own contract and to seek an alternative position.

The Court is satisfied that the constructive dismissal occurred due to circumstances amounting to discrimination . . ."

Notes

(1) This case provides evidence of the interpretation given to "reasonable" behaviour on the part of an employer with regard to accommodating the needs of individuals with disabilities, and the standards that an employer must meet as a result of this requirement. It is interesting to note that no cost issues arose, and that the situation simply required a considered response to the needs of the complainant.

(2) The Court held that the tasks allotted to the complainant were unsuited to her disability, and the employer had not responded sufficiently or appropriately to the concerns raised by the complainant. Amongst other things, the Court noted that the employer had not assessed at an early enough stage the effect of her disability; and that the employer could have addressed the problems raised at no cost by the existing policy of task rotation amongst workers and by making available an existing parking space.

(3) In this case, the failure to provide a reasonable accommodation grounded a claim of constructive dismissal.

A second Irish case decided under the Employment Equality Act 1998 provides further insight into how the Irish courts assessed whether an employer had done "all that was reasonable" to accommodate an employee with a disability.

Equality Tribunal, 4 February 2002[28]   **6.IE.7.**
Decision DEC-E/2002/4, An Employee (represented by IMPACT) v. *A Local
Authority*

FAILURE TO DO ALL THAT IS REASONABLE TO ACCOMMODATE AN
EMPLOYEE—FAILURE TO FOLLOW EXPERT ADVICE

An Employee v. A Local Authority

Facts: The complainant, who had brain damage, took up a position as a clerical officer with the respondent organisation. As a result of his disability, he experienced some functional limitations, including difficulty concentrating. The complainant nevertheless passed a medical examination prior to taking up work, and had been advised by an occupational therapist that he was suited to clerical work. The complainant's work was subsequently assessed as unsatisfactory by the respondent. A representative of the Irish National Training and Employment Authority (FÁS) (Mr A.) met with the respondent and suggested ways in which FÁS could assist the respondent to support the complainant in carrying out his work. The respondent did not feel any of the suggested options were suitable and offered the complainant alternative work in an industrial setting. The complainant submitted that the respondent discriminated against him, inter alia, by failing to provide him with a reasonable accommodation as provided in section 16(3) of the Employment Equality Act 1998.

Held: The respondent discriminated against the complainant when it failed to provide him with appropriate special treatment and facilities (reasonable accommodation) in the context of section 16 of the Employment Equality Act 1998.

Judgment: "6. EQUALITY OFFICER'S CONCLUSIONS
6.1 The issues for consideration by me are . . . (ii) whether or not the respondent failed to provide the complainant with a reasonable accommodation as provided in section 16(3) of the Act . . .

6.7 The Act . . . does not require an employer to recruit, train or retain in employment a person who is not fully competent or capable to undertake the duties attached to a post. However, it also provides that a person with a disability must not be regarded as other than fully competent and capable of performing the duties attached to a post if the provision of special treatment or facilities would assist this objective. An employer is obliged to do all that is reasonable to provide such treatment or facilities unless its provision would give rise to a cost to the employer which exceeds a nominal cost.

6.8 I propose to examine, in the first instance, the three initiatives suggested by FÁS to the respondent as possibly being of assistance in accommodating the complainant. I note that the respondent states that any contact it had with FÁS was not considered by it as professional advice, rather it was an outline of the services available. I also note that paragraph 31 of the Department of the Environment and Local Government's Code of Practice states that 'on questions of expert advice . . . local authorities should . . . directly approach the organisation . . . where the required expertise is most likely to be found'. I am satisfied that the personnel in the Local Authority who were involved in exploring the question of appropriate treatment and facilities for the complainant did not possess the relevant expertise in this area and consequently, they required external advice. I am of the opinion that the information provided by FÁS comprised such advice and that the Code of Practice placed an onus on the respondent to view and treat it as such, in the absence of any attempt by the respondent to obtain the advice elsewhere.

---

[28] Available on the website of the Equality Tribunal of Ireland, under the heading Employment Equality Decisions.

6.9 I propose to deal firstly with the suggestion from Mr A that the complainant might undergo an independent vocational assessment to identify his work strengths and weaknesses . . . I have examined the report prepared by the Senior Occupational Therapist at the National Rehabilitation Hospital . . .

6.11 I note with particular interest that the report states that the complainant demonstrated good work traits in, inter alia, application, concentration and persistence—the very character-istics the respondent alleges were significantly lacking by him. The results of this assessment, in my view, clearly indicate that the complainant possessed the basic capacity to undertake the duties attached to the post of Clerical Officer and I am satisfied, on balance, that the vocational assessment presents a more realistic outline of the complainant's capabilities than the views of the untrained staff involved with the complainant's performance evaluation within the respondent Authority. I note that whilst the respondent did not have any objection to a vocational assessment of the complainant, it only began to give active consideration to the idea in mid-November, 2000, some six weeks after it had decided that the complainant was not capable of performing his job as a Clerical Officer. I find therefore, that the respondent's conclusion that the complainant was not fully competent and capable to undertake his duties was a decision reached without proper consideration of all of the relevant factors and could not, therefore, have been reached in a reasonable and objective manner.

6.12 I shall now examine the second initiative suggested by Mr A—a personal Job Coach for the complainant. I note that the respondent states that following the Meeting between the complainant and two of his line managers on 15 August, 2000, the level of training afforded him increased to such an extent that it resembled coaching and that this coaching was performed on a one-to-one basis by the complainant's Staff Officer—without any success. I further note that the respondent states that the provision of a Job Coach did not seem appropriate to the complainant's circumstances as it was the respondent's understanding that such a Coach was more appropriate to a person with mental disability as distinct from a person with residual brain damage, which is what the respondent understood the complainant to suffer from. As I understand it the role of a Coach in these circumstances is to assist the individual concerned to identify the problems in relation to his/her work and through one-to-one tuition and instruction, enable the person to come to grips with these difficulties. It appears to me that to perform such a role effectively requires a significant degree of training—not least when dealing with an individual with a disability to have the necessary awareness of the special difficulties such a person might encounter. Whilst, I am not suggesting that the complainant's Staff Officer did not devote a high level of attention to him, her intervention did not prove successful and at that stage the involvement of a professional Coach might have been appropriate. I note that the complainant's vocational assessment, referred to in the previous paragraph, states that in certain circumstances the complainant may require some extra time with initial organisation of new work or a new process, but thereafter when a task is fully understood and a routine established he can manage independently. In the light of this comment, I am of the opinion that had a professional Job Coach been engaged by the respondent to assist the complainant, the complainant would have been able to carry out the functions attached to his post in a capable and competent manner. I find therefore, that the respondent did not reasonably assess this option, that its decision to dismiss it as not being possibly beneficial to the complainant was hasty and influenced by subjective factors and could therefore not be considered reasonable.

7. DECISION

7.1 In view of the foregoing I find that the respondent: . . .

(b) discriminated against the complainant when it failed to provide him with appropriate special treatment and facilities (reasonable accommodation) in the context of section 16 of the Employment Equality Act, 1998 during his tenure as a clerical officer with that organisation."

Notes

(1) According to this judgment, in determining what measures can reasonably be required, an employer should take account of specialist advice which has been received and medical reports which have been made available. The employer should not substitute its own opinion as to what an employee can achieve as result of a particular accommodation being made. To do so would be to fail to take a decision in a "reasonable and objective manner".

(2) In this particular case the employer acted unreasonably by failing to properly consider a variety of possible accommodations which had been recommended to it by a specialist from the Training and Employment Authority and did not accept the specialist medical advice it received following an individualised assessment of the employee.

A third Irish case, decided on the basis of the Equal Status Act 2000, reveals how the questions are addressed with regard to accommodations needed to access services.

Equality Tribunal, 1 August 2002[29]   **6.IE.8.**
Decision DEC-S2002-086, Mr John Roche v. *Alabaster Associates Limited t/a Madigans*

REFUSAL TO ALLOW ACCESS TO A RESTAURANT OF A GUIDE DOG AMOUNTS TO A FAILURE TO PROVIDE A REASONABLE ACCOMMODATION

Roche v. Alabaster

Facts: The complainant, who was visually impaired and used a guide dog, was refused access to a service in the respondent's premises (a pub). The complainant submitted that he was discriminated against on the grounds of his disability as the respondent failed to provide special treatment to accommodate his needs. The respondent argued that it would have been contrary to the Food Hygiene Regulations to allow the complainant's dog into the pub, which served food. The respondent submitted that it tried to accommodate the complainant's needs and it offered to allow him to leave the dog at the door in the company of the doorman while the complainant had refreshments, but this was not acceptable to the complainant.

Held: The respondent had failed to provide a reasonable accommodation to the complainant, namely allowing him to enter their premises whilst being accompanied by his guide dog, and had consequently discriminated against him on the grounds of disability.

Judgment: "5 Conclusions of Equality Officer . . .

5.4 Circumstances of Refusal of Service

. . . I note in this case the respondent applied the same rules to everyone accompanied by a dog and provided no exception for a person accompanied by a guide dog. In considering the case I

---

[29] Available on the website of the Equality Tribunal of Ireland, under the heading Equal Status Decisions.

have noted the Equality Officer's Decision in the case of Mr John Maughan v the Glimmerman Limited DEC-S2001-020. In that case the Equality Officer stated that:

'*I am satisfied that if a person brought a dog, which was not a guide dog, into the respondent's premises they would not have been served in line with the respondent's no dogs policy. On the face of it, therefore, the complainant was not treated less favourably because he was treated the same as anyone else with a dog would have been treated. However, because of his visual impairment the complainant was not in the same circumstances as someone else with a dog who was not visually impaired. This difference is important and to quote the European Court of Justice ruling in the case of Gillespie and others v Northern Health and Social Services Boards and others (Case no. C-342/93) "discrimination involves the application of different rules to comparable situations, or the application of the same rules to different situations . . ."*'

It is relevant therefore at this stage to examine the treatment of the complainant in the context of Section 4 of the Act which deals with the provision of special facilities for a person with a disability.

Reasonable Accommodation

5.6 . . . I am now going to examine if the respondent did '*all that is reasonable to accommodate the needs of a person with a disability by providing special treatment or facilities*'. [section 4(1) of the Equal Status Act].

The respondent submitted that he made an offer to the complainant to leave his guide dog at the door. The complainant said that this offer was not made to him and even if it was, it was not acceptable offer [sic] as his guide dog has to be with him at all times. It would present a danger to the dog to leave him in the care of a stranger on a busy street and in any event the proposition would be in contravention of the Guide Dog Association rules. The complainant's representative submitted that unnecessary obstacles are placed in the way of guide dog users which diminish the dignity, confidence and independence of those with visual impairments and the only special treatment the complainant required was the admission of his guide dog to the premises. They further submitted that it was impossible or unduly difficult for the complainant to avail of the service in question without the admission of his guide dog to the premises . . . Because a guide dog is '*the eyes*' for a visually impaired person I am satisfied that it would not be reasonable to expect the complainant to be separated from his dog in the manner suggested by the respondent. It is clear therefore that the complainant would have a need to have the guide dog with him at all times. In any case leaving a guide dog at the door of a busy pub on O'Connell Street in Dublin under the control of a stranger to the dog, in my view, would present a great danger to the dog and would have caused great upset and anxiety to the complainant. For the above reasons, I find that the respondent's offer to leave the dog at the door was not a reasonable offer to accommodate the needs of a person with a visual impairment. I find also that it would be unduly difficult for the complainant to avail of a service in the pub without the assistance of his guide dog.

. . .

Prohibition of Dogs in Food Premises

5.8 The respondent submitted that he relied on the Food Hygiene Regulations and that the Regulations take precedent over the Equal Status Act. Mr Keogh said that he believed he was complying with the legislation in relation to food hygiene . . .

In my view the Regulations do not apply to dogs visiting food premises with its owner . . . I am therefore satisfied that the respondent is not required by an enactment to exclude dogs which are leashed from his premises . . .

5.11 I find for the foregoing reasons that the respondent did unlawfully discriminate against the complainant contrary to the Equal Status Act, 2000 when he refused to allow him into his pub with his guide dog [emphasis in original].”

Notes

(1) It is interesting to note that the Equality Officer, in paragraph 5.4, reflected on the theoretical underpinning of the requirement to make a reasonable accommodation, and used this understanding in deciding whether the complainant had indeed been a victim of discrimination.

(2) No issue of cost arose in this case, and neither party sought to argue this. The question was whether the respondent had behaved in a reasonable way by denying the complainant access when accompanied by his guide dog, and allegedly offering, as an accommodation, to allow the dog to be left with the doorman. In finding that the respondent had acted unreasonably, the Equality Officer referred to the need of the complainant to be accompanied by his dog at all times, and the impact on both the complainant and the dog of leaving the dog with the doorman.

(3) The respondent sought to rely on the argument that to allow a guide dog onto the premises would have resulted in a breach of food health and safety legislation. The Equality Officer found that no such breach would have resulted. However, it is conceivable that the obligation to make a reasonable accommodation could at times clash with obligations provided for in other statutes. This factor was expressly recognised in the Preparatory Works to the Finnish Non-Discrimination Act cited above, which refers to “arrangements” which “could endanger compliance with workplace safety legislation”. Where this occurs the “arrangements” will no longer be reasonable under Finnish law. A similar reference to health and safety rules is also found in § 81 SGB IX of the German Social Law Code cited below.

(4) This case could conceivably have also been dealt with as an instance of indirect discrimination, in that it concerned an “apparently neutral provision, criterion or practice” (denial of access to dogs) which would place blind people with guide dogs at a “particular disadvantage” compared to other individuals who are accompanied by dogs. If the case had been dealt with in this way, the possible defence might have been different in nature. Under EC equality law the defence to a failure to provide a reasonable accommodation is that it would result in a disproportionate burden, which explicitly allows for factors such as cost to be considered. The defence to a complaint of indirect discrimination is that the challenged measure was objectively justified, and issues of cost are less likely to be regarded as meeting this test (see further above D. Schiek, Chapter Three: Indirect Discrimination).[30]

Belgian legislation adopts a different approach by specifically defining a “reasonable” accommodation as one that does not create a “disproportionate burden”, thereby limiting the nature of the obligation on the employer.

---

[30] This discussion is naturally hypothetical, since the Employment Equality Directive does not prohibit disability-related discrimination with regard to access to services.

Belgian Act of 25 February 2003 to Combat   **6.BE.9.**
Discrimination and to Amend the Act of 15 February 1993 to Establish
a Centre for Equal Opportunity and to Combat Racism

Article 2(3)
. . . A reasonable accommodation is an accommodation that does not create a disproportionate burden, or where the burden is sufficiently compensated for by existing measures.

Belgian Guide to . . . Reasonable Accommodations for Persons   **6.BE.10.**
with a Disability at Work, March 2005

"Inter-Ministerial initiative
This brochure is an initiative of the Inter-Ministerial Conference for persons with a disability.
Its practical implementation was entrusted to the Federal Government Department of
Employment, Labour and Social Dialogue.
. . .

3. The criteria that accommodations must comply with to be regarded as 'reasonable'

3.1 The financial and organisational burden on the employer . . . [see section 6.4.2.A. of this
chapter for extract]

3.1.1 The employer's financial capabilities . . . [see section 6.4.2.A of this chapter for extract]

3.1.2 The financial cost of the accommodation . . . [see section 6.4.2.A of this chapter for
extract]

3.1.3 Compensatory measures and subsidies . . . [see section 6.4.2.A of this chapter for extract]

3.1.4 Direct and indirect consequences
The consequences of the reasonable accommodation can also be measured and assessed.
Certain accommodations may offer support for a larger group of employees and/or for
external visitors. For example:

— Widening the entrance to the business to permit access by an employee in a wheelchair
also offers greater ease to other employees and visitors (persons in wheelchairs, persons
with prams, large persons, etc.).
— Installing a lift improves accessibility for persons in a wheelchair but also makes life
easier for other employees and visitors. Proper account must of course be taken of possible evacuation in the event of fire.

An accommodation that was originally intended for one person can also ultimately assist
future employees with a comparable disability. For example:

— An adjusted telephone switchboard for the hard of hearing.
— The conversion of work documents or courses in Braille or audiotape may have a multiple effect if more than one blind person is employed in the firm.

3.1.5 Job description and period for writing off the accommodation
Entrusting a colleague with minor additional tasks that the employee cannot execute independently without "expensive" accommodations may offer a reasonable accommodation. Clear job and task descriptions beforehand can offer clarity both to the employer and to the employees . . .

3.1.6 Work-related accommodations
A request for a reasonable accommodation at the workplace or on the shop floor must be connected with the execution of the work. A disabled employee can only request reasonable accommodations that are linked to discharge of the contract of employment. For example:

— An employee must acquire a wheelchair to overcome his movement problems. The employer need not contribute towards the purchase of this resource, as this is also put to private use. If on the other hand of the employee must be able to take specific action in the working context and consequently needs new equipment, the employer must cover the expense of this even if it can be used in the private sphere as well as the works clear
— A person working at home does not use a computer to do his job. He cannot ask for special adjustments to his own computer."

Notes
(1) Article 2(3), which covers employment-related accommodations, states that an accommodation is judged to be reasonable if it does not create a disproportionate burden for the employer. However, the preparatory texts relating to the Belgian statute specify that when determining whether any accommodation is reasonable, three criteria have to be considered:

— Are any accommodations possible which would allow a specific person with a disability to participate effectively in an equal way in a specific activity?
— Do these accommodations amount to a disproportionate burden for the person who must make them?
— Do there exist any measures that significantly reduce the burden on the person who is under the duty to provide accommodation?[31]

Given that only the last two criteria have been included in the Statute, one can criticise the drafting of the measure.
(2) The brochure from which the second extract above is taken is a result of an inter-ministerial initiative and should be of use in interpreting and applying all the provisions relating to reasonable accommodation for individuals with disabilities in the area of employment. These provisions are found in Federal, Regional and Community laws in Belgium.
(3) It is worth noting that the brochure does not specify that, amongst the criteria with which an accommodation must comply in order to be reasonable, the accommodation must be effective in allowing an individual with a disability to carry out

---

[31] Parl St 2001–2002, No. 1578/008, 30–1. See also Van den Langenbergh, "Discriminatie van Gehandicapten bij Aanwerving: Een Verkennende Analyse" in J. Velaers and J. Vrielink (eds.), *Vrijheid en Gelijkheid, De horizontale werking van het gelijkheidsbeginsel en de nieuwe antidiscriminatie wet* (Antwerp, Maklu, 2003) 604–5.

employment. The brochure lists this as a (separate) requirement which the accommodation must meet per se, and therefore distinguishes this requirement from the notion of "reasonableness". This is considered below in section 6.2.2.C.

(4) The extract from the brochure lists the factors that are to be considered when determining whether any accommodation is reasonable. The first four factors listed relate to the cost of the accommodation and the financial resources of the employer. In addition, three requirements, which will influence the determination of whether an accommodation is reasonable or not and which are not directly linked to the financing of the accommodation, are noted: the direct and indirect consequences of the accommodation, adaptations to the job description and non work-related accommodations.

(5) An adjustment or accommodation which is required in order to enable an individual to function in daily life and which is not connected to employment will not be regarded as reasonable. This is comparable to the requirement found in Article 16 of the Irish Employment Equality Act 1998–2004,[32] which specifies that employers are not required to provide accommodations which it can be expected that the individual with a disability should provide for him- or herself. Such an approach is also taken under UK law, where the Employment Appeals Tribunal has held that the duty to make reasonable adjustments is confined to work-related adjustments. In the case at issue this did not extend to personal care arrangements, such as assistance with use of a bathroom.[33] It is submitted that this principle is explicitly or implicitly recognised in all reasonable accommodation requirements related to employment.

The German Social Law Code imposes duties on employers with regard to accommodating severely disabled workers, but subjects this to the requirement that fulfilment of the worker's claim must be reasonable for the employer.

German Social Law Code, Book Nine (SGB IX)   **6.DE.11.**
Rehabilitation and Participation of disabled persons, of 19 June 2001,
§ 81 SGB IX[34]

Duties of employers and rights of severely disabled persons
(4) The severely disabled persons have a right against their employer

   1.   to be employed in a way that allows them to utilize and improve their skills and knowledge to the fullest extent possible,
   2.   to be preferentially considered for internal vocational training measures for furtherance of their professional progress,
   3.   to facilitations to a reasonable extent regarding participation in external vocational training measures,

---

[32] See section 6.2.1.B.
[33] *Kenny* v. *Hampshire Constabulary* [1999] IRLR 76.
[34] Federal Law Gazette I at 1046.

4. to adaptation and maintenance of the workplaces suitable to the disability, including operating equipment, machines and devices as well as the design of the workplace, the working environment, the work organisation and the working time, taking risk of accident particularly into consideration,

5. to equipment of the workplace with the necessary technical working aids taking the disability and its effects on the occupation into consideration. In implementing the measures described in numbers 1, 4 and 5 the employment and integration offices shall support the employer, taking into consideration the essential characteristics of the severely disabled persons. A claim according to sentence 1 does not exist if its fulfilment is not reasonable for the employer or if it would entail disproportionate burden or in as far as the occupational safety and health rules laid down by national law or by employer's liability insurance associations or rules governing members of the civil service are opposed.

Notes

(1) The reference to sentence 1 in paragraph 5 of the extract is to the first sentence of this sub-article, which ends in paragraph 5, and covers all items mentioned in the sub-article (1–5).

(2) The approach adopted in the German Social Law Code is unusual in that it is framed in terms of a positive right for a covered person with a disability, which allows the individual to claim an adaptation or other work-related benefit. Furthermore, this right is provided for in the Social Law Code, which is not a non-discrimination statute. In contrast, the General Equal Treatment Act of 2006, which was adopted to transpose the Equality Directives, and which covers disability discrimination in the areas of employment and civil law, makes no explicit reference to reasonable accommodations.

(3) According to the Social Law Code, only severely disabled people have the right to claim an accommodation as listed in sentence 1 of the above Article.

(4) German law requires that, in principle, employers must make an accommodation (in sentence 1 of § 81(4) SGB IX) and, quite separately, sets out the grounds on which an employer might justifiably refuse to make such an accommodation (in sentence 2). This approach, like the Dutch approach identified in the next section, has the advantage of providing for a two-stage process in deciding whether any accommodation must be made.

(5) According to paragraph 5, a severely disabled individual is not entitled to claim the right specified in paragraphs 1–5 if one (or more) of three conditions is met, namely, if the fulfilment of the claim would:

— be not reasonable for the employer;
— result in a disproportionate burden for the employer; or
— result in the breach of health and safety rules.

The concept of reasonableness is therefore used as a limitation on the actions that can be expected of the employer. In addition, the concept is distinct from two other defences to the requirement to make an accommodation—namely, that this would result in a disproportionate burden for the employer or breach health and safety rules.

The implication is that an accommodation might not result in a disproportionate burden or pose a threat to health and safety standards, but could still not be required of the employer on the grounds that it would be unreasonable. However, the exact requirements for determining whether making any accommodation would be unreasonable, or result in a disproportionate burden, are not set out in the legislation.

Finally, under this section, the statute which arguably provided the inspiration behind Article 5 of the Employment Equality Directive will be considered: the Americans with Disabilities Act (ADA) of 1990. It is worth noting that, in spite of the detailed statute and accompanying interpretative tools, the concept of reasonable accommodation in US law has been far from straightforward to interpret.
   The first extract considered contains the legislative requirement to make a reasonable accommodation for an individual with a disability.

Americans with Disabilities Act 42 U.S.C. § 12112(b)(5)(A)   **6.US.12.**

Discrimination under Title I includes that of a covered entity:
   (5)(A) not making reasonable accommodations to the known physical or mental limitations of an otherwise qualified individual with a disability who is an applicant or employee, unless such covered entity can demonstrate that the accommodation would impose an undue hardship on the operation of the business of such covered entity.

Note
The ADA clearly adopts a two-stage process. Under the statute an employer is obliged to make a reasonable accommodation (to the known physical or mental limitations of an otherwise qualified individual with a disability who is an applicant or employee) unless the employer can demonstrate that making the accommodation would result in undue hardship. The "reasonableness" of the accommodation is therefore assessed quite separately from the question of undue hardship.

The following extracts seek to explore how the term "reasonable" is interpreted.
   The Equal Employment Opportunity Commission (EEOC) regulations provide guidance on how the term "reasonable accommodation" should be interpreted, and define the term as follows:

Equal Employment Opportunity Commission (EEOC)   **6.US.13.**
Regulations on the ADA
EEOC Title I regulations, 29 C.F.R. §§ 1630.2(o) (1), 1630.9

(i)   Modifications or adjustments to a job application process that enable a qualified applicant with a disability to be considered for the position such qualified applicants desires; or

649

(ii)   Modifications or adjustments to the work environment, or to the manner or circumstances under which the position held or desired is customarily performed, that enable a qualified individual with a disability to perform the essential functions of that position; or

(iii) Modifications or adjustments that enable a covered entity's employee with a disability to enjoy equal benefits and privileges of employment as are enjoyed by its other similarly situated employees without disabilities.

Notes

(1) The EEOC is the Federal agency in charge of administrative and judicial enforcement of the federal civil rights laws with regard to employment.

(2) According to the Regulations, there are three categories of accommodation:

— those required to provide equal opportunities in the job application process;
— those required to enable an individual with a disability to perform the essential functions of a job; and
— those required to enable any employee with a disability to enjoy equal benefits and privileges of employment.

(3) In light of the EEOC Guidance, one could argue that an accommodation is reasonable if it allows a qualified individual with a disability to achieve one or more of the goals set out above. This interpretation is arguably supported by the House Labor Report on the ADA which stated:

"A reasonable accommodation should be effective for the employee . . . [and] should provide a meaningful equal employment opportunity . . . [that is] an opportunity to attain the same level of performance as is available to non-disabled employees having similar skills and abilities."[35]

(4) This interpretation of the term "reasonable" has been litigated before senior US courts, including the Supreme Court. In recent cases the courts have not endorsed the argument, referred to the preceding note, that a "reasonable" accommodation is an accommodation which is "effective" in allowing the employee with a disability to participate in employment, but rather perceived the term "reasonable" as a modification to the requirement which is imposed upon the employer, albeit a modification which is quite separate from the undue hardship defence. This is illustrated by the following two cases.

---

[35] H.R. Rep. No. 1001–485m pt. 2, at 66.

7th Circuit 1995, 44 F.3d 538   **6.US.14.**
Vande Zande v. State of Wisconsin Department of Administration

NO FAILURE TO MAKE A REASONABLE ACCOMMODATION BY NOT ALLOWING AN EMPLOYEE TO WORK FULL-TIME AT HOME AND BY NOT ADAPTING A KITCHEN

Vande Zande

Facts: The claimant, Vande Zande, alleged that her employer had failed to provide two forms of reasonable accommodation as required under the ADA. Vande Zande was a paraplegic and was periodically troubled by pressure ulcers as a result. Whilst she was experiencing such ulcers she requested permission to work full-time from home and that her employer provide her with a desktop computer for home work. Her employer declined, but did provide her with a significant amount of work she could do from home. In total, Vande Zande had to claim, and therefore lose any future entitlement to, 16.5 hours of sick leave. She requested restoration of the sick leave. Secondly, she requested that her employer lower a sink in a kitchenette at her place of work so she could use it. The employer lowered a shelf, but declined to lower the sink, arguing that Vande Zande could use a nearby accessible bathroom sink.

Held: It was not reasonable to expect the employer to make the accommodations requested, and there had been no breach of the requirement to make a reasonable accommodation.

Judgment: CHIEF JUDGE POSNER: ". . . It is plain enough what 'accommodation' means. The employer must be willing to consider making changes in its ordinary work rules, facilities, terms, and conditions in order to enable a disabled individual to work. The difficult term is 'reasonable'. The claimant in our case, a paraplegic, argues in effect that the term just means apt or efficacious. An accommodation is reasonable, she believes, when it is tailored to the particular individual's disability. A ramp or lift is thus a reasonable accommodation for a person who like this claimant is confined to a wheelchair. Considerations of cost do not enter into the term as the claimant would have us construe it. Cost is, she argues, the domain of 'undue hardship'—safe harbours for an employer that can show that it would go broke or suffer other excruciating financial distress were it compelled to make a reasonable accommodation in the sense of one effective in enabling the disabled person to overcome the vocational effects of the disability.

These are questionable interpretations both of 'reasonable' and of 'undue hardship'. To 'accommodate' a disability is to make some change that will enable the disabled person to work. An unrelated, inefficacious change would not be an accommodation of the disability at all. So 'reasonable' may be intended to qualify (in the sense of weaken) 'accommodation', in just the same way that if one requires a 'reasonable effort' of someone this means less than the maximum possible effort, or in law that the duty of 'reasonable care', the cornerstone of the law of negligence, requires something less than the maximum possible care. It is understood in that law that in deciding what care is reasonable the court considers the cost of increased care. Similar reasoning could be used to flesh out the meaning of the word 'reasonable' in the term 'reasonable accommodations'. It would not follow that the costs and benefits of altering a workplace to enable a disabled person to work would always have to be quantified, or even that an accommodation would have to be deemed unreasonable if the cost exceeded the benefit however slightly. But, at the very least, the cost could not be disproportionate to the benefit. Even if an employer is so large or wealthy—or, like the principal defendant in this case, is a state, which can raise taxes in order to finance any accommodations that it must make to disabled employees—that it may not be able to plead 'undue hardship', it would not be required to expend enormous sums in order to bring about a trivial improvement in the life of a disabled employee . . .

The concept of reasonable accommodation is at the heart of this case. The claimant sought a number of accommodations to her paraplegia that were turned down. The principal defendant as we have said is a state, which does not argue that the claimant's proposals were rejected because accepting them would have imposed undue hardship on the state or because they would not have done her any good. The district judge nevertheless granted summary judgment for the defendants on the ground that the evidence obtained in discovery, construed as favourably to the claimant as the record permitted, showed that they had gone as far to accommodate the claimant's demands as reasonableness, in a sense distinct from either aptness or hardship—a sense based, rather, on considerations of cost and proportionality—required. On this analysis, the function of the 'undue hardship' safe harbour, . . ., is to excuse compliance by a firm that is financially distressed, even though the cost of the accommodation to the firm might be less than the benefit to disabled employees.

So it seems that costs enter at two points in the analysis of claims to an accommodation to a disability. The employee must show that the accommodation is reasonable in the sense both of efficacious and of proportional to costs. Even if this prima facie showing is made, the employer has an opportunity to prove that upon more careful consideration the costs are excessive in relation either to the benefits of the accommodation or to the employer's financial survival or health . . .

[Regarding the claim that the employer should have allowed Vande Zande to work fulltime from home and provided her with a desktop computer for this purpose:] . . .

She argues that a jury might have found that a reasonable accommodation required the housing division either to give her the desktop computer or to excuse her from having to dig into her sick leave to get paid for the hours in which, in the absence of the computer, she was unable to do her work at home. No jury, however, could in our view be permitted to stretch the concept of 'reasonable accommodation' so far. Most jobs in organizations public or private involve team work under supervision rather than solitary unsupervised work, and team work under supervision generally cannot be performed at home without a substantial reduction in the quality of the employee's performance. This will no doubt change as communications technology advances, but is the situation today. Generally, therefore, an employer is not required to accommodate a disability by allowing the disabled worker to work, by himself, without supervision, at home . . . No doubt to this as to any generalization about so complex and varied an activity as employment there are exceptions, but it would take a very extraordinary case for the employee to be able to create a triable issue of the employer's failure to allow the employee to work at home . . .

[Regarding the claim that the employer lower a sink in a kitchenette at her place of work so that VandeZande could use it:] . . .

Apparently it would have cost only about $150 to lower the sink on Vande Zande's floor; to lower it on all the floors might have cost as much as $2,000, though possibly less. Given the proximity of the bathroom sink, Vande Zande can hardly complain that the inaccessibility of the kitchenette sink interfered with her ability to work or with her physical comfort. Her argument rather is that forcing her to use the bathroom sink for activities (such as washing out her coffee cup) for which the other employees could use the kitchenette sink stigmatized her as different and inferior; she seeks an award of compensatory damages for the resulting emotional distress. We may assume without having to decide that emotional as well as physical barriers to the integration of disabled persons into the workforce are relevant in determining the reasonableness of an accommodation. But we do not think an employer has a duty to expend even modest amounts of money to bring about an absolute identity in working conditions between disabled and nondisabled workers. The creation of such a duty would be the inevitable consequence of deeming a failure to achieve identical conditions 'stigmatizing'. That is merely an epithet. We conclude that access to a particular sink, when access to an equivalent sink, conveniently located, is provided, is not a legal duty of an employer. The duty of reasonable accommodation is satisfied when the employer does what is necessary to enable the disabled worker to work in reasonable comfort."

Notes

(1) The court rejected the argument that an accommodation is "reasonable" if it is effective and tailored to the needs of an individual with a disability. Instead, the court saw the term "reasonable" as serving to modify ("in the sense of weaken") the accommodation itself. In doing so, Judge Posner, who is a leading advocate of "law and economics", drew inspiration from the law of negligence and stated that the term "reasonable" implied that the cost of making the accommodation to the employer should not be disproportionate to the benefit. Therefore, even if making a particular accommodation would not result in a disproportionate burden for the employer, and if the accommodation would result in a benefit to the individual with the disability, the accommodation need not be made if it were unreasonable: the employer "would not be required to expend enormous sums in order to bring about a trivial improvement in the life of a disabled employee". The proportionality principle was therefore built into the calculation of whether any accommodation is reasonable or not.

(2) Whilst Judge Posner held that a proper assessment of what is a reasonable accommodation requires a cost–benefit analysis, meaning that the accommodation should be expedient and proportionate to the resulting benefits, he did not further elaborate on the formula to be applied.[36]

Supreme Court of the United States, 2002 535 U.S. 391   **6.US.15.**
US Airways, Inc. v. *Barnett*

AN ACCOMMODATION WHICH CONFLICTS WITH A SENIORITY RULE WILL
GENERALLY NOT BE REASONABLE

Barnett

Facts: The respondent, Barnett, injured his back while a cargo handler for US Airways. He was transferred to a less physically demanding position in the mailroom. His new position later became open to a seniority based employee bidding under US Airways' seniority system, and employees more senior to him planned to bid for his job. US Airways refused his request to accommodate his disability by allowing him to remain in the mailroom, and he lost his job. He challenged the decision on the grounds that US Airways had discriminated against him by failing to provide him with a reasonable accommodation. The case was litigated before a number of courts, before being heard by the US Supreme Court.

---

[36] For a thoughtful discussion as to how a law and economics approach can be used to analyse accommodation claims see M.A. Stein, "The Law and Economics of Disability Accommodations" (2004) 53 *Duke LJ* 79–191.

Held: An employer's showing that a requested accommodation conflicts with seniority rules is ordinarily sufficient to show, as a matter of law, that an "accommodation" is not "reasonable". However, the employee remains free to present evidence of special circumstances that makes a seniority rule exception reasonable in the particular case.

Judgment: JUSTICE BREYER:

"II

The parties interpret [the] statutory language as applied to seniority systems in radically different ways. In US Airways' view, the fact that an accommodation would violate the rules of a seniority system always shows that the accommodation is not a 'reasonable' one. In Barnett's polar opposite view, a seniority system violation never shows that an accommodation sought is not a 'reasonable' one. Barnett concedes that a violation of seniority rules might help to show that the accommodation will work 'undue' employer 'hardship', but that is a matter for an employer to demonstrate case by case. We shall initially consider the parties' main legal arguments in support of these conflicting positions.

A

. . . [The Court's discussion of the interpretation by US Airways is not included].

B

Barnett argues that the statutory words 'reasonable accommodation' mean only 'effective accommodation', authorizing a court to consider the requested accommodation's ability to meet an individual's disability-related needs, and nothing more. On this view, a seniority rule violation, having nothing to do with the accommodation's effectiveness, has nothing to do with its 'reasonableness'. It might, at most, help to prove an 'undue hardship on the operation of the business'. But, he adds, that is a matter that the statute requires the employer to demonstrate, case by case.

In support of this interpretation Barnett points to Equal Employment Opportunity Commission (EEOC) regulations stating that 'reasonable accommodation means . . . [m]odifications or adjustments . . . that *enable* a qualified individual with a disability to perform the essential functions of [a] position.' 29 CFR §1630(o)(ii) (2001) (emphasis added). See also H. R. Rep. No. 101-485, pt. 2, at 66; S. Rep. No. 101–116, at 35 (discussing reasonable accommodations in terms of 'effectiveness', while discussing costs in terms of 'undue hardship'). Barnett adds that any other view would make the words 'reasonable accommo-dation' and 'undue hardship' virtual mirror images—creating redundancy in the statute. And he says that any such other view would create a practical burden of proof dilemma.

The practical burden of proof dilemma arises, Barnett argues, because the statute imposes the burden of demonstrating an 'undue hardship' upon the employer, while the burden of proving 'reasonable accommodation' remains with the claimant, here the employee. This allocation seems sensible in that an employer can more frequently and easily prove the presence of business hardship than an employee can prove its absence. But suppose that an employee must counter a claim of 'seniority rule violation' in order to prove that an 'accommodation' request is 'reasonable'. Would that not force the employee to prove what is in effect an absence, i.e. an absence of hardship, despite the statute's insistence that the employer 'demonstrate' hardship's presence?

These arguments do not persuade us that Barnett's legal interpretation of 'reasonable' is correct. For one thing, in ordinary English the word 'reasonable' does not mean 'effective'. It is the word 'accommodation', not the word 'reasonable' that conveys the need for effectiveness. An *ineffective* 'modification' or 'adjustment' will not *accommodate* a disabled individual's

654

limitations. Nor does an ordinary English meaning of the term 'reasonable accommodation' make of it a simple, redundant mirror image of the term 'undue hardship'. The statute refers to an 'undue hardship on the operation of the business'. 42 U. S. C. §12112(b)(5)(A). Yet a demand for an effective accommodation could prove unreasonable because of its impact, not on business operations, but on fellow employees—say because it will lead to dismissals, relocations, or modification of employee benefits to which an employer, looking at the matter from the perspective of the business itself, may be relatively indifferent.

Neither does the statute's primary purpose require Barnett's special reading. The statute seeks to diminish or to eliminate the stereotypical thought processes, the thoughtless actions, and the hostile reactions that far too often bar those with disabilities from participating fully in the Nation's life, including the workplace . . . These objectives demand unprejudiced thought and reasonable responsive reaction on the part of employers and fellow workers alike. They will sometimes require affirmative conduct to promote entry of disabled people into the workforce . . . They do not, however, demand action beyond the realm of the reasonable.

Neither has Congress indicated in the statute, or elsewhere, that the word 'reasonable' means no more than 'effective.' The EEOC regulations do say that reasonable accommodations 'enable' a person with a disability to perform the essential functions of a task. But that phrasing simply emphasizes the statutory provision's basic objective. The regulations do not say that 'enable' and 'reasonable' mean the same thing . . .

Finally, an ordinary language interpretation of the word 'reasonable' does not create the 'burden of proof' dilemma to which Barnett points. Many of the lower courts, while rejecting both US Airways' and Barnett's more absolute views, have reconciled the phrases 'reasonable accommodation' and 'undue hardship' in a practical way.

They have held that a claimant/employee (to defeat a defendant/employer's motion for summary judgment) need only show that an 'accommodation' seems reasonable on its face, i.e. ordinarily or in the run of cases . . .

Once the claimant has made this showing, the defendant/employer then must show special (typically case-specific) circumstances that demonstrate undue hardship in the particular circumstances . . .

III

The question in the present case focuses on the relationship between seniority systems and the claimant's need to show that an 'accommodation' seems reasonable on its face, i.e. ordinarily or in the run of cases. We must assume that the claimant, an employee, is an 'individual with a disability'. He has requested assignment to a mailroom position as a 'reasonable accommodation'. We also assume that normally such a request would be reasonable within the meaning of the statute, were it not for one circumstance, namely, that the assignment would violate the rules of a seniority system. See §12111(9) ('reasonable accommodation' may include 'reassignment to a vacant position'). Does that circumstance mean that the proposed accommodation is not a 'reasonable' one?

In our view, the answer to this question ordinarily is 'yes'. The statute does not require proof on a case-by-case basis that a seniority system should prevail. That is because it would not be reasonable in the run of cases that the assignment in question trump the rules of a seniority system. To the contrary, it will ordinarily be unreasonable for the assignment to prevail.

A

Several factors support our conclusion that a proposed accommodation will not be reasonable in the run of cases. Analogous case-law supports this conclusion, for it has recognized the importance of seniority to employee-management relations . . . [The judgment refers to a number of earlier judgments]. All these cases discuss *collectively bargained* seniority systems, not systems (like the present system) which are unilaterally imposed by management. But the relevant seniority system advantages, and related difficulties that result from violations of seniority rules, are not limited to collectively bargained systems.

For one thing, the typical seniority system provides important employee benefits by creating, and fulfilling, employee expectations of fair, uniform treatment. These benefits include 'job security and an opportunity for steady and predictable advancement based on objective standards.' . . .

Most important for present purposes, to require the typical employer to show more than the existence of a seniority system might well undermine the employees' expectations of consistent, uniform treatment—expectations upon which the seniority system's benefits depend. That is because such a rule would substitute a complex case-specific 'accommodation' decision made by management for the more uniform, impersonal operation of seniority rules. Such management decision making, with its inevitable discretionary elements, would involve a matter of the greatest importance to employees, namely, layoffs; it would take place outside, as well as inside, the confines of a court case; and it might well take place fairly often. Cf. ADA, 42 U. S. C. §12101(a)(1) (estimating that some 43 million Americans suffer from physical or mental disabilities). We can find nothing in the statute that suggests Congress intended to undermine seniority systems in this way. And we consequently conclude that the employer's showing of violation of the rules of a seniority system is by itself ordinarily sufficient.

B

The claimant (here the employee) nonetheless remains free to show that special circumstances warrant a finding that, despite the presence of a seniority system (which the ADA may not trump in the run of cases), the requested 'accommodation' is 'reasonable' on the particular facts. That is because special circumstances might alter the important expectations described above . . . The claimant might show, for example, that the employer, having retained the right to change the seniority system unilaterally, exercises that right fairly frequently, reducing employee expectations that the system will be followed—to the point where one more departure, needed to accommodate an individual with a disability, will not likely make a difference. The claimant might show that the system already contains exceptions such that, in the circumstances, one further exception is unlikely to matter. We do not mean these examples to exhaust the kinds of showings that a claimant might make. But we do mean to say that the claimant must bear the burden of showing special circumstances that make an exception from the seniority system reasonable in the particular case. And to do so, the claimant must explain why, in the particular case, an exception to the employer's seniority policy can constitute a 'reasonable accommodation' even though in the ordinary case it cannot [emphasis in original]."

Notes

(1) *Barnett* was decided by the US Supreme Court and is the leading US judgment on the obligation to make a reasonable accommodation for an individual with a disability under the ADA.

(2) The claimant, Barnett, referred to the EEOC Regulations and the House Labor Report on the ADA to support his argument that an accommodation was

"reasonable" if it was "effective". The Court explicitly rejected his interpretation of the EEOC Guidelines (Section B of judgment). The relevant extracts from both the EEOC Guidelines and the House Labor Report were included at the beginning of this section.

(3) Many lower courts in the US have reconciled the phrases "reasonable accommodation" and "undue hardship" by holding that a claimant/employee need only show that an "accommodation" seems reasonable on its face, i.e. ordinarily or in the run of cases. The defendant/employer then must show special (typically case-specific) circumstances demonstrating undue hardship in the particular circumstances. Neither US Airways' position—that no accommodation violating a seniority system's rules is reasonable—nor Barnett's position—that "reasonable accommodation" authorises a court to consider only the requested accommodation's ability to meet an individual's disability-related needs—was regarded as a proper interpretation of the Act by the Supreme Court.

(4) In this case the question was whether a proposed accommodation that would normally be reasonable was rendered unreasonable if it would violate a seniority system's rules. The Court held that ordinarily the answer is "yes". The statute does not require proof on a case-by-case basis that a seniority system should prevail because it would not be reasonable in most cases that the accommodation trumps such a system's rules. The relevant seniority system advantages, and related difficulties resulting from violations of seniority rules, are not limited to collectively bargained systems, but also apply to many systems (like the one at issue) unilaterally imposed by management. A typical seniority system provides important employee benefits by creating, and fulfilling, employee expectations of fair, uniform treatment—e.g. job security and an opportunity for steady and predictable advancement based on objective standards—that might be undermined if an employer were required to show more than the system's existence.

(5) The claimant (here the employee) remains free to show that special circumstances warrant a finding that, despite the seniority system's presence, the requested accommodation is reasonable on the particular facts. Special circumstances might alter the important expectations created by a seniority system. These circumstances include that the employer already frequently makes unilateral changes to the system, thereby reducing employee expectations that the system will be followed. The claimant might also show that the system already contains exceptions and that, in the circumstances, one further exception is unlikely to matter. The claimant has the burden of showing special circumstances and must explain why, in the particular case, an exception to the seniority system can constitute a reasonable accommodation even though in the ordinary case it cannot.

(6) *Vande Zande* and *Barnett* are the only cases included in this chapter in which employers successfully argued that, although it was technically possible to make an accommodation to meet the needs of an individual with a disability, this was not required under the law. Furthermore, the defence relied on by the employers was not that making the accommodation would result in "undue hardship" or be a "disproportionate burden" (because, for example, the cost of the accommodation was so high), but that the accommodation required was not "reasonable". The absence of

further cases in which employers have successfully raised a defence to the accommodation requirement reflects the fact that, in the case of qualified individuals with a
disability, the law arguably provides very limited opportunities for justifying a failure
to make an accommodation.

The goal of the extracts in this section has been to demonstrate how the term
"reasonable" can be used to modify the requirement on employers or other covered
parties to make an accommodation. In this context the term signifies that the
accommodation should not result in excessive difficulties or costs for the covered
party.

6.2.1.B. AN ACCOMMODATION THAT IS EFFECTIVE

In this section an alternative understanding of the term is considered, namely that an
accommodation is regarded as reasonable if it is effective in allowing the beneficiary
to carry out (employment-related) tasks. Given that the term "reasonable" is not
easily capable of conveying such a meaning, legislators generally opt to use an
alternative term or elaborate on the meaning of the term "reasonable" if they favour
such an approach.

   The requirement that any accommodation must be effective is illustrated by the
Dutch extracts set out below.

Dutch Act on Equal Treatment on the Grounds of Disability   6.NL.16.
or Chronic Illness 2003

Article 2
The prohibition of making distinction also includes the duty for the person to whom the prohibition is addressed, to make effective accommodations in accordance to the need for this,
unless doing so would constitute a disproportionate burden upon her.

Notes
   (1) Instead of the term "reasonable", which is the term used in Article 5 of the
Directive, Article 2 of the Act on Equal Treatment on the Grounds of Disability or
Chronic Illness employs the term "effective". According to the Dutch government,
the latter term is preferable as it better reflects the fact that an accommodation has to
achieve the pursued effect.[37]

---

[37] Gelijke behandeling op grond van handicap of chronische ziekte, memorie van toelichting, Tweede
Kamer 2001/02, 28 169, nr. 3, 25 [Equal treatment on the ground of disability and chronic disease,
Explanatory Memorandum, Second Chamber of Parliament, 2001–2002, 28 169, nr. 3, at 25]. See also
M. Gijzen, "Het nieuwe gelijkebehandelingsrecht voor gehandicapten en chronisch zieken" in D.J.B. de
Wolff *et al.* (eds.), *Oordelenbundel* (Utrecht, CGB, 2003) 105.

(2) This approach has the advantage of establishing a clearly defined two-stage test to establish whether an employer is obliged to make an accommodation. One must first establish whether any "effective accommodation" is possible and then, quite separately, consider whether making such an accommodation would amount to a "disproportionate burden".

(3) The term "effective accommodation" is not defined in the Act on Equal Treatment on the Grounds of Disability or Chronic Illness. However, based on the Explanatory Memorandum that accompanied the adoption of the Act, one can conclude that the first stage of the test to establish whether an employer, or other covered entity, is under an obligation to provide an accommodation involves asking two separate questions:

(1) Is the accommodation that is being considered suitable and appropriate, i.e. does it enable the individual with a disability to carry out the job?
(2) Is the accommodation that is being considered necessary, i.e. is it a pre-condition to do the job?

If both of these questions have been answered in the affirmative, the "(dis)proportionality" of the burden on the part of the employer can be assessed.

(4) In most cases, "the person to whom the prohibition is addressed" will be the employer. However, as revealed below, this obligation also falls on organisations providing, or testing, vocational training courses.

The following opinions show how this requirement has been interpreted and applied by the Dutch Equal Treatment Commission.

Equal Treatment Commission (Commissie Gelijke Behandeling) **6.NL.17.**
Opinion 2004-140

FAILURE TO PROVIDE ACCOMMODATED EXAMS AT THE SAME PRICE AS ORDINARY
EXAMS AMOUNTED TO DISCRIMINATION

Dutch Exam case 1

Facts: A complaint was lodged by an Anti-Discrimination Bureau before the Equal Treatment Commission concerning the respondent organisation, which organised examinations for the hotel and restaurant branches. The respondent offered "accommodated" examinations to candidates who had a reading disability. However, exam candidates were required to pay €90 extra for an "accommodated" exam. It was alleged that this amounted to an unlawful distinction on the grounds of disability.

Held: By charging extra for the "accommodated" exams, the respondent made an unlawful distinction on the grounds of disability.

Opinion: "5 Consideration of the application

Effective accommodation
5.11 According to Article 2 WGB h/cz [Act on Equal Treatment on the Grounds of Disability or Chronic Illness] the ban on distinction also implies that a person at whom this ban is

directed is required to make effective accommodations in line with the requirements, unless they impose an unreasonable burden on him. This is a self-contained form of distinction which does not occur (as yet) in other equal treatment laws.

5.12 An accommodation must be effective. This means that the accommodation must be appropriate and necessary in order to enable the disabled or chronically ill person to participate like any other in social life or a particular aspect thereof. An accommodation is appropriate if it can eliminate these impediments of whatever kind and can promote the independence and full participation and integration of the disabled or chronically ill person (Parliamentary documents II 2001/02, 28 169, No. 3, p. 25).

5.13 An accommodation is necessary if the same objective cannot be achieved with another, possibly less expensive, provision (Parliamentary documents II 2001/02, 28 169, No. 3, p. 25). When considering what accommodation is effective in a specific case, medical or ergonomic advice will play an important role. The contribution by the disabled person himself is also important (Parliamentary documents II 2001/02, 28 169, No. 3, p. 26).

5.14 The respondent offers examination candidates with a reading disability and/or concentration difficulties an opportunity to take the examination in a separate room, with 15 minutes' additional time. These examination candidates can thereby take the examination without being disturbed. The combination of a separate room and additional time makes up for the disadvantages that they experienced during the examination as a result of their impairments, as the respondent also confirms. The Commission therefore considers this accommodation appropriate to eliminate the obstacles that the normal group examination method entails for this group of disabled persons. Since the Commission has not found that alternatives exist with which the same objective can be achieved and that are less expensive, it concludes that the accommodation is one that is appropriate and necessary."

Notes

(1) Whilst this case did not concern an alleged failure to make an effective accommodation (the respondent was already providing such an accommodation), the Equal Treatment Commission nevertheless took the opportunity to examine the meaning of this requirement. This may well have been because this was one of the first cases dealt with by the Commission under the Act on Equal Treatment on the Grounds of Disability or Chronic Illness 2004.

(2) The Commission stressed that any accommodation must be effective, meaning that it must be appropriate and necessary in order to enable the person who is disabled or chronically ill to participate in social life or a particular aspect thereof on par with non-disabled/healthy individuals. These goals seem to go beyond the mere elimination of employment-related distinctions on the ground of disability, and embrace an agenda for social change.

(3) An accommodation is appropriate if it can eliminate impediments to participation in social life and can promote the independence and full participation and integration of the person who is disabled or chronically ill.

(4) An accommodation is necessary if the same objective cannot be achieved with another, possibly less expensive, provision.

(5) The Commission noted that in determining whether any accommodation was effective a number of factors could be considered, including medical or ergonomic

advice and the contribution of the person with a disability. The Equality Officer took the same approach in the Irish case *An Employee* v. *A Local Authority* cited above, when the Officer held that, in determining what measures could reasonably be required of an employer, account should be taken of specialist advice and medical reports.

Equal Treatment Commission (Commissie Gelijke Behandeling) **6.NL.18.**
Opinion 2005-18

REQUIREMENT TO REACT IN AN ADEQUATE AND TIMELY MANNER TO REQUEST FOR
AN ACCOMMODATION

Dutch Exam Case 2

Facts: The applicant had dyslexia. During 2003–2004, the applicant followed the course to become a physiotherapist at the school of the respondent. The applicant failed a number of exams, and subsequently asked the respondent to check whether the failed exams were the result of his lack of knowledge or were connected with his dyslexia. If the latter, he requested that an alternative form of examination be considered.

Held: The respondent failed to react in an adequate and timely manner to the applicant's request to examine the possibilities for an alternative form of assessment.

Opinion: "5 Consideration of the application

5.1 At issue is whether a distinction was made on grounds of disability or chronic disease by neglecting to make effective accommodations for the applicant, namely to make an effective effort to investigate the need and possibility of an alternative form of exam.

5.3 By virtue of Article 2 WGBh/cz [Act on Equal Treatment on the Grounds of Disability or Chronic Illness], the ban on distinction as defined in Article 1 WGBh/cz further implies that the person at whom this ban is directed is required to make effective accommodations depending on requirements, unless this presents him with a disproportionate burden.

5.10 . . . The Commission . . . considers in the given circumstances that the efforts made and promised by the respondent fell short of the obligation to make effective accommodations (or to investigate this possibility). As a study was concerned in this case to which a lottery system applies where binding advice is given at the end of the first year of study and the applicant had already submitted a request for an accommodation (or investigation into this) after the first ICT [exam], the respondent might have been expected to have acted more thoroughly when dealing with the applicant's request, having regard also to the requirement that the accommodations concerned must be made within a reasonable period . . .

5.11 The Commission draws a conclusion from the progress of the case that the respondent inadequately realised that a request for investigation into the need and possibility of an effective accommodation must be followed by an effective response in line with such request. The respondent should have realised on the basis of the facts and circumstances that the existing accommodations for dyslexic students were considered insufficient by the applicant. A characteristic of an effective accommodation is precisely one tailored to the individual (or his situation) (. . . Article 5 EC Directive 2000/78/EC . . .). If the respondent took the view for reasons it considered justified, including the risk of making a precedent, that the adequacy of the existing facilities should first be examined, this should have been done within a reasonably delimited period. However, there has been no sign of a clear timetable in the present case, so that relations between the parties were needlessly put under stress.

5.12 Having regard to the above, the Commission takes the view that the respondent did not take the effort that might have been expected of it under article 2 WGBh/cz, so that it acted in conflict with the latter act."

Notes

(1) The Commission held that an effective accommodation in this instance implied that action be taken in response to the request from the individual seeking the accommodation within a reasonable period.

(2) The Commission also stressed that "a characteristic of an effective accommodation is precisely one tailored to the individual (or his situation)". An effective accommodation therefore involves an individualised response. In reaching this conclusion the Commission referred, inter alia, to Article 5 of the Employment Equality Directive.

(3) A further issue, which is not raised by these cases or any of the other examination cases considered in this chapter, is the phenomenon of "flagging" exam papers and scores, i.e. specifying that the exam was taken under special conditions (namely that some form of reasonable accommodation was provided), thereby identifying the examinee as having some form of disability. This issue has already attracted the attention of the US courts,[38] and it may do so in Europe in the future.

The adoption of the Employment Equality Directive required the amendment of Irish employment non-discrimination legislation. In doing so the Irish legislator redefined a reasonable accommodation as "appropriate measures".

Irish Equality Act 2004   **6.IE.19.**

Introductory note

The original section 16 of the Employment Equality Act 1998, which was amended by the following provision, is cited above under section **6.2.1.A.**

Amendment of section 16

9. Section 16 (nature and extent of employer's duties in certain cases) of the Act of 1998 is amended—

(a) by the substitution of the following subsection for subsection (3):

---

[38] See, e.g. *Breimhorst, et al* v. *ETS* (2001), US District Court, Northern District of California, Case No. C-99-3387. Under the settlement related to this case the Educational Testing Service, a major US standardised testing organisation, agreed to cease flagging scores on exams which had been taken with an extended time. However, some other US testing organisations continue to flag scores.

'(3)(a) For the purposes of this Act a person who has a disability is fully competent to undertake, and fully capable of undertaking any duties if the person would be so fully competent and capable on reasonable accommodation (in this subsection referred to as "appropriate measures") being provided by the person's employer.

(b) The employer shall take appropriate measures, where needed in a particular case, to enable a person who has a disability—
(i)   to have access to employment,
(ii) to participate more advanced in employment, or
(iii) to undergo training
unless the measures would impose a disproportionate burden on the employer.

(b) and in subsection (4) . . . by inserting the following definition:
"appropriate measures", in relation to a person with a disability—

(a)   means effective and practical measures, where needed in a particular case, to adapt the employer's place of business to the disability concerned,
(b)   without prejudice to the generality of paragraph (a), includes the adaptation of premises and equipment, patterns of working time, distribution of tasks or the provision of training or integration resources, but
(c)   does not include any treatment, facility or thing that the person might ordinarily or reasonably provide for himself or herself.'

Notes

(1) The amendment to section 16 defines a "reasonable accommodation" as an "appropriate measure". A measure is regarded as appropriate if it is effective in allowing an individual with a disability to have access to employment-related activities. An appropriate measure is not required if it would result in a disproportionate burden for an employer. However, the existence of a disproportionate burden does not detract from the fact that the measure would still be appropriate.

(2) A measure which the individual with the disability might be expected to provide for him- or herself is not regarded as "appropriate". It is submitted that such a measure might include the provision of a wheelchair, where the individual is a permanent wheelchair user, or the provision of help with washing or toileting. However, if a wheelchair is only needed for employment-related tasks, its provision would be regarded as an "appropriate measure".

(3) This definition of a "reasonable accommodation" contrasts with the previous definition found in the original section 16 of the Employment Equality Act 1998. The latter Act was adopted prior to the Employment Equality Directive, and was amended in light of the Directive. The amended Act is cited as the Employment Equality Act 1998–2004.

The French legislator has also opted to refer to an obligation to take appropriate measures ("measures appropriées") rather than reasonable accommodations ("aménagements raisonnables") when amending the Labour Code to render it compliant with the Employment Equality Directive.

French Labour Code (Legislative Part)   **6.FR.20.**

Subsection 1: General provisions
Article L. 323-9-1 (inserted by Law Nº. 2005-102 of 11 February, 2005, Art. 24 IV, Official Journal of 12 February, 2005)
In order to guarantee respect for the principle of equal treatment for disabled workers mentioned in article L. 323-3, employers shall take the appropriate measures as a function of concrete needs, to allow the workers mentioned in items 1, 2, 3, 4, 9, 10 and 11 of Article L. 323-3 access to a job or to keep a job corresponding to their qualifications, to carry out or progress towards the same or to allow the same workers to receive training adapted to their needs, subject to the provision that expenses resulting from the implementation of these measures are not disproportionate, considering the assistance which may compensate the expenses incurred by the employer in this capacity in whole or in part.

This assistance may notably relate to the adaptation of machines or equipment, the provision of jobs, including the individual support or equipment necessary for disabled workers to occupy these positions, and the access to their workplaces.

A refusal to take the appropriate measures pursuant to the first paragraph may constitute discrimination, pursuant to Article L. 122-45-4.

A REASONABLE ACCOMMODATION WITH REGARD TO RELIGIOUS PRACTICES

Mention will also be made briefly of the meaning of the term "reasonable" in the context of religious accommodations. Since European material is limited in this respect, reference once again will be made to US developments. Section 701 of the Civil Rights Act 1964 requires that employers reasonably accommodate an employee's or prospective employee's religious observance or practice unless this would result in undue hardship. The concept of reasonable religious accommodation has been elaborated by the Equal Employment Opportunity Commission.

The US Equal Employment Opportunity Commission[39]   **6.US.21.**

"Employers must reasonably accommodate employees' sincerely held religious practices unless doing so would impose an undue hardship on the employer. A reasonable religious accommodation is any adjustment to the work environment that will allow the employee to practice his religion. An employer might accommodate an employee's religious beliefs or practices by allowing: flexible scheduling, voluntary substitutions or swaps, job reassignments and lateral transfers, modification of grooming requirements and other workplace practices, policies and/or procedures."

Note
According to this definition, a reasonable religious accommodation is any adjustment that will allow an employee to practise his religion.

---

[39] Available via the homepage of the US Equal Employment Opportunity Commission.

6.2.1.C.   BOTH AN ACCOMMODATION WHICH DOES NOT RESULT IN EXCESSIVE
             DIFFICULTIES FOR THE EMPLOYER AND AN "EFFECTIVE
             ACCOMMODATION"

The extracts examined in the two previous sections have considered how the term
"reasonable", or a substitute term, can either imply that the accommodation must
not result in excessive costs or difficulties for the employer, or can signify that the
accommodation must be effective or appropriate. This section considers extracts in
which the term "reasonable" is used to convey the dual meaning that any accommodation must both not result in excessive difficulties for the employer and be effective.

THE EMPLOYMENT EQUALITY DIRECTIVE

Introductory note

The Employment Equality Directive does not clearly elaborate on the meaning of the
term "reasonable" in the context of making a "reasonable accommodation".
However, a number of provisions in the Directive suggest that the intention may have
been that the term "reasonable" be understood to mean that any accommodation
must be effective in allowing an individual with a disability to participate in
employment-related activities whilst not resulting in an excessive burden for the
employer.

Council Directive 2000/78/EC of 27 November 2000 establishing **6.EC.22.**
a general framework for equal treatment in employment and occupation

Preamble, Recital 20
Appropriate measures should be provided, i.e. effective and practical measures to adapt the
workplace to the disability, for example adapting premises and equipment, patterns of working
time, the distribution of tasks or the provision of training or integration resources . . .

Article 5
. . . This means that employers shall take appropriate measures, where needed in a particular
case, to enable a person with a disability to have access to, participate in, or advance in
employment, or to undergo training, unless such measures would impose a disproportionate
burden on the employer . . .

Notes
  (1) Article 5 defines the obligation to make a reasonable accommodation as meaning:

  (a) the employer must take "appropriate measures";
  (b) unless this would result in a disproportionate burden.

It is submitted that this reflects poor drafting, as the defence for failing to make a reasonable accommodation (disproportionate burden) is included within the definition of the obligation to make such an accommodation. Matters would have been clarified if the Directive had clearly stated what the obligation to make a "reasonable accommodation" involved and separately specified that employers could rely on the defence that making such an accommodation amounted to a "disproportionate burden".

(2) Nevertheless, one can extract from the text of Article 5, in combination with Recital 20, that a "reasonable accommodation" is any "appropriate measure". A "measure" will be "appropriate" if it is "effective and practical . . . to adapt the workplace to the disability", meaning that it should "enable a person with a disability to have access to, participate in, or advance in employment or to undergo training". One could argue that the "reasonableness" requirement therefore initially relates to the "effectiveness" of the accommodation in allowing employment participation by an individual with a disability. If such an accommodation can be made, the question then arises whether it would amount to a "disproportionate burden". If such a burden will result, then, by definition, the accommodation will not be "reasonable". This interpretation implies that under the Directive the "reasonable" requirement is seen as a modifier to both the accommodation itself and the obligation to make an accommodation, by requiring that the measure is both "effective" and not a "disproportionate burden".

LEGISLATIVE PROVISIONS IN EU MEMBER STATES BASED ON ARTICLE 5 OF THE FRAMEWORK DIRECTIVE

Latvian Labour Law, amended 7 May 2005[40]   **6.LV.23.**

Article 7(3)
To ensure implementation of the principle of equal rights in relation to the disabled persons it is the duty of the employer to take measures required by the circumstances in order to adapt the working environment, promote the possibilities of the disabled persons to establish labour relationships, fulfil work duties, be promoted or undergo professional training to the extent that such measures do not create a disproportionate burden for the employer.

---

[40] In G. Feldhune, "Report on Measures to Combat Discrimination: Directive 2000/43/EC and 2000/78/EC. Country Report Latvia" (European Commission, 2004), available on the website of Directorate-General for Employment, Social Affairs and Equal Opportunities.

Decree (Flemish Community), 8 May 2002 concerning   **6.BE.24.**
balanced participation in the labour market

Article 5
§ 4. Reasonable adjustments are required to ensure that the principle of equal treatment is observed. This entails the intermediary organisations and employer taking suitable steps in a concrete situation, according to requirement, to ensure access to work, participation in work or advancement therein unless these measures impose a disproportionate burden on the employer. This burden will not be regarded as disproportionate if sufficiently offset by existing measures.

Notes
(1) The inspiration of Article 5 of the Employment Equality Directive is clearly evident in both of these provisions. They define a reasonable accommodation or adjustment as "measures", or "suitable steps", which allow an individual (with a disability) access to employment or employment-related activities, but which do not result in a "disproportionate burden" for the employer.
(2) As noted above, with regard to Article 5 of the Employment Equality Directive, it is submitted that this approach reflects poor drafting as it merges what should, arguably, be a clearly defined two-stage approach to establish whether any accommodation should be made. Such an approach seems to be embraced by, for example, both Dutch and German legislation.
(3) With regard to Latvia, no more detailed provisions exist clarifying the relevant statutory provision.
(4) With regard to the Decree of the Flemish Community, reference should also be made to the *Belgian Guide to . . . Reasonable Accommodations for Persons with a Disability at Work* resulting from the inter-ministerial initiative which is referred to above (**6.2.1.A.**).

UNITED KINGDOM

The UK has the longest history, and most experience, of legislating to combat disability discrimination and providing for a duty to make reasonable accommodations within Europe.

The Disability Discrimination Act 1995, as amended   **6.UK.25.**

3A Meaning of 'discrimination'
. . .
(2) For the purposes of this Part, a person also discriminates against a disabled person if he fails to comply with a duty to make reasonable adjustments imposed on him in relation to the disabled person.

...

4A Employers: duty to make adjustments
(1) Where—

    (a)   a provision, criterion or practice applied by or on behalf of an employer, or
    (b)   any physical feature of premises occupied by the employer,

places the disabled person concerned at a substantial disadvantage in comparison with persons who are not disabled, it is the duty of the employer to take such steps as it is reasonable, in all the circumstances of the case, for him to have to take in order to prevent the provision, criterion or practice, or feature, having that effect.

   ...

18B Reasonable adjustments: supplementary
(1) In determining whether it is reasonable for a person to have to take a particular step in order to comply with a duty to make reasonable adjustments, regard shall be had, in particular, to—

    (a)   the extent to which taking the step would prevent the effect in relation to which the duty is imposed;
    (b)   the extent to which it is practicable for him to take the step;
    (c)   the financial and other costs which would be incurred by him in taking the step and the extent to which taking it would disrupt any of his activities;
    (d)   the extent of his financial and other resources;
    (e)   the availability to him of financial or other assistance with respect to taking the step;
    (f)   the nature of his activities and the size of his undertaking;
    (g)   where the step would be taken in relation to a private household, the extent to which taking it would—
        (i)   disrupt that household, or
        (ii) disturb any person residing there.

Notes

(1) The British Disability Discrimination Act 1995 was adopted prior to the Employment Equality Directive, and was subsequently amended by statutory regulation in order to ensure full compliance.

(2) Of the points listed under section 18B, only the first relates to the effectiveness of the adjustment. All the remaining points address the difficulty an employer might experience in making the accommodation.

(3) The Disability Discrimination Act also requires that reasonable adjustments are made in order to allow people with a disability to access a service.[41] The DDA does not provide any guidance on what might be regarded as reasonable in this context, although the relevant Code of Practice contains a list of factors similar to those found in section 18B relating to employment—effectiveness, practicability, cost, disruption, resources, amount already spent on adjustments and availability of other sources of assistance.[42]

---

[41] Sections 21 (service provision generally) and 21E (services provided by public authorities).
[42] Code of Practice, Goods, Facilities, Services, and Premises (DRC 2002), para. 4.22.

(4) The detail of the British legislation concerning the concept of "reasonableness" contracts starkly with the brevity found in the other domestic legislation designed to implement the Directive considered under this section.

6.2.1.D.   COMPARATIVE OVERVIEW

The analysis has revealed that there are three different approaches according to which the term "reasonable" can be understood. In the first approach, an accommodation will only be regarded as "reasonable" if it does not impose excessive difficulties or costs on the employer or other covered party. Generally this requirement exists alongside the separate defence that making an accommodation would result in a disproportionate burden or undue hardship.[43] This implies that an accommodation can be regarded as "unreasonable" and therefore not required, and, in such situations, the (stricter) disproportionate burden test will not be considered. It possibly also implies that an accommodation could be regarded as "reasonable" but still not required because it would result in a disproportionate burden. However, in practice, under this approach, it is difficult to conceive of such a situation.

According to the second approach, an accommodation will be regarded as "reasonable" if it is effective in allowing the relevant individual to carry out the necessary (employment-related) tasks. Given that the term "reasonable" cannot easily convey this meaning, European jurisdictions that have followed this approach have sensibly used alternative terms. Dutch legislation makes no reference to a "reasonable" accommodation but instead requires an "effective" accommodation, whilst the Irish Employment Equality Act 1998–2004 defines a "reasonable" accommodation as "appropriate measures", which is also the term found in the French Labour Code. The difficulties of using the term "reasonable" to convey this meaning are illustrated by US legislation and case-law. In both *Vande Zande* and *Barnett* the complainants sought to argue that a "reasonable" accommodation was one that was "apt or efficacious" (*Vande Zande*) or "effective" (*Barnett*). Barnett relied on the extracts from the EEOC Regulations, which are also cited in this chapter, to support his claim. However, in both instances the courts rejected this interpretation, and held that an accommodation has to be "reasonable", meaning that it should be expedient and proportionate to the resulting benefits (*Vande Zande*), or "reasonable on its face, i.e. ordinarily or in the run of cases" (*Barnett*). This experience suggests that the Dutch, Irish and French legislatures have wisely opted to use alternative language to convey the meaning that an accommodation must be effective.

What both approaches outlined above have in common is that they require a two-stage test to establish whether any accommodation must be made. First, in principle the employer or other covered party is obliged to make an accommodation. Generally the legislation sets out the objective of any accommodation. On occasions

---

[43] Although the Finnish legislation only makes use of the "reasonableness" requirement in establishing the limits to making an accommodation.

this objective is broad and relatively unelaborated, e.g. Finnish law requires that the accommodation must "help a person with disabilities to gain access to work or training, to cope at work and to advance their career", whilst other legal provisions provide more detail with regard to the objectives pursued, e.g. the German legislation lists five separate rights which could be met through making an accommodation. In contrast, Dutch and Irish law stress the effectiveness or appropriateness of any accommodation when setting out the general obligation.

At the second stage the question of whether any defence to the requirement to make an accommodation as defined in the legislation exists. Most legal systems described in these two sections make use of the disproportionate burden defence. However, those described in section 6.2.1.A also combine this with the additional test of "reasonableness", whilst those considered under section 6.2.1.B rely exclusively on the disproportionate burden defence. In contrast, Finnish legislation refers to the "reasonableness" of the accommodation only in this context. Nevertheless, in effect, it can be expected that the "reasonableness" requirement under Finnish law will be interpreted in the same way as the disproportionate burden and "reasonableness" requirements found in other jurisdictions.

The last way is which the term "reasonable" is used in legislation is to convey both that the accommodation must be effective and that it must not impose significant inconvenience or cost on the employer or covered party. This is the approach adopted in the UK, which has the longest standing reasonable accommodation requirement within the EU. Given that this approach is also adopted in Article 5 of the Employment Equality Directive, the European Court of Justice will be confronted with the task of interpreting, and thereby enabling national courts to apply, this dual meaning in the future. The Court may draw inspiration from the legal systems identified in the first two sections of this heading, which have opted for a two-staged approach to determining whether any accommodation is required. However, in doing so, the Court will have to delineate clearly the two different meanings of the term "reasonable" in its case-law.

6.2.2. THE MEANING OF THE TERM "ACCOMMODATION" AND THE KINDS OF ACCOMMODATIONS THAT ARE REQUIRED

The goal of any accommodation under Article 5 of the Employment Equality Directive is to enable a person with a disability "to have access to, participate in, or advance in employment". Assessing what kind of accommodation will achieve this goal, and therefore what kind of accommodation is required, involves an individual analysis taking into account the situation of the individual and the employment or training at issue. A similar analysis must frequently also be undertaken where the goal is to allow an individual with a disability to access goods or services,[44] or where the

---

[44] However, see section 6.6.2, which discusses the "anticipatory" nature of the duty to provide reasonable adjustments to allow access for disabled people as a group with regard to services under British law.

beneficiary of the accommodation is defined by another characteristic, such as religious belief. The reasonable accommodation requirement therefore generally involves an individual analysis and a tailored individual solution. Furthermore, this is true not only with regard to determining what kind of accommodation is required, but also with regard to other elements of the provision, such as assessing whether making any particular accommodation would amount to a "disproportionate burden". As a consequence, it is not possible for legislation to provide a definitive list of appropriate and required accommodations (or define "disproportionate burden" in absolute financial terms). Legislation can, however, provide a generic definition accompanied by an illustrative list of appropriate kinds of accommodation. Furthermore, case-law that establishes the duty to (not) make certain accommodations in specific circumstances can also clarify the requirement. These points are illustrated by the selected extracts.

6.2.2.A.   GENERAL CLASSIFICATIONS OF ACCOMMODATION

In spite of the very diverse nature of possible accommodations, one can nevertheless develop a number of classification systems to describe the kind of accommodations which can be required.

EMPLOYMENT-RELATED ACCOMMODATIONS—"HARD" AND "SOFT" COSTS

As Stein has pointed out, writing in the context of US law, employment-related accommodations can fall into one or both of two categories depending on the nature of the costs they impose:

M. A. Stein, "The Law and Economics of Disability   **6.US.26.**
Accommodations"[45]

"Reasonable accommodations can encompass a wide range of individualized adjustments to existing workplace conditions, but are mainly conceptualized as falling into one or both of two categories. The first category requires the alteration or provision of a physical plant, such as ramping a stair to accommodate the needs of an employee who uses a wheelchair. These type of accommodations involve 'hard' costs, meaning that they invoke readily quantifiable out-of-pocket expenses. Purchasing and installing a ramp, for example, is usually a one-time expenditure with a fixed and knowable cost.

The second type of accommodation involves the alteration of the way in which a job is performed. This might mean not requiring a wheelchair-using store clerk to stack high shelves. These sort of accommodations bring into play 'soft' costs, which are more difficult to quantify. This hypothetical employee might require a fellow worker to stack the high shelves while she

[45] (2003) 53 *Duke LJ* 88–9.

staffed the register. Her circumstance might also necessitate that a human resource manager meet with other employees to explain the change in their daily duties, or that a supervisor be required to learn how to take these alterations into consideration when evaluating overall job performance [references omitted]."

STAGE WITHIN THE EMPLOYMENT PROCESS

A second way of classifying employment-related accommodations focuses on the stage within the employment process at which the need for an accommodation arises. Broadly speaking, accommodations can be required at the recruitment stage (including accommodations related to information made available to applicants, interview procedures and aptitude/knowledge testing or assessment); during employment (including working conditions, job tasks, training, promotion and employee benefits); and after the employment contract has come to an end (including dismissal procedures and benefits provided to ex-employees). The extent of the obligation to make an accommodation is unlikely to be the same with regard to these different stages, and an employer can be expected to owe the most extensive duty to current employees. This is reflected in the extracts from the GB Disability Rights Commission Code of Practice which are found below (section 6.2.2.C).

CHARACTERISTICS OF BENEFICIARIES

Lastly, accommodations can be classified according to the characteristics of the (potential) beneficiary. The assessment and selection of an appropriate accommodation for an individual with a disability may differ from the approach followed where the accommodation is directed at an individual with other characteristics, such as a follower of minority religions. The kind of appropriate accommodations may also differ. In addition, where legal systems do establish an accommodation requirement to benefit individuals other than people with disabilities, evidence suggests that the standard required is frequently lower than that required for disability-related accommodations, meaning that it is far easier to justify a failure to make an accommodation.

6.2.2.B.   TERMINOLOGY

As was the case with the term "reasonable", in some jurisdictions the word "accommodations" has been replaced with another term. In the UK, legislation requires the making of reasonable "adjustments"; Finnish law refers to reasonable "steps"; whilst the Irish Employment Equality Act 1998–2004 and the French Labour Code, drawing their inspiration from the preamble to the Directive, define a reasonable accommodation as an "appropriate measure". This latter term is also found in the Lithuanian Law on Equal Treatment[46] and the Slovakian Act on Equal Treatment in Certain Areas and Protection Against Discrimination.[47] However, unlike the case with regard to the term "reasonable", it is submitted that the use of an alternative term with regard to "accommodations" is of no legal significance, and that in essence all of the terms referred to above convey the same meaning. This meaning is examined in the following three sub-sections.

6.2.2.C.   THE QUALITIES REQUIRED FOR ANY ACCOMMODATION

In some legal systems the qualities required of any accommodation—or the standards that an accommodation must meet—are set out in the legislation or accompanying guidelines. In such situations any possible accommodation should be measured against the set standards to determine if it is suitable. A particularly good example of this approach is found in the Belgian inter-ministerial brochure that has been issued to provide guidance on the meaning of the term "reasonable accommodation" in the various domestic laws.

Belgian Guide to . . . Reasonable Accommodations for Persons   **6.BE.27.**
with a Disability at Work, March 2005

"2. The criteria that an 'accommodation' must meet
An accommodation must meet three conditions: it must be effective and ensure equivalent and independent participation by disabled people

2.1 Effectiveness
Reasonable accommodations must be effective. They must effectively enable the person with a disability to participate in an activity. If an accommodation results in little specific improvement, the conclusion must be that it is not effective in that case.
    Example:

—No effective accommodations are possible for persons with a visual disability who wish to become an airline pilot.

2.2 Equivalence
Persons with a disability must be able to make equivalent use of facilities and services in the establishment.
    Examples:

—Employees with a disability must be able to eat together with their colleagues in the works canteen rather than in a separate room or at their desk.
—Employees with a disability must be able to attend all meetings and participate in other activities associated with their work.

[46] Art. 5.
[47] § 7.

2.3 Independence

The degree of independence is a decisive factor. Accommodations that ensure that a disabled person is enabled to participate without third party assistance are preferred.

Example:

— A person with a disability must be able to open the door for himself without having to wait for assistance from a chance passer-by.

Example:

— A workplace must be so rearranged that an employee can move independently in a wheelchair and has access to the essential sources of information in the immediate neighbourhood."

Notes

(1) As was seen in section 6.2.1.B, under Dutch and Irish legislation the requirement that the accommodation be "effective" (Dutch law) or "appropriate" (Irish Employment Equality Act 1998–2004) is statutory. Adopting a similar position—though based on a different set of legal provisions—Judge Posner, in the US case *Vande Zande*, simply stated that an "inefficacious change" that would not enable a person with a disability to work should not be regarded as an accommodation at all (see section 6.2.1.A). These approaches concur with the position adopted in paragraph 2.1 of the inter-ministerial brochure.

(2) The Belgian brochure is notable in that it sets out two additional requirements which should be met by any accommodation—namely, that the accommodation should enable persons with a disability to make equivalent use of facilities and services, and that the accommodation should promote independence for persons with a disability. The first example provided to illustrate the "equivalence" requirement (access to works' canteen) shows that the reasonable accommodation requirement extends beyond measures needed to allow an individual with a disability to carry out his or her work, and also includes access to benefits and services provided to all employees. This is also true of other jurisdictions with regard to the reasonable accommodation requirement. In contrast, whilst "independence" is clearly a desirable characteristic of an accommodation designed to benefit an individual with a disability, it is not clear how far the requirement that any accommodation should provide the maximum degree of independence is a principle common to other jurisdictions.

An alternative approach is found in Article 5 of the Directive and, for example, the Irish Employment Equality Act 1998–2004, which sets out the qualities any accommodation should have in relation to the employment-related goals that must be achieved.

Irish Employment Equality Act 1998–2004, Amended Section 16   **6.IE.28.**

. . .(b) The employer shall take appropriate measures, where needed in a particular case, to enable a person who has a disability—

(i)   to have access to employment,
(ii)   to participate or advance in employment, or
(iii) to undergo training,

unless the measures would impose a disproportionate burden on the employer.

Note
Given that this approach is adopted in Article 5 of the Employment Equality Directive, it is not surprising to find it reflected in a number of European statutory provisions, e.g. Finnish Non-Discrimination Act 21/2004, section 5; Greek Anti-Discrimination Law n.3304/2005, Article 10; Decree of the Flemish Community of 8 May 2002 concerning proportionate participation in the labour market, Article 5; and Lithuanian Law on Equal Treatment, Article 5.

Where accommodations serve non-employment-related purposes, a different set of goals must obviously be set. This is illustrated by the following extract.

Slovakian Act No. 29/1984 Coll. on the system of primary and   **6.SK.29.**
secondary schools (the School Act) as amended

§ 32b
(1) An integrated pupil shall mean a pupil with special educational and training needs admitted to a primary or secondary school . . .
    (3) Prior to pupil's admission the headmaster of the school shall in cooperation with the school special education teacher [section 25 paragraph 2 of Act No. 2 Coll. on school facilities as amended] or specialised educational counselling institution [section 22 of Act No. 279/1993 Coll. on school facilities as amended] create conditions for integrated education of the pupil, make adjustments in the classroom and the school, arrange for compensatory devices, or take other measures in order to ensure the required level of integrated education and training for the pupil.

§ 32c
The rights and duties of participants in school integration
(1) Pupils with special educational and training needs shall have the right to individual approach in education and training respecting their capabilities and health status, to instructions by a teacher having the necessary specialised and teaching skills, to education and training in safe and healthy environment, to respect for them and to ensured protection against physical and mental violence.

Notes

(1) In addition to requiring employment-related reasonable accommodations for people with disabilities[48] as required by the Directive, Slovakian law also requires that adjustments are made for children with disabilities in order to allow them to receive an integrated education. The goals of the relevant adjustments are to ensure the required level of integrated education and training for the pupil.

(2) Unlike the employment-related provisions, the law does not establish a limitation to the obligation to make adjustments based on a disproportionate burden requirement.

(3) Slovakia is not unique in this respect. A number of other EU Member States have adopted legal provisions requiring adjustments for children with disabilities in order to allow them to follow mainstream education, e.g. UK and Malta.

An interesting and alternative approach is adopted under Spanish law with regard to non-employment-related accommodations. The law defines a reasonable accommodation as:

Spanish Law 51/2003 For Equal Opportunities and Against the   **6.ES.30.**
Discrimination of Disabled Persons

Article 7
. . . measures to adapt the physical, social, and attitudinal environment to the specific needs of persons with disability which effectively and practically, without involving a disproportionate burden, facilitate accessibility or participation for a person with disability on the same terms as for other citizens.[49]

Notes

(1) The goal of any accommodation is to allow access or participation of persons with disabilities "on the same terms as for other citizens". The material scope of this law, and therefore the scope of the obligation to make accommodations, is telecommunications, built-up public spaces and buildings, transport, goods and services available to the public and relations with public administration.

(2) This goal can be compared to the goal of reasonable adjustments in the more limited area of access to services found under the UK Disability Discrimination Act (to ensure a practice, policy or procedure does not make it impossible or unreasonably difficult for disabled persons to use services, section 21(1)), which is discussed in more detail below in section 6.2.2.D.

---

[48] § 7, Act No. 365/2004 Coll. on Equal Treatment in Certain Areas and Protection against Discrimination, amending and supplementing certain other laws (Anti-discrimination Act).
[49] L. Cachón, "Report on Measures to Combat Discrimination: Directive 2000/43/EC and 2000/78/EC. Country Report Spain" (European Commission, 2005), available on the website of Directorate-General for Employment, Social Affairs and Equal Opportunities.

(3) In addition to this "equality of opportunity"-oriented goal, the Spanish statute explicitly requires that adaptations must be made not only to the physical environment, but also to the social and attitudinal environment. In adopting this approach, the statute explicitly embraces a social model of disability. This model is based on a socio-political analysis that argues that disability stems primarily from the failure of the social environment to adjust to the needs and aspirations of people with impairments, rather than from the inability of people with impairments to adapt to the environment. According to this perspective, the difficulties confronting disabled people arise from the disabling environment rather than from the individual's impairment. At its most extreme, this model holds that disability is purely a social construction. This model also implies that society has the responsibility to adapt to meet the needs of people with impairments.[50]

(4) The reasonable accommodation requirement with regard to people with disabilities and employment is found in a second Spanish statute (Article 37.2 bis of Law 13/1982 on the Social Integration of the Disabled as amended by Law 62/2003 transposing the Employment Equality Directive), and closely mirrors Article 5 of the Directive.

6.2.2.D.   THE KINDS OF ACCOMMODATIONS WHICH ARE REQUIRED

Illustrative lists providing information on the kind of accommodations required can be found in both statutory provisions and their accompanying Codes of Practice or Guidelines. In addition, case-law provides further guidance.

STATUTORY PROVISIONS

United Kingdom

The Disability Discrimination Act 1995 (as amended)   **6.UK.31.**
[relating to employment]

18B Reasonable adjustments: supplementary
. . .
(2) The following are examples of steps which a person may need to take in relation to a disabled person in order to comply with a duty to make reasonable adjustments—

   (a) making adjustments to premises;
   (b) allocating some of the disabled person's duties to another person;

---

[50] There is a wealth of literature addressing theoretical models of disability and justice can most certainly not be done to the relevant arguments and models here. See, e.g. M. Oliver, *Understanding Disability: from Theory to Practice* (Basingstoke, Macmillan Press, 1996) and M. Priestley, "Constructions and Creations: Idealism, Materialism and Disability Theory" (1998) 13 *Disability & Society* 75–94.

(c)   transferring him to fill an existing vacancy;
(d)   altering his hours of working or training;
(e)   assigning him to a different place of work or training;
(f)   allowing him to be absent during working or training hours for rehabilitation, assess-
      ment or treatment;
(g)   giving, or arranging for, training or mentoring (whether for the disabled person or any
      other person);
(h)   acquiring or modifying equipment;
(i)   modifying instructions or reference manuals;
(j)   modifying procedures for testing or assessment;
(k)   providing a reader or interpreter;
(l)   providing supervision or other support.

Notes
   (1) This is only an illustrative list of the kinds of employment-related accommodations which can be required.
   (2) This list has been supplemented by a Code of Practice, extracts of which
appear below under "Guidelines Accompanying Legislation", which provides further
guidance and, in particular, concrete illustrations of suitable adjustments.

Disability Discrimination Act 1995 as amended   **6.UK.32.**
[relating to service provision][51]

21.—(1) Where a provider of services has a practice, policy or procedure which makes it impossible or unreasonably difficult for disabled persons to make use of a service which he provides,
or is prepared to provide, to other members of the public, it is his duty to take such steps as it is
reasonable, in all the circumstances of the case, for him to have to take in order to change that
practice, policy or procedure so that it no longer has that effect.
(2) Where a physical feature (for example, one arising from the design or construction of a
building or the approach or access to premises) makes it impossible or unreasonably difficult
for disabled persons to make use of such a service, it is the duty of the provider of that service
to take such steps as it is reasonable, in all the circumstances of the case, for him to have to take
in order to—

(a)   remove the feature:
(b)   alter it so that it no longer has that effect;
(c)   provide a reasonable means of avoiding the feature; or
(d)   provide a reasonable alternative method of making the service in question available to
      disabled persons.

. . .

(4) Where an auxiliary aid or service (for example, the provision of information on audio tape
or of a sign language interpreter) would—

_____
[51] Similar obligations apply to public authorities under s. 21E of the Act.

(a)   enable disabled persons to make use of a service which a provider of services provides, or is prepared to provide, to members of the public, or

(b)   facilitate the use by disabled persons of such a service,

it is the duty of the provider of that service to take such steps as it is reasonable, in all the circumstances of the case, for him to have to take in order to provide that auxiliary aid or service.

Notes

(1) The kinds of accommodations envisaged in this provision involve changes to practices, policies or procedures (to ensure that it is not impossible or unreasonably difficult for a person with a disability to make use of a service); the removal or altering of a physical feature of a building; provision of a reasonable means of avoiding the feature or a reasonable alternative method of making use of the service; and the provision of auxiliary aids or services—e.g. information on audio tape or sign language interpretation.

(2) These provisions have been brought into force gradually. Those relating to practices, policies and procedures, auxiliary aids and services came into force in October 1999, and the remaining duties relating to physical features came into force in October 2004.

Ireland

Irish Equal Status Act 2000   **6.IE.33.**

4.—(1) For the purposes of this Act discrimination includes a refusal or failure by the provider of a service to do all that is reasonable to accommodate the needs of a person with a disability by providing special treatment or facilities, if without such special treatment or facilities it would be impossible or unduly difficult for the person to avail himself or herself of the service.

Notes

(1) The Irish statute requires that service providers provide "special treatment or facilities". This terminology has been criticised by Gooding and Casserley on the grounds that it "undermines the principle of inclusivity". They argue that it detracts from the obligation to ensure access and focuses instead on a conception of people with disabilities as "special" and, as such, in need of "special treatment", rather than adjustments which may benefit the whole of society and which are required in the interests of broad inclusivity.[52]

(2) One of the few Irish cases concerning reasonable accommodation and access to services is *Roche* v. *Alabaster*, cited in section 6.2.1.A, where the Equality Officer held

---

[52] C. Gooding and C. Casserley, "Discrimination Laws and Goods and Services" in Lawson and Gooding, above n. 9, 154.

that a reasonable accommodation in the form of allowing the complainant to enter a restaurant in the company of his guide dog should have been made.

GUIDELINES ACCOMPANYING LEGISLATION

In some jurisdictions, such as the UK and Belgium, the authorities have sought to assist those obliged to make accommodations by providing (lengthy and detailed) guidance on suitable measures, sometimes with specific case studies. These documents provide a good overview of the kinds of action that can be required with regard to disability-related employment accommodations, both within the jurisdictions in question and more generally. In addition, the extracts from the US and UK below illustrate the kind of accommodations that can be required with regard to individuals who wish to follow religious practices.

United Kingdom

Disability Discrimination Act 1995—Code of Practice— **6.GB.34.**
Employment and Occupation[53]

"What adjustments might an employer have to make when arranging or conducting interviews?
    Employers should think ahead for interviews. Depending upon the circumstances, changes may need to be made to arrangements for interviews or to the way in which interviews are carried out . . .
    An employer arranges a British Sign Language (BSL) interpreter to attend an interview with a deaf candidate who uses BSL to communicate. The interviewer also allows extra time for the interview . . . These are likely to be reasonable adjustments for the employer to make . . .
    An employer allows a candidate who has a learning disability to bring a supportive person to an interview to assist when answering questions that are not part of the assessment itself. This is likely to be a reasonable adjustment to the selection process.
    . . .
    What about aptitude or other tests in the recruitment process?
    The Act does not prevent employers carrying out aptitude or other tests, including psychological tests. However, routine testing of all candidates may still discriminate against particular individuals or substantially disadvantage them. In those cases, the employer would need to revise the tests—or the way the results are assessed—to take account of a disabled candidate. This does not apply, however, where the nature and form of the test is necessary to assess a matter relevant to the job. The following are examples of adjustments which may be reasonable:

    — allowing a disabled person extra time to complete the test
    — permitting a disabled person the assistance of a reader or scribe during the test

---

[53] UK Disability Rights Commission (London, TSO, 2004).

— accepting a lower 'pass rate' for a person whose disability inhibits performance in such a test.

The extent to which such adjustments might be required would depend on how closely the test is related to the job in question and what adjustments the employer might have to make if the applicant were given the job.

. . .

What adjustments might an employer have to make?

The Act gives a number of examples of adjustments, or 'steps', which employers may have to take, if it is reasonable for them to have to do so. Any necessary adjustments should be implemented in a timely fashion, and it may also be necessary for an employer to make more than one adjustment. It is advisable to agree any proposed adjustments with the disabled person in question before they are made . . . Steps other than those listed here, or a combination of steps, will sometimes have to be taken. However, the steps in the Act are:

— making adjustments to premises

An employer makes structural or other physical changes such as widening a doorway, providing a ramp or moving furniture for a wheelchair user; relocates light switches, door handles or shelves for someone who has difficulty in reaching; or provides appropriate contrast in décor to help the safe mobility of a visually impaired person.

— allocating some of the disabled person's duties to another person

An employer reallocates minor or subsidiary duties to another employee as a disabled person has difficulty doing them because of his disability. For example, the job involves occasionally going onto the open roof of a building but the employer transfers this work away from an employee whose disability involves sever vertigo.

— transferring the person to fill an existing vacancy

An employer should consider whether a suitable alternative post is available for an employee who becomes disabled (or whose disability worsens), where no reasonable adjustment would enable the employee to continue doing the current job. Such a post might also involve retraining or other reasonable adjustments such as equipment for the new post.

— altering the person's hours of working or training

This could include allowing a disabled person to work flexible hours to enable him to have additional breaks to overcome fatigue arising from his disability. It could also include permitting part time working, or different working hours to avoid the need to travel in the rush hour if this is a problem related to an impairment. A phased return to work with a gradual build-up of hours might also be appropriate in some circumstances.

— assigning the person to a different place of work or training

An employer relocates the work station of a newly disabled employee (who now uses a wheel-chair) from an inaccessible third floor office to an accessible one on the ground floor. It would be reasonable to move his place of work to other premises of the same employer if the first building is inaccessible.

— allowing the person to be absent during working or training hours for rehabilitation, assessment or treatment

An employer allows a person who has become disabled more time off during work than would be allowed to non-disabled employees to enable him to have rehabilitation training. A similar adjustment would be appropriate if a disability worsens or if a disabled person needs occasional treatment anyway.
. . .

As mentioned above, it might be reasonable for employers to have to take other steps, which are not given as examples in the Act. These steps could include:

— conducting a proper assessment of what reasonable adjustments may be required
— permitting flexible working
— allowing a disabled employee to take a period of disability leave . . .
— participating in supported employment schemes . . .
— employing a support worker to assist a disabled employee . . .
— modifying disciplinary or grievance procedures . . .
— adjusting redundancy selection criteria . . .
— modifying performance-related pay arrangements . . .

In some cases a reasonable adjustment will not work without the co-operation of other employees. Employees may therefore have an important role in helping to ensure that a reasonable adjustment is carried out in practice. Subject to considerations about confidentiality, employers must ensure that this happens. It is unlikely to be a valid defence to a claim under the Act that staff were obstructive or unhelpful when the employer tried to make reasonable adjustments. An employer would at least need to be able to show that it took such behaviour seriously and dealt with it appropriately . . .

The inclusion of unnecessary or marginal requirements in a job description or person specification can lead to discrimination . . ."

Belgium

Belgian Guide to . . . Reasonable Accommodations for Persons   **6.BE.35.**
with a Disability at Work, March 2005

"The various forms of reasonable accommodations
It is of course impossible to provide an exhaustive list of all existing and conceivable measures that could involve an accommodation for a disabled person. Every individual is unique and has his own qualities and limitations. Accommodations can therefore take various forms. They are grouped into the following categories.

3.2.1 Adjusted equipment
The purchase of new equipment or the adjusting of existing equipment can be a reasonable accommodation.

3.2.2 Accessible instructions
Written instructions and codes of conduct must be provided in accessible form.

3.2.3 Material adjustments to the workplace
Making certain structural adjustments to the shop floor or changes in the material fitting out of a workplace can also be a reasonable accommodation.

3.2.4 Reorganisation of duties
This entails permitting a change as from the point when and/or the way in which a task is completed. Certain tasks that cannot be undertaken by an employee because of his/her disability may also be transferred to another employee.

3.2.5 Home Working
Through the progress in communications technology (computers, email, fax, telephone, etc.) part of the job or the entire job can in certain cases be undertaken at home.

3.2.6 Adjusted timetable
This accommodation may mean offering the employee an opportunity to work part-time, starting or finishing work at a different time, permitting periodic interruptions or rearranging the period by which a certain task must be completed.

3.2.7 Policy changes
Changing particular rules or provisions to cope with an employee's disability may also constitute a reasonable accommodation.

3.2.8 Allocating a new position
If an employee is no longer able to discharge his/her duties because of a disability, another vacant position may be offered that will suit the employee.

3.2.9 Assistance and monitoring
Disabled persons may be able to discharge their duties more easily with additional monitoring or assistance. Such support may come from within the firm (colleagues, etc.) or outside."

Note

These extracts only address employment-related accommodations for people with disabilities, but they reveal the breadth of the accommodations which can be required. Some of the accommodations referred to above, e.g. altering the person's hours of working or training, may be suitable for individuals who request an accommodation in order to allow them to practise their religion (where the law requires such accommodations), but in most instances this will not be the case. Again, in such instances, an individualised analysis will be required to identify an appropriate accommodation. In addition, accommodations can be required to allow people with disabilities access to goods and services, and these extracts do not address such accommodations.

GUIDELINES RELATED TO ACCOMMODATING RELIGIOUS PRACTICES—US AND UK

Whilst legal provisions requiring the accommodation of religious practices do exist in Europe, they are far less developed than they are in the US. For this reason, reference will be made here to US EEOC Guidelines on Discrimination because of religion,[54] which includes, inter alia, an illustrative list of suitable accommodations and the British Guidelines relating to the obligation not to indirectly discriminate against individuals on the grounds of religion or belief. It can be expected that similar accommodations will be relevant in Europe where the obligation exists to accommodate religious practices.

Code of Federal Regulations, Title 29, Volume 4, Part 1605, **6.US.36.**
Guidelines on Discrimination because of Religion, 29 CFR § 1605.2[55]

" . . .d. Alternatives for accommodating religious practices
(1) Employees and prospective employees most frequently request an accommodation because their religious practices conflict with their work schedules. The following subsections are some means of accommodating the conflict between work schedules and religious practices which the Commission believes that employers and labor organizations should consider as part of the obligation to accommodate and which the Commission will consider in investigating a charge. These are not intended to be all-inclusive. There are often other alternatives which would reasonably accommodate an individual's religious practices when they conflict with a work schedule. There are also employment practices besides work scheduling which may conflict with religious practices and cause an individual to request an accommodation . . . The principles expressed in these Guidelines apply as well to such requests for accommodation.

(i) Voluntary Substitutes and 'Swaps'.
Reasonable accommodation without undue hardship is generally possible where a voluntary substitute with substantially similar qualifications is available. One means of substitution is the voluntary swap. In a number of cases, the securing of a substitute has been left entirely up to the individual seeking the accommodation. The Commission believes that the obligation to accommodate requires that employers and labor organizations facilitate the securing of a voluntary substitute with substantially similar qualifications. Some means of doing this which employers and labor organizations should consider are: to publicize policies regarding accommodation and voluntary substitution; to promote an atmosphere in which such substitutions are favorably regarded; to provide a central file, bulletin board or other means for matching voluntary substitutes with positions for which substitutes are needed.

(ii) Flexible Scheduling.
One means of providing reasonable accommodation for the religious practices of employees or prospective employees which employers and labor organizations should consider is the creation of a flexible work schedule for individuals requesting accommodation. The following list is an example of areas in which flexibility might be introduced: flexible arrival and departure times; floating or optional holidays; flexible work breaks; use of lunch time in exchange for early

[54] These guidelines have been codified in the US Code of Federal Regulations, which are the collected statutory instruments of the US Federal Agencies.
[55] At 193–4, available on the website of the US Government Printing Office.

departure; staggered work hours; and permitting an employee to make up time lost due to the observance of religious practices.

(iii) Lateral Transfer and Change of Job Assignments.
When an employee cannot be accommodated either as to his or her entire job or an assignment within the job, employers and labor organizations should consider whether or not it is possible to change the job assignment or give the employee a lateral transfer . . ."

British law does not establish a clear duty to provide reasonable accommodations or reasonable adjustments with regard to religion or belief. However, the Employment Equality (Religion or Belief Regulations) 2003,[56] which transpose the relevant provisions of the Employment Equality Directive, do prohibit indirect discrimination on the grounds of religion or belief, and the Advisory Conciliation and Arbitration Service (ACAS) Guidelines on the Regulations[57] also discuss some of the kinds of requests which employees may make in this context. These areas would also be of relevance where an obligation to accommodate exists.

Advisory, Conciliation and Arbitration Service (ACAS),   6.GB.37.
"A Guide for Employers and Employees. Religion or Belief and the Workplace"

"Religious Observance in the Workplace
4.1 The Regulations do not say that employers must provide time and facilities for religious or belief observance in the workplace. However, employers should consider whether their policies, rules and procedures indirectly discriminate against staff of particular religions or beliefs and if so whether reasonable changes might be made.

4.2 Many religions or beliefs have special festival or spiritual observance days. A worker may request holidays in order to celebrate festivals or attend ceremonies. An employer should sympathetically consider such a request where it is reasonable and practical for the employee to be away from work, and they have sufficient holiday entitlement in hand. While it may be practical for one or a small number to be absent it might be difficult if numerous such requests are made. In these circumstances the employer should discuss the matter with the employees affected, and with any recognised trade union, with the aim of balancing the needs of the business and those of other employees.

Employers should carefully consider whether their criteria for deciding who should and who should not be granted leave may indirectly discriminate . . .

4.3 Employers who operate a holiday system whereby the organisation closes for specific periods when all staff must take their annual leave should consider whether such closures are justified as they may prevent individuals taking annual leave at times of specific religious significance to them. Such closures may be justified by the business need to undertake machinery maintenance for instance. However, it would be good practice for such employers to consider how they might balance the needs of the business and those of their staff.

---

[56] Employment Equality (Religion or Belief) Regulation 2003, SI 2003, No. 1660.
[57] *Advisory Conciliation and Arbitration Service (ACAS) Guidelines,* available on the website of ACAS.

4.4 Organisations should have clear, reasonable procedures for handling requests for leave and ensure that all staff are aware of and adhere to the procedures. Staff should give as much notice as possible when requesting leave and in doing so should also consider that there may be a number of their colleagues who would like leave at the same time. Employers should be aware that some religious or belief festivals are aligned with lunar phases and therefore dates change from year to year; the dates for some festivals do not become clear until quite close to the actual day. Discussion and flexibility between staff and managers will usually result in a mutually acceptable compromise.

Organisations should take care not to disadvantage those workers who do not hold any specific religion or belief.

4.5 Some religions or beliefs have specific dietary requirements. If staff bring food into the workplace they may need to store and heat food separately from other food, for example Muslims will wish to ensure their food is not in contact with pork (or anything that may have been in contact with pork, such as cloths or sponges). It is good practice to consult your employees on such issues and find a mutually acceptable solution to any dietary problems . . .

4.6 Some religions require their followers to pray at specific times during the day. Staff may therefore request access to an appropriate quiet place (or prayer room) to undertake their religious observance. Employers are not required to provide a prayer room. However, if a quiet place is available and allowing its use for prayer does not cause problems for other workers or the business, organisations should agree to the request. Where possible, it is good employee relations practice for organisations to set aside a quiet room or area for prayer or private contemplation. In consultation with staff, it may be possible to designate an area for all staff for the specific purpose of prayer or contemplation rather than just a general rest room. Such a room might also be welcomed by those for whom prayer is a religious obligation and also by those who, for example, have suffered a recent bereavement. Organisations should consider providing separate storage facilities for ceremonial objects.

4.7 Employers are not required to enter into significant expenditure and/or building alterations to meet religious needs. In any event many needs will involve little or no change. For instance some religions or beliefs require a person to wash before prayer. This is often done symbolically or by using the existing facilities. However, it is good practice to consult with staff and to consider whether there is anything reasonable and practical which can be done to help staff meet the ritual requirements of their religion. It may help, for example, if all workers understand the religious observances of their colleagues thus avoiding embarrassment or difficulties for those practicing their religious obligations.

4.8 Some religions or beliefs do not allow individuals to undress or shower in the company of others. If an organisation requires its staff, for reasons of health and safety, to change their clothing and/or shower, it is good employee relations practice to explore how such needs can be met. Insistence upon same-sex communal shower and changing facilities could constitute indirect discrimination (or harassment) as it may disadvantage or offend staff of a particular religion or belief whose requirement for modesty extend to changing their clothing in the presence of others, even of the same sex.

4.9 Some religions require extended periods of fasting. Employers may wish to consider how they can support staff through such a period. However, employers should take care to ensure that they do not place unreasonable extra burdens on other workers which may cause conflict between workers or claims of discrimination.

4.10 If it is practical and safe to do so, staff may welcome the opportunity to wear clothing consistent with their religion. Where organizations adopt a specific dress code, careful consideration should be given to the proposed code to ensure it does not conflict with the dress requirements of some religions. General dress codes which have the effect of conflicting with religious requirements may constitute indirect discrimination unless they can be justified for example, on the grounds of health and safety.

4.11 If organisations have a policy on the wearing of jewellery, having tattoos or other markings, they should try and be flexible and reasonable concerning items of jewellery and markings which are traditional within some religions or beliefs. Unjustifiable policies and rules may constitute indirect discrimination."

EXAMPLES FROM CASE-LAW—TRANSFER OF EMPLOYEE TO ANOTHER POSITION

The following two cases, from the Netherlands and the UK, along with the US case *Barnett* considered under section 6.2.1.A, all involve the question of whether transferring a disabled employee to another position, when, as a result of a disability, he or she is no longer able to continue in the original position, can be regarded as a reasonable or effective accommodation. As can be seen from the UK Code of Practice ("transferring the person to fill an existing vacancy"), the Belgian inter-ministerial brochure ("allocating a new position") and the US ADA ("reassignment to a vacant position"),[58] such an accommodation can, in principle, be required. However, as was clear from *Barnett*, courts are not always prepared to require that an employer take such action. The following cases, and *Barnett*, explore the limits of the obligation to transfer a disabled employee to a new position.

Equal Treatment Commission (Commissie Gelijke Behandeling) **6.NL.38.**
Opinion 2004-21

TRANSFER TO ANOTHER POSITION CAN BE AN EFFECTIVE ACCOMMODATION

Civil servant Case

Facts: The applicant, a civil servant who worked for the City Council of Rotterdam (the respondent), had a visual disability. He requested an adapted work place, but the respondent refused to make the requested accommodations. The applicant did not work for 5 years and the respondent fired the applicant in December 2003. In the applicant's view he had been dismissed by reason of his disability and he also claimed that the respondent had refused to bring about effective accommodations or to offer him another job within the organisation. In the respondent's view the applicant had not been offered another job within the same organisation as a result of his own behaviour.

Held: To the extent that the applicant's claim was admitted, the Equal Treatment Commission found a breach of the Equal Treatment Act on the grounds of Disability or Chronic Illness. It held that the respondent, by refusing to transfer him and by dismissing him, failed in its duty to bring about effective accommodations and acted in contravention of the Act.

Opinion: "5.1 The question is at issue whether the respondent has made a distinction based on a disability and/or chronic disease by:
— refusing to implement accommodations at the workplace and to transfer the applicant following illness; . . .

---

[58] Americans with Disabilities Act 42 U.S.C. § 12111(9) (B).

Transfer following illness

5.17 The applicant has argued that the respondent made a distinction based on disability in the discharge of the obligation to take steps to transfer him. On an internal transfer, the respondent had to make accommodations on account of the applicant's disability.

. . .

5.21 The facts adduced by the applicant lead one to suspect that following the period of his illness he was not transferred because of his disability. It is now up to the respondent to prove that it did not act in conflict with the WGB h/cz [Equal Treatment Act on the grounds of Disability or Chronic Illness].

5.22 The respondent has pointed out that the applicant apparently had no faith in the municipal career advisory centre. In addition, it has argued that the obligation to take steps to transfer the applicant did not mean that the respondent is obliged to transfer the applicant but that the respondent must simply attempt to achieve a transfer. The respondent further asserted that the applicant no longer wished to return to his old workplace. The respondent holds it against the applicant that he was open only to jobs in salary class 9.

5.23 The Commission considers that the respondent has not thereby succeeded in proving that it did not act in conflict with the WGB h/cz.

5.24 The documents submitted by the parties and the investigation made at the hearing have shown that the respondent offered the applicant no internal position—of any kind whatever—and took no action on his applications. The facts have further shown that the respondent did not itself follow the recommendations of the career advisory centre. The respondent moreover withdrew the career itinerary set out in the action plan, and which was expected to continue until September 2003.

. . .

5.27 Internal transfer of the applicant requires necessary adjustments in connection with the applicant's disability. The parties have made the making of accommodations by means of a confirmatory agreement dependent on an internal transfer. By neglecting to transfer the applicant internally, the respondent has avoided its obligation to make accommodations.

5.28 The Commission considers that the respondent has made an illegal distinction on grounds of the WGB h/cz."

Notes

(1) It is not clear from this case why the disabled employee requested a transfer to another position—and specifically whether this was a result of a disability which could not be accommodated and which prevented him from carrying out his original position. Both *Archibald* v. *Fife* (see below **6.GB.39.**) and *Barnett* did involve such a scenario.

(2) In this case the employer made no attempt to offer the disabled individual an alternative position, and did not respond appropriately to the efforts made by the disabled individual when applying for alternative positions within the employer's organisation. The defence raised by the employer, that the disabled individual displayed a lack of trust in the organisation and that the employer was not obliged to arrange a transfer but simply to attempt to arrange such a transfer, were rejected by the Commission in light of the fact that the employer had made no attempts to arrange a transfer. This case can be contrasted with the UK case, *Archibald* v. *Fife*, which raised more complex issues, and where the employer did

enable the disabled employee to train for an alternative position, but failed actually to offer her such a position.

House of Lords, Session 2003-04[59]   **6.UK.39.**
Archibald v. *Fife*

TRANSFER TO ANOTHER POSITION WITHOUT REQUIRING STANDARD COMPETITIVE
INTERVIEW CAN BE A REASONABLE ADJUSTMENT

Archibald v. Fife

Facts: The complainant worked as a road sweeper for Fife Council. As a result of an operation she became disabled and was no longer able to continue in this position. She received retraining from her employer and subsequently applied for over 100 internal vacancies involving junior level office work. However, because all office positions were assessed as being at a higher grade than her previous manual position, the Council applied its standard redeployment policy, which meant that she had to undertake a competitive interview. She failed to obtain any of the posts and was subsequently dismissed. The complainant submitted a series of appeals arguing that she had been the victim of disability discrimination and that she should not have been required to go through the competitive interviews if she could show she was qualified and suitable for the job in question. The lower courts all found in favour of the employer, and the case eventually reached the House of Lords. In writing the lead judgment, Baroness Hale referred to section 6 of the Disability Discrimination Act 1995, which was in force at the time,[60] which provided, inter alia:

"(1) Where—

    (a)   any arrangements made by or on behalf of an employer, . . .,

place the disabled person concerned at a substantial disadvantage in comparison with persons who are not disabled, it is the duty of the employer to take such steps as it is reasonable, in all the circumstances of the case, for him to have to take in order to prevent the arrangements or feature having that effect . . .

(3) The following are examples of steps which an employer may have to take in relation to a disabled person in order to comply with subsection (1)—. . .

    (c)   transferring him to fill an existing vacancy;

(4) In determining whether it is reasonable for an employer to have to take a particular step in order to comply with subsection (1), regard shall be had, in particular, to—

    (a)   the extent to which taking the step would prevent the effect in question;
    (b)   the extent to which it is practicable for the employer to take the step;
    (c)   the financial and other costs which would be incurred by the employer in taking the step and the extent to which taking it would disrupt any of his activities;
    (d)   the extent of the employer's financial and other resources;
    (e)   the availability to the employer of financial or other assistance with respect to taking the step."

Held: The appeal was allowed and the case was remitted to the Employment Tribunal to consider whether the council had fulfilled its duty to take such steps as it was reasonable in all the circumstances.

---

[59] [2004] IRLR 651.
[60] The equivalent (slightly amended) provisions can now be found in ss. 4A and 18B of the Disability Discrimination Act 1995 as amended.

Judgment: BARONESS HALE OF RICHMOND: "65. The duty is to take such steps as it is reasonable in all the circumstances of the case for the employer to have to take. Could this ever include transferring her [the complainant] to fill an existing vacancy at a slightly higher grade without competitive interview? It is noteworthy that the council did do a great deal to help Mrs Archibald. They arranged retraining for her. They kept her on the books for a great deal longer than they normally would have done while she retrained and then looked for alternative posts. They automatically short-listed her for the posts for which she applied. They went rather beyond their normal policies in cases of redundancy or ill-health. They were behaving as if they did have a duty towards her under section 6(1) even if they did not think that they did. They would have been prepared to transfer her without competitive interview to another job at the same or a lower grade, even though there might be others better qualified to do it. But as she was at the bottom of the manual grade and all office jobs were nominally at a higher grade, there was no equal or lower grade job to which she could be transferred.

66. Section 6(3)(c) merely refers to 'an existing vacancy'. It does not qualify this by any words such as 'at the same or a lower grade'. It does refer to 'transferring' rather than 'promoting' her, but as a matter of language a transfer can be upwards as well as sideways or downwards. Furthermore, transferring her 'to fill' an existing vacancy is clearly more than merely allowing her to apply, short-listing or considering her for an existing vacancy. If that were all it meant, it would add nothing to the existing non-discrimination requirements: the employer is already required by section 4(2)(b) not to discriminate against a disabled employee in the opportunities afforded for promotion, transfer, training or any other benefit.

67. On the face of it, therefore, transferring Mrs Archibald to a sedentary position which she was qualified to fill was among the steps which it might have been reasonable in all the circumstances for the council to have to take once she could no longer walk and sweep. Is there any reason to hold to the contrary?

. . .

70. This will depend upon all the circumstances of the case, having regard in particular to the factors laid down in section 6(4). An important component in the circumstances must be the council's redeployment policy. This currently distinguishes between transfer to a post at the same or a lower grade and transfer to a post at a higher grade. Generally it must be reasonable for a council to maintain this distinction. But it might be reasonable to expect a small modification either in general or in the particular case to meet the needs of a well-qualified and well-motivated employee who has become disabled. Manual grades are often technically lower than non-manual grades even if the difference in pay is minimal. The possibility of transfer to fill an existing vacancy might become completely illusory for a manual worker who became incapable of manual work but was assessed as very well fitted for low grade sedentary work if that person was always up against the problem presented by her background. We are not talking here of high grade positions where it is not only possible but important to make fine judgments about who will be best for the job. We are talking of positions which a great many people could fill and for which no one candidate may be obviously 'the best'. There is no law against discriminating against people with a background in manual work, but it might be reasonable for an employer to have to take that difficulty into account when considering the transfer of a disabled worker who could no longer do that type of work. I only say 'might' because it depends upon all the circumstances of the case. While the 1995 Act clearly lays great emphasis on the circumstances of the individual case, the general policy of achieving fairness and transparency in local government appointments is also extremely important. The real question may be whether this case should have been seen as a sideways rather than an upwards move."

Notes

(1) This case can be contrasted with the US case *Barnett* (see section 6.2.1.A), in which the US Supreme Court held that the requirement to make a reasonable accommodation did not, in general, oblige an employer to take action which conflicted with seniority rules, on the grounds that such action would not be "reasonable". In that case the Court held that a job reassignment, which would normally be reasonable within the meaning of the statute, would become unreasonable when it conflicted with a unilaterally imposed seniority system. Amongst the reasons given for this decision, the Court held that "the typical seniority system provides important employee benefits by creating, and fulfilling, employee expectations of fair, uniform treatment". In addition, the accommodation "would substitute a complex case-specific 'accommodation' decision made by the management for the more uniform, impersonal operation of seniority rules".

(2) The UK House of Lords adopted a different approach in holding that the general merit-based appointment-making system, which could arguably be viewed as creating expectations amongst other employees as was the case in *Barnett*, could be adapted to provide for a reasonable adjustment for a disabled employee by allowing her to be appointed directly to a slightly more senior (sedentary) position once she became unable to carry our her previously held manual job as a result of disability.

(3) Where an employer follows the approach favoured by the House of Lords in *Archibald* v. *Fife*, no identifiable (non-disabled) individual will be disadvantaged by being denied a job opportunity. The opportunity lost would be that of applying for a particular job (that was awarded to a specific individual with a disability), rather than the job itself, which could always have been awarded to another (unknown) individual on the basis of merit. In contrast, in *Barnett* identifiable individuals would have lost out, in that they would otherwise have been entitled to claim the desired job on the basis of seniority, if the Supreme Court had found that awarding such positions to persons with disabilities was a required reasonable accommodation.

(4) Having said that, it is unlikely that a European court would have the option of following the precedent of the US Supreme Court if called upon to decide in a *Barnett*-like scenario. Under Article 16(b) of the Employment Equality Directive Member States are required to ensure that

> "any provisions contrary to the principle of equal treatment which are included in contracts or collective agreements, internal rules of undertakings or rules governing the independent occupations and professions and workers' and employers' organisations are, or may be, declared null and void or are amended."[61]

Should a European court nevertheless be confronted with such a measure, it is arguable that it would be obliged to interpret it in line with this Article.

---

[61] See section 6.4 of this chapter for further commentary.

Finally, under this heading, it is worth noting that retaining a disabled employee in a position which she is able to do, rather than transferring her to another position, can also be a form of accommodation.

Court of Pistoia, Labour Section, 30 September 2005   **6.IT.40.**
Laura Neri v. *Ministry of Justice*

FAILURE TO ALLOW A DISABLED EMPLOYEE TO CONTINUE WORKING NEAR TO HER PLACE OF RESIDENCE AND TO INSIST ON A TRANSFER TO ANOTHER OFFICE CAN BE A FORM OF DISCRIMINATION

The Court Officer Case

Facts: The claimant was a woman with a disability who worked as a court officer in Italy. As a result of her (mobility) disability, it was necessary for her to work near to her place of residence. She was employed at a court in Monsummano Terme which met these conditions. Her employer then decided to move her to a new workplace in Pistoia, further away from her residence, and she appealed against this decision.

Held: The employer acted in a discriminatory way by deciding to relocate the employee and was required to continue to employ her in Monsummano Terme.

Judgment: "Moving on to examine the claimant's claim, it must be considered that pursuant to Art. 2, 1st Paragraph, item b) of Legislative Decree 216/2003, indirect discrimination takes place when an apparently neutral provision, criterion, practice, act, agreement or action may place individuals professing a given religion or ideology of another nature, disabled individuals, or individuals of a certain age or sexual orientation in a situation of particular disadvantage with regard to other individuals.

On this point, it should be considered that Legislative Decree 216/2003 implemented Directive 2000/78/EC on equal treatment regarding employment and working conditions, so that for the purposes of a correct exegesis of internal regulations, it appears to be necessary to compare these with the purposes and content of European Community regulations.

The 6th Recital of the directive recalls that the Community Charter of the Fundamental Social Rights of Workers recognises the importance of fighting any form of discrimination, including the need to undertake appropriate actions for the social and economic integration of older and disabled individuals; the 9th Recital adds that employment and *working conditions* are key elements for guaranteeing equal opportunities to all citizens, and contribute notably to the full participation of the same individuals in economic, cultural and social life and to their personal realisation; that developing this indication, the 20th Recital adds that it is opportune to foresee appropriate measures, or efficient and practical measures intended to arrange the workplace as a function of the disability, e.g. arranging premises or adapting equipment, work times, the allocation of tasks or providing means of training or organisation.

To this must be added that Art. 5 of the directive is expressly concerned with reasonable solutions to guarantee respect for the principle of equal treatment for disabled individuals. The regulation adds that this means that the employer shall take the appropriate measures as a function of the demands of concrete situations, in order to allow disabled individuals access to jobs, to carry out the same, to receive promotion or to allow them to receive training, unless these provisions impose a disproportionate financial burden on the employer.

692

This solution is not disproportionate, whenever the burden is compensated to a sufficient degree by existing measures within the framework of the policy on disabled individuals of the member state.

It follows in absolutely guaranteed fashion from such regulatory indicators that the initiatives relating to the place of employment which translate into a notable deterioration of the position of the worker, or into *a particular disadvantage* for the same individual, must be considered as objectively discriminatory.

Furthermore, Legislative Decree 216/2003, for the purpose of mitigating conflicting interests, stipulates in Art. 3, 6th Paragraph that differences of treatment which, while being indirectly discriminatory, are objectively justified by legitimate objectives pursued through appropriate and necessary means do not constitute cases of discrimination pursuant to Art. 2.

It nevertheless appears clear that the deduction of the aims which justify the decision taken represent a burden on the employer. The question arises prior to the one concerning the burden of proof and relates to the demarcation of the issue to be decided.

In the case in question, since the public authority chose not to express the reasons for the secondment of the claimant to the office of the Small Claims Court of Pistoia, instead of the section of Monsummano Terme, which is evidently closer to the residence of Mrs Neri (Larciano) and this in both the administrative and the jurisdictional phases, it is not made clear in which direction the judge should direct his own powers of investigation. On reflection, it is indeed not a case of determining facts but of understanding (and subsequently of criticising the consistency of) evaluations which are currently mysterious.

From this follows the order to the Public Authority to cease the discriminatory behaviour, through the secondment of the claimant for the period stipulated by the measure of 29 July, 2005, at the Court of Pistoia, Division Monsummano Terme [emphasis in original]."

Notes

(1) The Italian Decree which is designed to transpose the Employment Equality Directive (Legislative Decree 216/2003) fails to explicitly provide for a requirement to provide a reasonable accommodation to disabled people and in this respect is in breach of the Directive.

(2) Given the absence of a requirement to provide a reasonable accommodation, the Court in this judgment appears to regard the decision to relocate the employee as a form of indirect discrimination ("indirect discrimination takes place when an apparently neutral provision, criterion, practice, act, agreement or action may place . . . disabled individuals . . . in a situation of particular disadvantage with regard to other individuals").

(3) In reaching this conclusion, the Court refers to Article 5 of the Directive and related recitals from the preamble, and thereby acts in accordance with the principle of interpreting national legislation in conformity with EC law.

6.2.2.E.   CHOICE AS TO THE APPROPRIATE ACCOMMODATION

The German extract in this section considers the obligation imposed on an employer where a choice exists amongst a variety of possible suitable accommodations.

RIGHT TO REASONABLE ACCOMMODATION/RIGHT TO BE EMPLOYED IN A WAY THAT
ALLOWS A SEVERELY DISABLED EMPLOYEE TO UTILISE AND IMPROVE SKILLS AND
KNOWLEDGE TO THE FULLEST EXTENT POSSIBLE—VARIETY OF MEANS OF
ACHIEVING THIS GOAL

The Lathe Case

Facts: The claimant, who was severely disabled, was employed as a lathe operator by the defendant in 1989. From 1994 the claimant worked as a CNC lathe operator on an RNC2 machine. In 1996 he was transferred to a conventional lathe. The claimant then applied to the Labour Court to order his employer to employ him on the RNC2 machine again as work on the conventional lathe was not suitable for his disability. In 1997 an agreement was reached whereby the defendant undertook to employ the claimant on a "Spinner" CNC lathe and to adapt the workplace in such a way that the claimant could be employed at the machine in a manner suitable for a severely disabled person. As of 2000, the claimant was employed at a drilling machine. He requested that he be transferred to the "Spinner", and argued that he had a contractual right to be employed on this machine as a result of the settlement reached in 1997, that work on the drilling machine did not correspond to his employment contract, and that this workplace was not suitable for a disabled person. The defendant argued that the claimant had agreed to be employed at the drilling machine. The Labour Court of First Instance rejected the claimant's claim, so the claimant appealed to State Labour Court. He applied for the initial judgment to be revoked and for the defendant to be ordered to employ him on the "Spinner" CNC lathe, or to employ him on the RNC2 CNC machine or another CNC machine.

Held: According to Section 81 paragraph 4 SGB IX, a severely disabled employee not only has a right to a workplace designed and adapted so as to be suitable for a severely disabled person, he or she also has a right to employment which is specifically defined. He or she has the right to be allocated employment, taking his or her education and training and state of health into consideration, that allows him or her to utilise and improve skills and knowledge to the fullest extent possible. The employer must fulfil this right to employment within the limits of what can reasonably be expected.

The defendant was ordered by the court to employ the claimant as a CNC lathe operator on a CNC lathe available in the factory.

Judgment: "38. The appeal is justified in part. The complaint is permissible (1.) [not considered further below]. The claimant does not have a right to employment on the 'Spinner' lathe (2.). Neither does he have a right to employment on the RNC2. However, he does have a right to employment as a CNC lathe operator at a CNC lathe available in the factory (3.)

. . .

43 (2.) The claimant does not have a right to employment on the 'Spinner' lathe.

. . .

50. A right to employment at the 'Spinner' workplace is . . . not justified according to Section 81 paragraph 4 SGB IX. The workplace was a single-operator workplace suitable for a disabled person because the defendant did not always have to stand, but was able to carry out part of the work sitting down, particularly the auxiliary tasks. Because of reorganisation, two-machine operation, disappearance of the auxiliary work at this workplace, the 'Spinner' workplace is no longer suitable for a disabled person. There are no more work processes which could be carried out sitting, while standing and alternating between the machines is stressful from a physical point of view.

51. (3.) The claimant does not have a right to employment at the RNC2 CNC lathe (1st alternative application). According to the contract he only has a right to be employed as a CNC lathe operator at a CNC lathe available in the factory (2nd alternative application), and to this extent the complaint is justified . . .

54. According to Section 81 paragraph 4 SGB IX severely disabled employees not only have a right to a workplace designed and adapted so as to be suitable for the severely disabled, he or she also has a right to employment which is specifically defined. He or she has the right to be allocated employment, taking his or her education and training and state of health into consideration, that allows him or her to utilise and improve skills and knowledge to the fullest extent possible. The employer must fulfil this right to employment within the limits of what can reasonably be expected . . . To this extent, the employer may also be obliged by means of reorganisation to create a workplace which is suitable to the needs of a disabled person and where the right to employment as described in the contract can be fulfilled.

55. According to the contract of employment and according to Section 81 paragraph 4 SGB IX, the claimant has a right to employment as a CNC lathe operator. He was employed as a lathe operator. He has been employed as a lathe operator since 1994 and has achieved corresponding qualifications and skill by means of induction and training. The object of the contract of employment is therefore a duty to provide performance and, accordingly, a right to employment as a CNC lathe operator. The claimant must be mainly employed on corresponding activities.

. . .

58. As a final result this means: the claimant has a contractual right and a right arising from Section 81 paragraph 4 SGB IX to be mostly employed at a CNC automatic lathe. However, in addition other tasks can be allocated to him, e.g. drilling work. The workplaces allocated to him must be designed so as to be suitable for a disabled person, and it may be that the defendant must implement a reasonable reorganisation in order to create such a CNC lathe operator workplace which is suitable for a disabled person. The right to employment of the claimant can be fulfilled by employment at the RNC2; however the claimant does not have a right to this specific workplace. The defendant can also reorganise and for example employ the claimant at the 'Spinner' again, having made this a workplace suitable for disabled persons. However, the defendant can also allocate a CNC workplace at another automatic lathe, in so far as this workplace is suitable for a disabled person. Because the defendant has several possible ways of fulfilling the right to employment of the claimant according to the aforementioned rules by means of decisions regarding the organisation of his works, it was not possible to issue a judgment to the effect that the defendant has the duty to employ the claimant at a specific workplace. The defendant could only be ordered to employ the claimant as a CNC lathe operator at a CNC lathe available in the factory."

Notes

(1) The text of Section 81 paragraph 4 SGB IX can be found under section 6.2.1.A of this chapter.

(2) The last paragraph of this judgment in particular makes it clear that the employer can fulfil its obligation to "accommodate" the disabled employee in a number of ways, and the choice as to which exact accommodation to make lies with the employer. The employer is not obliged per se to make the exact accommodation requested by the employee (or any representative of the employee or an accommodation suggested by a relevant expert). However, the accommodation chosen must achieve the goal set by the relevant legislation (in casu, inter alia, a right to a workplace designed and adapted so as to be suitable for a severely disabled person). This implies that the employer need not make an expensive accommodation if a cheaper alternative exists, nor need the employer make the "best" accommodation if

an alternative will meet (although not equally well) the relevant standard. It is submitted that this is a principle which applies to the reasonable accommodation requirement in general, and is not confined to German law.

6.2.2.F.   COMPARATIVE OVERVIEW

Given the very diverse nature of the accommodations that can be required, it is not possible for legislation to provide an overview of all the measures which can amount to an appropriate accommodation. This is also a consequence of the fact that, in general, an accommodation is an individualised response which is designed to meet the needs of a particular person in a specific situation. Codes of Practice or Guidelines, such as those produced in the UK and Belgium, can significantly help to clarify the nature of the obligation to make an accommodation on employers and the kinds of actions that can be required. In addition, or alternatively, such documents and the original statutes can seek to provide clarification through elaborating on the criteria any accommodation should meet, or the (employment-related) goals that it should serve. Terminological differences, whereby accommodations are referred to as "adjustments", "steps" or "measures" under domestic law, seem to be of little significance, and all terms reflect a similar requirement.

   The form of accommodation examined through the case-law extracts in this section, namely the transfer of a disabled employee to an alternative position when, as a result of disability, the employee is unable to carry out the original position, is generally recognised as a suitable form of reasonable accommodation. However, as the *Barnett* case shows, courts will not always be willing to find that such an accommodation is "reasonable" or that it does not amount to a disproportionate burden. Nevertheless, it is submitted that, particularly in the case of a large employer which employs people to perform many different functions, it will be very difficult for a European employer to argue that such an accommodation is not required.

6.3. ENTITLEMENT TO CLAIM A REASONABLE ACCOMMODATION AND OBLIGATIONS ON BOTH PARTIES

This section will examine both the question of who is entitled to claim an accommodation and what conditions they must meet when doing so, as well as considering the obligations which are imposed on the party from whom an accommodation is claimed.

   A distinction must be made between the category of potential claimants (a generic group) and the facts that a specific individual who falls into a generic category must prove in a particular case in order to claim entitlement to an accommodation.

6.3.1. THE GENERIC CATEGORIES

6.3.1.A. PEOPLE WITH DISABILITIES

Article 5 of the Employment Equality Directive requires only that reasonable accommodations be made for "persons with disabilities", and the right to claim an accommodation under EC law is confined to this group as a result. In most Member States the category of people with disabilities who are potentially able to claim an accommodation is the same as the category of people with disabilities who are entitled to protection under non-discrimination law. However, in a few instances, such as the Netherlands (where disability non-discrimination law protects both individuals with, and without, a disability from discrimination), the latter group is defined more broadly, and the reasonable accommodation is far more targeted (only at people with disabilities).

Examples of provisions which specify that the duty to make an accommodation is owed to the general group of people with disabilities can be found under section 6.2 of this chapter, and include the Finnish Non-Discrimination Act 21/2004, section 5 and the Greek Anti-Discrimination Law n. 3302/2005, Article 10 (both "persons with disabilities"), the Irish Equal Status Act, section 4 ("a person with a disability"), the Latvian Labour Law, Article 7(3) ("disabled persons") and the Lithuanian Law on Equal Treatment, Article 5 ("the disabled"). In contrast, § 81 SGB IX of the German Social Law Code, Book Nine, confines the right to obtain an accommodation to the (much) narrower group of "severely disabled persons".

6.3.1.B. MEMBERS OF RELIGIOUS MINORITIES AND INDIVIDUALS WISHING TO MANIFEST THEIR RELIGION

A limited number of European States provide for an obligation to make an accommodation to allow an individual to practise his or her religion or for measures which have an equivalent effect.

Bulgarian Protection against Discrimination Act **6.BG.42.**
(effective as of 1 January 2004)

Article 13(2)
Where this would not result in excessive difficulty for the organisation and implementation of the production process, and where there are possible ways to compensate for any potential unfavourable consequences of this on the overall production outcome, an employer shall ensure work conditions in terms of working hours and days of rest in accordance with the requirement of the religion or faith professed by an employee.

Notes

(1) Any employee who professes a religion or faith is entitled to request such an accommodation. In practice, working arrangements are likely to be such that they already accommodate the religious practices of followers of the majority or established religion, and only followers of minority religions will need to request an accommodation.

(2) The obligation is limited to "working hours and days of rest in accordance with the requirements of the religion or faith professed by an employee" (and not, for example, dress or dietary requirements resulting from (manifesting) a religion or faith). In addition, the obligation only applies when it "would not result in excessive difficulty for the organisation and implementation of the production process, and where there are possible ways to compensate for any potential unfavourable consequences of this on the overall production outcome". It is not clear whether the obligation to compensate for "unfavourable consequences" lies with the employee who has requested the accommodation or not.

(3) A similar provision is found in Polish law, whereby members of churches or religious associations can obtain time off work or study in order to celebrate religious holidays.[62]

In contrast, in Spain Cooperation Agreements between the state and three religious communities (Evangelical, Jewish and Islamic) contain specific regulations to ensure the reasonable accommodation for employees of particular religions.

L. Cachón, "Report on measures to combat discrimination: **6.ES.43.**
Directive 2000/43/EC and 2000/78/EC. Country report Spain"[63]
Spanish Cooperation Agreements

"The Cooperation Agreements with the various religious communities (Evangelical, Jewish and Islamic) [FN 12: *Law 24/1992, of 10 November, adopting the cooperation agreement between the State and the Federation of Evangelical Religious Entities of Spain; Law 25/1992, of 10 November, adopting the cooperation agreement between the State and the Jewish Communities of Spain; and Law 26/1992, of 10 November, adopting the cooperation agreement between the State and the Islamic Commission of Spain*] contain specific regulations to ensure reasonable accommodation for employees of particular religions. The three Agreements contain provisions on religious holidays and special diets. The weekly days of rest of the Seventh Day Adventists (Friday evening and all of Saturday) and Jewish communities (Friday evening and all of Saturday) can be granted instead of the day provided by article 37.1 of the Workers' Statute as the general rule (Saturday afternoon or Monday morning and all of Sunday), but only with the agreement of all the parties, which case-law has

---

[62] Art. 42 Ustawa z 17 maja 1989 r. o gwarancjach sumienia i wyznania (Act of 17 May 1989 on Guarantees of the Freedom of Conscience and Religion).

[63] (European Commission, 2005) 15, available on the website of Directorate-General for Employment, Social Affairs and Equal Opportunities.

interpreted as being possible only if this is asked for by the employee before the signing of the contract. [FN 13: *The Constitutional Court (19/1985, 13 February) provided on the subject of the weekly day of rest for a Seventh Day Adventist employee (albeit before the signature of the Cooperation Agreement with the Federation of Evangelical Religious Entities of Spain) that one party to the contract cannot impose modifications in working conditions on the other party, and also that the consideration of Sunday as the general day of weekly rest (article 37.1 of the Workers' Statute) is based not on a religious rule but on a secular tradition.*]

Moreover, members of the Islamic communities belonging to the Islamic Commission may request to stop work every Friday from 13.30 to 16.30 and one hour before sundown during Ramadan. This right is also subject to an agreement with the employer, and the hours not worked must be made up. [FN 14: *There is an interesting doctrine on this subject in the Judgment of the Madrid High Court of 27 October 1997. In this case, pursuant to a request for adaptation of working hours, the Court—not referring once to the Cooperation Agreement—states that although the courts of first instance should make employers adapt working hours, thus allowing their employees properly to meet their religious obligations, as well as not making them behave in a way incompatible with their beliefs, the worker must show loyalty and good faith, indicating his or her religious faith and the special working hours arising from it when applying for the job.*]

In the case of the Islamic Commission and the Jewish community, there is a list of religious holidays that can replace those established in article 37 of the Workers' Statute, again with the agreement of both parties.

As for special diet (adaptation of food to Islamic religious precepts and mealtimes during the Ramadan fast), this possibility is provided only for Muslims interned in public centres or establishments and on military premises, as well as in public and subsidized private schools, where requested, and not as an obligation, since article 14.4 of the Agreement clearly states only that in this case 'attempts shall be made'. In the field of employment, therefore, there are no provisions on this issue."

Notes

(1) The Spanish approach is targeted at followers of (specific) minority religions, and does not amount to a general accommodation obligation owed to all individuals who require accommodations in order to practise their religion.

(2) As with the Bulgarian legislation, the focus is on accommodations regarding working time, although, in the context of Islamic dietary requirements, some further action is also recommended.

Whilst British legislation does not explicitly provide for a duty to accommodate the religious needs of employees and job applicants, Rix LJ of the Court of Appeal seemed to suggest that such an obligation could be read into UK law, and specifically the requirements relating to unfair dismissal, in the *Copsey* case.

Court of Appeal, 25 July 2005[64]   **6.GB.44.**
Copsey v. *WBB Devon Clays Ltd*

EMPLOYERS MIGHT BE OBLIGED TO ACCOMMODATE NEEDS OF RELIGIOUS
EMPLOYEES IN CERTAIN CIRCUMSTANCES

Copsey

Facts: The appellant was dismissed following his refusal to work on Sundays. He claimed his employer had violated his rights to religious freedom under Article 9 of the European Convention of Human Rights and that his dismissal was unfair. He made no claim relating to discrimination and the relevant provisions transposing the Employment Equality Directive had not come into force at the time.

Held: The Court found that the dismissal was based not on the appellant's religious beliefs, but on his refusal to agree to new employment terms and conditions. The dismissal was based on the economic needs of the employer and the need to have similar working conditions for all employees following an agreement reached with the trade union. The Court took into account that the employer had offered the appellant alternative employment.

Judgment: RIX LJ: ". . . 67. It is common ground that there is no element of discrimination in Mr Copsey's case. All his fellow employees were required to work on Sundays . . . That a different analysis of similar situations is, nevertheless, possible is illustrated by the Canadian authorities . . . the effect of which, on essentially similar facts albeit different constitutional texts, required the employers to discharge a burden of proving, on a strict test (to the point of undue hardship), its attempts to accommodate the complainant . . .

68. Nevertheless, the concept of reasonable accommodation is not foreign to either Convention jurisprudence or English law . . .

69. I would therefore prefer to say, limiting myself to the facts of this case, that, where an employer seeks to change the working hours and terms of his contract of employment with his employee in such a way as to interfere materially with the employee's right to manifest his religion, then article 9(1) of the Convention is potentially engaged. One solution is to find a reasonable accommodation with the employee. If this is found, then there will in the event be no material interference. If a reasonable solution is offered to the employee, but not accepted by him, then I think it remains possible to say that there is no material interference; alternatively, one can speak of justification under article 9(2).

. . .

It seems to me that it is possible and necessary to contemplate that an employer who seeks to change an employee's working hours so as to prevent that employee from practising his sincere adherence to the requirements of his religion in the way of Sabbath observance may be acting unfairly if he makes no attempt to accommodate his employee's needs. I cannot conceive that a decent employer would not attempt to do so. To say in such a situation that the employee's religious needs simply lie outside the scope of what the law requires of the fair employer ought not to be acceptable. I do not think that this places any burden on a decent employer that he does not already observe in practice, as is illustrated on the particular facts of this case. Such a requirement would, I venture to think, be easily fitted into the general law of unfair dismissal. An employer who had sought to find a reasonable accommodation for his employee would have nothing to fear. Provided his solution was one which a reasonable employer could require, in that it lay within the range of reasonable responses to the problem, it would not be for an Employment Tribunal to second-guess the employer . . ."

[64] [2005] EWCA Civ 932.

Notes

(1) Rix LJ seemed to read into the requirements relating to dismissal resulting from an employee's refusal, for religious reasons, to comply with new working terms or conditions an obligation on the employers' part to make some form of effort to accommodate the employee. Therefore, in deciding whether the dismissal was unfair, the Court considered what efforts the employer made to accommodate the employee.

(2) Rix LJ followed the terminology found in Canadian legislation and case-law,[65] and US provisions relating to religious accommodations, by speaking of "reasonable accommodations". He did not use the language of the UK Disability Discrimination Act which speaks of "reasonable adjustments".

(3) The Court of Appeal was divided over the correct way to approach this case and each judge issued a different opinion. Rix LJ's judgment therefore was not the majority view.

6.3.1.C.   OTHER GROUPS

In Europe there is little evidence thus far that individuals belonging to other groups are legally entitled to claim a reasonable accommodation.[66] However, this statement is subject to three provisos: Article 5 of the Decree of the Flemish Community in Belgium of 8 May 2002 concerning balanced participation in the labour market contains a general right to claim "reasonable adjustments" with regard to employment, and this right is not confined to people with disabilities. This Article is cited in section 6.2.1.C.

Secondly, the French Labour Code does extend the right to one specific form of reasonable accommodation, namely individualised working hour arrangements, to family members of people with disabilities under certain circumstances:

French Labour Code (Legislative Part)					**6.FR.45.**

Paragraph 1: Individualised working hours
Article L. 212-4-1-1 (inserted by Law N°. 2005-102 of 11 February, 2005, Art. 24 IV, Official Gazette of 12 February, 2005)
With regard to the appropriate measures established in Article L. 323-9-1, the disabled employees mentioned in items 1, 2, 3, 4, 9, 10 and 11 of Article L. 323-3 may benefit, at their request, from individualised adjustments of working hours, suitable for aiding their access to work, their professional activities or the maintenance of their jobs.

[65] Para. 67 of judgment *Copsey* v. *WBB Devon Clays Ltd.*
[66] However, this is not to say that other legal tools do not exist which, de facto, achieve similar results in terms of recognising and providing for adaptations for other individuals/groups. Space does not allow for a thorough examination of such legal tools, although reference is made to various approaches in the conclusion to this chapter.

Family helpers and relatives of the disabled person shall benefit under the same conditions from individualised adjustments of working hours intended to facilitate the support of the same disabled individual.

Note
Both "disabled employees" and "family helpers and relatives of the disabled person" are entitled to claim this form of accommodation. However, in the latter case, the goal of the accommodation is to allow the covered individuals to "facilitate the support" of the individual with a disability.

Lastly, there is evidence that in some instances a successful claim of indirect (sex, race or religious) discrimination can result in what is, de facto, the entitlement to claim a form of accommodation.[67]

6.3.2. SPECIFIC REQUIREMENTS—PEOPLE WITH DISABILITIES

This section considers what requirements must be met by an individual with a disability who, first, wishes to claim an accommodation in the context of employment, and secondly an accommodation enabling access to services. It will also consider what obligations are imposed on employers who receive a request for a disability-related accommodation, or are otherwise aware that an accommodation may be required.

6.3.2.A. EMPLOYMENT

PERSON WITH DISABILITY MUST BE QUALIFIED FOR THE JOB/EMPLOYMENT-RELATED ACTIVITIES

As noted in the introductory section to this chapter, the reasonable accommodation requirement should be situated within the non-discrimination framework. As a consequence, the requirement should not be regarded as a tool to confer additional benefits on people with disabilities or other covered individuals; nor should it not be regarded as a tool to require the employment of individuals who are not qualified or able to perform the work in question. Instead, as an element of the non-discrimination requirement, the reasonable accommodation is designed to remove the discriminatory barriers which impede (disabled) individuals' chances on the labour market. Therefore, only qualified individuals should be able to claim a reasonable accommodation—but, in the absence of such an accommodation, those individuals will be unqualified. To overcome this vicious circle,

---

[67] See above D. Schiek, Chapter Three: Indirect Discrimination.

non-discrimination legislation generally provides that only those individuals with a disability (or other covered individuals) who are "otherwise competent, capable and available" to carry out the job, with or without an accommodation, are entitled to claim a "reasonable accommodation". This assessment presupposes that the core or essential elements of the work in question have been identified, since the individual with a disability should only be judged on his/her ability to carry out such tasks.

Employment Equality Directive

This is the position of the Directive, which states in recital 17:

> "It does not require the recruitment, promotion, maintenance in employment or training of an individual who is not competent, capable and available to perform the essential functions of the post concerned or to undergo the relevant training, without prejudice to the obligation to provide 'reasonable accommodation' for people with disabilities."

This position has been clarified by the first decision of the European Court of Justice concerning the disability provisions of the Directive.

ECJ, 11 July 2006   **6.EC.46.**
Case C–13/05, Sonia Chacón Navas v. Eurest Colectividades

DISCRIMINATION OCCURS WHERE AN INDIVIDUAL WITH A DISABILITY IS DISMISSED WHERE THEY WOULD BE COMPETENT, CAPABLE AND AVAILABLE TO PERFORM THE ESSENTIAL FUNCTIONS OF THE POST FOLLOWING THE MAKING OF A REASONABLE ACCOMMODATION

Chacón Navas

Facts: The claimant was dismissed on the grounds that she had been absent from work for a lengthy period of time as a result of illness. The Spanish court referred a preliminary reference to the ECJ to establish whether, inter alia, the Directive included "within its protective scope a . . . [worker] who has been dismissed by her employer solely because she is sick". In addressing this question, the Court also considered the role which the obligation to make a reasonable accommodation played when considering whether an individual with a disability was protected from dismissal.

Held (regarding the reasonable accommodation issue): The Directive prohibited dismissal of an individual with a disability where, following the making of a reasonable accommodation, the individual would be competent, capable and available to perform the essential functions of the post in question.

Judgment: "Protection of disabled persons as regards dismissal

48 Unfavourable treatment on grounds of disability undermines the protection provided for by Directive 2000/78 only in so far as it constitutes discrimination within the meaning of Article 2(1) of that directive.

49 According to Recital 17 in the preamble to Directive 2000/78, that directive does not require the recruitment, promotion or maintenance in employment of an individual who is not competent, capable and available to perform the essential functions of the post concerned, without prejudice to the obligation to provide reasonable accommodation for people with disabilities.

703

50 In accordance with Article 5 of Directive 2000/78, reasonable accommodation is to be provided in order to guarantee compliance with the principle of equal treatment in relation to persons with disabilities. That provision states that this means that employers are to take appropriate measures, where needed in a particular case, to enable a person with a disability to have access to, participate in, or advance in employment, unless such measures would impose a disproportionate burden on the employer.

51 The prohibition, as regards dismissal, of discrimination on grounds of disability contained in Articles 2(1) and 3(1)(c) of Directive 2000/78 precludes dismissal on grounds of disability which, in the light of the obligation to provide reasonable accommodation for people with disabilities, is not justified by the fact that the person concerned is not competent, capable and available to perform the essential functions of his post."

Notes

(1) The Directive therefore only prohibits discrimination against "qualified individuals", i.e. those who are "competent, capable and available to perform the essential functions of the post" (or "undergo the relevant training"). Two groups of individuals fall into this category:

(a) A person (with a disability) who can perform the job in its current form.
(b) A person with a disability whose impairment prevents them from performing the job in its current form, but who could perform the job if it were adapted in an appropriate fashion through the making of a "reasonable accommodation".

(2) Generally, recently adopted domestic legislation designed to transpose the Employment Equality Directive is particularly vague on the means by which "essential functions of the post" can be identified, and the European Court of Justice provided no elaboration in the *Chacón Navas* decision.

(3) The qualification and ability of the individual should be assessed on the basis of their expected performance following, if necessary, the making of the reasonable accommodation, with the latter element playing no further role in the assessment of suitability. An employer cannot therefore argue that the cost of the accommodation is a relevant consideration at the recruitment stage (unless cost is defined as one of the elements involved in assessing whether an accommodation is "reasonable").[68]

(4) In making this assessment the question as to whether any particular function of a particular job is "essential" to that job may be one area likely to be contested. The "essential functions of the post" can be changed by job restructuring, which is a possible "reasonable accommodation". Arguably, since virtually any job can be changed to compensate for any disability—by tailoring its requirements to what the individual with a disability can do—the crucial question is whether some particular job modification is reasonable[69] or whether job restructuring would cause a

[68] Although the cost will be relevant in assessing whether making the accommodation amounts to a disproportionate burden.
[69] The meaning of the term "reasonable" has been discussed above in section 6.2.1.

disproportionate burden to the employer.[70] These issues are considered below in the Irish case *A Computer Component Company* v. *A Worker*.

Ireland

Irish legislation requires that an individual must be qualified for a position in order to benefit from an accommodation.

Employment Equality Act 1998–2004   6.IE.47.

16.—(1) Nothing in this Act shall be construed as requiring any person to recruit or promote an individual to a position, to retain an individual in a position, or to provide training or experience to an individual in relation to a position, if the individual—

(a) will not undertake (or, as the case may be, continue to undertake) the duties attached to that position or will not accept (or, as the case may be, continue to accept) the conditions under which those duties are, or may be required to be, performed, or

(b) is not (or, as the case may be, is no longer) fully competent and available to undertake, and fully capable of undertaking, the duties attached to that position, having regard to the conditions under which those duties are, or may be required to be, performed.

. . .

(3) (a) For the purposes of this Act a person who has a disability is fully competent to undertake, and fully capable of undertaking, any duties if the person would be so fully competent and capable on reasonable accommodation (in this subsection referred to as 'appropriate measures') being provided by the person's employer.

Notes

(1) Irish legislation refers not to "essential functions", but rather to "the duties attached to the position".[71] Nevertheless, as is illustrated by the following case, this does not imply that a disabled individual must be able to undertake all the "duties attached to the position", and the courts do distinguish between core tasks, which must be carried out, and ancillary tasks, which can be excused within the framework of a reasonable accommodation.

(2) The Irish legislation clearly distinguishes between two groups of disabled people who should be regarded as qualified under the legislation, in accordance with the approach outlined under the previous note under (1)—namely, a person with a disability who can perform the job in its current form and a person with a disability whose impairment prevents them from performing the job in its current form but who could perform the job if it were adapted in an appropriate fashion through the making of a reasonable accommodation. Section 16(3)(a) emphasizes that an

---

[70] The concept of disproportionate burden is discussed below in section 6.4.
[71] The Irish Commission on the Status of Persons with Disabilities has argued that a reference to "essential functions" should be included in the non-discrimination legislation.

individual is qualified ("fully competent" and "fully capable") if the making of a reasonable accommodation by the employer would render the individual so.

The following Irish case involves the key question whether excusing an individual from carrying out certain job-related tasks can be regarded as a reasonable accommodation, and the circumstances under which an individual who cannot carry out all elements of a job will be regarded as qualified. It should be recalled that the purpose of the Irish Employment Equality Act (and other [disability] non-discrimination legislation) is not to oblige employers to create positions which are suitable for a particular individual with a disability—but rather, inter alia, to oblige an employer to adapt an existing position so that it can be carried out by a specific individual with a disability. In other words, whilst in the former scenario the focus is on creating a work-related activity which an individual with a disability can do, in the latter the focus is on adapting an existing position so that it can be carried out by an individual with a disability. Therefore, in any case in which it is argued that a person with a disability should be excused certain job-related tasks, the question is whether this falls within the realms of a reasonable accommodation or whether it goes beyond that, and, in turn, this determines whether the individual is qualified or not.

An Chúirt Oibreachais (Labour Court),   **6.IE.48.**
ED/00/8 Determination No. 013, 18 July 2001[72]
A Computer Component Company v. *A Worker*

AN EMPLOYEE WITH A DISABILITY NOT REQUIRED TO BE ABLE TO CARRY OUT
MINOR TASKS RELATED TO FUNCTION/AN INDIVIDUAL WITH A DISABILITY IS
FULLY COMPETENT AND CAPABLE IF SHE CAN CARRY OUT THE CORE FUNCTIONS
OF THE JOB

A Computer Company v. A Worker

Facts: The complainant was employed by the respondent as a packer on a temporary basis. She had epilepsy, but her condition was well controlled by medication. At the time of her initial employment, the claimant told the employment agency of her medical condition. She was subsequently informed that her work performance was very satisfactory and that the respondent would like to take her on in a permanent position. Having completed an application form, she attended a medical examination at the employer's request. Immediately following the examination, the doctor spoke with the respondent's personnel officer by telephone and told her that the complainant had epilepsy. As a result of this conversation, the respondent's personnel officer decided not to offer the complainant a permanent post and to terminate her temporary appointment with immediate effect. The doctor subsequently submitted a written report to the respondent.

The respondent admitted that it dismissed the complainant because she had epilepsy. It claimed that it did so on medical advice. However, the doctor's report, while advising that the complainant was not fit to operate heavy machinery, stated that the complainant's condition was well controlled with no seizures for the previous two years. The doctor advised that the complainant's condition would present no problem for

---

[72] Available on the website of the Irish Labour Court.

the type of work in which she was engaged.

The complainant claimed she was discriminated against on the grounds of disability and that the dismissal was unfair.

Note: This judgment was decided on the basis of the unamended Employment Equality Act 1998. Section 16(1) of the Act was not amended by the Equality Act 2004; however, slight changes were made to section 16(3)(a) of the Act. The provision in force at the time read:

"For the purposes of this Act, a person who has a disability shall not be regarded as other than fully competent to undertake, and fully capable of undertaking, any duties if, with the assistance of special treatment or facilities, such person would be fully competent to undertake, and be fully capable of undertaking, those duties."

Held: The complainant was dismissed by the respondent by reason of her disability, and this dismissal constituted an act of discrimination.

Judgment: "The respondent terminated the complainant's employment because she suffered from epilepsy. This, prima facie, constituted an act of discrimination on the disability ground. The respondent can only be relieved of liability if it can be shown that, by reason of her disability, the complainant was not fully competent and fully capable of performing the duties of her employment, having regard to the conditions under which those duties were to be performed and could not have had her needs reasonably accommodated.

The respondent told the Court that it is Company policy that employees should be competent to undertake all tasks associated with the production function in which they are employed. It said that in the case of the complainant this would involve the operation of machinery. It told the Court that the decision to terminate the complainant's employment was taken because, on medical advice, it believed that this working environment posed a danger to a person with epilepsy.

Whilst the respondent does have some machinery which could be classified as heavy, its use is a minor part of the production system and it is clear that not all production employees are required to use this machinery all of the time. It appears to the Court that if a problem existed in relation to the complainant, arrangements could have been put in place whereby she would not be required to use this machinery.

If the respondent did conclude that the complainant lacked full capacity to safely undertake the duties of her employment, it appeared to have done so precipitously. The decision was taken and implemented before the Doctor's written report was received. As already observed this written report does not definitively point to an insurmountable medical or safety impediment to the complainant's continued employment and could be read as leaning to the opposite conclusion.

The respondent did not consider undertaking any form of safety assessment which could have identified the extent, if any, to which the working environment presented a danger to the complainant, and how any such danger could be ameliorated. Further, the respondent did not discuss its concerns with the complainant and did not advise her to obtain a second opinion from a neurologist as had been suggested by the Doctor.

On the evidence, the Court does not accept that the respondent could reasonably and objectively have come to the conclusion that the complainant was not fully competent or capable of performing the duties of her employment. Even if the respondent did reach such a conclusion, it is abundantly clear that it did not give the slightest consideration to providing the complainant with reasonable special facilities which would accommodate her needs and so overcome any difficulty which she or the respondent might otherwise experience.

In all of these circumstances, the Court does not accept that the respondent can avail of the provisions of Section 16 (1) so as to avoid liability under the Act."

Notes

(1) If the Labour Court had held that working on heavy machinery was a key element of the complainant's work, the dismissal would have been justified.

(2) The Court did not explicitly find that the employer was required to accommodate the complainant by excusing her from working on heavy machinery, but did find that if problems existed in this request, alternative arrangements could have been made, i.e. a reasonable accommodation was possible.

(3) This case and others such as *An Employee* v. *A Local Authority* found under section 6.2.1, reveal the heavy weight given to medical assessments regarding the fitness for work of a disabled individual under Irish law.

(3) In this case the employer (the personnel officer) gave more weight to its own opinion as to what the individual with a disability was capable of, and whether the working environment posed a threat to the individual's safety, than the opinion of the relevant health professional and the person with a disability herself, who both felt that the employee was capable of carrying out the work safely (with slight modifications). In addition, the Court found the employer's response wanting in that it did not properly investigate the situation, e.g. by carrying out a safety assessment or considering possible adaptations, prior to taking the decision to dismiss the complainant on the grounds that she was not competent to carry out the work. These elements of the decision reveal the kinds of measures employers can reasonably be expected to take to determine whether an employee is (not) competent and capable, and whether any accommodation is (in)appropriate.

The Netherlands

A Dutch case, decided by the Equal Treatment Commission, reveals the approach taken where the complainant is not qualified, in the sense that the requested accommodation will not render the individual able to complete the necessary task, or where there is uncertainty as to whether the accommodation would result in the complainant being able to carry out the tasks.

Equal Treatment Commission (Commissie Gelijke Behandeling) **6.NL.49.**
Opinion 2004-59

NO OBLIGATION TO MAKE AN ACCOMMODATION WHERE IT IS UNCLEAR THAT THIS
WOULD ENABLE AN INDIVIDUAL TO SUCCESSFULLY COMPLETE EXAMS

Dutch Exam Case 3

Facts: The applicant was a university student with dyslexia. He argued that, as a result of his disability, he needed additional time to sit his exams. In his first year of study the applicant sat all exams without being granted additional time and met the required threshold of 50% or more study credits. In his second year of study, and prior to his first examination period of that year, the applicant presented a declaration stating that he had dyslexia to the coordinator of educational affairs. However, the latter refused to accept the declaration, given that it was more than three years old. As a consequence, the applicant was denied extra time in the relevant exam. Although he asked for it, no additional time was granted to him in any subsequent exam. Allegedly, due to the denial of additional time, the applicant failed his fiscal economics exam and consequently did not obtain his diploma. The applicant argued that the university acted in conflict with the Act by failing to allow him extra time to complete his exams.

Held: It could not be established that the granting of additional time would have led to a higher mark being obtained by the applicant for the fiscal economics exam and no unlawful distinction on the grounds of disability had occurred.

Opinion: "5.1 The question at issue is whether the respondent made a distinction based on disability or chronic illness by neglecting to make an effective accommodation for the applicant, namely by not giving him extra time to take exams, whereupon the applicant's studies were delayed.

5.5 Pursuant to the rules concerning the distribution of the burden of proof as stated in Article 10 WGB h/cz, [Act on Equal Treatment on grounds of Disability or Chronic Illness] the applicant must put forward facts that may establish a suspicion of distinction on grounds of disability or chronic disease. In the event of an effective accommodation as in the present case, this presumes that the applicant adduces facts that lead one to suspect that he was in principle suitable to take part in vocational education, and the respondent was aware of his need for an accommodation and that with the accommodation he can participate equally in the studies. If the applicant is successful, the respondent must prove that it did not act in conflict with the Act. The respondent can for this purpose prove that the applicant was ineligible to participate in the studies or was unaware of the need for an accommodation, or that the accommodation requested did not comply with the requirements as to 'appropriate' and 'necessary', or the accommodation formed a disproportionate burden for the respondent. ...

5.7 The Commission considers that the facts put forward by the applicant are normally sufficient to arouse a suspicion of distinction in the sense that the respondent neglected to make an effective accommodation, namely to grant extra time for completing exams ...

5.9 It is impossible to say whether a time extension for, amongst other things, the fiscal economics exam would have resulted in a higher mark for this subject. This is all the more uncertain since the applicant obtained half of his study points in his first study year without resorting to the possibility of a time extension for exams. On the other hand, the applicant passed his introductory examination only in his fourth study year. An added fact is that the applicant took some 10% of his exams without a time extension. Having regard to the above, it is hardly plausible that the time extension not obtained during certain exam periods over a stretch of more than three years resulted in the delayed studies claimed by the applicant ...

5.10 The Commission concludes on the grounds of the above considerations that the facts that the applicant has put forward were insufficiently able to arouse a suspicion that failure to obtain a time extension resulted in distinction."

Notes

(1) Paragraph 5.5 of this judgment contains a clear and brief description of the elements which a complainant must prove when arguing that he or she was entitled to a reasonable accommodation and, where a prima facie case has been made by the complainant, the elements that a respondent must prove in order to remove itself from the liability for making such an accommodation.

(2) The procedural process for allocating the burden of proof between the individual with a disability and an employer (or other covered party) may be of relevance for negotiations concerning a "reasonable accommodation". The individual with a

disability should arguably bear the burden of showing that a "reasonable accommodation" is possible. Once such an accommodation is identified, the employer should bear the burden of showing that it would result in a disproportionate burden, or that an accommodation is not required for some other reason. This reflects the differences in the parties' access to information. The individual with a disability is better acquainted with how his disabilities can be overcome; the employer will know (or can find out) how much various accommodations cost. Apart from the procedural consequences of allocating the burden of proof on these issues, an important goal might be to encourage the parties to share this information in negotiations over possible accommodations. Negotiations relating to identifying a suitable reasonable accommodation are considered in more detail in the following two sections (under headings *The Obligation on the person with a disability to inform the employer* and *The Obligation on the employer to consider and identify a reasonable accommodation*).

(3) In this case the Commission did not assess the question, or conclude, that the complainant was not qualified—in that, even with the extra exam time, he would still have been unable to achieve sufficiently high marks—but instead found that he had failed to meet the burden of proof to establish that the requested accommodation would have resulted in the necessary improvements.

THE OBLIGATION ON THE PERSON WITH A DISABILITY TO INFORM THE EMPLOYER

A successful accommodation often requires ongoing negotiation and cooperation between the employer and the employee. According to the ADA Interpretive Guidance, the focus should be on a flexible, interactive process of employer– employee negotiation and liberal modification of physical, logistic and attitudinal barriers that preclude full equality of opportunity when determining an appropriate "reasonable accommodation".[73] In addition, some European statutes make it clear that an employer can only be required to make an accommodation if he or she has been informed of the individual's disability, and case-law has helpfully elaborated this point.

United Kingdom

Under UK law an employer must be aware that the individual concerned has a disability.

Disability Discrimination Act 1995 as amended   **6.UK.50.**

S. 4A (2)
(2) In subsection (1) [establishing the duty to make a reasonable adjustment], 'the disabled person concerned' means—

---

[73] 29 C.F.R. app.pt. 1630 (1995) para. 1630.9.

710

(a) in the case of a provision, criterion or practice for determining to whom employment should be offered, any disabled person who is, or has notified the employer that he may be, an applicant for that employment;

(b) in any other case, a disabled person who is—

(i) an applicant for the employment concerned, or

(ii) an employee of the employer concerned.

(3) Nothing in this section imposes any duty on an employer in relation to a disabled person if the employer does not know, and could not reasonably be expected to know—

(a) in the case of an applicant or potential applicant, that the disabled person concerned is, or may be, an applicant for the employment; or

(b) in any case, that that person has a disability and is likely to be affected in the way mentioned in subsection (1).

Note

The British statute clearly requires that the employer be aware that the individual concerned has a disability and that a need exists to consider whether a reasonable adjustment is required or possible. However, the Act does not explicitly specify that the individual with a disability must inform the (potential) employer of the disability.

The Netherlands

Opinions of the Equal Treatment Commission have also made it clear that the employer or other covered party must be aware of the need for an accommodation. Since accommodations can only be claimed by individuals with disabilities, this implies that the covered party also had to be aware that the claimant was disabled. This position is elaborated in the following case, which resulted from a student asking the respondent college to check whether the reason for his failure to pass exams was his lack of knowledge or was connected to his dyslexia.

Equal Treatment Commission (Commissie Gelijke Behandeling) **6.NL.51.**
Opinion 2005-18

A CLAIMANT IS OBLIGED TO ENSURE HIS EMPLOYER OR VOCATIONAL TRAINER IS
AWARE OF THE NEED FOR ACCOMMODATION

Dutch Exam Case 2

Facts: The applicant had dyslexia. During 2003–2004, the applicant followed the course to become a physiotherapist at the school of the respondent. The applicant failed a number of exams, and subsequently asked the respondent to check whether the failed exams were the result of his lack of knowledge or were connected with his dyslexia. If the latter, he requested that an alternative form of examination be considered.

Held: The respondent failed to react in an adequate and timely manner to the applicant's request to examine the possibilities for an alternative form of assessment.

Opinion: "5.4 In accordance with the rules regarding the onus of proof (Article 10 WGBh/cz [Act on Equal Treatment on grounds of Disability or Chronic Illness]), on recourse to the ban on distinction on account of disability or chronic disease it is up to the applicant party to adduce facts that may give rise to a suspicion of distinction based on disability or chronic disease. In the case of an effective accommodation regarding vocational education, as in the present case, this implies that the applicant party adduces facts that may lead one to suspect that he was in principle suitable to participate in vocational education, that the respondent party was aware of the need for an accommodation, and that the applicant party would be able to participate in education with the accommodation. If the applicant is successful in this, it is up to the respondent party to show that it did not act in conflict with the law. For this purpose, the respondent party may prove that the applicant party was unsuitable to participate in education or that the respondent party was unaware of the need for an accommodation or that the accommodation requested did not comply with the requirement that this should be suitable and necessary or that the adjustment was disproportionately burdensome for the respondent party.

5.5 The parties do not dispute that the applicant indicated at various times that a link between his dyslexia and the results of the ICT [exams] could not be dismissed. More particularly, the applicant asked the respondent whether he could take the ICT in an alternative way in order to test his assumptions. Although this does not (as yet) amount to asking for a specific, effective accommodation, such a request must nonetheless be regarded as one for an effective accommodation, after all, making an effective accommodation usually presupposes that the interested party is essentially dealing with a restriction, in this case when participating in examinations. This is followed by the stage of considering whether a suitable, necessary accommodation exists, whereupon the contribution from the party concerned is important (Parliamentary documents II 2001/02, 28 169, No. 3, p. 25-26). Although the Act does not mention a period within which the request for effective accommodations has been made and the accommodations must have been implemented, this must "obviously" occur within a reasonable period". (Parliamentary Documents II 2001/02, 28 169, No. 5, p. 13)."

Notes

(1) Where legal challenges are made arguing that a covered party failed to provide an effective accommodation, it is up to the claimant to present a prima facie case showing that the respondent was aware of the need for an accommodation. This implies that it is the claimant's responsibility to bring such a request to the attention of the covered party, or to ensure that the covered party is aware of the need through some other means.

(2) The above Opinion makes it clear that the claimant does not have to request a specific accommodation, but only to ensure that the covered party is aware that an accommodation may be required.

(3) The Commission's Opinion in this case is also mirrored in *Dutch Exam Case 3*, referred to in excerpt number **6.NL.49.** above.

Latvia

In a slightly different context, the Latvian Labour Law imposes a duty on job applicants to inform employers of any disabilities which might impact on job performance.

Latvian Labour Law   **6.LV.52.**

—Article 33 Job Interviews
An applicant has a duty to provide information to the employer regarding the state of his or her health and occupational preparedness insofar as this is of significance for entering into an employment contract and for performance of the intended work.

Notes
(1) There are no consequences for failing to comply with this requirement. However, under Latvian law, where a disability does not result in the inability to perform the job, but does affect performance, the employer can request that the court terminates the employment relationship if he "has good cause", which includes "considerations of morality and fairness". This could presumably apply where the employee has failed to disclose the required information concerning his or her health. It is up to the court to determine whether good cause exists.
(2) Under German law severely disabled persons are required by law to inform the employer about their disability. If they lie, the employer has the right to request a court to declare the contract void (refutation because of wilful deceit).[74]

THE OBLIGATION ON THE EMPLOYER TO CONSIDER AND IDENTIFY A REASONABLE ACCOMMODATION

United Kingdom

Case-law in the UK and Ireland in particular has elaborated on the steps which an employer is required to take to identify the need for, and the suitability of, an accommodation. In the UK a key case in this respect is *Morse* v. *Wiltshire City Council*,[75] which established guidelines for Employment Tribunals in dealing with "reasonable adjustment cases".
 The guidelines developed in *Morse* v. *Wiltshire County Council* outlining the steps to be gone through in considering a claim by an employee with a disability that his employer failed to make reasonable adjustments are as follows:

---

[74] Bürgerliches Gesetzbuch: §126 (1) Anfechtbarkewit wegen Täuschung oder Drohung. See also Bundesarbeitsgericht Urteil vom 5. Oktober 1995 file No. 2 AZR 923/94.
[75] [1998] IRLR 352.

— Was there a duty on the employer to make adjustments in the circumstances of the particular case?

— If yes, did the employer take reasonable steps to comply with the duty?[76]

Notes

(1) Whilst these guidelines were developed with Employment Tribunals in mind, in essence they establish the steps which employers are required to go through in identifying the need for an adjustment and fulfilling that duty or, alternatively, justifying a failure to make an adjustment.

(2) This case was decided prior to the amendment of the Disability Discrimination Act to render it compliant with the Employment Equality Directive.

An additional important British case establishing the standard of behaviour expected of employers is *Cosgrove*, which was also decided under the unamended DDA 1995.

Employment Appeals Tribunal, 6 June 2001[77]   **6.UK.53.**
Cosgrove v. Caesar & Howie

OBLIGATION TO CONSIDER WHETHER ANY REASONABLE ADJUSTMENT IS POSSIBLE
LIES WITH THE EMPLOYER, AND AN EMPLOYER WHO FAILS TO CONSIDER MAKING
ADJUSTMENTS CANNOT ESCAPE LIABILITY SIMPLY ON THE BASIS THAT THE
EMPLOYEE WITH A DISABILITY WAS UNABLE TO SUGGEST AN APPROPRIATE
ADJUSTMENT

Cosgrove

Facts: Ms. Cosgrove worked as a legal secretary. Following a long period of absence from work as a result of depression, she was dismissed. She challenged the dismissal under the Disability Discrimination Act. She was initially unsuccessful, and submitted an appeal to the Employment Appeals Tribunal.

Held: An employer who fails to consider making adjustments as required by DDA 1995 cannot escape liability for that failure simply on the basis that the employee with the disability was unable to suggest an appropriate adjustment.

Judgment: "There will, no doubt, be cases where the evidence given on the applicant's side alone will establish a total unavailability of reasonable and effective adjustments. But it does not seem to us to follow that because a former secretary, long absent from the firm and clinically depressed to the point of disability and her general practitioner also (the latter, at least, being unlikely to know what office or other practicabilities were open to the employer) could postulate no useful adjustment, that the section 6 duty [to make reasonable adjustments]

---

[76] A third step referred to in the judgment was: if the employer did not take reasonable steps to comply with the duty, did he have a reason justifying the failure which was "both material to the circumstances of the particular case and substantial" within the meaning of DDA 1995, s. 5(4).

[77] [2001] IRLR 653.

on the employer should, without more, be taken to have been satisfied. Indeed, in the course of argument before us, Mr Millar accepted that the doctor and the applicant were not the most appropriate persons to be asked as to what adjustments could be made. The Tribunal said:—

'Perhaps most importantly both the applicant and Dr. Brook [her general practitioner] stated in evidence that the applicant's condition could not have responded to any adjustments to the workplace. She could not think of anything that the respondents could have done which would have improved the situation.'

That relates only to Ms Cosgrove's ability to discern some adjustment and to the possibility of adjustment *to* the workplace (and not, be it noted, *at* the workplace). But if the employer had turned its mind to adjustments, might a transfer to another office of the firm have been a possibility? . . . Would a very gradual return, building slowly from part-time working in gentle duties to full-time working on her erstwhile duties, have materially facilitated a return? . . . We do not suggest that there would necessarily have been a positive answer to such questions but there can be no assurance at all that there would not have been since, unfortunately, such questions were not asked at or around the time of dismissal, or indeed, as it would seem, even at the Tribunal. It cannot, it seems to us, be as *decisive* as the Tribunal took it to be on the issue of whether any reasonable adjustments were available that might have prevented Ms Cosgrove's inability to work by reason of her medical condition that neither she, a mentally disabled person could, at the Tribunal itself, suggest any, nor that her doctor, who, as far as we can tell, had no such questions posed to him and could not, presumably, in any event be expected to know what office possibilities the employer could offer, had, at the Tribunal, not been able to suggest any either.

In the circumstances there was, in our judgment, a . . . material error of law, namely in regarding Ms Cosgrove's views and those of her general practitioner as decisive on the issue of adjustments, where the employer himself had given no thought to the matter whatsoever. [emphasis in original]."

Notes

(1) This case clearly establishes that the duty is on the employer to consider whether any accommodations are possible. Whilst one can expect that it is good practice for an employer to discuss such matters with the employee and, if appropriate, medical specialists,[78] the employer will not be excused of its liability if, where the other interested parties are unable to suggest an accommodation or where the employer receives no advice from such parties, it fails to consider the question itself.

(2) This position can be contrasted with the approach of the Dutch Equal Treatment Commission, as elaborated in the *Dutch Exam Cases 2* and *3* cited above (above **6.NL.18.**, **6.NL.49.** and **6.NL.51.**), in which the Commission held that it is for the individual claiming the accommodation to show that he or she would be qualified (i.e. in these cases, able to pass the relevant exams) should an accommodation be made. This burden of proof rule establishes that it is for the individual with a disability to show that an effective accommodation can be made, whereupon it is up to the employer to justify any failure or refusal to make the accommodation. There would seem to be some tension between this burden of proof rule and the UK

---

[78] However, one should note that this may raise questions related to confidentiality.

approach, which requires an employer to consider an accommodation even where the individual with a disability cannot think of any appropriate accommodation themselves. However, *Dutch Exam Case 2* (above **6.NL.18.** and **6.NL.51.**) also makes it clear that the individual with a disability does not have to identify a specific accommodation which would achieve the set goal—but simply indicate that an accommodation may be required. "This is followed by the stage of considering whether a suitable, necessary accommodation exists, whereupon the contribution from the party concerned is important" (paragraph 5.5).

Ireland

Irish case-law has also elaborated on the standard of behaviour required of employers.

An Chúirt Oibreachais (Labour Court),   **6.IE.54.**
ED/02/59 Determination No. 037, 18 February 2003[79]
A Health and Fitness Club v. A Worker

AN EMPLOYER IS OBLIGED TO ENGAGE IN A TWO-STAGE ENQUIRY PROCESS TO ESTABLISH WHETHER AN EMPLOYEE IS CAPABLE OF CARRYING OUT WORK, AND WHETHER THE EMPLOYEE REQUIRES A REASONABLE ACCOMMODATION

A Health and Fitness Club v. A Worker

Facts: The complainant worked as a childcare assistant in a crèche facility operated by the respondent. Her duties involved the care of young children. She had anorexia, which later developed into bulimia. It was accepted that this disorder constituted a disability for the purposes of the Employment Equality Act.

The complainant took a number of periods of unpaid sick leave, during which she received treatment. The complainant became ill again and requested additional sick leave. By this point the respondent had come to the conclusion that it was not suitable for the complainant to work with children and they terminated the employment. The respondent did not obtain any medical or psychiatric advice in relation to the complainant's disorder, nor did they undertake any form of risk assessment in relation to her condition prior to taking the decision to dismiss the complainant.

The complainant alleged that the dismissal was unfair.

Held: The complainant was dismissed wholly or mainly because of her disability. Further, it was not shown to the satisfaction of the Court that the complainant was not fully capable of continuing to perform the duties for which she was employed within the meaning of Section 16(3) of the Employment Equality Act.

Judgment: "In the present case it is clear . . . that her dismissal arose wholly or mainly from the respondents belief that the disorder from which she suffered impaired her ability to carry out the duties for which she was employed. Thus she was treated less favourably than a person who did not suffer from a similar disability, resulting in the same perceived impairment, would have been treated. It follows that the dismissal was prima facie discriminatory and unlawful.

---

[79] Available on the website of the Irish Labour Court.

However a dismissal which appears to be discriminatory ... may be saved by Section 16 ... This Section, on which the respondent relies, can provide a complete defence to a claim of discrimination on the disability ground if it can be shown that the employer formed the bona fide belief that the complainant is not fully capable, within the meaning of the section, of performing the duties for which they are employed. However, before coming to that view the employer would normally be required to make adequate enquiries so as to establish fully the factual position in relation to the employee's capacity.

The nature and extent of the enquiries which an employer should make will depend on the circumstances of each case. At a minimum, however, an employer, should ensure that he or she in full possession [sic] of all the material facts concerning the employee's condition and that the employee is given fair notice that the question of his or her dismissal for incapacity is being considered. The employee must also be allowed an opportunity to influence the employer's decision.

In practical terms this will normally require a two-stage enquiry, which looks firstly at the factual position concerning the employee's capability including the degree of impairment arising from the disability and its likely duration. This would involve looking at the medical evidence available to the employer either from the employee's doctors or obtained independently.

Secondly, if it is apparent that the employee is not fully capable Section 16(3) of the Act requires the employer to consider what if any special treatment or facilities may be available by which the employee can become fully capable ...

Finally, such an enquiry could only be regarded as adequate if the employee concerned is allowed a full opportunity to participate at each level and is allowed to present relevant medical evidence and submissions.

Conclusions of the Court
In this case the respondent was faced with an employee who was suffering from a disorder which had both psychiatric and physical manifestations. The respondent became concerned that she might not be suitable to remain in charge of young children. The Court accepts that an employer is entitled to take account of possible dangers occasioned by a disability from which an employee suffers (and may be obliged to do so in certain circumstances).

However, in the instant case the respondent made no effort to obtain a prognosis of the complainant's condition. They did not discuss the situation with her before taking a decision on her future. They came to the conclusion that she could not be retained because of her disability without the benefit of any form of professional advice or assessment of the risks associated with her condition.

There were a number of courses of action open to the respondent. They could have had the situation assessed professionally and considered the most appropriate approach to adopt in consultation with the complainant and her medical advisor. Further, the complainant intimated her desire to re-enter hospital for further treatment. A decision on her future could have been deferred and she could have been given a further period of sick leave to undergo this treatment.

Had the complainant been given further leave her progress could have been monitored and her return to work made conditional upon medical certification that she was fully fit to resume her duties. Such evidence could have been required from either her own doctors or nominees of the respondent. The complainant was not paid during absences on sick leave and the respondent accepted that they could have employed a temporary replacement without additional costs."

Note

In this case the Court set out a two-stage test or enquiry process which employers should follow to establish whether a worker is unable to carry out the required job-related tasks and whether an accommodation is required.

First, the employer must establish "the factual position concerning the employee's capability including the degree of impairment arising from the disability and its likely duration". In line with other Irish case-law, which places a heavy emphasis on expert medical advice, the Court noted that this would involve looking at medical advice.

Secondly, if it is apparent that the employee is not "fully capable" of carrying out the employment as it stands, the employer must consider whether any reasonable accommodation ("any special treatment or facilities") could be made which would allow the employee to become "fully capable".

In addition, at both stages, the employee must be given "a full opportunity to participate" and be "allowed to present relevant medical evidence and submissions". If this does not occur, the employer's enquiry will not be regarded as adequate.

6.3.2.B.   SERVICES

Given that the goals of any accommodation designed to provide access to services differ from the goals of employment-related accommodations, claimants of the former must meet different requirements.

IMPOSSIBLE OR UNREASONABLY DIFFICULT TO ACCESS SERVICES

United Kingdom

As noted above, a number of disability non-discrimination statutes establish a duty for service providers to make a reasonable accommodation or adjustment to enable access for disabled individuals. The British Disability Discrimination Act 1995 establishes such a duty where "a provider of services has a practice, policy or procedure which makes it impossible or unreasonably difficult for disabled persons to make use of a service which he provides, or is prepared to provide, to other members of the public" and "where a physical feature (for example, one arising from the design or construction of a building or the approach or access to premises) makes it impossible or unreasonably difficult for disabled persons to make use of such a service".[80] In order for the obligation to make adjustments to arise it has to be established that, under the status quo, it is "impossible or unreasonably difficult" for

---

[80] Section 21.

a disabled person or persons to access the service in question. The following commentaries examine this requirement:

B. J. Doyle, Disability Discrimination, Law and Practice[81]   **6.UK.55.**

". . . the DDA 1995 does not define what is meant by 'impossible or unreasonably difficult' in the context of the effect upon accessibility of a service to a disabled person as a result of a reasonable adjustment. [FN 6: *The DRC recommends that the DDA 1995 should be amended to require adjustments either where they would enable and/or facilitate the use of a service or where a disabled customer is at a substantial disadvantage in accessing a service: DRC Legislative Review, recommendation 25.*] Instead the Code [The Rights of Access Code of Practice 2002] offers some factors (such as time, inconvenience, effort, discomfort or loss of dignity entailed in using a service) which go to the question of what would be unreasonably difficult for a disabled person to have to endure when attempting to use a service [reference omitted]."

C. Gooding and C. Casserley, "Disability Discrimination Laws   **6.UK.56.**
and Goods and Services"[82]

"The trigger of 'impossible or unreasonably difficult', however, is a potentially highly one to meet; it means that, in effect, a service can be reasonably difficult to use and a disabled person may have no remedy. [FN 63: *It contrasts with the trigger used in both the employment and education provisions—that of a substantial disadvantage, where substantial is said by the Employment Code of Practice to mean something 'not a minor or trivial': para4.17, Code of Practice for the Elimination of Discrimination in the field of employment against disabled persons or persons who have had a disability (London, Department for Education and Employment, 1996).*] This trigger has been the subject of criticism and the DRC [Disability Rights Commission] has highlighted the need for it to be changed. [reference omitted] These concerns appeared to be substantiated by two negative decisions by county courts. *Alistair Appleby v Department for Work and Pensions (DWP)* [reference omitted] concerned a man who had a hearing impairment and who applied for a national insurance number, which required his attendance at a DWP office. His claim of discrimination included a claim that there had been a failure to make a reasonable adjustment. The visual display unit in the office was out of order with the result that he could not tell when it was his turn to go into the office. Staff refused to notify him directly when his turn arose. Instead, he had to rely upon members of the public to assist him. The court held that the practice of having to ask a member of the public to notify him of when it was his turn did not make it 'unreasonably difficult' for Mr Appleby to use the service. The District Judge observed that:

> 'Indeed with commendable imagination and improvisation he enlisted without apparent difficulty the help of two members of the public who, it would appear, were more than willing to assist and he was thus able to ascertain when it was his turn.'

---

[81] Fifth edition (Bristol, Jordans, 2005) 151–2.
[82] In Lawson and Gooding, above n. 9, 152.

This demonstrates the danger of this trigger being interpreted so as to allow service providers to continue to provide a second-class service, which leaves the onus on the disabled person to cope with it [reference omitted].

Baggeley v Kingston-upon-Hull Council [reference omitted] saw a similar approach taken in relation to a wheelchair user who was unable to attend a pop concert. However, the Court of Appeal, in the case of *Roads v Central Trains Ltd* [reference omitted], stated that the policy of the DDA is what it was held to be by *Mynors Ch in Re Holy Cross, Pershore* [2002] 1 Fam 105: 'to provide access to a service as close as it is reasonably possible to get to the standard normally offered to the public at large.' This approach will hopefully guide courts on this issue in future."

Note

The obligation to make a reasonable accommodation in order to ensure access to services under the Irish Equal Status Act[83] is triggered by a similar situation—namely that, in the absence of "special treatment", it would be impossible or unduly difficult for the person with a disability to avail him- or herself of the service. For further information on the provision under Irish law, see section 6.2.1.A above and, in particular, the extract from *Roche* v. *Alabaster* and related notes.

A REACTIVE DUTY OWED TO INDIVIDUALS OR AN ANTICIPATORY DUTY OWED TO THE GROUP OF PEOPLE WITH DISABILITIES?

In principle, the duty to make a reasonable accommodation is owed to a specific person with a disability who meets the necessary criteria which entitle him or her to claim an accommodation. Employers are therefore never obliged to make accommodations in anticipation of the future employment of an unspecified individual with a particular disability, but are only obliged to meet the needs of specific individuals as and when those needs arise. In some jurisdictions which provide for an obligation to accommodate people with disabilities with regard to accessing services, such as Ireland, the duty also only arises in response to the needs of a specific individual. In contrast, in the UK the duty to accommodate in the context of access to services refers to "disabled persons" and is owed to people with disabilities as a whole (see above section 6.3.2.B). The duty is anticipatory in that service providers are expected to have made their services accessible in advance of customers who have a disability notifying them of specific needs.

---

[83] Section 6.4.

United Kingdom

Code of Practice—Rights of Access: **6.GB.57.**
services to the public,public authority functions, private clubs and premises[84]

"To whom is the duty to make reasonable adjustments owed?
6.14 A service provider's duty to make reasonable adjustments is a duty owed to disabled people at large. It is not simply a duty that is weighed in relation to each individual disabled person who wants to access a service provider's services. Disabled people are a diverse group with different requirements that service providers need to consider.
6.15 No single aspect of the way in which a service is delivered will obstruct access to the service for all disabled people, or, in most cases, for disabled people generally. A policy, or a feature of the premises, which obstructs access to a service for persons with a particular type of disability may present no difficulties for others with a different disability. The phrase 'disabled persons', which is used in relation to the duty, means that service providers need to consider features that impede people with one or more kinds of disability—for example, those with visual impairments or those with mobility impairments.

At what point does the duty to make reasonable adjustments arise?
6.16 Service providers should not wait until a disabled person wants to use a service that they provide before they give consideration to their duty to make reasonable adjustments. They should be thinking now about the accessibility of their services to disabled people. Service providers should be planning continually for the reasonable adjustments they need to make, whether or not they already have disabled customers. They should anticipate the requirements of disabled people and the adjustments that may have to be made for them. In many cases, it is appropriate to ask customers to identify whether they have any particular requirements and, if so, what adjustments may need to be made. Failure to anticipate the need for an adjustment may render it too late to comply with the duty to make the adjustment. Furthermore, it may not in itself provide a defence to a claim that it was reasonable to have provided one."

C. Gooding and C. Casserley, "Disability Discrimination Laws   **6.UK.58.**
and Goods and Services"[85]

"Because the wording of the duty refers specifically to 'disabled persons', it is said in the statutory Code of Practice to be 'anticipatory': service providers are said to owe duties to disabled people as a whole and, as a result, should ensure that they have considered and taken steps to ensure the accessibility of their services in advance of disabled customers notifying them of problems. This has been regarded as immensely significant in Britain: as a major driver in encouraging service providers to think in advance about removing barriers experienced by disabled customers or potential customers. It helps to avoid a situation in which a provider

---

[84] Available on the website of the UK Disability Rights Commission.
[85] In Lawson and Gooding, above n. 9, 151.

claims that, because they did not know in advance that an adjustment was required, it was not reasonable to provide one."

Note

The nature of this requirement to accommodate is substantially different from the individualised obligation owed to specific individuals with a disability in the employment context. However, as noted above, in other jurisdictions—notably Ireland—the legislator has opted to follow the individualised reactive approach to the duty to accommodate with regard to access to services.

6.3.3. SPECIFIC REQUIREMENTS—RELIGION

6.3.3.A. AN INDIVIDUAL MAY NEED TO PROVE THAT HE OR SHE IS OF A PARTICULAR FAITH

Subject to the comments made under section 6.3.1.B above, there is very little European material which establishes what specific requirements must be met by individuals who request an accommodation in order to practise their religion and other individuals who are not requesting a disability based accommodation. However, a 2006 case of the European Court of Human Rights, decided in the context of Article 9 and 14 ECHR,[86] is of some relevance.

ECtHR, 13 April 2006   **6.CoE.59.**
Kosteski v. *The Former Yugoslav Republic of Macedonia*

AN INDIVIDUAL WHO CLAIMS A RIGHT TO TAKE A PUBLIC HOLIDAY TO CELEBRATE A MUSLIM HOLIDAY CAN BE REQUIRED TO PROVIDE EVIDENCE THAT HE IS A MUSLIM

Kosteski v. Macedonia

Facts: The applicant took a number of days' leave from his place of employment without receiving permission from his employer. He justified his absence by stating he was celebrating Muslim religious holidays, which were public holidays for Macedonian citizens of Muslim faith under the Constitution and the respective law. The applicant was fined on a number of occasions for being absent without authorisation, and he challenged these decisions before the Macedonia courts. All the courts dismissed his appeal on the grounds that he did not adduce any evidence to prove that he was really of the Muslim faith.

Held: It was not unreasonable for the applicant to be required to substantiate his claim that he was a Muslim. No breach of Articles 9 and 14 ECHR.

Judgment: "39. Insofar as the applicant has complained that there was an interference with the inner sphere of belief in that he was required to prove his faith, the Court recalls that the

---

[86] These Arts concern respectively the right to freedom of thought, conscience and religion and the right to manifest one's religion; and the right to non-discrimination with regard to the enjoyment of the rights set out in the Convention.

courts' decisions on the applicant's appeal against the disciplinary punishment imposed on him made findings effectively that the applicant had not substantiated the genuineness of his claim to be a Muslim and that his conduct on the contrary cast doubt on that claim in that there were no outward signs of his practising the Muslim faith or joining collective Muslim worship. While the notion of the State sitting in judgment on the state of a citizen's inner and personal beliefs is abhorrent and may smack unhappily of past infamous persecutions, the Court observes that this is a case where the applicant sought to enjoy a special right bestowed by Macedonian law which provided that Muslims could take holiday on particular days . . . In the context of employment, with contracts setting out specific obligations and rights between employer and employee, the Court does not find it unreasonable that an employer may regard absence without permission or apparent justification as a disciplinary matter. Where the employee then seeks to rely on a particular exemption, it is not oppressive or in fundamental conflict with freedom of conscience to require some level of substantiation when that claim concerns a privilege or entitlement not commonly available and, if that substantiation is not forthcoming, to reach a negative conclusion . . . The applicant however was not prepared to produce any evidence that could substantiate his claims. To the extent therefore that the proceedings disclosed an interference with the applicant's freedom of religion, this was not disproportionate and may, in the circumstances of this case, be regarded as justified in terms of the second paragraph, namely, as prescribed by law and necessary in a democratic society for the protection of the rights of others."

Notes

(1) As such, this case did not concern a claim to a reasonable accommodation, but rather the right to benefit from a public holiday reserved for individuals of a particular faith. Such an exemption from work could, however, be regarded as a form of accommodation where the law allows for generic accommodations in order to allow individuals to manifest their religion.

(2) Since religious accommodations are designed to allow individuals to manifest their religion, one can envisage that, in cases of doubt, the claimant of the accommodation could be required to produce evidence of their faith. However, in many cases such evidence will already have been provided by their lifestyle and worshipping habits.

6.3.4. COMPARATIVE OVERVIEW

As a result of the inclusion of Article 5 in the Employment Equality Directive, virtually all EU Member States have established a duty on employers to accommodate the needs of individuals with disabilities. In addition, some Member States have also provided for a similar duty with regard to access to services and, less frequently, for employment-related accommodations for individuals who wish to practise their religion.

In order to claim any accommodation, an individual with a disability must be qualified for the job in question. An individual will be judged to be qualified if he or she can perform, with or without an accommodation, what are referred to in a Recital to the Directive as "essential functions of the post". This implies that the "essential functions" must be separated from those which are not "essential"—inability to perform the latter, either with or without an accommodation, is not a ground for differential treatment, as was shown in *A Computer Company* v. *A Worker*. However, where an individual with a disability is not capable of carrying out the "essential functions", an employer is required to consider if any accommodation is possible which will render the individual so able. If no accommodation is available which would achieve this result, the employer is not obliged to continue employing the person in the position in question. However, as demonstrated by the *Dutch Civil Servant Case* and the British case *Archibald* v. *Fife Council* examined in section 6.2.2.D, in this situation an employer would still be obliged to make a reasonable accommodation by transferring an individual with a disability to a different function that they can perform.

In order to activate the accommodation requirement, the employer or other covered party must be aware first that the individual concerned has a disability (or possesses some other characteristic, such as being a follower of a particular religion, which gives entitlement to an accommodation), and secondly requires some form of accommodation. The individual (with a disability) does not necessarily have to request a specific accommodation, although this will frequently be the case. An exception to this requirement exists where the duty to accommodate is "anticipatory" and owed to people with disabilities as a group, as is the case with regard to disability-related accommodations concerning access to services under UK law.

The obligation on the employer or other covered party to consider whether any accommodation is possible is far-reaching, as demonstrated by the UK case of *Cosgrove* and the Irish case, *A Health and Fitness Club* v. *A Worker*. It is submitted that the approach favoured by the court in the latter case, involving a two-stage process whereby, in the first instance, the factual position—relating to the existence and extent of the disability and its impact on job performance—is established, and secondly, a consideration as to the need and appropriateness of an accommodation occurs, is a good model which can be followed in other jurisdictions.

6.4. LIMITATIONS ON THE DUTY TO ACCOMMODATE

6.4.1. INTRODUCTION AND EXPLORATION OF THE ISSUES

Two limitations are imposed on the requirement to make an employment-related accommodation for individuals with disabilities: first, employers are only required to make a *"reasonable"* accommodation; and secondly, a failure to make such an accommodation can only be justified if it would result in the employer experiencing undue hardship or a disproportionate burden. Similar limitations exist with regard to the making of accommodations governing access to services.

The first issue has been extensively discussed under section 6.2.1 of this chapter. It is worth recalling that in some jurisdictions an accommodation is defined as reasonable if it does not result in (inter alia) a disproportionate burden, whilst in other jurisdictions the question of reasonableness has a different con-notation, and is not directly related to the issue of undue hardship or disproportionate burden.

With regard to the second limitation, based around the concept of "dispro-portionate burden", preamble recital 21 of the Employment Equality Directive states:

> "To determine whether the measures in question give rise to a disproportionate burden, account should be taken in particular of the financial and other costs entailed, the scale and financial resources of the organisation or undertaking and the possibility of obtaining public funding or any other assistance."

On the basis of this paragraph, Katie Wells has argued that under the Directive the financial cost of the accommodation is the primary factor in determining whether a "disproportionate burden" exists. She argues that the Directive frames the duty to accommodate by weighing two elements: on one side, the effectiveness of the accommodation in enabling the disabled person to access employment, and on the other side, the financial cost of the accommodation for the employer. Wells regards it as unfortunate that the Directive does not also point to the potential benefits that could accrue to employers from adapting their workplaces to facilitate the employment of disabled people.

> "This polar opposition of individual gain versus employer cost is not conducive to tackling attitudinal and systemic forms of disability discrimination, and it may reinforce the perception that the principal result of accommodation of disabled people is expense and not benefit."[87]

Since Wells wrote her article, the European Court of Justice has decided its first case relating to disability and the Employment Equality Directive. In his opinion in *Chacón Navas*, Advocate General Geelhoed seemed to touch on the limitations on the obligation to making a reasonable accommodation, including the relevance of the cost of the accommodation.

---

[87] K. Wells, "The Impact of the Framework Employment Directive on UK Disability Discrimination Law" (2003) 32 *ILJ* 264.

ECJ, 16 March 2006   **6.EC.60.**
Case C–13/05, Sonia Chacón Navas v. Eurest Colectividades

DISCRIMINATION OCCURS WHERE AN INDIVIDUAL WITH A DISABILITY IS DISMISSED
WHERE THEY WOULD BE COMPETENT, CAPABLE AND AVAILABLE TO PERFORM THE
ESSENTIAL FUNCTIONS OF THE POST FOLLOWING THE MAKING OF A REASONABLE
ACCOMMODATION

Chacón Navas

Facts: The claimant was dismissed on the grounds that she had been absent from work for a lengthy period of time as a result of illness. The Spanish court referred a preliminary reference to the ECJ to establish whether, inter alia, the Directive included "within its protective scope a . . . [worker] who has been dismissed by her employer solely because she is sick". In addressing this question, the Court also considered the role which the obligation to make a reasonable accommodation played when considering whether an individual with a disability was protected from dismissal.

Held (regarding the reasonable accommodation issue): The Directive prohibited dismissal of an individual with a disability where, following the making of a reasonable accommodation, the individual would be competent, capable and available to perform the essential functions of the post in question.

Opinion: ADVOCATE GENERAL GEELHOED [discussing the justification of a hypothetical dismissal on the grounds of disability]
"81. I would add, to complete the picture, that in that hypothesis the dismissal may none the less be justified if the functional limitations—the disability—make impossible or seriously restrict the pursuit of the occupation or business concerned.

82. However, that justification is admissible only if the employer has no reasonable means of alleviating or compensating for the disability concerned in such a way that the disabled person is able to continue pursuing his occupation or business [reference: see Article 4(1) of Directive 2000/78 (concerning genuine and determining occupational requirements)].

83. What is reasonable is also determined by the cost of appropriate resources, the proportionality of those costs if they are not reimbursed by the authorities, the reduction of or compensation for the disability thus made possible and the accessibility of the disabled person concerned to other occupation or forms of business where his disability will be no obstacle or far less of an obstacle. [reference: see Article 5 of Directive 2000/78]"

Notes
(1) The Advocate General did not refer explicitly to the concepts of reasonable accommodation or disproportionate burden in this part of his opinion. Nevertheless, given the footnote reference to Article 5 of the Directive in paragraph 83, one can assume that he is commenting on the limitations on the obligation to make a reasonable accommodation, and specifically the scope of the disproportionate burden defence.

(2) The reference to "the reduction of or compensation for the disability thus made possible [by the accommodation]" in paragraph 83 is confusing. It could simply be a reference to the fact that the accommodation must enable the person with a disability to perform the essential functions of the job; alternatively, it could convey the meaning that, quite separately from the former requirement, the effectiveness of the accommodation is also a relevant factor in determining whether it should be required.

Therefore, an accommodation which only just allows a person with a disability to perform the essential functions and which results in only a small improvement in capacity of the individual may not be regarded as "reasonable" for an employer, whilst an accommodation which brings with it the same costs but which results in a large improvement in capacity and enables a person with a disability to easily carry out the essential functions of the post would be required. There is no authority in the Directive or elsewhere for this latter interpretation, and it was not repeated by the Court in its judgment.

(3) The question as to how far "the accessibility of the disabled person concerned to other occupation or forms of business where his disability will be no obstacle or far less of an obstacle" (paragraph 83) is relevant in determining whether an employer is obliged to make an accommodation is addressed in more detail below.

Returning to the issue of cost of an accommodation identified by Wells, and the potential financial benefit to the employer of making an accommodation, one can note that a "reasonable accommodation" may pay for itself in the greater productivity of the worker with a disability. Alternatively it may have externalities beyond that particular worker, by, for example, enabling other workers to be more productive, or by attracting customers who would otherwise not have been able or inclined to patronise the firm. "Reasonable accommodations" in such cases would accord with the model of economic efficiency. One of the few European provisions which seem to recognise this is the non-binding *Belgian Guide to . . . Reasonable Accommodations for Persons with a Disability at Work*. The Guide notes that, amongst the criteria which must be considered in determining whether any accommodation is "reasonable", are the direct and indirect consequences of the accommodation.[88] These include whether the accommodation will offer support to a larger group of employees and/or external visitors, and whether the accommodation will assist future employees with a comparable disability. However, not all accommodations can be justified by this model. Some accommodations are simply economically inefficient. Furthermore, the justification for the duty of "reasonable accommodation" is not economic efficiency but equality of opportunity for people with disabilities. This presupposes a comparison with individuals who are not disabled.

Adopting a very different perspective, Kelman[89] argues that the accommodation "right" is a claim to receive treatment that disregards some (though not all) differential input costs. He regards the accommodation norm as establishing a distributive claim, rather than a right. He argues that those seeking accommodations are making claims on real social resources that compete with all other social resource claimants and that all such claims cannot be met. Thus a particular claimant's claim to have his "right" to accommodation met is subject to claims that his demands are "unreasonable" in the sense that the resources that would have to be devoted to meeting them could be spent in a better fashion.

---

[88] In para. 3.1.4 of the Guide. See section 6.2.1.A above for the relevant extract and further comments.
[89] M .Kelman, "Market Discrimination and Groups, Stanford Law School" (2000) Stanford Public Law and Legal Theory Working Paper Series, Working Paper No. 8.

He argues that the main reason we distribute the resources needed to accommodate otherwise excluded workers in kind, in the form of "inclusionary" services rather than in cash, is to break down the hierarchical segregation of social groups. If the basic goal of an accommodation requirement is to transfer resources, in kind, to increase social inclusion, there are certain limits on the accommodation requirement. These limits are relevant in determining what accommodations are reasonable and should be covered. According to Kelman, people who do not face something resembling social exclusion in the absence of legal intervention should perhaps not be entitled to employer subsidised accommodation.

As a consequence, he concludes that the added input the claimant seeks is unreasonable if it would benefit (large numbers of) other potential employees (nearly as much) as it would benefit the claimant. In this sense, the accommodation obligation is limited to those who are thought to be as "meritorious" as those who can work without the accommodation. Kelman concludes that accommodation arguably takes preference over more conventional redistributive transfers only in situations in which the transferees would otherwise suffer particular harm associated with being relegated to an outsider status.

A number of other factors may be relevant to establishing the limits of the obligation to accommodate. In some cases, should no accommodation duty exist, the individual with a disability would be unable to find any comparable job (or, in the extreme case, no job at all). The question then arises whether the extreme consequences for the individual, in terms of marginalisation or exclusion from the paid workforce, should be factored into the equation, or whether the individual consequences are irrelevant. In addition, successful employment in a particular line of work or with a particular employer may require an expensive accommodation, whilst an alternative employment or employer may require no accommodation, or only a modest one. In this situation, one can consider what weight should be placed on the career preferences of the individual. Advocate General Geelhoed, in paragraph 83 of his opinion in the *Chacón Navas*[90] case, seemed to consider that this was a relevant factor in determining whether an employer should be obliged to make any particular (expensive or difficult) accommodation.

Further problems are likely to arise where an individual's impairment is general, rather than firm or occupation specific. As a consequence, the jobs the individual can perform without accommodation, or with the accommodations that employers are willing to offer, may be far less lucrative or rewarding than a job that would require a costly accommodation. At the extreme, there may be an all-or-nothing choice. If this particular employer is not required to accommodate, then no employer is, and the entire cost of adjusting to the disability is borne by the individual with the disability; conversely, if the employer is required to accommodate, it bears the entire cost, subject to the availability of public support, solely because of a unilateral choice of the individual to apply for one of its jobs.

---

[90] Case *Sonia Chacón Navas* v. *Eurest Colectividades*, see above **6.EC.60.**

On the other hand, one could argue that the disproportionate burden test should allow no further room for such considerations. Employers should be expected to do all that is possible to accommodate individuals with disabilities in each and every case, and the disproportionate burden defence, which should only successfully be relied upon in cases of genuine and severe hardship, should not be further weakened even in such extreme situations. The reasonable accommodation requirement should already factor in the extreme scenarios described above, and the disproportionate burden defence, which should not be easily met, should always be the absolute limit of the employer's obligation.

A further relevant factor might appear to be the extent to which any accommodation breaches pre-existing collective bargaining agreements or other employment-related rules or procedures. In some jurisdictions collective bargaining agreements can restrict the obligation to make certain "reasonable accommodations". In the US, as revealed by the *Barnett* case, even the existence of unilaterally imposed rules by the employer can result in an accommodation which clashes with those rules being classified as "unreasonable" and therefore not required. However, in light of the wording of Article 16 (b) of the Employment Equality Directive, these possibilities seem to have been closed off.

Council Directive 2000/78/EC of 27 November 2000   **6.EC.61.**
establishing a general framework for equal treatment in employment and occupation[91]

—Article 16 Compliance
Member States shall take the necessary measures to ensure that:

(a) any laws, regulations and administrative provisions contrary to the principle of equal treatment are abolished;

(c) any provisions contrary to the principle of equal treatment which are included in contracts or collective agreements, internal rules of undertakings or rules governing the independent occupations and professions and workers' and employers' organisations are, or may be, declared null and void or are amended.

Finally, one set of costs which may be particularly difficult to quantify is the potential conflict that may arise with regard to the interests of other employees if an accommodation is granted. Kelman's arguments already reveal that, as a result of expenditure on accommodations, fewer funds may be available to provide benefits or meet the needs of other employees who are not entitled to claim accommodations. However, accommodations can also result in non-pecuniary negative consequences for other employees—for example, excusing a disabled employee from a physically demanding task, such as carrying a heavy post bag, which in principle all employees are required

---

[91] [2000] OJ L303/16.

to undertake, implies that the other employees must undertake that task more regularly. Alternatively always excusing an employee from working on Saturday or Sunday for religious reasons increases the likelihood that other employees must work on those days, which may clash with their family commitments or preferred days of rest. In these situations the employer has the difficult task of balancing conflicting interests, and the disproportionate burden test does not always readily lend itself to interpretation or application in such cases.

6.4.2. NATIONAL LEGISLATIVE PROVISIONS

6.4.2.A.   FINANCIAL CONSIDERATIONS

In many European jurisdictions legislative guidance as to what amounts to a disproportionate burden is brief or non-existent. Examples which can be found in section 6.2.1.A of this chapter, where they are accompanied by more extensive commentary provided by the relevant authorities, include Belgium (Article 2 (3) of Federal Law Act Combat Discrimination of 25 February 2003: ". . . A reasonable accommodation is an accommodation that does not create a disproportionate burden, or where the burden is sufficiently compensated for by existing measures.") and Finland (Finnish Non-Discrimination Act 21/2004, Section 5, ". . . In assessing what constitutes reasonable, particular attention shall be devoted to the costs of the steps, the financial position of the person commissioning work or arranging training, and the possibility of support from public funds or elsewhere towards the costs involved."). A further example, not referred to elsewhere in this chapter, can be found in Bulgarian legislation.

Bulgarian Protection Against Discrimination Act   **6.BG.62.**
(effective as of 1 January 2004)

Article 16
Upon recruitment, or where disability occurs during employment, an employer shall adapt the workplace to the needs of a person with disabilities, unless the cost is excessive and would seriously burden the employer.

As can be seen from these measures, the financial cost of any accommodation is an important factor in determining whether a disproportionate burden exists. This is examined and commented on in more detail in the following extract, taken from a brochure prepared by an inter-ministerial group in Belgium.

"3. The criteria that accommodations must comply with to be regarded as 'reasonable'

3.1 The financial and organisational burden on the employer

An adjustment is regarded as reasonable when its implementation does not imply a disproportionate burden on the employer or when the burden is adequately offset by the existing
measures. With each request for an application, consideration will have to be given to whether
it is reasonable by nature. When making this evaluation, account will also have to be taken of
the potential direct and indirect consequences. Use can be made of various criteria when
assessing the reasonableness of an accommodation.

3.1.1 The employer's financial capabilities
When considering whether an accommodation is reasonable or not, the financial capabilities
and organisational potential of the business or the employer must also be taken into consideration. In doing so, the size or extent of the business will also play an important role. Expensive
reconstruction may be reasonable for large firms or multinationals, while the same accommodations could mean a disproportionate burden for a small or medium-sized business. For
example:

— It may be unreasonable in certain cases to expect a firm with four employees to have various doors widened to permit access by a person in a wheelchair.
— It may be reasonable for a small or medium-sized business to have a ramp installed to
   make the workplace accessible.

3.1.2 The financial cost of the accommodation
The cost to the employer will differ according to the accommodation to be made.
   A reasonable accommodation need not always be very expensive. As both American
and European studies have shown (e.g. the calculations by the 'Job Accommodation
Network' in America (http://janweb.icdi.wvu.edu/) or the studies by the CRETH) the price
tag for a necessary accommodation for quality integration of a disabled person rarely exceeds
$ 500. In addition, there is nothing to prevent an employer with various options at his
disposal from making the cheapest choice provided, however, that it remains effective. For
example:

— An employer need not have a door widened for an employee in a wheelchair if there is a
   wide door close by that he can use.
— Instead of fully rebuilding the workplace for an employee suffering from a serious disability through a road accident, the employer can suggest that the employee does his
   work at home.

Certain adjustments require human investment. The financial cost associated with this
generally coincides with the staff costs and will also have to be taken into account. For
example:

— The recruitment of an additional person to support or monitor a person with a disability
   could by nature be an unreasonable accommodation if the additional cost cannot be
   offset.

3.1.3 Compensatory measures and subsidies

Subsidies and measures that can reduce the burden on the employer will affect the assessment of reasonableness. Assistance from various regional and community institutions e.g. for adjustments to the workplace and a contribution by insurers towards the cost of an accommodation following an accident may largely reduce the cost of the accommodation.

NB: Subsidies towards the pay and social security for potential loss of yield from disabled employees are not reasonable accommodations in themselves. However, they can be regarded as an additional factor to demonstrate that the necessary accommodation does not constitute a disproportionate burden.

3.1.4 Direct and indirect consequences [see extract in section 6.2.1.A. of this chapter]
. . .

3.1.5 Job description and period for writing off the accommodation [see extract in section 6.2.1.A of this chapter]
. . .

3.1.6 Work-related accommodations [see extract in section 6.2.1.A of this chapter] . . .”

Notes

(1) It is clear from the above references and extracts that, in determining whether any particular accommodation amounts to a disproportionate burden, an individualised analysis of the situation of the employer or other covered party must be made. In this context, the size and resources of the employer as well as the cost of the accommodation are all relevant.

(2) It has been suggested by Wells (see above) that the potential financial benefit of making the accommodation should also be taken into account. This is indeed considered under the Belgian Guide under paragraph 3.1.4 (“Direct and indirect consequences”). These may include benefits resulting from the accommodation accruing to a number of employees (with or without disabilities), rather than one specific individual, and greater accessibility to the business premises for customers and visitors who have disabilities. However, statutory provisions are generally silent with regard to such matters.

(3) Whilst the focus in the Directive and the legislation cited above is on the cost of the accommodation, it is not always possible to easily quantify the financial cost of any accommodation. Stein[92] has made a distinction between accommodations involving “hard” costs, meaning that they invoke readily quantifiable out-of-pocket expenses, and accommodations involving the alteration of the way in which a job is performed, or alterations to procedures, where the actual cost is far more difficult to measure, which he refers to as “soft” costs. The approach adopted in the legislation is generally suitable for addressing “hard” costs, but is far from clear as to how to deal with more intangible “soft” costs.

---

[92] Stein, above n. 36 See section 6.2.2.A. for relevant extract.

(4) As is clear from the Directive and legislation, the role of public subsidies is important. Costs which can be offset against the public purse will, by definition, not result in a disproportionate burden. However, it is frequently not clear whether employers are obliged to apply for public funding if such is available and, in particular, at what point the availability of public funding should be factored into the equation—when such funding is theoretically available but has not been applied for; when an application has been made but no definitive grant has been made; or only when an application for funding has been approved. One example of a jurisdiction in which this point has been clarified is Sweden. According to the Disability Ombudsman, the mere possibility of obtaining a government subsidy will not be taken into account in assessing the reasonableness of any measure. The subsidy should be taken into account, however, if it becomes apparent during the recruitment process that it will be granted.[93]

(5) *The Belgian Guide*, in paragraph 6.3.1.B, notes that an employer who has various options at his disposal when it comes to making an accommodation is free to choose the cheapest or easiest solution, as long as the accommodation is effective. This mirrors the finding of the German State Labour Court (Lower Saxony) in the *Lathe Case* cited under 6.2.2.E excerpt number **6.DE.41.**

6.4.2.B.   IRELAND—FINANCIAL ISSUES AND THE IMPACT OF THE
            EMPLOYMENT EQUALITY DIRECTIVE

Experience in Ireland is interesting in that it reveals the impact the Employment Equality Directive has had in framing legislative justifications for a failure to make an accommodation and, in particular, the extent to which the financial costs of any accommodation are now relevant. Prior to the adoption of the Employment Equality Act, which preceded the adoption of the Directive, a reference was made to the Irish Supreme Court to establish the compatibility of the then Bill with the Constitution. For the purposes of this chapter only the considerations of the Court with regard to the limitations on the requirement to make a reasonable accommodation are relevant.

---

[93] A. Numhauser-Henning, "Report on Measures to Combat Discrimination: Directive 2000/43/EC and 2000/78/EC. Country Report Sweden" (European Commission, 2005), available on the website of Directorate-General for Employment, Social Affairs and Equal Opportunities.

In the matter of Article 26 of the Constitution and in the matter of the Employment Equality Bill, 1996

OBLIGATION TO MAKE AN ACCOMMODATION UNLESS THIS AMOUNTED TO AN UNDUE HARDSHIP BREACHED THE RIGHT TO CARRY ON A BUSINESS AND EARN A LIVELIHOOD AS PROTECTED BY THE IRISH CONSTITUTION

Irish Constitution and Right to Property

Facts: The Employment Equality Bill, following approval by the Irish Parliament (*Oireachtas*), was submitted to the Irish Supreme Court to establish the compatibility of the Bill with the Constitution. One of the issues considered by the Court was the obligation to make a reasonable accommodation unless this amounted to a undue hardship.

Held: The obligation to make an accommodation unless this amounted to an undue hardship breached the right to carry on a business and earn a livelihood protected by the Irish Constitution and this provision of the Bill was unconstitutional.

Judgment: "Section 35 provides that:— . . .

(4) Nothing in this Part or Part II applies to discrimination against a person on the disability ground in relation to employment of any description if—. . .

(b)   the employer does all that is reasonable to accommodate the needs of that person,

unless, having regard to all the relevant circumstances, including, without prejudice to the generality, the matters specified in subsection (5), the cost of the provision of such treatment or facilities for that person would give rise to undue hardship to the employer.

(5) The matters referred to in subsection (4) are—

(a)   the nature of the treatment or facilities that would be required;
(b)   the cost of the treatment or facilities and the number of persons who would benefit from them;
(c)   the financial circumstances of the employer;
(d)   the disruption that would be caused by the provision of the treatment or facilities; and
(e)   the nature of any benefit or detriment which would accrue to any persons likely to be affected by the provision of the treatment or facilities.

. . .

The Court is satisfied that the provisions under consideration constitute a delimitation of the exercise by employers of a right protected by that Article [Article 43], i.e. the right to carry on a business and earn a livelihood. It is also satisfied that these limitations have been imposed by the Oireachtas with a view to reconciling the exercise of the rights in question with a specific aspect of the common good i.e. the promotion of equality in the workplace between the disabled and their more fortunate fellow citizens. The issue which the Court has to resolve is as to whether the abridgement of those rights effected by these provisions constitutes an 'unjust attack' on those rights in the case of individual employers, having regard to the manner in which it has been effected.

It is clear that, in determining whether the absence of any provision in the legislation under consideration for the payment of compensation constitutes such a 'unjust attack', the Court

---

[94] [1997] 2 IR 321.

may have regard to whether the restriction, in the form in which it was imposed, is consistent with the requirements of 'social justice' within the meaning of Article 43, s. 2, sub-section 1 . . . It is because the rights of private property 'ought' in civil society to be regulated by 'the principles of social justice' that the State may, as occasion requires, delimit their exercise with a view to reconciling it with the 'exigencies of the common good'. It is because such a delimitation, to be valid, must be not only reconcilable with the exigencies of the common good but also with the principles of social justice that it cannot be an unjust attack on a citizen's private property pursuant to the provisions of Article 40, s. 3 of the Constitution (see judgment of Walsh J in *Dreher v Irish Land Commission* [1984] ILRM 94).

Needless to say what is or is not required by the principles of social justice or by the exigencies of the common good is primarily a matter for the Oireachtas and this Court will be slow to interfere with the decision of the Oireachtas in this area. But it is not exclusively a matter for the Oireachtas. Otherwise, as was pointed out in the Buckley v The Attorney General [1950] IR 67 [sic], Article 43 would appear, with Article 45, in the section of the Constitution devoted to the directive principles of social policy the application of which by the Oireachtas in the making of laws is withdrawn from the consideration of the courts.

The Bill has the totally laudable aim of making provision for such of our fellow citizens as are disabled. Clearly it is in accordance with the principles of social justice that society should do this. But, *prima facie*, it would also appear to be just that society should bear the cost of doing it. It is important to distinguish between the proposed legislation and legislation to protect the health and safety of workers. It is entirely proper that the State should insist that those who profit from an industrial process should manage it as safely, and with as little danger to health, as possible. The cost of doing the job safely and in a healthy manner is properly regarded as part of the industrialist's costs of production. Likewise it is proper that he should pay if he pollutes the air the land or the rivers. It would be unjust if he were allowed to take the profits and let society carry the cost. Likewise it is just that the State, through its planning agencies, should insist that the public buildings and private buildings to which the general public are intended to have access for work or play should be designed in such a way as to be accessible by the disabled as well as by the able-bodied.

But the difficulty with the section now under discussion is that it attempts to transfer the cost of solving one of society's problems on to a particular group. The difficulty the Court finds with the section is not that it requires an employer to employ disabled people, but that it requires him to bear the cost of all special treatment or facilities which the disabled person may require to carry out the work unless the cost of the provision of such treatment or facilities would give rise to 'undue hardship' to the employer.

There is no provision to exempt small firms or firms with a limited number of employees, from the provisions of the Bill. The wide definition of the term 'disability' in the Bill means that it is impossible to estimate in advance what the likely cost to an employer would be. The Bill does provide that one of the matters to be taken into consideration in estimating whether employing the disabled person would cause undue hardship to the employer is 'the financial circumstances of the employer' but this in turn implies that the employer would have to disclose his financial circumstances and the problems of his business to an outside party.

It therefore appears to the Court that the provisions of the Bill dealing with disability, despite their laudable intention, are repugnant to the Constitution for the reasons stated."

Following the decision of the Supreme Court, the Employment Equality Bill was amended and the obligation to make a reasonable accommodation was much reduced.

Section 16

. . . (3) (a) For the purposes of this Act, a person who has a disability shall not be regarded as other than fully competent to undertake, and fully capable of undertaking, any duties if, with the assistance of special treatment or facilities, such person would be fully competent to undertake, and be fully capable of undertaking, those duties.

(b) An employer shall do all that is reasonable to accommodate the needs of a person who has a disability by providing special treatment or facilities to which paragraph (a) relates.

(c) A refusal or failure to provide for special treatment or facilities to which paragraph (a) relates shall not be deemed reasonable unless such provision would give rise to a cost, other than a nominal cost, to the employer.

Notes

(1) The impression is that the concept of "a nominal cost" is not relative to the size or resources of the employer, but absolute. However, in *An Employee* v. *A Local Authority* (see section 6.2.1.A and **6.IE.7.**) the term nominal cost was analysed and the following principles were enunciated:

— the size of the enterprise is relevant when determining whether an accommodation gives rise to a nominal cost or not;

— the status of the enterprise (public or private) is relevant when determining whether an accommodation gives rise to a nominal cost or not;

— all employers are not to be treated in an identical manner when determining whether an accommodation gives rise to a nominal cost or not.

(2) As has been seen from the cases examined in section 6.3 of this chapter, in spite of the limited nature of the obligation to provide an accommodation under pre-Directive Irish law, individuals with disabilities have been able to successfully argue that an employer or other covered party was under an obligation to make an accommodation.

(3) Following the adoption of the Employment Equality Directive, and specifically Article 5 and the relevant recitals thereof, it proved necessary to amend the Employment Equality Act 1998 on the grounds that the justification for a failure to make an accommodation—that it amounted to more than a nominal cost—was not compatible with the Directive.

For further information, including the text of the amended Article 16 of the Irish Equality Act 2004, see section 6.2.1.A.

6.4.2.C.   NON-FINANCIAL ISSUES WHICH JUSTIFY A FAILURE TO MAKE
            ACCOMMODATION

An example of a legislative provision which refers to matters other than costs as justifying a failure to make an accommodation can be found in the German Social

Law Code, Book Nine (SGB IX), Rehabilitation and Participation of disabled persons, of 19 June 2001, § 81 SGB IX[95] (see section 6.2.1.A), which states:

> "A claim [to an accommodation] . . . does not exist if its fulfilment is not reasonable for the employer or if it would entail disproportionate burden or in as far as the occupational safety and health rules laid down by national law or by employer's liability insurance associations or rules governing members of the civil service are opposed."

Therefore, in addition to the financial consequences of making an accommodation, the statute also gives priority to health and safety rules and rules relating to the civil service over the right of an individual to claim a reasonable accommodation. Likewise, the extract from the Preparatory Works to the Finnish Non-Discrimination Act (also found in section 6.2.1.A of this chapter) states that an "arrangement" might be unreasonable if it could "endanger compliance with workplace safety legislation". In addition, the Preparatory Works state that "arrangements" can be unreasonable if they "would excessively change the activities of the workplace". This is a rather vague exception which is not further elaborated.

Two further national statutes which provide for additional (non-financial) factors to be considered in determining the extent of the obligation to accommodate workers with disabilities can be found in Slovakia and Austria.

Slovakian Act No. 365/2004 Coll. on Equal Treatment   **6.SK.66.**
in Certain Areas and Protection against Discrimination, amending and
supplementing certain other laws (Anti-discrimination Act) of 20 May 2004

§ 7
(1) Refusal or omission of the employer to take appropriate measures to enable a person with a disability to have access to employment, to the work of certain type, to promotion or other advance or to training shall be also deemed to constitute indirect discrimination based on disability; this does not apply if the adoption of such measures would impose a disproportionate burden on the employer.
(2) To determine whether the measures referred to in paragraph 1 give rise to a disproportionate burden, account shall be taken of

    a)   the benefit that the adoption of the measure would mean for the disabled person,
    b)   financial resources of the employer, including the possibility of obtaining funding or any other assistance for the adoption of the measure, and
    c)   the possibility of attaining the purpose of the measure referred to in paragraph 1 in a different, alternative manner.

(3) The measure shall not be considered as giving rise to disproportionate burden if its adoption by the employer is mandatory under separate provisions.

---

[95] Federal Law Gazette I at 1046.

Note

The separate provisions referred to under § 7(3) include the obligation of the employer, as stipulated by Act No. 5/2006 Coll. on Employment Services, to employ an employee for a specified period of time if the state contributed to the creation of the job or the establishment of a protected workshop, and the obligation to observe the requirements relating to the construction of buildings for people with a reduced mobility as stipulated by regulation No. 523/2002 Coll.

Austrian Act on the Employment of People with Disabilities   **6.AT.67.**
(effective as of 1 January 2006)[96]

§ 7c

It shall not be deemed indirect discrimination if the removal of conditions which constitute disadvantage, especially of barriers, would be illegal or would pose an unreasonable and disproportionate burden on the employer. When testing whether a burden is disproportionate, especially the following has to be taken into account:

— the necessary effort to eliminate the conditions constituting the disadvantage
— the economic capacity of the employer
— public financial assistance available for the necessary improvements
— the time span between the coming into force of this Act and the alleged discrimination.

In case the removal of conditions which constitute disadvantage turns out to be a disproportionate burden in this sense it shall still be deemed discrimination if the employer failed to improve the situation of the affected person at least in a considerable way in order to reach the best possible approximation to equal treatment.

When assessing whether certain conditions constitute indirect discrimination it has to be taken into account whether relevant legislation exists in regard to accessibility and to what extent they have been obeyed. Premises or other facilities, means of transport, technical equipment, information systems or other dedicated spheres of life shall be deemed accessible if they can be accessed and used by people with disabilities in a customary way, unassisted and without extra difficulty.

Note

Both the Slovakian and Austrian statutes in essence state that an employer or other covered party cannot argue that an accommodation or removal of conditions would amount to a disproportionate burden if the accommodation or adaptation is required under separate legislation. This is an important principle. All Member States have enacted legislation establishing technical standards which are designed to ensure accessibility of disabled people to certain facilities, and such provisions are frequently derived from EC standards. Such legislation includes building regulations which make

---

[96] In D. Schindlauer, "Report on Measures to Combat Discrimination: Directive 2000/43/EC and 2000/78/EC. Country Report Austria" (European Commission, 2005), available on the website of Directorate-General for Employment, Social Affairs and Equal Opportunities.

mandatory the inclusion of certain design features in new or renovated buildings, such as lifts with wide doorways, to ensure accessibility for people with disabilities. Companies providing public transport are also under an obligation to ensure that all new vehicles comply with accessibility standards.[97] Whilst such technical standards have existed for some time, their relationship to the reasonable accommodation requirement has yet to be clarified in many jurisdictions. It can be increasingly expected that individuals with disabilities, when making a claim for a reasonable accommodation which involves a physical adaptation to a building, will refer to the failure to comply with pre-existing accessibility standards as evidence of both the need for an accommodation and the "reasonableness" of their claim or the lack of a disproportionate burden. Austrian and Slovakian legislation has established how the courts should respond in such a situation, and both statutes bring clarity to the situation.

6.4.3. COMPARATIVE OVERVIEW

In essence, two general limitations to the obligation to make an accommodation can be identified: that an accommodation must be reasonable and that it must not amount to a disproportionate burden. However, these concepts, and particularly the requirement of reasonableness, are interpreted differently in various jurisdictions.

With regard to the disproportionate burden limitation, which has been the focus of this section, the Directive makes it clear that the cost of any accommodation is a key factor (the key factor?) in determining the scope of the obligation. However, it can be difficult to quantify the exact cost of any accommodation. This should be less of a problem for what Stein has called "hard" costs—but can create problems regarding "soft" costs, which are far more intangible. Nevertheless, if an employer can show that "soft" costs—such as changing a production process to accommodate a worker with a disability—would result in a disproportionate burden, this will also justify a failure to make such an accommodation. Reflecting the individualised nature of the accommodation requirement, more can be expected of a wealthy and large employer—in both cost terms and in respect of other elements causing inconvenience—than a smaller or financially stricken employer.

In addition to cost, this section has identified jurisdictions which explicitly provide for a limitation to the accommodation requirement based on other factors— including health and safety requirements, as stated in the German Social Law Code.

More generally, the Directive provides that collective bargaining agreements, contracts, national laws and regulations, etc. should be abolished or declared null and void where they are contrary to the principle of equal treatment, including

---

[97] For information on EU rules relating to accessibility standards and public transport see L. Waddington, *From Rome to Nice in a Wheelchair, The Development of a European Disability Policy* (Groningen, Europa Law Publishing, 2006) 32–4.

presumably the reasonable accommodation requirement. Some statutes also specific-ally state that certain factors cannot amount to a justification for failing to make an accommodation. These include the fact that the accommodation is already required under separate legislation, as is stated in Austrian and Slovakian statutes.

In some cases it is clear that the general (financial) benefits accruing from any accommodation, such as greater access for visitors who have a disability to the employer's premises, or (potential) use of an accommodation by a number of individuals with disabilities, should also be considered. The greater the identified benefits of any accommodation, the greater the justification for imposing costs or initial inconvenience on an employer.

Finally, the Advocate General in *Chacón Navas* has suggested that the consequences for the individual with the disability of failing to make the accommo-dation should also be considered—if the individual could obtain an alternative position where the accommodation costs are lower, this would seem to make it less appropriate to require an employer to make an expensive accommodation, thereby bearing the cost of the personal choice made by the individual with the disability. This principle is not reflected in the national legislation or case-law which has been examined.

Given the scarcity of case-law from the ECJ on this topic, it is too early to say if any of these principles will be interpreted as applying to the reasonable accommo-dation requirement in the Directive, or whether they will remain peculiarities of specific Member States.

6.5. FITTING THE DUTY TO ACCOMMODATE INTO THE NON-DISCRIMINATION FRAMEWORK[98]

As noted elsewhere in this book, most jurisdictions make a distinction between direct and indirect discrimination. This is certainly the case in the European Union, where the provisions covering gender and race discrimination, as well as the Employment Equality Directive, make a clear distinction between these two forms of discrimination.

The question at issue in this section is how the concept of reasonable accommo-dation fits into this dual framework. Can the unjustified refusal to make a reasonable accommodation be regarded as a form of discrimination, and, if so, should it be regarded as direct or indirect discrimination, an aspect of both or, alternatively, a third and different form of discrimination?

[98] Sections of this section draw on Waddington and Hendriks, above n, 13.

6.5.1.   FAILURE TO MAKE A REASONABLE ACCOMMODATION AS A FORM OF DIRECT DISCRIMINATION

Direct discrimination generally involves intent on the part of the discriminator, or at least the intention to make a distinction on a specific ground.[99] In the case of the alleged failure to provide a reasonable accommodation, one could argue that such intent can be established where the employer has been made aware of the need for an adaptation to assist a specific individual, which can be made without excessive effort or cost, and has refused to make that adaptation. Such an approach could be fitted into the European Community framework mentioned above by explicitly providing for the "disproportionate burden" defence with regard to a directly discriminatory act involving a denial of a reasonable accommodation. However, in order to bring the failure to make a reasonable accommodation within the definition of direct discrimination as laid down in the Employment Equality Directive, one must establish that an individual requiring an accommodation is in "a comparable situation" to those who do not require such an accommodation.[100] The latter is often difficult to demonstrate, given that an accommodation typically seeks to take away a barrier which impedes an individual from placing him- or herself in "a comparable situation" to others. Unless one is willing to extend the meaning of direct discrimination to include the failure to create equal employment opportunities, the notion of direct discrimination can only rarely be invoked to redress a failure to make a reasonable accommodation.

Swedish law nevertheless adopts this approach with respect to disability.

Swedish Prohibition of Discrimination in Working Life   **6.SE.68.**
of People with Disability Act (1999:132)

Direct discrimination
Section 3
An employer may not disfavour a job applicant or an employee with a disability by treating her or him less favourably than the employer treats or would have treated persons without such a disability in a similar situation, if the disfavourable treatment has a connection with the disability.
. . .

Support and adaptation measures
Section 6
The prohibition contained in Section 3 also applies when an employer upon employment, promotion or training for promotion, by providing support and adaptation measures, can

---

[99] For a discussion of the difference between intent and motive in the context of direct discrimination, see above M. Bell, Chapter Two: Direct Discrimination, section 2.3.2.

[100] An alternative would be to make a comparison between two individuals who both require a (similar) accommodation, where one has received the accommodation and the other has not. However, such a restrictive interpretation would limit the relevance of the direct discrimination test.

create a situation for a person with a disability that is similar to that for persons without such a disability and it may reasonably be required that the employer implements such measures.

Notes

(1) This provision was adopted prior to the Employment Equality Directive.

(2) A further legal provision which classifies an unjustified failure to make a reasonable accommodation as a form of direct discrimination is the Maltese Equal Opportunities (Persons with Disability) Act 2000, Article 7.

Furthermore, EC laws regard pregnancy discrimination in this light, automatically classifying a decision based on pregnancy which results in disadvantage as a form of direct sex discrimination.[101] The European Court of Justice has therefore held that, in determining whether a failure to employ a woman on the grounds of pregnancy could be regarded as direct sex discrimination, "The answer depends on whether the fundamental reason for the refusal of employment is one which applies without distinction to workers of either sex or, conversely, whether it applies exclusively to one sex".[102] Applying this test, the Court found that discrimination on the grounds of pregnancy was a form of direct sex discrimination, since only women could be refused employment for this reason. Equally, under EC law, only people who have a disability can be disadvantaged by being denied a reasonable accommodation.[103] Whether the Court is willing to apply a similar test with respect to disability remains to be seen. It cannot be denied that disability is a more complex concept than pregnancy, not only with respect to the type of accommodations needed but also with respect to the nature and duration of an impairment. At the same type, the exclusion mechanisms are highly similar and, from an equal rights perspective, equally problematic.

6.5.2. FAILURE TO MAKE A REASONABLE ACCOMMODATION AS A FORM OF INDIRECT DISCRIMINATION

With regard to indirect discrimination, no intention to differentiate between protected groups is commonly required. The claimant generally has to demonstrate a difference in the effect of a seemingly neutral differentiation criterion which results in a disadvantage for members of the group the claimant pertains to compared with members of another—usually the "opposite"—group. However, the definition of indirect discrimination found in the Employment Equality Directive—analogous to

---

[101] Case C–177/88 *Dekker* [1990] ECR I–3941.

[102] *Ibid.*, para. 10.

[103] However, one must note that, in contrast to pregnancy discrimination, which can only be experienced by women, discrimination on the grounds of a failure to make a reasonable accommodation could potentially be experienced by other individuals, such as followers of minority religions, if the law provided for such a right. Nevertheless, as EC law currently stands, the right to a reasonable accommodation is only available to individuals with disabilities.

the Racial Equality Directive—is slightly different in that it focuses on a comparison between persons with a particular named characteristic and other persons, to identify if the former have been placed at a particular disadvantage. Seen in this way, the seemingly neutral physical organisation of the work or workplace, or working schedules, could, for example, disadvantage certain groups, e.g. people with mobility impairments or followers of a particular minority religion, and therefore be regarded as indirectly discriminatory.

Given that the Employment Equality Directive allows for a comparison of one individual (who belongs to the group of "persons having . . . a particular disability") with "other persons",[104] this suggests that the appropriate comparator depends on the given situation. But does this imply that the claimant is free to compare him/herself with any real or imaginary group of persons? This question is particularly relevant for people with disabilities in need of a job adaptation. The exclusionary effect of seemingly neutral job qualification requirements—e.g. fluency in foreign languages—and the availability of effective job accommodations is highly individualistic and dependent on environmental circumstances. In such cases, the assignment of an appropriate comparator may be particularly difficult and give rise to specific legal questions.

In spite of these difficulties a number of jurisdictions have chosen to classify an unjustified failure to make an accommodation as a form of indirect discrimination.

Slovakian Act No. 365/2004 Coll. on Equal Treatment   6.SK.69.
in Certain Areas and Protection against Discrimination, amending and
supplementing certain other laws (Anti-discrimination Act)

§ 7
(1) Refusal or omission of the employer to take appropriate measures to enable a person with a disability to have access to employment, to the work of a certain type, to promotion or other advance or to training shall be also deemed to constitute indirect discrimination based on disability; this does not apply if the adoption of such measures would impose a disproportionate burden on the employer.

Note
Another legal provision which defines an unjustified failure to make a reasonable accommodation as a form of indirect discrimination is the Spanish Law 13/1982 on Social Integration of Disabled People (LISMI) as amended by Law 62/2003, Article 37.3.

One problem with fitting the reasonable accommodation requirement into the framework of indirect discrimination under EC law, is that it would open the door to a further justification for a failure to make an accommodation—namely that the refusal to make the accommodation "is objectively justified by a legitimate aim and

---

[104] Art. 2(2)(b).

743

the means of achieving that aim are appropriate and necessary". The current Directive does not seem to allow for such an approach.

6.5.3. FAILURE TO MAKE A REASONABLE ACCOMMODATION AS A *SUI GENERIS* FORM OF DISCRIMINATION

In the light of the above, and given the prevailing notions about direct and indirect discrimination, in some jurisdictions reasonable accommodation discrimination is perceived as a form of discrimination *sui generis*.

An example of the *sui generis* approach can be found in the Netherlands. Whilst the relevant statute simply states that "the prohibition of making a distinction also includes the duty for the person to whom this prohibition is addressed, to make effective accommodations . . .",[105] without specifying how to classify a breach of the duty, the Equal Treatment Commission has provided further elaboration. In Opinion 2004-140 the Commission stated that reasonable accommodation discrimination "concerns an independent form of discrimination which does not (currently) exist in the other equal treatment laws", thereby clearly identifying such actions as a *sui generis* form of discrimination.

This approach is also adopted in the UK, where, under section 3A of the Disability Discrimination Act, three forms of disability discrimination are recognised, including discrimination by virtue of an unjustified failure to comply with the duty to make reasonable adjustments.[106]

6.5.4. FAILURE TO ELABORATE ON THE STATUS OF AN UNJUSTIFIED FAILURE TO MAKE A REASONABLE ACCOMMODATION

Many Member States have followed the lead of the Employment Equality Directive and have not explicitly acknowledged the status of an unjustified failure to make a reasonable accommodation. Whilst Article 5 of the Directive clearly locates the reasonable accommodation requirement within the paradigm of equal treatment ("in order to guarantee compliance with the principle of equal treatment . . ."), it does not explicitly define a failure to comply with the duty as a form of discrimination. Indeed, the concept of discrimination is addressed in Article 2 of the Directive, which refers to four types of action that are classified as discrimination: direct discrimination, indirect discrimination, harassment and an instruction to discriminate. This ambiguous situation is mirrored in many national transposition measures.

[105] Act on the Equal Treatment on the Grounds of Disability or Chronic Illness, Art. 2.
[106] The two other concepts of disability discrimination are: discrimination for a reason relating to a disabled person's disability (with a justification defence) and direct discrimination (with no justification defence). The UK Disability Discrimination Act does not provide for a prohibition of indirect discrimination.

6.5.5.   COMPARATIVE OVERVIEW

The analysis has revealed no common approach to the question of how an unjustified failure to make a reasonable accommodation should be classified. It has been argued that the duty does not readily fit within the existing constructions of direct and indirect discrimination—although it has also been noted that a number of jurisdictions have opted for one or other of these approaches. However, it is submitted that, different from direct and indirect discrimination, reasonable accommodation discrimination typically emerges in response to the failure to make an adaptation to ensure equal opportunities and commonly does not follow from differentiation on a forbidden or seemingly neutral ground—a distinction which is sometimes difficult to apply with respect to groups or individuals in need of accommodations.[107]

Reasonable accommodation discrimination can also be different from direct and indirect discrimination given that a disadvantage is not necessarily experienced by all or most members of a particular group, but is, as noted above, experienced on the individual level, depending on both individual and environmental factors. Such individual forms of disadvantage can only rarely be revealed by making a group comparison, which is characteristic for both direct and indirect discrimination standards. Reasonable accommodation discrimination therefore requires a different approach to do justice to the particularities of an individual in a given situation—or, as was held by the Canadian Supreme Court, "Accommodation ensures that each person is assessed according to his or her own personal abilities rather than presumed group characteristics".[108]

6.6. REASONABLE ACCOMMODATION AND POSITIVE ACTION

6.6.1.   INTRODUCTION AND EXPLORATION OF THE ISSUES[109]

It has been argued in previous sections of this chapter that the obligation to make a reasonable accommodation should be perceived as an element of the non-discrimination requirement. However, one should note that some commentators have argued that the concept is better regarded as a form of positive or affirmative action. Doyle,[110] writing in the British context some years ago, has argued that the duty to

---

[107] E.g. excluding dogs, thus using the criterion "having a dog" can be considered to constitute both direct discrimination (having a guide dog is inherent to some blind persons) and indirect discrimination (disproportionately affecting blind persons). See also *Roche* v. *Alabaster*, discussed in section 6.2.1.A, excerpt **6.IE.8.**

[108] *Grismer* v. *The British Columbia Council of Human Rights* [1999] 3 S.C.R. 868.

[109] Sections of this paragraph draw on Waddington and Hendriks, above n. 13.

[110] B. Doyle, "Enabling Legislation or Dissembling Law? The Disability Discrimination Act 1995" (1997) 60 *MLR* 74.

make a reasonable adjustment "is an example of legally mandated positive action rather than a requirement of reverse or positive discrimination". Meanwhile, Karlan and Rutherglen[111] have described the "reasonable accommodation" requirement in the ADA as conferring a right to "insist upon discrimination in their (persons with disabilities) favour" and regard the obligation as a form of affirmative action, albeit an unusual and distinct form. Tucker also argues that "reasonable accommodations" are one form of affirmative action, in that entities are required to spend money and/or reorganise their policies to treat a person with a disability differently—i.e. to take affirmative action on the behalf of people with a disability.[112] She regards the perception of the obligation to make "reasonable accommodations" in the ADA as a form of affirmative action (which is a justified perception in her opinion) as problematic for the Act's enforcement. She argues that courts view the ADA as going beyond the traditional civil rights approach to combating discrimination, and as imposing costs on employers in the form of affirmative "reasonable accommodation" requirements. These obligations are perceived as unjustified, and courts have responded by seeking to limit the scope of the ADA in a variety of ways, including through the development of a restricted definition of a person with a disability. Given the many instruments providing public support to finance accommodations which are available in the Member States of the EU, it is submitted that this problem is less likely to arise in Europe.

Authors who regard "reasonable accommodations" as a form of positive or affirmative action sometimes recognise that, unlike most forms of positive action which are aimed at members of a vulnerable or under-represented group, "reasonable accommodations" possess an individualised character. For this reason, statistical data revealing a numerical imbalance of a particular group of workers, such as women or ethnic minorities, in a particular employer's workforce are largely irrelevant for decisions concerning "reasonable accommodations". In addition, individuals generally have no legal standing to demand that they benefit from a positive action measure, whilst the reverse is true with regard to reasonable accommodations. Also, accommodations can involve regular and ongoing expenditure, such as a provision of personal assistance, rather than a one-off decision to award a woman or a member of an ethnic minority a job or training. For these reasons, the "reasonable accommo-dation" obligation is not susceptible to the problems of under- or over-inclusiveness which can dog classical positive action measures. In addition, the failure to render the obstacle or barrier irrelevant by adapting the environment can actually be regarded as a form of discrimination where it is possible for the employer to make such an accommodation.[113]

Karlan and Rutherglen argue that a revised model of affirmative action can be developed from an understanding of jobs as contingent assemblies of tasks and responsibilities that can be changed to accommodate the needs of individual

---

[111] Karlan and Rutherglen, above n. 16, 1.
[112] B. Poitras Tucker, "The ADA's Revolving Door: Inherent Flaws in the Civil Rights Paradigm" (2001) 62 *Ohio St LJ* at 335.
[113] See above section 6.5. for further discussion.

employees. The individualised adjustments required by the duty of "reasonable accommodations" leads away from the formalities and generalisations that have plagued traditional forms of affirmative action on the basis of race and sex and does not perpetuate the stereotypes.

In spite of these arguments, and the plea for a revised approach to positive action with regard to reasonable accommodation put forward by authors such as Karlan and Rutherglen, it seems generally inappropriate to view the reasonable accommodation requirement found in the Employment Equality Directive, or European domestic legislation, in this light. Even though the Directive does not explicitly define a failure to make a reasonable accommodation as a form of discrimination, or enunciate on the relationship between "reasonable accommodation" and positive action, it seems implicit in its wording that the two kinds of instruments are regarded as distinct. This can be surmised from the fact that "reasonable accommodation" is a requirement under the Directive, whilst Member States are given the freedom (but not the obligation) to allow for, and adopt, positive action measures in favour of people with disabilities under Article 7 of the Directive. This distinction arguably strengthens the argument that the obligation to make a "reasonable accommodation" should be fitted into the non-discrimination framework.

This argument is reinforced by a theoretical analysis of the concept of and motivation behind reasonable accommodation norms. It is recalled that the reasonable accommodation requirement is designed to secure the removal of barriers which would otherwise prevent individuals with a disability and other covered individuals from benefiting from employment opportunities.[114] Such barriers arise because, on occasions, the interaction between the physical or social environment and an individual's impairment or other relevant characteristic results in the inability to perform a particular function or job in the conventional manner. Ignoring (by failing to accommodate) the impairment or characteristic would result in denying a person equal employment opportunities. The reasonable accommodation requirement therefore recognises that, where people's impairments or relevant characteristics result in them being differently situated regarding employment opportunities, identical treatment may be a source of discrimination, and different treatment may be required to eliminate it. Recognition of this need for real, not merely formal, equality is the basis of the obligation to make individualised adjustments to permit particular individuals to participate in particular employment-related activities. In this situation inaction, as opposed to action, can amount to discrimination, and this is expressly recognised in the reasonable accommodation requirement in the Directive which prohibits an employer from denying an individual with a disability an employment opportunity by failing to take account of the impairment when taking account of it—in terms of changing the job or physical environment of the workplace—would enable the individual to do the work.[115]

---

[114] See above section 6.1.1.
[115] Karlan and Rutherglen, above n. 16.

6.6.2.   A CLEAR SEPARATION OF REASONABLE ACCOMMODATION
         FROM POSITIVE ACTION

Extracts cited elsewhere in this chapter reveal that many European jurisdictions clearly specify that an unjustified failure to make a reasonable accommodation amounts to a form of discrimination. In some instances, this is classified as direct discrimination, in other instances, as a form of indirect discrimination, or alternatively as a form *sui generis* discrimination, or, as a fourth option, the form of discrimination is simply not specified. However, in all instances the message is clear—the obligation to make a reasonable accommodation falls within the non-discrimination requirement, and is unrelated to positive action.

In the UK the relationship of the duty to provide reasonable adjustments to positive action was considered by the House of Lords in *Archibald* v. *Fife Council*. At issue was the question of whether a worker who had become disabled and unable to carry out her job (which involved manual work) could be transferred to a slightly higher and better paid office job without undergoing a competitive interview. Such a transfer would have involved a departure from the Council's standard redeployment procedure. The Council argued that the requested transfer amounted to positive discrimination, whilst the Disability Rights Commission, which represented Mrs Archibald, argued that the purpose of the Disability Discrimination Act was to achieve equality of outcome, and this required differential treatment.

House of Lords, Session 2003-04[116]   **6.UK.70.**
Archibald v. *Fife Council*

REASONABLE ADJUSTMENTS CAN INVOLVE AN ELEMENT OF MORE FAVOURABLE
TREATMENT WHERE THIS IS NEEDED IN ORDER TO ACHIEVE EQUALITY

Archibald v. Fife

Facts: The complainant worked as a road sweeper for Fife Council. As a result of an operation she became disabled and was no longer able to continue in this position. She received retraining from her employer and subsequently applied for over 100 internal vacancies involving junior level office work. However, because all office positions were assessed as being at a higher grade than her previous manual position, the Council applied its standard redeployment policy, which meant that she had to undertake a competitive interview. She failed to obtain any of the posts and was subsequently dismissed. The complainant submitted a series of appeals arguing that she had been the victim of disability discrimination and that she should not have been required to go through the competitive interviews if she could show she was qualified and suitable for the job in question. The lower courts all found in favour of the employer, and the case eventually reached the House of Lords. In writing the lead judgment, Baroness Hale referred to section 6 of the Disability Discrimination Act 1995, which was in force at the time,[117] which provided, inter alia:

---

[116] [2004] UKHL 32. See also above **6.GB.39.**
[117] The equivalent (slightly amended) provisions can now be found in ss. 4A and 18B of the Disability Discrimination Act 1995 as amended.

"(1) Where—

    (a)   any arrangements made by or on behalf of an employer, . . .

place the disabled person concerned at a substantial disadvantage in comparison with persons who are not disabled, it is the duty of the employer to take such steps as it is reasonable, in all the circumstances of the case, for him to have to take in order to prevent the arrangements or feature having that effect . . .

(3) The following are examples of steps which an employer may have to take in relation to a disabled person in order to comply with subsection (1)—. . .

    (c)   transferring him to fill an existing vacancy;

(4) In determining whether it is reasonable for an employer to have to take a particular step in order to comply with subsection (1), regard shall be had, in particular, to—

    (a)   the extent to which taking the step would prevent the effect in question;
    (b)   the extent to which it is practicable for the employer to take the step;
    (c)   the financial and other costs which would be incurred by the employer in taking the step and the extent to which taking it would disrupt any of his activities;
    (d)   the extent of the employer's financial and other resources;
    (e)   the availability to the employer of financial or other assistance with respect to taking the step."

Held: The appeal was allowed and the case was remitted to the Employment Tribunal to consider whether the council had fulfilled its duty to take such steps as it was reasonable in all the circumstances.

Judgment: Baroness Hale "47. According to its long title, the purpose of the 1995 Act is 'to make it unlawful to discriminate against disabled persons in connection with employment, the provision of goods, facilities and services or the disposal or management of premises . . .' But this legislation is different from the Sex Discrimination Act 1975 and the Race Relations Act 1976. In the latter two, men and women or black and white, as the case may be, are opposite sides of the same coin. Each is to be treated in the same way. Treating men more favourably than women discriminates against women. Treating women more favourably than men discriminates against men. Pregnancy apart, the differences between the genders are generally regarded as irrelevant. The 1995 Act, however, does not regard the differences between disabled people and others as irrelevant. It does not expect each to be treated in the same way. It expects reasonable adjustments to be made to cater for the special needs of disabled people. It necessarily entails an element of more favourable treatment. The question for us is when that obligation arises and how far it goes.

[Applying the relevant section of the DDA, Baroness Hale found that transferring Mrs Archibald to a sedentary position was a reasonable step that could be expected of the Council.]

67. On the face of it, therefore, transferring Mrs Archibald to a sedentary position which she was qualified to fill was among the steps which it might have been reasonable in all the circumstances for the council to have to take once she could no longer walk and sweep. Is there any reason to hold to the contrary?

68. The Employment Tribunal thought that there was. They relied upon that part of section 6(7) [which established the duty to make reasonable adjustments] which provides that 'nothing in this Part is to be taken to require an employer to treat a disabled person more favourably than he treats or would treat others'. But this is prefaced by the words, 'Subject to the provisions of this section, . . .': so that, to the extent that the duty to make reasonable adjustments requires it, the employer is not only permitted but obliged to treat a disabled person more favourably than others."

P. Hughes, Disability Discrimination and the Duty to Make   **6.UK.71.**
Reasonable Adjustments: Recent Developments
[commenting on the Archibald v. Fife Council case][118]

"This is a very important finding and it is central to the way the duty to make reasonable adjustments operates. The nature of the duty is such that it requires a difference in treatment between a disabled person and a person who is not disabled. This is required in the field of disability because equality of treatment may not lead to equality of outcome—hence the need for reasonable adjustments."

Notes

(1) This judgment clarifies that a reasonable adjustment under UK law may result in more favourable treatment for an individual with a disability. However, that treatment should not be regarded as positive action, but rather as a means to achieve equality. Arguably the judgment is based on the understanding of the goals and need for reasonable accommodations or adjustments outlined in sections 6.1.1 and 6.1.2 of this chapter.

(2) However, one should also note that Baroness Hale stated in paragraph 57 that "It is common ground that the [Disability Discrimination] Act entails a measure of positive discrimination, in the sense that employers are required to take steps to help disabled people which they are not required to take for others". One can ask if this reference to "positive discrimination" suggests that she was less clear about the distinction between positive action and reasonable adjustments than the extract above suggests.

6.6.3.   AMBIGUITY OR CONFUSION

One example of a legal provision which is ambiguous with regard to the relationship between reasonable accommodations and positive action is the right to claim an accommodation for severely disabled people found in the German § 81 (4) SGB IX, which was cited in section 6.2.1.A. Historically, the right to claim a reasonable accommodation in German law has not been linked to the right not to be discriminated against. The right to reasonable accommodation as a subjective right of a severely disabled employee was already entailed in the Severely Disabled Act of 1974, which preceded the SGB IX and which did not contain an anti-discrimination provision. Thus, some commentators view this right as a form of positive action, referring directly to Article 7 of the Employment Equality Directive.[119] Others consider the duty to accommodate (especially the duty to provide technical aids and

[118] (2004) 33 *ILJ* 358, 361.
[119] Dopotka-Ritz, § 81 Randzeichen 35 in D. Bihr, H. Fuchs, D. Krauskopf and E. Lewering (eds.), *Sozialgesetzbuch—Neuntes Buch—(SGB IX) (Loseblatt)* (Munich, Stand, 2003).

accessible worksite) as a protection against indirect discrimination as it prohibits the employer from arguing that the employment of a worker with a disability is impossible because the workplace is inaccessible.[120] On the other hand, the right to an accommodation is located in the same sub-paragraph as the right to preferential treatment concerning internal vocational training designed to promote career development,[121] which could be regarded as positive action.

The situation has been rendered even more complicated by the adoption of the General Equal Treatment Act (*Allgemeines Gleichbehandlungsgesetz* (AGG)[122] in 2006 and related amendments to § 81. § 81 (2) SGB IX now provides: "Employers must not discriminate[123] against severely disabled employees on grounds of their disability. The provisions of the General Equal Treatment Act apply for specific issues."

However, in spite of the adoption of the General Equal Treatment Act, no changes were made to § 81 (4) SGB IX, which still contains the only explicit reasonable accommodation provision with regard to individuals with disabilities in German law. This exclusion of the reasonable accommodation provision from the General Equal Treatment Act reinforces the ambiguity of the law regarding the legal character of reasonable accommodation, and means that it is unclear whether this provision should be regarded as being located within or outside the non-discrimination framework in German law.

In Belgium a perceived link between reasonable obligation and positive action hampered the adoption of non-discrimination legislation at the federal level, where there was initially a reluctance to include any reasonable accommodation provision in the federal statute implementing the Employment Equality Directive. A proposal to include such a provision, the wording of which was heavily based on Article 5 of the Directive, was rejected. One of the reasons given for this by the Minister of Employment was that the proposal amounted to a form of positive action, whilst the national statute in question was only an anti-discrimination measure.[124] It is worth noting in this context that the Belgian federal government does not have the competence to legislate on positive action, and this perception of reasonable accommodation amounted to a significant hurdle to adopting legislation at the federal level (although would not have restricted implementation at other levels of government).[125] Ultimately a way was found round this impasse, and the legislation

---

[120] Düwell, § 81 Randzeichen 32 in H.D. Dau, F.J. Düwell and H. Haines (eds.), *Rehabilitation und Teilhabe behinderter Menschen, Lehr- und Praxiskommentar* (LPK—SGB IX) (Baden-Baden, Nomos, 2002).

[121] § 81 (4) nr. 2: "to be preferentially considered for internal vocational training measures for furtherance of their professional progress".

[122] AGG, BGBl. Teil I 17 August 2006, s. 1897.

[123] § 81 (2) SGB IX does not use the word "discriminate" (*Diskriminierung*), but rather "disadvantage" (*Benachteiligung*). This is also in line with the approach adopted in the General Equal Treatment Act.

[124] Parl. St. Senaat 2001–2002, nr. 2–12/15, 149–52. Further reasons included the future adoption of specific legislation on this topic, and the need to discuss the measure with the social partners. See also Van den Langenbergh, *Vrijheid en Gelijkheid, De horizontale werking van het gelijkheidsbeginsel en de nieuwe antidiscriminatiewet* (Antwerp, Maklu, 2003) 573, 601–4.

[125] The Belgian constitutional structure divides the task of promoting equal opportunities for people with disabilities between: the Federal level, which has the responsibility for defining non-discrimination requirements in criminal and labour law and by regulating the contract of employment; the Regional level,

simply defines the denial of a reasonable accommodation for a person with a disability as discrimination.[126]

6.6.4.   REASONABLE ACCOMMODATION AS AN EXCEPTION TO THE PRINCIPLE OF EQUAL TREATMENT

One example of a jurisdiction which takes a different approach can be found in Estonia. It should be noted that Estonian law does not currently provide for a clear duty to make reasonable accommodations in favour of people with disabilities, and is therefore in breach of the Directive in this respect. However, a 1992 statute does refer to the creation of a working environment suitable for workers with disabilities.

Law of Republic of Estonia on Employment Contracts,   **6.EE.72.**
Passed 15 April 1992 (RT 1992, 15/16, 241), entered into force
1 July 1992[127]

Article 10 Exceptions to prohibition on unequal treatment pursuant to law
For the purposes of this Law, the following shall not be deemed to be unequal treatment:
. . .
    3) grant of preferences to disabled workers, including creation of working environment taking account of the special needs of disabled workers; . . .

Notes
    (1) The statute specifies that measures, including the creation of a working environment suitable for workers with disabilities, should not be regarded as unequal treatment pursuant to the law.
    (2) This suggests that the making of such measures are not located within the non-discrimination framework, but are merely regarded as acceptable exceptions to the prohibition on unequal treatment, akin to (other) permitted forms of positive action.

which has the responsibility for promoting the professional integration of people disabilities in employment policy; and the Communities, which have the responsibility for promoting the rehabilitation and vocational training of people with disabilities. However, some recent developments have brought about more coherence at the Regional and Community level.

[126] Art. 2(3).

6.6.5.   REASONABLE ACCOMMODATION LABELLED AS A FORM OF POSITIVE ACTION

The heading preceding Article 74 of the Portuguese Labour Code ("Measures of positive action . . ."), which transposes Article 5 of the Employment Equality Directive, suggests that the national legislator might have regarded reasonable accommodations as a form of positive action.

Portuguese Labour Code   **6.PT.73.**

Article 74
Measures of positive action taken by the employer
1. The employer shall promote the adoption of appropriate measures to enable a person with a disability or a chronic disease to have access to, participate in, or advance in employment, or to provide training for such a person, unless such measures would impose a disproportionate burden on the employer.
   2. The State should stimulate and support, by the convenient means, the employer's action in achieving the goals described in the previous number.
   3. When the burden referred to in number one is to a sufficient extent, remedied by State measures as an element of disability or chronic diseases policies, it should not be considered disproportionate.

Note
Whilst the wording of Article 74 of the Labour Code closely follows the wording of Article 5 of the Directive,[128] the Article appears under the heading "Measures of positive action taken by the employer". It is also important in this respect that the first sentence of Article 5 of the Directive, which refers to the need for reasonable accommodations measures in order to "guarantee compliance with the principle of equal treatment", has been dropped during the transposition process. It is submitted that this form of transposition reflects a misunderstanding of the nature of the duty to accommodate.

6.6.6.   COMPARATIVE OVERVIEW

It is clear that the majority view, amongst European legislators, is that the obligation to make a reasonable accommodation in favour of individuals with disabilities should be located within the non-discrimination paradigm. It is probable that this consensus results, at least partially, from the stance taken in the Employment Equality Directive; however, those jurisdictions which had incorporated this requirement within their

---

[127] Translation provided by Estonian Legal Language Centre.

domestic legislation prior to the adoption of the Directive also adopted this approach. Nevertheless, in a few Member States—Estonia, Germany and Portugal have been identified—the matter does not seem to have been clearly resolved, and the relationship of the reasonable accommodation requirement to positive action is ambiguous.

6.7. COMPARATIVE ANALYSIS

Whilst this chapter has focused on the obligation to provide reasonable accommodations, there also exists a variety of provisions which, although they are not classified as reasonable accommodation duties, can de facto have the same result.[129] It has not been possible to consider these measures in depth in this chapter but, for the sake of completeness, they will be briefly mentioned at this point.

As implied at various locations within this chapter, the obligation not to discriminate indirectly against a worker or other individual can, on occasions, result in positive duties to accommodate difference[130]—for example, by requiring that standard dress codes be relaxed to allow followers of (minority) religions to manifest their faith. In certain circumstances this can also be the result of the application of Article 9 of the European Convention of Human Rights, which confers a right on individuals to, inter alia, manifest their religion; although, given the scope the Article allows for states to exercise discretion, the European Court of Human Rights has frequently been reluctant to find in favour of individuals who have claimed what were, de facto, religious accommodations.[131] Nevertheless, in some jurisdictions domestic courts have been willing to confer positive rights on employees to manifest their religion, thereby accommodating their needs.[132] There is also a possibility that, in the future, the European Court of Human Rights will interpret Article 8 of the Convention, which provides for a right to respect for private life, as requiring states to provide for positive duties to accommodate individuals with disabilities. The limited numbers of cases in which such issues have been raised so far have been unsuccessful,[133] but this may not necessarily continue. Legislation can also require

---

[128] Although, unlike the Directive, individuals with chronic diseases are covered and entitled to claim an accommodation.

[129] For further discussion on this point see Waddington and Hendriks, above n. 13. The article argues that the areas in EC law where most parallels can be found to the reasonable accommodation requirement, concern the protection of pregnant workers and workers who have recently given birth and the right to parental leave.

[130] For more details see above ch. 3.

[131] See ECtHR, *Leyla Sahin* v. *Turkey*, Application no. 44774/98, judgment of 10 November 2005.

[132] See, e.g. Opinions 1995–31 and 1996–16, in which the Dutch Equal Treatment Commission held that a direct reference to a Muslim headscarf was tantamount to a direct reference to the claimant's religion, and amounted to direct discrimination (distinction). In subsequent cases the Commission held that the prohibition of wearing a headscarf amounts to indirect discrimination (distinction) based on religion—see, e.g. Opinion 2003–53. For further commentary see M. Gijzen, *Selected Issues in Equal Treatment Law: a Multi-Layered Comparison of European, English and Dutch Law* (Antwerp, Intersentia, 2006).

that accommodations are made for pregnant workers and workers who have recently given birth. These accommodations are often, although perhaps not always, motivated by health and safety concerns. Finally, and of most general significance, at least in the employment setting, is the duty to act as a good employer or the duty of care found in certain (civil) law jurisdictions.[134] Such obligations are provided for, for example, in Article 611[135] of Book 7 of the Dutch Civil Code[136] and in Article 618[137] of the German Federal Law Book (*Bundesgesetzbuch*)[138] and related case-law. These provisions impose obligations on employers with respect to the health, safety and accessibility of the workplace and work environment, and have been interpreted as requiring the employer to accommodate the specific needs of individuals (with disabilities). Nevertheless, whilst all these provisions (possibly) can, in certain circumstances, have an impact which is similar to the obligation to provide reasonable accommodations, they do not have this specific aim in mind, and are a less well tuned and less reliable means of securing accommodations. For this reason, it remains necessary for jurisdictions to recognise the duty to accommodate.

This need has been partially recognised through the Employment Equality Directive, which has required the adoption of legislative obligations to provide reasonable accommodations for people with disabilities in the area of employment in all Member States of the European Union. This has had a significant impact on the extent to which such an obligation is recognised at the domestic level, given that only three Member States provided for such a duty prior to the adoption of the Directive. Today, whilst almost all Member States have explicitly established such a duty, most do not go beyond the minimal requirements of the Directive by extending the right to claim an accommodation to people with disabilities beyond the area of employment, or other individuals with regard to employment. Nevertheless, a limited number of European states do require reasonable accommodations for people with disabilities who wish to access facilities such as goods and services or education, whilst others have recognised a (limited) right to accommodations in the employment context for people who wish to practise their religion. These provisions, which have not been directly influenced by EC law, reflect a greater degree of divergence than is the case with regard to the measures providing for employment accommodations for people with disabilities.

As implied in the previous paragraph, the Employment Equality Directive has set the tone and the scope of the reasonable accommodation requirement in most Member States. Nevertheless, a situation of uniformity does not exist. This chapter has revealed that important differences exist with regard to a number of areas. These include the meaning and significance of the term "reasonable", and the use of

---

[133] See ECtHR, *Botta* v. *Italy* (24 February 1998) Reports and Decisions of the ECtHR 1998-I, No. 66 412 and *Zehnalová and Zehnal* v. *the Czech Republic* (14 May 2002) Application No. 38621/97. See also De Schutter, above n. 9.

[134] Although see comments by Rix LJ in the British case of *Copsey*, above **6.GB.44.**

[135] The Art. establishes as an "eis van het goed werkgeverschap" or requirement to act as a good employer.

[136] M.A.C. de Wit, *Het goed werkgeverschap als intermediair van normen in het arbeidsrecht* (Dordrecht, Kluwer, 1999).

alternative terms in relation to the duty to accommodate; the existence of non-cost related justifications for failing to make an accommodation; and the classification of an unjustified failure to make an accommodation as different forms of discrimination.

In spite of these important differences, legislative provisions providing for (employment-related) accommodations for people with disabilities generally have in common that they are not designed to place people with disabilities in a better position than non-disabled employees, job applicants or service users. In order to benefit from an accommodation an individual must be qualified for the job or be able to access the service, if necessary following the making of an accommodation. However, there are indications that a small number of Member States have misunderstood the requirement by not clearly separating the duty to accommodation from positive action obligations.

One can expect that case-law, and particularly decisions of the European Court of Justice, will help to elaborate the extent of the duty to accommodate and how key terms found within Article 5 of the Directive should be interpreted. Nevertheless, in certain areas, and particularly those which remain outside the scope of Community law, diversity will continue to exist.

Prof. Olivier De Schutter

7.1. INTRODUCTION

Positive action[1] is a legal technique variously described in international human rights law as including measures aimed at "accelerating *de facto* equality",[2] at "diminish[ing] or eliminate[ing] conditions which cause or help to perpetuate" prohibited discrimination,[3] or at "securing adequate advancement of certain . . . groups or individuals requiring such protection as may be necessary in order to ensure such groups or individuals equal enjoyment or exercise of human rights and fundamental freedoms".[4] Positive action starts from the finding that formal non-discrimination in many cases will not be sufficient to achieve substantive equality. It seeks therefore to promote substantive equality for categories of persons which suffer from discrimination and/or exclusion on grounds such as sex, race or ethnic origin, disability, religion or belief, sexual orientation, or age, by taking into account the specific situation of the members of these categories. Certain forms of positive action may thus operate at the expense of formal equality. This may be the case when measures take the form of preferential treatment, either by offering specific treatment to members of certain categories in order to combat de facto inequality or by compensating for past inequalities. Such measures are sometimes denounced as discriminatory, as the term "positive discrimination", sometimes used as a substitute for "positive action", indicates. Widely debated examples include "quotas" which set aside positions for members of certain groups, preferential rules demanding that members of certain groups be preferred or special advantages to members of certain groups. Some authors only refer to such preferential measures as positive action.[5] Other authors prefer a wider view, comprising also measures which do not result in formal preferences and are thus less

---

[1] This chapter will refer to "positive action" or "affirmative action", used respectively in the debates surrounding these instruments in Europe and in the US. In the international law of human rights, the expression "temporary special measures" is usually preferred.

[2] Art. 4(1) of the International Convention on the Elimination of All Forms of Discrimination against Women (18 December 1979).

[3] UN Human Rights Committee, General Comment 18, Non-discrimination (Thirty-seventh Session, 1989), in "Compilation of the General Comments or General Recommendations adopted by Human Rights Treaty Bodies", UN doc. HRI/GEN/1/Rev.7 (12 May 2004) 146, para. 10.

[4] Art. 1(4) of the International Convention on the Elimination of All Forms of Racial Discrimination, opened for signature by the UN General Assembly Res. 2106(XX) of 21 December 1965; entered into force on 4 January 1969.

[5] E.g. A. Epiney and M. Freiermuth-Abt, *Das Recht der Gleichstellung von Mann und Frau in der EU* (Baden-Baden, Nomos, 2003) 195.

controversial.[6] Examples of these less controversial positive action measures comprise monitoring of the situation of certain groups as regards access to social goods such as employment, education or housing, but also measures such as flexible working time regimes in order to accommodate the needs of caring parents, and of course all geerally applicable measures targeted at overcoming indirectly discriminatory practices.

This chapter seeks chiefly to present a definition of positive action, to propose a typology of positive action measures, and to analyse the approach under international law and case-law and other materials from the European Union and national jurisdictions in EU Member States.

Section 7.2 provides a first definition of positive action, albeit still at a fairly abstract and general level. Section 7.3 then offers a typology of positive action measures, supported by a number of examples for such measures. Section 7.4 describes the status of positive action under the relevant instruments of international and European human rights law, including at UN level the International Convention on the Elimination of All Forms of Racial Discrimination (ICERD) and the Convention on the Elimination of All Forms of Discrimination against Women (CEDAW), and at Council of Europe level the European Convention on Human Rights, the European Social Charter and the Framework Convention for the Protection of National Minorities. Section 7.5 examines the regime of positive action under European Union law, analysing how it has evolved in the only field—equal treatment between men and women in employment—where the European Court of Justice (ECJ) case-law has hitherto addressed the question. Whether this case-law can be transposed without major revision to the new grounds of prohibited discrimination under the Racial Equality and Employment Equality Directives—or, indeed, even in the field of equal treatment between men and women, beyond employment—is briefly addressed in the final part of section 7.5. Section 7.6 then reviews positions towards positive action in national jurisdictions of representative Member States, with a particular emphasis on highest judicial bodies.

Finally, section 7.7 examines questions of data protection law arising in relation to positive action. Positive action policies often take membership of certain groups as a proxy for being subject to disadvantage, which, in turn, may call for preventive or compensatory measures. This implies not only monitoring the situation of different groups in society in order to identify fields for positive action, but also classifying individuals according to certain characteristics, such as race or ethnic origin, religion or disability, in order for them to benefit from positive action. Such classification may, in other contexts, be highly suspicious, and has proven to remain controversial even in the context of positive action. The final section of this chapter does not pretend to solve the questions raised about the compatibility of positive action schemes with the right to respect for the private life of the individual in the processing of personal data. Instead, it seeks to shed at least some light on those issues which still are awaiting their solution.

---

[6] E.g. S. Fredman, *Discrimination Law* (Oxford, Oxford University Press, 2002) 125–36 with numerous further references; C. McCrudden, "Rethinking Positive Action" (1986) 15 *ILJ* 219.

7.2. THE DEFINITION OF POSITIVE ACTION

In his 2002 study on the concept of affirmative action prepared upon the request of the UN Sub-Commission on the Promotion and Protection of Human Rights, the special rapporteur Bossuyt defines "affirmative action" as consisting in "a coherent packet of measures . . . aimed specifically at correcting the position of members of a target group in one or more aspects of their social life, in order to obtain effective equality".[7]

This citation mirrors the spirit of positive action. Positive action measures seek to guarantee not only equality before the law, but also equality in effective access to certain social goods such as employment, education or health care. Positive action is premised on the idea that legal rules applicable to the allocation of certain social goods should take into account the fact that the members of different groups are not similarly situated in their ability to gain access to such goods. Thus, formally equal treatment is often not sufficient to achieve equal distribution of resources. In other words, the principle of equal treatment requires the specific situations of members of the disadvantaged group to be taken into account. In order to achieve *real* equality (as opposed to *formal* equality), they need to be made equal in the distribution of social goods such as education, housing or employment, and not simply equal before the law. However, in the broader understanding of positive action relied upon in this chapter, positive action may also serve the distinct purpose of establishing or maintaining diversity in specific settings, even in the absence of any inequalities to be remedied.[8]

The distinct character of positive action as it is understood here is that it always involves differences in treatment on the basis of otherwise suspect grounds. While, on the one hand, this approach is relatively broad, insofar as it includes positive action as a means to preserve diversity, this chapter on the other hand assumes a narrower conception of positive action than some authors in Europe. It does not consider as positive action measures that eliminate pre-existing discriminatory practices where this does not imply differential treatment based on group membership but consists simply in the removal of such practices. And it distinguishes positive action from

---

[7] "The Concept and Practice of Affirmative Action", final report submitted by Mr. Marc Bossuyt, Special Rapporteur, in accordance with resolution 1998/5 of the Sub-Commission for the Promotion and Protection of Human Rights, UN doc. E/CN.4/Sub.2/2002/21, 17 June 2002, para. 6.

[8] See, e.g. the judgment of the US Supreme Court in *Grutter* v. *Bollinger et al.*, 539 US 306 (2003) (in deciding to uphold an admissions policy of University of Michigan Law School that includes a commitment to diversity with special reference to the inclusion of African-American, Hispanic and Native-American students who otherwise might not be represented in the student body in meaningful numbers, the Court accepts that "the Law School has a compelling interest in attaining a diverse student body" since its admissions policy "promotes 'cross-racial understanding'", helps to break down racial stereotypes, "enables [students] to better understand persons of different races"', "promotes learning outcomes", "better prepares students for an increasingly diverse workforce and society, and better prepares them as professionals"). For a discussion of this case and the companion case of *Gratz* v. *Bollinger*, 539 US 244 (2003) see, inter alia, K. Karst, "The Revival of Forward-Looking Affirmative Action" (2004) 104 *Colum. L. Rev.* 60; H. Norton, "Stepping Through Grutter's Open Doors: What the University of Michigan Affirmative Action Cases Mean for Race-Conscious Government Decision-making" (2005) 78 *Temple L Rev.* 543.

measures that improve the situation of disadvantaged or underrepresented groups by reshaping the environment which they inhabit. While such measures recognise the specific needs of certain groups—as does reasonable accommodation[9]—they do not imply a form of treatment which is potentially detrimental to other groups. The distinction thus drawn between positive action and the accommodation of specific needs of certain groups is supported by Article 4 of CEDAW.

International Convention on the Elimination of All Forms of   **7.UN.1.**
Discrimination against Women

Article 4

1. Adoption by States Parties of temporary special measures aimed at accelerating *de facto* equality between men and women shall not be considered discrimination as defined in the present Convention, but shall in no way entail as a consequence the maintenance of unequal or separate standards; these measures shall be discontinued when the objectives of equality of opportunity and treatment have been achieved.

2. Adoption by States Parties of special measures, including those measures contained in the present Convention, aimed at protecting maternity shall not be considered discriminatory.

The Committee on the Elimination of Discrimination against Women clarifies that

> "The purpose of article 4, paragraph 1, is to accelerate the improvement of the position of women to achieve their *de facto* or substantive equality with men, and to effect the structural, social and cultural changes necessary to correct past and current forms and effects of discrimination against women, as well as to provide them with compensation"

while

> "Article 4, paragraph 2, provides for non-identical treatment of women and men due to their biological differences. These measures are of a permanent nature, at least until such time as the scientific and technological knowledge . . .would warrant a review."[10]

Similarly, the 1995 Council of Europe *Framework Convention for the Protection of National Minorities*[11] guarantees to persons belonging to national minorities the right of equality before the law and of equal protection of the law and prohibits any discrimination based on belonging to a national minority (Article 4(1)), but also entails a specific article on positive action measures as well as a provision prohibiting the forced assimilation of national minorities.

---

[9] See above L. Waddington, Chapter Six: Reasonable Accommodation.

[10] Committee on the Elimination of Discrimination against Women, General Recommendation No. 25: Art. 4, para. 1 of the Convention (temporary special measures), adopted at the thirtieth session of the Committee (2004), in "Compilation of the General Comments or General Recommendations adopted by Human Rights Treaty Bodies", above n. 3, 282, paras. 15–16.

[11] ETS, No. 157. The Framework Convention for the Protection of National Minorities was opened for signature on 1 February 1995 and entered into force on 1 February 1998.

Framework Convention for the Protection of National Minorities **7.CoE.2.**

Article 4

. . .

(2) The Parties undertake to adopt, where necessary, adequate measures in order to promote, in all areas of economic, social, political and cultural life, full and effective equality between persons belonging to a national minority and those belonging to the majority. In this respect, they shall take due account of the specific conditions of the persons belonging to national minorities.

(3) The measures adopted in accordance with paragraph 2 shall not be considered to be an act of discrimination.

Article 5

(1) The Parties undertake to promote the conditions necessary for persons belonging to national minorities to maintain and develop their culture, and to preserve the essential elements of their identity, namely their religion, language, traditions and cultural heritage.

(2) Without prejudice to measures taken in pursuance of their general integration policy, the Parties shall refrain from policies or practices aimed at assimilation of persons belonging to national minorities against their will and shall protect these persons from any action aimed at such assimilation.

Positive action measures thus deemed allowable under Article 4(2) of the Convention should not be confused with the prohibition of forced assimilation under Article 5(1). In particular, positive action measures will only be acceptable insofar as they are "adequate", that is proportionate. This will often imply a limit on their duration.[12] Instead, the prohibition of assimilation of members of national minorities against their will is permanent.

7.3. A TYPOLOGY OF POSITIVE ACTION AND OTHER MEASURES

As defined for the purposes of this chapter,[13] positive action measures involve differential treatment on the basis of certain characteristics which are taken as a proxy for disadvantage. However, positive action measures thus understood will often be combined with certain other policies which precede differential treatment in order to overcome differences or maintain diversity. These measures are thus included in the following typology. The focus of our examples will be on employment, because it is in

---

[12] According to the Explanatory Report to the Framework Convention, the special measures referred to in Art. 4(2) must be adopted "in conformity with the proportionality principle, in order to avoid violation of the rights of others as well as discrimination against others. This principle requires, among other things, that such measures do not extend, in time or in scope, beyond what is necessary in order to achieve the aim of full and effective equality" (para. 39).

[13] For different views, see n. 6.

this sector that our experience of positive action measures is greatest. However, positive action measures can be adopted in other fields, such as education, housing and health care, in which disadvantaged groups may be given priority in order to secure more equitable distribution of social goods.

7.3.1. TYPOLOGY

This categorisation of positive action measures and other measures aimed at improving the situation of disadvantages groups uses two intersecting criteria. First, the true positive action measures grant preferential treatment to the members of a disadvantaged group, thus creating the risk of a violation of the rule of non-discrimination, while other measures do not create such a risk. Secondly, certain positive action measures require that specific individuals be categorised as members of the disadvantaged group, while other schemes do not entail such a consequence.[14] The former schemes may be questionable in respect to data protection legislation. Following these two criteria, we may classify the measures to be described as follows:

Measure (in the employment field)	Implying preferential treatment	Implying processing of personal data
Monitoring the composition of the workforce in order to identify instances of underrepresentation and, possibly, to encourage the adoption of remedial action, for instance by the adoption of action plans and the setting of targets	No	Not necessarily
Redefining the standard criterion on the basis of which employment or promotion are allocated (in general, merit)	No	No
Outreach measures, consisting in general measures targeting underrepresented groups, such as the provision of training aimed at members of underrepresented groups or job announcements encouraging members of such groups to apply	No	Not necessarily
Outreach measures, consisting in individual measures such as the guarantee to members of underrepresented groups that they will be interviewed if they possess the relevant qualifications	Yes	Yes
Preferential treatment of equally qualified members of the underrepresented group, with or without exemption clause (also referred to as "flexible quotas")	Yes	Yes
Strict quotas, linked or not to objective factors beyond the representation of the target group in the general active population	Yes	Yes

[14] The reader is referred to section 7.7 below for a further discussion of this question.

7.3.2.   MEASURES NOT (NECESSARILY) IMPLYING PREFERENTIAL TREATMENT

7.3.2.A.   MONITORING

This category of measures consists in imposing certain procedural requirements on employers, in the form of the filing of reports breaking down the composition of the workforce by different categories in order to identify instances of underrepresentation of certain groups, the setting of targets in order to improve the presence of those underrepresented groups, and the adoption of measures which should contribute to meeting these targets. The employer is thus encouraged to reflect about the rules, procedures and practices it has established in the undertaking, and modify them to the extent that they appear to have an adverse effect on the representation of certain categories. While the adoption of positive action measures may result from this, it is neither a necessary outcome nor the primary aim of such a framework.

One example is the Dutch Law on the Promotion of Labour Participation of Ethnic Minorities (*Wet stimulering arbeidsdeelname Minderheden*, SAMEN), which was in force between 1998 and 2004. It was meant to improve on the earlier Law on the Promotion of Proportional Labour Participation of Ethnic Minorities (*Wet bevordering evenredige arbeidsdeelname allochtonen*, WBEAA), which came into force on 1 July 1994.[15] This legislation was originally aimed at removing obstacles impeding people from ethnic minorities from entering the labour market and at promoting their proportional representation in private companies under the threat of criminal sanctions. The employers, however, did not comply adequately with the WEBEAA 1994, as they considered it unworkable and resented the administrative burdens attached. The social partners thus agreed to modify the legislation by focusing on the sector level and, preferably, individual companies, and by privileging the use of civil law instead of criminal law. The SAMEN law was the result of this agreement.

> *Dutch law on the Promotion of Labour Participation of*   **7.NL.3.**
> *Ethnic Minorities (Wet stimulering ar-beidsdeelname minderheden)*[16]
> *SAMEN Legislation*

General Provisions
Article 1
1. In the framework of the provisions of this act the following definitions apply

    . . .

    h. minorities: those who coming from elsewhere have settled in the Netherlands and their offspring

    . . .

---

[15] Staatsblad, 1998 241. For a useful description, see V. Guiraudon, K. Phalet and J. ter Wal, "Monitoring Ethnic Minorities in the Netherlands" (2005) 183 *Int'l SSJ* 75.

[16] Staatsblad, 2001, 625.

Promoting Labour Participation of Minorities
Article 2
1. The employer strives for equal representation of persons belonging to one of the target groups specified under Article 3.

2. Equal representation as referred to in paragraph 1 is satisfied where the proportion of persons belonging to one of the target groups within the undertaking is equivalent to their proportion in the regional pool of employees, taking into account required qualifications and experience.

Target groups
Article 3
The target groups of this act include:
   a)   persons born in Turkey, Morocco, Surinam, the Dutch Antilles, Aruba, the former Republic of Yugoslavia or in another state from South or Latin America, Africa or Asia, excluding Japan and the former Dutch India.
   b)   . . . [referred to persons registered in accordance with a special Act under which persons brought over to the Netherlands under Dutch supervisions were to be registered specifically]
   c)   Offspring of persons specified under a and b

Registration
Article 4
1. The employer establishes a special person register of its employees in which he includes no other data then the following:
   a)   name
   b)   state of birth
   c)   state of birth of parents
   d)   if relevant the fact that the employee or one or both of his or her parents are registered in the register referred to under Article 3 b)
   e)   whether the employee, resulting from the data under a—d belongs to one of the target groups or not
   f)   the level of the job
   g)   whether or not employed under a fulltime contract
   . . .

3. Where an employee's state of birth does not correspond to that of one or both of his parents, . . . the employee may declare that he does not wish to be registered as belonging to the target group . . .

4. The employee makes available to his employer the data referred to under 1 a to d, except if he has declared in writing that he objects thereto

The public annual report
Article 5
1. The employer reports annually at least on
   a)   the representation of persons belonging to the target groups within his undertaking during the year preceding the report
   b)   the measures taken in order to achieve a more equal representation . . . in the following year
2. The annual report includes at least the following data:
   . . ..

   b.   the number of employees in the undertaking on 31 December of the report year
   1.   categorised per function and the representation of persons belonging to the target group
   2.   categorised per fulltime and non-fulltime employment and the representation of persons belonging to the target group
   c.   the number of persons employed and dismissed during the report year and the representations of persons belonging to the target group
   d.   the number of persons having objected to their data being processed under Article 3 (4)
   e.   the measures taken during the past year and foreseen for the next year
. . . .

3. the annual report does not contain data that could be related to an individual employee
4. the works council . . . are consulted before establishing the annual report.

Notes

(1) The SAMEN legislation was inspired in part by the 1995 Canadian Employment Equity Act, in particular by its section 9(1). That section provides for employers to collect information and conduct an analysis of the workforce, in order to determine the degree of the underrepresentation of persons of certain target groups (women, aboriginal peoples, persons with disabilities and members of visible minorities) in each occupational category. Employers shall also conduct a review of the employment systems, policies and practices, in order to identify employment barriers against persons in target groups that result from those systems, policies and practices. This technique, which consists in leaving it to the employer to set its own targets on the basis of a self-monitoring of the composition of the workforce in order to promote awareness about the impact on the representation of minorities of certain procedures or practices, is also a characteristic of the SAMEN legislation.

(2) The SAMEN legislation was finally abrogated on 1 January 2004, based on the consideration that its main objective was to raise awareness among the employers about the benefits of diversity, which objective had been fulfilled.[17] The relatively high level of compliance with the requirements of the SAMEN legislation seems to demonstrate a high support for the legislation among the employers: it is reported that, during the period 1998–2003, 70% of the employers had met the reporting requirements. In contrast, the evaluation made in 1996 of the earlier 1994 *Law on the Promotion of Proportional Labour Participation of Ethnic Minorities* showed that at that time only 14% of employers were complying fully with its stipulations.

[17] In its Concluding Observations adopted on 10 May 2004, the Committee on the Elimination of Racial Discrimination took note of the fact that the SAMEN legislation had ceased to exist on 31 December 2003, and expressed its concern about "possible negative consequences that may ensue, given that the *Wet Samen* was the only legislative instrument containing regulations on the participation of ethnic minorities in the labour market and requiring employers to register the number of members of ethnic minorities employed by them" (CERD/C/64/CO/7, para. 13).

Another prominent example of legislation fitting under the notion of monitoring is the *Fair Employment and Treatment (Northern Ireland) Order 1998* (FETO).[18] The FETO makes it unlawful to discriminate against someone on the ground of religious belief or political opinion,[19] but it also places a number of significant duties on employers, which may lead to adopting positive action measures (named affirmative action in the language of the FETO). First, all private sector employers with more than 10 full-time employees (working more than 16 hours per week) are required to register with the Northern Ireland Equality Commission (Article 48). Specified public sector employers are automatically deemed to be registered. All registered employers must submit annually to the Commission a "monitoring return" giving details of the community background of their workforce and of those applying to positions. The rules referring to affirmative action and the specific positive duties are spelled out below.

Fair Employment and Treatment (Northern Ireland) Order 1998   **7.NIR.4.**
FETO

PART I INTRODUCTORY
...
'Affirmative action'
4.—(1) In this Order 'affirmative action' means action designed to secure fair participation in employment by members of the Protestant, or members of the Roman Catholic, community in Northern Ireland by means including—

   (a)   the adoption of practices encouraging such participation; and
   (b)   the modification or abandonment of practices that have or may have the effect of restricting or discouraging such participation.

...

PART VII DUTIES OF EMPLOYERS IN RESPECT OF THEIR WORKFORCES
Monitoring the workforce
Monitoring returns
52.—(1) For the purpose of enabling the composition of—

   (a)   those employed in a registered concern in Northern Ireland; and
   (b)   those applying to fill vacancies for employment in Northern Ireland in such a concern,

---

[18] 1998 No. 3162 (N.I. 21), 16 December 1998. The FETO was amended by the Fair Employment and Treatment Order (Amendment) Regulations (Northern Ireland) 2003 which came into operation on 10 December 2003. These Regulations are made under s. 2(2)(a) and (b) of the European Communities Act 1972, and seek to implement Council Directive 2000/78/EC of 27 November 2000 establishing a general framework for equal treatment in employment and occupation ([2000] OJ L303/16) (the Employment Equality Directive) in so far as it relates to discrimination on grounds of religion or belief. The provisions on affirmative action are, however, left unchanged by the Regulations.

[19] This includes a person's supposed religious belief or political opinion and the absence of any, or any particular, religious belief or political opinion.

to be ascertained, the employer shall prepare for each year and serve on the [Northern Ireland Equality] Commission a return (in this Part referred to as a "monitoring return") in a form provided by or on behalf of the Department.

(2) A monitoring return shall contain such information about the employees of the employer and those applying for employment in the concern as may be prescribed.

(3) For the purpose of enabling the composition of those ceasing to be employed in any concern of a person who is a public authority for the purposes of this Article to be ascertained, the employer shall include in a monitoring return such information as may be prescribed.

(4) For the purpose of enabling the composition of those ceasing to be employed in any other registered concern in which more than 250 employees are employed to be ascertained, the employer shall include in a monitoring return such information as may be prescribed; and for the purposes of this paragraph where, at the beginning of or at any subsequent time in any prescribed period, more than 250 employees are employed in the concern, that condition is to be treated as satisfied for the whole or, as the case may be, the remainder of that period.

Regulations as to monitoring
53.—(1) The Department shall, by regulations made after consultation with the Commission, make provision for the purposes of Article 52.

. . .

(3) The regulations may authorise or require the employer to determine which community (if any) a person employed or applying for employment in or ceasing to be employed in the concern is to be treated as belonging to for the purposes of monitoring by applying the principal method pre-scribed or where that method does not enable him to make that determination, by applying the residuary method, or one of the residuary methods, prescribed; so that, for example—

(a) where an applicant has stated that he belongs to a particular community the employer may be required to determine that he is to be treated as belonging to the community concerned; and

(b) where, in any case not within sub-paragraph (a), the employer has information about the applicant, being information which the employer is authorised by the regulations to take into account as tending to show that the person to whom it relates has a connection with a particular community, the employer may be required to determine the community to which the applicant is to be treated as belonging by reference to that information.

. . .

Periodic reviews by employers
55. (1) In the case of each registered concern, the employer shall from time to time review the composition of those employed in and ceasing to be employed in the concern in Northern Ireland and the employment practices of the concern for the purposes of determining whether members of each community are enjoying, and are likely to continue to enjoy, fair participation in employment in the concern.

(2) In a case where it appears to the employer in the course of the review that members of a particular community are not enjoying, or are not likely to continue to enjoy, such participation, he shall as part of the review determine the affirmative action (if any) which would be reasonable and appropriate.

(3) In a case where the employer determines in the course of the review that affirmative action would be reasonable and appropriate he shall as part of the review—

    (a)   consider whether, assuming the action is taken, it is practicable to determine, by refer-
          ence to one or more periods, the progress towards fair participation in employment in
          the concern that can reasonably be expected to be made by members of a particular
          community; and
    (b)   if he considers that it is practicable to determine such progress, determine the period
          or periods concerned and, in respect of each period, the progress that, in his opinion,
          can reasonably be expected to be made towards fair participation by members of the
          community concerned—
          (i)   in employment in the concern in Northern Ireland or among those whose
               employment in the concern there begins after the determination; or
          (ii) among applicants to fill vacancies for employment in the concern there.

Notes

(1) Over 30 years have passed since the UK parliament originally passed the *Fair Employment (Northern Ireland) Act 1976* outlawing discrimination in employment on grounds of religious belief and political opinion, and eighteen years elapsed since the 1989 Fair Employment Act imposed specific obligations on employers, antici-pating in that respect what the Fair Employment and Treatment (NI) Order 1998 would concretise further. It has now been shown that the fair employment legislation introduced in Northern Ireland has led to a substantial improvement in the employment opportunities of the members of the Roman Catholic community, although they remain disproportionately affected by unemployment.[20]

(2) Most significantly, while segregation in housing between the communities remains strong, most people in Northern Ireland now work in integrated environments. The community background is now less decisive on social mobility than education; indeed, religion plays no independent role in the ability of individuals to achieve better than their parents. It has been highlighted, in particular, that affirmative action agreements between the Equality Commission and employers have helped redress both Catholic and Protestant underrepresentation, and that this has constituted a vital part of the process of change.[21]

These examples—except the amendments to the FETO of 2003[22]—do not relate to the implementation of the Directives adopted on the basis of Article 13 EC. However, the Flemish Community/Region of Belgium adopted the Decree of 8 May 2002 on proportionate participation in the employment market (*Decreet houdende evenredige participatie op de arbeidsmarkt*),[23] which inter alia aims to encourage the integration of target groups into the labour market by positive action measures in the spirit of

---

[20] These conclusions are developed in B. Osborne and I. Shuttleworth (eds.), *Fair Employment in Northern Ireland: A Generation On* (Blackstaff Press, 2004). See also B. Cohen, "Positive Obligations: Shifting the Burden in Order to Achieve Equality" (2005) 1 *RR* 5, 7.

[21] See C. McCrudden, R. Ford, A. Heath, "The Impact of Affirmative Action Agreements" in B. Osborne and I. Shuttleworth (eds.), *Fair Employment in Northern Ireland: A Generation On* (Blackstaff Press, 2004); C. McCrudden, R. Ford, A. Heath, "Legal Regulation of Affirmative Action in Northern Ireland: An Empirical Assessment" (2004) 24 *OJLS* 363.

[22] See above n. 18.

[23] Moniteur belge, 26 July 2002, 33262.

the *Canadian Employment Equity Act* and the Dutch *SAMEN* legislation. The Flemish government has defined as target groups benefiting from positive action measures "all categories of persons whose level of employment, defined as the percentage of the active population of that category who effectively work, are under the average level of employment for the total Flemish population".[24] These include persons of non-EU origin and background (*allochtonen*),[25] persons with a disability, workers above 45 years of age, persons who have not completed their secondary education and persons belonging to the underrepresented sex in a specific profession (Art. 2(2), al. 2). The public services of the Flemish-speaking community are to file annual reports and action plans on the progress they are making towards proportionate representation of all target groups in the workforce; to this effect, they are to keep records of the representation of these different groups within the workforce, a form of monitoring which closely resembles that imposed under the above-mentioned Dutch, Canadian and Northern Irish legislation.

The provisions introduced here encourage employers to monitor the composition of the workforce and to adopt remedial measures where certain imbalances are found. But they are without prejudice to which forms of positive action measures the employer could adopt, either on its own initiative or under the pressure of a body entrusted with the implementation of equal treatment legislation, in cases of manifest imbalance. It is at this second stage only that positive action measures in the strict sense of the expression come into play. The adoption of positive action measures may be seen as conditional upon an adequate monitoring, if possible by statistical means, of both the imbalances to be remedied and of the effectiveness in time of whichever remedial measures are adopted.[26] The identification of imbalances through such monitoring will not necessarily lead to the adoption of positive action measures that—as defined in this chapter—include differential treatment. Legislation combining both elements illustrates that monitoring and remedial positive action may be complementary. The Hesse Women Equality Act for the public administration[27]

---

[24] Art. 2(2), al. 1, of the Besluit [van 30 Januari 2004] van de Vlaamse regering tot uitvoering van het decreet van 8 mei 2002 houdende evenredige participatie op de arbeidsmarkt wat betreft de beroepskeuzevoorlichting, beroepsopleiding, loopbaanbegeleiding en arbeidsbemiddeling, Moniteur belge, 4 March 2004, 12050 (Order [of 30 January 2004] of the Flemish Government concerning the execution of the decree of 8 May 2002 on proportionate participation in the employment market concerning professional orientation, vocational training, career counselling and the action of intermediaries on the labour market).

[25] I.e. adults legally residing in Belgium with a socio-cultural background from a non-EU country who, because of their poor knowledge of the Dutch language and/or their weak socio-economic position, whether or not reinforced by their poor education, are disadvantaged.

[26] This view is supported by the Committee on the Elimination of Discrimination against Women in its General Recommendations Nos. 9 and 25 (General Recommendation No. 9: Statistical data concerning the situation of women, in "Compilation of the General Comments or General Recommendations adopted by Human Rights Treaty Bodies", above n. 3, 237; General Recommendation No. 25: Art. 4, para. 1 of the Convention (temporary special measures), adopted at the thirtieth session of the Committee (2004), in "Compilation of the General Comments or General Recommendations adopted by Human Rights Treaty Bodies", above n. 3, 282 at para. 35).

[27] Hessisches Gesetz über die Gleichberechtigung von Frauen und Männern und zum Abbau von Diskriminierungen von Frauen in der öffentlichen Verwaltung (Hessisches Gleichberechtigungsgesetz— HGlG) (Hesse Act on equal rights for women and men and the removal of discrimination against women

provides an example where an obligation to set targets and an obligation to grant preferential treatment were imposed in combination.

Hesse Women Equality Act for the public administration   **7.DE.5.**
(Hessisches Gesetz über die Gleichberechtigung von Frauen und Männern und zum Abbau von Diskriminierungen von Frauen in der öffentlichen Verwaltung)

Paragraph 5—Content of the women's advancement plan
. . .
3. The women's advancement plan shall contain binding targets, for two years at a time, with reference to the proportion of women in appointments and promotions, for increasing the proportion of women in sectors in which women are underrepresented. In defining the targets, the particular features of the sectors and departments concerned shall be decisive.
4. In each women's advancement plan, more than half of the posts to be filled in a sector in which women are underrepresented are to be designated for filling by women. That shall not apply if a particular sex is an indispensable condition for an activity. If it is convincingly demonstrated that not enough women with the necessary qualifications are available, a correspondingly smaller number of posts may be designated for filling by women. In the case of promotions without posts being filled in sectors in which women are underrepresented, a proportion of women is to be designated which corresponds at least to the proportion of women in the next lowest salary group in the sector. The third sentence shall apply by analogy. If measures of personnel organisation are provided for which block or abolish posts, it must be ensured by means of the women's advancement plan that the proportion of women in the sectors affected remains at least the same.
. . .

Paragraph 10—Selection decisions
1. In order to ensure equal rights for women and men in connection with appointment and promotion and to ensure fulfilment of the women's advancement plans, suitability, capability and professional performance (qualifications) are to be assessed in accordance with the requirements of the post to be filled or the office to be conferred . . .
4. If the targets of the women's advancement plan for each two years are not fulfilled, until they are fulfilled every further appointment or promotion of a man in a sector in which women are underrepresented shall require the approval of the body which has approved the women's advancement plan, and, within the scope of the women's advancement plans drawn up in ministries, the State chancellery and the Land staff office, the approval of the Land Government. . . . The first sentence shall not apply in cases within Article 127(3) of the Hesse Constitution.

This legislation does not leave the question whether to engage in positive action as defined in this chapter (see above section 7.2) to the discretion of the employer. If an employer wishes to fill a position, and if the targets of the women's advancement plan

in the public administration), adopted on 21 December 1993 (GBVBl. I, p. 729). This legislation is limited to 13 years' duration (since 31 December 1993) and expired on 31 December 2006. See, for its legal assessment discussion of ECJ, C–158/97 *Badeck and others* [2000] ECR I–1875, discussed below in section 7.5, **7.EC.30.**

cannot be met otherwise, a woman has to be employed. Although there is no individual right for any woman to claim preferential treatment,[28] the national authorities consider themselves under an objective obligation to prefer an equally qualified woman under these circumstances.[29]

Thus, within the broad category of schemes which encourage employers to monitor the composition of the workforce and to identify instances of underrepresentation of certain categories of workers, a distinction has to be made between (a) schemes whose only purpose is to raise awareness about certain imbalances—leaving it to the employer to decide which measures to adopt and, indeed, whether or not to adopt certain remedial measures—or, at best, to encourage a social dialogue with the employees' representatives by obliging the employer to report on the results of the monitoring; and (b) schemes which should lead to the adoption of positive action measures (as defined in this chapter) in order to remedy imbalances which the monitoring has revealed, either by the adoption of action plans setting certain targets or by measures which grant certain forms of preferential treatment to the members of underrepresented categories. As such, the requirement to monitor the composition of the workforce does not necessarily mean that such measures (and which measures precisely) will have to be adopted.

7.3.2.B.   REDEFINING MERIT

Another type of measure which, while not constituting positive action as defined above, may be included in a typology of measures aimed at achieving substantive equality or at promoting diversity is the redefinition of the criterion used to allocate a particular social good, such as employment, in order to ensure that the specific situation of disadvantaged or underrepresented categories will be better taken into account. There are few examples of national legislation aimed at redefining merit in the context of employment, i.e. considering criteria for assessing qualifications which are less exclusive than others. Although such a redefinition of the concept of merit will lead to more favourable assessment of the qualifications of members of traditionally excluded groups, which may be detrimental towards the members of the privileged class, it should not be considered as discriminatory on that basis alone, since there is not one possible understanding, but a variety of understandings, of what "being qualified" might mean in any particular occupational context.[30] One of the few examples which fall under this category is another paragraph of the Hesse Women Equality Act for the public administration.

---

[28] D. Schiek, "Sex Equality Law after *Kalanke* and *Marschall*" (1998) 4(2) *ELJ* 148, 150–1.
[29] See the position of the Hesse Constitutional Court in the *Badeck* case presented to the European Court of Justice (cited above n. 27), para. 12.
[30] See in this respect also below **7.EC.30.**, paras. 31 and 32 of the ECJ judgment in *Badeck*.

Paragraph 10 Selection
When qualifications are assessed, qualifications and experience which have been acquired by looking after children or persons requiring care in the domestic sector (family work) are to be taken into account, in so far as they are of importance for the suitability, performance and capability of applicants. That also applies where family work has been performed alongside employment.

7.3.2.C.   OUTREACHING

In order to remedy the underrepresentation of certain groups, it may be necessary first to publicise certain opportunities to the members of that group, for instance by the insertion of job advertisements in the media which they rely upon, or by making explicit the willingness of the employer to conduct a recruitment policy which is aimed at achieving diversity. In the UK, for instance, Section 48 of the *Sex Discrimination Act 1975* (as amended) and Section 38 of the *Race Relations Act* permit employers a policy of encouraging applications from persons of a particular sex or race, nationality or ethnic origin respectively. As a result, it is not unusual for advertisements in the public sector to contain statements such as:[31]

> "A local government office is an equal opportunities employer. Women are currently underrepresented in this employment sector and applications from women are particularly welcomed."

The important benefit of such form of advertising is that it may encourage certain individuals to apply for positions in undertakings where they may otherwise have feared meeting hostility or prejudice. A Stonewall brochure for employers notes:

> "Excellent potential applicants may not bother to apply for jobs in organisations they, rightly or wrongly, believe to be intolerant of LGB people. Research indicates organisations get a better field of applicants if they include positive and inclusive statements in their advertising literature, and the material they send to applicants. A Greater Manchester Police advertising campaign targeting LGB people not only encouraged people to apply, it also sent a clear signal to other staff and the wider public about the changing culture and leadership of the force."[32]

It will be noted that outreaching, thus conceived, does not imply preferential treatment in favour of the underrepresented category. The ambition of outreaching

---

[31] Example proposed by E. Szyszczak, "Positive Action as a Tool in Promoting Access to Employment" (2006) 1 *RRQuarterly* 25, 28.
[32] *The Employment Equality (Sexual Orientation) Regulations. Guidelines for Employers*, 2nd edn (London, Stonewall). Available on the website of Stonewall: Equality & Justice for Lesbians, Gay Men and Bisexuals.
* See also above **7.DE.5.**

measures is more modest, but crucial nevertheless: it indicates the commitment of the employer to conducting a fair recruitment policy, thus reassuring potential candidates from minority groups that they should overcome any hesitation they may have to join a sector or an employer where they have traditionally been underrepresented. By placing job advertisements in a paper read primarily by those of a specific ethnic community, an employer demonstrates a willingness to go beyond a non-discrimination policy in order to achieve a better balance within the workforce. The same applies for explicitly encouraging minorities or women to apply, or indicating that the undertaking has a nursery in order to attract applications from women. It is thus doubtful whether outreaching qualifies as positive action.[33] More suitable terms may be "affirmative mobilisation" or "affirmative fairness".[34]

The guarantee given to the members of an underrepresented category that they will be interviewed if they present the minimum qualifications required for the job offered may be seen as a variation upon outreach programmes. This was one of the provisions of the 1993 Hesse Women's Equality Act for Public Administrations (HGlG)[35] at stake in the case of *Badeck and Others.*

Hesse Women Equality Act for the public administration **7.DE.7.**[*]

Paragraph 9—Interviews
1. In sectors in which women are underrepresented, at least as many women as men, or all the women applicants, shall be called to interview, if interviews are carried out, if they satisfy the conditions laid down by law or otherwise for appointment to the post or the office to be conferred.

Such a measure does not question the allocation of jobs on the exclusive basis of merit[36] or qualifications. Rather, it seeks to ensure that candidates from the underrepresented group will be given the opportunity to convince the employer that he or she has the required profile to adequately perform the tasks allocated. It thus avoids that appreciation of qualifications will be tainted by prejudice or stereotyping against the members of the underrepresented category. It may be described as an outreach measure, to the extent that it seeks to ensure that a recruitment system based on qualifications will work for the benefit of the members of certain identified underrepresented groups, which in turn should encourage those members to apply for

---

[33] Outreach is considered as positive action by C. Crudden, "Redefining Positive Action" [1986] *ILJ* 219, 224, who concurs with the finding that such measures do not entail preferential treatment.
[34] See Bossuyt, above n. 7, paras. 72–4.
[35] See above n. 27..
[36] For a discussion of merit see below section 7.5.3.
[*] See also above **7.DE.5.** and **7.DE.6.**

the positions concerned, and to invest in the acquisition of the qualifications required.

The provision of specific training opportunities to the members of certain underrepresented categories may go beyond a strict definition of "outreaching measures", although it could be argued that such a measure does not go beyond seeking to reinforce the opportunities open to those individuals. Indeed, the British Sexual Orientation Regulations and Race, Belief Regulations explicitly link the provision of training to outreach measures.

The Employment Equality (Sexual Orientation) Regulations 2003   **7.GB.8.**

(1) Nothing in [the SO Regulations] shall render unlawful any act done in or in connection with—

    (a) affording persons of a particular sexual orientation access to facilities for training which would help fit them for particular work; or

    (b) encouraging persons of a particular sexual orientation to take advantage of opportunities for doing particular work, where it reasonably appears to the person doing the act that it prevents or compensates for disadvantages linked to sexual orientation suffered by persons of that sexual orientation doing that work or likely to take up that work.

A similar provision is to be found in the 1993 Hesse Women Equality Act for the public administration.

Hesse Women Equality Act for the public administration   **7.DE.9.**[*]

Paragraph 7—Allocation of training places
1. In trained occupations in which women are underrepresented, they are to be taken into account to the extent of at least one half in the allocation of training places. The first sentence shall not apply to training procedures in which the State exclusively provides training.
2. Suitable measures are to be taken to draw women's attention to vacant training places in occupations within the meaning of the first sentence of subparagraph 1 and to induce them to apply. If de-spite such measures there are not enough applications from women, more than half of the training places may be filled with men, contrary to the first sentence of subparagraph 1.

It will be noted, however, that the European Court of Justice qualified the latter rule as in need of being justified by Article 2 (4) of Directive 76/207/EEC and thus as preferential treatment.[37]

[37] *Badeck*, above n. 27; see above n. 27 and below **3.EC.30.**, para. 54.
[*] See also above **7.DE.5.**, **7.DE.6.** and **7.DE.7.**

7.3.3. POSITIVE ACTION MEASURES IMPLYING PREFERENTIAL TREATMENT

7.3.3.A. PREFERENTIAL TREATMENT OF EQUALLY QUALIFIED MEMBERS OF THE UNDERREPRESENTED GROUP

Another form of positive action may consist in granting preferential treatment to the members of the underrepresented category in any one professional sector or level of the hierarchy, *all other things being equal*. In this situation, positive action does not introduce an exception to the principle of recruitments or promotions being based on merit or qualification; neither does it impose quotas, i.e. set-asides for the members of the underrepresented category in order to remedy the imbalance.[38] Rather, this form of positive action introduces one supplementary criterion for the allocation of jobs, *where all the other (relevant) criteria appear insufficient to guide the decision-maker*. The objective of improving the representation of the underrepresented group will only become relevant if no decision can be reached by reference to merits and qualifications of different candidates, who appear equally qualified or deserving. Most well-known examples of this form of positive action have been subject to judicial review by the European Court of Justice.[39]

Bremen Act on Equal Treatment for Men and Women **7.DE.10.**
in the Public Service (Landesgleichstellungsgesetz) of 20 November 1990[40]

Paragraph 4: Appointment, assignment to an official post and promotion
(1) In the case of an appointment (including establishment as a civil servant or judge) which is not made for training purposes, women who have the same qualifications as men applying for the same post are to be given priority in sectors where they are underrepresented.
(2) In the case of an assignment to a position in a higher pay, remuneration and salary bracket, women who have the same qualifications as men applying for the same post are to be given priority if they are underrepresented. This also applies in the case of assignment to a different official post and promotion.
. . .
(5) There is underrepresentation if women do not make up at least half of the staff in the individual pay, remuneration and salary brackets in the relevant personnel group within a department. This also applies to the function levels provided for in the organization chart.

---

[38] Thus, the term "flexible quotas" is misleading; see M. Ferber, "In Defense of Affirmative Action" (1997) 50 *ILRR* 516.
[39] Cases C–450/93 *Kalanke v. Freie Hansestadt Bremen* [1995] ECR I–3051, C–409/95 *Marschall* [1997] ECR I–6363 and C–407/98 *Abrahamsson and Anderson* [2000] ECR I–5539, to be covered in more detail below in section 7.5.
[40] *Gesetzblatt*, 433.

Under such a scheme, the preference given to the member of the underrepresented category is absolute and unconditional: in the case of *Kalanke*, this led the European Court of Justice to consider that it went beyond what was admissible under Article 2(4) of Directive 76/207/EEC.[41] But such a scheme may also be combined with an exemption clause, allowing the member of the overrepresented category to put forward certain elements specific to his or her individual situation which could justify rebutting the presumption in favour of granting a preference to the member of the underrepresented category. In the view of the European Court of Justice, this may ensure that the scheme is compatible with the requirement of proportionality.[42]

German Law on Civil Servants of the Land   **7.DE.11.**
(Beamtengesetz für das Land Nordrhein-Westfalen)[43]

Para. 25
(5) Where, in the sector of the authority responsible for promotion, there are fewer women than men in the particular higher grade post in the career bracket, women are to be given priority for promotion in the event of equal suitability, competence and professional performance, unless reasons specific to an individual [male] candidate tilt the balance in his favour.

7.3.3.B.   STRICT QUOTAS

A second, and more extreme, form of positive action consists in granting preferential treatment for the members of the underrepresented group, even where they are not equally qualified. This may be done through schemes such as those at stake in the case of *Abrahamsson* presented to the European Court of Justice.[44]

Swedish Equality Act   **7.SE.12.**
(Jämställdhetslagen) 1991:433

Article 16
Point 2
Unlawful sexual discrimination shall be deemed to exist where an employer, at the time of recruitment, promotion or training with a view to promotion, appoints one person rather than another of the opposite sex even though the person not chosen better satisfies the objective conditions for holding that post or taking part in the training.

[41] *Kalanke*, above n. 39.
[42] *Marschall*, above n. 39.
[43] In the version published on 1 May 1981 (GVNW, 234), as last amended by para. 1 of the Seventh Law amending certain rules relating to the civil service of 5 February 1995 (GVNW, 102).
[44] *Abrahamsson and Anderson*, above n. 36.

Those conditions shall not apply where the employer can prove that:

. . .

(2)   the decision forms part of efforts to promote equality between men and women in the work-place, or . . .

Swedish Regulation concerning certain professors' and research   **7.SE.13.**
assistants' posts created with a view to promoting equality (Förordningen
(1995:936) om vissa anställningar som professor och forskarassistent vilka
in-rättas i jämställdhetssyfte)

Article 1
This regulation concerns the posts of professor and research assistant created and filled under special appropriations during the budgetary year 1995/96 in certain universities and higher educational institutions of the State in the context of efforts to promote equality in professional life.

. . .

Article 3
When appointments are made, the provisions of Article 15a of [the regulation applicable to all positions in universities nationwide] shall be replaced by the following provisions.

A candidate belonging to an underrepresented sex who possesses sufficient qualifications . . . must be granted preference over a candidate of the opposite sex who would otherwise have been chosen (positive discrimination) where it proves necessary to do so in order for a candidate of the underrepresented sex to be appointed.

Positive discrimination must, however, not be applied where the difference between the candidates' qualifications is so great that such application would give rise to a breach of the requirement of objectivity in the making of appointments.

The same result may be achieved by setting aside a certain number of positions for the members of groups identified as underrepresented in any particular professional sector or at a particular level of the hierarchy. Again we can distinguish two ways to define such quotas. Either such quotas are set according to a criterion closely linked to the particular employment opportunity offered, e.g. on the basis of the representation of different groups among the holders of a particular diploma or qualification, or they are set according to the idea that, within each professional sector or at each level of the professional hierarchy, different groups should be represented in proportions roughly equivalent to their representation in the whole society, so as to mirror this representation to the fullest extent possible. Such a distinction may be relevant because, insofar as a "quota" is defined on the basis of a more objective and refined criterion than the overall representation of each group within society, the imposition of a quota will be easier to justify. The Hesse Women Equality Act for the public administration[45] and the Northern Ireland Police Act 2000 provide examples of the first approach.

[45] For the evaluation of such a scheme by the European Court of Justice, see *Badeck*, above n. 27.

Hesse Women Equality Act for the public administration **7.DE.14.**[*]

Paragraph 5—Content of the women's advancement plan

. . . 7. Posts in the academic service which are filled for a fixed term under Paragraph 57a in conjunction with point 1 or 3 of Paragraph 57b(2) of the Hochschulrahmengesetz (Framework law on universities and colleges) are to be filled with at least the same proportion of women as the proportion of women among the graduates in the discipline in question. Posts in the academic service which are filled for a fixed term under Paragraph 48 of the Hochschulrahmengesetz are to be filled with at least the same proportion of women as the proportion of women among the holders of higher degrees in the discipline in question. The means applied for the employment of academic assistants without degrees must be applied at least to the same proportion of women as the proportion of women among the students in the discipline in question . . ..

Paragraph 14—Collective bodies

In making appointments to commissions, advisory boards, boards of directors and supervisory boards and other collective bodies, at least half the members should be women."

The above is an example of the first, more modest approach. The special recruitment mechanisms in the Northern Ireland Police Service, which are one of the measures resulting from the Belfast Agreement of 10 April 1998, may be cited as an example for the second approach.

Police (Northern Ireland) Act 2000[46] **7.NIR.15.**

Appointment of Police Trainees

39. The Chief Constable shall, in accordance with regulations under section 41(3), appoint police trainees.

. . .

44. (1) The Secretary of State shall by regulations prescribe the arrangements to be made, by the Chief Constable or a person appointed under section 43(1), for the recruitment of persons for appointment

. . .

(5) In relation to the recruitment of persons for appointment as police trainees, the regulations shall include provision for the selection of qualified applicants to form a pool of applicants for the purposes of section 46(1).

. . .

46. (1) In making appointments under section 39 on any occasion, the Chief Constable shall appoint from the pool of qualified applicants formed for that purpose by virtue of Section 44(5) an even number of persons of whom—

    (a)   one half shall be persons who are treated as Roman Catholic; and

    (b)   one half shall be persons who are not so treated.

. . .

---

[46] HMSO 2000, chapter 32.

[*] See also above **7.DE.5.**, **7.DE.5.**, **7.DE.6.** and **7.DE.9.**

(5) In making appointments to relevant posts in the police support staff under subsection (3) of section 4 on any occasion, the Chief Constable (acting by virtue of subsection (5) of that section) shall appoint from the pool of qualified applicants formed for that purpose by virtue of section 44(6) an even number of persons of whom-

(a)   one half shall be persons who are treated as Roman Catholic; and

(b)   one half shall be persons who are not so treated.

Notes

(1) The background is the following. As part of the 1998 Belfast Agreement, the "Patten Commission" was set up in order to advise on the measures necessary to achieve "a police service that can enjoy widespread support from, and is seen to be an integral part of, the community as a whole". One of its central recommendations was to adopt a special method of recruitment of police officers, in order to increase the number of Catholics serving in the force. The recommendation, enshrined in the Police (Northern Ireland) Act 2000, was that for at least 10 years the new intake of officers should comprise 50% Catholics and 50% Protestants or others. Indeed, the Commission noted that only about 8% of the Royal Ulster Constabulary was Catholic, although more than 40% of Northern Ireland's population was, at the time of the Commission's report, Catholic. Despite various initiatives, it had never proved possible to increase the number of Catholics in the force above 21%. The imbalance of representation was considered by the Commission to be "the most striking problem in the composition of the RUC", especially since the parties to the Belfast Agreement had recorded their view that the police service should be "representative of the society it polices".

(2) It was recognised, crucially, that the recruitment of Catholics should not be at the expense of the quality of those serving in the police force. The Patten Commission insisted that all candidates for membership should be required to reach a minimum standard of merit in the selection procedure, and only those fulfilling these standards would enter a pool from which the required number of recruits could be drawn. Thus, the means by which the Police Service of Northern Ireland is to become representative of the community it serves should be through the creation of a pool of candidates who are qualified for appointment as police trainees and then the selection from that pool of the same number from each category. The system is seen as temporary, as the mechanisms for the balanced recruitment of Catholics and Protestants in the police are to be reviewed on a triennial basis, and may be extended by the Secretary of State only having regard to the progress that has been made towards securing that membership of the police and the police support staff is representative of the community in Northern Ireland, and in consultation with the Policing Board.[47]

---

[47] For more detail see the discussion of the decision by the High Court of Justice in Northern Ireland (2002) NIQB 46 (below **7.NIR.31.**).

(3) Due to fears that these mechanisms might not be compatible with the Employment Equality Directive, even taking into account the permissibility of positive action measures under Article 7(1) of the Directive, the UK negotiated for an exemption, which is enshrined in Article 15, stating that

> "In order to tackle the underrepresentation of one of the major religious communities in the Police Service of Northern Ireland differences in treatment regarding recruitment into that Service including its support staff shall not constitute discrimination insofar as those differences are expressly authorised by national legislation."

7.3.4. POSITIVE ACTION REQUIRING PREFERENCE—AIMS AND SCRUTINY

Under section 7.3.1 a typology of different measures that may be employed in order to combat factual inequality was presented. Those measures which imply preferential treatment (included those in the three last rows of the typology under section 7.3.1) may have to be scrutinised for their compatibility *vel non* with the requirements of the principle of equal treatment. Two questions will matter in the performance of such scrutiny. First, it will be necessary to inquire into the aims pursued by such a policy, in order to decide whether these aims are legitimate and may justify the restriction to the right of each individual to be treated "equally", i.e. on the basis of his or her individual situation, rather than as a member of the group to which he or she belongs. Three distinct rationales may be invoked in this regard.[48] A first rationale is backward-looking. Affirmative action is presented, here, as compensatory: because the group to which A belongs has, in the past, been excluded or denied certain benefits, in comparison to the group to which B belongs, it will be justified to grant preferential treatment to A in order to overcome the legacy of this past discrimination. A second rationale focuses not on the past, but on the present. It sees affirmative action as a tool necessary to establish "equality in fact", rather than mere "formal equality", because the latter (equality before the law, i.e. non-discrimination) would remain blind to certain realities—conscious or unconscious prejudice or stereotypes—which, unless taken into account, will work to the disadvantage of the members of a defined category. The trait of the individual, which characterises that individual as the member of a group, is thus taken as a proxy for a disadvantage which it is the objective of the positive action policy to remedy. A third rationale may be said to be "forward-looking". It sees affirmative action as a tool to promote diversity or proportionate representation in sectors or at levels where it matters that all the sub-groups of the community are fairly represented.

Once the rationale justifying affirmative action as a restriction to the principle of (formal) equal treatment is identified, the second question will be which level of scrutiny should be applied. Whether affirmative action policies are subjected to a

---

[48] For a more systematic approach, see McCrudden, above n. 6, 243; or see Bossuyt, above n. 7.

strict scrutiny, requiring that they be demonstrated to be both appropriate and strictly proportionate, i.e. necessary, for the achievement of the aims pursued, or to a looser form of scrutiny will depend largely on the understanding of affirmative action either as a means to achieve equal treatment (complementing the requirement of formal equality as non-discrimination) or as a mere derogation to that principle. It may also depend on the more or less suspect character of the trait on which the affirmative action policy is based—for instance, race or ethnic origin will usually be considered highly suspect, while sex may be considered less suspect.

The following sections of this chapter examine the regime of positive action measures under the relevant instruments of international human rights law (section 7.4), under European Union law (section 7.5) and in certain most representative national jurisdictions within the European Union (section 7.6). The final section (section 7.7) examines the responses given to the questions positive action measures raise under the rules protecting the right to respect for private life vis-à-vis the processing of personal data.

7.4. POSITIVE ACTION UNDER INTERNATIONAL LAW

7.4.1.   UNITED NATIONS HUMAN RIGHTS INSTRUMENTS

Both the *International Convention for the Elimination of All Forms of Racial Discrimination* (ICERD) and the *International Convention for the Elimination of All Forms of Discrimination Against Women* (CEDAW) allow for the adoption of affirmative action, under certain conditions.

International Convention for the Elimination of All Forms   **7.UN.16.**
of Racial Discrimination[49]

Article 1(4). Special measures taken for the sole purpose of securing adequate advancement of certain racial or ethnic groups or individuals requiring such protection as may be necessary in order to ensure such groups or individuals equal enjoyment or exercise of human rights and fundamental freedoms shall not be deemed racial discrimination, provided, however, that such measures do not, as a consequence, lead to the maintenance of separate rights for different racial groups and that they shall not be continued after the objectives for which they were taken have been achieved . . .

Article 2(2). States Parties shall, when the circumstances so warrant, take, in the social, economic, cultural and other fields, special and concrete measures to ensure the adequate development and protection of certain racial groups or individuals belonging to them, for the

[49] See above n. 4.

purpose of guaranteeing them the full and equal enjoyment of human rights and fundamental freedoms. These measures shall in no case entail as a consequence the maintenance of unequal or separate rights for different racial groups after the objectives for which they were taken have been achieved.

While Article 1(4) ICERD appears to allow for the adoption of certain positive action measures by the States Parties to ICERD, Article 2(2) suggests that the adoption of such measures may be required under certain conditions. In its General Recommendation XXVII on discrimination against Roma adopted in 2000, the Committee for the Elimination of Racial Discrimination, although not making explicit reference to Article 2(2) ICERD, encourages the States Parties to "take special measures to promote the employment of Roma in the public administration and institutions, as well as in private companies", and to

> "adopt and implement, whenever possible, at the central or local level, special measures in favour of Roma in public employment such as public contracting and other activities undertaken or funded by the government, or training Roma in various skills and professions".[50]

Similarly, in its General Recommendation XXIX on Article 1, paragraph 1 of the Convention (Descent), adopted in 2002, the CERD Committee recommends the adoption of "special measures in favour of descent-based groups and communities in order to ensure their enjoyment of human rights and fundamental freedoms, in particular concerning access to public functions, employment and education", as well as to "educate the general public on the importance of affirmative action programmes to address the situation of victims of descent-based discrimination" and to take "special measures to promote the employment of members of affected communities in the public and private sectors".[51]

International Convention for the Elimination of All Forms   **7.UN.17.**
of Discrimination against Women

Article 4(1)
Adoption by States Parties of temporary special measures aimed at accelerating *de facto* equality between men and women shall not be considered discrimination as defined in the present Convention, but shall in no way entail as a consequence the maintenance of unequal or

---

[50] Committee for the Elimination of Racial Discrimination, General Recommendation XXVII on discrimination against Roma adopted at the fifty-seventh session (2000), in: "Compilation of the General Comments or General Recommendations adopted by Human Rights Treaty Bodies", above n. 3, at 219, paras. 28–9.

[51] Committee for the Elimination of Racial Discrimination, General Recommendation XXIX on Art. 1, para. 1 of the Convention (Descent), adopted at the sixty-first session (2002), in "Compilation of the General Comments or General Recommendations adopted by Human Rights Treaty Bodies", above n. 3, at 226, paras. 1 f) and h), and 7 j).

separate standards; these measures shall be discontinued when the objectives of equality of opportunity and treatment have been achieved.

The purpose of this provision, as described by the CEDAW Committee, is to

"accelerate the improvement of the position of women to achieve their *de facto* or substantive equality with men, and to effect the structural, social and cultural changes necessary to correct past and current forms and effects of discrimination against women, as well as to provide them with compensation".[52]

In its fifth General Recommendation, adopted in 1988, the Committee on the Elimination of Discrimination against Women encouraged States Parties to "make more use of temporary special measures such as positive action, preferential treatment or quota systems to advance women's integration into education, the economy, politics and employment".[53] The CEDAW Committee has been more specific in the context of participation of women in public and political life:

CEDAW Committee, General Recommendation No. 23: **7.UN.18.**
Political and public life, adopted at the sixteenth session of the Committee (1997)

"While removal of *de jure* barriers is necessary, it is not sufficient. Failure to achieve full and equal participation of women can be unintentional and the result of outmoded practices and procedures which inadvertently promote men. Under article 4, the Convention encourages the use of temporary special measures in order to give full effect to articles 7 [relating to the elimi-nation of discrimination against women in political and public life] and 8 [concerning the opportunity women must be provided to represent their Governments at the international level and to participate in the work of international organizations]. Where countries have developed effective temporary strategies in an attempt to achieve equality of participation, a wide range of measures has been implemented, including recruiting, financially assisting and training women candidates, amending electoral procedures, developing campaigns directed at equal participation, setting numerical goals and quotas and targeting women for appointment to public positions such as the judiciary or other professional groups that play an essential part in the everyday life of all societies. The formal removal of barriers and the introduction of temporary special measures to encourage the equal participation of both men and women in the public life of their societies are essential prerequisites to true equality in political life. In

---

[52] Committee on the Elimination of Discrimination against Women, General Recommendation No. 25: Art. 4, para. 1 of the Convention (temporary special measures), adopted at the thirtieth session of the Committee (2004), in "Compilation of the General Comments or General Recommendations adopted by Human Rights Treaty Bodies", above n. 3, at 282, para. 15. On this provision, see also I. Boerefijn, F. Coomans, J. Goldschmidt, R. Holtmaat and R. Wolleswinkel (eds.), *Temporary Special Measures. Accelerating De Facto Equality of Women under Article 4(1) UN Convention on the Elimination of All Forms of Discrimination against Women* (Antwerp, Intersentia, 2003) (following a roundtable discussion held in Maastricht in October 2002).

[53] Committee on the Elimination of Discrimination against Women, General Recommendation No. 5: Temporary special measures, adopted at the seventh session of the Committee (1988), in "Compilation of the General Comments or General Recommendations adopted by Human Rights Treaty Bodies", above n. 3, at 235.

order, however, to overcome centuries of male domination of the public sphere, women also require the encouragement and support of all sectors of society to achieve full and effective participation, encouragement which must be led by States parties to the Convention, as well as by political parties and public officials. States parties have an obligation to ensure that temporary special measures are clearly designed to support the principle of equality and therefore comply with constitutional principles which guarantee equality to all citizens."[54]

Under the *Convention for the Elimination of All Forms of Discrimination against Women*, the shift from the *possibility* to adopt positive action measures without this being considered discriminatory to an *obligation*, in certain instances, to adopt such measures in the name of real and effective equality is encouraged by three character-istics of this instrument. First, CEDAW does not simply prohibit discrimination on grounds of sex: it is aimed specifically at the protection of women. Other instruments such as, in particular, Article 26 of the *International Covenant on Civil and Political Rights* or Article 2(2) of the *International Covenant on Economic, Social and Cultural Rights*—the latter in the enjoyment of the rights guaranteed under the ICESCR—ensure a symmetrical protection of equality between women and men; in contrast, CEDAW focuses on discrimination against women, thus "emphasizing that women have suffered, and continue to suffer from various forms of discrimination because they are women".[55] Secondly, Article 24 CEDAW imposes on the States Parties to "adopt all necessary measures at the national level aimed at achieving the full realization of the rights recognised in the present Convention". It thus explicitly provides that states are under a positive obligation to realise the principle of equal treatment. Thirdly, a number of specific articles of the Convention also mention that states are to "take all appropriate measures" in order to fulfil the rights guaranteed. On the basis of these arguments, as well as of a dynamic interpretation of the Convention for the Elimination of All Forms of Discrimination against Women, the CEDAW Committee concludes, in the General Recommendation it adopted in 2004 on Article 4, paragraph 1 of the Convention, that the adoption of certain positive action measures may be required under that instrument. Since States Parties have an obligation to "improve the *de facto* position of women through concrete and effective policies and programmes",[56] they may have to

---

[54] Committee on the Elimination of Discrimination against Women, General Recommendation No. 23: Political and public life, adopted at the sixteenth session of the Committee (1997), in "Compilation of the General Comments or General Recommendations adopted by Human Rights Treaty Bodies", above n. 3, at 263, para. 15. See also the recommendation made in para. 43: "States parties should identify and implement temporary special measures to ensure the equal representation of women in all fields covered by articles 7 and 8."

[55] Committee on the Elimination of Discrimination against Women, General Recommendation No. 25: Art. 4, para. 1 of the Convention (temporary special measures), adopted at the thirtieth session of the Committee (2004), in "Compilation of the General Comments or General Recommendations adopted by Human Rights Treaty Bodies", above n. 3, at 282, para. 5.

[56] Committee on the Elimination of Discrimination against Women, General Recommendation No. 25: Art. 4, para. 1 of the Convention (temporary special measures), adopted at the thirtieth session of the Committee (2004), in "Compilation of the General Comments or General Recommendations adopted by Human Rights Treaty Bodies", above n. 3, at 282, para. 7.

"provide adequate explanations with regard to any failure to adopt temporary special measures. Such failures may not be justified simply by averring powerlessness, or by explaining inaction through predominant market or political forces, such as those inherent in the private sector, private organizations, or political parties" (paragraph 29).

Another important contribution of this Recommendation is that, far from being presented as derogation from the requirement of (formal) equality, the adoption of such positive action measures is seen as a contribution to the implementation of the principles of equality and non-discrimination:

"The Convention targets discriminatory dimensions of past and current societal and cultural contexts which impede women's enjoyment of their human rights and fundamental freedoms. It aims at the elimination of all forms of discrimination against women, including the elimination of the causes and consequences of their *de facto* or substantive inequality. Therefore, the application of temporary special measures in accordance with the Convention is one of the means to realize *de facto* or substantive equality for women, rather than an exception to the norms of non-discrimination and equality."[57]

A third important contribution of this Recommendation is to emphasise that the requirement under Article 4(1) CEDAW that "special measures" be "temporary" only applies to special measures which seek to accelerate the *de facto*, or substantive equality between women and men, and not to other measures of a general nature which seek to ensure that the environment will be transformed in order to eliminate the root causes of discrimination against women. All these elements are summarised in the following excerpts of General Recommendation No. 25:

Committee on the Elimination of Discrimination against Women, **7.UN.19.** *General recommendation No. 25: Article 4, paragraph 1, of the Convention (temporary special measures), adopted at the thirtieth session of the Committee (2004)*

"18. Measures taken under article 4, paragraph 1, by States parties should aim to accelerate the equal participation of women in the political, economic, social, cultural, civil or any other field. The Committee views the application of these measures not as an exception to the norm of non-discrimination, but rather as an emphasis that temporary special measures are part of a necessary strategy by States parties directed towards the achievement of *de facto* or substantive equality of women with men in the enjoyment of their human rights and fundamental freedoms. While the application of temporary special measures often remedies the effects of past discrimination against women, the obligation of States parties under the Convention to improve the position of women to one of *de facto* or substantive equality with men exists irrespective of any proof of past discrimination. The Committee considers that States parties

---

[57] Committee on the Elimination of Discrimination against Women, General Recommendation No. 25: Art. 4, para. 1 of the Convention (temporary special measures), adopted at the thirtieth session of the Committee (2004), in "Compilation of the General Comments or General Recommendations adopted by Human Rights Treaty Bodies", above n. 3, at 282, para. 14.

that adopt and implement such measures under the Convention do not discriminate against men.

19. States parties should clearly distinguish between temporary special measures taken under article 4, paragraph 1, to accelerate the achievement of a concrete goal for women of *de facto* or substantive equality, and other general social policies adopted to improve the situation of women and the girl child. Not all measures that potentially are, or will be, favourable to women are temporary special measures. The provision of general conditions in order to guarantee the civil, political, economic, social and cultural rights of women and the girl child, designed to ensure for them a life of dignity and non-discrimination, cannot be called temporary special measures.

20. Article 4, paragraph 1, explicitly states the "temporary" nature of such special measures. Such measures should therefore not be deemed necessary forever, even though the meaning of 'temporary' may, in fact, result in the application of such measures for a long period of time. The duration of a temporary special measure should be determined by its functional result in response to a concrete problem and not by a predetermined passage of time. Temporary special measures must be discontinued when their desired results have been achieved and sustained for a period of time.

21. The term 'special', though being in conformity with human rights discourse, also needs to be carefully explained. Its use sometimes casts women and other groups who are subject to discrimination as weak, vulnerable and in need of extra or 'special' measures in order to participate or compete in society. However, the real meaning of 'special' in the formulation of article 4, paragraph 1, is that the measures are designed to serve a specific goal.

22. The term 'measures' encompasses a wide variety of legislative, executive, administrative and other regulatory instruments, policies and practices, such as outreach or support programmes; allocation and/or reallocation of resources; preferential treatment; targeted recruitment, hiring and promotion; numerical goals connected with time frames; and quota systems. The choice of a particular 'measure' will depend on the context in which article 4, paragraph 1, is applied and on the specific goal it aims to achieve.

23. The adoption and implementation of temporary special measures may lead to a discussion of qualifications and merit of the group or individuals so targeted, and an argument against preferences for allegedly lesser-qualified women over men in areas such as politics, education and employment. As temporary special measures aim at accelerating achievement of *de facto* or substantive equality, questions of qualification and merit, in particular in the area of employment in the public and private sectors, need to be reviewed carefully for gender bias as they are normatively and culturally determined. For appointment, selection or election to public and political office, factors other than qualification and merit, including the application of the principles of democratic fairness and electoral choice, may also have to play a role.

24. Article 4, paragraph 1, read in conjunction with articles 1, 2, 3, 5 and 24, needs to be applied in relation to articles 6 to 16 which stipulate that States parties 'shall take all appropriate measures'. Consequently, the Committee considers that States parties are obliged to adopt and implement temporary special measures in relation to any of these articles if such measures can be shown to be necessary and appropriate in order to accelerate the achievement of the overall, or a specific goal of, women's *de facto* or substantive equality."

The view that, under certain conditions, preferential treatment will not be deemed to constitute discrimination under the general non-discrimination clause of Article 26 of the *International Covenant on Civil and Political Rights* has been confirmed in a communication in which the author complained of the preferential treatment, regarding reinstatement to the public service, of former public officials who had previously been unfairly dismissed on ideological, political, or trade union grounds. The author complained that this preferential treatment unfairly prejudiced his own chances of gaining a public service job. The Human Rights Committee, however, found the alleged discrimination to be permissible affirmative action in favour of a formerly disadvantaged group.

Human Rights Committee, Communication No. 198/1985[58]   **7.UN.20.**
Stalla Costa v. *Uruguay*

REINSTATEMENT IN THE URUGUAYAN PUBLIC SERVICE OF UNFAIRLY DISMISSED CIVIL SERVANTS

Stalla Costa v. Uruguay

Facts: After a democratic government came into power following the military dictatorship in Uruguay, it adopted legislation affording public officials dismissed under the dictatorship on ideological grounds a priority in access to the public service. The measure was challenged as a violation of Article 25(c) of the International Covenant on Civil and Political Rights, which guarantees to every citizen the right and the opportunity, "without any of the distinctions mentioned in article 2 and without unreasonable restrictions [to] have access, on general terms of equality, to public service in his country".

Held: The measure is compatible with the Covenant, as a remedy for past wrongs.

Judgment: "The main question before the Committee is whether the author of the communication is a victim of a violation of article 25 (c) of the Covenant because, as he alleges, he has not been permitted to have access to public service on general terms of equality. Taking into account the social and political situation in Uruguay during the years of military rule, in particular the dismissal of many public servants pursuant to Institutional Act No. 7, the Committee understands the enactment of Act No. 15.737 of 22 March 1985 by the new democratic Government of Uruguay as a measure of redress. Indeed, the Committee observes that Uruguayan public officials dismissed on ideological, political or trade-union grounds were victims of violations of article 25 of the Covenant and as such are entitled to have an effective remedy under article 2, paragraph 3 (a), of the Covenant. The Act should be looked upon as such a remedy. The implementation of the Act, therefore, cannot be regarded as incompatible with the reference to 'general terms of equality' in article 25 (c) of the Covenant. Neither can the implementation of the Act be regarded as an invidious distinction under article 2, paragraph 1, or as prohibited discrimination within the terms of article 26 of the Covenant."

A similar conclusion was reached by the Human Rights Committee in the case of *Jacobs* v. *Belgium*:

---

[58] Human Rights Committee, *R. D. Stalla Costa* v. *Uruguay*, U.N. Doc. Supp. No. 40 (A/42/40) 170 (1987) (final views of 9 July 1987).

COMPATIBILITY WITH ARTICLES 25(C) AND 26 ICCPR OF A
QUOTA IN FAVOUR OF THE UNDER-REPRESENTED SEX IN THE BELGIAN
PUBLIC SERVICE

Sex quotas in the Belgian High Judicial Council

Facts: Under the Belgian Act of 22 December 1998 amending certain provisions of part two of the Judicial Code concerning the High Council of Justice, the nomination and appointment of magistrates and the introduction of an evaluation system, the High Council of Justice is to comprise 44 members of Belgian nationality, divided into one 22-member Dutch-speaking college and one 22-member French-speaking college. Each college comprises 11 justices and 11 non-justices. It is also provided that the group of non-justices in each college shall have no fewer than four members of each sex (Article 259 bis-1, paragraph 3 of the Judicial Code). The author of the communication had applied to be elected as a non-justice to the High Council of Justice, but failed to be elected, following a second call for applications, since the first call had not led to a sufficient number of women applying. Mr. Jacobs claimed that the introduction of a gender requirement, namely that four non-justice seats in each college be reserved for women and four for men, made it impossible to carry out the required comparison of the qualifications of candidates for the High Council of Justice, and that, since such a condition meant that candidates with better qualifications may be rejected in favour of others whose only merit is that they meet the gender requirement, it constituted a form of discrimination on grounds of sex, in violation of Articles 25(c) and 26 of the International Covenant on Civil and Political Rights.[59]

Held: The facts presented to the Committee do not disclose any violation of the Covenant.

Judgment:[60] "9.3 The Committee recalls that, under article 25(c) of the Covenant, every citizen shall have the right and opportunity, without any of the distinctions mentioned in article 2 and without un-reasonable restrictions, to have access, on general terms of equality, to public service in his or her country. In order to ensure access on general terms of equality, the criteria and processes for appointment must be objective and reasonable. State parties may take measures in order to ensure that the law guarantees to women the rights contained in article 25 on equal terms with men. The Committee must therefore determine whether, in the case before it, the introduction of a gender requirement constitutes a violation of article 25 of the Covenant by virtue of its discriminatory nature, or of other provisions of the Covenant concerning discrimination, notably articles 2 and 3 of the Covenant, as invoked by the author, or whether such a requirement is objectively and reasonably justifiable. The question in this case is whether there is any valid justification for the distinction made between candidates on the grounds that they belong to a particular sex.

---

[59] Art. 25 of the ICCPR provides that "Every citizen shall have the right and the opportunity, without any of the distinctions mentioned in article 2 and without unreasonable restrictions: . . . (c) To have access, on general terms of equality, to public service in his country". Art. 26 ICCPR states: "All persons are equal before the law and are entitled without any discrimination to the equal protection of the law. In this respect, the law shall prohibit any discrimination and guarantee to all persons equal and effective protection against discrimination on any ground such as race, colour, sex, language, religion, political or other opinion, national or social origin, property, birth or other status."

[60] While the excerpts present the reasoning of the Human Rights Committee under Art. 25 c) of the Covenant, the reasoning under Art. 26 of the Covenant is not substantially different. No mention is made here of the other arguments raised by the author of the communication and of the answers of the Committee.

9.4 In the first place, the Committee notes that the gender requirement was introduced by Parliament under the terms of the Act of 20 July 1990 on the promotion of a balance between men and women on advisory bodies. The aim in this case is to increase the representation of and participation by women in the various advisory bodies in view of the very low numbers of women found there. On this point, the Committee finds the author's assertion that the insufficient number of female applicants in response to the first call proves there is no inequality between men and women to be unpersuasive in the present case; such a situation may, on the contrary, reveal a need to encourage women to apply for public ser-vice on bodies such as the High Council of Justice, and the need for taking measures in this regard In the present case, it appears to the Committee that a body such as the High Council of Justice could legitimately be perceived as requiring the incorporation of perspectives beyond one of juridical expertise only. Indeed, given the responsibilities of the judiciary, the promotion of an awareness of gender-relevant issues relating to the application of law, could well be understood as requiring that perspective to be included in a body involved in judicial appointments. Accordingly, the Committee cannot conclude that the requirement is not objective and reasonably justifiable.

9.5 Secondly, the Committee notes that the gender clause requires there to be at least four applicants of each sex among the 11 non-justices appointed, which is to say just over one third of the candidates selected. In the Committee's view, such a requirement does not in this case amount to a disproportionate restriction of candidates' right of access, on general terms of equality, to public office. Furthermore, and contrary to the author's contention, the gender requirement does not make qualifications irrelevant, since it is specified that all non-justice applicants must have at least 10 years' experience. With regard to the author's argument that the gender requirement could give rise to discrimination between the three categories within the group of non-justices as a result, for example, of only men being appointed in one category, the Committee considers that in that event there would be three possibilities: either the female applicants were better qualified than the male, in which case they could justifiably be appointed; or the female and male applicants were equally well qualified, in which case the priority given to women would not be discriminatory in view of the aims of the law on the promotion of equality between men and women, as yet still lacking; or the female candidates were less well qualified than the male, in which case the Senate would be obliged to issue a second call for candidates in order to reconcile the two aims of the law, namely, qualifications and gender balance, neither of which may preclude the other. On that basis, there would appear to be no legal impediment to reopening applications. Lastly, the Committee finds that a reasonable proportionality is maintained between the purpose of the gender requirement, namely to promote equality between men and women in consultative bodies; the means applied and its modalities, as described above; and one of the principal aims of the law, which is to establish a High Council made up of qualified individuals. Consequently, the Committee finds that paragraph 3 of article 295 bis-1 of the Act of 22 December 1998 meets the requirements of objective and reasonable justification."

Notes

(1) Although this is not cited by the Human Rights Committee, it is probable that the conclusion which it arrives at in the case of *Jacobs* has been influenced by the position of the Committee on the Elimination of Discrimination against Women, which, in the General Recommendation No. 23: Political and public life which it adopted in 1997, recommends to the States Parties "the adoption of a rule that

neither sex should constitute less than 40 per cent of the members of a public body".[61] Any other conclusion by the Human Rights Committee in *Jacobs* would have placed Belgium before two potentially conflicting requirements, at least if we consider the general recommendations adopted by the CEDAW as authoritative for the States Parties to CEDAW.

(2) Positive action measures such as the one adopted in Uruguay in favour of the reinstatement of public servants previously dismissed on discriminatory grounds, or the one adopted in Belgium in favour of a balanced representation of both sexes in the High Judicial Council, may therefore be considered justifiable in the view of the Human Rights Committee: they should not be seen as constituting a form of prohibited discrimination under either Article 2(1) or Article 26 of the Covenant. Moreover, the Human Rights Committee has suggested that, in certain cases, positive action may be not only allowable, but even obligatory.[62] If this is indeed the position which may be attributed to the Human Rights Committee, it is not isolated among the human rights treaty bodies. The UN Committee on Economic, Social and Cultural Rights similarly took the view in its first General Comment that "special attention [should] be given to any worse off regions or areas and to any specific groups or sub-groups which appear to be particularly vulnerable or disadvantaged".[63] It has reiterated this position in later General Comments.

> *UN Committee on Economic, Social and Cultural Rights,*   **7.UN.22.**
> *General Comment No. 5: The rights of persons with disabilities*

"The obligation of States parties to the Covenant to promote progressive realization of the relevant rights to the maximum of their available resources clearly requires Governments to do much more than merely abstain from taking measures which might have a negative impact on persons with disabilities. *The obligation in the case of such a vulnerable and disadvantaged group is to take positive action to reduce structural disadvantages and to give appropriate preferential treatment to people with disabilities in order to achieve the objectives of full participation and equality within society for all persons with disabilities.* This almost invariably means that

---

[61] Committee on the Elimination of Discrimination against Women, General Recommendation No. 23: Political and public life, adopted at the sixteenth session of the Committee (1997), in "Compilation of the General Comments or General Recommendations adopted by Human Rights Treaty Bodies", above n. 3, at 263.

[62] See Human Rights Committee, General Comment No. 18: Non-discrimination (1989), in "Compilation of the General Comments or General Recommendations adopted by Human Rights Treaty Bodies", above n. 3, at 146, para. 10 (". . . the principle of equality sometimes requires States parties to take affirmative action in order to diminish or eliminate conditions which cause or help to perpetuate discrimination prohibited by the Covenant. For example, in a State where the general conditions of a certain part of the population prevent or impair their enjoyment of human rights, the State should take specific action to correct those conditions. Such action may involve granting for a time to the part of the population concerned preferential treatment in specific matters as compared with the rest of the population. However, as long as such action is needed to correct discrimination in fact, it is a case of legitimate differentiation under the Covenant").

[63] Committee on Economic, Social and Cultural Rights, General Comment No. 1: Reporting by States Parties, adopted at the third session of the Committee (1989), in "Compilation of the General Comments or General Recommendations adopted by Human Rights Treaty Bodies", above n. 3, at 9, para. 3.

additional resources will need to be made available for this purpose and that a wide range of specially tailored measures will be required."[64]

Notes

(1) The Committee on Economic, Social and Cultural Rights confirms in this General Comment that "appropriate measures [may] need to be taken to undo existing discrimination and to establish equitable opportunities for persons with disabilities", and it considers that

> "such actions should not be considered discriminatory in the sense of article 2(2) of the International Covenant on Economic, Social and Cultural Rights as long as they are based on the principle of equality and are employed only to the extent necessary to achieve that objective" (paragraph 18).

This has traditionally been the doctrine of the Committee on Economic, Social and Cultural Rights.[65] For instance, it noted in its *General Comment No. 13: The right to education* (Article 13), that the adoption of "temporary special measures intended to bring about *de facto* equality for men and women and for disadvantaged groups" is not a violation of the right to non discrimination with regard to education, "so long as such measures do not lead to the maintenance of unequal or separate standards for different groups, and provided they are not continued after the objectives for which they were taken have been achieved".[66] It therefore considered—citing in this respect Article 2 of the UNESCO Convention against Discrimination in Education of 14 December 1960[67]—that separate educational systems or institutions for groups

---

[64] Committee on Economic, Social and Cultural Rights, General Comment No. 5: The rights of persons with disabilities (1994), in "Compilation of the General Comments or General Recommendations adopted by Human Rights Treaty Bodies", above n. 3, at 25, para. 9 [emphasis added].

[65] See, e.g. General Comment No. 4: The right to adequate housing (art. 11 (1) of the Covenant), adopted at the sixth session (1991), at para. 11 ("States parties must give due priority to those social groups living in unfavourable conditions by giving them particular consideration. Policies and legislation should correspondingly not be designed to benefit already advantaged social groups at the expense of others"). See, generally, M. Craven, *The International Covenant on Economic, Social and Cultural Rights, a perspective on its development* (Oxford, Clarendon Press, 1995) 126 (emphasising the obligation of States to focus their efforts on the most vulnerable and disadvantaged groups in society, which may include preferential treatment in favour of the members of these disadvantaged groups).

[66] Committee on Economic, Social and Cultural Rights, General Comment No. 13: The right to education (1999), in "Compilation of the General Comments or General Recommendations adopted by Human Rights Treaty Bodies", above n. 3, at 72, para. 32.

[67] This reference may, however, be inadequate. In its relevant part, this provision states that "The establishment or maintenance, for religious or linguistic reasons, of separate educational systems or institutions offering an education which is in keeping with the wishes of the pupil's parents or legal guardians [shall not constitute discrimination in the meaning of the Convention], if participation in such systems or attendance at such institutions is optional and if the education provided conforms to such standards as may be laid down or approved by the competent authorities, in particular for education of the same level" (Art. 2(b)). However, the separate educational systems or institutions referred to in this instrument in fact serve to protect the rights of minorities, especially religious or linguistic minorities, to a form of education which respects their specific needs. This may not be assimilated to the adoption of measures which seek integration as their end-goal, and whose reliance on differential treatment is simply a means to that end. M. Bossuyt correctly argues that this provision "does not refer to special measures, but only determines when separate educational systems will not be deemed to constitute discrimination" (above n. 7, para. 56).

defined by the grounds listed in Article 2(2) of the Covenant shall be deemed not to constitute a breach of that instrument.

(2) The Committee on Economic, Social and Cultural Rights, in the excerpt presented above, mentions not only an authorisation for states to adopt temporary special measures, but also the existence, in certain circumstances, of an obligation to do so. As noted above, Article 2(2) of ICERD implies that the adoption of positive action measures may be an obligation for the States Parties in certain settings. Indeed, the Committee on the Elimination of Discrimination against Women considered that

> "The practice of treaty monitoring bodies, including the Committee on the Elimination of Racial Discrimination, the Committee on Economic, Social and Cultural Rights, and the Human Rights Committee, shows that these bodies consider the application of temporary special measures as mandatory to achieve the purposes of the respective treaties. Conventions adopted under the auspices of the International Labour Organization, and various documents of the United Nations Educational, Scientific and Cultural Organization also explicitly or implicitly provide for such measures."[68]

It should come as no surprise, therefore, that, in the conclusions of his report to the UN Sub-commission for the promotion and protection of human rights, Mr. Bossuyt notes that

> "a persistent policy in the past of systematic discrimination of certain groups of the population may justify—*and in some cases may even require*—special measures intended to overcome the sequels of a condition of inferiority which still affects members belonging to such groups".[69]

At the same time, while the principle seems to be agreed that positive action measures may be required from the state in order to ensure real and effective equality under its jurisdiction, it will typically be difficult for any individual seeking to benefit from such a scheme to force the state to take an initiative in this regard, considering the broad margin of appreciation which the state authorities are left as regards the choice of the means through which to achieve substantive equality and the broad panoply of measures they have at their disposal. A deepening of the debate on the notion of "structural discrimination" might serve in the future to clarify the conditions under which, according to the international law of human rights, a state may be obliged to adopt positive action measures.[70] In the meaning

---

[68] Committee on the Elimination of Discrimination against Women, General Recommendation No. 25: Art. 4, para. 1 of the Convention (temporary special measures), adopted at the thirtieth session of the Committee (2004), in "Compilation of the General Comments or General Recommendations adopted by Human Rights Treaty Bodies", above n. 3, at 282, n. 3.

[69] See Bossuyt, above n. 7, para. 101 [emphasis added].

[70] In its most recent Concluding Observations relating to Kenya, which it adopted on 29 April 2005, the Human Rights Committee mentions the "systemic discrimination" of women in this country (ICCPR/CO/83/KEN, para. 10). See for a detailed exploration of this notion C. McCrudden, "Institutional Discrimination" (1982) 2 *OJLS* 303. For a use of this notion in order to address the situation of the Roma in Europe, see O. De Schutter and A. Verstichel, "Integrating the Roma into European Society: Time for a New Initiative" (2004/5) 4 *EYMI* 411. See also the reasoning behind the proposal for the adoption of an instrument aimed specifically at ensuring the desegregation of the Roma: EU Network of Independent

attached to this notion here, structural discrimination is not simply a particularly serious form of discrimination. Its defining characteristic would be, rather, that it cuts across different spheres (education, employment, housing and access to health care in particular), resulting in a situation where the prohibition of discrimination in any one of these spheres or, indeed, in all of them, will not suffice to ensure effective equality. For instance, it will not be sufficient to prohibit discrimination in employment if inequalities persist in access to education or vocational training, thus leading to a situation of underrepresentation of the group concerned in employment, in spite of the effective prohibition of (direct or indirect) discrimination in that sphere. And it will not be sufficient to prohibit discrimination in education if, due to segregated housing, the children of one particular minority community are disproportionately represented in certain educational establishments and never or almost never have access to other establishments attended by children from the majority group, for instance due to the lack of public transportation allowing these minority children to travel from their neighbourhood to the mainstream schools. Structural discrimination should be understood as a situation where, due to the extent of the discrimination faced by a particular segment of society, more is required in order to achieve effective equality than to outlaw direct and indirect discrimination.

7.4.2.   COUNCIL OF EUROPE HUMAN RIGHTS INSTRUMENTS

The regime of positive action under the relevant Council of Europe instruments is similar to that which has just been summarised above under United Nations human rights treaties: positive action is allowable within certain limits, which the requirement of proportionality broadly serves to define; and although it cannot be excluded that, in certain cases at least, the adoption of such measures may be required in order to ensure that real and effective equality will be achieved for all, including the most disadvantaged segments of society, the conditions under which such an obligation may be identified have not been defined with sufficient clarity, in the absence of a commonly agreed understanding of the concept of structural discrimination. The European instruments are, however, less explicit on these issues and only recently have the monitoring bodies they establish sought to move beyond the silence of the treaties these bodies monitor. This paragraph first surveys briefly the regime of positive action measures under the 1950 *European Convention on Human Rights*. It then examines positive action under the European Social Charter, originally adopted in 1961 and to which the 1996 R*evised European Social Charter* progressively succeeds following the ratification of this latter instrument by the Member States of the Council of Europe. Finally, it recalls the explicit authorisation to adopt positive

Experts on Fundamental Rights, Thematic Comment No. 3, "The Rights of Minorities in the European Union" (March 2005), available on the website of the European Commission, Directorate-General Freedom, Security and Justice.

action measures under the 1995 *Framework Convention for the Protection of National Minorities.*

7.4.2.A. THE EUROPEAN CONVENTION ON HUMAN RIGHTS

There exists no case-law of the European Court of Human Rights on the compatibility with the non-discrimination clause of the European Convention on Human Rights[71] of positive action measures.[72] This may be attributed to the fact that, until the entry into force on 1 April 2005 of Protocol No. 12 to the European Convention on Human Rights (ECHR),[73] the European Court of Human Rights had only a limited competence to receive applications alleging discrimination, as Article 14 ECHR only prohibits discrimination in the enjoyment of the rights and freedoms of the Convention and therefore does not constitute an independent or free-standing non-discrimination guarantee.[74] In any case, it would be wrong to conclude from the silence of the Court that positive action measures would be disallowed under the Convention. Individual opinions by members of the Court leave little doubt as to the permissibility of such measures and, indeed, it has been suggested by at least one member of the Court that Article 14 ECHR could impose on the States Parties an obligation to "make up for the differences" existing between the situation of certain minority groups and the majority.[75] The case-law of the Court moreover suggests, minimally, that the States Parties may be placed under a procedural obligation to monitor the impact of measures of general application in order to ensure that they will not disproportionately affect the most vulnerable segments of society.[76] In the preamble to Protocol No. 12—which seeks to extend the scope of application of the non-discrimination provision present in the Convention itself, but without modifying its substantive content—the signatories reaffirm that "the principle of

---

[71] Under Art. 14 of the European Convention on Human Rights (ETS, No. 5; signed in Rome on 4 November 1950 and in force since 3 September 1953): "The enjoyment of the rights and freedoms set forth in this Convention shall be secured without discrimination on any ground such as sex, race, colour, language, religion, political or other opinion, national or social origin, association with a national minority, property, birth or other status."

[72] See also J.-Fr. Flauss, "Discrimination positive et Convention européenne des droits de l'homme" in *Pouvoir et liberté. Mélanges offerts à Jacques Mourgeon* (Brussels, Bruylant, 1998) 415.

[73] CETS, No. 177. Signed in Rome on 4 November 2000 and in force since 1 April 2005.

[74] For a detailed exploration, see R.Wintemute, "'Within the Ambit': How Big Is the 'Gap' in Art. 14 European Convention on Human Rights?" (2004) *EHRLR* 366.

[75] See the dissenting opinion of Judge Cabral Barreto in ECtHR (2nd sect.), *D.H. and Others* v. *the Czech Republic*, Appl. n° 57325/00, judgment of 7 February 2006, at §§ 4–5 of the dissenting opinion (noting in particular that "pupils who, for various reasons—whether cultural, linguistic or other—find it difficult to pursue a normal school education should be entitled to expect the State to take positive measures to compensate for their handicap and to afford them a means of resuming the normal curriculum"). Compare with the position adopted in the same judgment by Judge Costa in § 7 of his concurring opinion (rejecting the notion that the States Parties to the Convention might be under an obligation to adopt positive action measures, referred to by Judge Costa as "positive discrimination", and citing as authority ECtHR (GC), *Chapman* v. *the UK*, judgment of 18 January 2001).

[76] See ECtHR (2nd sect.), *Kjartan Ásmundsson* v. *Iceland*, Appl. n° 60669/00, judgment of 12 October 2004 (final on 30 March 2005), at § 43.

non-discrimination does not prevent States Parties from taking measures in order to promote full and effective equality, provided that there is an objective and reasonable justification for those measures". The explanatory report of Protocol No. 12 specifies in this respect:[77]

European Convention on Human Rights,   **7.CoE.23.**
The Explanatory Report to Protocol 12

"The fact that there are certain groups or categories of persons who are disadvantaged, or the existence of *de facto* inequalities, may constitute justifications for adopting measures providing for specific advantages in order to promote equality, provided that the proportionality principle is respected . . . However, the present Protocol does not impose any obligation to adopt such measures. Such a programmatic obligation would sit ill with the whole nature of the Convention and its control system which are based on the collective guarantee of individual rights which are formulated in terms sufficiently specific to be justifiable."

Whether under Article 14 ECHR or under Article 1 of Protocol No. 12 to the ECHR, positive action should be considered admissible provided that the difference in treatment it results in is objectively and reasonably justified; in other words, provided it pursues a legitimate aim, and it does not pursue this aim by disproportionate means. Like the fight against other forms of discrimination, the fight against racism and xenophobia indisputably constitutes a very important objective for the European Court of Human Rights, which affirms that it is "particularly conscious of the vital importance of combating racial discrimination in all its forms and manifestations".[78] In certain cases, discrimination on grounds of race or other suspect characteristics can also constitute degrading treatment within the meaning of Article 3 of the Convention.[79] A fortiori, the need to combat racial discrimination is one of the legitimate aims which the States Parties to the Convention may want to pursue, even if this leads to certain restrictions on the rights and freedoms enumerated by the Convention, such as the right to non-discrimination (understood as the right to formal equality of treatment) in the enjoyment of the rights and freedoms of the Convention. This is not to say that affirmative action could be upheld only on the basis that it is combating discrimination, as a remedial or backward-looking measure. The Court views a "democratic society" as one based on the values of diversity and tolerance. This would seem to imply that it would allow forms of positive action which are not premised on the pre-existing discrimination they would seek to respond to or compensate for, but are justified by the aim of organising diversity. It is,

---

[77] Explanatory Report of Protocol No. 12 to the Convention for the Protection of Human Rights and Fundamental Freedoms, H (2000) 11 prov., 29 August 2000, § 16.

[78] ECtHR, *Jersild* v. *Denmark*, judgment of 23 September 1994, § 30.

[79] European Commission of Human Rights, case of *East African Asians (Patel et al.)*, decision of 10 October 1970, Ann. Conv., vol. 13, 995; ECtHR, *Abdulaziz, Cabales and Balkandali* v. *UK*, judgment of 28 May 1985, Series A No. 94, 42, §§ 90–1; ECtHR, *Smith and Grady* v. *UK*, judgment of 27 September 1999, § 121; ECtHR, *Cyprus* v. *Turkey*, judgment of 10 May 2001, §§ 306, 310 and 314.

however, likely that the European Court of Human Rights would consider positive action as a disproportionate restriction of the right to formal equality where it did not correspond to the criteria set forth in the relevant international human rights treaties, in particular where the measure was not temporary but risked leading, instead, to the creation and maintenance of separate rights.[80]

7.4.2.B.   THE EUROPEAN SOCIAL CHARTER

The European Social Charter of 1961[81] does not contain an explicit provision on equal treatment or non-discrimination,[82] although the preamble does mention that "the enjoyment of social rights should be secured without discrimination on grounds of race, colour, sex, religion, political opinion, national extraction or social origin". However, the States Parties to the ESC, at least if they have accepted Article 1(2) of the European Social Charter,[83] undertake thereby to "protect effectively the right of the worker to earn his living in an occupation freely entered upon". The Committee of Independent Experts, renamed since July 1999 as the European Committee on Social Rights (ECSR), has read this clause—in combination with the preamble of the Charter—as prohibiting all forms of discrimination in employment.[84] It considers that paragraph 2 of Article 1 of the Charter requires states to:

> "legally prohibit any discrimination, direct or indirect, in employment. Stronger protection may be provided in respect of certain grounds, such as gender or membership of a race or ethnic group. The discriminatory acts and provisions prohibited by this provision are all those which may occur in connection with recruitment and employment conditions in general (mainly remuneration, training, promotion, transfer, dismissal and other detrimental action)."[85]

Though necessary, legal measures may, however, not be sufficient in the view of the Committee: concrete measures should, moreover, be taken in order to encourage

---

[80] It is well established in the case-law of the European Court of Human Rights that it will seek to interpret the European Convention on Human Rights in the light of any relevant rules and principles of international law applicable in relations between the States Parties. The Court refers in that respect to Art. 31 § 3 (c) of the Vienna Convention on the Law of Treaties of 23 May 1969. See, e.g. ECtHR (GC), *Al-Adsani* v. *the UK* (Appl. No. 35763/97), § 55, ECHR 2001 XI; or ECtHR (GC), *Bosphorus Hava Yollarý Turizm ve Ticaret Anonim Þirketi* v. *Ireland* (Appl. No. 45036/98), § 150.

[81] ETS, No. 35. The European Social Charter was signed in Turin on 18 October 1961 and entered into force on 26 February 1965.

[82] Art. 4(3), however, recognises "the right of men and women workers to equal pay for work of equal value". Art. 1 of the Additional Protocol to the European Social Charter, 1988 (ETS, No. 128; entered into force on 4 September 1992) guarantees the right to equal opportunities and equal treatment in matters of employment and occupation without discrimination on the grounds of sex. This guarantee is detailed in terms closely inspired by the then existing acquis of the European Community.

[83] Para. 2 of Art. 1 of the Revised European Social Charter opened for signature on 3 May 1996 contains an identical clause. Therefore the commentary of this clause is valid under both instruments.

[84] See, e.g. Concl. 2002, 22–8 (France).

[85] See also Concl. XVI-1, vol. 2 (Luxembourg), 377–80, although those conclusions do not include a list of measures "promoting the full effectiveness of the efforts to combat discrimination" according to Art. 1 § 2 of the Revised Charter.

complete equal treatment in employment.[86] The Committee therefore encourages the States Parties to conduct an active labour policy seeking to promote the integration of minorities.[87] The ECSR has occasionally referred in that respect to the Guidelines adopted in the framework of the European Employment Strategy, one pillar of which concerns the integration of disadvantaged groups into the employment market.[88] The insistence by the Committee on this dimension of non-discrimination is based on its general understanding of the requirements of paragraph 2 of Article 1 of the Charter that:

> "although a necessary requirement, appropriate domestic legislation that is in conformity with the Charter is not sufficient to ensure the principles laid down in the Charter are actually applied in practice. It is not sufficient therefore merely to enact legislation prohibiting discrimination . . . as regards access to employment; such discrimination must also be eliminated in practice."[89]

Where the situation of the labour market of women or certain minorities remains unsatisfactory, the Committee considers that this demonstrates that the measures taken to date are not sufficient.

It should therefore not be surprising that already in its first cycle of control, the Committee of Independent Experts remarked that acceptance of paragraph 2 of Article 1 of the Charter "placed the Contracting States under an obligation, inter alia, to provide appropriate education and training to ensure the full exercise of the right guaranteed therein".[90] Indeed, as the ECSR examines on the basis of that provision of the Charter not only the adequacy of the legal framework prohibiting discrimination, but also the results which are achieved in the integration of certain target groups traditionally excluded from the labour market, providing training and education to the members of those groups constitutes a means for the States Parties to comply with their obligations under that provision.[91]

Finally, when the Revised European Social Charter was adopted in 1996, Article E was included in Part V of the Revised Charter, which contains "horizontal" clauses applicable to the generality of its substantive clauses. According to Article E:

---

[86] In its first conclusions adopted about Italy, the Committee of Independent Experts noted "regretfully" that it has been "unable to find in the first report of the Italian Government sufficient particulars on the admission of women to certain posts, notably in the civil service; it considered that the rights guaranteed by the Charter, especially in the matter of non-discrimination against women, required not only that the State remove all legal obstacles to admission to certain types of employment, but also that positive, practical steps be taken to create a situation which really ensured complete equality of treatment in this respect" (Concl. I (released on 1 January 1970), 15–16). See also the conclusions adopted during that same cycle of control on the UK: Concl. I (released on 1 January 1970), 16.

[87] See Concl. XVI-1, vol. 2 (Norway), 485–7.

[88] See, e.g. Concl. XVI-1, vol. 2 (Spain), 602–6; Concl. XVI-1, vol. 1 (Germany), 236–42. See also Concl. XVI-1, vol. 1 (Czech Republic), 125–9 (reference to the national employment action plan 1999–2000).

[89] Concl. XVI-1, vol. 2 (Spain), 602–6.

[90] Concl. I (released on 1 January 1970), 15.

[91] See, with respect to the need to provide training and education to the Roma population, underrepresented in the labour market, Concl. XVI-1, vol. 1, 125–9.

797

"The enjoyment of the rights set forth in this Charter shall be secured without discrimination on any ground such as race, colour, sex, language, religion, political or other opinion, national extraction or social origin, health, association with a national minority, birth or other status."

This provision might serve in time to impose the adoption of positive action. The decision adopted by the European Committee on Social Rights on the collective complaint 13/2002 *Autism-Europe* v. *France*[92] might be read in this way. The collective complaint concerned the access of autistic children to education in generalist or special schools. Their proportion in these institutions was much lower than in the case of other children, whether or not disabled. In addition, there was a chronic shortage of care and support facilities for autistic adults. The Committee considered these facts as decisive in finding for (indirect) discrimination.

7.4.2.C. THE FRAMEWORK CONVENTION ON THE PROTECTION OF NATIONAL MINORITIES

The case-law of the European Committee of Social Rights exhibits the continuity from the negative obligation not to discriminate to the positive obligation to take affirmative action in order to make progress towards substantive equality. Similar positive obligations to adopt measures in the face of entrenched inequalities may be derived from the Council of Europe *Framework Convention on the Protection of National Minorities*.[93] As already noted, under Article 4 of the Framework Convention, States Parties are to adopt "adequate measures in order to promote, in all areas of economic, social, political and cultural life, full and effective equality between persons belonging to a national minority and those belonging to the majority", taking due account in this respect of "the specific conditions of the persons belonging to national minorities" (Article 4(2)); such measures are specifically designated as not being discriminatory in character (Article 4(3)). The Advisory Committee of the Framework Convention encourages the introduction of positive measures in favour of members of minorities, which are particularly disadvantaged.[94] Thus, in an opinion on Croatia, the Advisory Committee:

"considers that one key to reaching full and effective equality for persons belonging to national minorities is the launching of additional positive measures in the field of employment and it sup-ports efforts to seek financing for such measures. In this regard, the situation of persons belonging to the Serb minority merits particular attention, taking into account the past discriminatory measures, stirred by the 1991-1995 conflict, aimed at curtailing their number in various fields of employment, ranging from law-enforcement to education."[95]

---

[92] See in more detail above D. Schiek, Chapter Three: Indirect Discrimination, excerpt **3.CoE.12.**

[93] ETS, No. 157. Signed in Strasbourg on 1 February 1995, and entered into force on 1 February 1998.

[94] See also, e.g. Opinion on Azerbaijan, 22 May 2003, ACFC/OP/I (2004)001, para. 28; Opinion on Ukraine, 1 March 2002, ACFC/OP/I (2002)010, para. 27; Opinion on Serbia and Montenegro, 27 November 2003, ACFC/OP/I(2004)002, para. 38.

[95] Opinion on Croatia, 6 February 2002, ACFC/INF/OP/I(2002)003, para. 26.

In an opinion on the Czech Republic, the Advisory Committee:

> "notes with deep concern that many Roma in the Czech Republic face considerable socio-economic difficulties in comparison to both the majority and other minorities, in particular in the fields of education, employment and housing . . . The situation calls for the preparation and implementation of specific measures to realise full and effective equality between Roma and persons belonging to the majority as well as to other minorities."[96]

A very similar observation was made with respect to the situation of the Roma in Hungary.[97] The Advisory Committee therefore welcomed the decision of the Hungarian authorities to develop medium- and long-term plans of action towards improving the living conditions of the Roma/Gypsy minority. It was encouraged by:

> "the determination of the Government to resolve the problems of the Roma/Gypsy minority and considers that this gives rise to high expectations. The Advisory Committee stresses that the commitment to long term approaches should not lead to a delay in achieving improvements that can be secured in a short or medium term. Furthermore, a long-term approach requires that a consistent and sustained policy is designed, implemented and evaluated throughout this period and that appropriate resources are made available and maintained, even where there may be setbacks and disappointments. In the view of the Advisory Committee the Hungarian Government is to be commended and to be taken seriously for its initiative and its intentions. It is only consistent with this view that the future results of Hungary are to be evaluated in the light of the standards it has committed itself to. Finally, the Advisory Committee underlines that, when implementing special measures, particular attention should be paid to the situation of Romany women."[98]

The opinion it adopted on Ireland on 22 May 2003[99] offers another example of this insistence of the Advisory Committee on combating identified instances of structural discrimination through positive action measures—in this case, in order to improve the situation of the Travellers' community:

---

[96] Opinion on the Czech Republic, 25 January 2002, ACFC/INF/OP/I(2002)002, para. 29. In para. 30, the Advisory Committee further "welcomes the decision of the Czech authorities to adopt the 'Concept of the Government policy towards the members of the Roma community, supporting their integration into society'" (Resolution of the Government of the Czech Republic No. 599 of 14 June 2000). It also welcomes the fact that the government has already launched a strategic action plan for the period 2001–2020, in order to implement the above-mentioned policy. The Advisory Committee is of the opinion that greater participation of Roma women should be ensured in that process.

[97] In an opinion on Hungary it adopted on 22 September 2000, the Advisory Committee "notes with concern, that, as the Government openly recognises, the Roma/Gypsies in Hungary face a broad range of serious problems to a disproportionate degree, be it in comparison to the majority or in comparison to other minorities. This state of affairs certainly justifies that specific measures be designed and implemented to tackle these problems" (ACFC/INF/OP/I(2001)004, at para. 18).

[98] *Ibid.*, para. 19.

[99] Opinion on Ireland, 22 May 2003, ACFC/INF/OP/I(2004)003.

Advisory Committee of the Framework Convention on the   **7.CoE.24.**
Protection of National Minorities
Opinion on Ireland, 22 May 2003

"34. The Advisory Committee notes . . . that progress in the area of legislation and institution building has not always been matched by implementation in practice. A number of important concerns remain, notably in relation to the Traveller community. Travellers continue to suffer discrimination in a wide range of societal settings including education (see under Article 12 below), employment, health care, accommodation (see under Article 5 below) and access to certain goods and services, including access to places of entertainment.

35. The Advisory Committee is particularly concerned about the high level of unemployment of persons belonging to the Traveller community. Travellers have also seen their traditional areas of economic livelihood (scrap metal, horse trading, market trading, etc.) hit by changing economic and social climates. They consider that certain aspects of changes in legislation (such as in the Control of Horses Act (1996) and the Casual Trading Act (1995)) unduly hinder their ability to earn a living. In view of the impact that this legislation has had on Travellers, the Advisory Committee considers that the Government should examine how to promote further both traditional and new economic activities of Travellers.

36. Notwithstanding the efforts made by the authorities to support the entrance of Travellers into the labour market, the Advisory Committee considers that more needs to be done in order to improve the situation. It is clear that the lack of statistics on Traveller employment makes it difficult to monitor the situation, and that such statistics are essential to the design, implementation and monitoring in this field (see comments under the General Remarks above).

37. Concerning employment in the public service, the Advisory Committee supports the recommendations in this field made by the Committee to Monitor and Co-ordinate the Implementation of the Recommendations of the Task Force on the Travelling Community and in particular the need for setting targets to include Travellers in general recruitment strategies."

Note
These statements by the Advisory Committee established under the Framework Convention for the Protection of National Minorities and by the European Committee of Social Rights monitoring the European Social Charter remain unclear as to the precise conditions under which the adoption of positive action measures may constitute an obligation for the States Parties to these instruments. In this respect, the Council of Europe bodies have not gone further than the human rights treaties bodies established within the United Nations. Insofar as these bodies primarily seek to facilitate the adoption by states of adequate strategies for the implementation of their international obligations, in a spirit of cooperation with those states, this may not be particularly problematic. It may become an impairment, however, when these bodies assume quasi-judicial functions, as when the United Nations human rights treaty bodies receive individual communications, or when the European Committee of Social Rights acts under the mechanism allowing non-governmental organisations or unions to file collective complaints. Moreover, a clarification of the circumstances under which the adoption of positive action schemes would not only be allowable, but would moreover constitute an obligation

for the state concerned, may impact decisively on the development of EU law in this area. It is to the regime of positive action under EU law that we now turn.

7.5. POSITIVE ACTION UNDER EUROPEAN UNION LAW

The legal regime of positive action in EU law has first developed in the context of equal treatment between men and women in employment. This section describes the initial approach adopted by the European Court of Justice towards this issue, on the basis of Council Directive 76/207/EEC of 9 February 1976 on the implementation of the principle of equal treatment for men and women as regards access to employment, vocational training and promotion, and working conditions (the Gender Employment Directive) (section 7.5.1). It then examines how the Court modified its attitude following the reactions to this initial approach, and which translated into an amendment being made in the Treaty of Rome to Article 141 EC (ex-Article 119 EEC) reaffirming the support of the Member States to the tool of positive action (section 7.5.2). Finally, it examines the questions raised by the extension of the notion of positive action beyond the area of equal treatment between men and women and beyond the sphere of employment (section 7.5.3).

7.5.1.   COUNCIL DIRECTIVE 76/207/EEC AND THE *KALANKE* RULING (1995)

The Gender Employment Directive in its original version of 9 February 1976 explicitly mentioned positive action.

> *Council Directive 76/207/EEC of 9 February 1976 on the*   **7.EC.25.**
> *implementation of the principle of equal treatment for men and women as regards*
> *access to employment, vocational training and promotion, and working conditions*[100]

Article 2

. . .

(4) This Directive shall be without prejudice to measures to promote equal opportunity for men and women, in particular by removing existing inequalities which affect women's opportunities

---

[100] [1976] OJ L 39/40.

The clause was inserted as an afterthought upon the suggestion of the UK, apparently without much debate.[101] On 13 December 1984, the Council adopted Recommendation 84/635/EEC on the promotion of positive action for women:

Recommendation 84/635/EEC on the promotion of positive action   **7.EC.26.**
for women[102]

The Council of the European Communities

. . .

Whereas existing legal provisions on equal treatment, which are designed to afford rights to individuals, are inadequate for the elimination of all existing inequalities unless parallel action is taken by governments, both sides of industry and other bodies concerned, to counteract the prejudicial effects on women in employment which arise from social attitudes, behaviour and structures

. . .

Hereby recommends Member States:

1. To adopt a positive action policy designed to eliminate existing inequalities affecting women in working life and to promote a better balance between the sexes in employment, comprising appropriate general and specific measures . . . in order:

(a) to eliminate or counteract the prejudicial effects on women in employment or seeking employment which arise from existing attitudes, behaviour and structures based on the idea of a traditional division of roles in society between men and women;

(b) to encourage the participation of women in various occupations in those sectors of working life where they are at present underrepresented, particularly in the sectors of the future, and at higher levels of responsibility in order to achieve better use of all human resources . . .

The Recommendation thus presents positive action as contributing towards implementing the principle of equal treatment between women and men. The European Court of Justice, when confronted with positive action measures adopted by Member States, read Article 2(4) Directive 76/207/EEC as an exception to the principle of equal treatment, although the provision might have been construed as a mere interpretation of what the prohibition of discrimination does *not* imply. In *Kalanke*, its first judgment on this issue, the Court arrived at the conclusion that paragraph 4 of the 1990 Bremen Act on Equal Treatment for Men and Women (see above **7.DE.10.**) went beyond what was authorised by Article 2(4) of Directive 76/207/EEC.

---

[101] C. Hoskyns, *Integrating Gender: Women, Law and Politics in the European Union* (London, Verso, 1996) 140.

[102] [1984] OJ L 331/34.

ECJ, 17 October 1995[103]   **7.EC.27.**

C-450/93, Eckhard Kalanke v. Freie Hansestadt Bremen

ADMISSIBILITY OF AN ABSOLUTE PREFERENCE IN FAVOUR OF THE MEMBER OF THE
UNDERREPRESENTED SEX ("FLEXIBLE QUOTA") UNDER THE GENDER EMPLOYMENT
DIRECTIVE

The Bremen scheme in favour of women in the public service

Facts: Mr. Kalanke challenged before the *Bundesarbeitsgericht* (BAG—the Federal Labour Court) the application of paragraph 4 of the Bremen Act on Equal Treatment (LGG), which had resulted in the promotion of Ms. Glissman instead of Mr. Kalanke from the shortlist for a post of Section Manager in the Bremen Parks Department. Mr. Kalanke claimed that he was better qualified than Ms. Glissmann, and that paragraph 4 LGG contravened German constitutional and statutory law. The BAG sought a preliminary ruling from the ECJ regarding whether this provision was compatible with Articles 2(1) and 2(4) of Directive 76/207.

Held: Articles 2(1) and (4) of the Gender Employment Directive preclude a national rule such as paragraph 4 LGG.

Judgment: "14 In its order for reference, the national court points out that a quota system such as that in issue may help to overcome in the future the disadvantages which women currently face and which perpetuate past inequalities, inasmuch as it accustoms people to seeing women also filling certain more senior posts. The traditional assignment of certain tasks to women and the concentration of women at the lower end of the scale are contrary to the equal rights criteria applicable today. In that connection, the national court cites figures illustrating the low proportion of women in the higher career brackets among city employees in Bremen, particularly if sectors, such as education, where the presence of women in higher posts is now established are excluded.

15 The purpose of the Directive is, as stated in Article 1(1), to put into effect in the Member States the principle of equal treatment for men and women as regards, inter alia, access to employment, including promotion. Article 2(1) states that the principle of equal treatment means that 'there shall be no discrimination whatsoever on grounds of sex either directly or indirectly'.

16 A national rule that, where men and women who are candidates for the same promotion are equally qualified, women are automatically to be given priority in sectors where they are underrepresented, involves discrimination on grounds of sex.

17 It must, however, be considered whether such a national rule is permissible under Article 2(4) . . .

18 That provision is specifically and exclusively designed to allow measures which, although discriminatory in appearance, are in fact intended to eliminate or reduce actual instances of

---

[103] [1995] ECR I–3051. See S. Prechal, "Case C–450/93, Kalanke v. Freie Hansestadt Bremen, [1995] ECR I–3051" (1996) 33 *CML. Rev.* 1245; D. Schiek, "Positive Action before the Court of Justice" [1996] *ILJ* 239; O. De Schutter and B. Renauld, "L'action affirmative devant la Cour de justice des Communautés européennes. A propos de l'arrêt Kalanke du 17 octobre 1995" (1996) 642 *Journal des tribunaux du travail* 125; S. Moore, "Nothing Positive from the Court of Justice" (1996) 21 *Eur. L. Rev.* 156; A. Donahue, "The Kalanke Ruling: Gender Equality in the European Labor Market" (1997/8) 18 *Northwestern Journal of International Law & Business* 730; R. Means, "Kalanke v. Freie Hansestadt Bremen: The Significance of the Kalanke Decision on Future Positive Action Programs in the European Union" (1997) 30 *Vanderbilt Journal of Transnational Law* 1087.

803

inequality which may exist in the reality of social life (see Case 312/86 Commission v France
. . . paragraph 15).

19 It thus permits national measures relating to access to employment, including
promotion, which give a specific advantage to women with a view to improving their ability to
compete on the labour market and to pursue a career on an equal footing with men.

20 As the Council considered in the third recital in the preamble to Recommendation
84/635/EEC . . . [above **7.EC.27.**].

21 Nevertheless, as a derogation from an individual right laid down in the Directive, Article
2(4) must be interpreted strictly (see Case 222/84 Johnston v Chief Constable of the Royal
Ulster Constabulary [1986] ECR 1651, paragraph 36).

22 National rules which guarantee women absolute and unconditional priority for
appointment or promotion go beyond promoting equal opportunities and overstep the limits
of the exception in Article 2(4) of the Directive.

23 Furthermore, in so far as it seeks to achieve equal representation of men and women in
all grades and levels within a department, such a system substitutes for equality of opportunity
as envisaged in Article 2(4) the result which is only to be arrived at by providing such equality
of opportunity.

24 The answer to the national court' s. questions must therefore be that Article 2(1) and (4)
of the Directive precludes national rules such as those in the present case . . ."

Notes

(1) The judgment follows the opinion delivered in that case by Advocate General
(AG) G. Tesauro. The Advocate General relied in his opinion, in particular, on the
only other case, decided in 1988, in which the European Court of Justice had
considered Article 2(4) of the Gender Employment Directive. In *Commission* v.
France,[104] France had sought to invoke that provision in order to justify maintaining a
provision of the French Labour Code which allowed employers to maintain special
benefits based on gender if these were of the kind that protected women by reason of
maternity, pregnancy or nursing. Thus, collective agreements could grant in favour of
women the extension of maternity leave, the shortening of working hours or special
leave when a child is ill, and similar measures. Although the provision in question was
discriminatory on its face, France alleged that its purpose was to provide equal
opportunity as allowed under Article 2(4). AG Sir Gordon Slynn considered that

> "the kind of right [benefiting women in the provision of the French Labour Code at issue]
> has never been enjoyed by men so that there exist no inequalities in favour of men which
> affect women's opportunities in the employment field. It is not permissible to argue, as
> France appears to argue, that because women in general have been discriminated against
> then any provisions in favour of women in the employment field are per se valid as part of
> an evening-up process".[105]

The Court followed this view, defining the scope of Article 2(4) as an exception to
equal treatment "specifically and exclusively designed to allow measures which,
although discriminatory in appearance, are in fact intended to eliminate or reduce

---

[104] Case 312/88, ECR [1988] 6315.
[105] *Ibid.*, 6328–9.

actual instances of inequality which may exist in the reality of social life". In *Kalanke*, AG Tesauro read this decision to imply that Article 2(4) of the Gender Employment Directive only allowed measures discriminatory in appearance but designed to "eliminate obstacles which prevent women from pursuing the same results as men on equal terms".[106]

(2) In his opinion in *Kalanke*, AG Tesauro distinguished three models of positive action: one in which disadvantage was compensated by improving the training for the disadvantaged group; a second, in which social conditions are made equal, for instance measures designed to balance the family and career life of working women; and a third, in which quotas and goals are designed to compensate for past discrimination, if necessary by granting preferential treatment to members of the disadvantaged class by affording them a priority even if they are less qualified. He then took the view that the third model went beyond Article 2(4) of Directive 76/207/EEC. This clause, he argued, only envisaged the equalisation of "opportunities" between women and men and could not be invoked in favour of a scheme guaranteeing equality of "results". Considering paragraph 4, LGG AG Tesauro remarked that it

> "is not designed to guarantee equality as regards starting points. The very fact that two candidates of different sex have equivalent qualifications implies in fact by definition that the two candidates have had and continue to have equal opportunities: they are therefore on an equal footing at the starting block."

Avoidance strategies followed the judgment delivered in *Kalanke*.[107] Such strategies were favoured by the lack of clarity of the judgment, which the doctrine heavily criticised: if promoting the member of the underrepresented sex could not be allowed in the presence of two equally qualified candidates of different sex, how, except by tossing a coin, could one decide on promotions in such situations, since the competing candidates per definition cannot be ranked on the basis of criteria strictly linked to the position offered?[108] On 27 March 1996, the European Commission issued a Communication to the Council and the European Parliament, taking the view that quota systems remained acceptable under Article 2(4) of the Gender Employment Directive, provided at least that they did not grant automatic and

---

[106] *Kalanke*, above n. 39, I-3061.

[107] As a result of the judgment, an exemption clause was inserted in the Bremen Law on Equal Treatment for Men and Women in the Public Service, following a judgment of 6 March 1996 by the Federal Labour Court (Bundesarbeidsgericht) (BAG, 1 AZR 590/92) that noted that "the ECJ had merely ruled upon the incompatibility of women's quotas without exemptions, and whilst no such clause might be read into the Bremen statute, therefore negating its preferential treatment, other less 'unconditional' equality measures remained unaffected" (152). For a commentary, see also the case note by Schiek, above n. 100.

[108] The resulting risk of using additional requirements more removed from the actual needs of the position offered may be illustrated by the postscript to the judgment delivered by the European Court of Justice in *Kalanke*. Ms. Glissmann retained the position, but only because her answer to a question concerning her proposed strategies for the position was considered by the public employer as more satisfactory than that offered by her male competitor (see D. Schiek, above n. 28, at 152, n. 10). The risk of subjectivity and thus arbitrariness grows, as we move from verifying whether the candidate presents the necessary qualifications to satisfactorily perform the job, to the verification of other factors that are less strictly job-related.

absolute preferential treatment.[109] The Commission listed a number of positive action schemes which, in its view, remained compatible with the requirements of Community law after *Kalanke*. Some confusion was created, however, by the proposal of the Commission, also made in its Communication, to amend the Directive in order to clarify the scope of the exception allowed in Article 2(4). The proposal of the Commission was to add one sentence to Article 2(4) of Directive 76/207/EC, which would read:

> "This Directive shall be without prejudice to measures to promote equal opportunity for men and women, in particular by removing existing inequalities which affect the opportunities of the underrepresented sex in the areas referred to in Article 1(1). Possible measures shall include the giving of preference, as regards access to employment or promotion, to a member of the underrepresented sex, provided that such measures do not preclude the assessment of the particular circumstances of an individual case."

Thus, the intent of the proposal was to modify the first sentence of this paragraph in order to adopt a formulation more neutral as to the sex which could benefit from positive action measures; and to add a second sentence, thus writing into the Directive the lesson from *Kalanke* as interpreted by the European Commission.

7.5.2.   POST-KALANKE

7.5.2.A.   CONSTITUTIONALISING POSITIVE ACTION BY CHANGING ARTICLE 141 EC (IGC AMSTERDAM)

It soon appeared that the *Kalanke* ruling could only be a provisional contribution to the debate on the legality of positive action under Community law. The tension was manifest between, on the one hand, the limitations to positive action imposed by the reading offered by the Court and, on the other hand, continued political support for positive action as a tool to encourage the professional integration of women. In this context, it should come as no surprise that the governments of the Member States considered that there was a need to reaffirm the freedom of the national authorities to adopt positive action schemes, despite the limits imposed by the *Kalanke* case-law. The Intergovernmental Conference (IGC) which opened on 29 March 1996 constituted an opportunity to do so. The IGC resulted in the signature by the Heads of State and governments of the European Union, on 2 October 1997, of the Treaty of Amsterdam, which entered into force on 1 May 1999. Article 119 EEC (now Article 141 EC) was substantially modified on that occasion. It now provides in paragraph 4 that:

> "With a view to ensuring full equality in practice between men and women in working life, the principle of equal treatment shall not prevent any Member State from maintaining or adopting measures providing for specific advantages in order to make it easier for the

---

[109]   COM(96)88.

underrepresented sex to pursue a vocational activity or to prevent or compensate for disadvantages in professional careers."[110]

Although the Court considered that the insertion of this provision in the Treaty of Rome might in principle lead to finding compatible with Community law a provision in the national law of a Member State which would conflict with Article 2(1) of Gender Employment Directive and would not be protected by Article 2(4) of that Directive,[111] in practice, and despite the differences in wording between the two provisions until the original text of the Directive was modified in 2002, they have been interpreted similarly by the Court of Justice.[112] This approach may have underestimated the potential of Article 141(4) EC.[113]

ECJ, 30 September 2004   **7.EC.28.**
Case C–319/03, Serge Briheche v. Ministère de l'intérieur, de la sécurité intérieure et des libertés locales[114]

COMPATIBILITY WITH ARTICLES 3(1) AND 2(4) OF THE GENDER EQUALITY DIRECTIVE OF A PROVISION RESERVING THE EXEMPTION FROM THE AGE LIMIT FOR OBTAINING ACCESS TO PUBLIC-SECTOR EMPLOYMENT TO WIDOWS WHO HAVE NOT REMARRIED WHO ARE OBLIGED TO WORK

The French widowers' access to public service

Facts: The applicant in the main proceedings, Mr. Serge Briheche, a 48-year-old widower who had not remarried with one dependent child, was denied the possibility to sit several competitive examinations organised for the recruitment of administrative assistants or secretaries on the ground that he did not fulfil the age requirement laid down by the French legislation for entry into those competitive examinations. The applicable legislation for entry to that examination (Article 1 of Decree No. 75-765 concerning age limits applicable to recruitment by competitive examination of civil servants classified in categories B, C and D, JORF of 19 August 1975, p. 8444) sets an age limit at 45 years, although exempting from this age limit (since 1979), if they are obliged to work, mothers with three or more children, widows who have not remarried, divorced women who have not remarried, legally separated women and unmarried women with at least one dependent child, as well as (since 2001) unmarried men with at least one dependent child who are obliged to work.

Held: Articles 3(1) and 2(4) of Council Directive 76/207/EEC of 9 February 1976 on the implementation of the principle of equal treatment for men and women as regards access to employment, vocational training and promotion, and working conditions preclude a national provision which reserves the exemption from

---

[110] The language in Art. 141(4) EC is symmetrical, applying identically to both women and men. However, Declaration No. 28 on Art. 141(4) (formerly Art. 119(4)) of the Treaty establishing the European Community, annexed to the Treaty of Amsterdam, states: "When adopting measures referred to in Article 141(4) of the Treaty establishing the European Community, Member States should, in the first instance, aim at improving the situation of women in working life."

[111] *Badeck*, above n. 27, para. 14.

[112] See *Abrahamsson and Anderson*, above n. 36, paras. 54–5 (where the Court appears to consider that a measure found disproportionate under Arts. 2(1) and (4) of Directive 76/207/EEC would also fail to be justified under Art. 141(4) EC); Case C–319/03 *Briheche* [2004] ECR I–8807, para. 31.

[113] J. Kenner, *EU Employment Law* (Oxford, Hart Publishing, 2003) 451.

[114] [2004] ECR I–8807.

807

the age limit for obtaining access to public-sector employment to widows who have not remarried who are obliged to work but excludes widowers who have not remarried who are in the same situation.

Opinion: ADVOCATE GENERAL POIARES MADURO

"48. It cannot be ruled out that positive measures which do not fall within the scope of Directive 76/207 could be authorised under this provision [Article 141 (4) EC]. In effect . . . one could argue that there is a distinction between measures aimed at reducing inequalities and measures aimed at compensating for past or existing inequalities suffered by a social group. It cannot be excluded that the reference in Article 141(4) EC to compensatory purposes is intended to provide the Member States with a broader discretion in adopting measures of positive discrimination. Such an interpretation must, however, always remain within the boundaries authorised by the general principle of equality. The question for the Court is not whether certain forms of positive discrimination would or would not lead to a more equal and just society but whether such forms of positive discrimination, if adopted by the legislature, can be reconciled with the general principle of equality and non-discrimination.

49. In this respect, the reference to compensation in Article 141(4) EC could be read as meaning either that the need to compensate for past or existing social inequalities can justify favouring individuals in those groups at the expense of discriminating against members of the overrepresented groups or that the adoption of measures of a compensatory type is necessary in view of the fact that the non-discriminatory application of the current societal rules is structurally biased in favour of the members of the overrepresented groups. The first reading makes individuals' rights not to be discriminated against subordinate to achieving equality between groups which is justified by the aim of compensating the members of the underrepresented groups for the past discrimination to which they were subject. Such a reading is hardly compatible with the priority which the Court has given to equality of opportunities and to its traditional understanding of the general principle of equal treatment.

50. The second reading may however be more easily reconciled with the principle of equal treatment as interpreted and applied by the Court. According to this view, equality of results is not the goal. Nor do the aims of positive discrimination necessarily justify discrimination between individuals. What is believed is that measures often associated with substantive equality which compensate for the underrepresentation of certain groups (for example quotas, automatic preferences) are the only ones that can effectively bring about long-term equality of opportunities. Measures favouring the members of certain groups are therefore not conceived as a means to achieve equality among groups or equality of results but, instead, as an instrument to bring about effective equality of opportunities. The purpose of compensatory measures of this type becomes that of re-establishing equality of opportunities by removing the effects of discrimination and promoting long-term maximisation of equality of opportunities. Compensation refers in this case to reinstating a balance between the opportunities given by society to the members of the different groups.

51. To base the acceptance of compensatory forms of positive discrimination on equality of opportunities and not on equality of results would still make equality among individuals prevail over equality among groups but would, in turn, impose certain limits and conditions on the forms of compensatory positive discrimination that could be acceptable in the light of Article 141(4) EC. The acceptability of such forms of positive discrimination would, for example, be closely linked to its transitional nature. Otherwise, such forms of positive discrimination may, in the long run, create entrenched rights even when the original conditions justifying them are no longer present. As a consequence, the purpose of creating long-term effective equality of opportunities would be compromised. Other conditions may be linked to the nature and extent of the burden imposed on the individuals of the overrepresented group,

the likelihood that increased prospects for the members of the underrepresented group can lead to real equality of opportunities and the requirement to show underrepresentation not only in general but in the specific sector or institution subject to forms of positive discrimination."

7.5.2.B.   THE *MARSCHALL* LINE OF CASE-LAW (1997–2002)

The Treaty of Amsterdam was not yet in force when the Court decided its second positive action case. The new wording of Article 141 EC may nevertheless have influenced the outcome, because of the strong signal sent to the Court that the Member States intended to maintain and develop positive action and did not consider that this should be seen as conflicting with equal treatment.

ECJ, 11 November 1997[115]   **7.EC.29.**
C-409/95, Hellmuth Marschall v. *Land Nordrhein-Westfalen*

WHETHER A PREFERENTIAL RULE WITH A "SAVINGS CLAUSE" IS COMPATIBLE WITH
THE GENDER EMPLOYMENT DIRECTIVE

Marschall

Facts: Hellmuth Marschall, a teacher, was not promoted at the time he had envisaged because a female colleague of equal qualification was preferred in line with paragraph 25 (5) LBG NRW (see above **7.DE.11.**). He considered that he had a right to promotion because he was older, had served for longer and had dependent children, which was in line with general practice in Germany before preferential rules were applied. The Administrative Court Gelsenkirchen referred to the ECJ questions relating to the interpretation of Article 2(4) of Directive 76/207/EEC.

Held: A preferential rule including a saving clause does not conflict with Article 2 (4) Directive 76/207/EEC.

Judgment: "24 . . . unlike the provisions in question in *Kalanke*, the provision in question in this case contains a clause ('Öffnungsklausel', hereinafter 'saving clause') to the effect that women are not to be given priority in promotion if reasons specific to an individual male candidate tilt the balance in his favour.

25 It is therefore necessary to consider whether a national rule containing such a clause is designed to promote equality of opportunity between men and women within the meaning of Article 2(4) of the Directive.

. . .

27 [Article 2 (4)] . . .authorizes national measures relating to access to employment, including promotion, which give a specific advantage to women with a view to improving their ability to compete on the labour market and to pursue a career on an equal footing with men (*Kalanke*, paragraph 19).

29 . . . it appears that even where male and female candidates are equally qualified, male candidates tend to be promoted in preference to female candidates particularly because of prejudices and stereotypes concerning the role and capacities of women in working life and the

[115] [1997] ECR I–6363.

fear, for example, that women will interrupt their careers more frequently, that owing to household and family duties they will be less flexible in their working hours, or that they will be absent from work more frequently because of pregnancy, childbirth and breastfeeding.

30 For these reasons, the mere fact that a male candidate and a female candidate are equally qualified does not mean that they have the same chances.

31 It follows that a national rule in terms of which, subject to the application of the saving clause, female candidates for promotion who are equally as qualified as the male candidates are to be treated preferentially in sectors where they are underrepresented may fall within the scope of Article 2(4) if such a rule may counteract the prejudicial effects on female candidates of the attitudes and behaviour described above and thus reduce actual instances of inequality which may exist in the real world.

32 However, since Article 2(4) constitutes a derogation from an individual right laid down by the Directive, such a national measure specifically favouring female candidates cannot guarantee absolute and unconditional priority for women in the event of a promotion without going beyond the limits of the exception laid down in that provision (*Kalanke*, paragraphs 21 and 22).

33 . . . .a national rule which . . . contains a saving clause does not exceed those limits if, in each individual case, it provides for male candidates who are equally as qualified as the female candidates a guarantee that the candidatures will be the subject of an objective assessment which will take account of all criteria specific to the individual candidates and will override the priority accorded to female candidates where one or more of those criteria tilts the balance in favour of the male candidate. In this respect, however, it should be remembered that those criteria must not be such as to discriminate against female candidates."

Notes

(1) *Marschall* has been described as a "silent revision" of the *Kalanke* judgment delivered only two years earlier.[116] This is an apt expression. On the one hand, the clear affirmation by the Court that the existence of a saving clause is sufficient to bring a preferential promotion programme within the protection of Article 2(4) of Directive 76/207/EEC corresponds to the reading made of *Kalanke* both by the European Commission and by the German courts to whom the answer of the Court was addressed. On the other hand, the judgment in *Marschall* was adopted against the opinion of Advocate General F.G. Jacobs, who had considered that the rule at stake in that case was not significantly different from that at issue in *Kalanke*. Indeed, the referring national court in *Kalanke* had expressly noted that paragraph 4 of the 1990 Bremen LGG (see above **7.DE.10.**)

"must be interpreted in accordance with the *Grundgesetz* with the effect that, even if priority for promotion is to be given in principle to women, exceptions must be made in appropriate cases".[117]

Therefore, one may legitimately wonder what significant difference there is between the *Marschall* hypothesis and the situation the European Court of Justice was presented with in the previous case of *Kalanke*.

---

[116] G.More, "Casenote" (1999) 36 *CMLRev* 443.
[117] See para. 9 of the *Kalanke* judgment of 17 October 1995, above **7.EC.27.**

(2) The most significant aspect of *Marschall*, however, resides less in its clarifi-cation (to put things euphemistically) of the *Kalanke* case-law than in the illustration it provides of the willingness of the Court to adopt a less formalistic stance towards the situation of women on the labour market and the virtues equalising opportunities. The Court's statement in paragraph 29 is an important one, when related to the typology of diverse forms of affirmative action presented by AG Tesauro in support of his conclusion in *Kalanke*. Far from agreeing with the idea that equally qualified candidates of a different sex per definition would have the same opportunities on the employment market, so that the only acceptable form of positive action could only be of an "educational" nature (consisting in the provision of training to the members of the underrepresented in order to ensure that they have equal opportunities to compete), the Court in *Marschall* recognises the existence of social prejudice and stereotyping, and therefore of the need to allow for certain forms of preferential treatment even in the presence of equally qualified individuals competing for the same position.

ECJ, 28 March 2000[118]   **7.EC.30.**
C-158/97, George Badeck and others

COMPATIBILITY WITH THE GENDER EMPLOYMENT DIRECTIVE OF PROVISIONS IMPOSING THE ADOPTION OF ADVANCEMENT PLANS AND OTHER MEASURES IN FAVOUR OF WOMEN

Badeck

Facts: The State Constitutional Court of the Land of Hesse refers to the European Court of Justice for a preliminary ruling questions on the interpretation of Article 2(1) and (4) of Directive 76/207/EEC in relation to the Hessen Act on Women's Equality (HGlG; see above **7.DE.5.**, **7.DE.6.**, **7.DE.7.**, **7.DE.9.** and **7.DE.14.**). These provisions comprise outreach measures in the form of an interview quota, obligations to install gender equality plans combined with an objective obligation to eventually prefer a member of the underrepresented sex, and strict quotas for training positions, PhD positions and for the members of committees.

Held: Such legislation is not in violation of Article 2(1) and (4) of Council Directive 76/207/EEC.

Judgment: "29 . . . [The] system introduced by the HGlG ensures that a candidate's sex is never decisive for the purposes of a selection procedure where that is not necessary in the particular case. That is so in particular where the initial evidence that a situation is unfavourable to women, based on the fact that they are underrepresented, is disproved.

30 [It] must be noted that, under Paragraph 10(1) to (3) of the HGlG, the selection procedure for candidates starts by assessing the candidates' suitability, capability and profes-sional performance (qualifications) with respect to the requirements of the post to be filled or the office to be conferred.

31 For the purposes of that assessment, certain positive and negative criteria are taken into account. Thus capabilities and experience which have been acquired by carrying out family work are to be taken into account in so far as they are of importance for the suitability,

---

[118] [2000] ECR I–1875.

811

performance and capability of candidates, whereas seniority, age and the date of last promotion are to be taken into account only in so far as they are of importance in that respect. Similarly, the family status or income of the partner is immaterial and part-time work, leave and delays in completing training as a result of looking after children or dependants in need of care must not have a negative effect.

32 Such criteria, although formulated in terms which are neutral as regards sex and thus capable of benefiting men too, in general favour women. They are manifestly intended to lead to an equality which is substantive rather than formal, by reducing the inequalities which may occur in practice in social life. Their legitimacy is not challenged in the main proceedings.

33 As the national court points out, it is only if a female candidate and a male candidate cannot be distinguished on the basis of their qualifications that the woman must be chosen where that proves necessary for complying with the objectives of the advancement plan in question and no reasons of greater legal weight are opposed . . .

36 Contrary to the submissions of the applicants in the main proceedings and the Land Attorney, it follows that the priority rule introduced by the HGlG is not absolute and uncondi-tional in the sense of paragraph 16 of *Kalanke*.

37 It is for the national court to assess, in the light of the above, whether the rule at issue in the main proceedings ensures that candidatures are the subject of an objective assessment which takes account of the specific personal situations of all candidates.

38 The answer must therefore be that Article 2(1) and (4) of the Directive does not preclude a national rule which, in sectors of the public service where women are underrepresented, gives priority, where male and female candidates have equal qualifications, to female candidates where that proves necessary for ensuring compliance with the objectives of the women's advancement plan, if no reasons of greater legal weight are opposed, provided that that rule guarantees that candidatures are the subject of an objective assessment which takes account of the specific personal situations of all candidates.

[The setting of binding targets in a women's advancement plan providing for a minimum percentage of women at least equal to the percentage of women among graduates, holders of higher degrees and students in each discipline]

41 On this point, it appears from the order for reference that Paragraph 5(7) of the HGlG limits the application of the principle of choosing the best in the same way with respect to selection decisions as with respect to all the se-lection decisions which have to be made taking into account the targets of the women's advancement plan. In any event, Paragraph 5(7) can influence a selection decision only where the candidates have equal qualifications. In that respect the general considerations as regards the binding nature of a women's advancement plan also apply.

42 As the Advocate General observes in point 39 of his Opinion, the special system for the academic sector at is-sue in the main proceedings does not fix an absolute ceiling but fixes one by reference to the number of persons who have received appropriate training, which amounts to using an actual fact as a quantitative criterion for giving preference to women.

43 It follows that the existence of such a special system for the academic sector encounters no specific objection from the point of view of Community law.

44 The answer must therefore be that Article 2(1) and (4) of the Directive does not preclude a national rule which prescribes that the binding targets of the women's advancement plan for temporary posts in the academic service and for academic assistants must provide for a minimum percentage of women which is at least equal to the percentage of women among graduates, holders of higher degrees and students in each discipline.

[The allocation of at least half the training places to women in sectors in which they are underrepresented and for which the State does not have a monopoly of training]

50 . . . [The] Hesse legislature, by introducing a strict result quota as regards professional training to facilitate such access, intended to establish a balanced allocation of training places at least in the public service.

51 That intention does not, however, necessarily entail total inflexibility. Paragraph 7(2) [HGlG] clearly provides that if, despite appropriate measures for drawing the attention of women to the training places available, there are not enough applications from women, it is possible for more than half of those places to be taken by men.

52 The provision at issue in the main proceedings forms part of a restricted concept of equality of opportunity. It is not places in employment which are reserved for women but places in training with a view to obtaining qualifications with the prospect of subsequent access to trained occupations in the public service.

53 Since the quota applies only to training places for which the State does not have a monopoly, and therefore concerns training for which places are also available in the private sector, no male candidate is definitively excluded from training. Taking an overall view of training (public and private sectors), the provision at issue there-fore merely improves the chances of female candidates in the public sector.

54 The measures provided for are thus measures which are intended to eliminate the causes of women's reduced opportunities of access to employment and careers, and moreover consist of measures regarding vocational orientation and training. Such measures are therefore among the measures authorised by Article 2(4) of the Directive, which are intended to improve the ability of women to compete on the labour market and to pursue a career on an equal footing with men.

55 The answer must therefore be that Article 2(1) and (4) of the Directive does not preclude a national rule which, in so far as its objective is to eliminate underrepresentation of women, in trained occupations in which women are underrepresented and for which the State does not have a monopoly of training, allocates at least half the training places to women, unless despite appropriate measures for drawing the attention of women to the training places available there are not enough applications from women.

[The guarantee to equally qualified female candidates that they will be called to interview in sectors where they are underrepresented]

57 The provision at issue in the main proceedings provides for two different approaches. With the first, all the qualified female candidates who satisfy all the conditions required are called to interview. In that case the number of male candidates to be interviewed may be equal to or greater or lesser than the number of female candidates. With the second, only a limited number of qualified female candidates are called to interview. In that case no more than the same number of male candidates may be called to interview . . .

60 As the Advocate General observes in point 41 of his Opinion, the provision at issue in the main proceedings does not imply an attempt to achieve a final result—appointment or promotion—but affords women who are qualified additional opportunities to facilitate their entry into working life and their career.

61 Next, it appears from the order for reference that that provision, although laying down rules on the number of interviews to be given to women, also provides that a preliminary examination of the candidatures must be made and that only qualified candidates who satisfy all the conditions required or laid down are to be called to interview.

62 This is consequently a provision which, by guaranteeing, where candidates have equal qualifications, that women who are qualified are called to interview, is intended to promote equal opportunity for men and women within the meaning of Article 2(4) of the Directive.

63 The answer must therefore be that Article 2(1) and (4) of the Directive does not preclude a national rule which, where male and female candidates have equal qualifications, guarantees

that qualified women who satisfy all the conditions required or laid down are called to interview, in sectors in which they are underrepresented.

[Recommendations concerning the appointments to employees' representative bodies and administrative and supervisory bodies]

65 It appears from the order for reference and from the statement of reasons that Paragraph 14 of the HGlG, which concerns the composition of collective bodies, is not compulsory, in that it is a non-mandatory provision which recognises that many bodies are established by legislative provisions and that full implementation of the requirement of equal membership of women on those bodies would in any event require an amendment to the relevant law. Moreover, it does not apply to offices for which elections are held. That would again require the relevant statutory bases to be amended. Finally, since the provision is not mandatory it permits, to some extent, other criteria to be taken into account.

66 The answer must therefore be that Article 2(1) and (4) of the Directive does not preclude a national rule relating to the composition of employees' representative bodies and administrative and supervisory bodies which recommends that the legislative provisions adopted for its implementation take into account the objective that at least half the members of those bodies must be women."

Notes

(1) The judgment confirms the lessons from the *Kalanke* and *Marschall* rulings. Faced with the above-mentioned provisions of the law of the *HGlG*, the ECJ begins by reiterating the validity of the criterion set in the *Marschall* judgment. Priority for women in positions where they are underrepresented is compatible with Article 2(1) and (4) of the Gender Employment Directive, insofar as it does not apply automatically and unconditionally, and the candidatures are the subject of an objective assessment which takes account of the specific personal situations of all candidates on the basis of "secondary" non-discriminatory criteria. However, the Court added several specifications to this criterion, three of which are of particular relevance to our purpose.

(2) First, even if, in principle, "automatic"—or "absolute and unconditional"— preferential treatment exceeds the limits of the exception to the individual right to equal treatment laid down in Article 2(4) of Directive 76/207/EEC, such an automatism may be justified when such preference is based on a quantitative criterion constituted by an "actual fact", for example referring to the number of appropriately qualified persons (paragraph 42).

(3) Secondly, when training positions are at issue, rather than actual employment positions, the imposition of an absolute preference aimed at achieving a balanced representation may be admissible, insofar as women are not applying in sufficient numbers despite appropriate outreach measures (paragraphs 51 and 55), and male candidates are not "definitively excluded from training", as places are also available in the private sector (paragraph 53).

(4) Thirdly, insofar as it aims to promote "equal opportunity for men and women" without guaranteeing a result, a set of rules which ensures that women with the necessary qualifications will be called to interview for jobs in public service sectors where they are underrepresented does not constitute a prohibited discrimination, but

instead should be considered a positive action measure covered by Article 2(4) of Directive 76/207/EEC (paragraphs 56–63).

ECJ, 6 July 2000[119]   **7.EC.31.**
Case C–407/98, Katarina Abrahamsson, Leif Anderson and Elisabet Fogelqvist

COMPATIBILITY WITH THE GENDER EMPLOYMENT DIRECTIVE OF A RULE PROVIDING
FOR THE AUTOMATIC RECRUITMENT OF A SUFFICIENTLY QUALIFIED MEMBER OF
THE UNDERREPRESENTED SEX, UNLESS THIS WOULD GIVE RISE TO A BREACH OF THE
REQUIREMENT OF OBJECTIVITY IN MAKING APPOINTMENTS

The University of Göteborg Women Quotas Case

Facts: The case was based on the Swedish Equality Act and the corresponding Regulations on positive action in filling professors' and research assistants' positions excerpted above (**7.SE.12.**). On 3 June 1996 the University of Göteborg announced a vacancy for an academic position, making explicit that the appointment should contribute to promotion of equality of the sexes in professional life and that positive discrimination might be applied in accordance with Regulation 1995:936. Eight candidates applied, including Ms. Abrahamsson, Ms. Destouni, Ms. Fogelqvist and Mr. Anderson. The selection board voted twice. In the first vote, based only on the candidates' academic qualifications, Mr. Anderson came first and Ms. Destouni second. On the second vote, taking into account both the academic merits and Regulation 1995:936, Ms. Destouni came first and Mr. Anderson second; Ms. Fogelqvist was ranked third. When Ms. Destouni withdrew her application, the Rector referred the matter back to the selection board. The board stated that they had already considered the question of equality and did not change the order. Despite this, the Rector of the University of Göteborg decided to appoint Ms. Fogelqvist, referring to Regulation 1995:936 and to the university's plan for equality between men and women. He stated that the difference between the respective merits of Mr. Anderson and Ms. Fogelqvist was not so considerable that positive discrimination in favour of the latter constituted a breach of the requirement of objectivity in the making of appointments. Mr. Anderson and Ms. Abrahamsson appealed against the decision be-fore the *Överklagandenämnden för Högskolan*, which requested a preliminary ruling from the ECJ regarding compatibility of the application of Regulation 1995:936 with Article 2(1) and (4) of the Gender Employment Directive.

Held: Article 2(1) and (4) of Directive 76/207 precludes national legislation under which a candidate for a public post belonging to the underrepresented sex and possessing sufficient qualifications must be preferred over a candidate of the opposite sex who would otherwise have been appointed, where this is necessary to secure the appointment of a candidate of the underrepresented sex and the difference between the respective merits is not so great as to give rise to a breach of the requirement of objectivity. National legis-lation of that kind is also precluded where it applies only to procedures for filling a predetermined number of posts or posts created as part of a specific programme of a particular higher educational institution allowing the application of positive discrimination measures.

Judgment: "45 In contrast to the national legislation on positive discrimination examined by the Court in its *Kalanke, Marschall* and *Badeck* judgments, the national legislation at issue in the main proceedings enables preference to be given to a candidate of the underrepresented sex who, although sufficiently qualified, does not possess qualifications equal to those of other candidates of the opposite sex.

46 As a rule, a procedure for the selection of candidates for a post involves assessment of their qualifications by reference to the requirements of the vacant post or of the duties to be performed.

---

[119] [2000] ECR I–5539.

47 In paragraphs 31 and 32 of *Badeck* . . ., the Court held that it is legitimate for the purposes of that assessment for certain positive and negative criteria to be taken into account which, although formulated in terms which are neutral as regards sex and thus capable of benefiting men too, in general favour women. Thus, it may be decided that seniority, age and the date of last promotion are to be taken into account only in so far as they are of importance for the suitability, qualifications and professional capability of candidates. Similarly, it may be prescribed that the family status or income of the partner is immaterial and that part-time work, leave and delays in completing training as a result of looking after children or dependants in need of care must not have a negative effect.

48 The clear aim of such criteria is to achieve substantive, rather than formal, equality by reducing *de facto* inequalities which may arise in society and, thus, in accordance with Article 141(4) EC, to prevent or compensate for disadvantages in the professional career of persons belonging to the underrepresented sex.

49 It is important to emphasise in that connection that the application of criteria such as those mentioned in paragraph 47 above must be transparent and amenable to review in order to obviate any arbitrary assessment of the qualifications of candidates.

50 As regards the selection procedure at issue in the main proceedings, it does not appear from the relevant Swedish legislation that assessment of the qualifications of candidates by reference to the requirements of the vacant post is based on clear and unambiguous criteria such as to prevent or compensate for disadvantages in the professional career of members of the underrepresented sex.

51 On the contrary, under that legislation, a candidate for a public post belonging to the underrepresented sex and possessing sufficient qualifications for that post must be chosen in preference to a candidate of the opposite sex who would otherwise have been appointed, where that measure is necessary for a candidate belonging to the underrepresented sex to be appointed.

52 It follows that the legislation at issue in the main proceedings automatically grants preference to candidates be-longing to the underrepresented sex, provided that they are sufficiently qualified, subject only to the proviso that the difference between the merits of the candidates of each sex is not so great as to result in a breach of the requirement of objectivity in making appointments.

53 The scope and effect of that condition cannot be precisely determined, with the result that the selection of a candidate from among those who are sufficiently qualified is ultimately based on the mere fact of belonging to the underrepresented sex, and that this is so even if the merits of the candidate so selected are inferior to those of a candidate of the opposite sex. Moreover, candidatures are not subjected to an objective assessment taking account of the specific personal situations of all the candidates. It follows that such a method of selection is not such as to be permitted by Article 2(4) of the Directive.

54 In those circumstances, it is necessary to determine whether legislation such as that at issue in the main proceedings is justified by Article 141(4) EC.

55 In that connection, it is enough to point out that, even though Article 141(4) EC allows the Member States to maintain or adopt measures providing for special advantages intended to prevent or compensate for disadvantages in professional careers in order to ensure full equality between men and women in professional life, it cannot be inferred from this that it allows a selection method of the kind at issue in the main proceedings which appears, on any view, to be disproportionate to the aim pursued.

56 The answer to the first question must therefore be that Article 2(1) and (4) of the Directive and Article 141(4) EC preclude national legislation under which a candidate for a public post who belongs to the underrepresented sex and possesses sufficient qualifications for

that post must be chosen in preference to a candidate of the opposite sex who would otherwise have been appointed, where this is necessary to secure the appointment of a candidate of the underrepresented sex and the difference between the respective merits of the candidates is not so great as to give rise to a breach of the requirement of objectivity in making appointments."

Notes

(1) In the proceedings which led to the referral, Mr. Anderson, one of the applicants against the appointment of Ms. Fogelqvist as a professor at the University of Göteborg, had in fact been ranked better than Ms. Fogelqvist, despite regard having been had to the equality plan of the university; yet Ms. Fogelqvist had been appointed in his place after the woman initially selected, Ms. Destouni—chosen in preference to Mr. Anderson in order to comply with the equality plan, despite the fact that Mr. Anderson was slightly better qualified—had withdrawn her application. The particular circumstances in which the reference was made, which seemed almost calculated to illustrate the risk of arbitrariness in the criteria applied to the appointments at the university and, at least, how these criteria could be manipulated, probably influenced the Court in its condemnation of the Swedish scheme.

(2) The EFTA Court delivered a judgment on similar legislation in Norway. This court applies the substantive law of the European Community in a number of fields, including equality of treatment between men and women in employment, taking into account the case-law of the European Court of Justice. In Case E-1/02,[120] the EFTA Surveillance Authority considered that Norway was in breach of its obligations under the EEA Agreement. On the basis of the positive action provision contained in the Norwegian University Act, a number of permanent and temporary academic positions were earmarked for women by direction of either the Norwegian government or the University of Oslo. The Norwegian government in 1998 allocated 40 so-called post-doctoral research grants, funded through the national budget, to universities and university colleges, 20 of which were assigned to the University of Oslo. Although such scholarships were designed to be a temporary position with a maximum duration of four years, they were intended to improve the recruitment base for high-level academic positions. Pursuant to Article 30(3) of the University Act, the university earmarked all of these positions for women. Moreover, of the 179 post-doctoral appointments at the university from 1998 to 2001, 29 were earmarked for women. Of the 227 permanent academic appointments during that period, four were earmarked for women. And under the university's Plan for Equal Treatment 2000–2004, another 10 postdoctoral positions and 12 permanent academic positions were to be earmarked for women. According to the Plan, the university intended to allocate the permanent positions to the faculties by way of an evaluation of, inter alia: academic fields where women in permanent academic positions are considerably underrepresented, giving priority to fields with less than 10% female academics; and academic fields where women in permanent academic positions are underrepresented

---

[120] [2004] *CMLRev* 245, annotated by C. Tobler.

as compared to the number of female students. While dismissing the quota regime, the EFTA Court recommended the reassessment of merit, remarking that:

> "the criteria for assessing the qualifications of candidates are essential. In such an assessment, there appears to be scope for considering those factors that, on empirical experience, tend to place female candidates in a disadvantaged position in comparison with male candidates. Directing awareness to such factors could reduce actual instances of gender inequality."[121]

Two further judgments from the European Court of Justice may be mentioned. In the case of *Lommers*[122], a scheme had been set up by a ministry in the Netherlands in order to tackle extensive underrepresentation of women, under which a limited number of subsidised nursery places made available by the ministry to its staff was to be reserved for female officials alone whilst male officials could have access to them only in cases of emergency, to be determined by the administration. The ECJ took the view that Article 2(1) and (4) of Directive 76/207/EEC does not preclude such a scheme, provided, however, that male employees placed in a situation similar to that of the female employees (who, under the scheme, are presumed to be the child-carers within the family) are recognised as having the same opportunities to benefit from the nursery services.[123] Finally, in *Briheche*,[124] the Court was confronted with the French legislation reserving to "widows who have not remarried" the benefit of the exemption from the age limit (45 years) for obtaining access to public-sector employment,[125] excluding widowers from the same advantage. This, says the Court, automatically and unconditionally gives priority to certain categories of women, including widows who have not remarried and who are obliged to work, reserving to them the benefit of the exemption from the age limit for obtaining access to public-sector employment and excluding widowers who have not remarried who are in the same situation.[126] The Court concludes that such legislation cannot be allowed under Article 2(4) of the Gender Employment Directive.[127]

Although the assessment which the Court of Justice has given of the various national rules that were submitted to it in the cases listed above may seem hard to reconcile with each other once we focus on the details of each case, the general

---

[121] Para. 57 of the judgment.

[122] Case C–476/99 *Lommers* [2002] ECR I–2891.

[123] Para. 50 of the judgment.

[124] *Briheche*, above n. 112.

[125] More precisely, Law No. 79-569 of 7 July 1979 abolishing the age limit for obtaining access to public-sector employment for certain categories of women (JORF of 8 July 1979) extended the exception (which initially was to benefit only "women who are obliged to work following the death of their husband") to make it applicable, if they are obliged to work, to mothers with three or more children, widows who have not remarried, divorced women who have not remarried, legally separated women and unmarried women with at least one dependent child.

[126] Although, as a result of an amendment introduced in 2000 (Art. 34 of Law No. 2001-397 of 9 May 2000 concerning equality at work for men and women (JORF of 10 May 2001, 7320)), the same exception also benefited unmarried men with at least one dependent child who are obliged to work.

[127] ECJ C–319/03, para. 24.

significance of the Court's approach seems fairly clear. This approach appears to be based on the idea that positive action in favour of women aimed at achieving equal "opportunity" for men and women cannot go beyond this objective and pursue equal "results". The latter objective would be contrary to the principle of equal treatment whereby each person has the right not to be disadvantaged on grounds of his or her sex.

According to the interpretation given by the Court, this limit is exceeded when positive action gives preference to women (or men) in the acquisition of a *result* (access to employment, obtaining a promotion) which has an *absolute* character, that is to say, which does not allow the rejected male (or female) candidate to bring forward any arguments that would be likely to tilt the balance in his (or her) favour. Absolute preference in this sense would be considered discriminatory, since it establishes a non-rebuttable presumption in favour of women or men in cases where the candidates from both sexes are equally qualified, unless it is based on an "actual fact", such as the proportion of men and women among the persons with such a qualification.

On the other hand, the preferential treatment that is accorded to women or men in terms of access to certain *opportunities* (vocational training, calls to job interviews) will be considered with less severity: even when absolute, such preferential treatment is aimed at achieving equal opportunity for men and women, and on this account should be considered as covered by the exception provided for in Article 2(4) of Directive 76/207/EEC—or, now, in Article 3 of the Recast Gender Employment Directive, which refers to Article 141(4) of the EC Treaty.

Upon closer examination, however, the distinction between equality of opportunities and equality of results, to which the Court attaches so much importance—and for which there is some textual support in the original version of Article 2(4) of Directive 76/207/EEC, which refers to "removing *existing inequalities* which affect women's opportunities" (emphasis added)—is not particularly helpful. It may even be a source of confusion, as it is used interchangeably either to distinguish measures which seek to provide chances to women from measures which seek to guarantee an outcome, or to distinguish measures which improve the access of women to training positions which prepare for the competition on the employment market from measures which favour women in the allocation of jobs proper. But access to a training programme may constitute an outcome, and the allocation of a job also provides an opportunity for further promotion.

Another way to approach the case-law of the Court of Justice in the positive action cases it has been presented with is by locating it within the framework outlined above (section 7.3.4). If we consider, first, the three possible justifications for the adoption of affirmative action measures (backward-looking or compensatory for past discrimination; as a tool to remove actual inequalities in fact; or forward-looking and aimed at proportionate representation or diversity), it is apparent that only the second rationale has to date been considered legitimate by the Court: the Court has hitherto read Article 2(4) of Directive 76/207/EEC as "specifically and exclusively designed to authorise measures which, although discriminatory in appearance, are in fact intended to eliminate or reduce *actual instances of inequality which may exist in the reality of social life*".[128]

The Court also considers that any positive action measure seeking to eliminate or reduce actual instances of inequality should be strictly proportionate to that end. This is the source of its suspicion towards rules guaranteeing preferential treatment to women which are absolute and unconditional, i.e. which do not provide for the possibility to objectively assess all competing candidates in order to take into account their specific personal situations. This is also why, for instance, the Court did not object in *Badeck* to a national rule for the public service which, in trained occupations in which women are underrepresented and for which the State does not have a monopoly of training, allocates at least half the training places to women: the Court reasoned that

> "the quota applies only to training places for which the State does not have a monopoly, and therefore concerns training for which places are also available in the private sector, [so that] no male candidate is definitively excluded from training".[129]

Many other examples could be given. What matters is that the requirement of proportionality imposed by the Court is in fact interpreted to ensure that the positive action measures developed by the Member States do not sacrifice individual justice (the right of each individual to be treated on the basis of his or her personal situation) in the name of group justice (the automatic and absolute preference given to the members of one group, e.g. women, simply because of that membership).

7.5.2.C.   ADAPTING DIRECTIVE 76/207/EEC TO ARTICLE 141(4) EC

Since the developments which led to the cases above, the Gender Employment Directive and the formulation in Article 141(4) EC have been reconciled: Directive 2002/73/EC of 23 September 2002 amending Council Directive 76/207/EEC[130] replaced Article 2 of that Directive with a new and more detailed provision, which stated in Article 2(8) that "Member States may maintain or adopt measures within the meaning of Article 141(4) of the Treaty with a view to ensuring full equality in practice between men and women". Furthermore, Article 2, paragraph 3 of Directive 76/207/EEC as amended by Directive 2002/73/EC provides that Member States shall communicate to the Commission, every four years, the texts of laws, regulations and administrative provisions of any measures adopted pursuant to Article 141(4) of the Treaty as well as reports on these measures and their implementation. This should

---

[128] *Kalanke*, above n. 39, para. 18 (citing Case 312/86 *Commission* v. *France* [1988] ECR 6315, para. 15); *Marschall*, above n. 39, para. 26; *Badeck*, above n. 27, para. 19 [emphasis added].

[129] *Badeck*, above n. 27, para. 53.

[130] Directive 2002/73/EC of the European Parliament and of the Council of 23 September 2002 amending Council Directive 76/207/EEC on the implementation of the principle of equal treatment for men and women as regards access to employment, vocational training and promotion, and working conditions [2002] OJ L269/15.

allow a more proactive verification of the compatibility with Community law of the positive action legislations and policies adopted by the Member States, and could lead to a more uniform interpretation of the Directive throughout the Union. Article 3 of the Recast Gender Employment Directive maintains the wording of Article 2 paragraph 3 Directive 76/207/EEC as amended.[131] There is no reason to believe that the ECJ will deviate from its reading the Directives on the basis of Article 141(4) EC to which Article 3 of the Recast Gender Employment Directive refers. On the contrary, it has already been noted that the Court considers that the proportionality test which it has applied on the basis of Article 2(4) of Directive 76/207/EC would apply in similar fashion under Article 141(4) EC itself.[132]

7.5.3. THE FUTURE OF POSITIVE ACTION UNDER EUROPEAN UNION LAW

How, then, may this case-law develop, when transposed to the new grounds of prohibited discrimination listed under Article 13 EC, and when applied to affirmative action measures developed in fields other than employment? Each of these Directives includes a positive action clause.

Directive 2000/78/EC establishing a general framework for equal **7.EC.32.**
treatment in employment and occupation [Employment Equality Directive][133]

Article 7—Positive Action
With a view to ensuring full equality in practice, the principle of equal treatment shall not prevent any Member State from maintaining or adopting specific measures to prevent or compensate for disadvantages linked to [religion or belief, disability, age or sexual orientation].[134]

When it proposed the insertion of these clauses in the directives, the Commission seemed to assume that the case-law of the European Court of Justice as it had begun to develop with *Kalanke* and *Marschall* would simply apply, *mutatis mutandis*, to the new grounds of prohibited discrimination.[135] However, given the differences between the grounds and the wider scope of application for the directives, it seems that there is a considerable gap between the questions which the Court has confronted hitherto and the challenges which lie ahead.

---

[132] Directive 2006/54/EC of the European Parliament and of the Council of 5 July 2006 on the implementation of the principle of equal opportunities and equal treatment of men and women in matters of employment and occupation (recast) [2006] OJ L204/23.

[132] See above **7.EC.30.**, paras. 54–5.

[133] [2000] OJ L303/16.

[134] Art. 5 of the Racial Equality Directive (Directive 2000/43/EC) contains a similar wording.

[135] See COM(1999) 565 final, of 25 November 1999, at 11: "as positive action measures are a derogation from the principle of equality, they should be interpreted strictly, in the light of the current case-law on sex discrimination".

First, while it has proven to be relatively open to the judgment of legislatures of the Member States according to which positive action measures in favour of women were desirable to move beyond merely formal equality, the European Court of Justice has never considered that the Member States may be *required* to adopt such measures in order to implement the principle of equal treatment. In the case presented to the EFTA Court, the Kingdom of Norway sought to justify a rule reserving a number of academic posts exclusively for women by the requirements of CEDAW.[136] This argument was dismissed by the EFTA Court, on the ground that neither CEDAW, nor other international instruments dealing with positive action measures in various circumstances, *impose* on States Parties an obligation to adopt such measures: these instruments, said the Court, are "permissive rather than mandatory" as regards positive action.[137]

It will be recalled, however, that Article 2(2) of the 1965 ICERD (see above **7.UN.1.**) is more precise than its equivalent in CEDAW (Article 3; see above **7.UN.16.**), which the EFTA Court probably had in view, together with Article 4(1) CEDAW, when it delivered its judgment in Case E-1/02. We have seen that the wording of Article 2(2) ICERD suggests that the adoption of affirmative action measures may in certain cases be compulsory, rather than simply optional, in circumstances where a particular racial or ethnic group is subjected to a form of structural discrimination. Similar positive obligations to adopt measures in the face of entrenched inequalities may be derived from Article 4 of the Council of Europe Framework Convention on the Protection of National Minorities, under which States Parties are to adopt "adequate measures in order to promote, in all areas of economic, social, political and cultural life, full and effective equality between persons belonging to a national minority and those belonging to the majority", taking due account in this respect of "the specific conditions of the persons belonging to national minorities"; such measures are specifically designated as not being discriminatory in character. With respect to persons with disabilities, the UN Committee on Economic, Social and Cultural Rights has considered, in its General Comment No. 5 on persons with disabilities, that the obligation imposed on the States Parties to progressively realise the rights of the International Covenant on Economic, Social and Cultural Rights to the maximum of their available resources extends "in the case of such a vulnerable and disadvantaged group" to the obligation

> "to take positive action to reduce structural disadvantages and to give appropriate preferential treatment to people with disabilities in order to achieve the objectives of full participation and equality within society for all persons with disabilities. This almost invariably means that additional resources will need to be made available for this purpose and that a wide range of specially tailored measures will be required".[138]

[136] On the status of positive action under the CEDAW, see above, section 7.4.1, at 782–786.

[137] Case E-1/02 *EFTA Surveillance Authority* v. *Kingdom of Norway*, judgment of 24 January 2003, para. 58.

[138] UN Committee on Economic, Social and Cultural Rights, General Comment No. 5: Persons with disabilities, adopted at its 11th session (1994) (UN doc. E/1995/22), para. 9. For a more detailed examination, see above, 790–793.

In addition, Article 27(1)(h) of the Convention on the Rights of Persons with Disabilities encourages the States Parties to "promote the employment of persons with disabilities in the private sector through appropriate policies and measures, which may include affirmative action programmes, incentives and other measures".[139] Therefore, it may be easier for the Member States to justify certain affirmative action measures benefiting racial or ethnic minorities, religious minorities, or persons with disabilities, than it has been to justify similar measures adopted in order to promote the professional integration of women.

A first challenge facing the Court in the interpretation of the Racial Equality and Employment Equality Directives therefore relates to the transposition of a body of case-law developed with respect to positive action measures benefiting women, to similar measures benefiting other groups which have been traditionally subject to discrimination and to the members of which the more recent directives adopted on the basis of Article 13 EC have extended the principle of equal treatment.

A second challenge concerns the transposition of a body of case-law developed in the field of employment to other domains, covered by Article 3 of the Racial Equality Directive or, more recently, by Article 3 of Council Directive 2004/113/EC of 13 December 2004 implementing the principle of equal treatment between men and women in the access to and supply of goods and services (Gender Goods and Services Directive).

Article 4(5) of the Gender Goods and Services Directive provides that it "shall not preclude differences in treatment, if the provision of the goods and services exclusively or primarily to members of one sex is justified by a legitimate aim and the means of achieving that aim are appropriate and necessary". The dissimilarity in wording illustrates that the authors of the directive were aware of the difficulties of transposing, *mutatis mutandis*, the existing case-law of the European Court of Justice as developed in the field of employment to the access to and supply of goods and services. The preamble of the Directive (16th Recital) nevertheless states that

> "Differences in treatment may be accepted only if they are justified by a legitimate aim . . .
> Any limitation should nevertheless be appropriate and necessary in accordance with the
> criteria derived from case-law of the Court of Justice of the European Communities".

The examples referred to, however, do not include positive action policies in the access to or provision of goods and services.

An acceptable justification for the allocation of scarce goods will always depend on the sphere in which we are situated. This is the reason why transposing case-law on positive action developed in the field of employment to other spheres such as education or housing may be less than straightforward. The use of positive action may be acceptable in a particular sphere, but may nevertheless be excluded in another sphere to ensure the allocation of another scarce social good: thus,

---

[139] See the Final Report of the Ad Hoc Committee on a Comprehensive and Integral International Convention on Protection and Promotion of the Rights and Dignity of Persons with Disabilities, UN doc. A/61/611, 6 December 2006. The Convention was adopted by the UN General Assembly on 13 December 2006 and has been opened for signature and ratification on 30 March 2007. It will enter into force after it will have been ratified by 20 countries.

the need to preserve a representation of all the cultural groups of a society in audiovisual programmes may justify certain restrictions to the principle of non-discrimination,[140] although a similar requirement might not be acceptable, for instance, in the context of recruitment processes in employment; and a positive action programme acceptable at the recruitment stage could be less acceptable in determining the order of layoffs, in collective layoff procedures.[141] It is therefore extremely difficult to establish admissibility criteria of positive action that can claim general validity. Such criteria must not be linked either to a particular "sphere", such as employment or education, or to certain specific contexts, such as the size of a company or the type of the market—local, national or global—where it sells its products. The identification of general criteria would be all the more difficult if, as the cases of the allocation of scholarships or social housing illustrate, social goods have to be distributed according to a combination of criteria (need, family situation, and academic merit as regards scholarships, for example; need, family situation and date of application in the case of social housing), rather than according to one single metric.

On the other hand, we should not underestimate the extent to which the precise significance we give to these criteria may be revised. This may be illustrated by the role which the notions of "merit" or "qualifications" have hitherto played in the case-law of the European Court of Justice. These notions operate to form the baseline of the Court's reasoning in the positive action cases it has decided, where access to employment or to employment-related benefits were at stake: procedures or criteria which reward "qualifications" relevant for the job are in principle valid, whereas any measures which seek to derogate from this baseline in order to achieve social justice (specifically, to improve the representation of women) are only allowable if they comply with the principle of proportionality. Thus, while it claims to combat certain effects resulting from the reliance on the mechanisms through which the market allocates its rewards to the individuals, positive action seems to acknowledge, without radically challenging it, the neutrality of these mechanisms. The technique of positive action allocates the roles. It is the role of market mechanisms to identify the "merits" and "skills"; in short, to locate the "most qualified". The instrument

---

[140] In cases where national legislation was challenged on the basis of the rules of the EC Treaty on the free movement of capital and the free provision of services, the European Court of Justice agreed that the need to safeguard, in the audiovisual sector, the freedom of expression of the different components, notably social, cultural, religious or philosophical, of society, should be considered a legitimate objective: see Case 353/89 *Commission* v. *the Netherlands* [1991] ECR 4089, para. 30 and Case 288/89 *Stichting Collectieve Antennevoorziening Gouda and others* v. *Commissariaat voor de Media* [1991] ECR 4007, para. 23. However, the obligation imposed on the national organisations of radio broadcasting to ensure that the different social, cultural, religious or philosophical components of the Dutch society are represented in their programmes through a national undertaking, the *Bedrijf*, was considered disproportionate to the objective pursued.

[141] See, e.g. *Wygant* v. *Jackson Board of Education* 476 US 267 (1986). Thus according to R.B. Ginsburg and D.J. Merritt, "Affirmative Action: An International Human Rights Dialogue" (1999) 21 *Cardozo L. Rev.* 253, 265, "the concern that affirmative action plans do not trench heavily on settled expectations has been salient in US affirmative action jurisprudence. Thus preferences permissible for hiring have been rejected when laying off workers is the issue; for layoffs, strict seniority systems prevail."

of positive action is then given the task of derogating from the outcome of these identifications, in order to grant "preferential" treatment to certain disadvantaged groups on account of the characteristics presented by its members.[142] Thus, far from subverting the dominant logic—the idea that the market will reward the most "qualified"—positive action may in fact reinforce it. As a result, the members of disadvantaged groups may find their negative stereotypes being further reinforced from the moment the law intervenes to compensate for the fact that they do not have—or are considered not to have—the qualities that would enable them to succeed without its help.

A more subversive approach then may consist in going a step further, which is to challenge not only the consequences of a market-based concept of "merit", but also the concept of "merit" itself—a concept which, convinced as we are of the natural character of the market mechanisms, we have such a strong tendency to fetishise.[143] The *Badeck* case precisely offers an illustration of the results which such an approach may lead to. The Hesse Women Equality Act (see above **7.DE.5., 7.DE.6., 7.DE.7., 7.DE.9.** and **7.DE.14.**) comprised a provision aimed at redefining merit (above **7.DE.6.**). The Court noted that such criteria, "although formulated in terms which are neutral as regards sex and thus capable of benefiting men too, in general favour women", but that they are "manifestly intended to lead to an equality which is substantive rather than formal, by reducing the inequalities which may occur in practice in social life".[144] It did not question their legitimacy.[145] In similar fashion, when it was confronted with the set-aside in favour of women in Norwegian academia, the EFTA Court remarked that

> ". . . the criteria for assessing the qualifications of candidates are essential. In such an assessment, there appears to be scope for considering those factors that, on empirical experience, tend to place female candidates in a disadvantaged position in comparison with male candidates. Directing awareness to such factors could reduce actual instances of gender inequality. Furthermore, giving weight to the possibility that in numerous academic disciplines female life experience may be relevant to the determination of the suitability and capability for, and performance in, higher academic positions, could enhance the equality of men and women, which concern lies at the core of the Directive".[146]

---

[142] In the *Abrahamsson and Anderson* judgment, which concerned the Swedish rule favouring the recruitment of women to university teaching posts, the Court of Justice of the European Communities clearly reasserted the principle: "As a rule, a procedure for the selection of candidates for a post involves assessment of their qualifications by reference to the requirements of the vacant post or of the duties to be performed" (*Abrahamsson and Anderson*, above n. 36, para. 46). It is significant that this assertion is made in a context where the Community court was asked to rule on the legitimacy of a recourse to positive action: its reasoning must be based on the initial position of a supposedly neutral concept of "merit", to the requirements of which affirmative action makes an exception.

[143] See further, on the need to unpack the concept of "merit" as it is used, in particular, in discussions concerning affirmative action policies in the field of employment, C. McCrudden, "Merit Principles" (1998) 18 *OJLS* 543.

[144] See above **7.EC.30.**, para. 32.

[145] The Court in fact did not have to adopt a position on the acceptability of these criteria, which the parties to the main proceedings did not challenge.

[146] Para. 57.

7.6. POSITIVE ACTION BEFORE THE NATIONAL COURTS

The question of positive action may present itself before national courts in Europe in a variety of ways. The most typical question arising before national courts is whether a particular positive action scheme is disproportionate and thus risks constituting discrimination against the members of the category not benefiting from the scheme. This question is illustrated in section 7.6.1. Typically also, the answer will be found in the protection against discrimination found in national law, especially in the equality clauses contained in the national constitutions: insofar as it also contains certain protections against discrimination, but does not at yet impose the adoption of positive action measures for the benefit of any particular group, European Community law will in general only be invoked insofar as such protection from discrimination is not already provided under national law. Other questions may arise, however. Section 7.6.2 envisages the situation of the individual litigant seeking to oblige an actor to adopt a positive action scheme which that litigant would benefit from. This is also a rather atypical situation, as in the vast majority of situations, even where the adoption of a positive action measure may be both legally allowable and opportune, it will not be obligatory as the only possible answer to instances of past, present or potential discrimination, which the positive action would seek to compensate for or prevent. Finally, section 7.6.3 illustrates why, once certain specific provisions are in place which seek to take into account factual inequalities by compensating the members of the disadvantaged group, the Legislature or the Executive are recognised a certain margin of appreciation in phasing out such provisions, as the needs which these provisions seek to respond to disappear progressively rather than all at once.

7.6.1. THE ADMISSIBILITY OF POSITIVE ACTION MEASURES

Typically, judicial decisions relating to positive action concern the limits to the adoption of positive action measures by the Legislature, the Executive or private parties, such as employers seeking to promote diversity within the undertaking. Private parties may act on an explicit legislative mandate, e.g. a statutory obligation to monitor the composition of the workforce and adopt remedial measures if imbalances are revealed (above **7.NL.3.** and **7.NIR.5.**), or on their own motion.

The case-law of the Belgian Constitutional Court (*Cour d'arbitrage*) for instance, has defined relatively strict conditions for the adoption of positive action measures to be allowable under Articles 10 and 11 of the Constitution, which guarantee equality and prohibit discrimination.

Court of Arbitration (Cour d'arbitrage), 27 January 1994 **7.BE.33.**
Case 9/94, A. Asztalos v. Office national des pensions

COMPATIBILITY WITH THE CONSTITUTIONAL REQUIREMENTS OF EQUALITY AND
NON-DISCRIMINATION OF A DIFFERENCE OF TREATMENT ON GROUNDS OF SEX IN
THE ALLOCATION OF BENEFITS TO THE ELDERLY

The Belgian guaranteed income to elderly case

Facts: The Employment Tribunal (*Tribunal du travail*) of Verviers requests from the Court of Arbitration a
preliminary ruling concerning the compatibility with the equality and non-discrimination provisions of the
Belgian Constitution of Article 1(1) of the Law of 1 April 1969 concerning a guaranteed revenue to the
elderly, which grants this benefit to women of 60 years of age and above, whereas men aged between 60 and
65 years are denied this benefit.

Held: Insofar as it grants a right to a guaranteed revenue to women of 60 years of age and above, while
denying this right to men aged between 60 and 65 years, Article 1(1) of the Law of 1 April 1969 concerning
a guaranteed revenue to the elderly violates the equality and non-discrimination clauses of the
Constitution.

Judgment: "B.6.1. The Council of Ministers [Belgian government] invokes the fact that because
of the 'burdens of the past', which disadvantage women, it is not in violation of the principle
of equal treatment between men and women to maintain certain differentiations in favour of
women for the period during which, according to a reason-able appreciation, will be required
in order to erase the disadvantages they have been subjected to.

B.6.2. It must be admitted that in certain circumstances, inequalities are not in violation
of the principle of equality and the prohibition of discrimination, where they seek precisely
to remedy existing inequalities. However, such corrective inequalities are compatible with the
principle of equality and the prohibition of discrimination, only to the extent that they are
imposed only where manifest inequalities are found to exist, where the legislator has
identified the abolishment of these inequalities as an objective to be promoted, where the
measures adopted are of a temporary nature, and are planned to disappear as soon as this
objective is attained, and where they do not unnecessarily restrict the rights of others. It is
the task of courts and tribunals, of the Council of State and of the Court of Arbitration, as
the case may be, to review the compatibility of such measures to the above-mentioned
conditions.

The Council of Ministers however only offers [in defence of the legislative provision alleged
to be discriminatory] a global comparison between the situation of men and that of women,
and fails to establish in which respect the challenged measure contributes to compensating for
a disadvantage if we consider the concrete situations of a man and a women aged between 60
and 65 years, and deprived of resources."

Note

The Court of Arbitration sees positive action, when it leads to imposing differences in
treatment between groups of people on the basis of a suspect characteristic, is seen as
a restriction imposed on the right to equal treatment—the right of each individual to
be judged according to his or her abilities, needs or merits, rather than on the basis of
characteristics such as sex, national origin or religious affiliation. The Constitutional
Court considers such positive action as discriminatory unless four conditions are

fulfilled.[147] First, the measure must be a response to situations of manifest inequality, i.e. it is based on a clear demonstration that a clear imbalance between the groups will remain in the absence of such action. Secondly, the legislator must have identified the need to remedy such imbalance—in other words, private parties may not introduce such positive action. Thirdly, the "corrective measures" must be of a temporary nature: since they are a response to a situation of demonstrated manifest imbalance, these measures must be abandoned as soon as their objective—to remedy this imbalance—is attained. Fourth, these corrective measures must not go further than is required, i.e. they must be restricted to what is strictly necessary, so that the limitation of the right to equality will remain within well-defined boundaries: the cure must not appear worse than the evil to be combated.

Another example is the position adopted by the French Constitutional Council (*Conseil constitutionnel*) regarding the Act on Equality of Wages between Women and Men (*Loi relative à l'égalité salariale entre les femmes et les homes*).

Constitutional Council (Conseil constitutionnel), 16 March 2006[148] **7.FR.34.**
Decision n°2006-533 DC

COMPATIBILITY WITH THE CONSTITUTION OF THE LAW ON EQUALITY OF WAGES
BETWEEN WOMEN AND MEN

The representation of women in France

Facts: Title III of the Law on equality of wages between women and men seeks to improve the representation of women within the boards and surveillance councils of both private and state-owned companies, as well as within the structures organised for the dialogue between management and workers and, inter alia, on the list of personnel representatives, by providing that these bodies should not include over 80% of persons of the same sex, and that, where this maximum is exceeded and the other sex therefore appears disproportionately underrepresented, the imbalance is to be remedied within five years following the entry into force of the Law on Equality of Wages between Women and Men. Title IV of the Law relates to access to vocational training and apprenticeship. It encourages the Regions to take into account the need to promote a balanced access of women and men to vocational training in the preparation of regional plans on this subject, which they are competent to adopt. Provisions from both these Titles of the Law are challenged as a violation of the Constitution.

Held: Title III of the Law on Equality of Wages between Women and Men violates the principle of equality before the law, insofar as it places considerations of sex above considerations relating to the capacities of the individual, in violation of Articles 1 and 6 of the 1789 Declaration on the Rights of Man and of the Citizen (*Déclaration des droits de l'homme et du citoyen*). Title IV is not contrary to the Constitution, provided that it does not lead to placing considerations of sex above considerations relating to the capacities of the individual.

Judgment: "11. Considering that Titles III and IV of the law under examination concern the access of women to deliberative and jurisdictional bodies as well as to vocational training and apprenticeship;

---

[147] The position expressed by the Court of Arbitration in Case No. 9/94 has been confirmed in its more recent case-law: see Case No. 157/04, judgment of 6 October 2004, recital B.79.

[148] JORF, 24 March 2006, at 4446.

Concerning Title III titled: 'Access of women to deliberative and jurisdictional bodies'

12. Considering that Article 1 of the 1789 Declaration [on the rights of the man and the citizen]: 'Men are born and remain free and equal in rights. Social distinctions may only be founded on common utility'; that alinea 3 of the Preamble of the Constitution of 27 October 1946 states: 'The law guarantees to the woman, in all fields, rights equal to those of the man'; that under Article 1 of the Constitution: 'France . . . ensures to all citizens equality be-fore the law, without distinction of origin, race or religion . . .';

13. Considering that under the terms of Article 6 of the Declaration of 1789: ' . . .All citizens have an equal access to all dignities, positions and employment in the public service, according to their capacity, and with no other distinction than those relating to their abilities and their talent'; that the second alinea of Article 3 of the Constitution states that 'no section of the people' may exercise the attributes of national sovereignty;

14. Considering that if, according to the fifth alinea of [Article 3 of the Constitution, inserted into this provision by the Constitutional Law No. 99-569 of 8 July 1999 (Official Journal, 9 July 1999)]: 'The law favours equal access of women and men to elective mandates and functions', it appears from the preparatory works that this alinea applies solely to elections to political mandates and functions;

15. Considering that, if the objective of ensuring a balanced access of women and men to responsibilities other than political elective functions is not in violation of the constitutional requirements recalled above, it may not, without violating these requirements, place consider-ations relating to gender above those relating to abilities and common utility; that, therefore, the Constitution does not allow the composition of executive or consultative bodies of legal (private or public) persons to be regulated by compulsory rules based on the sex of persons;

16. Considering that it follows that in imposing the respect of defined proportions between women and men in management and supervision boards of private and public companies, in undertakings' committees (*comités d'entreprise*), among employees' representatives, in the lists of candidates to *conseils de prud'hommes* [lower level jurisdictions specialized in labour disputes, comprising in their composition representatives of workers and of employers] and to paritary bodies in the public service [the law seeking to ensure a balanced representation of women and men by providing that each category will comprise a proportion of representatives of each sex not superior to 80%, and that, in the presence of an unequal representation of each sex in each category, this gap will be removed within five years following the entry into force of the Law on equality of wages between women and men], the provisions of Title III of the law under examination are in violation of the principle of equality before the law; that they should therefore be declared contrary to the Constitution; that the other provisions of that Title, being inseparable from the contested provisions, should also be declared unconstitutional;

Concerning Title IV: 'Access to vocational training and apprenticeship'

17. Considering that the provisions of Title IV of the law under examination also should be scrutinized under the 13th alinea to the Preamble of the Constitution of 1946 according to which 'The Nation guarantees the equal access to the child and the adult to education, vocational training and culture';

18. Considering that the provisions of Title IV which seek to favour a balanced access of women and men to the different vocational trainings and apprenticeships, by inviting the regions to take this objective into account in the formulation of the regional plan for the development of vocational training or in the preparation of contracts defining the objectives of the development of initial and continued vocational trainings, do not violate the requirements of the above-cited constitutional requirements; that, however, they should not result in placing considerations relative to gender above those relating to ability; that, with this reservation, Title IV is not contrary to the Constitution (. . .)."

829

Note

The French Constitutional Council thus takes the position that positive action implying preferential treatment is prohibited under the equality clauses of the Constitution unless explicitly provided for as an exception to those clauses. It may also be required that either the Constitution itself, or the legislator, define with sufficient precision under which conditions positive action measures may be adopted, in order to ensure a protection from arbitrariness. In the case presented below, the Slovak Constitutional Court was asked by the Slovak government to deliver an opinion on the compatibility with the Constitution of the Slovak Republic of § 8, paragraph 8 of the *antidiskriminaèný zákon* (Anti-discrimination Act),[149] implementing the Racial Equality Directive into Slovak legislation.

Constitutional Court of the Slovak Republic **7.SK.35.**
(Ústavný súd Slovenskej Republiky), 18 October 2005

COMPATIBILITY OF THE POSITIVE ACTION PROVISION OF THE ANTI-DISCRIMINATION ACT WITH THE CONSTITUTIONAL PRINCIPLES OF THE RULE OF LAW AND OF EQUALITY

The Slovak positive action case

Facts: The Slovak government challenges before the Slovak Constitutional Court § 8, paragraph 8 of the Anti-discrimination Act adopted by the National Council. This provision reads: "With a view to ensuring full equality in practice and in order to comply with the principle of equal treatment, specific measures for prevention and compensation of disadvantages linked to racial or ethnic origin may be adopted", which provides for the possibility of adopting specific measures in order to prevent or compensate for disadvantages linked to race or ethnic origin.

Held: The Slovak Republic, being governed by the rule of law according to Article 1 of the Constitution, is in violation of this constitutional requirement to provide for the possibility of positive action measures to be adopted without specifying the competent author for the adoption of such measures, the conditions under which such measures may be adopted, what such measures may consist of, and without ensuring that such measures will be of limited duration.

Judgment: "22. . . . The challenged provision of the Antidiscrimination Law does not contain . . . clear definitions necessary for the implementation in practice of this norm, especially the definition of the subject authorised to accept and adopt specific measures for the prevention and the compensation of disadvantages, the purpose, criteria and conditions of their admissibility, the scope and content of such measures, whereas such legislative approach promotes the possibility of arbitrary, purpose-oriented, non-uniform, hence undesirable interpretation and application.

[It] . . . is conceived according to the model of the substantive understanding of the principle of equality that would in itself be in accordance with principles of the rule of law

---

[149] *Zákon è. 365/2004 Z. z. o rovnakom zaobchádzaní v niektorých oblastiach a o ochrane pred diskrimináciou a o zmene a doplnení niektorých zákonov* (antidiskriminaèný zákon) [Act No. 365/2004 Coll. on Equal Treatment in Certain Areas and Protection against Discrimination, amending and supplementing certain other laws].

830

(Article 1, par. 1 of the Constitution). In a state functioning under the rule of law (*Rechtsstaat*), the equality of opportunities in the workplace, the principles of equal treatment as well as the means through which these principles are implemented in practice, including individual measures furthering equality that will prevent disadvantages perceived as discrimination, must be respected.

The challenged norm, however, fails to remain within the objective of securing equal opportunity in the workplace and to comply with principles of equal treatment, and it fails to establish the temporary character of these techniques (special equalizing measures) that are supposed to equalize or compensate for any disadvantages. Without the imposition of a strict time limit for such measures, the measures envisaged could lead to so-called reverse discrimination against individuals who do not benefit from such measures, even where the reasons for their acceptance, duration and application might have disappeared. Such measures could therefore be accepted only in order to achieve a well-defined goal, and once this goal has been achieved, they should be eliminated so that the measures intended to compensate for unequal starting positions would not result in breaching the general principles of equality against other groups of individuals.

The [legal provision allowing for the adoption of positive action measures] should also define the framework specifying the methods to be used in order to achieve this goal while not disrupting the balance towards other groups of individuals.

[The Court agrees with the position of the government according to which] the challenged provision of § 8, paragraph 8 of the Antidiscrimination Law does not include these limiting factors for the acceptability of special compensatory measures. [Indeed, the challenged provision defines neither] the kind of compensatory advantage that must be a legally permitted (financial, material or in form of a service), nor the criteria according to which the con-tent of the compensatory measures should be identified; therefore it does not ensure against the risk of arbitrariness in the definition of such special compensatory measures.

These flaws of the challenged provision of the Antidiscrimination Law—which does not contain a requirement of time limitation, and specifies neither the methodological framework which should be complied with in order to achieve the set goal, nor the allowable content of the compensatory measures and the criteria which should be re-lied upon to determine their content—, are not remedied even by interpreting this provision in conformity with Article 152, paragraph 4 of the Constitution, which sets out that the interpretation and application of the constitutional laws and other generally binding legal regulations must be in accordance with the Constitution. Such an interpretation would eventually also have to address the issue of the compatibility of the challenged provisions of the Antidiscrimination Law with Article 12 par. 1, first sentence, and with Article 12 par. 2 of the Constitution; how-ever, as the conclusion listed under Recitals 23 and 24 [below] indicates, such interpretation cannot be considered. (PL. Const. 19/18, PL Const. 17/02).

For this reason, the provision in question cannot be in accordance with the principle of the rule of law as described in Article 1, par. 1 of the Constitution, with a special consideration for legal certainty that is violated by the challenged provisions within the scope of questioned flaws of possible special compensatory measures.

This conclusion being reached, it is no longer necessary . . . to address the questions of the author which could adopt such special treatment measures, or that of the beneficiaries of such measures . . .

It is true that the circle of beneficiaries of special compensatory measures would be very vague and not closely specified. This circumstance would not be so significant were it not simultaneously tied to race or ethnicity, which is also the only determining criterion for the beneficiaries of these measures, and as the conclusion listed in Recital 24 of this decision [below] shows, this is a criterion that forms a basis for the conclusion regarding the conflict of the challenged provision with Article 12, par. 2 of the Constitution . . .

23. The method that according to § 8 par. 8 of the Antidiscrimination Law secures the objective of this norm are special compensatory measures. Such compensatory measures should be understood as positive measures relying on techniques widely resorted to in situations where the consequences of discrimination caused by objective circumstances or facts. The sole objective of such measures should be to compensate for the consequences of previous discrimination and unequal opportunities in order to achieve equal results. This suggests that special compensatory measures are to be understood as providing a specific advantage for a group of individuals by taking into account their previous disadvantage which impedes their equal access to employment opportunities. Such measures are complementary to the guarantee of an equal treatment which, with respect to disadvantaged groups of individuals, would not be in itself sufficient to ensure equal access to opportunities; such measures, however, cannot result in guaranteeing also an equality of outcomes.

24. The legal amendment allowing for the adoption of special compensatory measures could therefore be constitutionally acceptable in principle, from the viewpoint of equal opportunities and non-discrimination. [However, such a provision should fully respect] the general principles of equality and prohibition of discrimination, or would otherwise come into conflict with the constitutional order. Article 12, par. 2 of the Constitution, in its current interpretation by the constitutional court, implies that the Constitution prohibits both positive and negative discrimination for reasons that are stated in this Article, i.e. in regards to gender, race, skin colour, language, faith or creed, political and other opinions, national or social origin, affiliation to a nationality or ethnic group, property, ancestry or other status. Therefore, the acceptance of special compensatory measures, which otherwise constitute a widely used legislative technique for preventing disadvantage related to racial origin or ethnic origin, is in conflict with Article 12, par. 2 of the Constitution, and therefore also with Article 12, par. 1 of the Constitution.

This was moreover confirmed by a representative of the National Council, who stated during a public oral discussion: '*Article 12 clearly excludes any discrimination, be it positive or negative.*' Nevertheless, the National Council representative further added: '*Apparently, the constitutional regime is not so unambiguous, because the Constitution contains in Article 38 measures that are based on positive discrimination of a certain group of people.*' The Constitutional Court does not accept this argument, even though Article 38, par. 1 and 2 does establish special guarantees for women, juveniles and persons with disabilities in the exercise of their fundamental rights.[Article 38 of the Slovak Constitution reads:

'(1) Women, minors, and disabled persons shall enjoy more extensive health protection and special working conditions.

(2) Minors and disabled persons shall enjoy special protection in employment relations and special assistance in training.

(3) Further details of the rights defined in sections (1) and (2) of this Article shall be specified by law.'] The cited constitutional article has to be understood as a complementary constitutional norm to Article 12 par. 2 of the Constitution that allows for positive measures. In this context it should be noted that taking into account the factual inequality of women, juveniles and persons with disabilities [in accordance with Article 38 par. 1 and 2 of the Constitution] is a legitimate objective that cannot be achieved in any way other than by the chosen legislative solution containing also positive measures.

In this context, when examining the issue of constitutionality of student brigade work (PL. Const. 10/02), the Constitutional Court emphasized: 'A legal amendment that provides specific advantages for a certain group of people cannot be considered to be violating the equality principle solely for this reason. Regarding the agricultural, social, cultural and minority rights, such legislative interventions providing specific advantages within reasonable limits are not only acceptable, but sometimes also inevitable in order to remove natural inequalities between various groups of people.' Even in this decision, however, the Constitutional Court maintained that such legal amendment must be based on the Constitution, specifically in articles regulating the status of women, juveniles, and the disabled. Only in this case would such constitutional amendment not conflict with Article 12 par. 2 of the Constitution, but, on the contrary, would implement its purpose, essence and justification, however, exclusively on special constitutional basis (Article 38 of the Constitution).

These findings of the Constitutional Court determine that the constitutional order of the Slovak Republic recognizes as a widely accepted approach to ensuring equality in laws only such deviation from the universal under-standing of equality (prohibition of discrimination), that has an explicit constitutional foundation responding to natural inequalities among people which, if not met by the adoption of legal measures, could result in unnecessary hardship for certain groups of people (for instance juveniles, women, the disabled). In the opinion of the Constitutional Court, however, the challenged provisions of the Antidiscrimination Law do not have such constitutional foundation that would justify constitutionally allowed deviations from the universal principle of equality expressed in Article 12, par. 1, second sentence and in Article 12, par. 2 of the Constitution."

Notes

(1) While the arguments concerning the admissibility of positive action measures in the absence of an explicit constitutional authorisation therefore are similar to those put forward in the decision of the French Constitutional Council above, the original dimension of this case concerns the requirement that, in providing for the possibility of positive action measures, the legislator clarify with a sufficient degree of precision the conditions under which such measures may be adopted, from the points of view of both the content of such measures and their temporal applicability. This requirement is based on Article 1 of the Slovak Constitution, the first sentence of which states that "The Slovak Republic is a sovereign, democratic state governed by the rule of law". The principle of the "rule of law" is interpreted as excluding the adoption of a legislative provision abandoning an excessive margin of appreciation to the Executive, as this would create the risk of an arbitrary, and potentially discriminatory, reliance on such provision in order to adopt measures which could amount to forms of unallowable "reverse discrimination", i.e. forms of positive action which, because of their disproportionate character, would violate the right to equal treatment of the category of persons who are not benefiting from such measures.

(2) The judgment was met with concern from human rights bodies. The EU Network of Independent Experts on Fundamental Rights considered in March 2006 that:[150]

---

[150] Report on the situation of fundamental rights in the EU and its Member States in 2005, March 2006, at 176–7, available on the website of the European Commission, Directorate-General Freedom, Security and Justice.

"the adoption of positive action measures is not considered in international law a violation of the principle of non-discrimination, as confirmed for instance by Article 4(1) of the Convention for the Elimination of All Forms of Discrimination Against Women or by Article 1(4) of the International Convention on the Elimination of All Forms of Racial Discrimination. Moreover, in its resolution of April 2003 (*Uznesenie vlády è. 278/2003 z 23. apríla 2003* [Governmental Resolution no. 278/2003 of 23 April 2003]; see also the Resolution adopted in November 2003: *Uznesenie vlády è. 1117/2003 z 26.novembra 2003* [Governmental Resolution no. 1117/2003 of 26 November 2003]), the Slovak government adopted specific measures containing also programs of positive action towards Roma population, thus recognizing that *de facto* discrimination against Roma minority cannot be eliminated or even effectively combated without a reasonable use of positive action . . . [The judgment] contrasts with earlier decisions of the Constitutional Court in which it had declared 'positive discrimination' as an instrument of material (*de facto*) equality being consistent with the Slovak Constitution. For instance, in its ruling Ref. no. PL. ÚS 10/02 of 11 December 2003 the Constitutional Court said that 'preferential treatment of some group of natural persons for their specific, often disadvantageous attributes, as compared with other natural persons, by adoption of special legal regulations, is not a discrimination against other natural persons but on the contrary, it must be understood as a further implementation of the constitutional principle which is inherent in Article 12 paragraph 2 of the Constitution'. [In this case the Constitutional Court put under judicial review the provisions of Labour Code allowing the students, and only the students, to conclude special agreements on brigade-work with employers. The Court decided that although the challenged provisions constitute "positive discrimination" of students in comparison with other persons, the aim of these special agreements (enhancing the employability of students) is legitimate and consistent with the principle of equality and principle of non-discrimination]. The Network is concerned about the consequences this ruling may have, in particular, on the situation of the Roma minority in the Slovak Republic. It reaffirms its view that the widespread *de facto* discrimination of Roma minority may not be possible to reduce or eliminate without a reasonable use of positive action. The judgment adopted by the Constitutional Court in the Slovak Republic makes it even more urgent, not less, for the European Union to address affirmatively the situation of the Roma minority, by encouraging the Member States to go beyond the minimum requirements of the Racial Equality Directive, in particular by developing positive action schemes in favour of an effective integration of the Roma."

In the cases above, no direct reference is made to the position of the European Court of Justice on the admissibility of positive action measures. Indeed, such a reference is unnecessary where the equality provisions of the national constitution already suffice to identify the disproportionate or otherwise inadmissible character of provisions of national law allowing for the adoption of positive action measures. European Community law does not impose on the Member States the adoption of positive action measures but merely exempts from the definition of discrimination under Community law certain forms of positive action. The Member States may or may not choose to implement these. There is thus no need to rely on Community law where the positive action scheme or legislation allowing for its adoption is unconstitutional under national law. In contrast, the cases below rely on the European Community and on the case-law of the European Court of Justice.

Equal Treatment Commission (Commissie Gelijke Behandeling) **7.NL.36.**
Opinion 1996-97

COMPATIBILITY WITH NATIONAL LEGISLATION IMPLEMENTING THE GENDER
EMPLOYMENT DIRECTIVE OF A SCHEME AIMED AT IMPROVING THE
REPRESENTATION OF WOMEN IN THE POLICE FORCE

The Haarlem police scheme

Facts: The Kennemerland Police in Haarlem operate a policy implying preferential treatment of women in order to increase the number of women in the police service. According to this policy, while no targets have been set up for the administrative and technical positions in the service, such targets are set for executive positions, on the basis of a comparison between the number of women employed per type of position and per job scale, and the supply of women with the necessary skills on the labour market. The Haarlem Police ask the Equal Treatment Commission to deliver an opinion concerning the compatibility of such a scheme with the Equal Treatment of Men and Women Act (Wet gelijke behandeling van mannen en vrouwen, WGB). This legislation is to be interpreted in accordance with Council Directive 76/207/EEC of 9 February 1976 on the implementation of the principle of equal treatment for men and women as regards access to employment, vocational training and promotion, and working conditions (the Gender Employment Directive), which it implements.

Held: The judgment delivered by the European Court of Justice in the Case C–450/93 *Kalanke* v. *Freie Hansestadt Bremen* does not prohibit positive action establishing an absolute preference in favour of women, in so far as it is established that women are underrepresented in particular types of positions and at particular pay levels, in comparison with the proportion of women having the necessary qualifications on the labour market.

Opinion: "4.2. Article 1a WGB states that the competent authority may make no distinction in the public service between men and women when appointing a civil servant or making appointments by contract of employment under civil law, in the conditions of work, the provision of training, promotion and termination of the contract of employment.

Article 5 WGB states that this ban may be ignored if the distinction made is aimed at placing women in a preferential position in order to eliminate or reduce actual inequalities and the distinction is in reasonable proportion with the objective in view.

4.3. The Commission will test the preferential policy for recruitment and selection against the following criteria:

1) The arrears must be ascertained per type and level of duty, as corresponding to particular segments in the supply of labour. These arrears are determined by comparing the specific proportion of women therein with the number of women in the relevant potential supply on the labour market.

2) It must then be ascertained per type of duty whether, and if so, which preferential treatment is most appropriate, this also depending on the extent of arrears and the rate at which these can be eliminated.

3) The public announcement of a position must indicate that preferential treatment will apply.

The first criterion results in an organisation having to check what types and levels of duties attract a clear, specific inflow from the labour market within the organisation. Generally speaking, this means that jobs are distributed within an organisation according e.g. to job content and/or remuneration level. The specific labour supply is then examined.

4.4. The object aimed at by the applicant under the present scheme is to ensure and maintain an inflow of women.

By applying the preferential policy, the applicant made a distinction between the AT (Administrative and Technical jobs) jobs and the executive positions, in view of the differences in nature and admission requirements.

No targets have been set up for the AT positions having regard to the current reorganisation. For executive positions, a look is taken per type of position at the number of women employed per job scale and the supply of women with the necessary skills on the labour market.

. . . Since the request shows that the preferential policy has been worked up for the executive functions alone for the time being, the AT functions will be left further out of account. The Commission notes in the present case that the applicant proceeded with great diligence in laying down its preferential policy. The arrears have been deter-mined per type of duty and per level of duty from data concerning the supply of women on the labour market. What preferential treatment is best suited, was then examined. The applicant thereby conformed to the first two criteria mentioned. Perhaps unnecessarily, the Commission would comment that the applicant must in implementing its preferential policy also comply with criterion three. It must make the policy adopted known.

The Commission expresses its appreciation of the careful way in which not only the preferential policy was given shape but also how it was placed in a broader context, so that the positive effects of the preferential policy will not be dissipated when recruiting women through disproportionately many women leaving the service.

4.5. Since the judgement of the European Court of Justice (hereinafter called the 'Court') in [Case C–450/93, *Kalanke* v. *Freie Hansestadt Bremen*] partly induced the applicant to submit its preference policy to the Commission for consideration, the [Equal Treatment] Commission would like to draw further attention to the importance of this decision.

Kalanke v. *Bremen* was concerned, amongst other things, with whether a preferential policy could be adopted for women as long as at least half the personnel did not consist of women. The Court answered this query in the negative, because it cannot be automatically assumed that women are underrepresented if their proportion amongst the various salary groups of the personnel is less than 50%. The Court commented in this connection that a national provision that gives women absolute, unconditional precedence in appointments or promotions exceeds the limits of the exception provided in Article 2(4) of [the Gender Employment Directive].

The Commission finds that the significance of the judgement is not all that clear at first sight. After all, the Court is giving judgement in a specific case of preferential policy and one wonders what general consequences can be de-rived from it. And, the specific preferential policy that was submitted to the Court was one where there was no relationship between the preferential policy and the qualified supply on the labour market. On the other hand, the Court took it for granted that an absolute and unconditional precedence for women is unlawful. It is not clear how this finding must be interpreted. In determining its attitude to the precedents of the Court concerning the admissibility of preferential treatment, the [Equal Treatment] Commission subscribes to the Court's opinion. Here, it held in conflict with EC law that a national provision that 'where candidates of different sexes short listed for promotion are equally qualified, automatically give priority to women in sectors where they are underrepresented, underrepresentation being deemed to exist when women do not make up at least half of the staff in the individual pay brackets in the relevant personnel group or in the function levels provided for in the organization chart'. This opinion renders its relevance when testing preferential policy in the Netherlands fairly slight, insofar Dutch practice is characterised by a strict requirement of proportionality, as also contained in the test adopted by the Equal Treatment Commission.

The opaqueness of the Court's reasoning should not lead to the conclusion that preferential policy is a priori unjustified . . . The European Commission also feels that the Court decided only on the particular aspect of the Bremen Act, namely the automatic effect of the measure that grants women absolute, unconditional entitlement to appointment or promotion. The European Commission takes the view in this connection that only quota arrangements that offer no opportunity to take individual circumstances into account are illegal [COM (96) 88, see above n 110]. With regard to the latter point, the Equal Treatment Commission notes that while it certainly cannot be excluded that individual circumstances may stand in the way of the strict application of a preferential policy in certain (exceptional) cases, but in its opinion, introducing a general obligation to take account of individual circumstances is at odds with the essence of the provisions of Article 2(4) of [Gender Employment Directive], namely to promote equal opportunity. After all, almost any preferential treatment will affect other persons. Moreover, expectations are also aroused with regard to the policy to be adopted amongst those at whom the preferential policy is directed.

It may be concluded that the opinion expressed in the judgement in *Kalanke* v. *Bremen* does not call into question a careful preferential policy where it is determined per type of position on the basis of the available supply of labour whether there are arrears and where the most suitable of preferential treatment is also determined per type of job and job level. A policy of this kind should be made known to those concerned. Only in very incidental cases, where, for example, expectations have long been aroused regarding a third party, can departure from such a policy be justified.

Preferential policy as formulated by the applicant does not conflict with the WGB and AWGB [*Algemene Wet gelijke behandeling*—General Law on equal treatment] nor with the principle formulated by the Court in *Kalanke* v. *Bremen*, since the applicant has carefully examined per salary scale what the proportion is of women and has related this to the supply of qualified women in the labour market. The Commission expresses the opinion that the preferential policy of the Kennemerland Police in Haarlem in refuting and selecting for executive functions com-plies with articles 1a and 5 Equal Treatment of Men and Women Act [WGB]."

Notes

(1) The Dutch Equal Treatment Commission thus appears tempted to rely on an avoidance strategy. Its opinion distinguishes the case before it from the *Kalanke* setting and thus does not discuss the Community law aspects.

(2) The German Federal Labour Court also engaged in its own reading of *Kalanke*, even before the ECJ decided *Marschall*, noting that "the ECJ had merely ruled upon the incompatibility of women's quotas without exemptions, and whilst no such clause might be read into the Bremen statute, therefore negating its preferential treatment, other less 'unconditional' equality measures remained unaffected".[151]

Similarly, in its judgment reported below, the German Federal Labour Court draws conclusions from the ECJ's *Marschall* line of case-law,[152] relating it to the German constitution.

---

[151] *Bundesarbeitsgericht* (BAG), 1 AZR 590/92, AP Nr 226 zu Art 3 GG, no 55, English note by Schiek, above n. 100.

[152] Reported above section 7.5.2.B.

Federal Labour Court (Bundesarbeitsgericht), 21 January 2003[153] **7.DE.37.**
9 AZR 307/02, Anonymous v. Land Rheinland-Pfalz

COMPATIBILITY OF "FLEXIBLE QUOTAS", COMPRISING A "SAVINGS CLAUSE", WITH
THE GERMAN GRUNDGESETZ AND WITH EUROPEAN COMMUNITY LAW

The promotion of women in the Land of Rheinland-Pfalz

Facts: In the State of Rheinland-Pfalz a public employer in principle enjoys the discretion to choose when two equally qualified candidates apply for a job. The Equal Treatment Act of Rheinland-Pfalz (LGG), however, confers priority on women as long as they are underrepresented at the respective level of hierarchy within the public administration. A savings clause included in the legislation allows for an exception to be made in favour of the male candidate where circumstances personal to that candidate justify this. The months of professional experience may be taken into account in that respect, provided, however, that the male candidate has over 60 more months of professional experience than his female competitor.

Held: It is allowable, under both the German Basic Code (*Grundgesetz*) and European Community law, to provide that women who are equally qualified will be granted a preferential treatment in situations where they are underrepresented, provided that the priority accorded to female candidates may be overridden if criteria specific to the individual male candidate tilt the balance in his favour. Such criteria should not, however, be indirectly discriminatory against women. In this regard, it is allowable to refuse to take into account the supplementary months of professional experience of the male candidate unless he has at least 60 more months of professional experience than his female competitor.

Judgment: "In this case, discretion in the choice between equally qualified applicants in favour of applicant K. is restricted due to the legislative duty of the respondent to comply with § 7 Para. 1 LGG. According to this provision . . ., in cases where they are underrepresented female applicants are to be given preferential consideration, unless giving preference to a woman would result in a particular hardship for a male applicant. The plaintiff does not find himself in a situation of hardship as defined in § 9 LGG.

The preconditions for the claim of promotion in accordance § 7 Para. 1 LGG are met. As part of the indirect federal administration, the respondent has to apply LGG (§ 2 Para. 1 LGG) (Schiek, Women's Equality Acts at Federal and State Level, 2nd edn, § 2 LGG Rh-Pf Rn. 2596). Both applicants provided evidence of being equally qualified. The Regional Labour Court made a determination, which is binding for the appellate court, that underrepresentation in the meaning of § 4 Para. 3 LGG exists. It rightly did not distinguish between the employee groups of salaried staff and public servants (see Senate 2 December 1997—9 AZR 668/96—BAGE 87, 171).

Contrary to what the plaintiff asserts, there is no objection under constitutional law to the preference provided for in § 7 Para. 1 LGG in conjunction with § 9 LGG.

The preferential consideration of women follows from the prescription under Art. 3 Para. 2 GG [Grundgesetz—German Constitution] that the right to gender equality must be effectively implemented. Accordingly, existing disadvantages, which usually affect women, are to be redressed by affirmative action regulations (BVerfG 28 January 1992—1 BvR 1025/82—BVerfGE 85, 191).

Contrary to what the appeal made suggests, this kind of affirmative action in favor of women is not excluded by Art. 3 Para. 3 Clause 1 GG. The border line between a legitimate measure seeking to implement the right to equality (Art. 3 Para. 2 Clause 2 GG) and unlawful discrimination (Art. 3 Para. 3 Clause 1 GG) should be defined by means of practical concordance. [In the circumstances of this case, this requirement] is guaranteed through the

---

[153] BAGE 104, 264.

presupposition that the candidates present equal qualifications (§ 7 Para. 1 LGG), the fact of underrepresentation of women in line with § 4 Para. 3 LGG and the existence of a provision relating to undue hardship in § 9 LGG. As such, an unreasonable burden on male applicants is also excluded. Due to the clause on undue hardship, they can in individual cases successfully challenge women who have been given preferential treatment even in accordance with Art. 3 Para. 2 Clause 2 GG (see also BAG, 22 June 1993—1 AZR 590/92—BAGE 73, 269; Senate, 2 December 1997—9 AZR 668/96—BAGE 87, 171).

The regulation related to preferences specified in §§ 7 and 9 LGG is also compatible with European Community law. The hardship case regulation in § 9 LGG prevents female applicants from being automatically given preferential treatment.

Art. 2 (1) and Art. 3 of Council Directive 76/207/EEC of 9 February 1976 on the implementation of the principle of equal treatment for men and women as regards access to employment, vocational training and promotion, and working conditions prohibit discrimination on the basis of gender in the definition of conditions for access to employment including selection criteria. However, Art. 2(4) of Directive 76/207/EEC allows for the adoption of measures to promote equal opportunity for men and women, where the objective is to remove existing inequalities which affect women's opportunities. These measures are understood to include giving preference to women with equal qualifications in an area in which women are underrepresented (see also: the rationale behind the Council Recommendation 84/635/EEC of 13 December 1984 on the promotion of positive action for women, OJ 1984 L 331, p. 34). As Art. 2(4) of Directive 76/207/EEC provides for an exception to the prohibition of discrimination of paragraph 1, it must be strictly interpreted [reference to ECJ, *Kalanke*, above **7.EC.27.**]. Measures, which give an absolute and unqualified preference to women exceed the limits of this exception. They no longer serve to promote equality of opportunity. A national rule on the promotion of women, which automatically gives a preference to women applicants, contravenes European Community law, [ECJ, *Kalanke*, paras 21–22] A rule establishing preferential treatment only remains within the limits of legitimate positive action measures if it does not apply in situations where the priority accorded to female candidates may be overridden if criteria specific to the individual male candidate tilt the balance in his favour [reference to ECJ, *Marschall*, above **7.EC.29.** and *Badeck*, above **7.EC.30.**]. The hardship case rule in § 9 LGG represents a limitation to the promotion of women [ensuring that the preference granted to women is not absolute] as required by the Court of Justice of the European Communities; this is because the grounds in the person of the applicant are so serious that they outweigh the requirements of equality in favour of underrepresented women and the female applicant cannot be given preferential consideration.

The exception specified in § 7 LGG to the firm right to equal treatment for men and women in the directive is also proportionate [reference to ECJ, *Lommers*, above n 123]. It does not go beyond what is reasonable and required to achieve the objective pursued.

In selecting an applicant the respondent could ignore the plaintiff's 56 months of longer service.

aa) Whether the plaintiff's longer service is so important that it should be given greater weight than the equality of underrepresented women, has to be judged on the basis of the legitimate objectives pursued by equal treatment legislation under European and constitutional law.

bb) Determining the reasons that could weigh against preferential treatment of women is a task for the national courts to perform [reference to ECJ, *Marschall* and *Badeck*]. In performing this duty, they have to apply the case-law of the Court of Justice of the European Communities to interpret the directive and to make sure that their reasoning does not have any discriminatory effect on women ([reference to ECJ, *Marschall*, *Badeck* and *Abrahamsson*, above

7.EC.31.]; BAG 5 March 1996—1 AZR 590/92 (A)—BAGE 82, 211; Mallossek, The prerequisites for the Equal Treatment Directive 76/207/EEC and its repercussions on German
employment law, p. 161; Schiek, Women's Equality Acts at Federal and State Level, 2nd edn,
Rn 281 and ff., 2634).

cc) Taking length of service into consideration in the context of a hardship case ruling is
not excluded [reference to ECJ, *Badeck* and *Abrahamsson*]. However, it must not run counter to
the aims of the promotion of women as approved under Community law. The aim of the LGG
is to accelerate the filling of positions based on the requirement of gender equality. The precept
under European and constitutional law to implement equality for women in effective terms is
to be realised as soon as possible. This objective is incompatible with having to wait until the
length of service of suitable female applicants reaches that of male applicants. Taking a male
applicant's longer service into consideration without reservation would lead to indirect
discrimination against the other gender; in-deed, the factors that result in shorter length of
service, especially entering the workforce later or taking a leave from work in order to take care
of a child, mainly affect women.

dd) The respondent's application that only a length of service of at least 60 months should
be cited as a supporting criterion in favour of male applicants avoids this discrimination. It
redresses a typical disadvantage experienced by women.

ee) The appeal claims without success that it is unlawful to allow a hardship case to begin
only at a period of ser-vice longer than 59 months and to exclude it because it falls a few
months short of this. There is no objection in law to this principle of a cut-off date. It serves to
allow decisions on choosing applicants to be checked in objective terms and guarantees that,
on the whole, applicants are treated equally."

Notes

(1) This judgment also sheds light on the admissibility of positive action under the
German Basic Law (*Grundgesetz*, GG). Codifying the so-called "merit principle" in
access to public service—which the Court of Justice has referred to as "the constitutional principle of choosing the best"[154]—Article 33(2) GG states that "Every
German shall have, according to suitability, professional performance and aptitude
equal access to each civil service position". More generally, in its most recent version,
the Equal Protection Clause of Article 3 GG states:[155]

"(1) All persons are equal before the law.
(2) Men and women shall have equal rights. The State promotes the factual realisation of
equal rights of women and men and works towards the abolition of existing disadvantages.[156]

---

[154] *Badeck*, above n. 27, para. 11.
[155] Following the translation offered in A. Peters, *Women, Quotas and Constitutions. A Comparative
Study of Affirmative Action for Women under American, German, EC and International Law* (The Hague,
Kluwer Law International, 1999) 138.
[156] As underlined by Anne Peters, this clause, which was inserted into the GG in 1994 as a consequence
of the German unification, "does not embody a personal right, but a so-called government goal by virtue of
which the state is committed to promoting the factual realisation of equal rights" (above n 156, 138,
referring also on the context in which Article 3 GG was amended to J. Schumann, *Faktische
Gleichberechtigung: Die Grundgesetzerweiterung des Art. 3 II S. 2* (Frankfurt am Main-Berlin-Bern, Lang,
1997), and to D. König, "Die Grundgesetzänderung in Art. 3 Abs. 2 GG—Ein Fortschritt auf dem Weg
zur tatsächlichen Gliechberectigung?" (1995) 48 *Die öffentliche Verwaltung* 837.

"(3) No one may be disadvantaged or favoured because of his gender, his parentage, his race, his language, his homeland and origin, his faith, or his religious or political opinions. No one may be disadvantaged because of his disability."

(2) The precise interpretation of Article 3 (2) GG remains a subject of controversy.[157] J. Kokott, now an Advocate General at the European Court of Justice, has taken the view that this clause at the very least should be read as allowing "soft quotas", i.e. forms of preferential treatment in favour of equally qualified women in cases of underrepresentation.[158] This view is shared by a number of jurists,[159] but is not unanimously agreed on.

(3) At a minimum, Article 3(2) GG should influence the balancing exercise between the right of women to equal treatment (including by the abolition of existing disadvantages), on the one hand, and the right of men not to be discriminated against on the basis of their sex, on the other hand, in order to arrive at the "practical concordance" which—as theorised most explicitly in the work of the constitutional lawyer K. Hesse[160]—should be aimed at in situations of conflicting rights. In the judgment excerpted above, it is through this notion of "practical concordance" that the requirements of paragraphs 2 and 3 respectively of Article 3 of the Constitution are being reconciled.

A final example of the attitude adopted by national jurisdictions towards the implementation of positive action measures is borrowed from the case-law of the Dutch Equal Treatment Commission (*Commissie Gelijke Behandeling*).

It will be recalled the Act on the Promotion of Labour Participation of Ethnic Minorities entered into force in 1998 (*Wet Stimulering Arbeidsdeelname Minderheden*: SAMEN Act, above **7.NL.3.**). This Act sought, in part, to implement the obligations of the Netherlands under ICERD. The Act obliged employers to create a situation whereby the percentage of the workforce belonging to ethnic minorities within an organisation is approximately equivalent to the percentage of ethnic minorities within the region.

[157] On this controversy, see A. Peters, above n. 152, 178–90.

[158] J. Kokott, "Zur Gleichstellung von Mann und Frau—Deutsches Verfassungsrecht und Europäisches Gemeinschaftsrecht" (1995) 48 *Neue Juristische Wochenschrift* 1049.

[159] In particular, U. Berlit, "Die Reform des Grundgesetzes nach der staatlichen Einigung Deutschlands" (1996) 44 *Jahrbuch des Öffentlichen Rechts der Gegenwart—Neue Folge* 17.

[160] See, on this "Prinzip der praktischen Konkordanz" in K. Hesse, *Grundzüge des Verfassungsrechts der Bundesrepublik Deutschland*, 20th edn (Heidelberg, C.F. Müller), § 172, as cited by A. Peters, above n. 152, 190.

Equal Treatment Commission (Commissie Gelijke Behandeling)   **7.NL.38.**
Opinion 1999-32

COMPATIBILITY WITH THE GENERAL EQUAL TREATMENT ACT OF PREFERENTIAL
RECRUITMENT OF APPLICANTS OF IMMIGRANT ORIGIN

Preferential recruitment of applicants in South-East Amsterdam

Facts: The applicant complained about the text of a job advertisement made by the respondent. The contested text excludes the applicant de facto from applying to the position offered by the respondent. The text advertises for the post of "secretary project group Ganzenhoef male/female" and it reserves this post, without explanation, unconditionally for migrants. In the applicant's view this constitutes unlawful distinction on the ground of race.

Held: In the light of all the circumstances, the positive action measure at issue for migrant workers is justified and does not result in a breach of the principle of equal treatment.

Opinion: "The ban on distinction by race may be departed from only if one of the statutory exceptions referred to in article 2(3) and (4) AWGB [*Algemene Wet gelijke behandeling*— General Law on Equal Treatment] applies, namely in the event of preferential policy on behalf of ethnic minorities or in case of racial or sexual specificity of the job [where race or sex would constitute a genuine occupational requirement].

In this case, the exception under article 2 (3) AWGB is relevant. The text of article 2 (3) AWGB reads as follows:

> 'The ban imposed by this act on distinction does not apply if the distinction is aimed at granting women or persons belonging to a particular ethnic or cultural minority group a preferential position in order to remove or reduce actual inequalities and if the resource is in reasonable proportion to the object . . .'

4.4. The [defendant] adopts a preferential policy for those of immigrant origin. In this framework, the [defendant] has reserved the position of secretary to the Ganzenhoef project group to a resident of Amsterdam South-East of immigrant origin. The reasons for this are, first, the high unemployment amongst this group of the Amsterdam South-East population and, second, the fact that they did not find the normal preferential policy ('equal suitability') effective in this case. The question [to be answered by the Commission is] whether the acceptance policy adopted by the [defendant] meets the conditions made under article 2 (3) AWGB for conducting a preferential policy for persons belonging to a particular ethnic or cultural minority group.

The Commission finds as follows in this connection.

Various forms of preferential treatment are possible. Neither the wording of the AWGB nor that of the Explanatory Memorandum concerning this provision provides further indications on the application of specific forms of preferential treatment in particular cases. Reference is certainly made in this connection to the statutory requirement that the distinction (to which the preferential treatment gives rise) must be in reasonable proportion to the object, the so-called proportionality requirement. Apart from this proportionality requirement, the provision and its accompanying explanations provide no decisive answer as to what forms of preferential policy seen in that light are or are not permissible.

So far, the Commission has aligned itself on the case-law of the Court of Justice of the European Communities (ECJ) as far as the above question is concerned. This is relevant especially as far as preferential treatment of women is concerned because the Commission is under an obligation to interpret the WGB and AWGB (as far as distinction based on sex is concerned) in accordance with EC law and EC law is concerned with equal treatment for men and women. The ECJ has held in this connection that national authorities are required to interpret not only the national law that is of later date than the EC law concerned but also the national law of an earlier date than the EC law concerned, in the light of the text and objects of the directive(s) in question. The Commission is thereupon required to conform to the relevant precedents of the ECJ.

4.5. When the AWGB was enacted, reference was made regarding the preferential treatment under Article 2 (3) to the testing criteria applicable to preferential treatment under Article 5 (1) WGB.

The Commission has developed a consistent case-law on this point, with a test being made against particular criteria relating to the requirement for demonstrable, relative arrears, in connection with the available supply of labour, and the suitability and recognisability of the preferential treatment applied. This set of requirements follows not only from the WGB but also from the case-law of the Court of Justice of the European Communities.

Wherever possible, the same principles are therefore applied to questions concerning the admissibility of preferential treatment of persons originating from ethnic and/or cultural minority groups as in the case of sex.

These principles cannot, of course, always be applied in the same way, since this depends also on the legal and social context within which the preferential treatment is granted.

4.6. The result of the above is inter alia that in order to answer the question [presented to the Commission], the Act for the Stimulation of Minority Participation in Employment (*Wet stimulering arbeidsdeelname minderheden*—SAMEN Act), which entered into effect on 1 January 1988, is important in addition to the AWGB (which entered into effect on 1 September 1994).

Article 2 of the SAMEN Act states:

'1. The employer will seek to achieve a proportional representation within his business of members of the target groups referred to in Article 3.

2. Proportional representation within the meaning of paragraph 1 exists if the proportion of persons from the target groups within the business corresponds comparatively with their proportion in the regional working population. Account will also be taken of qualifications and suitability requirements.'

Article 3 of the SAMEN Act states that the target group under the act includes: persons born in Turkey, Morocco, Surinam, Dutch Antilles, Aruba, the former Yugoslavia or other countries of South or Central America, Africa or Asia, with the exception of Japan and the former Dutch Indies.

The Commission takes the view that questions concerning the admissibility of preferential policy for ethnic and/or cultural minorities must be answered also in the light of the SAMEN Act.

4.7. It is also important here that the SAMEN Act should be taken as an expression of one of the obligations placed on the government by article 1(4) and article 2(2) of the International Convention on the Elimination of All Forms of Racial Discrimination (CERD). These provisions impose on the States parties to take positive steps in the social fields that enjoy special protection under the CERD, including the field of employment. Preferential treatment is included as such amongst these obligations. This means that (with respect to groups of the population which are protected under the CERD) article 2 (3) AWGB must be interpreted in conformity with article 2 and article 3 of the SAMEN Act and Articles 1(4) and 2(2) CERD.

An employer may for the above reasons in principle adopt a preferential policy ensuring that proportional representation of the target groups is achieved within the organisation. Having regard also to the AWGB, the content and thrust of the preferential measure is justified by the degree of imbalance in representation (proportionality). The measure must therefore also have the actual effect of reducing or eliminating the arrears in question.

4.8. With regard to the actual arrears, the Commission considers as follows.

The [defendant] legitimates the adoption of a preferential policy by means of the particularly high unemployment figures amongst inhabitants of Amsterdam South-East, who are of non-Dutch origin, and the fact that immigrants are underrepresented amongst the civil servants employed there. Some 70% of the inhabitants of Amsterdam South-East are of non-Dutch origin (this proportion rises to 83% in the population living in apartments), while immigrants form some 50% of the local authority officers engaged in the Bijlmermeer. The vacancy in question arose in the Bijlmermeer Renewal Project Office which is chiefly concerned with urban renewal. Three persons of immigrant and six persons of non-immigrant origin work in the project office. By reserving the position in question for a person of immigrant origin, the proportion amongst the jobs concerned would change to 60% non-immigrant and 40% immigrant.

4.9. The Commission finds first of all that in the framework of a preferential policy it is reasonable for the arrears amongst those of immigrant origin amongst local government servants in an urban area to be related to the unemployment figures in the active population in the urban area concerned. This applies the more so because the [defendant] has also in fact in its recruitment centred on candidates residing in Amsterdam South-East.

As is clear from the above, figures concerning the regional labour supply are of essential importance in matters concerning the legitimacy of preferential policy. These figures are not in fact so detailed as to allow to ascertain the relevant labour supply for the position offered which exists in Amsterdam South-East. In the Commission's view however, the absence of these figures should not in this case be regarded as a reason for considering the preferential treatment unacceptable. It is well established by the Commission that exceptions to the equal treatment requirement should be interpreted restrictively. However, the interpretation should not be so strict that it would be at odds with the objectives aimed at by the introduction of an exception concerning the effective [de facto] equality of the population groups mentioned in the act.

Neither would a different approach be compatible with the objectives mentioned above of the SAMEN Act and the CERD. On the contrary, these provisions allow for the admissibility of preferential treatment to be based on more general considerations regarding the position of the protected groups on the labour market—in addition to the statistical data.

In this connection it is not only important that there is underrepresentation generally amongst the civil servants working in Amsterdam South-East. More generally, the fact that the unemployment rate is particularly high amongst these groups plays a part. In addition, it is generally known that the underrepresentation of groups protected by the Act increases the higher the position concerned, while it is precisely amongst the higher job levels that the positive side effects of proportional representation (such as the effects on and motivation for the population groups concerned) will play a greater role. Furthermore, the fact that the thresholds on the labour market are relatively high on recruitment and promotion amongst these population groups and only a small number of employers attempt to combat this with an effective preferential policy also has a bearing. Finally, surveys have high-lighted resistance amongst employers to recruiting employees of immigrant origin.

The job offered by the [defendant] is at higher national certificate/university level, so that when considering the admissibility of preferential treatment, importance must be attached not only to the single fact that underrepresentation of persons of immigrant origin cannot be established in this part of the service on the basis of the figures concerning the relevant labour supply. This is countered, after all, by the arguments already mentioned that concern the situation on the labour market in a broader sense.

With the above in mind, the Commission feels that the position on the labour market of the population groups concerned can justify a preferential policy on the part of the [defendant].

4.10. However, the above does not yet answer the question whether the preferential policy as applied by the [defendant] has in fact also remained within the bounds of the necessary proportionality as formulated in the AWGB and Samen Act.

The Commission considers the following in this connection.

The [defendant] has given as reasons for reserving the position for an immigrant resident of Amsterdam South-East the high unemployment amongst the immigrant population group in Amsterdam South-East, on the one hand, and the fact that the normal preferential policy ('equal suitability') has not proved effective in this case.

The Commission sees these arguments as compelling. It notes [that] despite measures to broaden work and economic growth, unemployment amongst minorities remains disturbingly high.

To combat the arrears concerned amongst the higher positions, far-reaching measures are necessary since earlier investigations—as mentioned under point 4.9—have highlighted the resistance amongst employers where the appointment of employees of immigrant origin is concerned. Having regard to the requirements mentioned above, this measure must therefore, after all, have the actual effect of reducing or eliminating the arrears in question.

Having regard to the limited effectiveness of less far-reaching forms of preferential treatment, the degree of the arrears amongst the protected population groups and the perpetuation of the thresholds on the labour market on recruitment and promotion, the Commission considers that the present preferential treatment does not go beyond the requirements of proportionality.

The Commission further comments in this connection that a form of preferential treatment of this kind should be limited to incidental cases and not constitute a general procedure. It is recommended, therefore, that other forms of recruitment be also examined before proceeding to this far-reaching form of preferential treatment.

4.11. The applicant in lodging his complaint also relied on the fact that the [defendant] gave no justification for the preferential policy adopted in the advertisement concerned. However, the absence of such justification does not in itself conflict with the equal treatment requirements since the [defendant] mentioned the preferential treatment in the advertisement. After all, neither the AWGB nor any other equal treatment provision obliges the [defendant] to give explicit reasons while the justification for the preferential policy can be taken as generally known.

In the light of the above, the Commission considers that the [defendant] does not in its preferential policy exceed the statutory limits imposed for it and is not therefore acting in conflict with the equal treatment provisions."

Notes

(1) The Equal Treatment Commission thus examines the positive action measure which it is asked to scrutinise in the light of the fact that unemployment amongst migrant workers in Amsterdam is particularly high, and that the underrepresentation of migrant workers in the workforce increases as the function level rises. It also takes

into account that the positive effects of an improved representation of migrant workers will be particularly important in such higher level positions, and that the thresholds for entering the labour market and for promotion once one has entered that market are rather high for migrant workers. Finally, the Commission gives weight to the fact that only a limited number of employers make a concrete attempt to combat this pattern of disadvantage. It is in the light of this full set of circumstances that the Dutch Equal Treatment Commission arrives at the conclusion that a positive action policy for migrant workers is justified, although it results in setting aside the position offered for a migrant worker. This, in the view of the Commission, constitutes an appropriate and proportionate measure to combat the under-representation of ethnic minorities.

(2) According to the case-law of the Equal Treatment Commission, positive action measures will be allowable if three conditions are satisfied: first, it must constitute the answer to a situation of actual disadvantage, which must be clearly identified; secondly, the positive action measures at stake must be both appropriate and necessary to compensate for these disadvantages; and finally, the Commission imposes a condition of transparency: the positive action measures must be made known clearly, so as to prevent any risk of arbitrariness in their application.[161]

(3) This case-law treats the adoption of positive action measures as an exception to the general norm of (formal) equal treatment. This is in conformity with the approach adopted by the Dutch legislator. The *Algemene Wet Gelijke Behandeling* (General Equal Treatment Act) (1994 as amended by the EC Implementation Act 2004) and the Disability Discrimination Act (2003 as amended by the EC Implemen-tation Act 2004) contain exceptions in favour of positive action measures. The General Equal Treatment Act prohibits differences in treatment in employment recruitment and selection, including vocational training, membership of employers' organisations and trade unions, access to self-employment, goods and services, including the giving of advice regarding the choice of an educational establishment or career. Moreover, with regard to the discrimination ground "race" the Act also applies in the area of social security, social advantages and health. Article 2(3) of the General Equal Treatment Act provides for the possibility of positive action measures on grounds on sex or race—positive action may be envisaged on no other grounds[162]—since the initial adoption of the Act in 1994. When, in 2003, Article 2(3) of the AGBW was revised in order to better comply with the requirements of European Community law (and specifically, with Article 5 of the Racial Equality Directive), it was acknowledged that the Dutch definition leaves less scope for affirmative action policies and programmes, since it does not allow for measures

---

[161] J.H. Gerards and A.W. Heringa, *Wetgeving Gelijke Behandeling* (Deventer, Kluwer, 2003) 125.

[162] The positive action exception in the General Equal Treatment Act (AWGB) only regards sex and race to the exclusion of any other ground. Moreover, positive action for women in the context of employment is covered by Art. 5(1) of the Act on Equal Treatment between Women and Men (Law Gazette 1989, 168) and Art. 6:646(4) of the Civil Code, to which the AWGB is without prejudice (Art. 4 AWGB).

which are aimed at *preventing* (potential) disadvantages, in addition to *removing* or *reducing* (existing) disadvantages.[163]

(4) In this and in other cases on the issue, the Dutch Equal Treatment Commission relies not only on the ECJ case-law in the field of equal treatment between men and women, but also on the International Convention for the Elimination of All Forms of Racial Discrimination.

As we have seen (see above, **7.NIR.15.**, in section 7.3.3.B, at 778–780), Article 15(1) of the Employment Equality Directive exempts from the requirements of the Directive the specific procedures put in place for the recruitment in the Police Service of Northern Ireland, in order to achieve in that service a balanced representation of Catholics and Protestants and, thus, a police better representative of the community it serves. The relevant provisions of the Police (Northern Ireland) Act 2000 have, however, been challenged as being in violation of Article 14 ECHR.

High Court of Justice in Northern Ireland,   **7.NIR.39.**
Queen's Bench Division (Judicial Review), 23 July 2002[164]
In the Matter of an Application by Mark Parsons for judicial review

COMPATIBILITY OF THE RECRUITMENT SYSTEM OF THE POLICE IN NORTHERN IRELAND WITH ARTICLE 14 ECHR

Parsons

Facts: Mark Parsons is a Protestant man who wanted to become an officer in the Police Service of Northern Ireland. He successfully passed each stage of the recruitment and assessment process and entered the final pool of qualified candidates on 13 September 2001. On 28 September 2001, however, he was informed that he was not being offered an appointment because the Chief Constable was required under section 46(1)(a) of the Police (Northern Ireland) Act 2000 to make appointments in equal numbers from the two communities in Northern Ireland. Mr. Parsons accordingly seeks a declaration that section 46(1)(a) of the Police (Northern Ireland) Act 2000 is incompatible with Articles 9 and 14 of the European Convention on Human Rights, which guarantee respectively freedom of religion and non-discrimination in the enjoyment of the rights and freedoms protected under the Convention; and he seeks judicial review of the decision not to offer him an appointment as a police officer.

Held: The application is dismissed. Specifically, the High Court, Kerr J, finds that the measure complained of does not impose a constraint on the applicant's freedom of religion under Article 9 ECHR; and that the section 46(1)(a) of the Police (Northern Ireland) Act 2000 meets a pressing social need, as demonstrated by the support of the voting population in Northern Ireland for the Belfast Agreement of which it is a part, and that no less restrictive alternative could be put forward in order to ensure that the police force would be representative of the community that it serves.

Judgment: KERR J: "[16] The recruitment exercise in which the applicant participated generated 7,843 applications. An initial selection test reduced the number of applicants to 1809. An assessment centre was designed for candidates to select those most suitable. The number of

---

[163] Memorie van Toelichting bij de EG Implementatiewet AWGB, Tweede Kamer, 2002–2003, 28 770, nr. 3, 9 [Explanatory Memorandum to the EC Implementation Act, Second Chamber of Parliament 2002–2003, 28 770, nr. 3, 9].
[164] (2002) NIQB 46.

847

applicants who passed the assessment was 884. These were graded in merit order. All were then required to undertake medical examinations, physical assessments, a firearms handling test and a vetting procedure. 553 candidates (including the applicant) were successful at that stage and they took with them into the pool of qualified candidates a merit score.

[17] The pool was then divided into two categories viz those who were treated as Catholic candidates and those who were not so treated. Of the pool of qualified candidates, 154 were treated as Catholics and 399 as other than Catholic. Offers of appointment were made to the 154 treated as Catholics and to the first 154 in the non-Catholic category.

[18] The applicant was number 514 in descending order of merit in terms of the pool as a whole. He was deemed to be in the non-Catholic category and was number 370 in that category. Of the 39 candidates below the applicant in the pool as a whole, 10 were in the Catholic category.

[On the compatibility of section 46(1)(a) of the 2000 Act with Article 9 ECHR: The holding on the question of the compatibility with Articles 9 and 14 ECHR, which is the only part of the opinion (paras 19-26) which is retained here, is based in particular on the position of the European Commission of Human Rights which had concluded that Article 9 ECHR may be complied with even in situations where an employee may be disadvantaged due to the exercise of freedom of religion. According to the decisions cited, the freedom of the applicant not to take up employment or to leave the position occupied ultimately ensure that the substance of his or her freedom of religion will be preserved: see in particular Stedman v. United Kingdom (Appl. No. 29107/95), 89-A Eur. Comm. HR Dec. & Rep. 104 (1997).]

[26] . . .In the present case the applicant has not been refused employment because he is a Protestant. He was not offered a post because he did not score sufficiently highly within the category that would have allowed him access to appointment. The action taken against him was not designed to restrict his religious freedom; it was because of his failure to achieve the required results in the various tests and assessments for appointment to the position that he sought. While it is true that others who scored less highly were appointed, this is because they had an attribute that he did not possess viz their Catholic status. That does not mean that the applicant's freedom to practise his religion or to adhere to the faith that he has espoused is diminished. The respondent has placed no constraint on that freedom. I am satisfied therefore that no violation of article 9 arises in this case.

[On the compatibility of section 46(1)(a) of the 2000 Act with Article 14 ECHR]

. . .

[30] . . .It appears to me that the applicant's application was treated differently from those who were perceived to be Catholic. All Catholic candidates who had passed the various tests were accepted, irrespective of the numbers of the non-Catholic candidates. The same cannot be said of the applicant.

. . .

[32] In Inze v Austria [1988] 10 EHRR 394, [the European Court of Human Rights] dealt with the ingredients of discrimination under article 14 in this way:

41. For the purposes of Article 14, a difference of treatment is discriminatory if it: 'has no objective and reason-able justification,' that is, if it does not pursue a 'legitimate aim' or if there is not a 'reasonable relationship of proportionality between the means employed and the aim sought to be realised' (see, *inter alia*, the Lithgow and others judgment of 8 July 1986, Series A no. 102, pp. 66–67, para. 177). The Contracting States enjoy a certain margin of appreciation in assessing whether and to what extent differences in otherwise similar situations justify a different treatment in law; the scope of this margin will vary according to the circumstances, the subject-matter and its background.

The measure must therefore have an objective and reasonable justification (in other words, it must pursue a legitimate aim), and it must be proportionate to that aim.

[33] Dealing with these two prerequisites, Lord Steyn in Regina v Secretary of State ex parte Daly [2001] 3 All ER 433, at paragraph 27 said:—

'The contours of the principle of proportionality are familiar. In de Freitas v Permanent Secretary of Ministry of Agriculture, Fisheries, Lands and Housing [1999] 1 AC 69, the Privy Council adopted a three-stage test. Lord Clyde observed that in determining whether a limitation (by an act, rule or decision) is arbitrary or excessive the court should ask itself:

"whether: (i) the legislative objective is sufficiently important to justify limiting a fundamental right; (ii) the measures designed to meet the legislative objective are rationally connected to it; and (iii) the means used to impair the right or freedom are no more than is necessary to accomplish the objective." (See [1999] 1 AC 69 at 80, [1998] 3 WLR 675 at 684.)

Clearly, these criteria are more precise and more sophisticated than the traditional grounds of review. What is the difference for the disposal of concrete cases? . . . First, the doctrine of proportionality may require the reviewing court to assess the balance which the decision maker has struck, not merely whether it is within the range of rational or reasonable decisions. Secondly, the proportionality test may go further than the traditional grounds of re-view in as much as it may require attention to be directed to the relative weight accorded to interests and considerations. Thirdly, even the heightened scrutiny test developed in R v Ministry of Defence, ex p Smith, [1996] QB 517 at 554 is not necessarily appropriate to the protection of human rights . . . In other words, the intensity of the review, in similar cases, is guaranteed by the twin requirements that the limitation of the right was necessary in a democratic society, in the sense of meeting a pressing social need, and the question whether the interference was really proportionate to the legitimate aim being pursued.'

Does section 46(1)(a) meet a pressing social need? If so, is the measure really proportionate to the aim being pursued?

[34] In my judgment both questions may be answered confidently in the affirmative. The need to correct the imbalance in the police force was undeniable. That had been recognised for a long time but earlier attempts to deal with it had foundered. It cannot seriously be disputed that a police force should be representative of the community that it serves. That had been recognised and endorsed by all the parties who supported the Belfast Agreement. That agreement had in turn been endorsed by 71% of the voting population of Northern Ireland. These circum-stances provide formidable support for a method of recruitment that would strike at the heart of the problem. They also distinguish the present case from one where a difference of treatment on the basis of gender is sought to be justified. The creation of a police force that can command the respect and support of the entire community in Northern Ireland is of an entirely different order from a measure that depends for its justification on an avowed difference of capacity of the two sexes.

[35] As to the proportionality of the provision it is significant that (i) various other initiatives have failed in the past; and (ii) no alternative method of achieving the aim could be suggested by the applicant. It is also of considerable importance that the measure was so firmly supported by the Equality Commission. Moreover all candidates must achieve a minimum standard of suitability and there is no reason to suppose that the calibre of police officer recruited in the way proposed by the legislation will be anything less than appropriate. Finally, the temporary nature of the arrangements and the opportunity to review them speak strongly in favour of the proposition that they are proportionate to the aim that they seek to fulfil."

Note

This case was appealed by Mr. Parsons before the Court of Appeal in Northern Ireland. The appeal, however, did not raise again the allegation that Article 14 ECHR was violated: instead, it invoked exclusively Article 9 ECHR, which guarantees freedom of thought, conscience and religion. The appeal was dismissed on the ground that the constraint could not be considered substantial.[165]

7.6.2.   THE POSITIVE OBLIGATION TO ADOPT A POSITIVE ACTION MEASURE

Under certain circumstances the adoption of positive action measures may appear obligatory—as a necessary component of a policy aimed at implementing the principle of equal treatment. Whether this confers a personal right to the potential beneficiaries is more doubtful, however, as the following case illustrates.

Equality Tribunal, 29 August 2003[166]   **7.IR.40.**
DEC-E/2003/035Gillen v. *Department of Health and Children*
(Represented by the Chief State Solicitor)

THE REFUSAL TO ADOPT A POSITIVE ACTION POLICY (ON THE GROUNDS OF AGE) AS
A FORM OF DISCRIMINATION

The Gillen Case

Facts: The claimant, Mr. J. Gillen, born in 1945, alleges that he was discriminated against by the Department of Health and Children on the ground of age contrary to the provisions of the Employment Equality Act, 1998 when he was unsuccessful in two competitions in 1999 for promotion to the grade of Principal Officer, despite having been deemed on several occasions in the past as being suitable for promotion, and although in his view the successful candidates all had significantly less service and experience than himself. He pointed out that section 33 of the Employment Equality Act, 1998 permitted employers to take measures to reduce or eliminate the effects of discrimination against certain persons, specifically including persons who have attained the age of 50 years.[167] Referring to the competitions he had taken part in and to other competitions where younger candidates were selected instead of those above 50 years, the complainant said that not only had the respondent department not taken any such measures as permitted by and within the spirit of the Act, but on the contrary, had followed a practice of discrimination against such persons. He thus submitted that he had been directly discriminated against by the respondent

---

[165] Court of Appeal in Northern Ireland, Parsons, re Application for Judicial Review [2003] NICA 20 (6 June 2003) (before Carswell LCJ, Nicholson LJ and Campbell LJ).

[166] Available on the website of the Equality Tribunal of Ireland, under the heading Employment Equality Decisions. The decision adopted on appeal by the Labour Court, decision EDA/0412 did not address this aspect of the case.

[167] Prior to its amendment in 2004, s. 33 of the 1998 Employment Equality Act stipulated that nothing in the Act prevented the taking of measures to facilitate the integration into employment, either generally or in particular areas or a particular workplace, of: persons who have attained the age of 50 years; persons with a disability or any class or description of such persons; or members of the Traveller community. Any measures taken under this section must have been intended to reduce or eliminate the effects of discrimination against any of the persons protected by this section.

department by reason of his age in competitions for promotion contrary to the provisions of section 8 of the Employment Equality Act, 1998, and indirectly by reasons of a practice of no promotion of persons over 50 years of age contrary to section 31 (1) of the Act.

Held: The argument that the respondent had been committing discrimination because of the absence of a positive action in place in favour of persons above 50 years of age is dismissed. The Equality Officer found the complainant's reference to section 33 of the Act to be unconvincing.

Judgment: "2.9 The complainant said he believed that these latter two competitions, together with those in which he participated, clearly demonstrated that there was a policy or practice within the respondent department which discriminated against older applicants and supported the case that he had been a victim of that policy. He pointed out that section 33 of the Employment Equality Act, 1998 permitted employers to take measures to reduce or eliminate the effects of discrimination against certain persons, specifically including persons who have attained the age of 50 years. The complainant said that not only had the respondent department not taken any such measures as permitted by and within the sprit of the Act, but on the contrary, had followed a practice of discrimination against such persons . . .

4.23 . . . Length of service per se cannot qualify a person for promotion, and while it could be argued that the quality and breadth of a person's experience are relevant to promotion, it is likely that seniority-based promotion would risk being indirectly discriminatory against younger applicants. Similarly, I do not find that the complain-ant's reference to section 33 of the Act to be convincing. Section 33 permits an employer to take positive action to facilitate the integration of into employment of persons aged 50 years, but does not require it, and the failure to take positive action may not be invoked as discriminatory. In any case, the complainant is already in employment, and failure to achieve promotion cannot be included in 'integration into employment'. As section 33 is an exception to the 1998 [Employment Equality] Act, it must be strictly construed".

Note

The decision above illustrates that the simple fact that an actor (for instance, an employer) may adopt positive action measures but has failed to do so should in principle not be construed as a form of discrimination against those who would have benefited from such a scheme being adopted: as not all positive action measures are adopted in order to prevent or compensate instances of discrimination, positive action may be allowed without its adoption being compulsory.

7.6.3.   PHASING OUT POSITIVE ACTION

It has been noted in section 7.4 that under international law, while positive action was in principle legitimate and should not be considered a form of discrimination, this was subject to the requirement that the difference in treatment be reasonably and objectively justified, in compliance with the requirement of proportionality. This in turn implies, in particular, that the difference in treatment should not be maintained for longer than is necessary to compensate for existing inequalities or to prevent such inequalities. If no permanent measures are needed to balance inequality, positive action should thus be considered as temporary, and should be removed after the objective it seeks to achieve has been realised. Indeed, under both Article 1(4) of

ICERD and Article 4(1) of CEDAW (see above **7.UN.16.**), positive action measures benefiting, respectively, persons defined by their race, colour, descent, or national or ethnic origin, or women, are specifically designated as *"temporary* special measures". Nevertheless, a wide margin of appreciation is left to the Legislature or to the Executive as to when such schemes should be removed.

House of Lords, 5 May 2005[168]   **7.GB.41.**

Regina v. *Secretary of State for Work and Pensions (Appellant) ex parte Hooper and others (FC) (Respondents), Regina* v. *Secretary of State for Work and Pensions (Respondent) ex parte Hooper (Appellant) and others, Regina* v. *Secretary of State for Work and Pensions (Respondent) ex parte Hooper and others (FC) (Appellants) (Conjoined Appeals)*

OBLIGATION TO PUT AN END TO WIDOW'S BENEFITS NOT RECOGNISED TO WIDOWERS, IN RESPONSE TO THE GRADUAL HISTORIC TREND TOWARDS GREATER ECONOMIC ACTIVITY BY WOMEN

Phasing out the discrimination against widowers

Facts: The four claimants are widowers; their wives died between 1995 and 2000. All except one (Mr. Naylor) had dependent children at the time of bereavement. If the claimants had been widows, they would have been entitled to claim widow's benefits: under section 36(1) of the Social Security Contributions and Benefits Act 1992 they would have been entitled to claim a widow's payment (WPt) of £1,000. Under section 37, all except Mr. Naylor would have been entitled to claim widowed mother's allowance (WMA), a weekly sum payable until such time as the children ceased to be dependent. Under section 38, Mr. Naylor would have been entitled to claim a widow's pension (WP). In the leading judgment it delivered on 11 June 2002 in the case of *Willis* v. *United Kingdom* (Appl. No. 36042/97 (2002) 35 EHRR 547) the European Court of Human Rights found that discrimination in the payment of WPt and WMA infringed the rights conferred by Article 14 of the European Convention on Human Rights read with Article 1 of Protocol No. 1 to the Convention but made no finding about WP. An end was put to these differences in treatment between widows and widowers after the Welfare Reform and Pensions Act 1999 abolished widow's benefits for widows whose husbands died on or after 9 April 2001. However, invoking the Human Rights Act 1998, the widowers submit that in denying them the benefits which would have been payable to widows between 2 October 2000 (when the Human Rights Act came into force) and 9 April 2001, the Secretary of State for Work and Pensions had acted in a way which is incompatible with their rights under Article 14 read with Article 1 of Protocol No. 1 and article 8 of the European Convention on Human Rights.

Held: The preservation of a widow's pension for widows bereaved before 9 April 2001 was objectively justified, and thus does not constitute discrimination within the meaning of Article 14 of the European Convention on Human Rights.

Judgment: "31. [The history of widows' pensions in the United Kingdom] demonstrates that the decision to achieve equality between men and women by levelling down survivors' benefits (subject to vested rights) was by no means easy or obvious. It is true that by 2000 the proportion of older women (50–59) who were 'economically active' was 65.9% against 72.5% for men. But those figures must be adjusted to reflect both greater part-time working by women (44% as against 9%) and the concentration of women in low-paid occupations. The comparative disadvantage of women in the labour market had by no means disappeared.

---

[168] [2005] UKHL 29.

32. The question then is whether the continued payment of WP to women in the period 1995-2001 and its continuation for women bereaved before 9 April 2001 was objectively justified. Moses J [2002] EWHC 191 (Admin) held that it was but the Court of Appeal [2003] EWCA Civ 813; [2003] 1 WLR 2623 thought otherwise. It is not in dispute that the jurisprudence of the European Court of Human Rights allows Member States to treat groups un-equally in order to 'correct factual inequalities' between them: see Belgian Linguistic Case (No 2) (1968) 1 EHRR 252, 284, para. 10. Furthermore, in making decisions about social and economic policy, particularly those concerned with the equitable distribution of public resources, the Strasbourg court allows Member States a generous margin of appreciation: see James v United Kingdom (1986) 8 EHRR 123, 142, para. 46. In a domestic system which (unlike the Strasbourg court) is concerned with the separation of powers, such decisions are ordinarily recognised by the courts to be matters for the judgment of the elected representatives of the people. The fact that the complaint concerns discrimination on grounds of sex is not in itself a reason for a court to impose its own judgment. Once it is accepted that older widows were historically an economically disadvantaged class which merited special treatment but were gradually becoming less disadvantaged, the question of the precise moment at which such special treatment is no longer justified becomes a social and political question within the competence of Parliament.

33. Why then did the Court of Appeal decide that by 1995 there was no longer any objective justification for WP? Their three reasons were brief. First, they examined the statistics of men and women in employment and noted, at para. 66, that 'the change between 1995 and 2000 can be seen to be relatively modest'. The figures did not span a watershed, that is to say, rise and then fall back to more or less the same level. The change was gradual, as it had been for many years.

34. Secondly, at para. 67, the Court of Appeal quoted statements by Government spokesmen during the passage of the 1999 Act through Parliament, stressing that the old system was outdated.

35. Thirdly, at para. 68, they drew attention to 14 European countries, together with Russia and Turkey, which had 'established equal entitlement to survivors' benefits by 1995.'

36. The first reason seems to mean that whenever Parliament decided to make the change to equalise survivors' benefits in response to the gradual historic trend towards greater economic activity by women, it would follow that for some years there had been no objective justification for the previous system. It would always be the case that the changes over the preceding few years had been relatively modest. In my respectful opinion, this proposition is fallacious. It contradicts the earlier acceptance by the Court of Appeal, at para. 63, that:

> 'in answering this question a very considerable margin of discretion must be accorded to the Secretary of State. Difficult questions of economic and social policy were involved, the resolution of which fell within the province of the executive and the legislature rather than the courts. In this context we revert to the fact that the issue was the point in time at which benefits which had long been enjoyed by widows should be withdrawn. No statistical formula or calculation could provide a precise answer to this question.'

37. The Court of Appeal seems to have treated the decision of Parliament in 1999 to abolish WP from 9 April 2001 as an acknowledgement that there could have been no possible reason for the legislature not taking such a step at that time and therefore as demonstrating that it should have taken the same step at an earlier date. But in my opinion the courts are not in a position to say that the 1999 decision was inescapably right or that a different decision, whether earlier or later, would have been inescapably wrong. It was a matter for legislative judgment.

38. The references to what Government spokesmen said in 1999 seem to me essentially debating points. Perhaps they represented the Government's opinion, although it is fair to point out, first, that they referred not to WP in particular but to the whole survivors' benefit system, part of which is not alleged to have been objectively justified, and, secondly, that they are couched in rhetoric characteristic of a new Government changing the previous system. But the question is not what the Government thought but whether Parliament could reasonably have taken a different view, then or five years earlier.

39. Finally, at para. 68, the Court of Appeal agreed with Moses J that the information available about the position in other Council of Europe countries did not enable the court to assess the 'overall economic impact of the measures taken.' In particular, we do not know whether the achievement of equality involved the withdrawal of a benefit which widows had enjoyed for half a century. Nevertheless, the Court of Appeal said that the evidence about other countries '[cut] the ground from the submission . . . that there were good reasons for the Government to take no steps to bring this country into line with our neighbours until 1998.' But we have no idea of the extent to which we are '[in] line with our neighbours' except in the content-free sense of not making a distinction between widows and widowers. That seems to me an inadequate basis for deciding that the widows' benefits should have been abolished earlier.

40. I therefore agree with Moses J that the preservation of WP for widows bereaved before 9 April 2001 was objectively justified. It involved no breach Convention rights."[169]

Note

The decision of the House of Lords explains that a certain margin of appreciation should be granted to the authors of positive action (the administration or the legislator) as to the choice of the precise moment at which to put an end to such measures as may have been adopted. It also reasons why such a margin of appreciation may be construed broadly.

7.7. POSITIVE ACTION POLICIES AND THE PROTECTION OF PRIVATE LIFE IN THE PROCESSING OF PERSONAL DATA

The rules relating to the protection of personal data are sometimes seen to create specific obstacles to the adoption of policies in favour of diversity by certain actors, in particular employers. A report presented in October 2003 to the European Commission (Directorate-General for Employment, Industrial Relations and Social Affairs) on the business case for diversity policies within the undertaking[170] notes that

---

[169] The excerpts are from the lead opinion by Lord Hoffmann. The opinion won the approval of Lord Nicholls of Birkenhead, Lord Hope of Craighead, Lord Scott of Foscote, and Lord Brown of Eaton-under-Heywood. The dimensions of the case which concern solely the interpretation of s. 6 of the 1998 Human Rights Act are not mentioned here.

[170] *The Costs and Benefits of Diversity. A Study on Methods and Indicators to Measure the Cost-Effectiveness of Diversity Policies in Enterprises*, report drawn up by the Centre for Strategy and Evaluation Service (CSES) on behalf of the European Commission. The report is based on a survey of 200 companies in 4 EU countries, on literature reviews, on eight case studies in six Member States, and on a

one specific obstacle to the adoption and implementation of workforce diversity policies is the existence of restrictions to the processing of sensitive data in the EU, which may make it impossible to measure the evolution of the workforce, according to sexual orientation, race or ethnic origin, or religion. Without returning to that difficulty, a more recent report identifies "workforce profiling" as a good practice of companies in monitoring progress towards diversity.[171] A study[172] commissioned under the Community action programme to combat discrimination (2001–2006) concluded from a comparative study on the 15 EU Member States, similarly, that data collection ought to be improved in order to gain a better understanding of discrimination in the EU Member States:

> "Data is needed to guide decision-makers, to facilitate awareness-raising activities, to enable the work of international human rights monitoring bodies, to facilitate legal action and to facilitate research on discrimination. Indeed, more than 90 % of the experts surveyed were convinced that data collection on discrimination helps to improve the situation of individuals and groups vulnerable to discrimination."

Among its recommendations, the report proposed that:

> "States should develop their social and economic statistics in such a manner that they would be more useful in disclosing data on the (potentially) disadvantaged economic and social position of members of groups vulnerable to discrimination. Data related to employment, housing, education and income should be broken down by the grounds of discrimination, e.g. national origin, disability, gender and age,"

and that

> "Larger companies, public and private, should keep track of their workforce so as to be able to assess their recruitment, promotion and firing policies and practices".

However, the survey prepared for that study also illustrated the high level of uncertainty about whether or not the existing rules on data protection represented an obstacle to the collection of data relating to discrimination, for the purposes recalled above.[173] The authors of the 2004 *Comparative Study on the Collection of Data to Measure the Extent and Impact of Discrimination within the United States, Canada,*

---

number of interviews with a range of actors. Available on the website of Directorate-General for Employment, Social Affairs and Equal Opportunities.

[171] This is defined thus: "Workforce Profiling Including Ethnicity, Nationalities, Religions, Languages Spoken, Gender and Age Mix to Enable Identification of Particular Areas of Underrepresentation, as well as to Enable Comparisons against Local Area Demographics" in *The Business Case for Diversity. Good Practices in the Workplace*, September 2005, European Commission, Directorate-General for Employment, Social Affairs and Equal Opportunities (Unit D3), at 26.

[172] Reuter *et al.*, *Study on Data Collection to Measure the Extent and Impact of Discrimination in Europe*, Final Report of 7 December 2004.

[173] Of the respondents to the survey 31% were of the view that the data protection legislation does limit data collection, 36% disagreed and 33% did not know. There were no major differences in views provided by NGOs and government representatives to this issue. See the report by Reuter *et al.*, above n. 172, 158–60.

Australia, Great Britain and the Netherlands noted the paradox underlying the debate in Europe on the implementation of anti-discrimination strategies:

> *Medis Projects (Measurement of Discriminations),*   **7.UN.42.**
> *Comparative Study on the collection of data to measure the extent and impact of discrimination within the United States, Canada, Australia, Great Britain and the Netherlands*[174]

"Although there is a lack of statistical indicators to assess the extent of discrimination in the Member States, the belief is widely shared that discrimination is widespread and that there is a need to mobilise all social institutions and stakeholders to reduce this discrimination. Nevertheless, the collection of statistics relating to ethnic or racial origin, religion, disability or sexual orientation has been the subject of strong resistance. The experience of the countries under study in this report demonstrates that the lack of sufficient statistics to illustrate and evaluate discrimination is not compatible with establishing an operational scheme whose main characteristic is the intensive use of statistical data. It appears necessary—and possible—to transcend the European paradox opposing the fight against discrimination and the production of 'sensitive' statistics."

It is therefore particularly important to clearly identify the limits imposed by data protection legislation on the use of statistical tools in order to monitor discrimination both in public policies and in private settings, including in particular within the workforce of private undertakings. This is required both for reasons of legal certainty, as the reluctance of both public and private actors to perform such monitoring may be attributed, in a number of cases, to misconceptions about the requirements of the rules relating to data protection, and in order to identify whether there may be a need to arbitrate a conflict between those requirements and effective anti-discrimination strategies.

The collection of statistical data constitutes an essential component of any positive action scheme: first, only by the collection of such data on the representation of different groups in employment, or on their access to education or housing, will it be possible to identify whether positive action is required in order to ensure real and effective equality; secondly, only through such monitoring will it be possible to evaluate the effectiveness of policies relying on the adoption of positive action measures, and thus, to ensure that such policies do not go beyond what is necessary and, in particular, that they be discontinued once they have fulfilled their objective. The first point is made clearly by the Advisory Committee established under the Council of Europe Framework Convention on the Protection of National Minorities in the following opinion it delivered on Germany:

---

[174] Coord. P. Simon (INED—Economie & Humanisme) (European Commission, August 2004) 87, available on the website of the Directorate General Employment and Social Affairs.

Advisory Committee on the Framework Convention on   **7.CoE.43.**
the Protection of National Minorities
Opinion on Germany, 1 March 2002[175]

" . . . 23. The Advisory Committee notes that in Germany official statistical data on the ethnic and linguistic breakdown of the population have not been collected since the second world war. It notes that there is a broad consensus in the country against the keeping of ethnic data. This is the result of the misuse of ethnic data during the Nazi period that facilitated the Holocaust. When it comes to estimating the number of members of a national minority the German authorities can base their estimations on various factors, such as the number of persons who are members of organisations representing minorities, or the number of pupils attending schools for minorities. In the absence of reliable statistics on national minorities and in spite of the fact that the figures used by the Government are not particularly challenged by the national minorities themselves, it can sometimes be difficult for the German authorities to monitor and take effective measures and for international monitoring bodies to ensure that Germany is honouring its commitments under the Framework Convention. The Advisory Committee therefore considers that the Government should seek means of obtaining more reliable statistics on national minorities. [See in this context also the second report on Germany of the European Commission against Racism and Intolerance (ECRI), adopted on 15 December 2000, paragraph 32.] If, in view of the historical context and the particularly sensitive nature of this information for persons belonging to national minorities, exhaustive statistical data pertaining to national minorities cannot be collected, other methods should be used, with the co-operation of the national minorities, such as estimates based on *ad hoc* studies, special surveys, polls or any other scientifically sound method . . . This data should be broken down by age, gender and location.

24. The lack of good statistical data makes it difficult for the German authorities to ensure that the full and effective equality of national minorities is promoted effectively. One example is where the German authorities state that they have no statistical data enabling them to evaluate the unemployment rate for each national minority or more elaborately broken down by age, gender, or geo-graphical differentials. The authorities assume that, in principle, membership of a national minority has no impact on a person's economic, social or cultural status. The Advisory Committee notes, however, that evidence presented to it indicates that members of the Roma/Sinti minority, in particular, find it significantly more difficult than the rest of the population to find work. In view of the preceding paragraph, the Advisory Committee considers that the German authorities should seek better to evaluate the socio-economic situation of persons belonging to this minority and, as appropriate, undertake measures in their favour to promote full and effective equality in the socio-economic field."

The processing of personal data within the EU Member States must comply with the guarantees stipulated by Article 8 of the European Convention on Human Rights[176]

---

[175] ACFC/INF/OP/I(2002)008.

[176] The European Court of Human Rights has interpreted this provision as protecting the individual from the processing of data, whether relating to his or her private or public activities, which may be traced back to an identified or identifiable individual [ECtHR, *Rotaru* v. *Romania* (Appl. No. 28341/95) judgment of 4 May 2000, at § 43 (noting in particular that "public information can fall within the scope of private life where it is systematically collected and stored in files held by the authorities")]. However, the Court has rejected an extensive understanding of this case-law which would have created an obstacle to the use of any information, even recent, concerning a specified individual, in order to adopt certain decisions affecting that individual: see the partial inadmissibility decision of 6 March 2003 in *Zdanoka* v. *Latvia* (Appl. No. 58278/00).

and by the Council of Europe Convention (No. 108) for the Protection of Individuals with regard to Automatic Processing of Personal Data.[177] Under this latter instrument, personal data undergoing automatic processing shall be "obtained and processed fairly and lawfully", "stored for specified and legitimate purposes" and processed by means "adequate, relevant and not excessive in relation to the purposes for which they are stored";[178] moreover, personal data cannot be used in a way incompatible with the purposes for which they are collected,[179] and states have to take the appropriate security measures for the protection of personal data stored in automated data files against unauthorised access, alteration or dissemination.[180] Under this same Convention, data relating to ethnic origin or the religion of an individual may not be automatically processed, unless domestic law provides for appropriate safeguards.[181] Within the European Union, Directive 95/46/CE of the European Parliament and the Council of 24 October 1995 on the protection of individuals with regard to the processing of personal data and on the free movement of such data (hereafter referred to as the "Personal Data Directive")[182] extends the protection offered by the 1981 Convention No. 108, in particular insofar as it applies also to the processing of personal data by non-automatic means. Moreover, Article 3(1) of the Council of Europe Framework Convention on National Minorities provides that every person shall have the right freely to choose to be treated or not to be treated as belonging to a national minority and that no disadvantage shall result from this choice.[183] Under a literal reading of this provision, state authorities thus would not be allowed to impose the quality of belonging to a national minority on individuals.[184] The European Parliament has summarised these principles in a resolution following the presentation by the Commission of a communication entitled "Non-discrimination and Equal Opportunities for All—a Framework Strategy".[185]

---

[177] This Convention was opened for signature on 28 January 1981; it has been ratified by all EU Member States.

[178] Art. 5(a), (b) and (c).

[179] Art. 5(b).

[180] See Art. 7. Appropriate security measures shall be taken as well for the protection of these personal data against accidental or unauthorised destruction or accidental loss.

[181] Art. 6. The Advisory Committee of the Framework Convention also emphasised the need to protect the confidentiality of the data relating to the membership to national (ethnic, religious, linguistic or cultural) minorities (Opinion on Italy, 14 September 2001, ACFC/OP/I(2002)007, para. 20).

[182] [1995] OJ L28/31.

[183] Therefore, an obligation to categorise oneself as member or non-member of a minority would contravene Art. 3(1) of the Framework Convention on National Minorities: see Opinion of the Advisory Committee of the Framework Convention on Estonia, 14 September 2001, ACFC/INF/OP/I(2002)005, para. 19; Opinion on Poland, 27 November 2003, ACFC/INF/OP/I(2004)005, para. 24.

[184] This right implies as well that each person shall have the liberty to request to stop being treated as belonging to a minority (see Opinion on Cyprus, 6 April 2001, ACFC/OP/I(2002)004, para. 18).

[185] COM(2005) 0224.

European Parliament, "European Parliament resolution on   **7.EC.44.**
non-discrimination and equal opportunities for all—a framework strategy"[186]

"H. . . .whereas it is important to define what is meant by positive action before deciding whether the law should change and if so how; whereas positive action comprises the measures to be taken to tackle inequality and unlawful discrimination and is a tool designed to promote balanced representation of people in areas and at levels where the population as a whole must be represented in equitable fashion; stressing that this concept must not be confined to the employment sector and must go beyond mere equality between the sexes,

. . .

J. aware of the fact that, in order to compensate for earlier injustices or discrimination, there may be a need for temporary recourse to positive measures based on a 'proactive' concept of justice and possibly taking very different forms; whereas the establishment of quotas must be regarded as an extreme measure which may be applied only in accordance with the case-law established by the European Court of Justice and with due regard to the proportionality criterion,

K. whereas in the case of certain particularly disadvantaged groups in society (such as Roma) or ones who are denied their rights (such as non-citizens), the adoption of positive measures—even of specific legislation—is essential if such people are to be able to participate actively in the life of their society (especially in political life) and hence to influence the decisions which affect them, . . .

General considerations

. . .

13. Considers that far from constituting an obstacle to the collection of data relating in particular to ethnic origin and to religion, Directive 95/46/EC provides necessary and desirable protection against any abuse of sensitive data collected for statistical purposes;

14. Considers that, notwithstanding cultural, historical or constitutional considerations, data collection on the situation of minorities and disadvantaged groups is critical and that policy and legislation to combat discrimination must be based on accurate data;

15. Considers that the Article 29 group set up pursuant to Directive 95/46/EC could usefully issue an opinion designed to clarify the provisions of the Directive which may hinder the collection of statistics relating to certain categories of individual and thus to ensure that those provisions are interpreted uniformly throughout the Member States;

16. Draws attention to the fact that once personal data have been rendered anonymous for statistical purposes, the information contained in the statistics is no longer to be regarded as personal data; points out that there are also reliable techniques which enable anonymity to be observed and are traditionally used in the social sciences and which should enable statistics based on criteria deemed sensitive to be established;

---

[186] 2005/2191(INI)), 8 May 2006 (rapp. T. Zdanoka). The resolution was strongly influenced by the positions adopted by the EU Network of Independent Experts on Fundamental Rights in its Thematic Comment No. 3 on the rights of minorities in the European Union, published in April 2005. That comment in turn resulted to a large extent from an attempt to develop an anti-discrimination agenda for the EU which would better take into account the principles from the Council of Europe Framework Convention on the Protection of National Minorities and from other instruments which protect minority rights in the international law of human rights.

17. Notes with satisfaction that the Commission intends to create (in cooperation with the Member States' authorities and other parties involved) statistics tools designed to assess the impact of discrimination; awaits with interest the publication of the data-collection handbook which is scheduled for 2006;

18. Points out that the concept of indirect discrimination is intrinsically linked to quantitative criteria and that it is therefore counter-productive to prevent statistics relating to certain characteristics from being gathered under the cover of legislation on the protection of personal data, since in the absence of such data the existence of indirect discrimination becomes impossible to prove;

19. Considers that if effective action is to be taken against all forms of indirect discrimination and if the Community directives on discrimination under which those forms are specifically prohibited are to be correctly transposed, it is essential that authorisation be granted for the supply of proof based on statistics;

20. Calls upon the Member States to develop their statistics tools with a view to ensuring that data relating to employment, housing, education and income are available for each of the categories of individual which are likely to suffer discrimination based on one of the criteria listed in Article 13 of the EC Treaty;

21. Draws attention to the fact that if an individual is to benefit from preferential treatment by virtue of his membership of a protected group, it must be possible for him to be identified as such, which means that sensitive data relating to him must be available; points out that such data must be processed in accordance with—in particular—the legislation relating to the protection of personal data and with Article 3(1) of the Framework Convention on the protection of national minorities . . ."

Directive 95/46/EC of the European Parliament and of the   **7.EC.45.**
Council of 24 October 1995 on the protection of individuals with regard to the
processing of personal data and on the free movement of such data
[Personal Data Directive][187]

Article 2—Definitions
For the purposes of this Directive:

(a) 'personal data' shall mean any information relating to an identified or identifiable natural per-son ('data subject'); an identifiable person is one who can be identified, directly or indirectly, in particular by reference to an identification number or to one or more factors specific to his physical, physiological, mental, economic, cultural or social identity.

b) 'processing of personal data' ('processing') shall mean any operation or set of operations which is performed upon personal data, whether or not by automatic means, such as collection, recording, organization, storage, adaptation or alteration, retrieval, consultation, use, disclosure by transmission, dissemination or otherwise making available, alignment or combination, blocking, erasure or destruction

. . .

[187] [1995] OJ L281/31.

Article 7
Member States shall provide that personal data may be processed only if:

  (a) the data subject has unambiguously given his consent; or

  . . .

  (e) the processing relates to data which are manifestly made public by the data subject or
       is necessary for the establishment, exercise or defence of legal claims.

Article 8
1. Member States shall prohibit the processing of personal data revealing racial or ethnic origin, political opinions, religious or philosophical beliefs, trade-union membership, and the processing of data concerning health or sex life.
2. Paragraph 1 shall not apply where:

  (a) the data subject has given his explicit consent to the processing of those data, except
       where the laws of the Member State provide that the prohibition referred to in para-
       graph 1 may not be lifted by the data subject's giving his consent; or
  (b) processing is necessary for the purposes of carrying out the obligations and specific
       rights of the controller in the field of employment law in so far as it is authorized by
       national law providing for adequate safeguards; or

  . . .

  (e) the processing relates to data which are manifestly made public by the data subject or
       is necessary for the establishment, exercise or defence of legal claims.

  . . .

4. Subject to the provision of suitable safeguards, Member States may, for reasons of substantial public interest, lay down exemptions in addition to those laid down in paragraph 2 either by national law or by decision of the supervisory authority . . .

The processing of personal data, relating, for instance, to the ethnic or religious affiliation of an individual or to his or her disability, will be required in order to grant to the individual members of minorities certain advantages or to offer them specific treatment. The relevant rules relating to the protection of personal data must be fully complied with in the framework of such a policy. In particular, the processing of "sensitive" data on racial origin, religious or other beliefs, health (disability) or sex life is subject to particularly strict conditions, in order to reflect the risk of discrimination involved in the use of such data.

  As the Personal Data Directive restricts the processing of sensitive data,[188] the consent of the "data subject" becomes decisive. Insofar as the processing of sensitive personal data in order to grant preferential treatment will be advantageous to the data subject, it will typically be possible to obtain the consent of that person to the processing of such data. In fact, at least with respect to the members of ethnic or religious minorities whose membership in those groups is defined by their ethnic origin or their religion, which are two "sensitive" traits, there may be a complementarity between that derogation to the principle according to which sensitive data

---

[188] See also Art. 6 of the Council of Europe Convention for the Protection of Individuals with regard to Automatic Processing of Personal Data (which says that sensitive data "may not be processed automatically unless domestic law provides appropriate safeguards").

may not be processed on the one hand, and the rule stipulated in Article 3(1) of the Framework Convention on the Protection of National Minorities, which provides that every person shall have the right freely to choose to be treated or not to be treated as belonging to a national minority and that no disadvantage shall result from this choice. The implication of these rules seems to be that, where a potential beneficiary of an affirmative action programme agrees to identify him- or herself as having a particular ethnicity or religious faith, that individual will be granted the preferential treatment afforded under the programme; if the potential beneficiary refuses to identify him- or herself as belonging to one ethnic or religious group, he or she should be considered to be exercising the right not to be treated as belonging to an ethnic or religious minority.

Whether this solution is workable in fact, however, may be doubted. First, the conditions under which the consent of the individual beneficiary of a position action measure may be said to be valid remain a subject of debate. In the context of the 1995 Personal Data Directive, the notion of "consent" is defined as the "freely given specific and informed indication of his wishes by which the data subject signifies his agreement to personal data relating to him being processed".[189] Two questions arise, however, even where the consent is free, informed and specific, as required by this definition. First, Article 3(1) of the Framework Convention on the Protection of National Minorities states that no disadvantage shall result from the choice of the individual not to be treated as a member of a minority. Would being denied benefit from a positive action policy not constitute precisely such a disadvantage? Secondly, in the specific context of the employment relationship, reliance on the consent of the worker either in order to legitimate the processing of personal data generally,[190] or in the context of the derogation to the processing of sensitive personal data, is generally considered highly suspicious, because of the power imbalance between the processor (the employer) and the data subject (the worker).[191]

These arguments against the reliance on the consent of the data subject who may benefit from a positive action policy would not seem to be decisive, however. The alternatives to this solution would consist either in not requesting the consent of the individual concerned for the processing of personal data in the context of a positive action programme or in renouncing the idea of such a programme altogether. But these alternatives are both unsatisfactory, and neither appears more favourable to the potential beneficiary of the positive action programme. Indeed, the first solution (to dispense with the consent of the data subject) would be in clear violation of Article 3(1) of the Framework Convention for the Protection of National Minorities, where ethnic or religious minorities are concerned, as well as of the interpretation given by the Committee on the Elimination of Racial Discrimination to Article 1(4) of

---

[189] Art. 2 h) of the Personal Data Directive.

[190] Art. 7 a) of the Personal Data Directive provides that if it is unambiguous, the consent of the data subject to the processing of personal data may legitimate this processing.

[191] This was one of the issues raised during the European Commission's social partner consultation regarding a directive on data protection in employment, see O. De Schutter, "La protection du travailleur vis-à-vis des nouvelles technologies dans l'emploi" (2003) 54 *RTDH* 627.

ICERD;[192] and the second solution would run counter to the consistent view of the Advisory Committee of the Framework Convention that affirmative action programmes seeking to contribute to the effective integration of minorities are in principle desirable.[193] As to the fragility of consent in the context of the employment relationship, it is a concern which has been expressed—most notably, by the Working Party created under Article 29 of the Personal Data Directive[194]—in the specific situation of the recruitment process, where, as a matter of course, a refusal by the candidate to a job to provide the employer with the information requested may lead the employer to deny the position to the individual concerned.[195] However, where the consent of the worker is requested in order to implement a positive action programme, it may not be presumed that it is coerced or particularly suspect: typically, the employer will seek this information from the employee in order to comply with the legal obligations imposed on the employer, and it will be in the interest of both that the employee identifies him- or herself with a particular group benefiting from the policy.

The framework presented above also raises a second and much more delicate question. Positive action schemes are a general measure adopted in order to substitute a notion of group justice for a notion of individual justice. The efficacy of such schemes can hardly be reconciled with the possibility, for each individual potentially concerned, not to be classified for instance according to race or ethnicity, or to religion—whether that individual belongs to the traditionally disadvantaged group which the scheme intends to benefit, or whether he or she belongs to the traditionally advantaged group, whose members will bear the cost of the positive action scheme. This is a real dilemma. It may point at the need to choose, in certain settings, between a literal reading of the Council of Europe Framework Convention for the Protection of National Minorities, especially its Article 3(1), on the one hand, and certain positive action schemes in favour of ethnic, religious or linguistic national minorities on the other hand. The difficulties raised in this regard by the implementation in Northern Ireland of the *Fair Employment and Treatment (Northern Ireland) Order 1998* (FETO)[196] are a perfect illustration. The modalities of assigning particular individuals to particular religious communities under the FETO have been described thus:

[192] The Committee on the Elimination of Racial Discrimination adopted General Recommendation VIII at its thirty-eighth session in 1990, in which it concluded that the identification of individuals as being members of a particular racial or ethnic group or groups "shall, if no justification exists to the contrary, be based upon self-identification by the individual concerned" (UN doc. A/45/18).

[193] See, e.g. Opinion on Azerbaijan, 22 May 2003, ACFC/OP/I(2004)001, para. 28; Opinion on Ukraine, 1 March 2002, ACFC/OP/I(2002)010, para. 27; Opinion on Serbia and Montenegro, 27 November 2003, ACFC/OP/I(2004)002, para. 38.

[194] Opinion No. 8/2001 on the processing of personal data in the employment context, WP 48, 5062/01, 13 September 2001.

[195] See p. 32 of Opinion No. 8/2001.

[196] See above, **7.NIR.4.** and nn. 18 *ff.* in this chapter.

C. McCrudden, "Consociationalism, Equality and Minorities   **7.NIR.46.**
in the Northern Ireland Bill of Rights Debate: The Role of the OCSE
High Commissioner on National Minorities"[197]

"As incorporated in the 1998 legislation, and subsequently set out in detail in subsidiary legislation [Fair Employment (Monitoring) Regulations (Northern Ireland) 1999, SRNI No. 148, as amended by the Fair Employment (Monitoring) (Amendment) Regulations (Northern Ireland) 2000, SR 2000 No. 228. The main difference between the old and new monitoring regulations as regards determining community affiliation is that the "principal method" in the old regulations al-lowed designation by virtue of school attended or direct question, whereas the new regulations permit only direct question as a "principal method", but do allow school attended to be taken into account in the application of the residuary method.], the employer is required to apply the 'principal method' to all employees and applicants. It provides for the community to which a person is treated as belonging to be determined by reference to his or her written answer to a direct question regarding his or her community affiliation.[1999 SR, Articles 8 and 9] Where the 'principal method' does not result in an employee or job applicant being treated as a member of the Protestant or Roman Catholic communities then the employer has the option of applying the 'residuary method' [1999 SR, Article 11]. The code of practice issued by the Equality Commission (the regulatory body with responsibility for the effectiveness of the legislation) recommends that 'in every case where an individual cannot be treated as belonging to a community under the principal method, [the employer is] strongly recommended to use the residuary method in order to determine the community background of the individual'. Where the employer chooses not to, or where this method produces no determination, the employee or applicant is to be treated as if the community to which he or she belongs cannot be determined.

What the 'residuary method' for discovering community affiliation involves is set out in some de-tail. Where an employee has provided the employer, in writing, with any relevant information about himself, then the employer is allowed (for the purposes of preparing a monitoring return) to treat that employee as belonging to the community with which the information tends to show he or she has a connection, or (if the information tends to show a connection with both communities) treat the employee as belonging to the community with which, in general, it tends to show he or she has the stronger connection. The following qualifies as relevant information: surname and other names; address; schools attended by the employee (whether in Northern Ireland or else-where); any course that the employee has undertaken in preparation for any recognised award or any examination conducted by the Department of Education for Northern Ireland; the employee's sporting or other leisure pursuits or interests; the clubs, societies or other organisations to which he or she belongs; or the occupation as a clergyman or minister of a particular religious denomination or as a teacher in a particular school, of any referee nominated by the employee when he or she applied for the job. These are all generally reliable ways of 'telling' religio-political origin in Northern Ireland. They provide reasonable methods of establishing identity that facilitates the implementation of the legislation.

Before sending in the monitoring return to the Commission the employer must give each employee a written notice telling him or her, the community to which he or she is regarded as belonging for the purposes of the return (or that the employee's community affiliation could not be determined) [1999 SR, Article 12]. If an employee believes that such a notice contains

---

[197] In J. Morison, K. Mcevoy and G.Anthony (eds.), *Judges, Transition and Human Rights Cultures* (Oxford University Press, 2006).

inaccurate information, he or she should tell the employer about this within seven days of receiving the notice. Where it appears to the employee that the employer has incorrectly designated the employee and draws this to the employer's attention, the employer is then obliged to correct the monitoring return to reflect this response [1999 SR, Article 13]. The law preserves the confidentiality of monitoring information under the main methods of monitoring [1999 SR, Article 16]. It does however allow the disclosure of otherwise confidential information to various official bodies: the Equality Commission, the Labour Relations Agency, the Fair Employment Tribunal, the courts and the employment tribunals. Nor is disclosure precluded to trade union officials and consultants assisting employers to develop equal opportunity policies. Anyone who supplies false information to someone filling in a monitoring return or who knowingly includes such false information in a return can be fined."

Whether this arrangement, which was largely supported as one of the key elements resulting from the 1998 Belfast Agreement, and which worked satisfactorily in practice, could be considered incompatible with the requirement of Article 3(1) of the Council of Europe Framework Convention for the Protection of National Minorities was intensely debated when the Northern Ireland Human Rights Commission proposed to include in the draft Bill of Rights for Northern Ireland a provision incorporating the substance of Article 3(1) of the Framework Convention. In the course of this debate, the Council of Europe was asked to provide an opinion on the issue. An ad hoc group of experts was set up for that purpose. It delivered an opinion where it stated:

> *A. W. Heringa, G. Malinverni and J. Marko, "Comments by*   **7.CoE.47.**
> *Council of Europe experts on certain aspects of a future Bill of Rights for*
> *Northern Ireland"*[198]

"61. The experts are aware that the inclusion of Clause 3 (7) in the Draft Bill of Rights has provoked much controversy. The current clause reads:
 'Everyone has the right freely to choose not to be treated as a member of a national, ethnic, religious, linguistic or cultural community and no disadvantage shall result from this choice or from the exercise of the rights which are connected to this choice.'
 62. This clause has its genesis in Article 3 of the Framework Convention for the Protection of National Minorities which concerns the right freely to choose to be treated or not to be treated as a person belonging to a national minority and that no disadvantage shall result from this choice.
 63. The concerns raised are primarily that the inclusion of such a clause could open the way for challenges to be made to current equality provisions that would undermine recent gains in equality over past years.
 64. Notwithstanding that the experts see that there may be an issue concerning the compatibility of certain equality provisions with the right to self-identification, they consider that this

---

[198] (Strasbourg, 3 February 2004) Council of Europe, DGII (2004) 4.

is not a matter that should be definitively solved in a bill of rights, but rather be addressed in ordinary legislation.

65. . . . [A] bill of rights should be the product of a broad societal consensus. From the discussions held in Belfast it is clear that there is no such broad societal consensus concerning the inclusion of this provision. Furthermore, it can be said that it is rare for a bill of rights or for a constitution to treat such matters . . .

66. The experts consider that it is important to note that the issue does not disappear if it is not specifically included in the Bill of Rights. The right remains to be implemented in the context of the application of Article 3 of the Framework Convention for the Protection of National Minorities. Furthermore, it can be argued that aspects of the right to self-identification may also be linked to Article 8 (right to privacy) of the ECHR for which redress procedures are already available under the Human Rights Act and under the ECHR itself . . .

67. The experts note that if a review of the legislation is to take place, it will require an examination of the application of positive measures to ensure equality as this is a central element of the issue in question. It can be noted that there could well be a clash of rights, for example between the right of self-identification on the one hand and the need to ensure equality on the other.

68. The experts consider that this issue could be better and more fully discussed or advanced, *inter alia*, in the con-text of discussions concerning the reform of the equality legislation and proposals to have a single equality act. There may also be other forums in which this matter can be raised, including the Advisory Committee on the Framework Convention during the second monitoring cycle under the Framework Convention for the Protection of National Minorities.

69. The experts are therefore of the view that the issue of self-identification should not be examined in the context of the Bill of Rights project, but rather outside of the project in a more appropriate forum."

Following in part what might be read as a call for caution from the Council of Europe experts, the Northern Ireland Human Rights Commission finally took the following view, which, precisely because of its ambiguity, exhibits clearly—as acknowledged by the Council of Europe experts themselves in paragraph 67 of their opinion—that a balance may be required between the need for effective equality legislation going beyond an anti-discrimination approach, on the one hand, and the right of each individual to be treated or not to be treated as a member of a national minority, on the other hand.

Northern Ireland Human Rights Commission,   **7.NIR.48.**
"Progressing a Bill of Rights for Northern Ireland: An Update"[199]

"The Commission understands that incorporation of Article 3(1) of the Framework Convention will not mean that the current requirements on employers in Northern Ireland to monitor the community background of their workforce, or of applicants for their workforce, will become unlawful. It will simply mean that employees and applicants, when being monitored, will be able to insist that their chosen community affiliation will be recorded, as

---

[199] April 2004, at 34.

well as any perceived community background. Under the existing Monitoring Regulations employees and applicants cannot be absolutely sure that the reality of their current community background is accurately recorded by the employer."

The debate continues on the question raised in this section. Personal data protection law and anti-discrimination law have developed hitherto in relative isolation from one another. And although minority rights—as codified in Europe by the Framework Convention for the Protection of National Minorities—lay in some respects at the intersection of these two bodies of rules, the terms of a compromise may still have to be worked out between what appear, in certain settings and under certain schemes, as conflicting requirements. Whether we should seek to define this compromise at the European level or at the level of each EU Member State[200] may be debated. The current situation, however, where different factions instrumentalise the existing legal requirements in order to serve their own agenda, is unsatisfactory: for the states concerned, it constitutes a source of legal uncertainty; and it may discourage a much-needed public debate on where such compromises should be struck, and what they should resemble.

7.8. COMPARATIVE ANALYSIS

As illustrated by the typology presented above (section 7.3), there exists a wide variety of schemes which seek to contribute to the realisation of substantive equality, although not all such schemes result in the preferential treatment of certain disadvantaged or underrepresented groups, or "positive action" per se. Certain schemes provide for the monitoring of the situation of categories defined, for instance, by sex, race or ethnicity, or religion, as regards access to social goods such as employment, education or housing. While such schemes are an important component of an anti-discrimination policy which seeks to go beyond mere formal equality, they do not necessarily lead to positive action measures as such, since they are without prejudice to the measures which will be adopted once an imbalance is found. Moreover, even within positive action measures, the typology includes outreaching measures; critical reflection on notions such as "merit" or "qualification", on which criteria for the allocation of social goods rely; the preferential treatment of equally qualified members of the underrepresented group (sometimes confusingly referred to as "flexible quotas" in German doctrine); or, finally, preferential measures for certain disadvantaged categories even where they are not equally situated according to the baseline criteria in use, or "strict quotas", i.e. set-asides in favour of members of the underrepresented group. These distinctions are essential. The debate on the desirability and the legitimacy of positive action has all too often developed at an exceedingly abstract level, comparing, for example, the virtues of "group justice" and "individual justice" or the acceptability of members of certain dominant groups

---

[200] Not only the EU Member States, of course, are facing this dilemma. The instruments of the Council of Europe broadly impose the same requirements as the relevant instruments of EU Law.

being made to pay for past acts of discrimination, where the different settings in which positive action measures are adopted and the various forms such measures may take ought to have been much more clearly distinguished. Moreover, the evaluation of the compatibility of positive action under international and European Union law depends not only on the legitimacy of the measure examined (whether it seeks to achieve a legitimate objective), but also on the proportionality of the measure examined (whether it is necessary for the realisation of the stated objective). The precise scope of the positive action scheme under scrutiny therefore will be decisive to evaluate its admissibility under general non-discrimination rules, where a conflict occurs.

Overall, the examination of the status of positive action under international human rights law shows that positive action is, within certain broad limits, allowed under the relevant anti-discrimination clauses. Indeed, the States Parties to these instruments are even occasionally encouraged to adopt such schemes, where this appears justified by the systemic discrimination to which a group is subjected. In comparison, European Union law appears relatively cautious, and even timid. Section 7.5 sought to provide a sense of how EU law has evolved in this area, in the only field—equal treatment between men and women in employment—where the case-law of the European Court of Justice has hitherto addressed the question. The initial *Kalanke* case of 1995 met not only with certain scepticism in legal doctrine, but also with a political response from the Member States, leading to an amendment to Article 141 of the EC Treaty brought about by the Treaty of Amsterdam. As a result, though without formally overruling its initial approach, the Court seems since 1997 to have adopted a more flexible position, allowing for a variety of schemes to be adopted or maintained, provided they do not establish an absolute and automatic preference based exclusively on sex in the attribution of certain advantages going beyond equal opportunities.

We have now arrived at a crucial moment in this development. As our understanding of the requirements of the principle of equal treatment develop, with positive action being seen more and more frequently as a necessary tool for the promotion of substantive equality, the tensions with other, potentially conflicting requirements—formal equality, of course, but also the requirements resulting from the protection of personal data (section 7.7)—become visible. Compromises need to be found. Arrangements need to be devised which ensure that a satisfactory balance is found between competing principles. Encouraging the search for such compromises at the level of each Member State would present a number of advantages. It would avoid having to opt, within a European Union in which different models for managing diversity coexist, for one of those models. The coexistence of approaches may encourage mutual correction. It may promote experimentation at local level, and mutual learning. It may ensure that no single model will be preferred over all the others, at the risk of rigidifying itself.

At the same time, however, the current framework of European Union law is not satisfactory. Lacking an authoritative interpretation of the requirements of the Personal Data Protection Directive in the context of positive action policies, the Member States may hesitate not only to develop schemes ensuring some form of monitoring of the situation of ethnic or religious minorities in employment, education or housing, but also and especially to adopt positive action policies where imbalances are found to exist. And it could be argued that, against the background of the developments of international human rights law, the current restrictions imposed by the case-law of the European Court of Justice on the adoption of positive action schemes are excessively restrictive. For experimentation at local level to take place, there must be room to experiment. Moreover, not only the specific characteristics of each positive action scheme adopted—of which there are in fact innumerable varieties, although typologies such as the one presented in section 7.3 necessarily tend to obfuscate this diversity—but also the local conditions and traditions should decisively influence the application of the proportionality test to such schemes,[201] so that national courts should be left with a broad margin of appreciation in the evaluation of the compatibility of positive action schemes with the general requirements of equal treatment, rather than this issue being decided at the level of European courts.

However, our current situation also presents us with an opportunity. At the end of section 7.5, doubts have been expressed as to whether the case-law developed by the European Court of Justice since its 1995 decision in *Kalanke* can be transposed without major revision to the new grounds of prohibited discrimination under the Racial Equality and Employment Equality Directives—or, indeed, even in the field of equal treatment between men and women, beyond employment. Thus, this is a time where new thinking is needed in this area. The question is not whether we see substantive equality as a desirable goal, for we do; but a debate needs to take place, on the basis of the variety of experiences we can benefit from, as to the best means to achieve this end.

---

[201] It is in that sense that the rule of equality may be said to be "empty" in the precise meaning that Peter Westen attributed to this expression: the rule of equality only takes on substantive content by the importation of external values. See P. Westen, "The Emply Idea of Equality" (1982) 95 *Harvard L. Rev.* 537–99. However, see A. D'Amato, "Is Equality a Totally Empty Idea?" (1983) 81 *Mich. L. Rev.* 600–3.

CHAPTER EIGHT
ENFORCEMENT BODIES

Gay Moon

8.1. INTRODUCTION

This chapter looks at the various types of equality bodies set up within the EU for the enforcement of equality norms. It starts by considering why equality bodies are needed and refers to the wide range of possible structures that have been adopted to meet this need. It will set out both the key norms for equality bodies in international law and the European requirements. It will then examine some of the powers and functions of equality bodies, and how these are defined by legislation at the state level. The chapter will then look at the need for equality bodies to be independent, explaining what changes the law requires in order to achieve true independence and how this can be protected in practice, and giving examples of ways in which independence is jeopardised.

It should be noted from the outset that equality bodies within Europe take a wide variety of forms and function in many different ways, and there is no precise formula for an equality body.

8.1.1. WHY DO WE NEED EQUALITY BODIES?

During the 1970s there was an increasing realisation in some European countries of the extent of gender and racial discrimination. With this came an increasing recognition that this was *not* a matter of purely private morality. Alongside this was a developing recognition that laws alone were insufficient to prohibit discrimination. To make anti-discrimination laws effective and to persuade discriminators to change their embedded patterns of behaviour, governments sought to provide institutions to promote the advantages of alternative behaviour. Equality bodies were identified as the means by which governments could secure a more widespread and more effective implementation of equality norms.

It is now well recognised that equality bodies are needed to promote the equal treatment of all persons without discrimination on one or more of the prohibited grounds.[1] Their common objective is to achieve cultural change within society by promoting equality values, by implementing those values throughout civil society and by assisting the victims of discrimination.

---

[1] Throughout this chapter "prohibited grounds" is taken to mean the grounds prohibited by any of the European Directives, namely sex, race or ethnic origin, religion or belief, disability, sexual orientation or age.

871

Equality bodies have the aim of securing the incremental implementation of equality norms and values within their geographical location. There are many steps that may be taken to achieve substantive equality beyond the passing of legislation to prohibit discrimination. Legislation only provides the first step towards a non-discriminatory society. Indeed, it has been said that

> "precisely because of the limitations of individual litigation, equality commissions need other distinctive powers. The primary purpose of an equality commission would not be seen to lie in the replication of activities undertaken by individuals but, instead, in the promotion of social change by different and idiosyncratic means."[2]

Equality bodies will also seek to change organisational policy and behaviour to reduce or eliminate under-representation, exclusion and institutional barriers to equal opportunities. This will usually be done by the provision of information on legal norms and best practice, by law enforcement, and by the encouragement of voluntary self-regulation or of economic incentives to encourage compliance with equal opportunities policies. Indeed, one of the main functions of equality bodies is often to provide information on the equality laws and help victims of discrimination with their claims.

8.1.2.   THE BROAD RANGE OF EUROPEAN EQUALITY BODIES

Most Member States of the European Union have now designated a specialised body for the promotion of equal treatment irrespective of racial or ethnic origin as required by Article 13 of the Racial Equality Directive, and although most of the Member States now have equality bodies, their shape, size, functions and effectiveness vary considerably.

There are many different types of organisations that fulfil some or all of the functions of an equality body. Some countries, such as Sweden, Cyprus and Lithuania have Ombuds.[3] Other countries, such as Ireland, Belgium, the UK and the Netherlands, have agencies called Commissions.

Most of the equality bodies set up by Member States deal with a number of different grounds for discrimination which are not limited to either race or gender.[4]

---

[2] N. O'Brien, "The Great Britain Disability Rights Commission and Strategic Law Enforcement: Transcending the Common Law Mind" in A. Lawson and C. Gooding (eds.), *Disability Rights in Europe. From Theory to Practice* (Oxford, Hart Publishing, 2005) 249.

[3] There is a variety of terminology used to refer to Ombuds, Ombudsmen and Ombudspersons. In this chapter we refer to specific institutions by their official names, but when referring to these bodies generically we have used the gender neutral term of "Ombud".

[4] The Austrian Equal Treatment Commission and Office for Equal Treatment, the Bulgarian Commission for the Protection against Discrimination (although Bulgaria is only an applicant state), the Cyprus Ombudsman, the Dutch Equal Treatment Commission, the Estonian Legal Chancellor, the French High Authority against Discrimination and for Equality, Greek Specialist Administrative bodies, the Hungarian Equal Treatment Authority, the Irish Equality Authority, the Latvian National Human Rights Office, the Lithuanian Equal Opportunities Ombudsman, the Equality Commission for Northern Ireland, the Romanian National Council for Combating Discrimination and the Slovenian Advocate for the Principle of Equality and Council for the Implementation of the Principle of Equal Treatment.

Other equality bodies, such as those in the UK,[5] Italy,[6] Finland,[7] Portugal[8] and Denmark,[9] cover single grounds.

Amongst those equality bodies set up to cover a single ground there is a trend towards amalgamation, with agencies covering the other grounds to create a single, larger agency covering all the prohibited grounds. Some countries which have had several different bodies for dealing with the grounds separately have now joined them together to make a single equality body, as in the case of the Dutch Equal Treatment Commission and the Equality Commission for Northern Ireland. The Belgian Centre for Equal Opportunities and Opposition to Racism was developed to take on all the grounds except gender, which is dealt with by the Institute for Equality of Women and Men. There are also some Member States which are in transition. Great Britain is in the process of transition towards a new Commission for Equality and Human Rights, which is due to commence operation in October 2007. The new body will cover discrimination on grounds of gender, race or ethnic origin, disability, religion or belief, sexual orientation and age, as well as human rights. Sweden is currently considering a proposal to join the offices of their different equality ombudsmen together.

Many of the countries setting up agencies for the first time, for example Romania, Hungary and Bulgaria, are setting up combined agencies rather than one body dealing with a single ground.

Some equality bodies operate within other organisations. Where this happens they are most commonly found within Human Rights Commissions. This is the case with the Danish Complaints Committee, which deals with issues of racial and ethnic origin within the Danish Institute for Human Rights. Two other countries in this situation, Latvia and Slovakia, have equality bodies that are located within the Latvian Human Rights Office and the Slovakian National Centre for Human Rights, respectively.

Another approach to equality bodies entails splitting their functions between several different agencies. For example, the Dutch Equal Treatment Commission does not assist victims in pursuing complaints because this would conflict with its primary task, namely that of considering complaints of unequal treatment in its quasi-judicial capacity. Consequently, the role of providing assistance to victims is met by the extensive "very competent infrastructure of local anti-discrimination agencies and a highly qualified independent National Bureau against Racial Discrimination, which, together with the ETC, can provide the structure required by the Directives".[10]

---

[5] Great Britain has the Equal Opportunities Commission for gender, the Commission for Racial Equality for race and ethnic origin and the Disability Rights Commission for disability.

[6] The Italian National Office against Racial Discrimination.

[7] The Finnish Ombudsman for Minorities deals with issues of racial and ethnic origin.

[8] The Portuguese Commission for Immigration and Ethnic Minorities.

[9] Denmark has a Danish Complaints Committee established within the Danish Institute for Human Rights to deal with issues of racial and ethnic origin and the Gender Equality Board to deal with issues of gender.

[10] See J. Goldschmidt, "Implementation of Equality Law: A Task for Specialists or for Human Rights Experts? Experiences and Developments in the Supervision of Equality Law in the Netherlands" (2006) 13 *MJ* 3, 324.

Germany currently has no federal equality body; however, a new General Equal Treatment Act which will set up a Federal Anti-Discrimination Agency has now been passed. This provides for the Federal Minister for Family Affairs, Senior Citizens, Women and Youth to appoint the Head of the Federal Anti-Discrimination Agency, acting on the suggestion of the federal government. The agency is to be provided "with any necessary human and material resources".[11] Additionally there are some equality bodies at Länder and more local levels.

Spain also has no equality body; however, the Spanish Council for the promotion of equal treatment of all persons without discrimination on grounds of racial or ethnic origin was due to be established before the end of 2006.

The Czech Republic only has a Governmental Council for Equal Opportunities for Women and Men, whose tasks are to advise the government on policy in relation to gender, to assess current problems in relation to the equality of women and men and to evaluate the implementation of policy initiatives in this area. It has no equality body to deal with the field of racial discrimination.

The way in which equality bodies provide assistance to victims of discrimination varies. Some provide support to individual claimants who wish to take legal action, others can consider complaints made to them and issue opinions on those complaints. These opinions may or may not be legally binding. Normally where the opinions are not legally binding in themselves the victim may take legal action before the courts in order to obtain a legal remedy if necessary.

Equality bodies need to be seen within their individual national context; differing political and legal circumstances inevitably affect the way that the equality body will make its impact felt.

In those countries that have a federal system of government it is important they ensure that they have a system which is comprehensive in its reach. If, as is typical, the relevant constitution separates the competency of the federal legislature from that of the provincial legislature, it will be necessary to ensure that the body is set up in such a way that it can review actions in both areas or to have a federal body and also a series of provincial bodies. Since such systems vary considerably, it is not possible to be entirely prescriptive as to how this is achieved. The key point is to ensure that there are no areas where there is an absence of an appropriate body.

From this short survey it can be seen that there is a very wide variety of bodies set up to assist the process of enabling equality norms to develop and that Member States have found that there is no single format for an equality body. These different formats reflect local circumstances, including the local legal structure. Some equality bodies have had a considerably longer existence than others. These bodies have therefore had time to develop more sophisticated procedures for tackling discrimination and inequality. This chapter will therefore pay more attention to the equality bodies of longer standing in order to benefit from the lessons that these bodies learnt.

---

[11] General Equal Treatment Act (*Allgemeines Gleichbehandlungsgesetz* (AGG)), 2006, ch. 8 para. 25(1), AGG, BGBl. Teil I 17.8.2006, S. 1897.

In order to share information and best practice, a group of European equality bodies have set up the European Network of Equality Bodies (Equinet).[12] Equinet aims to develop cooperation and facilitate information exchange between equality bodies across Europe to support the uniform implementation of EU anti-discrimination law and the levelling-up of legal protection for victims of discrimination.

The aim of Equinet is "to help Equality bodies fulfil their mandates by establishing a sustainable network and resource base for the exchange of legal expertise, enforcement strategies, training and best practice as well as a platform for dialogue with the European institutions."

Equinet has periodic meetings, discusses different ways of working and publishes reports to help build a body of information on good practice. This is useful as there is a richness of practice and experience that comes with this diversity of structure. Equality bodies are not static; Member States have let them grow and develop in order to adapt to changing needs or evolving ideas about best practice. Equinet assists this process.

In addition to the national equality bodies, the European Union has also set up the European Monitoring Centre on Racism and Xenophobia. This is a European equality body whose function is to collect objective, reliable and comparable information and data on racism, xenophobia, Islamophobia and anti-Semitism throughout the European Union in order to help both the EU and its Member States to develop policies to counter racial discrimination. Its role does not extend to offering any legal advice or assistance. The European Union has now extended its remit in order to turn it into a new Fundamental Rights Agency with a mandate to cover the fundamental rights of the European Union apart from gender. There will be a separate agency to deal with gender-related problems, the European Gender Institute.

8.2. SINGLE OR MULTIPLE EQUALITY BODIES?

European directives require the establishment of equality bodies to cover the areas of race discrimination and gender discrimination. Consequently, many Member States have been considering whether to set up a different body for each required field or a single body. A key question is which would be most effective. Would a body with jurisdiction to cover a number of different grounds for discrimination be better?

Member States with a longer tradition of equality bodies have usually set up one body for each ground, gender, race and sometimes disability, sexual orientation or religion. However, it is noticeable that in Great Britain a new combined equality body, the Commission for Equality and Human Rights, is being set up to operate from October 2007, and in Sweden active consideration is being given to amalgamating their ombudsmen into a single Office of the Ombudsman against Discrimination to cover each of the prohibited grounds for discrimination, gender, race, disability,

[12] For more information see the website of the Migration Policy Group.

religion or belief, sexual orientation and age, and sometimes other grounds such as marital status as well.

The arguments for amalgamation have often been driven by cost-saving, but also include the benefits of shared expertise and good practice. However, these moves have led to considerable controversy, with those committed to only one of the grounds fearing that their ground will become marginalised in any amalgamation. A key argument has been whether there is a hierarchy of inequalities. This argument points to the key place of gender equality in the main body of the EC Treaty, and the more extensive protection of race equality in the Race Equality Directive. The counter-argument points to the international statements on equality in the UN Declaration of Human Rights and the International Covenant on Civil and Political Rights.

A number of the more recently established equality bodies have been set up as single bodies to cover all the grounds prohibited by the race, employment equality and gender Directives. The High Authority in France, the Hungarian Authority of Equal Treatment and the Romanian National Council for Combating Discrimination are examples of single equality bodies that have been designed from their inception to cover all the prohibited grounds. These bodies are well placed to confront intersectional discrimination.

Equinet has considered the comparative benefits of single ground and multiple ground equality bodies. In their paper for Equinet Bjørn Jacobsen and Eddie Khawaja from the University of Copenhagen and the Danish Institute for Human Rights respectively consider that the advantages of a combined equality body include the more efficient use of limited resources and a better sharing of knowledge, the enhanced ability to deal with examples of multiple discrimination as well as structural discrimination affecting several different grounds, whilst they recognise the danger of the creation of a hierarchy of grounds for discrimination.

B.D. Jacobsen and E.O. Rosenberg Khawaja,   **8.EC.1.**
"Legal Assistance to Individuals. Powers and Procedures of Effective and
Strategic Individual Enforcement"[13]

"From the perspective of the individual complaints, it may be considered preferable to go beyond a minimum implementation of the directives, and establish equality bodies on all of the grounds of discrimination included in the Equality Directives. Indeed, the question arises as to what extent equality bodies that cover all grounds of discrimination provide, or have the potential to provide, more effective protection against discrimination than equality bodies that cover only a single ground of discrimination.

The first aspect of deploying a horizontal approach that should be highlighted is the possibility of a more effective utilisation of limited resources. The advantage of shared resources applies not only to the effective utilisation of limited financial resources, but also to the sharing of knowledge. Second, because the different grounds listed in the Racial Equality

---

[13] In Equinet Working Group 2 on Strategic Enforcement, "Report: Strategic Enforcement: Powers and Competences of Equality Bodies" (2006) 11–12, available on the website of the Migration Policy Group.

Directive and the Employment Equality Directive are to some extent inter-linked, the bodies that handle cases of discrimination on a range of grounds may more easily address all aspects of a given case. For instance, cases of religious discrimination regarding employment of women wearing religious headscarves include possible elements of discrimination on the grounds of religion, gender and ethnic origin. Third, equality bodies that cover all grounds of discrimination facilitate access in the sense that a victim of discrimination can have all aspects of his or her complaint heard without having to file several complaints with different organisations. Fourth, the possibility of uncovering structural and institutional discrimination that spans across several grounds, such as ethnic origin and gender, provides a substantial positive aspect of the horizontal approach. A fifth aspect of having harmonised and unified access to the assistance or decisions of quasi-judicial bodies that could be achieved through the horizontal approach is the same 'signal' effect of such an approach. When some groups and individuals do not have the same protection and possibilities as other groups or individuals, a possible unwanted effect could be that a hierarchy—both in the eyes of the victims and in general—is created between the different grounds of discrimination, rendering some groups or individuals less important.

The horizontal approach, however, does also require attention to the specific construction of the equality body. The different grounds of discrimination include different characteristics based on the nature, history and development of the given area. It is important to ensure that the equality body working with the horizontal approach pays attention to and upholds these differences when structuring its work, for instance through the creation of separate directorates or functional divisions within the body. Moreover, it is preferable that the body is equipped with similar powers when dealing with discrimination on different grounds. This will ensure that the beneficial effects of applying a horizontal approach are upheld because it is easier to make use of expertise and experiences from different areas if the body can conduct the same levels of investigations and apply the same procedural rules on all areas.

If such structures and powers are not in place when applying the horizontal approach in the equality body, there is a risk that the resources and the focus of the body will not be applied in a beneficial way to all areas. The danger exists in particular when several bodies with different life spans, resources and experiences are merged into one."

Christopher McCrudden, in writing on the proposal to develop a new European Fundamental Rights Agency, reflects on the UK experience in relation to the differing competencies of single and multiple bodies. In the following passage he examines the advantages and disadvantages of having a single equality body instead of a series of equality bodies each representing a different ground for discrimination:

C. McCrudden, "The contribution of the EU Fundamental Rights   8.UK.2.
Agency to Combating Discrimination and Promoting Equality"[14]

SINGLE OR MULTIPLE EQUALITY BODIES

"A second issue raised by the UK experience that may also be relevant for the debate on the role of the FRA [Fundamental Rights Agency] is the appropriateness of joining all the

[14] In P. Alston and O. De Schutter (eds.), *Monitoring Fundamental Rights in the EU* (Oxford, Hart Publishing, 2005) 148–51.

equality strands together in the context of a single body. In several jurisdictions which have adopted an agency regulation approach, the issue has arisen as to whether the preferable approach is to establish a single agency which is responsible for equality across a range of different groups, including race, gender, disability, sexual orientation, etc, or have several different agencies responsible.

One common argument in favour of a single agency approach covering all the separate equality strands is that particular equality agendas may gain in strength from being associated with other equality agendas. Two separable arguments recur. The first is that equality and non-discrimination are indivisible and that it strengthens each dimension of equality ideologically for it to be seen as part of a wider, broader movement. The second is that it strengthens those dimensions of equality that do not have the political priority of some other dimensions of equality for them to be associated with those dimensions that do have strong political support. In some jurisdictions, it is said, the movement against disability discrimination might have stronger political weight if it were associated with gender equality, which is perceived to be given greater political priority at the present time, and therefore benefit from greater financial resources. A more pragmatic argument in favour of a single agency is that, particularly from the point of view of organisations subject to regulation, a 'one-stop-shop' is desirable where advice on equality and discrimination across all grounds can be obtained and co-ordinated. This, it is said, saves time, money, and aggravation. It also avoids the perception of potentially inconsistent signals being sent on similar issues by different agencies. A similar argument, it is said, obtains in the context of victims of discrimination: it is not infrequent that a complainant comes to an equality body with a relatively broad sense of grievance which spans several possible areas of discrimination (for example, a complaint by an Afro-Caribbean woman) and it would be useful to be able to handle these issues in a co-ordinated way, dealing with the allegations in a way which recognises the overlapping nature of the jurisdictions involved.

The [UK] Government's justification for its decision to amalgamate the different equality commissions into one reflects these arguments. It is best summed up in the White Paper issued in 2004. A single body would be a strong and authoritative champion for equality and human rights. The CEHR [Commission for Equality and Human Rights] would be well positioned to drive change, making dignity and respect, fair treatment and social justice core values. The CEHR [Commission for Equality and Human Rights] would incorporate a depth of expertise on specific areas of discrimination, while also being able to cast a wide net across all equality and human rights issues. Through a cross-cutting approach, a single organisation would be better able to tackle barriers and inequalities affecting several groups, and identify and promote strategic solutions. A single organisation would benefit individuals seeking advice and support on all discrimination issues and information on human rights, in an accessible and user friendly way. Providing a single source of contact, for individuals and for the agencies and organisations to which they turn for advice, would deliver real benefits for everyone. In its policies and approach, a single organisation would be better equipped to address the reality of the many dimensions of an individual's identity, and therefore tackle discrimination on multiple grounds. A single organisation would be better able to meet the needs of employers and service providers, providing a single access point to information, advice and guidance on the full breadth of equality and human rights issues. A single organisation would be more effective at promoting improvements to the delivery of public services. It would provide guidance and support on human rights good practice and compliance, and can take a cross-cutting seamless approach on the full breadth of equality issues on a sector by sector basis with, for example, health authorities, local government and education providers. A single organisation would also provide the opportunity to pursue a more coherent approach to enforcing discrimination legislation. The CEHR [Commission for Equality and Human Rights] could ensure, for example, that when it takes action to tackle unlawful discrimination in one equality area it also takes the opportunity to ensure improvements in the other areas of discrimination. A single organisation would be able to work to promote good relations among different communities, building trust and understanding that will contribute to a more cohesive society. A single organisation would combine the strengths of the existing Commissions with the expertise from key organisations representing the new equality strands, identifying and promoting creative responses to the challenges and opportunities it will face.

There are four reasons for injecting a degree of caution, however, into this debate. The first is that the argument in favour of a single equality body covering many grounds assumes a relative degree of harmony in the allocation of resources within the single enforcement body. To the extent that the distribution of scarce resources involves tensions and conflicts, this harmony cannot be guaranteed. Indeed, experience from some countries has shown that agencies with such broad remits are not infrequently driven with in-fighting between the different 'constituencies'. One or other type of discrimination may be regarded by some as 'special': in the sense that the issue cannot be treated operationally as something that is submerged in the generality of [the] day to day work [of the body] [Summing up of the colloquy by Mr. Michael Head, Vice Chair, European Commission against Racism and Intolerance (ECRI) in ECRI. The Place and Role of National Specialised Bodies in Combating Racism, Lausanne, Switzerland 22–24 October 1998, Summary of the Proceedings, Council of Europe, Strasbourg, 1998, 8].

So, for example, the Vice Chairman has argued that there are three reasons for regarding racial discrimination as 'special' in this way:

'First, racial discrimination is at the root of a large proportion of human rights abuses. Second, the handling of such cases calls for a high level of expertise. Third, these sorts of cases tend to involve the most vulnerable groups in society; and fourth, they are frequently the most politically charged.'

Against this background, he says:

'it seems inconceivable to us in ECRI that any national body, irrespective of its precise form and remit, should not have within it at least a section dedicated to dealing with problems of discrimination on the grounds of race as defined in the International Convention [International Convention on the Elimination of all forms of Race Discrimination].'

This issue might be addressed in the context of the FRA by the allocation of earmarked budgets, and separate policy-making functions, for each area within the single agency.

A second reason for some caution regarding amalgamation is that part of the strength of separate agencies is the extent to which they are perceived as serving the needs of a specific group: women, or ethnic minorities, for example. This identification with the organisation may be a source of strength in the inevitable political disputes that arise, over funding for example. If these separate constituencies are seen as being submerged in some larger entity, there is a danger that this source of strength may be lost. Thirdly, the benefits of a 'one-stop shop' are largely illusory if there are significantly different statutory provisions dealing with race, gender, religion, disability, and so on. At the moment there are considerable differences in requirements between race, gender and disability discrimination legislation in the United Kingdom. Until there is a greater harmonisation of the various substantive requirements, the benefits of a single agency, at least in terms of being a 'one-stop-shop' may prove difficult to establish. In both Northern Ireland and Britain, pressure has grown for legislation (often termed a 'Single Equality Act') that would harmonise the different pieces of existing equality law into a more coherent whole. In the context of the EU, a single equality body is likely also to increase the already existing pressure for harmonisation of the Community's equality and non-discrimination directives."

European equality bodies have had little experience of dealing with multiple discrimination[15] so far. However, the various Canadian Human Rights Commissions (which deal predominantly with equality issues) have become increasingly aware that discrimination occurs on multiple grounds and consequently they found a need to develop an intersectional approach to address this.

For example, the Ontario Human Rights Commission found that, between April 1997 and December 2000, 48% of the complaints filed with them covered more than one ground. They argue that in such cases the discrimination experienced is different from that experienced on any of the individual grounds.[16] So, for example, the experience of discrimination suffered by a black woman is intrinsically different from that suffered by a black man, or a white woman. This has been described as:

> ". . . intersectional oppression [that] arises out of the combination of various oppressions which, together, produce something unique and distinct from any one form of discrimination standing alone . . ."[17]

This approach enables a person's particular experience to be both acknowledged and remedied. It is discussed more fully in Chapter One in section 1.5.

8.3. OVERVIEW OF MODELS FOR INTERVENTION

There is a wide range of types of equality bodies and it is not easy to compartmentalise them. However, one possible division can be made between Ombuds-type bodies and Commissions. These are not exclusive or watertight categories, and many of the roles undertaken by bodies which fall within the two broad categories will overlap.

---

[15] See above J. Gerards, Chapter One: Discrimination Grounds, section 1.5.

[16] Ontario Human Rights Commission, "An Intersectional Approach to Discrimination: Addressing Multiple Grounds in Human Rights Claims", discussion paper (2001) 11. Available on the website of the Ontario Human Rights Commission.

[17] M. Eaton, "*Patently Confused, Complex Inequality and Canada* v. *Mossop*" (1994) 1 *Rev. Cons. Stud.* 203, 229.

8.3.1. OMBUDS

8.3.1.A. SWEDEN

The term "ombudsman" originated in Sweden and was first introduced into the constitution in 1809. The term means "legal representative" or "commissioner".[18] An individual is appointed as Ombud and he or she will develop an office to support their work.

The first Member State to adopt an ombudsman system to counter discrimination was Sweden. The Ombudsman for Equal Opportunities between Men and Women, the JämO, was the first to be established in 1980, the Ombudsman for Ethnic Discrimination, the DO, was established in 1986, the Ombudsman for the Disabled, the HO, was established in 1994 and the Ombudsman for Sexual Orientation, the HomO, in 1999.

Initially their jurisdiction was limited to employment. However, in 2001 the Equal Treatment of Students at Universities Act (2001:1286) extended the powers of all the ombudsmen to cover students in higher education. The Prohibition of Discrimination Act (2003:307, as amended in 2005) extended the powers of the JämO, DO, HO and HomO to cover complaints arising in the field of goods and services, including housing, and in 2006 the Act on the Prohibition of Discrimination and other Degrading Treatment of Children and Pupils (2006:67) extended the powers of all the ombudsmen to cover the education of all children and pupils at pre-school or school.

A Parliamentary Government Commission Inquiry has presented a proposal to enact a single Equality Act and the Government has announced its intention to combine all the ombudsmen into a single ombudsman to deal with all the named forms of discrimination. The new single Ombudsman body would take up its work in 2008.

The ombudsmen can investigate complaints concerning discrimination and have the right to represent individuals in discrimination cases that he or she considers are of importance in terms of case-law or otherwise. The ombudsman must first try to settle the case without going to court, and any settlement that is reached is enforceable to the extent that they include financial compensation of the victim of discrimination. Ombudsmen can also give advice and support to individuals and institutions, as well as undertaking educational work, providing information, undertaking independent surveys and reports, making recommendations to government, whether in relation to legal or other measures to counter discrimination, and they can monitor international developments. They also do outreach work in the form of education and information activities to promote non-discrimination. The HO has published "Guidelines for an Accessible Public Service", although these guidelines are not legally enforceable.

The functions of the HO are typical of how the Swedish Ombuds work.

---

[18] *Chambers 21st Century Dictionary* (Edinburgh, Chambers Harrap, 2002).

The Swedish Disability Ombudsman Act of 9 June 1994 (1994:749)[19] **8.SE.3.**

"**Functions**

Section 1
The Disability Ombudsman has the function of monitoring the issues that relate to the rights and interests of people with disability. The objectives of the activities of the Disability Ombudsman shall be to ensure that people with disability are ensured full participation in the life of the community and equality of life conditions.
The activities of the Disability Ombudsman shall relate to the follow-up and evaluation of issues referred to in the first paragraph.
The Disability Ombudsman shall, in accordance with the Prohibition of Discrimination in Working Life of People with Disability Act (1999:132), Equal Treatment of Students at Universities Act (2001; 1286), the Prohibition of Discrimination Act (2003: 307) and the Prohibition of Discrimination and other Degrading treatment of Children and Pupils (2006: 67)ensure that this Act is complied with and is also empowered on behalf of an individual jobseeker or employee to present an action in disputes relating to the application of that Act.

Section 2
The Disability Ombudsman shall work to ensure that inadequacies in statutes and other enactments as regards people with disability are remedied.

Section 3
The Disability Ombudsman shall, when necessary, take initiatives for deliberations with authorities, businesses, organisations and others with the purpose of combating people owing to their disability being disfavoured or in other ways exposed to treatment that is unfair or violates integrity.
The Disability Ombudsman shall also, by information activities, and in other similar ways, work to ensure that nobody is owing to disability disfavoured or in another way exposed to treatment that is unfair or violates integrity.

Section 4
Authorities, county councils and municipalities that have an obligation to perform functions relating to people with disability shall, at the direction of the Disability Ombudsman, provide information to the Ombudsman about their activities. They are also under an obligation to attend deliberations with the Ombudsman if the Ombudsman so directs."

8.3.1.B.   OTHER COUNTRIES

Other countries with Ombuds-type organisations covering equality law include Cyprus (called either the Ombudsman or Commissioner for Administration); Estonia (the Legal Chancellor); Finland (the Office of the Ombudsman for Minorities); Greece (the Ombudsperson); Hungary (the Parliamentary Commissioners for

---

[19] Available on the website of the Swedish Disability Ombudsman.

National and Ethnic Minority Rights); Latvia (the National Human Rights Office); and Lithuania (the Office of the Equal Opportunities Ombudsman).

8.3.1.C.   SIGNIFICANT DIFFERENCE

The Ombud's offices tend to be more complaint-focused than those of Commissions; however, this does vary between different agencies, and a number of Ombuds have used their office to develop equality promotion work.[20]

8.3.2.   COMMISSIONS

8.3.2.A.   OVERVIEW

Equality Commissions are run by a committee of members often representing different aspects of society or grounds for discrimination. They are bodies entrusted by government with the performance of specified anti-discrimination duties. In some bodies Commission members are appointed by the state to represent a particular ground or interest, in other cases different organisations or officials are able to appoint one or more members, and in yet others there is no set criterion apart from interest in the equalities area.

However, most Commissions aim to use the diversity of skills and experience brought by their different Commissioners to reflect a broad spectrum of knowledge of the equalities area.

8.3.2.B.   EXAMPLES OF DIVERSITY IN COMMISSIONERS

In France the High Authority against Discrimination and For Equality has a board made up of political appointees (see **8.FR.53.**), the only provision being that they should overall provide a balance of men and women. The Irish Equality Authority has up to 12 members (including the Chairman) appointed by the Minister for Justice, Equality and Law Reform, of whom at least five shall be male and five female (**8.IE.54.**). The new Great Britain Commission for Equality and Human Rights will have between 10 and 15 members (Commissioners), who collectively will have experience and knowledge of the recognised grounds of discrimination and human rights. The Equality Act 2006 further specifies that one must be or have been a person with a disability, one is to be appointed "with the consent of the Scottish Minister who knows about conditions in Scotland" and one "with the consent of the National Assembly for Wales, who knows about conditions in Wales".[21] By comparison, the

[20] See, e.g. the work of the Swedish Ombudsmen.
[21] Equality Act 2006, sch. 1, para. 2(3).

Australian Human Rights and Equalities Commission has a President and five full-time Commissioners, each of whom represents a separate ground—namely, one each for Human Rights, Race, Sex, Disability and "Aboriginal and Torres Strait Islander Social Justice". However, there are currently only three Commissioners, so each one is taking on a dual role as Age has been added to the remit of the Sex Discrimination Commissioner. There is no similar example of this structure within European equality bodies.

8.4. LEGAL NORMS FOR ENFORCEMENT BODIES

8.4.1. INTERNATIONAL NORMS

There are important international recommendations as to the need for, and format of, national organisations to implement equality norms. Any equality body should be assessed for its effectiveness and utility against these principles.

8.4.1.A. THE PARIS PRINCIPLES

The United Nations for Human Rights Commissions set out in March 1992 the first important set of principles for human rights bodies; these are known as the "Paris Principles". They are widely referred to as setting the standard for equality bodies, even though these originally set out to provide a basic framework for Human Rights Commissions.

Office for the United Nations High Commissioner for Human Rights **8.UN.4.**
"Principles relating to the status and functioning of national institutions for protection and promotion of human rights" (known as the "Paris Principles")[22]

In October 1991, the Center for Human Rights convened an international workshop to review and update information on existing national human rights institutions. Participants included representatives of national institutions, states, the United Nations, its specialised agencies, and intergovernmental and non-governmental organisations.

In addition to exchanging views on existing arrangements, the workshop partic-ipants drew up a comprehensive series of recommendations on the role, composition, status and functions of national human rights instruments. These recommendations,

---

[22] Available on the website of the Office for the United Nations High Commissioner for Human Rights.

which were endorsed by the Commission on Human Rights in March 1992 (resolution 1992/54) and by the General Assembly in its resolution A/RES/48/134 of 20 December 1993, are summarised below:

"A. Competence and responsibilities
1. A national institution shall be vested with competence to protect and promote human rights.
2. A national institution shall be given as broad a mandate as possible, which shall be clearly set forth in a constitutional or legislative text, specifying its composition and its sphere of competence.
3. A national institution shall, inter alia, have the following responsibilities:

(a) To submit to the government, parliament and any other competent body, on an advisory basis either at the request of the authorities concerned or through the exercise of its power to hear a matter without higher referral, opinions, recommendations, proposals and reports on any matters concerning the protection and promotion of human rights. The national institution may decide to publicize them. These opinions, recommendations, proposals and reports, as well as any prerogative of the national institution, shall relate to the following areas:
  (i) Any legislative or administrative provisions, as well as provisions relating to judicial organization, intended to preserve and extend the protection of human rights. In that connection, the national institution shall examine the legislation and administrative provisions in force, as well as bills and proposals, and shall make such recommendations as it deems appropriate in order to ensure that these provisions conform to the fundamental principles of human rights. It shall, if necessary, recommend the adoption of new legislation, the amendment of legislation in force and the adoption or amendment of administrative measures;
  (ii) Any situation of violation of human rights which it decides to take up;
  (iii) The preparation of reports on the national situation with regard to human rights in general, and on more specific matters;
  (iv) Drawing the attention of the government to situations in any part of the country where human rights are violated and making proposals to it for initiatives to put an end to such situations and, where necessary, expressing an opinion on the positions and reactions of the government;
b) To promote and ensure the harmonization of national legislation, regulations and practices with the international human rights instruments to which the State is a party, and their effective implementation;
c) To encourage ratification of the above-mentioned instruments or accession to those instruments, and to ensure their implementation;
d) To contribute to the reports which States are required to submit to United Nations bodies and committees, and to regional institutions, pursuant to their treaty obligations, and, where necessary, to express an opinion on the subject, with due respect for their independence;
e) To cooperate with the United Nations and any other agency in the United Nations system, the regional institutions and the national institutions of other countries which are competent in the areas of the protection and promotion of human rights;
f) To assist in the formulation of programmes for the teaching of, and research into, human rights and to take part in their execution in schools, universities and professional circles;

g)   To publicize human rights and efforts to combat all forms of discrimination, in partic-
       ular racial discrimination, by increasing public awareness, especially through
       information and education and by making use of all press organs . . .

C. Methods of operation
Within the framework of its operation, the national institution shall:
1. Freely consider any questions falling within its competence, whether they are submitted by
the government or taken up by it without referral to a higher authority, on the proposal of its
members or of any petitioner;
2. Hear any person and obtain any information and any documents necessary for assessing
situations falling within its competence;
3. Address public opinion directly or through any press organ, particularly in order to publicize
its opinions and recommendations;
4. Meet on a regular basis and whenever necessary in the presence of all its members after they
have been duly consulted;
5. Establish working groups from among its members as necessary, and set up local or regional
sections to assist it in discharging its functions;
6. Maintain consultation with the other bodies, whether jurisdictional or otherwise, responsible for the protection and promotion of human rights (in particular, ombudsmen, mediators
and similar institutions);
7. In view of the fundamental role played by the non-governmental organizations in expanding
the work of the national institutions, develop relations with the non-governmental organizations devoted to protecting and promoting human rights, to economic and social development,
to combating racism, to protecting particularly vulnerable groups (especially children, migrant
workers, refugees, physically and mentally disabled persons) or to specialized areas."

8.4.1.B.   WIDER APPLICATION OF THE PARIS PRINCIPLES

Recommendation No. 17 of the UN Committee on the Elimination of Racial
Discrimination (CERD)[23] expressly applied the Paris Principles to its recommendations for race equality bodies. The Committee emphasised the specific importance
of these principles in the context of race discrimination, recommending that national
commissions or other appropriate bodies should promote respect for human rights
without discrimination, review government policy in relation to protection against
racial discrimination, monitor legislative compliance with the International
Convention on the Elimination of All Forms of Racial Discrimination (ICERD),
educate the public about the government's obligations under ICERD and assist the
government in the preparation of the periodic reports submitted to the CERD
committee.

[23] General Recommendation No. 17: Establishment of National Institutions to Facilitate Implementation of the Convention, 25 March 1993 (General Comments), 42nd session, 1993, A/48/18.

8.4.1.C.   ECRI RECOMMENDATIONS FOR EUROPEAN EQUALITY BODIES

These initiatives led the Council of Europe's European Commission against Racism and Intolerance (ECRI) to develop key recommendations for Member States on the establishment of equality bodies to counter discrimination on grounds of racism, xenophobia, anti-Semitism and intolerance at a national level. In turn, these recommendations then influenced the Council of the European Union when adopting the wording of Article 13 of the Racial Equality Directive. However, ECRI's recommendations are more detailed than those set out in Article 13 and hence are not open to the same criticisms of imprecision that have been made of the Racial Equality Directive (see **8.EC.7.**). Recommendation No. 2[24] in relation to race equality bodies sets out clear principles which could be applicable to equality bodies on any or all grounds. This recommendation makes it clear that the equality body itself must be independent, not just its functions. Consequently, with appropriate amendment they could provide a much better template for the framework of equality bodies.

8.4.2.   REQUIREMENTS FOR EQUALITY BODIES UNDER EUROPEAN
          LAW

8.4.2.A.   INTRODUCTION

There are several legislative provisions under the law of the European Union that are of specific importance. Member States will need to consider the requirements of Article 13 of the Racial Equality Directive (2000/43/EC),[25] Article 8a of the Gender Employment Directive (2002/73/EC),[26] Article 12 of the Gender Goods and Services Directive (2004/113/EC)[27] and Article 20(2) of the Recast Gender Employment Directive (2006/54/EC).[28] These impose requirements on Member States to establish equality bodies for race and gender. The race equality body duty, which came into operation in July 2003, may be taken as typical.

---

[24] ECRI General Policy Recommendation No. 2: Specialised Bodies to Combat Racism, Xenophobia, Antisemitism and Intolerance at National Level, adopted by ECRI on 13 June 1997, CRI (97) 36.
[25] [2000] OJ L180/22.
[26] [2002] OJ L269/15.
[27] [2004] OJ L373/37.
[28] [2006] OJ L204/23.

Council Directive 2000/43/EC of 29 June 2000 implementing the   **8.EC.5.**
principle of equal treatment between persons irrespective of racial or ethnic origin[29]

Article 13
1. Member States shall designate a body or bodies for the promotion of equal treatment of all persons without discrimination on the grounds of racial or ethnic origin. These bodies may form part of agencies charged at national level with the defence of human rights or the safeguard of individuals' rights.
2. Member States shall ensure that the competences of these bodies include:
    — without prejudice to the right of victims and of associations, organisations or other legal entities referred to in Article 7(2), providing independent assistance to victims of discrimination in pursuing their complaints about discrimination,
    — conducting independent surveys concerning discrimination,
    — publishing independent reports and making recommendations on any issue relating to such discrimination.

8.4.2.B.   MINIMUM STANDARDS

It should be noted that this Article sets a *minimum* requirement for Member States. It is possible and indeed desirable for equality bodies to have wider powers. However, the minimum for compliance with this Article is that these bodies be able to:

    — give *independent* advice and assistance;
    — conduct *independent* surveys and studies; and
    — publish *independent* reports and recommendations.

The requirement in the Article is not for the body itself to be independent; it only has to have the capacity to perform each of the named functions independently. This is somewhat surprising. The lack of more explicit requirements in the directive makes it difficult to ascertain whether the directive's requirements are being met. It seems to assume that the body is only to be judged by results and not by looking at the structure. The structure under which such tasks are carried out is very likely to indicate the extent of the independence of the body. It need hardly be said that if the body itself is not independent, the credibility of its work is likely to be very considerably diminished.

There are similar requirements for an equality body to deal with gender set out in Article 8a of the Gender Employment Directive.

---

[29] [2000] OJ L180/22.

Council Directive 2002/73/EC of 23 September 2002 amending   **8.EC.6.**
*Council Directive 76/207/EEC on the implementation of the principle of equal
treatment for men and women as regards access to employment, vocational training
and promotion and working conditions*[30]

Article 1(7) inserted as Article 8a
1. Member States shall designate and make the necessary arrangements for a body or bodies
for the promotion, analysis, monitoring and support of equal treatment of all persons without
discrimination on the grounds of sex. These bodies may form part of agencies charged at
national level with the defence of human rights or the safeguard of individuals' rights.
2. Member States shall ensure that the competences of these bodies include:
   (a) without prejudice to the right of victims and of associations, organisations or other
        legal entities referred to in Article 6(3), providing independent assistance to victims of
        discrimination in pursuing their complaints about discrimination;
   (b) conducting independent surveys concerning discrimination;
   (c) publishing independent reports and making recommendations on any issue relating to
        such discrimination.

An almost identical provision was enacted in Article 12 of the Gender Goods and
Services Directive, which extended the existing provisions in relation to gender
discrimination to access to and supply of goods and services. The Recast Gender
Employment Directive will replace the existing Gender Employment Directive (cited
in the extract above) and it must be implemented by 15 August 2008. It contains a
similar provision on equal treatment bodies in Article 20(2). However, it adds a fourth
competence required for a gender employment equality body, which is that they shall
have competence for "at the appropriate level exchanging available information with
corresponding European bodies such as any future European Institute for Gender
Equality".[31] It is not clear whether this means that gender employment equality
bodies are required to be able to exchange information only with Europe-wide gender
equality bodies or whether it extends to exchanges with national gender equality
bodies. If it does include national equality bodies, then this will reflect and include the
work already being done by Equinet (see above section 8.1.2) to exchange
information between equality bodies. This ambiguity may not be important as it is
surely helpful for equality bodies to exchange information with similar national
equality bodies and it would be difficult to imagine that any equality body would
consider that such a capacity was outside its remit.

---

[30] [2002] OJ L269/15.
[31] Directive 2006/54/EC of the European Parliament and of the Council of 5 July 2006 on the implementation of the principle of equal opportunities and equal treatment of men and women in matters of
employment and occupation (recast), [2006] OJ L204/23 Art. 20(2) [generally known as Recast Gender
Employment Directive].

8.4.3.   CRITICISMS OF EU REQUIREMENTS

8.4.3.A.   GENERAL COMMENTS

The wording of these directives in relation to equality bodies has been criticised as being overly vague and imprecise. The lack of detail in these Articles enables a range of steps to be taken in Member States but, while this diversity may facilitate a range of options, it leaves open many questions about the adequacy of compliance with European law. Questions left open include what level of help amounts to "independent assistance to victims"? Is it enough to just offer them some advice on the terms of the law over the telephone or to offer to send them an advisory leaflet? Does the equality body have to have any capacity for taking up cases for victims? What sort of "independent surveys" are required? Should they be national or local? While there is no clear provision about the way in which to use such surveys, at least the requirement to "publish independent reports" is linked to the requirement to make recommendations on any issue relating to such discrimination.

Such broad principles do not lend themselves to any form of enforcement. It appears that, as long as a Member State sets up one or two people in a small office able to send out leaflets to victims, conduct one or two small surveys and produce an annual report making one or two recommendations on race discrimination, the requirements under the Racial Equality Directive will be met. This would be to comply with the letter rather than the spirit of the directive, and it may well be that enforcement proceedings by the European Commission would then be upheld by the Court of Justice. Of course, to take this approach to the Directives would also constitute a substantial missed opportunity to help build a fairer and more equal society.

8.4.3.B.   THE RACIAL EQUALITY DIRECTIVE

In the passage below Colm O'Cinniede develops these points in relation to the Racial Equality Directive.

C. O'Cinneide, "The Race Equality Directive as a Basis for   **8.EC.7.**
Strategic Enforcement"[32]

"The language and wording of the Directive is vague in outlining these functions: for example, does 'providing assistance to individuals' include representing them in court or

---

[32] In J.Cormack (ed.), Strategic Enforcement and the EC Equal Treatment Directives. Towards the Uniform and Dynamic Implementation of EU Anti-Discrimination Legislation: The Role of Specialised Bodies, Report of the Sixth Experts' Meeting, hosted by the Irish Equality Authority, 4–5 March 2004, Migration Policy Group, 49.

before tribunals, or will the provision of advice be sufficient to satisfy the terms of the Directives? What exactly is required from states to ensure the independence of equality bodies? Also, the Directives' requirements are confined to the scope of their provisions: equality bodies established in line with the Directives may be given a role in combating other forms of discrimination, especially the types of discrimination in employment prohibited by the Framework Equality Directive [Employment Equality Directive], but cannot rely upon the terms of the Race and Gender Directives to argue that they should be given particular functions to deal with these other types of discrimination. (The Directives' requirement of independence may however continue to be of considerable importance.) Nevertheless, the Race and Gender Directives' provisions do provide to some degree a firm basis for equality bodies to take action against discrimination and prejudice, and also provide a formal guarantee of independence from government interference.

   How then should equality bodies set about fulfilling their functions under the Directives? It should be recognised that complex questions of tactics and strategy arise in trying to combat discrimination, especially when it is deep-rooted and systemic in nature. Equality bodies will inevitably have to struggle with limited resources and questions of how best to deploy these resources. They will also have to identify what areas and issues deserve priority treatment in their work, and how to use their finite resources to best effect to achieve the maximum return. Comparative experience from different countries as to which strategies work will be of great value in identifying appropriate approaches to combating inequality. Different approaches will inevitably have to be adopted in different national contexts: there is no single model of how an equality body should perform its functions. However, it is possible to identify several examples of good practice in strategic enforcement that are of relevance to any equality body in Europe."

8.5. FUNCTIONS

This section aims to examine the range of duties and powers that make up the functions of equality bodies and give some examples of good practice.

8.5.1.   LEGAL CASEWORK

There are a number of different ways in which an equality body can use legal casework to assist in the fight against discrimination. This section will look at the ways that equality bodies can use a combination of the provision of legal assistance to victims, mediation, taking action in its own name, interventions and situation testing to counter discrimination.

8.5.1.A.   PROVISION OF LEGAL ASSISTANCE TO VICTIMS

It is a key function of equality bodies that they should provide independent assistance to victims of discrimination. The Race and Gender Directives, whilst requiring equality bodies to provide "independent assistance to victims of discrimination in pursuing their complaints about discrimination", do not set out the nature or form of this assistance. It could be provided by the equality bodies' in-house legal department, it could be provided by a separate body possibly set up by the equality body as a linked organisation, or it could be met by legal aid or the provision of funds to enable the victim to purchase independent assistance from a lawyer.

The EC directives do not require that the equality body assist all cases where discrimination is alleged to have occurred.

It is perhaps not surprising that historically some of the early equality bodies which set out to provide assistance in all relevant discrimination cases did become substantially overloaded. The result has been very significant delay and this can be used by detractors to discredit the body concerned. Whilst this has not been the experience of any of the European equality bodies, the full impact of such policies were tested out in both Canada and America. From time to time this has been a feature of some of the Canadian Human Rights Commissions[33] (which deal almost exclusively with equality cases) and, more particularly, the American Equal Employment Opportunity Commission. This last body had a backlog in its case load in 1995 of 111,000 outstanding complaints.[34] It has now adopted a more systematic approach alongside an emphasis on precedent-establishing intensive litigation in relation to each ground.

On the other hand, for an equality body to assist too few cases also leads to a risk that it may become discredited. The Great Britain Commission for Racial Equality has in recent years received widespread criticism for supporting too few cases. This is particularly disappointing as in the past it has led the way in bringing important test cases.

The absence of a coherent case work strategy can lead to disengagement with the communities that ought to have most to gain from equality bodies. Such disengagement is a matter of concern as it could be seen as another occasion on which the state had failed them and so lead to greater and not less social exclusion. Equality bodies need to make decisions about which cases are important and which are less important in their current context. Decisions need to made about which cases they need to bring in order to establish a new legal precedent or to respond to a particular issue that has come to be seen as important.

Strategic litigation can have a range of important effects. It can help to define the reach and effect of the law or relevant legal duties, across the whole of a Member State, or a large organisation or particular sector, such as employment generally or local government or transport. Strategic legislation can ensure that particular working or business practices are exposed to independent judicial scrutiny, thereby

---

[33] See, e.g. *Promoting Equality: A New Vision 2000*, published by the Canadian Human Rights Act Review Panel under the authority of the Minister of Justice and the Attorney General of Canada.

[34] See P.M. Igasaki and P.D. Miller, *Priority Charge Handling Task Force* (Litigation Task Force Report, 1998), available on the website of the US Equal Employment Opportunity Commission—"The agency's pending charge inventory fell from 111,000 in 1995, immediately following introduction of charge processing reforms, to fewer than 66,000 at the end of the first quarter of FY [fiscal year] 1998. This represents a 40% reduction in charge inventory."

underlining the strategic importance of the relevant equality laws. It can provide new insights into how inequality works in practice and therefore how policies or practices might be framed to remedy such problems. Strategic litigation can perform a leavening role within an organisation, compelling a particular person or entity to look very closely at working or commercial policies, procedures and practices. It has a deterrent effect in relation to respondents who will inevitably have faced financial cost, inconvenience and perhaps adverse publicity, and also may in turn act as a deterrent to other employers or service providers, so prompting them to eradicate similar discriminatory practices in their own organisations. Further, when the equality body focuses its legal follow-up work around the strategic litigation, this can lead to effective changes being made in the wider context, thereby securing more lasting change through effective follow-up action and providing a basis for more incisive and specific actions by the equality body in other ways; thus in Great Britain, when a series of cases exposed discriminatory practices in a particular employment, the equality bodies undertook a formal investigation into that sector or business (see above 8.5.1.C.)

An example of the importance of test case litigation is provided by the European Court of Justice's ruling in Case 152/84 *Marshall* v. *Southampton and South West Hants Area Health Authority*.[35] This case tested the limits of a piece of UK legislation, the Sex Discrimination Act 1975, against the requirements of European law. It established that difference in treatment of men and women in relation to retirement ages was unlawful. Of even wider application was the second successful challenge, brought at a later stage of the same litigation.[36] In this second case the statutory limit for compensation for sex discrimination in the employment tribunal was ordered to be set aside. Now there are no such limits, and tribunals are expected to award compensation appropriate to the circumstances of each case.

It is important that equality bodies that do provide representation develop a strategic approach in order to maximise their effectiveness. Random litigation which follows no strategic priorities will not have much added value. It may also be difficult to ensure that associated promotional measures are effective in such a context. So equality bodies should litigate only those complaints that are strategically relevant. This requires prioritising the cases to be assisted. The following passage shows how thinking on this issue has been developing within European equality bodies in their discussions within Equinet and how solutions are being developed.

[35] [1986] ECR 723.
[36] Case C–271/91 *Marshall* v. *Southampton Area Health Authority (No.2)* [1993] ECR I–4367, in which the issue of what was necessary for an effective remedy for breach of a Community Law obligation was considered by the Court of Justice. This was just as much path-finding litigation supported by the Equal Opportunities Commission.

B.D. Jacobsen and E.O. Rosenberg Khawaja,   **8.EC.8.**
"Strategic Enforcement: Powers and Competences of Equality Bodies"[37]

"However, it has been the experience of equality bodies that handling individual complaints is a resource intensive process that is not always in proportion to the results achieved on a larger scale. It has also been the experience that some types of discrimination e.g. systemic discrimination, cannot be combated effectively solely by individual enforcement . . . this Article will focus on the powers and procedures that equality bodies apply when handling individual complaints, and how these powers and procedures may be used effectively- both in terms of providing the highest possible level of protection to individual victims given limited resources, and in terms of ensuring that the enforcement of an individual claim has general long-term effects beyond the results of any single case . . . [references omitted]."

The writers suggest some methods that equality bodies can adopt in order to ensure that the effect of their casework is maximised.

B.D. Jacobsen and E.O. Rosenberg Khawaja, *"Legal Assistance to*   **8.EC.9.**
*Individuals: Powers and Procedures of Effective and Strategic Individual
Enforcement"*[38]

"TRIAGING COMPLAINTS

Experiences with increasing caseloads
Some of the more well-established equality bodies have received so many complaints that it has caused a backlog of cases. This prolongs the review time, which often makes the complaints process less effective. Complaints about discrimination are best dealt with quickly: the sooner the conflict is addressed, the easier it tends to be to resolve it and the less resource intensive it is for the parties and the equality body . . . Based on the experiences of the more well-established equality bodies, it must be assumed that as an equality body becomes more established, the size of its caseload will become a challenge. The question is how to address the challenge so it does not prevent the equality bodies from dealing with the complaints effectively . . .

Considerations and recommendations
In order to meet the challenge of an increasing caseload, it is important to be able to triage complaints so they can be dealt with effectively and strategically. A possible approach to this is the strategic litigation approach, the main advantage of which is that it ensures that the resources of the equality body are used mainly on complaints that can lead to a wider impact. This approach is particularly useful for equality bodies that represent the complainant. Equality bodies that issue legally-binding decisions or non-legally binding statements as a neutral party must, as a general rule, handle all complaints that fall within the mandate of the equality bodies, that respect the time limits and that are not found to be manifestly ill-founded

---

[37] Equinet Working Group 2 on Strategic Enforcement, "Report: Legal Assistance to Individuals" (2006) 10.
[38] In Equinet, above n. 13, 14–16.

or better dealt with by another body. These equality bodies must deploy a case handling process that not only detects cases that may have a wider impact, but is also effective for all complaints.

Preliminary assessment may be an effective tool for speeding up the review process, primarily because it can lead to the quick settlement of complaints. However, applying informal procedures such as preliminary assessment is usually at the cost of the parties' right to due process. To ensure that parties do not feel pressured into settling their case without having exercised these rights, it is important that, as with the procedure followed by the Canadian Human Rights Commission, the parties are informed of their rights when the preliminary assessment is communicated i.e. that they are not bound by the assessment, that the assessment does not exclude a normal investigation, what the rights of the parties are under a normal investigation, and what influence the assessment may have on the final decision. Furthermore, one of the objectives of the individual undertaking the preliminary assessment may be to evaluate whether the situation described in the complaint constitutes discrimination. This assessment is made before any investigation is undertaken i.e. before the respondent has been heard. If the individual undertaking the assessment is to do any further work on the case, he/she may be influenced by his/her initial view of the case. If the equality body is to act as a neutral party when investigating a complaint and to issue objective decisions or statements, the question arises as to whether it is appropriate for the individual conducting the preliminary assessment to participate in the investigation and decision-making process.

The multi-disciplinary team review is recommended for enforcing individual complaints strategically because it focuses on the elements of single cases that can be used to promote equal treatment in general. The downside of this approach is that it costs more at the outset in terms of human resources and that it prolongs the review time. However, it has been the experience of the Canadian Human Rights Commission that the resources and time are well spent because the investigations tend to be shorter as a result [references omitted]."

The Irish Equality Authority has been very clear about the need to adopt a strategic approach to its litigation. It sees this as a key part of its work, as Niall Crowley, its Chief Executive, makes clear in its 2004 Annual Report.

N. Crowley, "Equality Authority, Annual Report 2004"[39]   **8.IE.10.**

"Strategic litigation
The Equality Authority provides legal advice and assistance to claimants in cases under the equality legislation on the basis of criteria established, and kept under review, by the board . . . These criteria ensure a strategic approach to litigation supported by the Equality Authority. This strategic approach ensures coordination between legal work and priorities established in the strategic plan. It pushes out boundaries in seeking to establish new legal precedents and to stimulate new practices in key sectors. It promotes a culture of compliance that ensures the legislation is seen to be relevant and effective by all concerned.

Significant successes are evident in casework supported by the Equality Authority during 2004 in both the settlements and the recommendations detailed in this report. Under the

[39] Chief Officer's Report, available on the website of the Irish Equality Authority, 11–12.

Employment Equality Acts the case of Campbell Catering Ltd v. Rasaq was particularly significant. The Labour Court found that in certain circumstances employers may have to take positive steps to ensure non discrimination on the race ground. In Citibank v. Ntoko the Labour Court provided an interesting interpretation of the use of a hypothetical comparator and affirmed the principle that awards for compensation for the effects of discrimination have to be effective, proportionate and dissuasive."

This view, that assistance in individual cases is an integral part of the process of "building a culture of compliance with the equality legislation", led to its continued explicit inclusion as a major objective when the Irish Equality Authority set its strategic plan for 2006–2008.[40]

To maximise the effectiveness of casework, promotional work must follow on from, and work hand in hand with, strategic litigation. The effect of successful cases can be maximised by ensuring that they receive wide publicity. Eilis Barry, Legal Advisor to the Equality Authority, Ireland, has commented on the usefulness of publicity:

> "In Ireland individual discrimination cases regularly receive considerable publicity and have prompted extensive national debate on a number of occasions. This has greatly heightened awareness of the legislation."[41]

In Great Britain the Commission for Racial Equality has developed an area of work which they call "legal follow up". This involves working with organisations on the practices and procedures following an adverse decision against them in the courts or tribunals. Such work can result in similar outcomes to those of an investigation, i.e. improved policies and cultural change.[42] The equality body can also use particular cases to publicise its recommendations as to good practice, showing employers how to avoid such discriminatory practices and work towards a real culture change.

The Dutch Equal Treatment Commission also sees the use of an active follow-up policy as a vital aspect of their work. The former President, Jenny Goldschmidt, has commented:

> "Since 2001, the results of the follow-up policy have been registered with the Commissions in its files . . . It is remarkable that, although these numbers refer mostly to individual cases, the measures taken in response often have an effect exceeding the individual case. Individual cases have resulted in e.g. amendment of discriminatory regulations, and thus the broader active follow-up policies seem to have a deeper structural impact than mere compliance by individual parties."[43]

---

[40] See further Irish Equality Authority, Strategic Plan 2006–8, Embedding Equality, Strategic Objective 2: to maintain and further develop a culture of compliance with the equality legislation, available on the website of the Irish Equality Authority.

[41] E. Barry, "Interventions and Amicus Curiae Applications Making Individual Enforcement More Effective" in Equinet, above n. 13.

[42] R. Karim, "A Legal Strategy to Combine and Coordinate Different Tools Available" in Cormack, above n. 32, 27–8.

[43] See Goldschmidt, above n. 10, 327.

The limitations of the individual enforcement model for equality bodies have frequently been noted. These are that strategic litigation is dependent on the willingness and ability of an individual to take a case; that groups experiencing discrimination are frequently disenfranchised and experience many barriers in accessing legal remedies, and may be very reluctant to be involved in litigation; and that litigation requires proof to a minimum standard—hence difficulties with gathering evidence and finding an appropriate comparator can cause cases to founder. Cases that appear at the outset to raise important points may be compromised before any resolution of the critical point in the case has taken place. Compromises may meet the needs of the complainant but may sometimes be on terms of confidentiality which provide no opportunity for publicity and promotion and hence little deterrent effect. Finally, litigation always carries a risk of victimisation both of the victim and of potential witnesses.

Nevertheless, it is clear that without litigation the rule of law cannot be vindicated. Equality bodies that operate in a system in which there is no effective remedy to vindicate the breach of equality rights will not meet the requirements either of the Paris Principles or of the EC Equality Directives.

8.5.1.B.   MEDIATION

Mediation or conciliation is a tool to which equality bodies are increasingly turning. It has important advantages over some kinds of litigation. It can be said that a mediated solution has no winner or loser, so it may be easier for an employee to return to work for the same employer. Additionally, the opportunity and motive for victimisation may be proportionately diminished. It may also be less time consuming. Both parties can retain ownership of the process and can control the outcome, the process can be made to focus on the future, rather than the past, and wider remedial agreements can be made than might be ordered by the courts: for example, for the employer to introduce new procedures to counter discrimination. The mediation approach highlights points of common interest and hence may ultimately be much less divisive. However, concerns have been expressed that the use of mediation can mean that legally binding decisions are reached without one or other of the parties understanding their full legal rights, that the role of an equality body in enforcing equality can be undermined, and tha the development and full enforcement of the law can be undermined by mediation because its essence lies in compromise. As Jenny Goldschmidt puts it,

> "[a]lthough mediation has the advantage that the relationship between parties is restored, and that, for example, a plaintiff may keep or resume his or her job, it also has disadvantages. From an equality law perspective, the main risk is that, in the process of negotiation, concessions have to be made which are not in line with the essentials of the law."[44]

---

[44] *Ibid.*, 328.

897

Moreover, there is a potential conflict between the policy advisory role of an equality body and the mediation role. Some of these problems can be partially overcome or avoided by the separation of the stage in which mediation is attempted from that in which litigation is pursued. Thus Great Britain's Disability Rights Commission has addressed the concern that a mediation function could undermine its role as a law enforcement agency by setting up an entirely separate body to offer mediation services to people with disabilities who wish to use mediation to resolve their problems.

The Swedish Ombudsman against Ethnic Discrimination explains how this process operates in Sweden and expresses some concerns about the role of mediation in achieving change in equality law and practice. Clearly, if legal decisions on the application of the law are not made, the parameters of the law are not developed.

European Commission, "Specialized bodies to promote equality **8.EC.11.**
and/or combat discrimination. Final report"[45]

"How the option of taking cases to court encourages out-of-court settlements
Before taking a case to court, the Swedish Ombudsman Against Ethnic Discrimination (DO) will suggest an out-of-court settlement. The law states that the first priority is to arrive at a voluntary settlement. Settlements are also less demanding of the DO's resources. The Ombudsman meets with the parties involved and seeks to reach agreement on financial compensation or some other relevant solution. While the DO interprets achieving a high number of such settlements as a criterion of success, it can also sometimes be important to obtain a court verdict and thereby establish a legal interpretation of an item of legislation. Since the law on measures against ethnic discrimination in the workplace came into force in 1999, the number of out of court settlements has increased. In 2001 there were about 32 settlements out of the 262 cases that were concluded the same year. This includes those settlements achieved with the assistance of trade unions. Often such a resolution is the preferred solution for both parties, e.g. because a complainant might prefer a job he/she had applied for than financial compensation. This would not be possible to achieve in court.

However, having the option of bringing cases to court might, according to the DO, apply a degree of pressure to the parties and serve as encouragement towards reaching a settlement."

In Ireland, the Equality Tribunal can offer both mediation and the ability to hear and issue a judgment on a case. Since 2004 every case is automatically allocated for mediation by an Equality Mediation Officer unless one of the parties objects. If mediation fails, either of the parties can ask for the case to be referred for a ruling. In such cases, a different Investigating Equality Officer will be allocated to the case so that the process of mediation and the process of adjudicating the case are kept

---

[45] Report on the Role, Structure and Functioning of Specialised Bodies to Promote Equality and/or Combat Discrimination—Final Report, May 2002, 77, available on the website of the European Commission, Directorate-General for Employment, Social Affairs and Equal Opportunities.

separate and the events surrounding the mediation should not influence the judgment. The effectivenenss of the mediation depends on the maintenance of confidence in an effective barrier between the Equality Mediation Officer and the Investigating Equality Officer hearing the case. The Irish Equality Tribunal (formerly called the Office of the Director of Equality Investigations (ODEI)) has an agreed set of procedures to regulate the way in which mediation is conducted.

European Commission, "Specialized bodies to promote equality **8.EC.12.** *and/or combat discrimination. Final report"*[46]

"The mediation method used by ODEI [Office of the Director of Equality Investigation—now the Equality Tribunal] is an internationally recognized process whereby a trained Mediation Officer who takes a neutral and impartial role assists the parties in exploring the areas of dispute, and where possible to assist them in reaching a mutually acceptable agreement. The process is voluntary and either party may end the process at any time. When a settlement is reached both parties sign a legally-binding agreement.

The mediation process is based on the following principles:

— Consent: this is sought independently from both parties
— Impartiality: the mediation service guarantees impartiality
— Voluntary process: the consent of both parties is necessary, and either party may withdraw from the process at any time
— Accessibility: the mediation is free of charge and intended to be universally accessible
— Participation: the process is based on the active participation of the parties involved in the case
— Power balance: the mediator will ensure balanced negotiations and will prevent manipulative or intimidatory negotiation techniques
— Third parties: these are welcome to be included in the process
— Advice: where the case involves rights and obligations other than those in which the mediator is trained, s/he will refer the parties to independent advice
— Confidentiality: the mediation is conducted in private, and the terms of the settlement are not published."

8.5.1.C.   TAKING ACTION IN ITS OWN NAME

Some equality bodies have explicit powers to take cases in the absence of individual litigants, so that if they find that they are receiving repeated complaints in relation to a particular issue but none of the victims who have been subjected to the particular discriminatory conduct in question wish to take an individual case, the equality body can bring a case in its own right (this can occur with the Irish Equality Authority, the Dutch Equal Treatment Commission and the Belgium Centre for Equal Opportunities and Opposition to Racism).

[46] *Ibid.*, 72.

In Belgium, where the alleged violation has an identifiable victim, the power of the Centre for Equal Opportunities and Opposition to Racism to take a case is dependent on the consent of the victim. However, in cases where there is no identifiable individual victim, the Centre may bring a case to challenge the actions in question in the public interest.

Belgian Act of 15 February 1993 pertaining to the foundation of **8.BE.13.**
a centre for equal opportunities and opposition to racism, modified on 13 April 1995,
20 January 2003, 25 February 2003 and 10 August 2005[47]

Art. 2
The Centre's task is to promote equal opportunities and to oppose any and all forms of distinction, exclusion, limitation or preference on the grounds of:

1° a so-called race, colour, descent, origin or nationality;
2° sexual orientation, marital status, birth, fortune, age, creed or philosophy of life, current and future state of health, disability or physical trait.

Art. 3
The Centre is completely independent in the fulfillment of its task.
The Centre is qualified to . . .

5° take legal action in any disputes that falls under the application the following acts . . .

Note
The Acts named are the principle Acts dealing with discrimination on any of the grounds listed in Article 2 together with Acts prohibiting holocaust denial, human trafficking and human trading. Gender issues are dealt with by the Belgian Federal Institute for the Equality of Men and Women.

A Centre for Equal Opportunities and Opposition to Racism report on civil actions brought in 2000 has highlighted a number of examples where these powers were used.

Centre for Equal Opportunities and Opposition to Racism, **8.BE.14.**
"Report: Fighting Racism in Belgium. Civil Actions brought in 2000"

"Since June 1999 press offences in Belgium can be brought before the magistrate's court if they constitute a violation of the law on racism. In a number of such cases, the Centre instituted civil proceedings.

[47] Moniteur belge of 19 February 1993, 25 April 1995, 12 February 2003, 17 March 2003 and 2 September 2005; also available on the website of the Centre for Equal Opportunities and Opposition to Racism.

The Centre brought a civil action following a complaint about a sticker campaign in Diest and surroundings, using the slogan 'hand in hand, back to your own land'.

The Centre also took action against a number of television programmes. Civil proceedings instituted against unknown persons for incitement to hatred on various programmes that were broadcast under the auspices of the Nationalistische Omroepstichting VZW [Nationalist Broadcasting Foundation, a non-profit-making organisation].

The Centre also brought a civil action against the publisher responsible for an 'Open letter to the people of Brussels' against which it had previously lodged an ordinary complaint.

Following the municipal elections on 8 October 2000, the Centre received a large number of complaints about the election propaganda. In a number of cases, the Centre's Board of Management decided to bring a civil action against the publishers of these pamphlets.

For instance, the Centre brought a civil action against two candidates of the Vlaams Blok political party on account of the nature of their election pamphlets. It depicted a plane taking off bearing the words 'hand in hand terug naar eigen land' [hand in hand back to your own land]. Another pamphlet included a drawing of an African hut with the words 'Reisbureau België, zijn dopgeld, zijn OCMW, zijn kindergeld' [Belgium travel agents: unemployment benefits, local social welfare services, family allowances]."

In Ireland the Equality Authority also has the power to instigate litigation in such circumstances; sections 85 and 86 of the Employment Equality Acts 1998–2004 provide that the Equality Authority has legal standing to bring complaints to the Equality Tribunal relating to patterns of discrimination, discriminatory advertising and the contents of collective agreements.

Irish Employment Equality Acts 1998–2004[48]   **8.IE.15.**

85.—(1) Where it appears to the Authority—

(a) that discrimination or victimisation is being generally practised against persons or that a practice referred to in section 8(4) is being applied or operated,

(b) that discrimination or victimisation has occurred in relation to a particular person who has not made a reference under section 77 in relation to the discrimination or victimisation and that it is not reasonable to expect that person to make such a reference,

(c) that there is a failure to comply with an equal remuneration term or an equality clause either generally in a business or in relation to a particular person who has not made a reference under section 77 in relation to the failure and whom it is not reasonable to expect to make such a reference,

(d) that a publication or display has been made in contravention of section 10,

(e) that, contrary to section 14, a person has procured or attempted to procure another to do anything which constitutes discrimination or victimisation, or

(f) that a person has procured or attempted to procure another to break an equal remuneration term or an equality clause, the Authority may refer the matter to the Director.

[48] Available on the website of the Irish Office of the Attorney General.

The Equality Authority exercised this power in the case of *Equality Authority* v. *Ryanair*[49] concerning discriminatory advertising. They took action against Ryanair after their publication of a discriminatory advertisement. The Authority was awarded damages and Ryanair was ordered to take action to implement appropriate equality training and policies within the company.

It is not always necessary to have explicit powers. It can sometimes be argued that the power to take action in its own name is implicit as part of the equality body's mandate. The Great Britain Equal Opportunities Commission has no such explicit right; however, it has used its duty to: "(a) to work towards the elimination of discrimination, and (b) to promote equality of opportunity between men and women generally" in order to justify taking action against the state and emanations of the state to challenge discriminatory laws and rules. Initially the Commission's power to take such actions was unchallenged. However, in *R.* v *Secretary of State for Employment ex parte Equal Opportunities Commission*, where the Equal Opportunities Commission (EOC) challenged the longer qualification period before part-time workers could bring unfair dismissal cases or claim a redundancy payment as being unfairly discriminatory against women as considerably more women than men worked part-time, this was challenged.

The EOC contended that this was contrary to Article 119 of the EEC Treaty (now Article 141 EC Treaty). The Secretary of State for Employment sought to challenge the EOC's power to bring these proceedings. The House of Lords ruled that the EOC's duties to work towards the elimination of discrimination and promote equality of opportunity between men and women generally gave them a sufficient interest in order to permit them to bring such actions.

House of Lords, 3 March 1994[50]   8.GB.16.
R. v. *Secretary of State for Employment ex parte Equal Opportunities Commission and another*

PART-TIME WORKERS RIGHTS TO CLAIM REDUNDANCY PAYMENTS

EOC part-time worker's case

Facts: The EOC challenged the Employment Protection (Consolidation) Act 1978, which provided that employees who worked for less than 16 hours per week were subject to different conditions in order to qualify for unfair dismissal protection or a redundancy payment compared to employees who worked for over 16 hours a week. The EOC argued that as a large proportion of employees who worked for less than 16 hours a week were women, hence this provision adversely affected women.

Held: The House of Lords held that the longer qualification period for part-time workers indirectly discriminated against women contrary to Article 119 TEC (now Article 141 EC). The government was not able to justify this provision and it was therefore unlawful.

[49] Irish Equality Tribunal, DEC-E2000-014.
[50] [1994] ICR 317, 326.

Judgment: LORD KEITH OF KINKEL, speaking for the majority, Lord Jauncey of Tullichettle dissenting on this issue:

> "Dealing first with the question of locus standi, R.S.C., Ord. 53, r. 3(7) provides that the court shall not grant leave to apply for judicial review 'unless it considers that the applicant has a sufficient interest in the matter to which the application relates.' Section 31(3) of the Supreme Court Act 1981 contains a provision in the same terms. The matter to which the EOC's application relates is essentially whether the relevant provisions of the Act of 1978 are compatible with European Community law regarding equal pay and equal treatment. Has the EOC a sufficient interest in that matter? Under section 53(1) of the Act of 1975 the duties of the EOC include
>
> '(a) to work towards the elimination of discrimination (b) to promote equality of opportunity between men and women generally . . .'
>
> If the admittedly discriminatory provisions of the Act of 1978 as regards redundancy pay and compensation for unfair dismissal are not objectively justified, then steps taken by the EOC towards securing that these provisions are changed may very reasonably be regarded as taken in the course of working towards the elimination of discrimination. The present proceedings are clearly such a step. In a number of cases the EOC has been the initiating party to proceedings designed to secure the elimination of discrimination . . . In my opinion it would be a very retrograde step now to hold that the EOC has no locus standi to agitate in judicial review proceedings questions related to sex discrimination which are of public importance and affect a large section of the population. The determination of this issue turns essentially upon a consideration of the statutory duties and public law role of the EOC as regards which no helpful guidance is to be gathered from decided cases. I would hold that the EOC has sufficient interest to bring these proceedings and hence the necessary locus standi."

8.5.1.D. INTERVENTIONS

Limitations in the added value obtained from individual cases has increasingly led equality bodies to consider alternative methods to promote the key equality standards. Taking action in their own name is obviously one solution; however, an alternative and often more cost-effective method is for the equality body to "intervene" or ask to be added as an interested party to an existing case. This method can work well so long as there are cases in which to "intervene", but it does not provide new opportunities to challenge or develop the law where the appropriate cases are not being brought by claimants. While the provisions of the Racial Equality Directive, the Gender Employment Directive, the Gender Goods and Services Directive and the Recast Gender Employment Directive all require Member States to designate a body or bodies to promote equal treatment in gender and race, as noted earlier, this requirement does not specify the nature and extent of the assistance to be provided to victims. However, it is noticeable that the Racial Equality Directive, the Employment Equality Directive, the Gender Employment Directive, the Gender Goods and Services Directive and the Recast Gender Employment Directive all require Member States to:

". . . ensure that associations, organisations or other legal entities, which have, in accordance with the criteria laid down by their national law, a legitimate interest in ensuring that the provisions of this Directive are complied with, may engage, either on behalf of or in support of the complainant, with his or her approval, in any judicial and/or administrative procedure provided for the enforcement of obligations under this Directive."[51]

This requirement has been thought to open the way to the use of interventions by equality bodies in litigation so that, rather than supporting any particular argument, they can make submissions as to how the law should be developed. In this way they undertake a role similar to that carried out by the European Commission in the submissions that it makes on a reference from a national court to the Court of Justice.

Interventions in this way are distinguished in the UK and Ireland from the role of amicus curiae,[52] however in other parts of Europe no such distinction exists. This section therefore refers to interventions in order to cover both interventions and the use of amicus curiae.

Although this is not yet widespread within Europe, other equality bodies do use powers to "intervene" in key cases in order to assist the court in reaching the right outcome. This practice has been extensively used in both Canada and the USA, and it is being increasingly used within the UK and to a lesser extent in Ireland, Belgium and France. The fact that it does not appear to have been utilised in other Member States may reflect that it is a procedure that is more obviously applicable to common law jurisdictions or one that is not applicable to the Ombuds-type bodies; or, alternatively, that a number of equality bodies are still in the early days of being set up and developing the most appropriate procedures. It is suggested that this is an important role that equality bodies ought to pursue since they clearly have a role in protecting the aims of the legislation in the area in which they work.

Within the UK interventions are increasingly being used in the appellate courts in public interest cases. In such cases bodies with "sufficient interest" can seek the court's consent to make an intervention which may be only written, or may be both oral and written. The British equality bodies have made use of these provisions in several important cases.

Most notable among recent cases is the joint intervention of all the British equality bodies in *Igen Ltd.* v. *Wong*.[53] Here the Court of Appeal heard three appeals from the Employment Appeals Tribunal concerning the application of the burden of proof provisions which had been introduced into domestic law as a result of the Racial Equality Directive, the Employment Equality Directive, the Burden of Proof Directive and the Gender Employment Directive. Thus the cases involved the

---

[51] Racial Equality Directive Art. 7(2), Employment Equality Directive Art. 9(2), Gender Employment Directive Art. 5, Gender Goods and Services Directive Art. 8(3) and the Recast Gender Employment Directive Art. 17(2).

[52] In England and Wales, a judge may ask for a barrister to argue as "a friend of the court", to assist the court with research and to offer a legal perspective which is unencumbered with partisan objective. This kind of amicus curiae is very different from that referred to in the jurisprudence of the US or of Canada, where the amicus argues a particular perspective defined by the party whose interest he or she represents.

[53] [2005] EWCA Civ 142, [2005] ICR 931.

interpretation of the burden of proof provisions in relation to sex discrimination, race discrimination and disability discrimination. Because of the importance of the issue and the extensive impact of any judgment, the three British Commissions—the Equal Opportunities Commission, the Commission for Racial Equality and the Disability Rights Commission—submitted a joint written intervention and were permitted to make oral submissions. Their submissions were broadly accepted and formed part of the guidelines issued by the Court for the future interpretation of the burden of proof. The judgment has already had a widespread impact within the UK courts, and has been considered by equality bodies in other Member States.

The Great Britain Disability Rights Commission has used its power to intervene on a number of occasions; in one case, *Burke* v. *General Medical Council*, Mr. Justice Munby commented on its role.

Queen's Bench Division, 30 July 2004[54]   **8.GB.17.**
Burke v. *General Medical Council*

GUIDANCE ON THE WITHDRAWAL OF ARTIFICIAL NUTRITION AND HYDRATION

Burke

Facts: Mr. Burke had a congenital degenerative brain condition known as spino-cerebellar ataxia. By reason of this condition, he anticipated that a time will come when he would be dependent on others for his care and survival. In particular, he would lose the ability to swallow and would require artificial nutrition and hydration by tube to survive. He was concerned that doctors would be able to make a decision as to whether he receives artificial nutrition and hydration on the basis of their opinion as to his quality of life. The General Medical Council (GMC) had issued guidelines to doctors on matters to consider when deciding whether to withdraw artificial nutrition and hydration. Mr. Burke sought declarations from the court that certain paragraphs of the GMC guidance, and the withholding or withdrawal of artificial nutrition and hydration in defined circumstances, are, or would be, unlawful as they are incompatible with the ECHR.

Held: The High Court held that it was hard to envisage any circumstances in which a withdrawal of artificial nutrition and hydration from a sentient patient, whether competent or incompetent, would be compatible with the Convention, however, this judgment was later set aside by the Court of Appeal.

Judgment: MR. JUSTICE MUNBY: "The DRC was joined in the proceedings as an interested party . . . in this case . . . I have been greatly assisted by the DRC . . .the DRC was able to deploy, to the greatest assistance of the court, a particular and highly relevant informed expertise which none of the other parties could bring to the task in hand. [This] case[s] illustrate[s] the important role that, in appropriate cases, bodies such as the DRC have to play in litigation, affording our courts the kind of valuable and valued assistance that courts in the United States of America have for so long been accustomed to receiving from those filing amicus curiae briefs."

In Ireland, there is a similar development. Interventions are being used to provide the court with a wider range of information with which to enable the court to reach a well-balanced judgment, taking account of factors that may not be immediately

---

[54] [2004] EWHC 1879.

relevant to the facts of the case at issue. Eilis Barry, Legal Advisor to the Equality Authority, has commented on their use of interventions and amicus curiae:

E. Barry, "Interventions and Amicus Curiae Applications.   **8.IE.18.**
Making Individual Enforcement More Effective"[55]

"Both the Equality Tribunal and the Labour Court are obliged to 'investigate the case and hear all persons appearing to the Director (or the Labour Court) to be interested and desiring to be heard'.
These provisions clearly envisage amicus curiae type applications. However, the extent to which this provision has been relied upon (if at all) is unknown.
The Irish Supreme Court has held that it does have an inherent jurisdiction to appoint an amicus curiae where it appears that this might be of assistance in determining an issue before the court:

'It is an unavoidable disadvantage of the adversarial system of litigation in common law jurisdictions that the courts are, almost invariably, confined in their consideration of the case to the submissions and other materials, such as relevant authorities, which the parties elect to place before the court. Since the resources of the court itself in this context are necessarily limited, there may be cases in which it would be advantageous to have the written and oral submissions of a party with a bona fide interest in the issue before the court which cannot be characterised as a meddlesome busybody. As the experience in other common law jurisdictions demonstrates, such intervention is particularly appropriate at the national appellate level in cases with a public law dimension.' [*H.I. v Minister for Justice, Equality and Law Reform on the Application of the United Nations High Commissioner for Refugees* [2003] 3 I.R. This principle has recently been reaffirmed in a case where the Equality Authority were permitted to appear as an amicus curiae—*P Doherty and B Doherty v. South Dublin County Council, the Minister for the Environment, Heritage and Local Government, Ireland and the Attorney General,* Supreme Court case no 233/2006, unreported, judgment given 31 October 2006.]

The Chief Justice also noted that the role of the amicus curiae in other jurisdictions has changed considerably over time:

'While it is still the case that an amicus curiae is allowed to appear because the court would be thereby assisted in coming to a correct resolution of an issue in dispute by being informed of all the relevant cases, statutes and other materials relevant to its determination, the amicus is no longer expected to be wholly disinterested in the outcome of the litigation' [references omitted]."

Eilis Barry also gave a recent example of the use of amicus curiae applications in relation to the discriminatory effect of a series of laws in their impact on the ability of Travellers to secure somewhere to live:

---

[55] In Equinet, above n. 13, 37.

E. Barry, "Interventions and Amicus Curiae Applications.   **8.IE.19.**
Making Individual Enforcement More Effective"[56]

"More recently, on 11th January 2006, the Equality Authority (the equality body in Ireland) was given liberty to appear as an amicus curiae in the High Court proceedings being brought by a Traveller family against a number of respondents including the local housing authorities, the Commissioner of An Garda Síochána, the Director of Public Prosecution, the District Justice, Ireland and the Attorney General. The case taken by the Traveller family raises a number of issues. These include the failure of the relevant housing authorities to meet the accommodation needs of the Traveller family. The claimants also contended that the Criminal Justice (Public Order) Act has a disproportionate and discriminatory impact on members of the Travelling community. This Act criminalises entry into and occupation of lands in certain situations. It gives members of An Garda Síochána broad powers including arrest and removal of caravans. The Equality Authority was given leave to appear as amicus curiae in relation to the application and interpretation of the Racial Equality Directive should it arise as part of the case. The Equality Authority sought to rely on the provisions of Article 13 of the Racial Equality Directive rather than Article 7(2), in making the application. This constitutes an important development for the Equality Authority, as it was not given explicit power in its legislation to apply to intervene as an amicus curiae."

This led Eilis Barry to conclude that the power to intervene should be part of the armoury of any equality body in seeking to eliminate discrimination and achieve real equality. She argues that this is a necessary addition to their powers to enable them to promote equal treatment without discrimination.

E. Barry, "Interventions and Amicus Curiae Applications.   **8.IE.20.**
Making Individual Enforcement More Effective"[57]

"The power to apply as an equality body to intervene as an amicus curiae in relevant cases would appear to be incidental to the required competencies of the equality body to provide independent assistance to victims of discrimination and make recommendations on any issue relating to such discrimination. If equality bodies have the function of promoting equal treatment without discrimination, it would seem to follow that they have competencies or capabilities to do things necessary to that end, including appearing as an amicus curiae in proceedings concerning the true meaning of the relevant directives. The courts of Member States must interpret domestic legislation in the light of the wording and purpose of the directives in order to achieve the result to be envisaged by the directives. It would be extraordinary if a body charged with promoting equal treatment did not have the capability of doing so by advocating a particular interpretation of a directive in a Court of Law given that this might be one of the most important and effective ways by which that principle could be promoted.

It is suggested therefore that equality bodies that are charged with the functions and capacities as envisaged by the directives have the capacity to act as an amicus curiae in a case

---

[56] *Ibid.*, 39.
[57] *Ibid.*, 41.

involving the interpretation of the relevant directive and such capacity implicitly arises under the provisions of the directives. Equality bodies should also be able to take part in litigation concerning the directive in support of a party: all of the relevant directives require Member States to ensure that associations, organisations or other legal entities, which have, in accordance with the criteria laid down by their national law, a legitimate interest in ensuring that the provisions of the directive are complied with, may engage, either on behalf of or in support of the complainant. Relevant procedural rules must comply with the principles of equivalence and effectiveness mentioned earlier.

Given the competencies that equality bodies must have, it is difficult to see how it could be maintained that they do not have a legitimate interest in ensuring that the provisions of the directive are complied with. The raison d'être of the equality bodies is the promotion of equal treatment.

Equality bodies under the relevant directives are partisan by the definition of their competencies. It is not suggested that equality bodies become 'meddlesome busybodies' and seek to intervene in every case concerning every aspect of the directives. While amicus curiae and intervention applications are clearly a strategic use of an equality body's resources, the equality body needs to be strategic about making such applications. It would be useful and important for equality bodies to develop and have transparent guidelines governing the decisions to make such applications. These guidelines could for example include:

— the importance of the equality issues raised in the proceedings,
— the extent to which there is significant case-law on the issue,
— the extent to which the proceedings are likely to have a beneficial impact for others covered under the same discrimination ground or other ground,
— the extent to which equality issues are central or peripheral to the case,
— the Court in which the proceedings are being heard (e.g. is it an appellate/Superior Court).

It is likely that equality bodies will not have resources to provide assistance to every individual. It is not always possible to predict a 'test case' in advance [references omitted]."

Similarly, in Belgium, the Centre for Equal Opportunities and Opposition to Racism has recently been given specific power to intervene.

> *Belgian Act of 25 February 2003 pertaining to the combat of*   **8.BE.21.**
> *discrimination and to the amendment of the Act of 15 February 1993 pertaining to*
> *the foundation of a centre for equal opportunities and opposition to racism*[58]

Art 31
The Centre for Equal Opportunities and Opposition to Racism may intervene in disputes to which this act may give rise.

Also in Hungary, the Equality Authority "in the case of a court review of a ruling made by another public administration body in respect of the requirements of

---

[58] Moniteur belge of 17 March 2003.

equal treatment, the Authority has the right to participate as the Intervening Party".[59]

In France, in civil law cases, either of the parties or the court can ask the High Authority against Discrimination and for Equality to intervene by transmitting its investigation file on the case to the court together with its opinion on the case, or, if they have not investigated the case, they can be asked to give their opinion on a case. In criminal cases they can respond to a request to intervene or they can intervene of their own volition.

French Act No. 2004-1486 dated 30 December 2004 concerning **8.FR.22.**
the creation of the high authority against discrimination and for equality[60]

Art 13
The civil, criminal or administrative courts may, when they are appraised of the facts relating to discrimination, on their authority or at the request of the parties, invite the high commission or its representative to present its observations. In the same circumstances, the criminal courts may, at the request of the high commission, invite it to present observations and also to expand on them orally in the course of the hearing.

In 2006 they were given additional powers to initiate an intervention.

French Act No. 2006-396 of 31 March 2006 on equality **8.FR.23.**
of opportunity[61]

Art 42
The second sentence of Article 13 of the abovementioned Act No. 2004-1486 of 30 December 2004 is worded as follows:

'The Authority may ask to be heard by these courts; in this event, the hearing will be lawful.'

8.5.1.E. SITUATION TESTING

Proving discrimination is widely recognised as presenting real difficulties in practice. It is in recognition of this that the burden of proof in discrimination cases has been shifted in the equality directives. However, even with shifting the burden of proof

---

[59] Government Decree 362/2004. (XII. 26.) Korm. on the Authority of Equal Treatment and the Detailed Rules of its Procedures, Section 15 (7).
[60] Loi 2004–1486 30 Décembre 2004 [*Loi portant création de la haute autorité de lutte contre les discriminations et pour l'égalité*].
[61] JO No. 79, 2 April 2006, 4950.

909

there can be grave difficulties in establishing that discrimination has occurred, and, in any event, it does not operate in criminal proceedings.

Another means that has been adopted in some Member States to secure the necessary evidence and to get behind the appearance to the reality has been to permit "situation testing".[62] Situation testing entails using two or more people who are matched for all relevant characteristics other than the one that is expected to give rise to discrimination. They then approach the same bar or discotheque in front of witnesses to see if they receive the same treatment. This technique can be applied to job applications, applications for tenancies or insurance, and a number of other similar situations. For some Member States this power is given to their equality body, in others it is a technique that could be used by any interested group. The following passage provides an overview of some of the issues that are involved:

I. Rorive, "Situation tests in Europe: myths and realities"[63]   **8.EC.24.**

"The use of situation testing
Situation tests aim to bring to light practices whereby a person who possesses a particular characteristic is treated less favourably than another person who does not possess this characteristic in a comparable situation. It means setting up a situation, a sort of role play, where a person is placed in a position to commit discrimination without suspecting that he or she is being observed. This person is presented with fictional 'candidates', some of whom possess a characteristic which may incite discriminatory behaviour. Observers aim to compare his or her attitude towards people bearing this characteristic compared to others without it. Situation testing allows direct discrimination, which is frequently hidden behind pretexts (such as the property has already been let, the job vacancy has already been filled, entrance is restricted to members), to be unmasked.

The most well known example of situation testing is that of different couples arriving at the entrance to a night club: if mixed couples or couples of foreign origin are systematically refused entry, yet 'native' couples who arrive before and after are admitted without difficulty, discrimination can be inferred. Similar experiments have been carried out with estate agencies or even with employers who are suspected of discriminatory recruitment practices."

In Belgium the 2003 Act of 25 February 2003 pertaining to the combat of discrimination and to the amendment of the Act of 15 February 1993 pertaining to the foundation of a centre for equal opportunities and opposition to racism Article 19(3) provided that:

"When the victim of discrimination or one of the groups referred to in Article 31 produces before the competent court facts such as statistical data or field trials that lead to the supposition of direct or indirect discrimination, the burden of proof that no discrimination has been committed shall fall on the defendant."

---

[62] The use of situation testing as an instrument to prove direct discrimination is discussed by M. Bell, above Chapter Two: Direct Discrimination.
[63] (2006) 3 *European Anti-discrimination Law Review* 33.

This would permit situation testing. However, as a result of public opposition, this provision was not confirmed by Royal Decree and so is not yet in force. As situation testing becomes more common it seems possible that this will be reconsidered.

In Hungary the Equality Authority has been given specific powers to undertake such tests.

Hungarian Government Decree 362/2004. (XII. 26.) Korm. **8.HU.25.**
on the Authority of Equal Treatment and the Detailed Rules of its Procedures

Specific rules of the testing procedure
Section 13
(1) The Authority may conduct a test to verify the compliance with the requirements of equal treatment. During such test the Authority exposes persons, who are only different in their position, properties or attributes (hereinafter: characteristics) stated in Section 8. of the Ebktv, but otherwise similar in all other characteristics, to a situation that is identical in respect of the conduct, measure, condition, a failure to take action, an instruction or practice (hereinafter together: the conditions) of the person subjected to the proceeding and examine the actions of the person subjected to the proceedings in terms of his/her compliance with the requirements of equal treatment.
(2) The result of such test may be used as evidence during the proceedings initiated on the basis of a violation of the requirements of equal treatment.

In France, the Court of Cassation has recognised that a situation test on restrictions to access to goods and services can provide valid evidence. For this purpose the Court can receive evidence from the potential clients or from the filing of a police or bailiff's report on the event. In a case in July 2005 the Criminal Chamber of the Court of Cassation ruled on the admissibility of situation testing in criminal cases of discrimination.[64] This case used telephone testing in order to establish discrimination in access to rental property. The Court admitted evidence of recordings of telephone conversations with an estate agent about the availability of apartments. The estate agent informed prospective clients that apartments were still available, or not, according to whether their names sounded "French". The Court decided that the weight to be attached to any such evidence was a matter for the trial judge; unfortunately, the ruling does not provide any guidance as to how such tests are to be conducted in order to be admitted as evidence.

New measures have now been introduced specifically to enable the High Authority against Discrimination to use situation testing procedures in order to establish the existence of discrimination. Once again, it is unfortunate that the power does not establish any guidelines as to how such tests are to be carried out.

---

[64] Cour de Cassation, Criminal Chamber No. 04-87354 of 7 June 2005.

"Article 45
Article 225-3-1 is inserted after Article 225-3 of the Criminal Code, worded as follows:

> '*Art. 225-3-1.*—The offences provided for under this Section will be established even if they are committed against one or more persons seeking any of the goods, acts, services or contracts mentioned in Article 225-2 for the purpose of proving the existence of discriminatory behaviour, where proof of such behaviour is established.'"

The issue of situation testing is also being raised in Sweden. In 2005, on the basis of situation testing in several clubs in Stockholm, Gothenburg and Malmö nine lawsuits were initiated. Some of these have been settled out of court. The Race Discrimination Report, *The Blue and Yellow Glass House: Structural Discrimination* (Stockholm, 2005), recommended that the Ombudsman for Ethnic Discrimination should be given the task of developing the use of situation testing as a method of establishing proof in discrimination cases.

It is important to consider how situation testing can be undertaken without creating a climate of suspicion and a backlash against the use of these measures. There is undoubtedly a need for a European protocol on the use of situation testing, both because its effectiveness and relevance is dependent on conformity with basic rules of fairness and because if not properly performed it can be seen as a provocative act. Olivier de Schutter comments on the implications of this:

O. de Schutter, "Methods of Proof in the context of   **8.EC.27.**
combating discrimination"[66]

"2.1. Added value of proving discrimination through situational tests
The use of situational tests is connected not to the concept of indirect discrimination, but to direct discrimination which is 'concealed', that is, not acknowledged by the person who turns out to be guilty of it. The aim of such tests is to expose behaviour whereby an individual is treated less favourably because of a particular characteristic, where another individual placed in a comparable situation who did not have this particular characteristic would not be treated in this way, although the perpetrator of this difference in treatment tries to prevent his/her conduct from being detected.

The situational test is in the same category as techniques which are employed to facilitate the exposure of other offences, particularly those linked to organised crime. The most obvious analogy is so-called 'pseudo purchasing' employed in combating drug trafficking. In both cases it is about surprising the perpetrator when s/he is in a situation of trust and does not suspect

---

[65] Above n. 61.
[66] In Migration Policy Group (ed.), Proving Discrimination. The Dynamic Implementation of EU-Anti Discrimination Law: The Role of Specialised Bodies, 2003, Report of the First Experts' Meeting, 14–15 January 2003, hosted by the Belgian Centre for Equal Opportunities and Opposition to Racism, 32–5, available on the website of the Belgian Centre for Equal Opportunities and Opposition to Racism.

that his/her actions are being observed, so that they may be used if necessary in legal proceedings.

2.2. The methodology for situational tests

The use of 'situational tests' assumes the greatest possible comparability between the 'experimental' group, which has a characteristic liable to give rise to discrimination, and the 'control' group, which is identical from the point of view of all the relevant characteristics (professional qualifications, age, clothing etc). In order for this method to be used to provide proof of discrimination, it is important to confirm this comparability on the basis of as comprehensive a list as possible of the elements likely to influence the decision made by someone responsible for recruitment or housing lets, or the manager of a restaurant, depending on the case in question . . .

This technique for exposing discrimination was used for a major international comparative study on ethnic discrimination in the hiring of employees conducted by the International Labour Office (Bureau international du travail—BIT) on the basis of Fr. Bovenkerk's methodological guidelines. The study was described as follows by B. Smeesters, in the context of the Belgian research carried out on behalf of the BIT:

Two researchers have identical characteristics in terms of the selection criteria which would be likely to appeal to an employer recruiting staff. They are the same age, have a similar 'background' with respect to their qualifications, but are of different ethnic origins. If just one of them is appointed, in principle, the difference cannot be attributed to any other characteristic apart from their ethnic origin.

This rationale assumes that ethnic origin should never be a relevant criteria for the selection of staff. If there is discrimination in the labour market, it will be proved through a sufficiently high number of similar situational tests . . .

The situational test conducted in this way facilitates the exposure of 'concealed' discrimination (whether unacknowledged or concealed behind neutral arguments which are merely pretexts), which is assumed to be a conscious action on the part of the perpetrator. By the very way they are constructed, situational tests may serve to identify the existence of indirect discrimination associated with the use of certain criteria or procedures which, applied to people who belong to different groups, lead to members of certain groups being particularly disadvantaged. The situational test works on the basis of a comparison between two candidacies which are identical in every respect, which generally prohibits the person responsible for the selection from deciding between rival candidates on any grounds other than on the basis of the only characteristic which distinguishes them from one another (for example, in the most common application of this technique, on the basis of their different national or ethnic origin). The identical nature of the two candidacies, ensured through the methodological framework of the test, means in principle that the suspect criteria or procedures, which are suspected of giving rise to indirect discrimination, should not influence the decision. Since there is nothing to distinguish the two candidates from one another except for a distinction made on the basis of a suspect characteristic, these criteria or procedures could not, in the usual course of events, influence the choice between the two candidates.

A possibly more troublesome weakness of the situational test method is found in the avoidance strategies to which it will give rise, as long as the tests are generalist. These strategies will exist in the mind of the perpetrator and involve, quite simply, the accumulation of sufficient information about the different competing candidates, in order to prove that the selection was made for reasons other than the inadmissible suspect characteristic . . .

2.3. The admissibility of situational tests in the context of legal proceedings

. . . The issue of the admissibility conditions for this method of proof is rather delicate, considering the risk of abuse involved. At the very least, this admissibility must be subject to strictly defined procedural conditions. Preferably, an individual able to provide certain guarantees of independence and credibility, such as a bailiff, could safeguard the conditions in which the evidence is gathered. The task of this person responsible for authenticating the situational test may be summarised in two points. First, s/he must ensure that nothing in the situational test process may give rise to a suspicion that the wrongful or negligent behaviour was provoked by those conducting the test. The test must simply be able to confirm or record an action which would have taken place even without this construction of an artificial situation. Secondly s/he must guarantee the methodological integrity of the situational test, in particular the comparability of the people in the 'experimental' group who have a suspect characteristic (for example, because they are of a particular ethnic origin or visibly wear a particular religious symbol) with the people of the 'control' group.

2.3.1. Private life and risk of provocation

. . . the Belgian Council of State expressed in particular its concern about the risks, which would be involved in the use of situational tests, of violation of the right to respect for private life. While the prohibition of discrimination must take account of the requirements of private life (which explains the fact that this prohibition will only be applied in the public or semi-public domain—employment, provision of goods and services, etc—and not in a purely private context), on the other hand, these requirements do not appear to represent an obstacle, in principle, to the lawfulness of using the situational test as the method of proof. In fact, in situations where the issue has arisen of using undercover agents in certain criminal milieux, especially in the area of drug trafficking, the European Court of Human Rights has considered that using an individual with a fictional identity for the sole purpose of exposing the illegal action does not constitute interference in the 'private life' of an individual [references omitted]."

Situation testing is likely to remain controversial. If the use of situation testing is to be used more widely it will be important to develop a clear set of rules or code of conduct for its operation to ensure that the testing is carried out fairly and there is no room for accusations of incitement or entrapment.

8.5.2.   QUASI-JUDICIAL FUNCTIONS

Several European equality bodies also operate as quasi-judicial bodies or have a quasi-judicial function. Some of these are able to issue legally binding rulings, some only issue recommendations and non-binding rulings. This section will look at the Netherlands as an example of a commission issuing non-binding rulings and the Irish Equality Tribunal which issues legally binding rulings, albeit ones which can be appealed. Other equality bodies sometimes have powers to issue legally enforceable decisions in defined areas, there is a continuum from the powers to hear cases to the powers to instigate investigations into the practices and procedures of national companies or government departments.

The United Nations Paris Principles recognise the utility of institutions with quasi-judicial powers. They made specific recommendations in respect of [human rights] commissions which had quasi-judicial competence. In making these recommendations, they stress the importance of considering conciliation as an option, ensuring that the petitioner is fully informed of their rights and making recommendations both to the government and to the institution concerned with the discriminatory act.

Office for the United Nations High Commissioner for   **8.UN.28.**
Human Rights
"Principles relating to the status and functioning of national institutions for
protection and promotion of human rights" (known as the "Paris Principles") [67]

"D. Additional principles concerning the status of commissions with quasi-jurisdictional competence
A national institution may be authorized to hear and consider complaints and petitions concerning individual situations. Cases may be brought before it by individuals, their representatives, third parties, non-governmental organizations, associations of trade unions or any other representative organizations. In such circumstances, and without prejudice to the principles stated above concerning the other powers of the commissions, the functions entrusted to them may be based on the following principles:

1. Seeking an amicable settlement through conciliation or, within the limits prescribed by the law, through binding decisions or, where necessary, on the basis of confidentiality;
2. Informing the party who filed the petition of his rights, in particular the remedies available to him, and promoting his access to them;
3. Hearing any complaints or petitions or transmitting them to any other competent authority within the limits prescribed by the law;
4. Making recommendations to the competent authorities, especially by proposing amendments or reforms of the laws, regulations or administrative practices, especially if they have created the difficulties encountered by the persons filing the petitions in order to assert their rights."

8.5.2.A.   THE NETHERLANDS

The Dutch Equal Treatment Commission (ETC)[68] is a commission which has semi-judicial functions and which issues non-binding opinions. Once it has issued an opinion, the claimant can still go to the relevant administrative or civil law court if he or she wishes to obtain a binding judgment, and the Commission's opinion will constitute part of the evidence. Professor Jenny Goldschmidt, a former President of

---

[67] Available on the website of the Office for the United Nations High Commissioner for Human Rights.
[68] The Dutch Equal Treatment commission is also known as *Commissie Gelijke Behandeling* (CGB). In this chapter, for the sake of consistency, it is referred to as the Equal Treatment Commission (ETC).

the Equal Treatment Commission, explains the rationale for the establishment of a commission with quasi-judicial powers.

J. Goldschmidt, "Implementation of Equality Law: **8.NL.29.**
a task for specialists or for human rights experts?"[69]

"The arguments to establish an ETC charged with the supervision of the implementation of the ETA were based on several considerations. First, it seemed appropriate to have an accessible procedure open for victims of discrimination, without undue financial or procedural barriers. Secondly, the problems complainants in discrimination cases face in gathering evidence comprised a good reason to establish a body with independent active investigatory powers. Finally, the recognition of the complex character of equality law and the background of persisting social inequality constituted an argument for an organ with specialist expertise . . . the Commission is entrusted with the general task of supervising the implementation of the equality laws, including an active advisory, monitoring and educational role. In the first years of its existence, the ETC gave priority to the interpretation of the law in order to clarify the specific concepts used, and thereafter more emphasis was put on increasing its effectiveness via a more active follow-up of cases and advisory activities, training and publicity.

Complaints and procedures
The primary task of the ETC is to consider concrete complaints of alleged unequal treatment based on the aforementioned specific laws, to investigate these complaints and to render a (non-binding) opinion. Requests can be lodged by individual complainants, organisations (class actions), or by corporations, bodies, etc. that wish to know whether their (proposed) actions or regulations are in conformity with the law. Finally, there is a possibility for judges to address the ETC, but thus far this possibility has not been used . . . The opinions of the Commission are not legally binding. The Commission has the power to add recommendations to its opinions. In case of non-compliance with the Commission's opinion or recommendations, or even simultaneously alongside the ETC procedure, the victim may take the case to court. The Commission itself is also entitled to go to court to enforce compliance with the law, but thus far this possibility has not been used.

The first instrument that the Commission uses in this regard is an active follow up policy. Following the issuing of every opinion which suggests the need for active measures to be taken the Commission keeps in touch with the parties and, if relevant, other organisations such as social partners, branch organisations, etc. Since 2001, the results of the follow-up policy have been registered by the Commission in its files, and in its second Evaluation Report the Commission notes that compliance with opinions of the Commission have increased from 60% in 2001 to 84% in the first half of 2004."

The PLS Ramboll Report describes how the Dutch Equal Treatment Commission hearings are conducted. They make the point that the chances of the parties obeying a decision are greater when they have been fully informed about the relevant laws.

---

[69] See Goldschmidt, above n. 10, 325–7.

Hence they see one of the objectives of the hearing as being to enable the parties to understand the purpose and provisions of the law, and persuade the parties to apply it appropriately.

European Commission, "Specialized bodies to promote equality **8.EC.30.**
and/or combat discrimination. Final report"[70]

"Hearings at the Dutch Equal Treatment Commission
The hearings are staged in a fairly informal setting to allow the commissioners to inform the parties on the laws and their implications. There is less at stake than at a court, and greater room for reconciliation. Hearings at the Commission should preferably take place within 6 months of a complainant submitting a written complaint to it.

The three commissioners and the juridical advisor have a pre-meeting where the content and format of the hearing are discussed. Generally the chairperson or the vice chair hosts the hearing. But instead of having only one commissioner asking questions during the hearing, they decide how to allocate the work among themselves and how to handle the case and their roles in it.

The Commissioners give considerable attention to how they communicate with the parties in the hearings. It is important for them to do so in open and positive terms to encourage the parties to co-operate and find solutions.

Therefore internal communication officials at the Commission provide feedback to individual Commissioners so that they can continuously improve their personal communication strategies."

It is always difficult to assess the full effects of a Commission's actions since ideally their effects will ripple widely throughout society. However, in 2005 an Equal Treatment Commission report reviewed the effectiveness of their follow-up procedures between 2001 and 2004.

Equal Treatment Commission (Commissie Gelijke Behandeling) **8.NL.31.**
"The Difference Made. Evaluation of the Equal Treatment Act and the Activities of the Equal Treatment Commission, 1999–2004"[71]

"Effectiveness of opinions: follow up by the parties
An important indication of the effectiveness of opinions is the extent to which the parties follow them. The ETC generally gives an opinion on request of a person who feels that a distinction is or has been made to his detriment. However, the [ETC] may also make recommendations at the request of private persons, legal entities or authorities, who wish to know whether they themselves have discriminatory. Such an opinion concerning own conduct has in

---

[70] Report on the Role, Structure and Functioning of Specialised Bodies, above n. 45, 86.
[71] ETC (CGB), *Het verschil gemaakt. Evaluatie AWGB en werkzaamheden CGB 1999–2004*, available on the website of the Dutch Equal Treatment Commission.

recent years been requested ever more frequently and may structurally promote awareness of and compliance with the equal treatment precept. This is so particularly because an [ETC] opinion on such a request usually attracts the attention of the entire social sector that it concerns.

It is therefore now possible to indicate almost precisely for the greater part of the evaluation period (1 January 2001 to 1 July 2004) to what extent the parties have followed up [ETC] opinions and what developments have occurred in this connection in the course of time. It should be noted for the sake of completeness that only the opinions are concerned where according to the [ETC] an (unlawful) distinction was made or another conflict with the Act occurred, and opinions where the [ETC] otherwise made recommendations.

The [ETC] held on a total of 315 occasions that the defendant acted in conflict with the law or made a recommendation. Apart from a slight fall in 2003, the follow-up percentage rose between 2001 and the first half of 2004.

The fact that three-quarters of negative opinions were followed by the parties in the first half of 2004 (75% and including arrangements even 84%) points to the opinions being reasonably effective. The more so, when one remembers that not all opinions can be followed up, e.g. because the applicant has found a different job in the meantime or because the applicant has subsequently enforced a number of opinions in a court of law (see also paragraph 6.5).

Individual and structural follow-up
Opinions are important not only to the case in hand but may more generally contribute to compliance with equal treatment law. An employer may, for example, adjust his recruitment and selection policy or introduce a complaints procedure. Opinions may also result in employers and providers of goods and services not concerned in the case changing their practices.

Opinions regarding own conduct
The number of requests for an opinion concerning own conduct (e.g. policy, collective agreements and other arrangements) has increased over the years. The proportion in 2001 was 1% of the total number of requests, in 2002 2%, in 2003 8% and in the first half of 2004 as much as 10% . . . The [ETC] considers this growth to be positive. An opinion regarding own conduct nearly always contributes structurally to observance of equal treatment law. Growth may additionally be taken as an indication of increased confidence in the [ETC].

Comparison with the previous evaluation
The average follow-up percentage has risen from 50% to 69%. As in the previous evaluation period, decisions appear to have greater effect at structural rather than individual level. And again opinions with a recommendation are followed up more effectively than those without."

It is unusual for the courts to have to consider the status of a ruling of the Commission; however, in the case of *St. Bavo* v. *Gielen* in 1987 the Supreme Court did consider the weight to be given to a Commission ruling and made it clear that considerable weight must be attached to its recommendations. This case concerned an equal pay claim in which the Commission had recommended that equal pay be paid.

Supreme Court (Hoge Raad), 13 November 1987[72]   **8.NL.32.**
St. Bavo v. Gielen

ROLE OF A COMMISSION DECISION IN AN EQUAL PAY CASE

St. Bavo

Facts: This case concerned an equal pay claim. Ms. Gielen was a member of the domestic service. She compared her wages to those paid to Mr. Aandewiel, who was employed as a member of the cleaning service. Normally only females were employed in the same position as Ms. Gielen whilst those employed in the same position as Mr. Aandewiel were exclusively male. The Commission for Equal Treatment of Men and Women, the predecessor of the Equal Treatment Commission, heard the case and concluded that Ms. Gielen was receiving unequal pay. St. Bavo appealed against this decision to the regional court.

Held: Sound reasons must be given for disagreeing with a decision of the Commission for Equal Treatment of Men and Women. The Commission's decision to recommend equal pay for Ms. Gielen was upheld and the appeal was dismissed.

Judgment: "3.1 This case is concerned with a claim within the meaning of Art. 2 Equal Pay for Women and Men Act (WGL), brought by Gielen, who was employed as a member of the domestic service on a wage paid basis at St. Bavo. Gielen relied on the wage paid to Mr. Aandewiel, employed by St. Bavo as a member of the cleaning service. The Court confirmed that the position held by Gielen at St. Bavo is held by women (except for certain months in 1981 when a male employee also did the job) and that members of the cleaning service were exclusively male. With regard to her pay, Gielen was allocated to group 3 and Aandewiel to group 5 . . .
3.4 . . .The regional court correctly assumed that, in view of the specific expertise of the Commission for Equal Treatment of Men and Women [hereafter GB Commission] and the weight attaching to its recommendations according to inter alia art. 16 WGL [Equal Pay for Women and Men Act] when assessing a claim such as the present, sound reasons must be given for advocating a decision departing from such a recommendation and, since the GB Commission had concluded 'work of the same or virtually the same value exists while in this case remuneration is divided into different groups', it was up to St. Bavo as employer to put forward such grounds. The regional court's opinion that what St. Bavo had put forward against the GB Commission's recommendation, insofar as not discussed in consideration 5.7, did not meet this requirement, does not indicate an incorrect interpretation of the law, is not beyond comprehension in the light of the court documents and cannot be examined further in cassation, as it is based on an interpretation of these documents . . .
3.4 . . .The Court correctly assumed that, in view of the specific expertise of the GB Commission and the weight attaching to its recommendations according to inter alia art. 16 WGL when assessing a claim such as the present, compelling reasons must be indicated for advocating such a decision departing from a recommendation and, since the Great Britain Commission had concluded 'work of the same or virtually the same value exists while in this case remuneration is divided into different groups', it was up to St. Bavo as employer to put forward such grounds. The Court's opinion that what St. Bavo had put forward against the GB Commission's recommendation, insofar as not discussed in consideration 5.7, did not meet this requirement, does not indicate an incorrect interpretation of the law, is not beyond comprehension in the light of the court documents . . .

[72] Nederlands Jurisprudentie 1989/698.

3.6 Section 5 cannot result in cassation because it is directed against an inessential consideration.
4. Decision: The Supreme Court: rejects the appeal . . ."

It appears that despite this ruling the Courts do not always give adequate weight to the Commission's rulings. This has also been recently re-evaluated by the Commission.

Equal Treatment Commission (Commissie Gelijke Behandeling) **8.NL.33.**
*"The Difference Made. Evaluation of the Equal Treatment Act and the
Activities of the Equal Treatment Commission, 1999–2004"*[73]

"Effectiveness of opinions: legal decisions following on opinions
On the first evaluation of the AWGB [General Equal Treatment Act 1994], it was noted amongst other things that the lower courts allowed themselves to be guided too little by the CGB's [ETC] opinion. The advice was therefore:

'. . . that parliament should strengthen the authority of a Commission opinion. This can simply be done by amending the act to include that the courts may depart from the Commission's opinion only on stated grounds.'

The government did not follow this advice because the obligation to state grounds under Article 121 of the Constitution in its opinion offered sufficient guarantees. Against this background, how the courts dealt with an [ETC] opinion in proceedings where the equal treatment legislation has a bearing was examined against this background for the period 1999–2004 . . .

Research and research method
On investigating the way in which the courts have dealt with [ETC] opinions, the first question is whether the court has taken note of the [ETC] opinion and, if so, whether it has included this in the judgment, or not. The most important question here is whether it is substantiated in the judgment whether or not the opinion has been followed. This has been investigated in the decisions by the cantonal courts, the ordinary courts, the appeal courts, the Supreme Court, the Central Appeals Council and the European Court of Justice.

To assess effectiveness, it is also important [to know] whether the [ETC's] way of reasoning has contributed towards the development of the law, e.g. by dealing with legal questions at the request of the judicial authorities or other mediators (under Article 12 (2) preamble and sub-paragraph c). In the ten years of the [ETC's] existence, no judicial authority has ever made such a request. The [ETC] will make this possibility better known in the future . . .

It is noticeable that the courts have departed from the [ETC's] opinion without substantiation in only four cases. Beside the 39 cases that followed on an [ETC] opinion that there was a distinction, the courts also dealt with four cases after the [ETC] had considered that there was *no* distinction. Amongst these four, the court followed the [ETC] with substantiation in three cases, while in the fourth case it did not consider the [ETC's] opinion.

Of the total of 43 cases (39+4), the court for various reasons did not consider the [ETC] opinion in 12 cases (11+1). Sometimes, other legal questions arose or no recourse was made to

---

[73] See above **8.NL.31.**

the equal treatment legislation any more.[37] Of the 31 cases where the court did consider the equal treatment question, it explicitly substantiated on 25 occasions why it did (17 times) or did not (8 times) follow the [ETC] opinion.

Although small numbers are concerned, some conclusions can nonetheless be drawn. First of all, that the courts in 81% of the cases (25 out of 31) explicitly took note of the [ETC] opinion in its decision, while in 61% of cases (19 out of 31) it followed the [ETC] opinion (see Figs. 16 and 17). In addition, it is noteworthy that the courts are increasingly following the [ETC's] opinions, except for 2001. Also worth mentioning is that the courts departed from the [ETC] opinion without substantiation in only 5 cases.

Requests for an opinion or advice by the courts
Since the courts usually take a positive view of the CGB's opinions, it is noteworthy that the courts have not once so far asked the CGB to issue an opinion . . . . The CGB can make its specific expertise available not only for legal decisions but also when considering the need to submit a request for a preliminary ruling to the European Court of Justice and the wording of these requests."

Note
As the Equal Treatment Commission does not make binding judgments, it is not able to refer cases to the Court of Justice. This has been described as a "serious lacuna" in the powers of the Equal Treatment Commission.[74] So, whilst the ETC deals with the vast majority of the cases concerning the equality directives, it is unable to refer questions to the Court of Justice.

8.5.2.B.   IRELAND

The Irish Equality Tribunal was set up in tandem with and at the same time as the Irish Equality Authority. It issues legally binding decisions. It is the forum for redress for claims of unfair discrimination on the grounds of gender, marital status, family status, sexual orientation, religion, disability, race, age and membership of the Traveller community, whether in relation to work or to the provision of goods and services. There are two exceptions to this provision: employment cases on the ground of gender may instead be initiated in the Circuit Court, and cases about discrimination in relation to licensed premises and registered clubs must be brought in the District Court. Originally cases concerning licensed premises and registered clubs could be brought in the Equality Tribunal. A considerable volume of litigation ensued, leading to protests from the trade body for licensed premises. The government subsequently introduced legislation that removed such cases from the jurisdiction of the Equality Tribunal and instead allocated such cases to the District Courts. This has resulted in a decrease in cases concerning licensed premises and registered clubs.

[74] See Goldschmidt, above n. 10, 333.

When an application is made to the Equality Tribunal a tribunal mediator will normally mediate between the two sides, leading to a Mediation Agreement. However, if either party objects to mediation or if the mediation fails, the tribunal will ask both sides to set out their evidence in writing. A different Equality Officer will then hold a joint hearing, in private, and issue a decision. Both Mediation Agreements and Decisions are legally binding. The Equality Officer has a wide range of powers as to the type of orders that can be made after a finding of discrimination. The Officer can, for example, order an employer to establish an equality policy or new procedures to deal with harassment, or instruct an employer to provide a lift or a ramp.

The Equality Tribunal 2004 Annual Report shows that, during 2004, 473 cases were dealt with by the Tribunal. Of these, 59 reached a mediated agreement, 227 were "otherwise closed" and 187 had a decision made. Those that were "otherwise closed" were found to be inadmissible, were settled or were withdrawn during the course of the investigation. The proportion of cases going to mediation has increased since this report as the procedure has now been changed so that it is assumed that all cases go to mediation unless one of the parties specifically requests otherwise.

During 2004 the Labour Court heard 19 appeals against Equality Tribunal cases. The Equality Tribunal reports that "of these 11 decisions were upheld in full and four were varied (part upheld, part overturned or had the award of compensation increased or decreased). The remaining four decisions were overturned."[75] Also during 2004, four appeals in respect of the Equal Status Acts 2000–2004 were dealt with by the Circuit Court. "[O]f these one Decision was upheld and one was overturned. One appeal was dismissed and one was struck out."[76]

8.5.3. INVESTIGATIONS AND INQUIRIES

Equality bodies receive many complaints (see section 8.5.1.A) and much information about discrimination occurring within their jurisdiction. It is not possible for them to take legal action in respect of each of these. Sometimes, particularly when there has been a series of complaints, a more effective solution is to undertake an investigation or inquiry into the area, business sector or business concerned.

Equality bodies' powers to conduct investigations and inquiries have proved to be a useful tool in countering discrimination in civil society. In Great Britain, these powers may be used in relation to a whole industrial sector (known as general inquiries) or to investigate a single body/employer, e.g. the Crown Prosecution Service or a particular prison (known as a specific investigation). In either situation, the result may lead to recommendations on future action.

---

[75] The Equality Tribunal, Annual Report 2004, 11, available on the website of the Irish Equality Tribunal.
[76] Ibid., 14.

In considering formal investigations and inquiries undertaken by equality bodies in Europe, Myra White of the Great Britain Disability Rights Commission (DRC) comments first on the use of these powers:

M. White, "Formal Investigations and Inquiries"[77]   8.EC.34.

"General inquiries
Inquiries are a useful tool for looking into a sector or theme without being required to have a specific named party (or parties) or to show a finding of reasonable belief that an unlawful act of discrimination has occurred. Inquiries must fall within the remit and scope of activity of the equality body undertaking the enquiry (for instance, the DRC's general duty to work towards the elimination of discrimination). In addition, in the case of the DRC the inquiry must be completed within a specified time (18 months). The basis for conducting inquiries provides greater flexibility in terms of the sector/sectors that equality bodies may examine. However, unlike for a named-party investigation, they may only make recommendations and may not issue a finding of unlawful discrimination. The DRC has completed one full general inquiry into website accessibility and is currently undertaking a second into health inequalities with a particular focus on those with learning difficulties and mental ill health. The Equal Opportunities Commission conducted three general inquiries in 2004–2005 on pregnancy discrimination, occupational segregation and flexible working practices respectively . . .

Formal investigations
In Great Britain the three main equality commissions may on their own initiative . . . undertake a formal investigation into areas connected with their explicit duties. This applies in a similar fashion to the race, gender and disability areas . . . once the Commission for Equality and Human Rights (CEHR) comes into being in late 2007, investigations on other grounds will also be possible. An investigation differs from an inquiry, as set out above, in that it requires the accusatory body to demonstrate a reasonable 'belief' that there is unlawful discrimination and that a particular body or bodies are targeted.

In addition to establishing 'belief', the accusatory party must also follow a specified process for the investigation, including allowing parties under investigation time to respond. The positive aspect of this type of investigation is that the process is kept in-house and can be controlled by the equality authority itself.

As mentioned previously, the DRC investigation power is subject to a time limit of 18 months. The limit was introduced by regulation to force the DRC to plan and research the investigation thoroughly prior to commencement in order to prevent the delays that were witnessed with some of the earlier Commission for Racial Equality and Equal Opportunities Commission investigations that dragged on for many years, consuming valuable resources and staff time.

Experience from British equality bodies has shown that formal 'belief' investigations are most effective in situations where the party under investigation is a repeat offender or in situations where prior litigation has been unsuccessful in instigating the desired cultural and organisational change, for example the Commission for Racial Equality's investigation into the Prison Service in 2000. These types of investigations are also useful where there is no victim, but where there is evidence of systemic or institutional discrimination . . .

---

[77] In Equinet, above n. 13; above n. 37, 27, available on the website of the Migration Policy Group.

Pros and cons of Inquiries and Investigations: a comparative approach

Criticisms of the conduct of formal 'named-party' or 'belief' investigations in the 70's and 80's were that they were overly adversarial and confrontational (in particular, the investigated parties would often challenge the investigation, taking up both time and resources in lengthy legal battles). Similarly, powers available by way of enforcement tools either before or following an investigation did not allow negotiation by way of a settlement, as is now the case under section 5 of the DRC Act which allows for a binding settlement agreement in lieu of other enforcement tools. Whilst this power has not been used in the context of an investigation thus far, the agreements brokered between the DRC and other parties in individual litigation cases have been deemed a useful tool in the range of available enforcement and resolution instruments.

. . . one of the key criticisms of undertaking an inquisitorial or investigative approach is the resources required. This was a common theme among all the equality bodies that responded to the survey. This was true both of organisations that have an existing inquiry power (Austria, Denmark, Sweden and Latvia, for example) and of those that do not have an inquiry power, as cost was said to be a prohibitive factor in permitting such powers . . .

Another area of common complaint across equality bodies (with some exceptions e.g. the Estonian Chancellor of Justice and the French High Authority against Discrimination and for Equality) was the inability to compel evidence in an inquiry or investigation (although this is a power which the UK equality commissions have) and/or follow up that investigation with any enforcement options, apart from general 'soft' recommendations, awareness raising or referral to a higher authority. An exception here was the French High Authority, which has powers to turn non-compliance over to the courts as a criminal matter.

The ability to compel evidence is a power possessed by all existing Great Britain equality bodies; it is built into their founding legislation and is a strong power that can be enforced by a court order. To date, the DRC has not had to use this power due to being a relative newcomer to such powers. The Commission for Racial Equality has used this power. Under their amended Race Relations legislation (2000) they are now required to serve a notice that may require respondents to provide the requested written information, give oral information, and/or produce any documents in their possession. Whilst it is not always necessary to use such a power, the fact that it exists assists in encouraging compliance."

Myra White then considers how similar investigations are undertaken in other European equality bodies. Here she is drawing on the responses that the Equinet members received from their survey of their members practice's and procedures.

M. White, "Formal Investigations and Inquiries"[78]   **8.EC.35.**

" . . . Other European examples have demonstrated that inquiries can be used to great effect as a means for promotion and lobbying. There are also some specific benefits of an inquiry-based approach, as noted by the Greek Ombudsman (GO) in the response to the Equinet questionnaire:

---

[78] *Ibid.*, 27–30.

'These powers allow the GO to examine in a systematic and general manner a specific service or sector, and to shed light in certain dark corners of public administration which may not be evident in a typical investigation of an individual complaint. As a result, these powers provide an important opportunity for the equality body to have a broad and constructive impact on the activities of public administration, particularly in cases where the issues are serious, the problems are widespread and the evidential documents or information insufficient to support an individual complaint.'

However there are some differences in application and scope when looking at examples across the EU. For example, the Estonian Chancellor of Justice and Greek Ombudsman can only undertake inquiries into public authorities or bodies that undertake functions of a public nature. This differs from the UK where the equality statutes do not restrict the scope of inquiries to either the public or private sectors . . .

There were also instances where investigative powers went further than Britain: for example the Commissioner for Administration in Cyprus can conduct investigations into human rights matters as well as equality areas (The new CEHR in Great Britain will be able to undertake human rights inquiries only and not 'named-party' or 'belief' investigations).

Conclusion
The results derived from initial evidence gathering demonstrate a diverse approach to inquiries and investigations amongst equality bodies in Europe. This is partly due to the complex nature of the terminology. Indeed, equality bodies in some countries made no distinction between an inquiry and an investigation (Latvia); others only had competence in one or the other. Whilst there were many similarities between bodies, no two countries had exactly matching powers or procedures, demonstrating the richness in approach to this area of strategic enforcement. The different approaches and the powers within the competence of the different specialised bodies is a result of the differing social and political contexts in which the organisations were established."

In Great Britain, it is the Commission for Racial Equality that has had the most extensive experience of conducting both general inquiries and formal investigations. Its Head of Legal Policy, Razia Karim, commented on some of the lessons that the Commission has learnt in the following passage:

R. Karim, *"A Legal Strategy to Combine and Coordinate* **8.GB.36.**
Different Tools available"[79]

"5.3 Formal Investigations
Sometimes seen as the jewel in the law enforcement crown, investigations can be a powerful force for change because of their ability to tackle endemic and systemic problems within organisations that have been resistant to change. While investigations may not immediately benefit individuals who have suffered racial discrimination, they can ensure that lasting beneficial changes are brought about in the long run. A formal investigation may lead the Commission to take further action such as:

[79] In Cormack, above n. 32, 49.

— recommending a change in policies and procedures in order to avoid unlawful discrimination
— issuing a non-discrimination notice requiring a person or organisation not to commit unlawful discrimination, to make changes to practices and other arrangements to avoid unlawful discrimination and to tell the Commission once these actions have been completed.

In formal investigations the Commission does not take legal action in a court of law but acts in effect as an investigative agency and makes findings. There is no risk of losing a case and no risk of having to pay costs of the other side. The final decision as to whether or not a body has behaved unlawfully remains with the CRE and not an outside judge or the judicial process. This means that we have control of the process from beginning to end.

In addition there are no time limitations on when we can begin or conclude an investigation although we cannot be unreasonably slow.

Thus, formal investigations may be more appropriate where:

— the discriminator is a repeat offender and litigation before the courts or tribunals has not resulted in a change in practice or procedures. For example, the CRE embarked on an investigation into the prison service in 2000 following findings of discrimination at an employment tribunal in a case taken by prison officer Claude Johnson against the prisoner service in relation to his treatment at Brixton Prison, the murder of Zahid Mubarek in Her Majesty's Young Offender Institution Feltham and a report from the Chief Inspector of Prisons about incidents of discrimination at another prison.
— There is evidence of institutional and systemic racism and discrimination within an organisation or sector. Usually, the evidence of institutional and systemic discrimination will come out during a case brought by a victim but in the case of the Household Cavalry it was remarks by Prince Charles that there were no Black guards which caused the Commission to consider an investigation into the Household Cavalry which subsequently developed into partnership work with the Ministry of Defence.
— A public authority has failed or is failing to comply with the racial equality duty (since there is no other means of enforcement other than judicial review). We have not yet embarked on such an investigation but it is part of the strategy around the racial equality duty.
— There is evidence of discriminatory practices but no 'victim' to bring proceedings. Examples of this are the early investigations into estate agents who were directing Black and Asian house buyers to areas of poorer quality houses. The evidence was obtained largely from discrimination testing by CRE officers.

The drawbacks to an investigation are:

— They can be overly complex. Investigations into a named body are governed by strict legal procedures which require terms of references and the opportunity for the organisation to make representations.
— The CRE can be challenged in court, particularly if we have not followed procedures. Challenges may also be made to the evidence to support the decision to embark on an investigation.
— A duty of confidentiality is owed to individuals and care is needed to maintain confidentiality where appropriate and relevant.

— Investigations are seen as confrontational. The business sector frequently alleges that it is difficult to work in partnership with us knowing that we could use our powers against them. In reality this has never arisen as a problem.
— Investigations can be resource intensive but again experience shows this be so with investigations into large public or national bodies or into sectors.
— Investigations do not clarify the law nor provide compensation for victims.

There is no moratorium on litigation during a formal investigation: we can provide assistance to an individual victim and carry out a formal investigation into the same discriminator but in practice we do not. I could not think of any examples where this was done. Usually a political decision is taken by Commissioners not to pursue litigation.

However, if it is necessary to clarify the law or seek a declaration as to whether a policy is discriminatory or not then we may resort to litigation.

Formal investigations tend to follow an adverse finding by a court or tribunal: for example the investigation into Ford Motor Company followed a couple of cases brought by employees who had suffered discrimination. This approach is largely the result of the narrow judicial interpretation of our powers to conduct investigations into named organisations.

An illustration of the links between litigation and other law enforcement powers is the work we have done on Gypsies and Travellers issues. Having supported two cases which established Romany Gypsies and Irish Travellers as ethnic groups protected by the Race Relations Act 1976, *CRE v Dutton* and *O'Leary v Allied Domecq* and others respectively, we are now moving away from providing individual support in such cases. Instead, we are now considering a formal investigation into local authority accommodation and site provision for Gypsies and Travellers. We are only able to be in this position as a result of the earlier cases and it was necessary to pursue litigation to establish these groups as protected groups under the 1976 Act."

Note
This passage shows the link between casework and investigations, as casework has frequently led to investigations where the casework has revealed a more structural or long-term problem.

In the Netherlands, the Equal Treatment Commission has commented on its powers to initiate investigations. Its power is only to undertake investigations in the public sector or against a whole sector of society; they cannot be undertaken against an individual organisation. And they can only be undertaken when the Commission can show that it has a suspicion of systemic discrimination. Here, as in Great Britain, there is a link between casework and investigations as individual cases can sometimes be the catalyst for an investigation. However, investigations are expensive and resource intensive, so the Commission's ability to undertake them is limited.

Equal Treatment Commission (Commissie Gelijke Behandeling)   **8.NL.37.**
"Equality law and the work of the Dutch Equal Treatment
Commission"[80]

"Investigation carried out on the commission's own initiative
The Commission does not have to wait for petitions to be filed. It is entitled to investigate on its own initiative in specific areas where systematic or persistent patterns of discrimination are suspected. According to Section 12, paragraph 1 of the AWGB [General Equal Treatment Act 1994], such an investigation is only possible in the public sector or in one or more sectors of society, not in an individual organisation or institution. An investigation may also cover various sectors when related to a specific subject, such as the essentials of home working contracts, for example. A suspicion of systematic discrimination is required to set up such an investigation.

Because of the restriction to investigate a complete sector, investigating public or societal sectors is a massive operation, and the Commission has only succeeded in completing just two such investigations during its first term (1994-2001). These concerned collective agreement provisions on pre-pension facilities and the access to fertility treatment through in vitro fertilisation in hospitals. However, its current budget and staffing levels are not sufficient to take on many of such projects.

However, individual complaints can also bring about large-scale investigations, covering a whole sector of society. Thus, the [ETC] has developed investigative and statistical methods for establishing unequal payment on the grounds of race and for gender. Using these methods, the Commission has, in several cases, been able to compare average wage levels and average career patterns of personnel doing work of equal value. These comparisons have brought to light a number of discriminatory pay practices.

In the first evaluation report on the AWGB [General Equal Treatment Act 1994], a recommendation has been given to extend the scope for investigation by the Commission on its own initiative of individual companies or a small group of companies."

The Swedish Ombudsmen also carry out investigations into broad areas that have given rise to concerns. During 2005, the Office of the Ombudsman against Discrimination on Grounds of Sexual Orientation (HomO) investigated the availability of artificial insemination to lesbians and the treatment of homosexuals within the prison and probation services, and reviewed three higher education institutions. The annual report for 2005 reflects how one of these investigations arose and how the HomO responded to it.

The Office of the Ombudsman against Discrimination on   **8.SE.38.**
Grounds of Sexual Orientation Report 2005[81]

"The prison and probation administration, the administration of justice and the police
During the year, the Ombudsman reviewed the operations of the National Prison and Probation Administration, with the object of preventing and countering discrimination and

---

[80] Available on the website of the Dutch Equal Treatment Commission, 12–13.
[81] HomO Ombudsmannen mot diskriminering på grund av sexuell läggning, Rapport 2005; available on the website of the Ombudsman against Discrimination on Grounds of Sexual Orientation, 95.

other offensive treatment on the grounds of sexual orientation. This review took place as a result of complaints by prisoners who felt that they had suffered discrimination or harassment for reasons linked to their sexual orientation. The review resulted, in particular, in criticism of the limited nature and vagueness of the Administration's measures vis-à-vis prisoners.

During 2005, the Office of the Ombudsman also continued its cooperation with the Public Prosecution Office and the National Courts Administration in the training of judges and prosecutors in questions involving human rights, homophobia, and non-discrimination rights, irrespective of sexual orientation."

It can be seen that investigations and inquiries are useful tools in the armoury of any equality body. They provide an alternative way for individual complaints to be resolved as they can make far-reaching recommendations to correct discriminatory practices. However, they are expensive and resource intensive, so equality bodies use them infrequently and normally only when there has been a series of complaints emanating from the same source.

8.5.4.   RESEARCH AND REPORTS

All countries seeking to eliminate discrimination need to understand more about where and how discrimination is operating in order to put in place the most effective measures to counter it. Accordingly, targeted research is a useful, even essential, tool in identifying problems and combating discrimination. Independent surveys and studies concerning the distribution of opportunities for employment or access to housing or health services play key roles in this respect.

Most equality bodies are able to conduct surveys and commission studies into the operation of discrimination in their area. The collection and analysis of data can cast new perspectives on current problems, whether by the juxtaposition of existing facts or the production of new materials. This research is sometimes carried out in-house, and sometimes universities and research institutes are commissioned to undertake surveys or studies.

Unless equality bodies and wider society have accurate information about the operation of discrimination in their society it is impossible to target equality work effectively. Hence most of the equality bodies have recognised the importance of conducting research into patterns of discrimination to inform their future work. This research can be used to justify further campaigns or information gathering, to make the case for further government action in particular areas and to identify specific areas where further anti-discrimination training is needed. Research is also useful to others outside the equality body working in the equality field, so part of the equality bodies' function is to make their research accessible to others both by hard copy publication and via the internet. Most equality bodies are now developing substantial websites to provide third parties with the means to access the information.

In 2004, recognising the importance of data collection for appropriately targeted anti-discrimination measures, the European Commission prepared a research report on data collection. The report comments on some of the uses to which such research can be put. Five different purposes are identified for which information is needed—to assist legislative decision making; to inform national and international monitoring bodies; to raise awareness; to back up litigation; and to help researchers understand the operation of discrimination.

N. Reuter, T. Makkonen, O. Oosi, "Study on Data Collection   **8.EC.39.**
to measure the extent and impact of discrimination in Europe"[82]

"Information is needed by different stakeholders and for different purposes. First, decision makers at the state and EU level need comprehensive and reliable data, when they are facing questions concerning appropriate policies, legislation and effective remedies for addressing the problem of discrimination and they need more information to guide policy and legal development. Second, information is needed by national and especially international monitoring bodies, such as the UN Committee on the Elimination of Racial Discrimination (CERD Committee) and the European Union Monitoring Centre on Racism (EUMC), in order to carry out their monitoring activities. Third, information is needed for awareness raising purposes. Scientific evidence on the extent and nature of discrimination serves as a compelling, factual baseline for national discussion on discrimination, benefiting governments and NGOs [non-government organisations] alike as they use this information for advocacy and awareness raising purposes. Fourth, victims of discrimination may make use of scientific evidence in bringing their cases to the courts. For instance in the USA, courts expect to see statistical evidence presented by the plaintiffs in employment discrimination cases, and the same is likely to happen in many EU countries as well. Fifth, information is indispensable for researchers seeking to improve our understanding of discrimination as a phenomenon, a task which again is a prerequisite for developing more effective policies countering discrimination."

8.5.5. MAKING RECOMMENDATIONS TO GOVERNMENT

As the national body entrusted with responsibility for equality, an equality body is in a strong position to make recommendations to the government for structural and institutional change. Some bodies, such as the Belgian Centre for Equal Opportunities and Opposition to Racism and the Swedish Ombudsmen, have a formal role in giving comments or opinions on existing or proposed legislation. So, for example, the Swedish Disability Ombudsman has a duty to "monitor the application of legislation that may be of importance for people with disability and propose to the Government such statutory amendments or other measures as are required to satisfy the rights and interests of people with disability".[83] In Hungary the Equal Treatment Authority has a duty to "submit their recommendations regarding the content of the legislation to

---

[82] Final Report, 7 December 2004, 14–15, available on the website of the European Commission, Directorate-General for Employment, Social Affairs and Equal Opportunities.
[83] Disability Ombudsman Instructions Ordinance (1994:949) s. 2(3).

the minister responsible for the preparation of the actual legislation and to the
Minister of Justice".[84] The Irish Equality Authority has a duty

> "to keep under review the working of this Act, the Maternity Protection Act, 1994, and
> the Adoptive Leave Act, 1995, and, whenever it thinks necessary, to make proposals to the
> Minister for amending any of those Acts; and . . . to keep under review the working of the
> Pensions Act, 1990, as regards the principle of equal treatment and, whenever it thinks
> necessary, to make proposals to the Minister for Social, Community and Family Affairs
> for amending that Act."[85]

The new British Commission for Equality and Human Rights "shall monitor the
effectiveness of the equality and human rights enactments"[86] and it may recommend
changes to the law or advise government about the likely effect of a proposed change
in the law.[87] The Parliamentary Commissioner for National and Ethnic Minority
Rights in Hungary has noted that a practice has evolved recently such that when new
acts are being developed the relevant ministry will seek the Ombudsman's
comments.[88] The French High Authority

> "may recommend any legislative or regulatory amendment. It is consulted by the
> Government on any draft legislation relating to the fight against discrimination and the
> promotion of equality. It may also be consulted by the Government on any issue relating
> to these areas."[89]

The Dutch Equal Treatment Commission notes that, although it has no explicit duty
to advise on legislation, it has developed a role in this area.

> *Equal Treatment Commission (Commissie Gelijke Behandeling)* **8.NL.40.**
> *"Equality law and the work of the Equal Treatment Commission in the Netherlands"*[90]

"The AWGB [General Equal Treatment Act 1994] does not explicitly confer the right or duty
on the Commission to advise the Government in matters concerning equal treatment legislation or equal opportunities policies. However, this advisory role has been recognised in
practice. This means the [ETC] has taken up this role as part of its general task to promote
adherence to equality law and in fact has often been requested to give such advice. In past
years, advice has been submitted in case of forthcoming legislation on age and disability. The
Commission has also given its opinions on proposed changes to European Community law
concerning non-discrimination and has issued commentaries on national policy plans, such as
the emancipation policy plan and policies concerning equal pay on the grounds of race and

---

[84] Government Decree 362/2004. (XII. 26.) Korm. on the Authority of Equal Treatment and the
Detailed Rules of its Procedures, s. 15.
[85] Employment Equality Acts 1998 to 2004, ss. 39(c) and (d).
[86] Equality Act 2006, s. 11(1).
[87] Equality Act 2006, s. 11(2).
[88] See ECRI, "Examples of Good Practices: Specialised Bodies to Combat Racism, Xenophobia,
Antisemitism and Intolerance at National Level" (January 2006) 32.
[89] Act No. 2004-1486 dated 30 December 2004 concerning the creation of the high commission against
discrimination and for equality (1) Art. 15.
[90] See above **8.NL.37.**, 18–19.

gender. On another level the Commission took part in a group consisting of the Mayor of the city of Utrecht, the Public Prosecutor, the police and branch-organisations in order to co-operate in the development of a policy for discos and bars to admit or refuse entrance to the public. Furthermore, the Commission developed an advice for the Ministry of Education containing rules for dress codes in education that can stand the anti-discrimination rules."

Although it has not been much developed, equality bodies can play an important role in equality-proofing new legislation. They are well placed to be able to review prospective legislation and report to governments on its likely impact with regard to equality.

8.5.6.   PROMOTING GOOD EQUALITY PRACTICE

There are many different ways of achieving the promotion of equality norms. Frequently equality bodies undertake awareness-raising campaigns, issue leaflets and set up websites to give information. They also undertake training, set up conferences, and identify and promote good practices in the field of equal treatment.

The Dutch Equal Treatment Commission is perhaps typical of many equality bodies in seeking to make equality norms as widely known as possible as a method of promoting equality.

Equal Treatment Commission (Commissie Gelijke Behandeling)   **8.NL.41.**
"Equality law and the work of the Equal Treatment Commission in the Netherlands"[91]

"Brochures, newsletters, websites and press releases
The Commission is committed to making its work and its judgments known both to the general public and to the legal profession. This means that it puts a lot of effort into its public relations activities. Brochures about the Commission's work have been published in Dutch and English as well as in Arabic and Turkish. The Commission also distributes a newsletter to organisations, institutions and civil service departments involved in the field of non-discrimination and equal treatment legislation. This newsletter appears three times a year and contains a summary of recent cases and follow-up reports.

The [ETC] has its own website on the Internet, where the full text of the AWGB [General Equal Treatment Act 1994] and the specific regulations based on the Act can be found. The site also contains the full text of the judgments and some background material about equal treatment legislation. An English section provides information to non-Dutch speaking persons.

Whenever a particularly important case has been completed, the Commission issues a press release. Radio, television, newspapers and journals are usually eager to interview the Chair of the Commission about 'revolutionary' cases."

---

[91] See above **8.NL.37.**, 20.

Equality bodies also have a valuable role in making recommendations to the business community about how they can promote equality in the management of their businesses and explaining the business benefits that can follow from this.

Some equality bodies publish Codes of Practice to assist with the application of the law in discrete areas. Codes of Practice can give practical, accessible advice, often with examples, on how to ensure that equality standards are being properly implemented. The Irish Equality Authority has produced a Code of Practice on sexual harassment and harassment at work. The UK Commissions have produced a series of different Codes of Practice aiming to cover each of the key areas.

The Parliamentary Commissioner for National and Ethnic Minority Rights in Hungary has published a manual "in order to promote cooperation between minority self-governments and local governments concerning the legal frameworks of their operations, including descriptions of concrete relevant cases".[92]

The Dutch Equal Treatment Commission has an unusual provision in that it can, and often does, make rulings at the request of organisations or employers about the lawfulness of their own practices or procedures.

Equal Treatment Commission (Commissie Gelijke Behandeling) **8.NL.42.**
"Equality law and the work of the Equal Treatment Commission in the Netherlands"[93]

"Request for an assessment of one's own practice or regulation
Individuals or organisations may also want to know whether their own conduct, policies or regulations fall within the scope of the equal treatment laws. Under Section 12 of the AWGB [General Equal Treatment Act 1994], they have the right to ask the Commission to give an expert opinion on such matters.

For example, an employer may ask whether a specific regulation on part-time work is permitted, or a car rental company may want to know whether it would be lawful to ask for additional guarantees from non-residents.

The Commission receives several such requests each year. The fact that every now and then individuals or organisations turn to the Commission for help and advice is a positive sign that the [ETC] is increasingly being seen as an authoritative and expert body."

8.5.7.   POSITIVE DUTIES TO PROMOTE EQUALITY

Another enforcement tool that equality bodies are beginning to use is the application of positive duties to promote equality. Within Great Britain, the use of positive duties in the field of race was introduced in 2000 when the Race Relations (Amendment) Act (RRAA) 2000 amended RRA 1976, section 71, to impose a new positive "general" duty on all public authorities in Great Britain to "have due regard to the

---

[92] See Examples of Good Practices: Specialised bodies to combat racism, xenophobia, antisemitism and intolerance at national level, above n 88 at 33.
[93] See above **8.NL.37.**, 12–13.

need to eliminate unlawful discrimination and promote equality of opportunity and good race relations in the carrying out of their functions". The authorities affected were most public authorities, including education authorities, health authorities, central and local government, and police authorities. The Home Secretary has imposed certain "specific" duties on specified public authorities to ensure the "better performance" of their general duties. Such authorities have a duty to prepare and publish racial equality schemes setting out how they intend to meet their general and specific duties. New duties are now being introduced in the fields of disability and gender. The Disability Equality Duty came into effect in December 2006 and the Gender Equality Duty in April 2007.

Lowri Griffiths from the Equal Opportunities Commission has reviewed the progress of positive duties to promote equality in Great Britain and Europe.

L. Griffiths, "Positive Duties to Promote Equality"[94]   **8.EC.43.**

"This paper is based on responses to the Questionnaire carried out by Equinet in the summer 2005. It looks at the extent to which positive duties to promote equality have been introduced in a number of European countries . . .

What Are Positive Duties?
A positive duty is a requirement that organisations promote equality and diversity in all aspects of their work, in a manner that involves employees, employers and service-users alike. It is a proactive approach, with an emphasis on achieving results backed by enforcement mechanisms and the measurement of outcomes.

The positive duties that have been, and are due to be, implemented in the public sector in the UK are based upon a legal requirement to eliminate unlawful discrimination and promote equality of treatment. This can be fulfilled by monitoring workforce composition, consulting with relevant groups, carrying out impact assessments to determine the impact of particular policies and practices upon disadvantaged groups, and by taking remedial action where necessary.

Why Positive Duties?
Anti-discrimination law has generated considerable cultural change in UK society, and has been effective in breaking down many visible barriers and prejudices. However, it often proves less than adequate in dealing with more complex and deep-rooted patterns of exclusion and inequality. There is too much reliance upon individual enforcement, legal technicalities of interpretation and complex adversarial litigation. It frequently suffers from lack of partici-pation and input of disadvantaged groups themselves. It also encourages a culture of passive compliance with legislation, rather than the taking of proactive action to encourage diversity . . .

[She also considers how far similar duties are operating in other European countries:]

---

[94] In Equinet, above n. 13, 44–6.

Are Positive Duties common across Europe?

In the Questionnaire carried out by Equinet in the summer 2005, a number of European equality bodies were asked whether the equality legislation in their countries imposes any legal obligations on public or private bodies to take action with regard to equality. There were a wide variety of responses to this question. Some countries reported that there were provisions in place that enabled positive action in both the public and private sphere. In the Slovak Republic, the constitutionality of provisions enabling positive action on the grounds of race and ethnic origin are currently being considered by the Constitutional Court. The Slovenian Office for Equal Opportunities reported that the Slovenian legislation sets out that the 'National Parliament, government, ministries and other state bodies and bodies of local communities shall establish conditions for equal treatment of all persons through awareness-raising and monitoring the situation in this field as well as through measures of a normative and political nature.' No details were given, however, of any enforcement mechanism to ensure that such measures are implemented.

The National Equality Body of Austria reported that, although equality legislation provides for the possibility of positive action, it does not require public or private bodies to implement positive action. However, Government contracts are only awarded to companies and individuals who observe the equality legislation.

The Office of the Commissioner for Administration in Cyprus reported that their equality legislation provides that positive duties can be imposed on both public and private sector organisations, but that so far no such duties have been imposed. Denmark has no positive duty for public or private bodies, although the Article 13 body has been given the task of promoting the principle of equality and non-discrimination on the grounds of race and ethnic origin. It does not, however, have the power to oblige private or public entities to eliminate discrimination in general or to promote equality.

In its response to the questionnaire, the Swedish Ombudsman against Ethnic Discrimination stated that there are positive duties in Sweden that cover both the public and private sector. These duties, however, apply only to employment in both the public and private sectors, and are only in force with regards to ethnicity, gender and religion. Only the Ombudsman against Ethnic Discrimination and the Equality Ombudsman have the right to enforce positive duties.

The Estonian Chancellor of Justice set out in detail legislative provisions introduced in the Gender Equality Act placing obligations on state and local government agencies, educational and research institutions and employers to promote gender equality of men and women. These obligations are wide-ranging. They require State and local government agencies to promote gender equality 'systematically and purposefully. Their duty is to change the conditions and circumstances which hinder achievement of gender equality.' The Estonian legislation requires State and local government agencies to 'take into account the different needs and social status of men and women' in the 'planning, implementation and assessment of national, regional and institutional strategies, policies and action plans'. The Minister of Social Affairs has responsibility for making recommendations concerning the implementation of these obligations. Educational institutions are required to 'ensure equal treatment for men and women in vocational guidance, acquisition of education, professional and vocational development and re-training.' They are also obliged to ensure that 'the curricula, study material used and research conducted shall facilitate abolition of the unequal treatment of men and women and promote equality.' The Estonian legislation goes further than the proposed positive duty in Great Britain, as it places a legal requirement on private sector employers to promote gender equality, including a requirement that employers 'create working conditions which are suitable for both women and men and support the combination of work and family life, taking into account the needs of employees.' Private sector employers are also required to 'collect statistical data concerning employment which are based on gender and which allow, if necessary, the relevant institutions to monitor and assess whether the principle of equal treatment is complied with in employment relationships. The procedure for the collection of data and a list of data shall be established by a regulation of the Government of the Republic.' A Gender Equality Commissioner will be appointed who will have responsibility for monitoring compliance with these positive requirements. The Commissioner does not appear to have enforcement powers [references omitted]."

The use of positive duties to promote equality is still a new tool in the armoury available to equality bodies. It aims to persuade organisations to build equality considerations into every aspect of their work. However, their enforcement often remains unclear, and this may lead to organisations ignoring them or adopting nominal compliance policies and not re-considering their policies and practices to eliminate inequalities.

8.6. PROTECTION OF INDEPENDENCE

The protection of the independence of equality bodies has already been referred to in the context of the requirements under both international and European law. It is rightly recognised by most Member States as key to the success of any equality body. Protection from discrimination can be a matter of acute political importance affecting either the state or very powerful actors. However, measuring or assessing independence is not straightforward, and independence itself is a relative matter. Nevertheless, there are a number of indicators that can signal the degree of independence enjoyed by an equality body so that the nearest that we can achieve to an absolute assessment is to look at some of these measures. This section will examine the statutes setting up some of the European equality bodies in order to see the extent to which their independence is preserved. Independence is difficult to measure even if we examine these indicators, as sometimes the true measure of actual independence will lie in the practice of the equality body rather than its strict legal construction.

   This section will also consider in some detail the discussions that have taken place in Britain prior to the setting up of a new Commission for Equality and Human Rights. This discussion has been included because it is a recent example of the way in which the concern that an equality body should have as much independence as possible influenced, or failed to influence, the wording of the legislation to establish a new equality body.

8.6.1.   INDEPENDENCE FROM GOVERNMENT

Lack of a strong foundation for the independence of equality bodies can be fatal when a conflict arises. That is why the extent to which such an organisation can withstand political pressure is seen as critical to the success of the body in fulfilling the Paris Principles (see **8.UN.4.** and **8.UN.44.**). These require that a national human rights institution "shall be given as broad a mandate as possible, which shall be clearly set forth in a constitutional or legislative text, specifying its composition and its sphere of competence".[95]

Although these principles were originally set out in respect of human rights institutions it is widely accepted that their principles are also applicable to equality bodies. The section of the Paris Principles dealing with the bodies' composition and independence focuses on the need for a proper appointment procedure for its ruling body, for representation of all the relevant sections of society and the need for a fixed period for the operation of their mandate, although this can be renewable. The principles make it clear that any governmental representatives on the ruling council should not have a vote and should be there in a purely advisory role. They also stress the importance of an appropriate structure as well as adequate funding to enable true independence to be enjoyed.

Office for the United Nations High Commissioner   **8.UN.44.**
for Human Rights
"Principles relating to the status and functioning of national institutions for protection and promotion of human rights" (known as the "Paris Principles")[96]

"B. Composition and guarantees of independence and pluralism
1. The composition of the national institution and the appointment of its members, whether by means of an election or otherwise, shall be established in accordance with a procedure which affords all necessary guarantees to ensure the pluralist representation of the social forces (of civilian society) involved in the protection and promotion of human rights, particularly by powers which will enable effective cooperation to be established with, or through the presence of, representatives of:
Non-governmental organizations responsible for human rights and efforts to combat racial discrimination, trade unions, concerned social and professional organizations, for example, associations of lawyers, doctors, journalists and eminent scientists; trends in philosophical or religious thought; universities and qualified experts; Parliament; Government departments (if they are included, these representatives should participate in the deliberations only in an advisory capacity).
2. The national institution shall have an infrastructure which is suited to the smooth conduct of its activities, in particular adequate funding. The purpose of this funding should be to enable it to have its own staff and premises, in order to be independent of the government and not be subject to financial control which might affect this independence.
3. In order to ensure a stable mandate for the members of the institution, without which there can be no real independence, their appointment shall be effected by an official act which shall establish the specific duration of the mandate. This mandate may be renewable, provided that the pluralism of the institution's membership is ensured."

[95] Para. A(2) of the Paris Principles.
[96] See the website of the Office for the United Nations High Commissioner for Human Rights.

The legal basis of each organisation will be a key determinant of its independence. Those set up by legislation are likely to have the most secure foundations and be less easy to dismantle than those set up merely by regulation or by administrative decision. The absence of full democratic legitimacy in this latter kind of body may well mean that the decision to set up such a body can be more easily reversed or subjected to interference. These points were explored in a report commissioned by the European Commission which was published in 2002. The report analyses the work of the existing bodies working to promote equality and combat discrimination.

European Commission, "Specialised bodies to promote equality   **8.EC.45.**
and/or combat discrimination"[97]

"A body's legal basis may have implications for its relative independence. With a firm legal basis in the form of a national act containing clear descriptions of its scope and a mandate passed by the parliament, it is more difficult for a government to alter the role and activities of an institution. Alterations in such cases will typically require parliamentary negotiations and the adoption of new legislation. Thus in situations where an institution acts or makes statements in a manner which conflicts with the government of the day, a firm legal basis may serve to counteract any intent of swift political interference and thereby lessen the possibility of political influence on the body in question. On the other hand, a body which is established by secondary legislation may be more prone to alterations in mandate and scope, since secondary legislation can be modified without involving the parliament . . . While the independence of the specialised body to promote equality may be best secured by law, this obviously will not protect the body if a parliamentary majority decides that it must be modified or removed.

Government decisions on the funding of the body may also have direct practical implications on the actual ability of an institution to implement its legal mandate . . . Though direct interference in the work of the institutions is seldom observed; institutional independence can be relative, such as when a government applies indirect pressure to it. As an example, one of the Dutch institutions referred to comments received from the Government questioning whether its choice of cases to present in its annual report did not suggest particular political associations. Though the institution in question rejected this notion, the example demonstrates how institutions might be exposed to indirect political interference."

As already noted, there has been a debate in Sweden on the amalgamation of its Ombudsmen. In this context, a Swedish Parliamentary Committee of Inquiry on Discrimination recently considered the future of its equality laws and whether to amalgamate their four Ombudsmen against discrimination into one authority the Office of the Ombudsman against Discrimination. The Committee tasked with considering this reached a very similar conclusion to the PLS Ramboll report.

[97] Report on the Role, Structure and Functioning of Specialised Bodies, above n. 45, 35.

Swedish report on coherent discrimination legislation,[98] *Part 1*   **8.SE.46.**
Final report of the parliamentary committee for non-discrimination

"We conclude that an important aspect of the issue of the Ombudsman's autonomy and independence is that the areas of responsibility and the functions of the Ombudsman should be clearly defined by statute and not by ordinance. It is consequently the Riksdag [Parliament] that should determine the mandate and the Government would thereby not be empowered to unilaterally change the functions of the Ombudsman. In accordance with this, the areas of responsibility and functions of the Ombudsman should be included within the Act. In this way a better safeguard is provided for the authority's autonomy and independence, as any amendments in the areas of responsibility and functions of the Ombudsman must be presented to the Riksdag. Through the areas of responsibility and functions of the Ombudsman being regulated by law, emphasis is also placed on the importance of the Ombudsman's activities, first for those who are subjected to discrimination, second for the government powers. The areas of responsibility and the functions of the Ombudsman should be regulated first in the new Prohibition and other Measures against Discrimination Act and second in a special Discrimination Ombudsman Act.

. . . The Ombudsman against Discrimination should for the time being be an authority reporting to the Government.

The Government should observe great restraint in the terms of reference for the Ombudsman . . . It is important that the new authority is given sufficient resources to ensure that the work against discrimination can be strengthened and improved [references omitted]."

In order to secure and maintain independence, there can be no doubt that it is important that equality bodies achieve and keep sufficient separation from the organs of government. Several of the European equality bodies operate as part of a government department. This seems regrettable. It is inevitable that it will be difficult for them to appear to civil society as wholly independent of government. Presentation of a visible independence matters. The report referred to below gives the example of the position in Portugal.

European Commission, "Specialised bodies to promote equality   **8.EC.47.**
and/or combat discrimination"[99]

"*Independence and the role of government*
The Commission for Equality and Against Racial Discrimination, which was recently established in Portugal, demonstrates an interesting contradiction in terms of the independence it enjoys. While on the one hand the law adopted by Parliament establishes the Commission for Equality and Against Racial Discrimination as an independent body, the same law states that the High Commissioner for Immigrants and Ethnic Minorities shall be its chair. The High Commissioner, who covers and co-ordinates a broad range of initiatives concerning minorities, is appointed by the prime minister, has the rank of a vice-secretary of state, and is subject to the authority of the Presidency of the Council of Ministers."

---

[98] *En Sammanhållen Diskrimineringslagstiftning, Del 1, Slutbetänkande av Diskrimineringskommitén* (Stockholm, SOU 2006: 22) 48–50.
[99] Report on the Role, Structure and Functioning of Specialised Bodies, above n. 45.

There is a similar problem in Italy, where the Italian National Office against Racial Discrimination has been set up within the Department for Equal Opportunities. The European Commission against Racism and Intolerance (ECRI) has therefore recommended that it should be made more independent.

European Commission against Racism and Intolerance,   **8.CoE.48.**
"Third report on Italy"[100]

"ECRI notes that legislative decree No. 215/200320 provides for the establishment of a National Office against Racial Discrimination (Ufficio Nazionale Antidiscriminazioni Razziali or UNAR). Established as part of the Department for Equal Opportunities of the Presidency of the Council of Ministers, UNAR has been entrusted with several functions, including: to provide assistance to victims of discrimination, including by investigating their complaints and assisting them in judicial and administrative proceedings; to raise general awareness of racism and racial discrimination, notably through training activities and research; and to report to Parliament and the Committee of Ministers on the implementation of the principle of equal treatment irrespective of racial or ethnic origin . . . ECRI invites the Italian authorities to keep the status, powers and duties of UNAR under review, in order to ensure that this Office provide victims of racial discrimination with the most effective protection possible . . . In particular, ECRI draws the attention of the Italian authorities to the need for such a body to be independent and to the guidelines it formulated on how to guarantee such independence."

There are two key ways in which governments may seek to influence equality bodies. Each needs to be kept well in mind whenever such a body is being scrutinised for its independence. These are (i) by the withdrawal or reduction of funding; and (ii) by the appointment of less than independent Commissioners, or even the failure to appoint Commissioners when they are needed.

So, in checking the independence of such bodies, key questions that must be asked are:

— How independent is the administrative control?
— How is the board appointed? For how long? Is there a fixed term of office?
— Who can dismiss the board and why?
— Do the members of the board serve a fixed term and if so for how long?
— Where is the financial control of the body?
— Is the allocation of resources to the body sufficient to secure an ability to operate independently?
— Is the body made accountable to parliament or to government?

There are also a number of subsidiary ways in which government can seek to influence equality bodies, ranging from requirements to undertake work required by

---

[100] CRI (2006) 19, adopted on 16 December 2005, made public on 16 May 2006, available on the website of the European Commission against Racism and Intolerance.

the government to requirements to obtain government consent in order to take a specific action.

8.6.1.A.   UNITED KINGDOM

The UK has a long tradition of establishing equality bodies known as "*Commissions*" to counter specific types of inequality and discrimination. In Great Britain there are three Commissions: in 1975 the Equal Opportunities Commission (EOC) was set up to deal with gender inequality; in 1976 the Commission for Racial Equality (CRE) was set up; and in 1999 the Disability Rights Commission (DRC) was established.

As a result of the implementation of the Employment Equality Directive, the UK government has decided to combine these three Commissions into one body that will also take responsibility for discrimination on grounds of sexual orientation, religion or belief and age, as well as human rights. The Equality Act 2006 established the powers for this new equality body to be set up and it is now proposed that it should be established by the end of 2007. It will be called the Commission for Equality and Human Rights (CEHR).

In Northern Ireland in 1999 the existing Northern Ireland Commissions were drawn together to create the Equality Commission for Northern Ireland (ECNI), with a remit to cover gender, race, religion and disability. Sexual orientation was added to its remit in 2003[101] and age was added in October 2006.

As the Equality Act 2006 made its progress through the UK Parliament, there were many discussions about the powers that the new Commission for Equality and Human Rights (CEHR) might be given. These are particularly instructive since they focused particularly on the independence of the proposed new body from state interference. The government published its proposals for a new equality body in the White Paper *Fairness for All: A new Commission for Equality and Human Rights*. The Parliamentary Joint Committee for Human Rights (JCHR) then considered both these proposals and later the proposals in the Equality Bill when it was introduced into Parliament. Their comments were strongly influenced by the requirements set out in the Paris Principles (see **8.UN.4.** and **8.UN.44.**) and show the practical outworking of these principles in considering the design of a new body.

UK Parliament, Joint Committee on Human Rights   **8.UK.49.**
Commission for Equality and Human Rights: the Government's White Paper
16th Report of Session 2003–2004[102]

"The time has come for the Government to recognise that there is a class of public bodies which have a distinctive constitutional role, and that these need to be designed with this special

---

[101] Equality Commission for Northern Ireland, Employment Equality (Sexual Orientation) Regulations (Northern Ireland) 2003, available on the website of the Equality Commission for Northern Ireland under the heading Publications.

[102] At paras 45 and 47, available on the website of the UK Parliament.

status in mind . . . The basic principles for the design of independent national institutions supporting democracy are that they should enjoy

— statutory guarantees of independence from both the executive and parliament;
— a system of funding independent of direct ministerial control;
— independent staffing arrangements;
— statutory involvement of a parliamentary body in approving and overseeing its budget and strategic plan;
— parliamentary involvement in key appointments;
— direct reporting to parliament . . .

[The JCHR concluded at paragraph 50:]
The essential elements [are] as follows:

— the Chair of the Commission should be defined in statute as an 'officer of Parliament'.
— dismissal of a commissioner within the fixed term of appointment should be effected only by a joint address of both Houses, or otherwise only on the recommendation of a statutory committee which includes parliamentary, non-executive, representatives;
— there should be no power of direction or veto over the commission, in relation to the promotion and protection of human rights, either by Ministers or by Parliament;
— the commission should be funded by moneys voted by the House of Commons directly, not through the voted expenditure of a ministerial department.;
— the commissioners and staff of the commission should not be crown servants (although they should have a statutory guarantee of broadly equivalent terms and conditions);
— there should be a statutory committee appointed to approve and oversee the commission's budget, and the strategic plan which it should be required by statute to present;
— the statutory committee should recommend commissioners for appointment, since there is no obvious way to reconcile differences of view between the two Houses;
— the commission should be required to make an annual report to Parliament, which should be laid before each House by its Clerk. The commission should be empowered to lay other reports before Parliament as it thinks fit, including those arising from general inquiries on matters of public policy relating to human rights;
— there should be a committee of both Houses charged with considering the reports of the commission (50)."

These recommendations show how the objectives of the Paris Principles (see **8.UN.4.** and **8.UN.44.**) and the ideal of independence from government could be achieved. These proposals were broadly not accepted by the government, although some changes to the original proposals were made. The main changes that were implemented related to the Secretary of State's power to require the new Commission to undertake specified work and the recognition that the Commission's powers should be constrained as little as possible. This led the JCHR to comment further in December 2005.

UK Parliament, Joint Committee on Human Rights   8.UK.50.
4th Report of Session 2005–2006[103]

"Throughout our consideration of the new Commission's status, we have consistently maintained that it should not be a creature of Parliament, any more than it should be a creature of Government. Nevertheless, we believe that it is right that, in comparison with the Government's proposals, the Commission's accountability to Parliament should be strengthened. This would be a logical reflection of the Commission's constitutional role as an independent watchdog over the executive's actions in relation to equalities and human rights.

22. The Government has not accepted the previous Committee's views on this, nor its package of recommendations, and has retained in the Bill the proposed status of an NDPB [non-departmental public body] for the Commission. However, a number of amendments have been made to the Bill to enhance the Commission's de facto independence from the Government. As well as the removal from the Bill of the Secretary of State's powers to require the Commission to advise on legislation or to conduct inquiries (see paragraphs 12 and 14 above), and the restriction of his power to require the Commission to issue codes of practice (see paragraph 13 above), there have been other important changes to the Bill. Notably there has been the insertion of a provision in Schedule 1 to the Bill stating that

'The Secretary of State shall have regard to the desirability of ensuring that the Commission is under as few constraints as reasonably possible in determining

(a)   its activities
(b)   its timetables, and
(c)   its priorities.'

In addition, the Secretary of State is now required to lay before Parliament the Commission's strategic plan, drawn up under clause 4 and setting out its activities, timetable and priorities.

23. The criteria for appointing Commissioners have been clarified to ensure that the Secretary of State must have regard to the experience and knowledge of individual appointees relating to the matters in respect of which the Commission has functions, as well as to the desirability of the Commissioners together having such knowledge and experience. Finally, the Secretary of State is now required to make funding available to the Commission which is 'reasonably sufficient' for the purpose of enabling it to perform its functions, rather than 'appropriate', as stated in the Bill as introduced this Session. This amended wording appears to us to be more consistent with the statement in the Paris Principles that national human rights institutions shall have 'adequate funding' to enable them to have their own staff and premises, in order to be independent of Government and not be subject to financial control which might affect their independence."

Some of the provisions ultimately approved by Parliament for the setting up and the constitution of the Commission for Equality and Human Rights are as follows:

---

[103]   The report is available on the website of the UK Parliament.

Equality Act 2006   **8.GB.51.**

Schedule 1   Section 2
Constitution
Membership

1 (1)   The Secretary of State shall appoint not less than 10 or more than 15 individuals as members of the Commission (to be known as Commissioners).

   (2)   The chief executive of the Commission (appointed under paragraph 7 below) shall be a Commissioner ex officio.

2 (1)   In appointing Commissioners the Secretary of State shall—

   (a)   appoint an individual only if the Secretary of State thinks that the individual—

      (i)   has experience or knowledge relating to a relevant matter, or

      (ii)   is suitable for appointment for some other special reason, and

   (b)   have regard to the desirability of the Commissioners together having experience and knowledge relating to the relevant matters.

   (2)   For the purposes of sub-paragraph (1) the relevant matters are those matters in respect of which the Commission has functions including, in particular

   (a)   discrimination (whether on grounds of age, disability, gender, gender reassignment, race, religion or belief, sexual orientation or otherwise), and

   (b)   human rights . . .

Tenure

3 (1)   A Commissioner shall hold and vacate office in accordance with the terms of his appointment (subject to this Schedule).

   (2)   The appointment of a Commissioner must be expressed to be for a specified period of not less than two years or more than five years.

   (3)   A Commissioner whose period of membership has expired may be reappointed.

   (4)   A Commissioner may resign by notice in writing to the Secretary of State.

   (5)   The Secretary of State may dismiss a Commissioner who is, in the opinion of the Secretary of State, unable, unfit or unwilling to perform his functions.

The Equality Act then provides for the Secretary of State to appoint one of the Commissioners as Chairman and another to be Deputy Chairman, and for the powers and functions of the Chair and Deputy Chair. Commissioners are appointed for a fixed period that can be between 2 and 5 years. The Commission itself has powers to appoint a Chief Executive and the other members of staff of the Commission.

8.6.1.B.   THE NETHERLANDS

The Equal Treatment Commission was established in 1994. It covers alleged discrimination on the grounds of religion, belief, political orientation, race, sex, nationality, sexual orientation or civil status, in both the employment and non-employment fields, and part-time or full-time work and temporary contracts in the employment field. It covers age in the employment field only and disability in relation to employment and public transport only. It is a semi-judicial body that issues non-binding opinions. The Commission consists of nine members who are appointed by the Minister of Justice in agreement with the Ministers of the Interior, Social and Labour Affairs, Education and Science and Welfare/Health and Culture (Article 16(3) below). A Commission member may be dismissed by the Dutch Supreme Court if it can be shown that the member has seriously impeded the course of the law or impeded the trust that has been put in him or her (Article 46). Members may be appointed for a maximum of six years and may be reappointed on the expiry of their term of office. In addition, there are at least nine Deputy Commissioners who are asked to substitute when there is a shortage of members to investigate cases.

The provisions in relation to the ETC are set out in the Equal Treatment Act 1994.

Dutch Equal Treatment Act 1994[104]   **8.NL.52.**

Chapter 2: The Equal Treatment Commission

Section 11
1. An Equal Treatment Commission shall be established, hereinafter referred to as the Commission.
2. The Commission may establish subcommittees from among its members for the performance of its duties . . .

Section 16
1. The Commission shall comprise nine members—including a chair and two assistant chairs—and the same number of deputy members.
2. The chair and the assistant chairs must fulfil the requirements laid down in section 1d of the Judiciary (Organisation) Act governing eligibility for appointment as a judge in a district court.
3. The members and deputy members shall be appointed by Our Minister of Justice, in consultation with Our Minister of the Interior, Our Minister of Employment & Social Security, Our Minister of Education & Science and Our Minister of Welfare, Health & Cultural Affairs . . .
5. The members and deputy members shall be appointed for a maximum of six years. They may be reappointed immediately. The Minister of Justice may accept their resignation, if tendered . . .

Section 17
1. An office shall be set up to assist the Commission in the performance of its duties.
2. Our Minister of Justice shall, on the recommendation of the Commission, appoint, promote, suspend and dismiss the staff of the office. Our Minister of Justice shall decide in what cases they shall be appointed, promoted, suspended and dismissed . . .

Section 20
1. The Commission shall issue an annual report of its activities, which shall be published. It shall forward this report in any event to such of Our Ministers as it may concern and to the advisory bodies concerned.

---

[104] (*Algemene wet gelijke behandeling*, AWGB) available on the website of the Dutch Equal Treatment Commission.

2. Every five years, calculated from the entry into force of this Act, the Commission shall draw up a report of its findings on the operation in practice of this Act, the Equal Opportunities Act or section 646 of Book 7 of the Civil Code. It shall forward this report to the Minister of the Interior.

8.6.1.C.   FRANCE

The High Authority against Discrimination and for Equality was set up in 2005. It is an independent administrative body. It has wide powers to counter discrimination on any of the grounds prohibited by law. Currently this covers race, ethnic origin, sex, disability, age, health, religion, sexual orientation, opinions, appearance and union activities. It is particularly interesting because of the broad range of different bodies who appoint members of the authority, and the importance of a balance between men and women.

French Act No. 2004-1486 dated 30 December 2004 concerning   **8.FR.53.**
the creation of the High Authority against Discrimination and for Equality[105]

Title I—Of the high authority against discrimination and for equality

Article 1
An independent administrative authority is to be set up known as the high authority against discrimination and for equality.
The high authority has the authority to discover all discrimination, direct or indirect, prohibited by law or by any international commitment to which France is a party.

Article 2
The high authority is made up of a board of eleven members appointed by decree by the President of the Republic:

— two members, including the Chairman, appointed by the President of the Republic;
— two members appointed by the President of the senate;
— two members appointed by the President of the National Assembly;
— two members appointed by the Prime Minister;
— one member appointed by the deputy Chairman of the Council of State;
— one member appointed by the First President of the Court of Cassation;
— one member appointed by the President of the Economic and Social Council.

The appointments by the President of the Republic, the President of the Senate, the President of the National Assembly and the Prime Minister shall provide a balanced representation of men and women.
    The chairman and the members of the high authority shall have a term of office of five years. This can neither be revoked nor renewed.

[105] JO No. 304 of 31 December 2004.

Half the members of the board, with the exception of the chairman, are to be replaced every thirty months.

In the event of a board member's seat becoming vacant for any reason whatever, it is provided that a new member shall be appointed for the remaining period of the term of office subject to the conditions set down in this Article. His term of office may be renewed if he has held this position as a replacement for less than two years.

The high authority shall create a consultative committee to work with it so as to involve in its work qualified persons selected from among representatives of associations, unions and professional organisations and any other persons involved in the field of the fight against discrimination and the promotion of equality.

It has departments placed under the authority of its chairman, for which it may recruit contractual agents.

The chairman represents the high authority and is empowered to act in its name.

In the event of a tied vote, the chairman of the high authority shall have the casting vote.

Article 16
Each year the high authority shall submit a report to the President of the Republic, the Parliament and the Prime Minister setting out how it has performed its duties. This report is made public.

Article 17
The funds required by the high authority for the performance of its duties are allocated to the budget of the minister responsible for social affairs. Its chairman is the controller of the receipts and expenses.

The high authority is subject to the control of the Court of Audit.

8.6.1.D.   IRELAND

The Equality Authority was established in 1999 by the Employment Equality Act 1998. It covers nine grounds for discrimination: gender, marital status, family status, age, disability, race, sexual orientation, religious belief and membership of the Traveller community in both the employment and non-employment areas.

Irish Employment Equality Acts 1998–2004   **8.IE.54.**

Part V—Equality authority: general

Membership
41. (1) Subject to subsection (2), the Authority shall consist of 12 members appointed by the Minister (one of whom shall be appointed as its chairperson) of whom at least 5 shall be male and 5 shall be female.
(2) For the 4 years immediately following the first appointment by the Minister of members of the Authority, the Authority shall consist of not more than 12 members so appointed (one of whom shall be its chairperson) of whom, other than 2, at least half shall be male and half shall be female . . .

Chairperson.

42. (1) The chairperson shall be appointed either in a whole-time or a part-time capacity and shall hold office for not more than 4 years on such terms and conditions as the Minister, with the consent of the Minister for Finance, may determine.

(2) The chairperson shall be paid, out of moneys provided by the Oireachtas [Parliament], such remuneration and allowances and expenses as the Minister, with the consent of the Minister for Finance, may determine.

(3) The chairperson may at any time resign that office by letter addressed to the Minister and the resignation shall take effect on the date of the receipt of the letter by the Minister.

(4) The Minister may at any time, for stated reasons, remove the chairperson from office . . .

Ordinary members.

44. (1) Of the ordinary members of the Authority

    (a)   two, one male and one female, shall be persons appointed on the nomination by such organisations representative of employees as the Minister considers appropriate,

    (b)   two, one male and one female, shall be persons appointed on the nomination by such organisations representative of employers as the Minister considers appropriate, and

    (c)   the remaining number shall be such persons as appear to the Minister to be persons who have knowledge of, or experience in—

        (i)   consumer, social affairs or equality issues, including issues related to the experience and circumstances of groups who are disadvantaged by reference to gender, marital status, family status, sexual orientation, religion, age, disability, race, colour, nationality, ethnic or national origin or membership of the traveller community,

        (ii)   issues related to the provision of goods or services, or

        (iii)   such other subject-matter (including law, finance, management or administration) as appears to the Minister to be relevant to the issues to which the functions of the Authority relate.

(2) Each ordinary member of the Authority shall be a part-time member and, subject to this Act, shall hold office for not more than 4 years on such terms and conditions as the Minister, with the consent of the Minister for Finance, may determine.

(3) The Minister may at any time, for stated reasons, remove an ordinary member of the Authority from office.

Note

Members can only be disqualified if they become a member of the Irish or European Parliaments, become bankrupt, are sentenced to a term of imprisonment or cease to be ordinarily resident in Ireland.

    The government retains a number of important powers which can be used to control the Equality Authority. The Authority has a duty to provide an annual report to the Minister for Justice, Equality and Law Reform on its activities during the previous year; this report is then submitted to Parliament. The Minister may at any time ask for specific information on any aspect of their policy or activities, on any specific matter or on the accounts prepared by the Authority. Whilst this may in practice be unproblematic, it could be misused to distract the Equality Authority from its primary function by requiring the production of unnecessary amounts of information or accounts.

The Equality Authority is subject to constraints on the way that it is able to appoint staff in that "The Minister may, 'after consultation with the Authority' appoint" staff;[106] their grades and the numbers of staff in each grade are determined by the Minister "after consultation with the Authority";[107] and the terms of their appointment are determined by "the Minister, with the consent of the Minister of Finance".[108] Currently, the staff of the Equality Authority consists mainly of civil servants on secondment: 40 of the 53 staff are appointed in this way, the remaining 13 staff, who are directly appointed, tend to occupy the more senior management roles within the organisation.[109] Whilst the Authority itself does not see this as a threat to its independence, it clearly affects the length of service, and hence continuity, of a substantial proportion of the staff. However, despite all the concerns noted here, the equality body is in fact highly effective and independent.

8.6.1.E.   HUNGARY

Hungary has appointed an Authority of Equal Treatment that has been operational since February 2005. It covers all the prohibited grounds of discrimination, whether in the field of employment, education or access to goods, facilities and services with "a very wide scope of authority".[110] It is an administrative organ functioning under the supervision of the government and has the right "to impose severe sanctions on persons and entities violating the ban on discrimination".[111] However, the Authority is stated to be "under the supervision of the Minister responsible for matters and issues relating to Equal Opportunities and the President of the Authority" (section 1(2)) and the President of the Authority "is appointed and discharged by the Prime Minister on the basis of the joint recommendation made by the Minister and the Minister of Justice" (section 2(1)). It would appear that these provisions could leave the Authority very vulnerable to government pressures. Indeed, in March 2005 a new bill was submitted to Parliament concerning the amendment of certain laws on taxes and fees. One provision of this bill removed the financial independence of the Authority of Equal Treatment and thus "(from a financial point of view) practically reduced the body to the level of a department within the Ministry [of]

---

[106] Employment Equality Acts 1998–2004, s. 51(1).

[107] *Ibid.*, s. 51(2).

[108] *Ibid.*, s. 51(3).

[109] Discussion between the author and Niall Crowley, Chief Executive Officer, Equality Authority, 2 May 2006.

[110] A. Kadar and L. Farkas, "Report on Measures to Combat Discrimination: Directive 2000/43/EC and 2000/78/EC. Country Report Hungary" (European Commission, 2005) 38, available on the website of the European Commission, Directorate-General for Employment, Social Affairs and Equal Opportunities.

[111] *Ibid.*

Youth, Social and Family Affairs and Equal Treatment".[112] This Act came into force on 10 May 2005.

The Act setting out the powers of the Authority of Equal Treatment provides for the President of the Authority to be appointed and discharged by the Prime Minister. He or she shall serve for "an unspecified period of time", and the Minister for Equal Opportunities "shall exercise the employers' rights in respect of the President". Clearly the government retains a considerable degree of control over the President of the Authority, and this is a danger to the independence of the Authority.

Hungarian Government Decree 362/2004. (XII. 26.) Korm. on   **8.HU.55.**
the Authority of Equal Treatment and the Detailed Rules of its Procedures

The Government . . . hereby decree as follows:

Section 1.
(1) The Authority of Equal Treatment (hereinafter: the Authority) shall supervise the completion of the requirements of equal treatment as a public administration body with nation-wide responsibility . . .
(2) The Authority shall be supervised by the Minister responsible for matters and issues relating to Equal Opportunities (hereinafter: the Minister).

The Organisation and the Leaders of the Authority

Section 2.
(1) The authority shall be led by a President, who is appointed and discharged by the Prime Minister on the basis of the joint recommendation made by the Minister and the Minister of Justice. The appointment shall be granted for an unspecified period of time and in accordance with the relevant provisions of Act XXIII. of 1992. (hereinafter: the Ktv.) on the legal status of civil servants . . .
(4) The Minister shall exercise the employers' rights in respect of the President, with the exception of his/her appointment and discharge . . .

Section 4.
(1) The President shall establish the organisational and procedural rules of the Authority, with the approval of the Minister . . .

The Equal Treatment Advisory Board, which was created to assist the Equal Treatment Authority with issues of strategic importance, was appointed on 30 June 2005. Advising the Equal Treatment Authority on their work, the Board has a right to see and comment on every "statement, recommendation and report relating to the completion of [the Equal Treatment Authorities'] tasks". Three members of the Equal Treatment Advisory Board are proposed by the Minister responsible for Equal

---

[112] In [2005] *European Anti-Discrimination Law Review*, issue no. 2, 61–2, available on the website of the Migration Policy Group.

Opportunities and three by the Minister for Justice, and they are appointed by the Prime Minister for a fixed period of six years.

8.6.2.   INDEPENDENCE FROM OTHER SOURCES OF INFLUENCE

Normally the main threat to the independence of an equality body comes from the government of the state concerned. However, there are a number of bodies who may have an interest in influencing the work of an equality body. When an equality body is considering undertaking an investigation into a particular sector or industry it could come under pressure not to proceed from those likely to be affected.

An unusual example can be found in Sweden, where trade unions play a distinctive role in the delivery of assistance to victims of discrimination. The Ombudsman can only take on a discrimination case if the victim is either not a member of a trade union or the trades union decides not to take on the case. This necessarily limits the role that the Ombudsman can take in relation to discrimination cases.

K. Linna, "The role of specialised bodies and of trade unions"[113]   **8.SE.56.**

"The Ombudsman's work in the area of working life is based on law. According to the law, the Ombudsman shall investigate and, as a final measure, bring cases before the Labour Court, when complaints have been submitted by individuals . . .

If the complainant is a union member, the Ombudsman must ask the union whether it is willing to take the case. If—and only if—the trades union decides not to take the case can the Ombudsman investigate the complaint and bring it to court. The trades unions thus have the primary responsibility for legal action.

The Ombudsman may bring a lawsuit on behalf of the employee or job applicant concerned, if the individual agrees, and the Ombudsman finds that a court judgment in the dispute would be of importance for the application of the law or there are other special reasons for bringing the case before the court. The proceedings are provided to the claimant free of charge. So far only a few court judgments have applied the ethnic discrimination legislation from 1999. Five to be exact, and the Ombudsman against Ethnic Discrimination brought all of them. For that reason you could say that most cases are still important for the application of the law. Trade Unions must act in the same way on behalf of their members, thus without any legal costs for the complainant/trade union member . . ."

It is inevitable that the role of the trades unions in taking cases must limit the choice of discrimination cases that the Ombudsmen can take and so inhibit the Ombudsman's ability to do strategic casework.

---

[113] In J. Cormack (ed.), Discrimination in Working Life. Remedies and Enforcement. Towards the uniform and dynamic implementation of EU Anti-Discrimination Legislation: The Role of Specialised Bodies, Report of the Fourth Experts' Meeting, hosted by the Swedish Ombudsman against Ethnic Discrimination, 14–15 October 2003, Migration Policy Group, 2004, 6, available on the website of the Migration Policy Group.

8.7. COMPARATIVE ANALYSIS

Over the past 30 years equality bodies have developed to assist in the delivery of equality and equal treatment at every level in society. As the range of possible work is huge, every equality body is forced to make a selection of tasks through which to deliver its programme for countering discrimination in society. It will always be difficult for equality bodies to make the right choices about where to focus their work. This requires good leadership, a profound knowledge of the society in which they work and a legal structure that is highly functional.

One means of providing some direction to their work is in the wording of the legislation used to establish them. Purpose clauses in the legislation setting up the equality body which reaffirm the purpose of the equality body are a means of providing direction for equality bodies. These clauses can also be useful when particular aspects of their work are challenged as being *ultra vires* their source powers. Purpose clauses can also play a valuable role in presenting and explaining the role of the equality body to civil society. Examples of such purpose clauses can be found in the provisions of the Employment Equality Acts 1998–2004 which set up the Irish Equality Authority and the Equality Act 2006 which sets up the Great Britain Commission for Equality and Human Rights.

This chapter shows that there is a broad range of possible models for equality bodies to adopt. Equality bodies can focus on a single ground for discrimination or on a number of grounds. They can be controlled by an Ombud or a Commission governed by a committee of members or Commissioners. Each equality body should evolve from its local circumstances in order to reflect local needs. Countries with a federal system of government need to develop both local and national bodies or to delegate authority to the national body in order for it to be able to deal with local issues.

Some Member States who have not previously had an equality body have taken the opportunity to go beyond the strict requirements of the race and gender directives and to set up equality bodies with a wider remit able to work to counter discrimination on all of the prohibited grounds. Additionally, other Member States that have had equality bodies responsible for only one prohibited ground have expanded their remit to enable them to take on further grounds or to amalgamate with equality bodies responsible for another ground to form a new agency to cover multiple grounds. Equality bodies that cover several grounds are able to use techniques developed in respect of one ground to the benefit of other grounds; they are also better equipped to counter multiple discrimination. On the other hand, critics have raised concern about the lack of focus of equality bodies with a multiple remit.

In reviewing these bodies it is neither possible nor appropriate to identify a single ideal structure for any equality body, although clearly there are important examples of good practice. There are several European and international recommendations about the structure and role of equality bodies. The most notable of these are, first, the "Paris Principles" of the United Nations, drawn up in 1991, which set out detailed requirements for national human rights institutions and are often referred to in the context of equality bodies; and, secondly, the provisions of the EC race and gender directives that require Member States to establish "bodies for the promotion of equal treatment". It is the latter requirement that has stimulated the establishment of equality bodies in most European countries. However, as the Directives provide little detail on the requirements for equality bodies, the Paris Principles are frequently referred to in order to fill this lacuna.

Recently, a number of European equality bodies have joined together to form Equinet in order to discuss and identify ways of working and good practices for the benefit of all. Their discussions have so far focused on legal assistance to individuals, formal investigations and inquiries, interventions and positive duties to promote equality, and have identified a number of areas of good practice. Equinet can be expected to continue to develop its analysis of the best practice for equality bodies and this will be of particular benefit to the newer equality bodies.

Lessons can be learnt both from the way in which the strategic use of their powers by the existing equality bodies has advanced the equality agenda and from the problems that such bodies have encountered. Of course, no agency can afford to take on every legal case within its jurisdiction, so legal casework has to be undertaken strategically. Strategic plans need to be adopted and reviewed regularly to ensure that they continue to meet the needs of the community. The use of mediation as a tool for resolving disputes is an increasingly popular and effective alternative to more formal processes. However, whilst this carries the advantage of enabling a relationship, such as that between an employer and an employee, to be preserved it can be at the price of making concessions about the full impact of the law. It also prevents the establishment of precedents that could be used to develop the law.

Additionally, equality bodies are developing new methods for challenging discrimination by taking action in their own name or intervening in existing cases in order to facilitate the clarification of the law. These can be cost-effective ways to establish legal precedents.

Alongside their legal powers, equality bodies also seek to educate and encourage good practice. To achieve this they use a variety of means from information websites and training to codes of practice. Newer developments include the use of mainstreaming and the implementation of positive duties. It has been found that an element of strong, external pressure is frequently needed as a catalyst to move an organisation from inertia in relation to equality towards real and effective action. Experience shows that, though change *can* be achieved through good practice and persuasion, often such change is only secured as a result of some "driver", such as an enquiry, a series of complaints from staff or customers, a legal case, a political or journalistic enquiry, or an obligation to report to an equality authority.

Promotion of good equality practice is important, but it should be only one part of a total approach. Good policies will not work without a back-up enforcement provision. Achieving the right balance between enforcement and promotion is key to the success of any equality body as it needs, so far as possible, to retain the confidence of all its stakeholders—individuals, the business community, NGOs and the government. Support of civil society and the NGO community can greatly enhance the work of a national equality body.

A key factor in the success of any equality body lies in its independence from outside interference, most importantly from governmental interference. This is why all the international and European recommendations for the establishment of equality bodies stress the need for independence to be built into the structure of the equality body when it is established. This chapter shows the varying degrees to which it is built into European equality bodies. As equality bodies are dependent on funding and must be publicly accountable for the use of their funds, total independence is not realistically achievable. However, there is a spectrum of independence that is illustrated here. This ranges from the Italian National Office against Racial Discrimination, which operates as part of a government department, to the relative independence of the Dutch and UK Commissions.

The search for more effective ways to achieve the full enforcement of equality norms throughout society continues. Equality bodies have the potential to bring far-reaching change in the equality field; however, to do this they need a clear focus and a balanced action plan. This involves adopting a clear set of values, an awareness of the needs of each of the prohibited grounds, flexible enforcement and promotion powers, and a clear recognition of its need for independence. Given the task they must undertake, there will continue to be a need for equality bodies in the foreseeable future.

Synopsis of the Content of the EU Anti-Discrimination Legislation

Directive 2000/43/EC: "Racial Equality Directive"
Directive 2000/78/EC: "Employment Equality Directive"
Directive 76/207/EEC amended by 2002/73/EC, to be replaced by Directive 2006/54/EC in 2009: "Gender Employment Directive"; in addition, Directives 79/7/EEC, 86/613/EEC will be mentioned, as they are to be integrated into Directive 2006/54/EC as well
Directive 2004/113/EC: "Gender Goods and Services Directive"

	2000/43/EC Racial Equality Directive	2000/78/EC Employment Equality Directive	76/207/EEC (amended by 2002/73/EC) Gender Employment Directive	2004/113/EC Gender Goods and Services Directive
1. Material scope	**Art. 3**			**Art. 3**
	Access to (self-)employment and occupation, promotion, vocational guidance and training, advanced vocational training and retraining, incl. practical work experience.			Persons who provide goods and services, which are available to the public irrespective of the person concerned as regards both the public and private sector, including public bodies, and which are offered outside the area of private and family life and the transactions carried out in this context.
	Employment- and working conditions, including dismissals and pay.		(...) and pay as defined by **Directive 75/117/EC.**	
	Membership of, and involvement in, an organisation of workers or employers, or any organisation whose members carry on a particular profession, including the benefits provided for by such organisations.			
	Social protection, including social security and healthcare.	Dir. does not apply to (...) state social security or social protection schemes.	(in other Directives to "gender") Dir. 79/7/EEC; Dir. 86/613/EEC (latter self-employed)	
	Social advantages, education.			
	Access to and supply of goods and services which are available to the public, including housing.			
2. Grounds of discrimination	**Art. 1** Racial or ethnic origin.	**Art. 1** Religion or belief, disability, age or sexual orientation.	**Art. 1** Sex (gender).	**Art. 1** Sex (gender).

3. Prohibited discrimination

Racial Equality Directive	Employment Equality Directive	Gender Employment Directive	Gender Goods and Services Directive
Art. 2 Direct and Indirect Discrimination.		**Art. 2** Identical, incl. less favourable treatment regarding pregnancy or maternity leave.	**Art. 2** Direct and indirect discrimination.
Harassment. Instruction to discriminate.	Harassment. Instruction to discriminate.	Harassment and sexual harassment. Instruction to discriminate.	Harassment and sexual harassment. Instruction to discriminate.
	Art. 5: Refusal to provide reasonable accommodation for a person with a disability (where needed in particular case, unless disproportionate burden)		

4. Definitions

(a) Direct discrimination

Racial Equality Directive	Employment Equality Directive	Gender Employment Directive	Gender Goods and Services Directive
Art. 2(2)a	**Art. 2(2)a**	**[2]Art. 2(2)1. / Art. 2(a)**	
Where one person on grounds of racial or ethnic origin	Where one person on any of the grounds referred to in Article 1	Where one person on grounds of sex	

is treated less favourably than another is, has been or would be treated in a comparable situation.

957

(b) Indirect discrimination

Racial Equality Directive	Employment Equality Directive	Gender Employment Directive	Gender Goods and Services Directive
Art. 2(2)b Where an apparently neutral provision, criterion or practice would put persons of a **racial or ethnic origin**	**Art. 2(2)b** Where an apparently neutral provision, criterion or practice would put persons **having a particular religion or belief, a particular disability, a particular age, or a particular sexual orientation**	**Art. 2(2)2. / Art. 2(b)** Where an apparently neutral provision, criterion or practice would put persons of one sex	

at a particular disadvantage compared with other persons unless that provision, criterion or practice is objectively justified by a legitimate aim and the means of achieving that aim are appropriate and necessary.

| | Art. 2. Abs. 2 ii: Particular objective justification for special measures for the integration of persons with disabilities. | | |

(c) Harassment

| Art. 2(3)
 Unwanted conduct related to racial or ethnic origin (Dir. 2000/78: any of the grounds referred to in Art. 1) which takes place with the purpose or effect of violating the dignity of a person and of creating an intimidating, hostile, degrading, humiliating or offensive environment. | | **Art. 2(2)3./Art. 2(c)**
 Unwanted conduct related to the sex of a person which occurs with the purpose or effect of violating the dignity of a person and of creating an intimidating, hostile, degrading, humiliating or offensive environment. | |

d) Sexual harassment

| | | **Art. 2(2)4. / Art. 2(d)**
 Any form of unwanted verbal, non-verbal or physical conduct of a sexual nature which occurs with the purpose or effect of violating the dignity of a person, in particular when creating an intimidating, hostile, degrading, humiliating or offensive environment. | |

958

5. Justification of different treatment

Racial Equality Directive	Employment Equality Directive	Gender Employment Directive	Gender Goods and Services Directive
Art. 4	**Art. 4**	**Art. 2(6)**	**Art. 4(5)**
Notwithstanding Art. 2(1) and (2) (direct and indirect discrimination) difference which is based on a characteristic related to racial or ethnic origin shall not constitute discrimination where, by reason of the nature of the particular occupational activities concerned or of the context in which they are carried out, such a characteristic constitutes a genuine and determining occupational requirement, provided that the objective is legitimate and the requirement is proportionate.	Notwithstanding Art. 2(1) and (2) (direct and indirect discrimination) difference which is based on a characteristic related to one of the listed grounds shall not constitute discrimination where, by reason of the nature of the particular occupational activities concerned or of the context in which they are carried out, such a characteristic constitutes a genuine and determining occupational requirement, provided that the objective is legitimate and the requirement is proportionate.	As regards access to employment including the training thereto, difference of treatment which is based on a characteristic related to sex may not constitute discrimination where, by reason of the nature of the particular occupational activities concerned or of the context in which they are carried out, such a characteristic constitutes a genuine and determining occupational requirement, provided that the objective is legitimate and the requirement is proportionate.	Dir. Shall not preclude differences in treatment, if the provision of the goods or service exclusively or primarily to members of one sex is justified by a legitimate aim and the means of achieving that aim are appropriate and necessary.

Racial Equality Directive	Employment Equality Directive	Gender Employment Directive	Gender Goods and Services Directive
	6. Special justification of different treatment		
	Art. 4(2) In case of occupational activities within churches or organisations the ethos of which is based on religion or belief **Art. 6 Age** **Differentiation justified**, if, within the context of national law, they are objectively and reasonably justified by a legitimate aim (i.e. appropriate and necessary). Aims include those from the field of employment policy, labour market and vocational training objectives. **Including (explicitly):** (a) Special conditions on access to employment and vocational training, employment and occupation, including dismissal and remuneration conditions for young people, older workers and persons with caring responsibilities in order to promote their vocational integration or ensure their protection.		**Art. 5 Actuarial factors** (2) MS may decide before 21.12.2007 to permit proportionate differences in individuals' premiums and benefits where the use of sex is a determining factor in the assessment of risk based on relevant and accurate actuarial and statistical data. (3) Costs related to pregnancy and maternity shall not result in differences in individuals' premiums and benefits.

Racial Equality Directive	Employment Equality Directive	Gender Employment Directive	Gender Goods and Services Directive
	(b) Fixing of minimum conditions of age, professional experience or seniority in service for access to employment or certain advantages linked to employment. (c) Fixing of a maximum age for recruitment which is based on the training requirements of the post in question or the need for a reasonable period of employment before retirement. (d) Fixing of ages for occupational social security schemes for admission or entitlement to retirement or invalidity benefits, including the use of age criteria in actuarial calculations, provided this does not result in discrimination on the ground of sex.		

7. Minimum requirement

Art. 6, Art. 8, Art. 8(e), Art. 7

The implementation of the Dir. shall under no circumstances constitute grounds for a reduction of the level of protection against discrimination already afforded by MS in the fields covered by the Directives. MS may introduce or maintain provisions which are more favourable.

8. Defence of rights

Art. 7 (2), Art. 9, Art. 6, Art. 8

Associations, organisations and other legal entities may engage, either on behalf or in support of the complainant, with his or her approval, in any judicial or administrative procedure.

961

Racial Equality Directive	Employment Equality Directive	Gender Employment Directive	Gender Goods and Services Directive
9. Burden of proof			
Art. 8(1)	**Art. 10 (1)**	**Art. 4 of Dir: 97/80/EC**	**Art. 9**
When persons establish, before a court or other competent authority, facts from which it may be presumed that there has been direct or indirect discrimination, it shall be for the respondent to prove that there has been no breach of the principle of equal treatment. This shall not apply to criminal procedures. MS need not apply the shift of the burden of proof to proceedings in which it is for the court or competent body to investigate the facts of the case.			
		Note: Directive 2006/54 repeals Dir. 97/80/EC. The Burden of Proof rule will then become Art. 19 of Dir 2006/54	
10. Sanctions			
Art. 15	**Art. 17**	**Art. 8(d)**	**Art. 14**
Sanctions, which may comprise the payment of compensation to the victim, must be effective, proportionate and dissuasive.			
		Art. 6(2)	
		Measures as are necessary to ensure real and effective compensation or reparation for the loss and damage sustained by a person injured as a result of discrimination – as the MS so determine – in a way which is dissuasive and proportionate to the damage suffered. Such compensation or reparation may only be restricted by the fixing of a prior upper limit where the employer can prove that the only damage suffered by the applicant as a result of discrimination is the refusal to take his/her job application into consideration	

Racial Equality Directive	Employment Equality Directive	Gender Employment Directive	Gender Goods and Services Directive
11. Victimisation			
Art. 9	**Art. 11**	**Art. 7**	**Art. 10**
Protection of individuals from any adverse treatment or adverse consequence as a reaction to a complaint or to proceedings aimed at enforcing compliance with the principle of equal treatment.	Protection of **employees** against **dismissal** or other adverse treatment **by the employer** as a reaction to a complaint **within the undertaking** or to any legal proceedings aimed at enforcing compliance with the principle of equal treatment.	Protection of employees including those who are <u>employees' representatives</u> provided for by national laws and/or practices, against dismissal or other adverse treatment by the employer as a reaction to a complaint within the undertaking or to any legal proceedings aimed at enforcing compliance with the principle of equal treatment.	Identical to Dir. 2000/43/EC
12. Social dialogue			
Art. 11, Art. 13, Art. 8(b) paras. 1 and 2			
Take adequate measures in accordance with national traditions and practices to promote the social dialogue between the two sides of industry with a view to fostering equal treatment, including through the monitoring of workplace practices, collective agreements, codes of conduct, research or exchange of experiences and *good practices*. Where consistent with national traditions and practices, both sides of industry are encouraged, without prejudice to their autonomy, to conclude at appropriate level, <u>agreements laying down anti-discrimination rules</u>, which fall within the scope of collective bargaining.			

Racial Equality Directive	Employment Equality Directive	Gender Employment Directive	Gender Goods and Services Directive

13. Dialogue with NGOs

Arts. 12, 13 and 14(8)c		**Art. 11**
Member States shall encourage dialogue with appropriate non-governmental organisations which have, in accordance with their national law and practices, a legitimate interest in contributing to the fight against discrimination on the respective ground with a view to promoting the principle of equal treatment.		MS shall encourage dialogue with relevant stakeholders that have, in accordance with national law and practice, a legitimate interest in contributing to the fight against discrimination on grounds of sex in the area of access to and supply of goods and services.

14. Special duties of employer

Art. 8(b)3

In accordance with national law, collective agreements or practice encourage employers to promote **equal treatment for men and women in the workplace** in a planned and systematic way.

Art. 8(b)4

Employers **should** be encouraged to provide at appropriate regular intervals employees and/or their representatives with appropriate information on equal treatment for men and women in the undertaking. Such **may** include statistics on proportions of men and women at different levels of the organisation and possible measures to improve the situation.

Racial Equality Directive	Employment Equality Directive	Gender Employment Directive	Gender Goods and Services Directive
15. Body (bodies) for the promotion of equal treatment			
Art. 13 A body or bodies for the promotion of equal treatment of all persons without discrimination on the grounds of racial or ethnic origin. These bodies may form part of agencies charged at national level with the defence of human rights or the safeguard of individuals' rights. Tasks/Competences: Independent assistance to victims in pursuing their complaints; Conducting independent surveys; Publishing independent reports.		**Art. 8(a), Art. 12** A body or bodies for the promotion, **analysis, monitoring and support** of equal treatment of all persons without discrimination **on the ground of sex.** These bodies may form part of agencies charged at national level with the defence of human rights or the safeguard of individuals' rights. **Tasks/Competences:** Independent assistance to victims in pursuing their complaints; Conducting independent surveys; Publishing independent reports.	
16. Special provisions			
		Art. 2(3) A person's rejection of, or submission to, sexual harassment may not be used as a basis for a decision affecting that person. **Art. 2(7)** A woman on maternity leave shall be entitled, after the end of her period of maternity leave, to return to her job or an equivalent post.	

17. Implementation

Racial Equality Directive	Employment Equality Directive	Gender Employment Directive	Gender Goods and Services Directive
19 July 2003	2 December 2003	5 October 2005	21 December 2007
	Additional period of 3 years to implement the provisions on age and disability.	(Note: date of implementation of Dir. 2006/54 is 15 August 2008)	

INDEX